Derivatives Markets

The Addison-Wesley Series in Finance

Copeland/Weston/Shastri
*Financial Theory
and Corporate Policy*

Dufey/Giddy
Cases in International Finance

Eakins
*Finance: Investments,
Institutions, and Management*

Eiteman/Stonehill/Moffett
Multinational Business Finance

Gitman
Principles of Managerial Finance

Gitman
*Principles of Managerial Finance
–Brief Edition*

Gitman/Joehnk
Fundamentals of Investing

Gitman/Madura
Introduction to Finance

Hughes/MacDonald
*International Banking:
Text and Cases*

Madura
Personal Finance

Marthinsen
*Risk Takers: Uses and Abuses
of Financial Derivatives*

McDonald
Derivatives Markets

Megginson
Corporate Finance Theory

Melvin
International Money and Finance

Mishkin/Eakins
Financial Markets and Institutions

Moffett
Cases in International Finance

Moffett/Stonehill/Eiteman
*Fundamentals of
Multinational Finance*

Rejda
*Principles of Risk Management
and Insurance*

Solnik/McLeavey
International Investments

Derivatives Markets

Second Edition

ROBERT L. McDONALD

Northwestern University

Kellogg School of Management

Boston San Francisco New York
London Toronto Sydney Tokyo Singapore Madrid
Mexico City Munich Paris Cape Town Hong Kong Montreal

Editor-in-Chief: Denise Clinton
Senior Sponsoring Editor: Donna Battista
Senior Project Manager: Mary Clare McEwing
Development Editor: Marjorie Singer Anderson
Senior Production Supervisor: Nancy Fenton
Executive Marketing Manager: Stephen Frail
Design Manager: Regina Hagen Kolenda
Text Designer: Regina Hagen Kolenda
Cover Designer: Rebecca Light
Cover and Interior Image: Private Collection/Art for After Hours/SuperStock
Senior Manufacturing Buyer: Carol Melville
Supplements Editor: Marianne Groth
Project Management: Elm Street Publishing Services, Inc.

Library of Congress Cataloging-in-Publication Data

McDonald, Robert L. (Robert Lynch), 1954–
    Derivatives markets, 2e / Robert L. McDonald.
      p. cm.
    Includes index.
    ISBN 0-321-28030-X
    1. Derivative securities. I. Title.
HG6024.A3 M3946 2006
332.64′5–dc21
ISBN 0-321-28030-X
    345678910–HT–09 08 07 06

For Irene, Claire, David, and Henry

CONTENTS

Preface   **xxi**

Chapter 1   Introduction to Derivatives   1
1.1 What Is a Derivative?   1
Uses of Derivatives   2
Perspectives on Derivatives   3
Financial Engineering and Security
    Design   3
1.2 The Role of Financial Markets   4
Financial Markets and the Averages   4
Risk-Sharing   5
1.3 Derivatives in Practice   6
Growth in Derivatives Trading   7
How Are Derivatives Used?   10
**1.4 Buying and Short-Selling Financial
    Assets   11**
Buying an Asset   11
Short-Selling   12
The Lease Rate of an Asset   14
Risk and Scarcity in Short-Selling   15
Chapter Summary   16
Further Reading   16
Problems   17

**PART ONE   INSURANCE,
HEDGING, AND SIMPLE STRATEGIES
19**

**Chapter 2   An Introduction to Forwards
and Options   21**
2.1 Forward Contracts   21
The Payoff on a Forward Contract   23
Graphing the Payoff on a Forward
    Contract   25

Comparing a Forward and Outright
    Purchase   26
Zero-Coupon Bonds in Payoff and Profit
    Diagrams   28
Cash Settlement Versus Delivery   30
Credit Risk   30
2.2 Call Options   31
Option Terminology   32
Payoff and Profit for a Purchased Call
    Option   33
Payoff and Profit for a Written Call
    Option   37
2.3 Put Options   38
Payoff and Profit for a Purchased Put
    Option   39
Payoff and Profit for a Written Put
    Option   40
The "Moneyness" of an Option   43
**2.4 Summary of Forward and Option
    Positions   43**
Long Positions   44
Short Positions   44
2.5 Options Are Insurance   45
Homeowner's Insurance Is a Put Option   45
But I Thought Insurance Is Prudent and Put
    Options Are Risky . . .   47
Call Options Are Also Insurance   47
2.6 Example: Equity-Linked CDs   48
Graphing the Payoff on the CD   49
Economics of the CD   50
Why Equity-Linked CDs?   51
Chapter Summary   52
Further Reading   53
Problems   54
*Appendix 2.A: More on Buying a Stock
    Option   56*
    Dividends   56*

Exercise   57

Margins for Written Options   57

Taxes   58

Chapter 3   Insurance, Collars, and Other Strategies   59

3.1   Basic Insurance Strategies   59

Insuring a Long Position: Floors   59

Insuring a Short Position: Caps   62

Selling Insurance   63

3.2   Synthetic Forwards   66

Put-Call Parity   68

3.3   Spreads and Collars   70

Bull and Bear Spreads   71

Box Spreads   72

Ratio Spreads   73

Collars   73

3.4   Speculating on Volatility   78

Straddles   78

Butterfly Spreads   81

Asymmetric Butterfly Spreads   82

3.5   Example: Another Equity-Linked Note   83

Chapter Summary   85

Further Reading   86

Problems   87

Chapter 4   Introduction to Risk Management   91

4.1   Basic Risk Management: The Producer's Perspective   91

Hedging with a Forward Contract   92

Insurance: Guaranteeing a Minimum Price with a Put Option   93

Insuring by Selling a Call   95

Adjusting the Amount of Insurance   96

4.2   Basic Risk Management: The Buyer's Perspective   98

Hedging with a Forward Contract   98

Insurance: Guaranteeing a Maximum Price with a Call Option   99

4.3   Why Do Firms Manage Risk?   100

An Example Where Hedging Adds Value   101

Reasons to Hedge   103

Reasons *Not* to Hedge   106

Empirical Evidence on Hedging   106

4.4   Golddiggers Revisited   108

Selling the Gain: Collars   108

Other Collar Strategies   112

Paylater Strategies   113

4.5   Selecting the Hedge Ratio   113

Cross-Hedging   114

Quantity Uncertainty   116

Chapter Summary   119

Further Reading   120

Problems   120

PART TWO   FORWARDS, FUTURES, AND SWAPS   125

Chapter 5   Financial Forwards and Futures   127

5.1   Alternative Ways to Buy a Stock   127

5.2   Prepaid Forward Contracts on Stock   128

Pricing the Prepaid Forward by Analogy   128

Pricing the Prepaid Forward by Discounted Present Value   129

Pricing the Prepaid Forward by Arbitrage   129

Pricing Prepaid Forwards with Dividends   131

5.3   Forward Contracts on Stock   133

Creating a Synthetic Forward Contract   135

Synthetic Forwards in Market-Making and Arbitrage   136

No-Arbitrage Bounds with Transaction Costs 138

Quasi-Arbitrage 139

Does the Forward Price Predict the Future Price? 140

An Interpretation of the Forward Pricing Formula 141

5.4 **Futures Contracts 142**

The S&P 500 Futures Contract 143

Margins and Marking to Market 144

Comparing Futures and Forward Prices 146

Arbitrage in Practice: S&P 500 Index Arbitrage 147

Quanto Index Contracts 149

5.5 **Uses of Index Futures 150**

Asset Allocation 150

Cross-hedging with Index Futures 151

5.6 **Currency Contracts 154**

Currency Prepaid Forward 155

Currency Forward 156

Covered Interest Arbitrage 156

5.7 **Eurodollar Futures 160**

Chapter Summary 160

Further Reading 162

Problems 162

Appendix 5.A: Taxes and the Forward Price 166

Appendix 5.B: Equating Forwards and Futures 166

Chapter 6 Commodity Forwards and Futures 169

6.1 **Introduction to Commodity Forwards 169**

6.2 **Equilibrium Pricing of Commodity Forwards 171**

6.3 **Nonstorability: Electricity 172**

6.4 **Pricing Commodity Forwards by Arbitrage: An Example 174**

An Apparent Arbitrage and Resolution 175

Pencils Have a Positive Lease Rate 176

6.5 **The Commodity Lease Rate 178**

The Lease Market for a Commodity 178

Forward Prices and the Lease Rate 179

6.6 **Carry Markets 181**

Storage Costs and Forward Prices 181

Storage Costs and the Lease Rate 182

The Convenience Yield 182

6.7 **Gold Futures 184**

Gold Investments 187

Evaluation of Gold Production 187

6.8 **Seasonality: The Corn Forward Market 188**

6.9 **Natural Gas 191**

6.10 **Oil 194**

6.11 **Commodity Spreads 195**

6.12 **Hedging Strategies 196**

Basis Risk 197

Hedging Jet Fuel with Crude Oil 199

Weather Derivatives 199

Chapter Summary 200

Further Reading 201

Problems 201

Chapter 7 Interest Rate Forwards and Futures 205

7.1 **Bond Basics 205**

Zero-Coupon Bonds 206

Implied Forward Rates 208

Coupon Bonds 210

Zeros from Coupons 211

Interpreting the Coupon Rate 212

Continuously Compounded Yields 213

7.2 **Forward Rate Agreements, Eurodollars, and Hedging 214**

Forward Rate Agreements 214

Synthetic FRAs 216

Eurodollar Futures 218

Interest Rate Strips and Stacks 223

7.3 Duration and Convexity 223
Duration 224
Duration Matching 227
Convexity 228

7.4 Treasury-Bond and Treasury-Note Futures 230

7.5 Repurchase Agreements 233
Chapter Summary 235
Further Reading 237
Problems 237
Appendix 7.A: Interest Rate and Bond Price Conventions 241
Bonds 242
Bills 244

Chapter 8 Swaps 247

8.1 An Example of a Commodity Swap 247
Physical Versus Financial Settlement 248
Why Is the Swap Price Not $20.50? 250
The Swap Counterparty 250
The Market Value of a Swap 253

8.2 Interest Rate Swaps 254
A Simple Interest Rate Swap 254
Pricing and the Swap Counterparty 255
Computing the Swap Rate in General 257
The Swap Curve 258
The Swap's Implicit Loan Balance 260
Deferred Swaps 261
Why Swap Interest Rates? 262
Amortizing and Accreting Swaps 263

8.3 Currency Swaps 264
Currency Swap Formulas 267
Other Currency Swaps 267

8.4 Commodity Swaps 268
The Commodity Swap Price 268
Swaps with Variable Quantity and Price 269

8.5 Swaptions 271

8.6 Total Return Swaps 272
Chapter Summary 274

Further Reading 275
Problems 275

PART THREE OPTIONS 279

Chapter 9 Parity and Other Option Relationships 281

9.1 Put-Call Parity 281
Options on Stocks 283
Options on Currencies 286
Options on Bonds 286

9.2 Generalized Parity and Exchange Options 287
Options to Exchange Stock 288
What Are Calls and Puts? 289
Currency Options 290

9.3 Comparing Options with Respect to Style, Maturity, and Strike 292
European Versus American Options 293
Maximum and Minimum Option Prices 293
Early Exercise for American Options 294
Time to Expiration 297
Different Strike Prices 299
Exercise and Moneyness 304
Chapter Summary 305
Further Reading 306
Problems 306
Appendix 9.A: Parity Bounds for American Options 310
Appendix 9.B: Algebraic Proofs of Strike-Price Relations 311

Chapter 10 Binomial Option Pricing: I 313

10.1 A One-Period Binomial Tree 313
Computing the Option Price 314
The Binomial Solution 315
Arbitraging a Mispriced Option 318

A Graphical Interpretation of the Binomial Formula 319

Risk-Neutral Pricing 320

Constructing a Binomial Tree 321

Another One-Period Example 322

Summary 322

10.2 Two or More Binomial Periods 323

A Two-Period European Call 323

Many Binomial Periods 326

10.3 Put Options 328

10.4 American Options 329

10.5 Options on Other Assets 330

Option on a Stock Index 330

Options on Currencies 332

Options on Futures Contracts 332

Options on Commodities 334

Options on Bonds 335

Summary 336

Chapter Summary 337

Further Reading 337

Problems 338

Appendix 10.A: Taxes and Option Prices 341

Chapter 11 Binomial Option Pricing: II 343

11.1 Understanding Early Exercise 343

11.2 Understanding Risk-Neutral Pricing 346

The Risk-Neutral Probability 346

Pricing an Option Using Real Probabilities 347

11.3 The Binomial Tree and Lognormality 351

The Random Walk Model 351

Modeling Stock Prices as a Random Walk 352

Continuously Compounded Returns 353

The Standard Deviation of Returns 354

The Binomial Model 355

Lognormality and the Binomial Model 355

Alternative Binomial Trees 358

Is the Binomial Model Realistic? 359

11.4 Estimating Volatility 360

11.5 Stocks Paying Discrete Dividends 361

Modeling Discrete Dividends 361

Problems with the Discrete Dividend Tree 362

A Binomial Tree Using the Prepaid Forward 363

Chapter Summary 365

Further Reading 366

Problems 366

Appendix 11.A: Pricing Options with True Probabilities 369

Appendix 11.B: Why Does Risk-Neutral Pricing Work? 369

Utility-Based Valuation 369

Standard Discounted Cash Flow 371

Risk-Neutral Pricing 371

Example 372

Why Risk-Neutral Pricing Works 373

Chapter 12 The Black-Scholes Formula 375

12.1 Introduction to the Black-Scholes Formula 375

Call Options 375

Put Options 378

When Is the Black-Scholes Formula Valid? 379

12.2 Applying the Formula to Other Assets 379

Options on Stocks with Discrete Dividends 380

Options on Currencies 381

Options on Futures 381

12.3 Option Greeks 382

Definition of the Greeks 382

Greek Measures for Portfolios 388

Option Elasticity 389

12.4 Profit Diagrams Before Maturity 395
Purchased Call Option 396
Calendar Spreads 397

12.5 Implied Volatility 400
Computing Implied Volatility 400
Using Implied Volatility 402

12.6 Perpetual American Options 403
Barrier Present Values 403
Perpetual Calls 404
Perpetual Puts 404
Chapter Summary 405
Further Reading 405
Problems 406
Appendix 12.A: The Standard Normal Distribution 409
Appendix 12.B: Formulas for Option Greeks 410
  Delta 410
  Gamma 410
  Theta 410
  Vega 411
  Rho 411
  Psi 411

Chapter 13   Market-Making and Delta-Hedging 413

13.1 What Do Market-Makers Do? 413

13.2 Market-Maker Risk 414
Option Risk in the Absence of Hedging 414
Delta and Gamma as Measures of Exposure 416

13.3 Delta-Hedging 417
An Example of Delta-Hedging for 2 Days 417
Interpreting the Profit Calculation 418
Delta-Hedging for Several Days 420
A Self-Financing Portfolio: The Stock Moves One σ 422

13.4 The Mathematics of Delta-Hedging 422
Using Gamma to Better Approximate the Change in the Option Price 423

Delta-Gamma Approximations 424
Theta: Accounting for Time 425
Understanding the Market-Maker's Profit 427

13.5 The Black-Scholes Analysis 429
The Black-Scholes Argument 429
Delta-Hedging of American Options 430
What Is the Advantage to Frequent Re-Hedging? 431
Delta-Hedging in Practice 432
Gamma-Neutrality 433

13.6 Market-Making as Insurance 436
Insurance 436
Market-Makers 437
Chapter Summary 438
Further Reading 438
Problems 438
Appendix 13.A: Taylor Series Approximations 441
Appendix 13.B: Greeks in the Binomial Model 441

Chapter 14   Exotic Options: I 443

14.1 Introduction 443

14.2 Asian Options 444
XYZ's Hedging Problem 445
Options on the Average 446
Comparing Asian Options 447
An Asian Solution for XYZ 448

14.3 Barrier Options 449
Types of Barrier Options 450
Currency Hedging 451

14.4 Compound Options 453
Compound Option Parity 454
Options on Dividend-Paying Stocks 455
Currency Hedging with Compound Options 456

14.5 Gap Options 457

14.6 Exchange Options 459
European Exchange Options 459
Chapter Summary 461
Further Reading 462

Problems 462

Appendix 14.A: Pricing Formulas for
  Exotic Options 466

  Asian Options Based on the Geometric
    Average 466

  Compound Options 467

  Infinitely Lived Exchange Option 468

PART FOUR FINANCIAL ENGINEERING AND APPLICATIONS 471

Chapter 15 Financial Engineering and Security Design 473

15.1 The Modigliani-Miller Theorem 473

15.2 Pricing and Designing Structured Notes 474

  Zero-Coupon Bonds 474

  Coupon Bonds 475

  Equity-Linked Bonds 476

  Commodity-Linked Bonds 478

  Currency-Linked Bonds 481

15.3 Bonds with Embedded Options 482

  Options in Coupon Bonds 482

  Options in Equity-Linked Notes 483

  Valuing and Structuring an Equity-Linked
    CD 483

  Alternative Structures 485

15.4 Engineered Solutions for Golddiggers 486

  Gold-Linked Notes 486

  Notes with Embedded Options 488

15.5 Strategies Motivated by Tax and Regulatory Considerations 490

  Capital Gains Deferral 490

  Tax-Deductible Equity 495

  Chapter Summary 498

  Further Reading 498

  Problems 498

Chapter 16 Corporate Applications 503

16.1 Equity, Debt, and Warrants 503

  Debt and Equity as Options 503

  Multiple Debt Issues 511

  Warrants 512

  Convertible Bonds 513

  Callable Bonds 516

  Bond Valuation Based on the Stock Price
    520

  Other Bond Features 520

  Put Warrants 522

16.2 Compensation Options 523

  Whose Valuation? 525

  Valuation Inputs 527

  An Alternative Approach to Expensing
    Option Grants 528

  Repricing of Compensation Options 531

  Reload Options 532

  Level 3 Communications 534

16.3 The Use of Collars in Acquisitions 538

  The Northrop Grumman–TRV Merger
    538

  Chapter Summary 542

  Further Reading 542

  Problems 543

Chapter 17 Real Options 547

17.1 Investment and the NPV Rule 548

  Static NPV 548

  The Correct Use of NPV 549

  The Project as an Option 550

17.2 Investment under Uncertainty 551

  A Simple DCF Problem 551

  Valuing Derivatives on the Cash Flow
    552

  Evaluating a Project with a 2-Year
    Investment Horizon 554

  Evaluating the Project with an Infinite
    Investment Horizon 558

17.3 **Real Options in Practice** 558
Peak-Load Electricity Generation 559
Research and Development 563

17.4 **Commodity Extraction as an Option** 565
Single-Barrel Extraction under Certainty 565
Single-Barrel Extraction under Uncertainty 569
Valuing an Infinite Oil Reserve 570

17.5 **Commodity Extraction with Shut-Down and Restart Options** 572
Permanent Shutting Down 574
Investment When Shutdown Is Possible 576
Restarting Production 578
Additional Options 578
Chapter Summary 579
Further Reading 580
Problems 580
Appendix 17.A: Calculation of Optimal Time to Drill an Oil Well 583
Appendix 17.B: The Solution with Shutting Down and Restarting 583

PART FIVE   ADVANCED PRICING THEORY   585

Chapter 18   The Lognormal Distribution   587

18.1 **The Normal Distribution** 587
Converting a Normal Random Variable to Standard Normal 590
Sums of Normal Random Variables 591

18.2 **The Lognormal Distribution** 593

18.3 **A Lognormal Model of Stock Prices** 595

18.4 **Lognormal Probability Calculations** 598
Probabilities 599

Lognormal Confidence Intervals 600
The Conditional Expected Price 602
The Black-Scholes Formula 604

18.5 **Estimating the Parameters of a Lognormal Distribution** 605

18.6 **How Are Asset Prices Distributed?** 608
Histograms 608
Normal Probability Plots 609
Chapter Summary 613
Further Reading 613
Problems 614
Appendix 18.A: The Expectation of a Lognormal Variable 615
Appendix 18.B: Constructing a Normal Probability Plot 616

Chapter 19   Monte Carlo Valuation   617

19.1 **Computing the Option Price as a Discounted Expected Value** 617
Valuation with Risk-Neutral Probabilities 618
Valuation with True Probabilities 619

19.2 **Computing Random Numbers** 621
Using Sums of Uniformly Distributed Random Variables 622
Using the Inverse Cumulative Normal Distribution 622

19.3 **Simulating Lognormal Stock Prices** 623
Simulating a Sequence of Stock Prices 623

19.4 **Monte Carlo Valuation** 624
Monte Carlo Valuation of a European Call 625
Accuracy of Monte Carlo 626
Arithmetic Asian Option 627

19.5 **Efficient Monte Carlo Valuation** 630
Control Variate Method 630
Other Monte Carlo Methods 632

19.6 **Valuation of American Options** 633

19.7 The Poisson Distribution   636

19.8 Simulating Jumps with the Poisson Distribution   639
Multiple Jumps   643

19.9 Simulating Correlated Stock Prices   643
Generating n Correlated Lognormal Random Variables   644
Chapter Summary   645
Further Reading   645
Problems   646
Appendix 19.A: Formulas for Geometric Average Options   648

Chapter 20   Brownian Motion and Itô's Lemma   649

20.1 The Black-Scholes Assumption about Stock Prices   649

20.2 Brownian Motion   650
Definition of Brownian Motion   650
Properties of Brownian Motion   652
Arithmetic Brownian Motion   653
The Ornstein-Uhlenbeck Process   654

20.3 Geometric Brownian Motion   655
Lognormality   655
Relative Importance of the Drift and Noise Terms   656
Correlated Itô Processes   657
Multiplication Rules   658

20.4 The Sharpe Ratio   659

20.5 The Risk-Neutral Process   660

20.6 Itô's Lemma   663
Functions of an Itô Process   663
Multivariate Itô's Lemma   665

20.7 Valuing a Claim on S^a 666
The Process Followed by S^a 667
Proving the Proposition   668
Specific Examples   669
Valuing a Claim on $S^a Q^b$ 670

20.8 Jumps in the Stock Price   672
Chapter Summary   674

Further Reading   674
Problems   675

Chapter 21   The Black-Scholes Equation   679

21.1 Differential Equations and Valuation under Certainty   679
The Valuation Equation   680
Bonds   680
Dividend-Paying Stocks   681
The General Structure   681

21.2 The Black-Scholes Equation   681
Verifying the Formula for a Derivative   683
The Black-Scholes Equation and Equilibrium Returns   686
What If the Underlying Asset Is Not an Investment Asset?   688

21.3 Risk-Neutral Pricing   690
Interpreting the Black-Scholes Equation   690
The Backward Equation   691
Derivative Prices as Discounted Expected Cash Flows   692

21.4 Changing the Numeraire   693

21.5 Option Pricing When the Stock Price Can Jump   696
Merton's Solution for Diversifiable Jumps   697
Chapter Summary   698
Further Reading   698
Problems   699
Appendix 21.A: Multivariate Black-Scholes Analysis   700
Appendix 21.B: Proof of Proposition 21.1   701

Chapter 22   Exotic Options: II   703

22.1 All-or-Nothing Options   703
Terminology   703
Cash-or-Nothing Options   704
Asset-or-Nothing Options   706

Ordinary Options and Gap Options   706

Delta-Hedging All-or-Nothing
  Options   707

22.2 All-or-Nothing Barrier Options   710
Cash-or-Nothing Barrier Options   710

Asset-or-Nothing Barrier Options   715

Rebate Options   716

22.3 Barrier Options   717
22.4 Quantos   718
The Yen Perspective   720

The Dollar Perspective   721

A Binomial Model for the
  Dollar-Denominated Investor   724

22.5 Currency-Linked Options   727
Foreign Equity Call Struck in Foreign
  Currency   728

Foreign Equity Call Struck in Domestic
  Currency   729

Fixed Exchange Rate Foreign Equity
  Call   730

Equity-Linked Foreign Exchange
  Call   731

22.6 Other Multivariate Options   732
Exchange Options   732

Options on the Best of Two Assets   733

Basket Options   735

Chapter Summary   736

Further Reading   736

Problems   737

Chapter 23   Volatility   741
23.1 Implied Volatility   741
**23.2 Measurement and Behavior of
Volatility   744**
Historical Volatility   744

Exponentially Weighted Moving Average
  746

Time-Varying Volatility: ARCH   747

The GARCH Model   751

Realized Quadratic Variation   755

23.3 Hedging and Pricing Volatility   757
Variance and Volatility Swaps   758

Pricing Volatility   759

**23.4 Extending the Black-Scholes Model
763**
Jump Risk and Implied Volatility   764

Constant Elasticity of Variance   766

The Heston Model   768

Evidence   771

Chapter Summary   773

Further Reading   773

Problems   774

Appendix 23.A   777

Chapter 24   Interest Rate Models   779
**24.1 Market-Making and Bond
Pricing   779**
The Behavior of Bonds and Interest
  Rates   780

An Impossible Bond Pricing Model   780

An Equilibrium Equation for Bonds   781

Delta-Gamma Approximations for
  Bonds   784

**24.2 Equilibrium Short-Rate Bond Price
Models   785**
The Rendelman-Bartter Model   785

The Vasicek Model   786

The Cox-Ingersoll-Ross Model   787

Comparing Vasicek and CIR   788

**24.3 Bond Options, Caps, and the Black
Model   790**
24.4 A Binomial Interest Rate Model   793
Zero-Coupon Bond Prices   794

Yields and Expected Interest Rates   796

Option Pricing   797

24.5 The Black-Derman-Toy Model   798
Verifying Yields   802

Verifying Volatilities   803

Constructing a Black-Derman-Toy
  Tree   804

Pricing Examples   805

Chapter Summary 808
Further Reading 808
Problems 809
*Appendix 24.A: The Heath-
  Jarrow-Morton Model 811*

Chapter 25 Value at Risk 813
25.1 Value at Risk 813
Value at Risk for One Stock 815
VaR for Two or More Stocks 817
VaR for Nonlinear Portfolios 819
VaR for Bonds 826
Estimating Volatility 830
Bootstrapping Return Distributions 831
25.2 Issues with VaR 832
Alternative Risk Measures 832
VaR and the Risk-Neutral Distribution
  835
Subadditive Risk Measures 837
Chapter Summary 838
Further Reading 839
Problems 839

Chapter 26 Credit Risk 841
26.1 Default Concepts and Terminology
  841
26.2 The Merton Default Model 843
Default at Maturity 843
Related Models 845
26.3 Bond Ratings and Default Experience
  847
Using Ratings to Assess Bankruptcy
  Probability 847
Recovery Rates 850
Reduced Form Bankruptcy Models 852
26.4 Credit Instruments 853
Collateralized Debt Obligations 853
Credit Default Swaps and Related
  Structures 858
Pricing a Default Swap 862
CDS Indices 864

Chapter Summary 866
Further Reading 867
Problems 867

PART SIX APPENDIXES 871

Appendix A The Greek Alphabet 873

Appendix B Continuous Compounding 875
B.1 The Language of Interest Rates 875
B.2 The Logarithmic and Exponential
  Functions 876
Changing Interest Rates 877
Symmetry for Increases and Decreases
  878
Problems 878

Appendix C Jensen's Inequality 881
C.1 Example: The Exponential Function
  881
C.2 Example: The Price of a Call 882
C.3 Proof of Jensen's Inequality 884
Problems 884

Appendix D An Introduction to
Visual Basic for Applications 885
D.1 Calculations without VBA 885
D.2 How to Learn VBA 886
D.3 Calculations with VBA 886
Creating a Simple Function 886
A Simple Example of a Subroutine 888
Creating a Button to Invoke a Subroutine
  888
Functions Can Call Functions 889
Illegal Function Names 889
Differences between Functions and
  Subroutines 890

D.4   **Storing and Retrieving Variables in a Worksheet**   890

     Using a Named Range to Read and Write Numbers from a Spreadsheet   891

     Reading and Writing to Cells That Are Not Named   892

     Using the Cells Functions to Read and Write to Cells   892

     Reading from within a Function   893

D.5   **Using Excel Functions from within VBA**   893

     Using VBA to Compute the Black-Scholes Formula   894

     The Object Browser   895

D.6   **Checking for Conditions**   896

D.7   **Arrays**   897

     Defining Arrays   897

D.8   **Iteration**   899

     A Simple *for* Loop   899

     Creating a Binomial Tree   900

     Other Kinds of Loops   901

D.9   **Reading and Writing Arrays**   901

     Arrays as Outputs   901

     Arrays as Inputs   903

D.10   **Miscellany**   904

     Getting Excel to Generate Macros for You   904

     Using Multiple Modules   905

     Recalculation Speed   905

     Debugging   906

     Creating an Add-In   906

Glossary   907

Bibliography   921

Index   935

FOREWORD

Derivatives have moved to the center of modern corporate finance, investments, and the management of financial institutions. They have also had a profound impact on other management functions such as business strategy, operations management, and marketing. A major drawback, however, to making the power of derivatives accessible to students and practitioners alike has been the relatively high degree of mathematical sophistication required for understanding the underlying concepts and tools.

With Robert McDonald's *Derivatives Markets,* we finally have a derivatives text that is a wonderful blend of the economics and mathematics of derivatives pricing and easily accessible to MBA students and advanced undergraduates. It is a special pleasure for me to introduce this new edition, since I have long had the highest regard for the author's professional achievements and personal qualities.

The book's orientation is neither overly sophisticated nor watered down, but rather a mix of intuition and rigor that creates an inherent flexibility for the structuring of a derivatives course. The author begins with an introduction to forwards and futures and motivates the presentation with a discussion of their use in insurance and risk management. He looks in detail at forwards and futures on stocks, stock indices, currencies, interest rates, and swaps. His treatment of options then follows logically from concepts developed in the earlier chapters. The heart of the text—an extensive treatment of the binomial option model and the Black-Scholes equation—showcases the author's crystal-clear writing and logical development of concepts. Excellent chapters on financial engineering, security design, corporate applications, and real options follow and shed light on how the concepts can be applied to actual problems.

The last third of the text provides an advanced treatment of the most important concepts of derivatives discussed earlier. This part can be used by itself in an advanced derivatives course, or as a useful reference in introductory courses. A rigorous development of the Black-Scholes equation, exotic options, and interest rate models are presented using Brownian Motion and Itô's Lemma. Monte Carlo simulation methods are also discussed in detail. New chapters on volatility and credit risk provide a clear discussion of these fast-developing areas.

Derivatives concepts are now required for every advanced finance topic. Therefore, it is essential to introduce these concepts at an early stage of MBA and undergraduate business or economics programs, and in a fashion that most students can understand. This text achieves this goal in such an appealing, inviting way that students will actually enjoy their journey toward an understanding of derivatives.

EDUARDO S. SCHWARTZ

PREFACE

Thirty years ago the Black-Scholes formula was new, and derivatives was an esoteric and specialized subject. Today, a basic knowledge of derivatives is necessary to understand modern finance. For example, corporations routinely hedge and insure using derivatives, finance activities with structured products, and use derivatives models in capital budgeting. This book will help you to understand the derivative instruments that exist, how they are used, who sells them, how they are priced, and how the tools and concepts are useful more broadly in finance.

Derivatives is necessarily an analytical subject, but I have tried throughout to emphasize intuition and to provide a common sense way to think about the formulas. I do assume that a reader of this book already understands basic financial concepts such as present value, and elementary statistical concepts such as mean and standard deviation. Most of the book should thus be accessible to anyone who has studied elementary finance. For those who want to understand the subject at a deeper level, the last part of the book develops the Black-Scholes *approach* to pricing derivatives and presents some of the standard mathematical tools used in option pricing, such as Itô's Lemma. There are also chapters dealing with applications: corporate applications, financial engineering, and real options.

In order to make the book accessible to readers with widely varying backgrounds and experiences, I use a "tiered" approach to the mathematics. Chapters 1–9 emphasize present value calculations, and there is almost no calculus until Chapter 18.

Most of the calculations in this book can be replicated using Excel spreadsheets on the CD-ROM that comes with the book. These allow you to experiment with the pricing models and build your own spreadsheets. The spreadsheets on the CD-ROM contain option pricing functions written in Visual Basic for Applications, the macro language in Excel. You can easily incorporate these functions into your own spreadsheets. You can also examine and modify the Visual Basic code for the functions. Appendix D explains how to write such functions in Excel and documentation on the CD-ROM lists the option pricing functions that come with the book. Relevant built-in Excel functions are also mentioned throughout the book.

PLAN OF THE BOOK

This book grew from my teaching notes for two MBA derivatives courses at Northwestern University's Kellogg School of Management. The two courses roughly correspond to the first two-thirds and last third of the book. The first course is a general introduction to derivative products (principally futures, options, swaps, and structured products), the markets in which they trade, and applications. The second course is for those wanting a deeper understanding of the pricing models and the ability to perform their own analysis. The advanced course assumes that students know basic statistics and have seen calculus, and from that point develops the Black-Scholes option-pricing framework as fully as possible. No one expects that a 10-week MBA-level course will produce rocket scientists, but mathematics is the language of derivatives and it would be cheating students to pretend otherwise.

You may want to cover the material in a different order than it occurs in the book, so I wrote chapters to allow flexible use of the material. I indicate several possible paths through the material below. In many cases it is possible to hop around. For example, I wrote the book expecting that the chapters on lognormality and Monte Carlo simulation might be used in a first derivatives course.

The book has five parts plus appendixes. **Part 1** introduces the basic building blocks of derivatives: forward contracts and call and put options. Chapters 2 and 3 examine these basic instruments and some common hedging and investment strategies. Chapter 4 illustrates the use of derivatives as risk management tools and discusses why firms might care about risk management. These chapters focus on understanding the contracts and strategies, but not on pricing.

Part 2 considers the pricing of forward, futures, and swaps contracts. In these contracts, you are obligated to buy an asset at a pre-specified price, at a future date. The main question is: What is the pre-specified price, and how is it determined? Chapter 5 examines forwards and futures on financial assets, Chapter 6 discusses commodities, and Chapter 7 looks at bond and interest rate forward contracts. Chapter 8 shows how swap prices can be deduced from forward prices.

Part 3 studies option pricing. Chapter 9 develops intuition about options prior to delving into the mechanics of option pricing. Chapters 10 and 11 cover binomial option pricing and Chapter 12, the Black-Scholes formula and option Greeks. Chapter 13 explains delta-hedging, which is the technique used by market-makers when managing the risk of an option position, and how hedging relates to pricing. Chapter 14 looks at a few important exotic options, including Asian options, barrier options, compound options, and exchange options.

The techniques and formulas in earlier chapters are applied in **Part 4.** Chapter 15 covers financial engineering, which is the creation of new financial products from the derivatives building blocks in earlier chapters. Debt and equity pricing, compensation options, and mergers are covered in Chapter 16. Chapter 17 studies real options—the application of derivatives models to the valuation and management of physical investments.

Finally, **Part 5** explores pricing and hedging in depth. The material in this part explains in more detail the structure and assumptions underlying the standard derivatives models. Chapter 18 covers the lognormal model and shows how the Black-Scholes formula is an expected value. Chapter 19 discusses Monte Carlo valuation, a powerful and commonly used pricing technique. Chapter 20 explains what it means to say that stock prices follow a diffusion process, and also covers Itô's Lemma, which is a key result in the study of derivatives. (At this point you will discover that Itô's Lemma has already been developed intuitively in Chapter 13, using a simple numerical example.)

Chapter 21 derives the Black-Scholes partial differential equation (PDE). Although the Black-Scholes *formula* is famous, the Black-Scholes *equation*, discussed in this chapter, is the more profound result. Chapter 22 covers exotic options in more detail than Chapter 14, including digital barrier options and quantos. Chapter 23 discusses volatility estimation and stochastic volatility pricing models. Chapter 24 shows how the Black-Scholes and binomial analysis apply to bonds and interest rate derivatives. Chapter 25 covers value-at-risk, and Chapter 26 discusses the burgeoning market in credit products.

WHAT IS NEW IN THE SECOND EDITION

There are two new chapters in this edition, covering volatility and credit risk:

- Chapter 23 covers empirical volatility models, such as GARCH and realized volatility; financial instruments that can be used to hedge volatility, such as variance swaps; and pricing models that incorporate jumps and stochastic volatility, such as the Heston model.

- Chapter 26 covers structural models of bankruptcy risk (the Merton model); tranched structures such as collateralized debt obligations; credit default swaps and credit indexes.

There are numerous changes and new examples throughout the book. Among the more important changes are the following:

- An expanded discussion of bond convexity

- An expanded treatment of computing hedge ratios

- An expanded treatment of convertible and callable bonds

- Discussion of the new option expensing rules in FAS 123R and the Bulow-Shoven expensing proposal

- Discussion of a variable prepaid forward on Disney stock issued by Roy Disney

- In-depth discussion of a mandatorily convertible bond issued by Marshall & Ilsley, including pricing and structuring

- The use of simulation to price American options

- Additional discussion of implied volatility

- Enhanced discussion of the link between discounted cash flow valuation and risk-neutral valuation

- An expanded discussion of value-at-risk

- New spreadsheet functions for pricing options with fixed dividends, CEV option pricing, the Merton jump model, and others

NAVIGATING THE MATERIAL

There are potentially many ways to cover the material in this book. The material is generally presented in order of increasing mathematical difficulty, which means that related material is sometimes split across distant chapters. For example, fixed income is covered in Chapters 7 and 24, and exotic options in Chapters 14 and 22. Each of these chapters is at the level of the neighboring chapters. As an illustration of one way to use the book, here is the material I cover in the courses I teach (within the chapters I skip some specific topics due to time constraints):

- Introductory course: 1–6, 7.1, 8–10, 11.1–11.2, 12, 13.1–13.3, 14, 15.4–15.5, 16, 17.

- Advanced course: 13, 18–22, 7, 8, 15.1–15.3, 23, 24, 25, 26.

The table on page xxv outlines some possible sets of chapters to use in courses that have different emphases. There are a few sections of the book that provide background on topics every reader should understand. These include short-sales (Section 1.4), continuous compounding (Appendix B), prepaid forward contracts (Sections 5.1 and 5.2), and zero-coupon bonds and implied forward rates (Section 7.1).

A NOTE ON EXAMPLES

Many of the numerical examples in this book display intermediate steps to assist you in following the calculations. In most cases it will also be possible for you to create a spreadsheet and compute the same answers starting from the basic assumptions. However, numbers displayed in the text are generally rounded to three or four decimal points, while spreadsheet calculations have many more significant digits. This creates a dilemma: Should results in the book match those you would obtain using a spreadsheet, or those you would obtain by computing the displayed equations?

As a general rule, the numerical examples in the book will provide the results you would obtain by entering the equations directly in a spreadsheet. The displayed calculations will help you follow the logic of a calculation, but a spreadsheet will be helpful in reproducing the final result.

SUPPLEMENTS

A robust package of ancillary materials for both instructors and students accompanies the text.

TABLE 1　　Possible chapters for different courses. Chapters marked with a "y" are strongly recommended, those marked with a "*" are recommended, and those with a "†" fit with the track, but are optional. The advanced course assumes students have already taken a basic course. Sections 1.4, 5.1, 5.2, 7.1, and Appendix B are recommended background for all introductory courses.

	Introductory				Advanced
	General	Futures	Options	Risk Management	
1. Introduction	y	y	y	y	
2. Intro. to Forwards and Options	y	y	y	y	
3. Insurance, Collars, and Other Strategies	y	y	y	y	
4. Intro. to Risk Management	*	*	y	y	
5. Financial Forwards and Futures	y	y	y	y	
6. Commodity Forwards and Futures	*	y	†	*	
7. Interest Rate Forwards and Futures	*	y		*	y
8. Swaps	y	y	†	y	y
9. Parity and Other Option Relationships	*	†	y	†	
10. Binomial Option Pricing: I	y	*	y	y	
11. Binomial Option Pricing: II	*		*		
12. The Black-Scholes Formula	y	*	y	y	
13. Market-Making and Delta-Hedging	†		y	*	y
14. Exotic Options: I	†		y	*	
15. Financial Engineering	*	*	*	y	*
16. Corporate Applications	†		*	*	
17. Real Options	†		*	*	
18. The Lognormal Distribution	†		*	*	y
19. Monte Carlo Valuation	†		*	*	y
20. Brownian Motion and Itô's Lemma					y
21. The Black-Scholes Equation					y
22. Exotic Options: II					y
23. Volatility					y
24. Interest Rate Models					y
25. Value at Risk				y	y
26. Credit Risk				*	y

Instructor's Resources

For instructors, an extensive set of online tools is available for download from the catalog page for *Derivatives Markets* at **www.aw-bc.com/finance**.

An online **Instructor's Solutions Manual** by Mark Cassano, University of Calgary, and Rüdiger Fahlenbrach, Ohio State University, contains complete solutions to all end-of-chapter problems in the text and spreadsheet solutions to selected problems.

The online **Test Bank** by Matthew W. Will, University of Indianapolis, features approximately ten to fifteen multiple-choice questions, five short-answer questions, and one longer essay question for each chapter of the book.

The Test Bank is available in both print and electronic formats, including Windows or Macintosh *TestGen* files and Microsoft Word files. The *TestGen* and Test Bank are available online at **http://www.aw-bc.com/irc**.

Online **PowerPoint slides,** developed by Charles Cao, Pennsylvania State University; Ufuk Ince, University of Washington; and Ekaterina Emm, Georgia State University, provide lecture outlines and selected art from the book. Copies of the slides can be downsized and distributed to students to facilitate note taking during class.

The Instructors Resource Disk contains the computerized Test Bank files (TestGen), the Instructor Manual files (Word), the Test Bank files (Word) and PowerPoint files.

Student Resources

A printed **Solutions Manual** by Mark Cassano, University of Calgary and Rüdiger Fahlenbrach, Ohio State University, provides answers to all the even-numbered problems in the textbook.

New to this edition, **Practice Problems and Solutions**, by Rüdiger Fahlenbrach, Ohio State University, contains additional problems and worked-out solutions for each chapter of the textbook.

Spreadsheets with user-defined option pricing functions in Excel are included on a CD-ROM packaged with the book. These Excel functions are written in VBA, with the code accessible and modifiable via the Visual Basic editor built into Excel. These spreadsheets and any updates are also posted on the book's Web site.

ACKNOWLEDGMENTS

Kellogg student Tejinder Singh catalyzed the book in 1994 by asking that the Kellogg Finance Department offer an advanced derivatives course. Kathleen Hagerty and I initially co-taught that course and my part of the course notes (developed with Kathleen's help and feedback) evolved into the last third of this book.

In preparing the second edition, I received invaluable assistance from Rüdiger Fahlenbrach, Ohio State University, who read much of the new material with a critical eye, and who both caught mistakes and offered valuable suggestions. Numerous other students, colleagues, and readers provided comments on the first edition. Colleagues in the Kellogg finance department who were generous with their time include Torben Andersen, Kathleen Hagerty, Ravi Jagannathan, Deborah Lucas, Mitchell Petersen, Ernst Schaumburg, Costis Skiadas, and David Stowell. Many Kellogg MBA and Ph.D. students helped, but I want to especially thank Arne Staal, Caroline Sasseville, and Alex

Wolf. Others who reviewed new material include David Bates, University of Iowa; Luca Benzoni, University of Minnesota; Mikhail Chernov, Columbia University; and Darrell Duffie, Stanford University. Mark Schroder, Michigan State University, kindly provided code to calculate the non-central chi-squared distribution, and Kellogg student Scott Freemon implemented this code in VBA.

A special note of thanks goes to David Hait, president of OptionMetrics, for permission to include options data on the CD-ROM.

I also received help and comments from George Allayanis, University of Virginia; Jeremy Bulow, Stanford University; Raul Guerrero, Dynamic Decisions; Darrell Karolyi, Compensation Strategies, Inc.; C. F. Lee, Rutgers University; David Nachman, University of Georgia; Anil Shivdasani, University of North Carolina; and Nicholas Wonder, Western Washington University.

I would like to particularly thank those who provided valuable feedback for the second edition, including Turan Bali, Baruch College, City University of New York; Philip Bond, Wharton School, University of Pennsylvania; Michael Brandt, Duke University; Charles Cao, Pennsylvania State University; Bruce Grundy, Melbourne Business School, Australia; Shantaram Hegde, University of Connecticut; Frank Leiber, Bell Atlantic; Ehud Ronn, University of Texas, Austin; Nejat Seyhun, University of Michigan; John Stansfield, University of Missouri, Columbia; Christopher Stivers, University of Georgia; Joel Vanden, Dartmouth College; Louis Charbonneau, Concordia University; and Guofu Zhou, Washington University, St. Louis.

I would be remiss not to acknowledge those who assisted with the first edition, including Tom Arnold, Louisiana State University; David Bates, University of Iowa; Luca Benzoni, University of Minnesota; Mark Broadie, Columbia University; Mark A. Cassano, University of Calgary; George M. Constantinides, University of Chicago; Kent Daniel, Northwestern University; Jan Eberly, Northwestern University; Virginia France, University of Illinois; Steven Freund, Suffolk University; Rob Gertner, University of Chicago; Kathleen Hagerty, Northwestern University; David Haushalter, University of Oregon; James E. Hodder, University of Wisconsin–Madison; Ravi Jagannathan, Northwestern University; Avraham Kamara, University of Washington; Kenneth Kavajecz, Wharton School, University of Pennsylvania; Arvind Krishnamurthy, Northwestern University; Dennis Lasser, State University of New York at Binghamton; Cornelis A. Los, Kent State University; Deborah Lucas, Northwestern University; Alan Marcus, Boston College; Mitchell Petersen, Northwestern University; Todd Pulvino, Northwestern University; Ernst Schaumburg, Northwestern University; Eduardo Schwartz, University of California–Los Angeles; David Shimko, Risk Capital Management Partners, Inc.; Anil Shivdasani, University of North Carolina-Chapel Hill; Costis Skiadas, Northwestern University; Donald Smith, Boston University; David Stowell, Northwestern University; Alex Triantis, University of Maryland; and Zhenyu Wang, Yale University. The following served as software reviewers: James Bennett, University of Massachusetts–Boston; Gordon H. Dash, University of Rhode Island; Adam Schwartz, University of Mississippi; and Robert E. Whaley, Duke University.

Special thanks are due to George Constantinides, Jennie France, Kathleen Hagerty, Ken Kavajecz, Alan Marcus, Costis Skiadas, and Alex Triantis for their willingness to read and comment upon some of the material multiple times and for class-testing. Mark Broadie generously provided his pricing software, which I used both to compute the Heston model and to double-check my own calculations.

I thank Rüdiger Fahlenbrach, Mark Cassano, Matt Will, and Charles Cao for their excellent work on the ancillary materials for this book. In addition, Rüdiger Fahlenbrach, Paskalis Glabadanidis, Jeremy Graveline, Dmitry Novikov, and Krishnamurthy Subramanian served as accuracy checkers for the book and Andy Kaplin provided programming assistance.

Among practitioners who helped, I thank Galen Burghardt of Carr Futures, Andy Moore of El Paso Corporation, Brice Hill of Intel, Alex Jacobson of the International Securities Exchange, and Blair Wellensiek of Tradelink, L.L.C.

With any book, there are many long-term intellectual debts. From the many, I want to single out two. I had the good fortune to take several classes from Robert Merton at MIT while I was a graduate student. Every derivatives book is deeply in his debt, and this one is no exception. His classic papers from the 1970s are as essential today as they were 30 years ago. I also learned an enormous amount working with Dan Siegel, with whom I wrote several papers on real options. Dan's death in 1991 at the age of 35 was a great loss to the profession, as well as to me personally.

The editorial and production team at Addison-Wesley made it clear from the outset that their goal was to produce a high-quality book. I was lucky to have the project overseen by Addison Wesley's talented and tireless Finance Editor, Donna Battista. Project Manager Mary Clare McEwing expertly kept track of myriad details and offered excellent advice when I needed a sounding board. Development Editor Marjorie Singer Anderson offered innumerable suggestions, improving the manuscript significantly. Production Supervisor, Nancy Fenton marshalled forces to turn manuscript into a physical book. Among those forces were the excellent teams at Elm Street Publishing Services and Techsetters. I received numerous compliments on the design of the first edition, which has been carried through ably into the second. Kudos are due to Gina Kolenda and Rebecca Light for their creativity in text and cover design.

The Addison-Wesley team and I have tried hard to minimize errors, including the use of the accuracy checkers noted above. Nevertheless, of course, I alone bear responsibility for remaining errors. Errata and software updates will be available at **www.aw-bc.com/mcdonald.** Please let us know if you do find errors so we can update the list.

I produced the original manuscript and revision using Gnu Emacs and MikTeX, extraordinarily powerful and robust tools for authors. I am deeply grateful to the worldwide community that produces and supports this software.

My deepest and most heartfelt thanks go to my family. Through both editions I have relied heavily on their understanding, love, support, and tolerance. This book is dedicated to my wife, Irene Freeman, and children Claire, David, and Henry.

RLM

Robert L. McDonald is Erwin P. Nemmers Distinguished Professor of Finance at North-western University's Kellogg School of Management, where he has taught since 1984. He is co-Editor of the Review of Financial Studies *and has been Associate Editor of the* Journal of Finance, Journal of Financial and Quantitative Analysis, Management Science, *and other journals. He has a BA in Economics from the University of North Carolina at Chapel Hill and a Ph.D. in Economics from MIT.*

CHAPTER 1

Introduction to Derivatives

Risk is the central element that influences financial behavior.

—Robert C. Merton (1999)

The world of finance and capital markets has undergone a stunning transformation in the last 30 years. Simple stocks and bonds now seem almost quaint alongside the dazzling, fast-paced, and seemingly arcane world of futures, options, swaps, and other "new" financial products. (The word "new" is in quotes because it turns out that some of these products have been around for hundreds of years.)

Frequently this world pops up in the popular press: Procter & Gamble lost $150 million in 1994, Barings bank lost $1.3 billion in 1995, Long-Term Capital Management lost $3.5 billion in 1998 and (according to some press accounts) almost brought the world financial system to its knees.[1] What is *not* in the headlines is that, most of the time, for most companies and most users, these financial products are an everyday part of business. Just as companies routinely issue debt and equity, they also routinely use swaps to fix the cost of production inputs, futures contracts to hedge foreign exchange risk, and options to compensate employees, to mention just a few examples.

1.1 WHAT IS A DERIVATIVE?

Options, futures, and swaps are examples of derivatives. A **derivative** is a financial instrument (or more simply, an agreement between two people) that has a value determined by the price of something else. For example, a bushel of corn is not a derivative; it is a commodity with a value determined by the price of corn. However, you could enter into an agreement with a friend that says: If the price of a bushel of corn in one year is greater than $3, you will pay the friend $1. If the price of corn is less than $3, the friend will pay you $1. This is a derivative in the sense that you have an agreement with a value depending on the price of something else (corn, in this case).

You might think: "That's not a derivative; that's just a bet on the price of corn." So it is: Derivatives can be thought of as bets on the price of something. But don't

---

[1] A readable summary of these and other infamous derivatives-related losses is in Jorion (2001).

automatically think the term "bet" is pejorative. Suppose your family grows corn and your friend's family buys corn to mill into cornmeal. The bet provides insurance: You earn $1 if your family's corn sells for a low price; this supplements your income. Your friend earns $1 if the corn his family buys is expensive; this offsets the high cost of corn. Viewed in this light, the bet hedges you both against unfavorable outcomes. The contract has reduced risk for both of you.

Investors could also use this kind of contract simply to speculate on the price of corn. In this case the contract is not insurance. And that is a key point: *It is not the contract itself, but how it is used, and who uses it, that determines whether or not it is risk-reducing.* Context is everything.

Although we've just defined a derivative, if you are new to the subject the implications of the definition will probably not be obvious right away. You will come to a deeper understanding of derivatives as we progress through the book, studying different products and their underlying economics.

Uses of Derivatives

What are reasons someone might use derivatives? Here are some motives:

Risk management   Derivatives are a tool for companies and other users to reduce risks. The corn example above illustrates this in a simple way: The farmer—a seller of corn—enters into a contract which makes a payment when the price of corn is low. This contract reduces the risk of loss for the farmer, who we therefore say is **hedging.** It is common to think of derivatives as forbiddingly complex, but many derivatives are simple and familiar. Every form of insurance is a derivative, for example. Automobile insurance is a bet on whether you will have an accident. If you wrap your car around a tree, your insurance is valuable; if the car remains intact, it is not.

Speculation   Derivatives can serve as investment vehicles. As you will see later in the book, derivatives can provide a way to make bets that are highly leveraged (that is, the potential gain or loss on the bet can be large relative to the initial cost of making the bet) and tailored to a specific view. For example, if you want to bet that the S&P 500 stock index will be between 1300 and 1400 one year from today, derivatives can be constructed to let you do that.

Reduced transaction costs   Sometimes derivatives provide a lower-cost way to effect a particular financial transaction. For example, the manager of a mutual fund may wish to sell stocks and buy bonds. Doing this entails paying fees to brokers and paying other trading costs, such as the bid-ask spread, which we will discuss later. It is possible to trade derivatives instead and achieve the same economic effect as if stocks had actually been sold and replaced by bonds. Using the derivative might result in lower transaction costs than actually selling stocks and buying bonds.

Regulatory arbitrage   It is sometimes possible to circumvent regulatory restrictions, taxes, and accounting rules by trading derivatives. Derivatives are often used, for example, to achieve the economic sale of stock (receive cash and eliminate the risk of holding the stock) while still maintaining physical possession of the stock. This transaction may allow the owner to defer taxes on the sale of the stock, or retain voting rights, without the risk of holding the stock.

These are common reasons for using derivatives. The general point is that derivatives provide an alternative to a simple sale or purchase, and thus increase the range of possibilities for an investor or manager seeking to accomplish some goal.

Perspectives on Derivatives

How you think about derivatives depends on who you are. In this book we will think about three distinct perspectives on derivatives:

The end-user perspective   End-users are the corporations, investment managers, and investors who enter into derivative contracts for the reasons listed in the previous section: to manage risk, speculate, reduce costs, or avoid a rule or regulation. End-users have a goal (for example, risk reduction) and care about how a derivative helps to meet that goal.

The market-maker perspective   Market-makers are intermediaries, traders who will buy derivatives from customers who wish to sell, and sell derivatives to customers who wish to buy. In order to make money, market-makers charge a spread: They buy at a low price and sell at a high price. In this respect market-makers are like grocers who buy at the low wholesale price and sell at the higher retail price. Market-makers are also like grocers in that their inventory reflects customer demands rather than their own preferences: As long as shoppers buy paper towels, the grocer doesn't care whether they buy the decorative or super-absorbent style. After dealing with customers, market-makers are left with whatever position results from accommodating customer demands. Market-makers typically hedge this risk and thus are deeply concerned about the mathematical details of pricing and hedging.

The economic observer   Finally, we can look at the use of derivatives, the activities of the market-makers, the organization of the markets, the logic of the pricing models, and try to make sense of everything. This is the activity of the economic observer. Regulators must often don their economic observer hats when deciding whether and how to regulate a certain activity or market participant.

These three perspectives are intertwined throughout the book, but as a general point, in the early chapters the book emphasizes the end-user perspective. In the late chapters, the book emphasizes the market-maker perspective. At all times, however, the economic observer is interested in making sense of everything.

Financial Engineering and Security Design

One of the major ideas in derivatives—perhaps *the* major idea—is that it is generally possible to create a given payoff in multiple ways. The construction of a given financial product from other products is sometimes called **financial engineering.** The fact that this is possible has several implications. First, since market-makers need to hedge their positions, this idea is central in understanding how market-making works. The market-maker sells a contract to an end-user, and then creates an offsetting position that pays him if it is necessary to pay the customer. This creates a hedged position.

Second, the idea that a given contract can be replicated often suggests how it can be customized. The market-maker can, in effect, turn dials to change the risk, initial premium, and payment characteristics of a derivative. These changes permit the creation of a product that is more appropriate for a given situation.

Third, it is often possible to improve intuition about a given derivative by realizing that it is equivalent to something we already understand.

Finally, because there are multiple ways to create a payoff, the regulatory arbitrage discussed above can be difficult to stop. Distinctions existing in the tax code, or in regulations, may not be enforceable, since a particular security or derivative that is regulated or taxed may be easily replaced by one that is treated differently but has the same economic profile.

A theme running throughout the book is that derivative products can generally be constructed from other products.

1.2   The Role of Financial Markets

We take for granted headlines saying that the Dow Jones Industrial Average has gone up 100 points, the dollar has fallen against the yen, and interest rates have risen. But why do we care about these things? Is the rise and fall of a particular financial index (such as the Dow Jones Industrial Average) simply a way to keep score, to track winners and losers in the economy? Is watching the stock market like watching sports, where we root for certain players and teams—a tale told by journalists, full of sound and fury, but signifying nothing?

Financial markets in fact have an enormous, often underappreciated, impact on everyday life. To help us understand the role of financial markets we will consider the Average family, living in Anytown. Joe and Sarah Average have 2.3 children and both work for the XYZ Co., the dominant employer in Anytown. Their income pays for their mortgage, transportation, food, clothing, and medical care. What is left over goes toward savings earmarked for their children's college tuition and their own retirement.

What role do global financial markets and derivatives play in the lives of the Averages?

Financial Markets and the Averages

The Averages are largely unaware of the ways in which financial markets affect their lives. Here are a few:

- The Average's employer, XYZ Co., has an ongoing need for money to finance operations and investments. It is not dependent on the local bank for funds because it can raise the money it needs by issuing stocks and bonds in global markets.

- XYZ Co. insures itself against certain risks. In addition to having property and casualty insurance for its buildings, it uses global derivatives markets to protect itself against adverse currency, interest rate, and commodity price changes. By being able to manage these risks, XYZ is less likely to go into bankruptcy, and less likely to throw the Averages into unemployment.

- The Averages invest in mutual funds. As a result they pay lower transaction costs than if they tried to achieve comparable diversification by buying individual stocks.

- Since both Averages work at XYZ, they run the risk that if XYZ does fall on hard times they will lose their jobs. The mutual funds in which they invest own stocks in a broad array of companies, ensuring that the failure of any one company will not wipe out their savings.

- The Averages live in an area susceptible to tornadoes and insure their home. If their insurance company were completely local, it could not offer tornado insurance because one disaster would leave it unable to pay claims. By selling tornado risk in global markets, the insurance company can in effect pool Anytown tornado risk with Japan earthquake risk and Florida hurricane risk. This pooling makes insurance available at lower rates.

- The Averages borrowed money from Anytown bank to buy their house. The bank sold the mortgage to other investors, freeing itself from interest rate and default risk associated with the mortgage, leaving that to others. Because the risk of their mortgage is borne by those willing to pay the highest price for it, the Averages get the lowest possible mortgage rate.

In all of these examples, particular financial functions and risks have been split up and parceled out to others. A bank that sells a mortgage does not have to bear the risk of the mortgage. An insurance company does not bear all the risk of a disaster. Risk-sharing is one of the most important functions of financial markets.

Risk-Sharing

Risk is an inevitable part of our lives and all economic activity. As we've seen in the example of the Averages, financial markets enable the financial losses from at least some of these risks to be shared. Risk arises from natural events, such as earthquakes, floods, and hurricanes, and from unnatural events such as wars and political conflicts. Drought and pestilence destroy agriculture every year in some part of the world. Some economies boom as others falter. On a more personal scale, people are born, die, retire, find jobs, lose jobs, marry, divorce, and become ill.

In the face of this risk, it seems natural to have arrangements where the lucky share with the unlucky. Risk-sharing occurs informally in families and communities. The insurance market makes formal risk-sharing possible. Buyers pay a premium to obtain various kinds of insurance, such as homeowner's insurance. Total collected premiums are then available to help those whose houses burn down. The lucky, meanwhile, did not need insurance and have lost their premium. The market makes it possible for the lucky to help the unlucky.

In the business world, changes in commodity prices, exchange rates, and interest rates can be the financial equivalent of a house burning down. If the dollar becomes expensive relative to the yen, some companies are helped and others are hurt. It makes sense for there to be a mechanism enabling companies to exchange this risk, so that the lucky can, in effect, help the unlucky.

Even insurers need to share risk. Consider an insurance company that provides earthquake insurance for California residents. A large earthquake could generate claims sufficient to bankrupt a stand-alone insurance company. Thus, insurance companies often use the *reinsurance market* to buy, from reinsurers, insurance against large claims. Reinsurers pool different kinds of risks, thereby enabling insurance risks to become more widely held.

In some cases, reinsurers further share risks by issuing **catastrophe bonds**—bonds that the issuer need not repay if there is a specified event, such as a large earthquake, causing large insurance claims. Bondholders willing to accept earthquake risk can buy these bonds, in exchange for greater interest payments on the bond if there is no earthquake. An earthquake bond allows earthquake risk to be borne by exactly those investors who wish to bear it.

Although there are mechanisms for sharing many kinds of risks, some have argued that significantly more risk-sharing is possible and desirable. The economist Robert Shiller (Shiller, 2003) envisions the creation of entirely new markets for risk-sharing, including home equity insurance (to trade risks associated with house prices), income-linked loans (personal loans that need not be fully repaid if wages decline in a particular occupation), and macro insurance (contracts with payments linked to national incomes). While these markets do not yet exist, there is a trend toward more inclusive markets for risk transfer. For example, Goldman Sachs and Deutsche Bank have recently created an "economic derivatives" market in which it is possible to buy claims with payouts based on economic statistics. The box on page 7 discusses this market.

You might be wondering what this discussion has to do with the notions of diversifiable and nondiversifiable risk familiar from portfolio theory. Risk is **diversifiable risk** if it is unrelated to other risks. The risk that a lightning strike will cause a factory to burn down, for example, is idiosyncratic and hence diversifiable. If many investors share a small piece of this risk, it has no significant effect on anyone. Risk that does not vanish when spread across many investors is **nondiversifiable risk.** The risk of a stock market crash, for example, is nondiversifiable.

Financial markets in theory serve two purposes. Markets permit diversifiable risk to be widely shared. This is efficient: By definition, diversifiable risk vanishes when it is widely shared. At the same time, financial markets permit nondiversifiable risk, which does not vanish when shared, to be held by those most willing to hold it. Thus, *the fundamental economic idea underlying the concepts and markets discussed in this book is that the existence of risk-sharing mechanisms benefits everyone.*

1.3 Derivatives in Practice

Derivatives use and the variety of derivatives have grown over the last 30 years.

Economic Derivatives

Government agencies in most countries periodically announce economic statistics, such as the number of jobs in the economy, production in different sectors, and the level of sales. These statistics provide information about the performance of the economy and—since policy makers rely upon them—can provide clues to future government policy. Consequently, money managers, dealers, and other market participants pay close attention to these statistics; their release often results in a flurry of trading activity and changes in stock and bond prices.

Because of the importance of these statistics for financial markets, Goldman Sachs and Deutsche Bank created a market in economic derivatives, in which it is possible to trade claims with payoffs based on these statistics. Specifically, beginning in late 2002, it became possible to trade claims based on employment (U.S. nonfarm payrolls), industrial production (the Purchasing Manager's Index), and U.S. retail sales. A European consumer price index was added in 2003. Participants can, in effect, bet on whether the statistics will be higher or lower than expected.

Whereas it is possible to trade stocks and bonds on any business day, the market for most economic derivatives is open only briefly before the government releases the statistic. Specifically, if the nonfarm payroll number is to be released on a Friday, on the day before there will be one hour during which participants can submit orders to buy or sell various derivatives based on the nonfarm payroll number. At the end of the hour, buyers are matched against sellers and prices are determined using a procedure known as a Dutch auction.[2] This market permits the trading of many different kinds of claims that we will discuss in later chapters, including forwards, calls, puts, spreads, straddles, strangles, and digital options.

Growth in Derivatives Trading

The introduction of derivatives in a market often coincides with an increase in price risk in that market. Currencies were officially permitted to float in 1971 when the gold standard was officially abandoned. OPEC's 1973 reduction in the supply of oil was followed by high and variable oil prices. U.S. interest rates became more volatile following inflation and recessions in the 1970s. The market for natural gas has been deregulated gradually since 1978, resulting in a volatile market in recent years. The deregulation of electricity began during the 1990s. Figures 1.1, 1.2, and 1.3 show the changes for oil prices, exchange rates, and interest rates. The link between price variability and the development of derivatives markets is natural—there is no need to manage risk when

[2]In a Dutch auction there is a single price that is paid by buyers who are willing to pay that price or more, and that is received by sellers who are willing to accept that price or less.

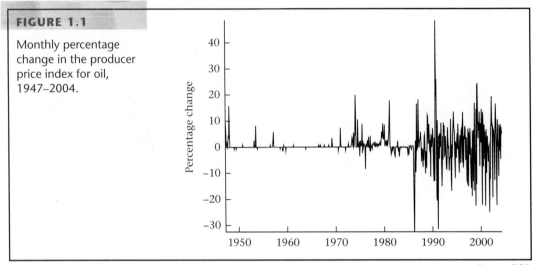

FIGURE 1.1

Monthly percentage change in the producer price index for oil, 1947–2004.

Source: DRI.

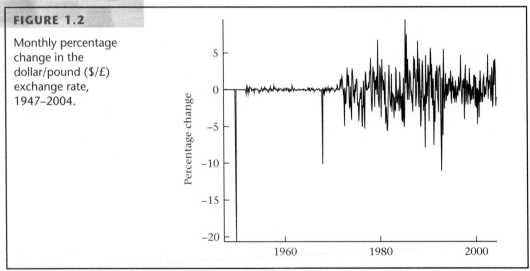

FIGURE 1.2

Monthly percentage change in the dollar/pound ($/£) exchange rate, 1947–2004.

Source: DRI.

there is no risk.[3] When risk does exist, we would expect that markets will develop to permit efficient risk-sharing. Investors who have the most tolerance for risk will bear more of it, and risk-bearing will be widely spread among investors.

....

[3]It is sometimes argued that the existence of derivatives markets can increase the price variability of the underlying asset or commodity. Without some price risk in the first place, however, the derivatives market is unlikely to exist.

FIGURE 1.3

Monthly change in
3-month Treasury bill
rate, 1947–2004.

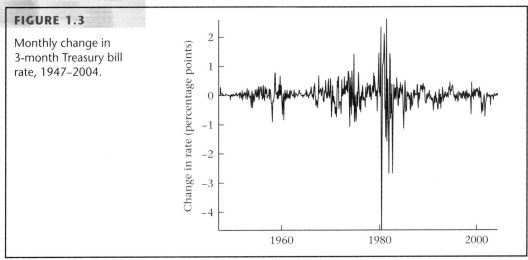

Source: DRI.

FIGURE 1.4

Millions of contracts
traded annually at the
Chicago Board of Trade
(CBT), Chicago
Mercantile Exchange
(CME), and the New
York Mercantile
Exchange (NYMEX),
1970–2002.

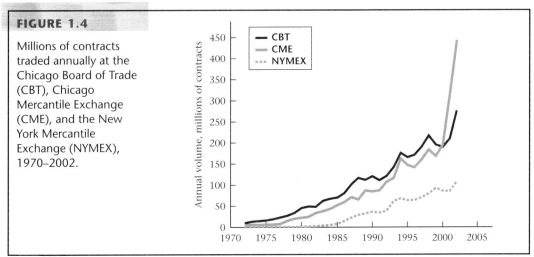

Source: CRB Commodity Yearbook.

A futures exchange is an organized and regulated marketplace for trading futures contracts, a kind of derivative. Figure 1.4 depicts futures contract volume for the three largest U.S. futures exchanges over the last 30 years. Clearly, the usage of futures contracts has grown significantly. Exchanges in other countries have generally experienced comparable or greater growth. In 2002, Eurex, an electronic exchange headquartered in Frankfurt, Germany, traded 528 million contracts, the largest trading volume of any futures exchange in the world.

TABLE 1.1		Examples of futures contracts traded on the Chicago Board of Trade (CBT), Chicago Mercantile Exchange (CME), and the New York Mercantile Exchange (NYMEX).

CBT	**CME**	**NYMEX**
30-day Average Federal Funds	S&P 500 index	Crude oil
10-year U.S. Treasury bonds	NASDAQ 100 index	Natural gas
Municipal Bond Index	Eurodollars	Heating oil
Corn	Nikkei 225	Gasoline
Soybeans	Pork bellies	Gold
Wheat	Heating and cooling degree-days	Copper
Oats	Japanese yen	Electricity

Table 1.1 provides examples of futures contracts traded at these exchanges.[4] Much commercial derivatives trading occurs in the **over-the-counter market,** where buyers and sellers transact with banks and dealers rather than on an exchange. It is difficult to obtain statistics for over-the-counter volume. However, in some markets, such as currencies, it is clear that the over-the-counter market is significantly larger than the exchange-traded market.

How Are Derivatives Used?

In recent years the U.S. Securities and Exchange Commission (SEC), Financial Accounting Standards Board (FASB), and the International Accounting Standard Board (IASB) have increased the requirements for corporations to report on their use of derivatives. Nevertheless, surprisingly little is known about how companies actually use derivatives to manage risk. The basic strategies companies use are well-understood—and will be described in this book—but it is not known, for example, what fraction of perceived risk is hedged by a given company, or by all companies in the aggregate. We frequently do not know a company's specific rationale for hedging or not hedging.

We would expect the use of derivatives to vary by type of firm. For example, financial firms, such as banks, are highly regulated and have capital requirements. They may have assets and liabilities in different currencies, with different maturities, and with

----

[4]The table lists only a fraction of the contracts traded at these exchanges. For example, in June 2004, the Chicago Mercantile Exchange Web page listed futures contracts on over 70 different underlying assets ranging from butter to the weather in Amsterdam.

different credit risks. Hence banks could be expected to use interest rate derivatives, currency derivatives, and credit derivatives to manage risks in those areas. Manufacturing firms that buy raw materials and sell in global markets might use commodity and currency derivatives, but their incentives to manage risk are less clear-cut because they are not regulated in the same ways as financial firms.

1.4 BUYING AND SHORT-SELLING FINANCIAL ASSETS

Throughout this book we will talk about buying and selling—and short-selling—assets such as stocks. These basic transactions are so important that it is worth describing the details. First, it is important to understand the costs associated with buying and selling. Second, a very important idea used throughout the book is that of short-sales. The concept of short-selling should be intuitive—a short-sale is just the opposite of a purchase—but for almost everyone it is hard to grasp at first. Even if you are familiar with short sales, you should spend a few minutes reading this section.

Buying an Asset

Suppose you want to buy 100 shares of XYZ stock. This seems simple: If the stock price is $50, 100 shares will cost $50 \times 100 = $5000. However, this calculation ignores transaction costs.

First, there is a commission, which is a transaction fee you pay your broker. A commission for the above order could be $15, or 0.3% of the purchase price.

Second, the term "stock price" is, surprisingly, imprecise. There are in fact two prices, a price at which you can buy, and a price at which you can sell. The price at which you can buy is called the **offer price** or **ask price,** and the price at which you can sell is called the **bid price.** Where do these terms come from?

To buy stock, you can pick up the phone and call a broker. If the stock is not too obscure and your order is not too large, your purchase will probably be completed in a matter of seconds. Have you ever wondered where the stock comes from that you have just bought? It is possible that at the exact same moment, another customer called the broker and put in an order to sell. More likely, however, a market-maker sold you the stock. Market-makers do what their name implies: They make markets. If you want to buy, they sell, and if you want to sell, they buy. In order to earn a living, market-makers sell for a high price and buy for a low price. If you deal with a market-maker, therefore, you buy for a high price and sell for a low price. This difference between the price at which you can buy and the price at which you can sell is called the **bid-ask spread.**[5] In practice the bid-ask spread on the stock you are buying may be $49.75 to $50. This means that you can buy for $50/share and sell for $49.75/share. If you were to buy

---

[5]If you think a bid-ask spread is unreasonable, ask what a world without dealers would be like. Every buyer would have to find a seller, and vice versa. The search would be costly and take time. Dealers, because they maintain inventory, offer an immediate transaction, a service called *immediacy*.

immediately and then sell, you would pay the commission twice, and you would pay the bid-ask spread.

Apparent rapid price fluctuations can occur because of the difference between the bid and ask prices. This is called "bid-ask bounce." If the bid is $49.75 and the ask is $50, a series of buy and sell orders will cause the price at which the stock was last traded to move between $49.75 and $50. The "true" price has not changed, however, because the bid and ask have not changed.

Example 1.1   Suppose XYZ is bid at $49.75 and offered at $50, and the commission is $15. If you buy 100 shares of the stock you pay ($50 × 100) + $15 = $5015. If you immediately sell them again, you receive ($49.75 × 100) − $15 = $4960. Your round trip transaction cost—the difference between what you pay and what you receive from a sale, not counting changes in the bid and ask prices—is $5015 − $4960 = $55.   ≷

Incidentally, this discussion reveals where the terms "bid" and "ask" come from. You might at first think that the terminology is backward. The bid price sounds like it should be what you pay. It is in fact what the *market-maker* pays; hence it is the price at which you sell. The offer price is what the market-maker will sell for—hence it is what you have to pay. The terminology reflects the perspective of the market-maker.

One last point: What happens to your shares after you buy them? Generally they are held by your broker. If you read the fine print on your brokerage contract carefully, your broker typically has the right to lend your shares to another investor. Why would anyone want to borrow your shares? The answer to that brings us to the next topic, short-sales.

Although we have focused here on shares of stock, there are similar issues associated with buying any asset.

Short-Selling

When we buy something, we are said to have a *long* position in that thing. For example, if we buy the stock of XYZ, we pay cash and receive the stock. Some time later, we sell the stock and receive cash. This transaction is *lending*, in the sense that we pay money today and receive money back in the future. The rate of return we receive may not be known in advance (if the stock price goes up a lot, we get a high return; if the stock price goes down, we get a negative return), but it is a kind of loan nonetheless.

The opposite of a long position is a short position. A **short-sale** of XYZ entails borrowing shares of XYZ and then selling them, receiving the cash. Some time later, we buy back the XYZ stock, paying cash for it, and return it to the lender. A short-sale can be viewed, then, as just a way of borrowing money. When you borrow money from a bank, you receive money today and repay it later, paying a rate of interest set in advance. This is also what happens with a short-sale, except that you don't necessarily know the rate you pay to borrow.

There are at least three reasons to short-sell:

1. **Speculation:** A short-sale, considered by itself, makes money if the price of the stock goes down. The idea is to first sell high and then buy low. (With a long position, the idea is to first buy low and then sell high.)

2. **Financing:** A short-sale is a way to borrow money, and it is frequently used as a form of financing. This is very common in the bond market, for example.

3. **Hedging:** You can undertake a short-sale to offset the risk of owning the stock or a derivative on the stock. This is frequently done by market-makers and traders.

These reasons are not mutually exclusive. For example, a market-maker might use a short-sale to simultaneously hedge and finance a position.

Because short-sales can seem confusing, here is a detailed example that illustrates how short-sales work.

Example: Short-selling wine There are markets for many collectible items, such as fine wines. Suppose there is a wine from a particular vintage and producer that you believe to be overpriced. Perhaps you expect a forthcoming review of the wine to be negative, or perhaps you believe that wines soon to be released will be of extraordinary quality, driving down prices of existing wines. Whatever the reason, you think the price will fall. How could you speculate based on this belief?

If you believe prices will rise, you would buy the wine on the market and plan to sell after the price rises. However, if you believe prices will fall, you would do the opposite: Sell today (at the high price) and buy sometime later (at the low price). How can you accomplish this?

In order to sell today, you must first obtain wine to sell. You can do this by borrowing a case from a collector. The collector, of course, will want a promise that you will return the wine at some point; suppose you agree to return it one week later. Having reached agreement, you borrow the wine and then sell it at the market price. After one week, you acquire a replacement case on the market, then return it to the collector from whom you originally borrowed the wine. If the price has fallen, you will have bought the replacement wine for less than the price at which you sold the original, so you make money. If the price has risen, you have lost money. Either way, you have just completed a *short-sale* of wine. The act of buying replacement wine and returning it to the lender is said to be *closing* or *covering* the short position.

Note that short-selling is a way to borrow money. Initially, you received money from selling the wine. A week later you paid the money back (you had to buy a replacement case to return to the lender). The rate of interest you paid was low if the price of the replacement case was low, and high if the price of the replacement case was high.

This example is obviously simplified. We have assumed several points:

- It is easy to find a lender of wine.

- It is easy to buy, at a fair price, satisfactory wine to return to the lender: The wine you buy after one week is a perfect substitute for the wine you borrowed.

TABLE 1.2   Cash flows associated with short-selling a share of IBM for 90 days. Note that the short-seller must pay the dividend, *D*, to the share-lender.

	Day 0	Dividend Ex-Day	Day 90
Action	Borrow shares	—	Return shares
Security	Sell shares	—	Purchase shares
Cash	$+S_0$	$-D$	$-S_{90}$

- The collector from whom you borrowed is not concerned that you will fail to return the borrowed wine.

Example: Short-selling stock   Now consider a short-sale of stock. As with the previous example, when you short-sell stock you borrow the stock and sell it, receiving cash today. At some future date you buy the stock in the market and return it to the original owner. You have cash coming in today, equal to the market value of the stock you short-sell. In the future, you repay the borrowing by buying the asset at its then-current market price and returning the asset—this is like the repayment of a loan. Thus, short-selling a stock is equivalent to borrowing money, except that the interest rate you pay is not known in advance. Rather, it is determined by the change in the stock price. The rate of interest is high if the security rises in price and low if the security falls in price. In effect, the rate of return on the security is the rate at which you borrow. With a short-sale, you are like the *issuer* of a security rather than the buyer of a security.

Suppose you want to short-sell IBM stock for 90 days. Table 1.2 depicts the cash flows. Observe in particular that if the share pays dividends, the short-seller must in turn make dividend payments to the share-lender. This issue did not arise with wine! This dividend payment is taxed to the recipient, just like an ordinary dividend payment, and it is tax-deductible to the short-seller.

Notice that the cash flows in Table 1.2 are exactly the opposite of the cash flows from purchasing the stock. Thus, *short-selling is literally the opposite of buying.*

The Lease Rate of an Asset

We have seen that when you borrow an asset it may be necessary to make payments to the lender. Dividends on short-sold stock are an example of this. We will refer to the payment required by the lender as the **lease rate** of the asset. This concept will arise frequently, and, as we will see, provides a unifying concept for our later discussions of derivatives.

The wine example did not have a lease payment. But under some circumstances it might be necessary to make a payment to borrow wine. Wine does not pay an explicit dividend but does pay an implicit dividend if the owner enjoys seeing bottles in the cellar. The owner might thus require a payment in order to lend a bottle. This would be a lease rate for wine.

Risk and Scarcity in Short-Selling

The preceding examples were simple illustrations of the mechanics and economics of short-selling, and they demonstrate the ideas you will need to understand our discussions of derivatives. It turns out, however, that some of the complexities we skipped over are easy to understand and are important in practice. In this section we use the wine example to illustrate some of these practical issues.

Credit risk   As the short-seller, you have an obligation to the lender to return the wine. The lender fears that you will renege on this obligation. This concern can be addressed with collateral: After you sell the wine, the lender can hold the money you received from selling the wine. You have an obligation to return the wine; the lender keeps the money in the event that you don't.

Holding on to the money will help the lender feel more secure, but after thinking the matter over, the lender will likely want more from you than just the current value of the wine. Suppose you borrow $5000 worth of wine. What happens, the lender will think, if the price of that particular wine rises to $6000 one week later? This is a $1000 loss on your short-sale. In order to return the wine, you will have to pay $6000 for wine you just sold for $5000. Perhaps you cannot afford the extra $1000 and you will fail to return the borrowed wine. The lender, thinking ahead, will be worried at the outset about this possibility and will ask you to provide *more* than the $5000 the wine is worth, say an extra $1000. This extra amount is called a **haircut,** and serves to protect the lender against your failure to return the wine when the price rises.[6]   In practice, short-sellers must have funds—called *capital*—to be able to pay haircuts. The amount of capital places a limit on their ability to short-sell.

Scarcity   As the short-seller, do you need to worry about the short-sale proceeds? The lender is going to have $6000 of your money. Most of this, however, simply reflects your obligation, and we could ask a trustworthy third party, such as a bank, to hold the money so the lender cannot abscond with it. However, when you return the wine, you are going to want your money back, *plus interest*. This raises the question: What rate of interest will the lender pay you? Over the course of the short-sale, the lender can invest your money, earning, say, 6%. The lender could offer to pay you 4% on the funds, thinking to keep as a fee the 2% difference between the 6% earned on the money and the 4% paid to you. What happens if the lender and borrower negotiate?

Here is the interesting point: The rate of interest the lender pays on the collateral is going to depend on how many people want to borrow wine from the particular vintage

---

[6]Note that the lender is not concerned about your failure to perform when the price goes down because the lender has the money!

and producer, and how many are willing to lend it! As a practical matter, it may not be easy to find a lender. If there is high demand for borrowed wine, the lender will offer a low rate of interest, essentially earning a fee for being willing to lend something that is scarce. However, if no one else wants to borrow the wine, the lender might conclude that a small fee is better than nothing and offer you a rate of interest close to the market rate.

The rate paid on collateral is called different things in different markets, the **repo rate** in bond markets and the **short rebate** in the stock market. Whatever it is called, the difference between this rate and the market rate of interest is another cost to your short-sale.

CHAPTER SUMMARY

Derivatives are financial instruments with a payoff determined by the price of something else. They can be used as a tool for risk management and speculation, and to reduce transaction costs or avoid taxes and regulation.

One important function of financial markets is to facilitate optimal risk-sharing. The growth of derivatives markets over the last 50 years has coincided with an increase in the risks evident in various markets. Events such as the 1973 oil shock, the abandonment of fixed exchange rates, and the deregulation of energy markets have created a new role for derivatives.

A short-sale entails borrowing a security, selling it, making dividend (or other cash) payments to the security lender, and then returning it. A short-sale is conceptually the opposite of a purchase. Short-sales can be used for speculation, as a form of financing, or as a way to hedge. Many of the details of short-selling in practice can be understood as a response to credit risk of the short-seller and scarcity of shares that can be borrowed. Short-sellers typically leave the short-sale proceeds on deposit with lenders, along with additional capital called a haircut. The rate paid on this collateral is called the short rebate, and is less than the interest rate.

FURTHER READING

The rest of this book provides an elaboration of themes discussed in this chapter. However, certain chapters are directly related to the discussion. Chapters 2, 3, and 4 introduce forward and option contracts, which are the basic contracts in derivatives, and show how they are used in risk management. Chapter 13 discusses in detail how derivatives market-makers manage their risk, and Chapter 15 explains how derivatives can be combined with instruments such as bonds to create customized risk-management products.

The derivatives exchanges have Web sites that list their contracts. The Web sites for the exchanges in Figure 1.4 are **www.cbot.com** (Chicago Board of Trade), **www.cme. com** (Chicago Mercantile Exchange), and **www.nymex.com** (New York Mercantile Exchange). Economic derivatives are discussed at **www.gs.com/econderivs**.

Jorion (1995) examines in detail one famous "derivatives disaster": Orange County in California. Bernstein (1992) presents a history of the development of financial markets, and Bernstein (1996) discusses the concept of risk measurement and how it evolved over the last 800 years. Miller (1986) discusses origins of past financial innovation, while Merton (1999) and Shiller (2003) provide a stimulating look at possible *future* developments in financial markets. Froot and O'Connell (1999) and Froot (2001) examine the market for catastrophe reinsurance. D'Avolio (2001) explains the economics and practices associated with short-sales. Finally, Lewis (1989) is a classic, funny, insider's account of investment banking, offering a different (to say the least) perspective on the mechanics of global risk-sharing.

PROBLEMS

1.1. Heating degree-day and cooling degree-day futures contracts make payments based on whether the temperature is abnormally hot or cold. Explain why the following businesses might be interested in such a contract:

    a. Soft-drink manufacturers.

    b. Ski-resort operators.

    c. Electric utilities.

    d. Amusement park operators.

1.2. Suppose the businesses in the previous problem use futures contracts to hedge their temperature-related risk. Who do you think might accept the opposite risk?

1.3. ABC stock has a bid price of $40.95 and an ask price of $41.05. Assume there is a $20 brokerage commission.

    a. What amount will you pay to buy 100 shares?

    b. What amount will you receive for selling 100 shares?

    c. Suppose you buy 100 shares, then immediately sell 100 shares with the bid and ask prices being the same in both cases. What is your round-trip transaction cost?

1.4. Repeat the previous problem supposing that the brokerage fee is quoted as 0.3% of the bid or ask price.

1.5. Suppose a security has a bid price of $100 and an ask price of $100.12. At what price can the market-maker purchase a security? At what price can a market-maker sell a security? What is the spread in dollar terms when 100 shares are traded?

1.6. Suppose you short-sell 300 shares of XYZ stock at $30.19 with a commission charge of 0.5%. Supposing you pay commission charges for purchasing the security to cover the short-sale, how much profit have you made if you close the short-sale at a price of $29.87?

1.7. Suppose you desire to short-sell 400 shares of JKI stock, which has a bid price of $25.12 and an ask price of $25.31. You cover the short position 180 days later when the bid price is $22.87 and the ask price is $23.06.

    a. Taking into account only the bid and ask prices (ignoring commissions and interest), what profit did you earn?

    b. Suppose that there is a 0.3% commission to engage in the short-sale (this is the commission to sell the stock) and a 0.3% commission to close the short-sale (this is the commission to buy the stock back). How do these commissions change the profit in the previous answer?

    c. Suppose the 6-month interest rate is 3% and that you are paid nothing on the short-sale proceeds. How much interest do you lose during the 6 months in which you have the short position?

1.8. When you open a brokerage account, you typically sign an agreement giving the broker the right to lend your shares without notifying or compensating you. Why do brokers want you to sign this agreement?

1.9. Suppose a stock pays a quarterly dividend of $3. You plan to hold a short position in the stock across the dividend ex-date. What is your obligation on that date? If you are a taxable investor, what would you guess is the tax consequence of the payment? (In particular, would you expect the dividend to be tax deductible?) Suppose the company announces instead that the dividend is $5. Should you care that the dividend is different from what you expected?

1.10. Short interest is a measure of the aggregate short positions on a stock. Check an online brokerage or other financial service for the short interest on several stocks of your choice. Can you guess which stocks have high short interest and which have low? Is it theoretically possible for short interest to exceed 100% of shares outstanding?

1.11. Suppose that you go to a bank and borrow $100. You promise to repay the loan in 90 days for $102. Explain this transaction using the terminology of short-sales.

1.12. Suppose your bank's loan officer tells you that if you take out a mortgage (i.e., you borrow money to buy a house) you will be permitted to borrow no more than 80% of the value of the house. Describe this transaction using the terminology of short-sales.

PART ONE

Insurance, Hedging, and Simple Strategies

*I*n this part of the book, Chapters 2–4, we examine the basic derivatives contracts: forward contracts, futures contracts, call options, and put options. All of these are contracts between two parties, with a payoff at some future date based on the price of an underlying asset (this is why they are called derivatives).

There are a number of things we want to understand about these instruments. What are they? How do they work and what do they cost? If you enter into a forward contract, futures contract, or option, what obligations or rights have you acquired? Payoff and profit diagrams provide an important graphical tool to summarize the risk of these contracts.

Once we understand what the basic derivatives contracts are, what can we do with them? We will see that, among other things, they can be used to provide insurance, to convert a stock investment into a risk-free investment and vice versa, and to speculate in a variety of ways. Derivatives can often be customized for a particular purpose. We will see how corporate risk managers can use derivatives, and some reasons for doing so.

In this part of the book we take the prices of derivatives as given; the underlying pricing models will be covered in much of the rest of the

book. The main mathematical tool is present and future value calcu-
lations. We do, however, develop one key pricing idea: put-call parity.
Put-call parity is important because it demonstrates a link among the dif-
ferent contracts we examine in these chapters, telling us how the prices of
forward contracts, call options, and put options are related to one another.

CHAPTER 2

An Introduction to Forwards and Options

T his chapter introduces the basic derivatives contracts: forward contracts, call options, and put options. These fundamental contracts are widely used, and serve as building blocks for more complicated derivatives that we discuss in later chapters. We explain here how the contracts work and how to think about their risk. We also introduce an extremely important tool for analyzing derivatives positions—namely, payoff and profit diagrams. The terminology and concepts introduced in this chapter are fundamental and will be used throughout this book.

2.1 FORWARD CONTRACTS

Suppose you wish to buy a share of stock. Doing so entails at least three separate steps: (1) setting the price to be paid, (2) transferring cash from the buyer to the seller, and (3) transferring the share from the seller to the buyer. With an outright purchase of stock, all three occur simultaneously. However, as a logical matter, a price could be set today and the transfer of shares and cash would occur at a specified date in the future.

This is in fact the definition of a **forward contract:** It sets today the terms at which you buy or sell an asset or commodity at a specific time in the future. A forward contract does the following:

- Specifies the quantity and exact type of the asset or commodity the seller must deliver.
- Specifies delivery logistics, such as time, date, and place.
- Specifies the price the buyer will pay at the time of delivery.
- Obligates the seller to sell and the buyer to buy, subject to the above specifications.

The time at which the contract settles is called the **expiration date.** The asset or commodity on which the forward contract is based is called the **underlying asset.** Apart from commissions and bid-ask spreads (see Section 1.4), a forward contract requires no initial payment or premium. The contractual forward price simply represents the price at which consenting adults agree today to transact in the future, at which time the buyer pays the seller the forward price and the seller delivers the asset.

Futures contracts are similar to forward contracts in that they create an obligation to buy or sell at a predetermined price at a future date. We will discuss the institutional and pricing differences between forwards and futures in Chapter 5. For the time being, think of them as interchangeable.

FIGURE 2.1

Index futures price listings.

Index Futures

	OPEN	HIGH	LOW	SETTLE	CHG	LIFETIME HIGH	LIFETIME LOW	OPEN INT
DJ Industrial Average (CBT)-$10 x index								
Sept	9953	10085	9950	10062	113	10557	9835	40,620
Dec	10072	10080	10005	10059	116	10575	8440	349
Est vol 7,149; vol Mon 8,914; open int 40,969, +132.								
Idx prl: Hi 10103.13; Lo 9963.54; Close 10085.14, +123.22.								
Mini DJ Industrial Average (CBT)-$5 x index								
Sept	9956	10087	9949	10062	113	10629	9840	48,695
Vol Tue 105,733; open int 48,789, +1,159.								
DJ-AIG Commodity Index (CBT)-$100 x index								
Aug	...	...	...	455.9	...	485.0	449.4	2,886
Est vol 0; vol Mon 0; open int 2,886, unch.								
Idx prl: Hi 144.743; Lo 144.024; Close 144.341, -.019.								
S&P 500 Index (CME)-$250 x index								
Sept	108310	109600	108300	109250	960	116080	78100	575,947
Dec	109350	109550	109300	109290	970	116010	78100	12,717
Est vol 39,263; vol Mon 37,876; open int 589,488, -1,470.								
Idx prl: Hi 1096.65; Lo 1084.07; Close 1094.83, +10.76.								
Mini S&P 500 (CME)-$50 x index								
Sept	108300	109600	108275	109250	950	114850	107500	596,759
Vol Tue 729,906; open int 642,116, +334.								
S&P Midcap 400 (CME)-$500 x index								
Sept	567.00	575.00	567.00	573.40	7.15	616.50	508.70	13,640
Est vol 496; vol Mon 700; open int 13,640, +49.								
Idx prl: Hi 574.85; Lo 566.31; Close 574.02, +7.63.								
Nasdaq 100 (CME)-$100 x index								
Sept	137300	139800	137250	139050	1750	156500	136000	70,024
Est vol 12,432; vol Mon 12,422; open int 72,319, -20.								
Idx prl: Hi 1395.95; Lo 1371.26; Close 1391.50, +23.10.								

Source: Wall Street Journal, July 28, 2004, p. C-16.

Figure 2.1 shows futures price listings from the *Wall Street Journal* for futures contracts on several stock indices, including the Dow Jones Industrial Average (DJ 30) and the Standard and Poor's 500 (S&P 500). The indices are the underlying assets for the contracts. (A **stock index** is the average price of a group of stocks. In these examples we work with this group price rather than the price of just one stock.) The first column of the listing gives the expiration month. The columns that follow show the price at the beginning of the day (the open), the high and low during the day, and the settlement price, which reflects the last transactions of the day.

The listing also gives the price change from the previous day, the high and low during the life of the futures contract, and open interest, which measures the number of contracts outstanding. (Since each trade of a contract has both a buyer and a seller, a buyer-seller pair counts as one contract.) Finally, the head of the listing tells us where the contracts trade (the Chicago Board of Trade [CBT] and Chicago Mercantile Exchange [CME]), and the size of the contract, which for the S&P 500 is $250 times the index value. We will discuss such futures contracts in more detail in Chapter 5. There are many more exchange-traded stock index futures contracts than those in Figure 2.1, both in the United States and around the world.

The price quotes in Figure 2.1 are from July. The September and December prices for the two contracts are therefore prices set in July for purchase of the index in later months. For example, the September S&P 500 futures price is $1092.50 and the December price is $1092.90.[1] By contrast, the current S&P index price that day is $1094.44. This is the **spot price** for the index—the market price for immediate delivery of the index.

There are many more exchange-traded futures contracts than just those listed in Figure 2.1. As we will see in Chapters 5, 6, and 7, there are also futures contracts on interest rates and commodities. Futures are widely used in risk management and as an alternative way to invest in the underlying asset. Agricultural futures (such as corn and soybeans) can be used by farmers and others to hedge crop prices. The box on page 24 discusses an unsuccessful proposal for a new futures contract that was in the news in 2003.

We will discuss in Chapter 5 how forward and futures prices are determined and more details about how futures contracts work. In this chapter we take prices as given and examine profit and loss on a forward contract. We will also see how a position in a forward contract is similar to and different from alternative investments, such as a direct investment in the underlying index.

The Payoff on a Forward Contract

Every forward contract has both a buyer and a seller. The term **long** is used to describe the buyer and **short** is used to describe the seller. Generally, a long position is one that makes money when the price goes up and a short is one that makes money when the price goes down. Because the long has agreed to buy at the fixed forward price, a long position profits if prices rise.

The **payoff** to a contract is the value of the position at expiration. The payoff to a long forward contract is

$$\text{Payoff to long forward} = \text{Spot price at expiration} - \text{forward price} \qquad (2.1)$$

Because the short has agreed to sell at the fixed forward price, the short profits if prices fall. The payoff to a short forward contract is

$$\text{Payoff to short forward} = \text{Forward price} - \text{spot price at expiration} \qquad (2.2)$$

To illustrate these calculations, consider a forward contract on a hypothetical stock index. Suppose the non-dividend-paying S&R ("Special and Rich") 500 index has a current price of $1000 and the 6-month forward price is $1020.[2] The holder of a long position in the S&R forward contract is obligated to pay $1020 in 6 months for one unit

---

[1] The use and nonuse of dollar signs for futures prices can be confusing. Many futures prices, in particular those for index futures, are in practice quoted without dollar signs, and multiplied by a dollar amount to determine the value of the contract. In this and the next several chapters, we will depart from this convention and use dollar signs for index futures prices. When we discuss the S&P 500 index futures contract in Chapter 5, however, we will follow practice and omit the dollar sign.

[2] We use a hypothetical stock index—the S&R—in order to avoid complications associated with dividends. We discuss dividends—and real stock indices—in Chapter 5.

Terrorism Futures?

Newspaper readers in July 2003 were undoubtedly startled to see the headline "Pentagon Prepares a Futures Market on Terror Attacks" (*New York Times*, July 29 2003, p. A1). The article continued:

> Traders bullish on a biological attack on Israel or bearish on the chances of a North Korean missile strike would have the opportunity to bet on the likelihood of such events on a new Internet site established by the Defense Advanced Research Projects Agency.

> The Pentagon called its latest idea a new way of predicting events and part of its search for the "broadest possible set of new ways to prevent terrorist attacks."

Critics immediately attacked the plan:

> Two Democratic senators who reported the plan called it morally repugnant and grotesque.... One of the two senators, Byron L. Dorgan of North Dakota, said the idea seemed so preposterous that he had trouble persuading people it was not a hoax. "Can you imagine," Mr. Dorgan asked, 'if another country set up a betting parlor so that people could go in ... and bet on the assassination of an American political figure?

The other critic, Senator Ron Wyden of Oregon, described the plan:

> You may think early on that Prime Minister X is going to be assassinated. So you buy the futures contracts for 5 cents each. As more people begin to think the person's going to be assassinated, the cost of the contract could go up, to 50 cents. The payoff if he's assassinated is $1 per future. So if it comes to pass, and those who bought at 5 cents make 95 cents. Those who bought at 50 cents make 50 cents.

Later the same day (July 29), this headline appeared on the *New York Times* web site: "Pentagon Abandons Plan for Futures Market on Terror."

Before dropping the plan, Defense officials defended it: "Research indicates that markets are extremely efficient, effective, and timely aggregators of dispersed and even hidden information. Futures markets have proven themselves to be good at predicting such things as elections results; they are often better than expert opinions."

A common concern about futures markets is the possibility that markets can be manipulated by better informed traders. The possibility of manipulation in this case was described as a "technical challenge and uncertainty." The natural worry was that terrorists would use the futures market to make money from attacks, or to mislead authorities about where they would attack.

---

of the index. The holder of the short position is obligated to sell one unit of the index for $1020. Table 2.1 lists the payoff on the position for various possible future values of the index.

TABLE 2.1	Payoff after 6 months from a long S&R forward contract and a short S&R forward contract at a forward price of $1020. If the index price in 6 months is $1020, both the long and short have a 0 payoff. If the index price is greater than $1020, the long makes money and the short loses money. If the index price is less than $1020, the long loses money and the short makes money.

| S&R Index | S&R Forward | |
in 6 Months	Long	Short
900	−$120	$120
950	−70	70
1000	−20	20
1020	0	0
1050	30	−30
1100	80	−80

Example 2.1   Suppose the index price is $1050 in 6 months. A holder who entered a long position at a forward price of $1020 is obligated to pay $1020 to acquire the index, and hence earns $1050 − $1020 = $30 per unit of the index. The short is likewise obligated to sell for $1020, and thus loses $30.

This example illustrates the mechanics of a forward contract, showing why the long makes money when the price rises and the short makes money when the price falls.

Graphing the Payoff on a Forward Contract

We can graph the information in Table 2.1 to show the payoff in 6 months on the forward contract as a function of the index. Figure 2.2 graphs the long and short positions, with the index price at the expiration of the forward contract on the horizontal axis and payoff on the vertical axis. As you would expect, the two positions have a zero payoff when the index price in 6 months equals the forward price of $1020. The graph for the short forward is a mirror image (about the x-axis) of the graph for the long forward. For a given value of the index, the payoff to the short is exactly the opposite of the payoff to the long. In other words, the gain to one party is the loss to the other.

This kind of graph is widely used because it summarizes the risk of the position at a glance.

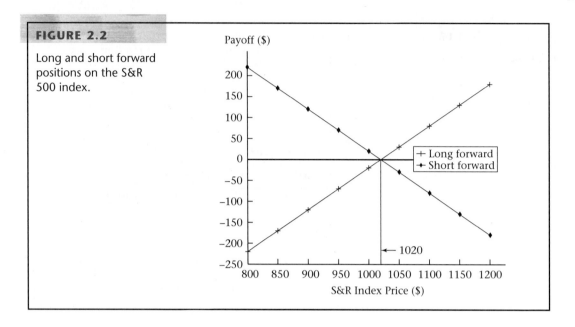

FIGURE 2.2

Long and short forward positions on the S&R 500 index.

Comparing a Forward and Outright Purchase

The S&R forward contract is a way to acquire the index by paying $1020 after 6 months. An alternative way to acquire the index is to purchase it outright at time 0, paying $1000. Is there any advantage to using the forward contract to buy the index, as opposed to purchasing it outright?

If we buy the S&R index today, it costs us $1000. The value of the position in 6 months is the value of the S&R index. The payoff to a long position in the physical S&R index is graphed in Figure 2.3. For comparison, the payoff to the long forward position, is graphed as well. Note that the axes have different scales in Figures 2.3 and 2.2.

To see how Figure 2.3 is constructed, suppose the S&R index price is $0 after 6 months. (This is just a thought experiment for the purpose of constructing the graph, but if you would like to be concrete, imagine that the S&R index contained Internet firms in the year 2000 which would be bankrupt in 2001.) If the index price is $0, the physical index will be worth $0; hence we plot a 0 on the y-axis against 0 on the x-axis. For all other prices of the S&R index, the payoff equals the value of the S&R index. For example, if we own the index and the price in 6 months is $750, the value of the position is $750.

If the index price in 6 months is $0, the payoff to the forward contract, using equation (2.1), is

$$\text{Payoff to long forward} = 0 - \$1020 = -\$1020$$

If instead the index price is $1020, the long index position will be worth $1020 and the forward contract will be worth $0.

FIGURE 2.3

Comparison of payoff after 6 months of a long position in the S&R index versus a forward contract in the S&R index.

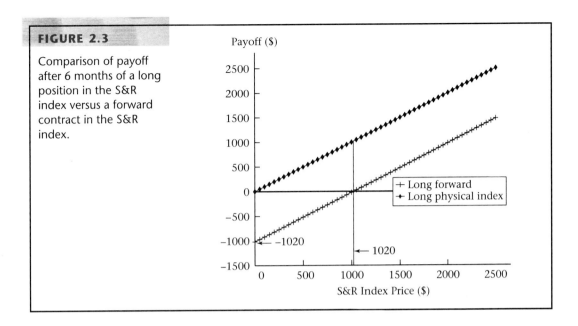

With both positions, we own the index after 6 months. What the figure does not reflect, however, is the different *initial* investments required for the two positions. With the cash index, we invest $1000 initially and then we own the index. With the forward contract, we invest $0 initially and $1020 after 6 months; then we own the index. The financing of the two positions is different. The payoff graph tells us how much money we end up with after 6 months, but does not account for the initial $1000 investment with the outright purchase. Figure 2.3 is accurate, but it does not answer our question—namely, whether there is an advantage to either a forward purchase or an outright purchase.

Both positions give us ownership of the S&R index after 6 months. We can compare them fairly if we equate the amounts initially invested and then account for interest earned over the 6 months. We can do this in either of two equivalent ways:

1. Invest $1000 in zero-coupon bonds (for example, Treasury bills) along with the forward contract, in which case each position initially costs $1000 at time 0.

2. Borrow to buy the physical S&R index, in which case each position initially costs $0 at time 0.

Suppose the 6-month interest rate is 2%. With alternative 1, we pay $1000 today. After 6 months the zero-coupon bond is worth $1000 \times 1.02 = $1020. At that point, we use the bond proceeds to pay the forward price of $1020. We then own the index. The net effect is that we pay $1000 initially and own the index after 6 months, just as if we bought the index outright. Investing $1000 and at the same time entering a long forward contract mimics the effect of buying the index outright.

With alternative 2, we borrow $1000 to buy the index, which costs $1000. Hence we make no net cash payment at time 0. After 6 months we owe $1000 plus interest. At that time we repay $1000 × 1.02 = $1020 for the borrowed money. The net effect is that we invest nothing initially, and after six months pay $1020. We also own the index. Borrowing to buy the stock therefore mimics the effect of entering into a long forward contract.[3]

We conclude that when the index pays no dividends, the only difference between the forward contract and the cash index investment is the timing of a payment that will be made for certain. Therefore, we can compare the two positions by using the interest rate to shift the timing of payments. In the above example, we conclude that the forward contract and the cash index are equivalent investments, differing only in the timing of the cash flows. Neither form of investing has an advantage over the other.

This analysis suggests a way to systematically compare positions that require different initial investments. We can assume that we borrow any required initial payment. At expiration, we receive the payoff from the contract, and repay any borrowed amounts. We will call this the **net payoff** or **profit.** Because this calculation accounts for differing initial investments in a simple fashion, we will primarily use profit rather than payoff diagrams throughout the book.[4] Note that the payoff and profit diagrams are the same for a forward contract because it requires no initial investment.

To summarize, a **payoff diagram** graphs the cash value of a position at a point in time. A **profit diagram** subtracts from the payoff the future value of the investment in the position.

This discussion raises a question: Given our assumptions, should we really expect the forward price to equal $1020, which is the future value of the index? The answer in this case is yes, but we defer a detailed explanation until Chapter 5.

Zero-Coupon Bonds in Payoff and Profit Diagrams

The preceding discussion showed that the long forward contract and outright purchase of the physical S&R index are essentially the same once we take time value of money into account. Buying the physical index is like entering into the forward contract and simultaneously investing $1000 in a zero-coupon bond. We can see this same point graphically by using a payoff diagram where we include a zero-coupon bond.

Suppose we enter into a long S&R index forward position, and at the same time purchase a $1000 zero-coupon bond, which will pay $1020 after 6 months. (This was

---

[3]If the index paid a dividend in this example, then we would receive the dividend by holding the physical index, but not when we entered into the forward contract. We will see in Chapter 5 how to take dividends into account in this comparison.

[4]The term "profit" is defined variously by accountants and economists. All of our profit calculations are for the purpose of *comparing* one position with another, not computing profit in any absolute sense.

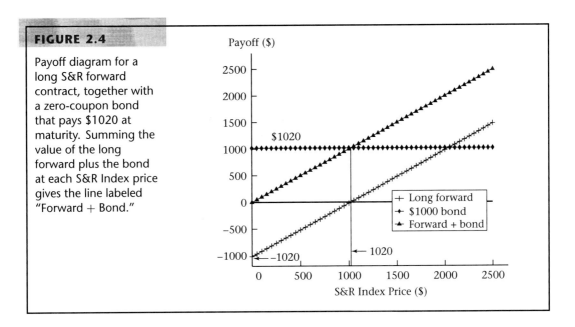

FIGURE 2.4

Payoff diagram for a long S&R forward contract, together with a zero-coupon bond that pays $1020 at maturity. Summing the value of the long forward plus the bond at each S&R Index price gives the line labeled "Forward + Bond."

alternative 1 in the previous section.) Algebraically, the payoff to the forward plus the bond is

$$\text{Forward} + \text{bond} = \underbrace{\text{Spot price at expiration} - \$1020}_{\text{Forward payoff}} + \underbrace{\$1020}_{\text{Bond payoff}}$$

$$= \text{Spot price at expiration}$$

This is the same as the payoff to investing in the physical index.

The payoff diagram for this position is an easy modification of Figure 2.3. We simply add a line representing the value of the bond after 6 months ($1000 × 1.02 = $1020), and then add the bond payoff to the forward payoff. This is graphed in Figure 2.4. The forward plus bond looks exactly like the physical index in Figure 2.3.

What is the profit diagram corresponding to this payoff diagram? For the forward contract, profit is the same as the payoff because there is no initial investment. Profit for the forward plus bond is obtained by subtracting the future value of the initial investment. The initial investment was the cost of the bond, $1000. Its future value is, by definition, $1020, the value of the bond after 6 months. Thus, the profit diagram for a forward contract plus a bond is obtained by *ignoring* the bond! Put differently, adding a bond to a position leaves a profit diagram unaffected.

Depending on the context, it can be helpful to draw either payoff or profit diagrams. Bonds can be used to shift payoff diagrams vertically, but do not change the profit calculation.

Cash Settlement Versus Delivery

The foregoing discussion assumed that at expiration of the forward contract, the contract called for the seller (the party short the forward contract) to deliver the cash S&R index to the buyer (the party long the forward contract). However, a physical transaction in a broad stock index will likely have significant transaction costs. An alternative settlement procedure that is widely used is **cash settlement.** Instead of requiring delivery of the actual index, the forward contract settles financially. The two parties make a net cash payment, which yields the same cash flow as if delivery had occurred, and both parties had then closed out their positions. We can illustrate this with an example.

Example 2.2   Suppose that the S&R index at expiration is $1040. Because the forward price is $1020, the long position has a payoff of $20. Similarly, the short position loses $20. With cash settlement, the short simply pays $20 to the long, with no transfer of the physical asset, and hence no transaction costs. It is as if the long paid $1020, acquired the index worth $1040, and then immediately sold it with no transaction costs.

If the S&R index price at expiration had instead been $960, the long position would have a payoff of −$60 and the short would have a payoff of $60. Cash settlement in this case entails the long paying $60 to the short.   ≹

Cash settlement is feasible only when there is an accepted reference price upon which the settlement can be based. Cash settlement is not limited to forward contracts—virtually any financial contract can be settled using cash rather than delivery.

Credit Risk

Any forward or futures contract—indeed, any derivatives contract—has **credit risk,** which means there is a possibility that the counterparty who owes money fails to make a payment. If you agree to sell the index in one year at a fixed price and the spot price turns out to be lower than the forward price, the counterparty is obligated to buy the index for more than it is worth. You face the risk that the counterparty will for some reason fail to pay the forward price for the index. Similarly the counterparty faces the risk that you will not fulfill the contract if the spot price in one year turns out to be higher than the forward price.

With exchange-traded contracts, the exchange goes to great lengths to minimize this risk by requiring collateral of all participants and being the ultimate counterparty in all transactions. We will discuss credit risk and collateral in more detail when we discuss futures contracts in Chapter 5. With over-the-counter contracts, the fact that the contracts are transacted directly between two parties means that each counterparty bears the credit risk of the other.[5]

Credit risk is an important problem with all derivatives, but it is also quite complicated. Credit checks of counterparties and credit protections such as collateral and bank letters of credit are commonly employed to guard against losses from counterparty default.

2.2 CALL OPTIONS

We have seen that a forward contract obligates the buyer (the holder of the long position) to pay the forward price at expiration, even if the value of the underlying asset at expiration is less than the forward price. Because losses are possible with a forward contract, it is natural to wonder: Could there be a contract where the buyer has the right to walk away from the deal?

The answer is yes; a **call option** is a contract where the buyer has the right to buy, but not the obligation to buy. Here is an example illustrating how a call option works at expiration.

Example 2.3   Suppose that the call buyer agrees to pay $1020 for the S&R index in 6 months but is not obligated to do so. (The buyer has purchased a call option.) If in 6 months the S&R price is $1100, the buyer will pay $1020 and receive the index. This is a payoff of $80 per unit of the index. If the S&R price is $900, the buyer walks away.

Now think about this transaction from the seller's point of view. The buyer is in control of the option, deciding when to buy the index by paying $1020. Thus, the rights of the option buyer are obligations for the option seller.

Example 2.4   If in 6 months the S&R price is $1100, the seller will receive $1020 and give up an index worth more, for a loss of $80 per unit of the index. If the S&R price is less than $1020, the buyer will not buy, so the seller has no obligation. Thus, at expiration, the seller will have a payoff which is zero (if the S&R price is less than $1020) or negative (if the S&R price is greater than $1020).

---

[5]Of course, credit risk also exists in exchange-traded contracts. The specific details of how exchanges are structured to minimize credit risk is a complicated and fascinating subject (see Edwards and Ma (1992), ch. 3, for details). In practice, exchanges are regarded by participants as good credit risks.

Does it seem as if something is wrong here? Because the buyer can decide whether to buy, the seller *cannot* make money at expiration. This situation suggests that the seller must, in effect, be "bribed" to enter into the contract in the first place. At the time the buyer and seller agree to the contract, the buyer must pay the seller an initial price, or **premium.** This initial payment compensates the seller for being at a disadvantage at expiration. Contrast this with a forward contract, for which the initial premium is zero.

Option Terminology

Here are some key terms used to describe options:

Strike price: The **strike price,** or **exercise price,** of a call option is what the buyer pays for the asset. In the example above, the strike price was $1020. The strike price can be set at any value.

Exercise: The **exercise** of a call option is the act of paying the strike price to receive the asset. In Example 2.3, the buyer decided after 6 months whether to exercise the option—that is, whether to pay $1020 (the strike price) to receive the S&R index.

Expiration: The **expiration** of the option is the date by which the option must either be exercised or it becomes worthless. The option in Example 2.3 had an expiration of 6 months.

Exercise style: The **exercise style** of the option governs the time at which exercise can occur. In the above example, exercise could occur only at expiration. Such an option is said to be a **European-style option.** If the buyer has the right to exercise at any time during the life of the option, it is an **American-style option.** If the buyer can only exercise during specified periods, but not for the entire life of the option, the option is a **Bermudan-style option.** (The terms "European" and "American," by the way, have nothing to do with geography. European, American, and Bermudan options are bought and sold worldwide.)

To summarize, a European call option gives the owner of the call the right, but not the obligation, to buy the underlying asset on the expiration date by paying the strike price. The option described in Examples 2.3 and 2.4 is a *6-month European-style S&R call with a strike price of $1020.* The buyer of the call can also be described as having a *long position* in the call.

Figure 2.5 presents a small portion of the option price listings for the S&P 500 Index option traded at the Chicago Board Options Exchange. Each row represents a different option, with the expiration month, strike price, a "c" or a "p" to denote call or put, the number of contracts traded that day, the premium at the last trade of the day, the change from the previous day, and open interest. As with futures, every option trade requires a buyer and a seller, so open interest measures the number of buyer-seller pairs. The box below discusses some of the mechanics of buying an option.

For the time being, we will discuss European-style options exclusively. We do this because European options are the simplest to discuss and are also quite common in

FIGURE 2.5

Closing options prices for S&P 500 index options from the Chicago Board Options Exchange.

STRIKE	VOL	LAST	NET CHG	OPEN INT
S & P 500(SPX)				
Aug 975 c	4	121	0.70	684
Aug 975 p	762	0.80	−0.50	66,643
Sep 975 c	1,000	116	2.50	1,210
Sep 975 p	311	3.70	−1.20	8,141
Sep 995 p	41	5	−1.90	29,641
Sep 1005 p	15	5.80	−2.60	27,684
Oct 1005 p	1	10.80	−2.00	1,496
Aug 1020 p	218	2.30	−1.10	941
Aug 1025 c	1,333	72	14.80	4,848
Aug 1025 p	1,020	2.45	−1.75	37,556
Sep 1025 c	1,255	77	9.50	4,065
Sep 1025 p	791	8.40	−2.30	51,851
Oct 1025 c	1	83	11.00	103
Oct 1025 p	5	16	−2.00	829
Sep 1030 c	15	70	2.50	15
Sep 1030 p	1,410	10.50	−1.20	27

Source: Wall Street Journal, July 28, 2004, p. C-15.

practice. While most exchange-traded options are American, the options in Figure 2.5 are European. Later in the book we will discuss American options in more detail.

Payoff and Profit for a Purchased Call Option

We can graph call options as we did forward contracts. The buyer is not obligated to buy the index, and hence will only exercise the option if the payoff is greater than zero. The algebraic expression for the *payoff* to a purchased call is therefore

$$\text{Purchased call payoff} = \max[0, \text{spot price at expiration} - \text{strike price}] \qquad (2.3)$$

The expression $\max[a, b]$ means take the greater of the two values a and b. (Spreadsheets contain a max function, so it is easy to compute option payoffs in a spreadsheet.)

Example 2.5 Consider a call option on the S&R index with 6 months to expiration and a strike price of $1000. Suppose the index in 6 months is $1100. Clearly it is worthwhile to pay the $1000 strike price to acquire the index worth $1100. Using equation (2.3), the call payoff is

$$\max[0, \$1100 - \$1000] = \$100$$

If the index is 900 at expiration, it is not worthwhile paying the $1000 strike price to buy the index worth $900. The payoff is then

$$\max[0, \$900 - \$1000] = \$0 \qquad ≋$$

As discussed before, the payoff does not take account of the initial cost of acquiring the position. For a purchased option, the premium is paid at the time the option is

---

How Do You Buy an Option?

How would you actually buy an option? The quick answer is that buying an option is just like buying a stock. Option premiums are quoted just like stock prices. Figure 2.5 provides an example. (For current quotes see, for example, **http://www.cboe.com;** this shows bid and ask prices at the Chicago Board Options Exchange.) Using either an online or flesh-and-blood broker, you can enter an order to buy an option. As with stocks, in addition to the option premium, you pay a commission, and there is a bid-ask spread.

Options on numerous stocks are traded on exchanges, and for any given stock or index, there can be over a hundred options available, differing in strike price and expiration date. (In July 2004, a quick count at the Chicago Board Options Exchange Web site showed over 500 options, with differing strikes and maturities, both puts and calls, with the S&P 500 index as the underlying asset.) Options may be either American or European. If you buy an American option, you have to be aware that exercising the option prior to expiration may be optimal. Thus, you need to have some understanding of why and when exercise might make sense.

You can also sell, or write, options. In this case, you have to post collateral (called margin) to protect others against the possibility you will default. See Appendix 2.A for a discussion of this and other issues.

---

acquired. In computing profit at expiration, suppose we defer the premium payment; then by the time of expiration we accrue 6 months' interest on the premium. The option *profit* is computed as

$$\text{Purchased call profit} = \max[0, \text{spot price at expiration} - \text{strike price}]$$
$$- \text{future value of option premium} \quad (2.4)$$

The following example illustrates the computation of the profit.

Example 2.6   Use the same option as in Example 2.5, and suppose that the risk-free rate is 2% over 6 months. Assume that the premium for this call is $93.81.[6] Hence, the future value of the call premium is $93.81 \times 1.02 = $95.68. If the S&R index price at expiration is $1100, the owner will exercise the option. Using equation (2.4), the call

------

[6]It is not important at this point how we compute this price, but if you wish to replicate the option premiums, they are computed using the Black-Scholes formula, which we discuss in Chapter 12. Using the BSCall spreadsheet function accompanying this book, the call price is computed as $\text{BSCall}(1000, 1000, 0.3, 2 \times \ln(1.02), 0.5, 0) = 93.81$.

profit is

$$\max[0, \$1100 - \$1000] - \$95.68 = \$4.32$$

If the index is 900 at expiration, the owner does not exercise the option. It is not worthwhile paying the $1000 strike price to buy the index worth $900. Profit is then

$$\max[0, \$900 - \$1000] - \$95.68 = -\$95.68,$$

reflecting the loss of the premium.

≷

We graph the call *payoff* by computing, for any index price at expiration, the payoff on the option position as a function of the price. We graph the call *profit* by subtracting from this the future value of the option premium. Table 2.2 computes the payoff and profit at different index values, computed as in Examples 2.5 and 2.6. Note that because the strike price is fixed, a higher market price at expiration of the S&R index benefits the call buyer.

Figure 2.6 graphs the call payoff that is computed in Table 2.2. The graph clearly shows the "optionality" of the option: Below the strike price of $1000, the payoff is zero, while it is positive and increasing above $1000.

TABLE 2.2

93.81 (1.02) - 95.68

Payoff and profit after 6 months from a purchased 1.000-strike S&R call option with a future value of premium of $95.68. The option premium is assumed to be $93.81 and the effective interest rate is 2% over 6 months. The payoff is computed using equation (2.3) and the profit using equation (2.4).

S&R Index in 6 months	Call Payoff	Future Value of Premium	Call Profit
800	$0	−$95.68	−$95.68
850	0	−95.68	−95.68
900	0	−95.68	−95.68
950	0	−95.68	−95.68
1000	0	−95.68	−95.68
1050	50	−95.68	−45.68
1100	100	−95.68	4.32
1150	150	−95.68	54.32
1200	200	−95.68	104.32

FIGURE 2.6

The payoff at expiration of a purchased S&R call with a $1000 strike price.

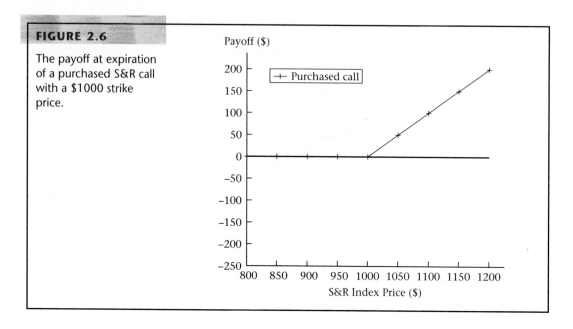

FIGURE 2.7

Profit at expiration for purchase of 6-month S&R index call with strike price of $1000 versus profit on long S&R index forward position.

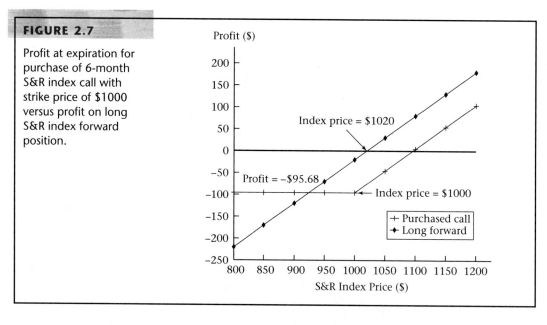

The last column in Table 2.2 computes the call profit at different index values. Because a purchased call and a forward contract are both ways to buy the index, it is interesting to contrast the two. Thus, Figure 2.7 plots the profit on both a purchased call and a long forward contract. Note that profit and payoff diagrams for an option differ by the future value of the premium, whereas for a forward contract they are the same.

If the index rises, the forward contract is more profitable than the option because it does not entail paying a premium. If the index falls sufficiently, however, the option is more profitable because the most the option buyer loses is the future value of the premium. This difference suggests that we can think of the call option as an *insured* position in the index. Insurance protects against losses, and the call option does the same. Carrying the analogy a bit further, we can think of the option premium as, in part, reflecting the cost of that insurance. The forward, which is free, has no such insurance, and potentially has losses larger than those on the call.

This discussion highlights the important point that there are always trade-offs in selecting a position. The forward contract outperforms the call if the index rises and underperforms the call if the index falls sufficiently. When all contracts are fairly priced, you will not find a contract that has higher profits for all possible index market prices.

Payoff and Profit for a Written Call Option

Now let's look at the option from the point of view of the seller. The seller is said to be the **option writer,** or to have a short position in a call option. The option writer is the counterparty to the option buyer. The writer receives the premium for the option and then has an obligation to sell the underlying security in exchange for the strike price if the option buyer exercises the option.

The payoff and profit to a written call are just the opposite of those for a purchased call:

$$\text{Written call payoff} = - \max[0, \text{spot price at expiration} - \text{strike price}] \qquad (2.5)$$

$$\text{Written call profit} = - \max[0, \text{spot price at expiration} - \text{strike price}]$$
$$+ \text{future value of option premium} \quad (2.6)$$

This example illustrates the option writer's payoff and profit. Just as a call buyer is long in the call, the call seller has a short position in the call.

Example 2.7 Consider a 1000-strike call option on the S&R index with 6 months to expiration. At the time the option is written, the option seller receives the premium of $93.81.

Suppose the index in 6 months is $1100. It is worthwhile for the option buyer to pay the $1000 strike price to acquire the index worth $1100. Thus, the option writer will have to sell the index, worth $1100, for the strike price of $1000. Using equation (2.5), the written call payoff is

$$- \max[0, \$1100 - \$1000] = -\$100.$$

The premium has earned 2% interest for 6 months and is now worth $95.68. Profit for the written call is

$$-\$100 + \$95.68 = -\$4.32.$$

FIGURE 2.8

Profit for writer of 6-month S&R call with strike of $1000 versus profit for short S&R forward.

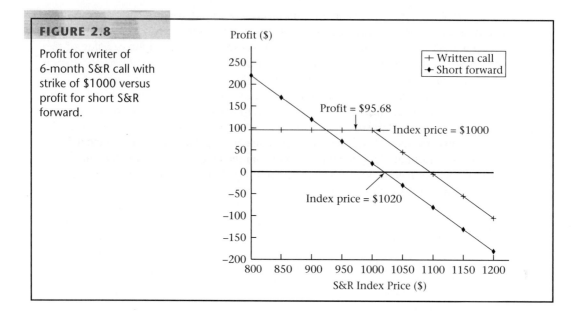

If the index is 900 at expiration, it is not worthwhile for the option buyer to pay the $1000 strike price to buy the index worth $900. The payoff is then

$$- \max[0, \$900 - \$1000] = \$0.$$

The option writer keeps the premium, for a profit after 6 months of $95.68.   ❧

Figure 2.8 depicts a graph of the option writer's profit, graphed against a short forward contract. Note that it is the mirror image of the call buyer's profit in Figure 2.7.

2.3 Put Options

We introduced a call option by comparing it to a forward contract in which the buyer need not buy the underlying asset if it is worth less than the agreed-to purchase price. Perhaps you wondered if there could also be a contract in which the *seller* could walk away if it is not in his or her interest to sell. The answer is yes. A **put option** is a contract where the seller has the right to sell, but not the obligation. Here is an example to illustrate how a put option works.

Example 2.8   Suppose that the seller agrees to sell the S&R index for $1020 in 6 months but is not obligated to do so. (The seller has purchased a put option.) If in 6 months the S&R price is $1100, the seller will not sell for $1020 and will walk away. If the S&R price is $900, the seller *will* sell for $1020 and will earn $120 at that time.

A put must have a premium for the same reason a call has a premium. The buyer of the put controls exercise; hence the seller of the put will never have a positive payoff at expiration. A premium paid by the put buyer at the time the option is purchased compensates the put seller for this no-win position.

It is important to be crystal clear about the use of the terms "buyer" and "seller" in the above example, because there is potential for confusion. The buyer of the put owns a contract giving the right to sell the index at a set price. Thus, *the buyer of the put is a seller of the index!* Similarly, the seller of the put is obligated to *buy* the index, should the put buyer decide to sell. Thus, the buyer of the put is potentially a seller of the index, and the seller of the put is potentially a buyer of the index. (If thinking through these transactions isn't automatic for you now, don't worry. It will become second nature as you continue to think about options.)

Other terminology for a put option is the same as for a call option, with the obvious change that "buy" becomes "sell." In particular, the strike price is the agreed-upon selling price ($1020 in Example 2.8), exercising the option means selling the underlying asset in exchange for the strike price, and the expiration date is that on which you must exercise the option or it is valueless. As with call options, there are European, American, and Bermudan put options.

Payoff and Profit for a Purchased Put Option

We now see how to compute payoff and profit for a purchased put option. The put option gives the put buyer the right to sell the underlying asset for the strike price. The buyer does this only if the asset is less valuable than the strike price. Thus, the payoff on the put option is

$$\text{Put option payoff} = \max[0, \text{strike price} - \text{spot price at expiration}] \qquad (2.7)$$

The put buyer has a long position in the put. Here is an example.

Example 2.9 Consider a put option on the S&R index with 6 months to expiration and a strike price of $1000.

Suppose the index in 6 months is $1100. It is not worthwhile to sell the index worth $1100 for the $1000 strike price. Using equation (2.7), the put payoff is

$$\max[0, \$1000 - \$1100] = \$0$$

If the index were 900 at expiration, it *is* worthwhile selling the index for $1000. The payoff is then

$$\max[0, \$1000 - \$900] = \$100 \qquad\qquad 🌲$$

As with the call, the payoff does not take account of the initial cost of acquiring the position. At the time the option is acquired, the put buyer pays the option premium to the put seller; we need to account for this in computing profit. If we borrow the premium amount, we must pay 6 months' interest. The option *profit* is computed as

$$\text{Purchased put profit} = \max[0, \text{strike price} - \text{spot price at expiration}]$$
$$- \text{future value of option premium} \quad (2.8)$$

The following example illustrates the computation of profit on the put.

Example 2.10   Use the same option as in Example 2.9, and suppose that the risk-free rate is 2% over 6 months. Assume that the premium for this put is $74.20.[7] The future value of the put premium is $74.20 \times 1.02 = \$75.68$.

If the S&R index price at expiration is $1100, the put buyer will not exercise the option. Using equation (2.8), profit is

$$\max[0, \$1000 - \$1100] - \$75.68 = -\$75.68$$

reflecting the loss of the premium.

If the index is $900 at expiration, the put buyer exercises the put, selling the index for $1000. Profit is then

$$\max[0, \$1000 - \$900] - \$75.68 = \$24.32$$

reflecting the payment of premium.   ≋

Table 2.3 computes the payoff and profit on a purchased put for a range of index values at expiration. Whereas call profit increases as the value of the underlying asset *increases*, put profit increases as the value of the underlying asset *decreases*.

Because a put is a way to sell an asset, we can compare it to a short forward position, which is a mandatory sale. Figure 2.9 graphs profit from the purchased put described in Table 2.3 against the profit on a short forward.

We can see from the graph that if the S&R index goes down, the short forward, which has no premium, has a higher profit than the purchased put. If the index goes up sufficiently, the put outperforms the short forward. As with the call, the put is like an insured forward contract. With the put, losses are limited should the index go up. With the short forward, losses are potentially unlimited.

Payoff and Profit for a Written Put Option

Now we examine the put from the perspective of the put writer. The put writer is the counterparty to the buyer. Thus, when the contract is written, the put writer receives the

---

[7]This price is computed using the Black-Scholes formula for the price of a put: BSPut($1000, 1000, 0.3, 2 \times \ln(1.02), 0.5, 0$) = 74.20. We will discuss this formula in Chapter 12.

| TABLE 2.3 | | | Profit after 6 months from a purchased 1000-strike S&R put option with a future value of premium of $75.68. |

S&R Index in 6 Months	Put Payoff	Future Value of Premium	Put Profit
$800	$200	−$75.68	$124.32
850	150	−75.68	74.32
900	100	−75.68	24.32
950	50	−75.68	−25.68
1000	0	−75.68	−75.68
1050	0	−75.68	−75.68
1100	0	−75.68	−75.68
1150	0	−75.68	−75.68
1200	0	−75.68	−75.68

FIGURE 2.9

Profit on a purchased S&R index put with strike price of $1000 versus a short S&R index forward.

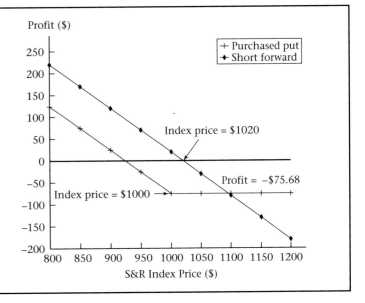

premium. At expiration, if the put buyer elects to sell the underlying asset, the put writer must buy it.

The payoff and profit for a written put are the opposite of those for the purchased put:

$$\text{Written put payoff} = -\max[0, \text{strike price} - \text{spot price at expiration}] \qquad (2.9)$$

Written put profit $= -\max[0,$ strike price $-$ spot price at expiration]

$$+ \text{future value of option premium} \quad (2.10)$$

The put seller has a short position in the put.

Example 2.11   Consider a 1000-strike put option on the S&R index with 6 months to expiration. At the time the option is written, the put writer receives the premium of $74.20.

Suppose the index in 6 months is $1100. The put buyer will not exercise the put. Thus, the put writer keeps the premium, plus 6 months' interest, for a payoff of 0 and profit of $75.68.

If the index is $900 in 6 months, the put owner will exercise, selling the index for $1000. Thus, the option writer will have to pay $1000 for an index worth $900. Using equation (2.9), the written put payoff is

$$-\max[0, \$1000 - \$900] = -\$100$$

The premium has earned 2% interest for 6 months, and is now worth $75.68. Profit for the written put is therefore

$$-\$100 + \$75.68 = -\$24.32 \qquad ❧$$

Figure 2.10 graphs the profit diagram for a written put. As you would expect, it is the mirror image of the purchased put.

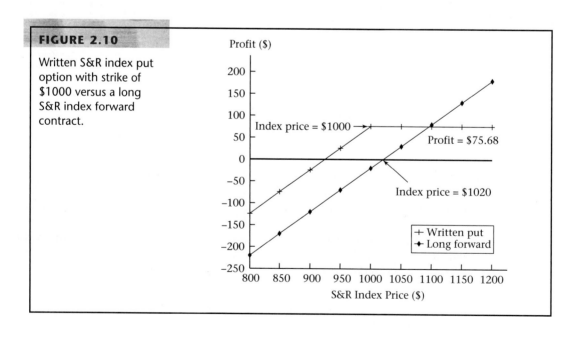

FIGURE 2.10

Written S&R index put option with strike of $1000 versus a long S&R index forward contract.

The "Moneyness" of an Option

Options are often described by their degree of *moneyness*. This term describes whether the option payoff would be positive if the option were exercised immediately. (The term is used to describe both American and European options even though European options cannot be exercised until expiration.) An **in-the-money option** is one which would have a positive payoff (but not necessarily positive profit) if exercised immediately. A call with a strike price less than the asset price and a put with a strike price greater than the asset price are both in-the-money.

An **out-of-the-money option** is one that would have a negative payoff if exercised immediately. A call with a strike price greater than the asset price and a put with a strike price less than the asset price are both out-of-the-money.

An **at-the-money option** is one for which the strike price is approximately equal to the asset price.

2.4 SUMMARY OF FORWARD AND OPTION POSITIONS

We have now examined six different positions: Short and long forwards, and purchased and written calls and puts. We can categorize these positions in at least two ways. One way is their potential for gain and loss. Table 2.4 summarizes the maximum possible gain and loss at maturity for forwards and European options.

Another way to categorize the positions is by whether the positions represent buying or selling the underlying asset. Those that represent buying are fundamentally *long* with respect to the underlying asset, while those that represent selling are fundamentally *short* with respect to the underlying asset.

TABLE 2.4	Maximum possible profit and loss at maturity for long and short forwards and purchased and written calls and puts. *FV(Premium)* denotes the future value of the option premium.

Position	Maximum Loss	Maximum Gain
Long forward	−Forward price	Unlimited
Short forward	Unlimited	Forward price
Long call	−FV(*premium*)	Unlimited
Short call	Unlimited	FV(*premium*)
Long put	−FV(*premium*)	Strike price −FV(*premium*)
Short put	FV(*premium*) − Strike price	FV(*premium*)

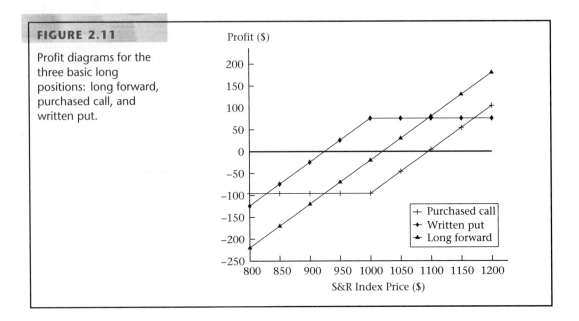

FIGURE 2.11

Profit diagrams for the three basic long positions: long forward, purchased call, and written put.

Long Positions

The following positions are long in the sense that there are circumstances in which they represent either a right or an obligation to *buy* the underlying asset:

Long forward: An *obligation* to buy at a fixed price.

Purchased call: The *right* to buy at a fixed price if it is advantageous to do so.

Written put: An obligation of the put writer to buy the underlying asset at a fixed price if it is advantageous to the option buyer to sell at that price. (Recall that the option *buyer* decides whether or not to exercise.)

Figure 2.11 compares these three positions. Note that the purchased call is long when the asset price is greater than the strike price, and the written put is long when the asset price is less than the strike price. *All three of these positions benefit from rising prices.*

Short Positions

The following positions are short in the sense that there are circumstances in which they represent either a right or an obligation to *sell* the underlying asset:

Short forward: An *obligation* to sell at a fixed price.

Written call: An obligation of the call writer to sell the underlying asset at a fixed price if it is advantageous to the option holder to buy at that price (recall that the option *buyer* decides whether to exercise).

Purchased put: The *right* to sell at a fixed price if it is advantageous to do so.

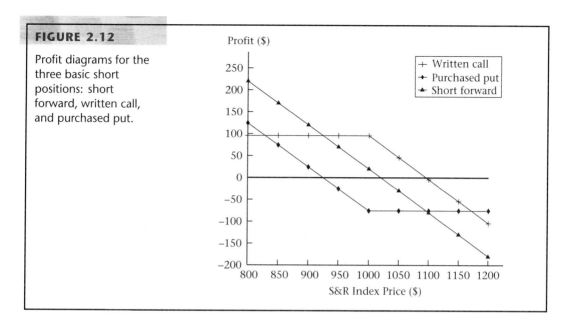

FIGURE 2.12

Profit diagrams for the three basic short positions: short forward, written call, and purchased put.

Figure 2.12 compares these three positions. Note that the written call is short when the asset price is greater than the strike price, and the purchased put is short when the asset price is less than the strike price. *All three of these positions benefit from falling prices.*

2.5 OPTIONS ARE INSURANCE

In many investment strategies using options, we will see that options serve as insurance against a loss. In what sense are options the same as insurance? In this section we answer this question by considering homeowner's insurance. You will see that options are literally insurance, and insurance is an option.

A homeowner's insurance policy promises that in the event of damage to your house, the insurance company will compensate you for at least part of the damage. The greater the damage, the more the insurance company will pay. Your insurance policy thus derives its value from the value of your house: It is a derivative.

Homeowner's Insurance Is a Put Option

To demonstrate how homeowner's insurance acts as a put option, suppose that you own a house that costs $200,000 to build. To make this example as simple as possible, we assume that physical damage is the only thing that can affect the market value of the house.

Let's say you buy a $15,000 insurance policy to compensate you for damage to the house. Like most policies, this has a deductible, meaning that there is an amount of damage for which you are obligated to pay before the insurance company pays anything. Suppose the deductible is $25,000. If the house suffers $4000 damage from a storm, you pay for all repairs yourself. If the house suffers $45,000 in damage from a storm, you pay $25,000 and the insurance company pays the remaining $20,000. Once damage occurs beyond the amount of the deductible, the insurance company pays for all further damage, up to $175,000. (Why $175,000? Because the house can be rebuilt for $200,000, and you pay $25,000 of that—the deductible—yourself.)

Let's graph the profit to you for this insurance policy. Put on the vertical axis the profit on the insurance policy—the payoff less the insurance premium—and on the horizontal axis, the value of the house. If the house is undamaged (the house value is $200,000) the payoff is zero, and profit is the loss from the unused insurance premium, $15,000. If the house suffers $50,000 damage, the insurance payoff is $50,000 less the $25,000 deductible, or $25,000. The profit is $25,000 − $15,000 = $10,000. If the house is completely destroyed, the policy pays $175,000, and your profit is $160,000.

Figure 2.13 graphs the profit on the insurance policy. Remarkably, the insurance policy in Figure 2.13 has the same shape as the put option in Figure 2.9. An S&R put is insurance against a fall in the price of the S&R index, just as homeowner's insurance insures against a fall in the price of the house. *Insurance companies are in the business of writing put options!* The $15,000 insurance premium is like the premium of a put, and the $175,000 level at which insurance begins to make payments is like the strike price on a put.

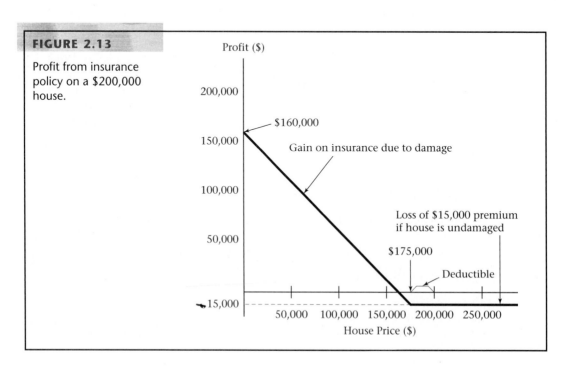

FIGURE 2.13

Profit from insurance policy on a $200,000 house.

The idea that a put option is insurance also helps us understand what makes a put option cheap or expensive. Two important factors are the riskiness of the underlying asset and the amount of the deductible. Just as with insurance, options will be more expensive when the underlying asset is riskier. Also, the option, like insurance, will be less expensive as the deductible gets larger (for the put option, this means lowering the strike price).

You have probably recognized that there are some practical differences between a financial put option and homeowner's insurance. One important difference is that the S&R put pays off no matter why the index price declines. Homeowner's insurance, on the other hand, pays off only if the house declines in value for specified reasons. In particular, a simple decline in real estate prices is not covered by typical homeowner's insurance policies. We avoided this complication by assuming at the outset that only damage could affect the value of the house.

But I Thought Insurance Is Prudent and Put Options Are Risky . . .

If we accept that insurance and put options are the same thing, how do we reconcile this with the common idea that buying insurance is prudent and buying put options is risky?

The risk of a derivative or any other asset or security can only be evaluated in context. Figure 2.13 depicts the risk of an insurance contract *without considering the risk of the insured asset*. This would be like owning insurance on your neighbor's house. It would be "risky" because you would buy the insurance policy, and you would lose your entire investment if there were no insurance claim.[8] We do not normally think of insurance like this, but it illustrates the point that an insurance policy is a put option on the insured asset.

In the same way, Figure 2.9 depicts the risk of a put option without considering the risk of any other positions an investor might be holding. In contrast to homeowner's insurance, many investors *do* own put options without owning the underlying asset. This is why options have a reputation for being risky while homeowner's insurance does not. With stock options it is possible to own the insurance without the asset. Of course, many investors who own put options also own the stock. For these investors, the risk is like that of insurance, which we normally think of as risk-reducing rather than risk-increasing.

Call Options Are Also Insurance

Call options can also be insurance. Whereas a put option is insurance for an asset we already own, a call option is insurance for an asset we plan to own in the future. Put differently, a put option is insurance for a *long* position while a call option is insurance for a *short* position.

---

[8]Of course, in real life no insurance company will sell you insurance on your neighbor's house. The reason is that you will then be tempted to cause damage in order to make your policy valuable. Insurance companies call this "moral hazard."

Return to the earlier example of the S&R index. Suppose that the current price of the S&R index is $1000 and that we plan to buy the index in the future. If we buy an S&R call option with a strike price of $1000, this gives us the right to buy S&R for a maximum cost of $1000/share. By buying a call, we have bought insurance against an *increase* in the price.

2.6 EXAMPLE: EQUITY-LINKED CDs

Although options and forwards are important in and of themselves, they are also commonly used as building blocks in the construction of new financial instruments. For example, banks and insurance companies offer investment products that allow investors to benefit from a rise in a stock index and that provide a guaranteed return if the market declines. We can "reverse-engineer" such equity-linked CDs and notes using the tools we have developed thus far.[9]

Other Equity-Linked Products

The equity-linked CD described in the text provides a zero return (a refund of the initial investment) if the index declines, and a return linked to the index if the index rises. In general, a combination of a bond and one or more equity options is called an **equity-linked note.** It is possible to specify the linkage to the index in different ways, leading to many variants on the basic structure.

MITTS (Market Index Target Term Securities), issued by Merrill Lynch, resemble the equity-linked note described in the text, except that they are traded on the American Stock Exchange. (CDs are issued by a bank and are generally not tradeable.) For example, MITTS issued in 2002 and maturing in 2009 provide a return linked to the Dow Jones Industrial Average. Specifically, the note promises approximately 86% of the simple appreciation of the Dow Jones average over the 7-year life of the note.

A common alternative is to compute the maturity payment of the note based on the average level of the index over the life of the CD. For example, State Farm Bank has offered to investors a Market Rate Certificate of Deposit. These have 5 years to maturity and have a payoff based on the arithmetic average of the quarter-end S&P index level for the 12 quarters prior to maturity. Instead of receiving 70% of the simple return, this particular CD pays 90% of the return based on the 12-quarter average. (The specific terms of the CD will vary with market conditions.) An option based on an average of prices over time, rather than a single price at maturity, is called an *Asian option.* We discuss Asian options in Chapter 14 and equity-linked notes in Chapter 15.

---

[9]A CD (certificate of deposit) is a kind of interest-bearing bank account. You can think of a CD as being the same as a note or a bond.

A simple 5 1/2 year CD with a return linked to the S&P 500 might have the following structure: At maturity, the CD is guaranteed to repay the invested amount, plus 70% of the simple appreciation in the S&P 500 over that time.[10]

We can ask several questions about the CD:

- Is the CD fairly priced?

- How can we decompose the product in terms of options and bonds?

- How does the issuing bank hedge the risk associated with issuing the product?

- How does the issuing bank make a profit?

To understand this product, suppose the S&P index is 1300 initially and an investor invests $10,000. If the index is below 1300 after 5.5 years, the CD returns to the investor the original $10,000 investment. If the index is above 1300 after 5.5 years, the investor receives $10,000 plus 70% of the percentage gain on the index. For example, if the index is 2200, the investor receives

$$\$10,000 \times [1 + (2200/1300 - 1) \times 70\%] = \$14,846$$

At first glance this product *appears* to permit gains but no losses. However, by now you are probably skeptical of a phrase like "gains but no losses"; the investor *must* pay something for an investment like this.

Graphing the Payoff on the CD

As a first step in analyzing the CD, we will draw a payoff diagram. If we invest $10,000, we receive at least $10,000. If the index rises to $S_{\text{final}} > 1300$, we also receive on our investment 70% of the rate of return

$$\frac{S_{\text{final}}}{1300} - 1$$

Thus, the CD pays

$$\$10,000 \times \left(1 + 0.7 \times \max\left[0, \frac{S_{\text{final}}}{1300} - 1\right]\right) \tag{2.11}$$

Figure 2.14 graphs the payoff at expiration to this investment in the CD.

Recall the discussion in Section 2.1 of incorporating a zero-coupon bond into a payoff diagram. Per unit of the index (there are $10,000/1300 = 7.69$ units of the index in a $10,000 investment), the CD buyer receives 0.7 of an index call option, plus a zero-coupon bond paying $1300 at expiration.

Table 2.5 computes the payoff to the equity-linked CD for different values of the index.

....

[10]This is the structure of a CD issued in 1999 by First Union National Bank.

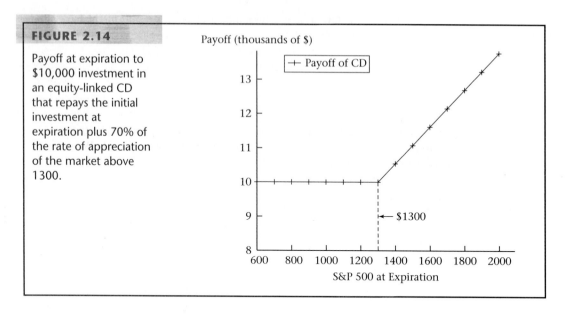

FIGURE 2.14

Payoff at expiration to $10,000 investment in an equity-linked CD that repays the initial investment at expiration plus 70% of the rate of appreciation of the market above 1300.

TABLE 2.5   Payoff of equity-linked CD at expiration.

S&P Index After 5.5 Years	CD Payoff
500	$10,000.00
1000	10,000.00
1500	11,076.92
2000	13,769.23
2500	16,461.54
3000	19,153.85

Economics of the CD

Now we are in a position to understand the economics of this product. Think about what happens if the index is below 1300 at expiration. We pay $10,000 and we receive $10,000 back, plus an option. Thus, we have forgone interest on $10,000 in exchange for the possibility of receiving 70% of the gains on the S&P. Suppose that the effective annual interest rate is 6%; after 5 1/2 years, the buyer has lost interest ~~of~~ *with a present value of*

$$\$10,000 \times (1.06)^{-5.5} - \$10,000 = -\$2,742$$

Essentially, the buyer forgoes interest in exchange for a call option on the index.

With this description we have reverse-engineered the CD, decomposing it in terms of an option and a bond. The question of whether the CD is fairly priced turns on whether the $2742 is a fair price for the index option implicit in the CD. Given information about the interest rate, the volatility of the index, and the dividend yield on the index, it is possible to price the option to determine whether the CD is fairly priced. We perform that analysis for this example in Chapter 15.

Why Equity-Linked CDs?

With reverse-engineering, we see that an investor could create the equivalent of an equity-linked CD by buying a zero-coupon bond and 0.7 call options. Why, then, do products like this exist?

Consider what must be done to replicate the payoff. If a retail investor were to insure an index investment using options, the investor would have to learn about options, decide what maturity, strike price, and quantity to buy, and pay transaction costs. Exchange-traded options have at most 3 years to maturity, so obtaining longer-term protection requires rolling over the position at some point.

An equity-linked CD provides a prepackaged solution. It may provide a pattern of market exposure that many investors could not otherwise obtain at such low transaction costs.

The idea that a prepackaged deal may be attractive should be familiar to you. Supermarkets sell whole heads of lettuce—salad building blocks, as it were—and they also sell, at a premium price, lettuce already washed, torn into bite-sized pieces, and mixed as a salad. The transaction cost of salad preparation leads some consumers to prefer the prepackaged salads.

What does the financial institution get out of this? Just as the supermarket earns profit on prepackaged salads, the issuing bank wants to earn a transaction fee on the CD. When it sells a CD, the issuing bank borrows money (the zero-coupon bond portion of the CD) and receives the premium for writing a call option. The cost of the CD to the bank is the cost of the zero-coupon bond plus the cost of the call option. Obviously the bank would not issue the equity-linked CD in the first place unless it was less expensive than alternative ways to attract deposits, such as standard CDs. The equity-linked CD is risky because the bank has written a call, but the bank can manage this risk in several ways, one of which is to purchase call options from a dealer to offset the risk of having written calls. Using data from the early 1990s, Baubonis et al. (1993) estimated that issuers of equity-linked CDs earned about 3.5% of the value of the CD as a fee, with about 1% as the transaction cost of hedging the written call.[11]

---

[11] A back-of-the-envelope calculation in Chapter 15 suggests the issuer fees for this product are in the neighborhood of 4% to 5%.

In this discussion we have viewed the equity-linked CD from several perspectives. The end-user is interested in the product and whether it meets a financial need at a fair cost. The market-maker (the bank in this case) is interested in making a profit without bearing risk from having issued the CD. And the economic observer is interested in knowing why equity-linked CDs exist. The three perspectives overlap, and a full explanation of the product touches on all of them.

CHAPTER SUMMARY

Forward contracts and put and call options are the basic derivative instruments that can be used directly and that serve as building blocks for other instruments. A long forward contract represents an obligation to buy the underlying asset at a fixed price, a call option gives its owner the right (but not the obligation) to buy the underlying asset at a fixed price, and a put option gives its owner the right (but not the obligation) to sell the underlying asset at a fixed price. Payoff and profit diagrams are commonly used tools for evaluating the risk of these contracts. Payoff diagrams show the gross value of a position at expiration, and profit diagrams subtract from the payoff the future value of the cost of the position.

Table 2.6 summarizes the characteristics of forwards, calls, and puts, showing which are long or short with respect to the underlying asset. The table describes the

TABLE 2.6	Forwards, calls, and puts at a glance: A summary of forward and option positions.		
Derivative Position	**Position with Respect to Underlying Asset**	**Asset Price Contingency**	**Strategy**
Long forward	Long (buy)	Always	Guaranteed price
Short forward	Short (sell)	Always	Guaranteed price
Long call	Long (buy)	> Strike	Insures against high price
Short call	Short (sell)	> Strike	Sells insurance against high price
Long put	Short (sell)	< Strike	Insures against low price
Short put	Long (buy)	< Strike	Sells insurance against low price

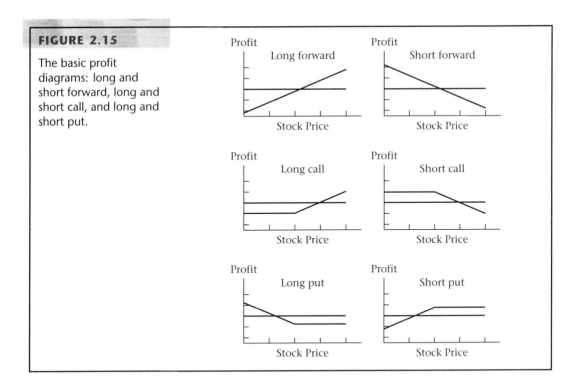

FIGURE 2.15

The basic profit diagrams: long and short forward, long and short call, and long and short put.

strategy associated with each: Forward contracts guarantee a price, purchased options are insurance, and written options are selling insurance. Figure 2.15 provides a graphical summary of these positions.

Options can also be viewed as insurance. A put option gives the owner the right to sell if the price declines, just as insurance gives the insured the right to sell (put) a damaged asset to the insurance company.

FURTHER READING

We use the concepts introduced in this chapter throughout the rest of this book. Chapter 3 presents a number of basic option strategies which are widely used in practice, including caps, collars, and floors. Chapter 4 presents the use of options in risk management.

A more general question raised implicitly in this chapter is how the prices of forwards and options are determined. Chapter 5 covers financial forwards and futures in detail, and Chapter 10 introduces the basic ideas underlying option pricing.

Brokerages routinely supply options customers with an introductory pamphlet about options entitled *Characteristics and Risks of Standardized Options*. This is available online from **http://www.cboe.com.** You can also obtain current option prices from Web sites such as the CBOE's and various brokerage sites.

The notion that options are insurance has been applied in practice. Sharpe (1976), for example, analyzed optimal pension funding policy taking into account pension insurance provided by the Pension Benefit Guaranty Corporation. Merton (1977a) observed that bank deposit insurance and in fact any loan guarantee can be modeled as a put option. Baubonis et al. (1993) discuss equity-linked CDs.

PROBLEMS

In the following problems, if the "effective annual interest rate" is r, a \$1 investment yields $1 + r$ after one year.

2.1. Suppose XYZ stock has a price of \$50 and pays no dividends. The effective annual interest rate is 10%. Draw payoff and profit diagrams for a long position in the stock. Verify that profit is 0 at a price in one year of \$55.

2.2. Using the same information as the previous question, draw payoff and profit diagrams for a short position in the stock. Verify that profit is 0 at a price in one year of \$55.

2.3. What position is the opposite of a purchased call? The opposite of a purchased put?

2.4.   **a.** Suppose you enter into a long 6-month forward position at a forward price of \$50. What is the payoff in 6 months for prices of \$40, \$45, \$50, \$55, and \$60?

   b. Suppose you buy a 6-month call option with a strike price of \$50. What is the payoff in 6 months at the same prices for the underlying asset?

   c. Comparing the payoffs of parts (a) and (b), which contract should be more expensive (i.e., the long call or long forward)? Why?

2.5.   **a.** Suppose you enter into a short 6-month forward position at a forward price of \$50. What is the payoff in 6 months for prices of \$40, \$45, \$50, \$55, and \$60?

   b. Suppose you buy a 6-month put option with a strike price of \$50. What is the payoff in 6 months at the same prices for the underlying asset?

   c. Comparing the payoffs of parts (a) and (b), which contract should be more expensive (i.e., the long put or short forward)? Why?

2.6. A default-free zero-coupon bond costs \$91 and will pay \$100 at maturity in 1 year. What is the effective annual interest rate? What is the payoff diagram for the bond? The profit diagram?

2.7. Suppose XYZ stock pays no dividends and has a current price of \$50. The forward price for delivery in 1 year is \$55. Suppose the 1-year effective annual interest rate is 10%.

   a. Graph the payoff and profit diagrams for a forward contract on XYZ stock with a forward price of \$55.

b. Is there any advantage to investing in the stock or the forward contract? Why?

c. Suppose XYZ paid a dividend of $2 per year and everything else stayed the same. Now is there any advantage to investing in the stock or the forward contract? Why?

2.8. Suppose XYZ stock pays no dividends and has a current price of $50. The forward price for delivery in one year is $53. *If* there is no advantage to buying either the stock or the forward contract, what is the 1-year effective interest rate?

2.9. An *off-market* forward contract is a forward where either you have to pay a premium or you receive a premium for entering into the contract. (With a standard forward contract, the premium is zero.) Suppose the effective annual interest rate is 10% and the S&R index is 1000. Consider 1-year forward contracts.

a. Verify that if the forward price is $1100, the profit diagrams for the index and the 1-year forward are the same.

b. Suppose you are offered a long forward contract at a forward price of $1200. How much would you need to be paid to enter into this contract?

c. Suppose you are offered a long forward contract at $1000. What would you be willing to pay to enter into this forward contract?

2.10. For Figure 2.7, verify the following:

a. The S&R index price at which the call option diagram intersects the x-axis is $1095.68.

b. The S&R index price at which the call option and forward contract have the same profit is $924.32.

2.11. For Figure 2.9, verify the following:

a. The S&R index price at which the put option diagram intersects the x-axis is $924.32.

b. The S&R index price at which the put option and forward contract have the same profit is $1095.68.

2.12. For each entry in Table 2.4, explain the circumstances in which the maximum gain or loss occurs.

2.13. Suppose the stock price is $40 and the effective annual interest rate is 8%.

a. Draw on a single graph payoff and profit diagrams for the following options:

(i) 35-strike call with a premium of $9.12.

(ii) 40-strike call with a premium of $6.22.

(iii) 45-strike call with a premium of $4.08.

b. Consider your payoff diagram with all three options graphed together. Intuitively, why should the option premium decrease with the strike price?

2.14. Suppose the stock price is $40 and the effective annual interest rate is 8%. Draw payoff and profit diagrams for the following options:

    a. 35-strike put with a premium of $1.53.

    b. 40-strike put with a premium of $3.26.

    c. 45-strike put with a premium of $5.75.

Consider your payoff diagram with all three options graphed together. Intuitively, why should the option premium increase with the strike price?

2.15. The profit calculation in the chapter assumes that you borrow at a fixed interest rate to finance investments. An alternative way to borrow is to short-sell stock. What complications would arise in calculating profit if you financed a $1000 S&R index investment by shorting IBM stock, rather than by borrowing $1000?

2.16. Construct a spreadsheet that permits you to compute payoff and profit for a short and long stock, a short and long forward, and purchased and written puts and calls. The spreadsheet should let you specify the stock price, forward price, interest rate, option strikes, and option premiums. Use the spreadsheet's max function to compute option payoffs.

Appendix 2.A: More on Buying a Stock Option

The box on page 34 discusses buying options. There are at least four practical issues that an option buyer should be aware of: Dividends, exercise, margins, and taxes. In this section we will focus on retail investors and exchange-traded stock options. Be aware that specific rules regarding margins and taxes change frequently. This section is intended to help you identify issues and is not intended as a substitute for professional brokerage, accounting, or legal advice.

Dividends

The owner of a standard call option has the right to buy a fixed number of shares of stock at a fixed price, but has no right to receive dividends paid on the underlying stock over the life of the option. When a stock pays a dividend, the stock price declines by approximately the amount of the dividend. This decline in the price lowers the return to the owner of a call option.

For exchange-traded options in the United States, there is typically no adjustment in the terms of the option if the stock pays an "ordinary" dividend (one that is typical for the stock). However, if the stock pays an unusual dividend, then officials at the Options Clearing Corporation (OCC) decide whether or not to make an adjustment.

In June 2003, Iomega Corporation declared a $5 dividend, payable on October 1. At the time of the declaration, Iomega's share price was $11.40. Since the dividend was 44% of the share price, the OCC reduced all Iomega option strike prices by $5, effective October 2.[12]

When we discuss option pricing, we will see that it is necessary to take dividends into account when pricing an option.

Exercise

Some options, for example those that are cash-settled, are automatically exercised at maturity; the option owner need not take any action. Suppose you own a traded option that is not cash-settled and not automatically exercised. In this case you must provide exercise instructions prior to the broker's deadline. If you fail to do so, the option will expire worthless. When you exercise the option, you generally pay a commission. If you do not wish to own the stock, exercising the option would require that you pay a commission to exercise and then a commission to sell the shares. It might be preferable to sell the option instead of exercising it. If you do wish to own the underlying asset, you can exercise the option. The option writer who is obligated to fulfill the option exercise (delivering the shares for a call or buying the shares for a put) is said to have been *assigned*. Assignment can involve paying a commission.

American-style options can be exercised prior to expiration. If you own an option and fail to exercise when you should, you will lose money relative to following the optimal exercise strategy. If you write the option, and it is exercised (you are assigned), you will be required to sell the stock (if you sold a call) or buy the stock (if you sold a put). Therefore, if you buy or sell an American option, you need to understand the circumstances under which exercise might be optimal. Dividends are one factor that can affect the exercise decision. We discuss early exercise in Chapters 9 and 11.

Margins for Written Options

Purchased options for which you fully pay require no margin, as there is no counterparty risk. With written option positions, however, you can incur a large loss if the stock moves against you. When you write an option, therefore, you are required to post collateral to insure against the possibility that you will default. This collateral is called margin.

Margin rules are beyond the scope of this book and change over time. Moreover, different option positions have different margin rules. Both brokers and exchanges can provide information about current margin requirements.

....

[12]Reducing the strike price by the amount of the dividend leaves call holders worse off, albeit better off than if no adjustment had been made. If S is the cum-dividend stock price and $S - D$ the ex-dividend stock price, Merton (1973b, p. 152) shows that to leave the value of a call position unchanged, it is necessary to reduce the strike price by the factor $(S - D)/S$, and give the option holder $S/(S - D) - 1$ additional options. An option with a value protected against dividends is said to be **payout-protected.**

Taxes

Tax rules for derivatives in general can be complicated, and they change frequently as the tax law changes. The taxation of simple option transactions is straightforward.

If you purchase a call option or stock and then sell it, gain or loss on the position is treated like gain or loss on a stock, and accorded long-term or short-term capital gains treatment depending on the length of time for which the position has been held. If you purchase a call option and then exercise it, the cost basis of the resulting stock position is the exercise price plus the option premium plus commissions. The holding period for the resulting stock position begins the day after the option is exercised. The time the option is held does not contribute to the holding period.

The rules become more intricate when forwards and options are held in tandem with the underlying asset. The reasons for this complexity are not hard to understand. Tax laws in the United States accord different tax treatment to different kinds of income. The tax code views interest income, dividend income, and capital gains income as distinct and subject to different tax rules. Futures also have special rules. However, using derivatives, one kind of income can be turned into another. We saw in this chapter, for example, that buying zero-coupon bonds and a forward contract mimics a stock investment.

One category of special rules governs a **constructive sale.** If you own a stock, entering into certain option or forward positions can trigger a constructive sale, meaning that even if you continue to own the stock, for tax purposes you are deemed to have sold it at the time you enter into the forward or option positions. By shorting a forward against the stock, for example, the stock position is transformed into a bond position. When you have no risk stemming from stock ownership, tax law deems you to no longer be an owner.

The so-called **straddle rules** are tax rules intended to control the recognition of losses for tax purposes when there are offsetting risks as with constructive sales. Such positions often arise when investors are undertaking tax arbitrage, which is why the positions are accorded special treatment. A stock owned together with a put is a tax straddle.[13] Generally, the straddle rules prevent loss recognition on only a part of the entire position. A straddle for tax purposes is not the same thing as an option straddle, discussed in Chapter 3.

It is probably obvious to you that if you are taxable and transact in options, and especially if you have both stock and offsetting option positions, you should be prepared to seek professional tax advice.

---

[13] For an illustration of the complexity, in this particular case, an exception to the straddle rules occurs if the stock and put are a "married put," meaning that the two are purchased together and the stock is delivered to settle the put.

CHAPTER 3

Insurance, Collars, and Other Strategies

In the last chapter we introduced forwards, calls, and puts; showed that options are insurance; and looked at an example of how options can be building blocks. In this chapter we continue these themes, showing how the use of options can be interpreted as buying or selling insurance. We also continue the building block approach, examining the link between forward prices and option prices, and looking at some common option strategies, including spreads, straddles, and collars. Among your goals in this chapter should be to understand the reasons for using one strategy instead of another and to become facile with drawing and interpreting profit and loss diagrams.

3.1 BASIC INSURANCE STRATEGIES

There are infinite ways to combine options to create different payoffs. In this section we examine two important kinds of strategies in which the option is combined with a position in the underlying asset. First, options can be used to insure long or short asset positions. Second, options can be written against an asset position, in which case the option writer is selling insurance. In this section we consider four positions: Being long the asset coupled with a purchased put or written call, and being short the asset coupled with a purchased call or written put.

In this section we continue to use the S&R index examples presented in Sections 2.2 and 2.3. We assumed a 2% effective 6-month interest rate, and premiums of $93.809 for the 1000-strike 6-month call and $74.201 for the 1000-strike 6-month put.

Insuring a Long Position: Floors

The analysis in Section 2.5 demonstrated that put options are insurance against a fall in the price of an asset. Thus, if we own the S&R index, we can insure the position by buying an S&R put option. The purchase of a put option is also called a **floor,** because we are guaranteeing a minimum sale price for the value of the index.

To examine this strategy, we want to look at the *combined* payoff of the index position and put. In the last chapter we graphed them separately; now we add them together to see the net effect of holding both positions at the same time.

Table 3.1 summarizes the result of buying a 1000-strike put with 6 months to expiration, in conjunction with holding an index position with a current value of $1000. The table computes the payoff for each position and sums them to obtain the total payoff.

TABLE 3.1		Payoff and profit at expiration from purchasing the S&R index and a 1000-strike put option. Payoff is the sum of the first two columns. Cost plus interest for the position is ($1000 + $74.201) × 1.02 = $1095.68. Profit is payoff less $1095.68.

Payoff at Expiration				
S&R Index	S&R Put	Payoff	−(Cost + Interest)	Profit
$900	$100	$1000	−$1095.68	−$95.68
950	50	1000	−1095.68	−95.68
1000	0	1000	−1095.68	−95.68
1050	0	1050	−1095.68	−45.68
1100	0	1100	−1095.68	4.32
1150	0	1150	−1095.68	54.32
1200	0	1200	−1095.68	104.32

The final column takes account of financing cost by subtracting cost plus interest from the payoff to obtain profit. "Cost" here means the initial cash required to establish the position. This is positive when payment is required, and negative when cash is received. We could also have computed profit separately for the put and index. For example, if the index is $900 at expiration, we have

$$\underbrace{\$900 - (\$1000 \times 1.02)}_{\text{Profit on S\&R Index}} + \underbrace{\$100 - (\$74.201 \times 1.02)}_{\text{Profit on Put}} = -\$95.68$$

This gives the same result as the calculation performed in Table 3.1. The level of the floor is −$95.68, which is the lowest possible profit.

Figure 3.1 graphs the components of Table 3.1. Panels (c) and (d) show the payoff and profit for the combined index and put positions. The combined payoff graph in panel (c) is created by adding at each index price the value of the index and put positions; this is just like summing columns 1 and 2 in Table 3.1.

Notice in Figure 3.1 that the combined position created by adding the index and the put looks like a call. Intuitively this equivalence makes sense. A call has a limited loss—the premium—and benefits from gains in the index above the strike price. Similarly, when we own the index and buy a put, the put limits losses, but it permits us to benefit from gains in the index. Thus, at a casual level, the call on the one hand and the insured index position on the other seem to have similar characteristics.

Panel (c), however, illustrates that the payoff to the combined position is *not* identical to the payoff from buying a call [compare panel (c) to Figure 2.6]. The difference stems from the fact that buying a call entails paying only the option premium, while buying the index and put entails paying for *both* the index and the put option, which together are more expensive than buying a call. The profit diagram in panel (d), however,

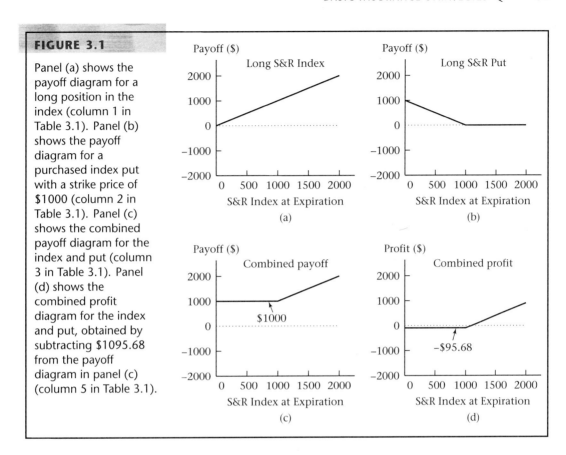

FIGURE 3.1

Panel (a) shows the payoff diagram for a long position in the index (column 1 in Table 3.1). Panel (b) shows the payoff diagram for a purchased index put with a strike price of $1000 (column 2 in Table 3.1). Panel (c) shows the combined payoff diagram for the index and put (column 3 in Table 3.1). Panel (d) shows the combined profit diagram for the index and put, obtained by subtracting $1095.68 from the payoff diagram in panel (c) (column 5 in Table 3.1).

does look like a call. We discussed in Section 2.1 that adding a bond to a payoff diagram shifts it vertically but leaves a profit diagram unaffected. The combined position of index plus put in panel (c) is actually equivalent to buying a 1000-strike call and buying a zero-coupon bond that pays $1000 at expiration of the option.

The profit diagram in panel (d) of Figure 3.1 does not merely resemble the profit diagram for buying an S&R index call with a strike price of $1000, graphed in Figure 2.7; it is identical. We can see this by comparing Table 2.2 with Table 3.1. The profit of −$95.68 for prices below $1000 is exactly the future value of the 1000-strike 6-month to expiration call premium above.

The zero-coupon bond thus affects the payoff in panel (c), but leaves profit in panel (d) unaffected. The cash flows in purchasing a call are different from the cash flows in buying an asset and insuring it, but the profit for the two positions is the same. If we had explicitly borrowed the present value of $1000 ($1000/1.02 = $980.39) to offset the cost of the index and put, then the payoff and profit diagrams, panels (c) and (d) in Figure 3.1, would be identical.

The point that buying an asset and a put generates a position that looks like a call can also be seen using the homeowner's insurance example from Section 2.5. There,

FIGURE 3.2

Payoff to owning a
house and owning
insurance. We assume a
$25,000 deductible and
a $200,000 house, with
the policy costing
$15,000.

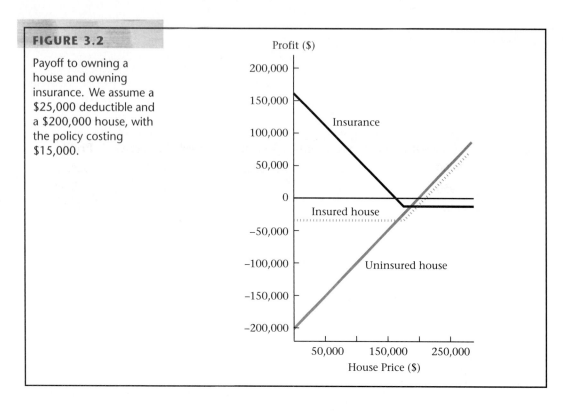

we examined the insurance policy in isolation. However, in practice, a buyer of home-owner's insurance also owns the insured asset (the house). Owning a home is analogous to owning the stock index, and insuring the house is like owning a put. Thus, owning a home plus insurance is like owning the index and owning a put. Figure 3.2 depicts the insurance policy from Figure 2.13, together with the uninsured house and the combined position. Interpreting the house as the S&R index and insurance as the put, Figure 3.2 looks exactly like Figure 3.1. *An insured house has a profit diagram that looks like a call option.*

Insuring a Short Position: Caps

If we have a short position in the S&R index, we experience a loss when the index rises. We can insure a short position by purchasing a call option to protect against a higher price of repurchasing the index.[1] Buying a call option is also called a **cap.**

....

[1] Keep in mind that if you have an obligation to buy the index in the future but the price is not fixed, then you have an *implicit* short position (if the price goes up, you will have to pay more). A call is insurance for both explicit and implicit short-sellers.

TABLE 3.2   Payoff and profit at expiration from short-selling the S&R index and buying a 1000 strike call option at a premium of $93.809. The payoff is the sum of the first two columns. Cost plus interest for the position is $(-\$1000 + \$93.809) \times 1.02 = -\$924.32$. Profit is payoff plus $924.32.

Payoff at Expiration				
Short S&R Index	S&R Call	Payoff	−(Cost + Interest)	Profit
−$900	$0	−$900	$924.32	$24.32
−950	0	−950	924.32	−25.68
−1000	0	−1000	924.32	−75.68
−1050	50	−1000	924.32	−75.68
−1100	100	−1000	924.32	−75.68
−1150	150	−1000	924.32	−75.68
−1200	200	−1000	924.32	−75.68

Table 3.2 presents the payoff and profit for a short position in the index coupled with a purchased call option. Because we short the index, we earn interest on the short proceeds less the cost of the call option, giving −$924.32 as the future value of the cost.

Figure 3.3 graphs the columns of Table 3.2. The payoff and profit diagrams resemble those of a purchased put. As with the insured index position in Figure 3.1, we have to be careful in dealing with cash flows. The *payoff* in panel (c) of Figure 3.3 is like that of a purchased put coupled with borrowing. In this case, the payoff diagram for shorting the index and buying a call is equivalent to that from buying a put and borrowing the present value of $1000 ($980.39). Since profit diagrams are unaffected by borrowing, however, the profit diagram in panel (d) is exactly the same as that for a purchased S&R index put. You can see this by comparing panel (d) with Figure 2.9. Not only does the insured short position look like a put, it has the same loss as a purchased put if the price is above $1000: $75.68, which is the future value of the $74.201 put premium.

Selling Insurance

We can expect that some investors want to purchase insurance. However, for every insurance buyer there must be an insurance seller. In this section we examine strategies in which investors *sell* insurance.

It is possible, of course, for an investor to simply sell calls and puts. Often, however, investors also have a position in the asset when they sell insurance. Writing an option when there is a corresponding long position in the underlying asset is called **covered writing, option overwriting,** or selling a covered call. All three terms mean

FIGURE 3.3

Panel (a) shows the payoff diagram for a short position in the index (column 1 in Table 3.2). Panel (b) shows the payoff diagram for a purchased index call with a strike price of $1000 (column 2 in Table 3.2). Panel (c) shows the combined payoff diagram for the short index and long call (column 3 in Table 3.2). Panel (d) shows the combined profit diagram for the short index and long call, obtained by adding $924.32 to the payoff diagram in panel (c) (column 5 in Table 3.2).

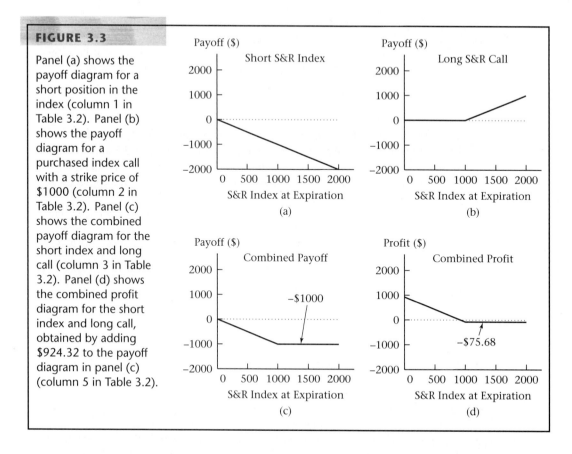

essentially the same thing.[2] In contrast, **naked writing** occurs when the writer of an option does not have a position in the asset.

In addition to the covered writing strategies we will discuss here, there are other insurance-selling strategies, such as delta-hedging, which are less risky than naked writing and are used in practice by market-makers. We will discuss these other strategies later in the book, particularly in Chapter 13.

Covered call writing   If we own the S&R index and simultaneously sell a call option, we have written a **covered call.** A covered call will have limited profitability if the index increases, because an option writer is obligated to sell the index for the strike price. Should the index decrease, the loss on the index is offset by the premium earned from

---

[2]Technically, "option overwriting" refers to selling a call on stock you already own, while a "covered write" entails simultaneously buying the stock and selling a call. The distinction is irrelevant for our purposes.

selling the call. A payoff with limited profit for price increases and potentially large losses for price decreases sounds like a written put.

Because the covered call looks like a written put, the maximum profit will be the same as with a written put. Suppose the index is $1100 at expiration. The profit is

$$\underbrace{\$1100 - (\$1000 \times 1.02)}_{\text{Profit on S\&R Index}} + \underbrace{(\$93.809 \times 1.02) - \$100}_{\text{Profit on Written Call}} = \$75.68$$

which is the future value of the premium received from writing a 1000-strike put.

The profit from writing the 1000-strike call is computed in Table 3.3 and graphed in Figure 3.4. If the index falls, we lose money on the index but the option premium partially offsets the loss. If the index rises above the strike price, the written option loses money, negating gains on the index.

Comparing Table 3.3 with Table 2.3, we can see that writing the covered call generates *exactly* the same profit as selling a put.

Why would anyone write a covered call? Suppose you have the view that the index is unlikely to move either up or down. (This is sometimes called a "neutral" market view.) If in fact the index does not move and you have written a call, then you keep the premium. If you are wrong and the stock appreciates, you forgo gains you would have had if you did not write the call.

Covered puts A covered put is achieved by writing a put against a short position on the index. The written put obligates you to buy the index—for a loss—if it goes down

---

TABLE 3.3   Payoff and profit at expiration from purchasing the S&R index and selling a 1000-strike call option. The payoff column is the sum of the first two columns. Cost plus interest for the position is ($1000 − $93.809) × 1.02 = $924.32. Profit is payoff less $924.32.

Payoff at Expiration				
S&R Index	**Short S&R Call**	**Payoff**	**−(Cost + Interest)**	**Profit**
$900	$0	$900	−$924.32	−$24.32
950	0	950	−924.32	25.68
1000	0	1000	−924.32	75.68
1050	−50	1000	−924.32	75.68
1100	−100	1000	−924.32	75.68
1150	−150	1000	−924.32	75.68
1200	−200	1000	−924.32	75.68

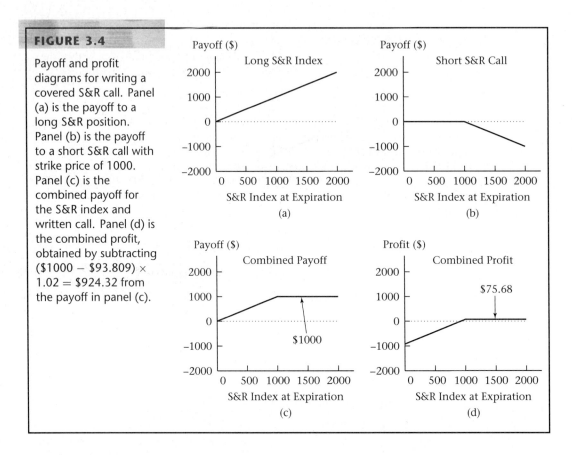

FIGURE 3.4

Payoff and profit diagrams for writing a covered S&R call. Panel (a) is the payoff to a long S&R position. Panel (b) is the payoff to a short S&R call with strike price of 1000. Panel (c) is the combined payoff for the S&R index and written call. Panel (d) is the combined profit, obtained by subtracting ($1000 − $93.809) × 1.02 = $924.32 from the payoff in panel (c).

in price. Thus, for index prices below the strike price, the loss on the written put offsets the short stock. For index prices above the strike price, you lose on the short stock.

A position where you have a constant payoff below the strike and increasing losses above the strike sounds like a written call. In fact, shorting the index and writing a put produces a profit diagram that is exactly the same as for a written call. Figure 3.5 shows this graphically, and Problem 3.2 asks you to verify this by constructing a payoff table.

3.2 SYNTHETIC FORWARDS

It is possible to mimic a long forward position on an asset by buying a call and selling a put, with each option having the same strike price and time to expiration. For example, we could buy the 1000-strike S&R call and sell the 1000-strike S&R put, each with 6 months to expiration. In 6 months we will be obliged to pay $1000 to buy the index, just as if we had entered into a forward contract.

For example, suppose the index in 6 months is at 900. We will not exercise the call, but we have written a put. The put buyer will exercise the right to sell the index

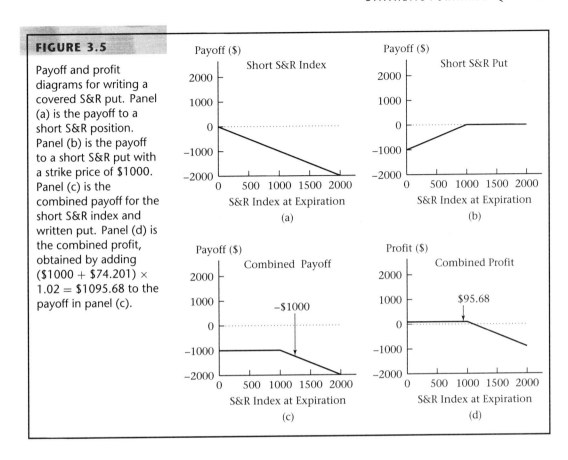

FIGURE 3.5

Payoff and profit diagrams for writing a covered S&R put. Panel (a) is the payoff to a short S&R position. Panel (b) is the payoff to a short S&R put with a strike price of $1000. Panel (c) is the combined payoff for the short S&R index and written put. Panel (d) is the combined profit, obtained by adding ($1000 + $74.201) × 1.02 = $1095.68 to the payoff in panel (c).

for $1000; therefore we are obligated to buy the index at $1000. If instead the index is at $1100, the put is not exercised, but we exercise the call, buying the index for $1000. Thus, whether the index rises or falls, when the options expire we buy the index for the strike price of the options, $1000.

The purchased call, written put, and combined positions are shown in Figure 3.6. The purchase of a call and sale of a put creates a *synthetic* long forward contract, which has two minor differences from the actual forward:

1. The forward contract has a zero premium, while the synthetic forward requires that we pay the net option premium.

2. With the forward contract we pay the forward price, while with the synthetic forward we pay the strike price.

If you think about it, these two considerations must be related. If we set the strike price low, we are obligated to buy the index at a discount relative to the forward price. Buying at a lower price than the forward price is a benefit. In order to obtain this benefit we have to pay the positive net option premium, which stems from the call being more

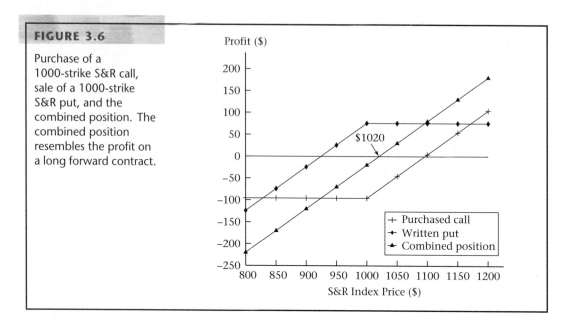

FIGURE 3.6

Purchase of a 1000-strike S&R call, sale of a 1000-strike S&R put, and the combined position. The combined position resembles the profit on a long forward contract.

expensive than the put. In fact, in Figure 3.6, the implicit cost of the synthetic forward—the price at which the profit on the combined call-put position is zero—is $1020, which is the S&R forward price.

Similarly, if we set the strike price high, we are obligated to buy the index at a high price relative to the forward price. To offset the extra cost of acquiring the index using the high strike options, it makes sense that we would receive payment initially. This would occur if the put that we sell is more expensive than the call we buy.

Finally, if we set the strike price equal to the forward price, then to mimic the forward the initial premium must equal zero. In this case, put and call premiums must be equal.

Put-Call Parity

We can summarize this argument by saying that *the net cost of buying the index using options must equal the net cost of buying the index using a forward contract.* If at time 0 we enter into a long forward position expiring at time T, we obligate ourselves to buying the index at the forward price, $F_{0,T}$. The present value of buying the index in the future is just the present value of the forward price, $PV(F_{0,T})$.

If instead we buy a call and sell a put today to guarantee the purchase price for the index in the future, the present value of the cost is the net option premium for buying the call and selling the put, $Call(K, T) - Put(K, T)$, plus the present value of the strike price, $PV(K)$. (The notations "$Call(K, T)$" and "$Put(K, T)$" denote the premiums of options with strike price K and with T periods until expiration.)

Equating the costs of the alternative ways to buy the index at time t gives us

$$PV(F_{0,T}) = [\text{Call}(K, T) - \text{Put}(K, T)] + PV(K)$$

We can rewrite this as

$$\boxed{\text{Call}(K, T) - \text{Put}(K, T) = PV(F_{0,T} - K)} \qquad (3.1)$$

In words, the present value of the bargain element from buying the index at the strike price [the right-hand side of equation (3.1)] must be offset by the initial net option premium [the left-hand side of equation (3.1)]. Equation (3.1) is known as **put-call parity,** and one of the most important relations in options.

Example 3.1 As an example of equation (3.1), consider buying the 6-month 1000-strike S&R call for a premium of $93.809 and selling the 6-month 1000-strike put for a premium of $74.201. These transactions create a synthetic forward permitting us to buy the index in 6 months for $1000. Because the actual forward price is $1020, this synthetic forward permits us to buy the index at a bargain of $20, the present value of which is $20/1.02 = $19.61. The difference in option premiums must therefore be $19.61. In fact, $93.809 − $74.201 = $19.61. This result is exactly what we would get with equation (3.1):

$$\$93.809 - \$74.201 = PV(\$1020 - \$1000) \qquad ◊$$

A forward contract for which the premium is not zero is sometimes called an **off-market forward.** This terminology arises since a true forward by definition has a zero premium. Therefore, a forward contract with a nonzero premium must have a forward price which is "off the market (forward) price." Unless the strike price equals the forward price, buying a call and selling a put creates an off-market forward.

Equivalence of different positions We have seen earlier that buying the index and buying a put generates the same profit as buying a call. Similarly, selling a covered call (buying the index and selling a call) generates the same profit as selling a put. Equation (3.1) explains why this happens.

Consider buying the index and buying a put, as in Section 3.1. Recall that, in this example, we have the forward price equal to $1020 and the index price equal to $1000. Thus, the present value of the forward price equals the index price. Rewriting equation (3.1) gives

$$PV(F_{0,T}) + \text{Put}(K, T) = \text{Call}(K, T) + PV(K)$$
$$\$1000 + \$74.201 = \$93.809 + \$980.39$$

That is, buying the index and buying the put cost the same, and generate the same payoff, as buying the call and buying a zero-coupon bond costing $PV(K)$. (Recall from Section 2.1 that a bond does not affect profit.)

Similarly, in the case of writing a covered call, we have

$$PV(F_{0,T}) - Call(K, T) = PV(K) - Put(K, T)$$

That is, writing a covered call has the same profit as lending $PV(K)$ and selling a put. Equation (3.1) provides a tool for constructing equivalent positions.

No arbitrage   In deriving equation (3.1), and in some earlier discussions, we relied on the idea that if two different investments generate the same payoff, they must have the same cost. This commonsensical idea is one of the most important in the book. If equation (3.1) did not hold, there would be both low-cost and high-cost ways to acquire the index at time T. We could simultaneously buy the index at low cost and sell the index at high cost. This transaction has no risk (since we both buy and sell the index) and generates a positive cash flow (because of the difference in costs). Taking advantage of such an opportunity is called arbitrage, and the idea that prices should not permit arbitrage is called "no-arbitrage pricing." We implicitly illustrated this idea earlier in showing how owning the index and buying a put has the same profit as a call, etc. No-arbitrage pricing will be a major theme in Chapter 5 and beyond.[3]

3.3 SPREADS AND COLLARS

There are many well-known, commonly used strategies that combine two or more options. In this section we discuss some of these strategies and explain the motivation for using them. The underlying theme in this section is that there are always trade-offs in designing a position: It is always possible to lower the cost of a position by reducing its payoff. Thus there are many variations on each particular strategy.

All the examples in this section will use the set of option prices in Table 3.4. We will assume the continuously compounded interest rate is 8%.

TABLE 3.4	Black-Scholes option prices assuming stock price = $40, volatility = 30%, effective annual risk-free rate = 8.33% (8%, continuously compounded), dividend yield = $0, and 91 days to expiration.

Strike	Call	Put
35	6.13	0.44
40	2.78	1.99
45	.97	5.08

----

[3]Another way to express the principle of no arbitrage is using profit diagrams. Given two profit diagrams, there is an arbitrage opportunity if one diagram is everywhere above the other.

Bull and Bear Spreads

An option **spread** is a position consisting of only calls or only puts, in which some options are purchased and some written. Spreads are a common strategy. In this section we define some typical spread strategies and explain why you might use a spread.

Suppose you believe a stock will appreciate. Let's compare two ways to speculate on this belief: entering into a long forward contract or buying a call option with the strike price equal to the forward price. The forward contract has a zero premium and the call has a positive premium. A difference in payoffs explains the difference in premiums. If the stock price at expiration is greater than the forward price, the forward contract and call have the same payoff. If the stock price is less than the forward price, however, the forward contract has a loss and the call is worth zero. Put-call parity tells us that the call is equivalent to the forward contract plus a put option. Thus, the call premium equals the cost of the put, which is insurance against the stock price being less than the forward price.

You might ask: Is there a lower-cost way to speculate that the stock price will rise, that still has the insurance implicit in the call? The answer is yes: You can lower the cost of your strategy if you are willing to reduce your profit should the stock appreciate. You can do this by selling a call at a higher strike price. The owner of this second call buys appreciation above the higher strike price and pays you a premium. You achieve a lower cost by giving up some portion of profit. A position in which you buy a call and sell an otherwise identical call with a higher strike price is an example of a **bull spread.**

Bull spreads can also be constructed using puts. Perhaps surprisingly, you can achieve the same result either by buying a low-strike call and selling a high-strike call, or by buying a low-strike put and selling a high-strike put.

Spreads constructed with either calls or puts are sometimes called **vertical spreads.** The terminology stems from the way option prices are typically presented, with strikes arrayed vertically (as in Table 3.4).

Example 3.2   To see how a bull spread arises, suppose we want to speculate on the stock price increasing. Consider buying a 40-strike call with 3 months to expiration. From Table 3.4, the premium for this call is $2.78. We can reduce the cost of the position—and also the potential profit—by selling the 45-strike call.

An easy way to construct the graph for this position is to emulate a spreadsheet: For each price, compute the profit of each option position and add up the profits for the individual positions. It is worth working through one example in detail to see how this is done.

The initial net cost of the two options is $2.78 − $.97 = $1.81. With 3 months interest, the total cost at expiration is $1.81 × (1.0833)^{0.25} = $1.85. Table 3.5 computes the cash flow at expiration for both options and computes profit on the position by subtracting the future value of the net premium.

Figure 3.7 graphs the position in Table 3.5. You should verify that if you buy the 40-strike put and sell the 45-strike put, you obtain exactly the same graph.   ≋

Stock Price at Expiration	Purchased 40-Call	Written 45-Call	Premium Plus Interest	Total
$35.0	$0.0	$0.0	−$1.85	−$1.85
37.5	0.0	0.0	−1.85	−1.85
40.0	0.0	0.0	−1.85	−1.85
42.5	2.5	0.0	−1.85	0.65
45.0	5.0	0.0	−1.85	3.15
47.5	7.5	−2.5	−1.85	3.15
50.0	10.0	−5.0	−1.85	3.15

TABLE 3.5 Profit at expiration from purchase of 40-strike call and sale of 45-strike call.

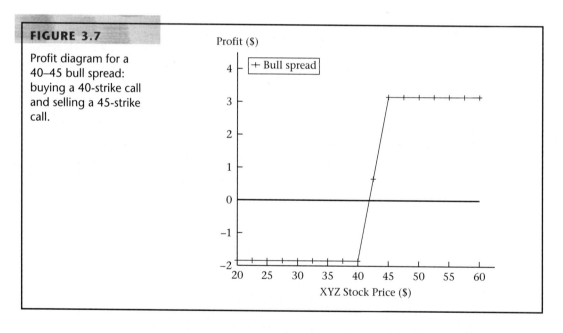

FIGURE 3.7

Profit diagram for a 40–45 bull spread: buying a 40-strike call and selling a 45-strike call.

The opposite of a bull spread is a **bear spread.** Using the options from the above example, we could create a bear spread by selling the 40-strike call and buying the 45-strike call. The profit diagram would be exactly the opposite of Figure 3.7.

Box Spreads

A **box spread** is accomplished by using options to create a synthetic long forward at one price and a synthetic short forward at a different price. This strategy guarantees a cash flow in the future. Hence, it is an option spread that is purely a means of borrowing or lending money: It is costly but has no stock price risk. The reasons for using a box spread are discussed in the box on page 74.

Example 3.3   Suppose we simultaneously enter into the following two transactions:

1. Buy a 40-strike call and sell a 40-strike put,

2. Sell a 45-strike call and buy a 45-strike put.

The first transaction is a synthetic forward purchase of a stock for $40, while the second transaction is the synthetic forward sale of the stock for $45. Clearly the payoff at expiration will be $5; hence, the transaction has no stock price risk. Using the assumptions in Table 3.4, the cost of the strategy should be

$$5 \times (1.0833)^{-0.25} = \$4.90$$

In fact, using the premiums in Table 3.4, the initial cash flow is

$$(\$1.99 - \$2.78) + (\$0.97 - \$5.08) = -\$4.90$$

Another way to view this transaction is that we have bought a 40–45 bull spread using calls (buy 40 call, sell 45 call), and bought a 40–45 bear spread using puts (sell 40 put, buy 45 put). 🜋

Ratio Spreads

A **ratio spread** is constructed by buying m calls at one strike and selling n calls at a different strike, with all options having the same time to maturity and same underlying asset. Ratio spreads can also be constructed with puts. You are asked to construct ratio spreads in problem 3.15. Also, a ratio spread constructed by buying a low-strike call and selling two higher-strike calls is one of the positions depicted in the chapter summary in Figure 3.17.

Since ratio spreads involve buying and selling unequal numbers of options, it is possible to construct ratio spreads with zero premium. The significance of this may not be obvious to you now, but we will see in Chapter 4 that by using ratio spreads we can construct paylater strategies: insurance that costs nothing if the insurance is not needed. The trade-off to this, as you might guess, is that the insurance is *more* costly if it *is* needed.

Collars

A **collar** is the purchase of a put option and the sale of a call option with a higher strike price, with both options having the same underlying asset and having the same expiration date. If the position is reversed (sale of a put and purchase of a call), the collar is written. The **collar width** is the difference between the call and put strikes.

The Use of Box Spreads

A box spread is an alternative to buying a bond. Option market-makers in particular have low transaction costs and can sell box spreads, which is equivalent to borrowing. Box spreads can therefore be a source of funds. In the past, box spreads also provided a tax benefit for some investors. Although a change in the tax law in 1993 ostensibly eliminated this use of box spreads, the issue provides an illustration of why derivatives create problems for the tax authorities.

Consider a taxable investor who has sold stock investments at a loss. This loss is classified for tax purposes as a capital loss. In the United States, capital gains are always taxed, but capital losses are only deductible against capital gains. (The exception to this is that individual investors are allowed to deduct a limited amount of capital losses against ordinary income.) Thus, a taxable investor with large capital losses would like to find a mechanism to generate income which can be labeled as capital gains. This is not as easy as it sounds. A risk-free zero-coupon bond—which is certain to appreciate over its life—generates interest income, which cannot be used to offset capital losses. A stock held to generate gains could instead go down in price, generating additional losses.

A box spread sounds as if it should enable investors to generate capital gains as needed: It is a synthetic bond, guaranteed to appreciate in value just like a bond. Moreover, the gain or loss on an option is a capital gain or loss. *If the change in value of a box spread were taxed as a capital gain, box spreads could be used to create risk-free capital gains income, against which capital losses could be offset.*

Lawmakers in the United States have anticipated strategies like this. Section 1258 of the U.S. Tax Code, enacted in 1993, explicitly states that capital income should be taxed as ordinary income if all expected return is due to time value of money on the investment (in other words, if the investment is equivalent to a bond). This would seem to eliminate the tax motive for entering into box spreads. The problem for the tax authorities, however, is how to identify taxpayers using box spreads for this purpose. There is nothing wrong with entering into a box spread; the law is only violated if the taxpayer reports the resulting income as a capital gain. This is difficult to detect. Tax rules may also differ internationally. In *Griffin* v. *Citibank Investments Ltd.* (2000), for example, British courts ruled that a box spread was not necessarily equivalent to a loan.

The fundamental problem is that the tax code calls for different taxation of bonds and options, but options can be used to create bonds. There are many similar illustrations of this problem.

Example 3.4 Suppose we sell a 45-strike call with a $0.97 premium and buy a 40-strike put with a $1.99 premium. This collar is shown in Figure 3.8. Because the purchased put has a higher premium than the written call, the position requires investment of $1.02. ≋

FIGURE 3.8

Profit diagram of a purchased collar constructed by selling a 45-strike call and buying a 40-strike put.

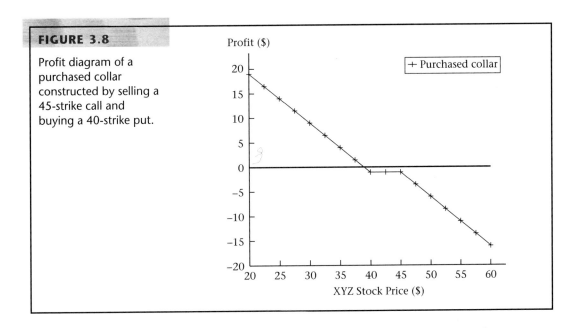

If you hold this book at a distance and squint at Figure 3.8, the collar resembles a short forward contract. Economically, it *is* like a short forward contract in that it is fundamentally a short position: The position benefits from price decreases in the underlying asset and suffers losses from price increases. A collar differs from a short forward contract in having a range between the strikes in which the expiration payoff is unaffected by changes in the value of the underlying asset.

In practice collars are frequently used to implement insurance strategies—for example, by buying a collar when we own the stock. This position, which we will call a *collared stock*, entails buying the stock, buying a put, and selling a call. It is an insured position because we own the asset and buy a put. The sale of a call helps to pay for the purchase of the put. The collared stock looks like a bull spread; however, it arises from a different set of transactions. The bull spread is created by buying one option and selling another. The collared stock begins with a position in the underlying asset that is coupled with a collar.

Example 3.5 Suppose that you own shares of XYZ for which the current price is $40, and you wish to buy insurance. You do this by purchasing put options. A way to reduce the cost of the insurance is to sell an out-of-the-money call. The profit calculations for this set of transactions—buy the stock, buy a 40-strike put, sell a 45-strike call—are shown in Table 3.6. Comparing this table to Table 3.5 demonstrates that profit on the collared stock position is identical to profit on the bull spread. Note that it is essential to account for interest as a cost of holding the stock. ◊

TABLE 3.6			Profit at expiration from purchase of 40-strike put and sale of 45-strike call.		
Stock Price at Expiration	Purchased 40-Put	Written 45-Call	Premium Plus Interest	Profit on Stock	Total
$35.00	$5.00	$0.00	−$1.04	−$5.81	−$1.85
37.50	2.50	0.00	−1.04	−3.31	−1.85
40.00	0.00	0.00	−1.04	−0.81	−1.85
42.50	0.00	0.00	−1.04	1.69	0.65
45.00	0.00	0.00	−1.04	4.19	3.15
47.50	0.00	−2.50	−1.04	6.69	3.15
50.00	0.00	−5.00	−1.04	9.19	3.15

If you have a short position in the stock, you can collar the position by buying a call for insurance and selling an out-of-the-money put to partially fund the call purchase. The result looks like a bear spread.

Zero-cost collars The collar depicted in Table 3.6 entails paying a net premium of $1.02: $1.99 for the purchased put, against $0.97 for the written call. It is possible to find strike prices for the put and call such that the two premiums exactly offset one another. This position is called a **zero-cost collar.**

To illustrate a zero-cost collar, suppose you buy the stock and buy the 40-strike put that has a premium of $1.99. Trial and error reveals that a call with a strike of $41.72 also has a premium of $1.99. Thus, you can buy a 40-strike put and sell a 41.72-strike call without paying any premium. The result is depicted in Figure 3.9. At expiration, the collar exposes you to stock price movements between $40 and $41.72, coupled with downside protection below $40. You pay for this protection by giving up gains should the stock move above $41.72.

For any given stock there is an infinite number of zero-cost collars. One way to see this is to first pick the desired put strike below the forward price. It is then possible to find a strike above the forward price such that a call has the same premium.

Understanding collars One aspect of the zero-cost collar that may seem puzzling is that you can finance the purchase of an at-the-money put by selling an out-of-the-money call. In the above example, with the stock at $40, you were able to costlessly buy a 40-strike put by also selling a 41.72-strike call. This makes it seem as if you have free insurance with some possibility of gain. Even if you are puzzled by this, you probably realize that "free" insurance is not possible, and something must be wrong with this way of thinking about the position.

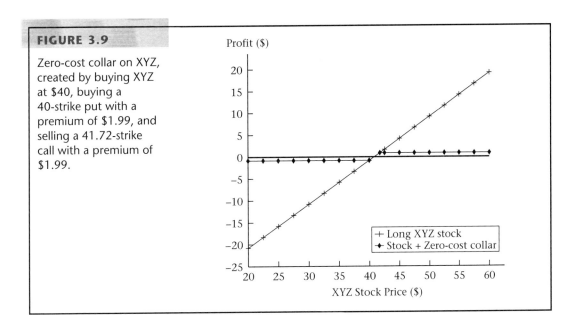

FIGURE 3.9

Zero-cost collar on XYZ, created by buying XYZ at $40, buying a 40-strike put with a premium of $1.99, and selling a 41.72-strike call with a premium of $1.99.

This puzzle is resolved by taking into account financing cost. Recall that if you pay $40 for stock and sell it for $40 in 91 days, *you have not broken even.* You have lost money, because you have forgone $40 × ((1.0833)$^{0.25}$ − 1) = $0.808 in interest. Thus, the true break-even stock price in this example is $40.808, about halfway between $40 and $41.72.

To illustrate the use and pricing of collars, consider an executive who owns a large position in company stock. Such executives frequently hedge their stock positions, using zero-cost collars with several years to maturity.[4] Suppose, for example, that Microsoft has a price of $30/share and an executive wishes to hedge 1 million shares. If the executive buys a 30-strike put with 3 years to maturity, what 3-year call will have the same premium? Assuming an effective annual risk-free rate of 6%, a zero dividend yield, and a 40% volatility, the Black-Scholes price is $5.298 for a 30-strike put with 3 years to maturity. Using trial and error (or a numerical solver), a call option with a strike of $47.39 has the same premium. Once again, the zero-cost collar seems highly asymmetric. However, this comparison does not take into account financing cost. The executive selling stock in three years for $30/share will in fact have lost three years' worth of interest: $30 × [(1.06)^3 − 1] = $5.73.

The cost of the collar and the forward price Suppose you try to construct a zero-cost collar in which you set the strike of the put option at the stock price plus financing

[4]For an account of this, see "Executive Relief," *The Economist,* April 3, 1999, p. 64.

cost—i.e., the future value of the stock price. In the 91-day example above, this would require that you set the put strike equal to $40.808, which gives a premium of $2.39. The call premium at this strike is also $2.39! *If you try to insure against all losses on the stock, including interest, then a zero-cost collar has zero width.*

This is an implication of put-call parity, equation (3.1). It turns out that $40.808 is also the theoretical forward price. If we set the strike equal to the forward price, the call premium equals the put premium.

3.4 SPECULATING ON VOLATILITY

collared stock

The positions we have just considered are all directional: A bull spread or a ~~collar~~ is a bet that the price of the underlying asset will increase. Options can also be used to create positions that are nondirectional with respect to the underlying asset. With a nondirectional position, the holder does not care whether the stock goes up or down, but only how much it moves. We now examine straddles, strangles, and butterfly spreads, which are examples of nondirectional speculations.

Straddles

Consider the strategy of buying a call and a put with the same strike price and time to expiration: This strategy is called a **straddle.** The general idea of a straddle is simple: If the stock price rises, there will be a profit on the purchased call, and if the stock price declines there will be a profit on the purchased put. Thus, the advantage of a straddle is that it can profit from stock price moves in both directions. The disadvantage to a straddle is that it has a high premium because it requires purchasing two options. If the stock price at expiration is near the strike price, the two premiums are lost. The profit diagram for a 40-strike straddle is graphed in Figure 3.10. The initial cost of the straddle at a stock price of $40 is $4.77: $2.78 for the call and $1.99 for the put.

Figure 3.10 demonstrates that a straddle is a bet that volatility will be high: The buyer of an at-the-money straddle is hoping that the stock price will move but does not care about the direction of the move. Because option prices reflect the market's estimate of volatility, the cost of a straddle will be greater when the market's perception is that volatility is greater. If at a given set of option prices all investors found it desirable to buy straddles, then option prices would increase. Thus, purchasing a straddle is really a bet that volatility is greater than the market's assessment of volatility, as reflected in option prices.

Strangle   The disadvantage of a straddle is the high premium cost. To reduce the premium, you can buy out-of-the-money options rather than at-the-money options. Such a position is called a **strangle.** For example, consider buying a 35-strike put and a 45-strike call, for a total premium of $1.41, with a future value of $1.44. These transactions reduce your maximum loss if the options expire with the stock near $40, but they also increase the stock-price move required for a profit.

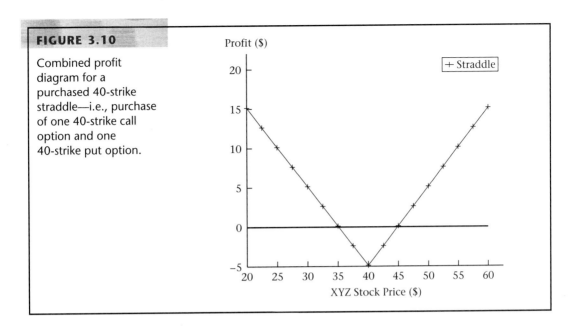

FIGURE 3.10

Combined profit diagram for a purchased 40-strike straddle—i.e., purchase of one 40-strike call option and one 40-strike put option.

Figure 3.11 shows the 40-strike straddle graphed against the 35–45 strangle. This comparison illustrates a key point: In comparing any two fairly priced option positions, there will always be a region where each outperforms the other. Indeed, this is necessary to have a fairly priced position.

In Figure 3.11, the strangle outperforms the straddle roughly when the stock price at expiration is between $36.57 and $43.43. Obviously, there is a much broader range in which the straddle outperforms the strangle. How can you decide which is the better investment? The answer is that unless you have a particular view on the stock's performance, you cannot say that one position is preferable to the other. An option pricing model implicitly evaluates the likelihood that one strategy will outperform the other, and it computes option prices so that the two strategies are equivalently fair deals. An investor might have a preference for one strategy over the other due to subjective probabilities that differ from the market's.

Written straddle   What if an investor believes that volatility is *lower* than the market's assessment? Because a purchased straddle is a bet that volatility is high (relative to the market's assessment), a **written straddle**—selling a call and put with the same strike price and time to expiration—is a bet that volatility is low (relative to the market's assessment).

Figure 3.12 depicts a written straddle, which is exactly the opposite of Figure 3.10, the purchased straddle. The written straddle is most profitable if the stock price is $40 at expiration, and in this sense it is a bet on low volatility. What is striking about Figure 3.12, however, is the potential for loss. A large change in the stock price in either direction leads to a large, potentially unlimited, loss.

FIGURE 3.11

40-strike straddle and strangle composed of 35-strike put and 45-strike call.

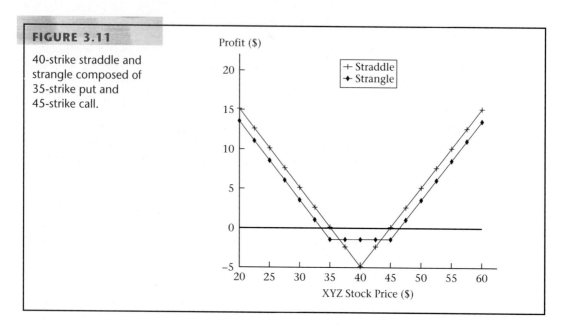

FIGURE 3.12

Profit at expiration from a written straddle—i.e., selling a 40-strike call and a 40-strike put.

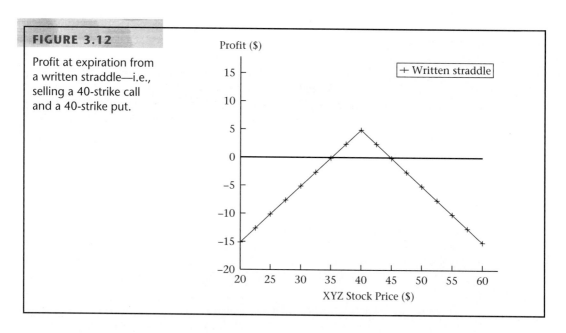

It might occur to you that an investor wishing to bet that volatility will be low could write a straddle and acquire insurance against extreme negative outcomes. That intuition is correct and leads to our next strategy.

Butterfly Spreads

The straddle writer can insure against large losses on the straddle by buying options to protect against losses on both the upside and downside. Buying an out-of-the-money put provides insurance on the downside, protecting against losses on the at-the-money written put. Buying an out-of-the-money call provides insurance on the upside, protecting against losses on the written at-the-money call.

Figure 3.13 displays the straddle written at a strike price of $40, along with the options to safeguard the position: A 35-strike put and a 45-strike call. The net result of combining these three strategies is an insured written straddle, which is called a **butterfly spread,** graphed in Figure 3.14. It can be thought of as a written straddle for the timid (or for the prudent!).

Comparing the butterfly spread to the written straddle (Figure 3.14), we see that the butterfly spread has a lower maximum profit (due to the cost of insurance) if the stock at expiration is close to $40, and a higher profit if there is a large move in the stock price, in which case the insurance becomes valuable.

We will see in Chapter 9 that by understanding the butterfly spread we gain important insights into option prices. Also, the butterfly spread can be created in a variety of ways: solely with calls, solely with puts, or by using the stock and a combination of calls and puts.[5] You are asked to verify this in Problem 3.18. The spread in Figure 3.14

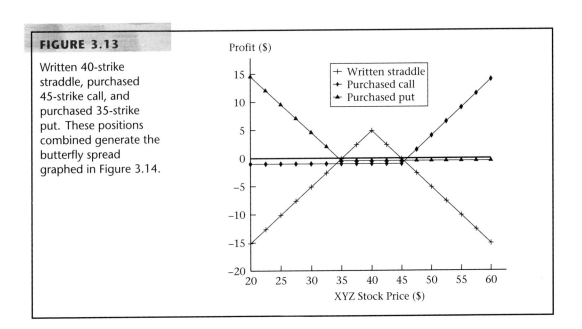

FIGURE 3.13

Written 40-strike straddle, purchased 45-strike call, and purchased 35-strike put. These positions combined generate the butterfly spread graphed in Figure 3.14.

[5]Technically, a true butterfly spread is created solely with calls or solely with puts. A butterfly spread created by selling a straddle and buying a strangle is called an "iron butterfly."

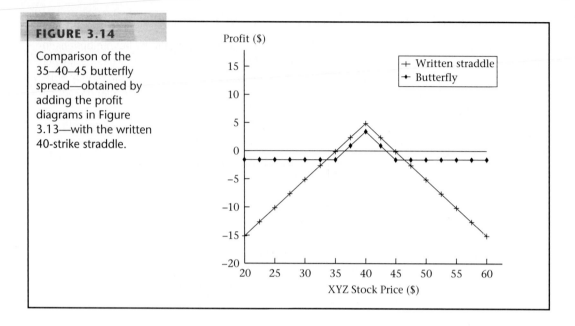

FIGURE 3.14

Comparison of the 35–40–45 butterfly spread—obtained by adding the profit diagrams in Figure 3.13—with the written 40-strike straddle.

can also be created by simultaneously buying a 35–40 bull spread and a 40–45 bear spread.

Asymmetric Butterfly Spreads

Examine Figure 3.15. It looks like a butterfly spread except that it is asymmetric: The peak is closer to the high strike than to the low strike. This picture was created by buying two 35-strike calls, selling ten 43-strike calls (with a premium of $1.525, using the assumptions in Table 3.4), and buying eight 45-strike calls. The position is like a butterfly in that it earns a profit if the stock stays within a small range, and the loss is the same for high and low stock prices. However, the profit diagram is now tilted to the right, rather than being symmetric.

Suppose you knew that you wanted a position that looks like Figure 3.15. How would you know how many options to buy and sell to construct this position? In order to obtain this position, the strikes clearly have to be at 35, 43, and 45. The total distance between 35 and 45 is 10. The number 43 is 80% ($= \frac{43-35}{10}$) of the way from 35 to 45. In fact, we can write 43 as

$$43 = (0.2 \times 35) + (0.8 \times 45)$$

This way of writing 43 tells us our call position: For every written 43-strike call, we want to buy 0.2 35 calls and 0.8 45 calls. Thus if we sell ten 43-strike calls, we buy two 35 calls and eight 45-strike calls.

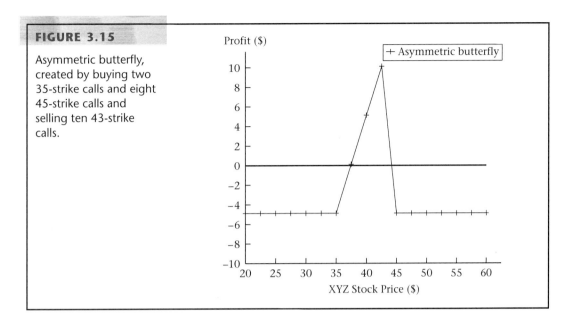

FIGURE 3.15

Asymmetric butterfly, created by buying two 35-strike calls and eight 45-strike calls and selling ten 43-strike calls.

In general, consider the strike prices K_1, K_2, and K_3, where $K_1 < K_2 < K_3$. Define λ so that

$$\lambda = \frac{K_3 - K_2}{K_3 - K_1}$$

or

$$K_2 = \lambda K_1 + (1 - \lambda) K_3$$

For example, if $K_1 = 35$, $K_2 = 43$, and $K_3 = 45$, then $\lambda = 0.2$, as in the above example. In order to construct an asymmetric butterfly, for every K_2 call we write, we buy λ K_1 calls and $1 - \lambda$ K_3 calls.

You should verify that if you buy two 35-strike puts, sell ten 43-strike puts, and buy eight 45-strike puts, you duplicate the profit diagram in Figure 3.15.

3.5 EXAMPLE: ANOTHER EQUITY-LINKED NOTE

In July 2004, Marshall & Ilsley Corp. (ticker symbol MI) raised $400 million by issuing bonds effectively maturing in August 2007.[6] Instead of making a maturity payment in cash, the bonds pay the holder in shares of Marshall & Ilsley's own stock. A bond that, under some circumstances, pays the holder in stock instead of cash is called a

---

[6]For simplicity we will refer here to the Marshall & Ilsley security as a "bond." As we will discuss in Chapter 15, it was actually a bond plus a forward contract.

convertible bond. The Marshall & Ilsley note *always* settles in stock; hence it is called a **mandatorily convertible bond.** We will discuss this particular bond more in Chapter 16, but the bond is interesting at this point because the payoff structure resembles a collar.

The bond pays an annual 6.5% coupon and at maturity makes payments in shares, with the number of shares dependent upon the firm's stock price. The specific terms of the maturity payment are in Table 3.7. To interpret this payoff, note that when the Marshall & Ilsley stock price at maturity is between $37.32 and $46.28, the payoff is a varying number of shares, selected so the bond is worth $25 (e.g., $0.5402 \times \$46.28 = \$25$).

Figure 3.16 graphs the maturity payoff of the bond as a function of the MI stock price in three years, against the payoff of owning 0.6699 shares of Marshall & Ilsley

TABLE 3.7 Number of shares paid at maturity to holders of Marshall & Ilsley bond. S_{MI} is the Marshall & Ilsley share price at maturity of the bond.

Marshall & Ilsley Share Price	Number of Shares Paid to Bondholders
$S_{MI} < 37.32$	0.6699
$37.32 \leq S_{MI} \leq 46.28$	$\$25/S_{MI}$
$46.28 < S_{MI}$	0.5402

FIGURE 3.16

Maturity payoff to the owners of the Marshall & Ilsley bond, compared to owning 0.6699 shares of Marshall & Ilsley common stock. The payoffs exclude the 6.5% distributions on the bond and dividends on Marshall & Ilsley common stock.

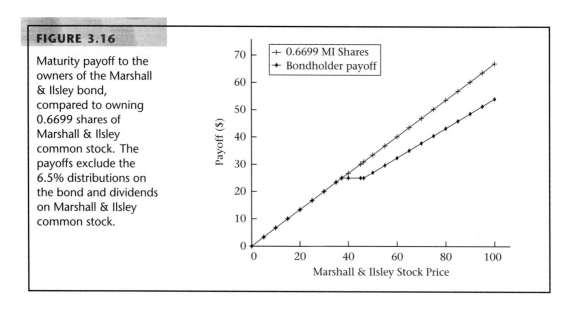

stock. Both graphs ignore dividends and other distributions. Based solely on comparing the maturity payoffs, investing in the bond is inferior to investing in the common stock. However, distributions on the bond (6.5% annually) are greater than on the stock (an annual dividend of about 2%); so without performing a valuation analysis it is impossible to say whether investors should prefer one or the other, or be indifferent. Accounting for the distributions would shift the payoff lines upward and would lead the bond to outperform 0.6699 shares of stock at low prices, with the stock outperforming the bond at high prices.

The Marshall & Ilsley share price was $37.32 on the day the bond was issued. The bond was designed so that, at issue, it would sell for $25, which is the same price as 0.6699 shares.

The bond was also designed so that bondholders would forgo 24% of the appreciation on the stock above $37.32. We have $37.32 \times 1.24 = \$46.28$, and $25/46.28 = 0.5402$. This accounts for the flat range in the payoff and the number of shares exchanged above a share price of $46.28.

Finally, in order for the bond to underperform the stock above $37.32, yet to sell at the share price, it is necessary to compensate bondholders with additional payments. The 6.5% coupon accomplishes this.

How would we price the bond? The graph in Figure 3.16 should remind you of a written collar. One way to construct the same graph is by (1) owning 0.6699 shares of stock (ignoring dividends), (2) selling 0.6699 calls with a strike price of $37.32, and (3) buying 0.5402 calls with a strike price of $46.28. The algebraic expression for the payoff is

$$\text{Payoff} = 0.6699 \times \left[S_{\text{MI}} - \max(0, S_{\text{MI}} - 37.32) + \frac{1}{1.24} \times \max(0, S_{\text{MI}} - 46.28) \right]$$
(3.2)

Note that the bond holder is implicitly selling a low strike call and buying 1/1.24 high strike calls, and is therefore owed option premium. The bondholder also forgoes dividends on the stock. These two factors explain the 6.5% distribution, which is effectively the dividend plus the amortized option premium. By pricing these options and valuing the 6.5% distribution, we can arrive at a fair price for the bond.

This discussion leaves unanswered the question of why Marshall & Ilsley would issue such a bond. We have also not discussed all the details of the bond's structure. We return to these issues in Chapter 15.

Chapter Summary

Puts are insurance against a price decline and calls are insurance against a price increase. Combining a long or short position in the asset with an offsetting position in options (for example, a long position in the asset is coupled either with a purchased put or written call) leads to the various possible positions and their equivalents in Table 3.8.

TABLE 3.8		Summary of equivalent positions from Section 3.1.
Position	**Is Equivalent To**	**And Is Called**
Index + Put	Zero-Coupon Bond + Call	Insured Asset (floor)
Index − Call	Zero-Coupon Bond − Put	Covered Written call
−Index + Call	−Zero-Coupon Bond + Put	Insured Short (cap)
−Index − Put	−Zero-Coupon Bond − Call	Covered Written Put

Buying a call and selling a put with the same strike price and time to expiration creates an obligation to buy the asset at expiration by paying the strike price. This is a synthetic forward. A synthetic forward must have the same cost in present value terms as a true forward. This observation leads to equation (3.1):

$$\text{Call}(K, T) - \text{Put}(K, T) = \text{PV}(F_{0,T} - K) \tag{3.1}$$

This relationship, called *put-call parity*, explains the difference in call and put premiums for otherwise identical options. It is one of the most important relationships in derivatives.

There are numerous strategies that permit speculating on the direction of the stock or on the size of stock price moves (volatility). Some of these positions are summarized graphically in Figure 3.17. We also categorize in Table 3.9 various strategies according to whether they reflect bullish or bearish views on the stock price direction or volatility.[7]

Netscape PEPS were equivalent to a bond coupled with an option spread, illustrating that the tools in this chapter have applicability beyond speculative investing.

FURTHER READING

In Chapter 4 we will see how firms can use these strategies to manage risk. We will further explore put-call parity in Chapter 9, in which we also will use bull, bear, and butterfly spreads to say more about what it means for an option to be fairly priced.

Put-call parity was first demonstrated in Stoll (1969). Merton (1973a) corrected the original analysis for the case of American options, for which, because of early exercise, parity need not hold. Ronn and Ronn (1989) provide a detailed examination of price bounds and returns on box spreads.

There are numerous practitioner books on option trading strategies. A classic practitioner reference is McMillan (1992).

----

[7]Table 3.9 was suggested by David Shimko.

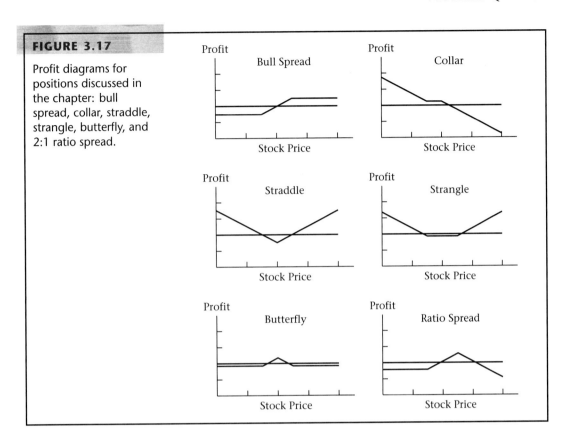

FIGURE 3.17

Profit diagrams for positions discussed in the chapter: bull spread, collar, straddle, strangle, butterfly, and 2:1 ratio spread.

TABLE 3.9 Positions consistent with different views on the stock price and volatility direction.

	Volatility Will Increase	**No Volatility View**	**Volatility Will Fall**
Price will fall	Buy puts	Sell underlying	Sell calls
No price view	Buy straddle	Do nothing	Sell straddle
Price will increase	Buy calls	Buy underlying	Sell puts

PROBLEMS

3.1. Suppose that you buy the S&R index for $1000, buy a 1000-strike put, and borrow $980.39. Perform a payoff and profit calculation mimicking Table 3.1. Graph the resulting payoff and profit diagrams for the combined position.

3.2. Suppose that you short the S&R index for $1000 and sell a 1000-strike put. Construct a table mimicking Table 3.1 which summarizes the payoff and profit of this position. Verify that your table matches Figure 3.5.

For the following problems assume the effective 6-month interest rate is 2%, the S&R 6-month forward price is $1020, and use these premiums for S&R options with 6 months to expiration:

Strike	Call	Put
$950	$120.405	$51.777
1000	93.809	74.201
1020	84.470	84.470
1050	71.802	101.214
1107	51.873	137.167

3.3. Suppose you buy the S&R index for $1000 and buy a 950-strike put. Construct payoff and profit diagrams for this position. Verify that you obtain the same payoff and profit diagram by investing $931.37 in zero-coupon bonds and buying a 950-strike call.

3.4. Suppose you short the S&R index for $1000 and buy a 950-strike call. Construct payoff and profit diagrams for this position. Verify that you obtain the same payoff and profit diagram by borrowing $931.37 and buying a 950-strike put.

3.5. Suppose you short the S&R index for $1000 and buy a 1050-strike call. Construct payoff and profit diagrams for this position. Verify that you obtain the same payoff and profit diagram by borrowing $1029.41 and buying a 1050-strike put.

3.6. Verify that you earn the same profit and payoff by (a) buying the S&R index for $1000 and (b) buying a 950-strike S&R call, selling a 950-strike S&R put, and lending $931.37.

3.7. Verify that you earn the same profit and payoff by (a) shorting the S&R index for $1000 and (b) selling a 1050-strike S&R call, buying a 1050-strike put, and borrowing $1029.41.

3.8. Suppose the premium on a 6-month S&R call is $109.20 and the premium on a put with the same strike price is $60.18. What is the strike price?

3.9. Construct payoff and profit diagrams for the purchase of a 950-strike S&R call and sale of a 1000-strike S&R call. Verify that you obtain exactly the same *profit* diagram for the purchase of a 950-strike S&R put and sale of a 1000-strike S&R put. What is the difference in the payoff diagrams for the call and put spreads? Why is there a difference?

3.10. Construct payoff and profit diagrams for the purchase of a 1050-strike S&R call and sale of a 950-strike S&R call. Verify that you obtain exactly the same *profit* diagram for the purchase of a 1050-strike S&R put and sale of a 950-strike S&R put. What is the difference in the initial cost of these positions?

3.11. Suppose you invest in the S&R index for $1000, buy a 950-strike put, and sell a 1050-strike call. Draw a profit diagram for this position. What is the net option premium? If you wanted to construct a zero-cost collar keeping the put strike equal to $950, in what direction would you have to change the call strike?

3.12. Suppose you invest in the S&R index for $1000, buy a 950-strike put, and sell a 1107-strike call. Draw a profit diagram for this position. How close is this to a zero-cost collar?

3.13. Draw profit diagrams for the following positions:

    a. 1050-strike S&R straddle.

    b. Written 950-strike S&R straddle.

    c. Simultaneous purchase of a 1050-strike straddle and sale of a 950-strike S&R straddle.

3.14. Suppose you buy a 950-strike S&R call, sell a 1000-strike S&R call, sell a 950-strike S&R put, and buy a 1000-strike S&R put.

    a. Verify that there is no S&R price risk in this transaction.

    b. What is the initial cost of the position?

    c. What is the value of the position after 6 months?

    d. Verify that the implicit interest rate in these cash flows is 2% over 6 months.

3.15. Compute profit diagrams for the following ratio spreads:

    a. Buy 950-strike call, sell two 1050-strike calls.

    b. Buy two 950-strike calls, sell three 1050-strike calls.

    c. Consider buying n 950-strike calls and selling m 1050-strike calls so that the premium of the position is zero. Considering your analysis in (a) and (b), what can you say about n/m? What exact ratio gives you a zero premium?

3.16. In the previous problem we saw that a ratio spread can have zero initial premium. Can a bull spread or bear spread have zero initial premium? A butterfly spread? Why or why not?

3.17. Construct an asymmetric butterfly using the 950-, 1020-, and 1050-strike options. How many of each option do you hold? Draw a profit diagram for the position.

3.18. Verify that the butterfly spread in Figure 3.14 can be duplicated by following transactions (use the option prices in Table 3.4):

    a. Buy 35 call, sell two 40 calls, buy 45 call.

    b. Buy 35 put, sell two 40 puts, buy 45 put.

    c. Buy stock, buy 35 put, sell two 40 calls, buy 45 call.

3.19. Here is a quote from an investment Web site about an investment strategy using options:

> One strategy investors are applying to the XYZ options is using "synthetic stock." A synthetic stock is created when an investor simultaneously purchases a call option and sells a put option on the same stock. The end result is that the synthetic stock has the same value, in terms of capital gain potential, as the underlying stock itself. Provided the premiums on the options are the same, they cancel each other out so the transaction fees are a wash.

Suppose, to be concrete, that the premium on the call you buy is the same as the premium on the put you sell, and both have the same strikes and times to expiration.

    a. What can you say about the strike price?

    b. What term best describes the position you have created?

    c. Suppose the options have a bid-ask spread. If you are creating a synthetic purchased stock and the net premium is zero *inclusive of the bid-ask spread*, where will the strike price be relative to the forward price?

    d. If you create a synthetic short stock with zero premium inclusive of the bid-ask spread, where will the strike price be relative to the forward price?

    e. Do you consider the "transaction fees" to really be "a wash"? Why or why not?

3.20. Construct a spreadsheet for which you can input up to five strike prices and quantities of put and call options bought or sold at those strikes, and which will automatically construct the total expiration payoff diagram for that position. Modify the spreadsheet to permit you to choose whether to graph a payoff or profit function.

CHAPTER 4
Introduction to Risk Management

Business, like life, is inherently risky. Firms convert inputs such as labor, raw materials, and machines into goods and services. A firm is profitable if the cost of what it produces exceeds the cost of the inputs. Prices can change, however, and what appears to be a profitable activity today may not be profitable tomorrow. Many instruments are available that permit firms to hedge various risks, ranging from commodity prices to weather. A firm that actively uses derivatives and other techniques to alter its risk and protect its profitability is engaging in **risk management.** In this chapter we take a look at how derivatives—such as forwards, calls, and puts—are used in practice to manage risk.

We begin by examining two hypothetical firms—Golddiggers, a gold-mining firm, and Auric Enterprises, a manufacturer using gold as an input—to see what risks they face and to demonstrate the use of derivatives strategies to manage those risks. After looking at these examples we will explore some reasons firms seek to manage risk in the first place.

4.1 BASIC RISK MANAGEMENT: THE PRODUCER'S PERSPECTIVE

Golddiggers is a gold-mining firm planning to mine and sell 100,000 ounces of gold over the next year. For simplicity, we will assume that they sell all of the next year's production precisely 1 year from today, receiving whatever the gold price is that day. The price of gold today is $405/oz. We will ignore production beyond the next year.

Obviously Golddiggers—like any producer—hopes that the gold price will rise over the next year. However, Golddiggers's management computes estimated net income for a range of possible prices of gold in 1 year (Table 4.1). The net income calculation shows that Golddiggers's profit is affected by gold prices.

Should Golddiggers simply shut the mine if gold prices fall enough to make net income negative? The answer depends on the extent to which costs are fixed. The firm incurs the fixed cost whether or not it produces gold. Variable costs are incurred only if the mine operates. Thus, for any gold price above the variable cost of $50/oz., it will make sense to produce gold.[1]

---

[1]Suppose the gold price is $350/oz. If Golddiggers produces no gold, the firm loses its fixed cost, $330/oz. If Golddiggers produces gold, the firm has fixed cost of $330/oz. and variable cost of $50/oz., and so loses $350 − ($330 + $50) = −$30/oz. It is better to lose only $30, so Golddiggers will produce even when they have negative net income. If the gold price were to fall below the variable cost of $50, then it would make sense to stop producing.

TABLE 4.1	Golddiggers's estimated net income one year from today, unhedged.

Gold Price in One Year	Fixed Cost	Variable Cost	Net Income
$350	−$330	−$50	−$30
$400	−$330	−$50	$20
$450	−$330	−$50	$70
$500	−$330	−$50	$120

Hedging with a Forward Contract

Golddiggers can lock in a price for gold in 1 year by entering into a short forward contract, agreeing today to sell its gold for delivery in 1 year. Suppose that gold to be delivered in 1 year can be sold today for $420/oz. and that Golddiggers agrees to sell forward all of its gold production in 1 year. We will assume in all examples that the forward contract settles financially. As noted earlier, the payoff to a forward is the same with physical or financial settlement.

Profit calculations when Golddiggers is hedged are summarized in Table 4.2. This table adds the profit on the forward contract to net income from Table 4.1. Figure 4.1 contains three curves showing the following:

- **Unhedged profit:** Since cost is $380/oz., the line labeled "unhedged seller" shows zero profit at $380, a loss at lower prices, and profit at higher prices. For example, at $420, profit is $40/oz. Since it has gold in the ground, Golddiggers has a long position in gold.

- **Profit on the short forward position:** The "short gold forward" line represents the profit from going short the gold forward contract at a forward price of $420/oz.

TABLE 4.2	Golddiggers's net income one year from today, hedged with a forward sale of gold.

Gold Price in One Year	Fixed Cost	Variable Cost	Profit on Short Forward	Net Income on Hedged Position
$350	−$330	−$50	$70	$40
$400	−$330	−$50	$20	$40
$450	−$330	−$50	−$30	$40
$500	−$330	−$50	−$80	$40

FIGURE 4.1

Producer profit in one year, assuming hedging with a short forward contract at a forward price of $420/oz.

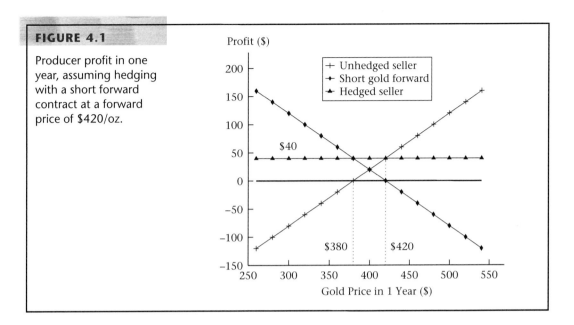

We profit from locking in the price if prices are lower than $420 and we lose if prices are higher.

- **Hedged profit:** The line labeled "hedged seller" is the sum of the other two lines, adding them vertically at every gold price. It is flat at $40/oz., as we would expect from Table 4.2. A quick way to add the lines together is to notice that the "unhedged seller" graph has a positive slope of 1, and the "short gold forward" graph has a slope of −1. Added together vertically, the two graphs will have a slope of 0, so the only question is the height of the line. A profit calculation at a single point tells us that it must be at $40/oz.

Insurance: Guaranteeing a Minimum Price with a Put Option

A possible objection to hedging with a forward contract is that if gold prices do rise, Golddiggers will still receive only $420/oz; there is no prospect for greater profit. Gold insurance—i.e., a put option—provides a way to have higher profits at high gold prices while still being protected against low prices. Suppose that the market price for a 420-strike put is $8.77/oz.[2] This put provides a *floor* on the price.

Since the put premium is paid 1 year prior to the option payoff, we must take into account interest cost when we compute profit in 1 year. The future value of the premium

....

[2]This uses the Black-Scholes formula for the put price with inputs $S = 420$, $K = 420$, $r = 4.879\%$, $\sigma = 5.5\%$, $\delta = 4.879\%$ and $t = 1$ (year).

is $8.77 \times 1.05 = \$9.21$. As with the forward contract, we assume financial settlement, although physical settlement would yield the same net income.

Table 4.3 shows the result of buying this put. If the price is less than $420, the put is exercised and Golddiggers sells gold for $420/oz. less the cost of the put. This gives net income of $30.79. If the price is greater than $420, Golddiggers sells gold at the market price.

The insurance strategy—buying the put—performs better than shorting the forward if the price of gold in 1 year is more than $429.21. Otherwise the short forward outperforms insurance. Figure 4.2 shows the unhedged position, profit from the put by itself, and the result of hedging with the put.

TABLE 4.3		Golddiggers's net income 1 year from today, hedged with a 420-strike put option.		
Gold Price in One Year	**Fixed Cost**	**Variable Cost**	**Profit on Put Option**	**Net Income**
$350	−$330	−$50	$60.79	$30.79
$400	−$330	−$50	$10.79	$30.79
$450	−$330	−$50	−$9.21	$60.79
$500	−$330	−$50	−$9.21	$110.79

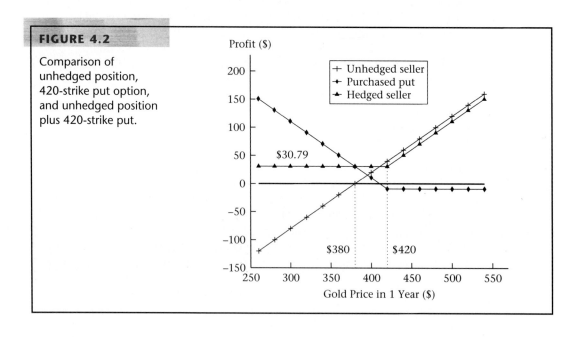

FIGURE 4.2

Comparison of unhedged position, 420-strike put option, and unhedged position plus 420-strike put.

What this analysis does not address is the *probability* that the gold price in 1 year will be in different regions; that is, how likely is it that the gold price will exceed $429.21? The price of the put option implicitly contains information about the likelihood that the gold price will exceed $420, and by how much. The *probability distribution* of the gold price is a key factor determining the pricing of the put. We will see in later chapters how the distribution affects the put price and how to use information about the probability distribution to help us assess risk.

Figure 4.3 compares the profit from the two protective strategies we have examined: Selling a forward contract and buying a put. As you would expect, neither strategy is clearly preferable; rather, there are trade-offs, with each contract outperforming the other for some range of prices.

The fact that no hedging strategy always outperforms the other will be true of all fairly priced strategies. In practice, considerations such as transaction costs and market views are likely to govern the choice of a strategy.

Insuring by Selling a Call

With the sale of a call, Golddiggers receives a premium, which reduces losses, but the written call limits possible profits. One can debate whether this really constitutes insurance, but our goal is to see how the sale of a call affects the potential profit and loss for Golddiggers.

Suppose that instead of buying a put, Golddiggers sells a 420-strike call and receives an $8.77 premium. Golddiggers in this case would be said to have sold a *cap*.

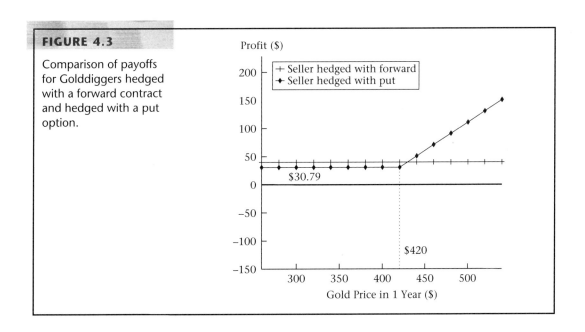

FIGURE 4.3

Comparison of payoffs for Golddiggers hedged with a forward contract and hedged with a put option.

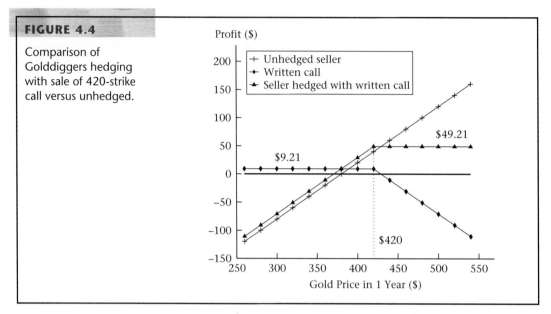

FIGURE 4.4

Comparison of Golddiggers hedging with sale of 420-strike call versus unhedged.

Figure 4.4 shows the ~~payoff~~ profit to this strategy. If we compute the actual profit 1 year from today, we see that if the gold price in 1 year exceeds $420, Golddiggers will show profits of

$$\$420 + \$9.21 - \$380 = \$49.21$$

That is, Golddiggers sells gold for $420 (since the written call is exercised by the holder), receives the future value of the premium, and has a cost of $380. If the price of gold is less than $420, Golddiggers will make

$$P_{\text{gold}} + \$9.21 - \$380$$

On the downside, Golddiggers has exposure to gold but keeps the option premium.

By writing the call, Golddiggers keeps the $8.77 call premium and 1 year later makes $9.21 more than an unhedged gold seller. On the other hand, if the gold price exceeds $420, the call is exercised and the price Golddiggers receives is thus capped at $420. Thus, for gold prices above $429.21, an unhedged strategy has a higher payoff than that of writing a 420-strike call. Also, for prices below $410.79, being fully hedged is preferable to having sold the call.

Adjusting the Amount of Insurance

Consider again Golddiggers's strategy of obtaining insurance against a price decline by purchasing a put option. A common objection to the purchase of insurance is that it is expensive. Insurance has a premium because it eliminates the risk of a large loss, while allowing a profit if prices increase. The cost of insurance reflects this asymmetry.

There are at least two ways to reduce the cost of insurance:

- Reduce the insured amount by lowering the strike price of the put option.
- Sell some of the gain.

Both of these strategies reduce the asymmetry between gains and losses, and hence lower the cost of insurance. The first strategy, lowering the strike price, permits some additional loss while the second, selling some of the gain, puts a cap on the potential gain.

Reducing the strike price lowers the amount of insurance; therefore the put option will have a lower premium. Figure 4.5 compares profit diagrams for Golddiggers's hedging using put options with strikes of \$400 (premium = \$2.21), \$420 (premium = \$8.77), and \$440 (premium = \$21.54). The 400-strike, low-premium option yields the highest profit if insurance is not needed (the price is high) and the lowest profit if insurance is needed (the price is low). The 440-strike, high-premium option yields the lowest profit if insurance is not needed, and the highest profit if insurance is needed.

The manager's view of the market and willingness to absorb risk will undoubtedly influence the choice among these alternatives. Managers optimistic about the price of gold will opt for low-strike-price puts, whereas pessimistic managers will more likely choose high-strike puts. While corporations *per se* may not be risk-averse, managers may be. Also, some managers may perceive losses to be costly in terms of the public's perception of the firm or the boss's perception of them.

This problem of choosing the appropriate strike price is not unique to corporate risk management. Safe drivers and more careful homeowners often reduce premiums

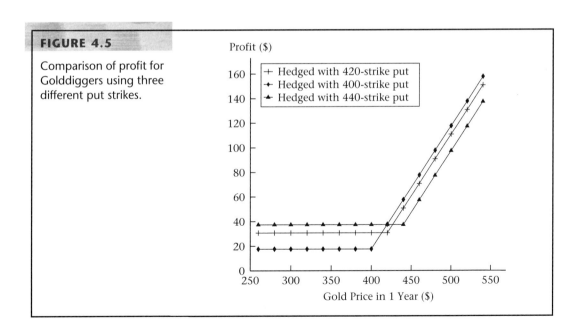

FIGURE 4.5

Comparison of profit for Golddiggers using three different put strikes.

by purchasing auto and homeowner's insurance with larger deductibles. This reflects their proprietary view of the likelihood that the insurance will be used. One important difference between gold insurance and property insurance, however, is that poor drivers would like smaller deductibles for their auto insurance; this differential demand by the quality of the insured is called *adverse selection* and is reflected in the premiums for different deductibles. A driver known to be good would face a lower premium for any deductible than a driver known to be bad. With gold, however, the price of the put is independent of who is doing the buying.[3]

4.2 BASIC RISK MANAGEMENT: THE BUYER'S PERSPECTIVE

Auric Enterprises is a manufacturer of widgets, a product that uses gold as an input. We will suppose for simplicity that the price of gold is the only uncertainty Auric faces. In particular, we assume that

- Auric sells each widget for a fixed price of $800, a price known in advance.
- The fixed cost per widget is $340.
- The manufacture of each widget requires 1 oz. of gold as an input.
- The nongold variable cost per widget is zero.
- The quantity of widgets to be sold is known in advance.

Because Auric makes a greater profit if the price of gold falls, Auric's gold position is implicitly short. As with Golddiggers, we will examine various risk-management strategies for Auric. The pro forma net income calculation for Auric is shown in Table 4.4.

Hedging with a Forward Contract

The forward price is $420 as before. Auric can lock in a profit by entering into a long forward contract. Auric thereby guarantees a profit of

$$\text{Profit} = \$800 - \$340 - \$420 = \$40$$

Note that whereas Golddiggers was *selling* in the forward market, Auric is *buying* in the forward market. Thus, Golddiggers and Auric are natural *counterparties* in an economic sense. In practice they need not be direct counterparties since they can enter into forward contracts through dealers or on exchanges. But in an economic sense, one firm's desire to sell forward has a counterpart in the other's desire to buy forward.

---

[3]You might think that a dealer would charge a higher price for a purchased option if the dealer knew that an option buyer had superior information about the market for gold. However, in general the dealer will quickly hedge the risk from the option and therefore has less concern than an ordinary investor about future movements in the price of gold.

TABLE 4.4		Auric estimated net income, unhedged, 1 year from today.		
Revenue per Widget	**Gold Price in 1 Year**	**Fixed Cost**	**Variable Cost**	**Net Income**
$800	$350	$340	$0	$110
$800	$400	$340	$0	$60
$800	$450	$340	$0	$10
$800	$500	$340	$0	−$40

FIGURE 4.6

Profit diagrams for unhedged buyer, long forward, and buyer hedged with long forward.

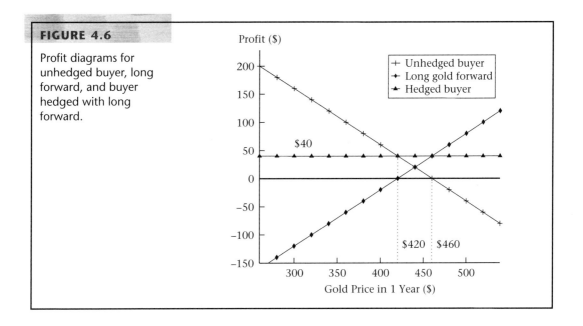

Figure 4.6 compares the profit diagrams for the unhedged buyer and a long forward position in gold. It also shows the profit for the hedged buyer, which is generated by summing up the forward position and the unhedged payoff. We see graphically that the buyer can lock in a profit of $40/oz.

Insurance: Guaranteeing a Maximum Price with a Call Option

Rather than lock in a price unconditionally, Auric might like to pay $420/oz. if the gold price is greater than $420/oz. but pay the market price if it is less. Auric can accomplish this by buying a call option. As a future buyer, Auric is naturally short; hence, a call is

TABLE 4.5		Auric net income 1 year from today, hedged with 420-strike call option.	
Gold Price in 1 Year	**Unhedged Net Income from Table 4.4**	**Profit on Call Option**	**Net Income**
$350	$110	−$9.21	$100.79
$400	$60	−$9.21	$50.79
$450	$10	$20.79	$30.79
$500	−$40	$70.79	$30.79

insurance. Suppose the call has a premium of $8.77/oz. (recall that this is the same as the premium on the put with the same strike price). The future value of the premium is $8.77 \times 1.05 = 9.21.

If Auric buys the insurance contract, net income on the hedged position will be as shown in Table 4.5. If the price is less than $420, the call is worthless at expiration and Auric buys gold at the market price. If the price is greater than $420, the call is exercised and Auric buys gold for $420/oz., less the cost of the call. This gives a profit of $30.79.

If the price of gold in 1 year is less than $410.79, insuring the price by buying the call performs better than locking in a price of $420. At low prices, the option permits us to take advantage of lower gold prices. If the price of gold in 1 year is greater than $410.79, insuring the price by buying the call performs worse than locking in a price of $420 since we have paid the call premium.

Figure 4.7 shows the profit from the call by itself, along with the results of hedging with the call. As before, the graph does not show the *probability* that the gold price in 1 year will be in different regions; hence, we cannot evaluate the likelihood of different outcomes.

4.3 WHY DO FIRMS MANAGE RISK?

The Golddiggers and Auric examples illustrate how the two companies can use forwards, calls, and puts to reduce losses in case of an adverse gold price move, essentially insuring their future cash flows. Why would a firm use these strategies?

In Chapter 1 we listed four reasons that firms might use derivatives: to hedge, to speculate, to reduce transaction costs, and to effect regulatory arbirage. In practice, more than one of these considerations may be important. We have already discussed the fact that market views—for example, opinions about the future price of gold—can affect the choice of a hedging strategy. Thus, the choice of a hedging strategy can have a speculative component. Managers often cite the accounting treatment of a transaction as important, and transaction costs are obviously a consideration.

In this section we discuss why firms might hedge, ignoring speculation, transactions costs, and regulation (but we do consider taxes). It seems obvious that managers would want to reduce risk. However, in a world with fairly priced derivatives, no trans-

FIGURE 4.7

Comparison of profit for unhedged gold buyer, gold buyer hedged with call, and stand-alone call.

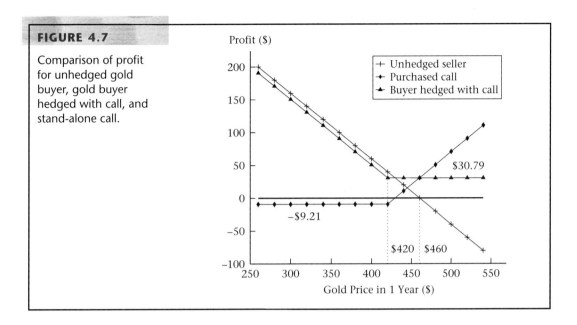

action costs, and no other market imperfections such as taxes, derivatives change the *distribution* of cash flows but do not increase the value of cash flows. Moreover, large publicly held firms are owned by diverse shareholders. These shareholders can, in theory, configure their own portfolios to bear risk optimally, suiting their own taste. In order to hedge, the firm must pay commissions and bid-ask spreads, and bear counterparty credit risk. Why incur these costs?

There are several reasons that firms might seek to manage risk. Before discussing them, let's think about what derivatives accomplish. To be concrete, suppose that Golddiggers sells gold forward at $420/oz. As we saw, this guarantees a net income of $40/oz.

When hedged with the forward, Golddiggers will have a profit of $40 whatever the price in 1 year. In effect, the value of the reduced profits, should the gold price rise, subsidizes the payment to Golddiggers should the gold price fall. If we use the term "state" to denote a particular gold price in 1 year, we can describe the hedging strategy as shifting dollars from more profitable states (when gold prices are high) to less profitable states (when gold prices are low).

This shifting of dollars from high gold price states to low gold price states will have value for the firm *if the firm values the dollar more in a low gold price state than in a high gold price state.* Why might a firm value a dollar differently in different states?

An Example Where Hedging Adds Value

Consider a firm that produces one unit per year of a good costing $10. Immediately after production, the firm receives a payment of either $11.20 or $9, with 50% probability. Thus, the firm has either a $1.20 profit or a $1 loss. On a pre-tax basis, the firm has an

TABLE 4.6   Calculation of after-tax net income in states where the output price is $9.00 and $11.20. Expected after-tax income is $(0.5 \times -\$1) + (0.5 \times \$0.72) = -\$0.14$.

		Price = $9	Price = $11.20
(1)	Pre-tax operating income	−$1	$1.20
(2)	Taxable income	$0	$1.20
(3)	Tax @ 40% [0.4 × (2)]	0	$0.48
	After-tax income [(2) − (3)]	−$1	$0.72

expected profit of

$$[0.5 \times (\$9 - \$10)] + [0.5 \times (\$11.20 - \$10)] = \$0.10$$

However, on an after-tax basis, the firm could have an expected loss.

    For example, suppose that when the firm reports a profit, 40% of the profit is taxed, but when the firm reports a loss, it pays no taxes and receives no tax refund. Table 4.6 computes expected after-tax profit under these circumstances. The taxation of profits converts an expected $0.10 pre-tax gain into an after-tax $0.14 loss.[4] Because of taxes, the firm values a dollar of profit at $0.60 ($0.40 goes to the government), but values a dollar of loss at $1. In this situation, it is desirable for the firm to trade pre-tax profits for pre-tax losses.

    Suppose that there is a forward market for the firm's output, and that the forward price is $10.10. If the firm sells forward, profit is computed as in Table 4.7. Instead of

TABLE 4.7   Calculation of hedged after-tax net income in states where the output price is $9.00 and $11.20. Expected after-tax income is $0.06.

		Price = $9	Price = $11.20
(1)	Pre-tax operating income	−$1.00	$1.20
(2)	Income from short forward	$1.10	−$1.10
(3)	Taxable income [(1) + (2)]	$0.10	$0.10
(4)	Tax @ 40% [0.4 × (3)]	$0.04	$0.04
	After-tax income [(3) − (4)]	$0.06	$0.06

....

[4]Problem 4.15 asks you to compute profit when losses are deductible.

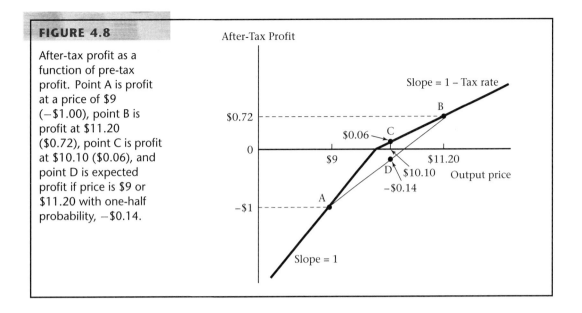

FIGURE 4.8

After-tax profit as a function of pre-tax profit. Point A is profit at a price of $9 (−$1.00), point B is profit at $11.20 ($0.72), point C is profit at $10.10 ($0.06), and point D is expected profit if price is $9 or $11.20 with one-half probability, −$0.14.

an expected loss of $0.14, we obtain a certain profit of $0.06. Hedging with a forward transfers net income from a less-valued to a more highly valued state, raising the expected value of cash flows.

Figure 4.8 depicts how the nondeductibility of losses affects after-tax cash flows. First, observe that after-tax profit (line ACB) is a concave function of the output price. (A **concave** function is one shaped like the cross section of an upside-down bowl.) When profits are concave, the expected value of profits is increased by reducing uncertainty. We can see this in the graph. If the price is certain to be $10.10, then profit will be given by point C. However, if price can be either $9 or $11.20, expected profit is at point D, on the line ADB at the expected price of $10.10. *Because ACB is concave, point D lies below point C, and hedging increases expected profits.*[5]

Some of the hedging rationales we discuss hinge on there being concave profits, so that value is increased by reducing uncertainty.

Reasons to Hedge

There are in fact a number of reasons why losses might be more harmful than profits are beneficial. We now discuss some of those reasons.[6]

---

[5]This is an illustration of *Jensen's inequality*, which is discussed in Appendix C, and which we will encounter often in this book.

[6]The following are discussed in Smith and Stulz (1985) and Froot et al. (1994).

Taxes   The previous example illustrating the effect of taxes was oversimplified in assuming that losses are completely untaxed, but it *is* typically the case that governments tax profits but do not give full credits for losses. Tax systems usually permit a loss to be offset against a profit from a different year. However, in present value terms, the loss will have a lower effective tax rate than that applied to profits, which still generates a motive to hedge.

There are other aspects of the tax code that can encourage firms to shift income using derivatives; such uses may or may not appear to be hedging and may or may not be approved of by tax authorities. Tax rules that may entice firms to use derivatives include the separate taxation of capital and ordinary income (derivatives can be used to convert one form of income to another), capital gains taxation (derivatives can be used to defer taxation of capital gains income as with collars), and differential taxation across countries (derivatives can be used to shift income from one country to another).

Bankruptcy and distress costs   An unusually large loss can threaten the survival of a firm. The most obvious reason is that a money-losing firm may be unable to meet fixed obligations, such as debt payments and wages. If a firm appears to be in distress, customers may be less willing to purchase its goods. (Would you buy a car or computer—both of which come with long-term warranties—from a company that appears likely to go out of business and would then be unable to honor its warranties?)

Actual or threatened bankruptcy can be costly; a dollar of loss can cost the company more than a dollar. As with taxes, this is a reason for firms to enter derivatives contracts that transfer income from profit states to loss states, thereby reducing the probability of bankruptcy or distress.

Costly external financing   Even if a loss is not large enough to threaten the survival of a firm, the firm must pay for the loss, either by using cash reserves or by raising funds externally (for example, by borrowing or issuing new securities).

Raising funds externally can be costly. There are explicit costs, such as bank and underwriting fees. There can also be implicit costs. If you borrow money, the lender may worry that you need to borrow because you are in decline, which increases the probability that you will not repay the loan. The lender's thinking this way raises the interest rate on the loan. The same problem arises even more severely with equity issues.

At the same time, cash reserves are valuable because they reduce a firm's need to raise funds externally in the future. So if the firm uses cash to pay for a loss, the reduction in cash increases the probability that the firm will need costly external financing in the future.

The fact that external financing is costly can even lead the firm to forgo investment projects it would have taken had cash been available to use for financing.

Thus, however the firm pays for the loss, a dollar of loss may actually cost the firm more than a dollar. Hedging can safeguard cash reserves and reduce the probability of costly external financing.

Increase debt capacity   Because of the deductibility of interest expense for tax purposes, firms may find debt to be a tax-advantaged way to raise funds.[7] However, lenders, fearful of bankruptcy, may be unwilling to lend to firms with risky cash flows. The amount that a firm can borrow is its **debt capacity.**

A firm that credibly reduces the riskiness of its cash flows should be able to borrow more, since for any given level of debt, bankruptcy is less likely. Such a firm is said to have raised its debt capacity. To the extent debt has a tax advantage, such a firm will also be more valuable.

Managerial risk aversion   While large, public firms are owned by well-diversified investors, firm managers are typically *not* well-diversified. Salary, bonus, and compensation options are all tied to the performance of the firm.

An individual who is unwilling to take a fair bet (i.e., one with an expected payoff equal to the money at stake) is said to be **risk-averse.** Risk-averse persons are harmed by a dollar of loss more than they are helped by a dollar of gain. Thus, they benefit from reducing uncertainty. The effect is analogous to that shown in Figure 4.8.

If managers are risk-averse and have wealth that is tied to the company, we might expect that they will try to reduce uncertainty. However, matters are not this simple: Managers are often compensated in ways that encourage them to take more risk. For example, options given to managers as compensation, which we discuss in Chapter 16, are more valuable, other things equal, when the firm's stock price is riskier. Thus, a manager's risk aversion may be offset by compensation that is more valuable if the firm is riskier.

Nonfinancial risk management   Firms make risk-management decisions when they organize and design a business. For example, suppose you plan to sell widgets in Europe. You can construct a plant in the United States and export to Europe, or you can construct the plant in Europe, in which case costs of construction, labor, interest rates, and other inputs will be denominated in the same currency as the widgets you sell. Exchange rate hedging, to take one example, would be unnecessary.

Of course, if you build in a foreign country, you will encounter the costs of doing business abroad, including dealing with different tax codes and regulatory regimes.

Risk can also be affected by such decisions as leasing versus buying equipment, which determines the extent to which costs are fixed. Firms can choose flexible production technologies that may be more expensive at the outset, but which can be reconfigured at low cost. Risk is also affected by the decision to enter a particular line of business in the first place. Firms making computer mice and keyboards, for example, have to consider the possibility of lawsuits for repetitive stress injuries.

---

[7]For a discussion of this issue, see Brealey and Myers (2003, ch. 17).

The point is that risk management is not a simple matter of hedging or not hedging using financial derivatives, but rather a series of decisions that start when the business is first conceived.

Reasons *Not* to Hedge

There are also reasons why firms might elect not to hedge:

- Transacting in derivatives entails paying transaction costs, such as commissions and the bid-ask spread.

- The firm must assess costs and benefits of a given strategy; this can require costly expertise.

- The firm must monitor transactions and have managerial controls in place to prevent unauthorized trading.

- The firm must be prepared for tax and accounting consequences of their transactions. In particular, this may complicate reporting.

Thus, while there are reasons to hedge, there are also costs. When thinking about costs and benefits, keep in mind that some of what firms do could be called risk management but may not obviously involve derivatives. For example, suppose Auric enters into a 2-year agreement with a supplier to buy gold at a fixed price. Will management think of this as a derivative? In fact this is a derivative under current accounting standards (it is a swap, which we discuss in Chapter 8), but it is exempt from derivatives accounting.[8] Finally, firms can face collateral requirements (the need to post extra cash with their counterparty) if their derivatives position loses money.

The box on page 108 illustrates an attempt to manage risk that backfired.

Empirical Evidence on Hedging

We know surprisingly little about the risk-management practice and derivatives use of firms in real life. It is difficult to tell, from publicly available information, the extent to which firms use derivatives. Beginning in 2000, Statement of Financial Accounting Standards (SFAS) 133 required firms to recognize derivatives as assets or liabilities on the balance sheet, to measure them at fair value, and to report changes in their market value.[9] This reporting does not necessarily reveal a firm's hedging position (forward contracts have zero value, for example). Prior to 2000, firms had to report notional exposure; hence much existing evidence relies on data from the 1990s.

Research tries to address two questions: How much do firms use derivatives and why? *Financial* firms—commercial banks, investment banks, broker-dealers, and other

---

[8]Current derivatives accounting rules contain a "normal purchases and sales" exemption. Firms need not use derivatives accounting for forward contracts with physical delivery, for quantities likely to be used or sold over a reasonable period in the normal course of business.

[9]See Gastineau et al. (2001) for a discussion of SFAS 133 and previous accounting rules.

financial institutions—transact in derivatives frequently. Risks are identifiable, and regulators encourage risk management. The more open question is the extent to which *nonfinancial* firms use derivatives. We can summarize research findings as follows:

- Roughly half of nonfinancial firms report using derivatives, with usage greater among large firms (Bodnar et al., 1998; Bartram et al., 2004).

- Among firms that do use derivatives, less than 25% of perceived risk is hedged, with firms likelier to hedge short-term risks (Bodnar et al., 1998).

- Firms with more investment opportunities are likelier to hedge (Géczy et al., 1997).

- Firms that use derivatives have a higher market value (Allayannis and Weston, 2001; Allayannis et al., 2004; Bartram et al., 2004) and more leverage (Graham and Rogers, 2002; Haushalter, 2000).[10]

Guay and Kothari (2003) verify many of these findings but conclude that for most firms, derivatives use is of minor economic significance. In their sample of large firms, slightly more than half report derivatives usage. Among derivatives users, the authors estimate that the *median* firm hedges only about 3% to 6% of exposure to interest rates and exchange rates.

Because data are hard to obtain, some studies have focused on particular industries and even firms. Tufano (1996), Petersen and Thiagarajan (2000), and Brown et al. (2003) have examined hedging behavior by gold-mining firms. Using a uniquely detailed data set, Tufano found that most gold firms use some derivatives, with the median firm in his sample (North American firms) selling forward about 25% of 3-year production. Fifteen percent of firms used no derivatives. Brown et al. found substantial variation over time in the amount hedging by gold firms. Firms tended to increase hedging as the price rose, and managers reported that they adjusted hedges based on their views about gold prices.

The currency-hedging operations of a U.S.-based manufacturing firm are examined in detail by Brown (2001), who finds that foreign exchange hedging is an integral part of firm operations, but the company has no clear rationale for hedging. For example, Brown reports one manager saying, "We do not take speculative positions, but the extent we are hedged depends on our views." Faulkender (2005) finds consistent evidence for interest-rate hedging in the chemical industry. These firms increase exposure to short-term interest rates as the yield curve becomes more upward-sloping,[11] but correlations between cash flows and interest rates do not affect behavior.

The varied evidence suggests that some use of derivatives is common, especially at large firms, but the evidence is weak that economic theories explain hedging.

---

[10]Graham and Smith (1999) find that after-tax profits are concave for a majority of firms, as in Figure 4.8. However, Graham and Rogers (2002) are unable to find a link between hedging and tax-induced concavity.

[11]An upward-sloping yield curve means that long-term bond yields are greater than short-term bond yields. This appears to make short-term financing less expensive. However, we will see in Chapters 7 and 8 that if a company hedges all of its future short-term financing costs, long-term and short-term financing will cost the same.

Ford: A Hedge Too Far

Ford Motor Co. stunned investors in January 2002 when it announced a $1 billion write-off on stockpiles of palladium, a precious metal Ford used in catalytic converters (devices that reduce polluting emissions from cars and trucks). Ironically, Ford sustained the loss while attempting to actively manage palladium risk.

According to the *Wall Street Journal* (see Gregory L. White, "A Mismanaged Palladium Stockpile Was Catalyst for Ford's Write-Off," February 6, 2002, p. A1), Ford in the late 1980s had begun to use palladium as a replacement for platinum. Palladium prices were steady until 1997, when Russia, a major supplier with a large stockpile of palladium, withheld supply from the market. Prices more than doubled to $350/oz. at a time when Ford was planning to increase its use of the metal. By early 2000, prices had doubled again, to $700. While GM had begun work several years earlier to reduce reliance on palladium, Ford continued to rely heavily on the metal.

In 2000, Ford management agreed to allow the purchasing staff to stockpile palladium. The purchasing staff evidently did not communicate with Ford's treasury department, which had hedging experience. Thus, for example, Ford did not buy puts to protect against a drop in palladium prices. The purchasing staff also did not communicate with Ford's research department, which was working to reduce reliance on palladium. Ford continued to buy palladium in 2001 as prices exceeded $1000. However, by the middle of the year, palladium prices had fallen to $350.

By the end of 2001, Ford had developed technology that would eventually reduce the need for palladium by 50%. The year-end price of palladium was $440/oz.

As a result of this experience, "Ford has instituted new procedures to ensure that treasury-department staffers with experience in hedging are involved in any major commodities purchases in the future, [Ford Chief Financial Officer Martin] Inglis says."

4.4 Golddiggers Revisited

We have looked at simple hedging and insurance strategies for buyers and sellers. We now examine some additional strategies that permit tailoring the amount and cost of insurance. For simplicity we will focus primarily on Golddiggers; however, in every case there are analogous strategies for Auric.

Table 4.8 lists premiums for three calls and puts on gold with 1 year to expiration and three different strikes. The examples use these values.

Selling the Gain: Collars

As discussed earlier, we can reduce the cost of insurance by reducing potential profit, i.e., by selling our right to profit from high gold prices. We can do this by selling a call. If the gold price is above the strike on the call, we are contractually obligated to sell at the strike. This caps our profits, in exchange for an initial premium payment.

TABLE 4.8		Call and put premiums for gold options.

Strike Price	Put Premium	Call Premium
440	21.54	2.49
420	8.77	8.77
400	2.21	21.26

Note: These prices are computed using the Black formula for options on futures, with a futures price of $420, effective annual interest rate of 5%, volatility of 5.5%, and 1 year to expiration.

A 420–440 collar Suppose that Golddiggers buys a 420-strike put option for $8.77 and sells a 440-strike call option for a premium of $2.49. If the price of gold in 1 year is $450/oz., the call owner will exercise and Golddiggers is obligated to sell gold at the strike price of $440, rather than the market price of $450. The $2.49 premium Golddiggers received initially compensates them for the possibility that this will happen.

Figure 4.9 depicts the combination of the purchased put and written call, while Figure 4.10 shows the two profit diagrams for Golddiggers hedged with a 420-strike put, as opposed to hedged with a 420-strike put plus writing a 440-strike call.

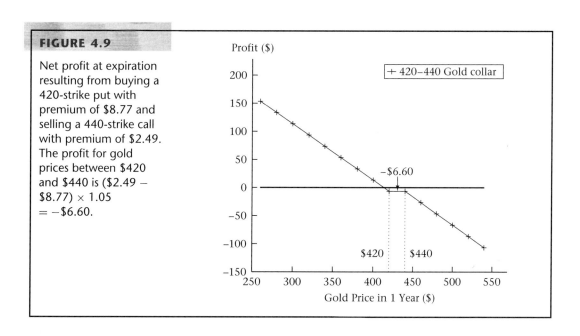

FIGURE 4.9

Net profit at expiration resulting from buying a 420-strike put with premium of $8.77 and selling a 440-strike call with premium of $2.49. The profit for gold prices between $420 and $440 is ($2.49 − $8.77) × 1.05 = −$6.60.

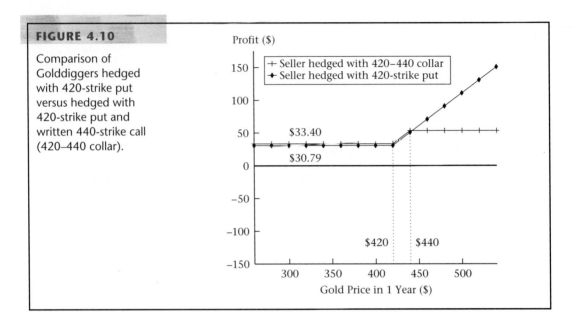

FIGURE 4.10

Comparison of Golddiggers hedged with 420-strike put versus hedged with 420-strike put and written 440-strike call (420–440 collar).

Note that the 420–440 collar still entails paying a premium. The 420 put costs $8.77, and the 440 call yields a premium of only $2.49. Thus, there is a net expenditure of $6.28. It is probably apparent, though, that we can tinker with the strike prices and pay a still lower net premium, including zero premium, if we wish. The trade-off is that the payoff on the collar becomes less attractive as we lower the required premium.

A zero-cost collar To construct a zero-cost collar, we could argue as follows: A 400-strike put and a 440-strike call are equally distant from the forward price of $420. This equivalence suggests that the options should have approximately the same premium. As we can see from the table of premiums for different strike options, the 400-strike put has a premium of $2.21, while the 440-strike call has a premium of $2.49. The net premium we would *receive* from buying this collar is thus $0.28. We can construct a true zero-cost collar by slightly changing the strike prices, making the put more expensive (raising the strike) and the call less expensive (also raising the strike). With strikes of $400.78 for the put and $440.78 for the call, we obtain a premium of $2.355 for both options.

In reality this zero-cost collar of width 40 would be sold at lower strike prices than $400.78 and $440.78. The reason is that there is a bid-ask spread: Dealers are willing to buy a given option at a low price and sell it at a high price.

The purchased put will be bought at the dealer's offer price and the call will be sold at the bid. The dealer can earn this spread in either of two ways: Selling the 400.78–440.78 collar and charging an explicit transaction fee, or lowering the strike prices appropriately and charging a zero transaction fee. Either way, the dealer earns the fee. One of the tricky aspects of the more complicated derivatives is that it is relatively

FIGURE 4.11

Comparison of unhedged profit for Golddiggers versus zero-cost collar obtained by buying 400.78-strike put and selling 440.78-strike call.

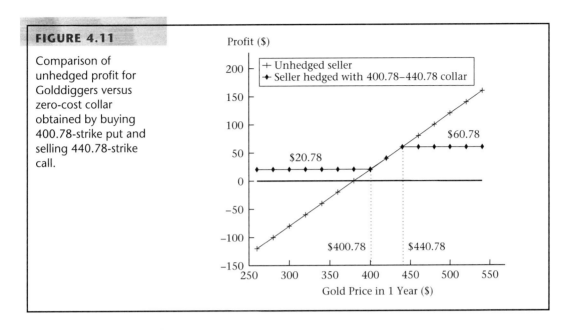

easy for dealers to embed fees that are invisible to the buyer. Of course a buyer can mitigate this problem by always seeking quotes from different dealers.

We can examine the payoffs by considering separately the three interesting regions of gold prices:

Price of gold < $400.78: In this region, Golddiggers can sell gold for $400.78 by exercising the put option.

Price of gold between $400.78 and $440.78: In this region, Golddiggers can sell gold at the market price.

Price of gold > $440.78: In this region, Golddiggers sells gold at $440.78. It has sold a call, so the owner of the call will exercise. This forces Golddiggers to sell gold to the call owner for the strike price of $440.78.

Figure 4.11 graphs the zero-cost collar against the unhedged position. Notice that between $400.78 and $440.78, the zero-cost collar graph is coincident with the unhedged profit. Above the 440.78-strike the collar provides profit of $60.78, and below the 400.78-strike, the collar provides profit of $20.78.

The forward contract as a zero-cost collar   Because the put and call with strike prices of $420 have the same premiums, we could also construct a zero-cost collar by buying the $420-strike put and selling the $420-strike call. If we do this, here is what happens:

Price of gold < $420: Golddiggers will exercise the put option, selling gold at the price of $420.

Price of gold > $420: Golddiggers has sold a 420-strike call. The owner of that call will exercise, obligating Golddiggers to sell gold for $420.

In either case, Golddiggers sells gold at $420. Thus, the "420–420 collar" is exactly like a forward contract. By buying the put and selling the call at the same strike price, Golddiggers has synthetically created a short position in a forward contract. Since a short forward and 420–420 collar have the same payoff, they must cost the same. *This is why the premiums on the 420-strike options are the same.* This example is really just an illustration of equation (3.1).

Synthetic forwards at prices other than $420   We can easily extend this example to understand the relationship between option premiums at other strike prices. In the previous example, Golddiggers created a synthetic forward sale at $420. You might think that you could benefit by creating a synthetic forward contract at a higher price such as $440. Other things being equal, you would rather sell at $440 than $420. To accomplish this you buy the 440 put and sell the 440 call. However, there is a catch: The 440-strike put is in-the-money and the 440-strike call is out-of-the-money. Since we would be buying the expensive option and selling the inexpensive option, we have to pay a premium.

How much is it worth to Golddiggers to be able to lock in a selling price of $440 instead of $420? Obviously, it is worth $20 1 year from today, or $20 ÷ (1.05) = $19.05 in present value terms. Since locking in a $420 price is free, it should therefore be the case that we pay $19.05 in net premium in order to lock in a $440 price. In fact, looking at the prices of the 440-strike put and call in Table 4.8, we have premiums of $21.54 for the put and $2.49 for the call. This gives us

$$\text{Net premium} = \$21.54 - \$2.49 = \$19.05$$

Similarly, suppose Golddiggers explored the possibility of locking in a $400 price for gold in 1 year. Obviously, Golddiggers would require compensation to accept a lower price. In fact, they would need to be paid $19.05—the present value of $20—today.

Again we compute the option premiums and we see that the 400-strike call sells for $21.26 while the 400-strike put sells for $2.21. Again we have

$$\text{Net premium} = \$2.21 - \$21.26 = -\$19.05$$

Golddiggers in this case receives the net premium for accepting a lower price.

Other Collar Strategies

Collar-type strategies are quite flexible. We have focused on the case where the firm buys one put and sells one call. However, it is also possible to deal with fractional options. For example, consider the 400.78–440.78 collar above. We could buy one put to obtain full downside protection, and we could vary the strike price of the call by selling fractional calls at strike prices other than $440.78. For example, we could lower the call strike price below $440.78, in which case we would obtain a higher premium per call. To offset the higher premium, we could ~~buy~~ sell less than one call. The trade-off is that we cap the gold price on part of production at a lower level, but we maintain some participation at any price above the strike.

Alternatively we could raise the cap level (the strike price on the call) and sell more than one call. This would increase participation in gold price increases up to the cap level, but also have the effect of generating a net short position in gold if prices rose above the cap.

Paylater Strategies

A disadvantage to buying a put option is that Golddiggers pays the premium even when the gold price is high and insurance was, after the fact, unnecessary. One strategy to avoid this problem is a **paylater** strategy, where the premium is paid only when the insurance is needed. While it is possible to construct exotic options in which the premium is paid only at expiration and only if the option is in the money, the strategy we discuss here is a ratio spread using ordinary put options. The goal is to find a strategy where if the gold price is high, there is no net option premium. If the gold price is low, there is insurance, but the effective premium is greater than with an ordinary insurance strategy.

If there is no premium when the gold price is high, we must have no initial premium. This means that we must sell at least one option. Consider the following strategy for Golddiggers: Sell a 434.6-strike put and buy two 420-strike puts. Using our assumptions, the premium on the 434.6-strike put is $17.55, while the premium on the 420-strike put is $8.77. Thus, the net option premium from this strategy is $17.55 − (2 × $8.775) = 0.

Figure 4.12 depicts the result of Golddiggers's hedging with a paylater strategy. When the price of gold is greater than $434.60, neither put is exercised, and Golddiggers's profit is the same as if it were unhedged. When the price of gold is between $420 and $434.60, because of the written $434.60 put, the firm loses $2 of profit for every $1 decline in the price of gold. Below $420 the purchased 420-strike puts are exercised, and profit becomes constant. The net result is an insurance policy that is not paid for unless it is needed.

Also depicted in Figure 4.12 is the familiar result from a conventional insurance strategy of hedging by purchasing a single 420-strike put. When the gold price is high, the paylater strategy with a zero premium outperforms the single put. When the gold price is low, the paylater strategy does worse because it offers less insurance. Thus, the premium is paid later, if insurance is needed.

4.5 SELECTING THE HEDGE RATIO

In the Golddiggers and Auric examples, we performed all calculations in terms of one unit of gold, and made two important assumptions. First, we assumed perfect correlation between the price of gold and the price of what each company wants to hedge. Second, we assumed that the companies knew for certain the quantity of gold they would sell and buy. As a result of these assumptions, we effectively assumed that the hedge ratio is one,

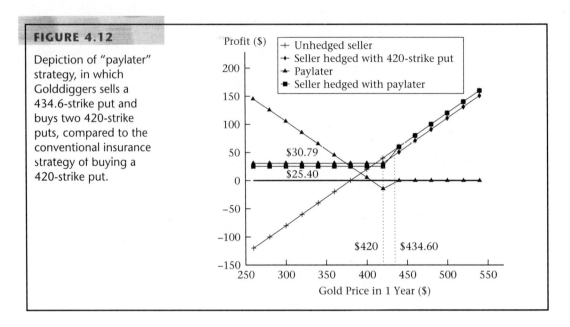

FIGURE 4.12

Depiction of "paylater" strategy, in which Golddiggers sells a 434.6-strike put and buys two 420-strike puts, compared to the conventional insurance strategy of buying a 420-strike put.

where the **hedge ratio** is defined as the ratio of the forward position to the underlying asset.

In practice, neither assumption may be valid. We first examine the effect of widget price uncertainty on hedging, and discuss *cross-hedging*. We then examine *quantity uncertainty* using an agricultural example.

Cross-Hedging

In the Auric example we assumed that widget prices are fixed. However, since gold is used to produce widgets, widget prices might vary with gold prices. If widget and gold prices vary one-for-one, Auric's profits would be independent of the price of gold and Auric would have no need to hedge.[12]

More realistically, the price of widgets could change with the price of gold, but not one-for-one; other factors could affect widget prices as well. In this case, Auric might find it helpful to use gold derivatives to hedge the price of the widgets it sells as well as the price of the gold it buys. Using gold to hedge widgets would be an example of **cross-hedging:** the use of a derivative on one asset to hedge another asset. Cross-hedging arises in many different contexts.

---

[12]"One-for-one" in this context means that if the price of gold rises by $1, the price of a widget rises by $1 times the amount of gold used to make the widget.

The hedging problem for Auric is to hedge the *difference* in the price of widgets and gold. Conceptually, we can think of hedging widgets and gold separately, and then combining those separate hedges into one net hedge.

To generalize the Auric example, suppose that buying N_g ounces of gold enables us to produce N_w widgets. Profit per ounce of gold, without hedging, is

$$\text{Profit} = N_w P_w - N_g P_{\text{gold}} \qquad (4.1)$$

where P_w is the widget price.

Suppose that we go long H gold futures contracts, each covering 1 oz. of gold. If F is the gold forward price, the return on the hedged position is

$$\text{Hedged profit} = N_w P_w - N_g P_{\text{gold}} + H(P_{\text{gold}} - F)$$

The variance of the return on the hedged position is given by

$$\sigma^2_{\text{hedged}} = N_w^2 \sigma_w^2 + (H - N_g)^2 \sigma_g^2 + 2(H - N_g)N_w \rho \sigma_w \sigma_g \qquad (4.2)$$

where σ_w is the standard deviation of the widget price, σ_g is the standard deviation of the gold price, and ρ is the price correlation between widgets and gold. Note that $\rho \sigma_w \sigma_g$ is the covariance between widget and gold prices.

The variance-minimizing hedge position, H^*, is[13]

$$H^* = N_g - N_w \frac{\rho \sigma_w}{\sigma_g} \qquad (4.3)$$

Equation (4.3) has a straightforward interpretation. The first term hedges costs—i.e., we enter into a long position on the amount of gold we use in production, N_g. The second term hedges revenue, providing the quantity of gold forwards we use to hedge widgets. The term $\rho \sigma_w / \sigma_g$ is the coefficient from regressing the widget price on the gold price.[14] This regression coefficient times the number of widgets, N_w, gives us the number of gold contracts to use in hedging widget price risk. The result is that the hedge quantity,

---

[13]This can be derived by differentiating equation (4.2) with respect to H^*.

[14]The term $\rho \sigma_w / \sigma_g$ measures the comovement of gold and widget prices, which is typically measured using a linear regression. A common approach is to regress price changes on price changes:

$$P_{w,t} - P_{w,t-1} = \alpha + \beta(P_{g,t} - P_{g,t-1}) + u_t$$

where the subscript t denotes the value at time t. Other specifications, including the use of percentage changes, or regressing levels on levels, are possible. The correct regression to use depends on context. In general, regressions using changes are more likely to give a correct hedge coefficient since the goal of the hedge is to have changes in the price of the asset matched by changes in futures price. In Chapters 5 and 6, we will present examples of hedging stocks and jet fuel, and the appropriate regressions will be returns on returns (stocks) and changes on changes (jet fuel). Regressions of level on level are problematic in many contexts. For example, in the case of stocks, asset pricing models tell us that stock *returns* are related, but we would not expect a stable relationship between two *prices*. The appropriate regression is returns on returns. A comprehensive discussion is Siegel and Siegel (1990, pp. 114–135).

H^*, is denominated in terms of units of gold. The net use of gold futures, H^*, is the difference in the number of contracts needed to hedge gold inputs and widget outputs.

Note that if gold and widgets are uncorrelated—i.e., $\rho = 0$—the hedge ratio is one (go long one forward ounce of gold per ounce purchased), while if $\rho > 0$, the hedge ratio is less than one because the widget price itself provides an implicit long position in gold that is a partial hedge.

When we hedge with H^* futures, σ^2_{hedged} is obtained by substituting H^* into equation (4.2):

$$\sigma^2_{hedged} = N_w^2 \sigma_w^2 \left(1 - \rho^2\right) \tag{4.4}$$

The uncertainty remaining in the hedged position is due to **basis risk**, which is risk due to the hedging instrument (gold) and the hedged price (widgets) not moving as predicted. The variance of profits ultimately depends upon the ability to hedge the price of widgets, which, since we are using gold to hedge, depends on the correlation, ρ, between widgets and gold. The larger that ρ is, the less is basis risk.

In this section we have shown that the ability to cross-hedge depends upon the correlation between the hedging instrument and the asset being hedged, and that we can determine the hedging amount as a regression coefficient. We will see in Section 5.4 that the same analysis obtains when we use stock index futures contracts to cross-hedge a stock portfolio.

Quantity Uncertainty

The quantity a firm produces and sells may vary with the prices of inputs or outputs. When this happens, using the "obvious" hedge ratio (for example, by hedging the expected quantity of an input) can increase rather than decrease risk. In this section we examine quantity uncertainty.

Agricultural producers commonly face quantity uncertainty because crop size is affected by factors such as weather and disease. Moreover, we expect there to be a correlation between quantity and price, because good weather gives rise to bountiful harvests. What quantity of forward contracts should a corn producer enter into to minimize the variability of revenue?

We will look at three examples of different relationships between price and quantity: The benchmark case where quantity is certain, an example where quantity and price are negatively correlated, and an example where quantity and price are positively correlated.[15]

In all the examples we suppose that the corn forward price is $2.50/bu and that there is a 50% probability that in one year the corn price will be $2/bu or $3/bu. In

---

[15]There are futures contracts intended to mitigate the problem of quantity uncertainty in an agricultural context. Corn yield futures, for example, traded at the Chicago Board of Trade, permit farmers to hedge variations in regional production quantity, and provide an agricultural example of a "quanto" contract. We discuss quantos further in Chapter 22.

TABLE 4.9	Three scenarios illustrating different correlations between price and quantity for an agricultural producer. Each row is equally likely. In scenario A, there is no quantity uncertainty. In scenario B, quantity is negatively correlated with price, and in scenario C, quantity is positively correlated with price.

	Production Scenario		
Corn Price ($)	**A (Uncorrelated)**	**B (Negative correlation)**	**C (Positive correlation)**
3	1.0m	1.0m	1.5m
3	1.0m	0.6m	0.8m
2	1.0m	1.5m	1.0m
2	1.0m	0.8m	0.6m

addition, for each possible price of corn there are two equally likely quantities, for a total of four possible price-quantity pairs. Table 4.9 illustrates the three scenarios. Note that in scenario B, average quantity is low when price is high (negative correlation), whereas in scenario C, average quantity is high when price is high (positive correlation).

First, consider scenario A where quantity is certain: The producer always produces 1m bushels. Let S and Q denote the price and quantity in 1 year. Revenue is SQ. Without hedging, revenue will be either $3m (if the corn price is $3) or $2m (if the corn price is $2).

On the other hand, if the producer sells forward 1m bushels at the forward price $F = 2.50$, revenue is

$$\text{Revenue} = (S \times 1m) - [1m \times (S - 2.50)] = 2.5m$$

We have guaranteed revenue in this case. The calculation is illustrated explicitly in Table 4.10.

TABLE 4.10	When the producer is sure to produce 1m bushels (Scenario A), revenue of $2.5m is assured by selling forward 1m bushels.

		Revenue	
Corn Price	**Quantity**	**Unhedged**	**Sell Forward 1m bu**
3	1.0m	3.0m	2.5m
2	1.0m	2.0m	2.5m

In general, if the producer enters into forward contracts on H units, hedged revenue, $R(H)$, will be

$$\text{Hedged revenue} = R(H) = (S \times Q) + [H \times (S - F)] \tag{4.5}$$

Using equation (4.5), when there is uncertainty, the variability of hedged revenue, $\sigma^2_{R(H)}$, is

$$\sigma^2_{R(H)} = \sigma^2_{SQ} + H^2 \sigma^2_S + 2H\rho_{SQ,S}\sigma_{SQ}\sigma_S \tag{4.6}$$

The standard deviation of total revenue, SQ, is σ_{SQ}, and the correlation of total revenue with price is $\rho_{SQ,S}$. As in the preceding discussion of cross-hedging, the H that minimizes the variance of hedged revenue will be

$$H = -\frac{\rho_{SQ,S}\sigma_{SQ}}{\sigma_S} \tag{4.7}$$

This is the same as the second term in equation (4.3). The formula for the variance-minimizing hedge ratio in equation (4.7) is the negative of the coefficient from a regression of unhedged revenue on price. We can therefore determine the variance-minimizing hedge ratios for the negative- and positive-correlation scenarios (scenarios B and C) in Table 4.9 either by using equation (4.7) directly, or else we can run a regression of revenue on price.

First, consider what happens in Scenario B if we hedge by shorting the expected quantity of production. As a benchmark, column 3 of Table 4.11 shows that unhedged revenue has variability of $0.654m. From Table 4.9, expected production in the negative

---

TABLE 4.11   Results in Scenario B (negative correlation between the price of corn and the quantity of production) from shorting 975,000 corn forwards (columns 4 and 5) and from selling forward 100,000 bushels (columns 6 and 7). Each price-quantity combination is equally likely, with a probability of 0.25. Standard deviations are computed using the population estimate of standard deviation.

Price	Quantity	Unhedged Revenue	Sell Forward 0.975m bu Futures Gain	Total	Sell Forward 0.100m bu Futures Gain	Total
$3	1.0m	$3.0m	−$0.488m	$2.512m	−$0.050m	$2.95m
$3	0.6m	$1.8m	−$0.488m	$1.312m	−$0.050m	$1.75m
$2	1.5m	$3.0m	$0.488m	$3.488m	$0.050m	$3.05m
$2	0.8m	$1.6m	$0.488m	$2.088m	$0.050m	$1.65m
	$\sigma_{\text{total revenue}}$	$0.654m		$0.814m		$0.652m

correlation scenario, B, is

$$0.25 \times (1 + 0.6 + 1.5 + 0.8) = 0.975$$

If we short this quantity of corn, column 5 of Table 4.11 shows that there is still variability in hedged revenue. Perhaps more surprising, the variability of total revenue actually *increases*. The reason is that price decreases when quantity increases, so nature already provides a degree of hedging: The increase in quantity partially offsets the decrease in price. Hedging by shorting the full expected quantity leaves us *overhedged*, with a commensurate increase in variability.

The variance-minimizing hedge can be obtained using equation (4.7). By direct calculation, we have $\rho_{SQ,S} = 0.07647$, $\sigma_S = \$0.5$, and $\sigma_{SQ} = \$0.654$m.[16] Thus, we have

$$H = -\frac{0.07647 \times \$0.654\text{m}}{\$0.5} = -0.100\text{m}$$

Column (7) of Table 4.11 shows that variability is reduced to $0.652m when hedging this amount. The optimal hedge quantity is closer to no hedging than to full hedging. In fact, we gain little by hedging optimally, but we increase the standard deviation of revenue by 25% if we adopt the plausible but incorrect hedging strategy of shorting 975,000 bushels. Problem 4.21 asks you to verify that you obtain the same answer by running a regression of revenue on price.

You might guess by now that when correlation is positive (Scenario C), the optimal hedge quantity exceeds expected quantity. The fact that quantity goes up when price goes up makes revenue that much more variable than when price alone varies, and a correspondingly larger hedge position is required. Problem 4.23 asks you to compute the optimal hedge in scenario C. The answer is to short almost 2 million bushels even though production is never that large.

CHAPTER SUMMARY

A producer selling a risky commodity, such as gold, has an inherent long position in the commodity. Assuming costs are fixed, the firm's profit increases when the price of the commodity increases. Such a firm can hedge profit with a variety of strategies, including selling forward, buying puts, and buying collars. A firm that faces price risk on inputs has an inherent short position in the commodity, with profit that decreases when the price of the input increases. Hedging strategies for such a firm include buying forward, buying calls, and selling collars. All of the strategies involving options can be customized by changing the option strike prices. Strategies such as a paylater can

---

[16]Because Table 4.11 presents the complete population of outcomes, which are equally likely, it is appropriate to use the population estimate of the standard deviation. In Excel, this is *STDEVP* as opposed to *STDEV*. The calculation for σ_{SQ} is obtained as *STDEVP*(3, 1.8, 3, 1.6) = 0.6538.

provide insurance with no initial premium, but on which the company has greater losses should the insurance be needed.

Hedging can be optimal for a company when an extra dollar of income received in times of high profits is worth less than an extra dollar of income received in times of low profits. Profits for such a firm are concave, in which case hedging can increase expected cash flow. Concave profits can arise from taxes, bankruptcy costs, costly external finance, preservation of debt capacity, and managerial risk aversion. Such a firm can increase expected cash flow by hedging. Nevertheless, firms may elect not to hedge for reasons including transaction costs of dealing in derivatives, the requirement for expertise, the need to monitor and control the hedging process, and complications from tax and accounting considerations.

Further Reading

In this and earlier chapters we have examined uses of forwards and options, taking for granted the pricing of those contracts. Two big unanswered questions are: How are those prices determined? How does the market for them work?

In Chapters 5 through 8, we will explore forward and futures contracts discussing pricing as well as how market-makers function. In Chapters 10 through 13, we will answer the same questions for options. Chapter 14 will discuss how exotic options can be used in risk-management strategies in place of the ordinary puts and calls discussed in this chapter.

Wharton and CIBC regularly survey nonfinancial firms to assess their hedging. A recent survey is summarized in Bodnar et al. (1998). Bartram et al. (2004) examine hedging behavior in an international sample of over 7000 firms. Tufano (1996, 1998), Petersen and Thiagarajan (2000), and Brown et al. (2003) have studied hedging practices in the gold-mining industry. Other papers examining hedging include Géczy et al. (1997), Allayannis and Weston (2001), Allayannis et al. (2003), and Allayannis et al. (2004). Guay and Kothari (2003) attempt to quantify derivatives usage using information in firm annual reports from 1997. Brown (2001) provides an interesting and detailed description of the hedging decisions by one (anonymous) firm and Faulkender (2005) examines interest rate hedging in the chemical industry.

Gastineau et al. (2001) discuss Statement of Financial Accounting Standards 133, which currently governs accounting for derivatives.

Finally, Fleming (1997) relates some of the history of (the fictitous) Auric Enterprises.

Problems

For the following problems consider the following three firms:

- *XYZ* mines copper, with fixed costs of $0.50/lb and variable cost of $0.40/lb.

- *Wirco* produces wire. It buys copper and manufactures wire. One pound of copper can be used to produce one unit of wire, which sells for the price of copper plus $5. Fixed cost per unit is $3 and noncopper variable cost is $1.50.

- *Telco* installs telecommunications equipment and uses copper wire from Wirco as an input. For planning purposes, Telco assigns a fixed revenue of $6.20 for each unit of wire it uses.

The 1-year forward price of copper is $1/lb. The 1-year continuously compounded interest rate is 6%. One-year option prices for copper are shown in the table below.[17]

Strike	Call	Put
0.9500	$0.0649	$0.0178
0.9750	0.0500	0.0265
1.0000	0.0376	0.0376
1.0250	0.0274	0.0509
1.0340	0.0243	0.0563
1.0500	0.0194	0.0665

In your answers, at a minimum consider copper prices in 1 year of $0.80, $0.90, $1.00, $1.10, and $1.20.

4.1. If XYZ does nothing to manage copper price risk, what is its profit 1 year from now, per pound of copper? If on the other hand XYZ sells forward its expected copper production, what is its estimated profit 1 year from now? Construct graphs illustrating both unhedged and hedged profit.

4.2. Suppose the 1-year copper forward price were $0.80 instead of $1. If XYZ were to sell forward its expected copper production, what is its estimated profit one year from now? Should XYZ produce copper? What if the forward copper price is $0.45?

4.3. Compute estimated profit in 1 year if XYZ buys a put option with a strike of $0.95, $1.00, or $1.05. Draw a graph of profit in each case.

4.4. Compute estimated profit in 1 year if XYZ sells a call option with a strike of $0.95, $1.00, or $1.05. Draw a graph of profit in each case.

4.5. Compute estimated profit in 1 year if XYZ buys collars with the following strikes:

    a. $0.95 for the put and $1.00 for the call.

    b. $0.975 for the put and $1.025 for the call.

    c. $1.05 for the put and $1.05 for the call.

Draw a graph of profit in each case.

4.6. Compute estimated profit in 1 year if XYZ buys paylater *puts* as follows (the net premium may not be exactly zero):

    a. Sell one 1.025-strike put and buy two 0.975-strike puts.

---

[17] These are option prices from the Black formula assuming that the risk-free rate is 0.06, volatility is 0.1, and time to expiration is one year.

b. Sell two 1.034-strike puts and buy three 1.00-strike puts.

Draw a graph of profit in each case.

4.7. If Telco does nothing to manage copper price risk, what is its profit 1 year from now, per pound of copper that it buys? If it hedges the price of wire by buying copper forward, what is its estimated profit 1 year from now? Construct graphs illustrating both unhedged and hedged profit.

4.8. Compute estimated profit in 1 year if Telco buys a call option with a strike of $0.95, $1.00, or $1.05. Draw a graph of profit in each case.

4.9. Compute estimated profit in 1 year if Telco sells a put option with a strike of $0.95, $1.00, or $1.05. Draw a graph of profit in each case.

4.10. Compute estimated profit in 1 year if Telco sells collars with the following strikes:

    a. $0.95 for the put and $1.00 for the call.

    b. $0.975 for the put and $1.025 for the call.

    c. $0.95 for the put and $0.95 for the call.

Draw a graph of profit in each case.

4.11. Compute estimated profit in 1 year if Telco buys paylater *calls* as follows (the net premium may not be exactly zero):

    a. Sell one 0.975-strike call and buy two 1.034-strike calls.

    b. Sell two 1.00-strike calls and buy three 1.034-strike calls.

Draw a graph of profit in each case.

4.12. Suppose that Wirco does nothing to manage the risk of copper price changes. What is its profit 1 year from now, per pound of copper? Suppose that Wirco buys copper forward at $1. What is its profit 1 year from now?

4.13. What happens to the variability of Wirco's profit if Wirco undertakes any strategy (buying calls, selling puts, collars, etc.) to lock in the price of copper next year? You can use your answer to the previous question to illustrate your response.

4.14. Golddiggers has zero net income if it sells gold for a price of $380. However, by shorting a forward contract it is possible to guarantee a profit of $40/oz. Suppose a manager decides not to hedge and the gold price in 1 year is $390/oz. Did the firm earn $10 in profit (relative to accounting break-even) or lose $30 in profit (relative to the profit that could be obtained by hedging)? Would your answer be different if the manager did hedge and the gold price had been $450?

4.15. Consider the example in Table 4.6. Suppose that losses are fully tax-deductible. What is the expected after-tax profit in this case?

4.16. Suppose that firms face a 40% income tax rate on all profits. In particular, losses receive full credit. Firm A has a 50% probability of a $1000 profit and a 50%

probability of a $600 loss each year. Firm B has a 50% probability of a $300 profit and a 50% probability of a $100 profit each year.

a. What is the expected pre-tax profit next year for firms A and B?

b. What is the expected after-tax profit next year for firms A and B?

4.17. Suppose that firms face a 40% income tax rate on positive profits and that net losses receive no credit. (Thus, if profits are positive, after-tax income is $(1 - 0.4) \times$ *profit,* while if there is a loss, after-tax income is the amount lost.) Firms A and B have the same cash flow distribution as in the previous problem. Suppose the appropriate effective annual discount rate for both firms is 10%.

a. What is the expected pre-tax profit for A and B?

b. What is the expected after-tax profit for A and B?

c. What would Firms A and B pay today to receive next year's expected cash flow for sure, instead of the variable cash flows described above?

For the following problems use the *BSCall* option pricing function with a stock price of $420 (the forward price), volatility of 5.5%, continuously compounded interest rate of 4.879%, dividend yield of 4.879%, and time to expiration of 1 year. The problems require you to vary the strike prices.

4.18. Consider the example of Auric.

a. Suppose that Auric insures against a price increase by purchasing a 440-strike call. Verify by drawing a profit diagram that simultaneously selling a 400-strike put will generate a collar. What is the cost of this collar to Auric?

b. Find the strike prices for a zero-cost collar (buy high-strike call, sell low-strike put) for which the strikes differ by $30.

4.19. Suppose that LMN Investment Bank wishes to sell Auric a zero-cost collar of width 30 without explicit premium (i.e., there will be no cash payment from Auric to LMN). Also suppose that on every option the bid price is $0.25 below the Black-Scholes price and the offer price is $0.25 above the Black-Scholes price. LMN wishes to earn their spread ($0.25 per option) without any explicit charge to Auric. What should the strike prices on the collar be? (*Note*: Since the collar involves two options, LMN is looking to make $0.50 on the deal. You need to find strike prices that differ by 30 such that LMN makes $0.50.)

4.20. Use the same assumptions as in the preceding problem, without the bid-ask spread. Suppose that we want to construct a paylater strategy using a ratio spread. Instead of buying a 440-strike call, Auric will sell one 440-strike call, and use the premium to buy two higher-strike calls, such that the net option premium is zero.

a. What higher strike for the purchased calls will generate a zero net option premium?

b. Graph the profit for Auric resulting from this strategy.

4.21. Using the information in Table 4.11, verify that a regression of revenue on price gives a regression slope coefficient of about 100,000.

4.22. Using the information in Table 4.9 about Scenario C:

    a. Compute $\sigma_{\text{total revenue}}$ when correlation between price and quantity is positive.

    b. What is the correlation between price and revenue?

4.23. Using the information in Table 4.9 about Scenario C:

    a. Using your answer to the previous question, use equation (4.7) to compute the variance-minimizing hedge ratio.

    b. Run a regression of revenue on price to compute the variance-minimizing hedge ratio.

    c. What is the variability of optimally hedged revenue?

4.24. Using the information in Table 4.9 about Scenario C:

    a. What is the expected quantity of production?

    b. Suppose you short the expected quantity of corn. What is the standard deviation of hedged revenue?

4.25. Suppose that price and quantity are positively correlated as in this table:

Price	Quantity	Revenue
$2	0.6m bu	$1.2m
$3	0.934m bu	$2.8m

There is a 50% chance of either price. The futures price is $2.50. Demonstrate the effect of hedging if we do the following:

    a. Short the expected quantity.

    b. Short the minimum quantity.

    c. Short the maximum quantity.

    d. What is the hedge position that eliminates variability in revenue? Why?

PART TWO

Forwards, Futures, and Swaps

$\mathcal{F}$orward contracts permit the purchase of an asset in the future at terms that are set today. In earlier chapters we took forward prices as given. In this part—Chapters 5–8—we explore in detail the pricing of forward and futures contracts on a wide variety of underlying assets: financial assets (such as stocks, currencies, and bonds) and commodities (such as gold, corn, and natural gas). We also examine swaps, which have multiple future settlement dates, as opposed to forward contracts, which settle on a single date. Swaps are in effect a bundle of forward contracts combined with borrowing and lending. As such, swaps are a natural generalization of forward contracts.

Forward contracts involve deferring receipt of, and payment for, the underlying asset. Thus, computing the forward price requires you to determine the costs and benefits of this deferral. As in Part 1, present and future value calculations are the primary pricing tool.

CHAPTER 5

Financial Forwards and Futures

Forward contracts—which permit firms and investors to guarantee a price for a future purchase or sale—are a basic financial risk management tool. In this chapter we continue to explore these contracts and study in detail forward and futures contracts on financial instruments, such as stocks, indexes, currencies, and interest rates. Our objectives are to understand more about the use of these contracts, how they are priced, and how market-makers hedge them.

Questions to keep in mind throughout the chapter include: Who might buy or sell specific contracts? What kinds of firms might use the contract for risk management? Why is the contract designed as it is?

5.1 ALTERNATIVE WAYS TO BUY A STOCK

The purchase of a share of XYZ stock has three components: (1) fixing the price, (2) the buyer making payment to the seller, and (3) the seller transferring share ownership to the buyer. If we allow for the possibility that payment and physical receipt can occur at different times, say time 0 and time T, then once the price is fixed there are four logically possible purchasing arrangements: Payment can occur at time 0 or T, and physical receipt can occur at time 0 or T. Table 5.1 depicts these four possibilities, along with their customary names. Let's discuss these different arrangements.[1]

Outright purchase: The typical way to think about buying stock. You simultaneously pay the stock price in cash and receive ownership of the stock.

Fully leveraged purchase: A purchase in which you borrow the entire purchase price of the security. Suppose you borrow the share price, S_0, and agree to repay the borrowed amount at time T. If the continuously compounded interest rate is r, at time T you would owe e^{rT} per dollar borrowed, or $S_0 e^{rT}$.

Prepaid forward contract: An arrangement in which you pay for the stock today and receive the stock at an agreed-upon future date.[2] The difference between a

---

[1]All of these arrangements can be reversed in the case of the seller. Problem 5.1 asks you to describe them from that perspective.

[2]The term *prepaid forward contract*, or *prepay*, is widely used in practice and such contracts are common. The Enron transaction discussed in Chapter 8 and a hedging transaction by Roy Disney, discussed in Chapter 15, used prepaid swaps and forwards.

127

| | | **TABLE 5.1** | Four different ways to buy a share of stock that has price S_0 at time 0. At time 0 you agree to a price, which is paid either today or at time T. The shares are received either at 0 or T. The interest rate is r. |

Description	Pay at Time	Receive Security at Time	Payment
Outright purchase	0	0	S_0 at time 0
Fully leveraged purchase	T	0	$S_0 e^{rT}$ at time T
Prepaid forward contract	0	T	?
Forward contract	T	T	? $\times e^{rT}$

prepaid forward contract and an outright purchase is that with the former, you receive the stock at time T. We will see that the price you pay is not necessarily the stock price.

Forward contract: An arrangement in which you both pay for the stock and receive it at time T, with the time T price specified at time 0.

From Table 5.1 it is clear that you pay interest when you defer payment. The interesting question is how deferring the *physical receipt* of the stock affects the price; this deferral occurs with both the forward and prepaid forward contracts. What should you pay for the stock in those cases?[3]

5.2 PREPAID FORWARD CONTRACTS ON STOCK

A prepaid forward contract entails paying today to receive something—stocks, a foreign currency, bonds—in the future. The sale of a prepaid forward contracts permits the owner to sell an asset while retaining physical possession for a period of time.

We will derive the prepaid forward price using three different methods: pricing by analogy, pricing by present value, and pricing by arbitrage.

Pricing the Prepaid Forward by Analogy

Suppose you buy a prepaid forward contract on XYZ. By delaying physical possession of the stock, you do not receive dividends and have no voting or control rights. (We ignore here the value of voting and control.)

....

[3]The arrangements also differ with respect to credit risk, which arises from the possibility that the person on the other side of the transaction will not fulfill his or her end of the deal. (And of course the person on the other side of the deal may be worried about *you* fulfilling your obligation.)

In the absence of dividends, whether you receive physical possession today or at time T is irrelevant: In either case you own the stock, and at time T it will be exactly as if you had owned the stock the whole time.[4] *Therefore, when there are no dividends, the price of the prepaid forward contract is the stock price today.* Denoting the prepaid forward price for an asset bought at time 0 and delivered at time T as $F_{0,T}^P$, the prepaid forward price for delivery at time T is

$$F_{0,T}^P = S_0 \tag{5.1}$$

Pricing the Prepaid Forward by Discounted Present Value

We can also derive the price of the prepaid forward using present value: We calculate the expected value of the stock at time T and then discount that value at an appropriate rate of return. The stock price at time T, S_T, is uncertain. Thus in computing the present value of the stock price, we need to use an appropriate risk-adjusted rate.

If the expected stock price at time T based on information we have at time 0 is $E_0(S_T)$, then the prepaid forward price is given by

$$F_{0,T}^P = E_0(S_T)e^{-\alpha T} \tag{5.2}$$

where α, the expected return on the stock, is determined using the CAPM or some other model of expected returns.

How do we compute the expected stock price? By definition of the expected return, we expect that in T years the stock will be worth

$$E_0(S_T) = S_0 e^{\alpha T}$$

Thus, equation (5.2) gives

$$F_{0,T}^P = E_0(S_T)e^{-\alpha T} = S_0 e^{\alpha T} e^{-\alpha T} = S_0$$

For a nondividend-paying stock, the prepaid forward price is the stock price.

Pricing the Prepaid Forward by Arbitrage

Classical **arbitrage** describes a situation in which we can generate a positive cash flow either today or in the future by simultaneously buying and selling related assets, with no net investment of funds and with no risk. Arbitrage, in other words, is free money. An extremely important pricing principle, which we will use often, is that *the price of a derivative should be such that no arbitrage is possible.*

Here is an example of arbitrage. Suppose that the prepaid forward price exceeds the stock price—i.e., $F_{0,T}^P > S_0$. The arbitrageur will buy low and sell high by buying

---

[4]Suppose that someone secretly removed shares of stock from your safe and returned them 1 year later. From a purely financial point of view you would never notice the stock to be missing.

| | **TABLE 5.2** | | Cash flows and transactions to undertake arbitrage when the prepaid forward price, $F_{0,T}^P$, exceeds the stock price, S_0. |

	Cash Flows	
Transaction	**Time 0**	**Time T (expiration)**
Buy stock @ S_0	$-S_0$	$+S_T$
Sell prepaid forward @ $F_{0,T}^P$	$+F_{0,T}^P$	$-S_T$
Total	$F_{0,T}^P - S_0$	0

the stock for S_0 and selling the prepaid forward for $F_{0,T}^P$. This transaction makes money and it is also risk-free: Selling the prepaid forward requires that we deliver the stock at time T and buying the stock today ensures that we have the stock to deliver. Thus, we earn $F_{0,T}^P - S_0$ today and at expiration we supply the stock to the buyer of the prepaid forward. We have earned positive profits today and offset all future risk. Table 5.2 summarizes this situation.

Now suppose on the other hand that $F_{0,T}^P < S_0$. Then we can engage in arbitrage by buying the prepaid forward and shorting the stock, earning $S_0 - F_{0,T}^P$. One year from now we acquire the stock via the prepaid forward and we use that stock to close the short position. The cash flows in the above table are simply reversed.

Throughout the book we will assume that prices are at levels that preclude arbitrage. This raises the question: If prices are such that arbitrage is not profitable, who can afford to become an arbitrageur, watching out for arbitrage opportunities? We can resolve this paradox with the insight that in order for arbitrageurs to earn a living, arbitrage opportunities must occur from time to time; there must be "an equilibrium degree of disequilibrium."[5] However, you would not expect arbitrage to be obvious or easy to undertake.

The transactions in Table 5.2 are the same as those of a market-maker who is hedging a position. A market-maker would sell a prepaid forward if a customer wished to buy it. The market-maker then has an obligation to deliver the stock at a fixed price and, in order to offset this risk, can buy the stock. The market-maker thus engages in the same transactions as an arbitrageur, except the purpose is risk management, not arbitrage. Thus, *the transaction described in Table 5.2—selling the prepaid forward and buying the stock—also describes the actions of a market-maker.*

The no-arbitrage arguments we will make thus serve two functions: They tell us how to take advantage of mispricings, and they describe the behavior of market-makers managing risk.

....

[5]The phrase is from Grossman and Stiglitz (1980), in which this idea was first proposed.

Pricing Prepaid Forwards with Dividends

When a stock pays a dividend, the prepaid forward price is less than the stock price. The owner of stock receives dividends, but the owner of a prepaid forward contract does not. This difference creates a financial distinction between owning the stock and holding the prepaid forward. It is necessary to adjust the prepaid forward price to reflect dividends that are received by the shareholder, but not by the holder of the prepaid forward contract.

Discrete dividends To understand the effects of dividends, we will compare prepaid forwards on two stocks: Stock A pays no dividend, and otherwise identical stock B pays a $5 dividend 364 days from today, just before the expiration of the prepaid forwards. We know that the prepaid forward price for stock A is the current stock price. What is the prepaid forward price for stock B?

Since the $5 dividend is paid just before the delivery date for the stock 1 year from today, on the delivery date stock B will be priced $5 less than stock A. Thus, the price we pay today for stock B should be lower than that for stock A by the present value of $5.

In general, the price for a prepaid forward contract will be the stock price less the present value of dividends to be paid over the life of the contract. Suppose there are multiple dividend payments made throughout the life of the forward contract: A stock is expected to make dividend payments of D_{t_i} at times t_i, $i = 1, \ldots, n$. A prepaid forward contract will entitle you to receive the stock at time T but without receiving the interim dividends. Thus, the prepaid forward price is

$$F_{0,T}^P = S_0 - \sum_{i=1}^{n} \mathrm{PV}_{0,t_i}(D_{t_i}) \tag{5.3}$$

where PV_{0,t_i} denotes the time 0 present value of a time t_i payment.

Example 5.1 Suppose XYZ stock costs $100 today and is expected to pay a $1.25 quarterly dividend, with the first coming 3 months from today and the last just prior to the delivery of the stock. Suppose the annual continuously compounded risk-free rate is 10%. The quarterly continuously compounded rate is therefore 2.5%. A 1-year prepaid forward contract for the stock would cost

$$F_{0,1}^P = \$100 - \sum_{i=1}^{4} \$1.25 e^{-0.025i} = \$95.30 \qquad ≹$$

The calculation in this example implicitly assumes that the dividends are certain. Over a short horizon this might be reasonable. Over a long horizon we would expect dividend risk to be greater, and we would need to account for this in computing the present value of dividends.

Continuous dividends For stock indexes containing many stocks, it is common to model the dividend as being paid continuously at a rate that is proportional to the level of the index; i.e., the dividend *yield* (the annualized dividend payment divided by the stock price) is constant. This is an approximation, but in a large stock index there can be dividend payments on a large proportion of days.[6] The dividend yield is not likely to be fixed in the short run: When stock prices rise, the dividend yield falls, at least temporarily. Nevertheless, we will assume a constant proportional dividend yield for purposes of this discussion.

To model a continuous dividend, suppose that the index price is S_0 and the annualized daily compounded dividend yield is δ. Then the dollar dividend over one day is

$$\text{Daily dividend} = \frac{\delta}{365} \times S_0$$

Now suppose that we reinvest dividends in the index. Because of reinvestment, after T years we will have more shares than we started with. Using continuous compounding to approximate daily compounding, we get

$$\text{Number of shares} = \left(1 + \frac{\delta}{365}\right)^{365 \times T} \approx e^{\delta T}$$

At the end of T years we have approximately $e^{\delta T}$ ~~more~~ times as many shares than initially.

Now suppose we wish to invest today in order to have one share at time T. We can buy $e^{-\delta T}$ shares today. Because of dividend reinvestment, at time T, we will have $e^{\delta T}$ more shares than we started with, so we end up with exactly one share. Adjusting the initial quantity in this way in order to offset the effect of income from the asset is called **tailing** the position. Tailing enables us to offset the effect of continuous dividends. We will encounter the concept of tailing frequently.

Since an investment of $e^{-\delta T} S_0$ gives us one share at time T, this is the time 0 prepaid forward price for delivery at time T:

$$\boxed{F_{0,T}^P = S_0 e^{-\delta T}} \tag{5.4}$$

where δ is the dividend yield and T the time to maturity of the prepaid forward contract.

Example 5.2 Suppose that the index is \$125 and the annualized daily compounded dividend yield is 3%. The daily dollar dividend is

$$\text{Dividend} = (0.03 \div 365) \times \$125 = \$0.01027$$

---

[6]There is significant seasonality in dividend payments, which can be important in practice. A large number of U.S. firms pay quarterly dividends in February, May, August, and November. German firms, by contrast, pay annual dividends concentrated in May, June, and July.

Low Exercise Price Options

In some countries, including Australia and Switzerland, it is possible to buy stock options with very low strike prices—so low that it is virtually certain the option will expire in-the-money. For example, in Australia, the strike price is a penny. Such an option is called a *low exercise price option* (LEPO). These often exist in order to avoid taxes or transaction fees associated with directly trading the stock. LEPOs do not pay dividends and do not carry voting rights. As with any call option, a LEPO is purchased outright, and entitles the option holder to acquire the stock at expiration by paying the (low) strike price. The payoff of a LEPO

expiring at time T is

$$\max(0, S_T - K)$$

However, if the strike price, K, is so low that the option is certain to be exercised, this is just

$$S_T - K$$

This option has a value at time 0 of

$$F_{0,T}^P - \text{PV}(K)$$

Since the strike price of the option is close to zero, a LEPO is essentially a prepaid forward contract.

or a little more than one penny per unit of the index. If we start by holding one unit of the index, at the end of 1 year we will have

$$e^{0.03} = 1.030455$$

shares. Thus, if we wish to end the year holding one share, we must invest in

$$e^{-0.03} = 0.970446$$

shares. The prepaid forward price is

$$\$125e^{-0.03} = \$121.306$$

5.3 FORWARD CONTRACTS ON STOCK

Now that we have analyzed prepaid forward contracts, it is easy to derive forward prices. The only difference between the prepaid forward and the forward is the timing of the payment for the stock. Thus, *the forward price is just the future value of the prepaid forward.*

Here are forward prices for the cases we have considered:

No dividends: Taking the future value of equation (5.1), for the time 0 forward price of a stock that is delivered at time T, we have

$$F_{0,T} = \text{FV}(F_{0,T}^P) = S_0 e^{rT} \tag{5.5}$$

This formula shows that the forward contract is a purchase of the stock, with deferred payment. The interest adjustment compensates for that deferral.

Discrete dividends: To obtain the forward price for a stock that pays discrete dividends, we take the future value of equation (5.3). The forward price is the future value of the prepaid forward.

$$F_{0,T} = S_0 e^{rT} - \sum_{i=1}^{n} e^{r(T-t_i)} D_{t_i} \qquad (5.6)$$

Whereas for the prepaid forward we subtract the present value of dividends from the current stock price, for the forward we subtract the future value of dividends from the future value of the stock price.

Continuous dividends: When the stock pays continuous dividends, we take the future value of equation (5.4):

$$F_{0,T} = e^{rT} S_0 e^{-\delta T}$$

or

$$F_{0,T} = S_0 e^{(r-\delta)T} \qquad (5.7)$$

It is important to distinguish between the *forward price* and the *premium* for a forward contract. Because the forward contract has deferred payment, *its initial premium is zero*; it is initially costless. The forward *price*, however, is the future value of the prepaid forward price. This difference between the forward price and premium is in contrast with the prepaid forward, for which price and the premium are the same: The prepaid forward price is the amount you pay today to acquire the asset in the future.

Occasionally it is possible to observe the forward price but not the price of the underlying stock or index. For example, the futures contract for the S&P 500 index trades at times when the NYSE is not open, so it is possible to observe the futures price but not the stock price. The asset price implied by the forward pricing formulas above is said to define **fair value** for the underlying stock or index. Equation (5.7) is used in this case to infer the value of the index.

The **forward premium** is the ratio of the forward price to the spot price, defined as

$$\text{Forward premium} = \frac{F_{0,T}}{S_0} \qquad (5.8)$$

We can annualize the forward premium and express it as a percentage, in which case we have

$$\text{Annualized forward premium} = \frac{1}{T} \ln\left(\frac{F_{0,T}}{S_0}\right)$$

For the case of continuous dividends, equation (5.7), the annualized forward premium is simply the difference between the risk-free rate and the dividend yield.

Creating a Synthetic Forward Contract

A market-maker or arbitrageur must be able to offset the risk of a forward contract. It is possible to do this by creating a *synthetic* forward contract to offset a position in the actual forward contract.

In this discussion we will assume that dividends are continuous and paid at the rate δ, and hence that equation (5.7) is the appropriate forward price. We can then create a synthetic long forward contract by buying the stock and borrowing to fund the position. To see how the synthetic position works, recall that the payoff at expiration for a long forward position on the index is

$$\text{Payoff at expiration} = S_T - F_{0,T}$$

In order to obtain this same payoff, we buy a tailed position in the stock, investing $S_0 e^{-\delta T}$. This gives us one share at time T. We borrow this amount so that we are not required to pay anything additional at time 0. At time T we must repay $S_0 e^{(r-\delta)T}$ and we sell the stock for S_T. Table 5.3 demonstrates that borrowing to buy the stock replicates the expiration payoff to a forward contract.

Just as we can use the stock and borrowing to synthetically create a forward, we can also use the forward to create synthetic stocks and bonds. Table 5.4 demonstrates that we can go long a forward contract and lend the present value of the forward price to synthetically create the stock. The expiration payoff in this table assumes that equation (5.7) holds. Table 5.5 demonstrates that if we buy the stock and short the forward, we create cash flows like those of a risk-free bond. The rate of return on this synthetic bond—the construction of which is summarized in Table 5.5—is called the **implied repo rate.**

To summarize, we have shown that

$$\text{Forward} = \text{Stock} - \text{zero-coupon bond} \tag{5.9}$$

TABLE 5.3	Demonstration that borrowing $S_0 e^{-\delta T}$ to buy $e^{-\delta T}$ shares of the index replicates the payoff to a forward contract, $S_T - F_{0,T}$.

	Cash Flows	
Transaction	**Time 0**	**Time T (expiration)**
Buy $e^{-\delta T}$ units of the index	$-S_0 e^{-\delta T}$	$+S_T$
Borrow $S_0 e^{-\delta T}$	$+S_0 e^{-\delta T}$	$-S_0 e^{(r-\delta)T}$
Total	0	$S_T - S_0 e^{(r-\delta)T}$

TABLE 5.4	Demonstration that going long a forward contract at the price $F_{0,T} = S_0 e^{(r-\delta)T}$ and lending the present value of the forward price creates a synthetic share of the index at time T.

	Cash Flows	
Transaction	**Time 0**	**Time T (expiration)**
Long one forward	0	$S_T - F_{0,T}$
Lend $S_0 e^{-\delta T}$	$-S_0 e^{-\delta T}$	$+S_0 e^{(r-\delta)T}$
Total	$-S_0 e^{-\delta T}$	S_T

TABLE 5.5	Demonstration that buying $e^{-\delta T}$ shares of the index and shorting a forward creates a synthetic bond.

	Cash Flows	
Transaction	**Time 0**	**Time T (expiration)**
Buy $e^{-\delta T}$ units of the index	$-S_0 e^{-\delta T}$	$+S_T$
Short one forward	0	$F_{0,T} - S_T$
Total	$-S_0 e^{-\delta T}$	$F_{0,T}$

We can rearrange this equation to derive other synthetic equivalents.

$$\text{Stock} = \text{Forward} + \text{zero-coupon bond}$$

$$\text{Zero-coupon bond} = \text{Stock} - \text{forward}$$

All of these synthetic positions can be reversed to create synthetic short positions.

Synthetic Forwards in Market-Making and Arbitrage

Now we will see how market-makers and arbitrageurs use these strategies. Suppose a customer wishes to enter into a long forward position. The market-maker, as the counterparty, is left holding a short forward position. He can offset this risk by creating a synthetic long forward position.

Specifically, consider the transactions and cash flows in Table 5.6. The market-maker is short a forward contract and long a synthetic forward contract, constructed as in Table 5.3. There is no risk because the total cash flow at time T is $F_{0,T} - S_0 e^{(r-\delta)T}$. All of the components of this cash flow—the forward price, the stock price, the interest rate, and the dividend yield—are known at time 0. The result is a risk-free position.

TABLE 5.6	Transactions and cash flows for a cash-and-carry: A market-maker is short a forward contract and long a synthetic forward contract.		
		Cash Flows	
Transaction		**Time 0**	**Time T (expiration)**
Buy tailed position in stock, paying $S_0 e^{-\delta T}$		$-S_0 e^{-\delta T}$	$+S_T$
Borrow $S_0 e^{-\delta T}$		$+S_0 e^{-\delta T}$	$-S_0 e^{(r-\delta)T}$
Short forward		0	$F_{0,T} - S_T$
Total		0	$F_{0,T} - S_0 e^{(r-\delta)T}$

TABLE 5.7	Transactions and cash flows for a reverse cash-and-carry: A market-maker is long a forward contract and short a synthetic forward contract.		
		Cash Flows	
Transaction		**Time 0**	**Time T (expiration)**
Short tailed position in stock, receiving $S_0 e^{-\delta T}$		$+S_0 e^{-\delta T}$	$-S_T$
Lend $S_0 e^{-\delta T}$		$-S_0 e^{-\delta T}$	$+S_0 e^{(r-\delta)T}$
Long forward		0	$S_T - F_{0,T}$
Total		0	$S_0 e^{(r-\delta)T} - F_{0,T}$

Similarly, suppose the market-maker wishes to hedge a long forward position. Then it is possible to reverse the positions in Table 5.6. The result is in Table 5.7.

A transaction in which you buy the underlying asset and short the offsetting forward contract is called a **cash-and-carry.** A cash-and-carry has no risk: You have an obligation to deliver the asset but also own the asset. The market-maker offsets the short forward position with a cash-and-carry. An arbitrage that involves buying the underlying asset and selling it forward is called a **cash-and-carry arbitrage.** As you might guess, a **reverse cash-and-carry** entails short-selling the index and entering into a long forward position.

If the forward contract is priced according to equation (5.7), then profits on a cash-and-carry are zero. We motivated the cash-and-carry in Table 5.6 as risk management by a market-maker. However, an arbitrageur might also engage in a cash-and-carry. If the forward price is too high relative to the stock price—i.e., if $F_{0,T} > S_0 e^{(r-\delta)T}$—then an arbitrageur or market-maker can use the strategy in Table 5.6 to make a risk-free profit.

An arbitrageur would make the transactions in Table 5.7 if the forward were underpriced relative to the stock—i.e., if $S_0 e^{(r-\delta)T} > F_{0,T}$.

As a final point, you may be wondering about the role of borrowing and lending in Tables 5.6 and 5.7. When you explicitly account for borrowing, you account for the opportunity cost of investing funds. For example, if we omitted borrowing from Table 5.6, we would invest $S_0 e^{-\delta T}$ today and receive $F_{0,T}$ at time T. In order to know if there is an arbitrage opportunity, we would need to perform a present value calculation to compare the time 0 cash flow with the time T cash flow. By explicitly including borrowing in the calculations, this time-value-of-money comparison is automatic.[7]

Similarly, by comparing the implied repo rate with our borrowing rate, we have a simple measure of whether there is an arbitrage opportunity. For example, if we could borrow at 7%, then there is an arbitrage opportunity if the implied repo rate exceeds 7%. On the other hand, if our borrowing rate exceeds the implied repo rate, there is no arbitrage opportunity.

No-Arbitrage Bounds with Transaction Costs

Tables 5.6 and 5.7 demonstrate that an arbitrageur can make a costless profit if $F_{0,T} \neq S_0 e^{(r-\delta)T}$. This analysis ignores transaction costs. In practice an arbitrageur will face trading fees, bid-ask spreads, different interest rates for borrowing and lending, and the possibility that buying or selling in large quantities will cause prices to change. The effect of such costs will be that, rather than there being a single no-arbitrage price, there will be a no-arbitrage *bound*: a lower price F^- and an upper price F^+ such that arbitrage will not be profitable when the forward price is between these bounds.

Suppose that the stock and forward have bid and ask prices of $S^b < S^a$ and $F^b < F^a$, a trader faces a cost k of transacting in the stock or forward, and the interest rates for borrowing and lending are $r^b > r^l$. In this example we suppose that there are no transaction costs at time T, when the forward is either settled by delivery or cash-settled.

We will first derive F^+. An arbitrageur believing the observed forward price, $F_{0,T}$, is too high, will undertake the transactions in Table 5.6: Sell the forward and borrow to buy the stock. For simplicity we will assume the stock pays no dividends. The arbitrageur will pay the transaction cost k to short the forward and pay $(S_0^a + k)$ to acquire one share of stock. The required borrowing to finance the position is therefore $S_0^a + 2k$. At time T, the payoff is

$$\underbrace{-(S_0^a + 2k)e^{r^b T}}_{\text{Repayment of borrowing}} + \underbrace{F_{0,T} - S_T}_{\text{Value of forward}} + \underbrace{S_T}_{\text{Value of stock}}$$

Arbitrage is profitable if this expression is positive, or

$$F_{0,T} > F^+ = (S_0^a + 2k)e^{r^b T} \tag{5.10}$$

....

[7] In general, arbitrageurs can borrow and lend at different rates. A pro forma arbitrage calculation needs to account for the appropriate cost of capital for any particular transaction.

Thus, the upper bound reflects the fact that we pay a high price for the stock (the ask price), pay transaction costs on both the stock and forward, and borrow at a high rate.

We can derive F^- analogously. Problem 5.14 asks you to verify that the bound below which arbitrage is feasible is

$$F_{0,T} < F^- = (S_0^b - 2k)e^{r^l T} \qquad (5.11)$$

~~This expression assumes that short-selling the stock does not entail costs other than bid-ask transaction costs when the short position is initiated.~~

Notice that in equations (5.10) and (5.11), the costs all enter in such a way as to make the no-arbitrage region as large as possible (for example, the low lending rate enters F^- and the high borrowing rate enters F^+). This makes economic sense: Trading costs cannot help an arbitrageur make a profit.

There are additional costs not reflected in equations (5.10) and (5.11). One is that significant amounts of trading can move prices, so that what appears to be an arbitrage may vanish if prices change when the arbitrageur enters a large order. Another challenge can be execution risk. If trades do not occur instantaneously, the arbitrage can vanish before the trades are completed.

It is likely that the no-arbitrage region will be different for different arbitrageurs at a point in time, and different across time for a given arbitrageur. For example, consider the trading transaction cost, k. A large investment bank sees stock order flow from a variety of sources and may have inventory of either long or short positions in stocks. The bank may be able to buy or sell shares at low cost by serving as market-maker for a customer order. It may be inexpensive for a bank to short if it already owns the stocks, or it may be inexpensive to buy if the bank already has a short position.

Borrowing and lending rates can also vary. For a transaction that is explicitly financed by borrowing, the relevant interest rates are the arbitrageur's marginal borrowing rate (if that is the source of funds to buy stocks) or lending rate (if stocks are to be shorted). However, at other times, it may be possible to borrow at a lower rate or lend at a higher rate. For example, it may be possible to sell T-bills being held for some other purpose as a source of short-term funds. This may effectively permit borrowing at a low rate. Finally, in order to borrow money or securities arbitrageurs must have available capital. Undertaking one arbitrage may prevent undertaking another.

The overall conclusion is not surprising: Arbitrage may be difficult, risky, and costly. Large deviations from the theoretical price may be arbitraged, but small deviations may or may not represent genuine arbitrage opportunities.

Quasi-Arbitrage

The previous section focused on explicit arbitrage. However, it can also be possible to undertake *implicit* arbitrage by substituting a low yield position for one with a higher return. We call this **quasi-arbitrage.**

Consider, for example, a corporation that can borrow at 8.5% and lend at 7.5%. Suppose there is a cash-and-carry transaction with an implied repo rate of 8%. There is no pure arbitrage opportunity for the corporation, but it would make sense to divert lending from the 7.5% assets to the 8% cash-and-carry. If we attempt explicit arbitrage by borrowing at 8.5% in order to earn 8% on the cash-and-carry, the transaction becomes unprofitable. We can arbitrage only to the extent that we are already lending; this is why it is "quasi"-arbitrage.

Does the Forward Price Predict the Future Price?

It is common to think that the forward price reflects an expectation of the asset's future price. However, from the formula for the forward price, equation (5.7), once we know the current asset price, risk-free rate, and dividend yield, the forward price conveys no additional information about the expected future stock price. Moreover, the forward price *systematically* errs in predicting the future stock price.

The reason is straightforward. When you buy a stock, you invest money that has an opportunity cost (it could otherwise have been invested in an interest-earning asset), and you are acquiring the risk of the stock. On average you expect to earn interest as compensation for the time value of money. You also expect an additional return as compensation for the risk of the stock—this is the risk premium. Algebraically, the expected return on a stock is

$$\alpha = \underbrace{r}_{\text{Compensation for time}} + \underbrace{\alpha - r}_{\text{Compensation for risk}} \tag{5.12}$$

When you enter into a forward contract, there is no investment; hence, you are not compensated for the time value of money. However, the forward contract retains the risk of the stock, so you must be compensated for risk. *This means that the forward contract must earn the risk premium.* If the risk premium is positive, then on average you must expect a positive return from the forward contract. The only way this can happen is if the forward price predicts too low a stock price. In other words *the forward contract is a biased predictor of the future stock price.*

We can see this algebraically. Let α be the expected return on a nondividend-paying stock and let r be the effective annual interest rate. Consider a 1-year forward contract. The forward price is

$$F_0 = S_0(1 + r)$$

The expected future spot price is

$$E_0(S_1) = S_0(1 + \alpha)$$

where E_0 denotes "expectation as of time 0." Thus, the difference between the forward price and the expected future spot price is

$$E_0(S_1) - F_0 = S_0(1 + \alpha) - S_0(1 + r) = S_0(\alpha - r)$$

The expression $\alpha - r$ is the *risk premium* on the asset—i.e., the amount by which the asset is expected to outperform the risk-free asset. This equation verifies that *the forward price is biased by the amount of the risk premium on the underlying asset.*

For example, suppose that a stock index has an expected return of 15%, while the risk-free rate is 5%. If the current index price is 100, then on average we expect that the index will be 115 in 1 year. The forward price for delivery in 1 year will be only 105, however. This means that a holder of the forward contract will on average earn positive profits, albeit at the cost of bearing the risk of the index.[8]

This bias does not imply that a forward contract is a good investment. Rather, it tells us that *the risk premium on an asset can be created at zero cost and hence has a zero value.* Though this seems surprising, it is a result from elementary finance that if we buy any asset and borrow the full amount of its cost—a transaction that requires no investment—then we earn the risk premium on the asset. Since a forward contract has the risk of a fully leveraged investment in the asset, it earns the risk premium. This proposition is true in general, not just for the example of a forward on a nondividend-paying stock.

An Interpretation of the Forward Pricing Formula

The forward pricing formula for a stock index, equation (5.7), depends on $r - \delta$, the difference between the risk-free rate and the dividend yield. This difference is called the **cost of carry.**

Suppose you buy a unit of the index that costs S and fund the position by borrowing at the risk-free rate. You will pay rS on the borrowed amount, but the dividend yield will provide offsetting income of δS. You will have to pay the difference, $(r - \delta)S$, on an ongoing basis. This difference is the net cost of carrying a long position in the asset; hence, it is called the "cost of carry."

Now suppose you were to short the index and invest the proceeds at the risk-free rate. You would receive S for shorting the asset and earn rS on the invested proceeds, but you would have to pay δS to the index lender. We will call δ the **lease rate** of the index; it is what you would have to pay to a lender of the asset. The lease rate of an asset is the annualized cash payment that the borrower must make to the lender. For a nondividend-paying stock, the lease rate is zero while for a dividend-paying stock, the lease rate is the dividend.

Here is an interpretation of the forward pricing formula:

$$\text{Forward price} = \text{Spot price} + \underbrace{\text{Interest to carry the asset} - \text{Asset lease rate}}_{\text{Cost of carry}} \qquad (5.13)$$

The forward contract, unlike the stock, requires no investment and makes no payouts and therefore has a zero cost of carry. One way to interpret the forward pricing formula is that, to the extent the forward contract saves our having to pay the cost of carry, we are willing to pay a higher price. This is what equation (5.13) says.

----

[8]Accounting for dividends in this example would not change the magnitude of the bias since dividends would lower the expected future price of the index and the forward price by equal amounts.

5.4 Futures Contracts

Futures contracts are essentially exchange-traded forward contracts. As with forwards, futures contracts represent a commitment to buy or sell an underlying asset at some future date. Because futures are exchange-traded, they are standardized and have specified delivery dates, locations, and procedures. Futures may be traded either electronically or in trading pits, with buyers and sellers shouting orders to one another (this is called **open outcry**). Each exchange has an associated **clearinghouse.** The role of the clearinghouse is to match the buys and sells that take place during the day, and to keep track of the obligations and payments required of the members of the clearinghouse, who are called *clearing members*. After matching trades, the clearinghouse typically becomes the counterparty for each clearing member.

Although forwards and futures are similar in many respects, there are differences.

- Whereas forward contracts are settled at expiration, futures contracts are settled daily. The determination of who owes what to whom is called **marking-to-market.** Frequent marking-to-market and settlement of a futures contract can lead to pricing differences between the futures and an otherwise identical forward.

- As a result of daily settlement, futures contracts are liquid—it is possible to offset an obligation on a given date by entering into the opposite position. For example, if you are long the September S&P 500 futures contract, you can cancel your obligation to buy by entering into an offsetting obligation to sell the September S&P 500 contract. If you use the same broker to buy and to sell, your obligation is officially cancelled.[9]

- Over-the-counter forward contracts can be customized to suit the buyer or seller, whereas futures contracts are standardized. For example, available futures contracts may permit delivery of 250 units of a particular index in March or June. A forward contract could specify April delivery of 300 units of the index.

- Because of daily settlement, the nature of credit risk is different with the futures contract. In fact, futures contracts are structured so as to minimize the effects of credit risk.

- There are typically daily price limits in futures markets (and on some stock exchanges as well). A **price limit** is a move in the futures price that triggers a temporary halt in trading. For example, there is an initial 5% limit on *down* moves in the S&P 500 futures contract. An offer to sell exceeding this limit can trigger a temporary trading halt, after which time a 10% price limit is in effect. If that is exceeded, there are subsequent 15% and 20% limits. The rules can be complicated, but it is important to be aware that such rules exist.

---

[9]Although forward contracts may not be explicitly marketable, it is generally possible to enter into an offsetting position to cancel the obligation to buy or sell.

Single Stock Futures

Futures contracts on individual stocks in the United States began trading in November 2002 on OneChicago, an electronic exchange owned jointly by the Chicago Board Options Exchange, the Chicago Board of Trade, and the Chicago Mercantile Exchange. Earlier, the trading of single stock futures had been stalled by disagreements among exchanges and by a regulatory turf battle between the Securities and Exchange Commission, which regulates stocks and stock options, and the Commodity Futures Trading Commission, which regulates commodity and equity index futures.

Single stock futures were controversial even before trading began, with disagreement about how successful the product would be. What need would single stock futures serve? There was already a well-established market for buying and short-selling stocks, and we saw in Chapter 3 that investors could create synthetic stock forwards using options. Would differences in margin requirements, transaction costs, or contract characteristics make the new product successful?

Since 2002, one competitor to OneChicago (NQLX) has entered and then exited the market for single stock futures in the United States. Trading volume has proved disappointing for some advocates (see Zwick and Collins, 2004).

We will illustrate futures contracts with the S&P 500 index futures contract as a specific example.

The S&P 500 Futures Contract

The S&P 500 futures contract has the S&P 500 stock index as the underlying asset. Futures on individual stocks have recently begun trading in the United States. See the box above. Figure 2.1 shows a newspaper quotation for the S&P 500 index futures contract along with other stock index futures contracts, and Figure 5.1 shows its specifications. The notional value, or size, of the contract is the dollar value of the assets underlying one contract. In this case it is by definition $250 \times 1300 = \$325,000$.[10]

The S&P 500 is an example of a cash-settled contract: Instead of settling by actual delivery of the underlying stocks, the contract calls for a cash payment that equals the profit or loss *as if* the contract were settled by delivery of the underlying asset. On the expiration day, the S&P 500 futures contract is marked-to-market against the actual cash index. This final settlement against the cash index guarantees that the futures price equals the index value at contract expiration.

....

[10]Because the S&P 500 index is a fabricated number—a value-weighted average of individual stock prices—the S&P 500 index is treated as a pure number rather than a price and the contract is defined at maturity to have a size of $250 \times$ S&P 500 index.

Underlying	S&P 500 index
Where traded	Chicago Mercantile Exchange
Size	$250 × S&P 500 index
Months	Mar, Jun, Sep, Dec
Trading ends	Business day prior to determination of settlement price
Settlement	Cash-settled, based upon opening price of S&P 500 on third Friday of expiration month

It is easy to see why the S&P 500 is cash-settled. A physical settlement process would call for delivery of 500 shares (or some large subset thereof) in the precise percentage they make up the S&P 500 index. This basket of stocks would be expensive to buy and sell. Cash settlement is an inexpensive alternative.

Margins and Marking to Market

Let's explore the logistics of holding a futures position. Suppose the futures price is 1100 and you wish to acquire a $2.2 million position in the S&P 500 index. The notional value of one contract is $250 × 1100 = $275,000; this represents the amount you are agreeing to pay at expiration per futures contract. To go long $2.2 million of the index, you would enter into $2.2 million/$0.275 million = 8 long futures contracts. The notional value of 8 contracts is 8 × $250 × 1100 = $2,000 × 1100 = $2.2 million.

A broker executes your buy order. For every buyer there is a seller, which means that one or more investors must be found who simultaneously agree to sell forward the same number of units of the index. The total number of open positions (buy/sell pairs) is called the **open interest** of the contract.

Both buyers and sellers are required to post a performance bond with the broker to ensure that they can cover a specified loss on the position.[11] This deposit, which can earn interest, is called **margin** and is intended to protect the counterparty against your failure to meet your obligations. The margin is a performance bond, not a premium. Hence, futures contracts are costless (not counting, of course, commissions and the bid-ask spread).

To understand the role of margin, suppose that there is 10% margin and weekly settlement (in practice, settlement is daily). The margin on futures contracts with a notional value of $2.2 million is $220,000.

If the S&P 500 futures price drops by 1, to 1099, we lose $2000 on our futures position. The reason is that 8 long contracts obligate us to pay $2000 × 1100 to buy

---

[11]The exchange's clearinghouse determines a minimum margin, but individual brokers can and do demand higher margins from individual customers. The reason is that the broker is liable to the clearing corporation for customer failure to pay.

2000 units of the index which we could now sell for only 2000×1099. Thus, we lose $(1099 - 1100) \times \$2000 = -\$2000$. Suppose that over the first week, the futures price drops 72.01 points to 1027.99, a decline of about 6.5%. On a mark-to-market basis, we have lost

$$\$2000 \times -72.01 = -\$144,020$$

We have a choice of either paying this loss directly, or allowing it to be taken out of the margin balance. It doesn't matter which we do since we can recover the unused margin balance plus interest at any time by selling our position.

    If the loss is subtracted from the margin balance, we have earned one week's interest and have lost $144,020. Thus, if the continuously compounded interest rate is 6%, our margin balance after one week is

$$\$220,000e^{0.06 \times 1/52} - \$144,020 = \$76,233.99$$

Because we have a 10% margin, a 6.5% decline in the futures price results in a 65% decline in margin. Were we to close out our position by entering into 8 short index futures contracts, we would receive the remaining margin balance of $76,233.99.

    The decline in the margin balance means the broker has signficantly less protection should we default. For this reason, participants are required to maintain the margin at a minimum level, called the **maintenance margin.** This is often set at 70% to 80% of the initial margin level. In this example, where the margin balance declines 65%, we would have to post additional margin. The broker would make a **margin call,** requesting additional margin. If we failed to post additional margin, the broker would close the position by selling 2000 units of the index, and return to us the remaining margin. In practice, marking-to-market and settling up are performed at least daily.

    Since margin you post is the broker's protection against your default, a major determinant of margin levels is the volatility of the underlying asset. The minimum margin on the S&P 500 contract has generally been less than the 10% we assume in this example. In August 2004, for example, the minimum margin on the S&P 500 futures contract was about 6% of the notional value of the contract.

    To illustrate the effect of periodic settlement, Table 5.8 reports hypothetical futures price moves and tracks the margin position over a period of 10 weeks, assuming weekly marking-to-market and a continuously compounded risk-free rate of 6%. As the party agreeing to buy at a fixed price, we make money when the price goes up and lose when the price goes down. The opposite would occur for the seller.

    The 10-week profit on the position is obtained by subtracting from the final margin balance the future value of the original margin investment. Week-10 profit on the position in Table 5.8 is therefore

$$\$44,990.57 - \$220,000e^{0.06 \times 10/52} = -\$177,562.60$$

What if the position had been a forward rather than a futures position, but with prices the same? In that case, after 10 weeks our profit would have been

$$(1011.65 - 1100) \times \$2000 = -\$176,700$$

TABLE 5.8		Mark-to-market proceeds and margin balance over 10 weeks from long position in 8 S&P 500 futures contracts. The last column does not include additional margin payments. The final row represents expiration of the contract.		
Week	Multiplier ($)	Futures Price	Price Change	Margin Balance($)
0	2000.00	1100.00	—	220,000.00
1	2000.00	1027.99	−72.01	76,233.99
2	2000.00	1037.88	9.89	96,102.01
3	2000.00	1073.23	35.35	166,912.96
4	2000.00	1048.78	−24.45	118,205.66
5	2000.00	1090.32	41.54	201,422.13
6	2000.00	1106.94	16.62	234,894.67
7	2000.00	1110.98	4.04	243,245.86
8	2000.00	1024.74	−86.24	71,046.69
9	2000.00	1007.30	−17.44	36,248.72
10	2000.00	1011.65	4.35	44,990.57

Why do the futures and forward profits differ? The reason is that with the futures contract, interest is earned on the mark-to-market proceeds. Given the prices in Table 5.8, the loss is larger for futures than forwards because prices on average are below the initial price and we have to fund losses as they occur. With a forward, by contrast, losses are not funded until expiration. Earning interest on the daily settlement magnifies the gain or loss compared to that on a forward contract. Had there been consistent gains on the position in this example, the futures profit would have exceeded the forward profit. Appendix 5.B demonstrates that the ultimate payoff to a forward and futures contract can be equated in this example by adjusting the number of futures contracts so as to undo the magnifying effect of interest.

Comparing Futures and Forward Prices

An implication of Appendix 5.B is that if the interest rate were not random, then forward and futures prices would be the same. However, what if the interest rate varies randomly? Suppose, for example, that on average the interest rate increases unexpectedly when the futures price increases; i.e., the two are positively correlated. Then the margin balance would grow (due to an increased futures price) just as the interest rate was higher. The margin balance would shrink as the interest rate was lower. On average in this case, a long futures position would outperform a long forward contract.

Conversely, suppose that the interest rate declined as the futures price rose. Then as the margin balance on a long position grew, the proceeds would be invested at a lower rate. Similarly, as the balance declined and required additional financing, this financing would occur at a higher rate. Here a long futures contract would on average perform worse than a long forward contract.

This comparison of the forward and futures payoffs suggests that when the interest rate is positively correlated with the futures price, the futures price will exceed the price on an otherwise identical forward contract: The investor who is long futures buys at a higher price to offset the advantage of marking-to-market. Similarly, when the interest rate is negatively correlated with the forward price, the futures price will be less than an otherwise identical forward price: The investor who is long futures buys at a lower price to offset the disadvantage of marking-to-market.

As an empirical matter, forward and futures prices are very similar.[12] The theoretical difference arises from uncertainty about the interest on mark-to-market proceeds. For short-lived contracts, the effect is generally small. However, for long-lived contracts, the difference can be significant, especially for long-lived interest rate futures, for which there is sure to be a correlation between the interest rate and the price of the underlying asset. For the rest of this chapter we will ignore the difference between forwards and futures.

Arbitrage in Practice: S&P 500 Index Arbitrage

The S&P 500 futures contract provides a context for illustrating practical issues that arise when we try to apply the theoretical pricing formulas to determine the fair price of a futures contract. In order to compute the theoretical forward price using equation (5.7), we need to determine three things: (1) the value of the cash index (S_0), (2) the value of dividends to be paid on the index over the life of the contract (δ), and (3) the interest rate (r).

We can use readily available information to see whether the observed futures price is close to that given by equation (5.7). On August 30, 2004, the closing S&P 500 index value was 1099.15 and the December futures price was 1099.30. The annualized dividend yield on the index was approximately 1.75%, which we will assume is expected to be constant over time. The December contract expires on December 17, hence there were 109 days ($T = 0.2986$) until expiration.

What interest rate is appropriate? Two interest rates that we can easily observe are the yield on U.S. Treasury bills and the London Interbank Offer Rate (LIBOR), which is a borrowing rate for large financial institutions. Ninety-day LIBOR can be inferred from Eurodollar futures, which we will discuss in Section 5.7. The yield to maturity on a Treasury bill maturing in December was 1.56%, while implied 90-day LIBOR was

---

[12] See French (1983) for a comparison of forward and futures prices on a variety of underlying assets.

1.86% from September to December. Using the T-bill rate,[13] the theoretical futures price is

$$S_0 e^{(r-\delta)T} = 1099.15 e^{(0.0156-0.0175)\times 109/365} = 1098.53$$

The theoretical price using LIBOR instead of the T-bill rate is

$$S_0 e^{(r-\delta)T} = 1099.15 e^{(0.0186-0.0175)\times 109/365} = 1099.51$$

There are *two* theoretical prices, depending upon which interest rate we use; the actual December futures price, 1099.30, is between these two prices. Does this mean that there is an arbitrage opportunity?

There are a number of considerations in interepreting these differences in prices:

- Future dividends on the S&P 500 stocks are uncertain. For pricing a 3-month futures contract, one could use equation (5.6), with actual recent cash dividends on the underlying stocks for D_{t_i} as proxies for forthcoming dividends. There is still a risk that dividends will change over the next 3 months. The risk is greater for longer-dated futures contracts.

- There are transaction costs of arbitrage. As illustrated by equations (5.10) and (5.11), transaction costs create no-arbitrage *regions*, rather than no-arbitrage prices. In practice, a representative bid-ask spread on the index futures contract might be 20 to 30 basis points (a basis point on the S&P futures contract is 0.01) and 0.25% to 0.5% on the stocks in the index when traded in significant quantities.

- Different interest rates will reflect differences in issuer credit risk. With margin requirements, daily settling up, and clearinghouse guarantees, the credit risk of a futures contract is not the same as that of either Treasury bills or LIBOR. In practice, LIBOR is frequently used to compute forward prices.

- Because of transaction costs, an arbitrageur will usually buy not the entire 500-stock index, but instead a subset of it.[14] The futures contract and the offsetting position in stocks may thus not move exactly together. When buying a large number of stocks, there is also execution risk—the possibility that prices move during the time between the order being placed and the stock being actually purchased.

---

[13]This example uses yields as if they were quoted as continuously compounded, which they are not. However, for short periods and low interest rates, there is almost no difference between effective annual and continuously compounded rates. For example, if the effective annual rate is 2%, the continuously compounded equivalent is $\ln(1.02) = 0.0198$, or 1.98%. In practice, interest rates are quoted using a variety of arcane conventions for annualizing the rate.

[14]Another way to trade the cash index is with the use of Standard and Poor's Depository Receipts (SPDRs). These are unit investment trusts that are backed by a portfolio intended to mimic the S&P 500. Investors can convert units of 50,000 SPDR shares into the actual stock and can convert stock into SPDRs. This keeps SPDRs close to the S&P 500 index, but in practice SPDRs may be mispriced relative to the cash S&P 500 just as futures are.

Arbitrageurs will need to take into account these considerations. Ultimately, the only way to know if arbitrage is profitable is to assess specific prices, trading costs, and borrowing and lending rates.

Quanto Index Contracts

At first glance the Chicago Mercantile Exchange's Nikkei 225 futures contract—see a newspaper quotation in Figure 5.2 and the details summarized in Figure 5.3—is a stock index contract like the S&P 500 contract. However, there is one very important difference: Settlement of the contract is in a different currency (dollars) than the currency of denomination for the index (yen).[15]

To see why this is important, consider a dollar-based investor wishing to invest in the Nikkei 225 cash index. This investor must undertake two transactions: changing dollars to yen and using yen to buy the index. When the position is sold, the investor reverses these transactions, selling the index and converting yen back to dollars. There are two sources of risk in this transaction: the risk of the index, denominated in yen, and the risk that the yen/dollar exchange rate will change. From Figure 5.3, the Nikkei 225

FIGURE 5.2

Listing for the Nikkei 225 futures contract from the *Wall Street Journal*, July 21, 2004.

	OPEN	HIGH	LOW	SETTLE	CHG	LIFETIME HIGH	LIFETIME LOW	OPEN INT
Nikkei 225 Stock Average (CME)-$5 x index								
Sept	11310.	11370.	11220.	11365.	55	12210.	9710.	31,205

Est vol 2,597; vol Mon 2,663; open int 31,302, –134.
Index: Hi 11318.14; Lo 11191.76; Close 11258.37, –177.63.

FIGURE 5.3

Specifications for the Nikkei 225 index futures contract.

Underlying	Nikkei 225 Stock Index
Where traded	Chicago Mercantile Exchange
Size	$5 × Nikkei 225 Index
Months	Mar, Jun, Sep, Dec
Trading ends	Business day prior to determination of settlement price
Settlement	Cash-settled, based upon opening Osaka quotation of the Nikkei 225 index on the second Friday of expiration month

---

[15]There is also a yen-denominated Nikkei 225 futures contract that trades at the Osaka exchange. Since it is purely yen-denominated, this contract *is* priced according to equation (5.7).

futures contract is denominated in dollars rather than yen. Consequently, the contract insulates investors from currency risk, permitting them to speculate solely on whether the index rises or falls. This kind of contract is called a *quanto*. Quanto contracts allow investors in one country to invest in a different country without exchange rate risk.

The dollar-denominated Nikkei contract provides an interesting variation on the construction of a futures contract. Because of the quanto feature, the pricing formulas we have developed do not work for the Nikkei 225 contract. We will discuss quantos and the necessary modification to price a quanto futures contract in Chapter 22.

5.5 Uses of Index Futures

An index futures contract is economically like borrowing to buy the index. Why use an index futures contract if you can synthesize one? One answer is that index futures can permit trading the index at a lower transaction cost than actually trading a basket of the stocks that make up the index. If you are taking a temporary position in the index, either for investing or hedging, the transaction cost saving could be significant.

In this section we provide two examples of the use of index futures: asset allocation and cross-hedging a related portfolio.

Asset Allocation

Asset allocation strategies involve switching investments among asset classes, such as stocks, money market instruments, and bonds. Trading the individual securities, such as the stocks in an index, can be expensive. Our earlier discussion of arbitrage demonstrated that we can use forwards to create synthetic stocks and bonds. The practical implication is that a portfolio manager can invest in a stock index without holding stocks, commodities without holding physical commodities, and so on.

Switching from stocks to T-bills As an example of asset allocation, suppose that we have an investment in the S&P 500 index and we wish to temporarily invest in T-bills instead of the index. Instead of selling all 500 stocks and investing in T-bills, we can simply keep our stock portfolio and take a short forward position in the S&P 500 index. This converts our cash investment in the index into a cash-and-carry, creating a synthetic T-bill. When we wish to revert to investing in stocks, we simply offset the forward position.

To illustrate this, suppose that the current index price, S_0, is $100, and the effective 1-year risk-free rate is 10%. The forward price is therefore $110. Suppose that in 1 year, the index price could be either $80 or $130. If we sell the index and invest in T-bills, we will have $110 in 1 year.

Table 5.9 shows that if, instead of selling, we keep the stock and short the forward contract, we earn a 10% return no matter what happens to the value of the stock. In this example 10% is the rate of return implied by the forward premium. If there is no arbitrage, this return will be equal to the risk-free rate.

| TABLE 5.9 | Effect of owning the stock and selling forward, assuming that $S_0 = \$100$ and $F_{0,1} = \$110$. |

		Cash Flows	
Transaction	**Today**	**1 year, $S_1 = \$80$**	**1 year, $S_1 = \$130$**
Own stock @ $100	−$100	$80	$130
Short forward @ $110	0	$110 − $80	$110 − $130
Total	−$100	$110	$110

General asset allocation   We can use forwards and futures to perform even more sophisticated asset allocation. Suppose we wish to invest our portfolio in Treasury bonds (long-term Treasury obligations) instead of stocks. We can accomplish this reallocation with two forward positions: Shorting the forward S&P 500 index and going long the forward T-bond. The first transaction converts our portfolio from an index investment to a T-bill investment. The second transaction converts the portfolio from a T-bill investment to a T-bond investment. This use of futures to convert a position from one asset category (stocks) to another (bonds) is called a **futures overlay.**

Futures overlays can have benefits beyond reducing transaction costs. Suppose an investment management company has portfolio managers who successfully invest in stocks they believe to be mispriced. The managers are judged on their performance relative to the S&P 500 stock index and consistently outperform the index by 2% per year (in the language of portfolio theory, their "alpha" is 2%). Now suppose that new clients of the company like the performance record, but want to invest in bonds rather than stocks. The investment management company could fire its stock managers and hire bond managers, but its existing investment managers are the reason for the company's success. The company can use a futures overlay to continue to invest in stocks, but to provide a bond return instead of a stock return to investors. By investing in stocks, shorting index futures, and going long bond futures, the managers continue to invest in stocks, but the client receives a bond return plus 2% rather than a stock return plus 2%. This use of futures to transform an outperforming portfolio on one asset class into an outperforming portfolio on a different asset class is called **alpha-porting.**

Cross-hedging with Index Futures

Index futures are often used to hedge portfolios that are not exactly the index. As discussed in Section 4.5, this is called *cross-hedging*.

Cross-hedging with perfect correlation   Suppose that we have a portfolio that is not the S&P 500, and we wish to shift the portfolio into T-bills. Can we use the S&P 500 futures contract to do this? The answer depends on the correlation of the portfolio with the S&P 500. To the extent the two are not perfectly correlated, there will be residual risk.

Suppose that we own $100 million of stocks with a beta relative to the S&P 500 of 1.4. Assume for the moment that the two indexes are perfectly correlated. Perfect correlation means that there is a perfectly predictable relationship between the two indexes, not necessarily that they move one-for-one. Using the Capital Asset Pricing Model (CAPM), the return on our portfolio, r_p, is related to its beta, β_p, by

$$r_p = r + \beta_p(r_{S\&P} - r)$$

Assume also that the S&P 500 is 1100 with a 0 dividend yield and the effective annual risk-free rate is 6%. Hence the futures price is $1100 \times 1.06 = 1166$.

If we wish to allocate from the index into Treasury bills using futures, we need to short some quantity of the S&P 500. There are two steps to calculating the short futures quantity:

1. *Adjust for the difference in the dollar amounts of our portfolio and the S&P 500 contract.* In this case, one futures contract has a value of $250 \times 1100 = \$275,000$. Thus, the number of contracts needed to cover $100 million of stock is

$$\frac{\$100 \text{ million}}{\$0.275 \text{ million}} = 363.636$$

2. *Adjust for the difference in beta.* Since the beta of our portfolio exceeds 1, it moves more than the S&P 500 in either direction. Thus we need to further increase our S&P 500 position to account for the greater magnitude moves in our portfolio relative to the S&P 500. This gives us

$$\text{Final hedge quantity} = \frac{\$100 \text{ million}}{\$0.275 \text{ million}} \times 1.4 = 509.09$$

Table 5.10 shows the performance of the hedged position. The result, as you would expect, is that the hedged position earns the risk-free rate, 6%.

TABLE 5.10	Results from shorting 509.09 S&P 500 index futures against a $100m portfolio with a beta of 1.4.		
S&P 500 Index	**Gain on 509 Futures**	**Portfolio Value**	**Total**
900	33.855	72.145	106.000
950	27.491	78.509	106.000
1000	21.127	84.873	106.000
1050	14.764	91.236	106.000
1100	8.400	97.600	106.000
1150	2.036	103.964	106.000
1200	−4.327	110.327	106.000

Cross-hedging with imperfect correlation   The preceding example assumes that the portfolio and the S&P 500 index are perfectly correlated. In practice, correlations between two portfolios can be substantially less than one. Using the S&P 500 to hedge such a portfolio would introduce basis risk, creating a hedge with residual risk.[16]

Denote the return and invested dollars on the portfolio as r_p and I_p. Assume that we short H futures contracts, each with a notional value N. The futures position earns the risk premium, $r_{S\&P} - r$. Thus, the return on the hedged position is

$$\text{Hedged return} = r_p I_p + H \times N \times (r_{S\&P} - r)$$

Repeating the analysis in Section 4.5 [in particular, see equation 4.2], the variance-minimizing hedge position, H^*, is

$$H^* = -\frac{I_p}{N} \frac{\text{Cov}(r_p, r_{S\&P})}{\sigma_{S\&P}^2} \tag{5.14}$$

$$= -\frac{I_p}{N} \beta_p$$

The hedge quantity is denominated in terms of a quantity of futures contracts. The second equality follows because $\text{Cov}(r_p, r_{S\&P})/\sigma_{S\&P}^2$ is the slope coefficient when we regress the portfolio return on the S&P 500 return; i.e., it is the portfolio beta with respect to the S&P 500 index. Equation (5.14) is also the formula we used in concluding that, with perfect correlation, we should short 509.09 contracts.

Notice that the hedge ratio in equation (5.14) depends on the ratio of the market value of the portfolio, I_p, to the notional value of the S&P 500 contract, N. Thus, as the portfolio changes value relative to the S&P 500 index, it is necessary to change the hedge ratio. This rebalancing is necessary when we calculate hedge ratios using a relationship based on returns, which are percentage changes.

When we add H^* futures to the portfolio, the variance of the hedged portfolio, σ_{hedged}^2, is

$$\sigma_{\text{hedged}}^2 = \sigma_p^2 I_p^2 \left(1 - \rho^2\right) \tag{5.15}$$

where ρ is the correlation coefficient between the portfolio and the S&P 500 index. This is the same as equation (4.4). The correlation coefficient, ρ, can be computed directly from r_p and $r_{S\&P}$, but it is also the square root of the regression r-squared (R^2) when we regress r_P on $r_{S\&P}$ in order to estimate β.

Example 5.3   Suppose we are optimistic about the performance of the NASDAQ index relative to the S&P 500 index. We can go long the NASDAQ index and short

---

[16]There is additional basis risk in such a hedge because, for reasons discussed in Section 5.4, the S&P 500 futures contract and the cash price of the S&P 500 index may not move perfectly together.

the S&P 500 futures. We obtain the variance-minimizing position in the S&P 500 by using equation (5.14). A 5-year regression (from June 1999 to June 2004) of the daily NASDAQ return on the S&P 500 return gives

$$r_{\text{NASD}} = \underset{(0.0003)}{-0.0001} + \underset{(0.0262)}{1.4784} \times (r_{\text{S\&P}} - r) \qquad R^2 = 0.7188$$

The regression beta tells us to short a dollar value of the S&P that is 1.4784 times greater than the NASDAQ position we hold. The correlation coefficient between the two returns, ρ, is $\sqrt{0.7188} = 0.8478$.[17] The daily standard deviation of the return on the NASDAQ over this period is 2.24%. Hence, using equation (5.15), for a $1 million investment, the variance of the hedged position is

$$\sigma^2_{\text{NASD}} I_p^2 \left(1 - \rho^2\right) = 0.0224^2 \times (\$1m)^2 \times (1 - 0.7188) = (\$11,878)^2$$

Thus, the daily standard deviation of the hedged return is $11,878. ⚡

Risk management for stock-pickers An asset manager who picks stocks is often making a bet about the relative, but not the absolute, performance of a stock. For example, XYZ might be expected to outperform a broad range of stocks on a risk-adjusted basis. If the economy suffers a recession, however, XYZ will decline in value even if it outperforms other stocks. Index futures can be used in this case to help isolate the *relative* performance of XYZ.

Suppose the return of XYZ is given by the CAPM:

$$r_{\text{XYZ}} = \alpha_{\text{XYZ}} + r + \beta_{\text{XYZ}}(r_m - r) \tag{5.16}$$

The term α_{XYZ} in this context represents the expected abnormal return on XYZ. If we use the S&P 500 as a proxy for the market, then we can select H according to equation (5.14). The result for the hedged position will be that, on average, we earn $\alpha_{\text{XYZ}} + r$. The risk of the position will be given by equation (5.15). Since the correlation of an individual stock and the index will not be close to 1, there will be considerable remaining risk. However, the portfolio will not have market risk.

5.6 CURRENCY CONTRACTS

Currency futures and forwards are widely used to hedge against changes in exchange rates. The pricing of currency contracts is a straightforward application of the principles we have already discussed. Newspaper listings for exchange-traded currency contracts are shown in Figure 5.4.

Many corporations use currency futures and forwards for short-term hedging. An importer of consumer electronics, for example, may have an obligation to pay the manufacturer ¥150 million 90 days in the future. The dollar revenues from selling these

----

[17]You can, of course, also compute the correlation coefficient directly from the time series of returns.

FIGURE 5.4

Listings for various currency futures contracts from the *Wall Street Journal*, July 21, 2004.

	OPEN	HIGH	LOW	SETTLE	CHG	LIFETIME HIGH	LIFETIME LOW	OPEN INT
Currency Futures								
Japanese Yen (CME)-¥12,500,000; $ per ¥								
Sept	.9268	.9272	.9216	.9234	−.0030	.9705	.8575	97,165
Dec	.9293	.9313	.9272	.9279	−.0030	.9740	.8800	10,385
Est vol 11,037; vol Mon 15,248; open int 107,558, +1,164.								
Canadian Dollar (CME)-CAD 100,000; $ per CAD								
Sept	.7640	.7644	.7583	.7608	−.0026	.7815	.6505	77,458
Dec	.7612	.7628	.7580	.7600	−.0026	.7800	.6940	4,531
Mr05	.7610	.7619	.7580	.7593	−.0026	.7775	.7150	737
June	.7600	.7600	.7568	.7586	−.0026	.7760	.7150	522
Est vol 7,847; vol Mon 14,867; open int 83,285, +1,209.								
British Pound (CME)-£62,500; $ per £								
Sept	1.8599	1.8599	1.8414	1.8437	−.0155	1.8712	1.6330	79,979
Dec	1.8357	1.8360	1.8260	1.8295	−.0155	1.8648	1.6850	415
Est vol 8,554; vol Mon 14,642; open int 80,400, −1,148.								
Swiss Franc (CME)-CHF 125,000; $ per CHF								
Sept	.8153	.8165	.8046	.8055	−.0096	.8209	.7110	58,413
Dec	.8102	.8118	.8080	.8080	−.0096	.8260	.7264	131
Est vol 9,948; vol Mon 8,936; open int 58,609, −901.								
Australian Dollar (CME)-AUD 100,000; $ per AUD								
Sept	.7281	.7296	.7225	.7243	−.0032	.7780	.5756	36,589
Dec	.7187	.7211	.7170	.7178	−.0032	.7705	.6150	258
Est vol 3,019; vol Mon 8,762; open int 36,937, +588.								
Mexican Peso (CME)-MXN 500,000; $ per MXN								
Aug	...	...	...	.08740	−.00027	.08760	.08730	400
Sept	.08730	.08730	.08670	.08690	−.00027	.08935	.08370	43,128
Est vol 7,247; vol Mon 18,659; open int 45,629, −222.								
Euro/US Dollar (CME)-€125,000; $ per €								
Sept	1.2430	1.2443	1.2306	1.2321	−.0102	1.2800	1.0500	145,614
Dec	1.2419	1.2430	1.2312	1.2314	−.0102	1.2781	1.0735	1,226
Mr05	1.2345	1.2360	1.2315	1.2314	−.0102	1.2720	1.1363	213
Est vol 28,053; vol Mon 44,073; open int 147,083, −2,866.								

products are likely known in the short run, so the importer bears pure exchange risk due to the payable being fixed in yen. By buying ¥150 million forward 90 days, the importer locks in a dollar price to pay for the yen, which will then be delivered to the manufacturer.

Currency Prepaid Forward

Suppose that 1 year from today you want to have ¥1. A prepaid forward allows you to pay dollars today to acquire ¥1 in 1 year. What is the prepaid forward price? Suppose the yen-denominated interest rate is r_y and the exchange rate today ($/¥) is x_0. We can work backward. If we want ¥1 in 1 year, we must have e^{-r_y} in yen today. To obtain that many yen today, we must exchange $x_0 e^{-r_y}$ dollars into yen.

Thus, the prepaid forward price for a yen is

$$F_{0,T}^P = x_0 e^{-r_y T} \tag{5.17}$$

where T is time to maturity of the forward.

The economic principle governing the pricing of a prepaid forward on currency is the same as that for a prepaid forward on stock. By deferring delivery of the underlying asset, you lose income. In the case of currency, if you received the currency immediately, you could buy a bond denominated in that currency and earn interest. The prepaid forward price reflects the loss of interest from deferring delivery, just as the prepaid forward price for stock reflects the loss of dividend income. This is why equation (5.17) is the same as that for a stock paying a continuous dividend, equation (5.4).

Example 5.4 Suppose that the yen-denominated interest rate is 2% and that the current exchange rate is 0.009 dollars per yen. Then in order to have 1 yen in 1 year, we would invest today

$$0.009\$/\yen \times \yen 1 \times e^{-0.02} = \$.008822$$ 🦋

Currency Forward

The prepaid forward price is the *dollar* cost of obtaining 1 yen in the future. Thus, to obtain the forward price, compute the future value using the dollar-denominated interest rate, r:

$$F_{0,T} = x_0 e^{(r-r_y)T} \tag{5.18}$$

The forward currency rate will exceed the current exchange rate when the domestic risk-free rate is higher than the foreign risk-free rate.[18]

Example 5.5 Suppose that the yen-denominated interest rate is 2% and the dollar-denominated rate is 6%. The current exchange rate is 0.009 dollars per yen. The 1-year forward rate is

$$0.009e^{0.06-0.02} = 0.009367$$ 🦋

Notice that equation (5.18) is just like equation (5.7), for stock index futures, with the foreign interest rate equal to the dividend yield. The interest rate difference $r - r_y$ is the cost of carry for a foreign currency (we borrow at the domestic rate r and invest the proceeds in a foreign money-market instrument, earning the foreign rate r_y as an offset to our cost). If we wish to borrow foreign currency, r_y is the lease rate.

Covered Interest Arbitrage

We can synthetically create a forward contract by borrowing in one currency and lending in the other. If we want to have 1 yen in the future, with the dollar price fixed today, we

----

[18] Of course if you think about it, every currency transaction can be expressed in terms of either currency, for example as yen/dollar or dollar/yen. If the forward price exceeds the current exchange rate viewed from the perspective of one currency, it must be less from the perspective of the other.

can pay today for the yen, and borrow in dollars to do so. To have 1 yen in 1 year, we need to invest

$$x_0 e^{-r_y T}$$

in dollars, and we obtain this amount by borrowing. The required dollar repayment is

$$x_0 e^{(r-r_y)T}$$

which is the forward exchange rate.

Example 5.6 Suppose that $x_0 = 0.009$, $r_y = 2\%$, and $r = 6\%$. The dollar cost of buying 1 yen today is $0.009 \times e^{-0.02} = 0.008822$. We defer the dollar payment by borrowing at 6%, for a cost 1 year from today of $0.008822 e^{0.06} = 0.009367$. This transaction is summarized in Table 5.11.   ⚛

The example shows that borrowing in one currency and lending in another creates the same cash flow as a forward contract. If we offset this borrowing and lending position with an actual forward contract, the resulting transaction is called **covered interest arbitrage.**

To summarize, a forward exchange rate reflects the difference in interest rates denominated in different currencies. Imagine that you want to invest $1 for 1 year. You can do so by buying a dollar-denominated bond, or you can exchange the dollar into another currency and buy a bond denominated in that other currency. You can then use currency forwards to guarantee the exchange rate at which you will convert the foreign currency back into dollars. The principle behind the pricing of currency forwards is that a position in foreign risk-free bonds, with the currency risk hedged, pays the same return as domestic risk-free bonds.

TABLE 5.11	Synthetically creating a yen forward contract by borrowing in dollars and lending in yen. The payoff at time 1 is ¥1 − $0.009367.

| | Cash Flows | | | |
| | Year 0 | | Year 1 | |
Transaction	$	¥	$	¥
Borrow $x_0 e^{-r_y}$ dollar at 6% ($)	+0.008822	—	−0.009367	—
Convert to yen @ 0.009 $/¥	−0.008822	+0.9802	—	—
Invest in yen-denominated bill (¥)	—	−0.9802	—	1
Total	0	0	−0.009367	1

5.7 Eurodollar Futures

Businesses and individuals face uncertainty about future interest rates. A manager may plan to borrow money 3 months from today but doesn't know today what the interest rate will be at that time. There are forward and futures contracts that permit hedging interest rate risk by allowing the manager to lock in now a borrowing rate for 3 months in the future.

The principles underlying interest rate contracts are exactly those we have been discussing, but interest rates seem more complicated because there are so many of them, depending upon whether you invest for 1 day, 1 month, 1 year, or 30 years. There are also implied forward interest rates between any two points in the future.[19] Because of this complexity, Chapter 7 is devoted to interest rates. However, the Eurodollar contract is so important that we discuss it briefly here. The Eurodollar strip (the set of futures prices with different maturities at one point in time) provides basic interest rate information that is commonly used to price other futures contracts and to price swaps. Figure 5.5 shows a newspaper listing for the Eurodollar futures contract and the companion 1-month LIBOR contract.

The Eurodollar contract, described in Figure 5.6, is based on a $1 million 3-month deposit earning LIBOR (the London Interbank Offer Rate), which is the average borrowing rate faced by large international London banks. The 1-month LIBOR contract is similar. Suppose that current LIBOR is 1.5% over 3 months. By convention, this is annualized by multiplying by 4, so the quoted LIBOR rate is 6%. Assuming a bank borrows $1 million for 3 months, a change in annualized LIBOR of 0.01% (one basis point) would raise its borrowing cost by $0.0001/4 \times \$1$ million = $25.

The Eurodollar futures price at expiration of the contract is

$$100 - \text{Annualized 3-month LIBOR}$$

Thus, if LIBOR is 6% at maturity of the Eurodollar futures contract, the final futures price will be $100 - 6 = 94$. It is important to understand that the Eurodollar contract settles based on current LIBOR, which is the interest rate quoted for the *next* 3 months. Thus, for example, the price of the contract that expires in June reflects the 3-month interest rate between June and September. With the futures contract, as with a $1 million LIBOR deposit, a change of 0.01% in the rate is worth $25.

Like most money-market interest rates, LIBOR is quoted assuming a 360-day year. Thus, the annualized 91-day rate, r_{91}, can be extracted from the futures price, F, by computing the 90-day rate and multiplying by 91/90. The quarterly effective rate is then computed by dividing the result by 4:

$$r_{91} = (100 - F) \times \frac{1}{100} \times \frac{1}{4} \times \frac{91}{90} \tag{5.19}$$

---

[19] In addition, there are different rates faced by different classes of borrower: government, private, and municipal. And of course there are different currencies of denomination.

FIGURE 5.5

Listing for the 1-month LIBOR and 3-month Eurodollar futures contract from the *Wall Street Journal*, July 21, 2004.

	OPEN	HIGH	LOW	SETTLE	CHG	LIFETIME HIGH	LOW	OPEN INT
1 Month Libor (CME)-$3,000,000; pts of 100%								
Aug	98.40	98.41	98.40	98.40	...	1.60	...	187,551
Sept	98.25	98.26	98.23	98.23	-.03	1.77	.03	28,150
Oct	98.13	98.14	98.11	98.11	-.03	1.89	.03	256,608
Est vol 15,694; vol Mon 5,902; open int 635,166, +1,332.								
Eurodollar (CME)-$1,000,000; pts of 100%								
Aug	98.23	98.24	98.20	98.21	-.02	1.79	.02	35,715
Sept	98.09	98.10	98.05	98.06	-.04	1.94	.04	864,712
Oct	97.93	97.93	97.90	97.90	-.04	2.10	.04	280
Dec	97.69	97.70	97.60	97.61	-.08	2.39	.08	877,744
Mr05	97.31	97.31	97.18	97.19	-.12	2.81	.12	822,610
June	96.94	96.94	96.79	96.80	-.14	3.20	.14	660,733
Sept	96.61	96.61	96.46	96.46	-.15	3.54	.15	549,699
Dec	96.32	96.31	96.16	96.17	-.15	3.83	.15	456,330
Mr06	96.09	96.08	95.93	95.95	-.14	4.05	.14	346,961
June	95.90	95.90	95.77	95.78	-.13	4.22	.13	211,752
Sept	95.73	95.74	95.62	95.63	-.13	4.37	.13	191,822
Dec	95.57	95.59	95.46	95.48	-.12	4.52	.12	144,923
Mr07	95.46	95.45	95.34	95.35	-.12	4.65	.12	147,495
June	95.33	95.32	95.21	95.23	-.11	4.77	.11	112,960
Sept	95.17	95.20	95.11	95.11	-.11	4.89	.11	93,133
Dec	95.05	95.08	94.98	94.99	-.10	5.01	.10	70,854
Mr08	94.95	94.97	94.88	94.89	-.10	5.11	.10	66,963
June	94.84	94.86	94.77	94.78	-.09	5.22	.09	67,755
Sept	94.78	94.78	94.68	94.68	-.09	5.32	.09	57,367
Dec	94.63	94.66	94.57	94.58	-.09	5.42	.09	47,027
Mr09	94.59	94.59	94.49	94.50	-.09	5.50	.09	41,223
June	94.47	94.48	94.40	94.41	-.08	5.59	.08	25,648
Sept	94.39	94.40	94.32	94.33	-.08	5.67	.08	9,428
Dec	94.30	94.31	94.24	94.24	-.08	5.76	.08	7,924
Mr10	94.23	94.24	94.17	94.17	-.08	5.83	.08	7,445
June	94.16	94.17	94.10	94.10	-.08	5.90	.08	7,590
Sept	94.09	94.10	94.03	94.03	-.08	5.97	.08	7,397
Dec	94.02	94.03	93.96	93.96	-.08	6.04	.08	5,468
Mr11	93.96	93.97	93.90	93.90	-.08	6.10	.08	5,519
June	93.90	93.91	93.84	93.84	-.08	6.16	.08	2,395
Sept	93.87	93.87	93.80	93.80	-.08	6.20	.08	2,144
Dec	93.82	93.82	93.75	93.75	-.08	6.25	.08	1,652
Mr12	93.78	93.78	93.71	93.71	-.08	6.29	.08	1,537
June	93.72	93.73	93.65	93.66	-.08	6.34	.08	891
Sept	93.69	93.70	93.62	93.63	-.08	6.37	.08	846
Dec	93.66	93.67	93.59	93.60	-.08	6.40	.08	536
Mr13	93.64	93.64	93.57	93.57	-.08	6.43	.08	409
Est vol 568,040; vol Mon 761,414; open int 6,035,024, -1,501.								

FIGURE 5.6

Specifications for the Eurodollar futures contract.

Where traded	Chicago Mercantile Exchange
Size	3-month Eurodollar time deposit, $1 million principal
Months	Mar, Jun, Sep, Dec, out 10 years, plus 2 serial months and spot month
Trading ends	5 A.M. (11 A.M. London) on the second London bank business day immediately preceding the third Wednesday of the contract month.
Delivery	Cash settlement
Settlement	100 − British Banker's Association Futures Interest Settlement Rate for 3-Month Eurodollar Interbank Time Deposits. (This is a 3-month rate annualized by multiplying by 360/90.)

Three-month Eurodollar contracts have maturities out to 10 years, which means that it is possible to use the contract to lock in a 3-month rate as far as 10 years in the future. The September 2007 futures price in Figure 5.5, for example, is 95.11. A position in this contract can be used to lock in an annualized rate of 4.89% from September 2007 to December 2007.

The Eurodollar contract can be used to hedge interest rate risk. For a borrower, for example, a short position in the contract is a hedge since it pays when the interest rate rises and requires payment when the interest rate falls. To see this, suppose that 7 months from today we plan to borrow $1 million for 90 days, and that our borrowing rate is the same as LIBOR. The Eurodollar futures price for 7 months from today is 94; this implies a 90-day rate of $(100 - 94) \times 90/360 \times 1/100 = 1.5\%$. Now suppose that 7 months hence, 3-month LIBOR is 8%, which implies a Eurodollar futures price of 92. The implied 90-day rate is 2%. Our extra borrowing expense over 90 days on $1 million will therefore be $(0.02 - 0.015) \times \$1m = \$5,000$.

This extra borrowing expense is offset by gains on the short Eurodollar contract. The Eurodollar futures price has gone down, giving us a gain of $25 per basis point, or $\$25 \times 100 \times (94 - 92) = \$5,000$. The short position in the futures contract compensates us for the increase in our borrowing cost.[20] In the same way, a long position can be used to lock in a lending rate.

The Eurodollar futures price is a construct, not the price of an asset. In this sense Eurodollar futures are different from the futures contracts we have already discussed. Although Eurodollar LIBOR is closely related to a number of other interest rates, there is no one specific identifiable asset that underlies the Eurodollar futures contract.

LIBOR is quoted in currencies other than dollars, and comparable rates are quoted in different locations. In addition to LIBOR, there are PIBOR (Paris), TIBOR (Tokyo), and Euribor (the European Banking Federation).

Finally, you might be wondering why we are discussing LIBOR rather than rates on Treasury bills. Business and bank borrowing rates move more in tandem with LIBOR than with the government's borrowing rate. Thus, these borrowers use the Eurodollar futures contract to hedge. LIBOR is also a better measure of the cost of funds for a market-maker, so LIBOR is typically used to price forward contracts. We will further discuss Eurodollar futures in Chapter 7.

Chapter Summary

The purchase of a stock or other asset entails agreeing to a price, making payment, and taking delivery of the asset. A forward contract fixes the price today, but payment and

---

[20]It might occur to you that the Eurodollar contract pays us at the time we borrow, but we do not pay interest until the loan matures, 91 days hence. Since we have time to earn interest on the change in the value of the contract, the hedge ratio should be less than 1 contract per $1 million borrowing. We discuss this complication in Chapter 7.

delivery are deferred. The pricing of forward contracts reflects the costs and benefits of this deferred payment and delivery. The seller receives payment later, so the price is higher to reflect interest owed the seller, and the buyer receives possession later, so the price is lower to reflect dividends not received by the buyer. A prepaid forward contract requires payment today; hence, it separates these two effects. The price of a prepaid forward is

$$\text{Prepaid forward price} = S_0 e^{-\delta T}$$

The prepaid forward price is below the asset spot price, S_0, due to dividends forgone by deferring delivery. The forward price also reflects deferral of payment, so it is the future value of the prepaid forward price:

$$\text{Forward price} = S_0 e^{(r-\delta)T}$$

In the case of a currency forward, the dividend yield forgone by holding the forward contract instead of the underlying asset, δ, is the interest rate you could earn by investing in foreign-currency denominated assets. Thus, for currencies, $\delta = r_f$, where r_f is the foreign interest rate.

A forward contract is equivalent to a leveraged position in an asset—borrowing to buy the asset. By combining the forward contract with other assets it is possible to create synthetic stocks and bonds. These equivalents are summarized in Table 5.12. Since a forward contract is risky but requires no investment, it earns the risk premium. The forward price is therefore a biased predictor of the future spot price of the asset, with the bias equal to the risk premium.

The fact that it is possible to create a synthetic forward has two important implications. First, if the forward contract is mispriced, arbitrageurs can take offsetting positions in the forward contract and the synthetic forward contract—in effect buying low and selling high—and make a risk-free profit. Second, dealers who make markets in the forward or in the underlying asset can hedge the risk of their position with a synthetic offsetting position. With transaction costs there is a no-arbitrage *region* rather than a single no-arbitrage price.

Futures contracts are similar to forward contracts, except that with futures there are margin requirements and daily settlement of the gain or loss on the position. The

---

TABLE 5.12 Synthetic equivalents assuming the asset pays continuous dividends at the rate δ.

Position	Synthetic Equivalent
Long forward	$= \text{Buy } e^{-\delta T} \text{ shares of stock} + \text{Borrow } S_0 e^{-\delta T}$
Bond paying $F_{0,T}$	$= \text{Buy } e^{-\delta T} \text{ shares of stock} + \text{Short forward}$
Synthetic stock	$= \text{Long forward} \qquad\qquad + \text{Lend } e^{-rT} F_{0,T}$

contractual differences between forwards and futures can lead to pricing differences, but in most cases forward prices and futures prices are very close.

In addition to hedging, forward and futures contracts can be used to synthetically switch a portfolio invested in stocks into bonds. A portfolio invested in Asset A can remain invested in Asset A but earn the returns associated with Asset B, as long as there are forward or futures contracts on A and B. This is called a futures overlay.

The Eurodollar futures contract, based on LIBOR (London Interbank Offer Rate) is widely used for hedging interest rate risk. Because the Eurodollar futures contract does not represent the price of an asset (at settlement it is $100 - \text{LIBOR}$), it cannot be priced using the formulas in this chapter.

FURTHER READING

Chapter 6 continues our exploration of forward markets by considering commodity forwards, which are different from financial forwards in important ways. Chapter 7 then examines interest rate forwards. Whereas forward contracts provide a price for delivery at one point in time, swaps, discussed in Chapter 8, provide a price for a series of deliveries over time. Swaps are a natural generalization of forward contracts.

The pricing principles discussed in this chapter will also play important roles when we discuss option pricing in Chapters 10, 11, and 12 and financial engineering in Chapter 15.

To get a sense of the range of traded contracts, look at the futures page of the *Wall Street Journal*, and also explore the Web sites of futures exchanges: the Chicago Board of Trade (**www.cbot.com**), the Chicago Mercantile Exchange (**www.cme.com**), the New York Mercantile Exchange (**www.nymex.com**), and the London International Financial Futures Exchange (**www.liffe.com**), among others. These sites typically provide current prices, along with information about the contracts: What the underlying asset is, how the contracts are settled, and so forth. The site for One Chicago (**www.onechicago.com**) provides information about single stock futures in the United States.

It is well accepted that forward prices are determined by the models and considerations in this chapter. Siegel and Siegel (1990) is a standard reference book on futures. Early papers that examined futures pricing include Modest and Sundaresan (1983), Cornell and French (1983), which emphasized tax effects in futures pricing (see Appendix 5.A), and French (1983), which compares forwards and futures when both exist on the same underlying asset. Brennan and Schwartz (1990) explore optimal arbitrage when there are transaction costs and Reinganum (1986) explores the arbitrage possibilities inherent in time travel. There is a more technical academic literature focusing on the difference between forward and futures contracts, including Black (1976a), Cox et al. (1981), Richard and Sundaresan (1981), and Jarrow and Oldfield (1981).

PROBLEMS

5.1. Construct Table 5.1 from the perspective of a seller, providing a descriptive name for each of the transactions.

5.2. A $50 stock pays a $1 dividend every 3 months, with the first dividend coming 3 months from today. The continuously compounded risk-free rate is 6%.

   a. What is the price of a prepaid forward contract that expires 1 year from today, immediately after the fourth-quarter dividend?

   b. What is the price of a forward contract that expires at the same time?

5.3. A $50 stock pays an 8% continuous dividend. The continuously compounded risk-free rate is 6%.

   a. What is the price of a prepaid forward contract that expires 1 year from today?

   b. What is the price of a forward contract that expires at the same time?

5.4. Suppose the stock price is $35 and the continuously compounded interest rate is 5%.

   a. What is the 6-month forward price, assuming dividends are zero?

   b. If the 6-month forward price is $35.50, what is the annualized forward premium?

   c. If the forward price is $35.50, what is the annualized continuous dividend yield?

5.5. Suppose you are a market-maker in S&R index forward contracts. The S&R index spot price is 1100, the risk-free rate is 5%, and the dividend yield on the index is 0.

   a. What is the no-arbitrage forward price for delivery in 9 months?

   b. Suppose a customer wishes to enter a short index futures position. If you take the opposite position, demonstrate how you would hedge your resulting long position using the index and borrowing or lending.

   c. Suppose a customer wishes to enter a long index futures position. If you take the opposite position, demonstrate how you would hedge your resulting short position using the index and borrowing or lending.

5.6. Repeat the previous problem, assuming that the dividend yield is 1.5%.

5.7. The S&R index spot price is 1100, the risk-free rate is 5%, and the dividend yield on the index is 0.

   a. Suppose you observe a 6-month forward price of 1135. What arbitrage would you undertake?

   b. Suppose you observe a 6-month forward price of 1115. What arbitrage would you undertake?

5.8. The S&R index spot price is 1100, the risk-free rate is 5%, and the continuous dividend yield on the index is 2%.

a. Suppose you observe a 6-month forward price of 1120. What arbitrage would you undertake?

b. Suppose you observe a 6-month forward price of 1110. What arbitrage would you undertake?

5.9. Suppose that 10 years from now it becomes possible for money managers to engage in time travel. In particular, suppose that a money manager could travel to January 1981, when the 1-year Treasury bill rate was 12.5%.

a. If time travel were costless, what riskless arbitrage strategy could a money manager undertake by traveling back and forth between January 1981 and January 1982?

b. If many money managers undertook this strategy, what would you expect to happen to interest rates in 1981?

c. Since interest rates *were* 12.5% in January 1981, what can you conclude about whether costless time travel will ever be possible?

5.10. The S&R index spot price is 1100 and the continuously compounded risk-free rate is 5%. You observe a 9-month forward price of 1129.257.

a. What dividend yield is implied by this forward price?

b. Suppose you believe the dividend yield over the next 9 months will be only 0.5%. What arbitrage would you undertake?

c. Suppose you believe the dividend yield will be 3% over the next 9 months. What arbitrage would you undertake?

5.11. Suppose the S&P 500 index futures price is currently 1200. You wish to purchase four futures contracts on margin.

a. What is the notional value of your position?

b. Assuming a 10% initial margin, what is the value of the initial margin?

5.12. Suppose the S&P 500 index is currently 950 and the initial margin is 10%. You wish to enter into 10 S&P 500 futures contracts.

a. What is the notional value of your position? What is the margin?

b. Suppose you earn a continuously compounded rate of 6% on your margin balance, your position is marked to market *weekly*, and the maintenance margin is 80% of the initial margin. What is the greatest S&P 500 index futures price 1 week from today at which will you receive a margin call?

5.13. Verify that going long a forward contract and lending the present value of the forward price creates a payoff of one share of stock when

a. The stock pays no dividends.

b. The stock pays discrete dividends.

c. The stock pays continuous dividends.

5.14. Verify that when there are transaction costs, the lower no-arbitrage bound is given by equation (5.11).

5.15. Suppose the S&R index is 800, and that the dividend yield is 0. You are an arbitrageur with a continuously compounded borrowing rate of 5.5% and a continuously compounded lending rate of 5%.

   a. Supposing that there are no transaction fees, show that a cash-and-carry arbitrage is not profitable if the forward price is less than 845.23, and that a reverse cash-and-carry arbitrage is not profitable if the forward price is greater than 841.02.

   b. Now suppose that there is a $1 transaction fee, paid at time 0, for going either long or short the forward contract. Show that the upper and lower no-arbitrage bounds now become 846.29 and 839.97.

   c. Now suppose that in addition to the fee for the forward contract, there is also a $2.40 fee for buying or selling the index. Suppose the contract is settled by delivery of the index, so that this fee is paid only at time 0. What are the new upper and lower no-arbitrage bounds?

   d. Make the same assumptions as in the previous part, except assume that the contract is cash-settled. This means that it is necessary to pay the stock index transaction fee (but not the forward fee) at both times 0 and 1. What are the new no-arbitrage bounds?

   e. Now suppose that transactions in the index have a fee of 0.3% of the value of the index (this is for both purchases and sales). Transactions in the forward contract still have a fixed fee of $1 per unit of the index at time 0. Suppose the contract is cash-settled so that when you do a cash-and-carry or reverse cash-and-carry you pay the index transaction fee both at time 1 and time 0. What are the new upper and lower no-arbitrage bounds? Compare your answer to that in the previous part. (*Hint:* To handle the time 1 transaction fee, you may want to consider tailing the stock position.)

5.16. Suppose the S&P 500 currently has a level of 875. The continuously compounded return on a 1-year T-bill is 4.75%. You wish to hedge an $800,000 portfolio that has a beta of 1.1 and a correlation of 1.0 with the S&P 500.

   a. What is the 1-year futures price for the S&P 500 assuming no dividends?

   b. How many S&P 500 futures contracts should you short to hedge your portfolio? What return do you expect on the hedged portfolio?

5.17. Suppose you are selecting a futures contract with which to hedge a portfolio. You have a choice of six contracts, each of which has the same variability, but with correlations of $-0.95, -0.75, -0.50, 0, 0.25$, and 0.85. Rank the futures contracts with respect to basis risk, from highest to lowest basis risk.

5.18. Suppose the current exchange rate between Germany and Japan is 0.02€/¥. The euro-denominated annual continuously compounded risk-free rate is 4% and the yen-denominated annual continuously compounded risk-free rate is 1%. What are the 6-month euro/yen and yen/euro forward prices?

5.19. Suppose the spot $/¥ exchange rate is 0.008, the 1-year continuously compounded dollar-denominated rate is 5% and the 1-year continuously compounded yen-denominated rate is 1%. Suppose the 1-year forward exchange rate is 0.0084. Explain precisely the transactions you could use (being careful about currency of denomination) to make money with zero initial investment and no risk. How much do you make per yen? Repeat for a forward exchange rate of 0.0083.

5.20. Suppose we wish to borrow $10 million for 91 days beginning next June, and that the quoted Eurodollar futures price is 93.23.

      a. What 3-month LIBOR rate is implied by this price?

      b. How much will be needed to repay the loan?

APPENDIX 5.A: TAXES AND THE FORWARD PRICE

Appendix available online at www.aw-bc.com/mcdonald.

APPENDIX 5.B: EQUATING FORWARDS AND FUTURES

Because the futures price exceeds the prepaid forward price, marking-to-market has the effect of magnifying gains and losses. For example, the futures price on a nondividend-paying stock is $F_{0,T} = S_0 e^{rT}$. If the stock price increases by $1 at time 0, the gain on the futures contract at time T is e^{rT}. Thus, in order to use futures to precisely hedge a position (with the hedge being settled at time T) it is necessary to hold fewer futures than forward contracts, effectively offsetting the extra volatility induced by the future value factor. In the example in Table 5.13, we can go long fewer than eight contracts, to make up for the effect of marking-to-market.

Table 5.13 shows the effect of this adjustment to the futures position and how it is adjusted over time. Initially, we go long

$$8 \times e^{-0.06 \times 9/52} = 7.91735$$

contracts. This number of contracts has a multiplier of $250 \times 7.91735 = 1979.34, the multiplier in the first row of the table. Reducing the number of contracts offsets the effect of earning interest. Each week there is less time until expiration, so we increase the number of index units we are long.

Profit on this position is

$$\$43,553.99 - \$217,727.21 e^{0.06 \times 10/52} = -\$176,700$$

| TABLE 5.13 | | Marking-to-market proceeds and margin balance from long position in the S&P 500 futures contract, where hedge is adjusted on a weekly basis. | | |

Week	Multiplier ($)	Futures Price	Price Change	Margin Balance ($)
0	1979.34	1100.00	—	217,727.21
1	1981.62	1027.99	−72.01	75,446.43
2	1983.91	1037.88	9.89	95,131.79
3	1986.20	1073.23	35.35	165,372.88
4	1988.49	1048.78	−24.45	117,001.17
5	1990.79	1090.32	41.54	199,738.33
6	1993.09	1106.94	16.62	233,055.86
7	1995.39	1110.98	4.04	241,377.01
8	1997.69	1024.74	−86.24	69,573.25
9	2000.00	1007.30	−17.44	34,813.80
10	2000.00	1011.65	4.35	43,553.99

which is exactly the same profit as a forward position. The example in Table 5.13 is unrealistic in the sense that the magnitude is too small for the adjustment to be worth the bother. However, it does demonstrate how to scale the position to offset the magnifying effect of marking-to-market, and the link between the profit on a forward and futures position.

CHAPTER 6
Commodity Forwards and Futures

Tolstoy observed that all happy families are all alike; each unhappy family is unhappy in its own way. An analogous idea in financial markets might be: Financial forwards are all alike; each commodity forward, however, has some unique economic characteristic that must be understood in order to appreciate forward pricing in that market. In this chapter we will see how commodity forwards and futures differ from, and are similar to, financial forwards and futures.

In our discussion of forward pricing for financial assets we relied heavily on the fact that for financial assets, the price of the asset today is the present value of the asset at time T, less the value of dividends to be received between now and time T. We will explore the extent to which this relationship also is true for commodities.

6.1 INTRODUCTION TO COMMODITY FORWARDS

Chapter 5 introduced the formula for a forward price on a financial asset:

$$F_{0,T} = S_0 e^{(r-\delta)T} \tag{6.1}$$

where S_0 is the spot price of the asset, r is the continuously compounded interest rate, and δ is the continuous dividend yield on the asset. The difference between the forward price and spot price reflects the cost and benefits of delaying payment for, and receipt of, the asset. In Chapter 5 we treated forward and futures prices as the same; we continue to ignore the pricing differences in this chapter.

On any given day, for many commodities there are futures contracts available that expire in a number of different months. The set of prices for different expiration dates for a given commodity is called the **forward curve** or the **forward strip** for that date. Table 6.1 displays futures prices with up to 6 months to maturity for several commodities. Let's consider these prices and try to interpret them using equation (6.1). To provide a reference interest rate, 3-month LIBOR on May 5, 2004, was 1.22%, or about 0.3% for 3 months. From May to July, the forward price of corn rose from 314.25 to 319.75. This is a 2-month increase of $319.75/314.25 - 1 = 1.75\%$, an annual rate of approximately 11%, far in excess of the 1.22% annual interest rate. In the context of the formula for pricing financial forwards, equation (6.1), we would need to have a continuous dividend yield, δ, of -9.19% in order to explain this rise in the forward price over time.

TABLE 6.1	Futures prices for various commodities, May 5, 2004. Corn and soybeans are from the CBOT and unleaded gasoline, oil, and gold from NYMEX.				
Expiration Month	Corn (cents/ bushel)	Soybeans (cents/ bushel)	Gasoline (cents/ gallon)	Crude Oil (dollars/ barrel)	Gold (dollars/ ounce)
May	314.25	1034.50	—	—	393.40
June	—	—	131.25	39.57	393.80
July	319.75	1020.00	127.15	39.36	394.30
August	—	959.00	122.32	38.79	394.80
September	316.75	845.50	116.57	38.13	—
October	—	—	109.64	37.56	395.90
November	—	786.50	105.49	37.04	—

Source: Futures data from Datastream.

In that case, we would have

$$F_{\text{July}} = 314.25e^{[0.0122-(-0.0919)]\times(1/6)} = 319.75$$

How do we interpret a negative dividend yield?

Perhaps even more puzzling, given our discussion of financial futures, is the subsequent drop in the corn futures price from July to September, and the behavior of soybean, gasoline, and crude oil prices, which all decline with time to expiration. It is possible to tell plausible stories about this behavior. Corn and soybeans are harvested over the summer, so perhaps the expected increase in supply accounts for the reduction over time in the futures price. In May 2004, the war in Iraq had driven crude oil prices to high levels. We might guess that producers would respond by increasing supply and consumers by reducing demand, resulting in lower expected oil prices in subsequent months. Gasoline is distilled from oil, so gasoline prices might behave similarly. Finally, in contrast to the behavior of the other commodities, gold prices rise steadily over time at a rate close to the interest rate.

It seems that we can tell stories about the behavior of forward prices over time. But how do we reconcile these explanations with our understanding of financial forwards, in which forward prices depend on the interest rate and dividends, and explicit expectations of future prices do not enter the forward price formula?

The behavior of forward prices can vary over time. Two terms often used by commodity traders are **contango** and **backwardation.** If on a given date the forward curve is upward-sloping—i.e., forward prices more distant in time are higher—then we say the market is in contango. We observe this pattern with corn in Table 6.1.

If the forward curve is downward sloping, as with gasoline, we say the market is in backwardation. Forward curves can have portions in backwardation and portions in contango, as does that for crude oil.

It would take an entire book to cover commodities in depth. Our goal here is to understand the *logic* of forward pricing for commodities and where it differs from the logic of financial forward pricing. What is the forward curve telling us about the market for the commodity?

6.2 EQUILIBRIUM PRICING OF COMMODITY FORWARDS

As with forward prices on financial assets, commodity forward prices are the result of a present value calculation. To understand this, it is helpful to consider synthetic commodities.

Just as we could create a synthetic stock with a stock forward contract and a zero-coupon bond, we can also create a synthetic commodity by combining a forward contract with a zero-coupon bond. Consider the following investment strategy: Enter into a long commodity forward contract at the price $F_{0,T}$ and buy a zero-coupon bond that pays $F_{0,T}$ at time T. Since the forward contract is costless, the cost of this investment strategy at time 0 is just the cost of the bond, or

$$\text{Time 0 cash flow} = -e^{-rT} F_{0,T} \tag{6.2}$$

At time T, the strategy pays

$$\underbrace{S_T - F_{0,T}}_{\text{Forward contract payoff}} + \underbrace{F_{0,T}}_{\text{Bond payoff}} = S_T$$

where S_T is the time T price of the commodity. This investment strategy creates a *synthetic commodity*, in that it has the same value as a unit of the commodity at time T. Note that, from equation (6.2), the cost of the synthetic commodity is the prepaid forward price, $e^{-rT} F_{0,T}$.

Valuing a synthetic commodity is easy if we can see the forward price. Suppose, however, that we do not know the forward price. Computing the time 0 value of a unit of the commodity received at time T is a standard problem: You discount the expected commodity price to determine its value today. Let $E_0(S_T)$ denote the expected time-T price as of time 0, and let α denote the appropriate discount rate for a time-T cash flow of S_T. Then the present value is

$$E_0(S_T)e^{-\alpha T} \tag{6.3}$$

The important point is that *expressions (6.2) and (6.3) represent the same value.* Both reflect what you would pay today to receive one unit of the commodity at time T. Equating the two expressions, we have

$$e^{-rT} F_{0,T} = E_0(S_T)e^{-\alpha T} \tag{6.4}$$

Rearranging this equation, we can write the forward price as

$$F_{0,T} = e^{rT} E_0(S_T) e^{-\alpha T} \tag{6.5}$$
$$= E_0(S_T) e^{(r-\alpha)T}$$

Equation (6.5) demonstrates the link between the expected commodity price, $E_0(S_T)$, and the forward price. As with financial forwards (see Chapter 5), the forward price is a biased estimate of the expected spot price, $E_0(S_T)$, with the bias due to the risk premium on the commodity, $\alpha - r$.[1]

Equation 6.4 deserves emphasis: *The time-T forward price discounted at the risk-free rate back to time 0 is the present value of a unit of commodity received at time T.* This calculation is useful when performing NPV calculations involving commodities for which forward prices are available. Thus, for example, an industrial producer who buys oil can calculate the present value of future oil costs by discounting oil forward prices at the risk-free rate. The present value of future oil costs is not dependent upon whether or not the producer hedges. We will see an example of this calculation later in the chapter.

If a commodity cannot be physically stored, the no-arbitrage pricing principles discussed in Section 5.2 cannot be used to obtain a forward price. Without storage, equation (6.5) determines the forward price. However, it is difficult to implement this formula, which requires forecasting the expected future spot price and estimating α. Moreover, even when physically possible, storage may be costly. Given the difficulties of pricing commodity forwards, our goal will be to interpret forward prices and to understand the economics of different commodity markets.

In the rest of the chapter, we will further explore similarities and differences between forward prices for commodities and financial assets. Some of the most important differences have to do with storage: whether the commodity can be stored and, if so, how costly it is to store. The next section provides an example of forward prices when a commodity cannot be stored.

6.3 NONSTORABILITY: ELECTRICITY

The forward market for electricity illustrates forward pricing when storage is not possible. Electricity is produced in different ways: from fuels such as coal and natural gas, or from nuclear power, hydroelectric power, wind power, or solar power. Once it is produced, electricity is transmitted over the power grid to end-users. Electricity has characteristics

------

[1]Historical commodity and futures data, necessary to estimate expected commodity returns, are relatively hard to obtain. Bodie and Rosansky (1980) examine quarterly futures returns from 1950 to 1976, while Gorton and Rouwenhorst (2004) examine monthly futures returns from 1959 to 2004. Both studies construct portfolios of synthetic commodities—T-bills plus commodity futures—and find that these portfolios earn the same average return as stocks, are on average negatively correlated with stocks, and are positively correlated with inflation. These findings imply that a portfolio of stocks and synthetic commodities would have the same expected return and less risk than a diversified stock portfolio alone.

| TABLE 6.2 | | Day-ahead price, by hour, for 1 megawatt-hour of electricity in New York City, September 7, 2004. | | | | | |

Time	Price	Time	Price	Time	Price	Time	Price
0000	$35.68	0600	$40.03	1200	$61.46	1800	$57.81
0100	$31.59	0700	$49.64	1300	$61.47	1900	$62.18
0200	$29.85	0800	$53.48	1400	$61.74	2000	$60.12
0300	$28.37	0900	$57.15	1500	$62.71	2100	$54.25
0400	$28.75	1000	$59.04	1600	$62.68	2200	$52.89
0500	$33.57	1100	$61.45	1700	$60.28	2300	$45.56

Source: Bloomberg.

that distinguish it not only from financial assets, but from other commodities as well. What is special about electricity?

First, electricity is difficult to store, hence it must be consumed when it is produced or else it is wasted.[2] Second, at any point in time the maximum supply of electricity is fixed. You can produce less but not more. Third, demand for electricity varies substantially by season, by day of week, and by time of day.

To illustrate the effects of nonstorability, Table 6.2 displays 1-day ahead hourly prices for 1 megawatt-hour of electricity in New York City. The 1-day ahead forward price is $28.37 at 3 A.M., and $62.71 at 3 P.M. Since you have learned about arbitrage, you are possibly thinking that you would like to buy electricity at the 3 A.M. price and sell it at the 3 P.M. price. However, there is no way to do so. Because electricity cannot be stored, its price is set by demand and supply at a point in time. There is also no way to buy winter electricity and sell it in the summer, so there are seasonal variations as well as intraday variations. Because of peak-load plants that operate only when prices are high, power suppliers are able to temporarily increase the supply of electricity. However, expectations about supply are already reflected in the forward price.

Given these characteristics of electricity, what does the electricity forward price represent? The prices in Table 6.2 are best interpreted using equation (6.5). The large price swings over the day primarily reflect changes in the expected spot price, which in turn reflects changes in demand over the day.

Notice two things. First, the swings in Table 6.2 could not occur with financial assets, which are stored. (It is so obvious that financial assets are stored that we usually don't mention it.) As a consequence, the 3 A.M. and 3 P.M. forward prices for a stock

---

[2]There are ways to store electricity. For example, it is possible to use excess electricity to pump water uphill and then, at a later time, release it to generate electricity. Storage is uncommon, expensive, and entails losses, however.

will be almost identical. If they were not, it would be possible to engage in arbitrage, buying low at 3 A.M. and selling high at 3 P.M. Second, whereas the forward price for a stock is largely redundant in the sense that it reflects information about the current stock price, interest, and the dividend yield, the forward prices in Table 6.2 provide information we could not otherwise obtain, revealing information about the future price of the commodity. This illustrates the forward market providing **price discovery,** with forward prices revealing information, not otherwise obtainable, about the future price of the commodity.

6.4 Pricing Commodity Forwards by Arbitrage: An Example

Electricity represents the extreme of nonstorability. However, many commodities are storable. To see the effects of storage, we now consider the very simple, hypothetical example of a forward contract for pencils. We use pencils as an example because they are familiar and you will have no preconceptions about how such a forward should work, because it does not exist.

Suppose that pencils cost $0.20 today and for certain will cost $0.20 in 1 year. The economics of this assumption are simple. Pencil manufacturers produce pencils from wood and other inputs. If the price of a pencil is greater than the cost of production, more pencils are produced, driving down the market price. If the price falls, fewer pencils are produced and the price rises. The market price of pencils thus reflects the cost of production. An economist would say that the supply of pencils is *perfectly elastic*.

There is nothing inherently inconsistent about assuming that the pencil price is expected to stay the same. However, before we proceed, note that a constant price would *not* be a reasonable assumption about the price of a nondividend-paying stock. A nondividend-paying stock must be expected to appreciate, or else no one would own it. At the outset, there is an obvious difference between this commodity and a financial asset.

One way to describe this difference between the pencil and the stock is to say that, in equilibrium, stocks and other financial assets must be held by investors, or *stored*. This is why the stock price appreciates on average; appreciation is necessary for investors to willingly store the stock.

The pencil, by contrast, need not be stored. The equilibrium condition for pencils requires that price equals marginal production cost. This distinction between a storage and production equilibrium is a central concept in our discussion of commmodities.[3]

---

[3]You may be thinking that you have pencils in your desk and therefore you do, in fact, store pencils. However, you are storing them to save yourself the inconvenience of going to the store each time you need a new one, not because you expect pencils to be a good financial investment akin to stock. When storing pencils for convenience, you will store only a few at a time. Thus, for the moment, suppose that no one stores pencils. We return to the concept of storing for convenience in Section 6.6.

Now suppose that the continuously compounded interest rate is 10%. What is the forward price for a pencil to be delivered in 1 year? Before reading any further, you should stop and decide what you think the answer is. (Really. Please stop and think about it!)

One obvious possible answer to this question, drawing on our discussion of financial forwards, is that the forward price should be the future value of the pencil price: $e^{0.1} \times \$0.20 = \$0.2210$. However, *common sense suggests that this cannot be the correct answer.* You *know* that the pencil price in one year will be $0.20. If you entered into a forward agreement to buy a pencil for $0.221, you would feel foolish in a year when the price was only $0.20.

Common sense also rules out the forward price being less than $0.20. Consider the forward seller. No one would agree to sell a pencil for a forward price of less than $0.20, knowing that the price will be $0.20.

Thus, it seems as if both the buyer and seller perspective lead us to the conclusion that the forward price must be $0.20.

An Apparent Arbitrage and Resolution

If the forward price is $0.20, is there an arbitrage opportunity? Suppose you believe that the $0.20 forward price is too low. Following the logic in Chapter 5, you would want to buy the pencil forward and short-sell a pencil. Table 6.3 depicts the cash flows in this reverse cash-and-carry arbitrage. The result seems to show that there is an arbitrage opportunity.

We seem to have reached an impasse. Common sense suggests a forward price of $0.20, but the application in Table 6.3 of our formulas suggests that any forward price less than $0.221 leads to an arbitrage opportunity, where we would make $0.221 - F_{0,1}$ per pencil.

TABLE 6.3	Apparent reverse cash-and-carry arbitrage for a pencil. These calculations *appear* to demonstrate that there is an arbitrage opportunity if the pencil forward price is below $0.221. However, there is a logical error in the table.

	Cash Flows	
Transaction	**Time 0**	**Time 1**
Long forward @ $0.20	0	$0.20 - F_{0,1}$
Short-sell pencil	+$0.20	−$0.20
Lend short-sale proceeds @ 10%	−$0.20	$0.221
Total	0	$0.221 - F_{0,1}$

Once again it is time to stop and think before proceeding. Examine Table 6.3 closely; there is a problem.

The arbitrage assumes that you can short-sell a pencil by borrowing it today and returning it in a year. However, recall that pencils cost $0.20 today and will cost $0.20 in a year. Borrowing one pencil and returning one pencil in a year is an interest-free loan of $0.20. *No one will lend you the pencil without charging you an additional fee.*

If you are to short-sell, there must be someone who is both holding the asset and willing to give up physical possession for the period of the short-sale. Unlike stock, nobody holds pencils in a brokerage account. It is straightforward to borrow a financial asset and return it later, in the interim paying dividends to the owner. However, if you borrow an unused pencil and return an unused pencil at some later date, the owner of the pencil loses interest for the duration of the pencil loan since the pencil price does not change.

Thus, *the apparent arbitrage in the above table has nothing at all to do with forward contracts on pencils.* If you find someone willing to lend you pencils for a year, you should borrow as many as you can and invest the proceeds in T-bills. You will earn the interest rate and pay nothing to borrow the money.

You might object that pencils do provide a flow of services—namely, making marks on paper. However, this service flow requires having physical possession of the pencil and it also uses up the pencil. A stock loaned to a short-seller continues to earn its return; the pencil loaned to the short-seller earns no return for the lender. Consequently, the pencil borrower must make a payment to the lender to compensate the lender for lost time value of money.

Pencils Have a Positive Lease Rate

How do we correct the arbitrage analysis in Table 6.3? We have to recognize that the lender of the pencil has invested $0.20 in the pencil. In order to be kept financially whole, *the lender of a pencil will require us to pay interest.* The pencil therefore has a *lease rate* of 10%, since that is the interest rate. With this change, the corrected reverse cash-and-carry arbitrage is in Table 6.4.

When we correctly account for the lease payment, this transaction no longer earns profits when the forward price is $0.20 or greater. If we turn the arbitrage around, buying the pencil and shorting the forward, the cash-and-carry arbitrage is depicted in Table 6.5. These calculations show that any forward price greater than $0.221 generates arbitrage profits.

Using no-arbitrage arguments, we have ruled out arbitrage for forward prices less than $0.20 (go long the forward and short-sell the pencil) and greater than $0.221 (go short the forward and long the pencil). However, what if the forward price is between $0.20 and $0.221?

If there is an active lending market for pencils, we can narrow the no-arbitrage price even further: We can demonstrate that the forward price *must* be $0.20. The lease rate of a pencil is 10%. Therefore a pencil *lender* can earn 10% by buying the pencil and lending it. The lease payment for a short seller is a dividend for the lender. Imagine that

TABLE 6.4

Reverse cash-and-carry arbitrage for a pencil. This table demonstrates that there is an arbitrage opportunity if the pencil forward price is below $0.20. It differs from Table 6.3 in properly accounting for lease payments.

Transaction	Cash Flows	
	Time 0	Time 1
Long forward @ $.20	0	$0.20 - F_{0,1}
Short-sell pencil @ lease rate of 10%	+$0.20	-$0.221
Lend short-sale proceeds @ 10%	-$0.20	$0.221
Total	0	$0.20 - F_{0,1}

TABLE 6.5

Cash-and-carry arbitrage for a pencil, showing that there is an arbitrage opportunity if the forward pencil price exceeds $0.221.

Transaction	Cash Flows	
	Time 0	Time 1
Short forward @ $.20	0	$F_{0,1} - $0.20
Buy pencil @ $.20	-$0.20	+$0.20
Borrow @ 10%	+$0.20	-$0.221
Total	0	$F_{0,1} - $0.221

the forward price is $0.21. We would buy a pencil and sell it forward, *and simultaneously lend the pencil*. To see that this strategy is profitable, examine Table 6.6.

Income from lending the pencil provides the missing piece: Any forward price greater than $0.20 now results in arbitrage profits. Since we also have seen that any forward price less than $0.20 results in arbitrage profits, we have pinned down the forward price as $0.20.

Finally, what about equation (6.5), which we claimed holds for all commodities and assets? To apply this equation to the pencil, recognize that the appropriate discount rate, α, for a risk-free pencil is r, the risk-free rate. Hence, we have

$$F_{0,T} = E_0(S_T)e^{(r-\alpha)T} = 0.20 \times e^{(0.10-0.10)} = 0.20$$

Thus, equation (6.5) gives us the correct answer.

TABLE 6.6   Cash and carry arbitrage with pencil lending. When the pencil is loaned, interest is earned and the no-arbitrage price is $0.20.

	Cash Flows	
Transaction	Time 0	Time 1
Short forward @ $0.20	0	$F_{0,1} - \$0.20$
Buy pencil @ $0.20	$-\$0.20$	$+\$0.20$
Lend pencil @ 10%	0	0.021
Borrow @ 10%	$+\$0.20$	$-\$0.221$
Total	0	$F_{0,1} - \$0.20$

The pencil is obviously a special example, but this discussion establishes the important point that in order to understand arbitrage relationships for commodity forwards, we have to think about the cost of borrowing and income from lending an asset. Borrowing and leasing costs also determine the pricing of financial forwards, but the cash flow associated with borrowing and lending financial assets is the dividend yield, which is readily observable. The commodity analogue to dividend income is *lease income*, which may not be directly observable. We now discuss leasing more generally.

6.5 THE COMMODITY LEASE RATE

The discussion of pencil forwards raises the issue of a lease market. How would such a lease market work in general?

The Lease Market for a Commodity

Consider again the perspective of a commodity lender, who in the previous discussion required that we pay interest to borrow the pencil. More generally, here is how a lender will think about a commodity loan: "If I lend the commodity, I am giving up possession of a unit worth S_0. At time T, I will receive a unit worth S_T. *I am effectively making an investment of S_0 in order to receive the random amount S_T.*"

How would you analyze this investment? Suppose that α is the expected return on a stock that has the same risk as the commodity; α is therefore the appropriate discount rate for the cash flow S_T. The NPV of the investment is

$$\text{NPV} = E_0(S_T)e^{-\alpha T} - S_0 \tag{6.6}$$

Suppose that we expect the commodity price to increase at the rate g, so that

$$E_0(S_T) = S_0 e^{gT}$$

Then from equation (6.6), the NPV of the commodity loan, without payments, is

$$\text{NPV} = S_0 e^{(g-\alpha)T} - S_0 \tag{6.7}$$

If $g < \alpha$, the commodity loan has a negative NPV. However, suppose the lender demands that the borrower return $e^{(\alpha-g)T}$ units of the commodity for each unit borrowed. If one unit is loaned, $e^{(\alpha-g)T}$ units will be returned. This is like a continuous proportional lease payment of $\alpha - g$ to the lender. Thus, the lease rate is the difference between the commodity discount rate and the expected growth rate of the commodity price, or

$$\delta_l = \alpha - g \tag{6.8}$$

With this payment, the NPV of a commodity loan is

$$\text{NPV} = S_0 e^{(\alpha-g)T} e^{(g-\alpha)T} - S_0 = 0 \tag{6.9}$$

Now the commodity loan is a fair deal for the lender. The commodity lender must be compensated by the borrower for the opportunity cost associated with lending. When the future pencil price was certain to be $0.20, the opportunity cost was the risk-free interest rate, 10%.

Note that if S_T were the price of a nondividend-paying stock, its expected rate of appreciation would equal its expected return, so $g = \alpha$ and no payment would be required for the stock loan to be a fair deal.[4] Commodities, however, are produced; as with the pencil, their expected price appreciation need not equal α.

Forward Prices and the Lease Rate

Suppose we have a commodity where there is an active lease market, with the lease rate given by equation (6.8). What is the forward price?

The key insight, as in the pencil example, is that *the lease payment is a dividend.* If we borrow the asset, we have to pay the lease rate to the lender, just as with a dividend-paying stock. If we buy the asset and lend it out, we receive the lease payment. Thus, the formula for the forward price with a lease market is

$$F_{0,T} = S_0 e^{(r-\delta_l)T} \tag{6.10}$$

Tables 6.7 and 6.8 verify that this formula is the no-arbitrage price by performing the cash-and-carry and reverse cash-and-carry arbitrages. In both tables we tail the position in order to offset the lease income.

The striking thing about Tables 6.7 and 6.8 is that on the surface they are *exactly* like Tables 5.6 and 5.7, which depict arbitrage transactions for a dividend-paying stock. In an important sense, however, the two sets of tables are quite different. With the stock, the dividend yield, δ, is an observable characteristic of the stock, reflecting payment received by the owner of the stock *whether or not the stock is loaned.*

....

[4]As we saw in Chapter 5, for a nondividend-paying stock, the present value of the future stock price is the current stock price.

TABLE 6.7   Cash-and-carry arbitrage with a commodity for which the lease rate is δ_l. The implied no-arbitrage restriction is $F_{0,T} \le S_0 e^{(r-\delta_l)T}$.

	Cash Flows	
Transaction	Time 0	Time T
Short forward @ $F_{0,T}$	0	$F_{0,T} - S_T$
Buy $e^{-\delta_l T}$ commodity units and lend @ δ_l	$-S_0 e^{-\delta_l T}$	$+S_T$
Borrow @ r	$+S_0 e^{-\delta_l T}$	$-S_0 e^{(r-\delta_l)T}$
Total	0	$F_{0,T} - S_0 e^{(r-\delta_l)T}$

TABLE 6.8   Reverse cash-and-carry arbitrage with a commodity for which the lease rate is δ_l. The implied no-arbitrage restriction is $F_{0,T} \ge S_0 e^{(r-\delta_l)T}$.

	Cash Flows	
Transaction	Time 0	Time T
Long forward @ $F_{0,T}$	0	$S_T - F_{0,T}$
Short $e^{-\delta_l T}$ commodity units with lease rate δ_l	$+S_0 e^{-\delta_l T}$	$-S_T$
Lend @ r	$-S_0 e^{-\delta_l T}$	$+S_0 e^{(r-\delta_l)T}$
Total	0	$S_0 e^{(r-\delta_l)T} - F_{0,T}$

With pencils, by contrast, the lease rate, $\delta_l = \alpha - g$, is income earned only if the pencil is loaned. In fact, notice in Tables 6.7 and 6.8 that the arbitrageur never stores the commodity! Thus, equation (6.10) holds whether or not the commodity can be, or is, stored.

One of the implications of Tables 6.7 and 6.8 is that the lease rate has to be consistent with the forward price. Thus, when we observe the forward price, we can infer what the lease rate would have to be if a lease market existed. Specifically, if the forward price is $F_{0,T}$, the annualized lease rate is

$$\delta_l = r - \frac{1}{T} ln(F_{0,T}/S) \tag{6.11}$$

If instead we use an effective annual interest rate, r, the effective annual lease rate is

$$\delta_l = \frac{(1+r)}{(F_{0,T}/S)^{1/T}} - 1 \tag{6.12}$$

The denominator in this expression annualizes the forward premium.

In some markets, consistent and reliable quotes for the spot price are not available, or are not comparable to forward prices. In such cases, the near-term forward price can be used as a proxy for the spot price, S.

By definition, contango—an upward-sloping forward curve—occurs when the lease rate is less than the risk-free rate. Backwardation—a downward-sloping forward curve—occurs when the lease rate exceeds the risk-free rate.

6.6 CARRY MARKETS

Sometimes it makes sense for a commodity to be stored, at least temporarily. Storage is also called **carry,** and a commodity that is stored is said to be in a **carry market.**

One reason for storage is seasonal variation in either supply or demand, which causes a mismatch between the time at which a commodity is produced and the time at which it is consumed. With some agricultural products, for example, supply is seasonal (there is a harvest season) but demand is constant over the year. In this case, storage permits consumption to occur throughout the year.

With natural gas, by contrast, there is high demand in the winter and low demand in the summer, but relatively constant production over the year. This pattern of use and production suggests that there will be times when natural gas is stored.

Storage Costs and Forward Prices

Storage is not always feasible (for example, fresh strawberries are perishable) and when technically feasible, storage is almost always costly. When storage is feasible, how do storage costs affect forward pricing? Put yourself in the position of a commodity merchant who owns one unit of the commodity and ask whether you would be willing to store this unit until time T. You face the choice of selling it today, receiving S_0, or selling it at time T. If you elect to sell at time T, you can sell forward (to guarantee the price you will receive), and you will receive $F_{0,T}$. This is a cash-and-carry.

The cash-and-carry logic with storage costs suggests that *you will store only if the present value of selling at time T is at least as great as that of selling today.* Denote the future value of storage costs for one unit of the commodity from time 0 to T as $\lambda(0, T)$. Indifference between selling today and at time T requires

$$\underbrace{S_0}_{\text{Revenue from selling today}} = e^{-rT} \underbrace{\left[F_{0,T} - \lambda(0, T)\right]}_{\text{Net revenue from selling at time } T}$$

This relationship in turn implies that if storage is to occur, the forward price is at least

$$F_{0,T} \geq S_0 e^{rT} + \lambda(0, T) \tag{6.13}$$

In the special case where storage costs are paid continuously and are proportional to the value of the commodity, storage cost is like a continuous negative dividend of λ, and we can write the forward price as

$$F_{0,T} = S_0 e^{(r+\lambda)T} \tag{6.14}$$

When there are no storage costs ($\lambda = 0$), equations (6.13) and (6.14) reduce to our familiar forward pricing formula from Chapter 5.

When there are storage costs, the forward price is higher. Why? The selling price must compensate the commodity merchant for both the financial cost of storage (interest) and the physical cost of storage. With storage costs, the forward curve can rise faster than the interest rate. We can view storage costs as a negative dividend in that, instead of receiving cash flow for holding the asset, you have to pay to hold the asset.

Example 6.1   Suppose that the November price of corn is $2.50/bushel, the effective monthly interest rate is 1%, and storage costs per bushel are $0.05/month. Assuming that corn is stored from November to February, the February forward price must compensate owners for interest and storage. The future value of storage costs is

$$\$0.05 + (\$0.05 \times 1.01) + (\$0.05 \times 1.01^2) = (\$0.05/.01) \times \left[(1 + 0.01)^3 - 1\right]$$
$$= \$0.1515$$

Thus, the February forward price will be

$$2.50 \times (1.01)^3 + 0.1515 = 2.7273$$

Problem 6.9 asks you to verify that this is a no-arbitrage price.   ❧

Keep in mind that just because a commodity *can* be stored does not mean that it *should* (or will) be stored. Pencils were not stored because storage was not economically necessary: A constant new supply of pencils was available to meet pencil demand. Thus, equation (6.13) describes the forward price *when storage occurs*. Whether and when a commodity is stored are peculiar to each commodity.

Storage Costs and the Lease Rate

Suppose that there is a carry market for a commodity, so that its forward price is given by equation (6.13). What is the lease rate in this case?

Again put yourself in the shoes of the commodity lender. If you lend the commodity, you are saved from having to pay storage cost. Thus, the lease rate should equal the *negative* of the storage cost. In other words, the lender will pay the borrower! In effect, the commodity borrower is providing "virtual storage" for the commodity lender, who receives back the commodity at a point in the future. The lender making a payment to the borrower generates a negative dividend.

The Convenience Yield

The discussion of commodities to this point has ignored business reasons for holding commodities. For example, suppose you are a food manufacturer for whom corn is an essential input. You will hold an inventory of corn. If you end up holding too much corn, you can sell the excess. However, if you hold too little and run out of corn, you must stop producing, idling workers and machines. Your physical inventory of corn in this case has value—it provides insurance that you can keep producing in case there is a disruption in the supply of corn.

In this situation, corn holdings provide an extra nonmonetary return that is sometimes referred to as the **convenience yield**.[5] You will be willing to store corn with a lower rate of return than if you did not earn the convenience yield. What are the implications of the convenience yield for the forward price?

Suppose that someone approached you to borrow a commodity from which you derived a convenience yield. You would think as follows: "If I lend the commodity, I am bearing interest cost, saving storage cost, and losing the value I derive from having a physical inventory. I was willing to bear the interest cost already; thus, I will pay a commodity borrower storage cost *less the convenience yield*."

Suppose the continuously compounded convenience yield is c, proportional to the value of the commodity. The commodity lender saves $\lambda - c$ by not physically storing the commodity; hence, the commodity borrower pays $\delta = c - \lambda$, compensating the lender for convenience yield less storage cost. Using an argument identical to that in Table 6.8, we conclude that the forward price must be no less than

$$F_{0,T} \geq S_0 e^{(r-\delta)T} = S_0 e^{(r+\lambda-c)T}$$

This is the restriction imposed by a reverse cash-and-carry, in which the arbitrageur borrows the commodity and goes long the forward.

Now consider what happens if you perform a cash-and-carry, buying the commodity and selling it forward. If you are an average investor, you will not earn the convenience yield (it is earned only by those with a business reason to hold the commodity). You could try to lend the commodity, reasoning that the borrower could be a commercial user to whom you would pay storage cost less the convenience yield. But those who earn the convenience yield likely already hold the optimal amount of the commodity. *There may be no way for you to earn the convenience yield when performing a cash-and-carry.* Those who do not earn the convenience yield will not own the commodity.

Thus, *for an average investor*, the cash-and-carry has the cash flows[6]

$$F_{0,T} - S_T + S_T - S_0 e^{(r+\lambda)T} = F_{0,T} - S_0 e^{(r+\lambda)T}$$

This expression implies that the forward price must be below $S_0 e^{(r+\lambda)T}$ if there is to be no cash-and-carry arbitrage.

....

[5]The term *convenience yield* is defined differently by different authors. Convenience yield generally means a return to physical ownership of the commodity. In practice it is sometimes used to mean the lease rate. In this book, the lease rate of a commodity can be inferred from the forward price using equation (6.11).

[6]In this expression, we assume we tail the holding of the commodity by buying $e^{\lambda T}$ units at time 0, and selling off units of the commodity over time to pay storage costs.

In summary, from the perspective of an arbitrageur, the price range within which there is no arbitrage is

$$S_0 e^{(r+\lambda-c)T} \leq F_{0,T} \leq S_0 e^{(r+\lambda)T} \tag{6.15}$$

The convenience yield produces a no-arbitrage *region* rather than a no-arbitrage *price*. The observed lease rate will depend upon both storage costs and convenience. Also, as in Section 5.3, bid-ask spreads and trading costs will further expand the no-arbitrage region in equation (6.15).

As another illustration of convenience yield, consider again the pencil example of Section 6.4. In reality, everyone stores a few pencils in order to be sure to have one available. You can think of this benefit from storage as the convenience yield of a pencil. However, because the supply of pencils is perfectly elastic, the price of pencils is fixed at $0.20. Convenience yield in this case does not affect the forward price, but it does explain the decision to store pencils.

The difficulty with the convenience yield in practice is that convenience is hard to observe. The concept of the convenience yield serves two purposes. First, it explains patterns in storage—for example, why a commercial user might store a commodity when the average investor will not. Second, it provides an additional parameter to better explain the forward curve. You might object that we can invoke the convenience yield to explain *any* forward curve, and therefore the concept of the convenience yield is vacuous. While convenience yield can be tautological, it is a meaningful economic concept and it would be just as arbitrary to assume that there is never convenience. Moreover, the upper bound in equation (6.15) depends on storage costs but not the convenience yield. Thus, the convenience yield only explains anomalously low forward prices, and only when there is storage.

We will now examine particular commodities to illustrate the concepts from the previous sections.

6.7 GOLD FUTURES

Gold is durable, relatively inexpensive to store (compared to its value), widely held, and actively produced through gold mining. Because of transportation costs and purity concerns, gold often trades in certificate form, as a claim to physical gold at a specific location. There are exchange-traded gold futures, specifications for which are in Figure 6.1.[7]

Figure 6.2 is a newspaper listing for the NYMEX gold futures contract. Figure 6.3 graphs the futures prices for all available gold futures contracts—the forward curve—for the first Wednesday in June, from 2001 to 2004. (Newspaper listings for most futures contracts do not show the full set of available expiration dates, so Figure 6.3

---

[7]Gold is usually denominated in troy ounces (480 grains), which are approximately 9.7% heavier than the more familiar avoirdupois ounce (437.5 grains). Twelve troy ounces make 1 troy pound, which weighs approximately 0.37 kg.

FIGURE 6.1

Specifications for the NYMEX gold futures contract.

Underlying	Refined gold bearing approved refiner stamp
Where traded	New York Mercantile Exchange
Size	100 troy ounces
Months	Feb, Apr, Aug, Oct, out two years. Jun, Dec, out 5 years
Trading ends	Third-to-last business day of maturity month
Delivery	Any business day of the delivery month

FIGURE 6.2

Listing for the NYMEX gold futures contract from the *Wall Street Journal*, July 21, 2004.

	OPEN	HIGH	LOW	SETTLE	CHG	LIFETIME HIGH	LIFETIME LOW	OPEN INT
Gold (CMX)-100 troy oz.; $ per troy oz.								
July	...	...	...	401.90	–3.70	400.20	380.50	4
Aug	406.00	407.10	399.70	402.10	–3.70	433.00	324.70	139,287
Oct	407.50	408.00	401.20	403.40	–3.70	432.00	332.00	11,310
Dec	408.50	409.90	402.00	404.80	–3.70	436.50	290.00	62,036
Fb05	408.50	408.50	405.00	406.40	–3.70	435.00	331.50	6,614
Aug	411.00	411.00	411.00	411.80	–3.70	416.50	379.00	2,290
Dec	420.00	420.00	420.00	415.90	–3.70	441.50	298.40	6,387
Est vol 52,000; vol Mon 31,225; open int 262,052, –1,522.								

FIGURE 6.3

The forward curve for gold on four dates, from NYMEX gold futures prices.

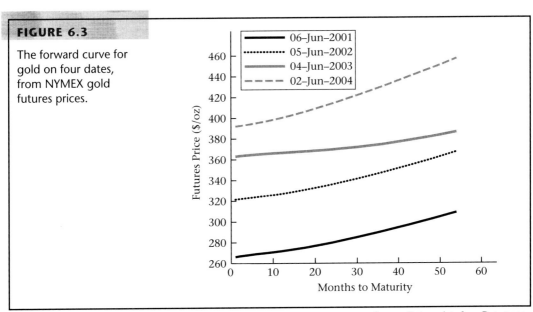

Source: Futures data from Datastream.

is constructed using more expiration dates than are in Figure 6.2.) What is interesting about the gold forward curve is how relatively uninteresting it is, with the forward price steadily increasing with time to maturity.

From our previous discussion, the forward price implies a lease rate. Short-sales and loans of gold are common in the gold market, and gold borrowers in fact have to pay the lease rate. On the lending side, large gold holders (including some central banks) put gold on deposit with brokers, in order that it may be loaned to short-sellers. The gold lenders earn the lease rate.

The lease rate for gold, silver, and other commodities is computed in practice using equation (6.12) and is reported routinely by financial reporting services. Table 6.9 shows the 6-month and 1-year lease rates for the four gold forward curves depicted in Figure 6.3, computed using equation (6.12).

Example 6.2   Here are the details of computing the 6-month lease rate for June 6, 2001. Gold futures prices are in Table 6.9. The June and September Eurodollar futures prices on this date were 96.09 and 96.13. Thus, 3-month LIBOR from June to September was $(100 - 96.09)/400 \times 91/90 = 0.988\%$, and from September to December was $(100 - 96.13)/400 \times 91/90 = 0.978\%$. The June to December interest rate was therefore $(1.00988) \times (1.00978) - 1 = 1.9763\%$, or 1.019736^2 annualized. Using equation (6.12), the annualized 6-month lease rate is therefore

$$\text{6-month lease rate} = \left(\frac{1.019763^2}{(269/265.7)^{(1/0.5)}} \right) - 1 = 1.456\%$$ ❧

TABLE 6.9   Six-month and 12-month gold lease rates for four dates, computed using equation (6.12). Interest rates are computed from Eurodollar futures prices.

	Gold Futures Prices ($)			Lease Rates	
Date	June	Dec	June	6 month	1 year
June 6, 2001	265.7	269.0	271.7	1.46%	1.90%
June 5, 2002	321.2	323.9	326.9	0.44%	0.88%
June 4, 2003	362.6	364.9	366.4	−0.14%	0.09%
June 2, 2004	391.6	395.2	400.2	−0.10%	0.07%

Source: Futures data from Datastream.

Gold Investments

If you wish to hold gold as part of an investment portfolio, you can do so by holding physical gold or synthetic gold—i.e., holding T-bills and going long gold futures. Which should you do? If you hold physical gold without lending it, and if the lease rate is positive, you forgo the lease rate. You also bear storage costs. With synthetic gold, on the other hand, you have a counterparty who may fail to pay so there is credit risk. Ignoring credit risk, however, synthetic gold is generally the preferable way to obtain gold price exposure.

Table 6.9 shows that the 6-month annualized gold lease rate is 1.46% in June 2001. Thus, by holding physical gold instead of synthetic gold, an investor would lose this 1.46% return.[8] In June 2003 and 2004, however, the lease rate was about −0.10%. If storage costs are about 0.10%, an investor would be indifferent between holding physical and synthetic gold. The futures market on those dates was compensating investors for storing physical gold.

Some nonfinancial holders of gold will obtain a convenience yield from gold. Consider an electronics manufacturer who uses gold in producing components. Suppose that running out of gold would halt production. It would be natural in this case to hold a buffer stock of gold in order to avoid a stock-out of gold, i.e., running out of gold. For this manufacturer, there *is* a return to holding gold—namely, a lower probability of stocking out and halting production. Stocking out would have a real financial cost, and the manufacturer is willing to pay a price—the lease rate—to avoid that cost.

Evaluation of Gold Production

Suppose we have an operating gold mine and we wish to compute the present value of future production. As discussed in Section 6.2, the present value of the commodity received in the future is simply the present value—computed at the risk-free rate—of the forward price. We can use the forward curve for gold to compute the value of an operating gold mine.

Suppose that at times t_i, $i = 1, \ldots, n$, we expect to extract n_{t_i} ounces of gold by paying an extraction cost $x(t_i)$. We have a set of n forward prices, F_{0,t_i}. If the continuously compounded annual risk-free rate from time 0 to t_i is $r(0, t_i)$, the value of the gold mine is

$$\text{PV gold production} = \sum_{i=1}^{n} n_{t_i} \left[F_{0,t_i} - x(t_i) \right] e^{-r(0,t_i)t_i} \tag{6.16}$$

This equation assumes that the gold mine is certain to operate the entire time and that the quantity of production is known. Only price is uncertain. (We will see in Chapter 17

[8]The cost of 1 ounce of physical gold is S_0. However, from equation (6.10), the cost of 1 ounce of gold bought as a prepaid forward is $S_0 e^{-\delta_l T}$. Synthetic gold is proportionally cheaper by the lease rate, δ_l.

TABLE 6.10	Gold forward and prepaid forward prices on 1 day for gold delivered at 1-year intervals, out to 6 years. The continuously compounded interest rate is 6% and the lease rate is assumed to be a constant 1.5%.	
Expiration Year	**Forward Price ($)**	**Prepaid Forward Price ($)**
1	313.81	295.53
2	328.25	291.13
3	343.36	286.80
4	359.17	282.53
5	375.70	278.32
6	392.99	274.18

how the possibility of mine closings due to low prices affects valuation.) Note that in equation (6.16), by computing the present value of the forward price, we compute the prepaid forward price.

Example 6.3   Suppose we have a mining project that will produce 1 ounce of gold every year for 6 years. The cost of this project is $1,100 today, the marginal cost per ounce at the time of extraction is $100, and the continuously compounded interest rate is 6%.

We observe the gold forward prices in the second column of Table 6.10, with implied prepaid forward prices in the third column. Using equation (6.16), we can use these prices to perform the necessary present value calculations.

$$\text{Net present value} = \sum_{i=1}^{6} \left[F_{0,i} - 100 \right] e^{-0.06 \times i} - \$1100 = \$119.56 \qquad (6.17)$$

≹

6.8 SEASONALITY: THE CORN FORWARD MARKET

Corn in the United States is harvested primarily in the fall, from September through November. The United States is a leading corn producer, generally exporting rather than importing corn. Figure 6.4 shows a newspaper listing for corn futures.

Given seasonality in production, what should the forward curve for corn look like? Corn is produced at one time of the year, but consumed throughout the year. In order to be consumed when it is not being produced, corn must be stored. Thus, to understand the forward curve for corn we need to recall our discussion of storage and carry markets.

FIGURE 6.4

Listing for the CBOT corn futures contract from the *Wall Street Journal*, July 21, 2004.

	OPEN	HIGH	LOW	SETTLE	CHG	LIFETIME HIGH	LIFETIME LOW	OPEN INT
Corn (CBT)-5,000 bu.; cents per bu.								
Sept	236.50	237.50	232.75	234.00	−3.00	341.00	229.75	162,000
Dec	244.75	246.00	240.75	242.00	−3.00	341.50	232.50	307,442
Mr05	252.25	254.00	248.75	250.25	−2.50	342.00	239.00	52,447
May	258.00	259.75	255.00	256.00	−3.00	344.00	243.50	16,608
July	262.00	263.25	259.00	260.00	−2.50	342.00	246.50	13,717
Sept	262.75	263.00	260.00	260.25	−2.75	299.00	260.00	3,058
Dec	262.50	262.75	260.00	260.50	−2.75	288.50	235.00	10,707
Est vol 74,710; vol Mon 71,892; open int 566,664, +1,488.								

As discussed in Section 6.6, storage is an economic decision in which there is a trade-off between selling today and selling tomorrow. If we can sell corn today for $2/bu and in 2 months for $2.25/bu, the storage decision entails comparing the price we can get today with the present value of the price we can get in 2 months. In addition to interest, we need to include storage costs in our analysis.

An equilibrium with some current selling and some storage requires that corn prices be expected to rise at the interest rate plus storage costs, which implies that there will be an upward trend in the price between harvests. While corn is being stored, the forward price should behave as in equation (6.14), rising at interest plus storage costs.

Once the harvest begins, storage is no longer necessary; if supply and demand remain constant from year to year, the harvest price will be the same every year. The corn price will fall to that level at harvest, only to begin rising again after the harvest.

The market conditions we have described are graphed in Figure 6.5, which depicts a hypothetical forward curve as seen from time 0. Between harvests, the forward price

FIGURE 6.5

A hypothetical forward curve for corn, assuming the harvest occurs at years 0, 1, 2, etc.

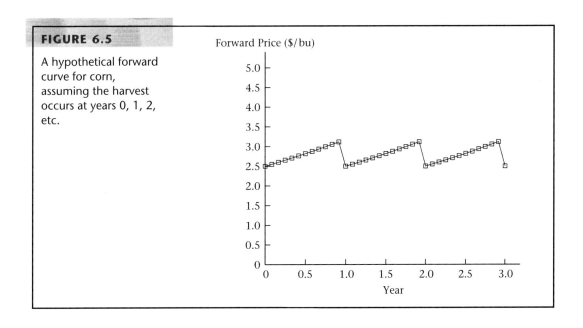

of corn rises to reward storage, and it falls at each harvest. Let's see how this graph was constructed.

The corn price is $2.50 initially, the continuously compounded interest rate is 6%, and storage cost is 1.5%/month. The forward price after n months (where $n < 12$) is

$$F_{0,n} = \$2.50 \times e^{(0.005 + 0.015) \times n}$$

Thus, the 12-month forward price is $\$2.50e^{0.06 + 0.18} = \$3.18$. After 1 year, the process starts over.

Farmers will plant in anticipation of receiving the harvest price, which means that it is the harvest price that reflects the cost of producing corn. The price during the rest of the year equals the harvest price plus storage. In general we would expect those storing corn to plan to deplete inventory as harvest approaches and to replenish inventory from the new harvest.

This is a simplified version of reality. Perhaps most important, the supply of corn varies from year to year. When there is a large crop, producers will expect corn to be stored not just over the current year, but into the next year as well. If there is a large harvest, therefore, we might see the forward curve rise continuously until year 2. To better understand the possible behavior of corn, let's look at real corn prices.

Table 6.11 shows the June forward curves for corn over a 10-year period. Some clear patterns are evident. First, notice that from December to March to May (columns 3–5), the futures price rises every year. We would expect there to be storage of corn

TABLE 6.11   Futures prices for corn (from the Chicago Board of Trade) for the first Wednesday in June, 1995–2004. The last column is the 18-month forward price. Prices are in cents per bushel.

| | Contract Expiration Month | | | | | | | |
| | Current Year | | | Following Year | | | | |
Date	July	Sept	Dec	Mar	May	July	Sept	Dec
07-Jun-1995	265.50	272.25	277.75	282.75	285.25	286.00	269.50	253.50
05-Jun-1996	435.00	373.25	340.75	346.75	350.50	348.00	298.00	286.50
04-Jun-1997	271.25	256.50	254.75	261.00	265.50	269.00	257.00	255.00
03-Jun-1998	238.00	242.25	245.75	253.75	259.00	264.00	261.00	268.00
02-Jun-1999	216.75	222.00	230.75	239.75	244.50	248.25	248.00	251.50
07-Jun-2000	219.75	228.50	234.50	239.25	242.50	248.50	254.50	259.00
06-Jun-2001	198.50	206.00	217.25	228.25	234.50	241.75	245.00	251.25
05-Jun-2002	210.25	217.25	226.75	234.50	237.25	240.75	235.00	239.00
04-Jun-2003	237.50	236.25	237.75	244.00	248.00	250.00	242.25	242.50
02-Jun-2004	321.75	319.75	319.25	322.50	325.50	324.50	296.50	279.00

Source: Futures data from Datastream.

during this period, with the futures price compensating for storage. A low current price suggests a large supply. Thus, when the near-July price is low, we might also expect storage across the coming harvest. Particularly in the years with the lowest July prices (1999–2002), there is a pronounced rise in price from July to December. When the price is unusually high (1996 and 2004), there is a drop in price from July to December. Behavior is mixed in the other years.[9] We can also examine the July-December price relationship in the following year. In 6 of the 10 years, the distant-December price (column 8) is below the distant July price (column 6). The exceptions occur in years with relatively low current prices (1998–2001). These patterns are generally consistent with storage of corn between harvests, and storage across harvests only occasionally.

Finally, compare prices for the near-July contract (the first column) with those for the distant-December contract (the last column). Near-term prices are quite variable, ranging from 216.75 to 435.00 cents per bushel. In December of the following year, however, prices range only from 239 to 286.50. In fact, in 7 of the 10 years, the price is between 251 and 268. The lower variability of distant prices is not surprising: It is difficult to forecast a harvest more than a year into the future. Thus, the forward price is reflecting the market's expectation of a normal harvest 1 year hence.

If we assume that storage costs are approximately \$0.03/month/bushel, the forward price in Table 6.11 never violates the no-arbitrage condition

$$F_{0,T+s} < F_{0,T}e^{rs} + \lambda(T, T+s) \tag{6.18}$$

which says that the forward price from T to $T + s$ cannot rise faster than interest plus storage costs.

6.9 NATURAL GAS

Natural gas is another market in which seasonality and storage costs are important. The natural gas futures contract, introduced in 1990, has become one of the most heavily traded futures contracts in the United States. The asset underlying one contract is 1 month's worth of gas, delivered at a specific location (different gas contracts call for delivery at different locations). Figure 6.6 shows a newspaper listing for natural gas futures, and Figure 6.7 details the specifications for the Henry Hub contract.

Natural gas has several interesting characteristics. First, gas is costly to transport internationally, so prices and forward curves vary regionally. Second, once a given well has begun production, gas is costly to store. Third, demand for gas in the United States is highly seasonal, with peak demand arising from heating in winter months. Thus, there is a relatively steady stream of production with variable demand, which leads to large and predictable price swings. Whereas corn has seasonal production and relatively constant demand, gas has relatively constant supply and seasonal demand.

[9] It is possible to have low current storage and a large expected harvest, which would cause the December price to be lower than the July price, or high current storage and a poor expected harvest, which would cause the July price to be below the December price.

FIGURE 6.6

Listing for the NYMEX natural gas futures contract from the *Wall Street Journal*, July 21, 2004.

	OPEN	HIGH	LOW	SETTLE	CHG	LIFETIME HIGH	LIFETIME LOW	OPEN INT
Natural Gas (NYM)-10,000 MMBtu.; $ per MMBtu								
Aug	5.815	5.960	5.797	5.837	.019	6.825	3.120	40,430
Sept	5.865	5.990	5.835	5.877	.013	6.780	3.100	60,098
Oct	5.910	6.040	5.898	5.934	.015	6.800	3.100	40,028
Nov	6.250	6.360	6.240	6.274	.016	6.940	3.270	19,225
Dec	6.560	6.660	6.530	6.584	.016	7.110	3.460	25,005
Ja05	6.740	6.835	6.730	6.757	.016	7.230	3.520	21,758
Feb	6.705	6.800	6.705	6.722	.017	7.145	3.400	15,510
Mar	6.575	6.650	6.560	6.592	.018	6.970	3.640	17,636
Apr	5.980	6.010	5.974	5.987	.013	6.200	3.400	13,388
May	5.890	5.900	5.870	5.874	.017	6.020	3.500	11,510
June	5.900	5.910	5.890	5.890	.017	6.030	3.530	8,340
July	5.960	5.960	5.935	5.927	.017	6.070	3.560	11,657
Aug	5.960	5.960	5.950	5.937	.008	6.080	3.230	8,036
Oct	5.990	5.990	5.990	5.952	.008	6.080	3.540	6,627
Nov	6.150	6.160	6.150	6.124	...	6.240	3.790	6,770
Dec	6.350	6.350	6.350	6.302	-.007	6.400	3.960	6,249
Jl06	5.520	5.520	5.520	5.488	-.012	5.520	3.580	3,074
Ap07	5.264	5.264	5.264	5.189	-.005	5.264	4.747	3,187
May	5.109	5.109	5.109	5.034	-.005	5.130	4.712	767
June	5.111	5.111	5.111	5.039	-.002	5.111	4.000	376
Oct	5.090	5.090	5.090	5.057	.013	5.090	4.891	312

Est vol 76,493; vol Mon 61,746; open int 380,824, +3,187.

FIGURE 6.7

Specifications for the NYMEX Henry Hub natural gas contract.

Underlying	Natural gas delivered at Sabine Pipe Lines Co.'s Henry Hub, Louisiana
Where traded	New York Mercantile Exchange
Size	10,000 million British thermal units (MMBtu)
Months	72 consecutive months
Trading ends	Third-to-last business day of month prior to maturity month
Delivery	As uniformly as possible over the delivery month

Figure 6.8 displays 3-year (2001) and 6-year (2002–2004) strips of gas futures prices for the first Wednesday in June from 1997 to 2000. Seasonality is evident, with high winter prices and low summer prices. The 2003 and 2004 strip shows seasonal cycles combined with a downward trend in prices, suggesting that the market considered prices in that year as anomalously high. For the other years, the average price for each coming year is about the same.

Gas storage is costly and demand for gas is highest in the winter. The steady rise of the forward curve during the fall months suggests that storage occurs just before the heaviest demand. Table 6.12 shows prices for October through December. The monthly increase in gas prices over these months ranges from $0.13 to $0.23. Assuming that the interest rate is about 0.15% per month and that you use equation (6.13), storage cost in November 2004, λ, would satisfy

$$6.947 = 6.759 e^{0.0015} + \lambda$$

FIGURE 6.8

Forward curves for natural gas for the first Wednesday in June from 2001 to 2004. Prices are dollars per MMBtu, from NYMEX.

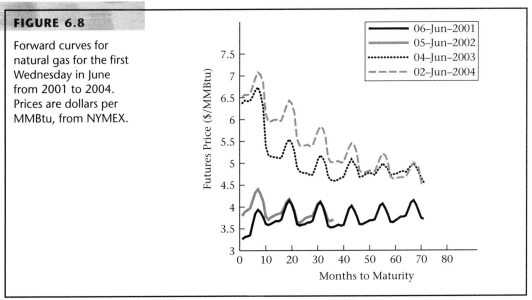

Source: Futures data from Datastream.

TABLE 6.12

June natural gas futures prices for October, November, and December in the same year, for 2001 to 2004.

Date	Oct	Nov	Dec
06-Jun-2001	2.173	2.305	2.435
05-Jun-2002	3.352	3.617	3.850
04-Jun-2003	6.428	6.528	6.658
02-Jun-2004	6.581	6.759	6.947

Source: Futures data from Datastream.

implying an estimated storage cost of $\lambda = \$0.178$ in November 2004. You will find different imputed marginal storage costs in each year, but this is to be expected if marginal storage costs vary with the quantity stored.

Because of the expense in transporting gas internationally, the seasonal behavior of the forward curve can vary in different parts of the world. In tropical areas where gas is used for cooking and electricity generation, the forward curve is relatively flat because demand is relatively flat. In the Southern hemisphere, where seasons are reversed from the Northern hemisphere, the forward curve will peak in June and July rather than December and January.

Recent developments in energy markets could alter the behavior of the natural gas forward curve in the United States. Power producers have made greater use of gas-fired peak-load electricity plants. These plants have increased summer demand for natural gas and may permanently alter seasonality.

6.10 Oil

Both oil and natural gas produce energy and are extracted from wells, but the different physical characteristics and uses of oil lead to a very different forward curve than that for gas. Oil is easier to transport than gas. Transportation of oil takes time, but oil has a global market. Oil is also easier to store than gas. Thus, seasonals in the price of crude oil are relatively unimportant. Specifications for the NYMEX light oil contract are shown in Figure 6.9. Figure 6.10 shows a newspaper listing for oil futures. The NYMEX forward curve on four dates is plotted in Figure 6.11.

FIGURE 6.9

Specifications for the NYMEX light, sweet crude oil contract.

Underlying	Specific domestic crudes delivered at Cushing, Oklahoma
Where traded	New York Mercantile Exchange
Size	1000 U.S. barrels (42,000 gallons)
Months	30 consecutive months plus long-dated futures out 7 years
Trading ends	Third-to-last business day preceding the 25th calendar day of month prior to maturity month
Delivery	As uniformly as possible over the delivery month

FIGURE 6.10

Listing for the NYMEX crude oil futures contract from the *Wall Street Journal*, July 21, 2004.

	OPEN	HIGH	LOW	SETTLE	CHG	LIFETIME HIGH	LIFETIME LOW	OPEN INT
Crude Oil, Light Sweet (NYM)-1,000 bbls.; $ per bbl.								
Aug	41.63	42.30	40.51	40.86	−0.78	42.30	20.84	29,478
Sept	41.41	41.75	40.31	40.44	−1.00	41.90	20.82	236,034
Oct	40.85	41.05	39.80	39.88	−1.00	41.30	23.75	68,764
Nov	40.38	40.45	39.52	39.45	−0.93	40.70	24.75	35,763
Dec	39.85	40.10	39.00	39.04	−0.89	40.30	16.35	60,672
Ja05	39.34	39.50	39.20	38.55	−0.86	39.50	23.25	23,149
Feb	38.89	39.05	38.65	38.13	−0.83	39.15	23.85	13,656
Mar	38.49	38.53	38.20	37.74	−0.80	38.65	23.05	14,312
Apr	38.05	38.20	37.85	37.37	−0.78	38.50	23.25	10,589
June	37.30	37.45	36.60	36.68	−0.73	37.55	22.40	22,138
Sept	36.65	36.65	36.65	35.96	−0.67	36.85	24.00	8,357
Dec	36.00	36.05	35.90	35.44	−0.61	36.30	17.00	47,774
Dc06	34.15	34.15	34.15	33.58	−0.58	34.15	19.10	34,365
Dc07	32.75	32.75	32.75	32.19	−0.55	32.75	19.50	12,536
Dc08	31.75	31.80	31.70	31.22	−0.55	32.00	19.75	11,967
Dc09	31.20	31.20	31.20	30.48	−0.55	31.20	22.50	10,916
Dc10	30.85	30.95	30.63	30.18	−0.55	31.00	27.15	15,928
Est vol 204,514, vol Mon 248,398; open int 708,255, −1,567.								

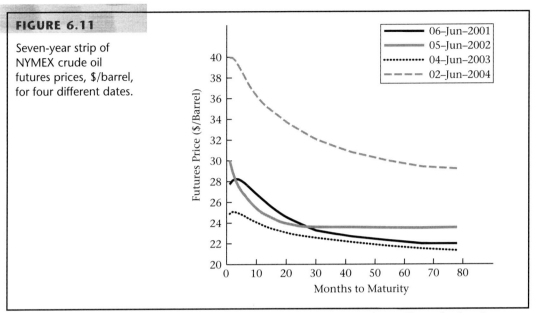

FIGURE 6.11

Seven-year strip of NYMEX crude oil futures prices, $/barrel, for four different dates.

Source: Futures data from Datastream.

On the four dates in the figure, near-term oil prices range from $25 to $40, while the 7-year forward price in each case is between $22 and $30. The long-run forward price is less volatile than the short-run forward price, which makes economic sense. In the short run, an increase in demand will cause a price increase since supply is fixed. A supply shock (such as production restrictions by the Organization of Petroleum Exporting Countries [OPEC]) will cause the price to increase. In the long run, however, both supply and demand have time to adjust to price changes with the result that price movements are attenuated. The forward curve suggests that market participants in June 2004 did not expect the price to remain at $40/barrel.

6.11 COMMODITY SPREADS

Some commodities are inputs in the creation of other commodities, which gives rise to **commodity spreads.** Soybeans, for example, can be crushed to produce soybean meal and soybean oil (and a small amount of waste). A trader with a position in soybeans and an opposite position in equivalent quantities of soybean meal and soybean oil has a **crush spread** and is said to be "trading the crush."

Similarly, crude oil is refined to make petroleum products, in particular heating oil and gasoline. The refining process entails distillation, which separates crude oil into different components, including gasoline, kerosene, and heating oil. The split of oil into these different components can be complemented by a process known as "cracking";

hence, the difference in price between crude oil and equivalent amounts of heating oil and gasoline is called the **crack spread.**

Oil can be processed in different ways, producing different mixes of outputs. The spread terminology identifies the number of gallons of oil as input, and the number of gallons of gasoline and heating oil as outputs. Traders will speak of "5-3-2," "3-2-1," and "2-1-1" crack spreads. The 5-3-2 spread, for example, reflects the profit from taking 5 gallons of oil as input, and producing 3 gallons of gasoline and 2 gallons of heating oil. A petroleum refiner producing gasoline and heating oil could use a futures crack spread to lock in both the cost of oil and output prices. This strategy would entail going long oil futures and short the appropriate quantities of gasoline and heating oil futures. Of course there are other inputs to production and it is possible to produce other outputs, such as jet fuel, so the crack spread is not a perfect hedge.

Example 6.4   Suppose we consider buying oil in July and selling gasoline and heating oil in August. On June 2, 2004, the July futures price for oil was $39.96/barrel, or $0.9514/gallon (there are 42 gallons per barrel). The August futures prices for unleaded gasoline and heating oil were $1.2427/gallon and $1.0171/gallon. The 3-2-1 crack spread tells us the gross margin we can lock in by buying 3 gallons of oil and producing 2 gallons of gasoline and 1 of heating oil. Using these prices, the spread is

$$(2 \times \$1.2427) + \$1.0171 - (3 \times \$0.9514) = \$0.6482$$

or $\$0.6482/3 = \$0.2161/$gallon. In this calculation we made no interest adjustment for the different expiration months of the futures contract.   ❧

There are crack spread options trading on NYMEX. Two of these options pay based on the difference between the price of heating oil and crude oil, and the price of gasoline and heating oil, both in a 1:1 ratio.

6.12 HEDGING STRATEGIES

In this section we discuss some of the complications that can arise when using commodity futures and forwards to hedge commodity price exposure. In Section 3.3 we discussed one such complication: the problem of quantity uncertainty, where, for example, a farmer growing corn does not know the ultimate yield at the time of planting. Other issues can arise. Since commodities are heterogeneous and often costly to transport and store, it is common to hedge a risk with a commodity contract that is imperfectly correlated with the risk being hedged. This gives rise to *basis risk*: The price of the commodity underlying the futures contract may move differently than the price of the commodity you are hedging. For example, because of transportation cost and time, the price of natural gas in California may differ from that in Louisiana, which is the location underlying the principal natural gas futures contract (see again Figure 6.7). In some cases, one commodity may be used to hedge another. As an example of this we discuss the use of crude oil to hedge jet fuel. Finally, weather derivatives provide another example of an instrument that can be used to cross-hedge. We discuss degree-day index contracts as an example of such derivatives.

Basis Risk

Exchange-traded commodity futures contracts call for delivery of the underlying commodity at specific locations and specific dates. The actual commodity to be bought or sold may reside at a different location and the desired delivery date may not match that of the futures contract. Additionally, the *grade* of the deliverable under the futures contract may not match the grade that is being delivered.

This general problem of the futures or forward contract not representing exactly what is being hedged is called *basis risk*. Basis risk is a generic problem with commodities because of storage and transportation costs and quality differences. Basis risk can also arise with financial futures, as for example when a company hedges its own borrowing cost with the Eurodollar contract.

Section 5.5 demonstrated how an individual stock could be hedged with an index futures contract. We saw that if we regressed the individual stock return on the index return, the resulting regression coefficient provided a hedge ratio that minimized the variance of the hedged position.

In the same way, suppose we wish to hedge oil delivered on the East Coast with the NYMEX oil contract, which calls for delivery of oil in Cushing, Oklahoma. The variance-minimizing hedge ratio would be the regression coefficient obtained by regressing the East Coast price on the Cushing price. Problems with this regression are that the relationship may not be stable over time or may be estimated imprecisely.

Another example of basis risk occurs when hedgers decide to hedge distant obligations with near-term futures. For example, an oil producer might have an obligation to deliver 100,000 barrels per month at a fixed price for a year. The natural way to hedge this obligation would be to buy 100,000 barrels per month, locking in the price and supply on a month-by-month basis. This is called a **strip hedge.** We engage in a strip hedge when we hedge a stream of obligations by offsetting each individual obligation with a futures contract matching the maturity and quantity of the obligation. For the oil producer obligated to deliver every month at a fixed price, the hedge would entail buying the appropriate quantity each month, in effect taking a long position in the strip.

An alternative to a strip hedge is a **stack hedge.** With a stack hedge, we enter into futures contracts with a *single* maturity, with the number of contracts selected so that changes in the *present value* of the future obligations are offset by changes in the value of this "stack" of futures contracts. In the context of the oil producer with a monthly delivery obligation, a stack hedge would entail going long 1.2 million barrels using the near-term contract. (Actually, we would want to tail the position and short less than 1.2 million barrels, but we will ignore this.) When the near-term contract matures, we

Metallgesellschaft A. G.

In 1992, a U.S. subsidiary of the German industrial firm Metallgesellschaft A. G. (MG) had offered customers fixed prices on over 150 million barrels of petroleum products, including gasoline, heating oil, and diesel fuel, over periods as long as 10 years. To hedge the resulting short exposure, MG entered into futures and swaps.

Much of MG's hedging was done using short-dated NYMEX crude oil and heating oil futures. Thus, MG was using stack hedging, rolling over the hedge each month.

During much of 1993, the near-term oil market was in contango (the forward curve was upward sloping). As a result of the market remaining in contango, MG systematically lost money when rolling its hedges and had to meet substantial margin calls. In December 1993, the supervisory board of MG decided to liquidate both its supply contracts and the futures positions used to hedge

those contracts. In the end, MG sustained losses estimated at between $200 million and $1.3 billion.

The MG case was extremely complicated and has been the subject of pointed exchanges among academics—see in particular Culp and Miller (1995), Edwards and Canter (1995), and Mello and Parsons (1995). While the case is complicated, several issues stand out. First, was the stack-and-roll a reasonable strategy for MG to have undertaken? Second, should the position have been liquidated when it was and in the manner it was liquidated (as it turned out, oil prices increased—which would have worked in MG's favor—following the liquidation). Third, did MG encounter liquidity problems from having to finance losses on its hedging strategy? While the MG case has receded into history, hedgers still confront the issues raised by this case.

reestablish the stack hedge by going long contracts in the new near month. This process of stacking futures contracts in the near-term contract and rolling over into the new near-term contract is called a **stack and roll.** If the new near-term futures price is below the expiring near-term price (i.e., there is backwardation), rolling is profitable.

Why would anyone use a stack hedge? There are at least two reasons. First, there is often more trading volume and liquidity in near-term contracts. With many commodities, bid-ask spreads widen with maturity. Thus, a stack hedge may have lower transaction costs than a strip hedge. Second, the manager may wish to speculate on the shape of the forward curve. You might decide that the forward curve looks unusually steep in the early months. If you undertake a stack hedge and the forward curve then flattens, you will have locked in all your oil at the relatively cheap near-term price, and implicitly made gains from not having locked in the relatively high strip prices. However, if the curve becomes steeper, it is possible to lose.

The box above recounts the story of Metallgesellschaft A. G. (MG), in which MG's large losses on a hedged position might have been caused, at least in part, by the use of a stack hedge.

Hedging Jet Fuel with Crude Oil

Jet fuel futures do not exist in the United States, but firms sometimes hedge jet fuel with crude oil futures along with futures for related petroleum products.[10] In order to perform this hedge, it is necessary to understand the relationship between crude oil and jet fuel prices. If we own a quantity of jet fuel and hedge by holding H crude oil futures contracts, our mark-to-market profit depends on the change in the jet fuel price and the change in the futures price:

$$(P_t - P_{t-1}) + H(F_t - F_{t-1}) \qquad (6.19)$$

where P_t is the price of jet fuel and F_t the crude oil futures price. We can estimate H by regressing the change in the jet fuel price (denominated in cents per gallon) on the change in the crude futures price (denominated in dollar per barrel). Doing so using daily data for January 2000–June 2004 gives (standard errors are in parentheses)

$$P_t - P_{t-1} = \underset{(0.069)}{0.009} + \underset{(0.094)}{2.037}(F_t - F_{t-1}) \qquad R^2 = 0.287 \qquad (6.20)$$

The futures price used in this regression is the price of the current near-term contract. The coefficient on the futures price change tells us that, on average, when the crude futures price increases by \$1, a gallon of jet fuel increases by \$0.02. Suppose that as part of a particular crack spread, 1 gallon of crude oil is used to produce 1 gallon of jet fuel. Then, other things equal, since there are 42 gallons in a barrel, a \$1 increase in the price of a barrel of oil will generate a \$1/42 = \$0.0238 increase in the price of jet fuel. This is approximately the regression coefficient.[11]

The R^2 in equation (6.19) is 0.287, which implies a correlation coefficient of about 0.50. The hedge would therefore have considerable residual risk.

Weather Derivatives

Weather derivatives provide another illustration of cross-hedging. Weather as a business risk can be difficult to hedge. For example, weather can affect both the prices of energy products and the amount of energy consumed. If a winter is colder than average, home-owners and businesses will consume extra electricity, heating oil, and natural gas, and the prices of these products will tend to be high as well. Conversely, during a warm winter, energy prices and quantities will be low. While it is possible to use futures markets to hedge prices of commodities such as natural gas, hedging the quantity is more difficult.

---

[10]For example, Southwest Airlines reportedly used a combination of crude oil and heating oil futures to hedge jet fuel. See Melanie Trottman, "Southwest Airline's Big Fuel-Hedging Call Is Paying Off," *Wall Street Journal*, January 16, 2004, p. B4.

[11]Recall that in Section 5.5 we estimated a hedge ratio for stocks using a regression based on percentage changes. In that case, we had an economic reason (an asset pricing model) to believe that there was a stable relationship based upon rates of return. With crude and jet fuel, crude is used to produce jet fuel, so it makes sense that dollar changes in the price of crude would be related to dollar changes in the price of jet fuel.

There are many other examples of weather risk: ski resorts are harmed by warm winters, soft drink manufacturers are harmed by a cold spring, summer, or fall, and makers of lawn sprinklers are harmed by wet summers. In all of these cases, firms could hedge their risk using **weather derivatives**—contracts that make payments based upon realized characteristics of weather—to cross-hedge their specific risk.

The payoffs for weather derivatives are based on weather-related measurements. An example of a weather contract is the degree-day index futures contract traded at the Chicago Mercantile Exchange. A **heating degree-day** is the maximum of zero and the difference between the average daily temperature and 65 degrees Fahrenheit. A **cooling degree-day** is the maximum of the difference between the average daily temperature and 65 degrees Fahrenheit, and zero. Sixty-five degrees is a moderate temperature. At higher temperatures, air conditioners may be used, while at lower temperatures, heating may be used. A monthly degree-day index is constructed by adding the daily degree-days over the month. The futures contract then settles based on the cumulative heating or cooling degree-days (the two are separate contracts) over the course of a month. The size of the contract is $100 times the degree-day index. As of September 2004, degree-day index contracts were available for over 20 cities in the United States, Europe, and Japan. There are also puts and calls on these futures.

With city-specific degree-day index contracts, it is possible to create and hedge payoffs based on average temperatures, or using options, based on ranges of average temperatures. If Minneapolis is unusually cold but the rest of the country is normal, the cooling degree-day contract for Minneapolis will make a large payment that will compensate the holder for the increased consumption of energy. Notice that in this scenario a natural gas price contract (for example) would not provide a sufficient hedge, since unusual cold in Minneapolis alone would not have much effect on national energy prices.

CHAPTER SUMMARY

At a general level, commodity forward prices can be described by the same formula as financial forward prices:

$$F_{0,T} = S_0 e^{(r-\delta)T} \tag{6.21}$$

For financial assets, δ is the dividend yield. For commodities, δ is the commodity *lease rate*—the return that makes an investor willing to buy and then lend a commodity. Thus, for the commodity owner who lends the commodity, it is like a dividend. From the commodity borrower's perspective, it is the cost of borrowing the commodity. As with financial forwards, commodity forward prices are biased predictors of the future spot price when the commodity return contains a risk premium.

While the dividend yield for a financial asset can typically be observed directly, the lease rate for a commodity can typically be estimated *only by observing the forward price*. The forward curve provides important information about the commodity.

Commodities are complex because every commodity market differs in the details. Forward curves for different commodities reflect different properties of storability, storage costs, production, and demand. Electricity, gold, corn, natural gas, and oil all have distinct forward curves, reflecting the different characteristics of their physical markets. These idiosyncracies will be reflected in the commodity lease rate. When there are seasonalities in either the demand or supply of a commodity, the commodity will be stored (assuming this is physically feasible), and the forward curve for the commodity will reflect storage costs. Some holders of a commodity receive benefits from physical ownership. This benefit is called the commodity's *convenience yield*. The convenience yield creates different returns to ownership for different investors, and may or may not be reflected in the forward price. The convenience yield can lead to no-arbitrage regions rather than a no-arbitrage price. It can also be costly to short-sell commodities with a significant convenience yield.

FURTHER READING

We will see in later chapters that the concept of a lease rate—which is a generalization of a dividend yield—helps to unify the pricing of swaps (Chapter 8), options (Chapter 10), and commodity-linked notes (Chapter 15). One particularly interesting application of the lease rate arises in the discussion of real options in Chapter 17. We will see there that if an extractable commodity (such as oil or gold) has a zero lease rate, it will never be extracted. Thus, the lease rate is linked in an important way with production decisions.

A useful resource for learning more about commodities is the Chicago Board of Trade (1998). The Web sites of the various exchanges (e.g., NYMEX and the CBOT) are also useful resources, with information about particular commodities and trading and hedging strategies.

Siegel and Siegel (1990) provide a detailed discussion of many commodity futures. There are numerous papers on commodities. Bodie and Rosansky (1980) and Gorton and Rouwenhorst (2004) examine the risk and return of commodities as an investment. Brennan (1991), Pindyck (1993b), and Pindyck (1994) examine the behavior of commodity prices. Schwartz (1997) compares the performance of different models of commodity price behavior. Jarrow and Oldfield (1981) discuss the effect of storage costs on pricing, and Routledge et al. (2000) present a theoretical model of commodity forward curves.

Finally, Metallgesellschaft engendered a spirited debate. Papers written about that episode include Culp and Miller (1995), Edwards and Canter (1995), and Mello and Parsons (1995).

PROBLEMS

6.1. The spot price of a widget is $70.00 per unit. Forward prices for 3, 6, 9, and 12 months are $70.70, $71.41, $72.13, and $72.86. Assuming a 5% continuously compounded annual risk-free rate, what are the annualized lease rates for each maturity? Is this an example of contango or backwardation?

6.2. The current price of oil is $32.00 per barrel. Forward prices for 3, 6, 9, and 12 months are $31.37, $30.75, $30.14, and $29.54. Assuming a 2% continuously compounded annual risk-free rate, what is the annualized lease rate for each maturity? Is this an example of contango or backwardation?

6.3. Given a continuously compounded risk-free rate of 3% annually, at what lease rate will forward prices equal the current commodity price? (Recall the pencil example in Section 6.4.) If the lease rate were 3.5%, would there be contango or backwardation?

6.4. Suppose that pencils cost $0.20 today and the continuously compounded lease rate for pencils is 5%. The continuously compounded interest rate is 10%. The pencil price in 1 year is uncertain and pencils can be stored costlessly.

    a. If you short-sell a pencil for 1 year, what payment do you have to make to the pencil lender? Would it make sense for a financial investor to store pencils in equilibrium?

    b. Show that the equilibrium forward price is $0.2103.

    c. Explain what ranges of forward prices are ruled out by arbitrage in the four cases where pencils can and cannot be short-sold and can and cannot be loaned.

6.5. Suppose the gold spot price is $300/oz., the 1-year forward price is 310.686, and the continuously compounded risk-free rate is 5%.

    a. What is the lease rate?

    b. What is the return on a cash-and-carry in which gold is not loaned?

    c. What is the return on a cash-and-carry in which gold is loaned, earning the lease rate?

For the next three problems, assume that the continuously compounded interest rate is 6% and the storage cost of widgets is $0.03 quarterly (payable at the end of the quarter). Here is the forward price curve for widgets:

2004			2005			2006	
Dec	Mar	Jun	Sep	Dec	Mar	Jun
3.000	3.075	3.152	2.750	2.822	2.894	2.968

6.6.   **a.** What are some possible explanations for the shape of this forward curve?

    b. What annualized rate of return do you earn on a cash-and-carry entered into in December 2004 and closed in March 2005? Is your answer sensible?

    c. What annualized rate of return do you earn on a cash-and-carry entered into in December 2004 and closed in September 2005? Is your answer sensible?

6.7. **a.** Suppose that you want to borrow a widget beginning in December 2004 and ending in March 2005. What payment will be required to make the transaction fair to both parties?

b. Suppose that you want to borrow a widget beginning in December 2004 and ending in September 2005. What payment will be required to make the transaction fair to both parties?

6.8. **a.** Suppose the March 2005 forward price were $3.10. Describe two different transactions you could use to undertake arbitrage.

b. Suppose the September 2005 forward price fell to $2.70 and subsequent forward prices fell in such a way that there is no arbitrage from September 2005 and going forward. Is there an arbitrage you could undertake using forward contracts from June 2005 and earlier? Why or why not?

6.9. Consider Example 6.1. Suppose the February forward price had been $2.80. What would the arbitrage be? Suppose it had been $2.65. What would the arbitrage be? In each case, specify the transactions and resulting cash flows in both November and February. What are you assuming about the convenience yield?

6.10. Using Table 6.10, what is your best guess about the current price of gold per ounce?

6.11. Suppose you know nothing about widgets. You are going to approach a widget merchant to borrow one in order to short-sell it. (That is, you will take physical possession of the widget, sell it, and return a widget at time T.) Before you ring the doorbell, you want to make a judgment about what you think is a reasonable lease rate for the widget. Think about the following possible scenarios.

a. Suppose that widgets do not deteriorate over time, are costless to store, and are always produced, although production quantity can be varied. Demand is constant over time. Knowing nothing else, what lease rate might you face?

b. Suppose everything is the same as in (a) except that demand for widgets varies seasonally.

c. Suppose everything is the same as in (a) except that demand for widgets varies seasonally and the rate of production cannot be adjusted. Consider how seasonality and the horizon of your short-sale interact with the lease rate.

d. Suppose everything is the same as in (a) except that demand is constant over time and production is seasonal. Consider how production seasonality and the horizon of your short-sale interact with the lease rate.

e. Suppose that widgets cannot be stored. How does this affect your answers to the previous questions?

CHAPTER 7

Interest Rate Forwards and Futures

Suppose you have the opportunity to spend $1 one year from today to receive $2 two years from today. What is the value of this opportunity? To answer this question, you need to know the appropriate interest rates for discounting the two cash flows. This comparison is an example of the most basic concept in finance: using interest rates to compute present values. Once we find a present value for one or more assets, we can compare the values of cash flows from those assets even if the cash inflows and cash outflows occur at different times. In order to perform these calculations, we need information about the set of interest rates prevailing between different points in time.

We begin the chapter by reviewing basic bond concepts—coupon bonds, yields to maturity, and implied forward rates. Any reader of this book should understand these basic concepts. We then look at interest rate forwards and forward rate agreements, which permit hedging interest rate risk. Finally, we look at bond futures and the repo market.

7.1 BOND BASICS

Table 7.1 presents information about current interest rates for bonds maturing in from 1 to 3 years. *Identical information is presented in five different ways in the table.* Although the information appears differently across columns, it is possible to take the information in any one column of Table 7.1 and reproduce the other four columns.[1]

Illustrating how similar information is presented in practice, Figure 7.1 reproduces a newspaper listing of information about outstanding U.S. government bonds. The listing reports a price per $100 of maturity value and a yield to maturity for each bond. A wide range of maturities exists at any point in time, but the U.S. government issues Treasury securities only at specific maturities—typically 3 months, 6 months, and 1, 2, 5, 10, and 30 years.[2] Government securities that are issued with less than 1 year to maturity and that make only a single payment, at maturity, are called Treasury *bills*. *Notes* and *bonds* pay

---

[1]Depending upon how you do the computation, you may arrive at numbers slightly different from those in Table 7.1. The reason is that all of the entries except those in column 1 are rounded in the last digit, and there are multiple ways to compute the number in any given column. Rounding error will therefore generate small differences among computations performed in different ways.

[2]Treasury securities are issued using an auction. In the past the government also issued bonds with maturities of 3 and 7. Between 2002 and 2005 the government issued no 30-year bonds.

TABLE 7.1			Five ways to present equivalent information about default-free interest rates. All rates but those in the the last column are effective annual rates.		
	(1)	(2)	(3)	(4)	(5) Continuously
Years to Maturity	Zero-Coupon Bond Yield	Zero-Coupon Bond Price	One-Year Implied Forward Rate	Par Coupon	Compounded Zero Yield
1	6.00%	0.943396	6.00000%	6.00000%	5.82689%
2	6.50	0.881659	7.00236	6.48423	6.29748
3	7.00	0.816298	8.00705	6.95485	6.76586

coupons and are issued at a price close to their maturity value (i.e., they are issued at par). Notes have 10 or fewer years to maturity and bonds have more than 10 years to maturity. The distinctions between bills, notes, and bonds are not important for our purposes; we will refer to all three as bonds. You will also see Treasury inflation protected securities (TIPS) in Figure 7.1. These are bonds for which payments are adjusted for inflation. Finally, the most recently issued government bonds are called **on-the-run;** other bonds are called **off-the-run.** These terms are used frequently in talking about government bonds since on-the-run bonds generally have lower yields and greater trading volume than off-the-run bonds. Appendix 7.A discusses some of the conventions used in bond price and yield quotations.

In addition to government bond information, there is also a listing for STRIPS. A **STRIPS**—Separate Trading of Registered Interest and Principal of Securities—is a claim to a single interest payment or the principal portion of a government bond. These claims trade separately from the bond. STRIPS are zero-coupon bonds since they make only a single payment at maturity. "STRIPS" should not be confused with the forward strip, which is the set of forward prices available at a point in time.

We need a way to represent bond prices and interest rates. Interest rate notation is, unfortunately and inevitably, cumbersome, because for any rate we must keep track of three dates: the date on which the rate is quoted, and the period of time (this has beginning and ending dates) over which the rate prevails. We will let $r_t(t_1, t_2)$ represent the interest rate from time t_1 to time t_2, prevailing on date t. If the interest rate is current—i.e., if $t = t_1$—and if there is no risk of confusion, we will drop the subscript.

Zero-Coupon Bonds

We begin by showing that the zero-coupon bond yield and zero-coupon bond price, columns (1) and (2) in Table 7.1, provide the same information. A **zero-coupon bond** is a bond that makes only a single payment at its maturity date. Our notation for zero-coupon bond prices will mimic that for interest rates. The price of a bond quoted at time

FIGURE 7.1

Government bond listing from the *Wall Street Journal*, July 21, 2004.

Treasury Bonds, Notes and Bills

July 20, 2004

Explanatory Notes

Representative Over-the-Counter quotation based on transactions of $1 million or more. Treasury bond, note and bill quotes are as of mid-afternoon. Colons in bid-and-asked quotes represent 32nds; 101:01 means 101 1/32. Net changes in 32nds. n-Treasury note. i-Inflation-Indexed issue. Treasury bill quotes in hundredths, quoted on terms of a rate of discount. Days to maturity calculated from settlement date. All yields are to maturity and based on the asked quote. Latest 13-week and 26-week bills are boldfaced. For bonds callable prior to maturity, yields are computed to the earliest call date for issues quoted above par and to the maturity date for issues below par. *When issued.

Source: eSpeed/Cantor Fitzgerald

U.S. Treasury strips as of 3 p.m. Eastern time, also based on transactions of $1 million or more. Colons in bid and asked quotes represent 32nds; 99:01 means 99 1/32. Net changes in 32nds. Yields calculated on the asked quotation. ci-stripped coupon interest. bp-Treasury bond, stripped principal. np-Treasury note, stripped principal. For bonds callable prior to maturity, yields are computed to the earliest call date for issues quoted above par and to the maturity date for issues below par.

Source: Bear, Stearns & Co. via Street Software Technology Inc.

Government Bonds & Notes

RATE	MATURITY MO/YR	BID	ASKED	CHG	ASK YLD
2.250	Jul 04n	100:00	100:01	...	0.54
2.125	Aug 04n	100:03	100:04	...	0.99
6.000	Aug 04n	100:10	100:11	...	0.97
7.250	Aug 04n	100:13	100:14	...	0.85
13.750	Aug 04	100:27	100:28	-1	0.95
1.875	Sep 04n	100:03	100:04	...	1.22
2.125	Oct 04n	100:05	100:06	-1	1.38
5.875	Nov 04n	101:11	101:12	-1	1.51
7.875	Nov 04n	102:00	102:01	...	1.44
11.625	Nov 04	103:06	103:07	-1	1.43
2.000	Nov 04n	100:05	100:06	...	1.47
1.750	Dec 04n	100:00	100:01	-1	1.64
1.625	Jan 05n	99:30	99:31	-1	1.65
7.500	Feb 05n	103:07	103:08	-2	1.73
1.500	Feb 05n	99:26	99:27	-2	1.73
1.625	Mar 05n	99:26	99:27	-3	1.83
1.625	Apr 05n	99:24	99:25	-3	1.89
6.500	May 05n	103:20	103:21	-3	1.95
6.750	May 05n	103:27	103:28	-3	1.95
12.000	May 05	108:05	108:06	-3	1.84
1.250	May 05n	99:12	99:13	-3	1.93
1.125	Jun 05n	99:05	99:06	-3	2.00
1.500	Jul 05n	99:13	99:14	-3	2.04
6.500	Aug 05n	104:20	104:21	-3	2.07
10.750	Aug 05	109:03	109:04	-4	2.07
2.000	Aug 05n	99:27	99:28	-3	2.11
1.625	Sep 05n	99:11	99:12	-4	2.14
1.625	Oct 05n	99:07	99:08	-4	2.21
5.750	Nov 05n	104:15	104:16	-5	2.25
5.875	Nov 05n	104:20	104:21	-5	2.25
1.875	Nov 05n	99:14	99:15	-4	2.27
1.875	Dec 05n	99:10	99:11	-4	2.34
1.875	Jan 06n	99:06	99:07	-5	2.39
5.625	Feb 06n	105:00	105:00	-5	2.36
9.375	Feb 06	110:22	110:23	-6	2.37
1.625	Feb 06n	98:23	98:24	-5	2.42
1.500	Mar 06n	98:12	98:13	-5	2.47
2.250	Apr 06n	99:16	99:17	-5	2.52
2.000	May 06n	99:00	99:01	-6	2.54
4.625	May 06n	103:20	103:21	-6	2.55
6.875	May 06n	107:19	107:20	-7	2.54
2.500	May 06n	99:26	99:27	-6	2.58
2.750	**Jun 06n**	**100:06**	**100:07**	**-6**	**2.63**
7.000	Jul 06n	108:10	108:11	-7	2.65
2.375	Aug 06n	99:12	99:13	-7	2.67
6.500	Oct 06n	108:00	108:01	-8	2.77
2.625	Nov 06n	99:18	99:19	-8	2.81
3.500	Nov 06n	101:16	101:17	-8	2.80
3.375	Jan 07i	107:06	107:07	-11	0.44
2.250	Feb 07n	98:12	98:13	-9	2.89
6.250	Feb 07n	108:07	108:08	-9	2.89
6.625	May 07n	109:22	109:23	-11	2.99
4.375	May 07n	103:21	103:22	-10	3.00
3.125	May 07n	100:10	100:11	-10	2.99
3.250	Aug 07n	100:15	100:16	-10	3.07
6.125	Aug 07n	108:24	108:25	-12	3.10
3.000	Nov 07n	99:14	99:15	-12	3.16
3.625	Jan 08i	109:15	109:16	-14	0.85
3.000	Feb 08n	99:04	99:05	-13	3.25
5.500	Feb 08n	107:16	107:17	-13	3.25
2.625	May 08n	97:13	97:14	-13	3.34
5.625	May 08n	108:03	108:04	-15	3.34
3.250	Aug 08n	99:10	99:11	-14	3.42
3.125	Sep 08n	98:23	98:24	-15	3.45
3.125	Oct 08n	98:19	98:20	-15	3.48
3.375	Nov 08n	99:15	99:16	-16	3.50
4.750	Nov 08n	105:00	105:01	-15	3.48
3.375	Dec 08n	99:11	99:12	-16	3.53
3.250	Jan 09n	98:23	98:24	-16	3.55
3.875	Jan 09i	111:23	111:24	-19	1.17
3.000	Feb 09n	97:17	97:18	-16	3.58
2.625	Mar 09n	95:26	95:27	-15	3.60
3.125	Apr 09n	97:26	97:27	-16	3.62
3.875	May 09n	101:00	101:01	-17	3.64
5.500	May 09n	108:11	108:12	-17	3.59
4.000	Jun 09n	101:16	101:17	-17	3.65
3.625	**Jul 09n**	**99:24**	**99:25**	**-17**	**3.67**
6.000	Aug 09n	110:18	110:19	-18	3.69
10.375	Nov 09	102:26	102:27	-2	1.37
4.250	Jan 10i	114:22	114:23	-22	1.45
6.500	Feb 10n	113:12	113:13	-19	3.81
11.750	Feb 10	105:18	105:19	-3	1.79
10.000	May 10	106:17	106:18	-4	1.85
5.750	Aug 10n	109:26	109:27	-20	3.91
12.750	Nov 10	113:15	113:16	-5	2.29
3.500	Jan 11i	111:12	111:13	-24	1.64
5.000	Feb 11n	105:19	105:20	-21	4.02
13.875	May 11	120:07	120:08	-7	2.41
5.000	Aug 11n	105:12	105:13	-22	4.11
14.000	Nov 11	125:08	125:09	-10	2.67
3.375	Jan 12i	111:03	111:04	-27	1.78
4.875	Feb 12n	104:10	104:11	-22	4.20
3.000	Jul 12i	108:14	108:15	-27	1.85
4.375	Aug 12n	100:22	100:23	-22	4.27
4.000	Nov 12n	98:00	98:00	-22	4.29
10.375	Nov 12	122:14	122:15	-14	3.18
3.875	Feb 13n	96:26	96:27	-21	4.32
3.625	May 13n	94:28	94:29	-22	4.32
1.875	Jul 13i	99:08	99:09	-28	1.96
4.250	Aug 13n	98:28	98:29	-24	4.40
12.000	Aug 13	132:12	132:13	-15	3.40
4.250	Nov 13n	98:21	98:22	-23	4.42
2.000	Jan 14i	99:30	99:31	-28	2.00
4.000	Feb 14n	96:18	96:19	-23	4.44
4.750	**May 14n**	**102:11**	**102:12**	**-24**	**4.45**
13.250	May 14	142:04	142:05	-18	3.63
2.000	Jul 14i	99:17	99:18	-29	2.05
12.500	Aug 14	140:08	140:09	-20	3.71
11.750	Nov 14	138:00	138:00	-21	3.79
11.250	Feb 15	156:01	156:02	-34	4.52
10.625	Aug 15	152:00	152:00	-34	4.58
9.875	Nov 15	145:23	145:24	-35	4.63
9.250	Feb 16	140:18	140:19	-34	4.67
7.250	May 16	122:17	122:18	-31	4.73
7.500	Nov 16	125:00	125:01	-32	4.78
8.750	May 17	137:13	137:14	-34	4.80
8.875	Aug 17	138:28	138:29	-36	4.82
9.125	May 18	142:08	142:09	-38	4.88
9.000	Nov 18	141:17	141:18	-37	4.92
8.875	Feb 19	140:10	140:11	-39	4.95
8.125	Aug 19	132:25	132:26	-37	5.00
8.500	Feb 20	137:06	137:07	-39	5.02
8.750	May 20	140:08	140:09	-39	5.03
8.750	Aug 20	140:13	140:14	-41	5.05
7.875	Feb 21	130:29	130:30	-39	5.09
8.125	May 21	134:00	134:00	-40	5.09
8.125	Aug 21	134:06	134:07	-40	5.10
8.000	Nov 21	132:30	132:31	-39	5.11
7.250	Aug 22	124:11	124:12	-38	5.16
7.625	Nov 22	129:00	129:01	-40	5.15
7.125	Feb 23	123:00	123:01	-38	5.18
6.250	Aug 23	112:13	112:14	-36	5.21
7.500	Nov 24	128:17	128:18	-41	5.20
7.625	Feb 25	130:08	130:09	-40	5.21
6.875	Aug 25	120:24	120:25	-39	5.23
6.000	Feb 26	109:17	109:18	-34	5.25
6.750	Aug 26	119:14	119:15	-37	5.25
6.500	Nov 26	116:07	116:08	-36	5.25
6.625	Feb 27	117:30	117:31	-36	5.25
6.375	Aug 27	114:24	114:25	-35	5.26
6.125	Nov 27	111:15	111:16	-36	5.26
3.625	Apr 28i	121:21	121:22	-52	2.42
5.500	Aug 28	103:03	103:04	-32	5.27
5.250	Nov 28	99:23	99:24	-32	5.27
5.250	Feb 29	99:25	99:26	-32	5.26
3.875	Apr 29i	127:05	127:06	-56	2.41
6.125	Aug 29	111:30	111:31	-35	5.26
6.250	May 30	114:00	114:00	-35	5.25
5.375	**Feb 31**	**102:24**	**102:25**	**-33**	**5.18**
3.375	Apr 32i	121:11	121:12	-58	2.32

U.S. Treasury Strips

MATURITY		TYPE	BID	ASKED	CHG	ASK YLD
Aug	04	ci	99:30	99:30	...	1.09
Aug	04	np	99:30	99:30	...	1.14
Nov	04	ci	99:18	99:18	...	1.41
Nov	04	bp	99:17	99:17	...	1.46
Nov	04	np	99:17	99:17	...	1.46
Jan	05	ci	99:12	99:12	-2	1.29
Feb	05	ci	99:02	99:02	-2	1.67
Feb	05	np	99:00	99:00	-2	1.77
May	05	ci	98:17	98:17	-3	1.81
May	05	bp	98:15	98:15	-3	1.91
May	05	np	98:14	98:14	-3	1.96
May	05	np	98:14	98:14	-3	1.94
Jul	05	ci	98:15	98:15	-3	1.60
Aug	05	ci	97:30	97:30	-3	1.98
Aug	05	bp	97:25	97:25	-3	2.12
Aug	05	np	97:25	97:25	-3	2.12
Nov	05	ci	97:05	97:05	-4	2.21
Nov	05	np	97:03	97:03	-4	2.26
Nov	05	np	97:03	97:03	-4	2.26
Jan	06	ci	97:02	97:02	-5	2.03
Feb	06	ci	96:11	96:11	-5	2.39
Feb	06	bp	96:12	96:12	-5	2.37
Feb	06	np	96:13	96:13	-5	2.35
May	06	ci	95:18	95:18	-6	2.52
May	06	np	95:16	95:16	-6	2.55
May	06	np	95:18	95:18	-6	2.52
Jul	06	ci	95:22	95:22	-6	2.23
Jul	06	np	94:30	94:30	-6	2.64
Aug	06	ci	94:26	94:26	-7	2.60
Aug	06	np	94:21	94:21	-7	2.68
Oct	06	np	94:01	94:01	-7	2.77
Nov	06	ci	93:27	93:27	-7	2.76
Nov	06	np	93:23	93:23	-7	2.82
Nov	06	np	93:24	93:24	-7	2.81
Feb	07	ci	92:25	92:25	-8	2.94
Feb	07	np	92:26	92:26	-8	2.93
May	07	ci	91:27	91:27	-9	3.05
May	07	np	91:27	91:27	-9	3.04
May	07	np	91:30	91:30	-9	3.01
Aug	07	ci	90:24	90:24	-9	3.19
Aug	07	np	90:28	90:28	-9	3.15
Aug	07	np	90:31	90:31	-9	3.11
Nov	07	ci	89:31	89:31	-10	3.21
Nov	07	np	90:00	90:00	-10	3.20
Feb	08	ci	88:31	88:31	-11	3.30
Feb	08	np	88:31	88:31	-11	3.31
Feb	08	np	89:01	89:01	-11	3.28
May	08	ci	87:28	87:28	-11	3.41
May	08	np	87:31	87:31	-11	3.39
Aug	08	ci	86:31	86:31	-12	3.47
Aug	08	np	87:02	87:02	-12	3.44
May	08	np	88:02	88:02	-11	3.36
Nov	08	ci	85:25	85:25	-13	3.58
Nov	08	np	85:30	85:30	-13	3.54
Nov	08	np	86:00	86:00	-13	3.53
Feb	09	ci	84:21	84:21	-13	3.68
Feb	09	np	84:29	84:29	-13	3.61
May	09	ci	83:20	83:20	-14	3.75
May	09	np	83:31	83:31	-14	3.66
May	09	np	83:27	83:27	-14	3.69
Aug	09	ci	82:19	82:19	-14	3.81
Aug	09	np	82:23	82:23	-14	3.78
Nov	09	ci	81:27	81:27	-15	3.80
Nov	09	bp	81:05	81:05	-15	3.97
Feb	10	ci	80:13	80:13	-14	3.96
Feb	10	np	80:23	80:23	-14	3.89
May	10	ci	79:13	79:13	-14	4.01
Aug	10	ci	78:12	78:12	-15	4.06
Aug	10	np	78:20	78:20	-15	4.01
Nov	10	ci	77:21	77:21	-15	4.05
Feb	11	ci	76:08	76:08	-16	4.17
Feb	11	np	76:18	76:18	-16	4.11
May	11	ci	75:06	75:06	-16	4.23
Aug	11	ci	74:05	74:05	-16	4.28
Aug	11	np	74:15	74:15	-16	4.22
Nov	11	ci	73:07	73:07	-17	4.31
Feb	12	ci	72:00	72:00	-15	4.39
Feb	12	np	72:15	72:15	-15	4.30
May	12	ci	70:31	70:31	-15	4.44
Aug	12	ci	69:28	69:28	-16	4.49
Aug	12	np	70:18	70:18	-16	4.37
Nov	12	ci	68:28	68:28	-16	4.53
Nov	12	np	69:23	69:23	-16	4.38
Feb	13	ci	67:29	67:29	-15	4.57
Feb	13	np	68:27	68:27	-16	4.41
May	13	ci	66:28	66:28	-16	4.62
May	13	np	68:02	68:02	-16	4.41
Aug	13	ci	65:28	65:28	-16	4.66
Aug	13	np	66:25	66:25	-16	4.50
Nov	13	ci	64:29	64:29	-16	4.70
Nov	13	np	65:26	65:26	-16	4.54
Feb	14	ci	63:30	63:30	-16	4.73
Feb	14	np	65:03	65:03	-17	4.54
May	14	ci	62:30	62:30	-16	4.77
May	14	np	64:06	64:06	-17	4.57
Aug	14	ci	61:31	61:31	-16	4.81
Nov	14	ci	61:00	61:00	-17	4.85

Treasury Bills

MATURITY	DAYS TO MAT	BID	ASKED	CHG	ASK YLD
Jul 22 04	1	1.02	1.01	0.02	1.02
Jul 29 04	8	1.07	1.06	0.04	1.07
Aug 05 04	15	1.14	1.13	0.03	1.15
Aug 12 04	22	1.14	1.13	0.02	1.15
Aug 19 04	29	1.19	1.18	0.03	1.20
Aug 26 04	36	1.18	1.17	0.04	1.19
Sep 02 04	43	1.19	1.18	0.03	1.20
Sep 09 04	50	1.20	1.19	0.02	1.21
Sep 16 04	57	1.20	1.19	0.03	1.21
Sep 23 04	64	1.21	1.20	0.02	1.22
Sep 30 04	71	1.23	1.22	0.02	1.24
Oct 07 04	78	1.29	1.28	0.02	1.30
Oct 14 04	85	1.33	1.32	0.02	1.34
Oct 21 04	**92**	**1.33**	**1.32**	**...**	**1.34**
Oct 28 04	99	1.35	1.34	0.02	1.36
Nov 04 04	106	1.41	1.40	0.02	1.43
Nov 12 04	114	1.44	1.43	0.02	1.46
Nov 18 04	120	1.44	1.43	0.01	1.46
Nov 26 04	128	1.45	1.44	0.03	1.47
Dec 02 04	134	1.49	1.48	0.03	1.51
Dec 09 04	141	1.52	1.51	0.02	1.54
Dec 16 04	148	1.55	1.54	0.02	1.57
Dec 23 04	155	1.58	1.57	0.01	1.60
Dec 30 04	162	1.55	1.53	0.01	1.56
Jan 06 05	169	1.62	1.59	0.01	1.62
Jan 13 05	176	1.65	1.63	0.02	1.66
Jan 20 05	**183**	**1.66**	**1.65**	**...**	**1.69**

Inflation-Indexed Treasury Securities

RATE	MAT	BID/ASKED	CHG	*YLD	ACCR PRIN
3.375	01/07	107-06/07	-11	0.452	1191
3.625	01/08	109-15/16	-14	0.854	1168
3.875	01/09	111-23/24	-19	1.178	1150
4.250	01/10	114-22/23	-22	1.449	1121
3.500	01/11	111-12/13	-24	1.639	1084
3.375	01/12	111-03/04	-27	1.781	1063
3.000	07/12	108-14/15	-27	1.854	1049
1.875	07/13	99-08/09	-28	1.963	1028
2.000	01/14	99-30/31	-28	2.004	1019
2.000	07/14	99-17/18	-29	2.049	1167
3.625	04/28	121-21/22	-52	2.419	1167
3.875	04/29	127-05/06	-56	2.409	1148
3.375	04/32	121-11/12	-58	2.325	1063

*Yield to maturity on accrued principal.

t_0, with the bond to be purchased at t_1 and maturing at t_2, is $P_{t_0}(t_1, t_2)$. As with interest rates, we will drop the subscript when $t_0 = t_1$.

The 1-year zero-coupon bond price of $P(0, 1) = 0.943396$ means that you would pay $0.943396 today to receive $1 in 1 year. You could also pay $P(0, 2) = 0.881659$ today to receive $1 in 2 years and $P(0, 3) = 0.816298$ to receive $1 in 3 years.

The **yield to maturity** (or *internal rate of return*) on a zero-coupon bond is simply the percentage increase in dollars earned from the bond. For the 1-year bond, we end up with $1/0.943396 - 1 = 0.06$ more dollars per $1 invested. If we are quoting interest rates as effective annual rates, this is a 6% yield.

For the zero-coupon 2-year bond, we end up with $1/0.881659 - 1 = 0.134225$ more dollars per $1 invested. We could call this a 2-year effective interest rate of 13.4225%, but it is conventional to quote rates on an annual basis. If we want this yield to be comparable to the 6% yield on the 1-year bond, we could assume annual compounding and get $(1 + r(0, 2))^2 = 1.134225$, which implies that $r(0, 2) = 0.065$. In general,

$$P(0, n) = \frac{1}{[1 + r(0, n)]^n} \tag{7.1}$$

Note from equation (7.1) that *a zero-coupon bond price is a discount factor*: A zero-coupon bond price is what you would pay today to receive $1 in the future. If you have a future cash flow at time t, C_t, you can multiply it by the price of a zero-coupon bond, $P(0, t)$, to obtain the present value of the cash flow. Because of equation (7.1), multiplying by $P(0, t)$ is the same as discounting at the rate $r(0, t)$, i.e.,

$$C_t \times P(0, t) = \frac{C_t}{[1 + r(0, t)]^t}$$

The inverse of the zero-coupon bond price, $1/P(0, t)$, provides a future value factor.

In contrast to zero-coupon bond prices, interest rates such as those in Figure 7.1 are subject to quoting conventions that can make their interpretation difficult (if you doubt this, see Appendix 7.A). Because of their simple interpretation, we can consider zero-coupon bond prices as the building block for all of fixed income.

A graph of annualized zero-coupon yields to maturity against time to maturity is called the zero-coupon **yield curve**. A yield curve shows us how yields to maturity vary with time to maturity. In practice, it is common to present the yield curve based on coupon bonds, not zero-coupon bonds.

Implied Forward Rates

We now see how column (3) in Table 7.1 can be computed from either column (1) or (2). The 1-year and 2-year zero-coupon yields are the rates you can earn from year 0 to year 1 and from year 0 to year 2. There is also an *implicit* rate that can be earned from year 1 to year 2 that must be consistent with the other two rates. This rate is called the **implied forward rate.**

Suppose we could today guarantee a rate we could earn from year 1 to year 2. We know that $1 invested for 1 year earns $[1 + r_0(0, 1)]$ and $1 invested for 2 years earns

FIGURE 7.2

An investor investing for 2 years has a choice of buying a 2-year zero-coupon bond paying $[1 + r_0(0, 2)]^2$ or buying a 1-year bond paying $1 + r_0(0,1)$ for 1 year, and reinvesting the proceeds at the implied forward rate, $r_0(1,2)$ between years 1 and 2. The implied forward rate makes the investor indifferent between these alternatives.

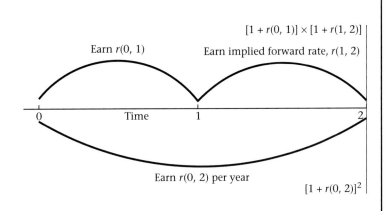

$[1 + r_0(0, 2)]^2$. Thus, the time 0 forward rate from year 1 to year 2, $r_0(1, 2)$, should satisfy

$$[1 + r_0(0, 1)][1 + r_0(1, 2)] = [1 + r_0(0, 2)]^2$$

or

$$1 + r_0(1, 2) = \frac{[1 + r_0(0, 2)]^2}{1 + r_0(0, 1)} \tag{7.2}$$

Figure 7.2 shows graphically how the implied forward rate is related to 1- and 2-year yields. If $r_0(1, 2)$ did not satisfy equation (7.2), then there would be an arbitrage opportunity. Problem 7.15 asks you to work through the arbitrage. In general, we have

$$\boxed{[1 + r_0(t_1, t_2)]^{t_2 - t_1} = \frac{[1 + r_0(0, t_2)]^{t_2}}{[1 + r_0(0, t_1)]^{t_1}} = \frac{P(0, t_1)}{P(0, t_2)}} \tag{7.3}$$

Corresponding to 1-year and 2-year interest rates, $r_0(0, 1)$ and $r_0(0, 2)$, we have prices of 1-year and 2-year zero-coupon bonds, $P_0(0, 1)$ and $P_0(0, 2)$. Just as the interest rates imply a forward 1-year interest rate, the bond prices imply a 1-year forward zero-coupon bond price. The implied forward zero-coupon bond price must be consistent with the implied forward interest rate. Rewriting equation (7.3), we have

$$P_0(t_1, t_2) = \frac{1}{[1 + r_0(t_1, t_2)]^{t_2 - t_1}} = \frac{[1 + r_0(0, t_1)]^{t_1}}{[1 + r_0(0, t_2)]^{t_2}} = \frac{P(0, t_2)}{P(0, t_1)} \tag{7.4}$$

The implied forward zero-coupon bond price from t_1 to t_2 is simply the ratio of the zero-coupon bond prices maturing at t_2 and t_1.

Example 7.1 Using information in Table 7.1, we want to compute the implied forward interest rate from year 2 to year 3 and the implied forward price for a 1-year zero-coupon bond purchased in year 2.

The implied forward interest rate, $r_0(2, 3)$, can be computed as

$$1 + r_0(2, 3) = \frac{[1 + r_0(0, 3)]^3}{[1 + r_0(0, 2)]^2} = \frac{(1 + 0.07)^3}{(1 + 0.065)^2} = 1.0800705$$

or equivalently as

$$1 + r_0(2, 3) = \frac{P_0(0, 2)}{P_0(0, 3)} = \frac{0.881659}{0.816298} = 1.0800705$$

The implied forward 1-year zero-coupon bond price is

$$\frac{P_0(0, 3)}{P_0(0, 2)} = \frac{1}{1 + r_0(2, 3)} = 0.925865$$

⚹

Coupon Bonds

Given the prices of zero-coupon bonds—column (1) in Table 7.1—we can price coupon bonds. We can also compute the **par coupon**—column (4) in Table 7.1—the coupon rate at which a bond will be priced at par. To describe a coupon bond, we need to know the date at which the bond is being priced, the start and end date of the bond payments, the number and amount of the payments, and the amount of principal. Some practical complexities associated with coupon bonds, not essential for our purposes, are discussed in Appendix 7.A.

We will let $B_t(t_1, t_2, c, n)$ denote the time t price of a bond that is issued at t_1, matures at t_2, pays a coupon of c per dollar of maturity payment, and makes n evenly spaced payments over the life of the bond, beginning at time $t_1 + (t_2 - t_1)/n$. We will assume the maturity payment is \$1. If the maturity payment is different than \$1, we can just multiply all payments by that amount.

Since the price of a bond is the present value of its payments, at issuance time t the price of a bond maturing at T must satisfy

$$B_t(t, T, c, n) = \sum_{i=1}^{n} c P_t(t, t_i) + P_t(t, T) \tag{7.5}$$

where $t_i = t + i(T - t)/n$, with i being the index in the summation. Using equation (7.5), we can solve for the coupon as

$$c = \frac{B_t(t, T, c, n) - P_t(t, T)}{\sum_{i=1}^{n} P_t(t, t_i)}$$

A par bond has $B_t = 1$, so the coupon on a par bond is given by

$$\boxed{c = \frac{1 - P_t(t, T)}{\sum_{i=1}^{n} P_t(t, t_i)}} \tag{7.6}$$

Example 7.2 Using the information in Table 7.1, the coupon on a 3-year coupon bond that sells at par is

$$c = \frac{1 - 0.816298}{0.943396 + 0.881659 + 0.816298}$$
$$= 6.95485\%$$

Equation (7.5) computes the bond price by discounting each bond payment at the rate appropriate for a cash flow with that particular maturity. For example, in equation (7.5), the coupon occuring at time t_i is discounted using the zero-coupon bond price $P_t(t, t_i)$. An alternative way to write the bond price is using the yield to maturity to discount all payments. Suppose the bond makes m payments per year. Denoting the per-period yield to maturity as y_m, we have

$$B_t(t, T, c, n) = \sum_{i=1}^{n} \frac{c}{(1 + y_m)^i} + \frac{1}{(1 + y_m)^n} \tag{7.7}$$

It is common to compute the quoted annualized yield to maturity, y, as $y = m \times y_m$. Government bonds, for example, make two coupon payments per year, so the annualized yield to maturity is twice the semiannual yield to maturity.

The difference between equation (7.5) and equation (7.7) is that in equation (7.5), each coupon payment is discounted at the appropriate rate for a cash flow occurring at that time. In equation (7.7), one rate is used to discount all cash flows. By definition, the two expresssions give the same price. However, equation (7.7) can be misleading, since the yield to maturity, y_m, is not the return an investor earns by buying and holding a bond. Moreover, equation (7.7) provides no insight into how the cash flows from a bond can be replicated with zero-coupon bonds.

Zeros from Coupons

We have started with zero-coupon bond prices and deduced the prices of coupon bonds. In practice, the situation is often the reverse: We observe prices of coupon bonds and must infer prices of zero-coupon bonds. This procedure in which zero coupon bond prices are deduced from a set of coupon bond prices is called **bootstrapping.**

Suppose we observe the par coupons in Table 7.1. We can then infer the first zero-coupon bond price from the first coupon bond as follows:

$$1 = (1 + 0.06) P(0, 1)$$

This implies that $P(0, 1) = 1/1.06 = 0.943396$. Using the second par coupon bond with a coupon rate of 6.48423% gives us

$$1 = 0.0648423 P(0, 1) + 1.0648423 P(0, 2)$$

Since we know $P(0, 1) = 0.943396$, we can solve for $P(0, 2)$:

$$P(0, 2) = \frac{1 - 0.0648423 \times 0.943396}{1.0648423}$$
$$= 0.881659$$

Finally, knowing $P(0, 1)$ and $P(0, 2)$, we can solve for $P(0, 3)$ using the 3-year par coupon bond with a coupon of 6.95485%:

$$1 = (0.0695485 \times P(0, 1)) + (0.0695485 \times P(0, 2)) + (1.0695485 \times P(0, 3))$$

which gives us

$$P(0, 3) = \frac{1 - (0.0695485 \times 0.943396) - (0.0695485 \times 0.881659)}{1.0695485}$$
$$= 0.816298$$

There is nothing about the procedure that requires the bonds to trade at par. In fact, we do not even need the bonds to all have different maturities. For example, if we had a 1-year bond and two different 3-year bonds, we could still solve for the three zero-coupon bond prices by solving simultaneous equations.

Interpreting the Coupon Rate

A coupon rate—for example the 6.95485% coupon on the 3-year bond—determines the cash flows the bondholder receives. However, except in special cases, it does not correspond to the rate of return that an investor actually earns by holding the bond.

Suppose for a moment that interest rates are certain; i.e., the implied forward rates in Table 7.1 are the rates that will actually occur in years 1 and 2. Imagine that we buy the 3-year bond and hold it to maturity, reinvesting all coupons as they are paid. What rate of return do we earn? Before going through the calculations, let's stop and discuss the intuition. We are going to invest an amount at time 0 and to reinvest all coupons by buying more bonds, and we will not withdraw any cash until time 3. *In effect, we are constructing a 3-year zero-coupon bond.* Thus, we should earn the same return as on a 3-year zero: 7%. This buy-and-hold return is different than the yield to maturity of 6.95485%. The coupon payment is set to make a par bond fairly priced, but it is not actually the return we earn on the bond except in the special case when the interest rate is constant over time.

Consider first what would happen if interest rates were certain, we bought the 3-year bond with a $100 principal and a coupon of 6.95485%, and we held it for 1 year. The price at the end of the year would be

$$B_1 = \frac{6.95485}{1.0700237} + \frac{106.95485}{(1.0700237)(1 + 0.0800705)}$$
$$= 99.04515$$

The 1-period return is thus

$$\text{1-period return} = \frac{6.95485 + 99.04515}{100} - 1$$
$$= 0.06$$

We earn 6%, since that is the 1-year interest rate. Problem 7.13 asks you to compute your 2-year return on this investment.

By year 3, we have received three coupons, two of which have been reinvested at the implied forward rate. The total value of reinvested bond holdings at year 3 is

$$6.95485 \times [(1.0700237)(1.0800705) + (1.0800705) + 1] + 100 = 122.5043$$

The 3-year yield on the bond is thus

$$\left(\frac{122.5043}{100}\right)^{1/3} - 1 = 0.07$$

As we expected, this is equal to the 7% yield on the 3-year zero and different from the coupon rate.

This discussion assumed that interest rates are certain. Suppose that we buy and hold the bond, reinvesting the coupons, and that interest rates are not certain. Can we still expect to earn a return of 7%? The answer is yes if we use interest rate forward contracts to guarantee the rate at which we can reinvest coupon proceeds. Otherwise, the answer in general is no.

The belief that the implied forward interest rate equals the expected future spot interest rate is a version of the **expectations hypothesis.** We saw in Chapters 5 and 6 that forward prices are biased predictors of future spot prices when the underlying asset has a risk premium; the same is true for forward interest rates. When you own a coupon bond, the rate at which you will be able to reinvest coupons is uncertain. If the resulting risk carries a risk premium, then the expected return to holding the bond will not equal the 7% return calculated by assuming interest rates are certain. The expectations hypothesis will generally not hold, and you should not expect implied forward interest rates to be unbiased predictors of future interest rates.

In practice you can guarantee the 7% return by using forward rate agreements to lock in the interest rate for each of the reinvested coupons. We discuss forward rate agreements in Section 7.2.

Continuously Compounded Yields

Any interest rate can be quoted as either an effective annual rate or a continuously compounded rate. (Or in a variety of other ways, such as a semiannually compounded rate, which is common with bonds. See Appendix 7.A.) Column (5) in Table 7.1 presents the continuously compounded equivalents of the rates in the "zero yield" column.

In general, if we have a zero-coupon bond paying $1 at maturity, we can write its price in terms of an annualized continuously compounded yield, $r^{cc}(0, t)$, as[3]

$$P(0, t) = e^{-r^{cc}(0,t)t}$$

....

[3] In future chapters we will denote continuously compounded interest rates simply as r, without the cc superscript.

Thus, if we observe the price, we can solve for the yield as

$$r^{cc}(0, t) = \frac{1}{t} \ln[1/P(0, t)]$$

We can compute the continuously compounded 3-year zero yield, for example, as

$$\frac{1}{3} \ln(1/0.816298) = 0.0676586$$

Alternatively, we can obtain the same answer using the 3-year zero yield of 7%:

$$\ln(1 + 0.07) = 0.0676586$$

Any of the zero yields or implied forward yields in Table 7.1 can be computed as effective annual or continuously compounded. The choice hinges on convention and ease of calculation.

7.2 FORWARD RATE AGREEMENTS, EURODOLLARS, AND HEDGING

We now consider the problem of a borrower who wishes to hedge against increases in the cost of borrowing. We consider a firm expecting to borrow $100m for 91 days, beginning 120 days from today, in June. This is the borrowing date. The loan will be repaid in September on the loan repayment date. In the examples we will suppose that the effective quarterly interest rate at that time can be either 1.5% or 2%, and that the implied June 91-day forward rate (the rate from June to September) is 1.8%. Here is the risk faced by the borrower, assuming no hedging:

	120 days	**211 days**	
		$r_{\text{quarterly}} = \mathbf{1.5\%}$	$r_{\text{quarterly}} = \mathbf{2\%}$
Borrow $100m	+100m	−101.5m	−102.0m

Depending upon the interest rate, there is a variation of $0.5m in the borrowing cost. How can we hedge this uncertainty?

Forward Rate Agreements

A **forward rate agreement** (FRA) is an over-the-counter contract that guarantees a borrowing or lending rate on a given notional principal amount. FRAs can be settled either at the initiation or maturity of the borrowing or lending transaction. If settled at maturity, we will say the FRA is settled in arrears. In the example above, the FRA could be settled on day 120, the point at which the borrowing rate becomes known and the borrowing takes place, or settled in arrears on day 211, when the loan is repaid.

FRAs are a forward contract based on the interest rate, and as such do not entail the actual lending of money. Rather, the borrower who enters an FRA is paid if a reference rate is above the FRA rate, and the borrower pays if the reference rate is below the FRA rate. The actual borrowing is conducted by the borrower independently of the FRA. We will suppose that the reference rate used in the FRA is the same as the actual borrowing cost of the borrower.

FRA settlement in arrears   First consider what happens if the FRA is settled in September, on day 211, the loan repayment date. In that case, the payment to the borrower should be

$$\left(r_{\text{quarterly}} - r_{\text{FRA}}\right) \times \text{notional principal}$$

Thus, if the borrowing rate is 1.5%, the payment under the FRA should be

$$(0.015 - 0.018) \times \$100m = -\$300,000$$

Since the rate is lower than the FRA rate, the borrower pays the FRA counterparty.

Similarly, if the borrowing rate turns out to be 2.0%, the payment under the FRA should be

$$(0.02 - 0.018) \times \$100m = \$200,000$$

Settling the FRA in arrears is simple and seems like the obvious way for the contract to work. However, settlement can also occur at the time of borrowing.

FRA settlement at the time of borrowing   If the FRA is settled in June, at the time the money is borrowed, payments will be less than when settled in arrears because the borrower has time to earn interest on the FRA settlement. In practice, therefore, the FRA settlement is tailed by the reference rate prevailing on the settlement (borrowing) date. (Tailing in this context means that we reduce the payment to reflect the interest earned between June and September.) Thus, the payment for a borrower is

$$\text{Notional principal} \times \frac{\left(r_{\text{quarterly}} - r_{\text{FRA}}\right)}{1 + r_{\text{quarterly}}} \tag{7.8}$$

If $r_{\text{quarterly}} = 1.5\%$, the payment in June is

$$\frac{-\$300,000}{1 + 0.015} = -\$295,566.50$$

By definition, the future value of this is $-\$300,000$. In order to make this payment, the borrower can borrow an extra \$295,566.50, which results in an extra \$300,000 loan payment in September. If on the other hand $r_{\text{quarterly}} = 2.0\%$, the payment is

$$\frac{\$200,000}{1 + 0.02} = \$196,078.43$$

The borrower can invest this amount, which gives \$200,000 in September, an amount that offsets the extra borrowing cost.

If the forward rate agreement covers a borrowing period other than 91 days, we simply use the appropriate rate instead of the 91-day rate in the above calculations.

Synthetic FRAs

Suppose that today is day 0 and we plan to lend money 120 days hence. By using a forward rate agreement, we can guarantee the lending rate we will receive on day 120. In particular, we will be able to invest $1 on day 120 and be guaranteed a 91-day return of 1.8%.

We can synthetically create the same effect as with an FRA by trading zero-coupon bonds. In order to accomplish this we need to guarantee cash flows of $0 on day 0, −$1 on day 120, and +$1.018 on day 211.[4]

First, let's get a general sense of the transaction. To match the FRA cash flows, we want cash going out on day 120 and coming in on day 211. To accomplish this, on day 0 we will need to borrow with a 120-day maturity (to generate a cash outflow on day 120) and lend with a 211 day maturity (to generate a cash inflow on day 211). Moreover, we want the day 0 value of the borrowing and lending to be equal so that there is no initial cash flow. This description tells us what we need to do.

In general, suppose that today is day 0, and that at time t we want to lend $1 for the period s, earning the implied forward rate $r_0(t, t + s)$ over the interval from t to $t + s$. To simplify the notation in this section, $r_0(t, t + s)$ will denote the *nonannualized* percent return from time t to time s. Recall first that

$$1 + r_0(t, t + s) = \frac{P(0, t)}{P(0, t + s)}$$

The strategy we use is to

1. Buy $1 + r_0(t, t + s)$ zero-coupon bonds maturing at time $t + s$.

2. Short-sell 1 zero-coupon bond maturing at time t.

The resulting cash flows are illustrated in Table 7.2, which shows that transactions made on day 0 synthetically create a loan commencing on day t and paying the implied forward rate, $r_0(t, t + s)$, on day $t + s$.

This example can be modified slightly to synthetically create the cash flows from a forward rate agreement that settles on the borrowing date, day t. To make this modification, we sell at time t the bond maturing at time $t + s$. The result is presented in Table 7.3. Note that if we reinvested the FRA proceeds at the market rate prevailing on day t, $r_t(t, t + s)$, we would receive $r_0(t, t + s) − r_t(t, t + s)$ on day $t+s$

Example 7.3   Consider the example above and suppose that $P(0, 211) = 0.95836$ and $P(0, 120) = 0.97561$, which implies a 120-day interest rate of 2.5%. In order to receive $1.018 on day 211, we buy 1.018 211-day zero-coupon bonds. The cost of this

....

[4]The example in the previous section considered locking in a borrowing rate, but in this section we lock in a lending rate; the transactions can be reversed for borrowing.

TABLE 7.2   Investment strategy undertaken at time 0, resulting in net cash flows of −$1 on day t, and receiving the implied forward rate, $1 + r_0(t, t + s)$ at $t + s$. This synthetically creates the cash flows from entering into a forward rate agreement on day 0 to lend at day t.

	Cash Flows		
Transaction	**0**	**t**	**$t + s$**
Buy $1 + r_0(t, t + s)$ zeros maturing at $t + s$	$-P(0, t + s) \times (1 + r_0(t, t + s))$	—	$1 + r_0(t, t + s)$
Short 1 zero maturing at t	$+P(0, t)$	-1	—
Total	0	-1	$1 + r_0(t, t + s)$

TABLE 7.3   Example of synthetic FRA. The transactions in this table are exactly those in Table 7.2, except that all bonds are sold at time t.

	Cash Flows	
Transaction	**0**	**t**
Buy $1 + r_0(t, t + s)$ zeros maturing at $t + s$	$-P(0, t + s) \times [1 + r_0(t, t + s)]$	$\frac{1+r_0(t,t+s)}{1+r_t(t,t+s)}$
Short 1 zero maturing at t	$+P(0, t)$	-1
Total	0	$\frac{r_0(t,t+s)-r_t(t,t+s)}{1+r_t(t,t+s)}$

is

$$1.018 \times P(0, 211) = \$0.97561$$

In order to have zero cash flow initially and a cash outflow on day 120, we borrow 0.97561, with a 120-day maturity. This entails borrowing one 120-day bond, since

$$\frac{0.97561}{P(0, 120)} = 1$$

The result on day 120 is that we pay $1 to close the short position on the 120-day bond, and on day 211 we receive $1.018 since we bought that many 211-day bonds.   🌊

To summarize, we have shown that an FRA is just like the stock and currency forwards we have considered, both with respect to pricing and synthesizing. If at time 0 we want to lock in a ~~borrowing~~ *lending* rate from time t to time $t + s$, we can create a rate forward synthetically by buying the underlying asset (the bond maturing at $t + s$) and borrowing (shorting) the bond maturing at day t.

In general, we have the following conclusions concerning a rate forward covering the period t_1 to t_2:

- The forward rate we can obtain is the implied forward rate—i.e., $r_{t_0}(t_1, t_2) = P_{t_0}(t_0, t_1)/P_{t_0}(t_0, t_2) - 1$.

- We can synthetically create the payoff to an FRA, $\frac{r_{t_0}(t_1,t_2)-r_{t_1}(t_1,t_2)}{1+r_{t_1}(t_1,t_2)}$, by borrowing to buy the ~~prepaid forward~~ *Bond maturing at $t=2$*, i.e., by

    1. Buying $1 + r_{t_0}(t_1, t_2)$ of the zero-coupon bond maturing on day t_2, and

    2. Shorting 1 zero-coupon bond maturing on day t_1.

Eurodollar Futures

Eurodollar futures contracts are similar to FRAs in that they can be used to guarantee a borrowing rate. There are subtle differences between FRAs and Eurodollar contracts, however, that are important to understand.

Let's consider again the example in which we wish to guarantee a borrowing rate for a \$100m loan from June to September. Suppose the June Eurodollar futures price is 92.8. Implied 3-month LIBOR is $\frac{100-92.8}{4} = 1.8\%$ over 3 months. As we saw in Chapter 5, the payoff on a single short Eurodollar contract at expiration will be[5]

$$[92.8 - (100 - r_{\text{LIBOR}})] \times 100 \times \$25$$

Thus, the payoff on the Eurodollar contract compensates us for differences between the implied rate (1.8%) and actual LIBOR at expiration.

To illustrate hedging with this contract we again consider two possible 3-month borrowing rates in June: 1.5% or 2%. If the interest rate is 1.5%, borrowing cost on \$100m will be \$1.5m, payable in September. If the interest rate is 2%, borrowing cost will be \$2m.

Suppose that we were to short 100 Eurodollar futures contracts. Ignoring marking-to-market prior to June, if the 3-month rate in June is 1.5%, the Eurodollar futures price will be 94. The payment is

$$[(92.8 - 94) \times 100 \times \$25] \times 100 = -\$300,000$$

We multiply by 100 twice: Once to account for 100 contracts, and the second time to convert the change in the futures price to basis points. Similarly, if the borrowing rate

---

[5]This calculation treats the Eurodollar contract as if it were a forward contract, ignoring the issues associated with daily settlement, discussed in Appendix 5.B.

is 2%, we have

$$[(92.8 - 92) \times 100 \times \$25] \times 100 = \$200,000$$

This is like the payment on an FRA paid in arrears, except that the futures contract settles in June, but our interest expense is not paid until September. Thus we have 3 months to earn or pay interest on our Eurodollar gain or loss before we actually have to make the interest payment.

Recall that when the FRA settles on the borrowing date, the payment is the *present value* of the change in borrowing cost. The FRA is thus tailed automatically as part of the agreement. With the Eurodollar contract, by contrast, we need to tail the position explicitly. We do this by shorting fewer than 100 contracts, using the implied 3-month Eurodollar rate of 1.8% as our discount factor. Thus, we enter into[6]

$$\text{Number of Eurodollar contracts} = -\frac{100}{1 + 0.018} = -98.2318$$

Now consider the gain on the Eurodollar futures position. If LIBOR = 6% ($r_{\text{quarterly}} = 1.5\%$), our total gain on the short contracts when we initiate borrowing on day 120 will be

$$98.2318 \times (92.8 - 94) \times \$2500 = -\$294,695$$

If LIBOR = 8% ($r_{\text{quarterly}} = 2.0\%$), our total gain on the contracts will be

$$98.2318 \times (92.8 - 92) \times \$2500 = \$196,464$$

Notice that the amounts are different than with the FRA: The reason is that the FRA payment is automatically tailed using the 3-month rate prevailing in June, whereas with the Eurodollar contract we tailed using 1.8%, the LIBOR rate implied by the initial futures price.

We can now invest these proceeds at the prevailing interest rate. Here are the results on day 211, when borrowing must be repaid. If LIBOR = 6% ($r_{\text{quarterly}} = 1.5\%$), we save \$300,000 in borrowing cost, and the proceeds from the Eurodollar contract are

$$-\$294,695 \times (1.015) = -\$299,115$$

If LIBOR = 8% ($r_{\text{quarterly}} = 2.0\%$), we owe an extra \$200,000 in interest and the invested proceeds from the Eurodollar contract are

$$\$196,464 \times (1.02) = \$200,393$$

Table 7.4 summarizes the result from this hedging position. The borrowing cost is close to 1.8%.

Convexity bias and tailing   In Table 7.4 the net borrowing cost appears to be a little less than 1.8%. You might guess that this is due to rounding error. It is not. Let's examine the numbers more closely.

---

[6]We assume here that it is possible to short fractional contracts in order to make the example exact.

| TABLE 7.4 | Results from hedging $100m in borrowing with 98.23 short Eurodollar futures. |

	Cash Flows			
	June		September	
Borrowing Rate:	1.5%	2%	1.5%	2%
Borrow $100m	+100m	+100m	−101.5m	−102.0m
Gain on 98.23 short Eurodollar contracts	−0.294695m	0.196464m		
Gain plus interest			−0.299115m	0.200393m
Net			−101.799m	−101.799m

If LIBOR = 6%, ($r_{quarterly}$ = 1.5%), we pay $1.5m in borrowing cost, and we lose $299,115 on the Eurodollar contract, for a net borrowing expense of $1.799115m. This is a "profit" from the Eurodollar hedge, relative to the use of an FRA, of $1.8m − $1.799115m = $884.

If LIBOR = 8% ($r_{quarterly}$ = 2.0%), we pay $2.0m in borrowing cost, but make $200,393 on the Eurodollar contract, for a net borrowing expense of $1.799607m. We make a profit, relative to an FRA, of $1.8m − $1.799607m = $393.

It appears that we systematically come out ahead by hedging with Eurodollar futures instead of an FRA. You are probably thinking that something is wrong.

As it turns out, what we have just shown is that *the rate implied by the Eurodollar contract cannot equal the prevailing FRA (implied forward) rate for the same loan.* To see this, consider the borrower perspective: When the interest rate turns out to be high, the short Eurodollar contract has a positive payoff and the proceeds can be reinvested until the loan payment date at the high realized rate. When the interest rate turns out to be low, the short Eurodollar contract has a negative payoff and we can fund this loss until the loan payment date by borrowing at a low rate. Thus the settlement structure of the Eurodollar contract works *systematically* in favor of the borrower. By turning the argument around, we can verify that it systematically works against a lender.

The reason this happens with Eurodollars and not FRAs is that we have to make the tailing decision *before* we know the 3-month rate prevailing on day 120. When we tail by a fixed amount (1.8% in the above example), the actual variations in the realized rate work in favor of the borrower and against the lender. The FRA avoids this by automatically tailing—paying the present value of the change in borrowing cost—using the actual interest rate on the borrowing date.

In order for the futures price to be fair to both the borrower and lender, the rate implicit in the Eurodollar futures price must be higher than a comparable FRA rate. This difference between the FRA rate and the Eurodollar rate is called **convexity bias.** For the most part in subsequent discussions we will ignore convexity bias and treat the

Eurodollar contract and FRAs as if they are interchangeable. The reason is that in many cases the effect is small. In the above example, convexity bias results in a profit of several hundred dollars out of a borrowing cost of $1.8m. For short-term contracts, the effect can be small, but for longer-term contracts the effect can be important.[7]

In practice, convexity bias also matters before the final contract settlement. We saw in Section 5.4 that marking-to-market a futures contract can lead to a futures price that is different from the forward price. When a futures contract is marked to market and interest rates are negatively correlated with the futures price, there is a systematic advantage to being short the futures contract. This leads to a futures price that is greater than the forward price. This is exactly what happens with the Eurodollar contract in this example. When interest rates rise, the borrower receives a payment that can be invested at the higher interest rate. When interest rates fall, the borrower makes a payment that can be funded at the lower interest rate. This works to the borrower's benefit. Marking-to-market prior to settlement is therefore another reason why the rate implied by the Eurodollar contract will exceed that on an otherwise comparable FRA.

LIBOR versus 3-month T-bills   The Eurodollar futures contract is based on LIBOR, but there are other 3-month interest rates. For example, the Treasury-bill futures contract is based on the price of the 3-month Treasury bill. A borrower could use either the Eurodollar contract or the Treasury-bill futures contract to hedge their borrowing rate. Which contract is preferable?

Banks that offer LIBOR time deposits have the potential to default. Thus, LIBOR includes a default premium. (The **default premium** is an increase in the interest rate that compensates the lender for the possibility the borrower will default.) Private companies that borrow can also default, so their borrowing rates will also include a default premium.

....

[7] If future interest rates were known for certain in advance, then it would be possible to perfectly tail the position. However, with uncertainty about rates, the error is due to interest on the difference between the realized rate, $\tilde{r}$, and the forward rate, r_{forward}. Given that we tail by the forward rate, the error is measured by

$$\frac{\tilde{r}\,(\tilde{r}-r_{\text{forward}})}{1+r_{\text{forward}}}$$

The expected error is

$$E\left[\frac{\tilde{r}\,(\tilde{r}-r_{\text{forward}})}{1+r_{\text{forward}}}\right] = \frac{1}{(1+r_{\text{forward}})}\left[E\left(\tilde{r}^2\right)-E\left(\tilde{r}r_{\text{forward}}\right)\right]$$

$$= \frac{\sigma^2}{(1+r_{\text{forward}})}$$

where σ^2 is the variance of the interest rate. Rates in our example can be 2% or 1.5%, so the standard deviation is approximately 25 basis points or 0.0025 and the variance is thus $0.0025^2 = 0.00000625$. Convexity bias is thus

$$\$100\text{m} \times \frac{0.00000625}{1.018^2} = \$603.09$$

The actual average convexity error in the example was ($884 + $393)/2, or $638.5.

The U.S. government, by contrast, is considered unlikely to default, so it can borrow at a lower rate than firms. In addition, in the United States and other countries, government bonds are more liquid than corporate bonds, and this results in higher prices—a *liquidity premium*—for government bonds.[8]

The borrower will want to use the futures contract that has a price that moves in tandem with its own borrowing rate. It makes sense that a private borrower's interest rate will more closely track LIBOR than the Treasury-bill rate. In fact, the spread between corporate borrowing rates and Treasuries moves around a great deal. The problem with hedging borrowing costs based on movements in the T-bill rate is that a private firm's borrowing costs could increase even as the T-bill rate goes down; this can occur during times of financial distress, when investors bid up the prices of Treasury securities relative to other assets (a so-called "flight to quality"). Thus, LIBOR is commonly used in markets as a benchmark, high-quality, private interest rate.

Figure 7.3 shows historical 3-month LIBOR along with the difference between LIBOR and the 3-month T-bill yield, illustrating this variability.[9] It is obvious that the spread varies considerably over time: Although the spread has been as low as a few basis points, twice in the 1990s it exceeded 100 basis points. In September of 1982, when Continental Bank failed, the spread exceeded 400 basis points. A private LIBOR-based

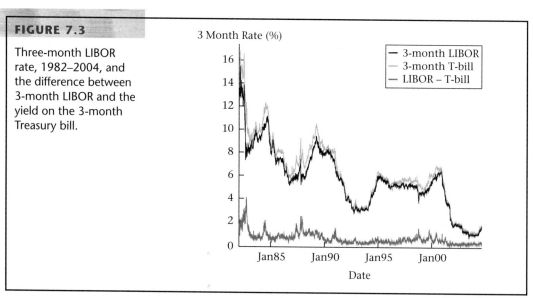

FIGURE 7.3

Three-month LIBOR rate, 1982–2004, and the difference between 3-month LIBOR and the yield on the 3-month Treasury bill.

Source: Datastream.

---

[8] In the United States, another reason for government bonds to have higher prices than corporate bonds is that government bond interest is exempt from state taxation.

[9] The TED spread ("T-Bills over Eurodollars") is obtained by going long T-bill futures and short the Eurodollar futures contract.

borrower who had hedged its borrowing rate by shorting T-bill futures in August of 1982 would by September have lost money on the T-bill contract as Treasury rates declined, while the actual cost of borrowing (LIBOR) would have remained close to unchanged. This example illustrates the value of using a hedging contract that reflects the actual cost of borrowing.

The Eurodollar futures contract is far more popular than the T-bill futures contract. Trading volume and open interest on the two contracts were about equal in the early 1980s. However, in August 2004, open interest on the Eurodollar contract exceeded 6 million contracts, while the T-bill contract had zero open interest. This is consistent with LIBOR being a better measure of private sector interest rates than the T-bill yield.

Interest Rate Strips and Stacks

Suppose a borrower plans to borrow $100m by rolling over 3-month debt for a period of 2 years, beginning in 6 months. Thus, the borrowing will take place in month 6, month 9, month 12, etc. The borrower in this situation faces eight unknown quarterly borrowing rates. We saw in Section 6.12 that an oil hedger could hedge each commitment individually (a strip) or could hedge the entire commitment using one near-dated contract (a stack). The same alternatives are available with interest rates.

One way to hedge is to enter into separate $100m FRAs for each future 3-month period. Thus, we would enter into one FRA for months 6–9, another for months 9–12, etc. This strip hedge should provide a perfect hedge for future borrowing costs.

Depending on market conditions, using a strip is not always feasible. For example, forward prices may not be available with distant maturities, or liquidity may be poor at distant maturities. Rather than individually hedging the borrowing cost of each quarter, an alternative in the context of this example is to use a "stack" of short-term FRAs or Eurodollar contracts to hedge the present value of future borrowing costs.

In the above example, we will be borrowing $100 million per quarter for eight quarters. To effect a stack, we would enter into forward agreements on the 3-month rate, maturing in 6 months, for slightly less than $800 million. (We enter into less than $800 million of forward rate agreements due to tailing for quarters 2 through 8.)

As with the oil example in Section 6.12, the obvious problem with a stacking strategy is basis risk: Quarterly borrowing costs in distant quarters may not move perfectly with borrowing costs in near quarters.

Once we reach the first quarter of borrowing, all of the forward agreements mature and we need to renew our hedge. We now face seven quarters with unknown borrowing costs and therefore we enter into forward agreements for slightly less than $700 million. The constant renewal of the hedging position necessary to effect a stack and roll is exactly like that in the oil example.

7.3 DURATION AND CONVEXITY

An important characteristic of a bond is the sensitivity of its price to interest rate changes, which we measure using **duration.** Duration tells us approximately how much the bond's price will change for a given change in the bond's yield. Duration is thus a summary measure of the risk of a bond, permitting a comparison of bonds with different coupons, times to maturity, and discounts or premiums relative to principal. In this section we also discuss **convexity,** which is another measure related to bond price risk.

Duration

Suppose a bond makes m coupon payments per year for T years in the amount C/m, and pays M at maturity. Let y/m be the per-period yield to maturity (by convention, y is the annualized yield to maturity) and $n = m \times T$ the number of periods until maturity. The price of the bond, $B(y)$, is given by

$$B(y) = \sum_{i=1}^{n} \frac{C/m}{(1+y/m)^i} + \frac{M}{(1+y/m)^n}$$

The change in the bond price for a unit change in the yield, y, is[10]

$$\frac{\text{Change in bond price}}{\text{Unit change in yield}} = -\sum_{i=1}^{n} \frac{i}{m} \frac{C/m}{(1+y/m)^{i+1}} - \frac{n}{m} \frac{M}{(1+y/m)^{n+1}}$$

$$= -\frac{1}{1+y/m} \left[\sum_{i=1}^{n} \frac{i}{m} \frac{C/m}{(1+y/m)^i} + \frac{n}{m} \frac{M}{(1+y/m)^n} \right] \quad (7.9)$$

Equation (7.9) tells us the *dollar* change in the bond price for a change of 1.0 in y. It is natural to scale this either to reflect a change per percentage point [in which case we divide equation (7.9) by 100] or per basis point [divide equation (7.9) by 10,000]. Equation (7.9) divided by 10,000 is also known as the **price value of a basis point** (PVBP). To interpret PVBP for a bond, we need to know the par value of the bond.

Example 7.4 Consider the 3-year zero-coupon bond in Table 7.1 with a yield to maturity of 7%. The bond price per $100 of maturity value is $\$100/1.07^3 = \$81.62979$. At a yield of 7.01%, one basis point higher, the bond price is $\$100/1.0701^3 = \$81.60691$, a change of $-\$0.02288$ per $100 of maturity value.

As an alternative way to derive the price change, we can compute equation (7.9) with $C = 0$, $M = \$100$, $n = 3$, and $m = 1$ to obtain

$$-\frac{1}{1.07} \times 3 \times \frac{\$100}{1.07^3} = -\$228.87$$

In order for this to reflect a change of 1 basis point, we divide by 10,000 to obtain $-\$228.87/10,000 = -\$0.02289$, almost equal to the actual bond price change. This illustrates the importance of scaling equation (7.9) appropriately. ❧

---

[10]This is obtained by computing the derivative of the bond price with respect to the yield, $dB(y)/dy$.

When comparing bonds with different prices and par values, it is helpful to have a measure of price sensitivity expressed *per dollar of bond price*. We obtain this by dividing equation (7.9) by the bond price, $B(y)$ and multiplying by -1. This gives us a measure known as **modified duration,** which is the *percentage* change in the bond price for a unit change in the yield:

$$\text{Modified duration} = -\frac{\text{Change in bond price}}{\text{Unit change in yield}} \times \frac{1}{B(y)}$$

$$= \frac{1}{B(y)} \frac{1}{1+y/m} \left[\sum_{i=1}^{n} \frac{i}{m} \frac{C/m}{(1+y/m)^i} + \frac{n}{m} \frac{M}{(1+y/m)^n} \right] \quad (7.10)$$

We obtain another measure of bond price risk—**Macaulay duration**—by multiplying equation (7.10) by $1 + y/m$.[11] This puts both bond price and yield changes in percentage terms and gives us an expression with a clear interpretation:

$$\text{Macaulay duration} = -\frac{\text{Change in bond price}}{\text{Unit change in yield}} \times \frac{1+y/m}{B(y)}$$

$$= \frac{1}{B(y)} \left[\sum_{i=1}^{n} \frac{i}{m} \frac{C/m}{(1+y/m)^i} + \frac{n}{m} \frac{M}{(1+y/m)^n} \right] \quad (7.11)$$

To interpret this expression, note that $(C/m)/(1+y/m)^i$ is the present value of the ith bond payment, which occurs in i/m years. The quantity $C/m/[(1+y/m)^i B(y)]$ is therefore the fraction of the bond value that is due to the ith payment. Macaulay duration is a *weighted average of the time (number of periods) until the bond payments occur,* with the weights being the percentage of the bond price accounted for by each payment. This interpretation of Macaulay duration as a time-to-payment measure explains why these measures of bond price sensitivity are called "duration."[12] For a zero-coupon bond, equation (7.11) implies that Macaulay duration equals time to maturity.

Macaulay duration illustrates why maturity alone is not a satisfactory risk measure for a coupon bond. A coupon bond makes a series of payments, each with a different maturity. Macaulay duration summarizes bond price risk as a weighted average of these different maturities.

....

[11] This measure of duration is named after Frederick Macaulay, who wrote a classic history of interest rates (Macaulay, 1938).

[12] The Excel duration functions are *Duration* for Macaulay duration and *MDuration* for modified duration.

Example 7.5   Returning to Example 7.4, using equation (7.11), Macaulay duration for the 7% bond is

$$-\frac{-\$228.87}{1} \times \frac{1.07}{\$81.62979} = +3.000$$

Example 7.6   Consider the 3-year coupon bond in Table 7.1. For a par bond, the yield to maturity is the coupon, 6.95485% in this case. For each payment we have

$$\%\text{Payment 1} \quad = \quad \frac{0.0695485}{1.0695485} \quad = 0.065026$$

$$\%\text{Payment 2} \quad = \quad \frac{0.0695485}{(1.0695485)^2} = 0.060798$$

$$\%\text{Payment 3} \quad = \quad \frac{1.0695485}{(1.0695485)^3} = 0.874176$$

Thus, with $n = 3$ and $m = 1$, Macaulay duration is

$$(1 \times 0.065026) + (2 \times 0.060798) + (3 \times 0.874176) = 2.80915$$

The interpretation of the duration of 2.81 is that the bond responds to interest rate changes as if it were a pure discount bond with 2.81 years to maturity. Modified duration is $2.80915/1.0695485 = 2.626482$.

      Since duration tells us the sensitivity of the bond price to a change in the interest rate, it can be used to compute the approximate bond price change for a given change in interest rates. Suppose the bond price is $B(y)$ and the yield on the bond changes from y to $y + \epsilon$, where ϵ is a small change in the yield. The formula for modified duration, D, can be written

$$D = -\frac{[B(y + \epsilon) - B(y)]}{\epsilon} \frac{1}{B(y)}$$

Letting Macaulay duration be denoted by D_{Mac}, we have $D_{\text{Mac}} = D(1 + y)$. We can therefore rewrite this equation to obtain the new bond price in terms of the old bond price and either duration measure:

$$B(y + \epsilon) = B(y) - [D \times B(y)\epsilon] = B(y) - [D_{\text{Mac}}/(1 + y) \times B(y)\epsilon] \qquad (7.12)$$

Example 7.7   Consider the 3-year zero-coupon bond with a price of $81.63 per $100 maturity value. The yield is 7% and the bond's Macaulay duration is 3.0. If the yield were to increase to 7.25%, the predicted price would be

$$B(7.25\%) = \$81.63 - (3/1.07) \times \$81.63 \times 0.0025 = \$81.058$$

The actual new bond price is $100/(1.0725)^3 = \$81.060$. The prediction error is about 0.02% of the bond price.

Although duration is an important concept and is frequently used in practice, it has a conceptual problem. We emphasized in the previous section that a coupon bond is a collection of zero-coupon bonds, and therefore each cash flow has its own discount rate. Yet both duration formulas are computed assuming that all cash flows are discounted by a single artificial number, the yield to maturity. In Chapter 24 we will examine alternative approaches to measuring bond price risk.

Duration Matching

Suppose we own a bond with time to maturity t_1, price B_1, and Macaulay duration D_1. We are considering a short position in a bond with maturity t_2, price B_2, and Macaulay duration D_2. We can ask the question: How much of the second bond should we short-sell in order that the resulting portfolio—long the bond with duration D_1 and short the bond with duration D_2—is insensitive to interest rate changes?

Equation (7.12) gives us a formula for the change in price of each bond. Let N denote the quantity of the second bond. The value of the portfolio is

$$B_1 + N B_2$$

and, using equation (7.12), the change in price due to an interest rate change of ϵ is

$$[B_1(y_1 + \epsilon) - B_1(y_1)] + N[B_2(y_2 + \epsilon) - B_2(y_2)]$$
$$= -D_1 B_1(y_1)\epsilon/(1 + y_1) - N D_2 B_2(y_2)\epsilon/(1 + y_2)$$

where D_1 and D_2 are Macaulay durations. If we want the net change to be zero, we choose N to set the right-hand side equal to zero. This gives

$$N = -\frac{D_1 B_1(y_1)/(1 + y_1)}{D_2 B_2(y_2)/(1 + y_2)} \qquad (7.13)$$

When a portfolio is duration-matched in this fashion, the net investment in the portfolio will typically not be zero. That is, either the value of the short bond is less than the value of the long bond, in which case additional financing is required, or vice versa, in which case there is cash to invest. This residual can be financed or invested in very short-term bonds, with duration approximately zero, in order to leave the portfolio duration matched.

Example 7.8 Suppose we own a 7-year, 6% coupon bond with a yield of 7%, and want to find the duration-matched short position in a 10-year, 8% coupon bond yielding 7.5%. Assuming annual coupon payments, the Macaulay duration and price of the two bonds is 5.882 years and $94.611, and 7.297 years and $103.432, respectively. Thus, if we own one of the 7-year bonds, we must hold

$$-\frac{5.882 \times 94.611/(1.07)}{7.297 \times 103.432/(1.075)} = -0.7408$$

units of the 10-year bond. The short position in the 10-year bond is not enough to pay for the 7-year bond; hence, investment in the portfolio is $1 \times 94.611 - 0.7408 \times 103.432 = 17.99$. If the yield on both bonds increases 25 basis points, the price change of the portfolio is

$$-1.289 + (-0.7408) \times -1.735 = -0.004 \qquad ❦$$

Convexity

The hedge in example 7.8 is not perfect because duration changes as the interest rate changes.[13] *Convexity* measures the extent to which duration changes as the bond's yield changes. The formula for convexity is[14]

$$\text{Convexity} = \frac{1}{B(y)} \left[\sum_{i=1}^{n} \frac{i(i+1)}{m^2} \frac{C/m}{(1+y/m)^{i+2}} + \frac{n(n+1)}{m^2} \frac{M}{(1+y/m)^{n+2}} \right]$$

(7.14)

We can use convexity in addition to duration to obtain a more accurate prediction of the new bond price. When we include convexity, the price prediction formula, equation (7.12), becomes[15]

$$B(y+\epsilon) = B(y) - [D \times B(y) \times \epsilon] + 0.5 \times \text{Convexity} \times B(y) \times \epsilon^2 \qquad (7.15)$$

where D is modified duration. Here is an example of computing a bond price at a new yield using both duration and convexity.

Example 7.9   Consider again example 7.7. We want to predict the new price of a 3-year zero-coupon bond when the interest rate changes from 7% to 7.25%. Using

---

[13]At the original yields, we computed a hedge ratio of 0.7408. Problem 7.19 asks you to compute the hedge ratio that would have exactly hedged the portfolio had both interest rates increased 25 basis points and decreased 25 basis points. The two hedge ratios are different, which means that one hedge ratio would not have worked perfectly.

[14]This is obtained by taking the second derivative of the bond price with respect to the yield to maturity, $d^2 B(y)/dy^2$, and normalizing the result by dividing by the bond price.

[15]If you recall calculus, you may recognize equation (7.12) as a Taylor series expansion of the bond price. See Appendix 13.A.

equation (7.14) with $C = 0$, $m = 1$, and $M = \$100$, convexity of the bond is

$$\text{Convexity} = 3 \times 4 \times \frac{100}{1.07^{(3+2)}} \times \frac{1}{81.63} = 10.4812$$

Using equation (7.15), the price at a yield of 7.25% is

$$B(7.25\%) = \$81.63 - (3/1.07) \times \$81.63 \times 0.0025 + 0.5 \times 10.4812 \times \$81.63 \times 0.0025^2$$
$$= \$81.060$$

The predicted price of \$81.060 is the same as the actual price at a yield of 7.25%, to an accuracy of three decimal points. In example 7.7, the predicted price was slightly lower (\$81.058) than the actual new price. The difference without a convexity correction occurs because the bond's sensitivity to the interest rate changes as the interest rate changes.[16] Convexity corrects for this effect.

Figure 7.4 illustrates duration and convexity by comparing three bond positions that have identical prices at a yield of 10%. Duration is the slope of the bond price graph at a given yield, and convexity is the curvature of the graph. The 10% 10-year bond has the lowest duration and is the shallowest bond price curve. The other two bonds have almost

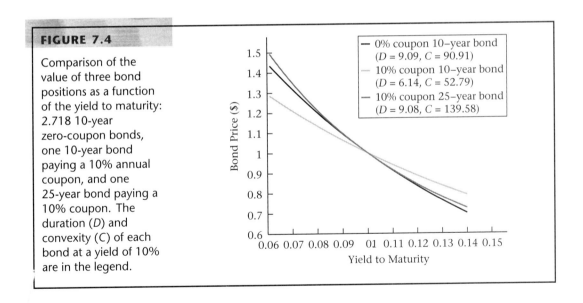

FIGURE 7.4

Comparison of the value of three bond positions as a function of the yield to maturity: 2.718 10-year zero-coupon bonds, one 10-year bond paying a 10% annual coupon, and one 25-year bond paying a 10% coupon. The duration (D) and convexity (C) of each bond at a yield of 10% are in the legend.

— 0% coupon 10-year bond ($D = 9.09$, $C = 90.91$)
— 10% coupon 10-year bond ($D = 6.14$, $C = 52.79$)
— 10% coupon 25-year bond ($D = 9.08$, $C = 139.58$)

[16]You might wonder about this statement since the bond in example 7.7 is a zero-coupon bond, for which Macaulay duration is constant. Notice, however, that the bond price prediction formula, equation (7.12), depends on *modified* duration, which is $D_{\text{Mac}}/(1 + y)$. Modified duration does change with the yield on the bond.

equal durations at a yield of 10% and their slopes are equal in the figure. However, the 25-year bond exhibits greater curvature: Its price is above the 10-year bond at both lower and higher yields. This greater curvature is what it means for the 25-year bond to have greater convexity.

The idea that using both duration and convexity provides a more accurate model of bond price changes is not particular to bonds, but it pertains to options as well. This is our first glimpse of a crucial idea in derivatives that will appear again in Chapter 13 when we discuss delta-gamma approximations, as well as throughout the book.

7.4 TREASURY-BOND AND TREASURY-NOTE FUTURES

The Treasury-note and Treasury-bond futures contracts are important instruments for hedging interest rate risk.[17] Figure 7.5 shows newspaper listings for these futures, and the specifications for the T-note contract are listed in Figure 7.6. The bond contract is similar except that the deliverable bond has a maturity of at least 15 years, or if the bond is callable, has 15 years to first call. The two contracts are similar; we will focus here on the T-note contract. In this discussion we will use the terms "bond" and "note" interchangeably.

The basic idea of the T-note contract is that a long position is an obligation to buy a 6% bond with between 6.5 and 10 years to maturity. To a first approximation we can think of the underlying as being like a stock with a dividend yield of 6%. The futures price would then be computed as with a stock index: The future value of the current bond price, less the future value of coupons payable over the life of the futures contract.

FIGURE 7.5

Treasury-bond and Treasury-note futures listings from the *Wall Street Journal*, July 21, 2004.

Interest Rate Futures

Treasury Bonds (CBT)-$100,000; pts 32nds of 100%

Sept	109-13	109-14	108-07	108-11	-32	114-30	101-24	504,177
Dec	107-28	108-00	107-01	107-04	-32	113-07	100-24	18,209

Est vol 220,782; vol Mon 136,287; open int 522,624, -11,075.

Treasury Notes (CBT)-$100,000; pts 32nds of 100%

Sept	11-115	11-125	110-16	10-185	-24.0	15-095	106-13	1,333,368
Dec	109-30	110-00	09-095	109-10	-24.0	13-045	105-14	35,374

Est vol 723,779; vol Mon 388,611; open int 1,368,752, -17,572.

5 Yr. Treasury Notes (CBT)-$100,000; pts 32nds of 100%

Sept	110-01	110-01	109-13	109-15	-17.0	112-15	106-29	1,162,334

Est vol 408,024; vol Mon 164,023; open int 1,235,146, +3,661.

2 Yr. Treasury Notes (CBT)-$200,000; pts 32nds of 100%

Sept	05-235	105-24	05-162	105-17	-6.7	106-01	04-187	187,818

Est vol 20,322; vol Mon 14,354; open int 187,818, -1,093.

---

[17]The interest rate on the 10-year Treasury note is a commonly used benchmark interest rate, hence the 10-year note futures are important.

FIGURE 7.6

Specifications for the Treasury-note futures contract.

Where traded	CBOT
Underlying	6% 10-year Treasury note
Size	$100,000 Treasury note
Months	Mar, Jun, Sep, Dec, out 15 months
Trading ends	Seventh business day preceding last business day of month. Delivery until last business day of month.
Delivery	Physical T-note with at least 6.5 years to maturity and not more than 10 years to maturity. Price paid to the short for notes with other than 6% coupon is determined by multiplying futures price by a conversion factor. The conversion factor is the price of the delivered note ($1 par value) to yield 6%. Settlement until last business day of the month.

This description masks a complication that may already have occurred to you. The delivery procedure permits the short to deliver any note maturing in 6.5 to 10 years. Hence, the delivered note can be one of many outstanding notes, with a range of coupons and maturities. Which bond does the futures price represent?

Of all bonds that *could* be delivered, there will generally be one that is the most advantageous for the short to deliver. This bond is called the **cheapest to deliver.** A description of the delivery procedure will demonstrate the importance of the cheapest-to-deliver bond.

In fulfilling the note futures contract, the short delivers the bond in exchange for payment. The payment to the short—the *invoice price* for the delivered bond—is the futures price times the conversion factor. The conversion factor is the price of the bond if it were priced to yield 6%. Thus, the short delivering a bond is paid[18]

Invoice price = (Futures price × conversion factor) + accrued interest

Example 7.10 Consider two bonds making semiannual coupon payments. Bond A is a 7% coupon bond with exactly 8 years to maturity, a price of 103.71, and a yield of 6.4%. This bond would have a price of 106.28 if its yield were 6%. Thus its conversion factor is 1.0628.

Bond B has 7 years to maturity and a 5% coupon. Its current price and yield are 92.73 and 6.3%. It would have a conversion factor of 0.9435, since that is its price at a 6% yield. ≩

[18]Appendix 7.A contains a definition of accrued interest.

Now suppose that the futures contract is close to expiration, the observed futures price is 97.583, and the only two deliverable bonds are Bonds A and B. The short can decide which bond to deliver by comparing the market value of the bond to its invoice price if delivered. For Bond A we have

$$\text{Invoice price} - \text{market price} = (97.583 \times 1.0628) - 103.71 = 0.00$$

For Bond B we have

$$\text{Invoice price} - \text{market price} = (97.583 \times 0.9435) - 92.73 = -0.66$$

These calculations are summarized in Table 7.5.

Based on the yields for the two bonds, the short breaks even delivering the 8-year 7% bond and would lose money delivering the 7-year 5% coupon bond (the invoice price is less than the market price). In this example, the 8-year 7% bond is thus the cheapest to deliver.

In general there will be a single cheapest-to-deliver bond. You might be wondering why both bonds are not equally cheap to deliver. The reason is that the conversion factor is set by a mechanical procedure (the price at which the bond yields 6%), taking no account of the current relative market prices of bonds. Except by coincidence, two bonds will not be equally cheap to deliver.

Also, all but one of the bonds must have a negative delivery value. If two bonds had a positive delivery value, then arbitrage would be possible. The only no-arbitrage configuration in general has one bond worth zero to deliver (Bond A in example 7.10) and the rest lose money if delivered. To avoid arbitrage, the futures price is

$$\text{Futures price} = \frac{\text{Price of cheapest to deliver}}{\text{Conversion factor for cheapest to deliver}} \qquad (7.16)$$

TABLE 7.5	Prices, yields, and the conversion factor for two bonds. The futures price is 97.583. The short would break even delivering the 8-year 7% bond, and lose money delivering the 7-year 5% bond. Both bonds make semiannual coupon payments.

Description	8-Year 7% Coupon, 6.4% Yield	7-Year 5%, 6.3% Yield
Market price	103.71	92.73
Price at 6% (conversion factor)	106.28	94.35
Invoice price (futures × conversion factor)	103.71	92.09
Invoice − market	0	−0.66

This discussion glosses over subtleties involving transaction costs (whether you already own a bond may affect your delivery profit calculation) and uncertainty before the delivery period about which bond will be cheapest to deliver. Also the T-note is deliverable at any time during the expiration month, but trading ceases with 7 business days remaining. Consequently, if there are any remaining open contracts during the last week of the month, the short has the option to deliver any bond at a price that might be a week out of date. This provides a delivery option for the short that is also priced into the contract. There are other complications, but suffice it to say that the T-bond and T-note contracts are complex.

The T-bond and T-note futures contracts have been extremely successful. The contracts illustrate some important design considerations for a futures contract. Consider first how the contract is settled. If the contract designated a particular T-bond as the underlying asset, that T-bond could be in short supply, and in fact it might be possible for someone to corner the available supply. (A **market corner** occurs when someone buys most or all of the deliverable asset or commodity.) A short would then be unable to obtain the bond to deliver. In addition, the deliverable T-bond would change from year to year and the contract would become more complicated, since traders would have to price the futures differently to reflect different underlying bonds for different maturity dates.

An alternative scheme could have had the contract cash-settle against a T-bond index, much like the S&P 500. This arrangement, however, introduces basis risk, as the T-bond futures contract might then track the index but fail to track any particular bond.

In the end, settlement procedures for the T-bond and T-note contracts permitted a range of bonds and notes to be delivered. Since a high-coupon bond is worth more than an otherwise identical low-coupon bond, there had to be a conversion factor, in order that the short is paid more for delivering the high-coupon bond.

The idea that there is a cheapest to deliver is not exclusive to Treasury bonds. The same issue arises with commodities, where a futures contract may permit delivery of commodities at different locations or of different qualities.

7.5 REPURCHASE AGREEMENTS

An extremely important kind of forward contract is a repurchase agreement, or **repo.**[19] A repo entails selling a security with an agreement to buy it back at a fixed price. It is effectively a reverse cash-and-carry—a sale coupled with a long forward contract. Like any reverse cash-and-carry, it is equivalent to borrowing. The particular twist with a repo is that the underlying security is held as collateral by the counterparty, who has bought the security and agreed to sell it at a fixed price. Thus, a repo is collateralized borrowing. Repos are common in bond markets, but in principle a repurchase agreement can be used for any asset.

---

[19]For a detailed treatment of repurchase agreements, see Steiner (1997).

Example 7.11   Suppose you enter into a 1-week repurchase agreement for a 9-month $1m Treasury bill. The current price of the T-bill is $956,938, and you agree to repurchase it in 1 week for $958,042. You have borrowed money at a 1-week rate of $958,042/956,938 - 1 = 0.115\%$, receiving cash today and promising to repay cash plus interest in a week. The security provides collateral for the loan.   ≷

The party who initiates the repo owns the asset when the transaction is completed and is therefore the financial owner of the security. During the repo, however, the counterparty owns the bond. Most repos are overnight. A longer-term repurchase agreement is called a **term repo.**

The counterparty is said to have entered into a reverse repurchase agreement, or **reverse repo,** and is short the forward contract. This is a loan of cash for the duration of the agreement with a security held as collateral. It can also be described as a cash-and-carry.

If the borrower does not repay the loan, the lender keeps the security. Thus, the counterparty's view of the risk of the transaction differs according to the quality of the collateral. Collateral with a more variable price and a less liquid market is lower quality from the perspective of the lender. Because collateral quality varies, every security can have its own market-determined repo rate.

Repurchase agreements are most common for government securities, and can be negotiated to require a specific security as collateral—called a *special collateral repurchase agreement*—or with any of a variety of government securities as collateral—called a *general collateral repurchase agreement*. General collateral repos have greater flexibility and hence lower transaction costs.

The repo rate on special collateral repos will generally be below that on general collateral repos. Suppose that there is demand for a specific bond as a speculative investment. The owner of such a bond can engage in a repurchase agreement, and high demand for the bond will drive the repo rate down. A low repo rate means that the original bondholder can earn interest on the cash received for the bond that exceeds the repo rate, thereby profiting from the specialness of the bond.

In addition to a repo rate that reflects collateral quality, dealers can also charge a **haircut,** which is the amount by which the value of the collateral exceeds the amount of the loan. The haircut reflects the credit risk of the borrower. A 2% haircut would mean that the borrower receives only 98% of the market value of the security, providing an additional margin of protection for the counterparty.

Repurchase agreements are frequently used by dealers to finance inventory. In the ordinary course of business a dealer buys and sells securities. The purchase of a security requires funds. A dealer can buy a bond from a customer and then repo it overnight. The money raised with the repo provides the cash needed to pay the seller. The dealer then has a cost of carrying the bond equal to the repo rate.[20] The counterparty on this

---

[20]The repurchase agreement in this example provides financing. The dealer still is the ultimate owner of the bond and thus has price risk that could be hedged with futures contracts.

transaction is an investor with cash to invest short-term, such as a corporation. The investor buys the bond, promising to sell it back. This is lending.

The same techniques can be used to finance speculative positions. Hedge funds, for example, use repurchase agreements. A hedge fund speculating on the price difference between two Treasury bonds can finance the transaction with repos. An example of this is discussed in the Long-Term Capital Management box on page 236.

How do we engage in a transaction like this—long bond A and short bond B—in practice? The answer is that we undertake the following two transactions simultaneously:

The long position: Buy bond A and repo it. Use the cash raised in the repo to pay for the bond (recall that dealers finance inventory in this fashion). When it is time to reverse the repo, sell the bond and use the cash raised from the sale to buy the bond back and close the repo position (think of the sale and close of the repo as happening simultaneously). Note that a low repo rate for this bond works to the arbitrageur's advantage, since it means that the repurchase price of the bond is low. The arbitrageur also benefits from a price increase on the bond.

The short position: Borrow bond B by entering into a reverse repurchase agreement. We receive the bond (collateral for the loan) via the reverse repo, sell it, and use the proceeds to pay the counterparty. At the termination of the agreement, buy the bond back in the open market and return it, being paid the repo rate. Since we receive interest in this transaction, a high repo rate works to our advantage as does a price decrease on the bond.

Since the investor is betting that there will be a reduction in the price difference between the two bonds, it is necessary to enter into both legs of the transaction. The arbitrageur would like a low repo rate on the purchased bond and a high repo rate on the sold bond, as well as a price increase of the purchased bond relative to the short-sold bond.

In practice, haircuts on both bond positions are a transaction cost. Haircuts are a capital requirement imposed by the counterparty, which means that an arbitrageur must have capital to undertake an otherwise self-financing arbitrage transaction. Differences in repo rates on the assets can be an additional transaction cost. Even if the price gap between the two bonds does not close, the arbitrage can be prohibitively costly if the difference in repo rates on the two bonds is sufficiently great. Cornell and Shapiro (1989) document that in one well-known episode of on-the-run/off-the-run arbitrage (see the box on page 236), the repo rate on an on-the-run (short-sold) bond went to zero, making arbitrage costly even though the price gap remained when the on-the-run bond became off-the-run.

CHAPTER SUMMARY

The price of a zero-coupon bond with T years to maturity tells us the value today of $1 to be received at time T. The set of these bond prices for different maturities is the zero-coupon yield curve and is the basic input for present value calculations. There are

Long-Term Capital Management

Repurchase agreements are a common financing strategy, but they achieved particular notoriety during the Long-Term Capital Management (LTCM) crisis in 1998. LTCM was a hedge fund with a luminous roster of partners, including star bond trader John Meriwether, former Federal Reserve Vice Chairman David Mullins, and academics Robert Merton and Myron Scholes, who won the Nobel Prize in Economics while associated with LTCM.

Many of LTCM's strategies involved so-called convergence trades, meaning that they were a bet that the prices of two assets would grow closer together. One well-known convergence trade involved newly issued on-the-run 30-year Treasury bonds, which typically sold at a lower yield than the almost identical off-the-run 29 $\frac{1}{2}$-year Treasury bond. One might bet that the yields of the 30-year and 29 $\frac{1}{2}$-year bonds would converge as the 30-year bond aged and became off-the-run. Traders made this bet by short-selling the on-the-run bond and buying the off-the-run bond. When the on-the-run bond became off-the-run, its yield should (in theory) have equaled that of the other off-the-run bond, and

the price of the two bonds should have converged. The trader would profit from the convergence in price, buying back the former on-the-run bond at its new, cheaper price.

In his book about LTCM, Lowenstein (2000, p. 45) described the trade like this: "No sooner did Long-Term buy the off-the-run bonds than it loaned them to some other Wall Street firm, which then wired cash to Long-Term as collateral. Then Long-Term turned around and used this cash as collateral on the bonds that *it* borrowed. The collateral it paid equaled the collateral it collected. In other words, Long-Term pulled off the entire $2 billion trade *without using a dime of its own cash*." (Emphasis in original.) Many forward contracts, of course, are entered into without a party "using a dime of its own cash." LTCM also reportedly paid small or no haircuts.

When LTCM failed in the fall of 1998, it had many such transactions and thus potentially many creditors. The difficulty of unwinding all of these intertwined positions was one of the reasons the Fed brokered a buyout of LTCM by other banks, rather than have LTCM explicitly declare bankruptcy.

equivalent ways to express the same information about interest rates, including the par coupon rate and implied forward rates.

Forward rate agreements (FRAs) permit borrowers and lenders to hedge the interest rate by locking in the implied forward rate. If the interest rate changes, FRAs require a payment reflecting the change in the value of the interest rate as of the loan's maturity day. Eurodollar contracts are an alternative to FRAs as a hedging mechanism. However, Eurodollar contracts make payment on the initiation date for the loan rather than the maturity date, so there is a timing mismatch between the Eurodollar payment and the interest payment date. This gives rise to convexity bias, which causes the rate implied by the Eurodollar contract to be greater than that for an otherwise equivalent FRA. Treasury bill contracts are yet another possible hedging vehicle, but suffer from basis risk since the change in the government's borrowing rate may be different from the change in the borrowing rate for a firm or individual.

Duration is a measure of a bond's risk. Modified duration is the percentage change in the bond price for a unit change in the interest rate. Macaulay duration is the percentage change in the bond price for a percentage change in the discount factor. Duration is not a perfect measure of bond price risk. A portfolio is said to be duration-matched if it consists of short and long bond positions with equal value-weighted durations. Convexity is a measure of the change in duration as the bond's yield to maturity changes.

Treasury-note and Treasury-bond futures contracts have Treasury notes and bonds as underlying assets. A complication with these contracts is that a range of bonds are deliverable, and there is a cheapest to deliver. The futures price will reflect expectations about which bond is cheapest to deliver.

Repurchase agreements and reverse repurchase agreements are synthetic short-term borrowing and lending, the equivalent of reverse cash-and-carry and cash-and-carry transactions.

FURTHER READING

Basic interest rate concepts are fundamental in finance and are used throughout this book. Some of the formulas in this chapter will appear again as swap rate calculations in Chapter 8. Chapter 15 shows how to price bonds that make payments denominated in foreign currencies or commodities, and how to price bonds containing options. While the bond price calculations in this chapter are useful in practice, concepts such as duration have conceptual problems. In Chapter 24, we will see how to build a coherent, internally consistent model of interest rates and bond prices.

Useful references for bond and money market calculations are Stigum (1990) and Stigum and Robinson (1996). Sundaresan (2002) and Tuckman (1995) are fixed-income texts that go into topics in this chapter in more depth. Convexity bias is studied by Burghardt and Hoskins (1995) and Gupta and Subrahmanyam (2000). Grinblatt and Longstaff (2000) discuss the market for STRIPS and study the pricing relationships between Treasury bonds and STRIPS. The repo market is discussed in Fleming and Garbade (2002, 2003, 2004).

PROBLEMS

7.1. Suppose you observe the following zero-coupon bond prices per $1 of maturity payment: 0.96154 (1-year), 0.91573 (2-year), 0.87630 (3-year), 0.82270 (4-year), 0.77611 (5-year). For each maturity year compute the zero-coupon bond yields (effective annual and continuously compounded), the par coupon rate, and the 1-year implied forward rate.

7.2. Using the information in the previous problem, find the price of a 5-year coupon bond that has a par payment of $1,000.00 and annual coupon payments of $60.00.

7.3. Suppose you observe the following effective annual zero-coupon bond yields: 0.030 (1-year), 0.035 (2-year), 0.040 (3-year), 0.045 (4-year), 0.050 (5-year). For each maturity year compute the zero-coupon bond prices, continuously compounded zero-coupon bond yields, the par coupon rate, and the 1-year implied forward rate.

7.4. Suppose you observe the following 1-year implied forward rates: 0.050000 (1-year), 0.034061 (2-year), 0.036012 (3-year), 0.024092 (4-year), 0.001470 (5-year). For each maturity year compute the zero-coupon bond prices, effective annual and continuously compounded zero-coupon bond yields, and the par coupon rate.

7.5. Suppose you observe the following continuously compounded zero-coupon bond yields: 0.06766 (1-year), 0.05827 (2-year), 0.04879 (3-year), 0.04402 (4-year), 0.03922 (5-year). For each maturity year compute the zero-coupon bond prices, effective annual zero-coupon bond yields, the par coupon rate, and the 1-year implied forward rate.

7.6. Suppose you observe the following par coupon bond yields: 0.03000 (1-year), 0.03491 (2-year), 0.03974 (3-year), 0.04629 (4-year), 0.05174 (5-year). For each maturity year compute the zero-coupon bond prices, effective annual and continuously compounded zero-coupon bond yields, and the 1-year implied forward rate.

7.7. Using the information in Table 7.1,

  a. Compute the implied forward rate from time 1 to time 3.

  b. Compute the implied forward price of a par 2-year coupon bond that will be issued at time 1.

7.8. Suppose that in order to hedge interest rate risk on your borrowing, you enter into an FRA that will guarantee a 6% effective annual interest rate for 1 year on $500,000.00. On the date you borrow the $500,000.00, the actual interest rate is 5%. Determine the dollar settlement of the FRA assuming

  a. Settlement occurs on the date the loan is initiated.

  b. Settlement occurs on the date the loan is repaid.

7.9. Using the same information as the previous problem, suppose the interest rate on the borrowing date is 7.5%. Determine the dollar settlement of the FRA assuming

  a. Settlement occurs on the date the loan is initiated.

  b. Settlement occurs on the date the loan is repaid.

CHAPTER 8

Swaps

Thus far we have talked about derivatives contracts that settle on a single date. A forward contract, for example, fixes a price for a transaction that will occur on a specific date in the future. However, many transactions occur repeatedly. Firms that issue bonds make periodic coupon payments. Multinational firms frequently exchange currencies. Firms that buy commodities as production inputs or that sell them make payments or receive income linked to commodity prices on an ongoing basis.

These situations raise the question: If a manager seeking to reduce risk confronts a risky payment *stream*—as opposed to a single risky payment—what is the easiest way to hedge this risk? One obvious answer to this question is that we can enter into a separate forward contract for each payment we wish to hedge. However, it might be more convenient, and entail lower transaction costs, if there were a single transaction that we could use to hedge a stream of payments.

A **swap** is a contract calling for an exchange of payments over time. One party makes a payment to the other depending upon whether a price turns out to be greater or less than a reference price that is specified in the swap contract. A swap thus provides a means to hedge a stream of risky payments. By entering into an oil swap, for example, an oil buyer confronting a stream of uncertain oil payments can lock in a fixed price for oil over a period of time. The swap payments would be based on the difference between a fixed price for oil and a market price that varies over time.

From this description, you can see that there is a relationship between swaps and forward contracts. In fact, a forward contract is a single-payment swap. It is possible to price a multi-date swap—determine the fixed price for oil in the above example—by using information from the set of forward prices with different maturities (i.e., the strip). We will see that swaps are nothing more than forward contracts coupled with borrowing and lending money.

8.1 AN EXAMPLE OF A COMMODITY SWAP

We begin our study of swaps by presenting an example of a simple commodity swap. Our purpose here is to understand the economics of swaps. In particular we wish to understand how a swap is related to forwards, why someone might use a swap, and how market-makers hedge the risk of swaps. In later sections we present swap-price formulas and examine interest rate swaps, total return swaps, and more complicated commodity swap examples.

An industrial producer, IP Inc., is going to buy 100,000 barrels of oil 1 year from today and 2 years from today. Suppose that the forward price for delivery in 1 year is $20/barrel and in 2 years is $21/barrel. We need interest rates in this discussion, so suppose that annual interest rates are as in Table 7.1 (see page 206): The 1- and 2-year zero-coupon bond yields are 6% and 6.5%.

IP can use forward contracts to guarantee the cost of buying oil for the next 2 years. Specifically, IP could enter into long forward contracts for 100,000 barrels in each of the next 2 years, committing to pay $20/barrel in 1 year and $21/barrel in 2 years. The present value of this cost is

$$\frac{\$20}{1.06} + \frac{\$21}{1.065^2} = \$37.383$$

IP could invest this amount today and ensure that it had the funds to buy oil in 1 and 2 years. Alternatively, IP could pay an oil supplier $37.383, and the supplier would commit to delivering one barrel in each of the next two years. A single payment today for a single delivery of oil in the future is a prepaid forward. A single payment today to obtain *multiple* deliveries in the future is a **prepaid swap.**

Although it is possible to enter into a prepaid swap, buyers might worry about the resulting credit risk: They have fully paid for oil that will not be delivered for up to 2 years. (The prepaid forward has the same problem.) For the same reason, the swap counterparty would worry about a postpaid swap, where the oil is delivered and full payment is made after 2 years. A more attractive solution for both parties is to defer payment until the oil is delivered, while still fixing the total price.

Note that there are many feasible ways to have the buyer pay; any payment stream with a present value of $37.383 is acceptable. Typically, however, a swap will call for equal payments in each year. The payment per year per barrel, x, will then have to be such that

$$\frac{x}{1.06} + \frac{x}{1.065^2} = \$37.383$$

To satisfy this equation, the payments must be $20.483 in each year. We then say that the 2-year swap price is $20.483. *However, any payments that have a present value of $37.383 are acceptable.*

Physical Versus Financial Settlement

Thus far we have described the swap as if the swap counterparty supplied physical oil to the buyer. Figure 8.1 shows a swap that calls for physical settlement. In this case $20.483 is the per-barrel cost of oil.

However, we could also arrange for *financial settlement* of the swap. With financial settlement, the oil buyer, IP, pays the swap counterparty the difference between $20.483 and the spot price (if the difference is negative, the counterparty pays the buyer), and the oil buyer then buys oil at the spot price. For example, if the market price is $25, the

FIGURE 8.1

Illustration of a swap where the oil buyer pays $20.483/year and receives one barrel of oil each year.

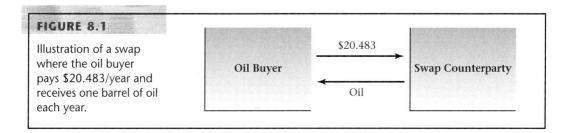

swap counterparty pays the buyer

$$\text{Spot price} - \text{swap price} = \$25 - \$20.483 = \$4.517$$

If the market price is $18, the spot price less the swap price is

$$\text{Spot price} - \text{swap price} = \$18 - \$20.483 = -\$2.483$$

In this case, the oil buyer makes a payment to the swap counterparty. Whatever the market price of oil, the net cost to the buyer is the swap price, $20.483:

$$\underbrace{\text{Spot price} - \text{swap price}}_{\text{Swap payment}} - \underbrace{\text{spot price}}_{\text{Spot purchase of oil}} = -\text{Swap price}$$

Figure 8.2 depicts cash flows and transactions when the swap is settled financially. *The results for the buyer are the same whether the swap is settled physically or financially.* In both cases, the net cost to the oil buyer is $20.483.

We have discussed the swap on a per-barrel basis. For a swap on 100,000 barrels, we simply multiply all cash flows by 100,000. In this example, 100,000 is the **notional amount** of the swap, meaning that 100,000 barrels is used to determine the magnitude of the payments when the swap is settled financially.

FIGURE 8.2

Cash flows from a transaction where the oil buyer enters into a financially settled 2-year swap. Each year the buyer pays the spot price for oil and receives spot price − $20.483. The buyer's net cost of oil is $20.483/barrel.

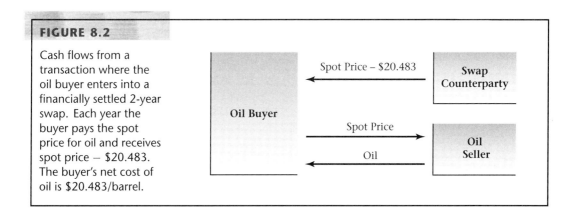

Why Is the Swap Price Not $20.50?

The swap price, $20.483, is close to the average of the two oil forward prices, $20.50. However, it is not exactly the same. Why?

Suppose that the swap price were $20.50. The oil buyer would then be committing to pay $0.50 more than the forward price the first year and would pay $0.50 less than the forward price the second year. Thus, *relative to the forward curve, the buyer would have made an interest-free loan to the counterparty.* There is implicit lending in the swap.

Now consider the actual swap price of $20.483/barrel. Relative to the forward curve prices of $20 in 1 year and $21 in 2 years, we are overpaying by $0.483 in the first year and we are underpaying by $0.517 in the second year. Therefore, the swap is equivalent to being long the two forward contracts, coupled with an agreement to lend $0.483 to the swap counterparty in 1 year, and receive $0.517 in 2 years. This loan has the effect of equalizing the net cash flow on the two dates.

The interest rate on this loan is $0.517/0.483 - 1 = 7\%$. Where does 7% come from? We assumed that 6% is the 1-year zero yield and 6.5% is the 2-year yield. Given these interest rates, 7% is the 1-year implied forward yield from year 1 to year 2. (See Table 7.1.) By entering into the swap, we are lending the counterparty money for 1 year beginning in 1 year. If the deal is priced fairly, the interest rate on this loan should be the implied forward interest rate.

The Swap Counterparty

The swap counterparty is a dealer, who hedges the oil price risk resulting from the swap. The dealer can hedge in several ways. First, imagine that an oil seller would like to lock in a fixed selling price of oil. In this case, the dealer locates the oil buyer and seller and serves as a go-between for the swap, receiving payments from one party and passing them on to the other. In practice the fixed price paid by the buyer exceeds the fixed price received by the seller. This price difference is a bid-ask spread and is the dealer's fee.

Figure 8.3 illustrates how this transaction would work with financial settlement. The oil seller receives the spot price for oil and receives the swap price less the spot price, on net receiving the swap price. The oil buyer pays the spot price and receives the spot price less the swap price. The situation where the dealer matches the buyer and seller is called a **back-to-back transaction** or "matched book" transaction. The dealer bears the credit risk of both parties but is not exposed to price risk.

A more interesting situation occurs when the dealer serves as counterparty and hedges the transaction using forward markets. Let's see how this would work.

After entering the swap with the oil buyer, the dealer has the obligation to pay the spot price and receive the swap price. If the spot price rises, the dealer can lose money. The dealer has a short position in 1- and 2-year oil.

The natural hedge for the dealer is to enter into long forward or futures contracts to offset this short exposure. Table 8.1 illustrates how this strategy works. As we discussed earlier, there is an implicit loan in the swap and this is apparent in Table 8.1. The net

FIGURE 8.3

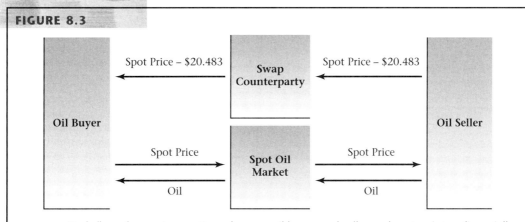

Cash flows from a transaction where an oil buyer and seller each enters into a financially settled 2-year swap. The buyer pays the spot price for oil and receives spot price − $20.483 each year as a swap payment. The oil seller receives the spot price for oil and receives $20.483 − spot price as a swap payment.

TABLE 8.1   Positions and cash flows for a dealer who has an obligation to receive the fixed price in an oil swap and who hedges the exposure by going long year 1 and year 2 oil forwards.

Year	Payment from Oil Buyer	Long Forward	Net
1	$20.483 − Year 1 spot price	Year 1 spot price − $20	$0.483
2	$20.483 − Year 2 spot price	Year 2 spot price − $21	−$0.517

cash flow for the hedged dealer is a loan, where the dealer receives cash in year 1 and repays it in year 2.

This example shows that *hedging the oil price risk in the swap does not fully hedge the position*. The dealer also has interest rate exposure. If interest rates fall, the dealer will not be able to earn a sufficient return from investing $0.483 in year 1 to repay $0.517 in year 2. Thus, in addition to entering oil forwards, it would make sense for the dealer to use Eurodollar contracts or forward rate agreements to hedge the resulting interest rate exposure.

The box on p. 252 shows an extreme example of a hedged transaction—allegedly used to hide debt and manipulate earnings—involving Enron and J. P. Morgan Chase.

Enron's Hidden Debt

When energy giant Enron collapsed in the fall of 2001, there were charges that other companies had helped Enron mislead investors. In July 2003, the Securities and Exchange Commission announced that J. P. Morgan Chase and Citigroup had each agreed to pay more than $100 million to settle allegations that they had helped Enron commit fraud. Specifically, the SEC alleged that both banks had helped Enron characterize loan proceeds as operating income.

The basic outline of the transaction with J. P. Morgan Chase is as follows. Enron entered into "prepaid forward sales contracts" (essentially a prepaid swap) with an entity called Mahonia; Enron received a lump-sum payment and agreed to deliver natural gas in the future. Mahonia in turn received a lump-sum payment from Chase and agreed to deliver natural gas in the future. Chase, which controlled Mahonia, then hedged its Mahonia transaction with Enron. With all transactions netted out, Enron had no commodity exposure, and received its lump-sum initial payment from Mahonia in exchange for making future fixed installment payments to Chase. In other words, Enron in effect had a loan with Chase. Not only did Enron not record debt from these transactions, but the company reported operating income. The transaction is illustrated in the figure below.

The SEC complaint included a revealing excerpt from internal Chase e-mail:

> WE ARE MAKING DISGUISED LOANS, USUALLY BURIED IN COMMODITIES OR EQUITIES DERIVATIVES (AND I'M SURE IN OTHER AREAS). WITH AFEW [sic] EXCEPTIONS, THEY ARE UNDERSTOOD TO BE DISGUISED LOANS AND APPROVED AS SUCH. (Capitalization in the original.)

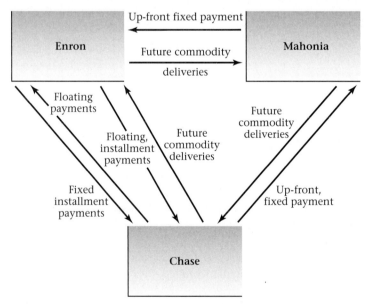

Source: Securities and Exchange Commission.

The Market Value of a Swap

When the buyer first enters the swap, its market value is zero, meaning that either party could enter or exit the swap without having to pay anything to the other party (apart from commissions and bid-ask spreads). From the oil buyer's perspective, the swap consists of two forward contracts plus an agreement to lend money at the implied forward rate of 7%. The forward contracts and forward rate agreement have zero value, so the swap does as well.

Once the swap is struck, however, its market value will generally no longer be zero, for two reasons. First, the forward prices for oil and interest rates will change over time. New swaps would no longer have a fixed price of $20.483; hence, one party will owe money to the other should one party wish to exit or *unwind* the swap.

Second, even if oil and interest rate forward prices do not change, the value of the swap will remain zero only *until the first swap payment is made*. Once the first swap payment is made, the buyer has overpaid by $0.483 relative to the forward curve, and hence, in order to exit the swap, the counterparty would have to pay the oil buyer $0.483. Thus, even if prices do not change, the market value of swaps can change over time due to the implicit borrowing and lending.

A buyer wishing to exit the swap could negotiate terms with the original counterparty to eliminate the swap obligation. An alternative is to leave the original swap in place and enter into an offsetting swap with whoever offers the best price. The original swap called for the oil buyer to pay the fixed price and receive the floating price; the offsetting swap has the buyer receive the fixed price and pay floating. The original obligation would be cancelled except to the extent that the fixed prices are different. However, the difference is known, so oil price risk is eliminated. (There is still credit risk when the original swap counterparty and the counterparty to the offsetting swap are different. This could be a reason for the buyer to prefer offsetting the swap with the original counterparty.)

To see how a swap can change in value, suppose that immediately after the buyer enters the swap, the forward curve for oil rises by $2 in years 1 and 2. Thus, the year-1 forward price becomes $22 and the year-2 forward price becomes $23. The original swap will no longer have a zero market value.

Assuming interest rates are unchanged, the new swap price is $22.483. (Problem 8.1 asks you to verify this.) The buyer could unwind the swap at this point by agreeing to sell oil at $22.483, while the original swap still calls for buying oil at $20.483. Thus, the net swap payments in each year are

$$\underbrace{(\text{Spot price} - \$20.483)}_{\text{Original swap}} + \underbrace{(\$22.483 - \text{spot price})}_{\text{New swap}} = \$2$$

The present value of this difference is

$$\frac{\$2}{1.06} + \frac{\$2}{(1.065)^2} = \$3.650$$

The buyer can receive a stream of payments worth $3.65 by offsetting the original swap with a new swap. Thus, $3.65 is the market value of the swap.

If interest rates had changed, we would have used the new interest rates in computing the new swap price.

The examples we have analyzed in this section illustrate the fundamental characteristics of swaps and their cash flows. In the rest of the chapter, we will compute more realistic swap prices for interest rates, currencies, and commodities and see some of the ways in which we can modify the terms of a swap.

8.2 INTEREST RATE SWAPS

Companies use interest rate swaps to modify their interest rate exposure. In this section we will begin with a simple example of an interest rate swap, similar to the preceding oil swap example. We will then present general pricing formulas and discuss ways in which the basic swap structure can be altered.

A Simple Interest Rate Swap

Suppose that XYZ Corp. has $200m of floating-rate debt at LIBOR—meaning that every year XYZ pays that year's current LIBOR—but would prefer to have fixed-rate debt with 3 years to maturity. There are several ways XYZ could effect this change.

First, XYZ could change their interest rate exposure by retiring the floating-rate debt and issuing fixed-rate debt in its place. However, an actual purchase and sale of debt has transaction costs.

Second, they could enter into a strip of forward rate agreements (FRAs) in order to guarantee the borrowing rate for the remaining life of the debt. Since the FRA for each year will typically carry a different interest rate, the company will lock in a different rate each year and, hence, the company's borrowing cost will vary over time, even though it will be fixed in advance.

A third alternative is to obtain interest rate exposure equivalent to that of fixed rate debt by entering into a swap. XYZ is already paying a floating interest rate. They therefore want to enter a swap in which they receive a floating rate and pay the fixed rate, which we will suppose is 6.9548%. This swap is illustrated in Figure 8.4. Notice the similarity to the oil swap.

In a year when the fixed 6.9548% swap rate exceeds 1-year LIBOR, XYZ pays 6.9548% − LIBOR to the swap counterparty. Conversely, when the 6.9548% swap rate is less than LIBOR, the swap counterparty pays LIBOR − 6.9548% to XYZ. On net, XYZ pays 6.9548%. Algebraically, the net interest payment made by XYZ is

$$\text{XYZ net payment} = - \underbrace{\text{LIBOR}}_{\text{Floating payment}} + \underbrace{\text{LIBOR} - 6.9548\%}_{\text{Swap payment}} = -6.9548\%$$

The notional principal of the swap is $200m: It is the amount on which the interest payments—and, hence, the net swap payment—is based. The life of the swap is the **swap term** or **swap tenor.**

There are timing conventions with a swap similar to those for a forward rate agreement. At the beginning of a year, the borrowing rate for that year is known.

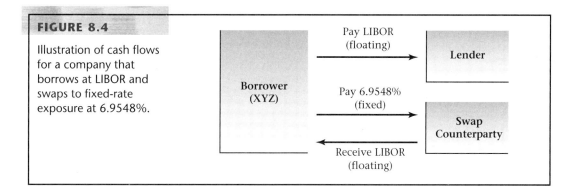

FIGURE 8.4

Illustration of cash flows for a company that borrows at LIBOR and swaps to fixed-rate exposure at 6.9548%.

However, the interest payment on the loan is due at the end of the year. The interest rate determination date for the floating interest payment would therefore occur at the beginning of the period. As with an FRA we can think of the swap payment being made at the end of the period (when interest is due).

With the financially settled oil swap, only net swap payments—in this case the difference between LIBOR and 6.9548%—are actually made between XYZ and the counterparty. If one party defaults, they owe to the other party at most the present value of net swap payments they are obligated to make at current market prices. This means that a swap generally has less credit risk than a bond: Whereas principal is at risk with a bond, only net swap payments are at risk in a swap.

The swap in this example is a construct, making payments *as if* there were an exchange of payments between a fixed-rate and floating-rate bond. In practice, a fund manager might own fixed-rate bonds and wish to have floating-rate exposure while continuing to own the bonds. A swap in which a fund manager receives a floating rate in exchange for the payments on bonds the fund continues to hold is called an **asset swap.**

Pricing and the Swap Counterparty

To understand the pricing of the swap, we will examine it from the perspective of both the counterparty and the firm. We first consider the perspective of the counterparty, who we assume is a market-maker.

The market-maker is a counterparty to the swap in order to earn fees, not to take on interest rate risk. Therefore, the market-maker will hedge the transaction. The market-maker receives the fixed rate from the company and pays the floating rate; the danger for the market-maker is that the floating rate will rise. The risk in this transaction can be hedged by entering into forward rate agreements. We express the time 0 implied forward rate between time t_i and t_j as $r_0(t_i, t_j)$ and the realized 1-year rate as $\tilde{r}_{t_i}$. The current 1-year rate, 6%, is known. With the swap rate denoted R, Table 8.2 depicts the risk-free (but time-varying) cash flows faced by the hedged market-maker.

How is R determined? Obviously a market-maker receiving the fixed rate would like to set a high swap rate, but the swap market is competitive. We expect R to be bid

TABLE 8.2		Cash flows faced by a market-maker who receives fixed and pays floating and hedges the resulting exposure using forward rate agreements.	

Year	Payment on Forward	Net Swap Payment	Net
1	—	$R - 6\%$	$R - 6\%$
2	$\tilde{r}_2 - 7.0024\%$	$R - \tilde{r}_2$	$R - 7.0024\%$
3	$\tilde{r}_3 - 8.0071\%$	$R - \tilde{r}_3$	$R - 8.0071\%$

down by competing market-makers until the present value of the hedged cash flows is zero. In computing this present value, we need to use the appropriate rate for each cash flow: The one-year rate for $R - 6\%$, the two-year rate for $R - 7.0024\%$, and so forth. Using the rate information from Table 7.1, we compute

$$\frac{R - 6\%}{1.06} + \frac{R - 7.0024\%}{1.065^2} + \frac{R - 8.0071\%}{1.07^3} = 0$$

This formula gives us an R of 6.9548%, which from Table 7.1 is the same as the par coupon rate on a 3-year bond! In fact, our swap-rate calculation is a roundabout way to compute a par bond yield. On reflection, this result should be no surprise. Once the borrower has entered into the swap, the net effect is exactly like borrowing at a fixed rate. Thus the fixed swap rate should be the rate on a coupon bond.

Notice that the unhedged net cash flows in Table 8.2 (the "net swap payment" column) can be replicated by borrowing at a floating rate and lending at a fixed rate. In other words, *an interest rate swap is equivalent to borrowing at a floating rate to buy a fixed-rate bond.*

The borrower's calculations are just the opposite of the market-maker's. The borrower continues to pay the floating rate on its floating-rate debt, and receives floating and pays fixed in the swap. Table 8.3 details the cash flows.

Since the swap rate is the same as the par 3-year coupon rate, the borrower is indifferent between the swap and a coupon bond, ignoring transaction costs. Keep in mind

TABLE 8.3		Cash flows faced by a floating-rate borrower who enters into a 3-year swap with a fixed rate of 6.9548%.	

Year	Floating-Rate Debt Payment	Net Swap Payment	Net
1	-6%	$6\% - 6.9548\%$	-6.9548%
2	$-\tilde{r}_2$	$\tilde{r}_2 - 6.9548\%$	-6.9548%
3	$-\tilde{r}_3$	$\tilde{r}_3 - 6.9548\%$	-6.9548%

that the borrower could also have used forward rate agreements, locking in an escalating interest rate over time: 6% the first year, 7.0024% the second, and 8.0071% the third. By using interest rate forwards the borrower would have eliminated uncertainty about future borrowing rates and created an uneven but certain stream of interest payments over time. The swap provides a way to both guarantee the borrowing rate and lock in a constant rate in a single transaction.

Computing the Swap Rate in General

We now examine more carefully the general calculations for determining the swap rate. We will use the interest rate and bond price notation introduced in Chapter 7. Suppose there are n swap settlements, occurring on dates t_i, $i = 1, \ldots, n$. The implied forward interest rate from date t_{i-1} to date t_i, known at date 0, is $r_0(t_{i-1}, t_i)$. [We will treat $r_0(t_{i-1}, t_i)$ as *not* having been annualized; i.e., it is the return earned from t_{i-1} to t_i.] The price of a zero-coupon bond maturing on date t_i is $P(0, t_i)$.

The market-maker can hedge the floating-rate payments using forward rate agreements. The requirement that the hedged swap have zero net present value is

$$\sum_{i=1}^{n} P(0, t_i)[R - r_0(t_{i-1}, t_i)] = 0 \qquad (8.1)$$

where there are n payments on dates $t_1, t_2, \ldots, t_n$. The cash flows $R - r_0(t_{i-1}, t_i)$ can also be obtained by buying a fixed-rate bond paying R and borrowing at the floating rate.

Equation (8.1) can be rewritten as

$$R = \frac{\sum_{i=1}^{n} P(0, t_i) r(t_{i-1}, t_i)}{\sum_{i=1}^{n} P(0, t_i)} \qquad (8.2)$$

The expression $\sum_{i=1}^{n} P(0, t_i) r(t_{i-1}, t_i)$ is the present value of interest payments implied by the strip of forward rates. The expression $\sum_{i=1}^{n} P(0, t_i)$ is just the present value of a $1 annuity when interest rates vary over time. Thus, the swap rate annuitizes the interest payments on the floating-rate bond.

We can rewrite equation (8.2) to make it easier to interpret:

$$R = \sum_{i=1}^{n} \left[\frac{P(0, t_i)}{\sum_{j=1}^{n} P(0, t_j)} \right] r(t_{i-1}, t_i)$$

Since the terms in square brackets sum to one, this form of equation (8.2) emphasizes that the fixed swap rate is a weighted average of the implied forward rates, where zero-coupon bond prices are used to determine the weights.

There is another, equivalent way to express the swap rate. Recall from Chapter 7, equation (7.4), that the implied forward rate between times t_1 and t_2, $r_0(t_1, t_2)$, is given by the ratio of zero-coupon bond prices, i.e.,

$$r_0(t_1, t_2) = P(0, t_1)/P(0, t_2) - 1$$

Therefore equation (8.1) can be rewritten

$$\sum_{i=1}^{n} P(0, t_i)[R - r(t_{i-1}, t_i)] = \sum_{i=1}^{n} P(0, t_i)\left[R - \frac{P(0, t_{i-1})}{P(0, t_i)} + 1\right]$$

Setting this equation equal to zero and solving for R gives us

$$R = \frac{1 - P_0(0, t_n)}{\sum_{i=1}^{n} P_0(0, t_i)} \tag{8.3}$$

You may recognize this as the formula for the coupon on a par coupon bond, equation (7.6), from Chapter 7. This in turn can be rewritten as

$$R \sum_{i=1}^{n} P(0, t_i) + P(0, t_n) = 1$$

This is the valuation equation for a bond priced at par with a coupon rate of R.

The conclusion is that *the swap rate is the coupon rate on a par coupon bond.* This result is intuitive since a firm that swaps from floating-rate to fixed-rate exposure ends up with the economic equivalent of a fixed-rate bond.

The Swap Curve

As discussed in Chapter 5, the Eurodollar futures contract provides a set of 3-month forward LIBOR rates extending out 10 years. It is possible to use this set of forward interest rates to compute equation (8.2) or (8.3). As discussed in Chapter 7, zero-coupon bond prices can be constructed from implied forward rates.

The set of swap rates at different maturities implied by LIBOR is called the *swap curve*. There is an over-the-counter market in interest rate swaps, which is widely quoted. The swap curve should be consistent with the interest rate curve implied by the Eurodollar futures contract, which is used to hedge swaps.[1]

Here is how we construct the swap curve using the set of Eurodollar prices.[2] Column 2 of Table 8.4 lists 2 years of Eurodollar futures prices from June 2004. The next column shows the implied 91-day interest rate, beginning in the month in column 1. For example, using equation (5.19), the June price of 98.5558 implies a June to

---

[1]The Eurodollar contract is a futures contract, while a swap is a set of forward rate agreements. Because of convexity bias, discussed in Chapter 7, the swap curve constructed from Eurodollar futures contracts following the procedure described in this section will be somewhat greater than the observed swap curve. This is discussed by Burghardt and Hoskins (1995) and Gupta and Subrahmanyam (2000).

[2]Collin-Dufresne and Solnik (2001) point out that the credit risk implicit in the LIBOR rate underlying the Eurodollar futures contract is different than the credit risk of an interest rate swap. LIBOR is computed as an average 3-month borrowing rate for international banks with good credit. Banks that experience credit problems are dropped from the sample. Thus, by construction, the pool of banks represented in the Eurodollar contract never experience a credit downgrade. A firm with a swap, by contrast, could be downgraded.

			Implied June 2004 Price of $1	
Maturity Date, t_i	**Eurodollar Futures Price**	**Implied Quarterly Rate, $r(t_i, t_{i+1})$**	**Paid on Maturity Date, t_i, $P(0, t_i)$**	**Swap Rate**
Jun-04	98.555	0.0037	—	1.4611%
Sep-04	98.010	0.0050	0.9964	1.7359%
Dec-04	97.495	0.0063	0.9914	2.0000%
Mar-05	97.025	0.0075	0.9851	2.2495%
Jun-05	96.600	0.0086	0.9778	2.4836%
Sep-05	96.235	0.0095	0.9695	2.6997%
Dec-05	95.910	0.0103	0.9603	2.8995%
Mar-06	95.650	0.0110	0.9505	3.0808%

TABLE 8.4   Three-month LIBOR forward rates implied by Eurodollar futures prices with maturity dates given in the first column. Prices are from June 2, 2004.

Source: Eurodollars futures prices from Datastream.

September quarterly interest rate of

$$(100 - 98.555)\frac{91}{90}\frac{1}{400} = 0.0037\%$$

Column 4 reports the corresponding implied zero-coupon bond price. In the second row, the price is the cost in June of $1 paid in September. The third row is the June cost of $1 paid in December, and so forth. The fourth row is

$$\frac{1}{1.0037} \times \frac{1}{1.0050} \times \frac{1}{1.0063} = 0.9851$$

which is the June cost of $1 paid in March. The December swap rate, expressed as a quarterly rate, is the fixed quarterly interest rate from June through March, with swap payments in June, September, and December (the months in which the quarterly rate prevailing over the *next* 3 months is known). This is computed using equation (8.3):

$$\frac{1 - 0.9851}{0.9964 + 0.9914 + 0.9851} = 0.50\%$$

Multiplying this by 4 to annualize the rate gives the 2.00% in the swap rate column of Table 8.4.

In Figure 8.5 we graph the entire swap curve against quarterly forward rates implied by the Eurodollar curve. The **swap spread** is the difference between swap rates and

FIGURE 8.5

Forward 3-month interest rate curve implied by the Eurodollar strip, swap rates, and constant maturity Treasury yields for June 2, 2004.

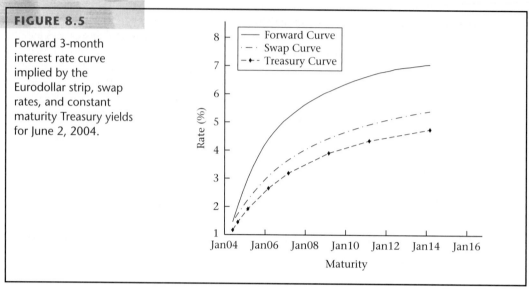

Source: Datastream.

Treasury-bond yields for comparable maturities. Thus, Figure 8.5 also displays yields on government bonds.

The Swap's Implicit Loan Balance

An interest rate swap behaves much like the oil swap in Section 8.1. At inception, the swap has zero value to both parties. If interest rates change, the present value of the fixed payments and, hence, the swap rate will change. The market value of the swap is the difference in the present value of payments between the old swap rate and the new swap rate. For example, consider the 3-year swap in Table 8.3 (see page 256). If interest rates rise after the swap is entered into, the value of the existing 6.9548% swap will fall for the party receiving the fixed payment.

Even in the absence of interest rate changes, however, the swap in Table 8.3 changes value over time. Once the first swap payment is made, the swap acquires negative value for the market-maker (relative to the use of forwards) because in the second year the market-maker will make a net cash payment. Similarly, the swap will have positive value for the borrower (again relative to the use of forwards) after the first payment is made. In order to smooth payments, the borrower pays "too much" (relative to the forward curve) in the first year and receives a refund in the second year. *The swap is equivalent to entering into forward contracts and undertaking some additional borrowing and lending.*

The 10-year swap rate in Figure 8.5 is 5.3986%. We can use this value to illustrate the implicit borrowing and lending in the swap. Consider an investor who pays fixed and receives floating. This investor is paying a high rate in the early years of the swap, and, hence, is lending money. About halfway through the life of the swap, the Eurodollar forward rate exceeds the swap rate and the loan balance declines, falling to zero by the end of the swap. The fixed rate recipient has a positive loan balance over the life of the swap because the Eurodollar futures rate is below the swap initially—so the fixed-rate recipient is receiving payments—and crosses the swap price once. The credit risk in this swap is therefore borne, at least initially, by the fixed-rate payer, who is lending to the fixed-rate recipient. The implicit loan balance in the swap is illustrated in Figure 8.6.

Deferred Swaps

We can construct a swap that begins at some date in the future, but for which the swap rate is agreed upon today. This type of swap is called a **deferred swap.** To demonstrate this type of swap, we can use the information in Table 7.1 to compute the value of a 2-period swap that begins 1 year from today. The reasoning is exactly as before: The swap rate will be set by the market-maker so that the present value of the fixed and

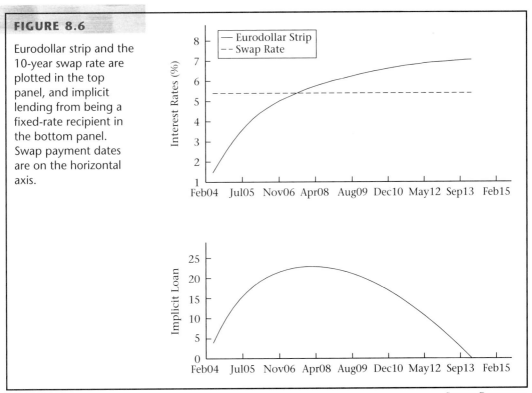

FIGURE 8.6

Eurodollar strip and the 10-year swap rate are plotted in the top panel, and implicit lending from being a fixed-rate recipient in the bottom panel. Swap payment dates are on the horizontal axis.

Source: Datastream.

floating payments is the same. This gives us

$$\frac{R - 0.070024}{1.065^2} + \frac{R - 0.080071}{1.07^3} = 0$$

Solving for R, the deferred swap rate is 7.4854%. In general, the fixed rate on a deferred swap beginning in k periods is computed as

$$R = \frac{\sum_{i=k}^{T} P_0(0, t_i) r_0(t_{i-1}, t_i)}{\sum_{i=k}^{T} P(0, t_i)} \tag{8.4}$$

This can also be written as

$$R = \frac{P(0, t_{k-1}) - P(0, t_n)}{\sum_{i=k}^{n} P(0, t_i)} \tag{8.5}$$

Equation (8.4) is equal to equation (8.2) when $k = 1$.

Why Swap Interest Rates?

Managers sometimes say that they would like to borrow short-term because short-term interest rates are on average lower than long-term interest rates. Leaving aside the question of whether this view makes sense theoretically, let's take for granted the desire to borrow at short-term interest rates. The problem facing the manager is that the firm may be unable to borrow significant amounts by issuing short-term debt.

When a firm borrows by issuing long-term debt, bondholders bear both interest rate risk and the credit risk of the firm. If the firm borrows short-term (for example, by issuing commercial paper), lenders primarily bear credit risk.

In practice, short-term lenders appear unwilling to absorb large issues from a single borrower because of credit risk. For example, money-market mutual funds that hold commercial paper will not hold large amounts of any one firm's commercial paper, preferring instead to diversify across firms. This diversification minimizes the chance that a single bankruptcy will significantly reduce the fund's rate of return.

Because short-term lenders are sensitive in this way to credit risk, a firm cannot borrow a large amount of money short-term without lenders demanding a higher interest rate. By contrast, long-term lenders to corporations—for example, pension funds and insurance companies—willingly assume both interest rate and credit risk. Thus there are borrowers who wish to issue short-term debt and lenders who are unwilling to buy it. Swaps provide a way around this problem, permitting the firm to separate credit risk and interest rate risk.

Suppose, for example, that a firm borrows long-term and then swaps into short-rate exposure. The firm receives the fixed rate, pays the fixed rate to bondholders, and pays the floating rate on the swap. The net payment is the short-term rate, which is the rate the firm wanted to pay.

Credit risk does not vanish; it is still mostly held by the long-term bondholders. The swap counterparty faces credit risk since the firm could go bankrupt when the value of the swap is positive to the counterparty (this would occur if interest rates had risen). The notional principal of the loan is not at risk for the swap counterparty, however, so the credit risk in the swap is less than for a short-term loan. Thus, by swapping its interest rate exposure, the firm pays the short-term interest rate, *but the long-term bondholders continue to bear most of the credit risk.*

If it seems odd to you that the firm can use a swap to convert a high fixed rate into a low floating rate, recognize that any time there is an upward-sloping yield curve, the short-term interest rate is below the long-term interest rate. If you reduce the period for which your borrowing rate is fixed (which happens when you swap fixed for floating), you borrow at the lower short-term interest rate instead of the higher long-term interest rate.

Swaps thus permit separation of two aspects of borrowing: credit risk and interest rate risk. To the extent these risks are acquired by those most willing to hold them, swaps increase efficiency.

Amortizing and Accreting Swaps

We have assumed that the notional value of the swap remains fixed over the life of the swap. However, it is also possible to engage in a swap where the notional value is changing over time. For example, consider a floating-rate mortgage, for which every payment contains an interest and principal component. Since the outstanding principal is declining over time, a swap involving a mortgage would need to account for this. Such a swap is called an **amortizing swap** because the notional value is declining over time. It is also possible for the principal in a swap to grow over time. This is called an **accreting swap.**

Let Q_t be the relative notional amount at time t. Then the basic idea in pricing a swap with a time-varying notional amount is the same as with a fixed notional amount: The present value of the fixed payments should equal the present value of the floating payments:

$$\sum_{i=1}^{n} Q_{t_i} P(0, t_i)[R - r(t_{i-1}, t_i)] = 0 \qquad (8.6)$$

where, as before, there are n payments on dates $t_1, t_2, \ldots, t_n$. Equation (8.6) can be rewritten as

$$R = \frac{\sum_{i=1}^{n} Q_{t_i} P(0, t_i) r(t_{i-1}, t_i)}{\sum_{i=1}^{n} Q_{t_i} P(0, t_i)} \qquad (8.7)$$

The fixed swap rate is still a weighted average of implied forward rates, only now the weights also involve changing notional principal.

Many other structures are possible for swaps based on interest rates or other prices. One infamous swap structure is described in the box on page 264, which recounts the 1993 swap between Procter & Gamble and Bankers Trust.

The Procter & Gamble Swap

In November 1993, consumer products company Procter & Gamble (P&G) entered into a 5-year $200m notional value swap with Bankers Trust. The contract called for P&G to receive a 5.3% fixed rate from Bankers Trust and pay the 30-day commercial paper rate less 75 basis points, plus a spread. Settlements were to be semiannual. The spread would be zero for the first settlement, and thereafter be fixed at the spread as of May 4, 1994.

The spread was determined by the difference between the 5-year constant maturity treasury (CMT) rate (the yield on a 5-year Treasury bond, but a constructed rate since there is not always a Treasury bond with exactly 5 years to expiration) and the price per $100 of maturity value of the 6.25% 30-year Treasury bond. The formula for the spread was

$$\text{Spread} = \max\left(\frac{\frac{5\text{-year CMT\%}}{0.0578} \times 98.5 - \text{price of 30-year bond}}{100}, 0\right)$$

At inception in November 1993, the 5-year CMT rate was 5.02% and the 30-year Treasury price was 102.57811. The expression in the max function evaluated to $-.17$ (-17 basis points), so the spread was zero.

If the spread were 0 on May 4, 1994, P&G would save 75 basis points per year on $200m for 4.5 years, an interest rate reduction worth approximately $7m. However, notice something important: If interest rates rise before the spread determination date, then the 5-year CMT goes up *and the price of the 30-year bond goes down*. Thus, the swap is really a bet on the *direction* of interest rates, not the difference in rates!

The swap is recounted in Smith (1997) and Srivastava (1998). Interest rates rose after P&G entered the swap. P&G and Bankers Trust renegotiated the swap in January 1994, and P&G liquidated the swap in March, with a loss of about $100m. P&G sued Bankers Trust, complaining in part that the risks of the swap had not been adequately disclosed by Bankers Trust.

In the end P&G and Bankers Trust settled, with P&G paying Bankers Trust about $35m. [Forster (1996) and Horwitz (1996) debate the implications of the trial and settlement.] The notion that Procter & Gamble might have been uninformed about the risk of the swap, and if so, whether this should have mattered, was controversial. U.S. securities laws are often said to protect "widows and orphans." Nobel-prize–winning economist Merton Miller wryly said of the case, "Procter is the widow and Gamble is the orphan."

8.3 CURRENCY SWAPS

Firms sometimes issue debt denominated in a foreign currency. A firm may do this as a hedge against revenues received in that currency, or because perceived borrowing costs in that currency are lower. Whatever the reason, if the firm later wants to change the currency to which they have exposure, there are a variety of ways to do so. The firm can use forward contracts to hedge exchange rate risk, or it can use a **currency swap,** in which payments are based on the difference in debt payments denominated in different currencies.

To understand these alternatives, let's consider the example of a dollar-based firm that has euro-denominated 3-year fixed-rate debt. The annual coupon rate is ρ. The firm is obligated to make a series of payments that are fixed in euro terms but variable in dollar terms.

Since the payments are known, eliminating euro exposure is a straightforward hedging problem using currency forwards. We have cash flows of $-\rho$ each year, and $-(1 + \rho)$ in the maturity year. If currency forward prices are $F_{0,t}$, we can enter into long euro forward contracts to acquire at a known exchange rate the euros we need to pay to the lenders. Hedged cash flows in year t are $-\rho F_{0,t}$.

As we have seen in other examples, the forward transactions eliminate risk but leave the firm with a variable (but riskless) stream of cash flows. The variability of hedged cash flows is illustrated in the following example.

Example 8.1 Suppose the effective annual euro-denominated interest rate is 3.5% and the dollar-denominated rate is 6%. The spot exchange rate is \$0.90/€. A dollar-based firm has a 3-year 3.5% euro-denominated bond with a €100 par value and price of €100. The firm wishes to guarantee the dollar value of the payments. Since the firm will make debt payments in euros, it buys the euro forward to eliminate currency exposure. Table 8.5 summarizes the transaction and reports the currency forward curve and the unhedged and hedged cash flows. The value of the hedged cash flows is

$$\frac{\$3.226}{1.06} + \frac{\$3.304}{1.06^2} + \frac{\$100.064}{1.06^3} = \$90$$ 🦑

Example 8.1 verifies what we knew had to be true: Hedging does not change the value of the debt. The initial value of the debt in euros is €100. Since the exchange rate is \$0.90/€, the debt should have a dollar value of \$90, which it has.

As an alternative to hedging each euro-denominated payment with a forward contract, a firm wishing to change its currency exposure can enter into a currency swap,

TABLE 8.5 Unhedged and hedged cash flows for a dollar-based firm with euro-denominated debt.

Year	Unhedged Euro Cash Flow	Forward Exchange Rate	Hedged Dollar Cash Flow
1	−€3.5	0.922	−\$3.226
2	−€3.5	0.944	−\$3.304
3	−€103.5	0.967	−\$100.064

which entails making debt payments in one currency and receiving debt payments in a different currency. There is typically an exchange of principal at both the start and end of the swap. Compared with hedging the cash flows individually, the currency swap generates a different cash flow stream, but with equivalent value. We can examine a currency swap by supposing that the firm in Example 8.1 uses a swap rather than forward contracts to hedge its euro exposure.

Example 8.2   Make the same assumptions as in Example 8.1. The dollar-based firm enters into a swap where it pays dollars (6% on a $90 bond) and receives euros (3.5% on a €100 bond). The firm's euro exposure is eliminated. The market-maker receives dollars and pays euros. The position of the market-maker is summarized in Table 8.6. The present value of the market-maker's net cash flow is

$$\frac{\$2.174}{1.06} + \frac{\$2.096}{1.06^2} - \frac{\$4.664}{1.06^3} = 0$$

❧

The market-maker's net exposure in this transaction is long a dollar-denominated bond and short a euro-denominated bond. Table 8.6 shows that after hedging there is a series of net cash flows with zero present value. As in all the previous examples, the effect of the swap is equivalent to entering into forward contracts, coupled with borrowing or lending. In this case, the firm is lending to the market-maker in the first 2 years, with the implicit loan repaid at maturity.

The fact that a currency swap is equivalent to borrowing in one currency and lending in the other is familiar from our discussion of currency forwards in Chapter 5. There we saw the same is true of currency forwards.

TABLE 8.6   Unhedged and hedged cash flows for a dollar-based firm with euro-denominated debt. The effective annual dollar-denominated interest rate is 6% and the effective annual euro-denominated interest rate is 3.5%.

Year	Forward Exchange Rate ($/€)	Receive Dollar Interest	Pay Hedged Euro Interest	Net Cash Flow
1	0.9217	$5.40	$-€3.5 \times 0.9217$	$2.174
2	0.9440	$5.40	$-€3.5 \times 0.9440$	$2.096
3	0.9668	$95.40	$-€103.5 \times 0.9668$	−$4.664

Currency Swap Formulas

Currency swap calculations are the same as those for the other swaps we have discussed. To see this, consider a swap in which a dollar annuity, R, is exchanged for an annuity in another currency, R^*. Given the foreign annuity, R^*, what is R?

We start with the observation that the present value of the two annuities must be the same. There are n payments and the time-0 forward price for a unit of foreign currency delivered at time t_i is F_{0,t_i}. This gives

$$\sum_{i=1}^{n} \left[R P_{0,t_i} - R^* F_{0,t_i} P_{0,t_i} \right] = 0$$

In calculating the present value of the payment R^*, we first convert to dollars by multiplying by F_{0,t_i}. We can then compute the present value using the dollar-denominated zero-coupon bond price, P_{0,t_i}. Solving for R gives

$$R = \frac{\sum_{i=1}^{n} P_{0,t_i} R^* F_{0,t_i}}{\sum_{i=1}^{n} P_{0,t_i}} \tag{8.8}$$

This expression is exactly like equation (8.2), with the implied forward rate, $r_0(t_{i-1}, t_i)$, replaced by the foreign-currency-denominated annuity payment translated into dollars, $R^* F_{0,t_i}$.

When coupon bonds are swapped, we have to account for the difference in maturity value as well as the coupon payment, which is an annuity. If the dollar bond has a par value of \$1, the foreign bond will have a par value of $1/x_0$, where x_0 is the current exchange rate expressed as dollars per unit of the foreign currency. If R^* is the coupon rate on the foreign bond and R is the coupon rate on the dollar bond, the present value of the difference in payments on the two bonds is

$$\sum_{i=1}^{n} \left[R P_{0,t_i} - R^* F_{0,t_i} P_{0,t_i} / x_0 \right] + P_{0,t_n} (1 - F_{0,t_n} / x_0) = 0$$

The division by x_0 accounts for the fact that a \$1 bond is equivalent to $1/x_0$ bonds with a par value of 1 unit of the foreign currency. The dollar coupon in this case is

$$R = \frac{\sum_{i=1}^{n} P_{0,t_i} R^* F_{0,t_i} / x_0 + P_{0,t_n} (F_{0,t_n} / x_0 - 1)}{\sum_{i=1}^{n} P_{0,t_i}} \tag{8.9}$$

The fixed payment, R, is the dollar equivalent of the foreign coupon plus the amortized value of the difference in the maturity payments of the two bonds. Problem 8.16 asks you to verify that equation (8.9) gives 6% using the assumptions in Tables 8.5 and 8.6.

Other Currency Swaps

There are other kinds of currency swaps. The preceding examples assumed that all borrowing was fixed rate. Suppose the dollar-based borrower issues a euro-denominated loan with a *floating* interest rate. In this case there are two future unknowns: the exchange rate at which interest payments are converted, and—because the bond is floating rate—the amount of the interest payment. Swapping this loan to a dollar loan is still straightforward, however; we just require one extra hedging transaction.

We first convert the floating interest rate into a fixed interest rate with a *euro* interest rate swap. The resulting fixed-rate euro-denominated exposure can then be hedged with currency forwards and converted into dollar interest rate exposure. Given the assumptions in Table 8.6, the euro-denominated loan would swap to a 3.5% floating-rate loan. From that point on, we are in the same position as in the previous example.

In general, we can swap fixed-to-fixed, fixed-to-floating, floating-to-fixed, and floating-to-floating. The analysis is similar in all cases.

One kind of swap that might on its face seem similar is a **diff swap,** short for differential swap. In this kind of swap, payments are made based on the difference in floating interest rates in two different currencies, with the notional amount in a single currency. For example, we might have a swap with a $10m notional amount, but the swap would pay in dollars, based on the difference in a euro-denominated interest rate and a dollar-denominated interest rate. If the short-term euro interest rate rises from 3.5% to 3.8% with the dollar rate unchanged, the annual swap payment would be 30 basis points on $10m, or $30,000. This is like a standard interest rate swap, only for a diff swap, the reference interest rates are denominated in different currencies.

Standard currency forward contracts cannot be used to hedge a diff swap. The problem is that we can hedge the change in the foreign interest rate, but doing so requires a transaction denominated in the foreign currency. We can't easily hedge the exchange rate at which the value of the interest rate change is converted *because we don't know in advance how much currency will need to be converted.* In effect there is quantity uncertainty regarding the foreign currency to be converted. We have seen this kind of problem before, in our discussion of crop yields in Chapter 4 and in our discussion of dollar-denominated Nikkei index futures in Chapter 5. The diff swap is an example of a quanto swap. We will discuss quantos in Chapter 22.

8.4 COMMODITY SWAPS

At the beginning of this chapter we looked at a simple two-date commodity swap. Now we will look at commodity swaps more generally, present the general formula for a commodity swap—showing that the formula is exactly the same as for an interest rate swap—and look at some ways the swap structure can be modified.

The Commodity Swap Price

The idea of a commodity swap, as discussed in Section 8.1, is that we use information in the commodity forward curve to fix a commodity price over a period of time. We can derive the swap price following the same logic as before.

Think about the position of the market-maker, who we suppose receives the fixed payment, $\bar{F}$, makes the floating payment, and hedges the risk of the floating payment. If there are n swap payments, the resulting hedged cash flow is

$$\text{Hedged cash flow for payment } i = \bar{F} - F_{0,t_i}$$

With competitive market-makers, the present value of the net *hedged* swap payments will be zero (ignoring bid-ask spreads):

$$\sum_{i=1}^{n} P(0, t_i) \left(\bar{F} - F_{0,t_i} \right) \tag{8.10}$$

As before, $P(0, t_i)$ is the price of a zero-coupon bond paying \$1 at time t_i. Equation (8.10) implies that the present value of the swap payments equals the present value of the forward curve:

$$\bar{F} \sum_{i=1}^{n} P(0, t_i) = \sum_{i=1}^{n} P(0, t_i) F_{0,t_i}$$

Solving for the swap price, we obtain

$$\bar{F} = \frac{\sum_{i=1}^{n} P(0, t_i) F_{0,t_i}}{\sum_{i=1}^{n} P(0, t_i)} \tag{8.11}$$

Compare equation (8.11) with equation (8.2) for an interest rate swap. *They are the same formula, except that the interest swap rate is a weighted average of implied forward interest rates and the commodity swap price is a weighted average of commodity forward prices.*

Because of seasonality in both price and quantity, natural gas provides an interesting context for examining commodity swaps. The swap curves for June 2002 and June 2004, computed using equation (8.11), are plotted in Figure 8.7.

Swaps with Variable Quantity and Price

It might make sense for a gas buyer with seasonally varying demand (for example, someone buying gas for heating) to enter into a swap in which quantities vary over time. For example, a buyer might want three times the quantity in the winter months as in the summer months. A buyer also might be willing to fix different prices in different seasons—for example, if there is seasonal variation in the price of the output produced using gas as an input. How do we determine the swap price with seasonally varying quantities?

Let Q_{t_i} denote the quantity of gas purchased at time t_i. Once again, we can think about this from the perspective of the competitive market-maker. The market-maker who hedges the swap will enter into varying quantities of forward contracts in different months to match the variable quantity called for in the swap. The zero-profit condition is still that the fixed and floating payments have zero present value, only in this case they

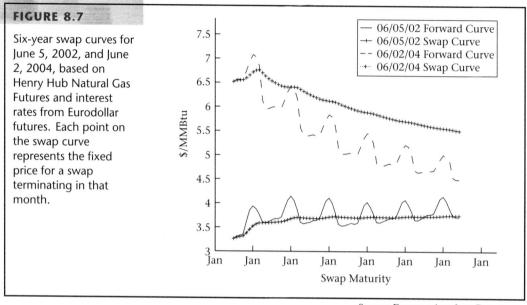

FIGURE 8.7

Six-year swap curves for June 5, 2002, and June 2, 2004, based on Henry Hub Natural Gas Futures and interest rates from Eurodollar futures. Each point on the swap curve represents the fixed price for a swap terminating in that month.

Legend:
— 06/05/02 Forward Curve
-+- 06/05/02 Swap Curve
-- 06/02/04 Forward Curve
·+· 06/02/04 Swap Curve

y-axis: \$/MMBtu (3, 3.5, 4, 4.5, 5, 5.5, 6, 6.5, 7, 7.5)

x-axis: Jan Jan Jan Jan Jan Jan Jan Jan — Swap Maturity

Source: Futures prices from Datastream.

must be weighted by the appropriate quantities. Thus, we have

$$\sum_{i=1}^{n} P(0, t_i) Q_{t_i} \left(\bar{F} - F_{0,t_i} \right)$$

The swap price is thus

$$\bar{F} = \frac{\sum_{i=1}^{n} Q_{t_i} P(0, t_i) F_{0,t_i}}{\sum_{i=1}^{n} Q_{t_i} P(0, t_i)} \tag{8.12}$$

This equation makes perfect sense: If we are going to buy more gas when the forward price is high, we have to weight more heavily the forward price in those months. When $Q_t = 1$, the formula is the same as equation (8.11), when the quantity is not varying.

We can also permit prices to be time-varying. If we let the summer swap price be denoted by $\bar{F}_s$ and the winter price by $\bar{F}_w$, then the summer and winter swap prices can be any prices that satisfy the market-maker's zero present value condition:

$$\bar{F}_s \sum_{i \in \text{summer}} P(0, t_i) Q_{t_i} + \bar{F}_w \sum_{i \in \text{winter}} P(0, t_i) Q_{t_i}$$

$$= \sum_{i \in \text{summer}} P(0, t_i) Q_{t_i} F_{0,t_i} + \sum_{i \in \text{winter}} P(0, t_i) Q_{t_i} F_{0,t_i}$$

The notations $i \in$ summer and $i \in$ winter mean to sum over only the months in those seasons. This gives us one equation and two unknowns, $\bar{F}_w$ and $\bar{F}_s$. Once we fix one of the two prices, the equation will give us the other.

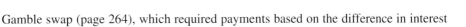

Gamble swap (page 264), which required payments based on the difference in interest rates and bond prices, as well as default swaps.

FURTHER READING

The same formulas used to price swaps will appear again in the context of structured notes, which we will encounter in Chapter 15. We will discuss default swaps in Chapter 25.

Litzenberger (1992) provides an overview of the swap market. Turnbull (1987) discusses arguments purporting to show that the use of swaps can have a positive net present value. Default swaps are discussed by Tavakoli (1998). Because of convexity bias (Chapter 7), the market interest rate swap curve is not exactly the same as the swap curve constructed from Eurodollar futures. This is discussed in Burghardt and Hoskins (1995) and Gupta and Subrahmanyam (2000). The SEC complaint against J. P. Morgan Chase is at **http://www.sec.gov/litigation/complaints/comp18252.htm**.

PROBLEMS

Some of the problems that follow use Table 8.9. Assume that the current exchange rate is $0.90/€.

8.1. Consider the oil swap example in Section 8.1 with the 1- and 2-year forward prices of $22/barrel and $23/barrel. The 1- and 2-year interest rates are 6% and 6.5%. Verify that the new 2-year swap price is $22.483.

8.2. Suppose that oil forward prices for 1 year, 2 years, and 3 years are $20, $21, and $22. The 1-year effective annual interest rate is 6.0%, the 2-year interest rate is 6.5%, and the 3-year interest rate is 7.0%.

    a. What is the 3-year swap price?

    b. What is the price of a 2-year swap beginning in one year? (That is, the first swap settlement will be in 2 years and the second in 3 years.)

8.3. Consider the same 3-year oil swap. Suppose a dealer is paying the fixed price and receiving floating. What position in oil forward contracts will hedge oil price risk

TABLE 8.9

Quarter	1	2	3	4	5	6	7	8
Oil forward price	21	21.1	20.8	20.5	20.2	20	19.9	19.8
Gas swap price	2.2500	2.4236	2.3503	2.2404	2.2326	2.2753	2.2583	2.2044
Zero-coupon bond price	0.9852	0.9701	0.9546	0.9388	0.9231	0.9075	0.8919	0.8763
Euro-denominated zero-coupon bond price	0.9913	0.9825	0.9735	0.9643	0.9551	0.9459	0.9367	0.9274
Euro forward price ($/€)	0.9056	0.9115	0.9178	0.9244	0.9312	0.9381	0.9452	0.9524

in this position? Verify that the present value of the locked-in net cash flows is zero.

8.4. Consider the 3-year swap in the previous example. Suppose you are the fixed-rate payer in the swap. How much have you overpaid relative to the forward price after the first swap settlement? What is the cumulative overpayment after the second swap settlement? Verify that the cumulative overpayment is zero after the third payment. (Be sure to account for interest.)

8.5. Consider the same 3-year swap. Suppose you are a dealer who is paying the fixed oil price and receiving the floating price. Suppose that you enter into the swap and immediately thereafter all interest rates rise 50 basis points (oil forward prices are unchanged). What happens to the value of your swap position? What if interest rates fall 50 basis points? What hedging instrument would have protected you against interest rate risk in this position?

8.6. Supposing the effective quarterly interest rate is 1.5%, what are the per-barrel swap prices for 4-quarter and 8-quarter oil swaps? (Use oil forward prices in Table 8.9.) What is the total cost of prepaid 4- and 8-quarter swaps?

8.7. Using the information about zero-coupon bond prices and oil forward prices in Table 8.9, construct the set of swap prices for oil for 1 through 8 quarters.

8.8. Using the information in Table 8.9, what is the swap price of a 4-quarter oil swap with the first settlement occurring in the third quarter?

8.9. Given an 8-quarter oil swap price of $20.43, construct the implicit loan balance for each quarter over the life of the swap.

8.10. Using the zero-coupon bond prices and oil forward prices in Table 8.9, what is the price of an 8-period swap for which two barrels of oil are delivered in even-numbered quarters and one barrel of oil in odd-numbered quarters?

8.11. Using the zero-coupon bond prices and natural gas swap prices in Table 8.9, what are gas forward prices for each of the 8 quarters?

8.12. Using the zero-coupon bond prices and natural gas swap prices in Table 8.9, what is the implicit loan amount in each quarter in an 8-quarter natural gas swap?

8.13. What is the fixed rate in a 5-quarter interest rate swap with the first settlement in quarter 2?

8.14. Using the zero-coupon bond yields in Table 8.9, what is the fixed rate in a 4-quarter interest rate swap? What is the fixed rate in an 8-quarter interest rate swap?

8.15. What 8-quarter dollar annuity is equivalent to an 8-quarter annuity of €1?

8.16. Using the assumptions in Tables 8.5 and 8.6, verify that equation (8.9) equals 6%.

8.17. Using the information in Table 8.9, what are the *euro-denominated* fixed rates for 4- and 8-quarter swaps?

8.18. Using the information in Table 8.9, verify that it is possible to derive the 8-quarter dollar interest swap rate from the 8-quarter euro interest swap rate by using equation (8.9).

PART THREE

Options

In earlier chapters we have seen how options work, and introduced some of the terminology related to options. In this part of the book we return to options, with the goal of understanding how they are priced.

Forward contracts (and futures and swaps) represent a binding commitment to buy or sell the underlying asset in the future. Because the commitment is binding, but deferred, time value of money is the main economic idea used in determining forward prices.

Options, on the other hand, need not be exercised. Intuitively, you would expect the probability distribution of the stock to affect the option price. Consequently, in discussing option pricing we will use some concepts from basic probability. However, it turns out that there is much to say about options without needing to think about the probability distribution of the stock. In Chapter 9 we explore concepts such as parity in more depth, and discuss some basic intuition about option prices that can be gleaned using only time value of money arguments.

Chapters 10 and 11 introduce the binomial option pricing model. This model assumes that the stock can move only in a very simple way, but provides the intuition underlying more complicated option pricing calculations. *Chapter 12 presents the Black-Scholes option pricing formula, which is one of the most important formulas in finance.*

As with forwards, futures, and swaps, option contracts are bought and sold by market-makers who hedge the risk associated with market-making. Chapter 13 looks at how market-makers hedge their option risk, and shows the precise sense in which the price of an option reflects the cost of synthetically creating it. Finally, Chapter 14 discusses exotic options, which are variants of the standard options we have been discussing.

CHAPTER 9

Parity and Other Option Relationships

With this chapter we begin to study option pricing. Up to this point we have primarily studied contracts entailing *firm commitments*, such as forwards, futures, and swaps. These contracts do not permit either party to back away from the agreement. Optionality occurs when it is possible to avoid engaging in unprofitable transactions. The principal question in option pricing is: *How do you value the right to back away from a commitment*?

Before we delve into pricing models, we devote this chapter to refining our common sense about options. For example, Table 9.1 contains call and put prices for IBM for four different strikes and two different expiration dates. These are American-style options. Here are some observations and questions about these prices:

- What determines the difference between put and call prices at a given strike?

- How would the premiums change if these options were European rather than American?

- It appears that, for a given strike, the January options are more expensive than the November options. Is this necessarily true?

- Do call premiums always decrease as the strike price increases? Do put premiums always increase as the strike price increases?

- Both call and put premiums change by less than the change in the strike price. Does this always happen?

These questions, and others, will be answered in this chapter, but you should take a minute and think about the answers now, drawing on what you have learned in previous chapters. While doing so, pay attention to *how* you are trying to come up with the answers. What constitutes a persuasive argument? Along with finding the answers, we want to understand how to think about questions like these.

9.1 PUT-CALL PARITY

Put-call parity is perhaps the single most important relationship among option prices. In Chapter 2 we argued that synthetic forwards (created by buying the call and selling the put) must be priced consistently with actual forwards. The basic parity relationship for

281

TABLE 9.1		IBM option prices, dollars per share, October 15, 2004. The closing price of IBM on that day was $84.85.			
		Calls		**Puts**	
Strike	**Expiration**	**Bid ($)**	**Ask ($)**	**Bid ($)**	**Ask ($)**
75	November	9.90	10.30	0.20	0.25
80	November	5.30	5.60	0.60	0.70
85	November	1.90	2.10	2.10	2.30
90	November	0.35	0.45	5.50	5.80
75	January	10.50	10.90	0.70	0.80
80	January	6.50	6.70	1.45	1.60
85	January	3.20	3.40	3.10	3.30
90	January	1.20	1.35	6.10	6.30

Source: Chicago Board Options Exchange (**www.cboe.com**).

European options with the same strike price and time to expiration is

$$\text{Call} - \text{put} = \text{PV(forward price} - \text{strike price)}$$

Equation (3.1) from Chapter 3 expresses this more precisely:

$$C(K, T) - P(K, T) = \text{PV}_{0,T}(F_{0,T} - K) \tag{9.1}$$
$$= e^{-rT}(F_{0,T} - K)$$

where $C(K, T)$ is the price of a European call with strike price K and time to expiration T, $P(K, T)$ is the price of a European put, $F_{0,T}$ is the forward price for the underlying asset, K is the strike price, T is the time to expiration of the options, and $\text{PV}_{0,T}$ denotes the present value over the life of the options. Note that $e^{-rT} F_{0,T}$ is the prepaid forward price for the asset and $e^{-rT} K$ is the prepaid forward price for the strike, so we can also think of parity in terms of prepaid forward prices.

The intuition for equation (9.1) is that buying a call and selling a put with the strike equal to the forward price ($F_{0,T} = K$) creates a synthetic forward contract and hence must have a zero price. If we create a synthetic long forward position at a price lower than the forward price, we have to pay $\text{PV}_{0,T}(F_{0,T} - K)$ since this is the benefit of buying the asset at the strike price rather than the forward price.

Parity generally fails for American-style options, which may be exercised prior to maturity. Appendix 9.A discusses a version of parity for American options.

We now consider the parity relationship in more detail for different underlying assets.

Options on Stocks

If the underlying asset is a stock and Div is the stream of dividends paid on the stock, then from Chapter 5, $e^{-rT}F_{0,T} = S_0 - PV_{0,T}(\text{Div})$. Thus, from equation (9.1), the parity relationship for European options on stocks is

$$C(K,T) = P(K,T) + [S_0 - PV_{0,T}(\text{Div})] - e^{-rT}K \qquad (9.2)$$

where S_0 is the current stock price and $PV_{0,T}(\text{Div})$ is the present value of dividends payable over the life of the stock. For index options, we know that $S_0 - PV_{0,T}(\text{Div}) = S_0 e^{-\delta T}$. Hence, we can write

$$C(K,T) = P(K,T) + S_0 e^{-\delta T} - PV_{0,T}(K)$$

Example 9.1 Suppose that the price of a nondividend-paying stock is $40, the continuously compounded interest rate is 8%, and options have 3 months to expiration. A 40-strike European call sells for $2.78 and a 40-strike European put sells for $1.99. This is consistent with equation (9.2) since

$$\$2.78 = \$1.99 + \$40 - \$40e^{-0.08 \times 0.25} \qquad ≸$$

Why does the price of an at-the-money call exceed the price of an at-the-money put by $0.79? We can answer this question by recognizing that buying a call and selling a put is a synthetic alternative to buying the stock, with different cash flows than an outright purchase.

Figure 9.1 represents the cash flows for a synthetic and outright purchase. Note that the synthetic purchase of the stock entails a cash outflow of $0.79 today and $40 at expiration, compared with an outright purchase that entails spending $40 today.

Also, both positions result in the ownership of the stock 3 months from today. With the outright purchase of stock, we still own the stock in 3 months. With the synthetic purchase, we will own the stock if the price is above $40 because we will exercise the call. We will also own the stock if the price is below $40, because we sold a put that

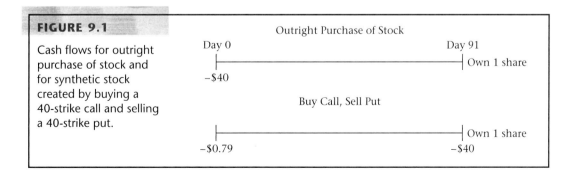

FIGURE 9.1

Cash flows for outright purchase of stock and for synthetic stock created by buying a 40-strike call and selling a 40-strike put.

Outright Purchase of Stock

Day 0 — Day 91 Own 1 share
−$40

Buy Call, Sell Put

Own 1 share
−$0.79 −$40

will be exercised; as the put-writer we have to buy the stock. In either case, in 3 months we pay $40 and acquire the stock.

Finally, the dollar risk of the positions is the same. In both cases, a $1 change in the stock price at 3 months will lead to a $1 change in the value of the position. In other words, both positions entail economic ownership of the stock. You can verify that the risk is the same by drawing a profit and loss diagram for the two positions.

Thus, by buying the call and selling the put we own the stock, but we have deferred the payment of $40 until expiration. To obtain this deferral we must pay 3 months of interest on the $40, the present value of which is $0.79. *The option premiums differ by interest on the deferral of payment for the stock.* Interest is the reason that at-the-money European calls on nondividend-paying stock always sell for more than at-the-money European puts with the same expiration.

Note that if we reverse the position by selling the call and buying the put, then we are synthetically short-selling the stock. In 3 months, the options will be exercised and we will receive $40. In this case, the $0.79 compensates us for deferring receipt of the stock price.

There are differences between the outright and synthetic positions. First, the stock pays dividends and the synthetic does not. This example assumed that the stock paid no dividends. If it did, the cost of the actual stock would exceed that of the synthetic by the present value of dividends paid over the life of the options. Second, the actual stock has voting rights, unlike the synthetic position.

Example 9.2   Make the same assumptions as in Example 9.1, except suppose that the stock pays a $5 dividend just before expiration. The price of the European call is $0.74 and the price of the European put is $4.85. These prices satisfy parity with dividends, equation (9.2):

$$\$0.74 - \$4.85 = (\$40 - \$5e^{-0.08 \times 0.25}) - \$40e^{-0.08 \times 0.25}$$

The call price is higher than the put price by interest on the strike ($0.79) and lower by the present value of the dividend ($4.90), for a net difference of $4.11.   ≋

In this example, the at-the-money call sells for less than an at-the-money put since dividends on the stock exceed the value of interest on the strike price.

It is worth mentioning a common but erroneous explanation for the higher premium of an at-the-money call compared to an at-the-money put. The profit on a call is potentially unlimited since the stock price can go to infinity, while the profit on a put can be no greater than the strike price. This explanation seems to suggest that the call should be more expensive than the put.[1] However, parity shows that the true reason for the call being more expensive (as in Example 9.1) is time value of money.

....

[1] In fact, the argument also seems to suggest that every stock is worth more than its price!

Synthetic stock Parity provides a cookbook for the synthetic creation of options, stocks, and T-bills.

The example above shows that buying a call and selling a put is like buying the stock except that the timing of the payment for the stock differs in the two cases. Rewriting equation (9.2) gives us

$$S_0 = C(K, T) - P(K, T) + \mathrm{PV}_{0,T}(\mathrm{Div}) + e^{-rT}K \qquad (9.3)$$

To match the cash flows for an outright purchase of the stock, in addition to buying the call and selling the put, we have to lend the present value of the strike and dividends to be paid over the life of the option. We then receive the stock in 91 days.

Example 9.3 In Example 9.1, $\mathrm{PV}_{0,0.25}(K) = \$40e^{-0.08\times0.25} = \$39.21$. Hence, by buying the call for \$2.78, selling the put for \$1.99, and lending \$39.21, we invest a total of \$40 today. In 91 days, we have the two options and a T-bill worth \$40. We acquire the stock via one of the exercised options, using the \$40 T-bill to pay the strike price.

Synthetic T-bills If we buy the stock, sell the call, and buy the put, we have purchased the stock and short-sold the synthetic stock. This transaction gives us a hedged position that has no risk but requires investment. Parity shows us that

$$S_0 + P(K, T) - C(K, T) = \mathrm{PV}_{0,T}(K) + \mathrm{PV}_{0,T}(\mathrm{Div})$$

We have thus created a position that costs $\mathrm{PV}(K) + \mathrm{PV}_{0,T}(\mathrm{Div})$ and that pays $K + FV_{0,T}(\mathrm{Div})$ at expiration. This is a synthetic Treasury bill.

Example 9.4 In Example 9.1, $\mathrm{PV}_{0,0.25}(K) = \$39.21$. Hence, by buying the stock, buying a put, and selling the call, we can create a T-bill that costs \$39.21 and pays \$40 in 91 days.

Since T-bills are taxed differently than stocks, the ability to create a synthetic Treasury bill with the stock and options creates problems for tax and accounting authorities. How should the return on this transaction be taxed—as a stock transaction or as interest income? Tax rules call for this position to be taxed as interest, but you can imagine taxpayers trying to skirt these rules.

The creation of a synthetic T-bill by buying the stock, buying a put, and selling a call is called a **conversion.** If we short the stock, buy a call, and sell a put, we have created a synthetic short T-bill position and this is called a **reverse conversion.**

Synthetic options Parity tells us that

$$C(K, T) = S_0 - \mathrm{PV}_{0,T}(\mathrm{Div}) - \mathrm{PV}_{0,T}(K) + P(K, T)$$

and that

$$P(K, T) = C(K, T) - S_0 + \text{PV}_{0,T}(K) + \text{PV}_{0,T}(\text{Div})$$

The first relation says that a call is equivalent to a leveraged position on the underlying asset $[S_0 - \text{PV}_{0,T}(\text{Div}) - \text{PV}(K)]$, which is insured by the purchase of a put. The second relation says that a put is equivalent to a short position on the stock, insured by the purchase of a call.

Options on Currencies

Suppose we have options to buy euros by paying dollars. From our discussion of currency forward contracts in Chapter 5, we know that the dollar forward price for a euro is $F_{0,T} = x_0 e^{(r - r_\euro)T}$, where x_0 is the current exchange rate denominated as \$/€, $r_\euro$ is the euro-denominated interest rate, and r is the dollar-denominated interest rate. The parity relationship for options to buy one euro by paying x_0 is then

$$C(K, T) - P(K, T) = x_0 e^{-r_\euro T} - K e^{-rT} \qquad (9.4)$$

Buying a euro call and selling a euro put is equivalent to lending euros and borrowing dollars. Equation (9.4) tells us that the difference in the call and put premiums simply reflects the difference in the amount borrowed and loaned, in the currency of the country in which the options are denominated.

Example 9.5   Suppose the current \$/€ exchange rate is 0.9, the dollar-denominated interest rate is 6%, and the euro-denominated interest rate is 4%. By buying a dollar-denominated euro call with a strike of \$0.92 and selling a dollar-denominated euro put with the same strike, we construct a position where in 1 year we will buy €1 by paying \$0.92. We can accomplish the same thing by lending the present value of €1 today (with a dollar cost of $\$0.9e^{-0.04} = \$0.8647$) and paying for this by borrowing the present value of \$0.92 ($\$0.92e^{-0.06} = \$0.8664$). The proceeds from borrowing exceed the amount we need to lend by \$0.0017. Equation (9.4) performs exactly this calculation, giving us a difference between the call premium and put premium of

$$
\begin{aligned}
x_0 e^{-r_\euro T} - K e^{-rT} &= 0.9\$/€ \times €e^{-0.04 \times 1} - \$0.92 \times e^{-0.06 \times 1} \\
&= \$0.8647 - \$0.8664 \\
&= -\$0.0017
\end{aligned}
$$

Options on Bonds

Finally, we can construct the parity relationship for options on bonds. The prepaid forward for a bond differs from the bond price due to coupon payments (which are like dividends). Thus if the bond price is B_0 we have

$$C(K, T) = P(K, T) + [B_0 - \text{PV}_{0,T}(\text{Coupons})] - \text{PV}_{0,T}(K) \qquad (9.5)$$

Note that for a pure-discount bond, the parity relationship is exactly like that for a nondividend-paying stock.

9.2 GENERALIZED PARITY AND EXCHANGE OPTIONS

The preceding section showed how the parity relationship works for different underlying assets. Now we will generalize parity to apply to the case where the strike asset is not necessarily cash but could be any other asset. This version of parity includes all previous versions as special cases.

Suppose we have an option to exchange one asset for another. Let the underlying asset, asset A, have price S_t, and the strike asset (the asset which, at our discretion, we surrender in exchange for the underlying asset), asset B, have the price Q_t. Let $F_{t,T}^P(S)$ denote the time t price of a prepaid forward on the underlying asset, paying S_T at time T, and let $F_{t,T}^P(Q)$ denote the time t price of a prepaid forward on asset B, paying Q_T at time T. We use the notation $C(S_t, Q_t, T - t)$ to denote the time t price of an option with $T - t$ periods to expiration, which gives us the right to give up asset B in exchange for asset A. $P(S_t, Q_t, T - t)$ is defined similarly as the right to give up asset A in exchange for asset B. Now suppose that the call payoff at time T is

$$C(S_T, Q_T, 0) = \max(0, S_T - Q_T)$$

and the put payoff is

$$P(S_T, Q_T, 0) = \max(0, Q_T - S_T)$$

Then for European options we have this form of the parity equation:

$$C(S_t, Q_t, T - t) - P(S_t, Q_t, T - t) = F_{t,T}^P(S) - F_{t,T}^P(Q) \qquad (9.6)$$

The use of prepaid forward prices in the parity relationship completely takes into account the dividend and time value of money considerations. This version of parity tells us that there is nothing special about an option having the strike amount designated as cash. In general, options can be designed to exchange any asset for any other asset, and the relative put and call premiums are determined by prices of prepaid forwards on the underlying and strike assets.

To prove equation (9.6) we can use a payoff table in which we buy a call, sell a put, sell a prepaid forward on A, and buy a prepaid forward on B. This transaction is illustrated in Table 9.2.

If the strategy in Table 9.2 does not pay zero at expiration, there is an arbitrage opportunity. Thus, we expect equation (9.6) to hold. All European options satisfy this formula, whatever the underlying asset.

		Expiration	
Transaction	**Time 0**	$S_T \leq Q_T$	$S_T > Q_T$
Buy call	$-C(S_t, Q_t, T-t)$	0	$S_T - Q_T$
Sell put	$P(S_t, Q_t, T-t)$	$S_T - Q_T$	0
Sell prepaid Forward on A	$F_{t,T}^P(S)$	$-S_T$	$-S_T$
Buy prepaid Forward on B	$-F_{t,T}^P(Q)$	Q_T	Q_T
Total	$-C(S_t, Q_t, T-t)$ $+P(S_t, Q_t, T-t)$ $+F_{t,T}^P(S) - F_{t,T}^P(Q)$	0	0

TABLE 9.2 Payoff table demonstrating that there is an arbitrage opportunity unless $-C(S_t, Q_t, T-t) + P(S_t, Q_t, T-t) + F_{t,T}^P(S) - F_{t,T}^P(Q) = 0$.

Example 9.6 Suppose that nondividend-paying stock A has a price of $20, and nondividend-paying stock B has a price of $25. Because neither stock pays dividends, their prepaid forward prices equal their prices. If A is the underlying asset and B is the strike asset, then put-call parity implies that

$$\text{Call} - \text{put} = \$20 - \$25 = -\$5$$

The put is $5 more expensive than the call for any time to expiration of the options.

Options to Exchange Stock

Executive stock options are sometimes constructed so that the strike price of the option is the price of an index, rather than a fixed cash amount. The idea is to have an option that pays off only when the company outperforms competitors, rather than one that pays off simply because all stock prices have gone up. As a hypothetical example of this, suppose Bill Gates, chairman of Microsoft, is given compensation options that pay off only if Microsoft outperforms Google. He will exercise these options if and only if the share price of Microsoft, S_{MSFT}, exceeds the share price of Google, S_{GOOG}, i.e., $S_{MSFT} > S_{GOOG}$. From Gates's perspective, this is a call option, with the payoff

$$\max(0, S_{MSFT} - S_{GOOG})$$

Now consider the compensation option for Eric Schmidt, CEO of Google. He will receive a compensation option that pays off only if Google outperforms Microsoft, i.e.,

$$\max(0, S_{GOOG} - S_{MSFT})$$

This is a call from Schmidt's perspective.

Here is the interesting twist: Schmidt's Google call looks to Gates like a Microsoft put! And Gates's Microsoft call looks to Schmidt like a Google put. Either option can be viewed as a put or call; it is simply a matter of perspective. *The distinction between a put and a call in this example depends upon what we label the underlying asset and what we label as the strike asset.*

What Are Calls and Puts?

The preceding discussion suggests that labeling an option as a call or put is always a matter of convention. It is an important convention because we use it all the time in talking about options. Nevertheless, in general we can interpret calls as being puts, and vice versa. We can see why by using an analogy.

When you go to the grocery store to obtain bananas, you typically say that you are *buying* bananas. The actual transaction involves handing cash to the grocer and receiving a banana. This is an exchange of one asset (cash) for another (a banana). We could also describe the transaction by saying that we are *selling cash* (in exchange for bananas). The point is that an exchange occurs, and we can describe it either as buying the thing we receive, or selling the thing we surrender.

Any transaction is an exchange of one thing for another. Whether we say we are buying or selling is a matter of convention. This insight may not impress your grocer, but it is important for options since it suggests that the labeling we commonly use to distinguish calls and puts is a matter of convention.

To see how a call could be considered a put, consider a call option on a stock. This is the right to exchange a given number of dollars, the strike price K, for stock worth S, if the stock is worth more than the dollars. For example, suppose that if $S > K$, we earn $S - K$. We can view this as either of two transactions:

- Buying one share of stock by paying K. In this case we exercise when $S > K$. This is a call option on stock.

- Selling K dollars in exchange for one share of stock. Again we exercise when $S > K$—i.e., when the dollars we sell are worth less than the stock. This is a put option on dollars, with a share of stock as the strike asset.

Under either interpretation, if $S < K$ we do not exercise the option. If the dollars are worth more than the stock, we would not sell them for the stock.

Now consider a put option on a stock. The put option confers the right to exchange one share of stock for a given number of dollars. Suppose $S < K$; we earn $K - S$. We can view this in either of two ways:

- Selling one share of stock at the price K.

- Buying K dollars by paying one share of stock. This is a call where we have the right to give up stock to obtain dollars.

If $S > K$ we do not exercise under either interpretation. If the dollars are worth less than the stock, we would not pay the stock to obtain the dollars.

Currency Options

The idea that calls can be relabeled as puts is not just academic; it is used frequently by currency traders. A currency transaction involves the exchange of one kind of currency for another. In this context, it is obvious to market participants that referring to a particular currency as having been bought or sold is a matter of convention. Labeling a particular option a call or a put depends upon which currency you regard as your home currency.

In the following example we will show that a dollar-denominated call option on euros, which gives you the right to pay dollars to receive euros, is equivalent to a euro-denominated put option on dollars, which gives the right to sell a dollar for euros. Obviously, the strike prices and option quantities must be chosen appropriately for there to be an equivalence.

We will say that an option is "dollar-denominated" if the strike price and premium are denominated in dollars. An option is "euro-denominated" if the strike price and premium are in euros.

Suppose the current exchange rate is $x_0 = 0.90\$/€$, and consider the following two options:[2]

1. A 1-year *dollar-denominated call option* on euros with a strike price of $0.92 and premium of $0.0337. In 1 year, the owner of the option has the right to buy €1 for $0.92. The payoff on this option, in dollars, is therefore

$$\max(0, x_1 - 0.92)$$

2. A 1-year *euro-denominated put option* on dollars with a strike of $\frac{1}{0.92} = €1.0870$. The premium of this option is €0.0407. In 1 year the owner of this put has the right to give up $1 and receive €1.0870; the owner will exercise the put when $1 is worth less than €1.0870. The euro value of $1 in 1 year will be $1/x_1$. Hence, the payoff of this option is

$$\max\left(0, \frac{1}{0.92} - \frac{1}{x_1}\right)$$

Since $x_1 > 0.92$ exactly when $\frac{1}{0.92} > \frac{1}{x_1}$, the euro-denominated dollar put will be exercised when, and only when, the dollar-denominated euro call is exercised.

---

[2]These are Black-Scholes prices with a current exchange rate of 0.90 $/€, a dollar-denominated interest rate of 6%, a euro-denominated interest rate of 4%, and exchange rate volatility of 10%.

Though they will be exercised under the same circumstances, the dollar-denominated euro call and the euro-denominated dollar put differ in two respects:

- The scale of the two options is different. The dollar-denominated euro call is based on one euro (which has a current dollar value of $0.90) and the euro-denominated dollar put is based on one dollar.

- The currency of denomination is different.

We can equate the scale of the two options by holding more of the smaller option or less of the larger option: We can either scale up the dollar-denominated euro calls, holding $\frac{1}{0.92}$ of them, or we can scale down the euro-denominated dollar puts, holding 0.92 of them. To see the equivalence of the euro call and the dollar put, consider the following two transactions:

1. Buy $\frac{1}{0.92}$ 1-year dollar-denominated euro call options with a strike of $0.92. If we exercise, we will give up $1 for €$\frac{1}{0.92}$. The cost is $\frac{1}{0.92} \times \$0.0337 = \$0.0366$.

2. Buy one 1-year euro-denominated put option on dollars with a strike of €1.0870. The cost of this in dollars is $0.90\$/€ \times €0.0407 = \$0.0366$. When the option expires, convert the proceeds back from euros to dollars.

Table 9.3 compares the payoffs of these two option positions. At exercise, each position results in surrendering $1 for €$\frac{1}{0.92}$ if $x_1 > 0.92$. Thus, the two positions must cost the same, or else there is an arbitrage opportunity.

We can summarize this result algebraically. The price of a dollar-denominated foreign currency call with strike K, when the current exchange rate is x_0, is $C_\$(x_0, K, T)$. The price of a foreign-currency–denominated dollar put with strike $\frac{1}{K}$, when the

TABLE 9.3		The equivalence of buying a dollar-denominated euro call and a euro-denominated dollar put. In transaction I, we buy $\frac{1}{0.92}$ dollar-denominated call options permitting us to buy €1 for a strike price of $0.92. In transaction II, we buy one euro-denominated put permitting us to sell $1 for a strike price of €$\frac{1}{0.92}$ = € 1.0870. The option premium is €0.0407.

| | | Year 0 | | Year 1 | | | |
| | | | | $x_1 < 0.92$ | | $x_1 \geq 0.92$ | |
	Transaction	$	€	$	€	$	€
I:	Buy $\frac{1}{0.92}$ Euro calls	−0.0366	—	0	0	−1	$\frac{1}{0.92}$
II:	Convert dollars to Euros	−0.0366	0.0407				
	Buy dollar put		−0.0407	0	0	−1	$\frac{1}{0.92}$

exchange rate is $\frac{1}{x_0}$, is $P_f(\frac{1}{x_0}, \frac{1}{K}, T)$. Adjusting for currency and scale differences, the prices are related by

$$C_\$(x_0, K, T) = x_0\, K\, P_f\left(\frac{1}{x_0}, \frac{1}{K}, T\right) \qquad (9.7)$$

This insight—that calls in one currency are the same as puts in the other—is common-place among currency traders. While this observation is interesting in and of itself, its generalization to *all* options provides a fresh perspective for thinking about what calls and puts actually are.

9.3 COMPARING OPTIONS WITH RESPECT TO STYLE, MATURITY, AND STRIKE

We now examine how option prices change when there are changes in option charac-teristics, such as exercise style (American or European), the strike price, and time to expiration. Remarkably, we can say a great deal without a pricing model and without making any assumptions about the distribution of the underlying asset.[3] Thus, *whatever* the particular option model or stock price distribution used for valuing a given option, we can still expect option prices to behave in certain ways.

Here is an example of the kind of questions we will address in this section. Suppose you have three call options, with strikes of \$40, \$45, and \$50. How do the premiums on these options differ? Common sense suggests that, with a call option on any underlying asset, the premium will go down as you raise the strike price; it is less valuable to be able to buy at a higher price.[4] Moreover, the decline in the premium cannot be greater than \$5. (The right to buy for a \$5 cheaper price cannot be worth more than \$5.)

Following this logic, the premium will drop as we increase the strike from \$40 to \$45, and drop again when we increase the strike further from \$45 to \$50. Here is a more subtle question: In which case will the premium drop more? It turns out that the decline in the premium from \$40 to \$45 *must* be greater than the decline from \$45 to \$50, or else there is an arbitrage opportunity.

In this section we will explore the following issues for stock options (some of the properties may be different for options on other underlying assets):

- How prices of otherwise identical American and European options compare.

....

[3]The so-called "theory of rational option pricing," on which this section is based, was first presented in 1973 by Robert Merton in an astonishing paper (Merton (1973b)). This material is also superbly exposited in Cox and Rubinstein (1985).

[4]If you are being fastidious, you will say the option premium *cannot increase* as the strike goes up. Saying that the option premium will *decrease* as the strike increases does not account for the possibility that all the premiums are zero, and hence the premium will not go down, but will remain unchanged, as the strike price increases.

- How option prices change as the time to expiration changes.
- How option prices change as the strike price changes.

A word of warning before we begin this discussion: If you examine option price listings in the newspaper, you can often find option prices that seemingly give rise to arbitrage opportunities. There are several reasons for this. One is that some reported option price quotes are stale, meaning that the comparison is among option prices recorded at different times of the day. Moreover, an apparent arbitrage opportunity only becomes genuine when bid-ask spreads (see Table 9.1), commissions, costs of short-selling, and market impact are taken into account. Caveat arbitrageur!

European Versus American Options

Since an American option can be exercised at any time, it must always be at least as valuable as an otherwise identical European option. (By "otherwise identical" we mean that the two options have the same underlying asset, strike price, and time to expiration.) Any exercise strategy appropriate to a European option can always be duplicated with an American option: The American option cannot be less valuable. Thus we have

$$C_{\text{Amer}}(S, K, T) \geq C_{\text{Eur}}(S, K, T) \qquad (9.8a)$$

$$P_{\text{Amer}}(S, K, T) \geq P_{\text{Eur}}(S, K, T) \qquad (9.8b)$$

We will see that there are times when the right to early-exercise is worthless, and, hence, American and European options have the same value.

Maximum and Minimum Option Prices

It is often useful to understand just how expensive or inexpensive an option can be. Here are some basic limits.

Calls   The price of a European call option

- Cannot be negative, because the call need not be exercised.
- Cannot exceed the stock price, because the best that can happen with a call is that you end up owning the stock.
- Must be at least as great as the price implied by parity with a zero put value.

Combining these statements, together with the result about American options never being worth less than European options, gives us

$$S \geq C_{\text{Amer}}(S, K, T) \geq C_{\text{Eur}}(S, K, T) \geq \max[0, \text{PV}_{0,T}(F_{0,T}) - \text{PV}_{0,T}(K)] \qquad (9.9)$$

where present values are taken over the life of the option.

Puts   Similarly, a put

- Cannot be worth more than the undiscounted strike price, since that is the most it can ever be worth (if the stock price drops to zero, the put pays K at some point).

- Must be at least as great as the price implied by parity with a zero call value.

   Also, an American put is worth at least as much as a European put. This gives us

$$\boxed{K \geq P_{\text{Amer}}(S, K, T) \geq P_{\text{Eur}}(S, K, T) \geq \max[0, \text{PV}(K) - \text{PV}(F_{0,T})]} \qquad (9.10)$$

Early Exercise for American Options

When might we want to exercise an option prior to expiration? An important result is that an American call option on a nondividend-paying stock should never be exercised prior to expiration. You may, however, rationally exercise an American-style put option prior to expiration.

Calls on a nondividend-paying stock   We can demonstrate in two ways that an American-style call option on a nondividend-paying stock should never be exercised prior to expiration. Early exercise is not optimal if the price of an American call prior to expiration satisfies

$$C_{\text{Amer}}(S_t, K, T - t) > S_t - K$$

If this inequality holds, you would lose money by early-exercising (receiving $S_t - K$) as opposed to selling the option (receiving $C_{\text{Amer}}(S_t, K, T - t) > S_t - K$).

   We will use put-call parity to demonstrate that early exercise is not rational. If the option expires at T, parity implies that

$$C_{\text{Eur}}(S_t, K, T) = \underbrace{S_t - K}_{\text{Exercise value}} + \underbrace{P_{\text{Eur}}(S_t, K, T - t)}_{\text{Insurance against } S_T < K}$$

$$+ \underbrace{K(1 - e^{-r(T-t)})}_{\text{Time value of money on } K} > S_t - K \qquad (9.11)$$

Since the put price, $P_{\text{Eur}}(S_t, K, T - t)$, and the time value of money on the strike, $K(1 - e^{-r(T-t)})$, are both positive, this equation establishes that the European call option premium on a nondividend paying stock always is at least as great as $S_t - K$. From equation (9.8), we also know that $C_{\text{Amer}} \geq C_{\text{Eur}}$. Thus we have

$$C_{\text{Amer}} \geq C_{\text{Eur}} > S_t - K$$

Since C_{Amer}, the American option premium, always exceeds $S - K$, we would lose money exercising an American call prior to expiration, as opposed to selling the option.

   Equation (9.11) is useful because it shows us precisely *why* we would never early-exercise. Early-exercising has two effects. First, we throw away the implicit put protection should the stock later move below the strike price. Second, we accelerate the payment of the strike price.

A third effect is the possible loss from deferring receipt of the stock. However, when there are no dividends, we lose nothing by waiting to take physical possession of the stock.

We have demonstrated that if a stock pays no dividends, you should never see an option selling for less than $S_t - K$. In fact, equation (9.11), like equation (9.9), actually implies the stronger result that you should never see a call on a nondividend-paying stock sell for less than $S_t - Ke^{-r(T-t)}$. What happens if you do observe an option selling for too low a price? If $C < S_t - K$ and the option is American, you can buy the option, exercise it, and earn $S_t - K - C_{\text{Amer}}(S_t, K, T - t) > 0$. However, what if the option is European and therefore cannot be exercised early? In this case the arbitrage is: Buy the option, short the stock, and lend the present value of the strike price. Table 9.4 demonstrates the arbitrage in this case. The sources of profit from the arbitrage are the same as those identified in equation (9.11).

It is important to realize that this proposition does *not* say that you must hold the option until expiration. It says that if you no longer wish to hold the call, you should sell it rather than early-exercising it.[5]

Exercising calls just prior to a dividend If the stock pays dividends, the parity relationship is

$$C(S_t, K, T - t) = P(S_t, K, T - t) + S_t - \text{PV}_{t,T}(\text{Div}) - \text{PV}_{t,T}(K)$$

Using this expression, we cannot always rule out early exercise as we did above. Early exercise is not optimal at any time where

$$K - \text{PV}_{t,T}(K) > \text{PV}_{t,T}(\text{Div}) \tag{9.12}$$

TABLE 9.4		Demonstration of arbitrage if a call option with price C sells for less than $S_t - Ke^{-r(T-t)}$. Every entry in the row labeled "total" is nonnegative.	

		Expiration or Exercise, Time T	
Transaction	Time t	$S_T < K$	$S_T > K$
Buy call	$-C$	0	$S_T - K$
Short stock	S_t	$-S_T$	$-S_T$
Lend $Ke^{-r(T-t)}$	$-Ke^{-r(T-t)}$	K	K
Total	$S_t - Ke^{-r(T-t)} - C$	$K - S_T$	0

[5]Some options, such as compensation options, cannot be sold. In practice it is common to see executives exercise options prior to expiration and then sell the stock. The discussion in this section demonstrates that such exercise would be irrational if the option could be sold, or if the stock could be sold short.

That is, if interest on the strike price (which induces us to delay exercise) exceeds the present value of dividends (which induces us to exercise), then we will for certain never early-exercise at that time. If inequality (9.12) is violated, this does not tell us that we *will* exercise, only that we cannot rule it out.

If dividends are sufficiently great, however, early exercise can be optimal. To take an extreme example, consider a 90-strike American call on a stock selling for $100, which is about to pay a dividend of $99.99. If we exercise—paying $90 to acquire the $100 stock—we have a net position worth $10. If we delay past the ex-dividend date, the option is worthless.

If dividends do make early exercise rational, it will be optimal to exercise at the last moment before the ex-dividend date. By exercising earlier than that, we pay the strike price prematurely and thus at a minimum lose interest on the strike price.

Early exercise for puts　When the underlying stock pays no dividend, a call will not be early-exercised, but a put might be. To see that early exercise for a put can make economic sense, suppose a company is bankrupt and the stock price falls to zero. Then a put that would not be exercised until expiration will be worth $PV_{t,T}(K)$. If we could early-exercise, we would receive K. If the interest rate is positive, $K > PV(K)$. Therefore, early exercise would be optimal in order to receive the strike price earlier.

We can also use a parity argument to understand this. The put will never be exercised as long as $P > K - S$. Supposing that the stock pays no dividends, parity for the put is

$$P(S_t, K, T - t) = C(S_t, K, T - t) - S_t + PV_{t,T}(K)$$

$P > K - S$ then implies

$$C(S_t, K, T - t) - S_t + PV_{t,T}(K) > K - S_t$$

or

$$C(S_t, K, T - t) > K - PV_{t,T}(K)$$

If the call is sufficiently valueless (as in the above example of a bankrupt company), parity cannot rule out early exercise. This does not mean that we *will* early-exercise; it simply means that we cannot rule it out.

We can summarize this discussion of early exercise. When we exercise an option, we receive something (the stock with a call, the strike price with a put). A necessary condition for early exercise is that we prefer to receive this something sooner rather than later. For calls, dividends on the stock are a reason to want to receive the stock earlier. For puts, interest on the strike is a reason to want to receive the strike price earlier. Thus, dividends and interest play similar roles in the two analyses of early exercise. In fact, if we view interest as the dividend on cash, then dividends (broadly defined) become the sole reason to early-exercise an option.

Similarly, dividends on the strike asset become a reason not to early-exercise. In the case of calls, interest is the dividend on the strike asset, and in the case of puts, dividends on the stock are the dividend on the strike asset.

The point of this section has been to make some general statements about when early exercise will not occur, or under what conditions it *might* occur. Early exercise is a trade-off involving time value of money on the strike price, dividends on the underlying asset, and the value of insurance on the position. In general, figuring out when to exercise requires an option pricing model. We will discuss early exercise further in Chapters 10 and 11.

Time to Expiration

How does an option price change as we increase time to expiration? If the options are American, the option price can never decline with an increase in time to expiration. If the options are European, the price can go either up or down as we increase time to expiration.

American options   An American call with more time to expiration is at least as valuable as an otherwise identical call with less time to expiration. An American call with 2 years to expiration, for example, can always be turned into an American option with 1 year to expiration by voluntarily exercising it after 1 year. Therefore, the 2-year call is at least as valuable as the 1-year call.

The same is true for puts: A longer-lived American put is always worth at least as much as an otherwise equivalent European put.

European options   A European call on a nondividend-paying stock will be at least as valuable as an otherwise identical call with a shorter time to expiration. This occurs because, with no dividends, a European call has the same price as an otherwise identical American call. With dividends, however, longer-lived European options may be less valuable than shorter-lived European options. Economic forces that make it optimal to exercise an option early can make a short-lived European option worth more than a long-lived European option.

To see this for calls, imagine a stock that will pay a liquidating dividend 2 weeks from today.[6] A European call with 1 week to expiration will have value since it is exercisable prior to the dividend. A European call with 3 weeks to expiration will have no value since the stock will have no value at expiration. This is an example of a longer-lived option being less valuable than a shorter-lived option. Note that if the options were American, we would simply exercise the 3-week option prior to the dividend.

Longer-lived European puts can also be less valuable than shorter-lived European puts. A good example of this is a bankrupt company. The put will be worth the present value of the strike price, with present value calculated until time to expiration. Longer-lived puts will be worth less than shorter-lived puts. If the options were American, they would all be exercised immediately and hence would be worth the strike price.

---

[6]A liquidating dividend occurs when a firm pays its entire value to shareholders. A firm is worthless after paying a liquidating dividend.

European options when the strike price grows over time In discussing the effect of changing time to maturity, we have been keeping the option strike price fixed. The present value of the strike price therefore decreases with time to maturity. Suppose, however, that we keep the present value of the strike constant by setting $K_t = Ke^{rt}$. When the strike grows at the interest rate, the premiums on European calls and puts on a nondividend-paying stock increase with time to maturity.[7] We will demonstrate this for puts; the demonstration is identical for calls.

To keep the notation simple, let $P(t)$ denote the time 0 price of a European put maturing at time t, with strike price $K_t = Ke^{rt}$. We want to show that $P(T) > P(t)$ if $T > t$. To show this, we will demonstrate an arbitrage if $P(T) \leq P(t)$.

If the longer-lived put is not more expensive—i.e., if $P(T) \leq P(t)$—buy the put with T years to expiration and sell the put with t years to expiration. At time t the written put will expire. If $S_t > K_t$ its value is zero and we can ignore the shorter-lived option from this point on. If $S_t < K_t$, the put holder will exercise the short-lived option and our payoff is $S_t - K_t$. Suppose that we keep the stock we receive and borrow to finance the strike price, holding this position until the second option expires at time T. Here is the important step: Notice that the time-T value of this time-t payoff is $S_T - K_t e^{r(T-t)} = S_T - K_T$.

Table 9.5 summarizes the resulting payoffs. By buying the long-lived put and selling the short-lived put, we are guaranteed not to lose money at time T. Therefore, if $P(t) \geq P(T)$ there is an arbitrage opportunity. A practical application of this result is discussed in the box on page 299.

TABLE 9.5

Demonstration that there is an arbitrage if $P(T) \leq P(t)$ with $t < T$. The strike on the put with maturity t is $K_t = Ke^{rt}$, and the strike on the put with maturity T is $K_T = Ke^{rt}$. If the option expiring at time t is in-the-money, the payoff, $S_t - K_t$, is reinvested until time T. If $P(t) \geq P(T)$, all cash flows in the "total" line are nonnegative.

		Payoff at Time T			
		$S_T < K_T$		$S_T > K_T$	
		Payoff at Time t			
Transaction	**Time 0**	$S_t < K_t$	$S_t > K_t$	$S_t < K_t$	$S_t > K_t$
Sell $P(t)$	$P(t)$	$S_T - K_T$	0	$S_T - K_T$	0
Buy $P(T)$	$-P(T)$	$K_T - S_T$	$K_T - S_T$	0	0
Total	$P(t) - P(T)$	0	$K_T - S_T$	$S_T - K_T$	0

---

[7]Dividends can easily be accommodated in the following way. Suppose that all dividends are reinvested in the stock. Call the resulting position a *total return portfolio* and let S_t be the price of this portfolio. Define the options so that the total return portfolio is the underlying asset. The result in this section then obtains for the total return portfolio. The reason is that the total return portfolio is a synthetic nondividend-paying stock.

Portfolio Insurance for the Long Run

Historically, the rate of return from investing in stocks over a long horizon has outperformed that from investing in government bonds in the United States (see, for example, Siegel (1998)). This observation has led some to suggest that if held for a sufficiently long period of time, stocks are a safe investment relative to risk-free bonds.

Bodie (1995) suggests using put option premiums to think about the claim that stocks are safe in the long run. Specifically, what would it cost to buy a put option insuring that after T years your stock portfolio would be worth at least as much as if you had instead invested in a zero-coupon bond? If your initial investment was S_0, you could provide

this insurance by setting the strike price on the put option equal to $K_T = S_0 e^{rT}$.

Bodie uses the Black-Scholes model to show that the premium on this insurance increases with T. As Bodie notes, however, this proposition must be true for any valid option pricing model. The payoffs in Table 9.5 demonstrate that the cost of this insurance *must* increase with T or else there is an arbitrage opportunity. Whatever the historical return statistics appear to say, the cost of portfolio insurance is increasing with the length of time for which you insure the portfolio return. Using the cost of insurance as a measure, stocks are riskier in the long run.

Different Strike Prices

We discussed at the beginning of this section some statements we can make about how option prices vary with the strike price. Here is a more formal statement of these propositions. Suppose we have three strike prices, $K_1 < K_2 < K_3$, with corresponding call option prices $C(K_1)$, $C(K_2)$, and $C(K_3)$ and put option prices $P(K_1)$, $P(K_2)$, and $P(K_3)$. Here are the propositions we discuss in this section:

1. A call with a low strike price is at least as valuable as an otherwise identical call with a higher strike price:

$$C(K_1) \geq C(K_2) \qquad (9.13)$$

   A put with a high strike price is at least as valuable as an otherwise identical put with a low strike price:

$$P(K_2) \geq P(K_1) \qquad (9.14)$$

2. The premium difference between otherwise identical calls with different strike prices cannot be greater than the difference in strike prices:

$$C(K_1) - C(K_2) \leq K_2 - K_1 \qquad (9.15)$$

The premium difference for otherwise identical puts also cannot be greater than the difference in strike prices:

$$\boxed{P(K_2) - P(K_1) \le K_2 - K_1}$$

(9.16)

3. Premiums decline at a decreasing rate as we consider calls with progressively higher strike prices. The same is true for puts as strike prices decline. This is called **convexity** of the option price with respect to the strike price:

$$\boxed{\frac{C(K_1) - C(K_2)}{K_2 - K_1} \ge \frac{C(K_2) - C(K_3)}{K_3 - K_2}}$$

(9.17)

$$\boxed{\frac{P(K_2) - P(K_1)}{K_2 - K_1} \le \frac{P(K_3) - P(K_2)}{K_3 - K_2}}$$

(9.18)

These statements are all true for both European and American options.[8] Algebraic demonstrations are in Appendix 9.B. It turns out, however, that these three propositions are equivalent to saying that there are no free lunches: If you enter into an option spread, there must be stock prices at which you would lose money on the spread net of your original investment. Otherwise the spread represents an arbitrage opportunity. These three propositions say that you cannot have a bull spread, a bear spread, or a butterfly spread for which you can never lose money. Specifically:

1. If equation (9.13) were not true, buy the low-strike call and sell the high-strike call (this is a call bull spread). If equation (9.14) were not true, buy the high-strike put and sell the low-strike put (a put bear spread).

2. If equation (9.15) were not true, sell the low-strike call and buy the high-strike call (a call bear spread). If equation (9.16) were not true, buy the low-strike put and sell the high-strike put (a put bull spread).

3. If either of equations (9.17) or (9.18) were not true, there is an asymmetric butterfly spread with positive profits at all prices.

We will illustrate these propositions with numerical examples.

Example 9.7 Suppose we observe the call premiums in Panel A of Table 9.6. These values violate the second property for calls, since the difference in strikes is 5 and the difference in the premiums is 6. If we observed these values, we could engage in

---

[8]In fact, if the options are European, the second statement can be strengthened: The difference in option premiums must be less than the *present value* of the difference in strikes.

TABLE 9.6	Panel A shows call option premiums for which the change in the option premium ($6) exceeds the change in the strike price ($5). Panel B shows how a bear spread can be used to arbitrage these prices. By lending the bear spread proceeds, we have a zero cash flow at time 0; the cash outflow at time T is always greater than $1.

Panel A

Strike	50	55
Premium	18	12

Panel B

| | | Expiration or Exercise | | |
Transaction	Time 0	$S_T < 50$	$50 \leq S_T \leq 55$	$S_T \geq 55$
Buy 55-strike call	-12	0	0	$S_T - 55$
Sell 50-strike call	18	0	$50 - S_T$	$50 - S_T$
Total	6	0	$50 - S_T$	-5

arbitrage by buying the 55-strike call and selling the 50-strike call, which is a bear spread. Note that we receive $6 initially and never have to pay more than $5 in the future. This is an arbitrage, whatever the interest rate. ≷

Now consider the third proposition, *strike price convexity*. There is a different way to write the convexity inequality, equation (9.17). Since K_2 is between K_1 and K_3, we can write it as a weighted average of the other two strikes, that is

$$K_2 = \lambda K_1 + (1 - \lambda)K_3$$

where

$$\lambda = \frac{K_3 - K_2}{K_3 - K_1} \qquad (9.19)$$

With this expression for λ, it is possible to rewrite equation (9.17) as

$$C(K_2) \leq \lambda C(K_1) + (1 - \lambda)C(K_3) \qquad (9.20)$$

Here is an example illustrating convexity.

Example 9.8 If $K_1 = 50$, $K_2 = 59$, and $K_3 = 65$, $\lambda = \frac{65-59}{65-50} = 0.4$; hence,

$$59 = 0.4 \times 50 + 0.6 \times 65$$

Call prices must then satisfy

$$C(59) \leq 0.4 \times C(50) + 0.6 \times C(65)$$

Suppose we observe the call premiums in Table 9.7. The change in the option premium per dollar of strike price change from 50 to 59 is $5.1/9 = 0.567$, and the change from 59 to 65 is $3.9/6 = 0.65$. Thus, prices violate the proposition that the premium decreases at a decreasing rate as the strike price increases.

To arbitrage this mispricing, we engage in an asymmetric butterfly spread: Buy four 50-strike calls, buy six 65-strike calls, and sell ten 59-strike calls.[9] By engaging in a butterfly spread, Panel B shows that a profit of at least $3 is earned. ≹

TABLE 9.7 The example in Panel A violates the proposition that the rate of change of the option premium must decrease as the strike price rises. The rate of change from 50 to 59 is 5.1/9, while the rate of change from 59 to 65 is 3.9/6. We can arbitrage this convexity violation with an asymmetric butterfly spread. Panel B shows that we earn at least $3 plus interest at time T.

Panel A

Strike	50	59	65
Call premium	14	8.9	5

Panel B

Transaction	Time 0	$S_T < 50$	$50 \leq S_T \leq 59$	$59 \leq S_T \leq 65$	$S_T > 65$
Buy four 50-strike calls	−56	0	$4(S_T - 50)$	$4(S_T - 50)$	$4(S_T - 50)$
Sell ten 59-strike calls	89	0	0	$10(59 - S_T)$	$10(59 - S_T)$
Buy six 65-strike calls	−30	0	0	0	$6(S_T - 65)$
Lend $3	−3	$3e^{rT}$	$3e^{rT}$	$3e^{rT}$	$3e^{rT}$
Total	0	$3e^{rT}$	$3e^{rT} + 4(S_T - 50)$	$3e^{rT} + 6(65 - S_T)$	$3e^{rT}$

[9]Note that we get exactly the same arbitrage with any number of calls as long as the ratio at the various strikes remains the same. We could also have bought 0.4 50 calls, sold one 59 call, and bought 0.6 65 calls.

The formula for λ may look imposing, but there is an easy way to figure out what λ is in any situation. In this example, we had the prices 50, 59, and 65. It is possible to express 59 as a weighted average of 50 and 65. The total distance between 50 and 65 is 15, and the distance from 50 to 59 is 9, which is $9/15 = 0.6$ of the total distance. Thus, we can write 59 as

$$59 = (1 - 0.6) \times 50 + 0.6 \times 65$$

This is the interpretation of λ in expression (9.20).

Here is an example of convexity with puts.

Example 9.9   See the prices in Panel A of Table 9.8. We have $K_1 = 50$, $K_2 = 55$, and $K_3 = 70$. $\lambda = 0.75$ and $55 = 0.75 \times 50 + (1 - 0.75) \times 70$. Convexity is violated since

$$P(55) = 8 > 0.75 \times 4 + (1 - 0.75) \times 16 = 7$$

To arbitrage this mispricing, we engage in an asymmetric butterfly spread: Buy three 50-strike puts, buy one 70-strike put, and sell four 55-strike puts. The result is in Panel B of Table 9.8.   ❧

TABLE 9.8   Arbitrage of mispriced puts using asymmetric butterfly spread.

Panel A

Strike	50	55	70
Put premium	4	8	16

Panel B

Transaction	Time 0	$S_T < 50$	$50 \leq S_T \leq 55$	$55 \leq S_T \leq 70$	$S_T > 70$
Buy three 50-strike puts	-12	$3(50 - S_T)$	0	0	0
Sell four 55-strike puts	32	$4(S_T - 55)$	$4(S_T - 55)$	0	0
Buy one 70-strike put	-16	$70 - S_T$	$70 - S_T$	$(70 - S_T)$	0
Lend \$4	-4	$4e^{rT}$	$4e^{rT}$	$4e^{rT}$	$4e^{rT}$
Total	0	$4e^{rT}$	$4e^{rT} + 3(S_T - 50)$	$4e^{rT} + 70 - S_T$	$4e^{rT}$

Column header "Expiration or Exercise" spans $S_T < 50$, $50 \leq S_T \leq 55$, $55 \leq S_T \leq 70$, $S_T > 70$.

In this case, we always make at least 4. Figure 9.2 illustrates the necessary shape of curves for both calls and puts relating the option premium to the strike price.

Exercise and Moneyness

If it is optimal to exercise an option, it is also optimal to exercise an otherwise identical option that is more in-the-money. Consider what would have to happen in order for this *not* to be true.

Suppose a call option on a dividend-paying stock has a strike price of $50, and the stock price is $70. Also suppose that it is optimal to exercise the option. This means that the option must sell for $70 − $50 = $20.

Now what can we say about the premium of a 40-strike option? We know from the discussion above that the change in the premium is no more than the change in the strike price, or else there is an arbitrage opportunity. This means that

$$C\,(40) \leq \$20 + (\$50 - \$40) = \$30$$

Since the 40-strike call is worth $30 if exercised, it must be optimal to exercise it.

Following the same logic, this is also true for puts.

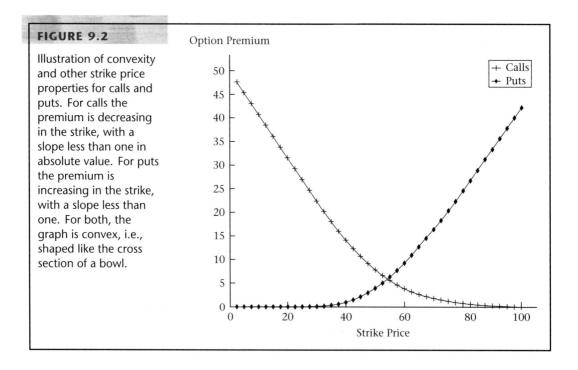

FIGURE 9.2

Illustration of convexity and other strike price properties for calls and puts. For calls the premium is decreasing in the strike, with a slope less than one in absolute value. For puts the premium is increasing in the strike, with a slope less than one. For both, the graph is convex, i.e., shaped like the cross section of a bowl.

CHAPTER SUMMARY

Put-call parity is one of the most important relations in option pricing. Parity is the observation that buying a European call and selling a European put with the same strike price and time to expiration is equivalent to making a leveraged investment in the underlying asset, less the value of cash payments to the underlying asset over the life of the option. Different versions of parity for different underlying assets appear in Table 9.9. In every case the value on the left-hand side of the parity equation is the price of the underlying asset less its cash flows over the life of the option. The parity relationship can be algebraically rearranged so that options and the underlying asset create a synthetic bond, options and a bond create a synthetic stock, and one kind of option together with the stock and bond synthetically create the other kind of option.

The idea of an option can be generalized to permit an asset other than cash to be the strike asset. This insight blurs the distinction between a put and a call. The idea that puts and calls are different ways of looking at the same contract is commonplace in currency markets.

Option prices must obey certain restrictions when we vary the strike price, time to maturity, or option exercise style. American options are at least as valuable as European options. American calls and puts become more expensive as time to expiration increases, but European options need not. European options on a nondividend-paying stock do become more expensive with increasing time to maturity if the strike price grows at the interest rate. Dividends are the reason to exercise an American call early, while interest is the reason to exercise an American put early. A call option on a nondividend-paying stock will always have a price greater than its value if exercised; hence, it should never be exercised early.

There are a number of pricing relationships related to changing strike prices. In particular, as the strike price increases, calls become less expensive with their price

TABLE 9.9 Versions of put-call parity. Notation in the table includes the spot currency exchange rate, x_0; the risk-free interest rate in the foreign currency, r_f; and the current bond price, B_0.

Underlying Asset	Parity Relationship
Futures contract	$e^{-rT} F_{0,T} = C(K, T) - P(K, T) + e^{-rT} K$
Stock, no-dividend	$S_0 = C(K, T) - P(K, T) + e^{-rT} K$
Stock, discrete dividend	$S_0 - \text{PV}_{0,T}(\text{Div}) = C(K, T) - P(K, T) + e^{-rT} K$
Stock, continuous dividend	$e^{-\delta T} S_0 = C(K, T) - P(K, T) + e^{-rT} K$
Currency	$e^{-r_f T} x_0 = C(K, T) - P(K, T) + e^{-rT} K$
Bond	$B_0 - \text{PV}_{0,T}(\text{Coupons}) = C(K, T) - P(K, T) + e^{-rT} K$

decreasing at a decreasing rate. The absolute value of the change in the call price is less than the change in the strike price. As the strike price decreases, puts become less expensive with their price decreasing at a decreasing rate. The change in the put price is less than the change in the strike price.

FURTHER READING

Two of the ideas in this chapter will prove particularly important in later chapters.

The first key idea is put-call parity, which tells us that if we understand calls we also understand puts. This equivalence makes it easier to understand option pricing since the pricing techniques and intuition about one kind of option are directly applicable to the other. The idea of exchange options—options to exchange one asset for another—also will show up again in later chapters. We will see how to price such options in Chapter 14.

A second key idea that will prove important is the determination of factors influencing early exercise. As a practical matter, it is more work to price an American than a European option, so it is useful to know when this extra work is not necessary. Less obviously, the determinants of early exercise will play a key role in Chapter 17, where we discuss real options. We will see that certain kinds of investment projects are analogous to options, and the investment decision is like exercising an option. Thus, the early-exercise decision can have important consequences beyond the realm of financial options.

Much of the material in this chapter can be traced to Merton (1973b), which contains an exhaustive treatment of option properties that must hold if there is to be no arbitrage. Cox and Rubinstein (1985) also provides an excellent treatment of this material.

PROBLEMS

9.1. A stock currently sells for $32.00. A 6-month call option with a strike of $35.00 has a premium of $2.27. Assuming a 4% continuously compounded risk-free rate and a 6% continuous dividend yield, what is the price of the associated put option?

9.2. A stock currently sells for $32.00. A 6-month call option with a strike of $30.00 has a premium of $4.29, and a 6-month put with the same strike has a premium of $2.64. Assume a 4% continuously compounded risk-free rate. What is the present value of dividends payable over the next 6 months?

9.3. Suppose the S&R index is 800, the continuously compounded risk-free rate is 5%, and the dividend yield is 0%. A 1-year 815-strike European call costs $75 and a 1-year 815-strike European put costs $45. Consider the strategy of buying the stock, selling the 815-strike call, and buying the 815-strike put.

    a. What is the rate of return on this position held until the expiration of the options?

    b. What is the arbitrage implied by your answer to (a)?

    c. What difference between the call and put prices would eliminate arbitrage?

    d. What difference between the call and put prices eliminates arbitrage for strike prices of $780, $800, $820, and $840?

9.4. Suppose the exchange rate is 0.95 $/€, the euro-denominated continuously compounded interest rate is 4%, the dollar-denominated continuously compounded interest rate is 6%, and the price of a 1-year 0.93-strike European call on the euro is $0.0571. What is the price of a 0.93-strike European put?

9.5. The premium of a 100-strike yen-denominated put on the euro is ¥8.763. The current exchange rate is 95 ¥/€. What is the strike of the corresponding euro-denominated yen call, and what is its premium?

9.6. The price of a 6-month dollar-denominated call option on the euro with a $0.90 strike is $0.0404. The price of an otherwise equivalent put option is $0.0141. The annual continuously compounded dollar interest rate is 5%.

    a. What is the 6-month dollar-euro forward price?

    b. If the euro-denominated annual continuously compounded interest rate is 3.5%, what is the spot exchange rate?

9.7. Suppose the dollar-denominated interest rate is 5%, the yen-denominated interest rate is 1% (both rates are continuously compounded), the spot exchange rate is 0.009 $/¥, and the price of a dollar-denominated European call to buy one yen with 1 year to expiration and a strike price of $0.009 is $0.0006.

    a. What is the dollar-denominated European yen put price such that there is no arbitrage opportunity?

    b. Suppose that a dollar-denominated European yen put with a strike of $0.009 has a premium of $0.0004. Demonstrate the arbitrage.

    c. Now suppose that you are in Tokyo, trading options that are denominated in yen rather than dollars. If the price of a dollar-denominated at-the-money yen call in the United States is $0.0006, what is the price of a yen-denominated at-the-money dollar call—an option giving the right to buy one dollar, denominated in yen—in Tokyo? What is the relationship of this answer to your answer to (a)? What is the price of the at-the-money dollar put?

9.8. Suppose call and put prices are given by

Strike	50	55
Call premium	9	10
Put premium	7	6

What no-arbitrage property is violated? What spread position would you use to effect arbitrage? Demonstrate that the spread position is an arbitrage.

9.9. Suppose call and put prices are given by

Strike	50	55
Call premium	16	10
Put premium	7	14

What no-arbitrage property is violated? What spread position would you use to effect arbitrage? Demonstrate that the spread position is an arbitrage.

9.10. Suppose call and put prices are given by

Strike	50	55	60
Call premium	18	14	9.50
Put premium	7	10.75	14.45

Find the convexity violations. What spread would you use to effect arbitrage? Demonstrate that the spread position is an arbitrage.

9.11. Suppose call and put prices are given by

Strike	80	100	105
Call premium	22	9	5
Put premium	4	21	24.80

Find the convexity violations. What spread would you use to effect arbitrage? Demonstrate that the spread position is an arbitrage.

9.12. In each case identify the arbitrage and demonstrate how you would make money by creating a table showing your payoff.

    a. Consider two European options on the same stock with the same time to expiration. The 90-strike call costs $10 and the 95-strike call costs $4.

    b. Now suppose these options have 2 years to expiration and the continuously compounded interest rate is 10%. The 90-strike call costs $10 and the 95-strike call costs $5.25. Show again that there is an arbitrage opportunity. (*Hint:* It is important in this case that the options are European.)

    c. Suppose that a 90-strike European call sells for $15, a 100-strike call sells for $10, and a 105-strike call sells for $6. Show how you could use an asymmetric butterfly to profit from this arbitrage opportunity.

9.13. Suppose the interest rate is 0 and the stock of XYZ has a positive dividend yield. Is there any circumstance in which you would early-exercise an American XYZ call? Is there any circumstance in which you would early-exercise an American XYZ put? Explain.

9.14. In the following, suppose that neither stock pays a dividend.

    a. Suppose you have a call option that permits you to receive one share of Apple by giving up one share of AOL. In what circumstance might you early-exercise this call?

b. Suppose you have a put option that permits you to give up one share of Apple, receiving one share of AOL. In what circumstance might you early-exercise this put? Would there be a loss from not early-exercising if Apple had a zero stock price?

c. Now suppose that Apple is expected to pay a dividend. Which of the above answers will change? Why?

9.15. The price of a nondividend-paying stock is $100 and the continuously compounded risk-free rate is 5%. A 1-year European call option with a strike price of $100 \times e^{0.05 \times 1} = \$105.127$ has a premium of $11.924. A $1\frac{1}{2}$ year European call option with a strike price of $100 \times e^{0.05 \times 1.5} = \$107.788$ has a premium of $11.50. Demonstrate an arbitrage.

9.16. Suppose that to buy either a call or a put option you pay the quoted ask price, denoted $C_a(K, T)$ and $P_a(K, T)$, and to sell an option you receive the bid, $C_b(K, T)$ and $P_b(K, T)$. Similarly, the ask and bid prices for the stock are S_a and S_b. Finally, suppose you can borrow at the rate r_H and lend at the rate r_L. The stock pays no dividend. Find the bounds between which you cannot profitably perform a parity arbitrage.

9.17. In this problem we consider whether parity is violated by any of the option prices in Table 9.1. Suppose that you buy at the ask and sell at the bid, and that your continuously compounded lending rate is 1.9% and your borrowing rate is 2%. Ignore transaction costs on the stock, for which the price is $84.85. Assume that IBM is expected to pay a $0.18 dividend on November 8 (prior to expiration of the November options). For each strike and expiration, what is the cost if you

a. Buy the call, sell the put, short the stock, and lend the present value of the strike price plus dividend?

b. Sell the call, buy the put, buy the stock, and borrow the present value of the strike price plus dividend?

9.18. Consider the January 80, 85, and 90 call option prices in Table 9.1.

a. Does convexity hold if you buy a butterfly spread, buying at the ask price and selling at the bid?

b. Does convexity hold if you *sell* a butterfly spread, buying at the ask price and selling at the bid?

c. Does convexity hold if you are a market-maker either buying or selling a butterfly, paying the bid and receiving the ask?

APPENDIX 9.A: PARITY BOUNDS FOR AMERICAN OPTIONS

The exact parity relationship discussed in Chapter 9 only holds for European options. However, American options often come close to obeying put-call parity, especially when options have short times to expiration.

With a nondividend-paying stock, the call will not be exercised early, but the put might be. The effect of early exercise for the put is to accelerate the receipt of the strike price. Since interest on the strike price is small for short times to maturity, parity will come close to holding for short-lived American options on nondividend-paying stocks.

We now let P and C refer to prices of American options. The American put can be more valuable than the European put, and we have

$$P \geq C + \mathrm{PV}(K) - S$$

However, suppose that the put were exercised early. Then it would be worth $K - S$. For example, if we think of synthetically creating the stock by buying the call and selling the put, there is a chance that we will pay K before expiration, in the event the stock price plummets and the put is early-exercised. Consequently, if we replace the present value of the strike with the undiscounted strike, we have a valid upper bound for the value of the put. It will be true (and you can verify with a no-arbitrage argument) that

$$P \leq C + K - S$$

When there are no dividends, we have $C + K - S$ as an upper bound on the put, and European parity as a lower bound (since an American put is always worth at least as much as a European put). The parity relationship can be written as a restriction on the put price or on the call price:

$$C + K - S \geq P \geq C + \mathrm{PV}(K) - S$$
$$P + S - \mathrm{PV}(K) \geq C \geq P + S - K$$

Thus, when there are no dividends, European parity can be violated to the extent of interest on the strike price. Since this will be small for options that are not long-lived, European parity can remain a good approximation for American options.

Dividends add the complication that the call as well as the put may be exercised early. There exists the possibility of a large parity violation because of the following "whipsaw" scenario: The call is exercised early to capture a large dividend payment, the stock price drops, and the put is then exercised early to capture interest on the strike price. The possibility that this can happen leads to a wider no-arbitrage band. With dividends, the parity relationship becomes (Cox and Rubinstein, 1985, p. 152)

$$C + K + \mathrm{PV}(D) - S \geq P \geq C + \mathrm{PV}(K) - S$$
$$P + S - \mathrm{PV}(K) \geq C \geq P + S - \mathrm{PV}(D) - K$$

The upper bound for the call is the same as in European parity, except without dividends. The intuition for the upper bound on the call option (the left-hand side) is that we can avoid the loss of dividends by early-exercising the call; hence, it is the same bound as in the European case with no dividends. The lower bound exists because it may not be optimal to exercise the call to avoid dividends, and it may be optimal to early-exercise the put.

Consider the worst case for the call. Suppose $K = \$100$ and $S = \$100$, and the stock is about to pay a liquidating dividend (i.e., $D = \$100$). We will not exercise the call, since doing so gives us nothing. The put will be exercised after the dividend is paid, once the stock is worthless. So $P = \$100$. The relationship then states

$$C \geq P + S - D - K = 100 + 100 - 100 - 100 = 0$$

And indeed, the call will be worthless in this case.

APPENDIX 9.B: ALGEBRAIC PROOFS OF STRIKE-PRICE RELATIONS

Appendix available online at www.aw-bc.com/mcdonald.

This is two equations in the two unknowns Δ and B. Solving for Δ and B gives

$$\Delta = e^{-\delta h}\frac{C_u - C_d}{S(u - d)} \tag{10.1}$$

$$B = e^{-rh}\frac{uC_d - dC_u}{u - d} \tag{10.2}$$

Note that when there are dividends, the formula adjusts the number of shares in the replicating portfolio, Δ, to offset the dividend income.

Given the expressions for Δ and B, we can derive a simple formula for the value of the option. The cost of creating the option is the net cash required to buy the shares and bonds. Thus, the cost of the option is $\Delta S + B$. Using equations (10.1) and (10.2), we have

$$\Delta S + B = e^{-rh}\left(C_u\frac{e^{(r-\delta)h} - d}{u - d} + C_d\frac{u - e^{(r-\delta)h}}{u - d}\right) \tag{10.3}$$

The assumed stock price movements, u and d, should not give rise to arbitrage opportunities. In particular, we require that

$$u > e^{(r-\delta)h} > d \tag{10.4}$$

To see why this condition must hold, suppose $\delta = 0$. If the condition were violated, we would short the stock to hold bonds (if $e^{rh} \geq u$), or we would borrow to buy the stock (if $d \geq e^{rh}$). Either way, we would earn an arbitrage profit. Therefore the assumed process could not be consistent with any possible equilibrium. Problem 10.21 asks you to verify that the condition must also hold when $\delta > 0$.

Note that because Δ is the number of shares in the replicating portfolio, it can also be interpreted as the sensitivity of the option to a change in the stock price. If the stock price changes by \$1, then the option price, $\Delta S + B$, changes by Δ. This interpretation will be quite important later.

Example 10.1 Here is the solution for Δ, B, and the option price using the stock price tree depicted in Figure 10.1. There we have $u = \$60/\$41 = 1.4634$, $d = \$30/\$41 = 0.7317$, and $\delta = 0$. In addition, the call option had a strike price of \$40 and 1 year to expiration—hence, $h = 1$. Thus $C_u = \$60 - \$40 = \$20$, and $C_d = 0$. Using equations (10.1) and (10.2), we have

$$\Delta = \frac{\$20 - 0}{\$41 \times (1.4634 - 0.7317)} = 2/3$$

$$B - e^{-0.08}\frac{1.4634 \times \$0 - 0.7317 \times \$20}{1.4634 - 0.7317} = -\$18.462$$

Hence, the option price is given by

$$\Delta S + B = 2/3 \times \$41 - \$18.462 = \$8.871$$ ❧

Note that *if we are interested only in the option price, it is not necessary to solve for Δ and B;* that is just an intermediate step. If we want to know only the option price, we can use equation (10.3) directly:

$$\Delta S + B = e^{-0.08} \left(\$20 \times \frac{e^{0.08} - 0.7317}{1.4634 - 0.7317} + \$0 \times \frac{1.4634 - e^{0.08}}{1.4634 - 0.7317} \right)$$
$$= \$8.871$$

Throughout this chapter we will continue to report Δ and B, since we are interested not only in the price but also in the replicating portfolio.

Arbitraging a Mispriced Option

What if the observed option price differs from the theoretical price? Because we have a way to replicate the option using the stock, it is possible to take advantage of the mispricing and fulfill the dream of every trader—namely, to buy low and sell high.

The following examples illustrate that if the option price is anything other than the theoretical price, arbitrage is possible.

The option is overpriced   Suppose that the market price for the option is \$9.00, instead of \$8.871. We can sell the option, but this leaves us with the risk that the stock price at expiration will be \$60 and we will be required to deliver the stock.

We can address this risk by buying a synthetic option at the same time we sell the actual option. We have already seen how to create the synthetic option by buying 2/3 shares and borrowing \$18.462. If we simultaneously sell the actual option and buy the synthetic, the initial cash flow is

$$\underbrace{\$9.00}_{\text{Receive option premium}} - \underbrace{2/3 \times \$41}_{\text{Cost of shares}} + \underbrace{\$18.462}_{\text{Borrowing}} = \$0.129$$

We earn \$0.129, the amount by which the option is mispriced.

Now we verify that there is no risk at expiration. We have

	Stock Price in 1 Year (S_1)	
	\$30	**\$60**
Written call	\$ 0	−\$20
2/3 Purchased shares	\$20	\$40
Repay loan of \$18.462	−\$20	−\$20
Total payoff	\$0	\$0

By hedging the written option, we eliminate risk.

The option is underpriced   Now suppose that the market price of the option is $8.25. We wish to buy the underpriced option. Of course, if we are unhedged and the stock price falls at expiration, we lose our investment. We can hedge by selling a synthetic option. We accomplish this by reversing the position for a synthetic purchased call: We short 2/3 shares and invest $18.462 of the proceeds in Treasury bills. The cost of this is

$$\underbrace{-\$8.25}_{\text{Option premium}} + \underbrace{2/3 \times \$41}_{\text{Short-sale proceeds}} - \underbrace{\$18.462}_{\text{Invest in T-bills}} = \$0.621$$

At expiration we have

	Stock Price in 1 Year (S_1)	
	$30	$60
Purchased call	$0	$20
2/3 short-sold shares	−$20	−$40
Sell T-bill	$20	$20
Total payoff	$0	$0

We have earned the amount by which the option was mispriced and hedged the risk associated with buying the option.

A Graphical Interpretation of the Binomial Formula

The binomial solution for Δ and B, equations (10.1) and (10.2), is obtained by solving two equations in two unknowns. Letting C_h and S_h be the option and stock value after one binomial period, and supposing $\delta = 0$, the equations for the portfolio describe a line with the formula

$$C_h = \Delta \times S_h + e^{rh} B$$

This is graphed as line AED in Figure 10.2, which shows the option payoff as a function of the stock price at expiration.

We choose Δ and B to yield a portfolio that pays C_d when $S_h = dS$ and C_u when $S_h = uS$. Hence, by construction this line runs through points E and D. We can control the slope of a payoff diagram by varying the number of shares, Δ, and its height by varying the number of bonds, B. It is apparent that a line that runs through both E and D must have slope $\Delta = (C_u - C_d)/(uS - dS)$. Also, the point A is the value of the portfolio when $S_h = 0$, which is the time-h value of the bond position, $e^{rh} B$. Hence, $e^{rh} B$ is the y-axis intercept of the line.

You can see by looking at Figure 10.2 that *any* line replicating a call will have a positive slope ($\Delta > 0$) and a negative intercept ($B < 0$). As an exercise, you can verify graphically that a portfolio replicating a put would have negative slope ($\Delta < 0$) and positive intercept ($B > 0$).

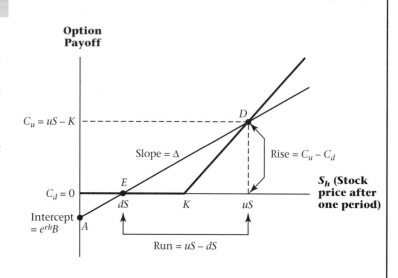

FIGURE 10.2

FIGURE 10.2

The payoff to an expiring call option is the dark heavy line. The payoff to the option at the points dS and uS are C_d and C_u (at point D). The portfolio consisting of Δ shares and B bonds has intercept $e^{rh}B$ and slope Δ, and by construction goes through both points E and D. The slope of the line is calculated as $\frac{\text{Rise}}{\text{Run}}$ between points E and D, which gives the formula for Δ.

Risk-Neutral Pricing

So far we have not specified the probabilities of the stock going up or down. In fact, probabilities were not used anywhere in the option price calculations. Since the strategy of holding Δ shares and B bonds replicates the option whichever way the stock moves, the probability of an up or down movement in the stock is irrelevant for pricing the option.

Although probabilities are not needed for pricing the option, there is a probabilistic interpretation of equation (10.3). Notice that in equation (10.3) the terms $(e^{(r-\delta)h} - d)/(u - d)$ and $(u - e^{(r-\delta)h})/(u - d)$ sum to 1 and are both positive (this follows from inequality 10.4). Thus, we can interpret these terms as probabilities. Let

$$p^* = \frac{e^{(r-\delta)h} - d}{u - d} \tag{10.5}$$

Equation (10.3) can then be written as

$$C = e^{-rh}[p^* C_u + (1 - p^*)C_d] \tag{10.6}$$

This expression has the appearance of a discounted expected value. It is peculiar, though, because we are discounting at the risk-free rate, even though the risk of the option is at least as great as the risk of the stock (a call option is a leveraged position in the stock since $B < 0$). In addition, there is no reason to think that p^* is the true probability that the stock will go up; in general it is not.

What happens if we use p^* to compute the expected *undiscounted* stock price? Doing this, we obtain

$$p^* u S + (1 - p^*) d S = e^{(r-\delta)h} S = F_{t,t+h} \tag{10.7}$$

When we use p^* as the probability of an up move, the expected stock price equals the forward price, $e^{(r-\delta)h} S$. (We derived this expression for the forward price of the stock in Chapter 5, equation 5.7.) Thus, *we can compute the forward price using the binomial tree.* In fact, one way to think about p^* is that it is the probability for which the expected stock price is the forward price.

We will call p^* the **risk-neutral probability** of an increase in the stock price. Equation (10.6) will prove very important and we will discuss risk-neutral pricing more in Chapter 11.

Constructing a Binomial Tree

We now explain the construction of the binomial tree.[3] Recall that the goal of the tree is to characterize future uncertainty about the stock price in an economically reasonable way.

As a starting point, we can ask: What if there were no uncertainty about the future stock price? Without uncertainty, the stock price next period must equal the forward price. Recall from Chapter 5 that the formula for the forward price is

$$F_{t,t+h} = S_t e^{(r-\delta)h} \tag{10.8}$$

Thus, without uncertainty we must have $S_{t+h} = F_{t,t+h}$. To interpret this, under certainty, the rate of return on the stock must be the risk-free rate. Thus, the stock price must rise at the risk-free rate less the dividend yield, $r - \delta$.

Now we incorporate uncertainty, but we first need to define what we mean by uncertainty. A natural measure of uncertainty about the stock return is the *annualized standard deviation of the continuously compounded stock return*, which we will denote by σ. The standard deviation measures how sure we are that the stock return will be close to the expected return. Stocks with a larger σ will have a greater chance of a return far from the expected return.

We incorporate uncertainty into the binomial tree by modeling the up and down moves of the stock price relative to the forward price, with the difference from the forward price being related to the standard deviation. We will see in Section 11.3 that if the annual standard deviation is σ, the standard deviation over a period of length h is $\sigma\sqrt{h}$. In other words, the standard deviation of the stock return is proportional to the *square root* of time.

We now model the stock price evolution as

$$\begin{aligned} u S_t &= F_{t,t+h} e^{+\sigma\sqrt{h}} \\ d S_t &= F_{t,t+h} e^{-\sigma\sqrt{h}} \end{aligned} \tag{10.9}$$

---

[3]This discussion is intended as a quick overview. Section 11.3 contains a more in-depth discussion.

Using equation (10.8), we can rewrite this as

$$u = e^{(r-\delta)h+\sigma\sqrt{h}}$$
$$d = e^{(r-\delta)h-\sigma\sqrt{h}} \tag{10.10}$$

This is the formula we will use to construct binomial trees. Note that if we set volatility equal to zero (i.e., $\sigma = 0$), we will have $u S_t = d S_t = F_{t,t+h}$. Thus, with zero volatility, the price will still rise over time, just as with a Treasury bill. Zero volatility does not mean that prices are *fixed;* it means that prices are *known in advance.*

We will refer to a tree constructed using equation (10.10) as a "forward tree." In Section 11.3 we will discuss alternative ways to construct a tree, including the Cox-Ross-Rubinstein tree.

Another One-Period Example

We began this section by assuming that the stock price followed the binomial tree in Figure 10.1. The up and down stock prices of $30 and $60 were selected to make the example easy to follow. Now we present an example where everything is the same except that we use equation (10.10) to construct the up and down moves.

Suppose volatility is 30%. Since the period is 1 year, we have $h = 1$, so that $\sigma\sqrt{h} = 0.30$. We also have $S_0 = \$41$, $r = 0.08$, and $\delta = 0$. Using equation (10.10), we get

$$uS = \$41 e^{(0.08-0)\times 1 + 0.3\times\sqrt{1}} = \$59.954$$
$$dS = \$41 e^{(0.08-0)\times 1 - 0.3\times\sqrt{1}} = \$32.903 \tag{10.11}$$

Because the binomial tree is different than in Figure 10.1, the option price will be different as well.

Using the stock prices given in equation (10.11), we have $u = \$59.954/\$41 = 1.4623$ and $d = \$32.903/\$41 = 0.8025$. With $K = \$40$, we have $C_u = \$59.954 - \$40 = \$19.954$, and $C_d = 0$. Using equations (10.1) and (10.2), we obtain

$$\Delta = \frac{\$19.954 - 0}{\$41 \times (1.4623 - 0.8025)} = 0.7376$$

$$B = e^{-0.08} \frac{1.4623 \times \$0 - 0.8025 \times \$19.954}{1.4623 - 0.8025} = -\$22.405$$

Hence, the option price is given by

$$\Delta S + B = 0.7376 \times \$41 - \$22.405 = \$7.839$$

This example is summarized in Figure 10.3.

Summary

We have covered a great deal of ground in this section, so we pause for a moment to review the main points:

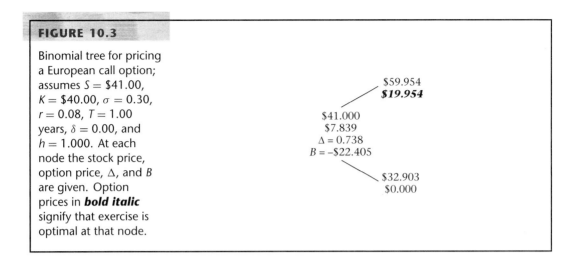

FIGURE 10.3

Binomial tree for pricing a European call option; assumes $S = \$41.00$, $K = \$40.00$, $\sigma = 0.30$, $r = 0.08$, $T = 1.00$ years, $\delta = 0.00$, and $h = 1.000$. At each node the stock price, option price, Δ, and B are given. Option prices in **_bold italic_** signify that exercise is optimal at that node.

$41.000
$7.839
$\Delta = 0.738$
$B = -\$22.405$

$59.954
_$19.954_

$32.903
$0.000

- In order to price an option, we need to know the stock price, the strike price, the standard deviation of returns on the stock (in order to compute u and d), the dividend yield, and the risk-free rate.

- Using the risk-free rate, dividend yield, and σ, we can approximate the future distribution of the stock by creating a binomial tree using equation (10.10).

- Once we have the binomial tree, it is possible to price the option using equation (10.3). The solution also provides the recipe for synthetically creating the option: Buy Δ shares of stock (equation 10.1) and borrow B (equation 10.2).

- The formula for the option price, equation (10.3), can be written so that it has the appearance of a discounted expected value.

There are still many issues we have to deal with. The simple binomial tree seems too simple to provide an accurate option price. Unanswered questions include how to handle more than one binomial period, how to price put options, how to price American options, etc. With the basic binomial formula in hand, we can now turn to those questions.

10.2 TWO OR MORE BINOMIAL PERIODS

We now see how to extend the binomial tree to more than one period.

A Two-Period European Call

We begin first by adding a single period to the tree in Figure 10.3; the result is displayed in Figure 10.4. We can use that tree to price a 2-year option with a $40 strike when the current stock price is $41, assuming all inputs are the same as before.

Since we are increasing the time to maturity for a call option on a nondividend-paying stock, then based on the discussion in Section 9.3 we expect the option premium

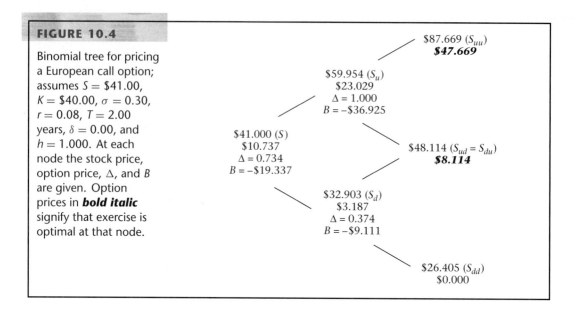

FIGURE 10.4

Binomial tree for pricing a European call option; assumes $S = \$41.00$, $K = \$40.00$, $\sigma = 0.30$, $r = 0.08$, $T = 2.00$ years, $\delta = 0.00$, and $h = 1.000$. At each node the stock price, option price, Δ, and B are given. Option prices in **bold italic** signify that exercise is optimal at that node.

$87.669 ($S_{uu}$)$
$47.669

$59.954 ($S_u$)$
$23.029
$\Delta = 1.000$
$B = -\$36.925$

$48.114 ($S_{ud} = S_{du}$)$
$8.114

$41.000 ($S$)$
$10.737
$\Delta = 0.734$
$B = -\$19.337$

$32.903 ($S_d$)$
$3.187
$\Delta = 0.374$
$B = -\$9.111$

$26.405 ($S_{dd}$)$
$0.000

to increase. In this example the two-period tree will give us a price of $10.737, compared to $7.839 in Figure 10.3.

Constructing the tree   To see how to construct the tree, suppose that we move up in year 1, to $S_u = \$59.954$. If we reach this price, then we can move further up or down according to equation (10.9). We get

$$S_{uu} = \$59.954e^{0.08+0.3} = \$87.669$$

and

$$S_{ud} = \$59.954e^{0.08-0.3} = \$48.114$$

The subscript *uu* means that the stock has gone up twice in a row and the subscript *ud* means that the stock has gone up once and then down.

Similarly if the price in one year is $S_d = \$32.903$, we have

$$S_{du} = \$32.903e^{0.08+0.3} = \$48.114$$

and

$$S_{dd} = \$32.903e^{0.08-0.3} = \$26.405$$

Note that an up move followed by a down move (S_{ud}) generates the same stock price as a down move followed by an up move (S_{du}). This is called a **recombining tree.** If an up move followed by a down move led to a different price than a down move followed by an up move, we would have a **nonrecombining tree.**[4] A recombining tree has fewer nodes, which means less computation is required to compute an option price. We will see examples of nonrecombining trees in Sections 11.5 and 24.4.

We also could have used equation (10.10) directly to compute the year-2 stock prices. Recall that $u = e^{0.08+0.3} = 1.462$ and $d = e^{0.08-0.3} = 0.803$. We have

$$S_{uu} = u^2 \times \$41 = e^{2\times(0.08+0.3)} \times \$41 = \$87.669$$

$$S_{ud} = S_{du} = u \times d \times \$41 = e^{(0.08+0.3)} \times e^{(0.08-0.3)} \times \$41 = \$48.114$$

$$S_{dd} = d^2 \times \$41 = e^{2\times(0.08-0.3)} \times \$41 = \$26.405$$

Pricing the call option How do we price the option when we have two binomial periods? The key insight is that we work *backward* through the binomial tree. In order to use equation (10.3), we need to know the option prices resulting from up and down moves in the subsequent period. At the outset, the only period where we know the option price is at expiration.

Knowing the price at expiration, we can determine the price in period 1. Having determined that price, we can work back to period 0.

Figure 10.4 exhibits the option price at each node as well as the details of the replicating portfolio at each node. Remember, however, when we use equation (10.3), it is not necessary to compute Δ and B in order to derive the option price.[5] Here are details of the solution:

Year 2, Stock Price = $87.669 Since we are at expiration, the option value is $\max(0, S - K) = \$47.669$.

Year 2, Stock Price = $48.114 Again we are at expiration, so the option value is $8.114.

Year 2, Stock Price = $26.405 Since the option is out of the money, the value is 0.

Year 1, Stock Price = $59.954 At this node we use equation (10.3) to compute the option value. (Note that once we are at this node, the "up" stock price, uS, is $87.669, and the "down" stock price, dS, is $48.114.)

$$e^{-0.08}\left(\$47.669 \times \frac{e^{0.08} - 0.803}{1.462 - 0.803} + \$8.114 \times \frac{1.462 - e^{0.08}}{1.462 - 0.803}\right) = \$23.029$$

....

[4]In cases where the tree recombines, the representation of stock price movements is also (and, some argue, more properly) called a *lattice*. The term *tree* would then be reserved for nonrecombining stock movements.

[5]As an exercise, you can verify the Δ and B at each node.

Year 1, Stock Price = $32.903 Again we use equation (10.3) to compute the option value:

$$e^{-0.08}\left(\$8.114 \times \frac{e^{0.08} - 0.803}{1.462 - 0.803} + \$0 \times \frac{1.462 - e^{0.08}}{1.462 - 0.803}\right) = \$3.187$$

Year 0, Stock Price = $41 Again using equation (10.3):

$$e^{-0.08}\left(\$23.029 \times \frac{e^{0.08} - 0.803}{1.462 - 0.803} + \$3.187 \times \frac{1.462 - e^{0.08}}{1.462 - 0.803}\right) = \$10.737$$

Notice the following:

- The option price is greater for the 2-year than for the 1-year option, as we would expect.

- We priced the option by working backward through the tree, starting at the end and working back to the first period.

- The option's Δ and B are different at different nodes. In particular, at a given point in time, Δ increases to 1 as we go further into the money.

- We priced a European option, so early exercise was not permitted. However, permitting early exercise would have made no difference. At every node prior to expiration, the option price is greater than $S - K$; hence we would not have exercised even if the option had been American.

- Once we understand the two-period option it is straightforward to value an option using more than two binomial periods. The important principle is to work backward through the tree.

Many Binomial Periods

The generalization to many binomial periods is straightforward. We can represent only a small number of binomial periods here, but a spreadsheet or computer program can handle a very large number of binomial nodes.

An obvious objection to the binomial calculations thus far is that the stock can only have two or three different values at expiration. It seems unlikely that the option price calculation will be accurate. The solution to this problem is to divide the time to expiration into more periods, generating a more realistic tree.

To illustrate how to do this, at the same time illustrating a tree with more than two periods, we will re-examine the 1-year European call option in Figure 10.3, which has a $40 strike and initial stock price of $41. Let there be three binomial periods. Since it is a 1-year call, this means that the length of a period is $h = \frac{1}{3}$. We will assume that other inputs stay the same, so $r = 0.08$ and $\sigma = 0.3$.

Figure 10.5 depicts the stock price and option price tree for this option. The option price is $7.074, as opposed to $7.839 in Figure 10.3. The difference occurs because

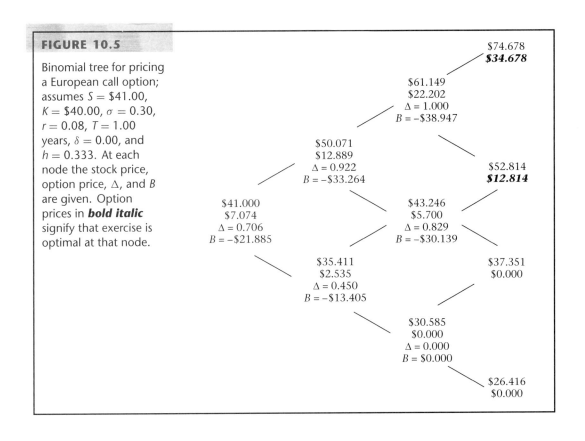

FIGURE 10.5

Binomial tree for pricing a European call option; assumes $S = \$41.00$, $K = \$40.00$, $\sigma = 0.30$, $r = 0.08$, $T = 1.00$ years, $\delta = 0.00$, and $h = 0.333$. At each node the stock price, option price, Δ, and B are given. Option prices in **bold italic** signify that exercise is optimal at that node.

the numerical approximation is different; it is quite common to see large changes in a binomial price when the number of periods, n, is changed, particularly when n is small.

Since the length of the binomial period is shorter, u and d are smaller than before (1.2212 and 0.8637 as opposed to 1.462 and 0.803 with $h = 1$). Just to be clear about the procedure, here is how the second-period nodes are computed:

$$S_u = \$41e^{0.08 \times 1/3 + 0.3\sqrt{1/3}} = \$50.071$$

$$S_d = \$41e^{0.08 \times 1/3 - 0.3\sqrt{1/3}} = \$35.411$$

The remaining nodes are computed similarly.

The option price is computed by working backward. The risk-neutral probability of the stock price going up in a period is

$$\frac{e^{0.08 \times 1/3} - 0.8637}{1.2212 - 0.8637} = 0.4568$$

The option price at the node where $S = \$43.246$, for example, is then given by

$$e^{-0.08 \times 1/3} \left([\$12.814 \times 0.4568] + [\$0 \times (1 - 0.4568)] \right) = \$5.700$$

Option prices at the remaining nodes are priced similarly.

10.3 PUT OPTIONS

Thus far we have priced only call options. The binomial method easily accommodates put options also, as well as other derivatives. We compute put option prices using the same stock price tree and in almost the same way as call option prices; the only difference with a European put option occurs at expiration: Instead of computing the price as $\max(0, S - K)$, we use $\max(0, K - S)$.

Figure 10.6 shows the binomial tree for a European put option with 1 year to expiration and a strike of $40 when the stock price is $41. This is the same stock price tree as in Figure 10.5.

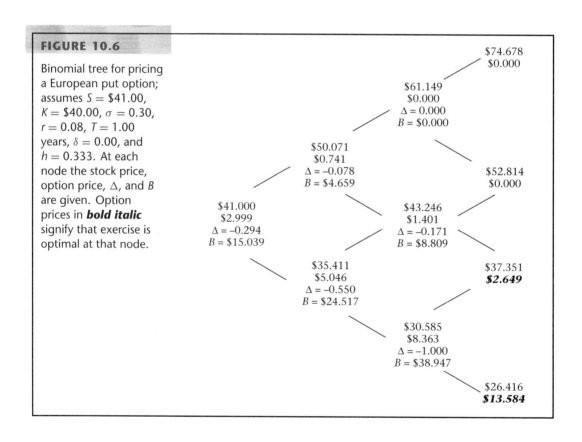

FIGURE 10.6

Binomial tree for pricing a European put option; assumes $S = \$41.00$, $K = \$40.00$, $\sigma = 0.30$, $r = 0.08$, $T = 1.00$ years, $\delta = 0.00$, and $h = 0.333$. At each node the stock price, option price, Δ, and B are given. Option prices in **bold italic** signify that exercise is optimal at that node.

$74.678
$0.000

$61.149
$0.000
$\Delta = 0.000$
$B = \$0.000$

$50.071
$0.741
$\Delta = -0.078$
$B = \$4.659$

$52.814
$0.000

$41.000
$2.999
$\Delta = -0.294$
$B = \$15.039$

$43.246
$1.401
$\Delta = -0.171$
$B = \$8.809$

$35.411
$5.046
$\Delta = -0.550$
$B = \$24.517$

$37.351
$2.649

$30.585
$8.363
$\Delta = -1.000$
$B = \$38.947$

$26.416
$13.584

To illustrate the calculations, consider the option price at the node where the stock price is \$35.411. The option price at that node is computed as

$$e^{-0.08 \times 1/3} \left(\$1.401 \times \frac{e^{0.08 \times 1/3} - 0.8637}{1.2212 - 0.8637} + \$8.363 \times \frac{1.2212 - e^{0.08 \times 1/3}}{1.2212 - 0.8637} \right) = \$5.046$$

Figure 10.6 does raise one issue that we have not previously had to consider. Notice that at the node where the stock price is \$30.585, the option price is \$8.363. If this option were American, it would make sense to exercise at that node. The option is worth \$8.363 when held until expiration, but it would be worth \$40 − \$30.585 = \$9.415 if exercised at that node. Thus, in this case the American option should be more valuable than the otherwise equivalent European option. We will now see how to use the binomial approach to value American options.

10.4 AMERICAN OPTIONS

Since it is easy to check at each node whether early exercise is optimal, the binomial method is well-suited to valuing American options. The value of the option if it is left "alive" (i.e., unexercised) is given by the value of holding it for another period, equation (10.3). The value of the option if it is exercised is given by $\max(0, S - K)$ if it is a call and $\max(0, K - S)$ if it is a put.

Thus, for an American put, the value of the option at a node is given by

$$P(S, K, t) = \\ \max \left(K - S, e^{-rh} \left[P(uS, K, t + h)p^* + P(dS, K, t + h)(1 - p^*) \right] \right) \quad (10.12)$$

where, as in equation (10.5),

$$p^* = \frac{e^{(r-\delta)h} - d}{u - d}$$

Figure 10.7 presents the binomial tree for the American version of the put option valued in Figure 10.6. The only difference in the trees occurs at the node where the stock price is \$30.585. The American option at that point is worth \$9.415, its early-exercise value. We have just seen in the previous section that the value of the option if unexercised is \$8.363.

The greater value of the option at that node ripples back through the tree. When the option price is computed at the node where the stock price is \$35.411, the value is greater in Figure 10.7 than in Figure 10.6; the reason is that the price is greater at the subsequent node S_{dd} due to early exercise.

The initial option price is \$3.293, greater than the value of \$2.999 for the European option. This increase in value is due entirely to early exercise at the S_{dd} node.

In general the valuation of American options proceeds as in this example. At each node we check for early exercise. If the value of the option is greater when exercised, we assign that value to the node. Otherwise, we assign the value of the option unexercised. We work backward through the tree as usual.

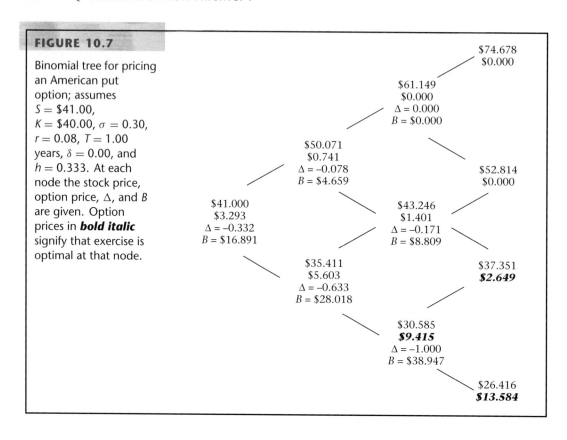

FIGURE 10.7

Binomial tree for pricing an American put option; assumes $S = \$41.00$, $K = \$40.00$, $\sigma = 0.30$, $r = 0.08$, $T = 1.00$ years, $\delta = 0.00$, and $h = 0.333$. At each node the stock price, option price, Δ, and B are given. Option prices in **bold italic** signify that exercise is optimal at that node.

10.5 Options on Other Assets

The model developed thus far can be modified easily to price options on underlying assets other than nondividend-paying stocks. In this section we present examples of how to do so. We examine options on stock indexes, currencies, and futures contracts. In every case the general procedure is the same: We compute the option price using equation (10.6). The difference for different underlying assets will be the construction of the binomial tree and the risk-neutral probability.

The valuation of an option on a stock that pays discrete dividends is more involved and is covered in Chapter 11.

Option on a Stock Index

Suppose a stock index pays continuous dividends at the rate δ. This type of option has in fact already been covered by our derivation in Section 10.1. The up and down index moves are given by equation (10.10), the replicating portfolio by equations (10.1) and

(10.2), and the option price by equation (10.3). The risk-neutral probability is given by equation (10.5).[6]

Figure 10.8 displays a binomial tree for an American call option on a stock index. Note that because of dividends, early exercise is optimal at the node where the stock price is $157.101. Given these parameters, we have $p^* = 0.457$; hence, when $S = \$157.101$, the value of the option unexercised is

$$e^{-0.05 \times 1/3} \left[0.457 \times \$87.747 + (1 - 0.457) \times \$32.779 \right] = \$56.942$$

Since $57.101 > 56.942$, we exercise the option at that node.

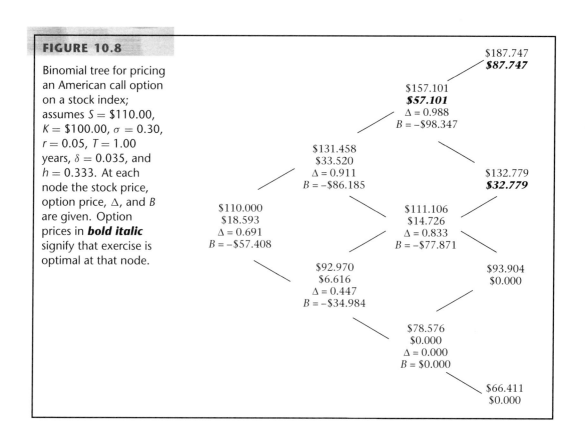

FIGURE 10.8

Binomial tree for pricing an American call option on a stock index; assumes $S = \$110.00$, $K = \$100.00$, $\sigma = 0.30$, $r = 0.05$, $T = 1.00$ years, $\delta = 0.035$, and $h = 0.333$. At each node the stock price, option price, Δ, and B are given. Option prices in **bold italic** signify that exercise is optimal at that node.

$187.747
$87.747

$157.101
$57.101
$\Delta = 0.988$
$B = -\$98.347$

$131.458
$33.520
$\Delta = 0.911$
$B = -\$86.185$

$132.779
$32.779

$110.000
$18.593
$\Delta = 0.691$
$B = -\$57.408$

$111.106
$14.726
$\Delta = 0.833$
$B = -\$77.871$

$92.970
$6.616
$\Delta = 0.447$
$B = -\$34.984$

$93.904
$0.000

$78.576
$0.000
$\Delta = 0.000$
$B = \$0.000$

$66.411
$0.000

---

[6]Intuitively, dividends can be taken into account either by (1) appropriately lowering the nodes on the tree and leaving risk-neutral probabilities unchanged, or (2) by reducing the risk-neutral probability and leaving the tree unchanged. The forward tree adopts the first approach.

Options on Currencies

With a currency with spot price x_0, the forward price is $F_{0,h} = x_0 e^{(r-r_f)h}$, where r_f is the foreign interest rate. Thus, we construct the binomial tree using

$$ux = xe^{(r-r_f)h + \sigma\sqrt{h}}$$
$$dx = xe^{(r-r_f)h - \sigma\sqrt{h}}$$

There is one subtlety in creating the replicating portfolio: Investing in a "currency" means investing in a money-market fund or fixed income obligation denominated in that currency. (We encountered this idea previously in Chapter 5.) Taking into account interest on the foreign-currency-denominated obligation, the two equations are

$$\Delta \times dxe^{r_f h} + e^{rh} \times B = C_d$$
$$\Delta \times uxe^{r_f h} + e^{rh} \times B = C_u$$

The risk-neutral probability of an up move in this case is given by

$$p^* = \frac{e^{(r-r_f)h} - d}{u - d} \tag{10.13}$$

Notice that if we think of r_f as the dividend yield on the foreign currency, these two equations look exactly like those for an index option. In fact the solution is the same as for an option on an index: Set the dividend yield equal to the foreign risk-free rate and the current value of the index equal to the spot exchange rate.

Figure 10.9 prices a dollar-denominated American put option on the euro. The current exchange rate is assumed to be \$1.05/€ and the strike is \$1.10/€. The euro-denominated interest rate is 3.1%, and the dollar-denominated rate is 5.5%.

Because volatility is low and the option is in-the-money, early exercise is optimal at three nodes prior to expiration.

Options on Futures Contracts

We now consider options on futures contracts. We assume the forward price is the same as the futures price. Since we build the tree based on the forward price, we simply add up and down movements around the current price. Thus, the nodes are constructed as

$$u = e^{\sigma\sqrt{h}}$$
$$d = e^{-\sigma\sqrt{h}}$$

Note that this solution for u and d is exactly what we would get for an option on a stock index if δ, the dividend yield, were equal to the risk-free rate.

In constructing the replicating portfolio, recall that in each period a futures contract pays the change in the futures price, and there is no investment required to enter a futures contract. The problem is to find the number of futures contracts, Δ, and the lending, B, that replicates the option. We have

$$\Delta \times (dF - F) + e^{rh} \times B = C_d$$
$$\Delta \times (uF - F) + e^{rh} \times B = C_u$$

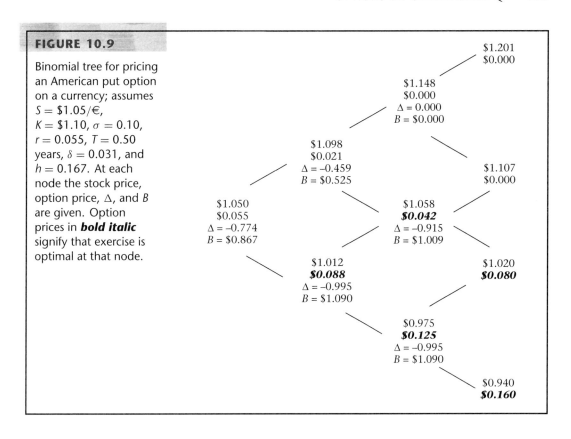

FIGURE 10.9

Binomial tree for pricing an American put option on a currency; assumes $S = \$1.05/€$, $K = \$1.10$, $\sigma = 0.10$, $r = 0.055$, $T = 0.50$ years, $\delta = 0.031$, and $h = 0.167$. At each node the stock price, option price, Δ, and B are given. Option prices in **bold italic** signify that exercise is optimal at that node.

Solving gives[7]

$$\Delta = \frac{C_u - C_d}{F(u - d)}$$

$$B = e^{-rh}\left(C_u\frac{1 - d}{u - d} + C_d\frac{u - 1}{u - d}\right)$$

While Δ tells us how many futures contracts to hold to hedge the option, the value of the option in this case is simply B. The reason is that the futures contract requires no

[7]The interpretation of Δ here is the number of futures contracts in the replicating portfolio. Another interpretation of Δ is the price sensitivity of the option when the price of the underlying asset changes. These two interpretations usually coincide, but not in the case of options on futures. The reason is that the futures price at time t reflects a price denominated in future dollars. The effect on the option price of a futures price change today is given by $e^{-rh}\Delta$. To see this, consider an option that is one binomial period

(*continued*)

investment, so the only investment is that made in the bond. We can again price the option using equation (10.3).

The risk-neutral probability of an up move is given by

$$p^* = \frac{1-d}{u-d} \tag{10.14}$$

Figure 10.10 shows a tree for pricing an American call option on a gold futures contract. Early exercise is optimal when the price is $336.720. The intuition for early exercise is that when an option on a futures contract is exercised, the option holder pays nothing, is entered into a futures contract, and receives mark-to-market proceeds of the difference between the strike price and the futures price. The motive for exercise is the ability to earn interest on the mark-to-market proceeds.

Options on Commodities

Many options exist on commodity futures contracts. However, it is also possible to have options on the physical commodity. If there is a market for lending and borrowing the commodity, then, in theory, pricing such an option is straightforward.

Recall from Chapter 6 that the *lease rate* for a commodity is conceptually similar to a dividend yield. If you borrow the commodity, you pay the lease rate. If you buy the commodity and lend it, you receive the lease rate. Thus, from the perspective of someone synthetically creating the option, the commodity is like a stock index, with the lease rate equal to the dividend yield.

Because this is conceptually the same as the pricing exercise in Figure 10.8 (imagine a commodity with a price of $110, a lease rate of 3.5%, and a volatility of 30%), we do not present a pricing example.

In practice, pricing and hedging an option based on the physical commodity can be problematic. If an appropriate futures contract exists, a market-maker could use it to hedge a commodity option. Otherwise, transactions in physical commodities often have greater transaction costs than for financial assets. Short-selling a commodity may not be possible, for reasons discussed in Chapter 6. Market-making is then difficult.

---

from expiration and for which $uF > dF > K$. Then

$$\Delta = \frac{uF - K - (dF - K)}{F(u-d)} = 1$$

But we also have

$$B = e^{-rh} \left[(uF - K)\frac{1-d}{u-d} + (dF - K)\frac{u-1}{u-d} \right]$$
$$= e^{-rh}(F - K)$$

From the second expression, you can see that if the futures price changes by $1, the option price changes by e^{-rh}.

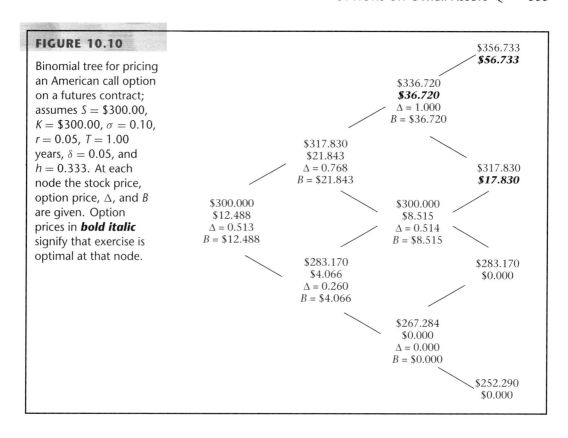

FIGURE 10.10

Binomial tree for pricing an American call option on a futures contract; assumes $S = \$300.00$, $K = \$300.00$, $\sigma = 0.10$, $r = 0.05$, $T = 1.00$ years, $\delta = 0.05$, and $h = 0.333$. At each node the stock price, option price, Δ, and B are given. Option prices in **bold italic** signify that exercise is optimal at that node.

Options on Bonds

Finally, we will briefly discuss options on bonds. We devote a separate chapter later to discussing fixed-income derivatives, but it is useful to understand at this point some of the issues in pricing options on bonds. As a first approximation we could just say that bonds are like stocks that pay a discrete dividend (a coupon), and price bond options using the binomial model.

However, bonds differ from the assets we have been discussing in two important respects.

1. The volatility of a bond decreases over time as the bond approaches maturity. The prices of 30-day Treasury bills, for example, are much less volatile than the prices of 30-year Treasury bonds. The reason is that a given change in the interest rate, other things equal, changes the price of a shorter-lived bond by less.

2. We have been assuming in all our calculations that interest rates are the same for all maturities, do not change over time and are not random. While these assumptions may be good enough for pricing options on stocks, they are logically inconsistent for pricing options on bonds: If interest rates do not change unexpectedly, neither do bond prices.

In some cases, it may be reasonable to price bond options using the simple binomial model in this chapter. For example, consider a 6-month option on a 29-year bond. The underlying asset in this case is a 29.5-year bond. As a practical matter, the volatility difference between a 29.5- and a 29-year bond is likely to be very small. Also, because it is short-lived, this option will not be particularly sensitive to the short-term interest rate, so the correlation of the bond price and the 6-month interest rate will not matter much.

On the other hand, if we have a 3-year option to buy a 5-year bond, these issues might be quite important. Another issue is that bond coupon payments are discrete, so the assumption of a continuous dividend is an approximation.

In general, the conceptual and practical issues with bonds are different enough that bonds warrant a separate treatment. We will return to bonds in Chapter 24.

Summary

Here is the general procedure covering the other assets discussed in this section.

- Construct the binomial tree for the price of the underlying asset using

$$uS_t = F_{t,t+h}e^{+\sigma\sqrt{h}} \quad \text{or} \quad u = \frac{F_{t,t+h}}{S_t}e^{+\sigma\sqrt{h}}$$

$$dS_t = F_{t,t+h}e^{-\sigma\sqrt{h}} \quad \text{or} \quad d = \frac{F_{t,t+h}}{S_t}e^{-\sigma\sqrt{h}}$$

(10.15)

  Since different underlying assets will have different forward price formulas, the tree will be different for different underlying assets.

- The option price at each node, if the option is unexercised, can then be computed as follows:

$$p^* = \frac{F_{t,t+h}/S_t - d}{u - d}$$

$$= \frac{e^{(r-\delta)h} - d}{u - d}$$

(10.16)

and, as before,

$$C = e^{-rh}\left(p^*C_u + (1 - p^*)C_d\right)$$

(10.17)

  where C_u and C_d are the up and down nodes relative to the current node. For an American option, at each node take the greater of this value and the value if exercised.

Pricing options with different underlying assets requires adjusting the risk-neutral probability for the borrowing cost or lease rate of the underlying asset. Mechanically, this means that we can use the formula for pricing an option on a stock index with an appropriate substitution for the dividend yield. Table 10.1 summarizes the substitutions.

TABLE 10.1	Substitutions for pricing options on assets other than a stock index.		
Underlying Asset	**Interest Rate**		**Dividend Yield**
Stock index	Domestic risk-free rate		Dividend yield
Currency	Domestic risk-free rate		Foreign risk-free rate
Futures contract	Domestic risk-free rate		Domestic risk-free rate
Commodity	Domestic risk-free rate		Commodity lease rate
Coupon bond	Domestic risk-free rate		Yield on bond

CHAPTER SUMMARY

In order to price options, we must make an assumption about the probability distribution of the underlying asset. The binomial distribution provides a particularly simple stock price distribution: At any point in time, the stock price can go from S up to uS or down to dS, where the movement factors u and d are given by equation (10.10).

Given binomial stock price movements, the option can be replicated by holding Δ shares of stock and B bonds. The option price is the cost of this replicating portfolio, $\Delta S + B$. For a call option, $\Delta > 0$ and $B < 0$, so the option is replicated by borrowing to buy shares. For a put, $\Delta < 0$ and $B > 0$. If the option price does not equal this theoretical price, arbitrage is possible. The replicating portfolio is dynamic, changing as the stock price moves up or down. Thus it is unlike the replicating portfolio for a forward contract, which is fixed.

The binomial option pricing formula has an interpretation as a discounted expected value, with the risk-neutral probability (equation 10.5) used to compute the expected payoff to the option and the risk-free rate used to discount the expected payoff. This is known as risk-neutral pricing.

The binomial model can be used to price American and European calls and puts on a variety of underlying assets, including stocks, indexes, futures, currencies, commodities, and bonds.

FURTHER READING

This chapter has focused on the *mechanics* of binomial option pricing. Some of the underlying concepts will be discussed in more detail in Chapter 11. There we will have more to say about risk-neutral pricing, the link between the binomial tree and the assumed stock price distribution, how to estimate volatility, and how to price options when the stock pays a discrete dividend.

The binomial model provides a foundation for much of what we will do in later chapters. We will see in Chapter 12, for example, that the binomial option pricing formula gives results equivalent to the Black-Scholes formula when h becomes small. Consequently, if you thoroughly understand binomial pricing, you also understand the Black-Scholes formula. In Chapter 22, we will see how to generalize binomial trees to handle two sources of uncertainty.

In addition to the original papers by Cox et al. (1979) and Rendleman and Bartter (1979), Cox and Rubinstein (1985) provides an excellent exposition of the binomial model.

PROBLEMS

In these problems, n refers to the number of binomial periods. Assume all rates are continuously compounded unless the problem explicitly states otherwise.

10.1. Let $S = \$100$, $K = \$105$, $r = 8\%$, $T = 0.5$, and $\delta = 0$. Let $u = 1.3$, $d = 0.8$, and $n = 1$.

    a. What are the premium, Δ, and B for a European call?

    b. What are the premium, Δ, and B for a European put?

10.2. Let $S = \$100$, $K = \$95$, $r = 8\%$, $T = 0.5$, and $\delta = 0$. Let $u = 1.3$, $d = 0.8$, and $n = 1$.

    a. Verify that the price of a European call is $\$16.196$.

    b. Suppose you observe a call price of $\$17$. What is the arbitrage?

    c. Suppose you observe a call price of $\$15.50$. What is the arbitrage?

10.3. Let $S = \$100$, $K = \$95$, $r = 8\%$, $T = 0.5$, and $\delta = 0$. Let $u = 1.3$, $d = 0.8$, and $n = 1$.

    a. Verify that the price of a European put is $\$7.471$.

    b. Suppose you observe a put price of $\$8$. What is the arbitrage?

    c. Suppose you observe a put price of $\$6$. What is the arbitrage?

10.4. Let $S = \$100$, $K = \$95$, $\sigma = 30\%$, $r = 8\%$, $T = 1$, and $\delta = 0$. Let $u = 1.3$, $d = 0.8$, and $n = 2$. Construct the binomial tree for a call option. At each node provide the premium, Δ, and B.

10.5. Repeat the option price calculation in the previous question for stock prices of $\$80$, $\$90$, $\$110$, $\$120$, and $\$130$, keeping everything else fixed. What happens to the initial option Δ as the stock price increases?

10.6. Let $S = \$100$, $K = \$95$, $\sigma = 30\%$, $r = 8\%$, $T = 1$, and $\delta = 0$. Let $u = 1.3$, $d = 0.8$, and $n = 2$. Construct the binomial tree for a European put option. At each node provide the premium, Δ, and B.

10.7. Repeat the option price calculation in the previous question for stock prices of $\$80$, $\$90$, $\$110$, $\$120$, and $\$130$, keeping everything else fixed. What happens to the inital put Δ as the stock price increases?

10.8. Let $S = \$100$, $K = \$95$, $\sigma = 30\%$, $r = 8\%$, $T = 1$, and $\delta = 0$. Let $u = 1.3$, $d = 0.8$, and $n = 2$. Construct the binomial tree for an American put option. At each node provide the premium, Δ, and B.

10.9. Suppose $S_0 = \$100$, $K = \$50$, $r = 7.696\%$ (continuously compounded), $\delta = 0$, and $T = 1$.

    a. Suppose that for $h = 1$, we have $u = 1.2$ and $d = 1.05$. What is the binomial option price for a call option that lives one period? Is there any problem with having $d > 1$?

    b. Suppose now that $u = 1.4$ and $d = 0.6$. Before computing the option price, what is your guess about how it will change from your previous answer? Does it change? How do you account for the result? Interpret your answer using put-call parity.

    c. Now let $u = 1.4$ and $d = 0.4$. How do you think the call option price will change from (a)? How does it change? How do you account for this? Use put-call parity to explain your answer.

10.10. Let $S = \$100$, $K = \$95$, $r = 8\%$ (continuously compounded), $\sigma = 30\%$, $\delta = 0$, $T = 1$ year, and $n = 3$.

    a. Verify that the binomial option price for an American call option is $\$18.283$. Verify that there is never early exercise; hence, a European call would have the same price.

    b. Show that the binomial option price for a European put option is $\$5.979$. Verify that put-call parity is satisfied.

    c. Verify that the price of an American put is $\$6.678$.

10.11. Repeat the previous problem assuming that the stock pays a continuous dividend of 8% per year (continuously compounded). Calculate the prices of the American and European puts and calls. Which options are early-exercised?

10.12. Let $S = \$40$, $K = \$40$, $r = 8\%$ (continuously compounded), $\sigma = 30\%$, $\delta = 0$, $T = 0.5$ year, and $n = 2$.

    a. Construct the binomial tree for the stock. What are u and d?

    b. Show that the call price is $\$4.110$.

    c. Compute the prices of American and European puts.

10.13. Use the same data as in the previous problem, only suppose that the call price is $\$5$ instead of $\$4.110$.

    a. At time 0, assume you write the option and form the replicating portfolio to offset the written option. What is the replicating portfolio and what are the net cash flows from selling the overpriced call and buying the synthetic equivalent?

b. What are the cash flows in the next binomial period (3 months later) if the call at that time is fairly priced and you liquidate the position? What would you do if the option continues to be overpriced the next period?

c. What would you do if the option is underpriced the next period?

10.14. Suppose that the exchange rate is $0.92/€. Let $r_\$ = 4\%$, and $r_€ = 3\%$, $u = 1.2$, $d = 0.9$, $T = 0.75$, $n = 3$, and $K = \$0.85$.

    a. What is the price of a 9-month European call?

    b. What is the price of a 9-month American call?

10.15. Use the same inputs as in the previous problem, except that $K = \$1.00$.

    a. What is the price of a 9-month European put?

    b. What is the price of a 9-month American put?

10.16. Suppose that the exchange rate is 1 dollar for 120 yen. The dollar interest rate is 5% (continuously compounded) and the yen rate is 1% (continuously compounded). Consider an at-the-money American dollar call that is yen-denominated (i.e., the call permits you to buy 1 dollar for 120 yen). The option has 1 year to expiration and the exchange rate volatility is 10%. Let $n = 3$.

    a. What is the price of a European call? An American call?

    b. What is the price of a European put? An American put?

    c. How do you account for the pattern of early exercise across the two options?

10.17. An option has a gold futures contract as the underlying asset. The current 1-year gold futures price is $300/oz., the strike price is $290, the risk-free rate is 6%, volatility is 10%, and time to expiration is 1 year. Suppose $n = 1$. What is the price of a call option on gold? What is the replicating portfolio for the call option? Evaluate the statement: "Replicating a call option always entails borrowing to buy the underlying asset."

10.18. Suppose the S&P 500 futures price is 1000, $\sigma = 30\%$, $r = 5\%$, $\delta = 5\%$, $T = 1$, and $n = 3$.

    a. What are the prices of European calls and puts for $K = \$1000$? Why do you find the prices to be equal?

    b. What are the prices of American calls and puts for $K = \$1000$?

    c. What are the time-0 replicating portfolios for the European call and put?

10.19. For a stock index, $S = \$100$, $\sigma = 30\%$, $r = 5\%$, $\delta = 3\%$, and $T = 3$. Let $n = 3$.

    a. What is the price of a European call option with a strike of $95?

    b. What is the price of a European put option with a strike of $95?

    c. Now let $S = \$95$, $K = \$100$, $\sigma = 30\%$, $r = 3\%$, and $\delta = 5\%$. (You have exchanged values for the stock price and strike price and for the interest rate and dividend yield.) Value both options again. What do you notice?

10.20. Repeat the previous problem calculating prices for American options instead of European. What happens?

10.21. Suppose that $u < e^{(r-\delta)h}$. Show that there is an arbitrage opportunity. Now suppose that $d > e^{(r-\delta)h}$. Show again that there is an arbitrage opportunity.

APPENDIX 10.A: TAXES AND OPTION PRICES

It is possible to solve for a binomial price when there are taxes. Suppose that each form of income is taxed at a different rate: interest at the rate τ_i, capital gains on a stock at the rate τ_g, capital gains on options at the rate τ_O, and dividends at the rate τ_d. We assume that taxes on all forms of income are paid on an accrual basis, and that there is no limit on the ability to deduct losses or to offset losses on one form of income against gains on another form of income.

    We then choose Δ_t and B_t by requiring that the *after-tax* return on the stock/bond portfolio equal the *after-tax* return on the option in both the up and down states. Thus we require that

$$\left[S_{t+h} - \tau_g(S_{t+h} - S_t) + \delta S_t(1 - \tau_d)\right]\Delta_t + [1 + r_h(1 - \tau)]\,B_t$$
$$= \phi_{t+h}(S_{t+h}) - \tau_O\left[\phi_{t+h}(S_{t+h}) - \phi_t(S_t)\right] \tag{10.18}$$

The solutions for Δ and B are then

$$\Delta = \frac{1 - \tau_O}{1 - \tau_g}\frac{\phi_1(S_1^+) - \phi_1(S_1^-)}{S_1^+ - S_1^-}$$

$$B = \frac{1}{1 + r_h\dfrac{1 - \tau_i}{1 - \tau_O}}\left(\frac{u\phi_1(S_1^-) - d\phi_1(S_1^+)}{u - d} - \frac{\Delta}{1 - \tau_O}S_0\left[\frac{\tau_g - \tau_O}{1 - \tau_g} + \delta(1 - \tau_d)\right]\right)$$

This gives an option price of

$$\phi_t = \frac{1}{1 + r_h\dfrac{1 - \tau_i}{1 - \tau_O}}\left[p^*\phi_{t+h}(S_{t+h}^+) + (1 - p^*)\phi_{t+h}(S_{t+h}^-)\right] \tag{10.19}$$

where

$$p^* = \frac{1 + r_h\dfrac{1 - \tau_i}{1 - \tau_g} - \delta\dfrac{1 - \tau_d}{1 - \tau_O} - d}{u - d} \tag{10.20}$$

In practice, dealers are marked-to-market for tax purposes and face the same tax rate on all forms of income. In this case taxes drop out of all the option-pricing expressions. When dealers are the effective price-setters in a market, taxes should not affect prices.

CHAPTER 11

Binomial Option Pricing: II

Chapter 10 introduced binomial option pricing, focusing on how the model can be used to compute European and American option prices for a variety of underlying assets. In this chapter we continue the discussion of binomial pricing, delving more deeply into the economics of the model and its underlying assumptions.

First, the binomial model can value options that may be early-exercised. We will examine early exercise in more detail, and see that the option pricing calculation reflects the economic determinants of early exercise discussed in Chapter 9.

Second, the binomial option pricing formula can be interpreted as the expected option payoff one period hence, discounted at the risk-free rate. In Chapter 10 we referred to this calculation as *risk-neutral pricing*. This calculation appears to be inconsistent with standard discounted cash flow valuation, in which expected cash flows are discounted at a risk-adjusted rate, not the risk-free rate. We show that, in fact, the binomial pricing formula (and, hence, risk-neutral valuation) is consistent with option valuation using standard discounted cash flow techniques.

Third, we modeled the stock price by using volatility (σ) to determine the magnitude of the up and down stock price movements. In this chapter we explain this calculation in more detail. What is the economic meaning of this assumption? In constructing the binomial tree, why is volatility multiplied by the square root of time ($\sigma \sqrt{h}$)? How should we estimate volatility?

Finally, we saw how to price options on stock indices where the dividend is continuous. In this chapter we adapt the binomial model to price options on stocks that pay discrete dividends.

11.1 UNDERSTANDING EARLY EXERCISE

In deciding whether to early-exercise an option, the option holder compares the value of exercising immediately with the value of continuing to hold the option, and exercises if immediate exercise is more valuable. This is the comparison we performed at each binomial node when we valued American options in Chapter 10.

We obtain an economic perspective on the early-exercise decision by considering the costs and benefits of early exercise. As discussed in Section 9.3, there are three economic considerations governing the decision to exercise early. By exercising, the option holder

- Receives the stock and therefore receives future dividends,

- Pays the strike price prior to expiration (this has an interest cost), and

- Loses the insurance implicit in the call. By holding the call instead of exercising, the option holder is protected against the possibility that the stock price will be less than the strike price at expiration. Once the option is exercised, this protection no longer exists.

Consider an example where a call option has a strike price of $100, the interest rate is 5%, and the stock pays continuous dividends of 5%. If the stock price is $200, the net effect of dividends and interest encourages early exercise. Annual dividends are approximately 5% of $200, or $0.05 \times \$200 = \$10$. The annual interest saved by deferring exercise is approximately $0.05 \times \$100 = \$5$. Thus, for a stock price of $200 (indeed, for any stock price above $100) dividends lost by not exercising exceed interest saved by deferring exercise.

The only reason in this case not to exercise early is the implicit insurance the option owner loses by exercising. This implicit insurance arises from the fact that the option holder could exercise and then the stock price could fall below the strike price of $100. Leaving the option unexercised protects against this scenario. The early-exercise calculation for a call therefore implicitly weighs dividends, which encourage early exercise, against interest and insurance, which discourage early exercise.

If volatility is zero, then the value of insurance is zero, and it is simple to find the optimal exercise policy as long as r and δ are constant. It is optimal to defer exercise as long as interest savings on the strike exceed dividends lost, or

$$rK > \delta S$$

It is optimal to exercise when this is not true, or

$$S > \frac{rK}{\delta}$$

In the special case when $r = \delta$ and $\sigma = 0$, any in-the-money option should be exercised immediately. If $\delta = 0.5r$, then we exercise when the stock price is twice the exercise price.

The decision to exercise is more complicated when volatility is positive. In this case the implicit insurance has value that varies with time to expiration. Figure 11.1 displays the price above which early exercise is optimal for a 5-year option with $K = \$100$, $r = 5\%$, and $\delta = 5\%$, for three different volatilities, computed using 500 binomial steps. Recall from Chapter 9 that if it is optimal to exercise a call at a given stock price, then it is optimal to exercise at all higher stock prices. Figure 11.1 thus shows the *lowest* stock price at which exercise is optimal. The oscillation in this lowest price, which is evident in the figure, is due to the up and down binomial movements that approximate the behavior of the stock; with an infinite number of binomial steps the early-exercise schedule would be smooth and continuously decreasing. Comparing the three lines, we observe a significant volatility effect. A 5-year option with a volatility of 50% should only be exercised if the stock price exceeds about $360. If volatility is 10%, the boundary

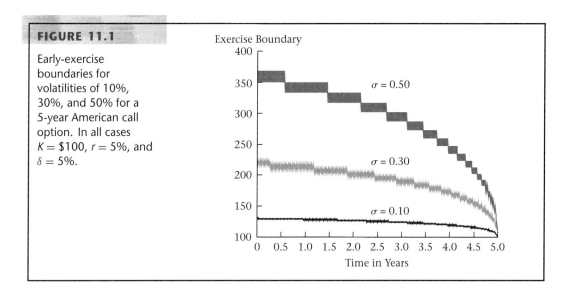

FIGURE 11.1

Early-exercise boundaries for volatilities of 10%, 30%, and 50% for a 5-year American call option. In all cases $K = \$100$, $r = 5\%$, and $\delta = 5\%$.

drops to \$130. This volatility effect stems from the fact that the insurance value lost by early-exercising is greater when volatility is greater.

Figure 11.2 performs the same experiment for put options with the same inputs. The picture is similar, as is the logic: The advantage of early exercise is receiving the strike price sooner rather than later. The disadvantages are the dividends lost by giving up the stock, and the loss of insurance against the stock price exceeding the strike price.

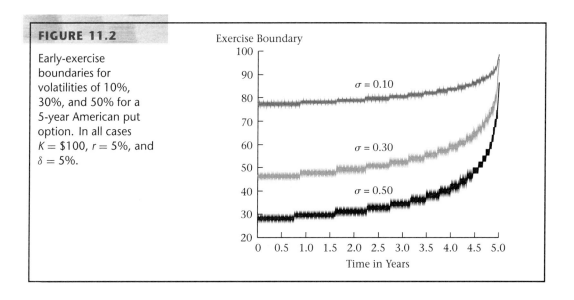

FIGURE 11.2

Early-exercise boundaries for volatilities of 10%, 30%, and 50% for a 5-year American put option. In all cases $K = \$100$, $r = 5\%$, and $\delta = 5\%$.

Figures 11.1 and 11.2 also show that, other things equal, early-exercise criteria become less stringent closer to expiration. This occurs because the value of insurance diminishes as the options approach expiration.

While these pictures are constructed for the special case where $\delta = r$, the overall conclusion holds generally.

11.2 Understanding Risk-Neutral Pricing

In Chapter 10, we saw that the binomial option pricing formula can be written

$$C = e^{-rh}[p^*C_u + (1 - p^*)C_d] \qquad (11.1)$$

where

$$p^* = \frac{e^{(r-\delta)h} - d}{u - d} \qquad (11.2)$$

We labeled p^* the *risk-neutral probability* that the stock will go up. Equation (11.1) has the appearance of a discounted expected value, where the expected value calculation uses p^* and discounting is done at the risk-free rate.

The idea that an option price is the result of a present value calculation is reassuring, but at the same time equation (11.1) is puzzling. A standard discounted cash flow calculation would require computing an expected value using the true probability that the stock price would go up. Discounting would then be done using the expected return on an asset of equivalent risk, not the risk-free rate. Moreover, what is p^*? Is it really a probability?

We will begin our exploration of risk-neutral pricing by interpreting p^*, showing that it is not the true probability that the stock goes up, but rather the probability that gives the stock an expected rate of return equal to the risk-free rate. We will then show that it *is* possible to compute an option price using standard discounted cash flow calculations using the true probability that the stock goes up, but that doing so is cumbersome.

The Risk-Neutral Probability

It is common in finance to emphasize that investors are risk averse. To see what risk aversion means, suppose you are offered either (a) $1000, or (b) $2000 with probability 0.5, and $0 with probability 0.5. A **risk-averse** investor prefers (a), since alternative (b) is risky and has the same expected value as (a). This kind of investor will require a premium to bear risk when expected values are equal.

A **risk-neutral** investor is indifferent between a sure thing and a risky bet with an expected payoff equal to the value of the sure thing. A risk-neutral investor, for example, will be equally happy with alternative (a) or (b).

Before proceeding, we need to emphasize that *at no point are we assuming that investors are risk-neutral. Now and throughout the book, the pricing calculations are consistent with investors being risk-averse.*

Having said this, let's consider what an imaginary world populated by risk-neutral investors would be like. In such a world, investors care only about expected returns and not about riskiness. Assets would have no risk premium since investors would be willing to hold assets with an expected return equal to the risk-free rate.

In this hypothetical risk-neutral world, we can solve for the probability of the stock going up, p^*, such that the stock is expected to earn the risk-free rate. In the binomial model we assume that the stock can go up to uS or down to dS. If the stock is to earn the risk-free return on average, then the probability that the stock will go up, p^*, must satisfy

$$p^*uSe^{\delta h} + (1 - p^*)dSe^{\delta h} = e^{rh}S$$

Solving for p^* gives

$$p^* = \frac{e^{(r-\delta)h} - d}{u - d}$$

This is exactly the definition of p^* in equation (11.2). This is why we refer to p^* as the *risk-neutral probability that the stock price will go up.* It is the probability that the stock price would increase in a risk-neutral world.

Not only would the risk-neutral probability, equation (11.2), be used in a risk-neutral world, but also all discounting would take place at the risk-free rate. Thus, the option pricing formula, equation (11.1), can be said to price options *as if* investors are risk-neutral. At the risk of being repetitive, we are not assuming that investors are actually risk-neutral, and we are not assuming that risky assets are actually expected to earn the risk-free rate of return. Rather, *risk-neutral pricing is an* interpretation *of the formulas above*. Those formulas in turn arise from finding the cost of the portfolio that replicates the option payoff.

Interestingly, this interpretation of the option-pricing procedure has great practical importance; risk-neutral pricing can sometimes be used where other pricing methods are too difficult. We will see in Chapter 19 that risk-neutral pricing is the basis for Monte Carlo valuation, in which asset prices are simulated under the assumption that assets earn the risk-free rate, and these simulated prices are used to value the option.

Pricing an Option Using Real Probabilities

We are left with the question: Is option pricing consistent with standard discounted cash flow calculations? The answer is yes. We can use the true distribution for the future stock price in computing the expected payoff to the option. This expected payoff can then be discounted with a rate based on the stock's required return.

Discounted cash flow is not used in practice to price options because there is no reason to do so: It is necessary to compute the option price in order to compute the correct discount rate. However, we present two examples of valuing an option using real probabilities to see the difficulty in using real probabilities, and also to understand how to determine the risk of an option.

Suppose that the continuously compounded expected return on the stock is α and that the stock does not pay dividends. Then if p is the true probability of the stock going up, p must be consistent with u, d, and α:

$$puS + (1 - p)dS = e^{\alpha h}S \tag{11.3}$$

Solving for p gives us

$$p = \frac{e^{\alpha h} - d}{u - d} \qquad (11.4)$$

For probabilities to be between 0 and 1, we must have $u > e^{\alpha h} > d$. Using p, the actual expected payoff to the option one period hence is

$$pC_u + (1 - p)C_d = \frac{e^{\alpha h} - d}{u - d}C_u + \frac{u - e^{\alpha h}}{u - d}C_d \qquad (11.5)$$

Now we face the problem with using real as opposed to risk-neutral probabilities: At what rate do we discount this expected payoff? It is not correct to discount the option at the expected return on the stock, α, because the option is equivalent to a leveraged investment in the stock and, hence, is riskier than the stock.

Denote the appropriate per-period discount rate for the option as γ. To compute γ, we can use the fact that the required return on any portfolio is the weighted average of the returns on the assets in the portfolio.[1] In Chapter 10, we saw that an option is equivalent to holding a portfolio consisting of Δ shares of stock and B bonds. The expected return on this portfolio is

$$e^{\gamma h} = \frac{S\Delta}{S\Delta + B}e^{\alpha h} + \frac{B}{S\Delta + B}e^{rh} \qquad (11.6)$$

We can now compute the option price as the expected option payoff, equation (11.5), discounted at the appropriate discount rate, given by equation (11.6). This gives

$$e^{-\gamma h}\left[\frac{e^{\alpha h} - d}{u - d}C_u + \frac{u - e^{\alpha h}}{u - d}C_d\right] \qquad (11.7)$$

It turns out that *this gives us the same option price as performing the risk-neutral calculation*. Appendix 11.A demonstrates algebraically that equation (11.7) is equivalent to the risk-neutral calculation, equation (11.1).

The calculations leading to equation (11.7) started with the assumption that the expected return on the stock is α. We then derived a consistent probability, p, and discount rate for the option, γ. You may be wondering if it matters whether we have the "correct" value of α to start with. The answer is that it does not matter: *Any* consistent pair of α and γ will give the same option price. Risk-neutral pricing is valuable because setting $\alpha = r$ results in the *simplest* pricing procedure.

A one-period example To see how to value an option using true probabilities, we will compute two examples. First, consider the one-period binomial example in Figure 11.3. Suppose that the continuously compounded expected return on XYZ is $\alpha = 15\%$. Then the true probability of the stock going up, from equation (11.4), is

$$p = \frac{e^{0.15} - 0.8025}{1.4623 - 0.8025} = 0.5446$$

---

[1] See, for example, Brealey and Myers (2003, ch. 9).

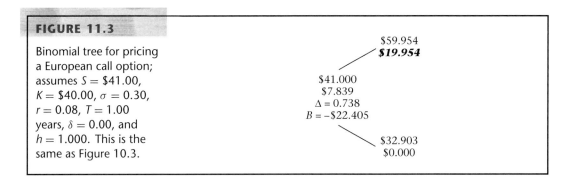

FIGURE 11.3

Binomial tree for pricing a European call option; assumes $S = \$41.00$, $K = \$40.00$, $\sigma = 0.30$, $r = 0.08$, $T = 1.00$ years, $\delta = 0.00$, and $h = 1.000$. This is the same as Figure 10.3.

$41.000
$7.839
$\Delta = 0.738$
$B = -\$22.405$

$59.954
$19.954

$32.903
$0.000

The expected payoff to the option in one period, from equation (11.5) is

$$0.5446 \times \$19.954 + (1 - 0.5446) \times \$0 = \$10.867$$

The replicating portfolio, Δ and B, does not depend on p or α. In this example, $\Delta = 0.738$ and $B = -\$22.405$. The discount rate, γ, from equation (11.6) is given by

$$e^{\gamma h} = \frac{0.738 \times \$41}{0.738 \times \$41 - \$22.405} e^{0.15} + \frac{-\$22.405}{0.738 \times \$41 - \$22.405} e^{0.08}$$
$$= 1.386$$

Thus, $\gamma = \ln(1.386) = 32.64\%$. The option price is then given by equation (11.7):

$$e^{-0.3264} \times \$10.867 = \$7.839$$

This is exactly the price we obtained before.

Notice that in order to compute the discount rate, we first had to compute Δ and B. But once we have computed Δ and B, we can simply compute the option price as $\Delta S + B$. There is no need for further computations. It can be helpful to know the actual expected return on an option, but for valuation it is pointless.

A multi-period example To demonstrate that this method of valuation works over multiple periods, Figure 11.4 presents the same binomial tree as Figure 10.5, with the addition that the true discount rate for the option, γ, is reported at each node. Given the 15% continuously compounded discount rate, the true probability of an up move in Figure 11.4 is

$$\frac{e^{0.15 \times 1/3} - 0.8637}{1.2212 - 0.8637} = 0.5247$$

To compute the price at the node where the stock price is $61.149, we discount the expected option price the next period at 26.9%. This gives

$$e^{-0.269 \times 1/3} \left[0.5247 \times \$34.678 + (1 - 0.5247) \times \$12.814 \right] = \$22.202$$

When the stock price is $43.246, the discount rate is 49.5%, and the option price is

$$e^{-0.495 \times 1/3} \left[0.5247 \times \$12.814 + (1 - 0.5247) \times \$0 \right] = \$5.700$$

FIGURE 11.4

Binomial tree for pricing
an American call
option; assumes
$S = \$41.00$,
$K = \$40.00$, $\sigma = 0.30$,
$r = 0.08$, $T = 1.00$
years, $\delta = 0.00$, and
$h = 0.333$. The
continuously
compounded true
expected return on the
stock, α, is 15%. At
each node the stock
price, option price, and
continuously
compounded true
discount rate for the
option, γ, are given.

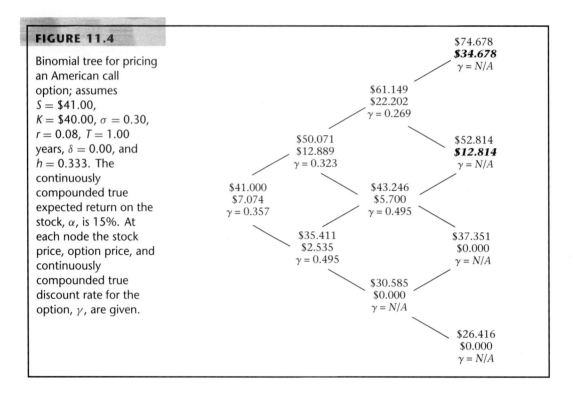

$74.678
$34.678
$\gamma = N/A$

$61.149
$22.202
$\gamma = 0.269$

$50.071
$12.889
$\gamma = 0.323$

$52.814
$12.814
$\gamma = N/A$

$41.000
$7.074
$\gamma = 0.357$

$43.246
$5.700
$\gamma = 0.495$

$35.411
$2.535
$\gamma = 0.495$

$37.351
$0.000
$\gamma = N/A$

$30.585
$0.000
$\gamma = N/A$

$26.416
$0.000
$\gamma = N/A$

These are both the same option prices as in Figure 10.5, where we used risk-neutral pricing.

We continue by working back through the tree. To compute the price at the node where the stock price is $50.071, we discount the expected option price the next period at 32.3%. Thus,

$$e^{-0.323 \times 1/3} \left[0.5247 \times \$22.202 + (1 - 0.5247) \times \$5.700 \right] = \$12.889$$

Again, this is the same price at this node as in Figure 10.5.

The actual discount rate for the option changes as we move down the tree at a point in time and also over time. The required return on the option is less when the stock price is $61.149 (26.9%) than when it is $43.246 (49.5%). The discount rate increases as the stock price decreases because the option is equivalent to a leveraged position in the stock, and the degree of leverage increases as the option moves out of the money.

These examples illustrate that it is possible to obtain option prices using standard discounted-cash-flow techniques. Generally, however, there is no reason to do so. Moreover, the fact that risk-neutral pricing works means that it is not necessary to estimate α, the expected return on the stock, when pricing an option. Since expected returns are hard to estimate precisely, this makes option pricing a great deal easier.

Appendix 11.B goes into more detail about risk-neutral pricing.

11.3 THE BINOMIAL TREE AND LOGNORMALITY

The usefulness of the binomial pricing model hinges on the binomial tree providing a reasonable representation of the stock price distribution. In this section we discuss the motivation for and plausibility of the binomial tree. We will define a lognormal distribution and see that the binomial tree approximates this distribution.

The Random Walk Model

It is often said that stock prices follow a random walk. In this section we will explain what a random walk is. In the next section we will apply the random walk model to stock prices.

To understand a random walk, imagine that we flip a coin repeatedly. Let the random variable Y denote the outcome of the flip. If the coin lands displaying a head, $Y = 1$. If the coin lands displaying a tail, $Y = -1$. If the probability of a head is 50%, we say the coin is fair. After n flips, with the ith flip denoted Y_i, the cumulative total, Z_n, is

$$Z_n = \sum_{i=1}^{n} Y_i \tag{11.8}$$

It turns out that the more times we flip, on average, the farther we will move from where we start. We can understand intuitively why with more flips the average distance from the starting point increases. Think about the first flip and imagine you get a head. You move to $+1$, and as far as the remaining flips are concerned, *this is your new starting point*. After the second flip, you will either be at 0 or $+2$. If you are at zero, it is as if you started over; however if you are at $+2$ you are starting at $+2$. Continuing in this way your average distance from the starting point increases with the number of flips.[2]

Another way to represent the process followed by Z_n is in terms of the *change* in Z_n:

$$Z_n - Z_{n-1} = Y_n$$

We can rewrite this more explicitly as

$$\text{Heads:} \quad Z_n - Z_{n-1} = +1 \tag{11.9}$$

$$\text{Tails:} \quad Z_n - Z_{n-1} = -1 \tag{11.10}$$

---

[2]After n flips, the average squared distance from the starting point will be n. Conditional on the first flip being a head, your average squared distance is $0.5 \times 0 + 0.5 \times 2^2 = 2$. If your first flip had been a tail, your average squared distance after two moves would also be 2. Thus, the unconditional average squared distance is 2 after 2 flips. If D_n^2 represents your squared distance from the starting point, then

$$D_n^2 = 0.5 \times (D_{n-1} + 1)^2 + 0.5 \times (D_{n-1} - 1)^2 = D_{n-1}^2 + 1$$

Since $D_0^2 = 0$, this implies that $D_n^2 = n$. This idea that with a random walk you drift increasingly farther from the starting point is an important concept later in the book.

With heads, the *change* in Z is 1, and with tails, the change in Z is −1. This random walk is illustrated in Figure 11.5.

The idea that asset prices should follow a random walk was articulated in Samuelson (1965). In efficient markets, an asset price should reflect all available information. By definition, new information is a surprise. In response to new information the price is equally likely to move up or down, as with the coin flip. The price after a period of time is the initial price plus the cumulative up and down movements due to informational surprises.

Modeling Stock Prices as a Random Walk

The idea that stock prices move up or down randomly makes sense; however, the description of a random walk in the previous section is not a satisfactory description of stock price movements. Suppose we take the random walk model in Figure 11.5 literally. Assume the beginning stock price is $100, and the stock price will move up or down $1 each time we flip the coin. There are at least three problems with this model:

1. If by chance we get enough cumulative down movements, the stock price will become negative. Because stockholders have limited liability (they can walk away from a bankrupt firm), a stock price will never be negative.

2. The magnitude of the move ($1) should depend upon how quickly the coin flips occur and the level of the stock price. If we flip coins once a second, $1 moves

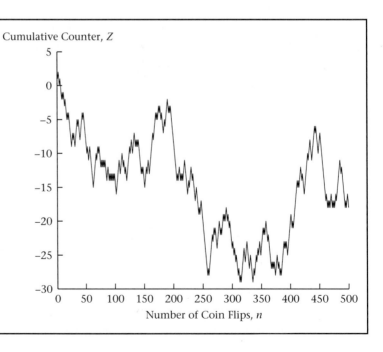

FIGURE 11.5

Illustration of a random walk, where the counter, Z, increases by one when a fair coin flip comes up heads, and decreases by one with tails.

Cumulative Counter, Z

Number of Coin Flips, n

are excessive; in real life, a $100 stock will not typically have 60 $1 up or down movements in 1 minute. Also, if a $1 move is appropriate for a $100 stock, it likely isn't appropriate for a $5 stock.

3. The stock on average should have a positive return. The random walk model taken literally does not permit this.

It turns out that the binomial model is a variant of the random walk model that solves all of these problems at once. The binomial model assumes that *continuously compounded returns are a random walk*. Thus, before proceeding, we first review some properties of continuously compounded returns.

Continuously Compounded Returns

Here is a summary of the important properties of continuously compounded returns. (See also Appendix B at the end of this book.)

The logarithmic function computes returns from prices Let S_t and S_{t+h} be stock prices at times t and $t + h$. The continuously compounded return between t and $t + h$, $r_{t,t+h}$ is then

$$r_{t,t+h} = \ln(S_{t+h}/S_t) \tag{11.11}$$

The exponential function computes prices from returns If we know the continuously compounded return, we can obtain S_{t+h} by exponentiating both sides of equation (11.11). This gives

$$S_{t+h} = S_t e^{r_{t,t+h}} \tag{11.12}$$

Continuously compounded returns are additive Suppose we have continuously compounded returns over a number of periods—for example, $r_{t,t+h}$, $r_{t+h,t+2h}$, etc. The continuously compounded return over a long period is the *sum* of continuously compounded returns over the shorter periods, i.e.,

$$r_{t,t+nh} = \sum_{i=1}^{n} r_{t+(i-1)h,t+ih} \tag{11.13}$$

Continuously compounded returns can be less than −100% A continuously compounded return that is a large negative number still gives a positive stock price. The reason is that e^r is positive for any r. Thus, if the log of the stock price follows a random walk, the stock price cannot become negative.

Here are some examples illustrating these statements.

Example 11.1 Suppose the stock price on four consecutive days is $100, $103, $97, and $98. The daily continuously compounded returns are

$\ln(103/100) = 0.02956$; $\ln(97/103) = -0.06002$; $\ln(98/97) = 0.01026$

The continuously compounded return from day 1 to day 4 is $\ln(98/100) = -0.0202$. This is also the sum of the daily continuously compounded returns:

$$r_{1,2} + r_{2,3} + r_{3,4} = 0.02956 + (-0.06002) + 0.01026 = -0.0202 \qquad ❧$$

Example 11.2 Suppose that the stock price today is $100 and that 1 year from today it is $10. The percentage return is $(10 - 100)/100 = -0.9 = -90\%$. However, the continuously compounded return is $\ln(10/100) = -2.30$, a continuously compounded return of -230%. ❧

Example 11.3 Suppose that the stock price today is $100 and that over 1 year the continuously compounded return is -500%. Using equation (11.12), the end-of-year price will be small but positive: $S_1 = 100e^{-5.00} = \$0.6738$. The percentage return is $0.6738/100 - 1 = -99.326\%$. ❧

The Standard Deviation of Returns

Suppose the continuously compounded return over month i is $r_{monthly,i}$. From equation (11.13), we can sum continuously compounded returns. Thus, the annual return is

$$r_{annual} = \sum_{i=1}^{12} r_{monthly,i}$$

The variance of the annual return is therefore

$$\text{Var}(r_{annual}) = \text{Var}\left(\sum_{i=1}^{12} r_{monthly,i}\right) \qquad (11.14)$$

Now suppose that returns are uncorrelated over time; that is, the realization of the return in one period does not affect the expected returns in subsequent periods. With this assumption, the variance of a sum is the sum of the variances. Also suppose that each month has the same variance of returns. If we let σ^2 denote the annual variance, then from equation (11.14) we have

$$\sigma^2 = 12 \times \sigma^2_{monthly}$$

Taking the square root of both sides and rearranging, we can express the monthly standard deviation in terms of the annual standard deviation:

$$\sigma_{monthly} = \frac{\sigma}{\sqrt{12}}$$

If we split the year into n periods of length h (so that $h = 1/n$), the standard deviation over the period of length h, σ_h, is

$$\boxed{\sigma_h = \sigma\sqrt{h}} \qquad (11.15)$$

The standard deviation therefore scales with the square root of time. This is why $\sigma\sqrt{h}$ appears in the binomial pricing model.

The Binomial Model

We are now in a position to better understand the binomial model, which is

$$S_{t+h} = S_t e^{(r-\delta)h \pm \sigma\sqrt{h}}$$

Taking logs, we obtain

$$\ln(S_{t+h}/S_t) = (r - \delta)h \pm \sigma\sqrt{h} \tag{11.16}$$

Since $\ln(S_{t+h}/S_t)$ is the continuously compounded return from t to $t + h$, $r_{t,t+h}$, the binomial model is simply a particular way to model the continuously compounded return. That return has two parts, one of which is certain $[(r - \delta)h]$, and the other of which is uncertain and generates the up and down stock price moves ($\pm\sigma\sqrt{h}$).

Let's see how equation (11.16) solves the three problems in the random walk discussed earlier:

1. The stock price cannot become negative. Even if we move down the binomial tree many times in a row, the resulting large, negative, continuously compounded return will give us a positive price.

2. As stock price moves occur more frequently, h gets smaller, therefore up and down moves get smaller. By construction, annual volatility is the same no matter how many binomial periods there are. Since returns follow a random walk, the percentage price change is the same whether the stock price is $100 or $5.

3. There is a $(r - \delta)h$ term, and we can choose the probability of an up move, so we can guarantee that the expected change in the stock price is positive.

To illustrate that the binomial tree can be thought of as a random walk, Figure 11.6 illustrates the stock price that results when the continuously compounded return follows a random walk. The figure is one particular path through a 500-step binomial tree, with the particular path generated by the same sequence of coin flips as in Figure 11.5.

Lognormality and the Binomial Model

The binomial tree approximates a lognormal distribution, which is commonly used to model stock prices.

First, what is the lognormal distribution? The lognormal distribution is the probability distribution that arises from the assumption that *continuously compounded returns on the stock are normally distributed*. When we traverse the binomial tree, we are implicitly adding up binomial random return components of $(r - \delta)h \pm \sigma\sqrt{h}$. In the limit (as $n \to \infty$ or, the same thing, $h \to 0$), the sum of binomial random variables is normally distributed. Thus, continuously compounded returns in a binomial tree are

FIGURE 11.6

Illustration of a particular path through a 500-step binomial tree, where the up and down moves are the same as in Figure 11.5. Assumes $S_0 = \$100$, $r = 6\%$, $\sigma = 30\%$, $T = 5$ years, and $h = 0.01$.

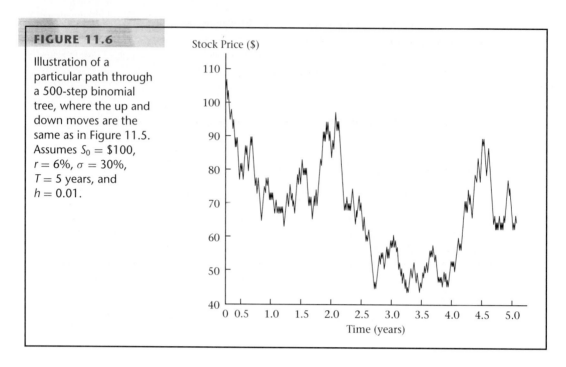

(approximately) normally distributed, which means that the stock is lognormally distributed. We defer a more complete discussion of this to Chapters 18 and 20, but we can see with an example how it works.

The binomial model implicitly assigns probabilities to the various nodes. Figure 11.7 depicts the construction of a tree for three binomial periods, along with the risk-

FIGURE 11.7

Construction of a binomial tree depicting stock price paths, along with risk-neutral probabilities of reaching the various terminal prices.

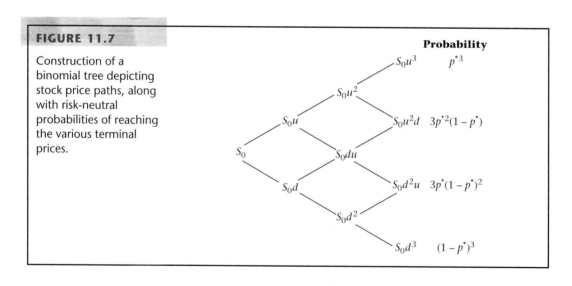

neutral probability of reaching each final period node. There is only one path—sequence of up and down moves—reaching the top or bottom node (*uuu* or *ddd*), but there are three paths reaching each intermediate node. For example, the first node below the top (S_0u^2d) can be reached by the sequences *uud*, *udu*, or *duu*. Thus, there are more paths that reach the intermediate nodes than the extreme nodes.

We can take the probabilities and outcomes from the binomial tree and plot them against a lognormal distribution with the same parameters. Figure 11.8 compares a three-period binomial approximation with a lognormal distribution assuming that the initial stock price is $100, volatility is 30%, the expected return on the stock is 10%, and the time horizon is 1 year. Because we need different scales for the discrete and continuous distributions, lognormal probabilities are graphed on the left vertical axis and binomial probabilities on the right vertical axis.

Suppose that a binomial tree has n periods and the risk-neutral probability of an up move is p^*. To reach the top node, we must go up n times in a row, which occurs with a probability of $(p^*)^n$. The price at the top node is Su^n. There is only one path through the tree by which we can reach the top node. To reach the first node below the top node, we must go up $n - 1$ times and down once, for a probability of $(p^*)^{n-1} \times (1 - p^*)$. The price at that node is $Su^{n-1}d$. Since the single down move can occur in any of the n periods, there are n ways this can happen. The probability of reaching the ith node below the top is $(p^*)^{n-i} \times (1 - p^*)^i$. The price at this node is $Su^{n-i}d^i$. The number of ways to reach this node is

$$\text{Number of ways to reach } i\text{th node} = \frac{n!}{(n-i)!\, i!} = \binom{n}{i}$$

where $n! = n \times (n - 1) \times \cdots \times 1$.[3]

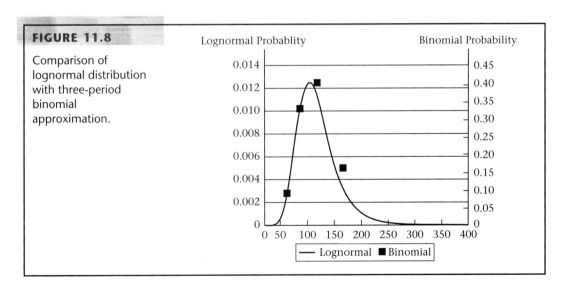

FIGURE 11.8

Comparison of lognormal distribution with three-period binomial approximation.

---

[3]The expression $\binom{n}{i}$ can be computed in Excel using the combinatorial function, *Combin(n, i)*.

We can construct the implied probability distribution in the binomial tree by plotting the stock price at each final period node, $Su^{n-i}d^i$, against the probability of reaching that node. The probability of reaching any given node is the probability of one path reaching that node times the number of paths reaching that node:

$$\text{Probability of reaching } i^{\text{th}} \text{ node} = p^{*n-i}(1-p^*)^i \frac{n!}{(n-i)!\, i!} \qquad (11.17)$$

Figure 11.9 compares the probability distribution for a 25-period binomial tree with the corresponding lognormal distribution. The two distributions appear close; as a practical matter, a 25-period approximation works fairly well for an option expiring in a few months.

Figures 11.8 and 11.9 show you what the lognormal distribution for the stock price looks like. The stock price is positive, and the distribution is skewed to the right; that is, there is a chance that extremely high stock prices will occur.

Alternative Binomial Trees

There are other ways besides equation (11.16) to construct a binomial tree that approximates a lognormal distribution. An acceptable tree must match the standard deviation of the continuously compounded return on the asset and must generate an appropriate distribution as the length of the binomial period, h, goes to 0. Different methods of constructing the binomial tree will result in different u and d stock movements. No matter how we construct the tree, however, we use equation (10.5) to determine the risk-neutral probability and equation (10.6) to determine the option value.

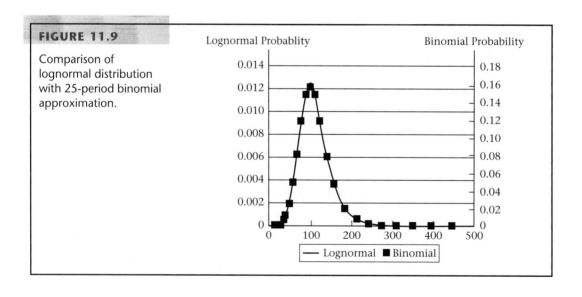

FIGURE 11.9

Comparison of lognormal distribution with 25-period binomial approximation.

The Cox-Ross-Rubinstein binomial tree The best-known way to construct a binomial tree is that in Cox et al. (1979), in which the tree is constructed as

$$u = e^{\sigma\sqrt{h}}$$
$$d = e^{-\sigma\sqrt{h}}$$

(11.18)

The Cox-Ross-Rubinstein approach is often used in practice. A problem with this approach, however, is that if h is large or σ is small, it is possible that $e^{rh} > e^{\sigma\sqrt{h}}$, in which case the binomial tree violates the restriction in equation (10.4). In real applications h would be small, so this problem does not occur. In any event, the tree based on the forward price never violates equation (10.4).

The lognormal tree Another alternative is to construct the tree using

$$u = e^{(r-\delta-0.5\sigma^2)h+\sigma\sqrt{h}}$$
$$d = e^{(r-\delta-0.5\sigma^2)h-\sigma\sqrt{h}}$$

(11.19)

This procedure for generating a tree was proposed by Jarrow and Rudd (1983) and is sometimes called the Jarrow-Rudd binomial model. It has a very natural motivation that you will understand after we discuss lognormality in Chapter 18. You will find in computing equation (10.5) that the risk-neutral probability of an up-move is generally close to 0.5.

All three methods of constructing a binomial tree yield different option prices for finite n, but approach the same price as $n \to \infty$. Also, while the different binomial trees all have different up and down movements, all have the same ratio of u to d:

$$\frac{u}{d} = e^{2\sigma\sqrt{h}} \qquad \text{or} \qquad \ln(u/d) = 2\sigma\sqrt{h}$$

This is the sense in which, however the tree is constructed, the proportional distance between u and d measures volatility.

Is the Binomial Model Realistic?

Any option pricing model relies on an assumption about the behavior of stock prices. As we have seen in this section, the binomial model is a form of the random walk model, adapted to modeling stock prices. The lognormal random walk model in this section assumes, among other things, that volatility is constant, that "large" stock price movements do not occur, and that returns are independent over time. All of these assumptions appear to be violated in the data.

We will discuss the behavior of volatility in Chapters 18 and 23. However, there is evidence that volatility changes over time (see Bollerslev et al., 1994). It also appears that on occasion stocks move by a large amount. The binomial model has the property that stock price movements become smaller as the period length, h, becomes smaller. Occasional large price movements—"jumps"—are therefore a feature of the data inconsistent with the binomial model. We will also discuss such moves in Chapters 19 and 21. Finally, there is some evidence that stock returns are correlated across time, with positive correlations at the short to medium term and negative correlation at long horizons (see Campbell et al., 1997, ch. 2).

The random walk model is a useful starting point for thinking about stock price behavior, and it is widely used because of its elegant simplicity. However, it is not sacrosanct.

11.4 ESTIMATING VOLATILITY

In practice we need to figure out what parameters to use in the binomial model. The most important decision is the value we assign to σ, which we cannot observe directly. One possibility is to measure σ by computing the standard deviation of continuously compounded historical returns. Volatility computed from historical stock returns is **historical volatility.**

Table 11.1 lists 13 weeks of Wednesday closing prices for the S&P 500 composite index and for IBM, along with the standard deviation of the continuously compounded returns, computed using the *StDev* function in Excel.[4]

Over the 13-week period in the table, the weekly standard deviation was 0.0309 and 0.0365 for the S&P 500 index and IBM, respectively. These are weekly standard deviations since they are computed from weekly returns; they therefore measure the variability in weekly returns. We obtain annualized standard deviations by multiplying the weekly standard deviations by $\sqrt{52}$, giving annual standard deviations of 22.32% for the S&P 500 index and 26.32% for IBM.

We can now use these annualized standard deviations to construct binomial trees with the binomial period, h, set to whatever is appropriate. Don't be misled by the fact that the standard deviations were estimated with weekly data. Once we annualize the estimated standard deviations by multiplying by $\sqrt{52}$, we can then multiply again by $\sqrt{h}$ to adapt the annual standard deviation to any size binomial step.

The procedure outlined above is a reasonable way to estimate volatility when continuously compounded returns are independent and identically distributed, as in the logarithmic random walk model in Section 11.3. However, if returns are not independent—as with some commodities, for example—volatility estimation becomes more complicated. If a high price of oil today leads to decreased demand and increased supply, we would expect prices in the future to come down. In this case, the volatility over T years will be less than $\sigma \sqrt{T}$, reflecting the tendency of prices to revert from extreme values. Extra care is required with volatility if the random walk model is not a plausible economic model of the asset's price behavior.

---

[4]We use weekly rather than daily data because computing daily statistics is complicated by weekends and holidays. In theory the standard deviation over the 3 days from Friday to Monday should be greater than over the 1 day from Monday to Tuesday. Using weekly data avoids this kind of complication. Further, using Wednesdays avoids most holidays.

| | **TABLE 11.1** | | | Weekly prices and continuously compounded returns for the S&P 500 index and IBM, from 3/5/03 to 5/28/03. | |

Date	S&P 500		IBM	
	Price	$\ln(S_t/S_{t-1})$	Price	$\ln(S_t/S_{t-1})$
03/05/03	829.85	—	77.73	—
03/12/03	804.19	−0.0314	75.18	−0.0334
03/19/03	874.02	0.0833	82.00	0.0868
03/26/03	869.95	−0.0047	81.55	−0.0055
04/02/03	880.90	0.0125	81.46	−0.0011
04/09/03	865.99	−0.0171	78.71	−0.0343
04/16/03	879.91	0.0159	82.88	0.0516
04/23/03	919.02	0.0435	85.75	0.0340
04/30/03	916.92	−0.0023	84.90	−0.0100
05/07/03	929.62	0.0138	86.68	0.0207
05/14/03	939.28	0.0103	88.70	0.0230
05/21/03	923.42	−0.0170	86.18	−0.0288
05/28/03	953.22	0.0318	87.57	0.0160
Std. deviation		0.0309	—	0.0365
Std. deviation $\times \sqrt{52}$		0.2232	—	0.2632

11.5 STOCKS PAYING DISCRETE DIVIDENDS

Although it may be reasonable to assume that a stock index pays dividends continuously, individual stocks pay dividends in discrete lumps, quarterly or annually. In addition, over short horizons it is frequently possible to predict the amount of the dividend. How should we price an option when the stock will pay a known dollar dividend during the life of the option? The procedure we have already developed for creating a binomial tree can accommodate this case. However, we will also discuss a preferable alternative due to Schroder (1988).

Modeling Discrete Dividends

When no dividend will be paid between time t and $t + h$, we create the binomial tree as in Chapter 10. Suppose that a dividend will be paid between times t and $t + h$ and that its future value at time $t + h$ is D. The time t forward price for delivery at $t + h$ is then

$$F_{t,t+h} = S_t e^{rh} - D$$

Since the stock price at time $t + h$ will be ex-dividend, we create the up and down moves based on the ex-dividend stock price:

$$\begin{aligned}S_t^u &= \left(S_t e^{rh} - D\right) e^{\sigma \sqrt{h}} \\ S_t^d &= \left(S_t e^{rh} - D\right) e^{-\sigma \sqrt{h}}\end{aligned} \qquad (11.20)$$

How does option replication work when a dividend is imminent? When a dividend is paid, we have to account for the fact that the stock earns the dividend. Thus, we have

$$\begin{aligned}\left(S_t^u + D\right) \Delta + e^{rh} B &= C_u \\ \left(S_t^d + D\right) \Delta + e^{rh} B &= C_d\end{aligned}$$

The solution is

$$\Delta = \frac{C_u - C_d}{S_t^u - S_t^d}$$

$$B = e^{-rh} \left[\frac{S_t^u C_d - S_t^d C_u}{S_t^u - S_t^d}\right] - \Delta D e^{-rh}$$

Because the dividend is known, we decrease the bond position by the present value of the certain dividend. (When the dividend is proportional to the stock price, as with a stock index, we reduce the stock position, equation (10.1).) The expression for the option price is given by equation (10.17).

Problems with the Discrete Dividend Tree

The practical problem with this procedure is that the tree does not completely recombine after a discrete dividend. In all previous cases we have examined, we reached the same price after a given number of up and down movements, regardless of the order of the movements.

Figure 11.10, in which a dividend with a period-2 value of $5 is paid between periods 1 and 2, demonstrates that with a discrete dividend, the order of up and down movements affects the price. In the third binomial period there are six rather than four possible stock prices.

To see how the tree is constructed, period-1 prices are

$$\$41 e^{0.08 \times 1/3 + 0.3 \times \sqrt{1/3}} = \$50.071$$

$$\$41 e^{0.08 \times 1/3 - 0.3 \times \sqrt{1/3}} = \$35.411$$

The period-2 prices from the $50.071 node are

$$\left(\$50.071 e^{0.08 \times 1/3} - 5\right) \times e^{0.3 \times \sqrt{1/3}} = \$55.203$$

$$\left(\$50.071 e^{0.08 \times 1/3} - 5\right) \times e^{-0.3 \times \sqrt{1/3}} = \$39.041$$

Repeating this procedure for the node $S = \$35.411$ gives prices of $37.300 and $26.380. You can see that there are now four prices instead of three after two binomial steps: The

FIGURE 11.10

The tree depicts a discrete $5 dividend paid between the first and second binomial periods. There are eight discrete terminal nodes (six of them distinct) rather than four. Assumes $S = \$41$, $\sigma = 0.3$, $r = 0.08$, $t = 1$ year, and $h = 0.333$.

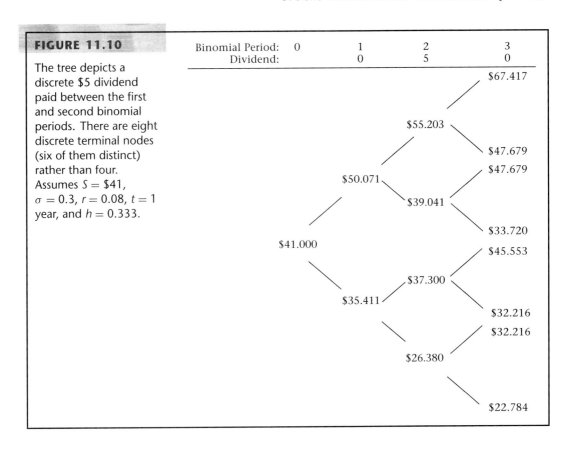

Binomial Period:	0	1	2	3
Dividend:		0	5	0

$67.417

$55.203

$47.679

$47.679

$50.071

$39.041

$33.720

$41.000

$45.553

$37.300

$35.411

$32.216

$32.216

$26.380

$22.784

ud and du nodes do not recombine. There are six distinct prices in the final period as each set of ex-dividend prices generates a distinct tree (three prices arise from the top two prices in period 2 and three prices arise from the bottom two prices in period 2). Each discrete dividend causes the tree to bifurcate.

There is also a conceptual problem with equation (11.20). Since the amount of the dividend is fixed, the stock price could in principle become negative if there have been large downward moves in the stock prior to the dividend.

This example demonstrates that handling fixed dividends requires care. We now turn to a method that is computationally easier than constructing a tree using equation (11.20) and that will not generate negative stock prices.

A Binomial Tree Using the Prepaid Forward

Schroder (1988) presents an elegant method of constructing a tree for a dividend-paying stock that solves both problems encountered with the method in Figure 11.10. The key insight for this method is that if we know for certain that a stock will pay a fixed dividend, then we can view the stock price as being the sum of two components: the dividend, which is like a zero-coupon bond with zero volatility, and the present value of the ex-dividend value of the stock—in other words, the prepaid forward price. Since the dividend is known, all volatility is attributed to the prepaid forward component of the stock price.

Suppose we know that a stock will pay a dividend D at time $T_D < T$, where T is the expiration date of the option. Then we base stock price movements on the prepaid forward price, $F_{t,T}^P = S_t - De^{-r(T_D-t)}$. The one-period forward price for the prepaid forward is $F_{t,t+h} = F_{t,T}^P e^{rh}$. As before, this gives us up and down movements of

$$u = e^{rh+\sigma\sqrt{h}} \qquad d = e^{rh-\sigma\sqrt{h}}$$

However, the actual stock price at each node is given by $S_t = F_{t,T}^P + De^{-r(T_D-t)}$.

Figure 11.11 shows the construction of the binomial tree for this case. Both the observed stock price and the stock price less the present value of dividends (the prepaid forward price) are included in the figure. Note that the volatility is 0.3392 rather than 0.3 as in Figure 10.5. The reason for this difference is that the random walk is assumed to apply to the prepaid forward price. If the actual stock price is observed to have a volatility of 30%, then the prepaid forward price, which is less than the stock price, must

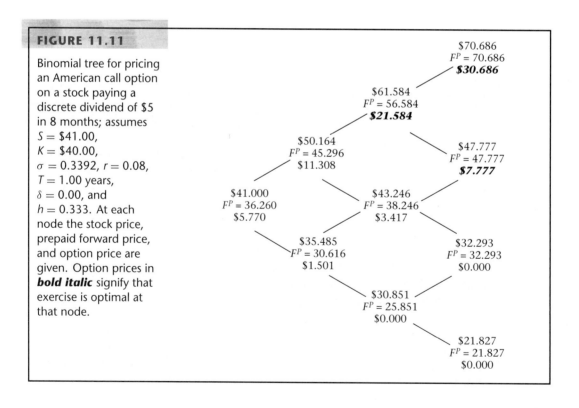

FIGURE 11.11

Binomial tree for pricing an American call option on a stock paying a discrete dividend of $5 in 8 months; assumes
$S = \$41.00$,
$K = \$40.00$,
$\sigma = 0.3392$, $r = 0.08$,
$T = 1.00$ years,
$\delta = 0.00$, and
$h = 0.333$. At each node the stock price, prepaid forward price, and option price are given. Option prices in **bold italic** signify that exercise is optimal at that node.

$41.000
$FP = 36.260$
$5.770

$50.164
$FP = 45.296$
$11.308

$35.485
$FP = 30.616$
$1.501

$61.584
$FP = 56.584$
$21.584

$43.246
$FP = 38.246$
$3.417

$30.851
$FP = 25.851$
$0.000

$70.686
$FP = 70.686$
$30.686

$47.777
$FP = 47.777$
$7.777

$32.293
$FP = 32.293$
$0.000

$21.827
$FP = 21.827$
$0.000

have a greater volatility. We use the approximate correction

$$\sigma_F = \sigma_S \times \frac{S}{F^P}$$

$$= 0.3 \times \frac{\$41}{\$36.26} = 0.3392$$

You may be wondering exactly how the dividend affects Figure 11.11. Note first that $u = 1.2492$. Look at the node where the stock price is $61.584. This is a *cum-dividend* price, just before the dividend is paid. The nodes in the last period are constructed based on the *ex-dividend* price, for example

$$(\$61.584 - \$5) \times 1.2492 = \$70.686$$

As a final point, we obtain risk-neutral probabilities for the tree in the same way as in the absence of dividends. It is important to realize that we construct the binomial tree for the *prepaid forward*, which pays no dividends. Thus, the risk-neutral probability of an up move in the prepaid forward price is given by equation (10.5), just as in the case of a nondividend paying stock.

CHAPTER SUMMARY

Both call and put options may be rationally exercised prior to expiration. The early-exercise decision weighs three considerations: dividends on the underlying asset, interest on the strike price, and the insurance value of keeping the option alive. Calls will be early-exercised in order to capture dividends on the underlying stock; interest and insurance weigh against early exercise. Puts will be early-exercised in order to capture interest on the strike price; dividends and insurance weigh against early exercise. For both calls and puts, the early-exercise criterion becomes less stringent as the option has less time to maturity.

Risk-neutral option valuation is consistent with valuation using more traditional discounted cash flow methods. With risk-neutral pricing it is not necessary to estimate the expected return on the stock in order to price an option. With traditional discounted cash flow methods, the correct discount rate for the option varies along the binomial tree; thus, valuation is considerably more complicated than with risk-neutral pricing.

The binomial model, which approximates the lognormal distribution, is a random walk model adapted to modeling stock prices. The model assumes that the continuously compounded return on the stock follows a random walk. The volatility needed for the binomial model can be estimated by computing the standard deviation of continuously compounded returns and annualizing the result.

The binomial model can be adapted to price options on a stock that pays discrete dividends. Discrete dividends can lead to a nonrecombining binomial tree. If we assume that the prepaid forward price follows a binomial process instead of the stock price, the tree becomes recombining.

Further Reading

The binomial model can be used to derive the Black-Scholes model, which we discuss in Chapter 12. The practical importance of risk-neutral pricing will become evident in Chapter 19, when we see that Monte Carlo valuation hinges upon risk-neutral pricing. In that chapter we will also reexamine Figure 11.4 and show how the option price may be computed as an expected value using only stock prices in the final period.

The issue of how the stock price is distributed will also arise frequently in later chapters. Chapter 18 discusses lognormality in more detail and presents evidence that stock prices are not exactly lognormally distributed. Chapter 20 will examine in more detail the question of how the stock price moves, in particular what happens when h gets very small in the binomial model.

We will return to the determinants of early exercise in Chapter 17, when we discuss real options.

The literature on risk-neutral pricing is fairly technical. Cox and Ross (1976) was the first paper to use risk-neutral pricing and Harrison and Kreps (1979) studied the economic underpinnings. Two good treatments of this topic are Huang and Litzenberger (1988, ch. 8)—their treatment inspired Appendix 11.B—and Baxter and Rennie (1996).

Campbell et al. (1997) and Cochrane (2001) summarize evidence on the distribution of stock prices. The original Samuelson work on asset prices following a random walk (Samuelson, 1965) remains a classic, modern empirical evidence notwithstanding.

Broadie and Detemple (1996) discuss the computation of American option prices, and also discuss alternative binomial approaches and their relative numerical efficiency.

Problems

Many (but not all) of these questions can be answered with the help of the *BinomCall* and *BinomPut* functions available on the spreadsheets accompanying this book.

11.1. Consider a one-period binomial model with $h = 1$, where $S = \$100$, $r = 0$, $\sigma = 30\%$, and $\delta = 0.08$. Compute American call option prices for $K = \$70$, $\$80$, $\$90$, and $\$100$.

    a. At which strike(s) does early exercise occur?

    b. Use put-call parity to explain why early exercise does not occur at the higher strikes.

    c. Use put-call parity to explain why early exercise is sure to occur for all lower strikes than that in your answer to (a).

11.2. Repeat Problem 11.1, only assume that $r = 0.08$. What is the greatest strike price at which early exercise will occur? What condition related to put-call parity is satisfied at this strike price?

11.3. Repeat Problem 11.1, only assume that $r = 0.08$ and $\delta = 0$. Will early exercise ever occur? Why?

11.4. Consider a one-period binomial model with $h = 1$, where $S = \$100$, $r = 0.08$, $\sigma = 30\%$, and $\delta = 0$. Compute American put option prices for $K = \$100$, $\$110$, $\$120$, and $\$130$.

      a. At which strike(s) does early exercise occur?

      b. Use put-call parity to explain why early exercise does not occur at the other strikes.

      c. Use put-call parity to explain why early exercise is sure to occur for all strikes greater than that in your answer to (a).

11.5. Repeat Problem 11.4, only set $\delta = 0.08$. What is the lowest strike price at which early exercise will occur? What condition related to put-call parity is satisfied at this strike price?

11.6. Repeat Problem 11.4, only set $r = 0$ and $\delta = 0.08$. What is the lowest strike price (if there is one) at which early exercise will occur? If early exercise never occurs, explain why not.

For the following problems, note that the *BinomCall* and *BinomPut* functions are array functions that return the option delta (Δ) as well as the price. If you know Δ, you can compute B as $C - S\Delta$.

11.7. Let $S = \$100$, $K = \$100$, $\sigma = 30\%$, $r = 0.08$, $t = 1$, and $\delta = 0$. Let $n = 10$. Suppose the stock has an expected return of 15%.

      a. What is the expected return on a European call option? A European put option?

      b. What happens to the expected return if you increase the volatility to 50%?

11.8. Let $S = \$100$, $\sigma = 30\%$, $r = 0.08$, $t = 1$, and $\delta = 0$. Suppose the true expected return on the stock is 15%. Set $n = 10$. Compute European call prices, Δ, and B for strikes of $\$70$, $\$80$, $\$90$, $\$100$, $\$110$, $\$120$, and $\$130$. For each strike, compute the expected return on the option. What effect does the strike have on the option's expected return?

11.9. Repeat the previous problem, except that for each strike price, compute the expected return on the option for times to expiration of 3 months, 6 months, 1 year, and 2 years. What effect does time to maturity have on the option's expected return?

11.10. Let $S = \$100$, $\sigma = 30\%$, $r = 0.08$, $t = 1$, and $\delta = 0$. Suppose the true expected return on the stock is 15%. Set $n = 10$. Compute European put prices, Δ, and B for strikes of $\$70$, $\$80$, $\$90$, $\$100$, $\$110$, $\$120$, and $\$130$. For each strike, compute the expected return on the option. What effect does the strike have on the option's expected return?

11.11. Repeat the previous problem, except that for each strike price, compute the expected return on the option for times to expiration of 3 months, 6 months, 1 year, and 2 years. What effect does time to maturity have on the option's expected return?

11.12. Let $S = \$100$, $\sigma = 0.30$, $r = 0.08$, $t = 1$, and $\delta = 0$. Using equation (11.17) to compute the probability of reaching a terminal node and $Su^i d^{n-i}$ to compute the price at that node, plot the risk-neutral distribution of year-1 stock prices as in Figures 11.8 and 11.9 for $n = 3$ and $n = 10$.

11.13. Repeat the previous problem for $n = 50$. What is the risk-neutral probability that $S_1 < \$80$? $S_1 > \$120$?

11.14. We saw in Section 10.1 that the undiscounted risk-neutral expected stock price equals the forward price. We will verify this using the binomial tree in Figure 11.4.

    a. Using $S = \$100$, $r = 0.08$, and $\delta = 0$, what are the 4-month, 8-month, and 1-year forward prices?

    b. Verify your answers in (a) by computing the risk-neutral expected stock price in the first, second, and third binomial period. Use equation (11.17) to determine the probability of reaching each node.

11.15. Compute the 1-year forward price using the 50-step binomial tree in Problem 11.13.

11.16. Suppose $S = \$100$, $K = \$95$, $r = 8\%$ (continuously compounded), $t = 1$, $\sigma = 30\%$, and $\delta = 5\%$. Explicitly construct an 8-period binomial tree using the Cox-Ross-Rubinstein expressions for u and d:

$$u = e^{\sigma\sqrt{h}} \qquad d = e^{-\sigma\sqrt{h}}$$

Compute the prices of European and American calls and puts.

11.17. Suppose $S = \$100$, $K = \$95$, $r = 8\%$ (continuously compounded), $t = 1$, $\sigma = 30\%$, and $\delta = 5\%$. Explicitly construct an 8-period binomial tree using the lognormal expressions for u and d:

$$u = e^{(r-\delta-.5\sigma^2)h+\sigma\sqrt{h}} \qquad d = e^{(r-\delta-.5\sigma^2)h-\sigma\sqrt{h}}$$

Compute the prices of European and American calls and puts.

11.18. Obtain at least 5 years' worth of daily or weekly stock price data for a stock of your choice.

    a. Compute annual volatility using all the data.

    b. Compute annual volatility for each calendar year in your data. How does volatility vary over time?

    c. Compute annual volatility for the first and second half of each year in your data. How much variation is there in your estimate?

11.19. Obtain at least 5 years of daily data for at least three stocks and, if you can, one currency. Estimate annual volatility for each year for each asset in your data.

What do you observe about the pattern of historical volatility over time? Does historical volatility move in tandem for different assets?

11.20. Suppose that $S = \$50$, $K = \$45$, $\sigma = 0.30$, $r = 0.08$, and $t = 1$. The stock will pay a $4 dividend in exactly 3 months. Compute the price of European and American call options using a four-step binomial tree.

APPENDIX 11.A: PRICING OPTIONS WITH TRUE PROBABILITIES

In this appendix we demonstrate algebraically that computing the option price in a consistent way using α as the expected return on the stock gives the correct option price. Using the definition of γ, equation (11.6), we can rewrite equation (11.7) as

$$(\Delta S + B)\left(\frac{1}{e^{\alpha h}\Delta S + e^{rh}B}\left[\frac{e^{rh} - d}{u - d}C_u + \frac{u - e^{rh}}{u - d}C_d + \frac{e^{\alpha h} - e^{rh}}{u - d}(C_u - C_d)\right]\right)$$

Since $\Delta S + B$ is the call price, we need only show that the expression in large parentheses is equal to one. From the definitions of Δ and B we have

$$\frac{e^{rh} - d}{u - d}C_u + \frac{u - e^{rh}}{u - d}C_d = e^{rh}(\Delta S + B)$$

We can rewrite (11.4) as

$$(\Delta S + B)\left(\frac{1}{e^{\alpha h}\Delta S + e^{rh}B}\left[e^{rh}(\Delta S + B) + (e^{\alpha h} - e^{rh})\Delta S\right]\right) = \Delta S + B$$

This follows since the expression in large parentheses equals one.

APPENDIX 11.B: WHY DOES RISK-NEUTRAL PRICING WORK?

There is a large and highly technical literature on risk-neutral pricing. The underlying economic idea is fairly easy to understand, however.

Utility-Based Valuation

The starting point is that the well-being of investors is not measured in dollars, but in *utility*. Utility is a measure of satisfaction. Economists say that investors exhibit *declining marginal utility*: Starting from a given level of wealth, the utility gained from adding $1 to wealth is less than the utility lost from taking $1 away from wealth. Thus, we expect that more dollars will make an investor happier, but that if we keep adding dollars, each additional dollar will make the investor less happy than the previous dollars.

Declining marginal utility implies that investors are risk-averse, which means that an investor will prefer a safer investment to a riskier investment that has the same expected return. Since losses are more costly than gains are beneficial, a risk-averse investor will avoid a fair bet, which by definition has equal expected gains and losses.[5]

To illustrate risk-neutral pricing, we imagine a world where there are two assets, a risky stock and a risk-free bond. Investors are risk-averse. Suppose the economy in one period will be in one of two states, a high state and a low state. How do we value assets in such a world? We need to know three things:

1. What utility value, expressed in terms of dollars today, does an investor attach to the marginal dollar received in each state in the future? Denote the values of $1 received in the high and low states as U_H and U_L, respectively.[6] Because the investor is risk-averse, $1 received in the high state is worth less than $1 received in the low state, hence, $U_H < U_L$.

2. How many dollars will an asset pay in each state? Denote the payoffs to the risky stock in each state C_H and C_L.

3. What is the probability of each state occurring? Denote the probability of the high state as p.

We begin by defining a state price as the price of a security that pays $1 only when a particular state occurs. Let Q_H be the price of a security that pays $1 when the high state occurs, and Q_L the price of a security paying $1 when the low state occurs.[7] Since U_H and U_L are the value today of $1 in each state, the price we would pay is just the value times the probability that state is reached:

$$Q_H = p \times U_H$$
$$Q_L = (1 - p) \times U_L \tag{11.21}$$

Since there are only two possible states, we can value any future cash flow using these state prices.

The price of the risky stock, S_0 is

$$\text{Price of stock} = Q_H \times C_H + Q_L \times C_L \tag{11.22}$$

---

[5]This is an example of *Jensen's Inequality* (see Appendix C at the end of this book). A risk-averse investor has a concave utility function, which implies that

$$E[U(x)] < U[E(x)]$$

The expected utility associated with a gamble, $E[U(x)]$, is less than the utility from receiving the expected value of the gamble for sure, $U[E(x)]$.

[6]Technically U_H and U_L are ratios of marginal utilities, discounted by the rate of time preference. However, you can think of them as simply converting future dollars in a particular state into dollars today.

[7]These are often called "Arrow-Debreu" securities, named after Nobel-prize–winning economists Kenneth Arrow and Gerard Debreu.

Since the risk-free bond pays \$1 in each state, we have

$$\text{Price of bond} = Q_H \times 1 + Q_L \times 1 \qquad (11.23)$$

We can calculate rates of return by dividing expected cash flows by the price. Thus, the risk-free rate is

$$1 + r = \frac{1}{\text{Price of bond}}$$
$$= \frac{1}{Q_H + Q_L} \qquad (11.24)$$

The expected return on the stock is

$$1 + \alpha = \frac{p \times C_H + (1 - p)C_L}{\text{Price of stock}}$$
$$= \frac{p \times C_H + (1 - p)C_L}{Q_H \times C_H + Q_L \times C_L} \qquad (11.25)$$

Standard Discounted Cash Flow

The standard discounted cash flow calculation entails computing the security price by discounting the expected cash flow at the expected rate of return. In the case of the stock, this gives us

$$\frac{p \times C_H + (1 - p)C_L}{1 + \alpha} = \text{Price of stock}$$

This is simply a rewriting of equation (11.25); hence, it is obviously correct. Similarly, the bond price is

$$\frac{1}{1 + r} = \text{Price of bond}$$

Risk-Neutral Pricing

The point of risk-neutral pricing is to sidestep the utility calculations above. We are looking for probabilities such that when we use those probabilities to compute expected cash flows *without* explicit utility adjustments, and discount that expectation at the risk-free rate, then we will get the correct answer.

The trick is the following: Instead of utility-weighting the cash flows and computing expectations, *we utility-weight the probabilities*, creating new "risk-neutral" probabilities. Now we will see how to perform risk-neutral pricing in this context. Use the state prices in equation (11.21) to define the risk-neutral probability of the high state, p^*, as

$$p^* = \frac{p \times U_H}{p \times U_H + (1 - p) \times U_L} = \frac{Q_H}{Q_H + Q_L}$$

Now we compute the stock price by using the risk-neutral probabilities to compute expected cash flow, and then discounting at the risk-free rate. We have

$$\frac{p^* C_H + (1 - p^*) C_L}{1 + r} = \frac{\frac{Q_H}{Q_H + Q_L} C_H + \frac{Q_L}{Q_H + Q_L} C_L}{1 + r}$$

$$= \frac{Q_H C_H + Q_L C_L}{(Q_H + Q_L)(1 + r)}$$

$$= Q_H C_H + Q_L C_L$$

which is the price of stock, from equation (11.22). This shows that we can construct risk-neutral probabilities and use them to price risky assets.

Example

Table 11.2 contains assumptions for a numerical example.

State prices Using equation 11.21, the state prices are $Q_H = 0.52 \times \$0.87 = \$0.4524$, and $Q_L = 0.48 \times \$0.98 = \$0.4704$.

Valuing the risk-free bond The risk-free bond pays \$1 in each state. Thus, using equation (11.23) the risk-free bond price, B_0, is

$$B_0 = Q_H + Q_L = \$0.4524 + \$0.4704 = \$0.9228 \tag{11.26}$$

The risk-free rate is

$$r = \frac{1}{0.9228} - 1 = 8.366\%$$

Valuing the risky stock using real probabilities Using equation (11.22) the price of the stock is

$$S_0 = 0.4524 \times \$180 + 0.4704 \times \$30 = \$95.544 \tag{11.27}$$

TABLE 11.2   Probabilities, utility weights, and equity cash flows in high and low states of the economy.

	High State	Low State
Cash flow to risk-free bond	$C_H = \$1$	$C_L = \$1$
Cash flow to stock	$C_H = \$180$	$C_L = \$30$
Probability	$p = 0.52$	$p = 0.48$
Value of \$1	$U_H = \$0.87$	$U_L = \$0.98$

The expected cash flow on the stock in one period is

$$E(S_1) = 0.52 \times \$180 + 0.48 \times \$30 = \$108$$

The expected return on the stock is therefore

$$\alpha = \frac{\$108}{\$95.544} - 1 = 13.037\%$$

By definition, if we discount $E(S_1)$ at the rate 13.037%, we will get the price $95.544.

Risk-neutral valuation of the stock   The risk-neutral probability is

$$p^* = \frac{\$0.4524}{\$0.4524 + \$0.4704}$$

$$= 49.025\%$$

Now we can value the stock using p^* instead of the true probabilities, and discount at the risk-free rate:

$$S_0 = \frac{0.49025 \times \$180 + (1 - 0.49025) \times \$30}{1.08366}$$

$$= \$95.544$$

We can also verify that a call option on the stock can be valued using risk-neutral pricing. Suppose the call has a strike of $130. Then the value computed using true probabilities and utility weights is

$$C = 0.52 \times 0.87 \times \max(0, \$180 - \$130) + 0.48 \times 0.98 \times \max(0, \$30 - \$130)$$

$$= \$22.62$$

Using risk-neutral pricing, we obtain

$$C = \frac{\left[0.49025 \times \max(0, \$180 - \$130) + (1 - 0.49025) \times \max(0, \$30 - \$130) \right]}{1.08366}$$

$$= \$22.62$$

Why Risk-Neutral Pricing Works

Risk-neutral pricing works in the above example because the same utility weights and probabilities are used to value both the stock and risk-free bond. As long as this is true, risk-neutral pricing formulas can be obtained simply by rewriting the more complicated valuation formulas that take account of utility.

A basic result from portfolio theory states that as long as investors are optimally choosing their portfolios, they will use the same utility weights for an additional dollar of investment in all assets. Thus, in an economy with well-functioning capital markets, risk-neutral pricing is possible for derivatives on traded assets.

When would risk-neutral pricing not work? Suppose you have an asset you cannot trade or hedge, or you have a nontradable asset with cash flows that cannot be replicated by the cash flows of traded assets. If you cannot trade or offset the risk of the asset, then there is no guarantee that the marginal utility you use to value payoffs from this asset in a given state will be the same as for other assets. In other words, U_H and U_L will differ across assets. If the same U_H and U_L are not used to value the stock and bond, the calculations in this appendix fail. Valuing the nontradable stream of cash flows then requires computing the utility value of the payoffs. The point of risk-neutral pricing is to avoid having to do this.

CHAPTER 12

The Black-Scholes Formula

I n 1973 Fischer Black and Myron Scholes (Black and Scholes, 1973) published a formula—the Black-Scholes formula—for computing the theoretical price of a European call option on a stock. Their paper, coupled with closely related work by Robert Merton, revolutionized both the theory and practice of finance. The history of the Black-Scholes formula is discussed in the box on page 376.

In this chapter we present the Black-Scholes formula for pricing European options, explain how it is used for different underlying assets, and discuss the so-called option Greeks—delta, gamma, theta, vega, rho, and psi—which measure the behavior of the option price when inputs to the formula change. We also show how observed option prices can be used to infer the market's estimate of volatility. Finally, while there is in general no simple formula comparable to Black-Scholes for valuing options that may be exercised early, perpetual options are an exception. We present the pricing formulas for perpetual American calls and puts.

12.1 INTRODUCTION TO THE BLACK-SCHOLES FORMULA

To introduce the Black-Scholes formula, we first return to the binomial model, discussed in Chapters 10 and 11. When computing a binomial option price, we can vary the number of binomial steps, holding fixed the time to expiration. Table 12.1 computes binomial call option prices, using the same inputs as in Figure 10.3, and increases the number of steps, n. Changing the number of steps changes the option price, but once the number of steps becomes great enough we appear to approach a limiting value for the price. The last row reports the call option price if we were to use an infinite number of steps. We can't literally have an infinity of steps in a binomial tree, but it is possible to show that as the number of steps approaches infinity, the option price is given by the Black-Scholes formula. Thus, the Black-Scholes formula is a limiting case of the binomial formula for the price of a European option.

Call Options

The Black-Scholes formula for a European call option on a stock that pays dividends at the continuous rate δ is

The History of the Black-Scholes Formula

The Black-Scholes formula was first published in the May/June 1973 issue of the *Journal of Political Economy* (*JPE*) (see Black and Scholes, 1973). By coincidence, the Chicago Board Options Exchange (CBOE) opened at almost the same time, on April 26, 1973. Initially, the exchange traded call options on just 16 stocks. Puts did not trade until 1977. In 2000, by contrast, the CBOE traded both calls and puts on over 1200 stocks.

Fischer Black told the story of the formula in Black (1989). He and Myron Scholes started working on the option-pricing problem in 1969, when Black was an independent consultant in Boston and Scholes an assistant professor at MIT. While working on the problem, they had extensive discussions with Robert Merton of MIT, who was also working on option pricing.

The first version of their paper was dated October 1970 and was rejected for publication by the *JPE* and subsequently by another prominent journal. However, in 1971, Eugene Fama and Merton Miller of the University of Chicago, recognizing the importance of their work, interceded on their behalf with the editors of the *JPE*. Later in 1973 Robert Merton published an important and wide-ranging follow-up paper (Merton, 1973b), which, among other contributions, established the standard no-arbitrage restrictions on option prices discussed in Chapter 9, significantly generalized the Black-Scholes formula and their derivation of the model, and provided formulas for pricing perpetual American puts and down-and-out calls.

In 1997, Robert Merton and Myron Scholes won the Nobel Prize in Economics for their work on option pricing. Fischer Black was ineligible for the Prize, having died in 1995 at the age of 57.

TABLE 12.1   Binomial option prices for different numbers of binomial steps. As in Figure 10.2, all calculations assume that the stock price $S = \$41$, the strike price $K = \$40$, volatility $\sigma = 0.30$, risk-free rate $r = 0.08$, time to expiration $T = 1$, and dividend yield $\delta = 0$.

Number of Steps (n)	Binomial Call Price ($)
1	7.839
4	7.160
10	7.065
50	6.969
100	6.966
500	6.960
∞	6.961

$$C(S, K, \sigma, r, T, \delta) = Se^{-\delta T} N(d_1) - Ke^{-rT} N(d_2) \qquad (12.1)$$

where

$$d_1 = \frac{\ln(S/K) + (r - \delta + \frac{1}{2}\sigma^2)T}{\sigma\sqrt{T}} \qquad (12.2a)$$

$$d_2 = d_1 - \sigma\sqrt{T} \qquad (12.2b)$$

As with the binomial model, there are six inputs to the Black-Scholes formula: S, the current price of the stock; K, the strike price of the option; σ, the volatility of the stock; r, the continuously compounded risk-free interest rate; T, the time to expiration; and δ, the dividend yield on the stock.

$N(x)$ in the Black-Scholes formula is the cumulative normal distribution function, which is the probability that a number randomly drawn from a standard normal distribution (i.e., a normal distribution with mean 0 and variance 1) will be less than x. Most spreadsheets have a built-in function for computing $N(x)$. In Excel, the function is "NormSDist." The normal and cumulative normal distributions are illustrated in Figure 18.2 on page 589.

Two of the inputs (K and T) describe characteristics of the option contract. The others describe the stock (S, σ, and δ) and the discount rate for a risk-free investment (r). All of the inputs are self-explanatory with the exception of volatility, which we discussed in Section 11.4. Volatility is the standard deviation of the rate of return on the stock—a measure of the uncertainty about the future return on the stock.

It is important to be clear about units in which inputs are expressed. Several of the inputs in equation (12.1) are expressed per unit time: The interest rate, volatility, and dividend yield are typically expressed on an annual basis. In equation (12.1), these inputs are all multiplied by time: The interest rate, dividend, and volatility appear as $r \times T$, $\delta \times T$, and $\sigma^2 \times T$ (or equivalently, $\sigma \times \sqrt{T}$). Thus, when we enter inputs into the formula, the specific time unit we use is arbitrary as long as we are consistent. If time is measured in years, then r, δ, and σ should be annual. If time is measured in days, then we need to use the daily equivalent of r, σ, and δ, and so forth. We will always assume inputs are per year unless we state otherwise.

Example 12.1 Let $S = \$41$, $K = \$40$, $\sigma = 0.3$, $r = 8\%$, $T = 0.25$ (3 months), and $\delta = 0$. Computing the Black-Scholes call price, we obtain[1]

$$\$41 \times e^{-0 \times 0.25} \times N\left(\frac{\ln(\frac{41}{40}) + (0.08 - 0 + \frac{0.3^2}{2}) \times 0.25}{0.3\sqrt{0.25}}\right)$$

$$- \$40 \times e^{-0.08 \times 0.25} \times N\left(\frac{\ln(\frac{41}{40}) + (0.08 - 0 - \frac{0.3^2}{2}) \times 0.25}{0.3\sqrt{0.25}}\right) = \$3.399 \qquad ⬥$$

---

[1] The call price here can be computed using the Black-Scholes formula call spreadsheet formula, BSCall:

$$\text{BSCall}(S, K, \sigma, r, t, \delta) = \text{BSCall}(41, 40, 0.3, 0.08, 0.25, 0) = \$3.399$$

There is one input which does *not* appear in the Black-Scholes formula, namely the expected return on the stock. You might guess that stocks with a high beta would have a higher expected return; hence, options on these stocks would have a higher probability of settlement in-the-money. The higher expected return would seem to imply a higher option price. However, as we saw in Section 11.2, a high stock beta implies a high option beta, so the discount rate for the expected payoff to such an option is correspondingly greater. The net result—one of the key insights from the Black-Scholes analysis—is that beta is irrelevant: The larger average payoff to options on high beta stocks is exactly offset by the larger discount rate.

Put Options

The Black-Scholes formula for a European put option is

$$P(S, K, \sigma, r, T, \delta) = Ke^{-rT}N(-d_2) - Se^{-\delta T}N(-d_1) \qquad (12.3)$$

where d_1 and d_2 are given by equations (12.2a) and (12.2b).

Since the Black-Scholes call and put prices, equations (12.1) and (12.3), are for European options, put-call parity must hold:

$$P(S, K, \sigma, r, T, \delta) = C(S, K, \sigma, r, T, \delta) + Ke^{-rT} - Se^{-\delta T} \qquad (12.4)$$

This version of the formula follows from equations (12.1) and (12.3), together with the fact that for any x, $1 - N(x) = N(-x)$. (This equation says that the probability of a random draw from the standard normal distribution being above x, $1 - N(x)$, equals the probability of a draw being below $-x$, $N(-x)$.)

Example 12.2 Using the same inputs as in Example 12.1, the put price is $1.607. We can compute the put price in two ways. First, computing it using equation (12.3), we obtain[2]

$$\$40e^{-0.08 \times 0.25} N\left(-\frac{\ln(\frac{41}{40}) + (0.08 - 0 - \frac{0.3^2}{2})0.25}{0.3\sqrt{0.25}}\right)$$

$$- \$41e^{-0 \times 0.25} N\left(-\frac{\ln(\frac{41}{40}) + (0.08 - 0 + \frac{0.3^2}{2})0.25}{0.3\sqrt{0.25}}\right) = \$1.607$$

Computing the price using put-call parity, equation (12.4), we have

$$P(41, 40, 0.3, 0.08, 0.25, 0) = 3.339 + 40e^{-0.08 \times 0.25} - 41$$

$$= \$1.607 \qquad \qquad \textit{❧}$$

---

[2]The put price here can be computed using the Black-Scholes put spreadsheet formula, BSPut:

$$\text{BSPut}(S, K, \sigma, r, t, \delta) = \text{BSPut}(41, 40, 0.3, 0.08, 0.25, 0) = \$1.607$$

When Is the Black-Scholes Formula Valid?

Derivations of the Black-Scholes formula make a number of assumptions that can be sorted into two groups: assumptions about how the stock price is distributed, and assumptions about the economic environment. For the version of the formula we have presented, assumptions about the distribution of the stock price include the following:

- Continuously compounded returns on the stock are normally distributed and independent over time. (As discussed in Chapter 11, we assume there are no "jumps" in the stock price.)

- The volatility of continuously compounded returns is known and constant.

- Future dividends are known, either as a dollar amount or as a fixed dividend yield.

Assumptions about the economic environment include these:

- The risk-free rate is known and constant.

- There are no transaction costs or taxes.

- It is possible to short-sell costlessly and to borrow at the risk-free rate.

Many of these assumptions can easily be relaxed. For example, with a small change in the formula, we can permit the volatility and interest rate to vary over time in a known way. In Appendix 10.A we discussed why, even though there are taxes, tax rates do not appear in the binomial formula; the same argument applies to the Black-Scholes formula.

As a practical matter, the first set of assumptions—those about the stock price distribution—are the most crucial. Most academic and practitioner research on option pricing concentrates on relaxing these assumptions. They will also be our focus when we discuss empirical evidence. You should keep in mind that almost *any* valuation procedure, including ordinary discounted cash flow, is based on assumptions that appear strong; the interesting question is how well the procedure works in practice.

12.2 APPLYING THE FORMULA TO OTHER ASSETS

The Black-Scholes formula is often thought of as a formula for pricing European options on stocks. Specifically, equations (12.1) and (12.3) provide the price of a call and put option, respectively, on a stock paying continuous dividends. In practice, we also want to be able to price European options on stocks paying discrete dividends, options on futures, and options on currencies. We have already seen in Chapter 10, Table 10.1, that the binomial model can be adapted to different underlying assets by adjusting the dividend yield. The same adjustments work in the Black-Scholes formula.

We can rewrite d_1 in the Black-Scholes formula, equation (12.2a), as

$$d_1 = \frac{\ln(Se^{-\delta T}/Ke^{-rT}) + \frac{1}{2}\sigma^2 T}{\sigma\sqrt{T}}$$

When d_1 is rewritten in this way, it is apparent that the dividend yield enters the formula *only* to discount the stock price, as $Se^{-\delta T}$, and the interest rate enters the formula *only* to discount the strike price, as Ke^{-rT}. Notice also that volatility enters only as $\sigma^2 T$.

The prepaid forward prices for the stock and strike asset are $F_{0,T}^P(S) = Se^{-\delta T}$ and $F_{0,T}^P(K) = Ke^{-rT}$. Then we can write the Black-Scholes formula, equation (12.1), entirely in terms of prepaid forward prices and $\sigma\sqrt{T}$:[3]

$$C(F_{0,T}^P(S), F_{0,T}^P(K), \sigma, T) = F_{0,T}^P(S)N(d_1) - F_{0,T}^P(K)N(d_2) \qquad (12.5)$$

$$d_1 = \frac{\ln[F_{0,T}^P(S)/F_{0,T}^P(K)] + \frac{1}{2}\sigma^2 T}{\sigma\sqrt{T}}$$

$$d_2 = d_1 - \sigma\sqrt{T}$$

This version of the formula is interesting because the dividend yield and the interest rate do not appear explicitly; they are implicitly incorporated into the prepaid forward prices.

To price options on underlying assets other than stocks, we can use equation (12.5) in conjunction with the forward price formulas from Chapters 5 and 6. For all of the examples in this chapter, we will have a strike price denominated in cash, so that $F_{0,T}^P(K) = Ke^{-rT}$.

Options on Stocks with Discrete Dividends

When a stock makes discrete dividend payments, the prepaid forward price is

$$F_{0,T}^P(S) = S_0 - PV_{0,T}(Div)$$

where $PV_{0,T}(Div)$ is the present value of dividends payable over the life of the option. Thus, using equation (12.5), we can price a European option with discrete dividends by subtracting the present value of dividends from the stock price, and entering the result into the formula in place of the stock price. The use of the prepaid forward price here should remind you of the approach to pricing options on dividend-paying stocks in Section 11.5.

Example 12.3 Suppose $S = \$41$, $K = \$40$, $\sigma = 0.3$, $r = 8\%$, and $T = 0.25$ (3 months). The stock will pay a $3 dividend in 1 month, but makes no other payouts over the life of the option (hence, $\delta = 0$). The present value of the dividend is

$$PV(Div) = \$3e^{-0.08 \times 1/12} = \$2.98$$

Setting the stock price in the Black-Scholes formula equal to $\$41 - \$2.98 = \$38.02$, the Black-Scholes call price is $\$1.763$. ≹

---

[3]We can also let $V(T) = \sigma\sqrt{T}$ represent total volatility—uncertainty about the relative time-T values of the underlying and strike assets—over the life of the option. The option price can then be written solely in terms of $F_{0,T}^P(S)$, $F_{0,T}^P(K)$, and $V(T)$. This gives us a minimalist version of the Black-Scholes formula: To price an option you need to know the prepaid forward prices of the underlying asset and the strike asset, and the relative volatility of the two.

Compared to the $3.399 price computed in Example 12.1, the dividend reduces the option price by about $1.64, or over half the amount of the dividend. Note that this is the price of a *European* option. An American option might be exercised just prior to the dividend, and hence would have a greater price.

Options on Currencies

We can price an option on a currency by replacing the dividend yield with the foreign interest rate. If the spot exchange rate is x (expressed as domestic currency per unit of foreign currency), and the foreign currency interest rate is r_f, the prepaid forward price for the currency is

$$F^P_{0,T}(x) = x_0 e^{-r_f T}$$

Using equation (12.5), the Black-Scholes formula becomes

$$C(x, K, \sigma, r, T, r_f) = xe^{-r_f T} N(d_1) - Ke^{-rT} N(d_2) \qquad (12.6)$$

$$d_1 = \frac{\ln(x/K) + (r - r_f + \frac{1}{2}\sigma^2)T}{\sigma\sqrt{T}}$$

$$d_2 = d_1 - \sigma\sqrt{T}$$

This formula for the price of a European call on currencies is called the Garman-Kohlhagen model, after Garman and Kohlhagen (1983).

The price of a European currency put is obtained using parity:

$$P(x, K, \sigma, r, T, r_f) = C(x, K, \sigma, r, T, r_f) + Ke^{-rT} - xe^{-r_f T}$$

Example 12.4 Suppose the spot exchange rate is $x = \$0.92/\text{€}$, $K = \$0.9$, $\sigma = 0.10$, $r = 6\%$ (the dollar interest rate), $T = 1$, and $r_f = 3.2\%$ (the euro-denominated interest rate). The price of a dollar-denominated euro call is $0.0606, and the price of a dollar-denominated euro put is $0.0172.

Options on Futures

The prepaid forward price for a futures contract is just the present value of the futures price. Thus, we price a European option on a futures contract by using the futures price as the stock price and setting the dividend yield equal to the risk-free rate. The resulting formula is also known as the **Black formula**:

$$C(F, K, \sigma, r, T, r) = Fe^{-rT} N(d_1) - Ke^{-rT} N(d_2) \qquad (12.7)$$

$$d_1 = \frac{\ln(F/K) + \frac{1}{2}\sigma^2 T}{\sigma\sqrt{T}}$$

$$d_2 = d_1 - \sigma\sqrt{T}$$

The put price is obtained using the parity relationship for options on futures:

$$P(F, K, \sigma, r, T, r) = C(F, K, \sigma, r, T, r) + Ke^{-rT} - Fe^{-rT}$$

Example 12.5 Suppose the 1-year futures price for natural gas is \$2.10/MMBtu and the volatility is 0.25. We have $F = \$2.10$, $K = \$2.10$, $\sigma = 0.25$, $r = 0.055$, $T = 1$, and $\delta = 0.055$ (the dividend yield is set to equal the interest rate). The Black-Scholes call price and put price are both \$0.197721. ⪼

12.3 OPTION GREEKS

Option Greeks are formulas that express the change in the option price when an input to the formula changes, taking as fixed all the other inputs.[4] One important use of Greek measures is to assess risk exposure. For example, a market-making bank with a portfolio of options would want to understand its exposure to stock price changes, interest rates, volatility, etc. A portfolio manager wants to know what happens to the value of a portfolio of stock index options if there is a change in the level of the stock index. An options investor would like to know how interest rate changes and volatility changes affect profit and loss.

Keep in mind that the Greek measures by assumption change only *one* input at a time. In real life, we would expect interest rates and stock prices, for example, to change together. The Greeks answer the question, what happens when *one and only one* input changes?

The actual formulas for the Greeks appear in Appendix 12.B. Greek measures can be computed for options on any kind of underlying asset, but we will focus here on stock options.

Definition of the Greeks

The units in which changes are measured are a matter of convention. Thus, when we define a Greek measure, we will also provide the assumed unit of change.

Delta (Δ) measures the option price change when the stock price increases by \$1.

Gamma (Γ) measures the change in delta when the stock price increases by \$1.

Vega measures the change in the option price when there is an increase in volatility of one percentage point.[5]

---

[4]Specifically, the Greeks are mathematical derivatives of the option price formula with respect to the inputs.

[5]"Vega" is not a Greek letter. "Kappa" and "lambda" are also sometimes used to mean the same thing as vega.

Theta (θ) measures the change in the option price when there is a decrease in the time to maturity of 1 day.

Rho (ρ) measures the change in the option price when there is an increase in the interest rate of 1 percentage point (100 basis points).

Psi (Ψ) measures the change in the option price when there is an increase in the continuous dividend yield of 1 percentage point (100 basis points).

A useful mnemonic device for remembering some of these is that "vega" and "volatility" share the same first letter, as do "theta" and "time." Also "r" is often used to denote the interest rate and is the first letter in "rho."

We will discuss each Greek measure in turn, assuming for simplicity that we are talking about the Greek for a purchased option. The Greek for a written option is opposite in sign to that for the same purchased option.

Delta   We have already encountered delta in Chapter 10, where we defined it as the number of shares in the portfolio that replicates the option. For a call option, delta is positive: As the stock price increases, the call price increases. Delta is also the sensitivity of the option price to a change in the stock price: If an option is replicated with 50 shares, the option should exhibit the price sensitivity of approximately 50 shares. You can think of delta as the *share-equivalent* of the option.

Figure 12.1 represents the behavior of delta for three options with different times to expiration. The figure illustrates that an in-the-money option will be more sensitive to the stock price than an out-of-the-money option. If an option is deep in-the-money (i.e., the stock price is high relative to the strike price), it is likely to be exercised and hence the option should behave much like a leveraged position in a full share. Delta approaches 1 in this case and the share-equivalent of the option is 1. If the option is out-of-the money, it is unlikely to be exercised and the option has a low price, behaving like a position with very few shares. In this case delta is approximately 0 and the share-equivalent is 0. An at-the-money option may or may not be exercised and, hence, behaves like a position with between 0 and 1 share. This behavior of delta can be seen in Figure 12.1. Note that as time to expiration increases, delta is less at high stock prices and greater at low stock prices. This behavior of delta reflects the fact that, for the depicted options that have greater time to expiration, the likelihood is greater that an out-of-the money option will eventually become in-the-money, and the likelihood is greater that an in-the-money option will eventually become out-of-the-money.

We can use the interpretation of delta as a share-equivalent to interpret the Black-Scholes price. The formula both prices the option and also tells us what position in the stock and borrowing is equivalent to the option. The formula for the call delta is

$$\Delta = e^{-\delta T} N(d_1)$$

If we hold $e^{-\delta t} N(d_1)$ shares and borrow $K e^{-rT} N(d_2)$ dollars, the cost of this portfolio is

$$S e^{-\delta T} N(d_1) - K e^{-rT} N(d_2)$$

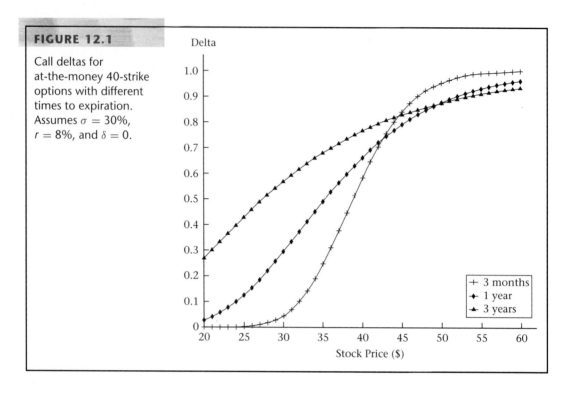

FIGURE 12.1

Call deltas for at-the-money 40-strike options with different times to expiration. Assumes $\sigma = 30\%$, $r = 8\%$, and $\delta = 0$.

This is the Black-Scholes price. Thus, the pieces of the formula tell us what position in the stock and borrowing synthetically recreates the call. Figure 12.1 shows that delta changes with the stock price, so as the stock price moves, the replicating portfolio changes and must be adjusted dynamically. We also saw this in Chapter 10.

Delta for a put option is negative, so a stock price increase reduces the put price. This relationship can be seen in Figure 12.2. Since the put delta is just the call delta minus $e^{-\delta T}$ (from put-call parity), Figure 12.2 behaves similarly to Figure 12.1.

Gamma Gamma—the change in delta as the stock price changes—is always positive for a purchased call or put. As the stock price increases, delta increases. This behavior can be seen in both Figures 12.1 and 12.2. For a call, delta approaches 1 as the stock price increases. For a put, delta approaches 0 as the stock price increases. Because of put-call parity, gamma is the same for a European call and put with the same strike price and time to expiration.

Figure 12.3 graphs call gammas for options with three different expirations. Deep in-the-money options have a delta of about 1, and, hence, a gamma of about zero. (If delta is 1, it cannot change much as the stock price changes.) Similarly deep out-of-the-money options have a delta of about 0 and, hence, a gamma of about 0. The large gamma for the 3-month option in Figure 12.3 corresponds to the steep increase in delta for the same option in Figure 12.1.

FIGURE 12.2

Put deltas for
at-the-money 40-strike
options with different
times to expiration.
Assumes $\sigma = 30\%$,
$r = 8\%$, and $\delta = 0$.

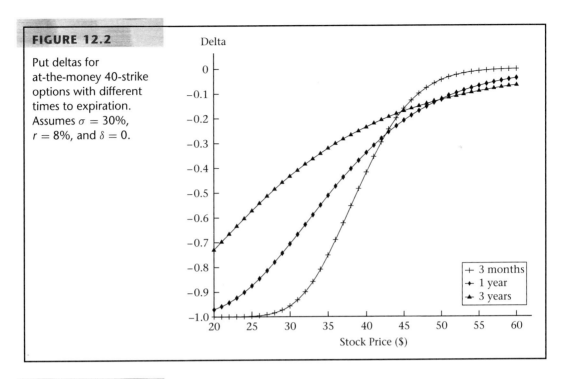

FIGURE 12.3

Call gammas for
at-the-money 40-strike
options with different
times to expiration.
Assumes $\sigma = 30\%$,
$r = 8\%$, and $\delta = 0$.

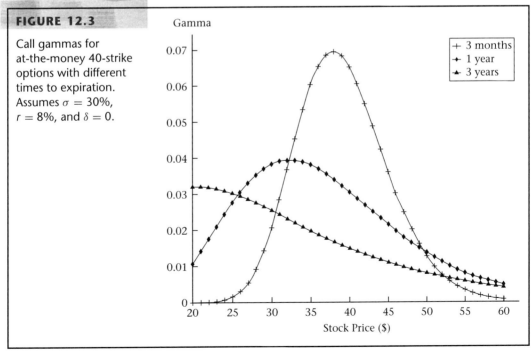

A derivative for which gamma is always positive is said to be *convex*. If gamma is positive, then delta is always increasing, and a graph of the price function will have curvature like that of the cross section of a bowl.

Vega   An increase in volatility raises the price of a call or put option. Vega measures the sensitivity of the option price to volatility. Figure 12.4 shows that vega tends to be greater for at-the-money options, and greater for options with moderate than with short times to expiration.[6] Because of put-call parity, vega, like gamma, is the same for calls and puts with the same strike price and time to expiration.

When calculating vega, it is important to be clear about units: How large is the assumed change in volatility? It is common to express vega as the change in option price for a *one percentage point* (0.01) change in volatility.[7] Figure 12.4 follows this convention.

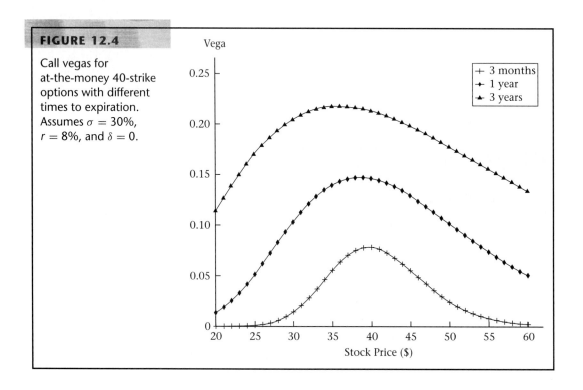

FIGURE 12.4

Call vegas for at-the-money 40-strike options with different times to expiration. Assumes $\sigma = 30\%$, $r = 8\%$, and $\delta = 0$.

---

[6]Be aware that neither result is true for very long-lived options. With a 20-year option, for example, vega is greatest for out-of-the-money calls and lower than that for a 3-year call for the range of prices in the figure.

[7]Vega is the derivative of the option price with respect to σ. It is expressed as the result of a percentage point change in volatility by dividing the derivative by 100.

Theta Options generally—but not always—become less valuable as time to expiration decreases. Figure 12.5 depicts the call price for out-of-the-money, at-the-money, and in-the-money options as a function of the time to expiration. For the at-the-money (strike = $40) option, time decay is most rapid at expiration. For the others, time decay is more steady. Figure 12.6 graphs theta explicitly for three different times to expiration, showing that time decay is greatest for the at-the-money short-term option.

Time decay can be positive for European options in some special cases. Deep-in-the-money call options on an asset with a high dividend yield and deep-in-the-money puts are two examples. In both cases we would want to exercise the options early if possible. Since we cannot, the option effectively becomes a T-bill, appreciating as it gets close to expiration. This effect is evident in Figure 12.7, in which the in-the-money (50-strike) put becomes more valuable, other things equal, as expiration approaches. Figure 12.8 on page 390 graphs the put theta explicitly, illustrating the positive theta.

When interpreting theta we need to know how long is the assumed change in time. Figures 12.6 and 12.8 are computed assuming a *1-day* change in time to expiration. It is also common in practice to compute theta over longer periods, such as 10 days.

Rho Rho is positive for an ordinary stock call option. Exercising a call entails paying the fixed strike price to receive the stock; a higher interest rate reduces the present value of the strike. Similarly, for a put, rho is negative, since the put entitles the owner to

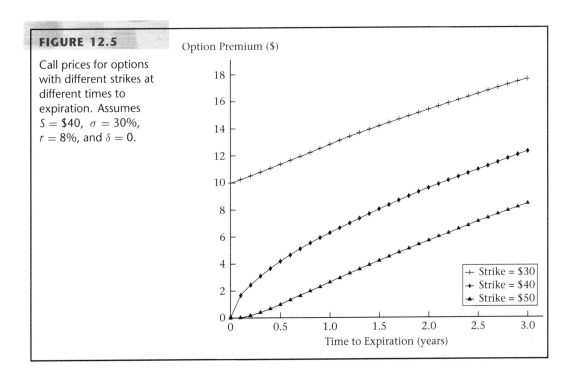

FIGURE 12.5

Call prices for options with different strikes at different times to expiration. Assumes $S = \$40$, $\sigma = 30\%$, $r = 8\%$, and $\delta = 0$.

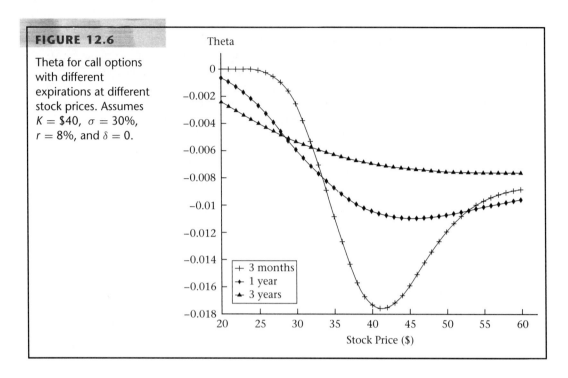

FIGURE 12.6

Theta for call options with different expirations at different stock prices. Assumes $K = \$40$, $\sigma = 30\%$, $r = 8\%$, and $\delta = 0$.

receive cash, and the present value of this is lower with a higher interest rate. Figure 12.9 shows that as the time to expiration increases and as a call option becomes more in-the-money, rho is greater.

Figure 12.9 assumes a one percentage point (100 basis point) change in the interest rate.

Psi Psi is negative for an ordinary stock call option. A call entitles the holder to receive stock, but without receiving the dividends paid on the stock prior to exercising the option. Thus, the present value of the stock to be received is lower, the greater the dividend yield. Owning a put entitles an obligation to deliver the stock in the future in exchange for cash. The present value of the stock to be delivered goes down when the dividend yield goes up, so the put is more valuable when the dividend yield is greater. Hence, psi for a put is positive.

Figure 12.10 shows that the absolute value of psi increases with time to expiration. An increase in the dividend yield has little effect with a short time to maturity, but dividends lost by not owning the stock increase with time to maturity. Note that Figure 12.10 is a mirror image of Figure 12.9.

Greek Measures for Portfolios

The Greek measure of a portfolio is the sum of the Greeks of the individual portfolio components. This relationship is important because it means that the risk of complicated

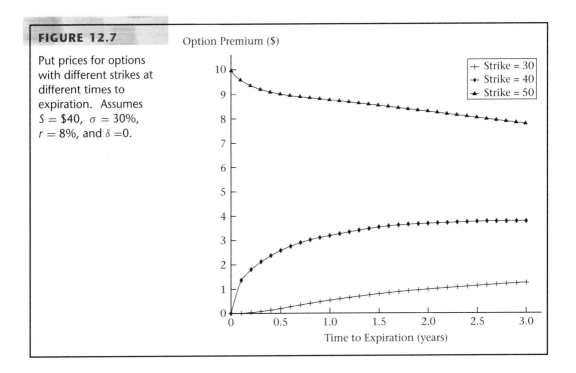

FIGURE 12.7

Put prices for options with different strikes at different times to expiration. Assumes $S = \$40$, $\sigma = 30\%$, $r = 8\%$, and $\delta = 0$.

option positions is easy to evaluate. For a portfolio containing n options with a single underlying stock, where the quantity of each option is given by ω_i, we have

$$\Delta_{\text{portfolio}} = \sum_{i=1}^{n} \omega_i \Delta_i$$

The same relation holds true for the other Greeks as well.

Example 12.6 Table 12.2 on page 392 lists Greek measures for a 40–45 bull spread. Greeks for the spread are Greeks for the 40-strike call less those for the 45-strike call.

Option Elasticity

An option is an alternative to investing in the stock. Delta tells us the dollar risk of the option relative to the stock: If the stock price changes by $1, by how much does the option price change? The option elasticity, by comparison, tells us the risk of the option relative to the stock in percentage terms: If the stock price changes by 1%, what is the percentage change in the value of the option?

FIGURE 12.8

Theta for put options with different expirations at different stock prices. Assumes $K = \$40$, $\sigma = 30\%$, $r = 8\%$, and $\delta = 0$.

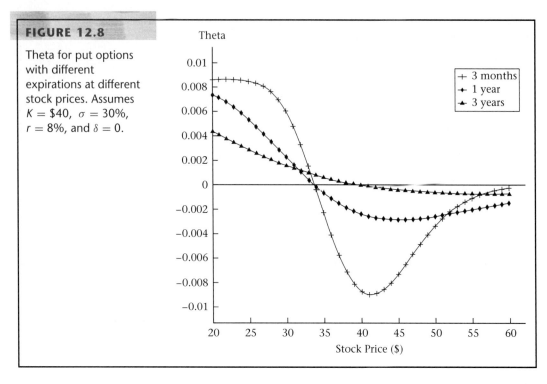

Dollar risk of the option If the stock price changes by ϵ, the change in the option price is

$$\text{Change in option price} = \text{Change in stock price} \times \text{option delta}$$
$$= \epsilon \times \Delta$$

Example 12.7 Suppose that the stock price is $S = \$41$, the strike price is $K = \$40$, volatility is $\sigma = 0.30$, the risk-free rate is $r = 0.08$, the time to expiration is $T = 1$, and the dividend yield is $\delta = 0$. As we saw earlier in the chapter, the option price is $\$6.961$. Delta is 0.6911. If we own options to buy 1000 shares of stock, the delta of the position is

$$1000 \times \Delta = 691.1 \text{ shares of stock}$$

Thus, the option position at this stock price has a "share-equivalent" of 691 shares. If the stock price changes by $\$0.50$, we expect an option price change of [8]

$$1000 \times \Delta \times \$0.50 = \$345.55$$

....

[8]A more accurate measure of the option price change is obtained by using both delta and gamma. This "delta-gamma approximation" is discussed in Chapter 13.

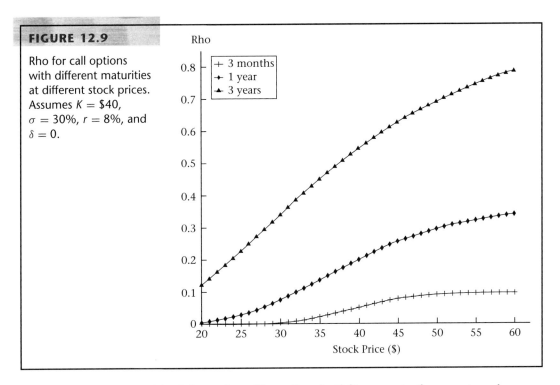

FIGURE 12.9

Rho for call options with different maturities at different stock prices. Assumes $K = \$40$, $\sigma = 30\%$, $r = 8\%$, and $\delta = 0$.

Percentage risk of the option The **option elasticity** computes the percentage change in the option price relative to the percentage change in the stock price. The percentage change in the stock price is simply ϵ/S. The percentage change in the option price is the dollar change in the option price, $\epsilon\Delta$, divided by the option price, C:

$$\frac{\epsilon\Delta}{C}$$

The option elasticity, denoted by Ω, is the ratio of these two:

$$\Omega \equiv \frac{\% \text{ change in option price}}{\% \text{ change in stock price}} = \frac{\frac{\epsilon\Delta}{C}}{\frac{\epsilon}{S}} = \frac{S\Delta}{C} \tag{12.8}$$

The elasticity tells us the percentage change in the option for a 1% change in the stock. It is effectively a measure of the leverage implicit in the option.

For a call, $\Omega \geq 1$. We saw in Chapter 10 that a call option is replicated by a levered investment in the stock. A levered position in an asset is always riskier than the underlying asset.[9] Also, the implicit leverage in the option becomes greater as the option is more out-of-the-money. Thus, Ω decreases as the strike price decreases.

For a put, $\Omega \leq 0$. This occurs because the replicating position for a put option involves shorting the stock.

....

[9]Mathematically, this follows since $S\Delta = Se^{-\delta t}N(d_1) > C(S)$.

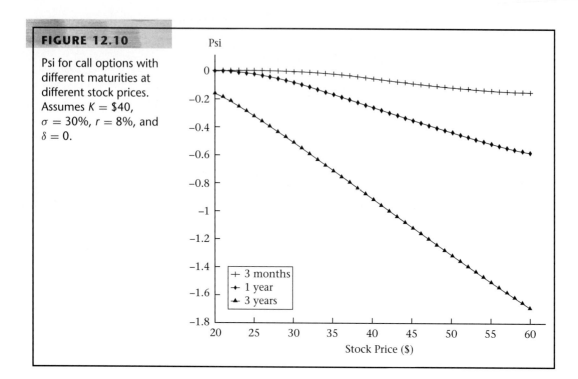

FIGURE 12.10

Psi for call options with different maturities at different stock prices. Assumes $K = \$40$, $\sigma = 30\%$, $r = 8\%$, and $\delta = 0$.

Psi

Legend:
+ 3 months
◆ 1 year
▲ 3 years

Stock Price ($)

TABLE 12.2

Greeks for the bull spread examined in Chapter 3, where $S = \$40$, $\sigma = 0.3$, $r = 0.08$, and $T = 91$ days, with a purchased 40-strike call and a written 45-strike call. The column titled "combined" is the difference between column 1 and column 2.

	Option 1	Option 2	Combined
ω_i	1	−1	—
Price	2.7804	0.9710	1.8094
Delta	0.5824	0.2815	0.3009
Gamma	0.0652	0.0563	0.0088
Vega	0.0780	0.0674	0.0106
Theta	−0.0173	−0.0134	−0.0040
Rho	0.0511	0.0257	0.0255

Example 12.8   Suppose $S = \$41$, $K = \$40$, $\sigma = 0.30$, $r = 0.08$, $T = 1$, and $\delta = 0$. The option price is $6.961 and $\Delta = 0.6911$. Hence, the call elasticity is

$$\Omega = \frac{\$41 \times 0.6911}{\$6.961} = 4.071$$

The put has a price of $2.886 and Δ of -0.3089; hence, the elasticity is

$$\Omega = \frac{\$41 \times -0.3089}{\$2.886} = -4.389$$

Figure 12.11 shows the behavior of elasticity for a call, varying both the stock price and time to expiration. The 3-month out-of-the-money calls have elasticities exceeding 8. For longer time-to-expiration options, elasticity is much less sensitive to the moneyness of the option.

The volatility of an option   The volatility of an option is the elasticity times the volatility of the stock:

$$\sigma_{\text{option}} = \sigma_{\text{stock}} \times |\Omega| \tag{12.9}$$

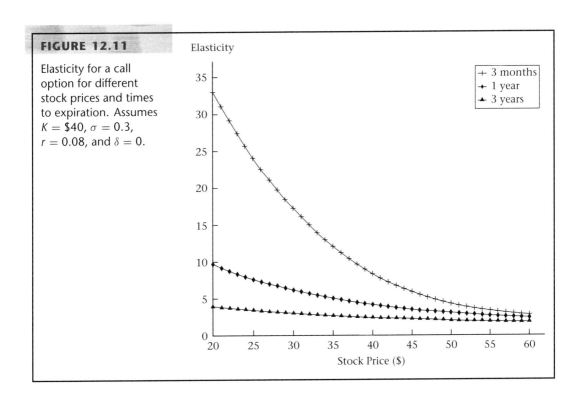

FIGURE 12.11

Elasticity for a call option for different stock prices and times to expiration. Assumes $K = \$40$, $\sigma = 0.3$, $r = 0.08$, and $\delta = 0$.

where $|\Omega|$ is the absolute value of Ω. Since elasticity is a measure of leverage, this calculation is analogous to the computation of the standard deviation of levered equity by multiplying the unlevered beta by the ratio of firm value to equity. Based on Figure 12.11, for a stock with a 30% volatility, an at-the-money option could easily have a volatility of 120% or more.

The risk premium of an option   Since elasticity measures the percentage sensitivity of the option relative to the stock, it tells us how the risk premium of the option compares to that of the stock. In Section 11.2, we computed the discount rate for an option. We were implicitly using option elasticity to do this.

At a point in time, the option is equivalent to a position in the stock and in bonds; hence, the return on the option is a weighted average of the return on the stock and the risk-free rate. Let α denote the expected rate of return on the stock, γ the expected return on the option, and r the risk-free rate. We have

$$\gamma = \frac{\Delta S}{C(S)}\alpha + \left(1 - \frac{\Delta S}{C(S)}\right)r$$

Since $\Delta S / C(S)$ is elasticity, this can also be written

$$\gamma = \Omega\alpha + (1 - \Omega)r$$

or

$$\gamma - r = (\alpha - r) \times \Omega \tag{12.10}$$

Thus, the risk premium on the option equals the risk premium on the stock times Ω.

Using our earlier facts about elasticity, we conclude that if the stock has a positive risk premium, then a call always has an expected return at least as great as the stock and that, other things equal, the expected return on an option goes down as the stock price goes up. In terms of the capital asset pricing model, we would say that the option beta goes down as the option becomes more in-the-money. For puts, we conclude that the put always has an expected return less than that of the stock.

The Sharpe ratio of an option   The Sharpe ratio for any asset is the ratio of the risk premium to volatility:

$$\text{Sharpe ratio} = \frac{\alpha - r}{\sigma} \tag{12.11}$$

Using equations (12.9) and (12.10), the Sharpe ratio for a call is

$$\text{Sharpe ratio for call} = \frac{\Omega(\alpha - r)}{\Omega\sigma} = \frac{\alpha - r}{\sigma} \tag{12.12}$$

Thus, the Sharpe ratio for a call equals the Sharpe ratio for the underlying stock. This equivalence of the Sharpe ratios is obvious once we realize that the option is always equivalent to a levered position in the stock, and that leverage *per se* does not change the Sharpe ratio.[10]

The elasticty and risk premium of a portfolio   The elasticity of a portfolio is the *weighted average* of the elasticities of the portfolio components. This is in contrast to the Greeks expressed in dollar terms (delta, gamma, etc.), for which the portfolio Greek is the *sum* of the component Greeks.

To understand this, suppose there is a portfolio of n calls with the same underlying stock, where the ith call has value C_i and delta Δ_i, and where ω_i is the fraction of the portfolio invested in the ith call. The portfolio value is then $\sum_{i=1}^{n} \omega_i C_i$. For a \$1 change in the stock price, the change in the portfolio value is

$$\sum_{i=1}^{n} \omega_i \Delta_i \qquad (12.13)$$

The elasticity of the portfolio is the percentage change in the portfolio divided by the percentage change in the stock, or

$$\Omega_{\text{portfolio}} = \frac{\frac{\sum_{i=1}^{n} \omega_i \Delta_i}{\sum_{j=1}^{n} \omega_j C_j}}{\frac{1}{S}} = \sum_{i=1}^{n} \left(\frac{\omega_i C_i}{\sum_{j=1}^{n} \omega_j C_j} \right) \frac{S\Delta_i}{C_i} = \sum_{i=1}^{n} \omega_i \Omega_i \qquad (12.14)$$

Using equation (12.10), the risk premium of the portfolio, $\gamma - r$, is just the portfolio elasticity times the risk premium on the stock, $\alpha - r$:

$$\gamma - r = \Omega_{\text{portfolio}} (\alpha - r) \qquad (12.15)$$

12.4 PROFIT DIAGRAMS BEFORE MATURITY

In order to evaluate investment strategies using options, we would like to be able to answer questions such as: If the stock price in 1 week is \$5 greater than it is today, what will be the change in the price of a call option? What is the profit diagram for an option position in which the options have different times to expiration? Our previous discussion of option strategies in Chapter 3 examined only expiration values. Now we will examine the behavior of option prices *prior* to expiration. To do this we need to use an option pricing formula.

....

[10]There is one subtlety: While the Sharpe ratio for the stock and option is the same at every point in time, it is not necessarily the same when measured using realized returns. For example, suppose you perform the experiment of buying a call and holding it for a year, and then evaluate the after-the-fact risk premium and standard deviation using historical returns. A standard way to do this would be to compute the average risk premium on the option and the average volatility and then divide them to create the Sharpe ratio. You would find that the call will have a lower Sharpe ratio than the stock. This is purely a result of dividing one *estimated* statistic by another.

Purchased Call Option

Consider the purchase of a call option. Just as with expiring options, we can ask what the value of the option is at a particular point in time and for a particular stock price. Table 12.3 shows the Black-Scholes value of a call option for five different stock prices at four different times to expiration. By varying the stock price for a given time to expiration, keeping everything else the same, we are able to graph the value of the call.

Figure 12.12 plots Black-Scholes call option prices for stock prices ranging from $20 to $60, including the values in Table 12.3. Notice that the value of the option prior to expiration is a smoothed version of the value of the option at expiration.

The payoff diagram depicted in Figure 12.12 does not show us how the value of the option compares to its original cost. In order to do that, we can subtract the cost of the option, plus interest.[11]

In order to determine profitability, we need to answer two questions that were unnecessary for the payoff diagram: What is the initial cost of the option position, and what is the holding period? To compute the profit, we take the value of the position and subtract the cost of the position, including interest.

Example 12.9 The 1-year option in Table 12.3 costs $6.285 at a stock price of $40. If after 1 day the stock price is still $40, the value of the option will have fallen to $6.274, and the 1-day holding period profit is $6.274 − $6.285 \times e^{0.08/365} = -\$0.012$. This loss reflects the theta of the option. If the stock price were to increase to $42, the option premium would increase to $7.655, and the 1-day holding period profit would be $7.655 − $6.285 \times e^{0.08/365} = \$1.369$.

TABLE 12.3	Value of 40-strike call option at different stock prices and times to expiration. Assumes $r = 8\%$, $\sigma = 30\%$, $\delta = 0$.			
	Time to Expiration			
Stock Price ($)	**12 Months**	**6 Months**	**3 Months**	**0 (Expiration)**
36	3.90	2.08	1.00	0
38	5.02	3.02	1.75	0
40	6.28	4.16	2.78	0
42	7.67	5.47	4.07	2
44	9.15	6.95	5.58	4

[11]As we discussed in Chapter 2, this is like assuming the option is financed by borrowing.

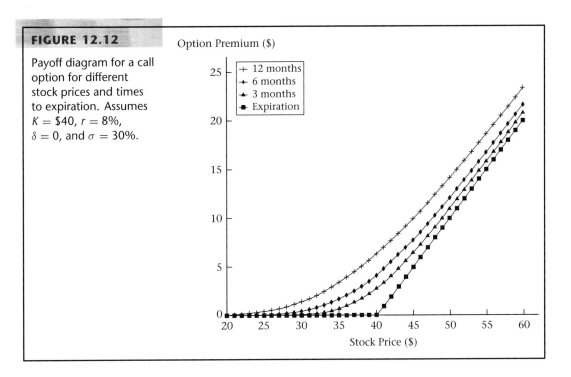

FIGURE 12.12

Payoff diagram for a call option for different stock prices and times to expiration. Assumes $K = \$40$, $r = 8\%$, $\delta = 0$, and $\sigma = 30\%$.

After 6 months, the holding period profit at a price of $40 would be $4.155 − $6.285 × $e^{0.08 \times 0.5}$ = −$2.386. Even if the stock price had risen to $42, the holding period return would still be a negative −$1.068. These profit calculations are illustrated in Figure 12.13.

The option premium graphs in Figures 12.12 and 12.13 can help us understand the behavior of delta and gamma discussed in Section 12.3. In all cases the slope of the call option graph is positive. This corresponds to a positive delta. In addition, the slope becomes greater as the stock price increases. Delta increasing with the stock price corresponds to a positive gamma. The fact that gamma is always positive implies that the graphs will be curved like the cross section of a bowl, i.e., the option price is *convex*. A positive gamma implies convex curvature. A negative gamma implies the opposite (concave) curvature.

Calendar Spreads

We saw in Chapter 3 that there are a number of option spreads that permit you to speculate on the volatility of a stock, including straddle, strangle, and butterfly spreads. These

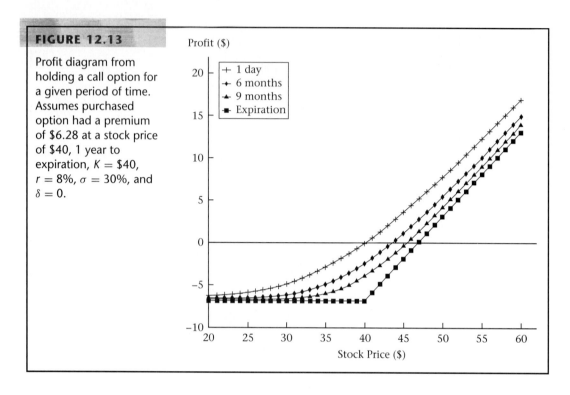

FIGURE 12.13

Profit diagram from holding a call option for a given period of time. Assumes purchased option had a premium of $6.28 at a stock price of $40, 1 year to expiration, $K = \$40$, $r = 8\%$, $\sigma = 30\%$, and $\delta = 0$.

spreads all contain options with the same time to expiration and different strikes. To speculate on volatility you could also enter into a **calendar spread**, in which the options you buy and sell have different expiration dates.

Suppose you want to speculate that XYZ's stock price will be unchanged over the next 3 months. An alternative to a written straddle or a written butterfly spread is simply to sell a call or put, in the hope that the stock price will remain unchanged and you will earn the premium. The potential cost is that if the option does move into the money, you can have a large loss.

To protect against a stock price increase when selling a call, you can simultaneously buy a call option with the same strike and greater time to expiration. This purchased calendar spread exploits the fact that the written near-to-expiration option exhibits greater time decay than the purchased far-to-expiration option, and therefore is profitable if the stock price does not move. For example, suppose you sell a 40-strike call with 91 days to expiration and buy a 40-strike call with 1 year to expiration. At a stock price of $40, the premiums are $2.78 for the 91-day call and $6.28 for the 1-year call. The profit diagram for this position for holding periods of 1 day, 45 days, and 91 days is displayed in Figure 12.14. You can see that you earn maximum profit over 91 days if the stock price does not change.

FIGURE 12.14

Profit diagram for a calendar spread. Assumes we sell a 91-day 40-strike call with premium of $2.78, and buy a 365-day 40-strike call with premium of $6.28. Assumes $S = \$40$, $\sigma = 30\%$, $r = 8\%$, and $\delta = 0$.

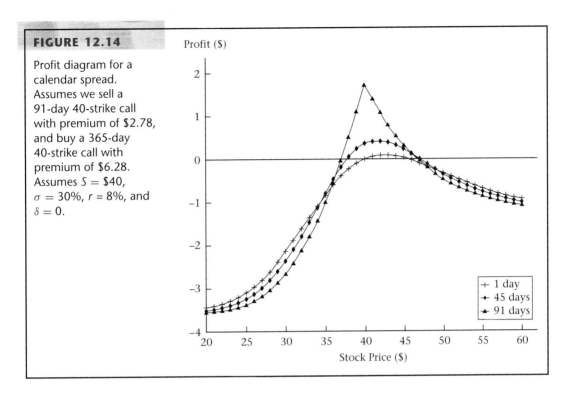

We can understand the behavior of profit for this position by considering the theta of the two options. Figure 12.6 shows that theta is more negative for the 91-day call (-0.0173) than for the 1-year call (-0.0104). Thus, if the stock price does not change over the course of 1 day, the position will make money since the written option loses more value than the purchased option. Over 91 days, the written 91-day option will lose its full value (its price declines from $2.78 to 0), while the 1-year option will lose only about $1 (its price declines from $6.28 to $5.28) if the stock price does not change. The difference in the rates of time decay generates profit of approximately $1.78.

The profit diagram also illustrates that at a stock price of $40, delta for the position is initially positive. Over 1 day, the maximum profit occurs if the stock price rises by a small amount. This reflects the fact that the delta of the written 91-day call is 0.5825 and that of the purchased 1-year call is 0.6615, for a net positive delta of 0.0790. With the 91-day holding period, the portion of the graph below 40 reflects the purchased 1-year option, which becomes increasingly unprofitable as the stock price falls. Above 40, the gain on the purchased 1-year option is offset by the loss on the expiring 91-day call. Since it is expiring, the delta of the 91-day call is -1 for stock prices above 40, which results in the graph turning back down to a negative slope above 40. As the stock price continues to increase, however, the delta of the purchased 1-year call increases toward 1, so the slope of the net position approaches zero.

12.5 IMPLIED VOLATILITY

Volatility is unobservable, and Figure 12.4 shows that option prices, particularly for near-the-money options, can be quite sensitive to volatility. Thus, choosing a volatility to use in pricing an option is difficult but also quite important.[12]

One approach to obtaining a volatility is to use the history of returns to compute historical volatility (see Section 11.4). A problem with historical volatility is that history is not a reliable guide to the future: Markets have quiet and turbulent periods and predictable events such as Federal Reserve Board Open Market Committee meetings can create periods of greater than normal uncertainty. There are sophisticated statistical models designed to improve upon simple volatility estimates, but no matter what you do, you cannot count on history to provide you with a reliable estimate of *future* volatility.

In many cases we can observe option prices for an asset. We can then invert the question: Instead of asking what volatility we should use to price an option, we can compute an option's **implied volatility**, which is the volatility that would explain the observed option price. Assuming that we observe the stock price S, strike price K, interest rate r, dividend yield δ, and time to expiration T, the implied call volatility is the $\hat{\sigma}$ that solves

$$\text{Market option price} = C(S, K, \hat{\sigma}, r, T, \delta) \qquad (12.16)$$

By definition, if we use implied volatility to price an option, we obtain the market price of the option. Thus, we cannot use implied volatility to assess whether an option price is correct, but implied volatility does tell us the market's assessment of volatility.

Computing Implied Volatility

Computing an implied volatility requires that we (1) observe a market price for an option and (2) have an option pricing model with which to infer volatility. Equation (12.16) cannot be solved directly for the implied volatility, $\hat{\sigma}$, so it is necessary to use an iterative procedure to solve the equation. Any pricing model can be used to calculate an implied volatility, but Black-Scholes implied volatilities are frequently used as benchmarks.

Example 12.10 Suppose we observe a 45-strike 6-month European call option with a premium of \$8.07. The stock price is \$50, the interest rate is 8%, and the dividend yield is zero. We can compute the option price as

$$\$8.07 = \text{BSCall}(50, 45, \sigma, 0.08, 0.5, 0).$$

[12] Of the five other inputs to the Black-Scholes formula, we also cannot observe dividends. Over short horizons, however, dividends are typically stable, so past dividends can be used to forecast future dividends.

By trial and error (or by using a tool such as Excel's Goalseek), we find that setting $\sigma = 28.7\%$ gives us a call price of $8.07.[13]

Table 12.4 lists ask prices of calls and puts on the S&P 500 index, along with implied volatilities computed using the Black-Scholes formula. These S&P options are European style, so the Black-Scholes model is appropriate. Notice that, although the implied volatilities in the table are not all equal, they are all in a range between 13% and 16%. We could describe the general level of S&P option prices by saying that the options are trading at about a 15% volatility level. There are typically numerous options on a given asset; implied volatility can be used to succinctly describe the general level of option prices for a given underlying asset.

There is one clear pattern in the implied volatilities in Table 12.4. For a given expiration month, volatilities decline as the strike price increases. This occurs with both the calls and puts. For example, the volatility for the November calls declines from 16.3% to 12.84% as the strike rises from 1100 to 1150. The decline is evident but smaller for the later expiration months. This systematic change in implied volatility across strike

TABLE 12.4					
Implied volatilities for S&P 500 options, 10/28/2004. Option prices (ask) from **www.cboe.com**; assumes $S = \$1127.44$, $\delta = 1.85\%$, $r = 2\%$.					
Strike ($)	**Expiration**	**Call Price ($)**	**Implied Volatility**	**Put Price ($)**	**Implied Volatility**
1100	11/20/2004	34.80	0.1630	6.80	0.1575
1125	11/20/2004	17.10	0.1434	14.70	0.1447
1150	11/20/2004	5.80	0.1284	29.20	0.1389
1100	12/18/2004	41.70	0.1559	13.80	0.1539
1125	12/18/2004	24.50	0.1396	22.50	0.1436
1150	12/18/2004	13.00	0.1336	35.50	0.1351
1100	1/22/2005	49.10	0.1567	20.40	0.1518
1125	1/22/2005	33.00	0.1463	29.40	0.1427
1150	1/22/2005	20.00	0.1363	41.50	0.1337

[13]An implied volatility function is available with the spreadsheets accompanying this book.

prices occurs generally for different underlying assets and is called **volatility skew**.[14] When you graph implied volatility against the strike price, the resulting line can take different shapes, often described as "smiles," "frowns," and "smirks." Explaining these patterns and modifying pricing models to account for them is a challenge for option pricing theory. We will discuss this important issue further in Chapter 23.

When examining implied volatilities, it is helpful to keep put-call parity in mind. If options are European, then *puts and calls with the same strike and time to expiration must have the same implied volatility*. This is true because prices of European puts and calls must satisfy the parity relationship or else there is an arbitrage opportunity. Thus, skew is not related to whether an option is a put or a call, but rather to differences in the strike price and time to expiration. Although call and put volatilities are not exactly equal in Table 12.4, they are close enough that parity arbitrage would not be profitable after transaction costs are taken into account. For example, for the in-the-money options in Table 12.4, bid-ask spreads are as wide as $2, a difference that can account for more than a percentage point of implied volatility on one option alone.

Using Implied Volatility

Implied volatility is important for a number of reasons. First, if you need to price an option for which you *cannot* observe a market price, you can use implied volatility to generate a price consistent with the prices of traded options. Market-makers, for example, will price options consistently with prices of similar options. Second, as we previously discussed, implied volatility is often used as a quick way to describe the level of option prices on a given underlying asset. Option prices are sometimes quoted in terms of volatility, rather than as a dollar price. Third, volatility skew provides a measure of how well option pricing models work. Because volatility is unobservable, a standard approach to testing the validity of the Black-Scholes model is to see whether, for a given underlying asset, implied volatilities are the same at all strike prices. The existence of volatility skew suggests that the Black-Scholes model and assumptions are not a perfect description of the world. We will discuss alternative pricing models in Chapter 23.

To better understand the importance of implied volatility, recognize that information about future volatility is uniquely provided by options markets. You can think of option markets as providing information about volatility that is not available elsewhere. In fact, there is now an exchange-traded futures contracts based on an index of implied volatility for the S&P 500. Just as stock markets provide information about stock prices and permit trading stocks, option markets provide information about volatility, and, in effect, permit the trading of volatility. Viewed from this perspective, we should expect information about volatility to be one of the most important things we can learn from option prices. We will discuss volatility in more depth in Chapter 23.

....

[14]The Black-Scholes formula is derived assuming that volatility is constant across strikes. Thus, it is internally inconsistent to use the Black-Scholes model to track changes in implied volatility. Nevertheless, it is a widely used benchmark.

12.6 PERPETUAL AMERICAN OPTIONS

The Black-Scholes formula prices options that are only exercised at expiration. In this section we present formulas, based on Merton (1973b), for the prices of calls and puts that never expire. We will call such options **perpetual options**. They are also known as expirationless options.

American options are harder to price than European options because it is difficult to characterize the optimal exercise strategy. Using the binomial model, we saw in Section 11.1 that for a finitely lived call option on a dividend-paying stock, the stock price at which it is optimal to exercise the option declines as the option approaches expiration. It is this changing optimal exercise price that makes it hard to derive a valuation formula.

With perpetual American options it *is* possible to derive a valuation formula because such an option always has the same time to expiration: infinity. Since time to expiration is constant, the option exercise problem will look the same today, tomorrow, and forever. Thus, the price at which it is optimal to exercise the option is constant. The optimal exercise strategy entails picking the right exercise barrier and exercising the option the first time the stock price reaches that barrier.

Barrier Present Values

As a prelude to valuing a perpetual option, consider computing the present value of $1 payable when the stock price reaches a level, H. We call H the barrier level and call the value today of $1 paid when the stock price reaches H the "barrier present value." It turns out there is a simple formula for this, which differs depending upon whether H is above or below the current stock value, S.

If H is above S (i.e., S has to rise to reach H), the value today of $1 received when S reaches H—the barrier present value—is

$$\text{Value of \$1 received when } S \text{ first reaches } H \text{ from below} = \left(\frac{S}{H}\right)^{h_1} \tag{12.17}$$

where

$$h_1 = \frac{1}{2} - \frac{r - \delta}{\sigma^2} + \sqrt{\left(\frac{r - \delta}{\sigma^2} - \frac{1}{2}\right)^2 + \frac{2r}{\sigma^2}}$$

If H is below S (i.e., S has to fall to reach H), the value of $1 received when S reaches H is

$$\text{Value of \$1 received when } S \text{ first reaches } H \text{ from above} = \left(\frac{S}{H}\right)^{h_2} \tag{12.18}$$

where

$$h_2 = \frac{1}{2} - \frac{r - \delta}{\sigma^2} - \sqrt{\left(\frac{r - \delta}{\sigma^2} - \frac{1}{2}\right)^2 + \frac{2r}{\sigma^2}}$$

Perpetual Calls

Suppose we have a perpetual American call with strike K. If we decide to exercise the option whenever S reaches the barrier H, then at exercise we receive $H - K$. From equation (12.17), the value of receiving $H - K$ when S reaches H is

$$(H - K)\left(\frac{S}{H}\right)^{h_1}$$

In order to finish computing the value of the call we need to specify H, the price at which the call should be exercised. We simply need to pick a value for H that makes the value of the call as great as possible. If we make H too small, then we prematurely throw away option value (i.e., protection against a subsequent price decline). If we make H too large, then we forgo dividends for too long while waiting to exercise. It is possible to show that the exercise level H^* that maximizes the value of the call is[15]

$$H^* = K\left(\frac{h_1}{h_1 - 1}\right)$$

Since $h_1 > 1$, we have $H^* > K$. Making this substitution, the value of the perpetual call is

$$\boxed{\text{Price of perpetual call} = \frac{K}{h_1 - 1}\left(\frac{h_1 - 1}{h_1}\frac{S}{K}\right)^{h_1}} \qquad (12.19)$$

If $\delta = 0$, then $H^* = \infty$; i.e., it is never optimal to exercise a call option on a nondividend-paying stock.

Perpetual Puts

For a perpetual put, using equation (12.18), the value if we exercise when $S = H$ is given by

$$(K - H)\left(\frac{S}{H}\right)^{h_2}$$

where

$$h_2 = \frac{1}{2} - \frac{r - \delta}{\sigma^2} - \sqrt{\left(\frac{r - \delta}{\sigma^2} - \frac{1}{2}\right)^2 + \frac{2r}{\sigma^2}}$$

---

[15]This is accomplished by differentiating the expression with respect to H, setting the derivative equal to zero, and solving for H.

Again selecting the exercise level H^* to maximize the value of the put, we get

$$H^* = K \frac{h_2}{h_2 - 1}$$

which implies that the price of the perpetual put is

$$\boxed{\text{Price of perpetual put} = \frac{K}{1 - h_2} \left(\frac{h_2 - 1}{h_2} \frac{S}{K} \right)^{h_2}}$$

(12.20)

CHAPTER SUMMARY

Under certain assumptions, the Black-Scholes formula provides an exact formula—approximated by the binomial formula—for pricing European options. The inputs to the Black-Scholes formula are the same as for the binomial formula: the stock price, strike price, volatility, interest rate, time to expiration, and dividend yield. As with the binomial formula, the Black-Scholes formula accommodates different underlying assets by changing the dividend yield (see Table 10.1 for a summary).

Option Greeks measure the change in the option price (or other option characteristic) for a change in an option input. Delta, gamma, vega, theta, rho, and psi are widely used in practice to assess the risk of an option position. The option elasticity is the percentage change in the option's price for a 1% change in the stock price. The volatility and beta of an option are the volatility and beta of the stock times the option elasticity. Thus, an option and the underlying stock have the same Sharpe ratio.

Of the inputs to the Black-Scholes formula, volatility is hardest to estimate. In practice it is common to use the formula in backward fashion to infer the market's estimate of volatility from the option price. This implied volatility is computed by finding the volatility for which the formula matches observed market prices for options. In theory, all options of a given maturity should have the same implied volatility. In practice, they do not, a phenomenon known as volatility skew.

Although there is no simple formula for valuing a finitely lived American option, there are simple formulas in the special case of perpetual puts and calls.

FURTHER READING

Chapter 13 will explore in more detail the market-maker's perspective on options, including how a market-maker uses delta to hedge option positions and the circumstances under which market-makers earn profits or make losses. Chapter 14 extends the discussion in this chapter to include exotic options.

In Chapters 15, 16, and 17, we will use option pricing to explore applications of option pricing, including the creation of structured products, issues in compensation options, capital structure, tax management with options, and real options.

Chapters 18 through 21 delve more into the mathematical underpinnings of the Black-Scholes model. The barrier present value calculations will be discussed again in Chapter 22. We will discuss volatility in much more detail in Chapter 23.

The classic early papers on option pricing are Black and Scholes (1973) and Merton (1973b). The details of how the binomial model converges to the Black-Scholes model are in Cox et al. (1979). The perpetual put formula is derived in Merton (1973b). The link between the perpetual call and put formulas is discussed by McDonald and Siegel (1986).

PROBLEMS

In answering many of these problems you can use the functions *BSCall*, *BSPut*, *CallPerpetual*, and *PutPerpetual* and the accompanying functions for the Greeks (see the spreadsheets on the CD-ROM accompanying this book).

12.1. Use a spreadsheet to verify the option prices in Examples 12.1 and 12.2.

12.2. Using the *BinomCall* and *BinomPut* functions, compute the binomial approximations for the options in Examples 12.1 and 12.2. Be sure to compute prices for $n = 8, 9, 10, 11$, and 12. What do you observe about the behavior of the binomial approximation?

12.3. Let $S = \$100$, $K = \$120$, $\sigma = 30\%$, $r = 0.08$, and $\delta = 0$.

    a. Compute the Black-Scholes call price for 1 year to maturity and for a variety of very long times to maturity. What happens to the option price as $T \to \infty$?

    b. Set $\delta = 0.001$. Repeat (a). Now what happens to the option price? What accounts for the difference?

12.4. Let $S = \$120$, $K = \$100$, $\sigma = 30\%$, $r = 0$, and $\delta = 0.08$.

    a. Compute the Black-Scholes call price for 1 year to maturity and for a variety of very long times to maturity. What happens to the price as $T \to \infty$?

    b. Set $r = 0.001$. Repeat (a). Now what happens? What accounts for the difference?

12.5. The exchange rate is ¥95/€, the yen-denominated interest rate is 1.5%, the euro-denominated interest rate is 3.5%, and the exchange rate volatility is 10%.

    a. What is the price of a 90-strike yen-denominated euro put with 6 months to expiration?

    b. What is the price of a 1/90-strike euro-denominated yen call with 6 months to expiration?

    c. What is the link between your answer to (a) and your answer to (b), converted to yen?

12.6. Suppose XYZ is a nondividend-paying stock. Suppose $S = \$100$, $\sigma = 40\%$, $\delta = 0$, and $r = 0.06$.

    a. What is the price of a 105-strike call option with 1 year to expiration?

    b. What is the 1-year forward price for the stock?

    c. What is the price of a 1-year 105-strike option, where the underlying asset is a futures contract maturing at the same time as the option?

12.7. Suppose $S = \$100$, $K = \$95$, $\sigma = 30\%$, $r = 0.08$, $\delta = 0.03$, and $T = 0.75$.

    a. Compute the Black-Scholes price of a call.

    b. Compute the Black-Scholes price of a call for which $S = \$100 \times e^{-0.03 \times 0.75}$, $K = \$95 \times e^{-0.08 \times 0.75}$, $\sigma = 0.3$, $T = 0.75$, $\delta = 0$, $r = 0$. How does your answer compare to that for (a)?

12.8. Make the same assumptions as in the previous problem.

    a. What is the 9-month forward price for the stock?

    b. Compute the price of a 95-strike 9-month call option on a futures contract.

    c. What is the relationship between your answer to (b) and the price you computed in the previous question? Why?

12.9. Assume $K = \$40$, $\sigma = 30\%$, $r = 0.08$, $T = 0.5$, and the stock is to pay a single dividend of $2 tomorrow, with no dividends thereafter.

    a. Suppose $S = \$50$. What is the price of a European call option? Consider an otherwise identical American call. What is its price?

    b. Repeat, only suppose $S = \$60$.

    c. Under what circumstance would you not exercise the option today?

12.10. "Time decay is greatest for an option close to expiration." Use the spreadsheet functions to evaluate this statement. Consider both the dollar change in the option value and the percentage change in the option value, and examine both in-the-money and out-of-the-money options.

12.11. In the absence of an explicit formula, we can estimate the change in the option price due to a change in an input—such as σ—by computing the following for a small value of ϵ:

$$\text{Vega} = \frac{BSCall(S, K, \sigma + \epsilon, r, t, \delta) - BSCall(S, K, \sigma - \epsilon, r, t, \delta)}{2\epsilon}.$$

    a. What is the logic behind this calculation? Why does ϵ need to be small?

    b. Compare the results of this calculation with results obtained from *BSCall-Vega*.

12.12. Suppose $S = \$100$, $K = \$95$, $\sigma = 30\%$, $r = 0.08$, $\delta = 0.03$, and $T = 0.75$. Using the technique in the previous problem compute the Greek measure corresponding to a change in the dividend yield. What is the predicted effect of a change of 1 percentage point in the dividend yield?

12.13. Consider a bull spread where you buy a 40-strike call and sell a 45-strike call. Suppose $S = \$40$, $\sigma = 0.30$, $r = 0.08$, $\delta = 0$, and $T = 0.5$. Draw a graph with stock prices ranging from $20 to $60 depicting the profit on the bull spread after 1 day, 3 months, and 6 months.

12.14. Consider a bull spread where you buy a 40-strike call and sell a 45-strike call. Suppose $\sigma = 0.30$, $r = 0.08$, $\delta = 0$, and $T = 0.5$.

    a. Suppose $S = \$40$. What are delta, gamma, vega, theta, and rho?

    b. Suppose $S = \$45$. What are delta, gamma, vega, theta, and rho?

    c. Are any of your answers to (a) and (b) different? If so, why?

12.15. Consider a bull spread where you buy a 40-strike put and sell a 45-strike put. Suppose $\sigma = 0.30$, $r = 0.08$, $\delta = 0$, and $T = 0.5$.

    a. Suppose $S = \$40$. What are delta, gamma, vega, theta, and rho?

    b. Suppose $S = \$45$. What are delta, gamma, vega, theta, and rho?

    c. Are any of your answers to (a) and (b) different? If so, why?

    d. Are any of your answers different in this problem from those in Problem 12.14? If so, why?

12.16. Assume $r = 8\%$, $\sigma = 30\%$, $\delta = 0$. In doing the following calculations, use a stock price range of $60–$140, stock price increments of $5, and two different times to expiration: 1 year and 1 day. Consider purchasing a 100-strike straddle, i.e., buying one 100-strike put and one 100-strike call.

    a. Compute delta, vega, theta, and rho of the call and put separately, for the different stock prices and times to expiration.

    b. Compute delta, vega, theta, and rho of the purchased straddle (do this by adding the Greeks of the individual options). As best you can, explain intuitively the signs of the straddle Greeks.

    c. Graph delta vega, theta, and rho of the straddle with 1 year to expiration as a function of the stock price. In each case explain why the graph looks as it does.

12.17. Assume $r = 8\%$, $\sigma = 30\%$, $\delta = 0$. Using 1-year-to-expiration European options, construct a position where you sell two 80-strike puts, buy one 95-strike put, buy one 105-strike call, and sell two 120-strike calls. For a range of stock prices from $60 to $140, compute delta, vega, theta, and rho of this position. As best you can, explain intuitively the signs of the Greeks.

12.18. Consider a perpetual call option with $S = \$50$, $K = \$60$, $r = 0.06$, $\sigma = 0.40$, and $\delta = 0.03$.

a. What is the price of the option and at what stock price should it be exercised?

b. Suppose $\delta = 0.04$ with all other inputs the same. What happens to the price and exercise barrier? Why?

c. Suppose $r = 0.07$ with all other inputs the same. What happens to the price and exercise barrier? Why?

d. Suppose $\sigma = 50\%$ with all other inputs the same. What happens to the price and exercise barrier? Why?

12.19. Consider a perpetual put option with $S = \$50$, $K = \$60$, $r = 0.06$, $\sigma = 0.40$, and $\delta = 0.03$.

a. What is the price of the option and at what stock price should it be exercised?

b. Suppose $\delta = 0.04$ with all other inputs the same. What happens to the price and exercise barrier? Why?

c. Suppose $r = 0.07$ with all other inputs the same. What happens to the price and exercise barrier? Why?

d. Suppose $\sigma = 50\%$ with all other inputs the same. What happens to the price and exercise barrier? Why?

12.20. Let $S = \$100$, $K = \$90$, $\sigma = 30\%$, $r = 8\%$, $\delta = 5\%$, and $T = 1$.

a. What is the Black-Scholes call price?

b. Now price a put where $S = \$90$, $K = \$100$, $\sigma = 30\%$, $r = 5\%$, $\delta = 8\%$, and $T = 1$.

c. What is the link between your answers to (a) and (b)? Why?

12.21. Repeat the previous problem, but this time for perpetual options. What do you notice about the prices? What do you notice about the exercise barriers?

APPENDIX 12.A: THE STANDARD NORMAL DISTRIBUTION

The *standard normal probability density function* is given by

$$\phi(x) \equiv \frac{1}{\sqrt{2\pi}}e^{-\frac{1}{2}x^2} \tag{12.21}$$

The *cumulative standard normal distribution function*, evaluated at a point x, for example, tells us the probability that a number randomly drawn from the standard normal distribution will fall below x, or

$$N(x) \equiv \int_{-\infty}^{x} \phi(x)dx \equiv \int_{-\infty}^{x} \frac{1}{\sqrt{2\pi}}e^{-\frac{1}{2}x^2}dx \tag{12.22}$$

Excel computes the cumulative distribution using the built-in function *NORMSDIST*. Note that $N'(x_1) = \phi(x_1)$.

APPENDIX 12.B: FORMULAS FOR OPTION GREEKS

In this section we present formulas for the Greeks for an option on a stock paying continuous dividends.[16] Greek measures in the binomial model are discussed in Appendix 13.B.

Delta (Δ)

Delta measures the change in the option price for a $1 change in the stock price:

$$\text{Call delta} = \frac{\partial C(S, K, \sigma, r, T - t, \delta)}{\partial S} = e^{-\delta(T-t)} N(d_1)$$

$$\text{Put delta} = \frac{\partial P(S, K, \sigma, r, T - t, \delta)}{\partial S} = -e^{-\delta(T-t)} N(-d_1)$$

Gamma (Γ)

Gamma measures the change in delta when the stock price changes:

$$\text{Call gamma} = \frac{\partial^2 C(S, K, \sigma, r, T - t, \delta)}{\partial S^2} = \frac{e^{-\delta(T-t)} N'(d_1)}{S\sigma\sqrt{T-t}}$$

$$\text{Put gamma} = \frac{\partial^2 P(S, K, \sigma, r, T - t, \delta)}{\partial S^2} = \text{Call gamma}$$

The second equation follows from put-call parity.

Theta (θ)

Theta measures the change in the option price with respect to calendar time (t), holding fixed time to expiration (T):

---

[16]If you wish to derive any of these formulas for yourself, or if you find that different authors use formulas that appear different, here are two useful things to know. The first is a result of the normal distribution being symmetric around 0:

$$N(x) = 1 - N(-x)$$

With some effort, the second can be verified algebraically:

$$Se^{-\delta T} N'(d_1) = Ke^{-rT} N'(d_2)$$

$$\text{Call theta} = \frac{\partial C(S, K, \sigma, r, T - t, \delta)}{\partial t}$$

$$= \delta S e^{-\delta(T-t)} N(d_1) - r K e^{-r(T-t)} N(d_2) - \frac{K e^{-r(T-t)} N'(d_2)\sigma}{2\sqrt{T-t}}$$

$$\text{Put theta} = \frac{\partial P(S, K, \sigma, r, T - t, \delta)}{\partial t}$$

$$= \text{Call theta} + r K e^{-r(T-t)} - \delta S e^{-\delta(T-t)}$$

If time to expiration is measured in years, theta will be the *annualized* change in the option value. To obtain a per-day theta, divide by 365.

Vega

Vega measures the change in the option price when volatility changes. Some writers also use the terms *lambda* or *kappa* to refer to this measure:

$$\text{Call vega} = \frac{\partial C(S, K, \sigma, r, T - t, \delta)}{\partial \sigma} = S e^{-\delta(T-t)} N'(d_1)\sqrt{T - t}$$

$$\text{Put vega} = \frac{\partial P(S, K, \sigma, r, T - t, \delta)}{\partial \sigma} = \text{Call vega}$$

It is common to report vega as the change in the option price *per percentage point* change in the volatility. This requires dividing the vega formula above by 100.

Rho (ρ)

Rho is the partial derivative of the option price with respect to the interest rate:

$$\text{Call rho} = \frac{\partial C(S, K, \sigma, r, T - t, \delta)}{\partial r} = (T - t) K e^{-r(T-t)} N(d_2)$$

$$\text{Put rho} = \frac{\partial P(S, K, \sigma, r, T - t, \delta)}{\partial r} = -(T - t) K e^{-r(T-t)} N(-d_2)$$

These expressions for rho assume a change in r of 1.0. We are typically interested in evaluating the effect of a change of 0.01 (100 basis points) or 0.0001 (1 basis point). To report rho as a change per percentage point in the interest rate, divide this measure by 100. To interpret it as a change per basis point, divide by 10,000.

Psi (ψ)

Psi is the partial derivative of the option price with respect to the continuous dividend yield:

$$\text{Call psi} = \frac{\partial C(S, K, \sigma, r, T - t, \delta)}{\partial \delta} = -(T - t)Se^{-\delta(T-t)}N(d_1)$$

$$\text{Put psi} = \frac{\partial P(S, K, \sigma, r, T - t, \delta)}{\partial \delta} = (T - t)Se^{-\delta(T-t)}N(-d_1)$$

To interpret psi as a price change per percentage point change in the dividend yield, divide by 100.

CHAPTER 13

Market-Making and
Delta-Hedging

At least as important as the Black-Scholes *formula* is the Black-Scholes *technique* for deriving the formula. In this chapter we explore the Black-Scholes technique by considering the market-maker perspective on options. What issues confront the market professionals who supply the options that customers want to buy? The insights we gain from studying this question apply not only to pricing call and put options but also to derivatives pricing and risk management in general.

The Black-Scholes approach to deriving the option pricing formula assumes that market-makers are profit-maximizers in a competitive market who want to hedge the risk of their option positions. As in Chapter 10, market-makers can hedge by taking a stock position that offsets the option's delta. Because option deltas change as the stock price changes, market-makers must continually review and modify their hedging decisions.

We will see that the costs of carrying a hedged option position can be expressed in terms of delta, gamma, and theta, option Greeks that were introduced in Chapter 12. On average, competitive market-makers should expect to break even by hedging. Under certain assumptions about the behavior of the stock price, the market-maker's break-even price is the Black-Scholes option price. Thus, as with any other good in a competitive market, the price of an option should equal the market-maker's cost of producing it.

13.1 WHAT DO MARKET-MAKERS DO?

A **market-maker** stands ready to sell to buyers and to buy from sellers. The owner of an appliance store, for example, is a market-maker. The store owner buys televisions at a low price (the wholesale price) and sells them at cost plus a markup (the retail price), earning the difference. The markup must at a minimum cover the cost of doing business—rent, salaries, utilities, and advertising—so that the retail price covers the cost of acquiring televisions plus all other costs of doing business. In the language of securities markets, we would say that the appliance dealer has both a bid price and an ask price. The bid price is the price at which the dealer buys the television, also known as the wholesale price. The ask price is the price at which the dealer will sell the television, also known as the retail price.

An appliance seller does not select which models to sell based on personal preference and does not expect to profit by speculating on the price of a television. Rather, the appliance dealer selects inventory based on expected customer demand and earns profit based on the markup. The store maintains an inventory, and the owner is able to satisfy customers who walk in and want to buy a television immediately. Market-makers supply *immediacy*, permitting customers to trade whenever they wish.

Proprietary trading, which is conceptually distinct from market-making, is trading to express an investment strategy. Customers and proprietary traders typically expect their positions to be profitable depending upon whether the market goes up or down. In contrast, market-makers profit by buying at the bid and selling at the ask. The position of a market-maker is the result of whatever order flow arrives from customers.

A difference between appliance sellers and financial market-makers is that an appliance store must possess a physical television in order to sell one. A financial market-maker, by contrast, can supply an asset by short-selling, thereby generating inventory as needed.

In some cases market-makers may trade as customers, but then the market-maker is paying the bid-ask spread and therefore not serving as a market-maker.

13.2 MARKET-MAKER RISK

Without hedging, an active market-maker will have an arbitrary position generated by fulfilling customer orders. An arbitrary portfolio has uncontrolled risk. An adverse price move has the potential to bankrupt the market-maker. Consequently, market-makers attempt to hedge the risk of their positions.

Market-makers can control risk by **delta-hedging.** As in Chapter 10, the market-maker computes the option delta and takes an offsetting position in shares. We say that such a position is *delta-hedged*. In general a delta-hedged position is not a zero-value position: The cost of the shares required to hedge is not the same as the cost of the options. Because of the cost difference, the market-maker must invest capital to maintain a delta-hedged position.

A key idea in derivatives is that such a hedged position should earn the risk-free rate: You have money tied up so you should earn a return on it, and you have no risk so you should earn the risk-free rate. We used this argument explicitly in our discussion of forward pricing in Chapter 5, and implicitly in binomial pricing in Chapter 10. The notion that a hedged position earns the risk-free rate is a linchpin of almost all derivative pricing models. It was the fundamental idea exploited by Black and Scholes in their derivation of the option pricing model.

With the help of a simple numerical example, we can understand not only the intuition of the Black-Scholes model, but the mathematics as well. Delta-hedging is key to pricing because it is the technique for offsetting the risk of an option position. If we think of option producers as selling options at cost, then delta-hedging provides us with an understanding of what the cost of the option is when it is replicated. Delta-hedging is thus both a technique widely used in practice, and a key to understanding option pricing.

Option Risk in the Absence of Hedging

If a customer wishes to buy a 91-day call option, the market-maker fills this order by selling a call option. To be specific, suppose that $S = \$40$, $K = \$40$, $\sigma = 0.30$,

$r = 0.08$ (continuously compounded), and $\delta = 0$. We will let T denote the expiration time of the option and t the present, so time to expiration is $T - t$. Let $T - t = 91/365$. The price, delta, gamma, and theta for this call are listed in Table 13.1.

Because the market-maker has written the option, the sign of the Greek measures for the position is opposite those of a purchased option. In particular, the written option is like shorting shares of stock (negative delta) and the option gains in value over time (positive theta). Because delta is negative, the risk for the market-maker who has written a call is that the stock price will rise.

Suppose that the market-maker does not hedge the written option and the stock price rises to $40.75. We can measure the profit of the market-maker by **marking-to-market** the position. Marking-to-market answers the question: If we liquidated the position today, what would be the gain or loss? In the case of an option price increase, the market-maker would need to buy the option back at a higher price than that at which it was sold, and therefore would lose money. At a stock price of $40.75, the call price would increase to $3.2352, so the market-maker profit on a per-share basis would be $2.7804 − $3.2352 = −$0.4548.[1]

Figure 13.1 graphs the overnight profit of the unhedged written call option as a function of the stock price, against the profit of the option at expiration. In computing overnight profit, we are varying the stock price holding fixed all other inputs to the Black-Scholes formula except for time to expiration, which decreases by 1 day. It is apparent from the graph that the risk for the market-maker is a rise in the stock price. Although it is not obvious from the graph, if the stock price does not change, the market-maker will profit because of time decay: It would be possible to liquidate the option position by buying options at a lower price the next day than the price at which they were sold originally.

TABLE 13.1	Price and Greek information for a call option with $S = \$40$, $K = \$40$, $\sigma = 0.30$, $r = 0.08$ (continuously compounded), $T - t = 91/365$, and $\delta = 0$.

	Purchased	**Written**
Call price	2.7804	−2.7804
Delta	0.5824	−0.5824
Gamma	0.0652	−0.0652
Theta	−0.0173	0.0173

---

[1]For simplicity, this calculation ignores the overnight interest that the market-maker can earn on the proceeds from selling the option. In this case, interest per share is $(\exp(.08/365) - 1) \times \$2.7804 = \$0.0006$. Later examples will account for interest.

FIGURE 13.1

Depiction of overnight and expiration profit from writing a call option on one share of stock, if the market-maker is unhedged.

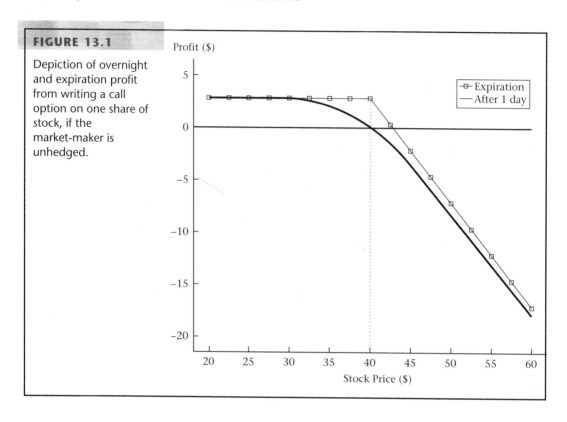

Delta and Gamma as Measures of Exposure

Since delta tells us the price sensitivity of the option, it also measures the market-maker's exposure. The delta of the call at a stock price of $40 is 0.5824, which suggests that a $1 increase in the stock price should increase the value of the option by approximately $0.5824. A $0.75 increase in the stock price would therefore increase the option price by $0.75 × 0.5824 = $0.4368. However, the actual increase in the option's value is $0.4548, greater by $0.0180.

This discrepancy occurs because delta varies with the stock price: As the stock price increases and the option moves more into the money, delta also increases. At a stock price of $40.75, delta is 0.6301. Thus, the delta at $40 will *understate* the actual change in the value of the option due to a price increase.

Similarly, delta will *overstate* the decline in the value of the option due to a stock price decrease. If the stock price had fallen $0.75 to $39.25, the option price would have declined to $2.3622, which would result in a gain of $0.4182 to the market-maker. Using delta, we would have predicted a price decline of −$0.75 × 0.5824 = −$0.4368, which is greater than the actual decline. This occurs because the option delta decreases as the stock price declines. The delta at this new price is 0.5326.

Gamma measures the change in delta when the stock price changes. In the example above, the gamma of 0.0652 means that delta will change by approximately 0.0652 if the stock price moves $1. This is why delta did not accurately predict the change in the option price: The delta itself was changing as the stock price changed. The ultimate change in the option price is a result of the *average* delta during the stock price change, not just the delta at the initial stock price. As you might guess, we can use gamma in addition to delta to better approximate the effect on the value of the option of a change in the stock price. We will discuss this adjustment later.

13.3 DELTA-HEDGING

Suppose a market-maker sells one call option and hedges the position with shares. With the sale of a call, the market-maker is short delta shares. To hedge this position, the market-maker can buy delta shares to delta-hedge the position.

We now will consider the risk of a delta-hedged position by assuming that the market-maker delta-hedges and marks-to-market daily. We first look at numerical examples and then in Section 13.4 explain the results algebraically.

An Example of Delta-Hedging for 2 Days

Day 0 Consider the 40-strike call option described above, written on 100 shares of stock. The market-maker sells the option and receives $278.04. Since $\Delta = 0.5824$, the market-maker also buys 58.24 shares. (We will permit fractional share purchases in this example.) The net investment is

$$(58.24 \times \$40) - \$278.04 = \$2051.56$$

At an 8% interest rate, the market-maker has an overnight financing charge of $2051.56 \times \left(e^{0.08/365} - 1\right) = \$0.45$.

Day 1: Marking-to-market Without at first worrying about rebalancing the portfolio to maintain delta-neutrality, we can ask whether the market-maker made money or lost money overnight. Suppose the new stock price is $40.50. The new call option price with 1 day less to expiration and at the new stock price is $3.0621. Overnight mark-to-market profit is a gain of $0.50, computed as follows:

Gain on 58.24 shares	$58.24 \times (\$40.50 - \$40)$	$=$	$29.12
Gain on written call option	$\$278.04 - \$306.21$	$=$	$-\$28.17
Interest	$-(e^{0.08/365} - 1) \times \$2051.56$	$=$	$-\$0.45
Overnight profit			**$0.50**

Day 1: Rebalancing the portfolio The new delta is 0.6142. Since delta has increased, we must buy $61.42 - 58.24 = 3.18$ additional shares. This transaction requires an investment of $40.50 \times 3.18 = \$128.79$. Since the readjustment in the number of shares

entails buying at the current market price, it does not affect the mark-to-market profits for that day.

Day 2: Marking-to-market The stock price now falls to $39.25. The market-maker makes money on the written option and loses money on the 61.42 shares. Interest expense has increased over the previous day because additional investment was required for the extra shares. The net result from marking-to-market is a loss of $-\$3.87$:

Gain on 61.42 shares	$61.42 \times (\$39.25 - \$40.50)$ $=$	$-\$76.78$
Gain on written call option	$\$306.21 - \$232.82$ $=$	$\$73.39$
Interest	$-(e^{0.08/365} - 1) \times \$2181.30$ $=$	$-\$0.48$
Overnight profit		$-\$3.87$

Interpreting the Profit Calculation

At the end of day 1, we show a $0.50 profit from the mark-to-market calculation. Conceptually, we can think of the profit or loss as measuring the extent to which the portfolio requires cash infusions in order to maintain a delta-neutral hedge. When we show a positive profit, as in this case, we can take cash out of the portfolio.

To see that mark-to-market profit measures the net cash infusions required to maintain the delta-neutral position, suppose that a lender is willing at all times to lend us the value of securities in the portfolio. Initially, we buy 58.24 shares of stock, which costs $2329.60, but this amount is offset by the $278.04 option premium, so the net cash we require is $2051.56. This is also the net value of our portfolio (stock less the option), so we can borrow this amount.[2]

As time passes, there are three sources of cash flow into and out of the portfolio:

1. **Borrowing:** Our borrowing capacity equals the market value of securities in the portfolio; hence, borrowing capacity changes as the net value of the position changes. On day 0, the net value of our securities was $2051.56. On day 1, the share price rose and we bought additional shares; the market value of the position was $61.42 \times \$40.50 - \$306.21 = \$2181.30$. Thus our borrowing capacity increased by $129.74. The change in the option value changes borrowing capacity, but there is no cash flow since we are not changing the number of options.

2. **Purchase or sale of shares:** We buy or sell shares as necessary to maintain delta-neutrality. In the above example, we increased shares in our portfolio from 58.24 to 61.42. The price at the time was $40.50, so we spent $3.18 \times \$40.50 = \$128.79$.

3. **Interest:** We pay interest on the borrowed amount. On day 1 we owed $0.45.

---

[2] In practice the market-maker would be able to borrow only part of the funds required to buy securities, with market-maker capital making up the difference.

Thus, we need \$128.79 to buy more shares and \$0.45 to pay interest expense. The change in our borrowing capacity—the extra amount the bank will lend us—is \$129.74. The difference between what the bank will lend us on the one hand and the cost of additional shares plus interest on the other is

$$\$129.74 - \$128.79 - \$0.45 = \$0.50$$

Since the bank is willing to lend us the value of our securities, we are free to pocket the \$0.50 that is left over.

This example demonstrates that the mark-to-market profit equals the net cash flow generated by always borrowing to fully fund the position. Another way to see the equality of mark-to-market profit and net cash flow is by examining the sources and uses of funds, and the extent to which it is necessary to inject additional cash into the position in order to maintain the delta-neutral hedge. We can calculate the net cash flow from the portfolio as

$$\text{Net cash flow} = \text{Change in borrowing capacity}$$
$$- \text{cash used to purchase additional shares}$$
$$- \text{interest}$$

Let Δ_i denote the option delta on day i, S_i the stock price, C_i the option price, and MV_i the market value of the portfolio. Borrowing capacity on day i is $MV_i = \Delta_i S_i - C_i$; hence, the change in borrowing capacity is

$$\text{MV}_i - \text{MV}_{i-1} = \Delta_i S_i - C_i - (\Delta_{i-1} S_{i-1} - C_{i-1})$$

The cost of purchasing additional shares is $S_i(\Delta_i - \Delta_{i-1})$, and interest owed on day i depends on the previous day's borrowing, $r\text{MV}_{i-1}$. Thus, on day i we have

$$\begin{aligned}
\text{Net cash flow} &= \text{MV}_i - \text{MV}_{i-1} - S_i(\Delta_i - \Delta_{i-1}) - r\text{MV}_{i-1} \\
&= \Delta_i S_i - C_i - (\Delta_{i-1} S_{i-1} - C_{i-1}) - S_i(\Delta_i - \Delta_{i-1}) - r\text{MV}_{i-1} \\
&= \Delta_{i-1}(S_i - S_{i-1}) - (C_i - C_{i-1}) - r\text{MV}_{i-1}
\end{aligned}$$

The last expression is the overnight gain on shares, less the overnight gain on the option, less interest; this result is identical to the profit calculation we performed above. In the numerical example, we have

$$\text{MV}_1 - \text{MV}_0 - S_1(\Delta_1 - \Delta_0) - r\text{MV}_0 = \$2181.30 - \$2051.56 - \$128.79 - \$0.45$$
$$= \$0.50$$

This value is equal to the overnight profit we calculated between day 0 and day 1.

Thus, we can interpret the daily mark-to-market profit or loss as the amount of cash that we can pocket (if there is a profit) or that we must pay (if there is a loss) in order to fund required purchases of new shares and to continue borrowing exactly the amount of our securities. When we have a positive profit, as on day 1, we can take money out of the portfolio, and when we have a negative profit, as on day 2, we must put money into the portfolio.

A hedged portfolio that never requires additional cash investments to remain hedged is **self-financing.** One of the questions we will answer is under what conditions a delta-hedged portfolio is self-financing.

Delta-Hedging for Several Days

We can continue the example by letting the market-maker rebalance the portfolio each day. Table 13.2 summarizes delta, the net investment, and profit each day for 5 days. The profit line in the table is *daily* profit, not cumulative profit.

What determines the pattern of gain and loss in the table? There are three effects, attributable to gamma, theta, and the carrying cost of the position.

1. **Gamma:** For the largest moves in the stock, the market-maker loses money. For small moves in the stock price, the market-maker makes money. The loss for large moves results from gamma: If the stock price changes, the position becomes unhedged. In this case, since the market-maker is short the option, a large move generates a loss. As the stock price rises, the delta of the call increases and the call loses money faster than the stock makes money. As the stock price falls, the delta of the call decreases and the call makes money more slowly than the fixed stock position loses money. In effect, the market-maker becomes unhedged net long as the stock price falls and unhedged net short as the stock price rises. The losses on days 2 and 4 are attributable to gamma. For all of the entries in Table 13.2, the gamma of the written call is about −0.06 per share.

2. **Theta:** If a day passes with no change in the stock price, the option becomes cheaper. This time decay works to the benefit of the market-maker who could unwind the position more cheaply. Time decay is especially evident in the profit on day 5, but is also responsible for the profit on days 1 and 3.

3. **Interest Cost:** In order to hedge, the market-maker must purchase stock. The net carrying cost is a component of the overall cost.

TABLE 13.2	Daily profit calculation over 5 days for a market-maker who delta-hedges.					
	Day					
	0	**1**	**2**	**3**	**4**	**5**
Stock ($)	40.00	40.50	39.25	38.75	40.00	40.00
Call ($)	278.04	306.21	232.82	205.46	271.04	269.27
Option delta	0.5824	0.6142	0.5311	0.4956	0.5806	0.5801
Investment ($)	2,051.58	2,181.30	1,851.65	1,715.12	2,051.35	2,051.29
Interest ($)		−0.45	−0.48	−0.41	−0.38	−0.45
Capital gain ($)		0.95	−3.39	0.81	−3.62	1.77
Daily profit ($)		0.50	−3.87	0.40	−4.00	1.32

Figure 13.2 graphs overnight market-maker profit on day 1 as a function of the stock price on day 1. At a stock price of $40.50, for example, the profit is $0.50, just as in the table. The graph is generated by recomputing the first day's profit per share for a variety of stock prices between $37 and $43. The graph verifies what is evident in the table: The delta-hedging market-maker who has written a call wants small stock price moves and can suffer a substantial loss with a big move. In fact, should the stock price move to $37.50, for example, the market-maker would lose $20.

If the market-maker had purchased a call and shorted delta shares, the profit calculation would be reversed. The market-maker would lose money for small stock price moves and make money with large moves. The profit diagram for such a position would be a mirror image of Figure 13.2.

FIGURE 13.2

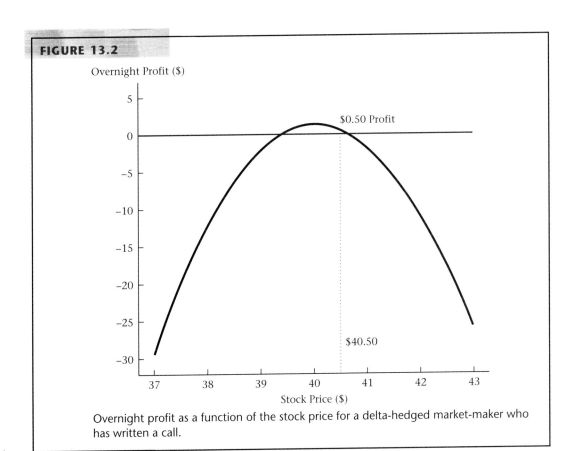

Overnight profit as a function of the stock price for a delta-hedged market-maker who has written a call.

TABLE 13.3		Daily profit calculation over 5 days for a market-maker who delta-hedges, assuming the stock price moves up or down 1 σ each day.				

	Day					
	0	**1**	**2**	**3**	**4**	**5**
Stock ($)	40.000	40.642	40.018	39.403	38.797	39.420
Call ($)	278.04	315.00	275.57	239.29	206.14	236.76
Option delta	0.5824	0.6232	0.5827	0.5408	0.4980	0.5406
Investment ($)	2,051.58	2,217.66	2,056.08	1,891.60	1,725.95	1,894.27
Interest ($)		−0.45	−0.49	−0.45	−0.41	−0.38
Capital gain ($)		0.43	0.51	0.46	0.42	0.38
Daily profit ($)		−0.02	0.02	0.01	0.01	0.00

A Self-Financing Portfolio: The Stock Moves One σ

In the previous example, the stock price changes by varying amounts and our daily profit varies substantially. However, in Figure 13.2, there is an up move and a down move for the stock such that the market-maker exactly breaks even in our profit calculations. If the stock always moved by this amount, the portfolio would be self-financing: No cash inflows are required to maintain delta-neutrality. It turns out that the portfolio is self-financing if the stock moves by one standard deviation.

In the binomial option pricing model in Chapter 10, we assumed that the stock moved up to $Se^{rh+\sigma\sqrt{h}}$ or down to $Se^{rh-\sigma\sqrt{h}}$, where $\sigma\sqrt{h}$ is the standard deviation per interval of the rate of return on the stock. Suppose we assume the stock moves up or down according to this binomial model. Table 13.3, which is otherwise the same as the previous example, shows the results of the stock moving up, down three times, and then up. You can see that the market-maker comes close to breaking even each day. If the stock moves according to the binomial model, therefore, the portfolio is approximately self-financing.

13.4 THE MATHEMATICS OF DELTA-HEDGING

Clearly, delta, gamma, and theta all play a role in determining the profit on a delta-hedged position. In this section we examine these relationships more closely in order to better understand the numerical example above. What we do here is a kind of financial forensics: Once we learn how the stock price changed, we seek to discover why we earned the profit we did.

Using Gamma to Better Approximate the Change in the Option Price

Delta alone is an inaccurate predictor of the change in the option price because delta changes with the stock price. When delta is very sensitive to the stock price (gamma is large), the inaccuracy will be relatively great. When delta is not sensitive to the stock price (gamma is small), the inaccuracy will be relatively small. Since gamma measures the change in delta, we can use gamma to develop a better approximation for the change in the option price.

If the stock price were \$40.75 instead of \$40, the option price would be \$3.2352 instead of \$2.7804. For the purpose of computing the change in the option price, we want to know the average rate of price increase between \$40 and \$40.75, which we can approximate by averaging the deltas at \$40 and \$40.75:

$$\Delta_{\text{Average}} = \frac{\Delta_{40} + \Delta_{40.75}}{2}$$

We could then approximate the option price at \$40.75 by computing

$$C(\$40.75) = C(\$40) + 0.75 \times \Delta_{\text{Average}} \tag{13.1}$$

When we average the deltas at \$40 and \$40.75, we have to compute deltas at two different stock prices. A different approach is to approximate the average delta by using only the delta evaluated at \$40 together with gamma. Since gamma measures the change in delta, we can approximate the delta at \$40.75 by adding $0.75 \times \Gamma$ to Δ_{40}:

$$\Delta_{40.75} = \Delta_{40} + 0.75 \times \Gamma$$

Using this relationship, the average delta is

$$\Delta_{\text{Average}} = \frac{\Delta_{40} + (\Delta_{40} + 0.75 \times \Gamma)}{2}$$

$$= \Delta_{40} + \frac{1}{2} \times 0.75 \times \Gamma$$

Using equation (13.1), we can then approximate the call price as

$$C(\$40.75) = C(\$40) + 0.75 \times \Delta_{\text{Average}}$$

$$= C(\$40) + 0.75 \times \left(\Delta_{40} + \frac{1}{2} \times 0.75 \times \Gamma \right)$$

$$= C(\$40) + 0.75 \times \Delta_{40} + \frac{1}{2} \times 0.75^2 \times \Gamma \tag{13.2}$$

The use of delta and gamma to approximate the new option price is called a **delta-gamma approximation**.[3]

---

[3]You may recognize that we have already encountered the idea of a delta-gamma approximation in Chapter 7, when we used duration (delta) and convexity (gamma) to approximate the price change of a bond.

Example 13.1 If the stock price rises from \$40 to \$40.75, the option price increases from \$2.7804 to \$3.2352. Using a delta approximation alone, we would estimate $C(\$40.75)$ as

$$C(\$40.75) = C(\$40) + 0.75 \times 0.5824 = \$3.2172$$

Using a delta-gamma approximation, we obtain

$$C(\$40.75) = C(\$40) + 0.75 \times 0.5824 + \frac{1}{2} \times 0.75^2 \times 0.0652 = \$3.2355$$

The delta-gamma approximation is significantly closer to the true option price at \$40.75 than is the delta approximation.

Similarly, for a stock price decline to \$39.25, the true option price is \$2.3622. The delta approximation gives

$$C(\$39.25) = C(\$40) - 0.75 \times 0.5824 = \$2.3436$$

The delta-gamma approximation gives

$$C(\$39.25) = C(\$40) - 0.75 \times 0.5824 + \frac{1}{2} \times 0.75^2 \times 0.0652 = \$2.3619$$

Again, the delta-gamma approximation is more accurate. ⟋

Delta-Gamma Approximations

We now repeat the previous arguments using algebra. For a "small" move in the stock price, we know that the rate at which delta changes is given by gamma. Thus, if over a time interval of length h the stock price change is

$$\epsilon = S_{t+h} - S_t$$

then gamma is the change in delta per dollar of stock price change, or

$$\Gamma(S_t) = \frac{\Delta(S_{t+h}) - \Delta(S_t)}{\epsilon}$$

Rewriting this expression, delta will change by approximately the magnitude of the price change, ϵ, times gamma, $\epsilon\Gamma$:

$$\Delta(S_{t+h}) = \Delta(S_t) + \epsilon\Gamma(S_t) \tag{13.3}$$

If the rate at which delta changes is constant (meaning that gamma is constant), this calculation is exact.

How does equation (13.3) help us compute the option price change? If the stock price changes by ϵ, we can compute the option price change if we know the *average* delta over the range S_{t+h} to S_t. If Γ is approximately constant, the average delta is

If σ is measured annually, then a one-standard-deviation move over a period of length h is $\sigma S_t \sqrt{h}$. Therefore a squared one-standard-deviation move is

$$\epsilon^2 = \sigma^2 S_t^2 h \tag{13.8}$$

Substituting this expression for ϵ^2, we can rewrite equation (13.7) as

$$\text{Market-maker profit} = -\left(\frac{1}{2}\sigma^2 S_t^2 \Gamma_t + \theta_t + r\left[\Delta_t S_t - C(S_t)\right]\right)h \tag{13.9}$$

This expression gives us market-maker profit when the stock moves one standard deviation. As an example, let $h = 1/365$ and $\sigma = 0.3$. Then $\sigma S \sqrt{h} = \$0.6281$. From Table 13.5, with this stock price move equation (13.9) is *exactly* zero! (Problem 13.13 asks you to verify this.) It is not an accident that equation (13.9) is zero for this price move. We explain this result in Section 13.5.

In Table 13.5, the loss from a $1 move is substantially larger in absolute value than the gain from no move. However, small moves are more probable than big moves. If we think of returns as being approximately normally distributed, then stock price moves greater than one standard deviation occur about one-third of the time. The market-maker thus expects to make small profits about two-thirds of the time and larger losses about one-third of the time. On average, the market-maker will break even.

13.5 THE BLACK-SCHOLES ANALYSIS

We have discussed how a market-maker can measure and manage the risk of a portfolio containing options. What is the link to pricing an option?

The Black-Scholes Argument

If a stock moves one standard deviation, then a delta-hedged position will exactly break even, taking into account the cost of funding the position. This finding is not a coincidence; it reflects the arguments Black and Scholes used to derive the option pricing formula.

Imagine, for example, that the stock always moves exactly one standard deviation every minute.[4] A market-maker hedging every minute will be hedged over an hour or over any period of time. Black and Scholes argued that the money invested in this hedged position should earn the risk-free rate since the resulting income stream is risk-free.

Equation (13.9) gives us an expression for market-maker profit when the stock moves one standard deviation. Setting this expression to zero gives

$$-\left(\frac{1}{2}\sigma^2 S_t^2 \Gamma_t + \theta + r\left[\Delta_t S_t - C(S_t)\right]\right)h = 0$$

....

[4]There are $365 \times 24 \times 60 = 525,600$ minutes in a year. Thus, if the stock's annual standard deviation is 30%, the per-minute standard deviation is $0.3/\sqrt{525,600} = 0.04\%$, or $\$0.016$ for a $40 stock.

If we divide by h and rearrange terms, we get

$$\frac{1}{2}\sigma^2 S_t^2 \Gamma_t + r S_t \Delta_t + \theta = rC(S_t) \qquad (13.10)$$

This is the equation Black and Scholes used to characterize the behavior of an option.
The Greeks Γ, Δ, and θ are partial derivatives of the option price. Equation (13.10) is the
well-known Black-Scholes partial differential equation, or just Black-Scholes equation
(as opposed to the Black-Scholes *formula* for the price of a European call). We will see
in later chapters that this relationship among the Greeks is as fundamental in valuing
risky cash flows as is e^{-rT} when valuing risk-free cash flows.

Equation (13.10) embodies numerous assumptions, among them that the underlying asset does not pay a dividend, the option itself does not pay a dividend, the interest
rate and volatility are constant, and the stock moves one standard deviation over a small
time interval. With these assumptions, equation (13.10) holds for calls, puts, American
options, European options, and most of the exotic variants we will consider in Chapter
14. With simple modifications, an equation like (13.10) will also hold for options on
dividend-paying stocks, currencies, futures, bonds, etc. The link between delta-hedging
and pricing is one of the most important ideas in finance.

Delta-Hedging of American Options

Equation (13.10) holds for American options as well as for European options, but it does
not hold at times when it is optimal to early-exercise the option. Consider a deep-in-
the-money American put option and suppose the option should be exercised early. Since
early exercise is optimal, the option price is $K - S$; hence, $\Delta = -1$, $\Gamma = 0$, and $\theta = 0$.
In this case, equation (13.10) becomes

$$[r \times (-1) \times S_t] + \left(\frac{1}{2} \times 0\right) + 0 = r \times (K - S_t)$$

Note that $-rS_t$ appears on both sides of the equation. Thus, we can rewrite the equation
as

$$0 = rK$$

Since this equation is false, something is wrong. We began by assuming that the put
was so far in-the-money that it should be early-exercised. From the discussion of early
exercise in Chapter 10, this means that interest received on the strike exceeds the loss
of the implicit call option. Thus, if the option should be exercised but you own it,
delta-hedge it, and *do not exercise it*, then you lose interest on the strike you are not
receiving. Similarly, if you have written the option and delta-hedged, and the owner
does not exercise, then you are earning arbitrage profit of rK.

Thus, equation (13.10) is only valid in a region where early exercise is not optimal.
If an option should be exercised but is not exercised, then behavior is irrational and there
is no reason why a delta-hedged position should earn the risk-free rate and thus no reason
that equation (13.10) should hold.

What Is the Advantage to Frequent Re-Hedging?

In practice, because of transaction costs, it is expensive for a market-maker to trade shares for every change in an option delta. Instead, a delta-hedger will wait for the position to become somewhat unhedged before trading to reestablish delta-neutrality. In the binomial model in Chapter 10, and in the preceding discussion, we assumed that market-makers maintain their hedged position and that stock prices move exactly one standard deviation. In real life the stock price will rarely move exactly one standard deviation over the course of a day. What does the market-maker lose by hedging less frequently?

Boyle and Emanuel (1980) considered a market-maker who delta-hedges at set intervals, rather than every time the stock price changes. Let x_i denote the number of standard deviations the stock price moves—we can think of x_i as being drawn randomly from the standard normal distribution. Also let $R_{h,i}$ denote the period-i return to a delta-hedged market-maker who, as in our earlier example, has written a call. Boyle and Emanuel show that this return can be written as[5]

$$R_{h,i} = \frac{1}{2}S^2\sigma^2\Gamma(x_i^2 - 1)h \tag{13.11}$$

where Γ is the option's gamma and h is the time interval between hedge readjustments. From Boyle and Emanuel, the variance of $x_i^2 - 1$ is 2; hence,

$$\text{Var}(R_{h,i}) = \frac{1}{2}\left(S^2\sigma^2\Gamma h\right)^2 \tag{13.12}$$

We assume—as in the binomial model—that the stock return is uncorrelated across time, so that x_i is uncorrelated across time.

Now let's compare hedging once a day against hedging hourly (suppose trading occurs around the clock). The daily variance of the return earned by the market-maker who hedges once a day is given by

$$\text{Var}(R_{1/365,1}) = \frac{1}{2}\left(S^2\sigma^2\Gamma/365\right)^2$$

The daily return of the market-maker who hedges hourly is the sum of the hourly returns. Assuming for the sake of simplicity that S and Γ do not change much, that variance is

$$\text{Var}\left(\sum_{i=1}^{24} R_{h,i}\right) = \sum_{i=1}^{24} \frac{1}{2}\left[S^2\sigma^2\Gamma/(24 \times 365)\right]^2$$

$$= \frac{1}{24} \times \text{Var}(R_{1/365,1})$$

Thus, by hedging hourly instead of daily the market-maker's total return variance is reduced by a factor of 24.

---

[5]This expression can be derived by assuming that the stock price move, ϵ, is normally distributed with variance $S\sigma\sqrt{h}$, and subtracting equation (13.9) from (13.7).

Here is the intuition for this result. Whatever the hedging interval, about two-thirds of the price moves will be less than a single standard deviation, whereas one-third will be greater. Frequent re-hedging does not avoid these large or small moves, since they can occur over any interval. However, frequent hedging does permit better *averaging* of the effects of these moves. Whether you hedge once a day or once an hour, the typical stock price move you encounter will likely not be close to one standard deviation. However, if you hedge every hour, over the course of a day you will have 24 moves and 24 opportunities to re-hedge. The *average* move over this period is likelier to be close to one standard deviation. The gains from small moves and losses from large moves will tend to average over the course of a day. In effect, the more frequent hedger benefits from diversification over time.[6]

Example 13.3 Using Boyle and Emanuel's formulas to study the market-maker problem in Section 13.3, the standard deviation of profit is about $0.075 for a market-maker who hedges hourly. Since hedging errors are independent from hour to hour, the daily standard deviation for an hourly hedger would be $0.075 \times \sqrt{24} = \$0.37$. If the market-maker were to hedge only daily as in our example, the daily standard deviation would be about $1.82. ◊

As you would expect, the *mean* return on a delta-hedged position is zero, even if the hedge is not frequently readjusted.

Delta-Hedging in Practice

The Black-Scholes analysis outlined here is the linchpin of modern option pricing theory *and* practice. Market-makers use equation (13.10) to price options, subject to qualifications mentioned above.

We have seen, however, that delta-hedging does not eliminate risk. One problem, which we emphasized above, is that a delta-hedged portfolio with negative gamma can sustain losses due to large moves in the price of the underlying asset. Consequently, a delta-hedging market-maker needs to worry about gamma. Another problem, discussed in the box on page 434, is that firms can unexpectedly change their dividend payments.

There are at least four ways a market-maker can try to reduce the risk of extreme price moves. Note that some of these strategies require the market-maker to acquire

---

[6]This resembles the problem faced by an insurance company. If the company insures one large asset, the standard deviation of the loss is $\sqrt{n}$ greater than if it insures n small assets, with the same total insured value in each case. Similarly, we can view the return over each hedging interval as being an independent draw from a probability distribution.

specific option positions, which means that the market-maker may have to pay the bid-ask spread. Since the bid-ask spread is revenue for the market-maker, paying the spread is undesirable.

First, just as market-makers can adopt a delta-neutral position, they can also adopt a gamma-neutral position. This position cannot be achieved with the stock alone, since the gamma of the stock is zero. Thus, to be gamma-neutral the market-maker must buy or sell options so as to offset the gamma of the existing position.[7] We provide an example of gamma-neutrality below.

Second, in a related strategy, market-makers can use **static option replication,** a strategy in which options are used to hedge options. In our delta-hedging example, the market-maker might not be able to buy an exactly offsetting call option to hedge the written call, but by selectively setting the bid and ask prices for related options, might be able to acquire an option position requiring only infrequent rebalancing. To take a simple example, if the market-maker were able to buy a put with the same strike price and maturity as the written call (e.g., by setting the bid price to attract any seller of that option), then by buying 100 shares to offset the risk of the position, the market-maker would have used put-call parity to create a hedge that is both gamma- and delta-neutral for the life of the options.

Third, a market-maker can buy out-of-the-money options as insurance. In our example of delta-neutral hedging of a written option, the market-maker could buy a deep-out-of-the-money put and a deep-out-of-the-money call. The two options would be relatively inexpensive and would protect against large moves in the stock. One problem with this solution is that, since option positions in the aggregate sum to zero, the market-making community as a whole can buy protective options only if investors in the aggregate are willing to sell them. Investors, however, are usually thought to be insurance buyers rather than insurance sellers.

Fourth, a market-maker can create a financial product by selling the hedging error, as discussed by Carr and Madan (1998). For example, to hedge a negative-gamma, delta-neutral position, the market-maker would make a payment to a counterparty if the stock makes a small move in either direction, and receive payment from the counterparty if the stock makes a large move in either direction. This is effectively a variance swap, which we will discuss in more detail in Chapter 23. The point is that the market-maker can potentially solve the delta-hedging problem by creating a new product.

Gamma-Neutrality

Let's explore gamma-hedging in more depth. Suppose we wish to both delta-hedge and gamma-hedge the written option described in Table 13.1. We cannot do this using just

---

[7]Market-makers sometimes buy and hold over-the-counter options issued by a firm. For example, in the late 1990s some firms sold put options on their own stock. These options were reportedly held by dealers and delta-hedged. One possible motivation for dealers to undertake such a transaction would be to acquire positive gamma. See McDonald (2004) for a discussion.

Dividend Risk

Market-makers price options taking into account the dividends they expect a stock to pay. If a firm announces a significant change in dividend policy, delta-hedgers can make or lose money depending on their position and depending on whether the derivatives they hold are protected against dividend changes.

In 1998, Daimler-Benz surprised option market-makers by announcing a special one-time dividend, creating a dividend payout of about 14%, or 10 times the usual dividend yield. The Deutsche Terminbörse (DTB), the exchange where Daimler options were traded, decided not to adust the terms of exchange-traded options to account for the dividend. The DTB was criticized for this, and some dealers were said to have sustained significant losses.

The stated policy of the Options Clearing Corporation (1994, 2003 supplement) in the United States is that typically there is adjustment only for "extraordinary" cash dividends or distributions, i.e., those exceeding "10% of the market value of the underlying security outstanding. Determinations . . . are made on a case-by-case basis."

In July 2004 Mocrosoft announced that it would make a special one-time payment of $3/share, a dividend yield in excess of 10% based on Microsoft's price at the time of the announcement. The Options Clearing Corporation in the United States responded by declaring that it would reduce strike prices on Microsoft options by $3 when the dividend was paid.

the stock, because the gamma of stock is zero. Hence, we must acquire another option in an amount that offsets the gamma of the written call. Table 13.6 presents information for the 3-month 40-strike call, and also for a 4-month 45-strike call. We will use the latter to gamma-hedge the former.

The ratio of the gamma of the two options is[8]

$$\frac{\Gamma_{K=40,t=0.25}}{\Gamma_{K=45,t=0.33}} = \frac{0.0651}{0.0524} = 1.2408 \tag{13.13}$$

Thus, we need to buy 1.2408 of the 45-strike 4-month options for every 40-strike 3-month option we have sold. The Greeks resulting from the position are in the last column of Table 13.6. Since delta is -0.1749, we need to buy 17.49 shares of stock to be both delta- and gamma-hedged.

Figure 13.4 compares this delta- and gamma-hedged position to the delta-hedged position, discussed earlier, in which the same call was written. The delta-hedged position has the problem that large moves always cause losses. The gamma-hedged position loses less if there is a large move down, and can make money if the stock price increases. Moreover, as Table 13.6 shows, the gamma-hedged position has a positive vega. Why would anyone *not* gamma-hedge?

....

[8]The gammas in equation (13.13) are rounded. The actual gammas are 0.065063 and 0.052438, the ratio of which is 1.2408.

TABLE 13.6	Prices and Greeks for 40-strike call, 45-strike call, and the (gamma-neutral) portfolio resulting from selling the 40-strike call for which $T - t = 0.25$ and buying 1.2408 45-strike calls for which $T - t = 0.33$. By buying 17.49 shares, the market-maker can be both delta- and gamma-neutral. Assumes $S = \$40$, $\sigma = 0.3$, $r = 0.08$, and $\delta = 0$.

	40-Strike Call	45-Strike Call	Sell 40-Strike Call, Buy 1.2408 45-Strike Calls
Price ($)	2.7847	1.3584	−1.0993
Delta	0.5825	0.3285	−0.1749
Gamma	0.0651	0.0524	0.0000
Vega	0.0781	0.0831	0.0250
Theta	−0.0173	−0.0129	0.0013
Rho	0.0513	0.0389	−0.0031

FIGURE 13.4
Comparison of 1-day holding period profit for delta-hedged position described in Table 13.2 and delta- and gamma-hedged position described in Table 13.6.

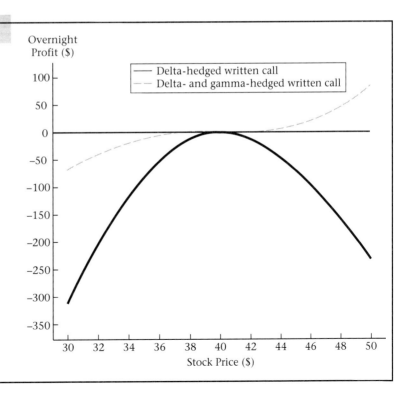

There are two reasons. First, as noted already, gamma-hedging requires the use of additional options. The market-maker will have to obtain the required option position from another market-maker, paying the bid-ask spread. In this example, all profits earned from writing the 40-strike call will go to pay the market-maker who sells the 45-strike call used in gamma-hedging. In a large portfolio, however, with many options bought and sold, naturally offsetting one another, gamma-hedging the net exposure would not require many option transactions.

The second reason is that if end-users on average buy puts and calls, then in the aggregate they have positive gamma (the end-users "buy gamma," to use market-making parlance). By definition, market-makers in the aggregate must then have negative gamma. Thus, while in principle any one market-maker could gamma-hedge, not all market-makers could be gamma-neutral. If investors want to buy insurance, they will not be gamma-neutral, and, hence, market-makers cannot in the aggregate be gamma-neutral.

In addition to gamma, other risks, such as vega and rho, can be hedged in the same fashion as delta.

13.6 MARKET-MAKING AS INSURANCE

The preceding discussion suggests that market-makers who write options can sustain large losses, even if they delta-hedge. This conclusion suggests that option market-making (and derivatives market-making more generally) has more in common with insurance than you might at first think.

Insurance

Insurance companies attempt to pool diversifiable risks. All insured individuals pay an insurance premium. The premiums are then used to compensate those who suffer losses, while those without losses lose the premium. Insurance thereby spreads the pain rather than forcing a few unlucky individuals to bear the brunt of inevitable losses.

In the classic model of an insurance company, risks are independent. Suppose an insurance company provides insurance for a large number of identical households, each of which has an independent 1% chance in any year of losing $100,000 in a fire. The expected loss for each house is $1\% \times \$100,000 = \$1,000$. This is the "actuarially fair" insurance premium, in the sense that if the insurance company collects this amount from each household, it will on average be able to pay annual insurance claims. In general insurance will be priced to cover the expected loss, plus costs of doing business, less interest earned on the premium.

However, even with diversification, there is a chance that actual insurance claims in a particular year will exceed $1000 per insured household, in which case the insurance company will not be able to fulfill its promises unless it has access to additional funds. Thus, the seller of a risk-management product—the insurance company—has a risk-management problem of its own—namely to be sure that it can meet its obligations to customers. Meeting such obligations is not just a matter of conscience for management;

if there is a significant chance that the insurance company will be bankrupted by claims, there will be no customers in the first place!

Insurance companies have two primary ways to ensure that they meet claims:

1. **Capital:** Insurance companies hold capital, i.e., a buffer fund in case there is an unusually large number of claims. Because of diversification, for any given bankruptcy probability insurers can use a smaller reserve fund per insured house as the number of insured houses grows. Capital in the form of reserves has traditionally been an important buffer for insurance companies against unexpectedly large claims.

2. **Reinsurance:** There is always the possibility of a loss that can exceed any *fixed* amount of capital. An insurance company can in turn buy insurance against large losses, in order to be able to make large payouts if necessary. Insurance for insurance companies is called reinsurance. Insurance companies buy insurance from reinsurance firms to cover the event that claims exceed a certain amount. Reinsurance is a put option: The reinsurance claim gives the insurance company the right to sell to the reinsurers claims that have lost money. Reinsurance does not change the aggregate need for capital, but it does permit further diversification.

Market-Makers

Now consider again the role of market-makers. Suppose that investors, fearful of a market crash, wish to buy out-of-the-money puts. Out-of-the-money put writers are selling insurance against large market moves. It is precisely when large market moves occur that delta-hedging breaks down. Just like an insurance company, a market-maker requires capital as a cushion against losses. Since capital has a cost, market-makers may also raise the cost of written options that require a disproportionately large commitment of capital per dollar of premium.

Reinsurance for a market-maker would entail buying out-of-the-money put options to move some risk to another market-maker, but ultimately if the financial industry is a net writer of insurance, there must be capital in the event of losses.

The importance of capital and the analogy to insurance becomes more obvious when we consider new derivatives markets. For example, think about weather derivatives. Financial institutions have hedged ski-resort operators against warm winters, soft-drink manufacturers against cold summers, and lawn sprinkler manufacturers against wet summers. Ultimately, the bank must find a counterparty willing to absorb the risk. If you think about the risks in weather insurance, on a *global* basis they are like traditional insurance. Weather contracts in the United States can be diversified with weather contracts in Asia, and ultimately the global capital committed to insurance absorbs the reinsurance risk. Global capital markets broadly defined are thus the natural party to absorb these risks.

Some risk, however, is not globally diversifiable. Consider writing puts on the S&P 500. If the U.S. stock market suffers a large decline, other markets around the world are likely to follow. Ultimately, it is capital that safeguards the financial industry.

Delta-hedging plays a key role, but in the end there is always risk that must be absorbed by capital.

CHAPTER SUMMARY

Market-makers buy and sell to satisfy customer demand. A derivatives market-maker can use the underlying stock to delta-hedge the resulting position. By definition, the return on a delta-hedged position does not depend on the *direction* in which the stock price moves, but it does depend on the *magnitude* of the stock price move. A position with zero delta and negative gamma makes money for small stock price moves and loses money for large stock price moves. If the gamma of the position is positive, it makes money for large moves and loses money for small moves. Either way, the delta-hedged position breaks even if the stock moves one standard deviation.

Using a delta-gamma-theta approximation to characterize the change in the value of the delta-hedged portfolio, we can demonstrate that there are three factors that explain the profitability of the portfolio. First, gamma measures the tendency of the portfolio to become unhedged as the stock price moves. Second, theta measures the gain or loss on the portfolio due to the passage of time alone. Third, the market-maker will have interest income or expense on the portfolio.

If we assume that the stock price moves one standard deviation and impose the condition that the market-maker earns zero profit, then a fair option price satisfies a particular relationship among delta, gamma, and theta. This relationship, equation (13.10), is the foundation of the Black-Scholes option pricing analysis and applies to derivatives in general, not just to calls and puts.

Ultimately, market-making is risky and requires capital. If customers on average buy puts and calls, and if we think of options as insurance, then market-makers are in the same business as insurance companies. This requires capital, since if an extreme event occurs, delta-hedging will fail.

FURTHER READING

The main example in this chapter assumed that the Black-Scholes formula provided the correct option price and illustrated the behavior of the formula, viewed from the perspective of a delta-hedging market-maker. In Chapters 20 and 21 we will start by building a model of how stock prices behave, and see how the Black-Scholes formula is derived. As in this chapter, we will conclude that equation (13.10) is key to understanding option pricing.

PROBLEMS

In the following problems assume, unless otherwise stated, that $S = \$40$, $\sigma = 30\%$, $r = 8\%$, and $\delta = 0$.

13.1. Suppose you sell a 45-strike call with 91 days to expiration. What is delta? If the option is on 100 shares, what investment is required for a delta-hedged portfolio? What is your overnight profit if the stock tomorrow is $39? What if the stock price is $40.50?

13.2. Suppose you sell a 40-strike put with 91 days to expiration. What is delta? If the option is on 100 shares, what investment is required for a delta-hedged portfolio? What is your overnight profit if the stock price tomorrow is $39? What if it is $40.50?

13.3. Suppose you buy a 40–45 bull spread with 91 days to expiration. If you delta-hedge this position, what investment is required? What is your overnight profit if the stock tomorrow is $39? What if the stock is $40.50?

13.4. Suppose you enter into a put ratio spread where you buy a 45-strike put and sell two 40-strike puts. If you delta-hedge this position, what investment is required? What is your overnight profit if the stock tomorrow is $39? What if the stock is $40.50?

13.5. Reproduce the analysis in Table 13.2, assuming that instead of selling a call you sell a 40-strike put.

13.6. Reproduce the analysis in Table 13.3, assuming that instead of selling a call you sell a 40-strike put.

13.7. Consider a 40-strike 180-day call with $S = \$40$. Compute a delta-gamma-theta approximation for the value of the call after 1, 5, and 25 days. For each day, consider stock prices of $36 to $44.00 in $0.25 increments and compare the actual option premium at each stock price with the predicted premium. Where are the two the same?

13.8. Repeat the previous problem for a 40-strike 180-day put.

13.9. Consider a 40-strike call with 91 days days to expiration. Graph the results from the following calculations.

  a. Compute the actual price with 90 days to expiration at $1 intervals from $30 to $50.

  b. Compute the estimated price with 90 days to expiration using a delta approximation.

  c. Compute the estimated price with 90 days to expiration using a delta-gamma approximation.

  d. Compute the estimated price with 90 days to expiration using a delta-gamma-theta approximation.

13.10. Consider a 40-strike call with 365 days to expiration. Graph the results from the following calculations.

  a. Compute the actual price with 360 days to expiration at $1 intervals from $30 to $50.

b. Compute the estimated price with 360 days to expiration using a delta approximation.

c. Compute the estimated price with 360 days to expiration using a delta-gamma approximation.

d. Compute the estimated price with 360 days to expiration using a delta-gamma-theta approximation.

13.11. Repeat Problem 13.9 for a 91-day 40-strike put.

13.12. Repeat Problem 13.10 for a 365-day 40-strike put.

13.13. Using the parameters in Table 13.1, verify that equation (13.9) is zero.

13.14. Consider a put for which $T = 0.5$ and $K = \$45$. Compute the Greeks and verify that equation (13.9) is zero.

13.15. You own one 45-strike call with 180 days to expiration. Compute and graph the 1-day holding period profit if you delta- and gamma-hedge this position using a 40-strike call with 180 days to expiration.

13.16. You have sold one 45-strike put with 180 days to expiration. Compute and graph the 1-day holding period profit if you delta- and gamma-hedge this position using the stock and a 40-strike call with 180 days to expiration.

13.17. You have written a 35–40–45 butterfly spread with 91 days to expiration. Compute and graph the 1-day holding period profit if you delta- and gamma-hedge this position using the stock and a 40-strike call with 180 days to expiration.

13.18. Suppose you enter into a put ratio spread where you buy a 45-strike put and sell two 40-strike puts, both with 91 days to expiration. Compute and graph the 1-day holding period profit if you delta- and gamma-hedge this position using the stock and a 40-strike call with 180 days to expiration.

13.19. You have purchased a 40-strike call with 91 days to expiration. You wish to delta-hedge, but you are also concerned about changes in volatility; thus, you want to *vega-hedge* your position as well.

a. Compute and graph the 1-day holding period profit if you delta- and vega-hedge this position using the stock and a 40-strike call with 180 days to expiration.

b. Compute and graph the 1-day holding period profit if you delta-, gamma-, and vega-hedge this position using the stock, a 40-strike call with 180 days to expiration, and a 45-strike put with 365 days to expiration.

13.20. Repeat the previous problem, except that instead of hedging volatility risk, you wish to hedge interest rate risk, i.e., to *rho-hedge*. In addition to delta-, gamma-, and rho-hedging, can you delta-gamma-rho-vega hedge?

APPENDIX 13.A: TAYLOR SERIES APPROXIMATIONS

We have seen that the change in the option price can be expressed in terms of delta, gamma, and theta. The resulting expression is really just a particular approximation to the option price, called a Taylor series approximation.

Let $G(x, y)$ be a function of two variables. Taylor's theorem says that the value of the function at the point $G(x + \epsilon_x, y + \epsilon_y)$ may be approximated using derivatives of the function, as follows:

$$G(x + \epsilon_x, y + \epsilon_y) =$$

$$G(x, y) + \epsilon_x G_x(x, y) + \epsilon_y G_y(x, y)$$

$$+ \frac{1}{2} \left[\epsilon_x^2 G_{xx}(x, y) + \epsilon_y^2 G_{yy}(x, y) + 2\epsilon_x \epsilon_y G_{x,y}(x, y) \right]$$

$$+ \frac{1}{6} \left[\epsilon_x^3 G_{xxx}(x, y) + 3\epsilon_x^2 \epsilon_y G_{xxy}(x, y) + 3\epsilon_x \epsilon_y^2 G_{xyy}(x, y) + \epsilon_y^3 G_{yyy} G(x, y) \right]$$

$$+ \cdots \tag{13.14}$$

The approximation may be extended indefinitely, using successively higher-order derivatives. The nth term in the expansion is

$$\frac{1}{n!} \sum_{i=0}^{n} \binom{n}{i} \epsilon_x^i \epsilon_y^{n-i} G_{x^i, y^{n-i}}(x, y)$$

where the notation $G_{x^i, y^{n-i}}(x, y)$ means take the ith derivative with respect to x and the $(n-i)$th derivative with respect to y. The Taylor series is useful when the approximation is reasonably accurate with few terms.

For our purposes, it is enough to note that the delta-gamma approximation, equation (13.6), looks like a Taylor series approximation that stops with the second derivative. You may wonder, however, why there is no second derivative with respect to time. You may also wonder why the approximation stops with the second derivative. These questions will arise again and be answered in Chapter 20.

APPENDIX 13.B: GREEKS IN THE BINOMIAL MODEL

The Black-Scholes Greeks are obtained by differentiating the option price. However, the general binomial option price calculation is not a formula but an algorithm. How can option Greeks be computed using the binomial tree? We can use some of the relations between delta, gamma, and theta discussed in this chapter to compute the binomial Greeks.

From Chapter 10, the option price and stock price for first two time steps in the binomial model can be represented as in Figure 13.5. We saw in Chapter 10 that delta

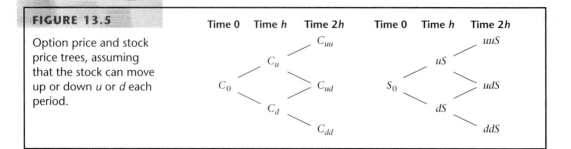

FIGURE 13.5

Option price and stock price trees, assuming that the stock can move up or down u or d each period.

at the initial node is computed using the formula

$$\Delta(S, 0) = e^{-\delta h} \frac{C_u - C_d}{uS - dS} \tag{13.15}$$

Gamma is the change in delta. We cannot compute the change in delta for the time-0 delta, since only one delta at a single stock price is defined at that point. But we can compute the change in delta at time h using the two deltas that are defined there. Thus, we have

$$\Gamma(S_h, h) = \frac{\Delta(uS, h) - \Delta(dS, h)}{uS - dS} \tag{13.16}$$

This is an approximation since we wish to know gamma at time 0, not at time h, and at the price S_0. However, even with a small number of binomial steps, the approximation works reasonably well.

With theta we are interested in the pure effect on the option price of changing time. We can calculate this using delta and gamma. Define

$$\epsilon = udS - S$$

Using the delta-gamma-theta approximation, equation (13.6), we can write the option price at time $2h$ and node udS as

$$C(udS, 2h) = C(S, 0) + \epsilon \Delta(S, 0) + \frac{1}{2} \epsilon^2 \Gamma(S, 0) + 2h\theta(S, 0)$$

Solving for $\theta(S, 0)$ gives

$$\theta(S, 0) = \frac{C(udS, 2h) - \epsilon \Delta(S, 0) - \frac{1}{2} \epsilon^2 \Gamma(S, 0) - C(S, 0)}{2h} \tag{13.17}$$

CHAPTER 14

Exotic Options: I

Thus far we have discussed standard options, futures, and swaps. By altering the terms of standard contracts like these, you obtain a "nonstandard" or "exotic" option. Exotic options can provide precise tailoring of risk exposures, and they permit investment strategies difficult or costly to realize with standard options and securities. In this chapter we discuss some basic kinds of exotic options, including Asian, barrier, compound, gap, and exchange options. In Chapter 22 we will consider other exotic options.

14.1 INTRODUCTION

Imagine that you are discussing currency hedging with Sally Smith, the risk manager of XYZ Corp., a dollar-based multinational corporation with sizable European operations. XYZ has a large annual inflow of euros that are eventually converted to dollars. XYZ is considering the purchase of 1-year put options as insurance against a fall in the euro but is also interested in exploring alternatives. You have already discussed with Smith the hedging variants from Chapters 2 and 3, including different strike prices, a collar, and a paylater strategy.

Suppose that Smith offhandedly mentions that XYZ receives large euro payments on a monthly basis, amounting to hundreds of millions of dollars per quarter. In thinking about how to hedge this position, you might reason as follows: "A standard 1-year put option would hedge the firm against the level of the euro *on the one day the option expires*. This hedge would have significant basis risk since the price at expiration could be quite different from the average price over the year. Buying a strip of put options in which one option expires every month would have little basis risk but might be expensive. Over the course of the year what really matters is the *average* exchange rate over this period; the ups and downs around the average rate cancel out by definition. I wonder if there is any way to base an option on the *average* of the euro/dollar exchange rate?"

This train of thought leads you to construct a new kind of option—based on the average price, rather than the price at a point in time—that addresses a particular business concern: It provides a more precise hedge against the risk that matters, namely the average exchange rate. This example demonstrates that exotic options can solve a particular business problem in a way that standard options do not. Generally, an **exotic option** (or **nonstandard option**) is simply an option with some contractual difference from standard options. Although we will focus on hedging examples, these products can also be used to speculate.

It is not hard to invent new kinds of options. The challenge is to invent new options that are potentially attractive to buyers (which we did in the preceding example) and that can be priced and hedged without too much difficulty. In Chapters 10 and 13, we saw how a market-maker can delta-hedge an option position. That analysis led us to see how the price of an option is equivalent to the cost of synthetically manufacturing the option. In particular, an option is fairly priced when there is a certain relationship among the Greeks of the option.

Options with exotic features can generally be priced and delta-hedged in the same way as ordinary options.[1] As a consequence, exotic derivative products are quite common in practice and the technology for pricing and hedging them is well understood. In fact, since many such options are in common use, the term "exotic" is an anachronism. We will continue to use it, however.

The goal in this chapter is *not* to master the mathematical details of particular products, but rather to gain an intuitive understanding of the trade-offs in design and pricing. Consequently, most of the formulas appear in the chapter appendix.

Since exotic options are often constructed by tweaking ordinary options in minor ways, ordinary options are useful as benchmarks for exotics. To understand exotic options you should ask questions like these:

- How does the payoff of the exotic compare to that of a standard option?

- Can the exotic option be approximated by some portfolio of other options?

- Is the exotic option cheap or expensive relative to standard options? Understanding the economics of the option is a critical step in understanding its pricing and use.

- What is the rationale for the use of the exotic option?

- How easily can the exotic option be hedged? An option may be desirable to a customer, but it will not be sold unless the risk arising from market-making can be controlled.

14.2 ASIAN OPTIONS

An **Asian option** has a payoff that is based on the average price over some period of time. An Asian option is an example of a **path-dependent option,** which means that the value of the option at expiration depends upon the path by which the stock arrived at its final price.[2] Such an option has the potential to solve XYZ's hedging problem.

----

[1] However, as we will see in Chapter 22, there are options that are quite difficult to hedge even though they are easy to price.

[2] You can think of path dependence in the context of a binomial pricing model. In the binomial model of Chapter 10, *udu* and *duu* are a series of up and down stock price moves—paths—occurring in a different order but which lead to the same final stock price. Thus, both yield the same payoff for a European option. However, with a path-dependent option, these two paths would yield different final option payoffs because the intermediate stock prices were different.

There are many practical applications in which we average prices. In addition to cases where the firm cares about the average exchange rate (as with XYZ), averaging is also used when a single price at a point in time might be subject to manipulation or price swings induced by thin markets. Bonds convertible into stock, for example, often base the terms of conversion on the average stock price over a 20-day period at the end of the bond's life. Settlement based on the average is called an **Asian tail,** since the averaging occurs only at the termination of the contract.

As we will see, Asian options are worth less at issuance than otherwise equivalent ordinary options. The reason is that the averaged price of the underlying asset is less volatile than the asset price itself, and an option on a lower volatility asset is worth less.

XYZ's Hedging Problem

Let's think more about XYZ's currency hedging problem. Suppose that XYZ has a monthly euro inflow of €100m, reflecting revenue from selling products in Europe. Its costs, however, are primarily fixed in dollars. Let x_i denote the dollar price of a euro in month i. At the end of the year, the converted amount in dollars is

$$€100\text{m} \times \sum_{i=1}^{12} x_i e^{r(12-i)/12} \tag{14.1}$$

We have numerous strategies available for hedging the end-of-year cash flow. Here are a few obvious ones:

- **Strip of forward contracts:** Sell euro forward contracts maturing each month over the year. The premium of this strategy is zero.

- **Euro swap:** Swap euros for dollars. We saw in Chapter 8 that, except for the timing of cash flows, a swap produces the same result as hedging with the strip of forwards. A swap also has a zero premium.

- **Strip of puts:** Buy 12 put options on €100m, each maturing at the end of a different month. The cost is the 12 option premiums.

As we saw in Chapter 2, the difference between the forward and option strategies is the ability to profit from a euro appreciation, but we pay a premium for the possibility of earning that profit. You can probably think of other strategies as well.

The idea of an Asian option stems from expression (14.1): What we really care about is the future value of the *sum* of the converted cash flows. This in turn depends on the sum of the month-end exchange rates. If for simplicity we ignore interest, what we are trying to hedge is

$$\sum_{i=1}^{12} x_i = 12 \times \left(\frac{\sum_{i=1}^{12} x_i}{12} \right) \tag{14.2}$$

The expression in parentheses is the month-end arithmetic average exchange rate, which motivates the idea of an option on the average.

Options on the Average

As a logical matter there are eight basic kinds of Asian options, depending upon whether the option is a put or a call, whether the average is computed as a geometric or arithmetic average, and whether the average asset price is used in place of the price of the underlying asset or the strike price. Here are details about some of these alternatives.

The definition of the average It is most common in practice to define the average as an *arithmetic average*. Suppose we record the stock price every h periods from time 0 to T; there are then $N = T/h$ periods. The arithmetic average is defined as

$$A(T) = \frac{1}{N} \sum_{i=1}^{N} S_{ih} \tag{14.3}$$

While arithmetic averages are typically used, they are mathematically inconvenient.[3] It is computationally easier, but less common in practice, to use the *geometric average* stock price, which is defined as

$$G(T) = (S_h \times S_{2h} \times \cdots \times S_{Nh})^{\frac{1}{N}} \tag{14.4}$$

There are easy pricing formulas for options based on the geometric average (see the chapter appendix).

Whether the average is used as the asset price or the strike The payoff at maturity can be computed using the average stock price either as the price of the underlying asset or as the strike price. When the average is used as the asset price, the option is called an *average price option.* When the average is used as the strike price, the option is called an *average strike option.* Here are the four variants of options based on the geometric average:

$$\text{Geometric average price call} = \max[0, G(T) - K] \tag{14.5}$$

$$\text{Geometric average price put} = \max[0, K - G(T)] \tag{14.6}$$

$$\text{Geometric average strike call} = \max[0, S_T - G(T)] \tag{14.7}$$

$$\text{Geometric average strike put} = \max[0, G(T) - S_T] \tag{14.8}$$

The terms "average price" and "average strike" refer to whether the average is used in place of the asset price or the strike price. In each case the average could also be computed as an arithmetic average, giving us our eight basic kinds of Asian options.

The following example illustrates the difference between an arithmetic and geometric average.

---

[3]Because the sum of lognormal variables is not lognormally distributed, there are no simple pricing formulas for options based on the arithmetic average.

Example 14.1 Suppose that we compute the average based on quarterly stock prices over 1 year. We observe stock prices of $55, $72, $61, and $85. The arithmetic average is

$$\frac{\$55 + \$72 + \$61 + \$85}{4} = \$68.250$$

The geometric average is

$$\left(\$55 \times \$72 \times \$61 \times \$85\right)^{0.25} = \$67.315$$

The chapter appendix has (relatively simple) formulas for pricing European options based on the geometric average. We further discuss options based on the arithmetic average in Chapter 19.

Comparing Asian Options

Table 14.1 shows values of geometric average price calls and puts. If the number of averages, N, is one, then the average is the final stock price. In that case the average price call is an ordinary call.

Intuitively, averaging reduces the volatility of $G(T)$ relative to the volatility of the stock price at expiration, S_T, and thus we should expect the value of an average price

TABLE 14.1	Premiums of at-the-money geometric average price and geometric average strike calls and puts, for different numbers of prices averaged, N. The case $N = 1$ for the average price options is equivalent to Black-Scholes values. Assumes $S = \$40$, $K = \$40$, $r = 0.08$, $\sigma = 0.3$, $\delta = 0$, and $t = 1$.

| | Average Price ($) | | Average Strike ($) | |
N	Call	Put	Call	Put
1	6.285	3.209	0.000	0.000
2	4.708	2.645	2.225	1.213
3	4.209	2.445	2.748	1.436
5	3.819	2.281	3.148	1.610
10	3.530	2.155	3.440	1.740
50	3.302	2.052	3.668	1.843
1000	3.248	2.027	3.722	1.868
∞	3.246	2.026	3.725	1.869

option to decrease with the number of stock prices used to compute the average. This is evident in Table 14.1, which shows the decline in value of the average price option as the frequency of averaging increases.

Table 14.1 also shows that, in contrast to average price calls, the price of an average strike call increases with the number of averaging periods. The average of stock prices between times 0 and T is positively correlated with the stock price at time T, S_T. If $G(T)$ is high, S_T is likely to be high as well. More frequent averaging makes the average strike option more valuable because it reduces the correlation between S_T and $G(T)$. To see this pattern, consider what happens if the average is computed only using the final stock price. The value of the call is

$$\max[0, S_T - G(T)]$$

If only one stock price observation is used, $G(T) = S_T$, and the value of the option is zero for sure. With more frequent averaging the correlation is reduced and the value of the average strike option increases.

When would an average strike option make sense? Such an option pays off when there is a difference between the average asset price over the life of the option and the asset price at expiration. Such an option could be used for insurance in a situation where we accumulated an asset over a period of time and then sold the entire accumulated position at one price.

An Asian Solution for XYZ

If XYZ receives euros and its costs are fixed in dollars, profits are reduced if the euro depreciates—that is, if the number of dollars received for a euro is lower. We could construct an Asian put option that puts a floor, K, on the average exchange rate received. The per euro payoff of this option would be

$$\max\left(0, K - \frac{1}{12}\sum_{i=1}^{12} x_i\right) \tag{14.9}$$

For example, if we wanted to guarantee an average exchange rate of $0.90 per euro, we would set $K = \$0.9$. If the average exchange rate was less than that, we would be paid the difference between $0.9 and the average. Since we repatriate €1.2b over the course of a year, we would buy contracts covering €1.2b.

Do you recognize the kind of option described by equation (14.9)? The average is arithmetic, the average is used in place of the asset price, and it is a put. Hence, it is an *arithmetic average price Asian put*.

There are other hedging strategies XYZ could use. Table 14.2 lists premiums for several alternatives. The single put expiring at year-end is the most expensive option. As discussed earlier, it has basis risk because the year-end exchange rate could be quite different from the average. Two other strategies have signficantly less basis risk: the strip of European puts expiring monthly and the arithmetic Asian put. The strip of puts protects against low exchange rates month-by-month, whereas the Asian option protects

TABLE 14.2	Comparison of costs for alternative hedging strategies for XYZ. The price in the second row is the sum of premiums for puts expiring after 1 month, 2 months, and so forth, out to 12 months. The first, third, and fourth row premiums are calculated assuming 1 year to maturity, and then multiplied by 12. Assumes the current exchange rate is $0.9/€, option strikes are 0.9, $r_\$ = 6\%$, $r_€ = 3\%$, and dollar/euro volatility is 10%.

Hedge Instrument	Premium ($)
Put option expiring in 1 year	0.2753
Strip of monthly put options	0.2178
Geometric average price put	0.1796
Arithmetic average price put	0.1764

the 12-month average. The Asian put is cheaper since there will be situations in which some of the individual puts are valuable (for example, if the exchange rate takes a big swing in one month that is reversed subsequently), but the Asian put does not pay off. The geometric option hedges less well than the arithmetic option since the quantity being hedged (equation 14.1) is an arithmetic, not a geometric, average.

Finally, be aware that this example ignores several subtleties. The option strikes, for example, might be made to vary with the forward curve for the exchange rate. The effect of interest in equation (14.1) could also be taken into account.

14.3 BARRIER OPTIONS

A **barrier option** is an option with a payoff depending upon whether, over the life of the option, the price of the underlying asset reaches a specified level, called the *barrier*. Barrier puts and calls either come into existence or go out of existence the first time the asset price reaches the barrier. If they are in existence at expiration, they are equivalent to ordinary puts and calls. It can be tricky to define what it means for the stock price to reach a barrier. See the box on page 450 for a discussion.

Since barrier puts and calls never pay more than standard puts and calls, they are no more expensive than standard puts and calls. Barrier options are another example of a path-dependent option.

Barrier options are widely used in practice. One appeal of barrier options may be their lower premiums, although the lower premium of course reflects a lower average payoff at expiration.

Types of Barrier Options

There are three basic kinds of barrier options:

1. **Knock-out options:** These go out of existence (are "knocked-out") if the asset price reaches the barrier. If the price of the underlying asset has to fall to reach the barrier, the option is a **down-and-out.** If the price of the underlying asset has to rise to reach the barrier, the option is an **up-and-out.**

2. **Knock-in options:** These come into existence (are "knocked-in") if the barrier is touched. If the price of the underlying asset has to fall to reach the barrier, the option is a **down-and-in.** If the asset price has to rise to reach the barrier, it is an **up-and-in.**

3. **Rebate options:** These make a fixed payment if the asset price reaches the barrier. The payment can occur either at the time the barrier is reached, or at the time the option expires, in which case it is a deferred rebate. Rebate options can be either "up rebates" or "down rebates," depending on whether the barrier is above or below the current price.

Figure 14.1 illustrates how a barrier option works. The stock price starts at around $100, ends at $80, and hits the barrier of $75 about halfway through the year. If the option were a 95-strike down-and-in put, the option would knock in and pay $15 ($95 − $80) at expiration. If the option were a down-and-out put, it would be worthless at expiration. If the option were a down-and-in call, it would knock-in at $75 but still be worthless at expiration because the stock price is below the strike price.

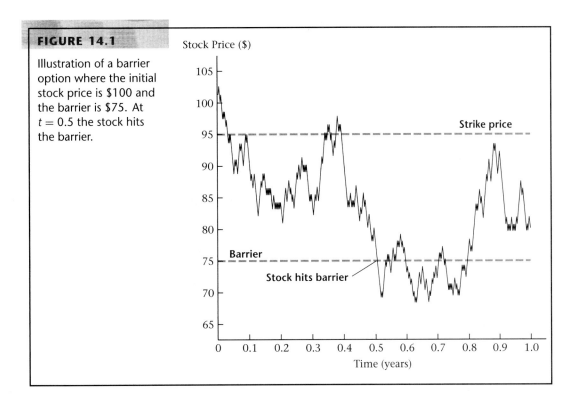

FIGURE 14.1

Illustration of a barrier option where the initial stock price is $100 and the barrier is $75. At $t = 0.5$ the stock hits the barrier.

The formulas for the various kinds of barrier options are discussed in Chapter 22. While we mention rebate options here for completeness, we will discuss them in more detail in Chapter 22.

The important parity relation for barrier options is

$$\boxed{\text{"Knock-in" option} + \text{"Knock-out" option} = \text{Ordinary option}} \qquad (14.10)$$

For example, for otherwise equivalent options, we have

$$\text{Down-and-in call} + \text{Down-and-out call} = \text{Standard call}$$

Since these option premiums cannot be negative, this equation demonstrates directly that barrier options have lower premiums than standard options.

Currency Hedging

Consider once again XYZ. Here we will focus on hedging only the cash flow occurring in 6 months to see how barrier puts compare to standard puts.

What kinds of barrier puts make sense in the context of XYZ's hedging problem? We are hedging against a decline in the exchange rate, which makes certain possibilities less attractive. A down-and-out put would be worthless when we needed it. Similarly, an

TABLE 14.3		Premiums of standard, down-and-in, and up-and-out currency put options with strikes K. The column headed "standard" contains prices of ordinary put options. Assumes $x_0 = 0.9$, $\sigma = 0.1$, $r_\$ = 0.06$, $r_€ = 0.03$, and $t = 0.5$.				

| | Standard | Down-and-In Barrier ($) | | Up-and-Out Barrier ($) | | |
Strike ($)	($)	0.8000	0.8500	0.9500	1.0000	1.0500
$K = 0.8$	0.0007	0.0007	0.0007	0.0007	0.0007	0.0007
$K = 0.9$	0.0188	0.0066	0.0167	0.0174	0.0188	0.0188
$K = 1.0$	0.0870	0.0134	0.0501	0.0633	0.0847	0.0869

up-and-in put would provide insurance only if, prior to the exchange rate falling below the strike, the exchange rate had risen so the option could knock-in.

This leaves down-and-ins and up-and-outs to consider. Table 14.3 presents prices of standard, down-and-in, and up-and-out puts with different strikes and different barriers. Consider first the row where $K = 0.8$. Notice that all options appear to have the same price. It is a useful exercise in the logic of barrier options to understand why they appear equally priced. In fact, here is an exercise to solve before reading further: Can you deduce which of the six premiums with $K = 0.8$ are exactly equal and which are merely close?

The option prices in Table 14.3 tell us something about the relative likelihood of different scenarios for the exchange rate. The ordinary put premium when the strike is 0.8 reflects the (risk-neutral) probability that the exchange rate will be below 0.8 at maturity. Both of the down-and-ins, having strikes below the starting exchange rate of 0.9 and at least 0.8, will necessarily have knocked-in should the exchange rate fall below 0.8. Described differently, a down-and-in put with a barrier above the strike is equivalent to an ordinary put. Therefore, the first three option premiums in the $K = 0.8$ row are identical.

Now consider the knock-out puts with $K = 0.8$. The difference between the ordinary put and the up-and-out put with a 0.95 barrier is that sometimes the exchange rate will drift from 0.9 to above 0.95, and then below 0.8. In this case, the ordinary put will have a payoff but the knock-out put will not.

How likely is this scenario? The low premium of 0.0007 for the ordinary put tells us that it is relatively unlikely the exchange rate will drift from 0.9 to 0.8 over 6 months. It is even less likely that the exchange rate will hit 0.95 *in those cases* when it does fall below 0.8. A knock-out may be likely, but it is rare to have a knock-out occur *in those cases when an ordinary put with a strike of 0.8 would pay off*. Thus, the knock-out feature is not subtracting much from the value of the option. This argument is even stronger for the knock-out barriers of 1.0 and 1.05. Nevertheless, since there is a chance these options will knock out and then end up in the money, the premiums are less than for the knock-in puts and are increasing with the barrier. Thus, the up-and-out prices in the $K = 0.8$ row are slightly less than the price of an ordinary put.

When the strike price is 1.0, the up-and-outs with barriers of 1.0 and 1.05 have substantially all the value of the ordinary put with the same strike. The interpretation is that most of the value of the puts comes from scenarios in which the option remains in-the-money; in those scenarios in which the option knocks out, the exchange rate on average does not fall enough for the option to be valuable.

14.4 COMPOUND OPTIONS

A **compound option** is an option to buy an option. If you think of an ordinary option as an asset—analogous to a stock—then a compound option is similar to an ordinary option.

Compound options are a little more complicated than ordinary options because there are two strikes and two expirations, one each for the underlying option and for the compound option. Suppose that the current time is t_0 and that we have a compound option which at time t_1 will give us the right to pay x to buy a European call option with strike K. This underlying call will expire at time $T > t_1$. Figure 14.2 compares the timing of the exercise decisions for this compound option with the exercise decision for an ordinary call expiring at time T.

If we exercise the compound call at time t_1, then the price of the option we receive is $C(S, K, T - t_1)$. At time T, this option will have the value $\max(0, S_T - K)$, the same as an ordinary call with strike K. At time t_1, when the compound option expires, the value of the compound option is

$$\max[C(S_{t_1}, K, T - t_1) - x, 0]$$

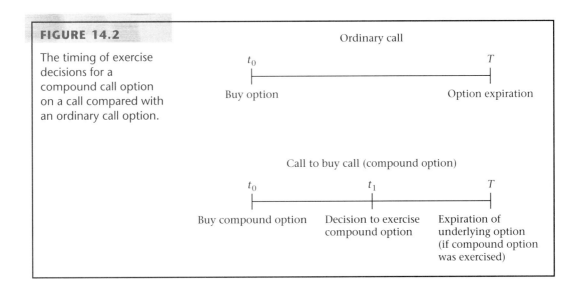

FIGURE 14.2

The timing of exercise decisions for a compound call option on a call compared with an ordinary call option.

Ordinary call

t_0 T

Buy option   Option expiration

Call to buy call (compound option)

t_0 t_1 T

Buy compound option   Decision to exercise   Expiration of compound option   underlying option (if compound option was exercised)

We only exercise the compound option if the stock price at time t_1 is sufficiently great that the value of the call exceeds the compound option strike price, x. Let S^* be the critical stock price above which the compound option is exercised. By definition, S^* satisfies

$$C(S^*, K, T - t_1) = x \qquad (14.11)$$

The compound option is exercised for $S_{t_1} > S^*$.

Thus, in order for the compound call to ultimately be valuable, there are two events that must take place. First, at time t_1 we must have $S_{t_1} > S^*$; that is, it must be worthwhile to exercise the compound call. Second, at time T we must have $S_T > K$; that is, it must be profitable to exercise the underlying call. Because two events must occur, the formula for a compound call contains a bivariate cumulative normal distribution, as opposed to the univariate distribution in the Black-Scholes formula.

Formulas for the four compound options—an option to buy a call (*CallOnCall*), an option to sell a call (*PutOnCall*), an option to buy a put (*CallOnPut*, and an option to sell a put (*PutOnPut*)—are in the chapter appendix. Valuing a compound option is different from valuing an ordinary option in part for mathematical rather than for conceptual reasons. The Black-Scholes formula assumes that the stock price is lognormally distributed. However, the price of an option—because there is a significant probability that it will be worthless—cannot be lognormally distributed. Thus, while an option on an option is conceptually similar to an option on a stock, it is mathematically different.[4] The trick in deriving a formula for the price of a compound option is to value the option based on the value of the stock, which *is* lognormally distributed, rather than the price of the underlying option, which is not lognormally distributed.

Compound Option Parity

As you might guess, there are parity relationships among the compound option prices. Suppose we buy a call on a call, and sell a put on a call, where both have the same strike, underlying option, and time to maturity. When the compound options expire, we will acquire the underlying option by paying the strike price x. If the stock price is high, we will exercise the compound call, and if the stock price is low, the compound put will be exercised and we will be forced to buy the call. Thus, the difference between the call on call and put on call premiums, plus the present value of x, must equal the premium to acquire the underlying option outright. That is,

$$\text{CallOnCall}(S, K, x, \sigma, r, t_1, t_2, \delta) - \text{PutOnCall}(S, K, x, \sigma, r, t_1, t_2, \delta) + xe^{-rt_1}$$
$$= \text{BSCall}(S, K, \sigma, r, t_2, \delta) \quad (14.12)$$

An analogous relationship holds for puts.

---

[4] Geske (1979) was the first to derive the formula for a compound option.

Options on Dividend-Paying Stocks

We saw in Chapter 11 that it is possible to price American options on dividend-paying stocks using the binomial model. It turns out that the compound option model also permits us to price an option on a stock that will pay a single discrete dividend prior to expiration.

Suppose that at time t_1 the stock will pay a dividend, D. We have a choice of exercising the option at the cum-dividend price,[5] $S_{t_1} + D$, or holding the call, which will have a value reflecting the ex-dividend price, S_{t_1}. Thus, at t_1, the value of the call option is the greater of its exercise value, $S_{t_1} + D - K$, and the option valued at the ex-dividend price, $C(S_{t_1}, T - t_1)$:

$$\max\left[C(S_{t_1}, T - t_1), S_{t_1} + D - K\right] \qquad (14.13)$$

By put-call parity, at time t_1 we can write the value of the ex-dividend unexercised call as

$$C(S_{t_1}, T - t_1) = P(S_{t_1}, T - t_1) + S_{t_1} - Ke^{-r(T-t_1)}$$

Making this substitution in equation (14.13) and rewriting the result, we obtain

$$S_{t_1} + D - K + \max\left(P[S_{t_1}, T - t_1] - \left[D - K(1 - e^{-r(T-t_1)})\right], 0\right) \qquad (14.14)$$

The value of the option is the present value of this expression.

Equation (14.14) tells us that we can value a call option on a dividend-paying stock as the sum of the following:

1. The stock, with present value S_0. (S_0 is the present value of $S_{t_1} + D$.)

2. Less the present value of the strike price, Ke^{-rt_1}.

3. Plus the value of a compound option—a call option on a put option—with strike price $D - K(1 - e^{-r(T-t_1)})$ and maturity date t_1, permitting the owner to buy a put option with strike price K and maturity date T.

In this interpretation, exercising the compound option corresponds to keeping the option on the stock unexercised. To see this, notice that if we exercise the compound option in equation (14.14), we give up the dividend and gain interest on the strike in order to acquire the put. The total is

$$S_{t_1} + P(S_{t_1}, T - t_1) - Ke^{-r(T-t_1)}$$

If we do not exercise the compound option, we receive the stock plus dividend, less the strike:

$$S_{t_1} + D - K$$

This valuation exercise provides a way to understand early exercise. We can view exercising an American call as *not* exercising the compound option to buy a put in

---

[5]The stock is *cum-dividend* if a purchaser of the stock will receive the dividend. Once the stock goes *ex-dividend*, the purchaser will not receive the dividend.

equation (14.14). The cost of not exercising is that we lose the dividend, less interest on the strike. This is exactly the intuition governing early exercise that we developed in Chapters 9 and 11.

Example 14.2   Suppose a stock with a price of $100 will pay a $5 dividend in 91 days ($t_1 = 0.249$). An option with a strike price of $90 will expire in 152 days ($T = 0.416$). Assume $\sigma = 0.3$ and $r = 0.08$. The value of a European call on the stock is

$$\text{BSCall} (\$100 - \$5e^{-(0.08 \times 0.249)}, \$90, 0.3, 0.08, 0.416, 0) = \$11.678$$

The value of an American call is computed as the present value of equation (14.14), with the exercise price for the compound option equal to $5 - 90(1 - e^{-0.08 \times (0.416 - 0.249)}) = 3.805$, and time to maturity 0.249 for the compound option and 0.416 for the underlying option. The price of the compound option is

$$\text{CallOnPut} (S, K, x, \sigma, r, t_1, T, \delta)$$
$$= \text{CallOnPut} (100, 90, 3.805, 0.30, 0.08, 0.249, 0.416, 0) = \$0.999$$

Thus, the value of the American option is

$$\$100 - \$90e^{-0.249 \times 0.08} + \$0.999 = \$12.774.$$

Moreover, the option should be exercised if the stock price cum-dividend is above $89.988.   ⚞

Currency Hedging with Compound Options

Compound options provide yet another variation on possible currency-hedging strategies. Instead of buying a 6-month put option on the euro, we could buy a call option on a put option. In effect, this compound option is giving us the opportunity to wait and see what happens.

Suppose that after 3 months we will decide whether to buy the put option. Here is one way to structure such a transaction. We could figure out what premium a 3-month put with a strike of $0.9 would have, if the exchange rate were still at 0.9. The Black-Scholes formula tells us that a 3-month at-the-money option with a strike of $0.9 would have a premium of $0.0146. (This value compares with the premium of $0.0188 for the 6-month option from Table 14.3.)

Now we can use the compound pricing formula to price a call on a put, setting the strike to equal $0.0146. The price of this compound call is $0.0093. So by paying less than two-thirds the premium of the 6-month at-the-money option, we can buy an option that permits us to pay $0.0146 for a 3-month option. By selecting this strike, we have constructed the option so that we will exercise it if the exchange rate is below 0.9. If the exchange rate goes up, we will not exercise the option and save the premium. If the exchange rate goes down, we will acquire an in-the-money option for the price of an at-the-money option. Many other structures are possible.

14.5 GAP OPTIONS

A call option pays $S - K$ when $S > K$. The strike price, K, here serves to determine both the range of stock prices where the option makes a payoff (when $S > K$) and also the size of the payoff $(S - K)$. However, we could imagine separating these two functions of the strike price. Consider an option that pays $S - 90$ when $S > 100$. Note that there is a difference between the prices that govern when there is a payoff ($100) and the price used to determine the size of the payoff ($90). This difference creates a discontinuity—or gap—in the payoff diagram, which is why the option is called a **gap option.**

Figure 14.3 shows a gap call option with payoff $S - 90$ when $S > 100$. The gap in the payoff occurs when the option payoff jumps from $0 to $10 as a result of the stock price changing from $99.99 to $100.01.

Figure 14.4 depicts a gap put that pays $90 - S$ when $S < 100$. This option demonstrates that a gap option can be structured to require, for some stock prices, a payout from the option holder at expiration. You should compare Figure 14.4 with Figure 4.12—the gap put looks very much like a paylater strategy.[6] Note that the owner of the put in Figure 14.4 is *required* to exercise the option when $S < 100$.[7]

The pricing formula for a gap call, which pays $S - K_1$ when $S > K_2$, is obtained by a simple modification of the Black-Scholes formula. Let K_1 be the strike price (the price

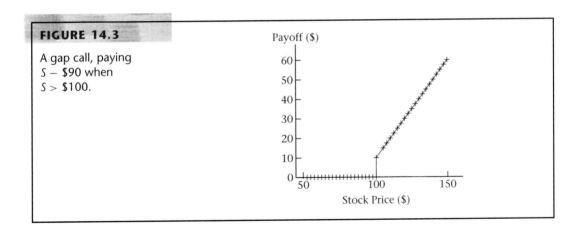

FIGURE 14.3

A gap call, paying $S - \$90$ when $S > \$100$.

---

[6]A gap option *must* be exercised when $S > K_1$ for a call or $S < K_1$ for a put. Since the owner can lose money at exercise, the term "option" is a bit of a misnomer.

[7]Recall that the paylater strategy for hedging a share of stock, discussed in Section 4.4, entails selling n puts at strike K_2 and buying $n + 1$ puts at strike $K_1 < K_2$, with n selected so that the net option premium is zero. It is possible to show that as $K_2 \to K_1$, there is a gap call that has the same profit diagram as the paylater strategy. In the limit, the paylater strategy is the same as a gap option.

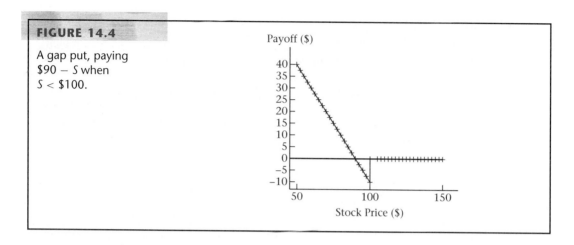

FIGURE 14.4

A gap put, paying $90 − S$ when $S < \$100$.

the option holder pays at expiration to acquire the stock) and K_2 the payment trigger (the price at which payment on the option is triggered). The formula is then

$$C(S, K_1, K_2, \sigma, r, T, \delta) = Se^{-\delta T} N(d_1) - K_1 e^{-rT} N(d_2) \tag{14.15}$$

$$d_1 = \frac{\ln(Se^{-\delta T}/K_2 e^{-rT}) + \frac{1}{2}\sigma^2 T}{\sigma\sqrt{T}}$$

$$d_2 = d_1 - \sigma\sqrt{T}$$

The modification to the put formula is similar.[8]

Returning to the XYZ currency hedging example, let's examine the use of gap options as a hedging instrument. The intuitive appeal of a gap option is that we can purchase insurance with which we are fully protected if the loss exceeds a certain amount.

Table 14.4 lists gap put premiums for different strikes and payment triggers. When the strike equals the payment trigger, the premium is the same as for an ordinary put. For a given strike, increasing the payment trigger reduces the premium. The reason is that when the payment trigger is above the strike, the option holder will have to make a payment to the option writer in some cases. For example, consider the case when the strike is $0.8 and the payment trigger is $1. If the exchange rate is 0.95, the gap put holder is obligated to sell euros worth $0.95 for only $0.8, a loss of $0.15. The option premium in this case is −$0.0888, reflecting the possibility that the option buyer will end up making a payment at maturity to the option seller. A hedger believing it highly likely that the exchange rate would be below 0.8 might be willing to receive a premium in exchange for the risk that the exchange rate would end up between 0.8 and 1.0.

....

[8]We will more fully discuss gap and related options in Chapter 22.

TABLE 14.4	Premiums of ordinary and gap put options with strikes K_1 and payment triggers K_2. Assumes $x_0 = 0.9$, $\sigma = 0.1$, $r_\$ = 0.06$, $r_\euro = 0.03$, and $t = 0.5$.			
		Payment Trigger (K_2) ($)		
Strike (K_1) ($)	**Put ($)**	**0.8**	**0.9**	**1.0**
0.8000	0.0007	0.0007	−0.0229	−0.0888
0.9000	0.0188	0.0039	0.0188	−0.0009
1.0000	0.0870	0.0070	0.0605	0.0870

Note that for a given strike, K_1, we can always find a trigger, K_2, to make the option premium zero. Thus, gap options permit us to accomplish something similar to the paylater strategy discussed in Section 4.4.

14.6 EXCHANGE OPTIONS

In Chapter 9 we discussed a hypothetical example of Microsoft and Google compensation options, in which the executives of each company were compensated only if their stock outperformed the other company's stock. An **exchange option**—also called an **outperformance option**—pays off only if the underlying asset outperforms some other asset, called the *benchmark*.

We saw in Section 9.2 that exercising any option entails exchanging one asset for another and that a standard call option is an exchange option in which the stock has to outperform cash in order for the option to pay off. In general, an exchange option provides the owner the right to exchange one asset for another, where both may be risky. The formula for this kind of option is a simple variant of the Black-Scholes formula.

European Exchange Options

Suppose an exchange call maturing T periods from today provides the right to obtain 1 unit of risky asset 1 in exchange for 1 unit of risky asset 2. (We could think of this as, for example, the right to obtain the Nikkei index by giving up the S&P 500.) Let S_t be the price of risky asset 1 and K_t the price of risky asset 2 at time t, with dividend yields δ_S and δ_K, and volatilities σ_S and σ_K. Let ρ denote the correlation between the continuously compounded returns on the two assets. The payoff to this option is

$$\max(0, S_T - K_t)$$

The formula for the price of an exchange option (see Margrabe, 1978) is

$$C(S, K, \sigma, r, T, \delta) = Se^{-\delta_S T} N(d_1) - Ke^{-\delta_K T} N(d_2) \qquad (14.16)$$

where

$$d_1 = \frac{\ln(Se^{-\delta_S T}/Ke^{-\delta_K T}) + \frac{1}{2}\sigma^2 T}{\sigma\sqrt{T}}$$

$$d_2 = d_1 - \sigma\sqrt{T}$$

$$\sigma = \sqrt{\sigma_S^2 + \sigma_K^2 - 2\rho\sigma_S\sigma_K} \tag{14.17}$$

The volatility, σ, is the volatility of $\ln(S/K)$ over the life of the option. Since $\ln(S/K) = \ln(S) - \ln(K)$, we have

$$\text{Var}[\ln(S/K)] = \text{Var}[\ln(S)] + \text{Var}[\ln(K)] - 2\text{Cov}[\ln(S), \ln(K)]$$
$$= \sigma_S^2 + \sigma_K^2 - 2\rho\sigma_S\sigma_K$$

The pricing formula for the exchange option turns out to be a simple variant of the Black-Scholes formula: The strike price is replaced by the price of the benchmark asset, the risk-free rate is replaced by the dividend yield on the benchmark asset, and the appropriate volatility is the volatility of the difference between continuously compounded returns on the two assets.

We can also interpret the pricing formula for an exchange option by considering the version of the Black-Scholes formula written in terms of prepaid forward prices, equation (12.1). Equation (14.16) is the same as equation (12.1), except that the volatility of the underlying asset is replaced by the volatility of the difference in continuously compounded returns of the underlying and strike assets. The expression $Ke^{-\delta_K T}$ is the prepaid forward price for the strike asset. The formula for an infinitely lived American exchange option is in the chapter appendix.

By setting the dividend yields and volatility appropriately, equation (14.16) yields the formulas for ordinary calls and puts:

- With a call, we give up cash to acquire stock. The dividend yield on cash is the interest rate. Thus, if we set $\delta_S = \delta$ (the dividend yield on stock), $\delta_K = r$ (the risk-free rate), and $\sigma_K = 0$ (asset 2 is risk-free), the formula reduces to the standard Black-Scholes formula for a call.

- With a put, we give up stock to acquire cash. Thus, if we set $\delta_S = r$, $\delta_K = \delta$ (the dividend yield on stock), and $\sigma_S = 0$, the formula reduces to the Black-Scholes formula for a put on stock. (Try this to verify that it works.)

Example 14.3   Consider an option to receive IBM shares by giving up Microsoft shares. We can view this as an IBM call with Microsoft as the strike asset. On November 15, 2004, the price of IBM was $95.92 and Microsoft was $27.39. Thus, one share of IBM had the same dollar value as $95.92/27.39 = 3.5020$ shares of Microsoft. For IBM and Microsoft, the most recent quarterly dividends were $0.18 and $0.08, giving annualized dividend yields of about 0.75% (IBM) and 1.17% (Microsoft). Their historical volatilities since January 2003 had been 20.30% for IBM and 22.27% for Microsoft, with a return correlation of 0.6869. The volatility of the relative prices, σ, is therefore

$$\sigma = \sqrt{0.2030^2 + 0.2227^2 - 2 \times .6869 \times .2030 \times .2227}$$
$$= 0.1694$$

Suppose the option permits exchanging equal values of Microsoft for IBM, based on the November 15 prices. We could then exchange 3.5020 shares of Microsoft for 1 share of IBM. The price of a 1-year "at-the-money" exchange call would be

BSCall ($95.92, 3.5020 × $27.39, 0.1694, 0.0117, 1, 0.0075) = $6.6133

Because Microsoft is the strike asset, we replace the risk-free rate with Microsoft's dividend yield. Assuming a risk-free rate of 2%, a plain 1-year at-the-money call on IBM would be worth

BSCall ($95.92, $95.92, 0.2030, 0.02, 1, 0.007) = $8.2545   ≋

Problem 14.19 asks you to think about the circumstances under which XYZ might hedge currency risk using exchange options.

CHAPTER SUMMARY

An exotic option is created by altering the contractual terms of a standard option. Exotic options permit hedging solutions tailored to specific problems and speculation tailored to particular views. Examples of exotic options include the following:

- *Asian options* have payoffs that are based on the average price of the underlying asset over the life of the option. The average price can be used in place of either the underlying asset (an *average price option*) or in place of the strike price (an *average strike option*). Averages can be arithmetic or geometric.

- *Barrier options* have payoffs that depend upon whether the price of the underlying asset has reached a barrier over the life of the option. These options can come into existence (*knock-in options*) or go out of existence (*knock-out options*) when the barrier is reached.

- *Compound options* are options on options: Put or call options with put or call options as the underlying asset.

- *Gap options* are options where the option payoff jumps at the price where the option comes into the money.

- *Exchange options* are options that have risky assets as both the underlying asset and the strike asset.

It is helpful in analyzing exotic options to compare them to standard options: In what ways does an exotic option resemble a standard option? How will its price compare to that of an ordinary option? When might someone use the exotic option instead of a standard option?

Further Reading

In Chapter 16 we will see some more applications of exotic options. In Chapter 21 we will discuss the underlying logic of pricing exotic options and in Chapter 22 we will discuss additional exotic options.

General books covering exotic options include Briys and Bellala (1998), Haug (1998), Wilmott (1998), and Zhang (1998). Rubinstein (1991b) discusses exchange options, Rubinstein (1991a) discusses compound options, and Rubinstein and Reiner (1991a) discuss barrier options.

Problems

To answer many of these questions you can use the exotic option functions in the spreadsheet accompanying this book.

14.1. Obtain monthly stock prices for 5 years for three stocks. Compute the arithmetic and geometric average month-end price for each stock. Which is greater?

14.2. Suppose you observe the prices {5, 4, 5, 6, 5}. What are the arithmetic and geometric averages? Now you observe {3, 4, 5, 6, 7}. What are the two averages? What happens to the difference between the two measures of the average as the standard deviation of the observations increases?

14.3. Suppose that $S = \$100$, $K = \$100$, $r = 0.08$, $\sigma = 0.30$, $\delta = 0$, and $T = 1$. Construct a standard two-period binomial stock price tree using the method in Chapter 10.

    a. Consider stock price averages computed by averaging the 6-month and 1-year prices. What are the possible arithmetic and geometric averages after 1 year?

    b. Construct a binomial tree for the *average*. How many nodes does it have after 1 year? (*Hint*: While the moves ud and du give the same year-1 price, they do *not* give the same average in year 1.)

    c. What is the price of an Asian arithmetic average price call?

    d. What is the price of an Asian geometric average price call?

14.4. Using the information in the previous problem, compute the prices of

    a. An Asian arithmetic average strike call.

    b. An Asian geometric average strike call.

14.5. Repeat Problem 14.3, except construct a *three*-period binomial tree. Assume that Asian options are based on averaging the prices every 4 months.

a. What are the possible geometric and arithmetic averages after 1 year?

b. What is the price of an Asian arithmetic average price call?

c. What is the price of an Asian geometric average price call?

14.6. Let $S = \$40$, $K = \$45$, $\sigma = 0.30$, $r = 0.08$, $T = 1$, and $\delta = 0$.

a. What is the price of a standard call?

b. What is the price of a knock-in call with a barrier of $44. Why?

c. What is the price of a knock-out call with a barrier of $44? Why?

14.7. Let $S = \$40$, $K = \$45$, $\sigma = 0.30$, $r = 0.08$, $\delta = 0$, and $T = \{0.25, 0.5, 1, 2, 3, 4, 5, 100\}$.

a. Compute the prices of knock-out calls with a barrier of $38.

b. Compute the ratio of the knock-out call prices to the prices of standard calls. Explain the pattern you see.

14.8. Repeat the previous problem for up-and-out puts assuming a barrier of $44.

14.9. Let $S = \$40$, $K = \$45$, $\sigma = 0.30$, $r = 0.08$, and $\delta = 0$. Compute the value of knock-out calls with a barrier of $60 and times to expiration of 1 month, 2 months, and so on, up to 1 year. As you increase time to expiration, what happens to the price of the knock-out call? What happens to the price of the knock-out call *relative to* the price of an otherwise identical standard call?

14.10. Examine the prices of up-and-out puts with strikes of $0.9 and $1.0 in Table 14.3. With barriers of $1 and $1.05, the .90-strike up-and-outs appear to have the same premium as the ordinary put. However, with a strike of 1.0 and the same barriers, the up-and-outs have lower premiums than the ordinary put. Explain why. What would happen to this pattern if we increased the time to expiration?

14.11. Suppose $S = \$40$, $K = \$40$, $\sigma = 0.30$, $r = 0.08$, and $\delta = 0$.

a. What is the price of a standard European call with 2 years to expiration?

b. Suppose you have a compound call giving you the right to pay $2 1 year from today to buy the option in part (a). For what stock prices in 1 year will you exercise this option?

c. What is the price of this compound call?

d. What is the price of a compound option giving you the right to *sell* the option in part (a) in 1 year for $2?

14.12. Make the same assumptions as in the previous problem.

a. What is the price of a standard European put with 2 years to expiration?

b. Suppose you have a compound call giving you the right to pay $2 1 year from today to buy the option in (a). For what stock prices in 1 year will you exercise this option?

c. What is the price of this compound call?

d. What is the price of a compound option giving you the right to *sell* the option in part (a) in 1 year for $2?

14.13. Consider the hedging example using gap options, in particular the assumptions and prices in Table 14.4.

   a. Implement the gap pricing formula. Reproduce the numbers in Table 14.4.

   b. Consider the option with $K_1 = \$0.8$ and $K_2 = \$1$. If volatility were zero, what would the price of this option be? What do you think will happen to this premium if the volatility increases? Verify your answer using your pricing model and explain why it happens.

14.14. Problem 12.11 showed how to compute approximate Greek measures for an option. Use this technique to compute delta for the gap option in Figure 14.3, for stock prices ranging from $90 to $110 and for times to expiration of 1 week, 3 months, and 1 year. How easy do you think it would be to hedge a gap call?

14.15. Consider the gap put in Figure 14.4. Using the technique in Problem 12.11, compute vega for this option at stock prices of $90, $95, $99, $101, $105, and $110, and for times to expiration of 1 week, 3 months, and 1 year. Explain the values you compute.

14.16. Let $S = \$40$, $\sigma = 0.30$, $r = 0.08$, $T = 1$, and $\delta = 0$. Also let $Q = \$60$, $\sigma_Q = 0.50$, $\delta_Q = 0.04$, and $\rho = 0.5$. What is the price of a standard 40-strike call with S as the underlying asset? What is the price of an exchange option with S as the underlying asset and $0.667 \times Q$ as the strike price?

14.17. Let $S = \$40$, $\sigma = 0.30$, $r = 0.08$, $T = 1$, and $\delta = 0$. Also let $Q = \$60$, $\sigma_Q = 0.50$, $\delta_Q = 0$, and $\rho = 0.5$. In this problem we will compute prices of exchange calls with S as the price of the underlying asset and Q as the price of the strike asset.

   a. Vary δ from 0 to 0.1. What happens to the price of the call?

   b. Vary δ_Q from 0 to 0.1. What happens to the price of the call?

   c. Vary ρ from -0.5 to 0.5. What happens to the price of the call?

   d. Explain your answers by drawing analogies to the effects of changing inputs in the Black-Scholes call pricing formula.

14.18. Let $S = \$40$, $\sigma = 0.30$, $r = 0.08$, $T = 1$, and $\delta = 0$. Also let $Q = \$40$, $\sigma_Q = 0.30$, $\delta_Q = 0$, and $\rho = 1$. Consider an exchange call with S as the price of the underlying asset and Q as the price of the strike asset.

   a. What is the price of an exchange call with S as the underlying asset and Q as the strike price?

   b. Now suppose $\sigma_Q = 0.40$. What is the price of the exchange call?

   c. Explain your answers to (a) and (b).

14.19. XYZ wants to hedge against depreciations of the euro and is also concerned about the price of oil, which is a significant component of XYZ's costs. However, there is a positive correlation between the euro and the price of oil: The euro appreciates when the price of oil rises. Explain how an exchange option based on oil and the euro might be used to hedge in this case.

14.20. A **chooser option** (also known as an **as-you-like-it option**) becomes a put or call at the discretion of the owner. For example, consider a chooser on the S&R index for which both the call, with value $C(S_t, K, T - t)$, and the put, with value $P(S_t, K, T - t)$, have a strike price of K. The index pays no dividends. At the choice date, t_1, the payoff of the chooser is

$$\max[C(S_{t_1}, K, T - t_1), P(S_{t_1}, K, T - t_1)]$$

    a. If the chooser option and the underlying options expire simultaneously, what ordinary option position is this equivalent to?

    b. Suppose that the chooser must be exercised at t_1 and that the underlying options expire at T. Show that the chooser is equivalent to a call option with strike price K and maturity T plus $e^{-\delta(T-t_1)}$ put options with strike price $Ke^{-(r-\delta)(T-t_1)}$ and expiration t_1.

14.21. Suppose that $S = \$100$, $\sigma = 30\%$, $r = 8\%$, and $\delta = 0$. Today you buy a contract which, 6 months from today, will give you one 3-month to expiration *at-the-money* call option. (This is called a **forward start** option.) Assume that r, σ, and δ are certain not to change in the next 6 months.

    a. Six months from today, what will be the value of the option if the stock price is $100? $50? $200? (Use the Black-Scholes formula to compute the answer.) In each case, what fraction of the stock price does the option cost?

    b. What investment *today* would guarantee that you had the money in 6 months to buy an at-the-money option?

    c. What would you pay today for the forward start option in this example?

    d. How would your answer change if the option were to have a strike price that was 105% of the stock price?

14.22. You wish to insure a portfolio for 1 year. Suppose that $S = \$100$, $\sigma = 30\%$, $r = 8\%$, and $\delta = 0$. You are considering two strategies. The *simple insurance strategy* entails buying one put option with a 1-year maturity at a strike price that is 95% of the stock price. The *rolling insurance strategy* entails buying one 1-month put option each month, with the strike in each case being 95% of the then-current stock price.

    a. What is the cost of the simple insurance strategy?

    b. What is the cost of the rolling insurance strategy? (*Hint*: See the previous problem.)

    c. Intuitively, what accounts for the cost difference?

Appendix 14.A: Pricing Formulas for Exotic Options

In this appendix we present formulas for some of the options discussed in this chapter.

Asian Options Based on the Geometric Average

The average can be used in place of either the asset price (an average price option) or the strike price (an average strike option).

Average price options   Suppose the risk-free rate is r and the stock has a dividend yield δ and volatility σ. We compute the average using N equally spaced prices from 0 to T, with the first observation at time T/N. A European geometric average price option can then be valued using the Black-Scholes formula for a call by setting the dividend yield and volatility equal to

$$\delta^* = \frac{1}{2}\left[r\frac{N-1}{N} + (\delta + 0.5\sigma^2)\frac{N+1}{N} - \frac{\sigma^2}{N^2}\frac{(N+1)(2N+1)}{6}\right] \qquad (14.18)$$

and

$$\sigma^* = \frac{\sigma}{N}\sqrt{\frac{(N+1)(2N+1)}{6}} \qquad (14.19)$$

With continuous sampling, i.e., $N = \infty$, the formulas reduce to

$$\delta^* = \frac{1}{2}\left(r + \delta + \frac{1}{6}\sigma^2\right)$$

and

$$\sigma^* = \sigma\sqrt{\frac{1}{3}}$$

Deriving these results is easier than you might guess, but requires some background covered in Chapters 18 and 19. The derivation is in Appendix 19.A.

Average strike options   In order to value the geometric average strike option, we need to know the correlation between the average, $G(T)$, and the terminal stock price, S_T. We also need to recognize that the strike asset is the average; hence, we value the option like an exchange option (see Section 14.6), in which we exchange the time-T stock price for its average.

In Appendix 19.A, we show that the average strike option can be valued using the Black-Scholes formula, with the following substitutions:

- Replace the risk-free rate with the "dividend yield," equation (14.18).

- Replace the volatility with

$$\sigma^{**} = \sigma\sqrt{T}\sqrt{1 + \frac{(N+1)(2N+1)}{6N^2} - 2\rho\sqrt{\frac{(N+1)(2N+1)}{6N^2}}}$$

where the correlation between $\ln(S_T)$ and $G(T)$ is given by

$$\rho = \frac{1}{2}\sqrt{\frac{6(N+1)}{2N+1}}$$

- Use the current stock price as the strike price.
- The dividend yield remains the same.

Compound Options

Letting ρ denote the correlation coefficient between normally distributed z_1 and z_2, we denote the cumulative bivariate standard normal distribution as

$$\text{Prob}(z_1 < a, z_2 < b; \rho) = \text{NN}(a, b; \rho)$$

This function is implemented in the spreadsheets as *BINORMSDIST.*

Suppose we have a compound call option to buy a call option. Let t_1 be the time to maturity of the compound option, and t_2 the time to maturity of the underlying option (obviously, we require that $t_2 > t_1$). Also let K be the strike price on the underlying option and x the strike price on the compound option; i.e., we have the right on date t_1 to pay x to acquire a call option with time to expiration $t_2 - t_1$. Define S^* as in equation (14.11); that is, S^* is the stock price at which the option is worth the strike that must be paid to get it.[9]

The formula for the price of a call option on a call option is

$$\text{CallOnCall}(S, K, x, \sigma, r, t_1, t_2, \delta) = Se^{-\delta t_2}\text{NN}\left(a_1, d_1; \sqrt{\frac{t_1}{t_2}}\right)$$

$$- Ke^{-rt_2}\text{NN}\left(a_2, d_2; \sqrt{\frac{t_1}{t_2}}\right) - xe^{-rt_1}N(a_2) \quad (14.20)$$

where

$$a_1 = \frac{\ln(S/S^*) + (r - \delta + 0.5\sigma^2)t_1}{\sigma\sqrt{t_1}}$$

$$a_2 = a_1 - \sigma\sqrt{t_1}$$

$$d_1 = \frac{\ln(S/K) + (r - \delta + 0.5\sigma^2)t_2}{\sigma\sqrt{t_2}}$$

$$d_2 = d_1 - \sigma\sqrt{t_2}$$

Notice that d_1 and d_2 are identical to the Black-Scholes d_1 and d_2, and relate to ultimate exercise of the underlying option, while a_1 and a_2 differ only in the strike price and time

---

[9]The spreadsheet function to compute S^* is called *BSCallImpS*, which is similar to the implied volatility function *BSCallImpVol*, except that it computes the stock price consistent with an option price, rather than the volatility.

to expiration and relate to exercise of the compound option. The last term in equation (14.20) reflects payment of the compound option strike price and the condition under which it is paid. The sign on the correlation term, $\sqrt{t_1/t_2}$, reflects whether exercise of the compound option is associated with an increase or decrease in the likelihood of exercising the underlying option. (The correlation is positive for a call on a call. For a call on a put, an increase in the stock price reduces the value of the put and also reduces the value of the option to buy the put; hence, the correlation is again positive.)

This discussion suggests that we can guess how the remaining compound option formulas will look. We would like to value puts on calls, calls on puts, and puts on puts.

The put on the call requires a positive sign on Ke^{-rt} and a negative sign on $Se^{-\delta t}$, since the option if ultimately exercised will require the owner to be a call writer. The underlying option is in-the-money if $S > K$; hence, we want positive d_1 and d_2. The compound option will be exercised and the strike x received if $S < S^*$, which requires negative a_1 and a_2 and a positive sign on x. Finally, if the stock price goes up, this increases the value of the call and decreases the value of the put on the call; hence, the correlation must be negatively signed. Thus, the formula is

$$\text{PutOnCall}(S, K, x, \sigma, r, t_1, t_2, \delta) = -Se^{-\delta t_2}\text{NN}\left(-a_1, d_1; -\sqrt{\frac{t_1}{t_2}}\right)$$

$$+ Ke^{-rt_2}\text{NN}\left(-a_2, d_2; -\sqrt{\frac{t_1}{t_2}}\right) + xe^{-rt_1}N(-a_2) \quad (14.21)$$

Similar arguments give us the following formulas:

$$\text{CallOnPut}(S, K, x, \sigma, r, t_1, t_2, \delta) = -Se^{-\delta t_2}\text{NN}\left(-a_1, -d_1; \sqrt{\frac{t_1}{t_2}}\right)$$

$$+ Ke^{-rt_2}\text{NN}\left(-a_2, -d_2; \sqrt{\frac{t_1}{t_2}}\right) - xe^{-rt_1}N(-a_2) \quad (14.22)$$

$$\text{PutOnPut}(S, K, x, \sigma, r, t_1, t_2, \delta) = Se^{-\delta t_2}\text{NN}\left(a_1, -d_1; -\sqrt{\frac{t_1}{t_2}}\right)$$

$$- Ke^{-rt_2}\text{NN}\left(a_2, -d_2; -\sqrt{\frac{t_1}{t_2}}\right) + xe^{-rt_1}N(a_2) \quad (14.23)$$

As an exercise, we can check that as t_1 approaches 0, the compound option formula simplifies to the greater of the value of the underlying option or zero.

Infinitely Lived Exchange Option

The logic of exchange options extends directly to the case of an infinitely lived American option. A key insight is that the optimal exercise level H really depends on the *ratio* of the values of the asset being received to the asset being given up; the absolute level is unimportant. Thus, if it is optimal to exchange stock A for stock B when the price of A is 100 and the price of B is 200, then it will be optimal to exchange A for B when their prices are 1 and 2. We therefore just need to find the *ratio* of prices at which exercise is optimal.

What payment would the bond have to make in order to sell for par ($20.90)?

b. Suppose that the oil payments are quarterly instead of annual. How large would they need to be for the bond to sell at par?

15.15. Using the information in Table 15.5, suppose we have a bond that after 2 years pays one barrel of oil plus $\lambda \times \max(0, S_2 - 20.90)$, where S_2 is the year-2 spot price of oil. If the bond is to sell for $20.90 and oil volatility is 15%, what is λ?

15.16. Using the information in Table 15.5, assume that the volatility of oil is 15%.

a. Show that a bond that pays one barrel of oil in 1 year sells today for $19.2454.

b. Consider a bond that in 1 year has the payoff $S_1 + \max(0, K_1 - S_1) - \max(0, S_1 - K_2)$. Find the strike prices K_1 and K_2 such that $K_2 - K_1 = \$2$, and the price of the bond is $19.2454. How would you describe this payoff?

c. Now consider a claim that in 1 year pays $S_1 - \$20.50 + \max(0, K_1 - S_1) - \max(0, S_1 - K_2)$, where K_1 and K_2 are from the previous answer. What is the value of this claim? What have you constructed?

15.17. Swaps often contain caps or floors. In this problem, you are to construct an oil contract that has the following characteristics: The initial cost is zero. Then in each period, the buyer pays the market price of oil if it is between K_1 and K_2; otherwise, if $S < K_1$, the buyer pays K_1, and if $S > K_2$, the buyer pays K_2 (there is a floor and a cap). Assume that $K_2 - K_1 = \$2$ and that oil volatility is 15%.

a. If there is a single settlement date in 1 year, what are K_1 and K_2?

b. If the swap settles quarterly for eight quarters, what are K_1 and K_2?

15.18. You have been asked to construct an oil contract that has the following characteristics: The initial cost is zero. Then in each period, the buyer pays $S - \overline{F}$, with a cap of $\$21.90 - \overline{F}$ and a floor of $\$19.90 - \overline{F}$. Assume oil volatility is 15%. What is $\overline{F}$?

15.19. Using Figure 3.16 on page 84 as the basis for a discussion, explain under what circumstances an investor might prefer a PEPS to the stock or vice versa.

15.20. Consider again the Netscape PEPS discussed in this chapter and assume the following: the price of Netscape is $39.25; Netscape is not expected to pay dividends; the interest rate is 7%; and the 5-year volatility of Netscape is 40%. What is the theoretical value of the PEPS?

15.21. A DECS contract pays two shares if $S_T < 27.875$, 1.667 shares if the price is above $S_T > 33.45$, and $27.875 and $55.75 otherwise. The quarterly dividend is $0.87. Value this DECS assuming that $S = \$26.70$, $\sigma = 35\%$, $r = 9\%$, and $T = 3.3$ and that the underlying stock pays a quarterly dividend of $0.10.

The next two problems are based on the M&I stock purchase contract.

15.22. A stock purchase contract with a zero initial premium calls for you to pay for one share of stock in 3 years. The stock price is $100 and the 3-year interest rate is 3%.

    a. If you expect the stock to have a zero dividend yield, what price in 3 years would you agree to pay for the stock?

    b. If the stock has a 2% dividend yield, what price in 3 years would you agree to pay for the stock?

    c. Now suppose that the stock purchase contract calls for you to pay $100 in 3 years for one share of stock. What annual payment on the stock purchase contract would be fair if the dividend yield on the stock is zero? What if it is 4%?

15.23. Value the M&I stock purchase contract assuming that the 3-year interest rate is 3% and the M&I volatility is 15%. How does your answer change if volatility is 35%?

CHAPTER 16

Corporate Applications

In this chapter we look at some contexts in which firms issue derivatives, either explicitly or implicitly. First, Black and Scholes (1973) observed that common debt and equity can be viewed as options, with the firm's assets as the underlying asset. We show how this insight can be used to price debt subject to default, as well as the implications for determining how leverage affects the expected return on equity. We also examine warrants, convertible debt, and callable debt as examples of securities that explicitly contain options.

Second, many firms grant options as compensation to employees. These options typically cannot be exercised for some period of time and cannot be sold, so they raise interesting valuation issues. In addition, compensation options often have nonstandard features.

Third, merger deals in which firm A offers their own stock to buy firm B sometimes offer price protection to firm B shareholders. This protection can take the form of a collar. We examine one merger—Northrop Grumman-TRW—that used a collar for this purpose.

16.1 EQUITY, DEBT, AND WARRANTS

Firms often issue securities that have derivative components. For example, firms issue options to employees for financing, and convertible debt is a bond coupled with a call option. However, even simple securities, such as ordinary debt and equity, can be viewed as derivatives. In this section we examine both implicit and explicit options issued by firms.

Debt and Equity as Options

Consider a firm with the following very simple capital structure. The firm has nondividend-paying equity outstanding, along with a single zero-coupon debt issue. Represent the time t values of the assets of the firm, the debt, and the equity as A_t, B_t, and E_t. The debt matures at time T and has maturity value $\overline{B}$.

We assume throughout this section that there are no taxes, bankruptcy costs, transaction costs, or other market imperfections.

The value of the debt and equity at time T will depend upon the value of the firm's assets. Equity-holders are the legal owners of the firm; in order for them to have unambiguous possession of the firm's assets, they must pay the debt-holders $\overline{B}$ at time T. If $A_T > \overline{B}$, equity-holders will pay $\overline{B}$ to the bondholders since equity will then be worth the value of the assets less the payment to bondholders, or $A_T - \overline{B} > 0$. However, if $A_T < \overline{B}$, equity-holders would have to inject additional funds in order to pay off the debt. In this case equity-holders would declare bankruptcy, permitting the bondholders to take possession of the assets. Therefore, the value of the equity at time T, E_T, is

$$E_T = \max(0, A_T - \overline{B}) \tag{16.1}$$

This expression is the payoff to a call option with the assets of the firm as the underlying asset and $\overline{B}$ as the strike price.

Because equity-holders control the firm, bondholders receive the *smallest* payment to which they are legally entitled. If the firm is bankrupt—i.e., if $A_T < \overline{B}$—the bond-holders receive A_T. If the firm is solvent—i.e., if $A_T \geq \overline{B}$—the bondholders receive $\overline{B}$. Thus the value of the debt is

$$B_T = \min(A_T, \overline{B}) \tag{16.2}$$

This expression can be written[1]

$$B_T = A_T + \min(0, \overline{B} - A_T)$$
$$= A_T - \max(0, A_T - \overline{B}) \tag{16.3}$$

Equation (16.3) says that the bondholders own the firm, but have written a call option to the equity-holders. This way of expressing the debt value explains where the call option in equation (16.1) comes from. Summing equations (16.1) and (16.2) gives the the total value of the firm—equity plus debt—as A_T.

A different way to write equation (16.2) is the following:

$$B_T = \overline{B} + \min(0, A_T - \overline{B})$$
$$= \overline{B} - \max(0, \overline{B} - A_T) \tag{16.4}$$

The interpretation of equation (16.4) is that the bondholders own risk-free debt with a payoff equal to $\overline{B}$, but have written a put option on the assets with strike price $\overline{B}$.[2]

Example 16.1　Suppose a firm has issued zero-coupon debt with a face value of $\overline{B} = \$6000$. The maturity value of the equity is given by equation (16.1) and the maturity value of the debt is given by equation (16.4). The two payoffs are graphed in Figure 16.1 as a function of corporate assets at maturity.　❧

---

[1] To follow these derivations, note that $\min(0, x - y) = -\max(0, y - x)$.

[2] A bond with a payoff specified as in equation (16.2) is a **debenture**—a bond for which payments are secured only by the general credit-worthiness of the company. Such a bond is said to be *unsecured*. It is also possible for bonds to be secured by specific collateral. For example, lenders to airlines may have an airplane as collateral for their bond.

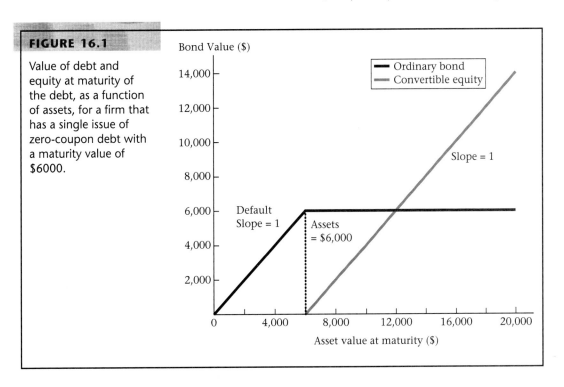

FIGURE 16.1

Value of debt and equity at maturity of the debt, as a function of assets, for a firm that has a single issue of zero-coupon debt with a maturity value of $6000.

If we assume that the assets of the firm are lognormally distributed, then we can use the Black-Scholes model to value the payoffs to the firm's equity and debt, equations (16.1) and (16.4). For purposes of option pricing, the firm's assets are the underlying asset, the strike price is the promised payment on debt, $\overline{B}$, the volatility of the firm's assets, σ, is volatility, and the payout rate from the firm becomes the dividend yield. If the risk-free rate is r and the debt matures at time T, we have

$$E_t = \text{BSCall}(A_t, \overline{B}, \sigma, r, T - t, \delta) \qquad (16.5)$$

$$B_t = A_t - E_t \qquad (16.6)$$

Assuming that the debt is zero-coupon, we can compute the yield to maturity on debt, ρ. By definition of the yield to maturity, we have $B_t = \overline{B}e^{-\rho(T-t)}$; hence we can solve for ρ to obtain

$$\rho = \frac{1}{T - t}\ln(\overline{B}/B_t) \qquad (16.7)$$

This model of the firm is very simple, in that there are no coupons or dividends, no refinancings or subsequent debt issues, etc. It is possible to create more complicated models of a firm's capital structure; nevertheless, this model provides a starting point for understanding how leverage affects returns on debt and equity and determines the yield on risky debt.

Viewing debt and equity as options also provides a framework for thinking about credit risk. Equation (16.4) shows that defaultable debt is equivalent to owning default-free debt plus a put option on the assets of the firm. An investor owning a corporate bond could buy such a put; the result would be economically equivalent to owning a default-free bond. Thus, the value of the put is the value of insurance to protect bondholders against default. We will examine credit risk more in Chapter 26.

Example 16.2   Suppose that $\overline{B} = \$100$, $A_0 = \$90$, $r = 6\%$, $\sigma = 25\%$, $\delta = 0$ (the firm makes no payouts), and $T = 5$ years. We have

$$E_0 = \text{BSCall}(\$90, \$100, 0.25, 0.06, 5, 0)$$
$$= \$27.07$$

The value of the debt is

$$B_0 = \$90 - \$27.07$$
$$= \$62.93$$

The debt-to-value ratio of this firm is therefore $\$62.93/\$90 = 0.699$. The yield to maturity on debt is

$$\rho = \frac{1}{5} \ln(100/62.93)$$
$$= 0.0926$$

The debt yield of 9.26% is 326 basis points greater than the risk-free rate.   ❧

Leverage and the Expected Return on Debt and Equity

Example 16.2 shows that, because of the possibility of bankruptcy, the yield to maturity on debt exceeds the risk-free rate. However, an investor in the bond earns the yield to maturity only if the firm does not go bankrupt. Accounting for the possibility of bankruptcy, the investor on average will earn a return less than the yield to maturity and greater than the risk-free rate. In effect, debt that can default bears some of the risk of the assets, sharing this risk with the equity-holders.

We can compute the expected return on both debt and equity using the concept of *option elasticity*, which we discussed in Chapter 12. Recall that the elasticity of an option tells us the relationship between the expected return on the underlying asset and that on the option. Using equation (12.10), we can compute the expected return on equity as

$$r_E = r + (r_A - r) \times \Omega_E \tag{16.8}$$

where r_A is the expected return on assets, r is the risk-free rate, and Ω_E is the elasticity of the equity. Using equation (16.5), elasticity is

$$\Omega_E = \frac{A_t \Delta_E}{E_t} \tag{16.9}$$

where Δ_E is the option delta.

We can compute the expected return on debt using the debt elasticty, Ω_B:

$$r_B = r + (r_A - r) \times \Omega_B \tag{16.10}$$

The elasticity calculation is slightly more involved for debt than for equity. Since we compute debt value as $B_t = A_t - E_t$, the elasticity of debt is a weighted average of the asset and equity elasticities:

$$\Omega_B = \frac{A_t}{A_t - E_t}\Omega_A - \frac{E_t}{A_t - E_t}\Omega_E \tag{16.11}$$

The elasticity of any asset with respect to itself is one, so we have $\Omega_A = 1$.

Using equations (16.8)–(16.11), you can verify that if you owned a proportional interest in the debt and equity of the firm, the expected return on your portfolio would be the expected return on the assets of the firm:

$$(\%\text{Equity} \times r_E) + (\%\text{Debt} \times r_B) = r_A \tag{16.12}$$

It bears emphasizing that this relationship requires that r_B represent the *expected return* on debt, not the yield to maturity.

Using the option model, we can also see how the dollar values of debt and equity change when there is a change in the value of the assets. In other words, we can ask what the *deltas* of debt and equity are. From equation (16.5), if assets increase in value by \$1, equity will increase by the delta of the call option. From equation (16.6), debt will increase by one less the equity delta.

It is instructive to compare the expected return calculation for equity in equation (16.8) with a common alternative calculation. If we assume the debt is risk-free, the expected return on equity is[3]

$$\hat{r}_E = r + (r_A - r)\frac{1}{\%\text{Equity}} \tag{16.13}$$

This is the familiar Modigliani-Miller expression for the expected return on levered equity. Equation (16.13) can be obtained from equation (16.8) by assuming that the delta of the equity is one, which implies that the delta of the debt is zero. Viewing debt and equity as options, by contrast, allows us take into the account the effects of possible bankruptcy. Equation (16.8) assumes that debt- and equity-holders share the risk of the assets, so equation (16.3) will give a higher r_E than equation (16.8).

---

[3]This expression is also sometimes written as $r_E = r_A + (r_A - r) \times D/E$.

Example 16.3   Use the same assumptions as in Example 16.2, and suppose that the expected return on assets, r_A, is 10%. The equity delta is

$$\text{BSCallDelta}(90, 100, 0.25, 0.06, 5, 0) = 0.735$$

The debt delta is $1 - 0.735 = 0.265$. Thus, if the asset value increases by \$1, the value of the debt increases by \$0.735 and the value of the debt increases by \$0.265.

Using equation (16.9), the equity elasticity is

$$\frac{90 \times 0.735}{27.07} = 2.443$$

The expected return on equity is therefore

$$r_E = 0.06 + (0.1 - 0.06) \times 2.443$$
$$= 0.1577$$

Using equation (16.11), the debt elasticity is

$$\frac{90}{90 - 27.07} \times 1 - \frac{27.07}{90 - 27.07} \times 2.443 = 0.3793$$

The expected return on debt is therefore

$$r_B = 0.06 + (0.1 - 0.06) \times 0.3793$$
$$= 0.0752$$

Note that the 7.52% expected return on debt is greater than the risk-free rate (6%) and less than the yield to maturity on debt (9.26%).

If we owned equity and debt in the same proportion in which they were issued by the firm, we would have a return of

$$\frac{27.07}{90} \times 0.1577 + \frac{90 - 27.07}{90} \times 0.0752 = 0.1000$$

Since 10% is the expected return on assets, this illustrates equation (16.12).

Finally, if we were to (erroneously) assume that debt is risk-free and use equation (16.13) to compute the expected return on equity, we would obtain

$$\hat{r}_E = 0.06 + \frac{1}{27.07/90}(0.1 - 0.06)$$
$$= 0.1929$$

This calculation gives an expected return on equity substantially greater than 15.77%.

❧

This example computes expected returns for a particular leverage ratio. As the firm becomes more levered, equity-holders bear more asset risk per dollar of equity. If assets have a positive beta, the expected return on equity will increase with leverage.

At the same time, debt also becomes riskier as leverage increases and there is increased chance of default on the debt.

Figure 16.2 graphs the debt-to-asset ratio (computed using equation 16.5) and the expected return on equity (computed using equation 16.8) as a function of the asset value of the firm, using the assumptions in Example 16.3. For very low asset values, the debt-to-asset ratio is almost 1 and the expected return on equity is almost 40%. As the asset value exceeds $200, the expected return on equity is about 12%.

For purposes of comparison, Figure 16.2 graphs the expected return on equity, computed assuming that the debt is risk-free. For asset values close to $200, the

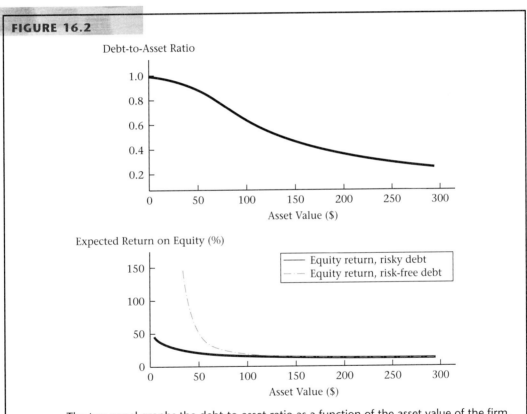

FIGURE 16.2

Debt-to-Asset Ratio

Expected Return on Equity (%)

— Equity return, risky debt
----- Equity return, risk-free debt

Asset Value ($)

The top panel graphs the debt-to-asset ratio as a function of the asset value of the firm, using the Black-Scholes formula to compute the value of the debt. The bottom panel graphs the expected return on equity as a function of the asset value of the firm, using equations (16.13) and (16.8). Both graphs assume that there is a single zero-coupon debt issue with maturity value $100 and 5 years to maturity, and also assume that $r = 6\%$, $\sigma = 25\%$ (for the assets), and $\delta = 0$.

difference is less than 20 basis points. For a very highly levered (low asset value) firm, however, the difference in Figure 16.2 is dramatic.

Conflicts between debt and equity   The idea that equity is a call option on the firm and that corporate bonds are risky provides insights into relations between debt- and equity-holders. Since equity-holders control the firm, bondholders may be concerned that equity-holders will take actions that would harm them, or may fail to take actions that would help them.

There are two decisions equity-holders make that affect the relative value of debt and equity. First, equity-holders can affect the volatility of assets. Equity-holders can increase asset volatility either by increasing the operating risk of existing assets, or by "asset substitution," replacing existing assets with riskier assets. An increase in volatility, other things equal, increases the value of the equity-holder's call option and therefore reduces the value of debt. In Example 16.2, the vega of the equity is 0.66, so an increase in asset volatility of 0.01 leads to an increase in the market value of equity of $0.66, which is $0.66/27.07 = 2.4\%$ of equity value. Debt value would decline by $0.66.

A second decision that equity-holders can make is the size of payouts to share-holders, such as dividends and share repurchases. To see why payouts are a potential problem for bondholders, suppose that the firm makes an unexpected one-time $1 payout to shareholders. This payout reduces assets by $1. The delta of the equity with respect to assets is less than one, so the value of equity declines by less than $1. Since the value of debt plus equity equals assets, *the value of the debt must decline by one less the delta of the equity.* Unanticipated payouts to equity-holders therefore can hurt bondholders.

Bondholders are well aware of the potentially harmful effects of asset substitution and dividends. Bond covenants (legal restrictions on the firm) often limit the ability of the firm to change assets or pay dividends. Viewing debt and equity as options makes it clear why such restrictions exist.

Bondholders also encounter problems from actions that shareholders fail to take. Suppose the firm has a project worth $2 that requires shareholders to make a $1 invest-ment. If shareholders make the investment, they pay $1, the value of the assets increases by $2 and the value of the shares rises by $2 \times \Delta$. The gain to shareholders is less than the increase in the value of assets. The difference of $2 - 2 \times \Delta$ goes to the bondholders. In making a positive NPV investment, shareholders help bondholders.

The shareholders in this example only will make the investment if the value of shares goes up by more than the $1 they invest, which will only occur if $\Delta > 0.5$. In order for shareholders to be willing to invest, the NPV must be great enough that shareholders gain after allowing for the value increase that is lost to debt-holders.[4] Thus, because of debt, the shareholders may fail to make positive NPV investments. A related problem is asset substitution: Shareholders might make negative NPV investments that increase asset risk, thereby transferring value from bondholders to stockholders.

....

[4]The idea that the debt may harm investment incentives is developed in Myers (1977).

Multiple Debt Issues

The option-based model of debt accommodates multiple issues of zero-coupon debt with different seniorities, as long as all debt expires on the same date. By definition, more senior debt has priority in the event of bankruptcy. Suppose that there are three debt issues, with maturity values of $30, $30, and $40, ranked in seniority from highest to lowest. We will refer to each distinct level of seniority as a *tranche*. The value of equity will be the same as in Example 16.2, since it is still necessary for equity-holders to pay $100 to receive ownership of the assets. However, the option pricing approach permits us to assign appropriate yields to each level of debt.

Senior debt-holders are the first in line to be paid. They own the firm and have written a call option permitting the next set of bondholders to buy the firm from them by paying the maturity value of the senior debt, $30. Intermediate debt-holders own a call option permitting them to buy the firm for $30, and have sold a call option permitting the junior bondholders to buy the firm for $60. Junior bondholders in turn own the call option to buy the firm for $60, and have written a call option permitting the equity-holders to buy the firm for $100. The values of these options are

$$\text{BSCall}(\$90, \$30, 0.25, 0.06, 5, 0) = \$67.82 \qquad (16.14)$$

$$\text{BSCall}(\$90, \$60, 0.25, 0.06, 5, 0) = \$47.25 \qquad (16.15)$$

$$\text{BSCall}(\$90, \$100, 0.25, 0.06, 5, 0) = \$27.07 \qquad (16.16)$$

Table 16.1 summarizes the value, yield to maturity, and expected return of each tranche of debt. The junior tranche has a yield to maturity of 13.69%, very close to the required return on equity. The senior tranche, according to the model, is almost risk-free.

The expected returns in Table 16.1 are computed using option elasticities. To illustrate the calculation, consider the junior bond, which is created by buying a 60-strike call on the assets of the firm and selling a 100-strike call. The two option elasticities are 1.7875 (60-strike) and 2.4432 (100-strike). Using the fact that the elasticity of a portfolio

TABLE 16.1 Market values, yields, and expected returns on three debt tranches.

Claim	Owns	Writes	Value ($)	Yield (%)	Expected Return (%)
Senior bonds	Assets	C(30)	22.18	6.04	6.04
Intermediate bonds	C(30)	C(60)	20.57	7.54	7.03
Junior bonds	C(60)	C(100)	20.18	13.69	9.63
Equity	C(100)		27.07		15.77

is a weighted average of the elasticities of the portfolio components, the elasticity of the junior bond is

$$\frac{47.25}{47.25 - 27.07} \times 1.7875 - \frac{27.07}{47.25 - 27.07} \times 2.4432 = 0.9077$$

The expected return on the junior debt is therefore

$$r_{\text{junior}} = 0.06 + (0.10 - 0.06) \times 0.9077 = 0.0963$$

Table 16.1 makes it clear why debt cannot be treated as a single homogeneous class when firms with complex capital structures enter bankruptcy. The interests of the most junior debt-holders may well resemble the interests of equity-holders more than those of senior debt-holders.

Warrants

Firms sometimes issue options explicitly. If a firm issues a call option on its own stock, it is known as a **warrant.** (The term "warrant" is used here to denote options on a firm issued by the firm itself, though in practice the term includes traded options issued in fixed supply.) When a warrant is exercised, the warrant-holder pays the firm the strike price, K, and receives a share worth more than K (or else the holder would not have exercised the warrant). Thus, the act of exercise is dilutive to other shareholders in the sense that the firm has sold a share for less than it is worth. Of course, existing shareholders are aware of warrants outstanding and can anticipate this potential exercise. The problem is how to value the warrant, and how to value the equity given the existence of warrants. This valuation problem does not arise with ordinary options, because they are traded by third parties and their exercise has no effect on the firm.

To see how to value a warrant, suppose the firm has n shares outstanding, and that the outstanding warrants are European, on m shares, with strike price K. The asset value is A.

At expiration, if warrant-holders exercise the warrants, they pay K per share and receive m shares. After the warrants are exercised, the firm has assets worth $A + mK$, hence exercised warrants are worth

$$\frac{A + mK}{n + m} - K = \frac{n}{n + m}\left(\frac{A}{n} - K\right) \tag{16.17}$$

The expression A/n is the value of a share of equity in the absence of warrants. Thus, equation (16.17) suggests that we can value a warrant in two steps. First, we compute an option price with A/n as the underlying asset and K as the strike price, ignoring dilution. Second, we multiply the result by a dilution correction factor, $n/(n + m)$. This second step accounts for the fact that warrant exercise changes the number of shares outstanding, with the new shares issued at a "below-market" price of K. The warrant can be valued by using the Black-Scholes formula:

$$\frac{n}{n + m}\text{BSCall}\left(\frac{A}{n}, K, \sigma, r, t, \delta\right) \tag{16.18}$$

Convertible Bonds

In addition to issuing warrants directly, firms can issue warrants embedded in bonds. A **convertible bond** is a bond that, at the option of the bondholder, can be exchanged for shares in the issuing company. A simple convertible bond resembles the equity-linked notes we studied in Chapter 15, except that the bond is convertible into the company's own shares rather than the shares of a third party. The call option in the bond gives the bondholder the right to surrender the bond's maturity payment, M, in exchange for q shares. The valuation of a convertible bond entails valuing both debt subject to default and a warrant.

Suppose there are m bonds with maturity payment M, each of which is convertible into q shares. The value of the firm at time T is A_T. If there are n original shares outstanding, then there will be $n + mq$ shares if the bond is converted. At expiration, the bondholders will convert if the value of per share of the assets after conversion, $A_T/(n + mq)$, exceeds the value per share of the maturity payment that bondholders would forgo:

$$\frac{A_T}{n + mq} > \frac{M}{q}$$

or

$$\frac{n}{n + mq}\left(\frac{A_T}{n} - \frac{M}{q}\frac{n + mq}{n}\right) > 0 \tag{16.19}$$

This expression is different from equation (16.12) for warrants, because rather than injecting new cash into the firm when they convert, the bondholders instead avoid taking cash out of the firm.

Conversion occurs if the assets increase sufficiently in value. If the assets decrease, the firm could default on the promised maturity payment. Assuming the convertible is the only debt issue, bankruptcy occurs if assets are worth less the promised payment to all convertible holders, or $A_T < mM$. The payoff of the convertible at maturity, time T, is

$$\underbrace{mM}_{\text{Bond}} - \underbrace{\max\left(0, mM - A_T\right)}_{\text{Written put}} + \underbrace{mq \times \frac{n}{n + mq} \times \max\left(0, \frac{A_T}{n} - \frac{M}{q}\frac{n + mq}{n}\right)}_{mq \text{ Purchased warrants}} \tag{16.20}$$

Thus, owning m convertibles can be valued as owning a risk-free bond with maturity payment mM, selling a put on the firm's assets, and buying mq warrants with strike $M/q \times (n + mq)/n$.

Equation (16.20) can be rewritten as

$$\max\left[\min\left(mM, A_T\right), \frac{mq}{n + mq}A_T\right] \tag{16.21}$$

This version of the convertible payoff can be interpreted as follows: Shareholders give bondholders the least they can ($\min[M, A_T/m]$); if it is optimal to do so, convertible holders can then exchange this amount for the conversion value, which is their proportionate share of the assets $(mq/[n + mq] \times A_T)$.

Example 16.4　Suppose a firm has issued $m = 6$ convertible bonds, each with maturity value $M = \$1000$ and convertible into $q = 50$ shares. The firm has $n = 400$ common shares outstanding. Figure 16.3 shows the maturity payoff for the aggregate value of the convertible bonds, comparing it with the maturity payoff of otherwise identical nonconvertible bonds issued by the same firm. The six bonds have a total promised maturity value of \$6000, so default occurs when assets are below that level. Equation (16.19) implies that conversion occurs when assets exceed $\$1000 \times 700/50 = \$14,000$. The slope of the convertible payoff above \$14,000 is $mq/(n + mq) = 3/7$, less than the slope in default, because convertible investors share gains with existing shareholders, but once in default, convertible bondholders bear additional losses alone (in default, shares are already worthless).　❦

Just as we valued ordinary zero-coupon bonds with the Black-Scholes formula, we can also use the Black-Scholes formula to value a bond convertible at maturity.

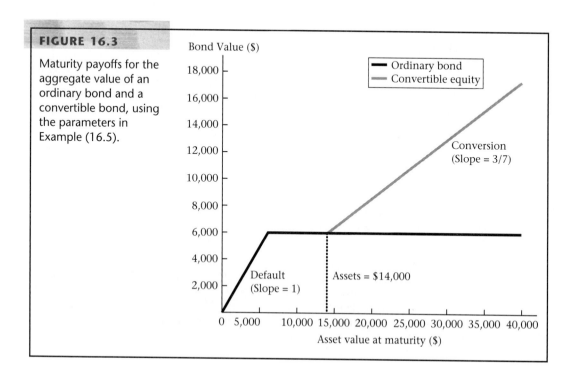

FIGURE 16.3

Maturity payoffs for the aggregate value of an ordinary bond and a convertible bond, using the parameters in Example (16.5).

the noncallable bonds are worth $4912.38, for a yield of 6%. (If assets reach that node, default will not occur.) The firm calls the callable bond at that node since it is now possible to issue default-free debt. The prospect of this call prevents the bondholders from receiving a capital gain. This in turn lowers the initial price of the bond. Problem 16.15 asks you to compute share prices at each node so that you can see the effect on shareholders of the different bonds.

Callable convertible bonds We now consider noncallable and callable convertible bonds, Panels E and F in Figure 16.4. Note first that, as in Example 16.5, the yield on the convertible noncallable bond (2.39%) is lower than that on the ordinary bond (7.29%) because convertible bondholders receive a call option and pay for this with a lower yield.

Using equation (16.21), the year 5 value for the convertible bond is

$$\max[\min(mM, A_5), \frac{mq}{n + mq} A_5]$$

In Panel E in Figure 16.3, bondholders convert at the top two nodes in year 5, receive the maturity payment in cash at the next node, and the firm defaults at the bottom node.

Prior to maturity, the convertible investor values the bond as the greater of its conversion value and the value of letting the bond live one more period:

$$B_t = \max [\text{ Continue to hold, convert }]$$

$$= \max \left[e^{-rh}(p B_{t+h}^{+} + (1 - p)B_{t+h}^{-}), \frac{mq}{n + mq} A_t \right] \qquad (16.23)$$

B_t is the total value of the bonds. You may recognize this expression as almost identical to equation (10.10) for valuing an American call option on a stock. The difference is that the payoff is the conversion value instead of $S_t - K$.

When the bond is both convertible and callable, there is a tug-of-war between the firm and the bond investors. We can imagine the bond value being determined as follows: The bondholders decide whether to hold or convert (maximizing the bond value). Given this decision, the firm decides whether to call (minimizing the bond value). If the firm calls, bondholders revisit their decision about whether or not to convert (again maximizing the bond value, conditional upon the behavior of the firm). This chain of reasoning implies the following valuation equation:

$$B_t = \max \{\min [\max(\text{ Continue to Hold, Convert}), \text{ Call }], \text{ Convert }\}$$

$$= \max \left\{ \min \left[\max \left(\underbrace{e^{-rh}[p B_{t+h}^{+} + (1 - p)B_{t+h}^{-}]}_{\text{Hold}}, \underbrace{\frac{mq}{n + mq} A_t}_{\text{Convert}} \right), \underbrace{K_t^{\text{call}}}_{\text{Call}} \right], \right.$$

$$\left. \underbrace{\frac{mq}{n + mq} A_t}_{\text{Convert}} \right\} \qquad (16.24)$$

As you would expect, the ability to call a convertible bond lowers its price, raising its yield from 2.39% to 4.01%. By comparing Panels E and F in Figure 16.4, you can see why this happens. In year 1.67 at the top node, it is optimal to wait to convert if the bond is noncallable. This gives a bond value in Panel E of $7578.78. However, if the bond is callable using the call schedule in Panel C, the firm will call at the top node in year 1.67. In response, the bondholders convert, giving them 50 shares worth $6976.66. The bond is worth less because shareholders cannot delay the conversion. The firm does not call at the lower node in year 1.67 because the credit quality of the bond deteriorates at that node.

Bond Valuation Based on the Stock Price

The binomial examples in Figure 16.4 assume that the assets of the firm follow a binomial process and use the resulting tree to value a convertible bond. This approach becomes complicated when the firm's capital structure contains multiple bonds and convertible securities.

An alternative approach, often used in practice, is to base valuation of a convertible bond on a binomial tree for the stock, rather than on assets. A standard binomial tree for the stock, however, will never reach a zero stock price, and thus a convertible bond valued on this tree will be priced as if it were default-free. This raises the question: How can we incorporate bond default risk into the pricing procedure?

Tsiveriotis and Fernandes (1998) suggest valuing separately the bond income and the stock income from an optimally managed convertible bond. Their procedure accounts for default by discounting bond income at a rate greater than the risk-free rate, while the component of the bond income related to conversion into stock is discounted at the risk-free rate.

Other Bond Features

It is possible to issue bonds that are considerably more complex than those we have considered. Conversion and call schedules can vary with time in complicated ways. Bonds can be *puttable*, meaning that the investor can sell them back to the firm at a predetermined price. Bonds can pay *contingent interest*, meaning that if a particular event occurs, the interest rate on the bond changes.

As we saw in Chapter 15, particular structures are often a response to tax and accounting considerations. Another example is the use of *contingent convertible* bonds, also known as "co-co's."

Firms report earnings on a *per-share* basis. For a firm that has issued only shares and ordinary debt, computing earnings per share (EPS) is straightforward since there is no ambiguity about the number of shares outstanding. However, if a firm has issued convertible debt or warrants, how many shares should the firm use in computing EPS? Under financial accounting rules in the United States, the firm must compute the worst-case fully diluted earnings per share. When the firm has issued a convertible security, this generally means adding back to earnings after-tax interest on the convertible, and adding the number of convertible shares to shares outstanding.

Co-Co Puffery?

Gм was taken by surprise in July 2004 when the FASB proposed new rules governing the accounting treatment of contingent convertibles:[6]

> The earnings of General Motors will be reduced by $1 per share, or 15 percent of the carmaker's target for the year, by new accounting rules for an increasingly popular type of bond expected to come into force this winter.
>
> John Devine, chief financial officer, said the change to the treatment of contingently convertible bonds would confuse investors, and GM would not have issued them if it had known it was coming. GM is thought to be the largest issuer of the "co-co" bonds, with over $8 billion outstanding....
>
> "To say the least, this is very disruptive to us," Mr. Devine said. "It has significant ramifications for how investors look at our business. It confuses investors."...
>
> Mr. Devine expects the new rules to come into force towards the end of the year, and GM would then have to restate its eps figures. Net income would be unaffected.

> Co-co securities were first introduced in 2000 and have become popular because of their accounting advantages. They make up the bulk of new issuance in the convertible market, but will be far less attractive under the new rules.
>
> "It will substantially decrease the number of co-cos," one convertible securities analyst said.

Two weeks later, GM had found a solution to its dilemma:[7]

> Devine ... said GM had found a solution to the problem that would meet the requirements of the Financial Accounting Standards Board, which oversees US accounting.
>
> "GM would waive its right to issue stock to settle at least the principal amount of debt," Mr. Devine told the Management Briefing Seminars, an annual automotive conference in Michigan.
>
> "This means we would use cash rather than stock and significantly limit the dilutive effect."...

Accounting for instruments like co-cos remains a confusing and contentious issue.

In recent years firms have issued **contingent convertible bonds,** which are securities that for a time received different accounting treatment than ordinary convertibles. Holders of such bonds can convert only when a contingency—such as the stock price

---

[6]"New Bond Rules to Dent GM Earnings," by James Mackintosh and Jenny Wiggins, *Financial Times,* London ed., July 22, 2004, p. 26.

[7]"GM acts on New Co-Co Bond Rules" by Jeremy Grant, *Financial Times,* London ed., August 6, 2004, p. 24.

being sufficiently high—has occurred. Prior to 2005, firms were permitted to ignore such bonds in computing fully diluted EPS. However, the FASB ruled that such bonds had to be treated as convertibles, and a number of firms that had issued such bonds were forced to change the way they accounted for them.

The box on page 521 discusses the reaction of one company to the FASB's new rule, and makes it clear that the accounting treatment of a security is important for issuers.

Put Warrants

When shares are used to pay employees (as for example with compensation options), there is an increase in the number of shares outstanding. Companies making heavy use of share compensation frequently buy shares back from other shareholders (a *share repurchase*) so there is no net increase in the number of shares outstanding.[8]

Many companies that repurchased shares during the 1990s also sold put options on their own stock; a commonly stated rationale for issuing such put warrants (see, for example, Thatcher et al., 1994) is that the put sales are a hedge against the cost of repurchasing shares. Intel, Microsoft, and Dell, for example, all sold significant numbers of puts, with Microsoft alone earning well over $1 billion in put premiums during the 1990s. Here is a quote from Microsoft's 1999 10-K describing the put program:

> Microsoft enhances its repurchase program by selling put warrants.... On June 30, 1999, 163 million warrants were outstanding with strike prices ranging from $59 to $65 per share. The put warrants expire between September 1999 and March 2002. The outstanding put warrants permit a net-share settlement at the Company's option and do not result in a put warrant liability on the balance sheet.

How do we think about this transaction? If Microsoft repurchases shares, via a written put or by any other means, nonselling shareholders are in effect buying shares from selling shareholders. It is common to say that managers should maximize shareholder value, but which set of shareholders do they care about? Despite this theoretical ambiguity, we will examine the transaction using a standard profit and loss calculation.

Figure 16.5 is a profit diagram for various alternatives. Suppose that the share price today is $100 and the firm will for certain buy one share back in 3 years. The firm has 3 years to earn interest on the $100 it could have spent today. The profit diagram shows that if the price is still $100 in 3 years, the firm has profited by the amount of this interest. The sale of a put expiring in 3 years generates the curve labeled "Written Put."

The third curve in Figure 16.5 shows the combined profit and loss for a short share and written put. (By put-call parity, this position looks like a written call.) Should the share price rise, the firm repurchases shares at a higher price but keeps the put premium. If the share price falls, the firm is obligated to pay the strike price to repurchase shares. This transaction is the mirror image of covered call writing, discussed in Chapter 3.

---

[8]Corporate finance theory offers no justification for this practice, but firms seem to believe that it is important.

FIGURE 16.5

Profit diagram for being short a share of stock, writing a put, and the combination of the two.

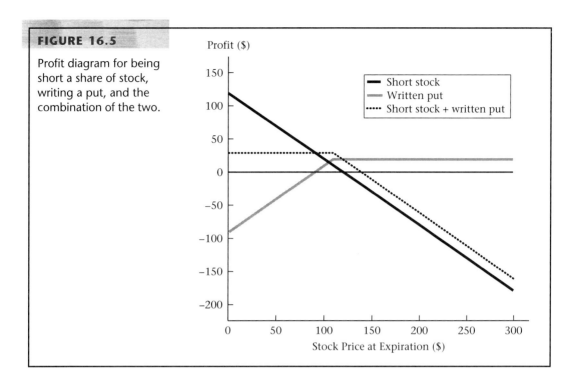

In practice, dealers have purchased the puts written by firms such as Microsoft, Intel, and Dell. The dealers reportedly hold the puts and delta-hedge the position, as in Chapter 13, thus reducing their risk. Moreover, the transactions, including the dealer's hedging trades, occur without any public announcement. In effect, put-selling firms transact with shareholders using the dealer as a conduit. When the share price rises, the delta of the dealer's purchased put, which is negative, increases toward zero and the dealer sells the shares it had purchased to hedge the put. When the share price falls, delta increases to negative one and the dealer buys additional shares to hedge its position. The dealer, acting on behalf of the firm, buys as the share price declines and sells as the share price rises.

Problem 16.19 asks you to examine a binomial example of this transaction, showing first that the firm could accomplish the same end as put-writing by transacting directly in its shares. Second, the problem asks you to show how the counterparty dealer delta-hedges the transaction.

16.2 COMPENSATION OPTIONS

Many firms compensate executives and other employees with call options on the company's own stock. The use of such *compensation options* is common and significant in many companies, but has declined since 2002.

Microsoft, for example, estimated in its 1999 annual report (10-K) that its grants that year of 78 million options were worth about $1.6 billion. This is approximately $52,000 per employee (Microsoft had 31,000 employees). Elsewhere in its 10-K, Microsoft reported that total outstanding options on 766 million shares (against 5 billion shares outstanding) had a market value on June 30, 1999, of $69 billion, or $2 *million* per employee.

Many other companies made significant use of compensation options. Eberhart (2005) found in a sample of 1800 firms using compensation options in 1999 that options were on average 12% of shares outstanding. Moreover, the use of options has not been restricted to executives: Core and Guay (2001) found in a sample of 750 companies that two-thirds of option grants were to nonexecutive employees.

The use of compensation options has declined in recent years. Several developments seem to be responsible for this change. First, the market decline in 2000 left many employees with deep out-of-the-money options and created morale problems for companies heavily dependent upon options. The box on page 526 discusses Microsoft's response to its overhang of out-of-the-money options.

Second, both the Financial Accounting Standards Board (FASB) in the United States and the International Accounting Standards Board (IASB) announced that they would require companies to recognize employee option grants as a compensation expense. Throughout the 1990s most companies had treated compensation options as worthless when computing earnings.[9] An attempt by the FASB to require option expensing in the early 1990s was defeated by companies opposed to expensing. Many of these companies were concerned about the decline in reported earnings that would result from expensing.

The logic behind requiring companies to expense option grants is straightforward. If a company pays cash to an employee, the company deducts the payment as an expense. If an otherwise identical company replaces some of the cash with an option grant, that company will report systematically higher earnings than the first *unless* the value of the option grant is also deducted as an expense.

To think about expensing, you can perform the following thought experiment: Imagine that a firm that issues options to employees were to hedge its obligations by buying a contract from a third party. Under the terms of this contract, the third party would pay the firm the value of the option when the employee exercises it. The firm could grant an option and buy the hedging contract, thereby insulating shareholders from the effect of the grant. The cost of this hedging contract is the cost to the firm of the option grant.

If a firm does not buy such a contract, it self-insures, meaning that shareholders bear the cost of the option grant. Either way, the cost of the insurance is the cost to shareholders of the compensation option. The problem of valuing a compensation option amounts to asking how much it would cost the firm to hedge its compensation commitments.

....

[9]SFAS 123 did require companies to report the value of options in a footnote. This value—frequently computed using the Black-Scholes formula—did not affect reported earnings.

In December 2004, the FASB issued Statement of Financial Accounting Standards (SFAS) 123R, which contained the final rules, effective in June 2005, for companies to follow in expensing options. The statement

> requires a public entity to measure the cost of employee services received in exchange for an award of equity instruments based on the grant-date fair value of the award (with limited exceptions). That cost will be recognized over the period during which an employee is required to provide service in exchange for the award—the requisite service period (usually the vesting period).[10]

A company might grant options that vest after three years and expire after seven years. Under SFAS 123R, the company could value these options using the Black-Scholes or the binomial formula, and then expense 1/3 of their value over each year of the vesting period.

The valuation of compensation options is complicated by the fact that there are many special considerations in valuing them:

- Compensation options cannot be sold and typically are not fully vested (i.e., the employee does not own them) for several years.

- The executive may resign, be fired, die, or become disabled, or the company may be acquired. Any of these may affect the value of the option grant, either by forcing early exercise (as may happen with a death) or requiring that the options be forfeited (in the event the executive is fired).

- The term of the options can be 10 years or more, which makes volatility and dividend estimates difficult.

- The company may not have a publicly traded stock, in which case the stock price must be estimated.

- There may be unusual contractual features of the compensation option contract. For example, the strike price may be an industry stock price index.

Such considerations make it harder to value compensation options than short-lived exchange-traded options. We will now discuss some of the issues that arise in option expensing.

Whose Valuation?

Compensation options cannot be traded. An employee who cannot sell options will typically discount their value. As a result, you can expect that firms and employees will value compensation options differently. Such a difference in valuation can occur for any compensation other than immediate cash.

---

[10]Statement of Financial Accounting Standards No. 123R, p. ii.

The End of Compensation Options?

In July 2003, the *Wall Street Journal* proclaimed: "The golden age of stock options is over." (See "Microsoft Ushers Out The Era of Options," by Robert A. Guth and Joann S. Lublin, *Wall Street Journal*, July 14, 2003.) Microsoft stock had fallen recently and many employees had out-of-the-money options. Employees expressed what CEO Steve Ballmer called "angst" about the low stock price, and the effect on option values.

Microsoft's CFO was quoted in the article as saying that employees could no longer expect to become wealthy from stock options:

> "If you think what happened in the nineties is going to happen again— it's not," said Microsoft Chief Financial Officer John Connors. In a recent interview he described the PC market boom as a "phenomenon" that "nobody will ever likely repeat."

Microsoft announced that it would eliminate the use of options as compensation, issuing restricted stock instead. (Restricted stock is stock that cannot be sold for a period of time.)

In addition, Microsoft entered into an agreement with JP Morgan Chase whereby the bank would, on a one-time basis, offer to buy employee options. The bank bought the options at modified terms; for example, maturities were reduced to a maximum of three years. As a result employees sold their options for a price that in many cases was significantly less than the unrestricted price for an otherwise equivalent traded option. JP Morgan Chase, which would hold the options it acquired, informed Microsoft employees that it would be short-selling shares in order to delta-hedge the option position. Slightly more than half of employee options were sold in this fashion.

Microsoft's avoidance of options appeared to be part of a general trend. One survey found a 50% reduction in the value of option grants between 2001 and 2003. ("Stock Option Awards Sharply Cut," by Ruth Simon, *Wall Street Journal*, December 14, 2004, p. D3.)

In 2005, Microsoft chairman Bill Gates even told a group of business writers, "I regret that we ever used stock options." (Reuters, "Gates Regrets Paying with Stock Options," www.cnn.com, May 3, 2005)

Accounting standards require that companies deduct the *cost to the company*. The goal is to measure cost to nonemployee shareholders, not value to employees. For example, suppose a company grants employees nontradable membership in a golf club costing $15,000 per year. No one would value the membership at more than $15,000, because it can be purchased for that amount. However, someone who does not play golf might value the membership at zero. Thus, while for one executive the membership might displace $15,000 of salary, for another, it might not displace any salary. However, in either case, shareholders bear the $15,000 cost. *The fact that the employee discounts the membership's value does not reduce the cost to the firm.* For shareholders, the key question is the cost to the company: How should shareholders value option grants, given the behavior of employees.

Valuation Inputs

SFAS 123R calls for the valuation to measure fair market value of the option. This requires that companies estimate the likely behavior of employees with respect to exercise and forfeiture of options, and also that the company estimate prospective volatility and dividends.[11] To illustrate several practical issues in measuring cost to the company, we again consider Microsoft as an example. In accord with SFAS 123, Microsoft in 1999 valued its options using Black-Scholes and disclosed this value in a footnote. The options vested in 4 1/2 years and expired after 7 years. Here is the discussion from Microsoft's 1999 10-K:

> [Option] value was estimated using an expected life of 5 years, no dividends, volatility of 0.32 in 1999 and 1998 and 0.30 in 1997, and risk-free interest rates of 6.5%, 5.7%, and 4.9% in 1997, 1998, and 1999.

Microsoft does not document how it chose volatilities, but these are close to historical volatilities in each year. Using weekly data, historical volatilities for Microsoft for July to June were 32% for 1996–1997, 30% for 1997–1998, and 39% for 1998–1999.

Why did Microsoft use a 5-year expiration to value options expiring in 7 years? We learned in Chapter 9 that it is never optimal to early-exercise a publicly traded call option on a nondividend-paying stock since it can be sold for more than its intrinsic value. However, compensation options cannot be sold. Thus, the value of the options *to the holder* may be less than intrinsic value. In this case, employees may exercise the options before expiration.[12] This is in fact how employees behave: In practice, executives frequently exercise a large fraction of their in-the-money options as soon as they vest.[13] In addition to exercise by continuing employees, options are often canceled due to death, termination, or retirement of the employee. Taxes can also potentially affect the exercise decision, although a common tax-motivated argument for early exercise is incorrect.[14] Finally, compensation options cannot be exercised until they vest. A realistic

----

[11] Since dividends reduce the value of an option, it is possible that widespread use of compensation options has resulted in a reduction in corporate dividends.

[12] See Kulatilaka and Marcus (1994) for a discussion of the employee's valuation of options.

[13] Huddart (1998) shows that options are disproportionately exercised on the first through fourth anniversaries of the grant, in blocks of 25% of the grant. Since it is common for grants to vest 25% annually, this finding suggests that many options are being exercised as soon as possible.

[14] An employee is taxed at ordinary income rates on the exercise of a nonqualified option, with subsequent gains on the stock being taxed at capital gains rate. Some have argued that employees optimistic about the share price should exercise compensation options early in order to maximize the percentage of income taxed at the favorable capital gains rate. This argument is incorrect. However, if the ordinary income rate is expected to increase, early exercise can be optimal. For a discussion see McDonald (2003).

valuation would account for the likelihood of these various factors. The assumed 5-year life is intended to account for the *expected* life of an option.[15]

It is possible to modify both the Black-Scholes and binomial models to account for complications due to early exercise. For example, suppose that 4-year options vest after 3 years. The company examines historical data and estimates that 5% of outstanding options will be forfeited each year during the vesting period. Furthermore, the company believes that half of the remaining options will be exercised at vesting, with the other half exercised at expiration. One could then value the option grant as being partially a 3-year option and partially a 4-year option:

$$(1 - 0.05)^3 \, [0.5 \times \text{3-year option} + (1 - 0.05) \times 0.5 \times \text{4-year option}] \qquad (16.25)$$

In this expression, each option price is weighted by the fraction of employees who historically exercised at that time. A problem with this approach is that it does not recognize that employee behavior depends on the stock price. If the option is deeply in the money in the early years, fewer employees are likely to resign before the options vest. If the option is out of the money in year 3, all employees who do not resign will wait before deciding whether to exercise, which lengthens option maturity. Thus, the assumptions about exercise behavior will generally be incorrect. Bodie et al. (2003) point out that for these reasons, equation (16.25) will undervalue the option. A binomial model or Monte Carlo valuation (which we will discuss in Chapter 19) permits a more flexible and realistic treatment of early exercise.

An Alternative Approach to Expensing Option Grants

There are alternative ways to account for option expense. For example, companies could fully deduct the market value of the option at exercise; this is the approach taken in taxing option grants. A deduction at exercise gives an expense with the correct present value. However, by waiting to deduct the expense, the firm's reported income in earlier years will not reflect the economic value of compensation in those years.

Another alternative is suggested by Bulow and Shoven (2004). They propose an option expense calculation that records an expense for each period that the option remains unexercised. Their approach neatly sidesteps many valuation difficulties and provides a correct present value of option deductions. Moreover, the method provides insight into why a long-term option grant is costly. We will illustrate the proposal in the specific context of compensation options, but the methodology is generally applicable to long-term contracts and contingent liabilities.

---

[15]If a company alters its assumption about the exercise behavior of employees, the estimated value of newly issued options will change. Cisco, for example, changed its assumed option life from 5.6 to 3.3 years, reducing the estimated value of its option grants by 23%, from $1.3 to $1.0 billion. See "Cisco May Profit on New Option Assumptions," by Scott Thurm, *Wall Street Journal*, December 7, 2004, p. C1.

Bulow and Shoven make the observation that most option contracts are exercisable after a vesting period, and that employees or heirs are typically required to exercise their options within 90 days of resignation or death. Thus, in practice, a 10-year option can be viewed as a renewable 90-day option, extendible (by the employee's continuing to work) for 39 additional 90-day periods. Bulow and Shoven propose taking the value of this extension as the deduction in each quarter.[16] The value of the extension is the market value of a 90-day option, less intrinsic value. The present value of expected option expense computed in this fashion is the fair market value for an option with the same time to expiration.

Figure 16.6 provides a binomial example illustrating how the Bulow-Shoven proposal works for a 3-year option that vests immediately, and for which recipients can exercise the option in year 1, 2, or 3, or one year after resignation. The binomal value of the three-year 100-strike option is $28.15; you can verify this by applying the binomial pricing method to the stock price tree in Panel A.

Panel D of Figure 16.6 shows the annual expense reported under the Bulow-Shoven scheme. To see how the entries in Panel D are calculated, consider the $4.88 expense in year 1 when the stock price is $134.99. From Panel C, the price of a one-year option at that node is $39.86. Option expense in that year is therefore fair market value less intrinsic value, or $39.86 − 34.99 = $4.88. Why do we deduct intrinsic value? The reason is that *the deduction for the year 2 intrinsic value was, in effect, already taken the previous year, when we deducted the value of a one-year option.* The price of a one-year option is the present value of the next year's intrinsic value. Therefore, the only *new* value to deduct in a given year is the value of a one-year option over and above that year's intrinsic value, which is the present value of *next* year's intrinsic value. In effect, the Bulow-Shoven scheme amortizes the value of the three-year option, where the amortization amount varies with the stock price.

You can compute the present value of all deductions in Panel D by using the binomial pricing method with the same parameters used to generate Panel A. As an exercise, you can verify that the present value of deductions in Panel D is $28.15, which is also the the binomial value of a 3-year option.

There are several points to make about this example. First, the full deductions with a present value of $28.15 are reported by the company only if the option is held unexercised until year 3. Thus, the proposal solves the problem of early exercise and the employee leaving the company. Second, the actual deductions are substantially less than the maximum possible value of the option at exercise. Third, expenses behave in what might appear to be a counterintuitive fashion, with reported option expense greatest when the option is at-the-money. In year 2, for example, expense is greatest when the stock price is $100. The reason is that the value of delaying exercise on a deep-in-the-money option is primarily the value of delaying the payment of the strike price. Thus, in Panel D, $4.88 is the one-year present value of interest on $100. When

---

[16]Consider the analogy with wages. An employee may have a long-term employment contract specifying wages for 10 years, but the firm on the income statement only deducts wages paid each quarter. The goal of the Bulow-Shoven proposal is to afford similar treatment to options.

FIGURE 16.6

Panel	Year:	0	1	2	3
A: Stock price process		100.00	134.99	182.21	245.96
			74.08	100.00	134.99
				54.88	74.08
					40.66
B: Intrinsic value (max[0, $S_t - K$])		0.00	34.99	82.21	145.96
			0.00	0.00	34.99
				0.00	0.00
					0.00
C: One period option value		16.96	39.86	87.09	0.00
			0.00	16.96	0.00
				0.00	0.00
					0.00
D: Reported expense (Panel C less Panel B)		16.96	4.88	4.88	0.00
			0.00	16.96	0.00
				0.00	0.00
					0.00

Option expense calculation under the Bulow-Shoven proposal. Assumes $K = \$100$, $\sigma = 0.30$, $r = 0.05$, $\delta = 0$, and $T = 3$ years. The risk-neutral probability of an up move is $p = 0.5097$. The CRR binomial stock price process is in Panel A. Panel B reports the option intrinsic value, max[0, $S_t - K$]. Panel C reports the one-period option value. Panel D reports the annual option expense.

the option is at-the-money, however, put-call parity tells us that the value of the implicit put option is also important, and this is why the at-the-money expense is greater. To say this differently, an employee who prematurely exercises an option that is near the money loses more economic value than an employee who prematurely exercises an option that is deep in the money. The option expense calculation in Figure 16.6 reflects this.

Suppose a firm must compute annual option expense and separated employees have *two* years to exercise their options. How does this change the calculation? In this case, by working one more year, the employee obtains a new two-year option and gives up the remaining one year on the previous year's two-year option. It is straightforward to calculate expense in this situation. Using the assumptions in Figure 16.6, Problem 16.24 asks you to verify that the present value of option expense in this case again equals the fair market value of $28.15.

Note that if we were to apply this methodology to a grant of stock, we would expense the entire grant initially. A share of stock is like a zero-exercise price option, and with no dividends, such an option is worth the share price. Price would therefore equal intrinsic value in every period, resulting in zero expense every period after the first.

Finally, note that this expensing method is generally applicable to contingent liabilities, and it thus has broad applicability beyond compensation options. In general, in order to record a current expense, it is necessary to value the liability only over a short horizon, and then to do so repeatedly.

Repricing of Compensation Options

Between July and December of 1997, the price of Oracle stock fell from a (split-adjusted) high of almost $14 in August to $7.25 on December 11. On December 12, Oracle's Board of Directors lowered the strike price on a number of Oracle's compensation options. This excerpt is from Oracle's 10-Q issued in January 1998:

> In December 1997, the Company reduced the exercise price of approximately 20% of the outstanding common stock options held by the Company's employees to the fair market value per share as of the date of the reduction in price. The Company repriced these employee stock options in an effort to retain employees at a time when a significant percentage of employee stock options had exercise prices that were above fair market value. The Company believes that stock options are a valuable tool in compensating and retaining employees. Executive officers and directors were excluded from this repricing.

Reducing the exercise price of compensation options in response to a decline in the stock price is called option **repricing.** The delta of a deep-out-of-the-money option is low, so that subsequent stock price changes will not have much effect on the value of employee options. Companies in this case often reprice options.[17]

If you expect that options will be repriced if the price falls, how valuable is the option grant in the first place? We can answer this question using barrier options, discussed in Chapter 14. An option that is going to be repriced if the stock price reaches a certain level can be modeled as a knock-out option (the originally granted option vanishes), plus a knock-in option (a new option replaces it) with the same barrier. Specifically, suppose that the option strike is K, and that at the barrier, H, a new at-the-money option will be issued in place of the original option. A repriceable option is then worth

$$\text{CallDownOut}(S, K, \sigma, r, T, \delta, H) + \text{CallDownIn}(S, H, \sigma, r, T, \delta, H) \qquad (16.26)$$

The second term reflects the knock-in call being at-the-money when it knocks in.

----

[17]Morgenson (1998) reported that in addition to Oracle, option repricing occurred at Netscape Communications, Apple Computer, Bay Networks, Best Buy, and Oxford Health Plans, among others.

Example 16.6 Suppose $S = \$100$, $\sigma = 0.4$, $r = 0.06$, $t = 10$, $\delta = 0.01$, and that options will be repriced if the stock price hits $60. The value of an option that will *not* be repriced is

$$\text{BSCall}(\$100, \$100, 0.4, 0.06, 10, 0.01) = \$54.43$$

The value of an otherwise equivalent option that will be repriced at $60 is

$$\text{CallDownOut}(\$100, \$100, 0.4, 0.06, 10, 0.01, 60)$$
$$+ \text{CallDownIn}(\$100, \$60, 0.4, 0.06, 10, 0.01, 60) = \$41.11 + \$20.30 = \$61.41$$

Thus, the possibility of repricing increases the value of the option by 13%. ≋

Reload Options

A **reload option** gives the option-holder new call options when existing call options are exercised. The idea is that the option-holder uses shares to pay for exercise, and new at-the-money options are granted for each share given up in this fashion. This type of option is best explained with an example. Assume that a 10-year option grant for 1000 shares with a strike price of $100 permits a single reload. Suppose the employee exercises the option when the stock price is $250, with 4 years of option life remaining. The exercise price requires a payment of $100 × 1000 = $100,000. This amount can be paid in cash or by surrendering $100,000/$250 = 400 shares. An executive paying the strike price by surrendering shares receives 400 new at-the-money options with 4 years to expiration.

Arnason and Jagannathan (1994) pointed out that there are two important characteristics of reload options. First, the reload feature is valuable: A reload option can be worth 30% more than an otherwise equivalent option without the reload feature. Second, reload options cannot be valued using the Black-Scholes formula because reload options may be early-exercised. However, they can be valued using the binomial option pricing model.

Reload options might seem esoteric, but Saly et al. (1999) show that 1135 reload options were granted, in 1997, out of a total of 9673 grants reported in the S&P Execucomp database. SFAS 123R accounts for reloads by ignoring the extra value of the reload feature when the option is granted, and accounting for the additional expense when the option is exercised and reloaded.[18] This treatment is in the spirit of the Bulow-Shoven expensing proposal, discussed above.

Reload options can be valued binomially. This is accomplished by replacing the exercise amount at the time of exercise, $S - K$, with the value of a new reload option. We will illustrate this in the simplest possible fashion, with a two-period binomial example.

---

[18] Saly et al. (1999) suggest that reload options may be a way to give management undisclosed compensation.

Figure 16.7 shows the binomial valuation of an ordinary option and a reload option with a single reload. The binomial price for an option without a reload provision is $38.28. (The Black-Scholes price for this option is $36.76.) The reload price, by contrast, is $42.25, and a reload optimally occurs in the second binomial period. Let's examine how this works.

First, consider the valuation without a reload. When $S = \$179.37$ in period 1, the value of the option left alive is $94.153, while the value exercised is $79.37. As we would expect since there are no dividends, the option is not exercised early; the value in period 0 is $38.28.

When a reload is permitted, the one candidate node for a reload is when $S = \$179.37$. (A reload would have no value at $S = \$100$ or in the final period.) If a reload occurs, the option-holder receives $79.37 for exercising the option, and 100/179.37 options are issued with a strike price of $179.37 and 2 years to maturity. Thus, we calculate the value of the option at this node as

$$\$79.37 + \frac{100}{179.37}e^{-0.08 \times 2}\left(0.395 \times \$142.36 + 0.605 \times \$0\right) = \$106.09 \quad (16.27)$$

From Figure 16.7, the value of the reload option is $42.25, 10.5% greater than in the absence of the reload.

In general, we can compute the value of the reload at every node by solving another binomial pricing problem valuing the appropriate number of newly issued options. The

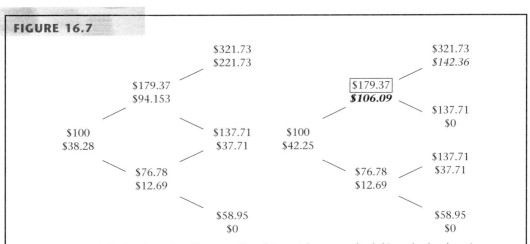

FIGURE 16.7

Binomial valuation of ordinary option (binomial tree on the left) and reload option (binomial tree on the right). The calculations assume that $S = \$100$, $K = \$100$, $\sigma = 0.3$, $r = 0.08$, $\delta = 0$, $T = 4$, $h = 2$, and that there is a single reload. Stock prices and option prices are shown at each node, with the reload value in italics. A reload occurs at the boxed stock price. In this example, we have $u = 1.794$, $d = 0.768$, and $p = 0.395$.

option-holder reloads if doing so is more valuable than not doing so, just like the exercise decision for an American option.[19]

Level 3 Communications

Level 3 Communications was one of the first companies to deduct the cost of compensation options in computing earnings. However, Level 3 also granted unusually complex and valuable options and did not take this complexity and extra value into account when expensing. In a June 1998 proxy statement, Level 3 described its outperform stock options (OSO), granted to employees. This is how they are described in the proxy:

> Participants in the OSO Program do not realize any value from awards unless the Level 3 Common Stock outperforms the Standard & Poor's 500 Index. When the stock price gain is greater than the corresponding gain on the Standard & Poor's 500 Index, the value received for awards under the OSO Program is based on a formula involving a Multiplier related to how much the Common Stock outperforms the Standard & Poor's 500 Index.

The multiplier is then described as follows:

> The Multiplier shall be based on the "Outperform Percentage" . . . for the Period, determined on the date of exercise. The Outperform Percentage shall be the excess of the annualized percentage change . . . in the Fair Market Value of the Common Stock over the Period . . . over the annualized percentage increase or decrease . . . in the Standard & Poor's 500 Index over the Period. . . .

The multiplier is computed based on the outperform percentage as follows:

Outperform Percentage	Multiplier
$x \leq 0$	0
$0 < x \leq 11\%$	$x \times \frac{8}{11} \times 100$
$x > 11\%$	8.0

Because of the multiplier, if Level 3 outperforms the S&P 500 index by at least an annual average of 11%, the option recipient will have the payoff of eight options. The options have a 4-year maturity and are exercisable and fully vested after 2 years.

Example 16.7   Suppose that at the grant of an option, the price of Level 3 is $100, and the S&P 500 index is at 1300. After 4 years, the price of Level 3 is $185, and the

---

[19]When n reloads are permitted, the problem can be solved by having the binomial pricing function call itself, along with the information that one less reload remains. This is simple to program but computationally very slow because of the large number of binomial valuations. See Saly et al. (1999) for a discussion.

S&P 500 index is at 1950. A "non-multiplied" outperformance option would have had a payoff of

$$\$185 - \$100 \times \frac{1950}{1300} = \$35$$

The (nonannualized) returns on Level 3 and the S&P 500 index are 85% and 50%. The outperform percentage is

$$1.85^{0.25} - 1.50^{0.25} = 5.957\%$$

The multiplier is therefore

$$0.05957 \times \frac{8}{11} \times 100 = 4.332$$

The payment on the option is

$$\left(\$185 - \$100 \times \frac{1950}{1300}\right) \times 4.332 = \$151.64$$

This option is worth between 0 and 8 times as much as an ordinary option. How can we get an intuitive sense for the value of the difference? We will first examine the effect of the outperformance feature and then consider the effect of the multiplier.

Valuing the outperformance feature First, what would be the value of an ordinary 4-year-to-maturity at-the-money call? Using a volatility of 25% (which Level 3 says in its 1999 Annual Report is the "expected volatility" of its common stock), and a risk-free rate of 6%, we obtain an option price of

$$\mathrm{BSCall}(\$100, \$100, 0.25, 0.06, 4, 0) = \$30.24$$

The Level 3 1999 Annual Report discusses the valuation of the outperformance option as follows:

> The fair value of the options granted was calculated by applying the Black-Scholes method with an S&P 500 expected dividend yield rate of 1.8% and an expected life of 2.5 years. The Company used a blended volatility rate of 24% between the S&P 500 expected volatility rate of 16% and the Level 3 Common Stock expected volatility rate of 25%. The expected correlation factor of 0.4 was used to measure the movement of Level 3 stock relative the S&P 500.

We saw in Section 14.6 that to value an outperformance option, we use the Black-Scholes formula but make the following substitutions:

$$\sigma_{\text{Level 3}} \rightarrow \hat{\sigma} = \sqrt{\sigma_{\text{Level 3}}^2 + \sigma_{\text{S\&P}}^2 - 2\rho\sigma_{\text{Level 3}}\sigma_{\text{S\&P}}}$$
$$r \quad \rightarrow \delta_{\text{S\&P}}$$

where ρ is the correlation between Level 3 and S&P 500 returns and r is the risk-free rate. The net effect on value of granting an outperformance call depends upon the effect of these substitutions. The "blended" volatility, $\hat{\sigma}$, can be greater or less than $\sigma_{\text{Level 3}}$. In recent years, $\delta_{\text{S\&P}}$ has been less than r. The calculation Level 3 makes for the blended volatility is

$$\hat{\sigma} = \sqrt{0.25^2 + 0.16^2 - 2 \times 0.4 \times 0.25 \times 0.16}$$
$$= 0.2368$$

which is rounded to 24%. The price of the outperformance option is therefore

$$\text{BSCall}(\$100, \$100, 0.2368, 0.018, 4, 0) = \$21.75$$

This is about $\frac{2}{3}$ of the value of the ordinary option. This reduction in value is primarily due to replacing the 6% interest rate with a 1.8% dividend yield. The volatility reduction by itself lowers the option price only to $29.44.

Adding the multiplier   Now consider the effect of the multiplier. We can approximate the value of the multiplied option using gap options (described in Section 14.5). The multiplier in effect provides additional options as outperformance increases. For every $\frac{11}{8} = 1\frac{3}{8}$% per year by which Level 3 outperforms the S&P 500, the multiplier increases by 1. Thus, we can approximate the effect of the multiplier by valuing a strip of gap outperformance options.

For example, the multiplier is 2 if over 4 years, Level 3 outperforms the S&P 500 by a factor of $1.0275^4 = 1.1146$, nonannualized. To approximate the value of the option, we can assume that if outperformance is between 0 and 1.375% per year, the option-holder receives nothing. Between 1.375% and 2.75%, the option-holder receives one option. At 2.75% per year, the option-holder receives a second option, etc. Above 11% per year, the option holder receives eight options. Each additional option can be valued as a gap option. For example, the option received if performance is above 2.75% per year would pay $S_{\text{Level3}} - S_{\text{S\&P}}$ if $S_{\text{Level3}} > 1.0275^4 \times S_{\text{S\&P}}$.

Figure 16.8 shows the payoff of a single nonmultiplied option, plotted against the exact payoff and the payoff approximated by gap options. Note that the exact and gap approximation are not identical, but they are quite close.

Table 16.2 shows that, using the gap option approximation, the value of the compensation option is about seven times the value of a single option. A more precise binomial valuation using 100 binomial steps gives a value for the option of $156.25, so the gap approximation of $153 is quite close. Monte Carlo valuation, which we will discuss in Chapter 19, provides an alternative way to value the Level 3 option.

Finally, it is interesting to note that it may be rational to exercise the Level 3 option early even in the absence of dividends. Suppose the option is close to expiration and the outperformance percentage is slightly above 11%. If the holder exercises, the multiplier is 8. If the share price rises further, the multiplier remains 8. However, if the share price falls, the multiplier may fall to 7; by waiting to exercise, the option-holder can lose options. This extra loss from a share price decline can provide an incentive to exercise early. For very high prices, there is no incentive to exercise early since the multiplier remains constant. For low prices, the potential increase in the multiplier offsets the

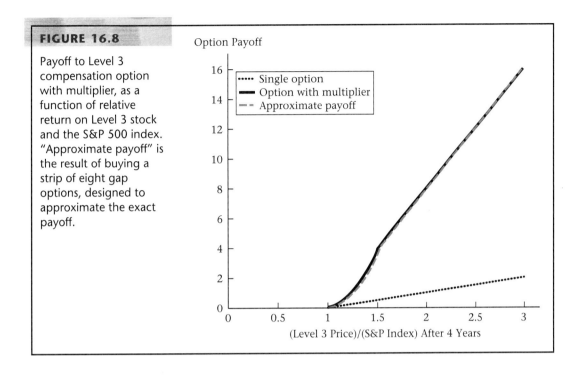

FIGURE 16.8

Payoff to Level 3 compensation option with multiplier, as a function of relative return on Level 3 stock and the S&P 500 index. "Approximate payoff" is the result of buying a strip of eight gap options, designed to approximate the exact payoff.

TABLE 16.2 Valuation of Level 3 option approximated as sum of gap options. For each row, the option value is computed as a gap call option (equation (14.15)), where $S = \$100$, $K_1 = \$100$, $K_2 = \$100\alpha$, $r = 0.018$, $\sigma = 0.2368$, $T = 4$, and $\delta = 0$.

Multiplier	Outperformance (α)	Gap Option Value ($)
1	1.056	21.63
2	1.115	21.28
3	1.175	20.72
4	1.239	19.96
5	1.305	19.04
6	1.373	17.98
7	1.444	16.81
8	1.518	15.58
Total		153.00

potential reduction in the multiplier. Thus, early exercise is potentially optimal only for intermediate prices and close to expiration.

16.3 The Use of Collars in Acquisitions

A common financial transaction is for one firm (the *acquirer*) to buy another (the *target*) by buying its common stock. The acquirer can pay for these shares with cash or by exchanging its own shares for target firm shares. Collarlike structures are frequently used in these transactions.

Suppose that under the purchase agreement, each target share will be exchanged for *x* shares of the acquirer (*x* is the *exchange ratio*). Once the target agrees to the purchase, the acquisition will generally take time to complete, often six months or more.[20] Target shareholders will be concerned that the acquirer's stock will drop before the merger is completed, in which case the dollar value of *x* acquirer shares will be lower. To protect against a price drop, it is possible to exchange whatever number of shares have a fixed dollar value. (For example, if the acquirer price is $100, exchange 1 share for each target share. If the acquirer price is $50, exchange 2 shares for each target share.) However, target shareholders may also wish to participate in share price gains that the acquirer experiences; this suggests fixing the exchange ratio rather than the dollar value. There are four common offer structures that address considerations such as these:[21]

- **Fixed stock offer:** A offers to pay B a fixed number of A shares per B share.

- **Floating stock offer:** A offers to pay B however many shares have a given dollar value, based on A's share price just before the merger is completed.

- **Fixed collar offer:** There is a range for A's share price within which the offer is a fixed stock offer. Outside this range the deal can become a floating stock offer or may be subject to cancellation.

- **Floating collar offer:** There is a range for A's share price within which the offer is a floating stock offer. Outside this range the deal can become a fixed stock offer or may be subject to cancellation.

Figure 16.9 illustrates these four types of acquisition offers. As this list shows, it is possible to modify the extent to which the target bears the risk of a change in the stock price of the acquirer. More complicated structures are also possible.

The Northrop Grumman—TRW merger

Northrop Grumman's 2002 bid for TRW is an example of a merger offer with a collar. In July 2002, Northrop Grumman and TRW agreed that Northrop would pay $7.8 billion for TRW. News headlines stated that Northrop offered "$60 per share," but the offer actually resembled a collar. The number of Northrop Grumman shares to be exchanged for each

---

[20]In many cases, for example, regulatory agencies examine the acquisition to see if it is anticompetitive.

[21]Fuller (2003) discusses the kinds of offers and the motives for using alternative kinds of collars.

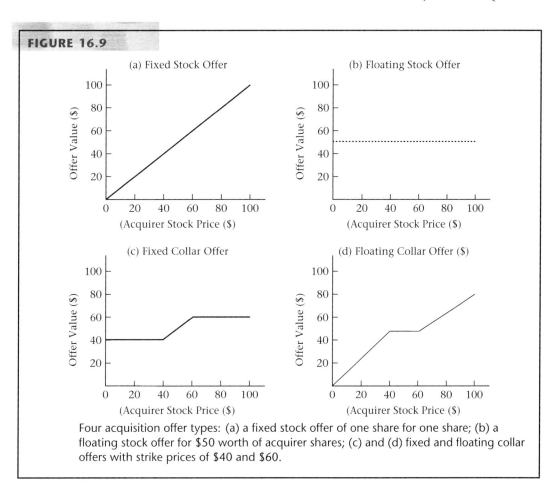

FIGURE 16.9

Four acquisition offer types: (a) a fixed stock offer of one share for one share; (b) a floating stock offer for $50 worth of acquirer shares; (c) and (d) fixed and floating collar offers with strike prices of $40 and $60.

TRW share would be determined by dividing $60 by the average Northrop Grumman price over the five days preceding the close of the merger, with the exchange ratio to be no less than 0.4348 ($60/$138) and no more than 0.5357 ($60/$112). Thus, if the price of Northrop Grumman at the merger closing was below $112, TRW shareholders would receive 0.5357 shares. If the price was above $138, TRW shareholders would receive 0.4348 shares. If the price, S, was in between $112 and $138, TRW shareholders would receive $60/S$, which is $60 worth of shares.[22] The deal closed on December 11, 2002, when the closing price of Northrop Grumman was $96.50; TRW shareholders therefore

[22]The acquisition terms changed between February and July. Initially, Northrop offered to exchange $47 worth of Northrop Grumman stock for each TRW share: The number of shares to be exchanged was to be no more than 0.4563 ($47/$103) or less than 0.4159 ($47/$113). In May, the value of the bid was increased to $53 (no more than 0.4690 shares ($53/$113) or less than 0.4309 ($53/$123) shares.)

received shares worth

$$0.5357 \times \$96.50 = \$51.69$$

How would TRW shareholders value the Northrop offer? Suppose that TRW shareholders were certain the merger would occur at time T, but uncertain about the future Norththrop Grumman stock price, S. TRW shareholders could then value the offer by noting that the offer is equivalent to buying 0.5357 shares of Northrop Grumman, selling 0.5357 112-strike calls, and buying 0.4348 138-strike calls. In addition, the TRW shareholders would not receive Northrop dividends paid prior to closing and would continue to receive TRW dividends. The time t value of TRW shares would then be

$$0.5357 \times \left[Se^{-\delta(T-t)} - \text{BSCall}(S, 112, \sigma, r, T - t, \delta) \right]$$
$$+ 0.4348 \times \text{BSCall}(S, 138, \sigma, r, T - t, \delta) + \text{PV}_{t,T}(\text{TRW Dividends}) \quad (16.28)$$

If the exchange ratio had been fixed, then the TRW share would simply be a fractional prepaid forward for Northrop, plus expected TRW dividends over the life of the offer.

Figure 16.10 graphs the value of the Northrop Grumman offer for one TRW share, as a function of the Northrop Grumman share price. The figure depicts the value of the offer both at closing and assuming there are 5 months to expiration.[23] Because of the structure of the offer, the value of a TRW share could either exceed or be less than the expiration value.

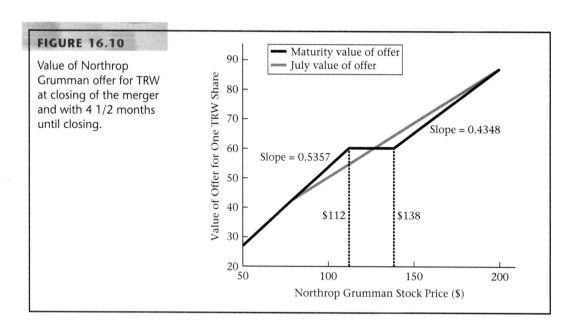

FIGURE 16.10

Value of Northrop Grumman offer for TRW at closing of the merger and with 4 1/2 months until closing.

---

[23]The calculation also assumes a risk-free rate of 1.5%, dividend yield of 1.25%, and volatility of 36%.

Figure 16.11 depicts equation (16.28) using the historical Northrop Grumman stock price from July to December 2002, assuming that the offer would close on December 11.[24] The theoretical value of a TRW share under the terms of the offer is consistently greater than the market price of a TRW share. This is what we would expect to see, since in order to induce the target company to accept an offer, the acquirer generally has to offer a price greater than the perceived value of the target as a stand-alone company. Since there is some chance the merger might not occur, the target share price is below the value of the offer. The difference between the value of a TRW share and the theoretical value of the offer declined toward zero as December approached. Had the merger been cancelled for some reason, the value of a TRW share would have diverged from the value under the terms of the offer.

Risk arbitrageurs take positions in the two stocks in order to speculate on the success or failure of the merger.[25] Equation (16.27) tells us that the offer is equivalent to a portfolio of Northrop shares and options. Thus, using the option replication technique of Chapter 10, we can hold Northrop shares and borrowing or lending to synthetically create a position equivalent to the offer. Because the price of TRW is less than the offer value, an arbitrageur speculating that the merger would succeed could then take a long position in TRW shares and a short position in the offer, short-selling delta shares of

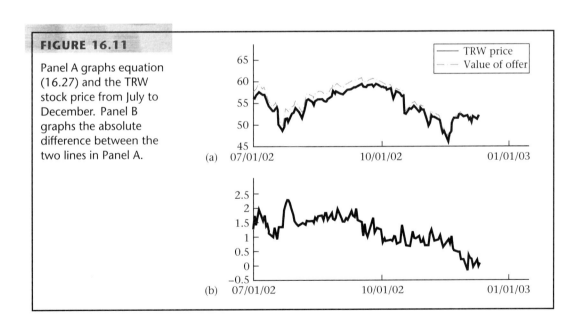

FIGURE 16.11

Panel A graphs equation (16.27) and the TRW stock price from July to December. Panel B graphs the absolute difference between the two lines in Panel A.

[24]It was necessary for Northrop Grumman and TRW to receive regulatory approval from European authorities, the U. S. Department of Defense and the U. S. Department of Justice. Final approval from the Department of Justice was on December 10 and the merger was completed on December 11.

[25]Mitchell and Pulvino (2001) examine the historical returns earned by risk arbitrageurs.

Northrop. If the offer succeeds, the position earns the difference in price depicted in Figure 16.11; if the offer fails, the difference should diverge and the arbitrageur would lose money.

CHAPTER SUMMARY

Three corporate contexts in which options appear, either explicitly or implicitly, are capital structure (debt, equity, and warrants), compensation, and acquisitions.

If we view the assets of the firm as being like a stock, then debt and equity can be valued as options with the assets of the firm as the underlying asset. Viewing corporate securities as options provides a natural way to measure bankruptcy risk, and illuminates conflicts between bondholders and stockholders.

Compensation options are an explicit use of options by corporations. They exhibit a variety of complications, some naturally occurring (early exercise decisions by risk-averse employees) and some created by the issuer (repricing, reloads, outperformance, and multipliers). For this reason they provide an interesting context in which to use the exotic pricing formulas from Chapter 14.

Offers by one firm to purchase another sometimes have embedded collars. The Grumman offer to buy TRW was an example of this.

FURTHER READING

The idea that debt and equity are options was first pointed out by Black and Scholes (1973). Merton (1974) and Merton (1977) analyzed the pricing of perpetual debt and demonstrated that the Modigliani-Miller theorem holds even with (costless) bankruptcy. Two principal applications of this idea are the determination of the fair yield on risky debt and the assessment of bankruptcy probabilities. Galai and Masulis (1976) derived the link between the return on assets and the return on the firm's stock.

The discussion of warrants and convertible bonds in this chapter assumes that the options are European. With American warrants the optimal exercise strategy can be more complicated than with European options. The reason is that exercise alters the assets of the firm. The problem of optimal American warrant exercise is studied by Emanuel (1983), Constantinides (1984), and Spatt and Sterbenz (1988). McDonald (2004) examines the tax implications of warrant issues, including put warrants. Complications also arise with convertible bonds, which in practice are almost always callable. Thus, valuing a convertible bond requires understanding the call strategy. Classic papers studying the pricing of convertibles include Brennan and Schwartz (1977) and Ingersoll (1977). Harris and Raviv (1985) discuss how asymmetric information affects the decision to call the bond, and Stein (1992) discusses the decision to issue convertibles in the first place. Finally, there is a large empirical literature on the convertible call decision; for example, see Asquith (1995). Güntay et al. (2004) examine the decision to issue callable bonds.

Papers on compensation options include Saly et al. (1999), Johnson and Tian (2000a), and Johnson and Tian (2000b). Repricing is studied by Chance et al. (2000) and Acharya et al. (2000). Petrie (2000) examines the use of collars in acquisitions.

PROBLEMS

For all problems, unless otherwise stated assume that the firm has assets worth $A = \$100$, and that $\sigma = 30\%$, $r = 8\%$, and the firm makes no payouts prior to the maturity date of the debt.

16.1. There is a single debt issue with a maturity value of $120. Compute the yield on this debt assuming that it matures in 1 year, 2 years, 5 years, or 10 years. What debt-to-equity ratio do you observe in each case?

16.2. There is a single debt issue. Compute the yield on this debt assuming that it matures in 1 year and has a maturity value of $127.42, 2 years with a maturity value of $135.30, 5 years with a maturity value of $161.98, or 10 years with a maturity value of $218.65. (The maturity value increases with maturity at a 6% rate.) What debt-to-equity ratio do you observe in each case?

16.3. There are four debt issues with different priorities, each promising $30 at maturity.

    a. Compute the yield on each debt issue assuming that all four mature in 1 year, 2 years, 5 years, or 10 years.

    b. Assuming that each debt issue matures in 5 years, what happens to the yield on each when you vary σ? When you vary r?

16.4. Suppose there is a single 5-year zero-coupon debt issue with a maturity value of $120. The expected return on assets is 12%. What is the expected return on equity? The volatility of equity? What happens to the expected return on equity as you vary A, σ, and r?

16.5. Repeat the previous problem for debt instead of equity.

16.6. In this problem we examine the effect of changing the assumptions in Example 16.1.

    a. Compute the yield on debt for asset values of $50, $100, $150, $200, and $500. How does the yield on debt change with the value of assets?

    b. Compute the yield on debt for asset volatilities of 10% through 100%, in increments of 5%.

For the next three problems, assume that a firm has assets of $100 and 5-year-to-maturity zero-coupon debt with a face value of $150. Assume that investment projects have the same volatility as existing assets.

16.7. The firm is considering an investment project costing $1. What is the amount by which the project's value must exceed its cost in order for shareholders to be willing to pay for it? Repeat for project values of $10 and $25.

16.8. Now suppose the firm finances the project by issuing debt that has *lower* priority than existing debt. How much must a $1, $10, or $25 project be worth if the shareholders are willing to fund it?

16.9. Now suppose the firm finances the project by issuing debt that has *higher* priority than existing debt. How much must a $10 or $25 project be worth if the shareholders are willing to fund it?

16.10. Assume there are 20 shares outstanding. Compute the value of the warrant and the share price for each of the following situations.

    a. Warrants for 2 shares expire in 5 years and have a strike price of $15.

    b. Warrants for 15 shares expire in 10 years and have a strike of $20.

16.11. A firm has outstanding a bond with a 5-year maturity and maturity value of $50, convertible into 10 shares. There are also 20 shares outstanding. What is the price of the warrant? The share price? Suppose you were to compute the value of the convertible as a risk-free bond plus an option, valued using the Black-Scholes formula and the share price you computed. How accurate is this?

16.12. Suppose a firm has 20 shares of equity, a 10-year zero-coupon debt with a maturity value of $200, and warrants for 8 shares with a strike price of $25. What is the value of the debt, the share price, and the price of the warrant?

16.13. Suppose a firm has 20 shares of equity and a 10-year zero-coupon convertible bond with a maturity value of $200, convertible into 8 shares. What is the value of the debt, the share price, and the price of the warrant?

16.14. Using the assumptions of Example 16.3, suppose you were to perform a "naive" valuation of the convertible as a risk-free bond plus 50 call options on the stock. How does the price you compute compare with that computed in the example?

16.15. Consider Panels B and D in Figure 16.4. Using the information in each panel, compute the share price at each node for each bond issue.

16.16. As discussed in the text, compensation options are prematurely exercised or canceled for a variety of reasons. Suppose that compensation options both vest and expire in 3 years and that the probability is 10% that the executive will die in year 1 and 10% in year 2. Thus, the probability that the executive lives to expiration is 80%. Suppose that the stock price is $100, the interest rate is 8%, the volatility is 30%, and the dividend yield is 0.

    a. Value the option by computing the expected time to exercise and plugging this into the Black-Scholes formula as time to maturity.

    b. Compute the expected value of the option given the different possible times until exercise.

    c. Why are the answers for the two calculations different?

16.17. XYZ Corp. compensates executives with 10-year European call options, granted at the money. If there is a significant drop in the share price, the company's board will reset the strike price of the options to equal the new share price. The maturity of the repriced option will equal the remaining maturity of the original option. Suppose that $\sigma = 30\%$, $r = 6\%$, $\delta = 0$, and that the original share price is $100.

a. What is the value at grant of an option that will not be repriced?

b. What is the value at grant of an option that is repriced when the share price reaches $60?

c. What repricing trigger maximizes the initial value of the option?

16.18. Suppose that top executives of XYZ are told they will receive at-the-money call options on 10,000 shares each year for the next 3 years. When granted, the options have 5 years to maturity. XYZ's stock price is $100, volatility is 30%, and $r = 8\%$. Estimate the value of this promise. (*Hint:* See Problem 14.21.)

16.19. Suppose that $S = \$100$, $\sigma = 30\%$, $r = 6\%$, $t = 1$, and $\delta = 0$. XYZ writes a European put option on one share with strike price $K = \$90$.

a. Construct a two-period binomial tree for the stock and price the put. Compute the replicating portfolio at each node.

b. If the firm were synthetically creating the put (i.e., trading to obtain the same cash flows as if it issued the put), what transactions would it undertake?

c. Consider the bank that buys the put. What transactions does it undertake to hedge the transaction?

d. Why might a firm prefer to issue the put warrant instead of borrowing and repurchasing shares?

16.20. Firm A has a stock price of $40 and has made an offer for firm B where A promises to pay $60/share for B, as long as A's stock price remains between $35 and $45. If the price of A is below $35, A will pay 1.714 shares, and if the price of A is above $45, A will pay 1.333 shares. The deal is expected to close in 9 months. Assume $\sigma = 40\%$, $r = 6\%$, and $\delta = 0$.

a. How are the values 1.714 and 1.333 arrived at?

b. What is the value of the offer?

c. How sensitive is the value of the offer to the volatility of A's stock?

16.21. Firm A has a stock price of $40, and has made an offer for firm B where A promises to pay 1.5 shares for each share of B, as long as A's stock price remains between $35 and $45. If the price of A is below $35, A will pay $52.50/share, and if the price of A is above $45, A will pay $67.50/share. The deal is expected to close in 9 months. Assume $\sigma = 40\%$, $r = 6\%$, and $\delta = 0$.

a. How are the values $52.50 and $67.50 arrived at?

b. What is the value of the offer?

c. How does the value of this offer compare with that in Problem 16.20?

16.22. The strike price of a compensation option is generally set on the day the option is issued. On November 10, 2000, the CEO of Analog Devices, Jerald Fishman, received 600,000 options. The stock price was $44.50. Four days later, the price rose to $63.25 after an earnings release:

> Maria Tagliaferro of Analog said the timing of the two events [option grant and earnings release] is irrelevant because company policy is that no option vests until at least three years from its granting date. "What happens to the stock price in the day, the hour, the year the option is granted is not relevant to that option," she said. "The stock price only becomes relevant after that option has vested."[26]

In its annual report for 2000, Analog Devices reported that the expected life of its options granted that year was 4.9 years, with a 56.6% volatility and 6% risk-free rate. The company paid no dividends until 2003.

   a. Using the inputs from the annual report, and assuming no dividends, estimate the value to the CEO of an at-the-money option grant at a stock price of $44.50.

   b. Estimate the value of an at-the-money grant at a price of $63.25.

   c. Estimate the value of a newly granted option at a strike of $44.50 when the stock price is $63.25.

   d. Do you agree with Maria Tagliaferro? Why or why not?

16.23. Four years after the option grant, the stock price for Analog Devices was about $40. Using the same input as in the previous problem, compute the market value of the options granted in 2000, assuming that they were issued at strikes of $44.50 and $63.25.

16.24. Suppose that a firm offers a 3-year compensation option that vests immediately. An employee who resigns has two years to decide whether to exercise the option. Compute annual compensation option expense using the stock price tree in Figure 16.6. Verify that the present value of the option deductions is $28.15.

---

[26] See "SEC Probes Analog Devices' Options," *Wall Street Journal*, December 2, 2004, p. B6.

CHAPTER 17

Real Options

T hus far we have primarily discussed financial assets, but many of the most important decisions that firms make concern *real assets*, a term that broadly encompasses factories, mines, office buildings, research and development, and other nonfinancial firm assets. In this chapter we will see that it is possible to analyze investment and operating decisions for real assets using pricing models we have developed for financial options.

To illustrate how it can be possible to evaluate an investment decision as an option, consider a firm that is deciding whether or not to build a factory. Compare the following two descriptions:

- A *call option* is the right to pay a *strike price* to receive the present value of a stream of future cash flows (represented by the *price of the underlying asset*).

- An *investment project* is the right to pay an *investment cost* to receive the present value of a stream of future cash flows (represented by the *present value of the project*).

Do you notice the similarities in these two statements? We have

Investment Project		**Call Option**
Investment cost	=	Strike price
Present value of project	=	Price of underlying asset

This comparison suggests that we can view any investment project as a call option, with the investment cost equal to the strike price and the present value of cash flows equal to the asset price. The exploitation of this and other analogies between real investment projects and financial options has come to be called **real options**, which we define as the application of derivatives theory to the operation and valuation of real investment projects. Note the phrase "operation *and* valuation." We will see in this chapter that you cannot value a real asset without also understanding how you will operate it. We have encountered this link before: You cannot value any option without understanding when you will exercise it.

17.1 INVESTMENT AND THE NPV RULE

We first consider a simple investment decision of the sort you would encounter in a basic finance course when studying net present value (NPV). Despite its simplicity, the example illustrates the issues that will arise again later in this chapter.

Suppose we can invest in a machine, costing $10, that will produce one widget a year forever. In addition, each widget costs $0.90 to produce. The price of widgets will be $0.55 next year and will increase at 4% per year. The effective annual risk-free rate is 5% per year. We can invest, at any time, in one such machine. There is no uncertainty.

Before reading further, you should try to answer this question: What is the most you would pay to acquire the rights to this project?

Static NPV

A natural first step is to compute the NPV if we invested in the project today. We obtain

$$\text{NPV}_{\text{Invest today}} \tag{17.1}$$

$$= \$0.55 \times \left(\frac{1}{1.05} + \frac{1.04}{1.05^2} + \frac{1.04^2}{1.05^3} + \cdots \right)$$

$$\quad - \$0.9 \times \left(\frac{1}{1.05} + \frac{1}{1.05^2} + \frac{1}{1.05^3} + \cdots \right) - \$10$$

$$= \frac{\$0.55}{1.04} \times \left(\frac{1}{\frac{1.05}{1.04} - 1} \right) - \frac{\$0.9}{0.05} - \$10 = \frac{\$0.55}{0.01} - \$28 = \$27$$

This calculation tells us that if widget production were to start next year, we would pay $27 for the project. For reasons that will become obvious, we call this the project's **static NPV.**

Notice that in the early years, the project has an operating loss. If we activate the project today, then next year we will have negative operating cash flows, spending $0.90 to produce a $0.55 widget. In addition, at a 5% rate of interest, the opportunity cost of the $10 investment is $0.50/year.

Why is NPV positive if we will be producing at a loss? Although the initial cash flows are negative, the widget price is growing. The project *will become* profitable in the future. This eventual profitability is why NPV is positive. This analysis suggests that we might consider waiting until later to invest.

Suppose we wait 5 years to invest instead of investing immediately. NPV is then

$$\text{NPV}_{\text{wait 5 years}} = \frac{1}{1.05^5} \left[(1.04)^5 \frac{\$0.55}{0.01} - \$28 \right]$$

$$= \$30.49$$

Thus, it is better to wait 5 years than to invest today. What is the maximum NPV we can attain?

Common sense points to an approximate answer: We should not invest until annual widget revenue covers marginal production cost ($0.90) plus the opportunity cost of the project ($0.50); i.e., cost is at least $1.40. The widget price will be $1.40 when n satisfies

$$(1 + .04)^n 0.55 = 1.40$$

Solving for n gives us $n = 23.82$.[1] After 23.82 years, the widget price will have reached a break-even level. The value today of waiting that long to invest in the project is

$$\left[\frac{(1.04)^{23.82}\$0.55}{0.01} - \frac{\$0.90}{0.05} - \$10 \right] \frac{1}{(1 + 0.05)^{23.82}} = \$35.03$$

Problem 17.4 asks you to verify this result. You will discover that 23.82 years is not exactly optimal. Rather, waiting approximately 24.32 years—not 23.82 years—maximizes NPV. At this point the widget price will be about $1.43.

We will see the reason for this slight difference in Section 17.4. It occurs because the effective annual interest and growth rates of 5% and 4% are not the relevant rates since the decision to put off the investment is made on a day-to-day basis. It is instead the equivalent *continuously compounded* rates that matter.

This example demonstrates the important point that making an investment decision requires thinking carefully about alternatives, even under certainty.

We are left with (at least) two questions:

- How do we approach this kind of problem in general?

- Why didn't the NPV rule work? Or did it?

The Correct Use of NPV

The NPV rule worked correctly in the above example. The NPV rule for making investment decisions entails two steps:

1. Compute NPV by discounting expected cash flows at the opportunity cost of capital.

2. Accept a project if and only if its NPV is positive *and it exceeds the NPV of all mutually exclusive alternative projects.*[2]

When we computed the widget machine's NPV in equation (17.1), we neglected to take into account the NPV of alternative mutually exclusive projects, namely investing in the project tomorrow or at some other future date. Static NPV—NPV if we accept the project today—ignores project delay. Because static NPV measures the value of an action we could take, namely investing today, it at least provides a lower bound on the value of the project.

---

[1] The price must increase by a factor of 1.40/0.55 to reach $1.40, so we have $\ln(1.40/.55)/\ln(1.04) = 23.82$.

[2] Introductory finance textbooks state the NPV rule correctly, but in casual discussions it is sometimes stated incorrectly.

In this example it would be correct to invest in the project today *if not activating the project today meant that we would lose it forever.* Under this assumption, the mutually exclusive alternative (never taking the project) has a value of 0, so taking it today would be correct.

To decide whether and when to invest in an arbitrary project, we need to be able to compute the value of delaying that investment. As suggested at the start of the chapter, option pricing theory can help us to value delay.

The Project as an Option

The decision to invest in the project involves a comparison of net present values. In what sense is this an option?

We can interpret equation (17.1) so as to make the option analogy more apparent. When we take the project, we pay $10 and we commit to paying $0.90/year forever. The present value of this stream of costs is

$$\text{Present value of costs} = \$10 + \frac{\$0.90}{0.05} = \$28$$

As we discussed earlier, we can view this present value as analogous to the exercise price in an option valuation. In return for paying $28, we receive a cash flow with a present value of

$$\text{Present value of widget revenue} = \frac{S_{+1}}{0.01}$$

where S_{+1} is the widget price the year after we make the investment. When $S_{+1} = \$0.55$, the present value of cash flow is $55. This present value of widget revenue is the price the revenue stream would have if it were traded separately. It is analogous to the stock price in an option valuation, and therefore it is sometimes called the the **twin security** or the **traded present value** of the project.

Now recall the discussion in Sections 9.3 and 11.1 about the three factors governing early exercise of a call option: the dividends forgone by not acquiring the asset today; the interest saved by deferring the payment of the strike price; and the value of the insurance that is lost by exercising the option. It turns out that the same three considerations govern the decision to invest in the widget project.

First, by delaying investment, we lose the cash flow from selling widgets. The cash flow we do not receive is analogous to stock dividends we do not receive by holding an option rather than the underlying stock. The first period cash flow is $0.55. The present value of future cash flows is $0.55/0.01 = \$55$. Thus, the dividend yield is approximately 1%. (We can also think of the dividend yield as the difference between the discount rate [5%] and the growth rate of the cash flows [4%].)

Second, once we begin widget production, we are committed to spending the present value of the marginal widget cost, $18, along with the $10 initial investment. The annual value of delaying investment is interest on the total investment cost, or $0.05 \times \$28 = \$1.40$ per year.

Third and finally, in the widget project, there is no uncertainty and therefore no insurance value to delaying investment.

We can compute the value of the widget project option using the perpetual call calculation discussed in Section 12.6. The formula assumes continuously compounded rates, so for the interest rate we use $\ln(1.05) = 4.879\%$, and for the dividend yield we use the difference between the continuously compounded interest rate and growth rate, or $\ln(1.05) - \ln(1.04) = 0.9569\%$.

With $S = \$55$ (the present value of revenue), $K = \$28$ (the present value of costs), $r = 0.04879$, $\sigma = 0$,[3] and $\delta = 0.009569$, equation (12.19) gives an option price of $\$35.03$ and investment when the widget price equals $\$1.4276$. We will call this price the **investment trigger price.** We reach this price after about 24.32 years, which verifies the answer we discussed earlier.

The example in this section illustrates the importance of thinking dynamically about a project and shows how this specific problem can be modeled as an option.

17.2 INVESTMENT UNDER UNCERTAINTY

In this section we discuss the valuation of real investment projects when cash flows are uncertain. With the widget project in the previous section, waiting to invest was optimal because project dividends were initially less than the interest gained from deferring the project. If we add uncertainty about project cash flows, the value of insurance (the implicit put option) also influences the decision to delay the project. In such a case, waiting to invest provides information about the value of the project. In this section we will use a binomial tree to value a project with uncertain cash flows.

As before, the decision to invest in such a project is like exercising an American option: We pay the investment cost (strike price) to receive the asset (present value of future cash flows).

A Simple DCF Problem

We first examine a particularly simple valuation problem in order to better understand the link between discounted cash flow (DCF), real options, and financial options.

Suppose an analyst is evaluating a project that will generate a single cash flow, X, occurring at time T. As with many investment projects, it is not possible to observe market characteristics of the project. There is no way to directly estimate project returns, project volatility, or the covariances of the project with the stock market. Instead, suppose the analyst considers the economic fundamentals of the project and makes educated inferences about these characteristics. The analyst might also look for public firms with a business resembling the project. The analyst could then use information about these public firms to infer characteristics (such as beta) of the project.

[3] It is necessary to set σ to a small positive number such as 0.00001 to avoid a zero-divide error.

After examining all available data, the analyst estimates that the cash flow will be X_u if the economy is doing well—an event with the probability p—and X_d if the economy is doing poorly. The project requires expenditures of I_0 at time 0 and I_T at time T. The analyst determines that projects with comparable risk have an effective annual expected rate of return of α.

We can use this description to compute the value of the project, V. The standard discounted cash flow methodology calls for computing the expected cash flow, and using as a discount rate the expected return on a project of comparable risk:

$$V = \frac{pX_u + (1-p)X_d}{(1+\alpha)^T} \tag{17.2}$$

Assuming that we either take the project now or never, we invest in the project if $V \geq I_0 + I_T/(1+r)^T$.

Example 17.1   Suppose that the risk-free rate is $r = 6\%$, the expected return on the market is $r_M = 10\%$, the project beta is $\beta = 1.25$, $p = 0.60$, $T = 1$, $X_u = \$120$, and $X_d = \$80$. The expected return on an asset with the same risk as the project is

$$\alpha = 0.06 + 1.25 \times (0.10 - 0.06) = 0.11$$

The expected cash flow is

$$E(X) = 0.60 \times \$120 + 0.40 \times \$80 = \$104$$

Using (17.2), the present value of the project cash flows is

$$V = \frac{\$104}{1 + 0.11} = \$93.694$$

Suppose that $I_0 = \$10$ and $I_1 = \$95$ and that the manager commits at time 0 to paying the $95 at time 1. Then net present value is

$$V - I_0 - I_1/(1+r) = 93.694 - \$10 - \$95/1.06$$
$$= -\$5.929 \qquad ≹$$

Valuing Derivatives on the Cash Flow

The calculation in Example 17.1 is standard but it is nevertheless based on strong assumptions: We have specified the future cash flows in different states, the probabilities of those states, and the comparability of the project to a traded asset.[4] It turns out that in

....

[4]The last assumption in particular deserves some additional comment. We are assuming that the returns of the project are *spanned* by existing traded assets; in other words, the addition of the project to the universe of assets does not materially change the opportunities available to investors. If this were not true, we would have to know more about the preferences of investors in order to evaluate the project.

valuing the project *we have already made all the assumptions we need to make in order to value derivatives related to the project.*

To see how to perform capital budgeting calculations involving options, suppose that if we invest I_0 to start the project, the subsequent investment of I_1 is optional: We make this further investment only if the project at time 1 has sufficient value. Since the project has a good and bad outcome, it is natural to think about using binomial option valuation. In order to do so, we need to know the risk-neutral probability of the high outcome.[5]

Fortunately, we can easily compute risk-neutral probabilities for this project. Recall from Chapter 10 that the expected risk-neutral price is the forward price. We have computed V, which is the price of an asset paying a single cash flow at time T. The forward price is

$$F_{0,T} = V(1+r)^T$$

The risk-neutral probability must therefore satisfy

$$p^* X_u + (1 - p^*) X_d = F_{0,T}$$

Thus, we have

$$p^* = \frac{F_{0,T} - X_d}{X_u - X_d}$$

This gives us the binomial tree (X_u and X_d) and the risk-neutral probability of a high outcome (p^*). Notice that if we value the project using the risk-neutral distribution, then *by construction* we will obtain the original project value, V.

Example 17.2 Consider the same parameters as in Example 17.1. The forward price for the project is

$$F_{0,1} = \$93.694 \times (1.06) = \$99.315$$

The risk-neutral probability of the good outcome is

$$p^* = \frac{99.315 - 80}{120 - 80} = 0.4829$$

If we value the project using the risk-neutral probability, we obtain

$$\frac{0.4829 \times \$120 + (1 - 0.4829) \times \$80}{1.06} = \$93.694$$

Now make the same assumptions as in Example 17.1, except that we decide at time 1 whether to incur the $95 cost. We will choose to produce output in time 1 only

---

[5] In general we also need to know volatility to value an option. As we discussed in Chapter 10, volatility determines the vertical *distance* between binomial nodes. Thus, in specifying the tree, we implicitly specified volatility.

when the cash flow is \$120, since we would lose \$15 by paying \$95 to produce when the output sells for \$80. The value of the project is

$$\frac{p^* \max[0, X_u - I_1] + (1 - p^*) \max[0, X_L - I_1]}{1 + r} - I_0$$

$$= \frac{0.4829 \times \$25 + (1 - 0.4829) \times 0}{1.06} - \$10 = \$1.389 \quad 🦢$$

Given the risk-neutral probability and the cash flow distribution, we can value projects with options or other nonlinear cash flows.[6]

You may be thinking that there appears to be little difference between standard discounted cash flow valuation and real options valuation. Recognize that *any* financial valuation entails assigning a dollar value today to a (possibly uncertain) cash flow that occurs in the future. This description applies to the valuation of a project, as well as to valuing a bond, a stock, or an option.

When we value an option on a stock, we rely on the market to have already performed part of the valuation—namely, valuing the stock. When we value an option on a project, we have to estimate the value of the project since we cannot observe it. *This is true whether or not the project contains options.*

This discussion illustrates the point we made before in Section 11.2, that risk-neutral pricing and discounted cash flow are alternative means of valuing a future cash flow. If done using the same assumptions, the two methods give the same answer. In practice, of course, it is common to make simplifying assumptions for tractability. Answers may differ because the simplifying assumptions for different valuation methods are inconsistent.

Evaluating a Project with a 2-Year Investment Horizon

We now consider the problem of when to invest in a risky project. As before, the decision to invest in such a project is like exercising an American option: We pay the investment cost (strike price) to receive the asset (present value of future cash flows). The widget project in the previous section had cash flows that were certain.

Suppose a project costs \$100 and begins producing an infinite stream of cash flows 1 year after investment. Expected annual cash flows for the first year are \$18, and are expected to grow annually at a rate of 3%. Suppose further that the risk-free rate is 7%, the risk premium on the market is 6%, and the beta of the project is 1.33. Using the Capital Asset Pricing Model (CAPM), we compute the discount rate for the project in

----

[6]Problem 17.9 asks you to value a project paying the squared cash flow.

the usual way:

$$r_{\text{project}} = r_{\text{risk-free}} + \beta(r_{\text{market}} - r_{\text{risk-free}})$$
$$= 0.07 + 1.33(0.06)$$
$$= 0.15$$

To value the project, we perform a standard discounted cash flow calculation. Since the project lives forever, we treat it as a perpetual growing annuity. The present value is

$$PV = \frac{E(CF_1)}{r_{\text{project}} - \text{growth rate}}$$
$$= \frac{\$18}{0.15 - 0.03}$$
$$= \$150$$

Static NPV is therefore $150 - $100 = $50.

Suppose we have 2 years in which to decide whether to accept the project; at the end of that time, we either invest in the project or lose it. (Imagine, for example, that the licensing rights for a technology will revert at that time to the original owner). The static NPV rule will apply after two years because further deferral is not possible. However, at time 0, we must evaluate the option to wait.

The forgone initial cash flow (the dividend on the project) is $18 and the interest saving is $7 (7% × 100). Thus, considering only dividends and interest, it makes sense to start the project immediately. However, the project also has implicit insurance that we lose by investing in the project. To value the insurance we need to know the project volatility.

A tree for project value Suppose that cash flows are lognormally distributed with a 50% volatility. Figure 17.1 uses the Cox-Ross-Rubinstein approach to construct a

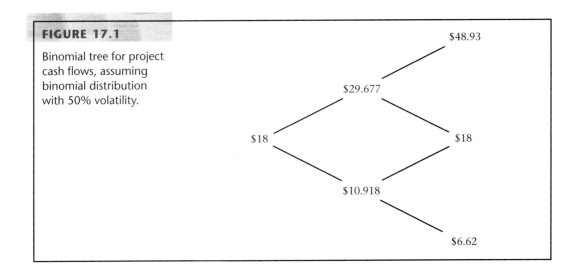

FIGURE 17.1

Binomial tree for project cash flows, assuming binomial distribution with 50% volatility.

$18 $29.677 $48.93

$18 $10.918 $6.62

binomial tree for the evolution of cash flows with a binomial period of 1 year. If we wait to take the project, initial cash flows in 1 year will be either $18e^{0.5} = \$29.677$ or $18e^{-0.5} = \$10.918$. Since the project value is proportional to cash flows, the value of the project is also lognormally distributed with a 50% volatility.

In 1 year, project value will be either $\$29.677/(0.15 - 0.03) = \$247.31$ or $\$10.918/(0.15 - 0.03) = \$91$. If we will continue to learn about the project at the same rate over time, we can build a binomial tree with constant volatility that shows the evolution of project value. This tree, constructed by discounting at each node the cash flows in Figure 17.1, is in Figure 17.2.

The act of investing creates the project, therefore the value at each node in Figure 17.2 is the value of the project *if we were to invest at that node*. Figure 17.2 describes the evolution of the project's present value. The project does not exist prior to investment, but the tree provides the information we need in order to decide whether to invest. The tree in Figure 17.2 is exactly the same tree we would construct for the stock price of a company that had the project as its only asset and that paid dividends equal to the cash flow of the project. Such a stock would have an initial price of $150 and a 50% volatility.

It may trouble you that in valuing this project, option pricing formulas are being used in a context where literal replication of the option is not possible because the twin security does not exist. As we saw in Chapter 11, however, *the binomial procedure also works in a setting where we perform valuation using the CAPM or other pricing model.* Thus, we are using option pricing formulas to create *fair prices*, not *arbitrage-free* prices.

Solving for the optimal investment decision   We can use Figure 17.2 to solve the investment problem exactly as we would use it in a binomial option pricing problem. The inputs are initial project value, $S = \$150$; investment cost, $K = \$100$; continuously compounded risk-free rate, $r = \ln(1.07) = 6.766\%$; volatility, $\sigma = 0.50$; and time to

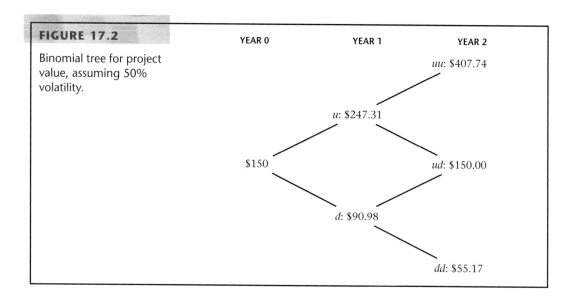

FIGURE 17.2

Binomial tree for project value, assuming 50% volatility.

	YEAR 0	YEAR 1	YEAR 2
			uu: $407.74
		u: $247.31	
	$150		ud: $150.00
		d: $90.98	
			dd: $55.17

the curve to the left of a, denoted $N(a)$, equals this probability, $Prob(z < a)$. We call $N(a)$ the **cumulative normal distribution function.** The integral from $-\infty$ to a is the area under the density over that range; it is cumulative in that it sums the probabilities from $-\infty$ to a. Mathematically, this is accomplished by integrating the standard normal density, equation (18.1) with $\mu = 0$ and $\sigma = 1$, from $-\infty$ to a:

$$N(a) \equiv \int_{-\infty}^{a} \frac{1}{\sqrt{2\pi}} e^{-\frac{1}{2}x^2} dx \qquad (18.2)$$

As an example, $N(0.3)$ is shown in Figure 18.2. In the top panel, $N(0.3)$ is the area under the normal density curve between $-\infty$ and 0.3. In the bottom panel, $N(0.3)$ is a point on the cumulative distribution. The range $-\infty$ to $+\infty$ covers all possible outcomes for a single draw from a normal distribution. The probability that a randomly drawn number will be less than ∞ is 1; hence, $N(\infty) = 1$. As you may already have surmised, the $N(a)$ defined above is the same $N()$ used in computing the Black-Scholes formula.

There is no simple formula for the cumulative normal distribution function, equation (18.2), but as we mentioned in Chapter 12, it is a frequent-enough calculation that modern spreadsheets have it as a built-in function. (In Excel the function is called

FIGURE 18.2

Top panel: Area under the normal curve to the left of 0.3. *Bottom panel:* Cumulative normal distribution. The height at $x = 0.3$, given by $N(0.3)$, is 0.6179.

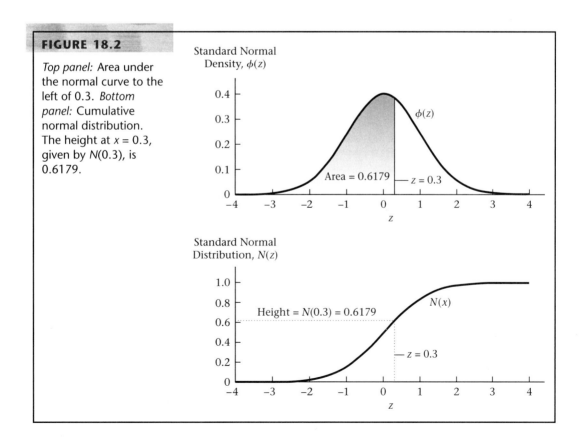

NormSDist.) The area under the normal density from $-\infty$ to 0.3 is 0.6179. Thus, if you draw a number from the standard normal distribution, 61.79% of the time the number you draw will be less than 0.3.

Suppose that we wish to know the probability that a number drawn from the standard normal distribution will be between a and $-a$. We have

$$\text{Prob}(z < -a) = N(-a)$$
$$\text{Prob}(z < a) = N(a)$$

These relationships imply that

$$\text{Prob}(-a < z < a) = N(a) - N(-a)$$

The area under the curve between $-a$ and a equals the difference between the area below a and the area below $-a$. Since the standard normal distribution is symmetric about 0, the area under the curve *above* a equals the area under the curve *below* $-a$. Thus,

$$N(-a) = 1 - N(a) \tag{18.3}$$

Example 18.1   The probability that a number drawn from the standard normal distribution will be between -0.3 and $+0.3$ is

$$\begin{aligned}
\text{Prob}(-0.3 < z < 0.3) &= N(0.3) - N(-0.3) \\
&= N(0.3) - [1 - N(0.3)] \\
&= 2 \times 0.6179 - 1 = 0.2358
\end{aligned}$$ ❧

Finally, if a variable obeys the standard normal distribution, it is extremely unlikely to take on large positive or negative values. The probability that a single draw will be below -3 or above 3 is only 0.0027. If you drew from a standard normal distribution every day, you would draw above 3 or below -3 only about once a year. The probability of being below -4 or above 4 is 0.000063, which, with daily draws, would occur on average about once every 43.25 years.

Converting a Normal Random Variable to Standard Normal

If we have an arbitrary normal random variable, it is easy to convert it to standard normal. Suppose

$$x \sim \mathcal{N}(\mu, \sigma^2)$$

Then we can create a standard normal random variable, z, by subtracting the mean and dividing by the standard deviation:

$$z = \frac{x - \mu}{\sigma} \tag{18.4}$$

Using this fact, we can compute the probability that x is less than some number b:

$$\text{Prob}(x < b) = \text{Prob}\left(\frac{x - \mu}{\sigma} < \frac{b - \mu}{\sigma}\right)$$

$$= N\left(\frac{b - \mu}{\sigma}\right) \tag{18.5}$$

Using equation (18.3), the complementary probability is

$$\text{Prob}(x > b) = 1 - \text{Prob}(x < b)$$

$$= 1 - N\left(\frac{b - \mu}{\sigma}\right)$$

$$= N\left(\frac{\mu - b}{\sigma}\right) \tag{18.6}$$

This result will be helpful in interpreting the Black-Scholes formula.

If we have a standard normal random variable z, we can generate a variable $x \sim \mathcal{N}(\mu, \sigma^2)$, using the following:

$$x = \mu + \sigma z \tag{18.7}$$

Example 18.2 Suppose that $x \sim \mathcal{N}(3, 25)$ and $z \sim \mathcal{N}(0, 1)$. Then

$$\frac{x - 3}{5} \sim \mathcal{N}(0, 1),$$

and

$$3 + 5 \times z \sim \mathcal{N}(3, 25)$$ ❧

Sums of Normal Random Variables

Suppose we have n random variables x_i, $i = 1, \ldots, n$, with mean and variance $E(x_i) = \mu_i$, $Var(x_i) = \sigma_i^2$, and covariance $Cov(x_i, x_j) = \sigma_{ij}$. (The covariance between two random variables measures their tendency to move together. We can also write the covariance in terms of ρ_{ij}, the correlation between x_i and x_j: $\sigma_{ij} = \rho_{ij}\sigma_i\sigma_j$.) Then the weighted sum of the n random variables has mean

$$E\left(\sum_{i=1}^{n} \omega_i x_i\right) = \sum_{i=1}^{n} \omega_i \mu_i \tag{18.8}$$

and variance

$$\text{Var}\left(\sum_{i=1}^{n} \omega_i x_i\right) = \sum_{i=1}^{n}\sum_{j=1}^{n} \omega_i \omega_j \sigma_{ij} \tag{18.9}$$

where ω_i and ω_j represent arbitrary weights. These formulas for the mean and variance are true for any distribution of the x_i.

In general, the distribution of a sum of random variables is different from the distribution of the individual random variables. However, the normal distribution is an example of a **stable distribution.** A distribution is stable if sums of random variables have the same distribution as the original random variables. In this case, the sum of normally distributed random variables is normal. Thus, for normally distributed x_i,

$$\sum_{i=1}^{n} \omega_i x_i \sim \mathcal{N} \left(\sum_{i=1}^{n} \omega_i \mu_i, \sum_{i=1}^{n} \sum_{j=1}^{n} \omega_i \omega_j \sigma_{ij} \right) \qquad (18.10)$$

A familiar special case of this occurs with the sum of two random variables:

$$ax_1 + bx_2 \sim \mathcal{N} \left(a\mu_1 + b\mu_2, a^2\sigma_1^2 + b^2\sigma_2^2 + 2ab\rho\sigma_1\sigma_2 \right)$$

The central limit theorem Why does the normal distribution appear in option pricing (and frequently in other contexts)? The normal distribution is important because it arises naturally when random variables are added. The normal distribution was originally discovered by mathematicians studying series of random events, such as gambling outcomes and observational errors.[2] Suppose, for example, that a surveyor is making observations to draft a map. The measurements will always have some error, and the error will differ from measurement to measurement. Errors can arise from observational error, imprecise use of the instruments, or simply from recording the wrong number. Whatever the reason, the errors will in general be accidental and, hence, *uncorrelated*. If you were using such error-prone data, you would like to know the statistical distribution of these errors in order to assess the reliability of your conclusions for a given number of observations, and also to decide how many observations to make to achieve a given degree of reliability. It would seem that the nature of the errors would differ depending on who made them, the kind of equipment used, and so forth. The remarkable result is that sums of such errors are approximately normal.

The normal distribution is therefore not just a convenient, aesthetically pleasing distribution, but it arises in nature when outcomes can be characterized as sums of independent random variables with a finite variance. The distribution of such a sum approaches normality. This result is known as the **central limit theorem.**[3]

In the context of asset returns, the continuously compounded stock return over a year is the sum of the daily continuously compounded returns. If news and other factors are the shocks that cause asset prices to change, and if these changes are independent, then it is natural to think that longer-period continuously compounded returns are normally

---

[2] The history of statistics—including the story of the normal distribution—is entertainingly related in Bernstein (1996).

[3] Most statistics books discuss one or more versions of the central limit theorem. See, for example, DeGroot (1975, pp. 227–231) or Mood et al. (1974, pp. 233–236).

distributed. Since the central limit theorem is a theorem about what happens in the limit, sums of just a few random variables may not appear normal. But the normality of continuously compounded returns is a reasonable starting point for thinking about stock returns.

18.2 THE LOGNORMAL DISTRIBUTION

A random variable, y, is said to be **lognormally distributed** if $\ln(y)$ is normally distributed. Put another way, if x is normally distributed, y is lognormal if it can be written in either of two equivalent ways:

$$\ln(y) = x$$

or

$$y = e^x$$

This last equation is the link between normally distributed continuously compounded returns and lognormality of the stock price.

By definition, the continuously compounded return from 0 to t is

$$R(0, t) = \ln(S_t/S_0) \tag{18.11}$$

Suppose $R(0, t)$ is normally distributed. By exponentiating both sides, we obtain

$$S_t = S_0 e^{R(0,t)} \tag{18.12}$$

Equation (18.12) shows that if continuously compounded returns are normally distributed, then the stock price is lognormally distributed. Exponentiation converts the continuously compounded return, $R(0, t)$, into one plus the effective total return from 0 to t, $e^{R(0,t)}$. Notice that because S_t is created by exponentiation of $R(0, t)$, *a lognormal stock price cannot be negative.*

We saw that the sum of normal variables is normal. For this reason, the *product* of lognormal random variables is lognormal. If x_1 and x_2 are normal, then $y_1 = e^{x_1}$ and $y_2 = e^{x_2}$ are lognormal. The product of y_1 and y_2 is

$$y_1 \times y_2 = e^{x_1} \times e^{x_2} = e^{x_1+x_2}$$

Since $x_1 + x_2$ is normal, $e^{x_1+x_2}$ is lognormal. Thus, because normality is preserved by addition, lognormality is preserved by multiplication. However, just as the product of normal random variables is not normal, the sum of lognormal random variables is not lognormal.

We saw in Section 11.3 that the binomial model generates a stock price distribution that appears lognormal; this was an example of the central limit theorem. In the binomial model, the continuously compounded stock return is binomially distributed. Sums of binomial random variables approach normality. Thus, in the binomial model, the continuously compounded return approaches normality and the stock price distribution approaches lognormality.

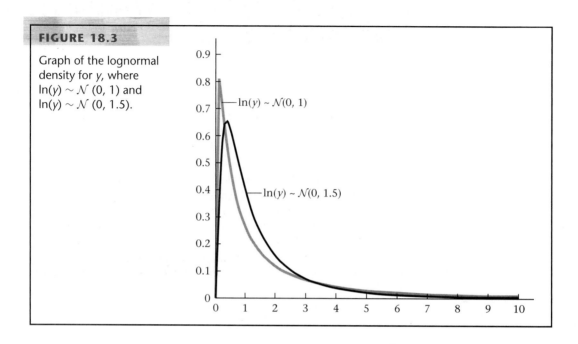

FIGURE 18.3

Graph of the lognormal density for y, where $\ln(y) \sim \mathcal{N}(0, 1)$ and $\ln(y) \sim \mathcal{N}(0, 1.5)$.

If $\ln(y) \sim \mathcal{N}(m, v^2)$, the lognormal density function is given by

$$g(y; m, v) \equiv \frac{1}{yv\sqrt{2\pi}} e^{-\frac{1}{2}\left(\frac{\ln(y)-m}{v}\right)^2}$$

Figure 18.3 is a graph of the lognormal distribution as a function of y, assuming $\mu = 0$, and for both $\sigma = 1$ and $\sigma = 1.5$. Notice that the lognormal distribution is non-negative and skewed to the right. Figure 18.3 is based upon exponentiating the distributions in Figure 18.1.

We can compute the mean and variance of a lognormally distributed random variable. If $x \sim \mathcal{N}(m, v^2)$, then the expected value of e^x is given by

$$E(e^x) = e^{m+\frac{1}{2}v^2} \tag{18.13}$$

We prove this in Appendix 18.A, but it is intuitive that the mean of the exponentiated variable will be greater than the exponentiated mean of the underlying normal variable. Exponentiation is asymmetric: A positive random draw generates a bigger increase than an identical negative random draw does a decrease. To see this, consider a mean zero binomial random variable that is 0.5 with probability 0.5 and −0.5 with probability 0.5. You can verify that $e^{0.5} = 1.6487$. Thus, $\frac{e^{0.5}+e^{-0.5}}{2} = \frac{1.6487+0.6065}{2} = 1.128$, which is obviously greater than $e^0 = 1$.

This is a specific example of **Jensen's inequality** (see Appendix C at the end of this book): The expectation of a function of a random variable is not generally equal to the function evaluated at the expectation of the random variable. In the context of this example, $E(e^x) \neq e^{E(x)}$. Since the exponential function is convex, Jensen's inequality implies that $E(e^x) > e^{E(x)}$. Derivatives theory is replete with examples of Jensen's inequality.

The variance of a lognormal random variable is

$$\text{Var}(e^x) = e^{2m+v^2}\left(e^{v^2} - 1\right) \qquad (18.14)$$

While we can compute the variance of a lognormal variable, it is much more convenient to use only the variance of $\ln(y)$, which is normal. We will not use equation (18.14) in the rest of this book.

18.3 A LOGNORMAL MODEL OF STOCK PRICES

How do we implement lognormality as a model for the stock price? If the stock price S_t is lognormal, we can write

$$\frac{S_t}{S_0} = e^x$$

where x, the continuously compounded return from 0 to t, is normally distributed. We want to find a specification for x that provides a *useful* way to think about stock prices.

Let the continuously compounded return from time t to some later time s be $R(t, s)$. Suppose we have times $t_0 < t_1 < t_2$. By the definition of the continuously compounded return, we have

$$S_{t_1} = S_{t_0} e^{R(t_0, t_1)}$$
$$S_{t_2} = S_{t_1} e^{R(t_1, t_2)}$$

The stock price at t_2 can therefore be expressed as

$$\begin{aligned} S_{t_2} &= S_{t_1} e^{R(t_1, t_2)} \\ &= S_{t_0} e^{R(t_0, t_1)} e^{R(t_1, t_2)} \\ &= S_{t_0} e^{R(t_0, t_1) + R(t_1, t_2)} \end{aligned}$$

Thus, the continuously compounded return from t_0 to t_2, $R(t_0, t_2)$, is the sum of the continuously compounded returns over the shorter periods:

$$R(t_0, t_2) = R(t_0, t_1) + R(t_1, t_2) \qquad (18.15)$$

Example 18.3 Suppose the stock price is initially \$100 and the continuously compounded return on a stock is 15% one year and 3% the next year. The price after 1 year is $\$100e^{0.15} = \$116.1834$, and after 2 years is $\$116.1834e^{0.03} = \$119.722$. This equals $100e^{0.15+0.03} = 100e^{0.18}$. ❦

As we saw in Section 11.3, equation (18.15), together with the assumption that returns are independent and identically distributed over time, implies that the mean and variance of returns over different horizons are proportional to the length of the horizon. Take the period of time from 0 to T and carve it up into n intervals of length h, where $h = T/n$. We can then write the continuously compounded return from 0 to T as the sum of the n returns over the shorter periods:

$$R(0, T) = R(0, h) + R(h, 2h) + \cdots + R[(n-1)h, T]$$

$$= \sum_{i=1}^{n} R[(i-1)h, ih]$$

Let $E(R[(i-1)h, ih]) = \alpha_h$ and $\text{Var}(R[(i-1)h, ih]) = \sigma_h^2$. Then over the entire period, the mean and variance are

$$E[R(0, T)] = n\alpha_h \tag{18.16}$$

$$\text{Var}[R(0, T)] = n\sigma_h^2 \tag{18.17}$$

Thus, if returns are independent and identically distributed, *the mean and variance of the continuously compounded returns are proportional to time.* This result corresponds with the intuition that both the mean and variance of the return should be greater over long horizons than over short horizons.

Now we have enough background to present an explicit lognormal model of the stock price. Generally we will let t be denominated in years and α and σ be the annual mean and standard deviation, with δ the annual dividend yield on the stock. We will assume that the continuously compounded capital gain from 0 to t, $\ln(S_t/S_0)$, is normally distributed with mean $(\alpha - \delta - 0.5\sigma^2)t$ and variance $\sigma^2 t$:

$$\boxed{\ln(S_t/S_0) \sim \mathcal{N}[(\alpha - \delta - 0.5\sigma^2)t, \sigma^2 t]} \tag{18.18}$$

This gives us two equivalent ways to write an expression for the stock price.

First, recall from equation (18.7) that we can convert a standard normal random variable, z, into one with an arbitrary mean or variance by multiplying by the standard deviation and adding the mean. We can write

$$\ln(S_t/S_0) = (\alpha - \delta - \frac{1}{2}\sigma^2)t + \sigma\sqrt{t}z \tag{18.19}$$

Second, we can exponentiate equation (18.19) to obtain an expression for the stock price:

$$\boxed{S_t = S_0 e^{(\alpha - \delta - \frac{1}{2}\sigma^2)t + \sigma\sqrt{t}z}} \tag{18.20}$$

We will use equation (18.20) often in what follows.

You may be wondering how to interpret equations (18.18), (18.19), and (18.20). The subtraction of the dividend yield, δ, is necessary since, other things equal, a higher dividend yield means a lower future stock price. But why do we subtract $\frac{1}{2}\sigma^2$ in the mean?

To understand equation (18.20) it helps to compute the expected stock price. We can do this by breaking up the right-hand side of equation (18.20) into two terms, one of which contains the random variable z and the other of which does not:

$$S_t = S_0 e^{(\alpha - \frac{1}{2}\sigma^2)t} e^{\sigma\sqrt{t}z}$$

Next, evaluate the expectation of $e^{\sigma\sqrt{t}z}$ using equation (18.13). Since $z \sim \mathcal{N}(0, 1)$, we have

$$E\left(e^{\sigma\sqrt{t}z}\right) = e^{\frac{1}{2}\sigma^2 t}$$

This gives us

$$E(S_t) = S_0 e^{(\alpha - \delta - \frac{1}{2}\sigma^2)t} e^{\frac{1}{2}\sigma^2 t} \qquad (18.21)$$

or

$$\boxed{E(S_t) = S_0 e^{(\alpha - \delta)t}} \qquad (18.22)$$

The expression $\alpha - \delta$ is the expected continuously compounded rate of appreciation on the stock. If we did not subtract $\frac{1}{2}\sigma^2$ in equation (18.20), then the expected rate of appreciation would be $\alpha - \delta + \frac{1}{2}\sigma^2$. This is fine (we can define things as we like), except that it renders α difficult to interpret.

Thus, the issue is purely one of creating an expression where it is easy to interpret the parameters. If we want $\alpha - \delta$ to have an interpretation as the expected continuously compounded capital gain on the stock, then because of equation (18.13), we need to subtract $\frac{1}{2}\sigma^2$.

The median stock price—the value such that 50% of the time prices will be above or below that value—is obtained by setting $z = 0$ in equation (18.20). The median is thus

$$S_0 e^{(\alpha - \delta - \frac{1}{2}\sigma^2)t} = E(S_t)e^{-\frac{1}{2}\sigma^2 t}$$

This equation demonstrates that the median is below the mean. *More than 50% of the time, a lognormally distributed stock will earn below its expected return.* Perhaps more surprisingly, if σ is large, a lognormally distributed stock will lose money ($S_t < S_0$) more than half the time!

Example 18.4 Suppose that the stock price today is \$100, the expected rate of return on the stock is $\alpha = 10\%$/year, and the standard deviation (volatility) is $\sigma = 30\%$/year. If the stock is lognormally distributed, the continuously compounded 2-year return is 20% and the 2-year volatility is $0.30 \times \sqrt{2} = 0.4243$. Thus, we have

$$S_2 = \$100 e^{(0.1 - \frac{1}{2}0.3^2) \times 2 + \sigma\sqrt{2}z}$$

The expected value of S_2 is

$$E(S_2) = \$100 e^{(0.1 \times 2)} = \$122.14$$

The median stock price is

$$\$100e^{(0.1-0.5\times0.3^2)\times2} = \$111.63$$

If the volatility were 60%, the expected value would still be $122.14, but the median would be

$$\$100e^{(0.1-0.5\times0.6^2)\times2} = \$85.21$$

Half the time, after 2 years the stock price would be below this value. ❧

We can also define a "one standard deviation move" in the stock price. Since z has the standard normal distribution, then if $z = 1$, the continuously compounded stock return is the mean plus one standard deviation, and if $z = -1$, the continuously compounded stock return is the mean minus one standard deviation.

Example 18.5 Using the same assumptions as in Example 18.4, a one standard deviation move up over 2 years is given by

$$S_2 = \$100e^{(0.1-\frac{1}{2}0.3^2)\times2+\sigma\sqrt{2}\times1} = \$170.62$$

A one standard deviation move down is given by

$$S_2 = \$100e^{(0.1-\frac{1}{2}0.3^2)\times2-\sigma\sqrt{2}\times1} = \$73.03$$

We can think of these prices as logarithmically centered around the mean price of $122.14.

This discussion also shows us where the binomial models in Chapter 11 come from. In Section 11.3, we presented three different ways to construct a binomial model. All had up and down stock price moves of the form

$$S_u = Se^{\alpha h+\sigma\sqrt{h}}; \qquad S_d = Se^{\alpha h-\sigma\sqrt{h}}$$

where α differed for the three models. In all cases, we generated up and down moves by setting $z = \pm1$. As $h \to 0$ the three models converge; the effects of the different α's in the three cases are offset by the different risk-neutral probabilities.

18.4 LOGNORMAL PROBABILITY CALCULATIONS

If S_t is lognormally distributed, we can use this fact to compute a number of probabilities and expectations. For example, we can compute the probability that an option will expire in the money, and, given that it expires in the money, the expected stock price. In this section we will present formulas for these calculations.

Probabilities

If the stock price today is S_0, what is the probability that $S_t < K$, where K is some arbitrary number? Note that $S_t < K$ exactly when $\ln(S_t) < \ln(K)$. Since $\ln(S)$ is normally distributed, we can just use the normal calculations we developed above. We have

$$\ln(S_t/S_0) \sim \mathcal{N}[(\alpha - \delta - 0.5\sigma^2)t, \sigma^2 t]$$

or, equivalently,

$$\ln(S_t) \sim \mathcal{N}\left[\ln(S_0) + (\alpha - \delta - 0.5\sigma^2)t, \sigma^2 t\right]$$

We can create a standard normal number random variable, z, by subtracting the mean and dividing by the standard deviation:

$$z = \frac{\ln(S_t) - \ln(S_0) - (\alpha - \delta - 0.5\sigma^2)t}{\sigma\sqrt{t}}$$

We have $\text{Prob}(S_t < K) = \text{Prob}[\ln(S_t) < \ln(K)]$. Subtracting the mean from both $\ln(S_t)$ and $\ln(K)$ and dividing by the standard deviation, we obtain

$$\text{Prob}(S_t < K) =$$

$$\text{Prob}\left[\frac{\ln(S_t) - \ln(S_0) - (\alpha - \delta - 0.5\sigma^2)t}{\sigma\sqrt{t}} < \frac{\ln(K) - \ln(S_0) - (\alpha - \delta - 0.5\sigma^2)t}{\sigma\sqrt{t}}\right]$$

Since the left-hand side is a standard normal random variable, the probability that $S_t < K$ is

$$\text{Prob}(S_t < K) = \text{Prob}\left[z < \frac{\ln(K) - \ln(S_0) - (\alpha - \delta - 0.5\sigma^2)t}{\sigma\sqrt{t}}\right]$$

Since $z \sim \mathcal{N}(0, 1)$, $\text{Prob}(S_t < K)$ is

$$\text{Prob}(S_t < K) = N\left[\frac{\ln(K) - \ln(S_0) - (\alpha - \delta - 0.5\sigma^2)t}{\sigma\sqrt{t}}\right]$$

This can also be written

$$\boxed{\text{Prob}(S_t < K) = N(-\hat{d}_2)} \qquad (18.23)$$

where $\hat{d}_2$ is the standard Black-Scholes argument (see equation (12.1)) with the risk-free rate, r, replaced with the actual expected return on the stock, α. We can also perform the complementary calculation. We have $\text{Prob}(S_t > K) = 1 - \text{Prob}(S_t < K)$, so

$$\boxed{\text{Prob}(S_t > K) = N(\hat{d}_2)} \qquad (18.24)$$

The expression $N(\hat{d}_2)$ contains the true expected return on the stock, α. If we replace α with r, the risk-free rate in equations (18.23) and (18.24), we obtain the risk-neutral probabilities that S_t is above or below K. It is exactly these risk-neutral versions of equations (18.23) and (18.24) that appear in the Black-Scholes call and put option pricing formulas.

Lognormal Confidence Intervals

We can now answer questions about future prices, such as "what is the range of prices such that there is a 95% probability that the stock price will be in that range 1 year from today?" To answer this question, we compute the 95% confidence intervals for a number of different time horizons.

Suppose we would like to know the prices S_t^L and S_t^U such that $\text{Prob}(S_t^L < S_t) = p/2$ and $\text{Prob}(S_t^U > S_t) = p/2$. If the stock price is S_0, we can generate S_t^L and S_t^U as follows. We know from equation (18.23) that

$$\text{Prob}(S < S_t^L) = N(-\hat{d}_2)$$

where

$$\hat{d}_2 = [\ln(S_0/S_t^L) + (\alpha - \delta - 0.5\sigma^2)t]/\sigma\sqrt{t}$$

Thus, we want to find the S_t^L such that the probability that S_t is less than S_t^L is $p/2$, or

$$p/2 = N(-\hat{d}_2)$$

In order to do this, we need to invert the cumulative standard normal distribution function—i.e., ask what number $\hat{d}_2$ corresponds to a given probability. We can write this inverse cumulative normal probability function as $N^{-1}(p)$. Then by definition, $N^{-1}[N(x)] = x$. Fortunately, this is a standard calculation, and Excel and other spreadsheets contain a built-in function that does this. (In Excel it is *NormSInv*.) We have

$$N^{-1}(p/2) = -d_2$$

Solving explicity for S_t^L gives us

$$S_t^L = S_0 e^{(\alpha - \delta - \frac{1}{2}\sigma^2)t + \sigma\sqrt{t}N^{-1}(p/2)}$$

Similiarly, we solve for the S_t^U such that

$$N^{-1}(1 - p/2) = \hat{d}_2$$

This gives us

$$S_t^U = S_0 e^{(\alpha - \delta - \frac{1}{2}\sigma^2)t + \sigma\sqrt{t}N^{-1}(1-p/2)}$$

Thus, to generate a confidence interval for a lognormal price, we need only find the values of z corresponding to the same confidence interval for a $\mathcal{N}(0, 1)$ variable, and then substitute those values into the expression for the lognormal price.

Example 18.6 If $p = 5\%$, $N^{-1}(0.025) = -1.96$ and $N^{-1}(0.975) = 1.96$. That is, there is a 5% probability that a standard normal random variable will be outside the range $(-1.96, 1.96)$. Thus, if $S_0 = \$100$, $t = 2$, $\alpha = 0.10$, $\delta = 0$, and $\sigma = 0.30$, we have

$$S_t^L = S_0 e^{(\alpha - \delta - \frac{1}{2}\sigma^2)t - \sigma\sqrt{t}1.96}$$

$$= S_0 e^{(0.10 - \frac{1}{2}0.3^2) \times 2 - 0.3 \times \sqrt{2} \times 1.96}$$

$$= \$48.599$$

Similarly, for S_t^U we have

$$S_t^U = S_0 e^{(\alpha - \delta - \frac{1}{2}\sigma^2)t + \sigma\sqrt{t}1.96}$$

$$= \$256.40$$

Example 18.7 Suppose we have a lognormally distributed $50 stock with a 15% continuously compounded expected rate of return, a zero dividend yield, and a 30% volatility. Consider a horizon of 1 month ($t = \frac{1}{12}$). The monthly continuously compounded mean return is

$$(\alpha - \delta - \frac{1}{2}\sigma^2)t = \left(0.15 - 0 - \frac{1}{2}0.3^2\right)\frac{1}{12}$$

$$= 0.00875$$

and the monthly standard deviation is

$$\sigma\sqrt{t} = 0.3\sqrt{\frac{1}{12}}$$

$$= .0866$$

For the standard normal distribution, there is a 68.27% probability of drawing a number in the interval $(-1, +1)$, and a 95.45% probability of drawing a number in the interval $(-2, +2)$. Thus, over a 1-month horizon, there is a 68.27% chance that the continuously compounded return on the stock will be 0.00875 ± 0.0866 (i.e., the return is between -7.88% and 9.54%), and a 95.45% chance that the return will be $0.00875 \pm 2 \times 0.0866$ (the return will be between -16.44% and 18.19%):

$$-.0788 \leq \ln\left(\frac{S_{\text{one month}}}{50}\right) \leq 0.0954 \qquad \text{prob} = 68.27\%$$

$$-.1644 \leq \ln\left(\frac{S_{\text{one month}}}{50}\right) \leq 0.1819 \qquad \text{prob} = 95.45\%$$

Equivalently, by exponentiating all of these terms (for example, $\$50e^{-0.0788} = \$46.22$, $e^{\ln\left(\frac{S_{\text{one month}}}{50}\right)} = S_{\text{one month}}/50$, etc.), we can express the confidence interval in terms of prices

$$\$46.22 \leq S_{\text{one month}} \leq \$55.06 \qquad \text{prob} = 68.27\%$$

$$\$42.35 \leq S_{\text{one month}} \leq \$62.09 \qquad \text{prob} = 95.45\%$$

TABLE 18.1		Stock prices (\$) corresponding to -2, -1, 1, and 2 standard deviations from the inital stock price of 50.				
Horizon	**Fraction of a Year**	-2σ	-1σ	$+1\sigma$	$+2\sigma$	
1 Day	0.0027	48.47	49.24	50.81	51.61	
1 Month	0.0849	42.35	46.22	55.06	60.09	
1 Year	1	30.48	41.14	74.97	101.19	
2 Years	2	26.40	40.36	94.28	144.11	
5 Years	5	22.10	43.22	165.31	323.33	

Using this same logic, we can compute one standard deviation and two standard deviation intervals over different horizons. This will give us 68.27% and 95.45% confidence intervals over those horizons, which are displayed in Table 18.1. For example, there is a 95.45% chance over a 1-day horizon that a \$50 stock will be between \$48.47 and \$51.61. Over a 5-year horizon, there is a 95.45% chance that the stock price will be between \$22.10 and \$323.33. ⧚

The calculation in Example 18.7 is often used to compute loss probabilities and risk exposure. We will see in Chapter 25 that this is how value at risk (VaR) is calculated. The idea behind VaR is to assess the magnitude of a possible loss on a position that can occur with a given probability over a given horizon. So, for example, if we examine the 1-day horizon in Table 18.1, there is a 2.275% probability that over a 1-day horizon the stock price will drop below \$48.47.[4] In practice, it is common to evaluate the magnitude of moves of 1.96σ since this corresponds to a 5% ("once in 20 days") probability of occurrence.

The box on page 603 illustrates how the probability calculations in this section can be used to analyze the cost of portfolio insurance over time, previously discussed in Chapter 9.

The Conditional Expected Price

Given that an option expires in the money, what is the expected stock price? The answer to this question is the *conditional* expected stock price. For a put with strike price K, we want to calculate $E(S_t|S_t < K)$, the expected stock price conditional on $S_t < K$. To compute this expectation, we need to take into account only the portion of the probability density representing stock prices below K.

---

[4]You can verify the 2.275% probability by computing $N(-2)$.

Portfolio Insurance for the Long Run, Revisited

In the box on page 299, we discussed the result that the cost of insuring a stock portfolio so that it performs at least as well as a zero-coupon bond is increasing with the time to maturity of the insurance. The demonstration of this in Chapter 9 relies on the absence of arbitrage, which is incontrovertible but does not always provide intuition about the result. Using the results in this section, we can reconcile the historical low probability of stocks underperforming bonds with the increasing cost of insurance as we insure over a longer horizon.

The probability that $S_T < K$ is given by equation (18.23). By setting the strike price to equal the forward price, i.e., $K_T = S_0 e^{rT}$, we can use equation (18.23) to calculate the probability that stocks bought at time 0 will have underperformed bonds at time T. After simplification, equation (18.23) can be written

$$\text{Prob}(S_T < K_T) = N\left(\frac{\frac{1}{2}\sigma^2 - (\alpha - r)}{\sigma}\sqrt{T}\right)$$

Thus, if the stock is lognormally distributed, the probability of the stock underperforming a zero-coupon bond depends on the size of the risk premium on stocks, $\alpha - r$, relative to one-half the variance, $\frac{1}{2}\sigma^2$. If the risk premium is high, puts will be increasingly less likely to pay off in the long run, even though the put price is increasing with horizon.

The put price depends in part on the *risk-neutral* probability that the stock will underperform bonds, $\text{Prob}^*(S_T < K)$. This is obtained by setting $\alpha = r$, and we then have

$$\text{Prob}^*(S_T < K_T) = N\left(\frac{1}{2}\sigma\sqrt{T}\right)$$

The *risk-neutral* probability that the put will pay off is increasing with time. This fact does not by itself explain the price of the put increasing with time, since the put price also depends on the conditional expectation of the stock price when the put is in the money. However, this example does illustrate how historical *true* probabilities can mislead about the price of insurance.

To understand the calculations we are going to perform in this section, consider a binomial model in which the strike price is $50, and the stock price at expiration can be $20, $40, $60, or $80, with probabilities 1/8, 3/8, 3/8, and 1/8. If a put is in the money at expiration, the stock price is either $20 or $40. Suppose that for these two values we sum the stock price times the probability. We obtain

$$\sum_{S_t < 50} \text{Prob}(S_t) \times S_t = \left(\frac{1}{8} \times \$20\right) + \left(\frac{3}{8} \times \$40\right) = \$17.50 \qquad (18.25)$$

The value $17.50 is clearly not an expected stock price since it is below the lowest possible price ($20). We call $17.50 the **partial expectation** of the stock price conditional upon $S_t < \$50$. When we compute a conditional expectation, we are conditioning upon the event $S_t < \$50$, which occurs with probability 0.5. We can convert a partial expectation into a conditional expectation by dividing by the probability of the conditioning event ($S_t < \$50$). Thus, the conditional expectation is

$$\frac{1}{\text{Prob}(S_t < 50)} \sum_{S_t < 50} \text{Prob}(S_t) \times S_t = \frac{1}{0.5}\left[\left(\frac{1}{8} \times \$20\right) + \left(\frac{3}{8} \times \$40\right)\right]$$

(18.26)

$$= \$35$$

The calculations for a lognormally distributed price are analogous, using integrals rather than summations.

The partial expectation of S_t, conditional on $S_t < K$, is

$$\int_0^K S_t g(S_t; S_0)dS_t = S_0 e^{(\alpha-\delta)t} N\left(\frac{\ln(K) - [\ln(S_0) + (\alpha - \delta + 0.5\sigma^2)t]}{\sigma\sqrt{t}}\right) \quad (18.27)$$

$$= S_0 e^{(\alpha-\delta)t} N(-\hat{d}_1)$$

where $g(S_t; S_0)$ is the probability density of S_t conditional on S_0, and $\hat{d}_1$ is the Black-Scholes d_1 (equation (12.1)) with α replacing r.

The probability that $S_t < K$ is $N(-\hat{d}_2)$. Thus, the expectation of S_t conditional on $S_t < K$ is

$$\boxed{E(S_t|S_t < K) = S e^{(\alpha-\delta)t} \frac{N(-\hat{d}_1)}{N(-\hat{d}_2)}}$$

(18.28)

For a call, we are interested in the expected price conditional on $S > K$. The partial expectation of S_t conditional on $S_t > K$ is

$$\int_K^\infty S_t g(S_t; S_0)dS_t = S e^{(\alpha-\delta)t} N\left(\frac{\ln(S_0) - \ln(K) + (\alpha - \delta + 0.5\sigma^2)t}{\sigma\sqrt{t}}\right) \quad (18.29)$$

$$= S_0 e^{(\alpha-\delta)t} N(\hat{d}_1)$$

As before, except for the fact that it contains the expected rate of return on the stock, α, instead of the risk-free rate, the second term is just the Black-Scholes expression, $N(d_1)$. The conditional expectation is

$$\boxed{E(S_t|S_t > K) = S e^{(\alpha-\delta)t} \frac{N(\hat{d}_1)}{N(\hat{d}_2)}}$$

(18.30)

The Black-Scholes Formula

Using equations (18.23), (18.24), (18.28), and (18.30), we can now heuristically derive the Black-Scholes formula. Recall that the Black-Scholes formula can be derived by assuming risk-neutrality. In this case, the expected return on stocks, α, will equal r, the risk-free rate. If we let g^* denote the risk-neutral lognormal probability density, E^* denote the expectation taken with respect to risk-neutral probabilities, and Prob* denote those probabilities, the price of a European call option on a nondividend-paying stock will be

$$C(S, K, \sigma, r, t, \delta) = e^{-rt} \int_K^\infty (S_t - K) g^*(S_t; S_0) dS_t$$

$$= e^{-rt} E^*(S - K | S > K) \times \text{Prob}^*(S > K)$$

We can rewrite this as

$$C(S, K, \sigma, r, t, \delta) = e^{-rt} E^*(S | S > K) \times \text{Prob}^*(S > K)$$
$$- e^{-rt} E^*(K | S > K) \times \text{Prob}^*(S > K)$$

Using (18.23) and (18.30), with $\alpha = r$, this becomes

$$C(S, K, \sigma, r, t, \delta) = e^{-\delta t} S N(d_1) - K e^{-rt} N(d_2)$$

which is the Black-Scholes formula.

Similarly, the formula for a European put option on a nondividend-paying stock is derived by computing

$$P(S, K, \sigma, r, t, \delta) = e^{-rt} E^*(K - S | K > S) \times \text{Prob}^*(K > S)$$

We can rewrite this as

$$P(S, K, \sigma, r, t, \delta) = e^{-rt} E^*(K | K > S) \times \text{Prob}^*(K > S)$$
$$- e^{-rt} E^*(S | K > S) \times \text{Prob}^*(K > S)$$

and using (18.24) and (18.28), with $\alpha = r$, this becomes

$$P(S, K, \sigma, r, t, \delta) = K e^{-rt} N(-d_2) - e^{-\delta t} S N(-d_1)$$

18.5 ESTIMATING THE PARAMETERS OF A LOGNORMAL DISTRIBUTION

In this section we will see how to estimate the mean and variance of lognormally distributed price data.

When stocks are lognormally distributed, a price S_t evolves from the previous price observed at time $t - h$, according to

$$S_t = S_{t-h} e^{(\alpha - \delta - \sigma^2/2)h + \sigma \sqrt{h} z}$$

Suppose we have daily observations. How would we estimate the mean and standard deviation? We have

$$\ln(S_t) = \ln(S_{t-h}) + (\alpha - \delta - \sigma^2/2)h + \sigma \sqrt{h} z$$

Thus

$$E[\ln(S_t/S_{t-h})] = (\alpha - \delta - \sigma^2/2)h$$

$$\text{Var}[\ln(S_t/S_{t-h})] = \sigma^2 h$$

By using the log ratio of prices at adjacent points in time, we can compute the continuously compounded mean and variance. Note that to estimate α, we have to add one-half the estimate of the variance to the estimate of the mean.

Example 18.8 Table 18.2 contains seven weekly stock price observations along with continuously compounded returns computed from those observations. You can compute the mean and standard deviation of the values in the third column (for example, using the *Average* and *Stdev* functions in Excel). Since these are weekly observations, we are estimating the *weekly* mean of the log price ratio and the *weekly* standard deviation.

The mean of the second column in Table 18.2 is 0.006745 and the standard deviation is 0.038208. The annualized standard deviation is

$$\text{Annualized standard deviation} = 0.038208 \times \sqrt{52} = 0.2755$$

Two adjustments are needed to interpret the mean. First, we have to annualize it. Second, since we computed the mean of the log returns, we have to add back one-half the variance. Thus, we obtain

$$\text{Annualized expected return} = 0.006745 \times 52 + 0.5 \times 0.2755^2 = 0.3887$$

The prices were generated randomly assuming using a standard deviation of 30% and a mean of 10%. Despite having only six observations, the standard deviation estimate is quite close to the true value of 30%. The estimated mean, however, is quite far off. ❧

We used hypothetical data in this example in order to compare the estimates to the true underlying parameters, something we cannot do with real data. As this example

| TABLE 18.2 | Hypothetical weekly stock price observations and corresponding weekly continuously compounded returns, $\ln(S_t/S_t - 1)$. |

Week	Price (\$)	$\ln(S_t/S_{t-1})$
1	100	—
2	105.04	0.0492
3	105.76	0.0068
4	108.93	0.0295
5	102.50	−0.0608
6	104.80	0.0222
7	104.13	−0.0064

illustrates, mean returns are hard to estimate precisely because the mean is determined by the difference between where you start and where you end. If you start at a price of $100 and end at a price of $104, the in-between prices are irrelevant: If you had a big negative weekly return (say −20%), it must have been offset by a big positive return (on the order of +20%), or you would not have ended up at 104! Having many frequent observations is not helpful in estimating mean returns. What is helpful is having a long time interval, and seven weeks is not long.

Statistical theory tells us the precision of our estimate of the mean. With a normally distributed random variable, the standard deviation of the estimated mean is the standard deviation of the variable divided by the square root of the number of observations. The data in this example were generated using an actual weekly σ of $0.3/\sqrt{52} = 0.0416$. Divide this by $\sqrt{6}$ (since there are six return observations) to get 0.017. Thus, one standard deviation for our estimate of the mean is 1.7% on a weekly basis, or 12.25% annualized. There is a 68% probability that the annualized continuously compounded mean falls in the range 38% ± 12.25%! A 95% confidence interval is 38% ± 24.5%. This is a wide range. Even with 10 years of weekly data, one standard deviation for our estimated annualized mean would be $30\%/\sqrt{520} = 1.3\%$.

When we estimate a standard deviation, we are interested in the movement of the price. The more observations we have, the more precisely we can estimate movement. With six observations, an approximate 95% confidence interval for the standard deviation is approximately ±18 percentage points.[5] With only 26 weekly observations, the 95% confidence interval shrinks to ±8 percentage points. Moreover, unlike the mean, we can increase the precision of our estimate of the standard deviation by making more frequent observations. In general, standard deviations are easier to estimate than means.

In this discussion we have assumed that the variance is not changing over time. There is good evidence, however, that the variance does change over time, and sophisticated statistical methods can be used to estimate changing variances.

You should also be aware that, in practice, using data from very tiny intervals (e.g., hourly prices) may not increase precision. Over short time periods, factors such as bid-ask bounce—the movement of the price between the bid and ask spreads due to some orders being sells and others being buys—can introduce into prices noise that is not related to the values we are trying to measure.

....

[5] The variability of the variance estimate is described by the chi-squared distribution. (The chi-squared distribution is the distribution of sums of squared independent standard normal variables; hence, it describes the distribution of the estimated variance when observations are independent.) Suppose we wish to test the null hypothesis that our variance estimate $s^2 = \sigma_0^2$ and that we have n observations. The variable $(n-1)s^2/\sigma_0^2$ has the chi-squared distribution with $n-1$ degrees of freedom. If we wish to perform a two-tailed test when we have six observations, the critical values for 0.975 and 0.025 confidence are 0.831 and 12.832. If our null hypothesis is that $\sigma_0^2 = 0.09$, then the 95% confidence interval is $0.01496 - 0.23097$. This corresponds to a range of standard deviations of $12.23\% - 48.06\%$, or approximately 30% ± 18%. The calculation for 26 observations is similar.

18.6 How Are Asset Prices Distributed?

The lognormal model assumes that stock returns are independent over time (today's return does not affect future returns), that mean and volatility are constant over time, and that the distribution of continuously compounded returns is normal. However, we saw in Chapter 12 that implied volatilities differ for options with different strikes. One possible explanation is that stock prices are not lognormally distributed. How can we tell whether lognormality (or some other particular distribution) is a reasonable approximation for actual stock prices?

Histograms

One way to assess lognormality is simply to plot the continuously compounded returns as a histogram and see whether the resulting distribution appears normal. The top row of Figure 18.4 presents histograms for daily returns over a 10-year period for the S&P

FIGURE 18.4

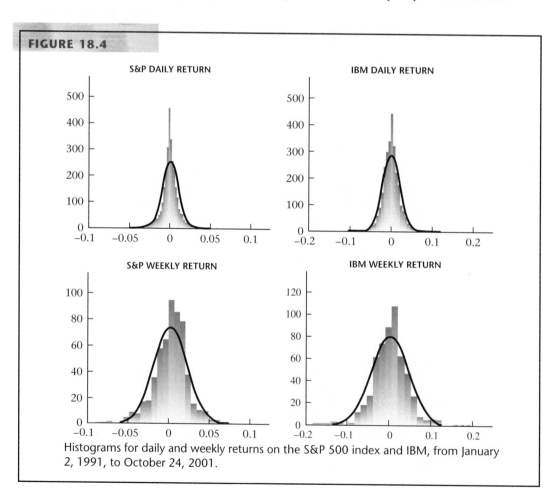

Histograms for daily and weekly returns on the S&P 500 index and IBM, from January 2, 1991, to October 24, 2001.

500 index and for IBM. The bottom row is histograms for weekly returns. Also plotted on each graph is a normal distribution, computed using the historical mean and standard deviation for each return series.[6] Several observations are pertinent.

None of the histograms appears exactly normal. All of the histograms exhibit a peak around zero; the presence or absence of this peakedness is referred to as *kurtosis* (a measure of how "sharp" the peak of the distribution is), and the graph displays *leptokurtosis* (lepto meaning "small, thin, delicate").[7] For a normally distributed random variable, kurtosis is 3. For the data plotted in Figure 18.4, kurtosis for the S&P and IBM are 8.03 and 9.54 for daily returns, and 4.68 and 5.21 for weekly returns. Accompanying the peaks are *fat tails*, large returns that occur more often than would be predicted by the lognormal model. These shapes are typical for stock returns.

There are several possible explanations for returns appearing nonnormal. One is that stock prices can jump discretely from time to time. We will discuss jumps in subsequent chapters. Another explanation is that returns are normally distributed, but with a variance that changes over time. If actual daily returns are drawn from a distribution that has a 1% volatility half the time and a 2% volatility half the time, the stock price histogram will appear fat-tailed. This blend of two distributions is commonly referred to as a **mixture of normals** model. Long-horizon returns, which result from summing short-horizon returns, will still appear normal.

Normal Probability Plots

Figure 18.5 presents normal probability plots for the same data as Figure 18.4. These plots are an alternative to histograms for assessing normality. We will examine normal probability plots as a tool for assessing normality and also to introduce a technique that we will encounter again in discussing Monte Carlo simulation.

The interpretation of these plots is straightforward: If the data points (plotted with a "+") lie along the straight line in the graph, the data are consistent with a normal distribution. If the data plot is curved, the data are less likely to have come from a normal distribution. In both cases it appears the data are not normal. There are too many points to the left of the line for low values and to the right of the line for high values. The interpretation of the plots is that extreme low and high returns occur more often than with a normal distribution.

For both the S&P index and IBM, the weekly returns appear more normal than daily returns, in that the observations more closely resemble the straight line. This is the relationship we would expect from the central limit theorem. Weekly returns are the sum of daily returns. If daily returns are independent and identically distributed, the summed daily returns will tend toward normality.

---

[6]An equivalent approach would be to normalize returns by subtracting the estimated mean and dividing by the estimated standard deviation. The resulting series should then be standard normal if returns are truly lognormal.

[7]The kurtosis of a distribution is the fourth central moment (i.e., $E[(x - \mu)^4]$, where μ is the mean) divided by σ^4.

FIGURE 18.5

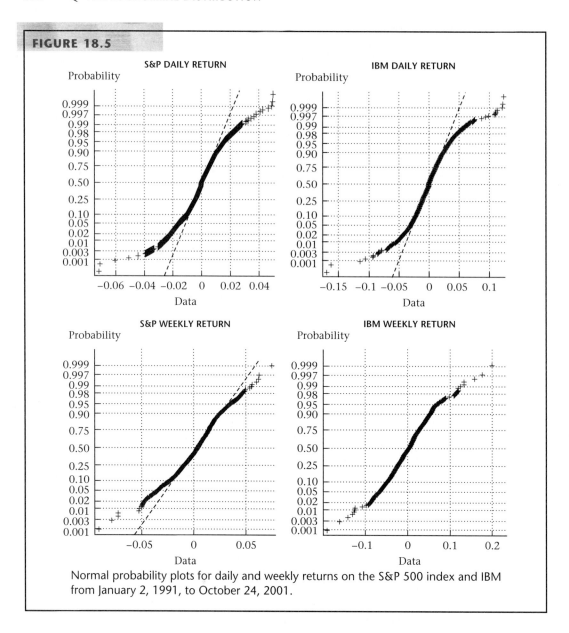

Normal probability plots for daily and weekly returns on the S&P 500 index and IBM from January 2, 1991, to October 24, 2001.

We will consider a simple example to see how a normal plot is constructed. First we have to define two concepts, *order statistics* and *quantiles*. Suppose that we randomly draw n random variables $x_i, i = 1, \ldots, n$, from some distribution with the cumulative distribution function $F(x)$. (For the normal distribution, $F(x) = N(x)$). If we sort the data in ascending order, the sorted data are called **order statistics.**

Example 18.9 Suppose we draw from a distribution five times and obtain the values $\{7, 3, 11, 5, 4\}$. The order statistics are $\{3, 4, 5, 7, 11\}$.   ⨼

The qth **quantile** of the distribution F is the smallest value x such that $F(x) \geq q$. In words, the qth quantile is the x such that there is at least probability q of drawing a value from the distribution less than or equal to x.

Example 18.10 Suppose z is standard normal. The 10% quantile is the value such that there is a 10% chance that a draw from the standard normal distribution is less than that number. Using the inverse cumulative distribution, $N^{-1}(0.10) = -1.282$. Thus, the 10% quantile is -1.281. The 30% quantile is $N^{-1}(0.3) = -0.524$.   ⨼

The idea of the normal probability plot (which can be done for any distribution, not just normal) is to compare the distance between the quantiles of the data with the distance between the quantiles of the normal distribution. If they are the same, the normal probability plot is a straight line.

To see how this works, suppose we have the five values in Example 18.9. We want to assign quantiles to the data points, so with five data points we need five quantiles. Divide the range $0 - 100\%$ into $0 - 20\%$, $20\% - 40\%$, and so forth. Assign the order statistics (the ordered data points) to the midpoints of these ranges, so that 3 is assigned a quantile value of 10%, 4 a quantile value of 30%, 5 to 50%, 7 to 70%, and 11 to 90%.[8] The normal probability plot then graphs these points against the points from the corresponding quantiles of the standard normal distribution.

The top left panel of Figure 18.6 presents the normal plot for the data in Example 18.9 with the data points plotted against the corresponding z-values of the standard normal distribution. Appendix 18.B explains the construction of this plot. The top right panel is exactly the same, except that the y-axis is labeled with probabilities corresponding to the z-values. The data do not appear normal, though with only five points there is a large possibility for error.

The bottom row of Figure 18.6 presents normal probability plots with two different y-axes for 1000 randomly generated points from a $\mathcal{N}(0, 1)$ distribution. In this case the data lie along the line and, hence, appear normal. In all of the normal probability plots, the straight line is drawn connecting the 25% and 75% quantiles of the data.[9] In essence, the normal probability plot *changes the scale on the y-axis so the cumulative normal distribution is a straight line rather than an S-shaped curve.*

---

[8]With six data points, we would have assigned quantile ranges of $0 - 16.67$, $16.67 - 33.33$, etc., and the order statistics would then be assigned to the quantiles 8.333, 25, 41.67, etc.

[9]The straight line can be fitted in numerous ways. For example, Matlab connects the quartiles. In the case of the sample data, the 10% and 30% quantiles are 3 and 4, so by interpolation the 25% quantile is 3.75. Similarly, the 70% and 90% quantiles are 7 and 11, so by interpolation the 75% quantile is 8.

FIGURE 18.6

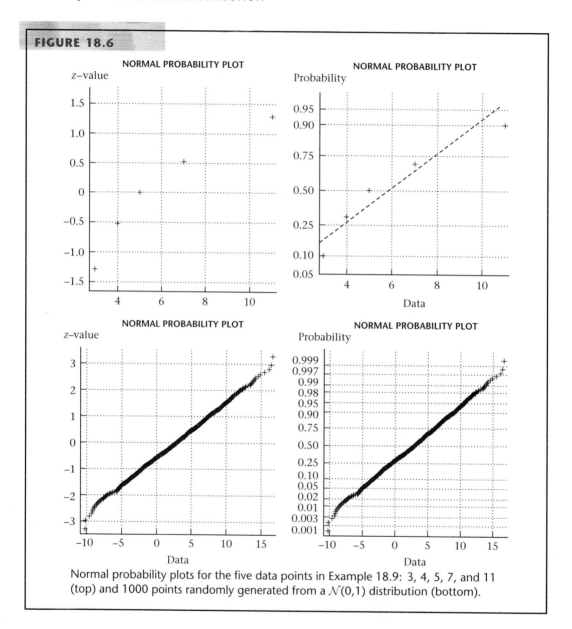

Normal probability plots for the five data points in Example 18.9: 3, 4, 5, 7, and 11 (top) and 1000 points randomly generated from a $\mathcal{N}(0,1)$ distribution (bottom).

CHAPTER SUMMARY

The normal distribution has these characteristics:

- It is symmetric; i.e., the right and left sides are mirror images of each other.
- It runs to plus and minus infinity, which means it is possible (albeit perhaps unlikely) that *any* number could occur when you draw from the distribution.
- It is unimodal; i.e., it has a single hump, which occurs at the mean.
- Sums of normal random variables are normal.

The lognormal distribution arises from assuming that continuously compounded returns are normally distributed. The lognormal distribution has these characteristics:

- It is skewed to the right.
- It runs from zero to plus infinity, which means that negative outcomes are impossible.
- It is unimodal (i.e., it has a single hump), which occurs to the left of the mean.
- Products of lognormal random variables are lognormal.

The Black-Scholes formula arises from a straightforward lognormal probability calculation using risk-neutral probabilities. The contribution of Black and Scholes was not the particular formula but rather the appearance of the risk-free rate in the formula.

From examining histograms and normal probability plots for daily and weekly continuously compounded returns, we can see that there are too many large returns relative to normally distributed returns. Although continuously compounded returns do not appear to be exactly normal, the Black-Scholes model and the accompanying assumption of lognormality is used frequently and we will continue to use and develop this model in the rest of the book. We will also explore extensions that are consistent with departures from normality we have seen in this chapter.

FURTHER READING

In Chapter 19 we will use simulation to price options assuming lognormal stock prices. We will also extend lognormality by allowing stock prices to jump discretely. In Chapter 20 we will introduce the continuous time model of stock returns used by Black and Scholes, which is the basis for modern option pricing and which, with their assumptions, generates lognormal stock prices.

Both the histogram and normal probability plot verify that continuously compounded returns in practice are not normally distributed. The question is whether this matters for pricing, and if so, how to modify the assumed price distributions and pricing formulas to obtain more accurate derivative prices. Two modifications we will examine in later chapters are to allow the stock to jump discretely and to permit volatility to be stochastic.

An excellent discussion of the basic characteristics of stock returns is Campbell et al. (1997, chs. 1 and 2). The history of the normal distribution is entertainingly recounted in Bernstein (1996). (See in particular the accounts of DeMoivre, Gauss, and Galton.)

PROBLEMS

18.1. You draw these five numbers randomly from a normal distribution with mean -8 and variance 15: $\{-7, -11, -3, 2, -15\}$. What are the equivalent draws from a standard normal distribution?

18.2. You draw these five numbers from a standard normal distribution: $\{-1.7, 0.55, -0.3, -0.02, .85\}$. What are the equivalent draws from a normal distribution with mean 0.8 and variance 25?

18.3. Suppose $x_1 \sim \mathcal{N}(1, 5)$ and $x_2 \sim \mathcal{N}(-2, 2)$. The covariance between x_1 and x_2 is 1.3. What is the distribution of $x_1 + x_2$? What is the distribution of $x_1 - x_2$?

18.4. Suppose $x_1 \sim \mathcal{N}(2, 0.5)$, and $x_2 \sim \mathcal{N}(8, 14)$. The correlation between x_1 and x_2 is -0.3. What is the distribution of $x_1 + x_2$? What is the distribution of $x_1 - x_2$?

18.5. Suppose $x_1 \sim \mathcal{N}(1, 5)$, $x_2 \sim \mathcal{N}(2, 3)$ and $x_3 \sim \mathcal{N}(2.5, 7)$, with correlations $\rho_{1,2} = 0.3$, $\rho_{1,3} = 0.1$, and $\rho_{2,3} = 0.4$. What is the distribution of $x_1 + x_2 + x_3$? $x_1 + (3 \times x_2) + x_3$? $x_1 + x_2 + (0.5 \times x_3)$?

18.6. If $x \sim \mathcal{N}(2, 5)$, what is $E(e^x)$? What is the median of e^x?

18.7. Suppose you observe the following month-end stock prices for stocks A and B:

	Day				
	0	**1**	**2**	**3**	**4**
Stock A	100	105	102	97	100
Stock B	100	105	150	97	100

For each stock:

a. Compute the mean monthly continuously compounded return. What is the annual return?

b. Compute the mean monthly standard deviation. What is the annual standard deviation?

c. Evaluate the statement: "The estimate of the mean depends only on the beginning and ending stock prices; the estimate of the standard deviation depends on all prices."

For the following five problems, unless otherwise stated, assume that $S_0 = \$100$, $\alpha = 0.08$, $\sigma = 0.30$, and $\delta = 0$.

18.8. What is Prob($S_t > \$105$) for $t = 1$? How does this probability change when you change t? How does it change when you change σ?

18.9. What is $E(S_t | S_t > \$105)$ for $t = 1$? How does this expectation change when you change t, σ, and r?

18.10. What is Prob($S_t < \$98$) for $t = 1$? How does this probability change when you change t?

18.11. Let $t = 1$. What is $E(S_t | S_t < \$98)$? What is $E(S_t | S_t < \$120)$? How do both expectations change when you vary t from 0.05 to 5? Let $\sigma = 0.1$. Does either answer change? How?

18.12. Let $K_T = S_0 e^{rT}$. Compute Prob($S_T < K_T$) and Prob($S_T > K_T$) for a variety of Ts from 0.25 to 25 years. How do the probabilities behave? How do you reconcile your answer with the fact that *both* call and put prices increase with time?

18.13. Consider Prob($S_t < K$), equation (18.23), and $E(S_t | S_t < K)$, equation (18.28). Verify that it is possible to pick parameters such that changes in t can have ambiguous effects on Prob($S_t < K$) (experiment with very short and long times to maturity, and set $\alpha > 0.5\sigma^2$). Is the effect of t on $E(S_t | S_t < K)$ ambiguous?

18.14. Select a stock or index and obtain at least 5 years of daily or weekly data. Estimate the annualized mean and volatility, using all data and 1 year at a time. Compare the behavior of your estimates of the mean with those of the standard deviation.

18.15. Select a stock that has at least 5 years of daily data. Create data sets consisting of daily data and weekly data, Wednesday to Wednesday. (The *weekday* function in Excel will tell you the day of the week corresponding to a date. Wednesday is 4.) For both data sets, create a histogram of returns and a normal plot. Are the stock prices lognormal?

APPENDIX 18.A: THE EXPECTATION OF A LOGNORMAL VARIABLE

In this appendix we verify equation (18.13). Suppose that $y \sim \mathcal{N}(\mu, \sigma^2)$; hence, e^y is lognormally distributed. The normal distribution is given by

$$\phi(x; \mu, \sigma^2) \equiv \frac{1}{\sigma\sqrt{2\pi}} e^{-\frac{1}{2}\left(\frac{x-\mu}{\sigma}\right)^2}$$

Hence, we can directly compute the expectation:

$$E(e^y) = \int_{-\infty}^{\infty} e^x \frac{1}{\sigma\sqrt{2\pi}} e^{-\frac{1}{2}\left(\frac{x-\mu}{\sigma}\right)^2} dx$$

Collect the exponentiated terms under the integral. This gives us

$$E(e^y) = \int_{-\infty}^{\infty} \frac{1}{\sigma\sqrt{2\pi}} \, e^{-\frac{1}{2\sigma^2}[(x-\mu)^2 - 2\sigma^2 x]} dx \qquad (18.31)$$

Now focus on the exponentiated term in the square brackets. We have

$$
\begin{aligned}
(x - \mu)^2 - 2\sigma^2 x &= x^2 + \mu^2 - 2x(\mu + \sigma^2) \\
&= x^2 + (\mu + \sigma^2)^2 - 2x(\mu + \sigma^2) + \mu^2 - (\mu + \sigma^2)^2 \\
&= [x - (\mu + \sigma^2)]^2 - \sigma^4 - 2\mu\sigma^2
\end{aligned}
$$

We can now substitute this expression into (18.31), obtaining

$$
\begin{aligned}
E(e^y) &= \int_{-\infty}^{\infty} \frac{1}{\sigma\sqrt{2\pi}} \, e^{-\frac{1}{2\sigma^2}([x-(\mu+\sigma^2)]^2 - \sigma^4 - 2\mu\sigma^2)} dx \\
&= e^{\mu + \frac{1}{2}\sigma^2} \int_{-\infty}^{\infty} \frac{1}{\sigma\sqrt{2\pi}} \, e^{-\frac{1}{2\sigma^2}([x-(\mu+\sigma^2)]^2)} dx \\
&= e^{\mu + \frac{1}{2}\sigma^2}
\end{aligned}
$$

The last equality follows because the integral expression is one: It is the total area under a normal density with mean $\mu + \sigma^2$ and variance σ^2. Thus we obtain equation (18.13).

APPENDIX 18.B: CONSTRUCTING A NORMAL PROBABILITY PLOT

Appendix available online at www.aw-bc.com/mcdonald.

CHAPTER 19

Monte Carlo Valuation

So far we have primarily discussed derivatives for which there is a (relatively simple) valuation formula, or which can be valued binomially. For many common derivatives, however, a different approach is necessary. For example, consider arithmetic Asian options (see Section 14.2). There is no simple valuation formula for such options, and the binomial pricing approach is difficult because the final payoff depends on the specific path the stock price takes through the tree—i.e., the payoff is path-dependent. A pricing method that can be used in such cases is **Monte Carlo valuation.** In Monte Carlo valuation we simulate future stock prices and then use these simulated prices to compute the discounted expected payoff of the option. The idea that an option price is a discounted expected value is familiar from our discussion of the binomial model in Chapter 11 and the Black-Scholes formula in Chapter 18.

Monte Carlo valuation is performed using the risk-neutral distribution, where we assume that assets earn the risk-free rate on average, and we then discount the expected payoff using the risk-free rate. We will see in this chapter that risk-neutral pricing is a cornerstone of Monte Carlo valuation; using the actual distribution instead would create a complicated discounting problem.

Since with Monte Carlo you simulate the possible future values of the security, as a byproduct you generate the *distribution* of payoffs. The distribution can be extremely useful when you want to compare two investment strategies that have different distributions of outcomes. Computing value-at-risk for complicated portfolios is a common use of Monte Carlo.

In this chapter we will see why risk-neutral valuation is important for Monte Carlo, see how to produce normal random numbers, discuss the efficiency of Monte Carlo, introduce the Poisson distribution to help account for nonlognormal patterns in the data, and see how to create correlated random stock prices.

19.1 COMPUTING THE OPTION PRICE AS A DISCOUNTED EXPECTED VALUE

The concept of risk-neutral valuation is familiar from earlier Chapters 15. We saw that option valuation can be performed *as if* all assets earned the risk-free rate of return and investors performed all discounting at this rate. Monte Carlo valuation exploits this insight. We *assume* that assets earn the risk-free rate of return and simulate their returns.

For example, for any given stock price 3 months from now, we can compute the payoff on a call. We perform the simulation many times and average the outcomes. Since we use risk-neutral valuation, we then discount the average payoff at the risk-free rate in order to arrive at the price.

As a practical matter, Monte Carlo valuation depends critically on risk-neutral valuation. In order to see why this is so, we will compute an option price as an expected value with both risk-neutral and true probabilities, using an example we discussed in Chapters 10 and 11.

Valuation with Risk-Neutral Probabilities

We saw in equation (10.6) that we can interpret the one-period binomial option pricing calculation as an expected value, in which the expectation is computed using the risk-neutral probability p^*, and discounting is at the risk-free rate.

In a multiperiod tree, we repeat this process at each node. For a European option, the result obtained by working backward through the tree is equivalent to computing the expected option price in the final period, and discounting at the risk-free rate.

If there are n binomial periods, equation (11.17) gives the probability of reaching any given stock price at expiration. Let n represent the number of binomial steps and i the number of stock price down moves. We can value a European call option by computing the expected option payoff at the final node of the binomial tree and then discounting at the risk-free rate. For example, for a European call,

European call price =

$$e^{-rT} \sum_{i=1}^{n} \max[0, Su^{n-i}d^i - K](p^*)^{n-i}(1 - p^*)^i \frac{n!}{(n - i)! \, i!} \quad (19.1)$$

To illustrate this calculation, Figure 19.1 shows the stock price tree from Figure 10.5, with the addition of the total risk-neutral probabilities of reaching each of the terminal nodes. Figure 19.1 demonstrates that the option can be priced by computing the expected payoff at expiration using the probability of reaching each final node, and then discounting at the risk-free rate. You can verify that the option price in Figure 19.1 is the same as that in Figure 10.5.

We can also use the tree in Figure 19.1 to illustrate Monte Carlo valuation. Imagine a gambling wheel divided into four unequal sections, where each section has a probability corresponding to one of the option payoffs in Figure 19.1: 9.5% ($34.678), 34% ($12.814), 40.4% (0), and 16% (0). Each spin of the wheel therefore selects one of the final stock price nodes and option payoffs in Figure 19.1. If we spin the wheel numerous times and then average the resulting option values, we will have an estimate of the expected payoff. Discounting this expected payoff at the risk-free rate provides an estimate of the option value.

It is easy to compute the actual expected payoff for the option in Figure 19.1 without using a gambling wheel. However, the example illustrates how random trials can be used to perform valuation.

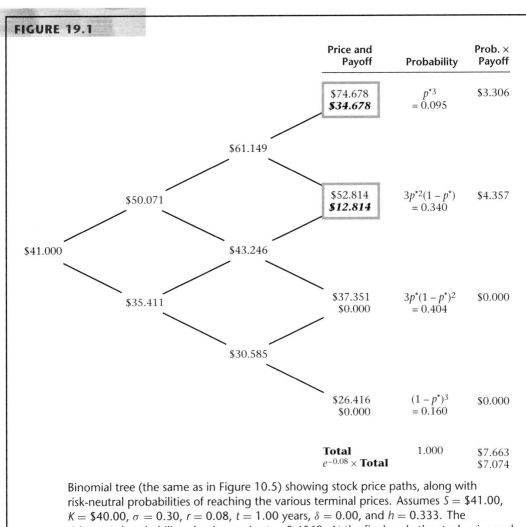

FIGURE 19.1

Binomial tree (the same as in Figure 10.5) showing stock price paths, along with risk-neutral probabilities of reaching the various terminal prices. Assumes $S = \$41.00$, $K = \$40.00$, $\sigma = 0.30$, $r = 0.08$, $t = 1.00$ years, $\delta = 0.00$, and $h = 0.333$. The risk-neutral probability of going up is $p^* = 0.4568$. At the final node the stock price and terminal option payoff (beneath the price) are given.

Valuation with True Probabilities

The simple procedure we used to discount payoffs for the risk-neutral tree in Figure 19.1 *does not work* when we use actual probabilities. We analyzed the pricing of this option using true probabilities in Chapter 11, in Figure 11.4. We saw there that when using true probabilities to evaluate the option, the discount rate is different at different nodes on the tree. In fact, if we are to compute an option price as an expected value using true probabilities, we need to compute the discount rate *for each path*. There are eight possible paths for the stock price, four of which result in a positive option payoff. All of these paths have a first-period annualized continuously compounded discount rate of 35.7%. The subsequent discount rates depend on the path the stock takes. Table 19.1 verifies that discounting payoffs at path-dependent discount rates gives the correct option price. To take just the first row, the discounted expected option payoff for that row is computed as follows:

$$e^{-(0.357\times\frac{1}{3}+0.323\times\frac{1}{3}+0.269\times\frac{1}{3})} \times (0.5246)^3 \times (\$74.678 - \$40) = \$3.649$$

This calculation uses the fact that the actual probability that the stock price will move up in any period is 52.46%.

As Table 19.1 illustrates, it is necessary to have a different cumulative discount rate along each *path* the stock can take. A call option is a high-beta security when it

TABLE 19.1   Computation of option price using expected value calculation and true probabilities. The stock price tree and parameters are the same as in Figure 11.4. The column entitled "Discount Rates Along Path" reports the node-specific true annualized continuously compounded discount rates from that figure. "Discount Rate for Path" is the compound annualized discount rate for the entire path. "Prob. of Path" is the probability that the particular path will occur, computed using the true probability of an up move (52.46%). The last column is the probability times the payoff, discounted at the continuously compounded rate for the path.

Path	Discount Rates Along Path			Discount Rate for Path	Prob. of Path	Payoff ($)	Discounted ($) (Prob. × Payoff)
uuu	35.7%	32.3%	26.9%	31.64%	0.1444	34.678	3.649
uud	35.7%	32.3%	26.9%	31.64%	0.1308	12.814	1.222
udu	35.7%	32.3%	49.5%	39.18%	0.1308	12.814	1.133
duu	35.7%	49.5%	49.5%	44.91%	0.1308	12.814	1.070
udd	—	—	—	—	—	0	0
dud	—	—	—	—	—	0	0
ddu	—	—	—	—	—	0	0
ddd	—	—	—	—	—	0	0
					Sum		7.074

is out-of-the-money and it has a lower beta (but still higher than the stock) when it is in-the-money. This variation in the discount rate complicates discounting if we are using the true distribution of stock prices.[1]

Risk-neutral valuation neatly sidesteps the hardest problem about using discounted cash flow valuation techniques with an option. While it is easy to compute the expected payoff of an option if the stock is lognormally distributed, it is hard to compute the discount rate. If we value options *as if* the world were risk-neutral, this complication is avoided.

19.2 COMPUTING RANDOM NUMBERS

In this section we discuss how to compute the normally distributed random numbers required for Monte Carlo valuation. We will take for granted that you can compute a uniformly distributed random number between 0 and 1. The uniform distribution is defined on a specified range, over which the probability is 1, and assigns equal probabilities to every interval of equal length on that range. A random variable, u, that is uniformly distributed on the interval (a, b), has the distribution $\mathcal{U}(a, b)$. The uniform probability density, $f(x; a, b)$, is defined as

$$f(x; a, b) = \frac{1}{b - a}; a \leq x \leq b \tag{19.2}$$

and is 0 otherwise. When $a = 0$ and $b = 1$, the uniform distribution is a flat line at a height of 1 over the range 0 to 1.

Drawing uniformly distributed random variables is very common; virtually all programming languages and spreadsheets have a way to do this.[2] The *Rand* built-in function in Excel does this, for example. It turns out that once we have a way to compute uniformly distributed random variables, there are two common ways to compute a normally distributed random variable. Many programs also have functions to compute normal random numbers directly, in which case it is not necessary to use these methods. However, the second method we will discuss can be used to compute random numbers drawn from *any* distribution.

....

[1] Here is why a single discount rate does not work. Suppose we represent the terminal option price associated with a particular pattern of stock price up and down movements by $C_i(T)$ and the compound discount factor for that path by β_i. Since both the payoff and the discount rates are uncertain, we need to compute $E[C_i(T)/(1 + \beta_i)]$. However, if we average the payoff and then separately average the discount factors, we are computing the ratio of the averages, $E[C_i(T)]/E[(1 + \beta_i)]$, rather than the average of the ratios. Jensen's inequality tells us that these are not the same calculation.

[2] Since computers are ultimately deterministic devices, it is virtually impossible to compute "true" random numbers. See Judd (1998, pp. 285–287) for a discussion and additional references.

Using Sums of Uniformly Distributed Random Variables

One standard technique to compute normally distributed random variables is to sum 12 uniform (0,1) random variables and subtract 6. Thus, we compute the $\mathcal{N}(0, 1)$ random variable $\tilde{Z}$ as

$$\tilde{Z} = \sum_{i=1}^{12} u_i - 6$$

where the u_i are distributed uniformly on (0,1).

This technique works because the variance of a variable that is uniformly distributed between 0 and 1 is 1/12 and the mean is 1/2. Thus, if you sum 12 uniformly distributed random variables and subtract 6, you get a random variable with a variance of 1 and a mean of 0. The sum of 12 uniform variables is not precisely normal, but it is close. This technique is an application of the central limit theorem.

Using the Inverse Cumulative Normal Distribution

It is also possible to draw a *single* uniformly distributed random number and convert it to a normally distributed random number. Suppose that $u \sim \mathcal{U}(0, 1)$ and $z \sim \mathcal{N}(0, 1)$. As we saw in Chapter 18, the *cumulative distribution function*, denoted $U(w)$ for the uniform and $N(y)$ for the normal, is the probability that $u < w$ or $z < y$, i.e.,

$$U(w) = \text{Prob}(u \leq w)$$
$$N(y) = \text{Prob}(z \leq y)$$

As discussed in Chapter 18, w is the $U(w)$ quantile and y is the $N(y)$ quantile of the two distributions. If we randomly draw a uniform number u, how can we use u to construct a corresponding normal random number, z?

It turns out that the same idea we used to construct normal plots in Section 18.6 permits us to generate a normal random number from a uniform random number. Instead of interpreting a random draw from the uniform distribution as a *number*, we interpret it as a *quantile*. So, for example, if we draw 0.7 from a $\mathcal{U}(0, 1)$ distribution, we interpret this as a draw corresponding to the 70% quantile. We then use the inverse distribution function, $N^{-1}(u)$, to find the value from the normal distribution corresponding to that quantile.[3] This technique works because, for any distribution, quantiles are uniformly

---

[3]The Excel function *NormSInv* computes the inverse cumulative normal distribution. Unfortunately, there is a serious bug in this function in Office 97 and Office 2000. In both versions of Excel, *NormSInv*(0.9999996) = 5.066, and *NormSInv*(0.9999997) = 5,000,000. Because of this, Excel will on occasion produce a randomly drawn normal value of 5,000,000, which ruins a Monte Carlo valuation. I thank Mark Broadie for pointing out this problem with using Excel to produce random normal numbers.

distributed: If you draw from a distribution, by definition any quantile is equally likely to be drawn.

The algorithm is therefore as follows:

1. Generate a uniformly distributed random number between 0 and 1. Say this is 0.7.

2. Ask: What is the value of z such that $N(z) = 0.7$? The answer to this question is computed using the *inverse cumulative distribution function*. In this case we have $N^{-1}(0.7) = 0.5244$. This value is a single draw of a standard normal random variable (0.5244).

3. Repeat.

This procedure simulates draws from a normal distribution. To simulate a log-normal random variable, simulate a normal random variable and exponentiate the draws.

This procedure of using the inverse cumulative probability distribution is valuable because it works for any distribution for which you can compute the inverse cumulative distribution.

19.3 SIMULATING LOGNORMAL STOCK PRICES

Recall from Chapter 18 that if $Z \sim \mathcal{N}(0, 1)$, a lognormal stock price can be written

$$S_T = S_0 e^{(\alpha - \delta - \frac{1}{2}\sigma^2)T + \sigma\sqrt{T}Z} \tag{19.3}$$

Suppose we wish to draw random stock prices for 2 years from today. From equation (19.3), the stock price is driven by the normally distributed random variable Z. Set $T = 2$, $\alpha = 0.10$, $\delta = 0$, and $\sigma = 0.30$. If we then randomly draw a set of standard normal Z's and substitute the results into equation (19.3), the result is a random set of lognormally distributed S_2's. The continuously compounded mean return will be 20% (10% per year) and the continuously compounded standard deviation of $\ln(S_2)$ will be $0.3 \times \sqrt{2} = 42.43\%$.

Simulating a Sequence of Stock Prices

There is another way to create a random set of prices 2 years from now. We can also generate *annual* random prices and compound these to get a 2-year price. This will give us exactly the same distribution for 2-year prices. Here is how to do it:

- Compute the 1-year price, S_1 as

$$S_1 = S_0 e^{(0.1 - \frac{1}{2}0.3^2) \times 1 + \sigma\sqrt{1}Z(1)}$$

- Using this S_1 as the starting price, compute S_2:

$$S_2 = S_1 e^{(0.1 - \frac{1}{2}0.3^2) \times 1 + 0.3\sqrt{1}Z(2)}$$

In these expressions, $Z(1)$ and $Z(2)$ are two draws from the standard normal distribution.

If we substititute the expression for S_1 into S_2, we get

$$S_2 = S_0 e^{(0.1 - \frac{1}{2}0.3^2) \times 2 + 0.3\sqrt{1}[Z(1) + Z(2)]} \qquad (19.4)$$

The difference between this expression and equation (19.3) is that instead of the term $\sqrt{2}Z$, we have $[Z(1) + Z(2)]$. Note that

$$\text{Var}(\sqrt{2}Z) = 2$$

and

$$\text{Var}[Z(1) + Z(2)] = 2$$

Therefore, equations (19.3) and (19.4) generate S_2's with the same distribution.

If we really want to simulate a random stock price after 2 years, there is no reason to draw two random variables instead of one. But if we want to simulate the *path* of the stock price over 2 years (for example, to price a path-dependent option), then we can do so by splitting up the 2 years into multiple periods.

In general, if we wish to split up a period of length T into intervals of length h, the number of such intervals will be $n = T/h$. We have

$$S_h = S_0 e^{(\alpha - \delta - \frac{1}{2}\sigma^2)h + \sigma\sqrt{h}Z(1)}$$
$$S_{2h} = S_h e^{(\alpha - \delta - \frac{1}{2}\sigma^2)h + \sigma\sqrt{h}Z(2)}$$

and so on, up to

$$S_{nh} = S_{(n-1)h} e^{(\alpha - \delta - \frac{1}{2}\sigma^2)h + \sigma\sqrt{h}Z(n)}$$

These n stock prices can be intepreted as equally spaced points on the stock price path between times 0 and T. Note that if we substitute S_h into the expression for S_{2h}, the expression for S_{2h} into that for S_{3h}, and so on, we get

$$S_T = S_0 e^{(\alpha - \delta - \frac{1}{2}\sigma^2)T + \sigma\sqrt{h}[\sum_{i=1}^{n} Z(i)]}$$
$$= S_0 e^{(\alpha - \delta - \frac{1}{2}\sigma^2)T + \sigma\sqrt{T}\left[\frac{1}{\sqrt{n}}\sum_{i=1}^{n} Z(i)\right]} \qquad (19.5)$$

Since $\frac{1}{\sqrt{n}}\sum_{i=1}^{n} Z(i) \sim \mathcal{N}(0, 1)$, we get the same distribution at time T with equation (19.5) as if we had drawn a single $\mathcal{N}(0, 1)$ random variable, as in equation (19.3). The important difference is that by splitting up the problem into n draws, we simulate the path taken by S. The simulation of a path is useful in computing the value of path-dependent derivatives, such as Asian and barrier options, the value of which depend on the path by which the price arrives at S_T.

19.4 MONTE CARLO VALUATION

In Monte Carlo valuation, we perform a calculation similar to that in equation (19.1). The option payoff at time T is a function of the stock price, S_T. Represent this payoff as $V(S_T, T)$. The time-0 Monte Carlo price, $V(S_0, 0)$, is then

$$V(S_0, 0) = \frac{1}{n} e^{-rT} \sum_{i=1}^{n} V(S_T^i, T) \qquad (19.6)$$

where $S_T^1, \ldots, S_T^n$ are n randomly drawn time-T stock prices. For the case of a call option, for example, $V(S_T^i, T) = \max(0, S_T^i - K)$.

Both equations (19.1) and (19.6) use approximations to the time-T stock price distribution to compute an option price. Equation (19.1) uses the binomial distribution to approximate the lognormal stock price distribution, while equation (19.6) uses simulated lognormal prices to approximate the lognormal stock price distribution.

As an illustration of Monte Carlo techniques, we will first work with a problem for which we already know the answer. Suppose we have a European option that expires in T periods. The underlying asset has volatility σ and the risk-free rate is r. We can use the Black-Scholes option pricing formula to price the option, but we will price the option using *both* Black-Scholes and Monte Carlo so that we can assess the performance of Monte Carlo valuation.

Monte Carlo Valuation of a European Call

We assume that the stock price follows equation (19.3), with $\alpha = r$. We generate random standard normal variables, Z, substitute them into equation (19.3), and generate many random future stock prices. Each Z creates one trial. Suppose we compute N trials. For each trial, i, we compute the value of a call as

$$\max(0, S_T^i - K) = \max\left(0, S_0 e^{(r-\delta-0.5\sigma^2)T+\sigma\sqrt{T}Z_i} - K\right); \qquad i = 1, \ldots, N$$

Average the resulting values:

$$\frac{1}{N} \sum_{i=1}^{N} \max(0, S_T^i - K)$$

This expression gives us an estimate of the expected option payoff at time T. We discount the average payoff back at the risk-free rate in order to get an estimate of the option value:

$$\overline{C} = e^{-rT} \frac{1}{N} \sum_{i=1}^{N} \max(0, S_T^i - K)$$

Example 19.1 Suppose we wish to value a 3-month European call option where the stock price is \$40, the strike price is \$40, the risk-free rate is 8%, the dividend yield is zero, and the volatility is 30%. We draw random 3-month stock prices by using the expression

$$S_{3\,\text{months}} = S_0 e^{(0.08-0.3^2/2)\times 0.25 + 0.3\sqrt{0.25}Z}$$

TABLE 19.2	Results of Monte Carlo valuation of European call with $S = \$40$, $K = \$40$, $\sigma = 30\%$, $r = 8\%$, $t = 91$ days, and $\delta = 0$. The Black-Scholes price is $2.78. Each trial uses 500 random draws.

Trial	Computed Price ($)
1	2.98
2	2.75
3	2.63
4	2.75
5	2.91
Average	2.804

For each stock price, we compute

$$\text{Option payoff} = \max(0, S_{3 \text{ months}} - \$40)$$

We repeat this procedure many times, average the resulting option payoffs, and discount the average back 3 months at the risk-free rate. With a single estimate using 2500 draws, we get an answer of $2.804 (see Table 19.2), close to the true value of $2.78. ⬩

In this example we priced a European-style option. We will discuss in Section 19.6 the use of Monte Carlo simulation to value American-style options.

Accuracy of Monte Carlo

There is no need to value a European call using Monte Carlo methods, but doing so allows us to assess the accuracy of Monte Carlo valuation for a given number of simulated stock price paths. The key question is how many simulated stock prices suffice to value an option to a desired degree of accuracy. Monte Carlo valuation is simple but relatively inefficient. There are methods that improve the efficiency of Monte Carlo; we discuss several of these in Section 19.5.

To assess the accuracy of a Monte Carlo estimate, we can run the simulation different times and see how much variability there is in the results. Of course in this case, we also know that the Black-Scholes solution is $2.78.

Table 19.2 shows the results from running five Monte Carlo valuations, each containing 500 random stock price draws. The result of 2500 simulations is close to the correct answer ($2.804 is close to $2.78). However, there is considerable variation among the individual trials of 500 simulations.

To assess accuracy, we need to know the standard deviation of the estimate. Let $C(\tilde{S}_i)$ be the call price generated from the randomly drawn $\tilde{S}_i$. If there are n trials, the Monte Carlo estimate is

$$\overline{C}_n = \frac{1}{n} \sum_{i=1}^{n} C(\tilde{S}_i)$$

Let σ_C denote the standard deviation of one draw and σ_n the standard deviation of n draws. The variance of a mean, given independent and identically distributed $\tilde{S}_i$'s, is

$$\sigma_n^2 = \frac{1}{n} \sigma_C^2$$

or

$$\sigma_n = \frac{1}{\sqrt{n}} \sigma_C$$

Thus, the standard deviation of the Monte Carlo estimate is inversely proportional to the square root of the number of draws.

In the Monte Carlo results reported in Table 19.2, the standard deviation of a draw is about $4.05. (This value is computed by taking the standard deviation of the 2500 price estimates used to compute the average.) For 500 draws, the standard deviation is

$$\frac{\$4.05}{\sqrt{500}} = \$0.18$$

Given that the correct price is $2.78, a $0.18 standard deviation is a substantial percentage of the option price (6.5%). With 2500 observations, the standard deviation is cut to $0.08, suggesting that the $2.80 estimate from averaging the five answers was only accidentally close to the correct answer. In order to have a 1% ($0.028) standard deviation, we would need to have 21,000 trials.

Arithmetic Asian Option

In the previous example of Monte Carlo valuation we valued an option that we already could value with the Black-Scholes formula. In practice, Monte Carlo valuation is useful under these conditions:

- Where the number of random elements in the option valuation problem is too great to permit direct numerical solution.

- Where underlying variables are distributed in such a way that direct solutions are difficult.

- Where options are path-dependent, i.e., the payoff at expiration depends upon the path of the underlying asset price.

For the case of a path-dependent option, the use of Monte Carlo estimation is straightforward. As discussed above, we can simulate the path of the stock as well as its terminal value. For example, consider the valuation of a security that at the end of 3 months makes a payment based on the arithmetic average of the stock price at the end of months 1, 2, and 3. As discussed in Chapter 14, this is an arithmetic average price Asian option: "Asian" because the payoff is based on an average, and "arithmetic average price" because the arithmetic average stock price replaces the actual stock price at expiration.

How will the value of an option on the average compare with an option that settles based on the actual expiration-day stock price? Intuitively, averaging should reduce the likelihood of large gains and losses. Any time the stock ends up high (in which case the call will have a high value at expiration), it will have traversed intermediate stock prices in the process of reaching a high value. The payoff to the Asian option will reflect these lower intermediate prices, and, hence, large payoffs will be much less likely.

We compute the 1-month, 2-month, and 3-month stock prices as follows:

$$S_1 = 40e^{(r-\delta-\sigma^2/2)T/3+\sigma\sqrt{T/3}Z(1)}$$

$$S_2 = S_1e^{(r-\delta-\sigma^2/2)T/3+\sigma\sqrt{T/3}Z(2)}$$

$$S_3 = S_2e^{(r-\delta-\sigma^2/2)T/3+\sigma\sqrt{T/3}Z(3)}$$

where $Z(1)$, $Z(2)$, and $Z(3)$ are independent draws from a standard normal distribution. We repeat the trial many times and draw many Z_i's. The value of the security is then computed as

$$C_{\text{Asian}} = e^{-rT} E\left(\max[(S_1 + S_2 + S_3)/3 - K, 0]\right) \tag{19.7}$$

Example 19.2 Let r = 8%, σ = 0.3, and suppose that the initial stock price is $40. Figure 19.2 compares histograms for the actual risk-neutral stock price distri-

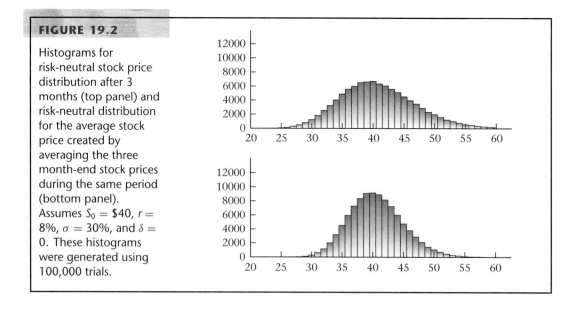

FIGURE 19.2

Histograms for risk-neutral stock price distribution after 3 months (top panel) and risk-neutral distribution for the average stock price created by averaging the three month-end stock prices during the same period (bottom panel). Assumes $S_0 = \$40$, $r = 8\%$, $\sigma = 30\%$, and $\delta = 0$. These histograms were generated using 100,000 trials.

bution after 3 months and that for the average stock price created by averaging the three month-end prices. As expected, the nonaveraged distribution has significantly higher tail probabilities and a lower probability of being close to the initial stock price of $40. ❧

Table 19.3 lists prices of Asian options computed using 10,000 Monte Carlo trials each.[4] The first row (where a single terminal price is averaged) represents the price of an ordinary call option with 3 months to expiration. The others represent more frequent averaging. The Asian price declines as the averaging frequency increases, with the largest price decline obtained by moving from no averaging (the first row in Table 19.3) to monthly averaging (the second row of Table 19.3).

Note also in Table 19.3 that, in any row, the arithmetic average price is always above the geometric average price. This is Jensen's inequality at work: Geometric

TABLE 19.3	Prices of arithmetic average-price Asian options estimated using Monte Carlo and exact prices of geometric average price options. Assumes option has 3 months to expiration and average is computed using equal intervals over the period. Each price is computed using 10,000 trials, assuming $S = \$40$, $K = \$40$, $\sigma = 30\%$, $r = 8\%$, $T = 0.25$, and $\delta = 0$. In each row, the same random numbers were used to compute both the geometric and arithmetic average price options. σ_n is the standard deviation of the estimated prices, divided by $\sqrt{10{,}000}$.

| Number of | Monte Carlo Prices ($) | | Exact | |
Averages	Arithmetic	Geometric	Geometric Price ($)	σ_n
1	2.79	2.79	2.78	0.0408
3	2.03	1.99	1.94	0.0291
5	1.78	1.74	1.77	0.0259
10	1.70	1.66	1.65	0.0241
20	1.66	1.61	1.59	0.0231
40	1.63	1.58	1.56	0.0226

....

[4]A trial in this case means the computation of a single option price at expiration. When 40 prices are averaged over 3 months, each trial consists of drawing 40 random numbers; hence, 400,000 random numbers are drawn in order to compute the price.

averaging produces a lower average stock price than arithmetic averaging, and hence a lower option price.

19.5 Efficient Monte Carlo Valuation

We have been describing what might be called "naive" Monte Carlo, making no attempt to reduce the variance of the simulated answer for a given number of trials. There are a number of methods to achieve faster Monte Carlo valuations.[5]

Control Variate Method

We have seen that naive Monte Carlo estimation of an arithmetic Asian option requires many simulations. In Table 19.3, even with 10,000 simulations, there is still a standard deviation of several percent in the option price.

In each row of Table 19.3, the same random numbers are used to estimate the option price. As a result, the errors in the estimated arithmetic and geometric prices are correlated: When the estimated price for the geometric option is high, this occurs because we have had high returns in the stock price simulation. This should result in a high arithmetic price as well.

This observation suggests the **control variate method** to increase Monte Carlo accuracy. The idea underlying this method is to estimate the error on each trial by using the price of a related option that does have a pricing formula. The error estimate obtained from this control price can be used to improve the accuracy of the Monte Carlo price on each trial.

Asian options provide an effective illustration of this idea.[6] Because we have a formula for the price of a geometric Asian option (see Section 14.2), we know whether the geometric price from a Monte Carlo valuation is too high or too low. For a given set of random stock prices, the arithmetic and geometric prices will typically be too high or too low in tandem, so we can use information on the error in the geometric price to adjust our estimate of the arithmetic price, for which there is no formula.

To be specific, we use simulation to estimate the arithmetic price, $\overline{A}$, and the geometric price, $\overline{G}$. Let G and A represent the true geometric and arithmetic prices. The error for the Monte Carlo estimate of the geometric price is $(G - \overline{G})$. We want to use this error to improve our estimate of the arithmetic price.

Consider calculating

$$A^* = \overline{A} + \left(G - \overline{G}\right) \tag{19.8}$$

---

[5]Excellent overviews are Boyle et al. (1997) and Glasserman (2004). See also Judd (1998, ch. 8), which in turn contains other references, and Campbell et al. (1997, ch. 9).

[6]This example follows Kemna and Vorst (1990), who used the control variate method to price arithmetic Asian options.

This is a control variate estimate. Since Monte Carlo provides an unbiased estimate, $E(\overline{G}) = G$. Hence, $E(A^*) = E(\overline{A}) = A$. Moreover, the variance of A^* is

$$\text{Var}(A^*) = \text{Var}(\overline{A}) + \text{Var}(\overline{G}) - 2\text{Cov}(\overline{A}, \overline{G}) \qquad (19.9)$$

As long as the estimate $\overline{G}$ is highly correlated with the estimate $\overline{A}$, the variance of the estimate A^* can be less than the variance of $\overline{A}$.

In practice, the variance reduction from the control variate method can be dramatic. Figure 19.3 graphs the results from the first 200 simulations in pricing an arithmetic Asian option. The control variate estimate converges in just a few trials to the correct value of about $1.98. For example, the very first draw in the graphed simulation gave an arithmetic option price of $0.80 and a geometric price—using the same random prices—of $0.75. The correct geometric price is $1.94. Correcting the estimate gives a price of

$$\text{Control variate price} = \$0.80 + (\$1.94 - \$0.75) = \$1.99$$

This example illustrates that if the correlation between the two estimates is high, the control variate method works very well.

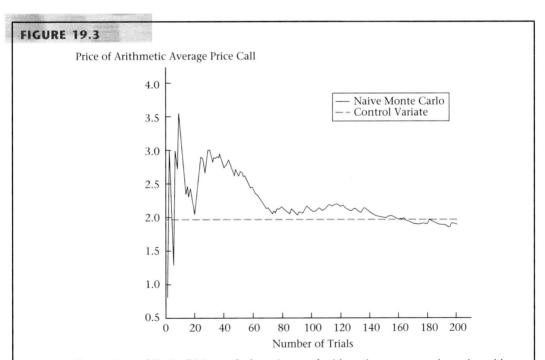

FIGURE 19.3

Price of Arithmetic Average Price Call

Comparison of "naive" Monte Carlo estimate of arithmetic average option price with control variate method. Graph depicts first 200 simulations for an option with $S = \$40$, $K = \$40$, $\sigma = 0.3$, $r = 0.08$, $T = 0.25$, $\delta = 0$, and the final price computed with three averages.

Boyle et al. (1997) point out that equation (19.8) does not in general provide the minimum variance Monte Carlo estimate, and in some cases can even increase the variance of the estimate. They suggest that instead of estimating equation (19.8), you estimate

$$A^* = \overline{A} + \beta \left(G - \overline{G} \right) \tag{19.10}$$

The variance of this estimate is

$$\text{Var}(A^*) = \text{Var}(\overline{A}) + \beta^2 \text{Var}(\overline{G}) - 2\beta \text{Cov}(\overline{A}, \overline{G}) \tag{19.11}$$

The variance $\text{Var}(A^*)$ is minimized by setting $\beta = \text{Cov}(\overline{A}, \overline{G})/\text{Var}(\overline{G})$. One way to obtain β is to perform a small number of Monte Carlo trials, run a regression of equation (19.10) to obtain $\hat{\beta}$, and then use $\hat{\beta}$ for the remaining trials. The optimal value of β will vary depending on the application.

Other Monte Carlo Methods

The control variate example is just one method for improving the efficiency of Monte Carlo valuation. The **antithetic variate method** uses the insight that for every simulated realization, there is an opposite and equally likely realization. For example, if we draw a random normal number of 0.5, we could just as well have drawn −0.5. By using the opposite of each normal draw we can get two simulated outcomes for each random path we draw. This seems as if it would help, since it doubles the number of draws. But drawing a random number is often not the time-consuming part of a Monte Carlo calculation.

There can be an efficiency gain because the two estimates are negatively correlated; adding them reduces the variance of the estimate. In practical terms, this means that if you draw an extreme estimate from one tail of the distribution, you will also draw an extreme estimate from the other tail, balancing the effect of the first draw. Boyle et al. (1997) find modest benefits from using the antithetic variate method.

Another important class of methods controls the region in which random numbers are generated. **Stratified sampling** is an example of this kind of method. Suppose you have 100 uniform random numbers, $u_i, i = 1, \ldots, 100$. With naive Monte Carlo you would compute $z_i = N^{-1}(u_i)$. This calculation treats each random number as representing a random draw from the cumulative distribution. However, because of random variation, 100 uniform random numbers will not be exactly uniformly distributed and therefore the z_i will not be exactly normal. We can improve the distribution of the u_i, and therefore of the z_i, if we treat each number *as a random draw from each percentile of the uniform distribution*. Thus, take the first draw, u_1, and divide it by 100. The resulting $\hat{u}_1$ is now uniformly distribtuted over [0,0.01]. Take the second draw, divide it by 100, and add 0.01. The resulting $\hat{u}_2$ is uniformly distributed over (0.01,0.02). For the ith draw, compute $\hat{u}_i = (i - 1 + u_i)/100$. This value is uniformly distributed over the ith percentile. Proceeding in this way we are guaranteed to generate a random number for each percentile of the normal distribution. You can select a number of intervals different from 100, and you can repeat the simulation multiple times. A generalization of this technique when the payoff depends on more than one random variable is *Latin hypercube sampling,* discussed by Boyle et al. (1997).

There are other techniques for improving the efficiency of Monte Carlo. The approach called *importance sampling* concentrates the generation of random numbers where they have the most value for pricing a particular claim. *Low discrepancy sequences* use carefully selected deterministic points to create more uniform coverage of the distribution. Boyle et al. (1997) provide an excellent summary and comparison of the different methods.

If you are performing a one-time calculation, the simplicity of naive Monte Carlo is appealing. However, if you are performing a Monte Carlo valuation repeatedly, you may achieve large efficiency gains by analyzing the problem and using one or more variance reduction techniques to increase efficiency.

19.6 VALUATION OF AMERICAN OPTIONS

It is generally more difficult to value American-style options than to value European-style options, and this remains true when using Monte Carlo valuation. Standard Monte Carlo entails simulating stock price paths *forward*, then averaging and discounting the maturity payoffs. In American option valuation, the difficulty is knowing when to exercise the option; this requires working *backward* to determine the times at which the option should be exercised. Recently, Broadie and Glasserman (1997) and Longstaff and Schwartz (2001) have demonstrated feasible methods for using Monte Carlo to value American options.

We will discuss pricing a 3-year put option with a strike of $1.10, the example used in Longstaff and Schwartz (2001). In order to analyze early exercise we need to consider times before maturity, so we must simulate stock price *paths*. Figure 19.4, taken from Longstaff and Schwartz (2001), illustrates eight hypothetical simulation paths, with intermediate stock prices generated annually. The in-the-money nodes (those for which

FIGURE 19.4		Stock Price Paths			
Assumes $S_0 = 1.0$,	Path	$t = 0$	$t = 1$	$t = 2$	$t = 3$
$K = 1.1$, and $r = 6\%$.	1	1.00	**1.09**	**1.08**	1.34
Prices in **bold** are nodes	2	1.00	1.16	1.26	1.54
where early exercise	3	1.00	1.22	**1.07**	**1.03**
might be optimal.	4	1.00	**0.93**	**0.97**	**0.92**
	5	1.00	1.11	1.56	1.52
	6	1.00	**0.76**	**0.77**	**0.90**
	7	1.00	**0.92**	**0.84**	**1.01**
	8	1.00	**0.88**	1.22	1.34

Source: Longstaff and Schwartz (2001).

$S < \$1.10$) are candidate nodes for exercise of the option; in Figure 19.4 they are in bold (this ignores exercise at time 0). How do we determine at which of these nodes early exercise is optimal?

The idea underlying any method of American option valuation is to compare the value of immediate exercise to the **continuation value** of the option—i.e., the value of keeping the option alive.[7] The problem is therefore to estimate the continuation value at each point in time.

It is worth noting one potential problem in estimating continuation value, which stems from the use of future stock prices on a given path to decide whether to exercise on that path. Consider path 1 in Figure 19.4. The option is out-of-the-money, and therefore worthless, at $t = 3$. Therefore, on this path we would be better off at $t = 2$ exercising rather than waiting. However, in deciding to exercise by looking ahead on the path, we are using knowledge of the future stock price, which is information we will not have in real life. Valuing the option assuming we know the future price will give us too high a value. The way to mitigate such "lookahead bias" is to base an exercise decision on *average* outcomes from a given point forward. There are at least two ways to characterize the average outcome from a given point. One is to use a regression to characterize the continuation value based on analysis of multiple paths. This is the method proposed by Longstaff and Schwartz (2001). Another is create additional branches from each node, providing multiple outcomes that we can average to characterize continuation value at that node. This is the basis for the Broadie and Glasserman (1997) procedure.

To price the option using regression analysis, we work backward through the columns of Figure 19.4, running a regression at each time to estimate continuation value as a function of the stock price. We work backward because the continuation value at $t = 1$ will depend upon whether exercise is optimal on a given path at $t = 2$. At $t = 2$, there are five paths (1, 3, 4, 6, and 7) where the option is in-the-money and exercise could be optimal. For each of these paths, we know the value of exercising immediately and the value of waiting. Longstaff and Schwartz run a regression of the present value of waiting to exercise (i.e., the continuation value) against the stock price and stock price squared. At time 2, we obtain the following result:

$$\text{Continuation value at time 2} = -1.07 + 2.98 \times S - 1.81 \times S^2$$

where S is the time 2 stock price. Now for each node where exercise could be optimal, we insert the stock price at that node into the regression equation and obtain an estimate of continuation value. By comparing this to intrinsic value, we decide whether to exercise at that node. For example, when $S = 1.08$ in row 1, the esimated value of waiting to exercise is

$$-1.07 + 2.98 \times 1.08 - 1.81 \times 1.166 = 0.037 \qquad (19.12)$$

---

[7]For example, this is the comparison in the binomial valuation in equation (10.10).

Since the immediate exercise value is $1.10 - 1.08 = 0.02$, which is less the 0.037, we wait at that node. Table 19.4 summarizes the results.

We then repeat the analysis at $t = 1$, using the results at $t = 2$. The final decision about where to exercise the option is summarized in Figure 19.5. We can value the option by computing the present value of cash flows based on exercising at the nodes where doing so is optimal. The final American put value is $0.1144, compared with $0.0564 for a European value computed using the same simulated paths.

A problem with the regression approach is that it is not obvious how to select an appropriate functional form for the continuation regression. Longstaff and Schwartz (2001) report obtaining similar results for a variety of functional forms, but for each new problem it will be desirable to experiment with different functions.

Broadie and Glasserman (1997) adopt a different approach, pointing out that American option valuations are subject to different kinds of biases. As we discussed above, an estimator will give too high a valuation to the extent it uses information about the future to decide whether to exercise at a given time. Estimators will be biased low to the extent that early exercise is suboptimal (since optimal exercise maximizes the value

TABLE 19.4		Exercise analysis at $t = 2$ for those nodes in Figure 19.4 where $S < \$1.10$ at $t = 2$.				
Path	PV(Wait)	S	S^2	Exercise	Continuation	Result
1	0.000	1.08	1.166	0.02	0.037	Wait
3	0.066	1.07	1.145	0.03	0.046	Wait
4	0.170	0.97	0.941	0.13	0.118	Exercise
6	0.188	0.77	0.593	0.33	0.152	Exercise
7	0.085	0.84	0.706	0.26	0.156	Exercise

FIGURE 19.5	Stock Price Paths			
	Path	$t = 0$	$t = 1$	$t = 2$	$t = 3$

Summary of results showing the nodes at which exercise is optimal (in **bold**) for the paths in Figure 19.4.

Path	$t = 0$	$t = 1$	$t = 2$	$t = 3$
1	1.00	1.09	1.08	1.34
2	1.00	1.16	1.26	1.54
3	1.00	1.22	1.07	**1.03**
4	1.00	**0.93**	0.97	0.92
5	1.00	1.11	1.56	1.52
6	1.00	**0.76**	0.77	0.90
7	1.00	**0.92**	0.84	1.01
8	1.00	**0.88**	1.22	1.34

of the option). To address the two errors, Broadie and Glasserman use two estimators, one with high bias and one with low bias. In constructing these estimators, they create sample paths in which there are multiple branches from each node. The resulting set of paths resembles a nonrecombining binomial tree with more than two branches from each node.

The high bias estimator assesses the continuation value by averaging the discounted values on branches emanating from a point and exercising if the value of doing so is greater than the value of continuing. Because the subsequent branches are constructed by simulation, there will be sampling error. To see the effects of such error, suppose exercise is optimal at a node. If the subsequent branches are too high due to sampling error, we will not exercise and assign an even higher value to the node than would be obtained by (optimally) exercising. Now suppose that exercise is not optimal at a node but subsequent branches are too low due to sampling error. We will then exercise and again assign a higher value to the node than we should, given the subsequent branch values.[8]

The low bias estimator is obtained by splitting the branches from each node into two sets. Using the first set, we estimate the value of continuation and decide whether to exercise. If it is optimal to continue, we use the second set of nodes to estimate the continuation value. By using separate sets of nodes to make the exercise decision and to estimate continuation value, this estimator avoids the "high bias" discussed above. But to the extent the exercise decision is suboptimal, the inferred option value will be too low. Both estimators are biased, but both also converge to the true option value as the number of paths increases.

The Broadie and Glasserman approach is computationally involved, but provides a general method for accomodating early exercise in a simulation model.

19.7 THE POISSON DISTRIBUTION

We have seen that the lognormal distribution assigns a low probability to large stock price moves. One approach to generating a more realistic stock price distribution is to permit large stock price moves to occur randomly. Occasional large price moves can generate the fat tails observed in the data in Section 18.6.

The **Poisson distribution** is a discrete probability distribution that counts the number of events—such as large stock price moves—that occur over a period of time. The Poisson distribution is summarized by the parameter λ, where λh is the probability that one event occurs over the short interval h. A Poisson-distributed event is very

---

[8] Note that the other two kinds of sampling errors do not matter for assessing the value of early exercise. If it is not optimal to exercise and subsequent branches are too high, we will not exercise and therefore not erroneously attribute value to exercising. Similarly, if it is optimal to exercise and subsequent values are too low, we will exercise, giving the correct value to early exercise.

unlikely to occur more than once over a sufficiently short interval. Thus, λ is like an annualized probability of the event occurring over a short interval.[9]

Over a longer period of time, t, the probability that the event occurs exactly m times is given by

$$p(m, \lambda t) = \frac{e^{-\lambda t}(\lambda t)^m}{m!}$$

The cumulative Poisson distribution is then the probability that there are m or fewer events from 0 to t.[10]

$$\mathcal{P}(m, \lambda t) = \text{Prob}(x \leq m; \lambda t) = \sum_{i=0}^{m} \frac{e^{-\lambda t}(\lambda t)^i}{i!}$$

Given an expected number of events, the Poisson distribution tells us the probability that we will see a particular number of the events over a given period of time.[11] The mean of the Poisson distribution is λt.

Example 19.3 Suppose the probability of a market crash is $\lambda = 2\%$ per year. Then the probability of seeing no market crashes in any given year can be computed as $p(0, 0.02 \times 1) = 0.9802$. The probability of seeing no crashes over a 10-year period would be $p(0, 0.02 \times 10) = 0.8187$. The probability of seeing exactly two crashes over a 10-year period would be $p(2, 0.02 \times 10) = 0.0164$. ≋

Figure 19.6 graphs the Poisson distribution for three values of the Poisson parameter, λt. Suppose we are interested in the number of times an event will occur over a

---

[9]By definition, the number of occurrences of an event is Poisson-distributed if four assumptions are satisfied:

1. The probability that one event will occur in a small interval h is proportional to the length of the interval.

2. The probability that more than one event will occur in a small interval h is substantially smaller than the probability that a single event will occur.

3. The number of events in nonoverlapping time intervals is independent.

4. The expected number of events between time t and time $t + s$ is independent of t.

The Poisson distribution can be derived from these four assumptions. See Casella and Berger (2002).

[10]In Excel, you can compute $p(m, \lambda t)$ as $\text{Poisson}(m, \lambda t, false)$, and the cumulative distribution, $\mathcal{P}(m, \lambda t)$, as $\text{Poisson}(m, \lambda t, true)$.

[11]The probability that no event occurs between time 0 and time t is $p(0, \lambda t) = e^{-\lambda t}$. The probability that one or more events occurs between 0 and t is therefore $1 - e^{-\lambda t}$. This expression is also the cumulative distribution of the **exponential distribution,** which models the time until the first event. The density function of the exponential distribution is $f(t, \lambda) = \lambda e^{-\lambda t}$.

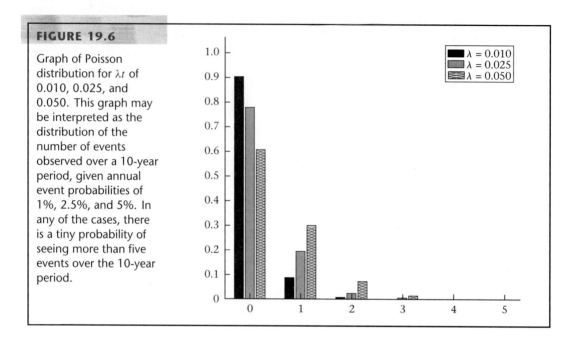

FIGURE 19.6

Graph of Poisson distribution for λt of 0.010, 0.025, and 0.050. This graph may be interpreted as the distribution of the number of events observed over a 10-year period, given annual event probabilities of 1%, 2.5%, and 5%. In any of the cases, there is a tiny probability of seeing more than five events over the 10-year period.

10-year period. Figure 19.6 shows us the distribution for $t = 10$ and $\lambda = 0.01$ (1% per year), $\lambda = 0.025$ (2.5% per year), and $\lambda = 0.05$ (5% per year). The likeliest occurrence in all three scenarios is that no events occur. It is also extremely unlikely that four or more events occur.

The Poisson distribution only counts the number of events. If an event occurs, we need to determine the magnitude of the jump as an independent draw from some other density; the lognormal is frequently used. Thus, in those periods when a Poisson event occurs, we would draw a separate random variable to determine the magnitude of the jump.

Using the inverse cumulative distribution function for a Poisson random variable, it is easy to generate a Poisson-distributed random variable. Even without the inverse cumulative distribution function (which Excel does not provide), we can construct the inverse distribution function from the cumulative distribution function.

Table 19.5 calculates the Poisson distribution for a mean of 0.8. Using this table we can easily see how to randomly draw a Poisson event. First we draw a uniform (0,1) random variable. Then we use the values in the table to decide how many events occur. If the uniform random variable is less than 0.4493, for example, we say that no events occur. If the value is between 0.4493 and 0.8088, we say that one event occurs, and so forth.

These properties imply that $Z(t)$ is a **martingale:** a stochastic process for which $E[Z(t + s)|Z(t)] = Z(t)$. The process $Z(t)$ is also called a **diffusion process.**

To represent this process mathematically, we can focus on the *change* in $Z(t)$, which we model as binomial, times a scale factor that makes the change in $Z(t)$ small over a small period of time. Brownian motion is then the limit of a sum of infinitesimal increments over a period of time. Denote the short period of time as h, and let $Y(t)$ be a random draw from a binomial distribution, where $Y(t)$ is ± 1 with probability 0.5. Note that $E[Y(t)] = 0$ and $\text{Var}[Y(t)] = 1$. We can write

$$Z(t + h) - Z(t) = Y(t + h)\sqrt{h} \tag{20.2}$$

Over any period of time longer than h, Z will be the sum of the binomial increments specified in equation (20.2). Let $n = T/h$ be the number of intervals of length h between 0 and T. We have

$$Z(T) - Z(0) = \sum_{i=1}^{n}(Z[ih] - Z[(i - 1)h]) = \sum_{i=1}^{n} Y(ih)\sqrt{h}$$

Since $h = T/n$, we can also write this as

$$Z(T) - Z(0) = \sqrt{T}\left[\frac{1}{\sqrt{n}}\sum_{i=1}^{n} Y(ih)\right] \tag{20.3}$$

To understand the properties of $Z(T)$, we must first understand the properties of the term in square brackets in equation (20.3). Since $E[Y(ih)] = 0$, we have

$$E\left[\frac{1}{\sqrt{n}}\sum_{i=1}^{n} Y(ih)\right] = 0$$

Also, since $\text{Var}[Y(ih)] = 1$, and the Y's are independent, we have

$$\text{Var}\left[\frac{1}{\sqrt{n}}\sum_{i=1}^{n} Y(ih)\right] = \frac{1}{n}\sum_{i=1}^{n} 1 = 1$$

Thus, the term in square brackets has mean 0 and variance 1, since it is the sum of n independent random variables with mean 0 and variance 1, divided by $\sqrt{n}$.

By the Central Limit Theorem, the distribution of the sum of independent binomial random variables approaches normality. We have

$$\lim_{n\to\infty} \frac{1}{\sqrt{n}}\sum_{i=1}^{n} Y(ih) \sim \mathcal{N}(0, 1)$$

The division by $\sqrt{n}$ in this expression prevents the variance from going to infinity as n goes to infinity.

Returning to equation (20.3), the multiplication by $\sqrt{T}$ on the right-hand side multiplies the variance by T. Thus, in the limit we have

$$Z(T) - Z(0) \to \mathcal{N}(0, T)$$

To summarize, we have verified that the $Z(T)$ we have constructed has some of the characteristics of Brownian motion: it is normally distributed with mean zero and variance T, and increments to $Z(T)$ are independent.

We have not verified that the $Z(T)$ defined in equation (20.3) is a continuous process, hence we have not demonstrated that it is true Brownian motion. However, it is plausible that $Z(T)$ is continuous because the magnitude of the increments is $\sqrt{h} = \sqrt{T/n}$, and $h \to 0$ as $n \to \infty$.

It is common to write down expressions denoting the Brownian increments. As h becomes small, rename h as dt and the change in Z as $dZ(t)$. We then have

$$dZ(t) = Y(t)\sqrt{dt} \tag{20.4}$$

This representation of the Brownian process is mathematically informal but surprisingly useful. Equation (20.4) is just like equation (20.2), except that $Z(t + h) - Z(t)$ is now called $dZ(t)$, and $\sqrt{h}$ is now $\sqrt{dt}$.[2] Equation (20.4) is a mathematical way to say: "Over small periods of time, changes in the value of the process are normally distributed with a variance that is proportional to the length of the time period."

Although expressions like equation (20.4) appear in the derivatives literature, it is mathematically more convenient to deal with sums of increments rather than increments. These sums are written as integrals, for example:

$$Z(T) = Z(0) + \lim_{n\to\infty} \sqrt{T}\left[\frac{1}{\sqrt{n}}\sum_{i=1}^{n} Y(ih)\right] \to Z(0) + \int_0^T dZ(t) \tag{20.5}$$

The integral in expression (20.5) is called a stochastic integral.[3]

Properties of Brownian Motion

We now use equation (20.3) to understand some of additional properties of Brownian motion. The following derivations will be informal, intended to provide intuition rather than actual proofs. In particular, we continue to use the binomial approximation to the Brownian process.

The **quadratic variation** of a process is defined as the sum of the squared increments to the process. Thus, the quadratic variation of the Brownian process $Z(t)$ is

$$\lim_{n\to\infty} \sum_{i=1}^{n} (Z[ih] - Z[(i-1)h])^2 = \lim_{n\to\infty} \sum_{i=1}^{n} \left(\sqrt{h}Y_{ih}\right)^2 = \lim_{n\to\infty} \sum_{i=1}^{n} hY_{ih}^2$$

....

[2] Should we think of $Y(t)$ as being binomially or normally distributed? For any t and ϵ, $Z(t+\epsilon) - Z(t)$ is the sum of infinitely many $dZ(t)$'s. Therefore, we can think of $Y(t)$ as binomial or normal; either way, $Z(t)$ is normal for any finite interval.

[3] Because $dZ(t)$ is a random variable, considerable care is required in defining equation (20.5). See Neftci (2000, ch. 9) for a discussion of stochastic integration. Karatzas and Shreve (1991) provide a more advanced treatment.

Since we are treating Y_i as binomial, taking on the values ± 1, we have $Y_{ih}^2 = 1$ and hence

$$\lim_{n \to \infty} \sum_{i=1}^{n} h Y_{ih}^2 = \lim_{n \to \infty} \sum_{i=1}^{n} \frac{T}{n} = T$$

In other words,

$$\lim_{n \to \infty} \sum_{i=1}^{n} (Z[ih] - Z[(i-1)h])^2 = T \tag{20.6}$$

Surprisingly, the quadratic variation of a Brownian process from time 0 to time T is not a random variable, but it is finite and equal to T. An important implication of the fact that quadratic variation is finite, is that higher-order variations are zero. Thus, for example, the sum of the cubed increments is zero. The finite quadratic variation of a Brownian process turns out to be an extremely important result that we will encounter again.

The **total variation** of the Brownian process is

$$\lim_{n \to \infty} \sum_{i=1}^{n} |\sqrt{h} Y_{ih}| = \lim_{n \to \infty} \sum_{i=1}^{n} \sqrt{h} |Y_{ih}|$$

Again, treating Y_i as binomial, we have $|Y_{ih}| = 1$, and hence

$$\lim_{n \to \infty} \sum_{i=1}^{n} \sqrt{h} |Y_{ih}| = \lim_{n \to \infty} \sqrt{T} \sum_{i=1}^{n} \frac{1}{\sqrt{n}} = \sqrt{T} \lim_{n \to \infty} \sqrt{n} = \infty$$

This means that the absolute length of a Brownian path is infinite over any finite interval. In order for a path to have infinite length over a finite interval of time, it must move up and down rapidly. This behavior implies the *infinite crossing* property, which states that a Brownian path will cross its starting point an infinite number of times in an interval of any finite length.

Arithmetic Brownian Motion

The Brownian motion process described above is a building block for more elaborate and realistic processes. With pure Brownian motion, the expected change in Z is 0, and the variance per unit time is 1. We can generalize this to allow an arbitrary variance and a nonzero mean. To make this generalization, we can write

$$X(t+h) - X(t) = \alpha h + \sigma Y(t+h)\sqrt{h}$$

This equation implies that $X(T)$ is normally distributed. Since $h = T/n$, we have

$$X(T) - X(0) = \sum_{i=1}^{n} \left(\alpha \frac{T}{n} + \sigma Y(ih)\sqrt{\frac{T}{n}} \right)$$

$$= \alpha T + \sigma \left(\sqrt{T} \sum_{i=1}^{n} \frac{Y(ih)}{\sqrt{n}} \right)$$

We have seen that as $n \to \infty$, the term in parentheses on the right-hand side has the distribution $\mathcal{N}(0, T)$. We can write

$$X(T) - X(0) = \alpha T + \sigma Z(T) \tag{20.7}$$

The differential form of this expression is

$$dX(t) = \alpha dt + \sigma dZ(t) \tag{20.8}$$

This process is called **arithmetic Brownian motion.** We say that α is the instantaneous mean per unit time and σ^2 is the instantaneous variance per unit time. The variable $X(t)$ is the sum of the individual changes dX. An implication of equation (20.8) is that $X(T)$ is normally distributed, or

$$X(T) - X(0) \sim \mathcal{N}(\alpha T, \sigma^2 T)$$

As before, there is an integral representation of equation (20.8):

$$X(T) = X(0) + \int_0^T \alpha dt + \int_0^T \sigma dZ(t)$$

This expression is equivalent to equation (20.7).

Here are some of the properties of the process in equation (20.8):

- $X(t)$ is normally distributed because it is a scaled Brownian process.

- The random term has been multiplied by a scale factor that enables us to change variance. Since $dZ(t)$ has a variance of 1 per unit time, $\sigma dZ(t)$ will have a variance of σ^2 per unit time.

- The αdt term introduces a nonrandom *drift* into the process. Adding αdt has the effect of adding α per unit time to $X(0)$.

Being able to adjust the drift and variance is a big step toward a more useful model, but arithmetic Brownian motion has several drawbacks:

- There is nothing to prevent X from becoming negative, so it is a poor model for stock prices.

- The mean and variance of changes in dollar terms are independent of the level of the stock price. In practice if a stock doubles, we would expect both the dollar expected return and the dollar standard deviation of returns to approximately double.

We will eliminate both of these criticisms with geometric Brownian motion, which we consider in Section 20.3.

The Ornstein-Uhlenbeck Process

Another modification of the arithmetic Brownian process permits mean reversion. It is natural to consider mean reversion when modeling commodity prices or interest rates. For example, if the interest rate becomes sufficiently high, it is likely to fall, and if the value is sufficiently low, it is likely to rise. Commodity prices may also exhibit this tendency to revert to the mean. We can incorporate mean reversion by modifying the drift term:

$$dX(t) = \lambda[\alpha - X(t)]dt + \sigma dZ(t) \qquad (20.9)$$

When $\alpha = 0$, equation (20.9) is called an **Ornstein-Uhlenbeck process.**

Equation (20.9) has the implication that if X rises above α, the drift, $\lambda[\alpha - X(t)]$, will become negative. If X falls below α, the drift becomes positive. The parameter λ measures the speed of the reversion: If λ is large, reversion happens more quickly. In the long run, we expect X to revert toward α. As with arithmetic Brownian motion, X can still become negative.

20.3 GEOMETRIC BROWNIAN MOTION

In general we can write both the drift and volatility as functions of X (or other variables):

$$dX(t) = \alpha[X(t)]dt + \sigma[X(t)]dZ(t) \qquad (20.10)$$

This equation, in which the drift, α, and volatility, σ, depend on the stock price, is called an **Itô process.**

Suppose we modify arithmetic Brownian motion to make the instantaneous mean and standard deviation proportional to $X(t)$:

$$dX(t) = \alpha X(t)dt + \sigma X(t)dZ(t)$$

This is an Itô process that can also be written

$$\frac{dX(t)}{X(t)} = \alpha dt + \sigma dZ(t) \qquad (20.11)$$

This equation says that the dollar mean and standard deviation of the stock price change are $\alpha X(t)$ and $\sigma X(t)$, and they are proportional to the level of the stock price. Thus, *the percentage change in the asset value is normally distributed with instantaneous mean α and instantaneous variance σ^2.* The process in equation (20.11) is known as **geometric Brownian motion.** For the rest of the book, we will frequently assume that prices of stocks and other assets follow equation (20.11).

The integral representation for equation (20.11) is

$$X(T) - X(0) = \int_0^T \alpha X(t)dt + \int_0^T \sigma X(t)dZ(t)$$

Lognormality

We now circle back to our discussion of lognormality because of this fact: A variable that follows geometric Brownian is lognormally distributed. Suppose we start a process at $X(0)$ and it follows geometric Brownian motion. Because the mean and variance at time t are proportional to $X(t)$, the evolution of X implied by equation (20.11) generates compounding (the change in X is proportional to X) and, hence, nonnormality.

However, while X is not normal, $\ln[X(t)]$ is normally distributed:

$$\ln[X(t)] \sim \mathcal{N}(\ln[X(0)] + (\alpha - 0.5\sigma^2)t, \sigma^2 t) \qquad (20.12)$$

As a result, we can write

$$X(t) = X(0)e^{(\alpha - 0.5\sigma^2)t + \sigma\sqrt{t}Z} \tag{20.13}$$

where $Z \sim \mathcal{N}(0, 1)$. This is the link between Brownian motion and lognormality. If a variable is distributed in such a way that instantaneous percentage changes follow geometric Brownian motion, then over discrete periods of time, the variable is lognormally distributed.

Given that X follows (20.11), we can compute the expected value of X at a point in the future. It follows from the discussion in Section 18.2 that

$$
\begin{aligned}
E[X(t)] &= X(0)e^{(\alpha - 0.5\sigma^2)t} E_0(e^{\sigma\sqrt{t}Z}) \\
&= X(0)e^{(\alpha - 0.5\sigma^2)t} e^{0.5\sigma^2 t} \\
&= X(0)e^{\alpha t}
\end{aligned}
\tag{20.14}
$$

Thus, α in equation (20.11) is the expected, continuously compounded return on X.

Relative Importance of the Drift and Noise Terms

Consider the discrete counterpart for geometric Brownian motion:

$$X(t + h) - X(t) = \alpha X(t)h + \sigma X(t)Y(t)\sqrt{h}$$

Over a short interval of time, there are two components to the change in X: a deterministic component, $\alpha X(t)h$, and a random component, $\sigma X(t)Y(t)\sqrt{h}$. An important fact is that *over short periods of time, the character of the Brownian process is determined almost entirely by the random component.* The drift can be undetectable amid all the up and down movement generated by the random term.

To understand why the random term is important over short horizons, consider the ratio of the standard deviation to the drift:

$$\frac{\sigma X(t)\sqrt{h}}{\alpha X(t)h} = \frac{\sigma}{\alpha\sqrt{h}}$$

This ratio becomes infinite as h approaches dt.

A numerical example shows this more concretely. Suppose $\alpha = 10\%$ and $\sigma = 10\%$. Over a year, the mean and standard deviations are the same. Table 20.1 shows that the ratio increases as the time interval becomes smaller. Over a period of 1 day, the standard deviation is 19 times larger than the mean. This is important in practice since it means that when you look at daily returns, you are primarily seeing the movement of a random variable following pure Brownian motion.[4] The deterministic drift (the expected return) is virtually undetectable.

----

[4]There are other considerations when you look at prices over short periods of time, including the bouncing of prices between the bid and the ask, and the effects of trades such as large blocks that may temporarily depress prices. Brownian motion implies that even in the absence of these effects, prices would still bounce around significantly.

TABLE 20.1		The last column computes the ratio of the per-period standard deviation to the per-period mean for different time intervals. The ratio becomes infinite as the time interval goes to zero.		
Period Length	h	αh	$\sigma\sqrt{h}$	$\dfrac{\sigma\sqrt{h}}{\alpha h}$
Five years	5	0.5	0.2236	0.447
One year	1	0.10	0.10	1.00
One month	0.0833	0.0083	0.0289	3.464
One day	0.0027	0.00027	0.0052	19.105
One minute	0.000002	0.0000002	0.00014	724.98

As the time interval becomes longer than a year, the reverse happens: The mean becomes more important than the standard deviation. Since the mean is proportional to h while the standard deviation is proportional to $\sqrt{h}$, the mean comes to dominate over longer horizons. Since we take the ratio of the instantaneous standard deviation to the instantaneous mean, Table 20.1 also holds for arithmetic Brownian motion.

Correlated Itô Processes

Suppose that we have the Itô process

$$dQ(t) = \alpha_Q[Q(t)]dt + \sigma_Q[Q(t)]dZ'(t) \qquad (20.15)$$

where $Z'(t)$ is a Brownian motion. The Brownian motion $Z'(t)$ in equation (20.15) can be correlated with $Z(t)$ in equation (20.10). For example, if X and Q represent stock prices, X and Q will typically be correlated. Let $W_1(t)$ and $W_2(t)$ be independent Brownian motions. We can then write

$$
\begin{aligned}
Z(t) &= W_1(t) \\
Z'(t) &= \rho W_1(t) + \sqrt{1 - \rho^2}\, W_2(t)
\end{aligned}
\qquad (20.16)
$$

You may recognize this is as the Cholesky decomposition, which we discussed in Section 19.9. Using equation (20.16), the correlation between $Z(t)$ and $Z'(t)$ is

$$
\begin{aligned}
E[Z(t)Z'(t)] &= \rho E[W_1(t)^2] + \sqrt{1 - \rho^2}\, E[W_1(t)W_2(t)] \\
&= \rho t + 0
\end{aligned}
$$

The second term on the right-hand side is zero because $W_1(t)$ and $W_2(t)$ are independent. We then say the correlation between dZ and dZ' is ρdt.

Multiplication Rules

The dominance of the noise term over short intervals has another implication. Since the behavior of dX is dominated by the noise term, the squared return, $(dX)^2$, reflects primarily the noise term. We have

$$[X(t+h) - X(t)]^2 = \left[\alpha X(t)h + \sigma X(t)Y(t)\sqrt{h}\right]^2$$

Expanding this expression and simplifying, we have

$$[X(t+h) - X(t)]^2 = \alpha^2 X(t)^2 h^2 + 2\alpha\sigma X(t)^2 Y(t)h^{1.5} + \sigma^2 X(t)^2 Y(t)^2 h$$

Suppose that h is 1 day. Then $h = 0.00274$, $h^{1.5} = 0.000143$, and $h^2 = 0.0000075$. If h is 1 hour, then $h = 0.000114$, $h^{1.5} = 0.0000012$, and $h^2 = 0.00000001$. Clearly, the relative magnitude of the term multiplied by h is much greater than the other terms as h becomes very small. In addition, if we think of Y as binomial, then $Y(t)^2 = 1$. This leads us to write

$$[X(t+h) - X(t)]^2 \approx \sigma^2 X(t)^2 h$$

or

$$[dX(t)]^2 = \sigma^2 X(t)^2 dt$$

essentially ignoring all terms that are higher powers of h. This equation tells us that if we look at the squared stock price change over a small interval, all we are seeing is the effect of the variance.

We can also consider terms like

$$[X(t+h) - X(t)]h$$

Rewriting this expression gives us

$$\left[\alpha X(t)h + \sigma X(t)Y(t)\sqrt{h}\right]h = \alpha X(t)h^2 + \sigma X(t)Y(t)h^{1.5}$$

Since the smallest power of h is 1.5, this entire term vanishes relative to h as h goes to zero.

Suppose we have two different Itô processes such as equations (20.10) and (20.15). We can write $dZ'(t) = Y'\sqrt{dt}$ where $E[Y(t)Y'(t)] = \rho$. Thus, ρ is the correlation between $Y(t)$ and $Y'(t)$. We have

$$E\left([X(t+h) - X(t)][Q(t+h) - Q(t)]\right)$$
$$= E\left([\alpha X(t)h + \sigma X(t)Y(t+h)\sqrt{h}][\alpha_Q Q(t)h + \sigma_Q Q(t)Y'(t+h)\sqrt{h}]\right)$$
$$= \sigma\sigma_Q\rho X(t)Q(t)h + \text{(terms with power} \geq \tfrac{3}{2})$$

One way to make these calculations mechanical is to use the following so-called "multiplication rules" for terms containing dt and dZ:

$$dt \times dZ = 0 \qquad\qquad (20.17a)$$

$$(dt)^2 = 0 \qquad\qquad (20.17b)$$

$$(dZ)^2 = dt \qquad (20.17c)$$
$$dZ \times dZ' = \rho dt \qquad (20.17d)$$

The reasoning behind these multiplication rules is that the multiplications resulting in powers of dt greater than 1 vanish in the limit.

20.4 THE SHARPE RATIO

If asset i has expected return α_i, the risk premium is defined as

$$\text{Risk premium}_i = \alpha_i - r$$

where r is the risk-free rate. A basic idea in finance is that the return on an asset is linked to its risk, where risk is measured as the covariance between the return on the asset and investor utility.[5] In the Capital Asset Pricing Model (CAPM), the risk that matters is the covariance between a stock and the market return since investor utility depends on the market return. There are other models of risk, but for our purposes we need not take a stand on a particular model.

The **Sharpe ratio** for asset i is the risk premium, $\alpha_i - r$, per unit of volatility, σ_i:

$$\text{Sharpe ratio}_i = \frac{\alpha_i - r}{\sigma_i} \qquad (20.18)$$

The Sharpe ratio is commonly used to compare well-diversified portfolios and is not intended to compare individual assets. In particular, if diversifiable risk is different, two assets with the same σ can have different risk premiums (and hence different Sharpe ratios) if they have different covariances with the market. However, we *can* use the Sharpe ratio to compare two perfectly correlated claims, such as a derivative and its underlying asset. The main point of this section is that two assets that are perfectly correlated will have the same Sharpe ratio.

To see that two perfectly correlated assets must have the same Sharpe ratio, consider the processes for two nondividend paying stocks:

$$dS_1 = \alpha_1 S_1 dt + \sigma_1 S_1 dZ \qquad (20.19)$$
$$dS_2 = \alpha_2 S_2 dt + \sigma_2 S_2 dZ \qquad (20.20)$$

Because the two stock prices are driven by the same dZ, it must be the case that $(\alpha_1 - r)/\sigma_1 = (\alpha_2 - r)/\sigma_2$, or else there will be an arbitrage opportunity.

Before we examine the arbitrage, let's explore the intuition. For example, in the CAPM, the risk premium of asset i, $\alpha_i - r$, is

$$\alpha_i - r = \beta_i (\alpha_M - r) \qquad (20.21)$$

---

[5] See Appendix 11.B.

where α_M is the expected return on the market portfolio. The beta of asset i is

$$\beta_i = \frac{\rho_{i,M}\sigma_i}{\sigma_M} \qquad (20.22)$$

where $\rho_{i,M}$ is the correlation of asset i with the market, σ_i is the volatility of the asset, and σ_M is the market volatility. Using equation (20.22), we can rewrite equation (20.21) as

$$\frac{\alpha_i - r}{\sigma_i} = \rho_{i,M}\frac{\alpha_M - r}{\sigma_M} \qquad (20.23)$$

Thus, if two assets have the same correlation with the market ($\rho_{i,M}$), they will have the same Sharpe ratios. In equations (20.19) and (20.20), the fundamental uncertainty driving the processes for both S_1 and S_2 is dZ. Thus, both assets have the same correlation with the market, and in the CAPM would have equal Sharpe ratios.

We will now demonstrate an arbitrage if the Sharpe ratios in equations (20.19) and (20.20) are different. Suppose that the Sharpe ratio for asset 1 is greater than that for asset 2. We then buy $1/(\sigma_1 S_1)$ shares of asset 1 and short $1/(\sigma_2 S_2)$ shares of asset 2. These two positions will generally have different costs, so we invest (or borrow) the cost difference, $1/\sigma_1 - 1/\sigma_2$, by buying (or borrowing) the risk-free bond, which has the rate of return rdt. The return on the two assets and the risk-free bond is

$$\frac{1}{\sigma_1 S_1}dS_1 - \frac{1}{\sigma_2 S_2}dS_2 + \left(\frac{1}{\sigma_2} - \frac{1}{\sigma_1}\right)rdt = \left(\frac{\alpha_1 - r}{\sigma_1} - \frac{\alpha_2 - r}{\sigma_2}\right)dt \qquad (20.24)$$

This demonstrates that if the Sharpe ratio of asset 1 is greater than that of asset 2, we can construct a zero-investment portfolio with a positive risk-free return. Therefore, to preclude arbitrage, assets 1 and 2 must have the same Sharpe ratio.[6]

This link between volatility and risk premiums for perfectly correlated assets arose in Chapter 12 when we discussed option elasticity. There we saw that the Sharpe ratio for a stock and an option on the stock are the same. The reason is that the stock and option have the same underlying source of risk—the same dZ. They do not have the same volatility—the volatility of a call option is greater than that of the stock—and, hence, they do not have the same risk premium. Nevertheless, they do have the same Sharpe ratio.

20.5 THE RISK-NEUTRAL PROCESS

We saw in Chapters 10 and 11 that we can interpret the binomial model either as representing a risk-neutral stock price process, in which case we set probabilities so that assets earn the risk-free rate and we discount cash flows at the risk-free rate, or as representing the true stock price process, in which case we use true probabilities and discount at an appropriate (not risk-free) interest rate. In valuing options using Monte Carlo simulation in Chapter 19, we again used the risk-neutral approach, assuming that stocks on average

---

[6]Problem 20.12 asks you to consider the case where two assets are perfectly *negatively* correlated.

earn the risk-free rate and discounting expected payoffs at that rate. The risk-neutral pricing method arises from no-arbitrage pricing, but there is underlying economic intuition that we discuss in this section.

The notion of a risk-neutral process for the stock arises with Itô processes, just as in the binomial tree. We saw in Section 20.2 that Brownian motion is a process for which $E[Z(t + s)] = Z(t)$. In other words, Brownian motion is a martingale. In order to make such a statement, we must specify a probability distribution, or *measure*, for $Z(t + s)$, conditional on $Z(t)$. This point requires emphasis: in order to say whether a stochastic process is a martingale, we need to specify a probability distribution for the process.

Suppose the true price process is

$$\frac{dS(t)}{S(t)} = (\alpha - \delta)dt + \sigma dZ(t) \tag{20.25}$$

where δ is the dividend yield on the stock. This process represents the stock price we observe in the world, with $dZ(t)$ the unexpected portion of the stock return. On average we expect the stock to appreciate at the rate $\alpha - \delta$, and the deviations from this return should have mean zero. In other words, $Z(t)$ should be a martingale under the true probability distribution.

Now let's consider how a risk-averse investor assesses the stock price process. In utility terms, a risk-averse investor by definition values \$1 of gain less than \$1 of loss. When such an investor receives the return on an asset, the portion of the return that is a martingale will have negative expected value in utility terms: The gain from an increase in $Z(t + h)$ will be worth less than the loss from an equal decrease in $Z(t + h)$. In equilibrium, this lower expected utility is offset by the asset paying a risk premium, $\alpha - r$.

This description suggests that there might be another way to write the return on the asset. Suppose we create a new process $\tilde{Z}(t)$, such that $\tilde{Z}(t)$ *does* generate a martingale in utility terms for a risk-averse investor. (Note that this implies that $\tilde{Z}(t)$ is *not* a martingale with respect to the true probability distribution.) In order to offset risk aversion, we must modify the distribution for $Z(t + h)$ so that positive outcomes are more likely than negative outcomes. However, if we want to substitute $d\tilde{Z}(t)$ for $dZ(t)$ in equation (20.25), the transformed process will not give us the correct stock price unless we reduce the drift term to compensate for the greater expected value of $d\tilde{Z}(t)$. It turns out that if $\tilde{Z}(t)$ is a martingale when evaluated in terms of the investor's utility, the appropriate offsetting change in the drift is to remove the risk premium. This gives us the risk-neutral price process

$$\frac{dS(t)}{S(t)} = (r - \delta)dt + \sigma d\tilde{Z}(t) \tag{20.26}$$

In this equation, we subtract the risk premium, $\alpha - r$, from the drift $\alpha - \delta$, and we replace $dZ(t)$ with $d\tilde{Z}(t)$. As in the binomial model, when we replace α with r, we must also modify the probabilities associated with stock price movements. Also here and in the binomial model, when we switch to the risk-neutral process, the volatility remains the same.

The probability distribution associated with the risk-neutral process, $d\tilde{Z}(t)$, is said to be the **risk-neutral measure.** When we perform risk-neutral pricing, we will implicitly assume that we are using the risk-neutral measure. With this revised price process, we can perform valuation *as if* the investor were risk-neutral, because we have transformed $Z(t)$ to $\tilde{Z}(t)$ in order to make the investor behave risk-neutrally with respect to the revised process. Thus, using equation (20.26), we can perform valuation as if $\tilde{Z}(t)$ were a martingale, because a risk-averse investor will treat it as such in valuation.

It is important to emphasize that in the applications we have discussed to this point, we need not do any extra work in order to use equation (20.26) for pricing.[7] In particular, we do not need to worry about how to construct $\tilde{Z}(t)$ from $Z(t)$. For example, when we perform Monte Carlo valuation of a derivative with a stock as the underlying asset, we draw mean zero random variables to simulate $\tilde{Z}(t)$ and we use those random variables for pricing—discounting expected payoffs at the risk-free rate—without any further adjustment.

The technical result underlying the transformation from equation (20.25) to equation (20.26) is called **Girsanov's theorem.**[8] Girsanov's theorem states that a Brownian process, $Z(t)$, can be transformed into a new process, $d\tilde{Z}(t) = dZ(t) + \eta dt$, that is a martingale under a transformed probability distribution.[9] Girsanov's theorem explains how to create the transformed probability distribution. In the case we are discussing, the transformation is based on the Sharpe ratio: set $\eta = (\alpha - r)/\sigma$. Thus, we have

$$(\alpha - \delta)dt + \sigma dZ(t) = (r - \delta)dt + \sigma \left(dZ(t) + \frac{\alpha - r}{\sigma}dt \right)$$

$$= (r - \delta)dt + \sigma d\tilde{Z}(t)$$

The economic intuition behind the change of measure is that investors in equilibrium are indifferent to a small change in the allocation of their portfolio between risky

---

[7]We will see in later chapters, particularly when discussing fixed income, that in some contexts we need to take account of the risk premium on the underlying asset when moving from equation (20.25) to equation (20.26).

[8]References on Girsanov's theorem include Karatzas and Shreve (1991, sec. 3.5), Baxter and Rennie (1996) and Neftci (2000, ch. 14).

[9]A simplified version of Girsanov's theorem states that if $Z(t)$ is a Brownian motion under the probability density $f(t)$, then $\tilde{Z}(t) = Z(t) + \eta t$, is a Brownian motion under the probability density $\zeta(t)f(t)$, where $\zeta(t) = \exp(-\eta Z(t) - 0.5\eta^2 t)$. The probability density function for a normal variable with variance t is

$$f(t) = \exp\left[-\frac{1}{2t}Z^2 \right] \frac{1}{\sqrt{2\pi t}}$$

You can see how the Girsanov transformation works by examining $\zeta(t)f(t)$. Writing out $\zeta(t)$ and combining terms, we obtain

$$\zeta(t)\exp\left[-\frac{1}{2t}Z(t)^2 \right] \frac{1}{\sqrt{2\pi t}} = \exp\left[-\frac{1}{2t}(Z + \eta t)^2 \right] \frac{1}{\sqrt{2\pi t}}$$

The last expression is the probability density for a normally distributed variable with mean $-\eta t$.

and risk-free assets. The Sharpe ratio appears in the transformation because it measures the equilibrium return investors require to absorb additional risk.

20.6 ITÔ'S LEMMA

Suppose a stock with an expected instantaneous return of $\hat{\alpha}$, dividend yield of $\hat{\delta}$, and instantaneous volatility $\hat{\sigma}$ follows geometric Brownian motion:

$$dS(t) = \left\{ \hat{\alpha}[S(t), t] - \hat{\delta}[S(t), t] \right\} dt + \hat{\sigma}[S(t), t] dZ(t) \qquad (20.27)$$

In this equation, α, δ, and σ can be functions of the stock price. When $S(t)$ follows geometric Brownian motion, we have $\hat{\alpha}[S(t), t] = \alpha S(t)$, $\hat{\delta}[S(t), t] = \delta S(t)$, and $\hat{\sigma}[S(t), t] = \sigma S(t)$.

Now suppose that we have a derivative claim that is a function of the stock price. Express the value of this claim as $V[S(t), t]$. Given that we know how the stock behaves, how does the claim behave? In particular, how can we describe the behavior of the claim in terms of the behavior of S?

Functions of an Itô Process

Recall that dS is a geometric random walk with drift. Suppose for a moment that the drift is zero, in which case S obeys a geometric random walk with equal probabilities of up and down moves.

Now look at Figure 20.1. Notice that equal changes up and down in S do not give rise to equal changes in $V(S, t)$. Since V is an increasing convex function of S, a change to $S + \epsilon$ increases V by more than a change to $S - \epsilon$ decreases V. Thus, if the expected change in S is zero, the expected change in V will not be zero. The actual expected change will depend on the curvature of V and the probability distribution of S, which tells us the expected size of the up and down moves.

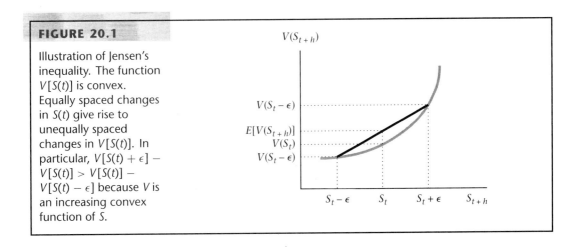

FIGURE 20.1

Illustration of Jensen's inequality. The function $V[S(t)]$ is convex. Equally spaced changes in $S(t)$ give rise to unequally spaced changes in $V[S(t)]$. In particular, $V[S(t) + \epsilon] - V[S(t)] > V[S(t)] - V[S(t) - \epsilon]$ because V is an increasing convex function of S.

In Figure 20.1, the second derivative is positive; that is, the slope of V becomes greater as S increases. As is evident in the figure, the expected change in V will then be positive. The figure illustrates Jensen's inequality: $V[E(S)] \leq E[V(S)]$ if V is convex (see Appendix C).

Using a Taylor series expansion (see Appendix 13.A), we can see how V depends on S. We have

$$V(S + dS, t + dt) = V(S, t) + V_S dS + V_t dt$$

$$+ \tfrac{1}{2}V_{SS}(dS)^2 + \tfrac{1}{2}V_{tt}(dt)^2 + V_{St}dSdt$$

$$+ \text{ terms in } (dt)^{3/2} \text{ and higher}$$

The multiplication rules already discussed in Section 20.3 tell us that since S is an Itô process, the terms $(dt)^2$ and $dS \times dt$ vanish, along with all higher-order terms. Intuitively, since the interval of time is short, the noise term dominates, and the squared noise term is the same order of magnitude as the drift.[10] This result stems from the quadratic variation property we discussed in Section 20.2. If we integrate the Taylor expansion with respect to time, then the term containing squared changes will be proportional to time. Higher-order terms will sum to zero. This calculation is the basis for Itô's Lemma.

Proposition 20.1 (Itô's Lemma)   Let the change in the stock price be given by equation (20.27). If $C[S(t), t]$ is a twice-differentiable function of $S(t)$, then the change in C, $dC[S(t), t]$, is

$$dC(S, t) = C_S dS + \tfrac{1}{2}C_{SS}(dS)^2 + C_t dt \tag{20.28}$$

$$= \left\{ [\hat{\alpha}(S, t) - \hat{\delta}(S, t)]C_S + \tfrac{1}{2}\hat{\sigma}(S, t)^2 C_{SS} + C_t \right\} dt + \hat{\sigma}(S, t)C_S dZ$$

(We use the notation $C_S = \partial C/\partial S$, $C_{SS} = \partial^2 C/\partial S^2$, and $C_t = \partial C/\partial t$.) The terms in braces are the expected change in the option price.

In the case where $S(t)$ follows geometric Brownian motion, we have $\hat{\alpha}[S(t), t] = \alpha S(t)$, $\hat{\delta}[S(t), t] = \delta S(t)$, and $\hat{\sigma}[S(t), t] = \sigma S(t)$, hence

$$dC(S, t) = \left[(\alpha - \delta)SC_S + \tfrac{1}{2}\sigma^2 S^2 C_{SS} + C_t \right] dt + \sigma SC_S dZ \qquad ❧$$

If there is no uncertainty—that is, if $\sigma = 0$—then Itô's Lemma reduces to the calculation of a total derivative familiar from ordinary calculus:

$$dC(S, t) = C_S dS + C_t dt$$

---

[10] See Karatzas and Shreve (1998) or Merton (1990) for more details.

The extra term involving the variance arises from $(dS)^2$ and is the Jensen's inequality correction due to the uncertainty of the stochastic process.

We encountered Itô's Lemma—without naming it—when we discussed delta-gamma approximations in Chapter 13. Equation (13.6) stated

$$C[S(t+h), t+h] - C[S(t), t] \approx [S(t+h) - S(t)]\Delta[S(t), t]$$
$$+ \tfrac{1}{2}[S(t+h) - S(t)]^2\Gamma[S(t), t] + \theta[S(t), t]h$$

Make the substitutions $h \to dt$ and $S(t+h) - S(t) \to dS$, and recall that Γ, Δ, and θ are just partial derivatives of the option price:

$$\Delta \equiv C_S; \quad \Gamma \equiv C_{SS}; \quad \theta = C_t$$

The delta-gamma approximation over a very short period of time is Itô's Lemma.

We can use Itô's Lemma to verify that the expression for a lognormal stock price satisfies the equation for geometric Brownian motion, equation (20.27).

Example 20.1   The expression for a lognormal stock price is

$$S(t) = S(0)e^{(\alpha-\delta-\frac{1}{2}\sigma^2)t+\sigma Z(t)} \tag{20.29}$$

The stock price is a function of the Brownian process $Z(t)$. We can use Itô's Lemma to characterize the behavior of the stock as a function of $Z(t)$. We have

$$\frac{\partial S(t)}{\partial t} = \left(\alpha - \delta - \frac{1}{2}\sigma^2\right)S(t); \quad \frac{\partial S(t)}{\partial Z(t)} = \sigma S(t); \quad \frac{\partial^2 S(t)}{\partial Z(t)^2} = \sigma^2 S(t)$$

Itô's Lemma states that $dS(t)$ is given as

$$dS(t) = \frac{\partial S(t)}{\partial t}dt + \frac{\partial S(t)}{\partial Z(t)}dZ(t) + \frac{1}{2}\frac{\partial^2 S(t)}{\partial Z(t)^2}[dZ(t)]^2$$
$$= \left(\alpha - \delta - \frac{1}{2}\sigma^2\right)S(t)dt + \sigma S(t)dZ(t) + \frac{1}{2}\sigma^2 S(t)dt$$
$$= (\alpha - \delta)S(t)dt + \sigma S(t)dZ(t)$$

In going from the second line to the third we have used the fact that $dZ(t)^2 = dt$. This calculation demonstrates that by using Ito's Lemma to differentiate equation (20.29), we recover equation (20.27).

Multivariate Itô's Lemma

So far we have considered the case where the value of an option depends on a single Itô process. A derivative may have a value depending on more than one price, in which case we can use a multivariate generalization of Itô's Lemma.

Proposition 20.2 (Multivariate Itô's Lemma)   Suppose we have n correlated Itô processes:

$$\frac{dS_i(t)}{S_i(t)} = \alpha_i dt + \sigma_i dz_i, \qquad i = 1, \ldots, n$$

Denote the pairwise correlations as $E(dz_i \times dz_j) = \rho_{i,j} dt$. If $C(S_1, \ldots, S_n, t)$ is a twice-differentiable function of the S_i's, we have

$$dC(S_1, \ldots, S_n, t) = \sum_{i=1}^{n} C_{S_i} dS_i + \frac{1}{2} \sum_{i=1}^{n} \sum_{j=1}^{n} dS_i dS_j C_{S_i S_j} + C_t dt$$

The expected change in C per unit time is

$$\frac{1}{dt} E[dC(S_1, \ldots, S_n, t)] = \sum_{i=1}^{n} \alpha_i S_i C_{S_i} + \frac{1}{2} \sum_{i=1}^{n} \sum_{j=1}^{n} \sigma_i \sigma_j \rho_{ij} S_i S_j C_{S_i S_j} + C_t \qquad ❧$$

Example 20.2   Suppose $C(S_1, S_2) = S_1 S_2$. Then by Itô's Lemma we have

$$d(S_1 S_2) = S_2 dS_1 + S_1 dS_2 + dS_1 dS_2$$

This implies that

$$\frac{1}{dt} E(dC) = (\alpha_1 + \alpha_2 + \rho \sigma_1 \sigma_2) S_1 S_2$$

Note that since $C(S_1, S_2)$ does not depend explicitly on time, $C_t = 0$. ❧

Example 20.2 is interesting because we know that the product of lognormal variables is lognormal. Hence, we might expect that the drift for the product of two lognormal variables would just be the sum of the drifts. However, Example 20.2 shows that the drift has an extra term, stemming from the term $dS_1 dS_2$, due to the covariation between the two variables. The intuition for this result will be explored further in the discussion of quantos in Chapter 22.

20.7 Valuing a Claim on S^a

Suppose we have a claim with a payoff depending on S raised to some power. For example, we may have a claim that pays $S(T)^2$ at time T. In this section we examine this claim with two goals. First, we want to compute the price of such a claim. Second, we want to understand the different ways to approach the problem of valuing the claim.

The following proposition gives us the forward and prepaid forward prices for this claim.

Proposition 20.3 Suppose S follows the process given by equation (20.27). The value at time 0 of a claim paying $S(T)^a$—the prepaid forward price—is

$$F_{0,T}^P[S(T)^a] = e^{-rT}S(0)^a e^{[a(r-\delta)+\frac{1}{2}a(a-1)\sigma^2]T} \qquad (20.30)$$

The forward price for $S(T)^a$ is

$$F_{0,T}[S(T)^a] = S(0)^a e^{[a(r-\delta)+\frac{1}{2}a(a-1)\sigma^2]T} \qquad (20.31)$$

The lease rate for a claim paying S^a is $\delta^* = r - a(r-\delta) - \frac{1}{2}a(a-1)\sigma^2$. ≸

To prove this proposition, we will first use Itô's Lemma to determine the process followed by S^a. We will then use three different arguments to obtain the pricing formula, equation (20.30).

The Process Followed by S^a

Consider a claim maturing at time T that pays $C[S(T), T] = S(T)^a$. If S follows equation (20.27), then we can use Ito's Lemma to determine the process followed by S^a. We obtain

$$dS^a = aS^{a-1}dS + \frac{1}{2}a(a-1)S^{a-2}(\sigma S)^2 dt$$
$$= aS^a\frac{dS}{S} + \frac{1}{2}a(a-1)S^a\sigma^2 dt$$

Dividing by S^a, we get

$$\frac{dS^a}{S^a} = \left[a(\alpha-\delta) + \frac{1}{2}a(a-1)\sigma^2\right]dt + a\sigma dZ \qquad (20.32)$$

Thus, S^a follows geometric Brownian motion with drift $a(\alpha-\delta) + \frac{1}{2}a(a-1)\sigma^2$ and risk $a\sigma dZ$. Hence, if α is the expected return for S, the expected return of a claim with price S^a will be

$$a(\alpha-r)+r \qquad (20.33)$$

Thus, the risk premium is $a(\alpha-r)$.

There is another way to obtain the drift term in equation (20.32) that does not require the use of Itô's Lemma. We can write

$$S(T)^a = S(0)^a e^{a(\alpha-\delta-0.5\sigma^2)T+a\sigma Z(T)}$$

Using equation (18.13) to compute the expectation of a lognormal variable, we have

$$E[S(T)^a] = S(0)^a e^{a(\alpha-\delta-0.5\sigma^2)T+0.5a^2\sigma^2 T}$$
$$= S(0)^a e^{[a(\alpha-\delta)+0.5a(a-1)\sigma^2]T}$$

Thus, the expected continuously compounded return on S^a is $a(\alpha - \delta) + 0.5a(a-1)\sigma^2$, as in equation (20.32).

Proving the Proposition

Given equations (20.32) and (20.33), there are three arguments we can use to compute the time-0 value of a claim that pays $S(T)^a$ at time T. All three methods will confirm Proposition 20.3.

Risk-neutral pricing   First we use risk-neutral pricing. Subtract the risk premium, $a(\alpha - r)$, from the drift, $a(\alpha - \delta)$, to obtain the following as the risk-neutral process for dS^a:

$$\frac{dS^a}{S^a} = \left[a(r - \delta) + \frac{1}{2}a(a-1)\sigma^2 \right] dt + a\sigma dZ^* \tag{20.34}$$

Using the drift term in equation (20.34), the expected value of the claim at time T under the risk-neutral measure, which we denote E^*, is

$$E_0^* [S(T)^a] = S(0)^a e^{[a(r-\delta) + \frac{1}{2}a(a-1)\sigma^2]T} \tag{20.35}$$

We saw in Section 10.1 that the expected price under the risk-neutral measure is the forward price. Thus, equation (20.35) gives the forward price. Discounting this expression at the risk-free rate gives us the prepaid forward price, equation (20.30).

Discounted cash flow   We can also value the claim on S^a by discounting the true (nonrisk-neutral) expected value. To do this we must compute the expected value of the claim and discount the expected payoff appropriately. From equation (20.14), the expected value of $S(T)^a$ is

$$E_0 [S(T)^a] = S(0)^a e^{[a(\alpha-\delta) + \frac{1}{2}a(a-1)\sigma^2]T}$$

The discount rate is expression (20.33). The price at time 0 of a claim paying $S(T)^a$ at time T is the prepaid forward price, which we will denote $F_{0,T}^P(S^a)$:

$$\begin{aligned} F_{0,T}^P(S^a) &= e^{-[r+a(\alpha-r)]T} E(S(T)^a) \\ &= e^{-[r+a(\alpha-r)]T} S(0)^a e^{[a(\alpha-\delta) + \frac{1}{2}a(a-1)\sigma^2]T} \\ &= S(0)^a e^{-rT} e^{[a(r-\delta) + \frac{1}{2}a(a-1)\sigma^2]T} \end{aligned}$$

Note that the risk premium on the stock, $\alpha - r$, drops out. The forward price for S^a, which we will denote $F_{0,T}(S^a)$, is just the future value of the prepaid forward:

$$\begin{aligned} F_{0,T}(S^a) &= e^{rT} F_{0,T}^P(S^a) \\ &= S(0)^a e^{[a(r-\delta) + \frac{1}{2}a(a-1)\sigma^2]T} \end{aligned}$$

The use of a single discount rate works in this case because the payoff to the claim is simple. In general, computing a price as a nonrisk-neutral discounted expected value is more difficult than this.

Finding the lease rate   Finally, we value the claim by finding its lease rate. We ask what cash payment the claim would have to make in order for us to willingly hold it, or equivalently, what payment we would have to make to short-sell it. We can then treat the lease rate as the dividend yield and compute the forward price.

From equation (20.32), the claim has risk $a\sigma dZ$ and so must be expected to earn a rate of return of $a(\alpha - r) + r$. Equation (20.32) also tells us that the actual expected capital gain on this security is $a(\alpha - \delta) + \frac{1}{2}a(a - 1)\sigma^2$.

In order to hold the security, we would need to earn the difference between the expected return and expected capital gain as a cash payment. Thus, the payment would have to be

$$\delta^* = a(\alpha - r) + r - \left[a(\alpha - \delta) + \tfrac{1}{2}a(a - 1)\sigma^2\right]$$
$$= r - a(r - \delta) - \tfrac{1}{2}a(a - 1)\sigma^2$$

The value δ^* is the lease rate of the claim paying S^a. The prepaid forward price is then

$$F_{0,T}^P(S^a) = S(0)^a e^{-\delta^* T}$$
$$= S(0)^a e^{[-r+a(r-\delta)+\frac{1}{2}a(a-1)\sigma^2]T}$$

This is the same as equation (20.30).

Specific Examples

We now examine four special cases of equations (20.30) and (20.31): $a = -1, 0, 1,$ and 2.

Claims on S   First, suppose $a = 1$. Equation (20.30) then gives us

$$V(0) = S(0)e^{-\delta T}$$

This equation is just the prepaid forward price on a stock.

Claims on S^0   If $a = 0$, the claim does not depend on the stock price; rather since $S^0 = 1$, it is a bond. Setting $a = 0$ gives us

$$V(0) = e^{-rT}$$

which is the price of a T-period pure discount bond.

Claims on S^2   When $a = 2$ the claim pays $S(T)^2$. From equation (20.31), the forward price is

$$F_{0,T}(S^2) = e^{rT}S(0)^2 e^{-[-r+2\delta-\sigma^2]T}$$
$$= S(0)^2 e^{2(r-\delta)T} e^{\sigma^2 T} \tag{20.36}$$
$$= \left[F_{0,T}(S)\right]^2 e^{\sigma^2 T}$$

Thus, the forward price on the squared stock price is the squared forward price times a variance term. The squared forward price is intuitive, but the variance term requires some discussion.

One way to think about equation (20.36) is to perform the following thought experiment. Suppose that we have an ordinary stock with a price denominated in dollars. Now imagine that we have a second stock that is identical to the first *except* that instead of receiving dollars when we sell the stock, we receive one share of ordinary stock for each dollar in the quoted price of the second stock. This conversion from dollars to shares is what it means to have a squared security.

With the squared stock, when the stock price goes up, we not only receive the extra dollars a share of stock is worth, but we also receive the appreciated value of each share we receive in lieu of dollars. We therefore receive an extra gain when the stock price goes up.

The effect works in reverse when the price goes down. In that case, we receive fewer dollars per share, and each share received in lieu of dollars is worth less as well. However, the lower price per share hurts us less because we receive fewer shares! Thus, on average, the extra we receive when the price goes up exceeds the loss when the price goes down. This effect becomes more important as the variance is greater, since large losses and large gains become more likely.

The result is that we will pay extra for the security, and the extra amount we pay is positively related to the variance. This example provides another illustration of Jensen's inequality.

Claims on 1/S Finally, let $a = -1$, so the claim pays $1/S$. Using equation (20.31) with $a = -1$, we get

$$F_{0,T}(1/S) = [1/S(0)] e^{(\delta-r)T} e^{\sigma^2 T}$$
$$= F_{0,T}^{-1} e^{\sigma^2 T}$$

As with the squared security, the forward price is increasing in volatility.

The payoffs for both the S^2 and $1/S$ securities are convex; hence, Jensen's inequality tells us that the price is higher when the asset price is risky than when it is certain. In both cases the forward price contains a volatility term, and in both cases the price is increasing in volatility. If we considered a concave claim, for example $\sqrt{S}$, the effect of increased volatility would be to lower the value of the claim. End-of-chapter problems 20.5–20.8 provide examples.

Valuing a Claim on $S^a Q^b$

Now we generalize the previous example by having two prices. Consider a claim paying $S(T)^a Q(T)^b$ where S follows

$$\frac{dS}{S} = (\alpha_S - \delta_S)dt + \sigma_S dZ_S \tag{20.37}$$

and Q follows

$$\frac{dQ}{Q} = (\alpha_Q - \delta_Q)dt + \sigma_Q dZ_Q \tag{20.38}$$

where

$$dZ_S dZ_Q = \rho dt$$

Proposition 20.4 Suppose that S and Q follow the processes given by equations (20.37) and (20.38). The forward prices for S^a and Q^b are given by Proposition 20.3. The forward price for $S^a Q^b$ is the product of those two forward prices times a covariance correction factor:

$$F_{t,T}(S^a Q^b) = F_{t,T}(S^a)F_{t,T}(Q^b)e^{ab\rho\sigma_S\sigma_Q(T-t)}$$

The variance of $S^a Q^b$ is given by

$$a^2\sigma_S^2 + b^2\sigma_Q^2 + 2ab\rho\sigma_S\sigma_Q \qquad\qquad ❧$$

Note that the squared security, S^2, is a special case of Proposition 20.4. When $S = Q$, $a = b = 1$, and $\rho = 1$ (since a variable is perfectly correlated with itself), the covariance term becomes

$$ab\rho\sigma_S\sigma_Q = \sigma_S^2$$

This gives us the same result as equation (20.36) for the forward price for a squared stock.

Using multivariate Ito's Lemma, the process for $S^a Q^b$ is

$$\frac{d\left(S^a Q^b\right)}{S^a Q^b} = \Big[a(\alpha_S - \delta_S) + b(\alpha_Q - \delta_Q) + \tfrac{1}{2}a(a-1)\sigma_S^2 + \tfrac{1}{2}b(b-1)\sigma_Q^2$$

$$+ ab\rho\sigma_S\sigma_Q\Big]dt + a\sigma_S dZ_S + b\sigma_Q dZ_Q \tag{20.39}$$

The expected return on this claim depends on the risk premiums for both S and Q:[11]

$$r + a(\alpha_S - r) + b(\alpha_Q - r)$$

As before, there are three ways to find the price of a prepaid forward on this claim. Here we use risk-neutral pricing. Problem 20.13 asks you to use the discounting and lease-rate methods to find the answer.

....

[11] Problem 20.11 asks you to verify that this expression gives the expected return.

The risk-neutral process for $dS^a Q^b$ is obtained by subtracting the risk premium, $a(\alpha_S - r) + b(\alpha_Q - r)$, from the drift in equation (20.39). This gives

$$
\frac{d\left(S^a Q^b\right)}{S^a Q^b} = \left[a(r - \delta_S) + b(r - \delta_Q) + \tfrac{1}{2}a(a-1)\sigma_S^2 + \tfrac{1}{2}b(b-1)\sigma_Q^2 \right.
$$
$$
\left. + ab\rho\sigma_S\sigma_Q \right] dt + a\sigma_S dZ_S^* + b\sigma_Q dZ_Q^*
$$

The expected time-T value of $S^a Q^b$ under the risk-neutral measure is

$$
E^*[S(T)^a Q(T)^b] = S(0)^a Q(0)^b e^{[a(r-\delta_S)+b(r-\delta_Q)+\tfrac{1}{2}a(a-1)\sigma_S^2+\tfrac{1}{2}b(b-1)\sigma_Q^2+ab\rho\sigma_S\sigma_Q]T}
$$

Using Proposition 20.3, in particular equation (20.31), this expression can be rewritten as

$$
F_{0,T}(S^a Q^b) = F_{0,T}(S^a) F_{0,T}(Q^b) e^{ab\rho\sigma_S\sigma_Q T} \tag{20.40}
$$

The expression on the right is the product of the forward prices times a factor that accounts for the covariance between the two assets.

This is an important result: The price that results when we multiply two prices together requires a correction for the covariance. We will see this result again in Chapters 21 and 22.

Proposition 20.4 can be generalized. Suppose there are n stocks, each of which follows the process

$$
\frac{dS_i}{S_i} = (\alpha_i - \delta_i)dt + \sigma_i dz_i \tag{20.41}
$$

where $dz_i dz_j = \rho_{ij} dt$. Let

$$
V(t) = \prod_{i=1}^n S_i^{a_i} \tag{20.42}
$$

The forward price for V is then

$$
F_{0,T}(V) = \prod_{i=1}^n [F_{0,T}(S_i)]^{a_i} e^{\sum_{i=1}^{n-1} \sum_{j=i+1}^n \rho_{ij}\sigma_i\sigma_j a_i a_j T} \tag{20.43}
$$

20.8 JUMPS IN THE STOCK PRICE[12]

A practical objection to the Brownian process as a model of the stock price is that Brownian paths are continuous—there are no discrete jumps in the stock price. In practice, asset prices occasionally do seem to jump; a famous example is October 19, 1987, when the Dow Jones index fell 22% in one day. A move of this size is exceedingly unlikely

---

[12]This section follows Merton (1976).

in the lognormal model. On a smaller scale, consider the stock price of a company that reports unexpectedly favorable earnings. To account for such nonlognormal behavior, Merton (1976) proposed modeling the stock price as lognormal with an occasional discrete jump. One way to model such jumps is by using the Poisson distribution mixed with a standard Brownian process, as we did in Chapter 19.

As discussed in Chapter 19, the Poisson distribution counts the number of jumps that occur in any interval. Conditional on a jump occurring, we assign some distribution to the change in the stock price. It is convenient to use the lognormal density to compute the price change if the jump occurs.

We can write a stock price process with jumps as follows. With the Poisson process, the probability of a jump event is proportional to the length of time. Furthermore, for an infinitesimal interval dt, the probability of more than a single jump is zero (this is part of the definition of the Poisson process). Let $q(t)$ represent the cumulative jump and dq the change in the cumulative jump. Most of the time, there is no jump and $dq = 0$. When there is a jump, we let the random variable Y denote the magnitude of the jump, and $k = E(Y) - 1$ is then the expected percentage change in the stock price. If λ is the expected number of jumps per unit time over an interval dt, then

$$\text{Prob(jump)} = \lambda dt$$

$$\text{Prob(no jump)} = 1 - \lambda dt$$

We can then write the stock price process as

$$dS(t)/S(t) = (\alpha - \lambda k)dt + \sigma dZ + dq \tag{20.44}$$

where

$$dq = \begin{cases} 0 & \text{if there is no jump} \\ Y - 1 & \text{if there is a jump} \end{cases}$$

and $E(dq) = \lambda k dt$. The drift term contains $-\lambda k dt$ for the reason discussed in Chapter 19: The dq term has a nonzero expectation, so we subtract $\lambda k dt$ in order to preserve the interpretation of α as the expected return on the stock. We have

$$E(dS/S) = (\alpha - \lambda k)dt + E(\sigma dZ) + E(dq) = \alpha dt$$

Thus, for example, if there is on average a downward jump, then $k < 0$, and, when no jump is occurring, we need extra drift of $-\lambda k dt > 0$ to compensate for the occasional bad times due to the jump.

The upshot of this model is that when no jump is occurring, the stock price S evolves as geometric Brownian motion. When the jump occurs, the new stock price is YS. The fact that it is straightforward to model jumps does not necessarily mean that it is easy to price options when there are jumps. We will discuss this further in Chapter 21.

Proposition 20.5 Suppose an asset follows equation (20.44). If $C(S, t)$ is a twice continuously differentiable function of the stock price, the process followed by C is

$$dC(S, t) = C_S dS + \tfrac{1}{2}C_{SS}\sigma^2 S^2 dt + C_t dt + \lambda E_Y[C(SY, t) - C(S, t)] \tag{20.45}$$

The last term in equation (20.45) is the expected change in the option price conditional on the jump times the probability of the jump. ≋

The last term in equation (20.45) accounts for the jump. That term is not present in the version of Itô's Lemma for a stock that cannot jump, equation (20.28).

CHAPTER SUMMARY

A stochastic process $Z(t)$ is a Brownian motion if it is normally distributed, changes independently over time, has variance proportional to time, and is continuous. The change in Brownian motion is denoted $dZ(t)$. The process $Z(t)$ and its change $dZ(t)$ provide the foundation for modern derivatives pricing models. The Brownian process $Z(t)$ by itself would be a poor model of an asset price, but its change, $dZ(t)$, provides a model for asset risk. By multiplying $dZ(t)$ by a scale factor and adding a drift term, we can control the variance and mean, and thereby construct more realistic processes. Such processes are called Itô processes or diffusion processes. Black and Scholes used just such a process in their original derivation of the option pricing model.

Given that a stock follows a particular Itô process, Itô's Lemma permits us to compute the process followed by an option or other claim on the stock. The pricing of claims with payoffs S^a and $S^a Q^b$, where S and Q follow geometric Brownian motion, illustrates the use of Itô's Lemma.

An important objection to Brownian motion as a driving process for a stock is the continuity of its path. It is possible to add jumps to a Brownian process, and there is a version of Itô's Lemma for such cases.

FURTHER READING

We will use the concepts in this chapter throughout the rest of the book. In the next chapter we will directly apply the concepts of this chapter, in particular Itô's Lemma, showing that prices of derivatives must satisfy a particular partial differential equation. In later chapters we will use these concepts to discuss the pricing of exotic options (Chapter 22), options based on interest rates (Chapter 24), and risk assessment (Chapter 25).

Many books cover the material in this chapter at a more advanced level. Merton (1990) in particular is an outstanding introduction. Other good sources include Neftci (2000), Duffie (1996), Wilmott (1998), Karatzas and Shreve (1991), and Baxter and Rennie (1996).

PROBLEMS

For the following four problems, use Itô's Lemma to determine the process followed by the specified equation, assuming that $S(t)$ follows (a) arithmetic Brownian motion, equation (20.8); (b) a mean reverting process, equation (20.9); and (c) geometric Brownian motion, equation (20.27).

20.1. Use Itô's Lemma to evaluate $d[\ln(S)]$.

20.2. Use Itô's Lemma to evaluate dS^2.

20.3. Use Itô's Lemma to evaluate dS^{-1}.

20.4. Use Itô's Lemma to evaluate $d(\sqrt{S})$.

20.5. Suppose that S follows equation (20.37) and Q follows equation (20.38). Use Itô's Lemma to find the process followed by $S^2 Q^{0.5}$.

20.6. Suppose that S follows equation (20.37) and Q follows equation (20.38). Use Itô's Lemma to find the process followed by $\ln(SQ)$.

20.7. Suppose $S(0) = \$100$, $r = 0.06$, $\sigma_S = 0.4$ and $\delta = 0$. Use equation (20.30) to compute prices for claims that pay the following:

    a. S^2

    b. $\sqrt{S}$

    c. S^{-2}

Compare your answers to the answers you obtained to Problem 19.6.

20.8. Suppose that $\ln(S)$ and $\ln(Q)$ have correlation $\rho = -0.3$ and that $S(0) = \$100$, $Q(0) = \$100$, $r = 0.06$, $\sigma_S = 0.4$ and $\sigma_Q = 0.2$. Neither stock pays dividends. Use equation (20.40) to find the price today of claims that pay

    a. SQ

    b. S/Q

    c. $\sqrt{SQ}$

    d. $1/(SQ)$

    e. $S^2 Q$

Compare your answers to the answers you obtained to Problem 19.7.

20.9. Suppose that $X(t)$ follows equation (20.9). Use Itô's Lemma to verify that a solution to this differential equation is

$$X_t = X(0)e^{-\lambda t} + \alpha \left(1 - e^{-\lambda t}\right) + \sigma \int_0^t e^{\lambda(s-t)} dZ_s$$

(Hint: Note that when t increases by a small amount, the integral term changes by $dZ(t)$.)

20.10. The formula for an infinitely lived call is given in equation (12.19). Suppose that S follows equation (20.27), with α replaced by r and that $E^*(dV) = rVdt$. Use Itô's Lemma to verify that the value of the call, $V(S)$, satisfies this equation:

$$\tfrac{1}{2}\sigma^2 S^2 V_{SS} + (r - \delta)SV_S - rV = 0$$

20.11. Suppose that the processes for S_1 and S_2 are given by these two equations:

$$dS_1 = \alpha_1 S_1 dt + \sigma_1 S_1 dZ_1$$
$$dS_2 = \alpha_2 S_2 dt + \sigma_2 S_2 dZ_2$$

Note that the diffusions dZ_1 and dZ_2 are different. In this problem we want to find the expected return on Q, α_Q, where Q follows the process

$$dQ = \alpha_Q Q dt + Q \left(\eta_1 dZ_1 + \eta_2 dZ_2 \right)$$

Show that, to avoid arbitrage,

$$\alpha_Q - r = \frac{\eta_1}{\sigma_1}(\alpha_1 - r) + \frac{\eta_2}{\sigma_2}(\alpha_2 - r)$$

(Hint: Consider the strategy of buying one unit of Q and shorting $Q\eta_1/S_1\sigma_1$ units of S_1 and $Q\eta_2/S_2\sigma_2$ units of S_2. Finance any net cost using risk-free bonds.)

20.12. Suppose that S follows equation (20.27) with $\delta = 0$. Consider an asset that follows the process

$$dQ/Q = \alpha_Q dt - \eta dZ$$

What is α_Q, expressed in terms of α? (*Hint:* Find a zero-investment position in S and Q that eliminates risk.)

20.13. Suppose that S and Q follow equations (20.37) and (20.38). Derive the value of a claim paying $S(T)^a Q(T)^b$ by each of the following methods:

    a. Computing the expected value of the claim and discounting at an appropriate rate. (*Hint:* The expected return on the claim can be derived using the result of Problem 20.11.)

    b. Computing the lease rate and substituting this into the formula for the forward price.

20.14. Assume that one stock follows the process

$$dS/S = \alpha dt + \sigma dZ \tag{20.46}$$

Another stock follows the process

$$dQ/Q = \alpha_Q dt + \sigma dZ + dq_1 + dq_2 \tag{20.47}$$

(Note that the σdZ terms for S and Q are identical.) Neither stock pays dividends. dq_1 and dq_2 are both Poisson jump processes with Poisson parameters λ_1 and λ_2. Conditional on either jump occurring the percentage change in the stock price is $Y_1 - 1$ or $Y_2 - 1$.

Consider the two stock price processes, equations (20.46) and (20.47).

a. If there were no jump terms (i.e., $\lambda_1 = \lambda_2 = 0$), what would be the relation between α and α_Q?

b. Suppose there is just one jump term ($\lambda_2 = 0$) and that $Y_1 > 1$. In words, what does it mean to have $Y_1 > 1$? What can you say about the relation between α and α_Q?

c. Write an expression for α_Q when both jump terms are nonzero. Explain intuitively why α_Q might be greater or less than α.

CHAPTER 21

The Black-Scholes Equation

In deriving the option pricing formula, Black and Scholes studied the problem faced by a delta-hedging market-maker. As we saw in Chapter 13, the market-maker who sells a call option buys shares to offset the risk of the written call. To analyze this situation it is necessary to characterize the risk of the position as a function of the share price. Itô's Lemma, discussed in Chapter 20, provides a tool that permits us to see how the option price changes in response to the stock price.

Black and Scholes assumed that the stock follows geometric Brownian motion and used Itô's Lemma to describe the behavior of the option price. Their analysis yields a partial differential equation, which the correct option pricing formula must satisfy.

In this chapter we study the Black-Scholes approach to pricing options.[1] This methodology is important not only for pricing European call options; it provides the intellectual foundation for pricing virtually all derivatives, and also underpins the risk-management practices of modern financial institutions.

21.1 DIFFERENTIAL EQUATIONS AND VALUATION UNDER CERTAINTY

The end result of the Black-Scholes derivation is a partial differential equation that describes the price of an option. At first glance the idea of using a differential equation to perform valuation may seem perplexing and special to options. However, differential equations can also be used to motivate even very simple calculations that appear in an elementary finance course. The valuation of stocks and bonds when payouts are known provides simple examples. We will demonstrate this in order to provide some context for the discussion of the Black-Scholes model.

---

[1]Robert Merton also contributed fundamentally to understanding the option pricing problem. As a result, the analysis in this chapter can also appropriately be referred to as the "Black-Scholes-Merton" methodology.

679

The Valuation Equation

A familiar equation from introductory finance is the following:

$$S(t) = \frac{D(t+h)h + S(t+h)}{(1+r_h)} \qquad (21.1)$$

This equation says that the stock price today, $S(t)$, is the discounted value of the future stock price, $S(t+h)$, plus dividends paid over the period of length h, $D(t+h)h$. The discount rate over a period of length h is r_h. We can also interpret $S(t)$ as the price of a bond and $D(t)$ as the coupon payment.

Whatever the interpretation, we can rewrite equation (21.1) as

$$\underbrace{S(t+h) - S(t)}_{\text{Change in Stock Price}} + \underbrace{D(t+h)h}_{\text{Cash Payout}} = \underbrace{r_h S(t)}_{\text{Return on Stock}} \qquad (21.2)$$

Written in this form, the equation says that the change in the stock price plus cash payouts (such as dividends) equals the return on the stock. Equation (21.2) is written to emphasize how the stock price should *evolve* over time, rather than the value of the stock at a point in time.

Dividing by h and letting $h \to 0$ in equation (21.2), we obtain

$$\frac{dS(t)}{dt} + D(t) = r S(t) \qquad (21.3)$$

Equation (21.3) is a differential equation stating the condition that the stock must appreciate to earn an appropriate rate of return. The transformation from equation (21.1) to equation (21.3) illustrates the sense in which an equation describing the evolution of the price is linked to valuation.

Bonds

Let $S(t)$ represent the price of a zero-coupon bond that pays \$1 at time T. Since the bond makes no payouts, the evolution of the bond price satisfies equation (21.3) with $D = 0$. The interpretation is that at every time, t, the percentage change in the price of the bond $[\frac{dS(t)}{dt}/S(t)]$ equals the interest rate. This is a familiar condition that the bond should satisfy if it is fairly priced. The general solution to this equation is[2]

$$S(t) = Ae^{-r(T-t)} \qquad (21.4)$$

where A can be any number. You can check that this is in fact a solution by differentiating it to be sure that it satisfies the differential equation.

The differential equation describes the bond's behavior over time but does not tell us what A is. In order to price the bond we also need to know the bond price at some particular point in time. This price is called a **boundary condition.** If the bond is worth \$1 at maturity, we have the boundary condition $S(T) = \$1$. Examining equation (21.4)

---

[2]You might wish to verify that $S(t) = Ae^{-r(T-t)} + a$ satisifies the differential equation only if $a = 0$.

shows that $S(T)$ can equal $1 only if $A = \$1$. Thus, the bond price is

$$S(t) = \$1 \times e^{-r(T-t)}$$

The condition $S(T) = \$1$ is called a terminal boundary condition because it sets the bond price at its maturity date. If instead we knew the bond price today, $S(0)$, we could set A so that the equation gave the correct value for $S(0)$. That value would be an initial boundary condition.

The solution confirms what you already know: The price of the bond is the present value of $1.

Dividend-Paying Stocks

We can interpret $S(t)$ as the price of a risk-free stock that pays a continuous fixed dividend of D and has a price of $\bar{S}$ at time T. Equation (21.3) then says that at every time, t, dividends plus capital gains on the stock provide the risk-free rate of return.

Since we know the value at time T will be $\bar{S}$, we also have the boundary condition

$$S(T) = \bar{S}$$

Equation (21.3) with this boundary condition has the solution

$$S(t) = \int_t^T De^{-r(s-t)}ds + \bar{S}e^{-r(T-t)}$$

The stock price today is the discounted value of dividends to be paid between now and time T, plus the present value of the stock at time T. Again, the discrete time version of this equation is the standard present value formula taught in every introductory finance class.

The General Structure

Under certainty, a bond or stock will be priced so that the owner receives a risk-free return. The differential equation in these examples describes how the security *changes* from a given point. The boundary condition describes the price at some point in the security's life (such as at a bond's maturity date). By combining the differential equation and the boundary condition, we can determine the price of the bond at any point in time.

By analogy, if at every point you know an automobile's speed and direction, and if you know where it stops, you can work backward to figure out where it started. Essentially the same idea is used to price options: We know the price of the option at maturity (for a call it is max[0, $S - K$]), and we then need to know how the option price changes over time.

21.2 THE BLACK-SCHOLES EQUATION

Consider the problem of owning an option and buying or selling enough shares to create a riskless position. Assume that the stock price follows geometric Brownian motion:

$$\frac{dS}{S} = (\alpha - \delta)dt + \sigma dZ \tag{21.5}$$

where α is the expected return on the stock, σ is the stock's volatility, and δ is the continuous dividend yield on the stock. The option value depends on the stock price, $S(t)$, and time, t, so we write it as $V[S(t), t]$. Also suppose there are risk-free bonds that pay the return r. If we invest W in these bonds, the change in the value of the bond position is

$$dW = rWdt \tag{21.6}$$

Let I denote the total investment in the option, stocks, and the risk-free bond. Suppose that we buy N shares of stock to hedge the option and invest W in risk-free bonds so that our total investment is zero. Then we have

$$I = V(S, t) + NS + W = 0 \tag{21.7}$$

The zero-investment condition ensures that we keep track of financing costs. It imposes the requirement that in order to buy more of one asset we have to sell something else. To buy stock, for example, we can short-sell bonds.

Applying Itô's Lemma to equation (21.7), we have

$$dI = dV + N(dS + \delta S dt) + dW$$
$$= V_t dt + V_S dS + \tfrac{1}{2}\sigma^2 S^2 V_{SS} dt + N(dS + \delta S dt) + rW dt \tag{21.8}$$

If we own the physical stock, we receive dividends; this accounts for the $N\delta S dt$ term.[3]

As in Chapter 13, we delta-hedge the position to eliminate risk. The option's delta (Δ) is V_S. We delta-hedge by setting

$$N = -V_S$$

Holding this number of shares has two results. First, the dS and, hence, dZ terms in equation (21.8) vanish, so the portfolio is no longer affected by changes in the stock price—the portfolio is risk-free. Second, because we are also maintaining zero investment (equation 21.7) our holding of bonds is whatever is necessary to finance the net purchase or sale of the option and the hedging position in stock:

$$W = V_S S - V \tag{21.9}$$

Substituting $N = -V_S$ and this expression for W into equation (21.8) gives

$$dI = V_t dt + \tfrac{1}{2}\sigma^2 S^2 V_{SS} dt - V_S \delta S dt + r(V_S S - V)dt \tag{21.10}$$

With a zero-investment, zero-risk portfolio, we should expect to earn a zero return or else there is arbitrage, so that $dI = 0$. Imposing this condition in equation (21.10) and dividing by dt gives

$$\boxed{V_t + \tfrac{1}{2}\sigma^2 S^2 V_{SS} + (r - \delta)S V_S - rV = 0} \tag{21.11}$$

---

[3] Similarly, if we short the stock we have to pay the dividends.

This is the famous Black-Scholes partial differential equation (PDE), which we will call the Black-Scholes *equation*.[4] (We will refer to the formula giving us the price of a European call as the Black-Scholes *formula*.) Appendix 21.A derives the generalization of equation (21.11) when the value of V depends on more than one underlying asset.

The significance of equation (21.11) is that the price of an option must satisfy this equation, or else there is an arbitrage opportunity. In fact you may recall this equation from Chapter 13. There we examined delta-hedging and saw that the delta, gamma, and theta of a fairly priced option had to be related in a certain way. Since V_{SS} is the option's gamma, V_S the option's delta, and V_t the option's theta, equation (21.11) describes the same relationship among the Greeks.

We started this discussion by supposing that we owned an option that we wished to delta-hedge. Nothing in the derivation uses the fact that V is the price of a call option or indeed any particular kind of option at all. Thus, equation (21.11) *describes the change in value of any contingent claim for which the underlying assumptions are met*.[5] To be sure, we have assumed a great deal: That (a) the underlying asset follows geometric Brownian motion with constant volatility, (b) the underlying asset pays a continuous proportional dividend at the rate δ (this can be zero), (c) the contingent claim itself pays no dividend and has a payoff depending on S, (d) the interest rate is fixed, with equal borrowing and lending rates, and (e) there are no transaction costs.

These assumptions are unquestionably violated in practice. There are transaction costs, volatility and interest rates change over time, asset prices can jump, etc. However, our goal is to have a thorough understanding of how derivatives pricing and hedging works in this basic setting. This is a starting point for developing more realistic models.

Verifying the Formula for a Derivative

We can now answer the main question of option pricing: Given that asset prices follow geometric Brownian motion (equation 21.5) what is the correct formula for the price of an option? As discussed in Section 21.1, there are two conditions. The pricing formula must satisfy the Black-Scholes equation, (21.11), and it must also satisfy the appropriate boundary conditions for the option. If we satisfy both conditions, we have the correct option price.

Almost all of the nonstandard option formulas we looked at in Chapter 14 solve the Black-Scholes equation.[6] The pricing formulas seem different, but they differ only

---

[4]When the derivative claim makes a payout, $D(t)dt$, then equation (21.11) becomes

$$V_t + \tfrac{1}{2}\sigma^2 S^2 V_{SS} + (r - \delta)SV_S + D(t) - rV = 0$$

[5]Equation (21.11) holds for unexercised American options as well as for European options.

[6]The exception is Asian options. Since the Asian option payoff is based on the average stock price, prices of those options solve a different partial differential equation, in which there is a term reflecting the evolution of the average.

in the boundary conditions. Appendix 21.C discusses a general set of solutions. Here, we discuss several particular solutions in order to convey the basic idea of how the Black-Scholes equation works.

Simple present value calculations   Let's begin by considering two familiar calculations: the price of a zero-coupon bond and the prepaid forward contract for a stock.

Suppose the bond matures at time T and pays \$1. The boundary condition is that it must be worth \$1 at time T. In addition it must satisfy the Black-Scholes equation, equation (21.11). Consider this formula for the price of the bond:

$$V^1(t, T) = e^{-r(T-t)} \qquad (21.12)$$

First, this satisfies the boundary condition since $V^1(T, T) = \$1$. Second, the price of the bond does not depend on the price of a stock. Thus, $V_S = 0$ and $V_{SS} = 0$. Equation (21.11) then becomes

$$V_t^1 = rV^1$$

Equation (21.12) satisfies this equation, with the boundary condition $V^1(T, T) = \$1$.

Now consider the prepaid forward contract for a share of stock. We know the value is

$$V^2[S(t), t] = S(t)e^{-\delta(T-t)} \qquad (21.13)$$

Since this contract pays a share at maturity, the boundary condition is that it is worth a share at maturity:

$$V^2[S(T), T] = S(T)$$

We will verify that equation (21.13) solves the Black-Scholes equation. We have

$$V_S^2 = e^{-\delta(T-t)}$$
$$V_{SS}^2 = 0$$
$$V_t^2 = \delta S(t)e^{-\delta(T-t)}$$

Substituting these into the Black-Scholes equation gives

$$\tfrac{1}{2}\sigma^2 S(t)^2 \times 0 + (r - \delta)S(t) \times e^{-\delta(T-t)} + \delta S(t)e^{-\delta(T-t)} - rS(t)e^{-\delta(T-t)} = 0$$

Equation (21.13) thus satisfies the Black-Scholes equation and the boundary condition.

Notice that for both claims, $V_{SS} = 0$; their gamma is zero. We already saw in Chapter 5 that we can replicate a prepaid forward by buying a tailed position in the stock. No further trading is necessary. This static hedging strategy works because gamma is zero.

Call option   A European call option has the boundary condition

$$V[S(T), T] = \max[0, S(T) - K] \qquad (21.14)$$

Let's verify that the Black-Scholes formula does satisfy the boundary condition. We can examine the behavior of the formula as t approaches T, the option expiration date. From equation (12.1), the value of the call is

$$Se^{-\delta(T-t)}N(d_1) - Ke^{-r(T-t)}N(d_2)$$

For an option at expiration, since $t = T$, the terms $e^{-\delta(T-t)}$ and $e^{-r(T-t)}$ are both equal to 1. What happens to $N(d_1)$ and $N(d_2)$?

We will rewrite slightly the definitions of d_1 and d_2:

$$d_1 = \frac{\ln(S/K)}{\sigma\sqrt{T-t}} + \left(r - \delta + \tfrac{1}{2}\sigma^2\right)\frac{\sqrt{T-t}}{\sigma}$$

$$d_2 = d_1 - \sigma\sqrt{T-t}$$

As t approaches T, the difference between d_1 and d_2 goes to zero, since the term $-\sigma\sqrt{T-t}$ goes to zero. Moreover, the term $(r - \delta + \tfrac{1}{2}\sigma^2)\sqrt{T-t}$ also goes to zero. Thus, both d_1 and d_2 are governed by the term $\ln(S/K)/\sigma\sqrt{T-t}$.

If $S > K$, then the option is in-the-money and $\ln(S/K) > 0$. If $S < K$, the option is out-of-the-money and $\ln(S/K) < 0$. Thus, as $t \to T$, we have

$$S > K \quad\Rightarrow\quad \ln(S/K) > 0 \quad\Rightarrow\quad \frac{\ln(S/K)}{\sigma\sqrt{T-t}} \to +\infty \quad\Rightarrow\quad N(d_1) = N(d_2) = 1$$

$$S < K \quad\Rightarrow\quad \ln(S/K) < 0 \quad\Rightarrow\quad \frac{\ln(S/K)}{\sigma\sqrt{T-t}} \to -\infty \quad\Rightarrow\quad N(d_1) = N(d_2) = 0$$

Thus, at expiration the Black-Scholes formula for a call evaluates to $S - K$ if $S > K$, and 0 if $S < K$, so it satisfies the boundary condition, equation (21.14). The call formula also satisfies equation (21.11), but we will not verify that here.

Puts can be analyzed just like calls. European puts have the boundary condition

$$V[S(T), T] = \max[0, K - S(T)]$$

The put formula contains $N(-d_1)$ and $N(-d_2)$; as a result, the $N()$ expressions at maturity equal 1 when $S < K$, and 0 when $S > K$.

All-or-nothing options It turns out that both terms in the Black-Scholes formula *individually* satisfy the Black-Scholes equation. Consequently, each of the two expressions

$$V^3[S(t), t] = e^{-\delta(T-t)}S \times N\left(\frac{\ln[S(t)/K] + [r - \delta + 0.5\sigma^2][T-t]}{\sigma\sqrt{T-t}}\right) \qquad (21.15)$$

$$V^4[S(t), t] = e^{-r(T-t)} \times N\left(\frac{\ln[S(t)/K] + [r - \delta - 0.5\sigma^2][T-t]}{\sigma\sqrt{T-t}}\right) \qquad (21.16)$$

on its own is a legitimate price of a derivative. What are they the prices of?

An **asset-or-nothing option** pays one share of stock if $S(T) > K$, and nothing otherwise.[7] Examine V^3 closely. We have $V^3[S(T), T] = 0$ if $S(T) < K$, and $V^3[S(T), T] = S(T)$ if $S(T) > K$. Thus, at time T, V^3 has the same value as an asset-or-nothing option. Moreover, because V^3 satisfies the Black-Scholes equation, it gives the correct value at time t for this payoff. Thus, V^3 is the value of an asset-or-nothing option.

A cash or nothing option pays $1 at time T if $S(T) > K$, and nothing otherwise.[8] Equation (21.16) has the same value at maturity as a cash-or-nothing option and satisifies the Black-Scholes equation. Thus, equation (21.16) gives us the time-t value of a cash-or-nothing option. Both asset-or-nothing and cash-or-nothing options are examples of all-or-nothing options, which pay a discrete amount or nothing.

A European call option is equivalent to buying one asset-or-nothing option and selling K cash-or-nothing options, both maturing at time T. The price of a European call is the cost of this strategy:

$$V^3[S(t), t] - K \times V^4[S(t), t]$$

You should verify that this is in fact the Black-Scholes formula. (See Problem 21.7.)

The fact that V^3 and V^4 solve the Black-Scholes equation gives us pricing formulas for two new derivatives, asset-or-nothing and cash-or-nothing options. Also, however, because V^4 by itself solves the Black-Scholes equation, we could have sold any number of cash-or-nothing options and still had a valid price for a derivative claim. In order to create a standard call, we buy one asset-or-nothing option and sell K cash-or-nothing options. However, suppose we had instead sold $0.5K$ cash-or-nothing options. The resulting claim would have paid $S(T) - 0.5K$ if $S(T) > K$ and 0 otherwise. This is a *gap option*, discussed in Chapter 14. This analysis verifies that equation (14.15) gives the correct price for a European gap call.[9]

The boundary conditions we have considered thus far are all *terminal* boundary conditions, meaning that they are satisfied by an option at expiration. American options and some nonstandard options have a boundary condition that must be satisfied prior to expiration. For example, barrier options have boundary conditions prior to expiration related to knocking in or out. Nevertheless, their price still solves equation (21.11).

The Black-Scholes Equation and Equilibrium Returns

In the foregoing derivation of the option pricing formula we required that a delta-hedged position earn the risk-free rate of return. A different approach to pricing an option is to impose the condition that the actual expected return on the option must equal the

---

[7]This claim is also called a **digital share.**

[8]This claim is also called **digital cash.**

[9]In practice, all-or-nothing and gap options are difficult to delta-hedge. We will discuss this further in Chapter 22.

equilibrium expected return.[10] As we saw in Section 11.2 in the context of the binomial model, the expected return on the option changes as the option moves into or out of the money.

We can decompose the return on the option into expected and unexpected components. Using Itô's Lemma, we have

$$dV = \underbrace{\left[\frac{1}{2}\sigma^2 S^2 V_{SS} + (\alpha - \delta)SV_S + V_t\right]dt}_{\text{Expected return}} + \underbrace{SV_S\sigma dZ}_{\text{Unexpected return}}$$

Thus, the instantaneous expected return on the option is

$$\frac{1}{dt}\frac{E(dV)}{V} = \frac{1}{dt}\frac{\left[\frac{1}{2}\sigma^2 S^2 V_{SS} + (\alpha - \delta)SV_S + V_t\right]dt}{V} \tag{21.17}$$
$$\equiv \alpha_{\text{option}}$$

The unexpected portion of the return is

$$\frac{E(dV)}{V} - \frac{dV}{V} = \frac{SV_S}{V}\sigma dZ \tag{21.18}$$
$$\equiv \sigma_{\text{option}}dZ \tag{21.19}$$

In interpreting this expression, recall that SV_S/V is the option's elasticity, Ω. Thus, we have

$$\sigma_{\text{option}} = \Omega\sigma \tag{21.20}$$

This is a result we presented in Chapter 12.

We know from Chapter 20 that two assets with returns generated by the same dZ must have the same Sharpe ratio. Thus, we have

$$\frac{\alpha - r}{\sigma} = \frac{\alpha_{\text{option}} - r}{\sigma_{\text{option}}} \tag{21.21}$$

Using equation (21.20), we can rewrite equation (21.21) to give

$$\alpha_{\text{option}} - r = \frac{SV_S}{V}(\alpha - r) \tag{21.22}$$

In words, the risk premium on the option is the risk premium on the stock times the option elasticity. We can interpret equation (21.22) as stating an *equilibrium* condition that the option must obey. In other words, if we view the option as just another asset, it must be priced so that its expected return is related to the expected return on the stock in a particular way.

---

[10]Black and Scholes also used this method to solve for the option price in their original paper.

Using equation (21.17), substitute for α_{option} in equation (21.22). This gives

$$\frac{1}{dt}\frac{\left[\frac{1}{2}\sigma^2 S^2 V_{SS} + (\alpha - \delta)S V_S + V_t\right]dt}{V} - r = \frac{S V_S}{V}(\alpha - r) \tag{21.23}$$

When we multiply both sides by V and rearrange terms, the expected return on the stock, α, vanishes: We once again obtain the Black-Scholes PDE, equation (21.11). Thus, an interpretation of the Black-Scholes equation is that the option is priced so as to earn its equilibrium expected return.

When we equate expected and actual returns, we can interpret the result as giving us a *fair* price for the option, as opposed to a no-arbitrage price. This is *equilibrium* pricing. The no-arbitrage and equilibrium prices are the same. The equilibrium approach makes clear that determining a fair price for the option using the Black-Scholes equation does not depend upon the assumption that hedging is actually possible.

What If the Underlying Asset Is Not an Investment Asset?

So far we have been discussing option pricing when the underlying asset is an investment asset, meaning that the asset is priced so as to be held by investors. Stocks and bonds are investment assets. Many commodities are not (see Chapter 6, especially Sections 6.3 and 6.4). Suppose that widgets generate no dividends, and that the price of widgets, S, follows the process

$$\frac{dS}{S} = \mu dt + \sigma dZ \tag{21.24}$$

From this equation, widget price risk is generated by the term dZ. Let ϕ represent the Sharpe ratio associated with dZ and let $\hat{\alpha}$ represent the expected return for an asset with σdZ risk. Since the Sharpe ratio is $\phi = (\hat{\alpha} - r)/\sigma$, we have

$$\hat{\alpha} = r + \sigma\phi$$

The important characteristic of an investment asset is that $\mu = \hat{\alpha}$. What happens if an asset is not an investment asset and $\mu < \hat{\alpha}$?

Consider again equation (21.20), which says that the expected return on the option equals the actual return on the option. When we derive this equation again using $\hat{\alpha}$ as the equilibrium expected return for an asset with risk dZ and μ as the actual expected return for widgets, we obtain

$$\frac{V_t + \frac{1}{2}\sigma^2 S^2 V_{SS} + \mu S V_S}{V} - r = \frac{S V_S}{V}(\hat{\alpha} - r) \tag{21.25}$$

Rearranging this equation, we obtain

$$V_t + \frac{1}{2}\sigma^2 S^2 V_{SS} + [r - (\hat{\alpha} - \mu)]S V_S - rV = 0 \tag{21.26}$$

If you compare equation (21.26) with (21.11), the dividend yield, δ, has been replaced with $\hat{\alpha} - \mu$, the difference between the equilibrium expected return and the actual expected return on noninvestment widgets.[11]

Let $\hat{\delta} = \hat{\alpha} - \mu$. We can interpret $\hat{\delta}$ as follows: μ is the return you get from holding a widget and $\hat{\alpha}$ is the return you must expect if you are to voluntarily hold a widget. Thus, in order for you to hold a widget you would need an additional return of $\hat{\delta} = \hat{\alpha} - \mu$. Given the expected widget price change, μ, the only way to receive the extra return is through a dividend. This is the reason that $\hat{\alpha} - \mu$ replaces the dividend yield in the Black-Scholes equation.

We have encountered this concept before: $\hat{\delta}$ is the *lease rate* for the widget, or more generally the lease rate for an asset with expected capital gain μ and risk σdZ. When you lend a commodity, you receive its capital gains. The lease rate is the extra income you need to make you willing to buy and lend the asset. In the same way, $\hat{\delta}$ is the extra income you need to make you willing to hold a widget as an investment asset.

In practice, a widget-linked bond could be used to hedge the risk of a widget option. If the widget bond were constructed so that its price equalled the widget price today and at maturity, we saw in Chapter 15 that the bond would pay the widget lease rate as a coupon. This coupon, being a cash payment on the underlying asset, would play the role in the option pricing formula of a dividend on the underlying asset. This idea of a hypothetical lease-rate-paying, widget-linked security is also like the *twin security* mentioned in Chapter 17. It provides an investment vehicle for owning the risk dZ. If such a twin security existed, we could use it to hedge the risk of the option, and its dividend yield, $\hat{\delta}$, would appear in the option price.

An equivalent way to write equation (21.26) is to replace $\hat{\alpha}$ with $r + \phi\sigma$. We then obtain

$$V_t + \tfrac{1}{2}\sigma^2 S^2 V_{SS} + (\mu - \phi\sigma)SV_S - rV = 0 \qquad (21.27)$$

In this version, the coefficient on the SV_S term is the drift on the widget less the risk premium appropriate for widgets.

Note that when the asset is an investment asset, $\hat{\alpha} = \alpha$ and $\mu = \alpha - \delta = r + \phi\sigma - \delta$. Both equations (21.26) and (21.27) reduce to equation (21.11).

To summarize, the Black-Scholes PDE, equation (21.11), also characterizes derivative prices for assets that are not investment assets. In the case of an asset that is not an investment asset, the dividend yield, δ, is replaced with the lease rate of the asset, $\hat{\delta}$.

Example 21.1 To see how to use equation (21.26), suppose we have an option for which the maturity payoff is based upon the stock price raised to a power, S^a. This type

[11] This modification to the Black-Scholes equation is discussed in Constantinides (1978) and McDonald and Siegel (1984).

of option is called a **power option.** For example, we could have a call option with a payoff of

$$\max(S^a - K^a, 0)$$

We have already seen in Proposition 20.3 that the lease rate on an asset paying S^a is $\delta^* = r - a(r - \delta) - \frac{1}{2}a(a-1)\sigma^2$. From Itô's Lemma the volatility is $a\sigma$. Thus, using equation (21.26), we can price the option by using S^a as the stock price, K^a as the strike price, δ^* as the dividend yield, and $a\sigma$ as the volatility. ☙

21.3 RISK-NEUTRAL PRICING

The expected return on the stock, α, does not appear in the Black-Scholes equation, equation (21.11). Thus, when pricing derivatives on investment assets, only the risk-free rate matters; the actual expected return on a stock is irrelevant for pricing an option on the stock. The binomial pricing formula (see Chapter 10) also depends only on the risk-free rate.

   This observation led Cox and Ross (1976) to the following important observation: Since only the risk-free rate appears in the Black-Scholes PDE, it must be consistent with any possible world in which there is no arbitrage. If we are trying to value an option, we can assume that we are in the world in which it is easiest to value the option. Valuation will be easiest in a risk-neutral world, in which (if it actually existed) all assets would earn the risk-free rate of return and we would discount expected future cash flows at the risk-free rate. Thus, we can value options and other derivative claims by *assuming* that the stock earns the risk-free rate of return and calculate values based on that premise. We assume that the stock in this world follows the process

$$\frac{dS}{S} = (r - \delta)dt + \sigma d\tilde{Z} \tag{21.28}$$

As we keep emphasizing, the risk-neutral distribution is *not* an assumption about investor risk preferences. It is a device that can be used when pricing by arbitrage is possible (see Appendix 11.B for a discussion).

Interpreting the Black-Scholes Equation

The actual expected change in the option price is given by

$$\frac{1}{dt}E(dV) = V_t + \frac{1}{2}\sigma^2 S^2 V_{SS} + (\alpha - \delta)SV_S \tag{21.29}$$

Let E^* represent the expectation with respect to the risk-neutral distribution. Under the risk-neutral distribution, the expected change in the stock price is $E^*(dS) = (r - \delta)dt$. The drift in the option price can thus be written

$$\frac{1}{dt}E^*(dV) = V_t + \frac{1}{2}\sigma^2 S^2 V_{SS} + (r - \delta)SV_S \tag{21.30}$$

The Black-Scholes equation, (21.11), can therefore be rewritten as

$$\frac{1}{dt} E^*(dV) = rV \qquad (21.31)$$

Under the risk-neutral process, the option appreciates on average at the risk-free rate.

The Backward Equation

Closely related to equation (21.31) are the following equations, which characterize both the actual and risk-neutral probability distributions:

$$\frac{1}{dt} E(dV) = 0 \qquad (21.32)$$

$$\frac{1}{dt} E^*(dV) = 0 \qquad (21.33)$$

For the risk-neutral process, equation (21.33) is

$$\boxed{V_t + \tfrac{1}{2}\sigma^2 S^2 V_{SS} + (r - \delta)S V_S = 0} \qquad (21.34)$$

Equation (21.34) is called the **Kolmogorov backward equation** for the geometric Brownian motion process given by equation (21.28). Whereas the Black-Scholes PDE characterizes prices, the backward equation characterizes probabilities. The backward equation is just like the Black-Scholes PDE except that there is no rV term.[12]

The Black-Scholes equation can be interpreted as saying that the expected return on the option must equal the risk-free rate. The backward equation pertains to probabilities of events, such as the probability that an option will expire in-the-money. To understand how such probabilities should behave, suppose we decide that the probability is 0.65 that the stock price 1 year from today will be greater than $100. We know today that if the stock price goes up tomorrow, we will then assign a greater probability to this event. If the stock price goes down tomorrow, our estimate of the probability will go down. However, we should not expect our estimate of the probability to change on average: Our expectation *today*, of *tomorrow's* probability, must also be 0.65. If today's estimate of tomorrow's probability were not 0.65, then 0.65 could not have been the correct probability today.

Thus, whereas the price of a financial asset is expected to change over time, the expected change in the probability of an event is zero. This is why the backward equation does not have the rV term.

If $f(S_T; S_t)$ is the probability density for S_T given that the price today is S_t, both of these expressions would satisfy the backward equation:

....

[12] The backward equation is covered in detail in standard texts (see, for example, Cox and Miller (1965), and Karlin and Taylor (1981)). Wilmott (1998, ch. 10) contains a particularly clear heuristic derivation of equation (21.34).

$$\int_K^\infty f(S_T; S_t)dS_T$$

$$\int_K^\infty S_T f(S_T; S_t)dS_T$$

The first is the *probability* a call is in-the-money at time T. The second is the *partial expectation* of the stock price, conditional on $S_T > K$. Both are undiscounted. The backward equation holds for both the true and risk-neutral distributions generated by Itô processes.

Derivative Prices as Discounted Expected Cash Flows

The solution to equation (21.31) is equivalent to computing an expected value of the derivative payoff under the risk-neutral probability distribution and discounting at the risk-free rate. The specific form of the integral depends upon boundary conditions and payouts. We can see how this works with our assumptions (in particular a constant risk-free interest rate) by considering a simple European call option on a stock that pays continuous dividends at the rate δ. In that case, equation (21.11), along with the boundary condition that the option at expiration is worth $\max[0, S(T) - K]$, is equivalent to the discounted expectation

$$C[S(t), K, \sigma, r, T - t, \delta] = e^{-r(T-t)} \int_K^\infty [S(T) - K]f^*[S(T), \sigma, r, \delta; S(t)]dS(T)$$

where $f^*[S(T), \sigma, r, \delta; S(t)]$ is the *risk-neutral* probability density for $S(T)$, conditional on the time-t price being $S(t)$. In general it is possible to write the solution to equation (21.11), with appropriate boundary conditions, as an explicit integral.[13]

If a probability $W(S, t)$ satisfies the backward equation under the risk-neutral distribution, expression (21.33), then $V(S, t) = e^{-r(T-t)}W(S, t)$, the present value of $W(S, t)$, will satisfy the Black-Scholes equation, equation (21.31). To see this, suppose that $W(S, t)$ satisfies the backward equation, i.e.,

$$\frac{1}{dt}E^*[dW(S, t)] = 0$$

Since $V = e^{-r(T-t)}W$, we have

$$\frac{1}{dt}E^*[dV(S, t)] = \frac{1}{dt}E^* \left\{ d\left[e^{-r(T-t)}W(S, t)\right]\right\}$$

$$= rV + e^{-r(T-t)}\frac{1}{dt}E^*[dW(S, t)]$$

$$= rV$$

This is the Black-Scholes PDE, equation (21.11).

---

[13] See for example Cox et al. (1985a, Lemma 4). The integral form of the Black-Scholes equation is also called the Feynman-Kac solution. See Karlin and Taylor (1981, pp. 222–224) and Duffie (1996, Chapter 5).

This result means that *discounted risk-neutral probabilities and partial expectations* are prices of derivatives. Thus, any risk-neutral probability or partial expectation also has a corresponding derivative price. As an example of this, we saw in Chapter 18 that the Black-Scholes term $N(d_2)$ is the risk-neutral probability that an option is in-the-money at expiration. The discounted probability, $e^{-r(T-t)} N(d_2)$, is therefore the price of a derivative that pays \$1 if the option is in-the-money at expiration.

21.4 CHANGING THE NUMERAIRE

Now we consider what happens when the number of options (or other derivative contracts) that we receive at expiration is random, determined by some asset price. This odd-sounding payoff is common. Consider the following example.

Example 21.2 The price today of a nondividend-paying stock is \$100, and the forward price is \$106.184. Joe bets Sarah that in 1 year the stock price will be greater than \$106.184. Joe wants the loser to pay one share to the winner. Sarah wants the loser to pay \$106.184 to the winner.

The share received by Joe would be worth more than \$106.184 if he wins. Similarly, Sarah's desired payoff of \$106.184 is worth more than one share if she wins. Are either of these fair bets? If not, who has the more valuable side of the bet if it is denominated in shares? Who has the more valuable side of the bet if it is denominated in cash? 🗲

If Sarah wins (i.e., the share price is below \$106.184), a payment of \$106.184 will exceed the value of one share. If Joe wins (i.e., the share price is greater than \$106.184), a payment of one share will be worth more than \$106.184. However, it is not obvious which bet has a greater fair value given a current stock price of \$100. Assuming no inside information about the stock, would an investor pay a greater price for Joe's desired bet or Sarah's desired bet?

We can describe the two forms of the bet as each having a different **numeraire** or *unit of denomination*. Joe's desired bet is denominated in shares, whereas Sarah's desired bet is denominated in dollars. You can interpret the share-denominated bet as paying either a fixed number of shares (one) or a variable number of dollars (the dollar price of one share). The dollar-denominated bet pays a fixed number of dollars (\$106.184) or a variable number of shares (the number of shares with the value \$106.184). The general question we want to answer is how a change in the numeraire (unit of denomination) for a derivative changes the price of the derivative.

Here are some other examples where a change of denomination is relevant:

- **Currency translation:** A cash flow originating in yen (for example) can be valued in yen, or in some other currency. We will discuss this example in depth in Chapter 22.

- **Quantity uncertainty:** An agricultural producer who wants to insure production of an entire field must hedge total revenue—the product of price and quantity—rather than quantity alone.

- **All-or-nothing options:** All-or-nothing options, which we briefly discussed earlier, can be structured either to pay cash if a certain event occurs (such as the stock price exceeding the strike) or shares. The payoffs to the stock price bets above are in fact all-or-nothing payoffs; thus, the bets can be valued as all-or-nothing options.

To see what happens when we change the denomination of an option, suppose Q is the price of an asset that follows

$$\frac{dQ}{Q} = (\alpha_Q - \delta_Q)dt + \sigma_Q dZ_Q \tag{21.35}$$

Let $V(S, t)$ represent the price of an option denominated in cash, where S follows the process in equation (21.5). The correlation between dZ_Q and dZ is ρ. Suppose we receive the time-T payoff

$$Y[Q(T), S(T), T] = Q(T)^b V[S(T), K, \sigma, r, T, \delta] \tag{21.36}$$

Equation (21.36) represents a random number, Q^b, of claims, V. The value of this payoff is given in the following proposition.

Proposition 21.1   Suppose the process for S is given by equation (21.5) and the process for Q by equation (21.35), with ρ the correlation between dS and dQ. Let $V(S, K, \sigma_S, r, T-t, \delta_S)$ represent the price of a European derivative claim on S expiring at time T. The price of a claim paying $Q^b V$ is given by

$$Q(t)^b e^{(r-\delta^*)(T-t)} V[S(t), K, \sigma_S, r, T - t, \eta] \tag{21.37}$$

where $\eta = \delta - b\rho\sigma\sigma_Q$ and $\delta^* = r - b(r - \delta_Q) - \frac{1}{2}b(b-1)\sigma_Q^2$. In other words, to value Q^b claims, each with value V, we replace the dividend yield on S, δ, by η, and multiply the resulting price by $Q(t)^b e^{(r-\delta^*)(T-t)}$.   ⚹

The proof is in Appendix 21.B. Equation (21.37) is quite important and deserves further comment. We encountered δ^* in Section 20.7, in Proposition 20.3; it is the lease rate for Q^b. Thus $Q(t)^b e^{(r-\delta^*)(T-t)}$ is the forward price for a claim paying Q^b. The value of a claim paying $Q^b V$ is thus the forward price for Q^b times V evaluated at a modified dividend yield. We know from Section 20.7 that if Q and S are correlated (in which case Q and V are correlated), there must also be a covariance term. The term η replaces the dividend yield δ to account for this covariance.

Example 21.3   We will now value the share-price bets described in Example 21.2. Let V^+ denote the value of a bet that pays \$1 at time T if $S(T) > K$, and V^- the value of a bet that pays \$1 at time T when $S(T) < K$. Both bets are cash-or-nothing options, therefore from equation (21.16) we have that

$$V^+[S(0), K, \sigma, r, T, \delta] = e^{-rT} N \left(\frac{\ln[S(0)/K] + [r - \delta - 0.5\sigma^2]T}{\sigma\sqrt{T}} \right)$$

$$= e^{-rT} N(d_2)$$

This expression is the discounted risk-neutral probability that the bet pays off; it is also the second term in the Black-Scholes formula. If you hold both a bet that pays $1 when $S(T) > K$ and a bet that pays $1 when $S(T) < K$ then for certain you will receive $1 at time T. Therefore, $V^+ + V^- = e^{-rT}$, and we have

$$V^-[S(0), K, \sigma, r, T, \delta] = e^{-rT} - V^+[S(0), K, \sigma, r, T, \delta]$$

$$= e^{-rT}[1 - N(d_2)]$$

Now consider the bets denominated in shares. Let Y^+ denote value a bet that pays one share when $S(T) > K$ and Y^- the value of a bet paying one share when $S(T) < K$. Holding a share-denominated bet is like having a random number, $S(T)$, of cash bets. By Proposition 21.1, the value of the share bet is obtained by multiplying V by the forward price for S, and replacing δ with $\delta - \sigma^2$ (we have $b = 1$ and $\rho = 1$ since S multiplies a claim based on S). Making these substitutions, the value of the share bet is $S(0)e^{(r-\delta)T} V[S(0), K, \sigma, r, T, \delta - \sigma^2]$, or

$$Y^+[S(0), K, \sigma, r, T, \delta] = S(0)e^{-\delta T} N \left(\frac{\ln[S(0)/K] + [r - \delta + 0.5\sigma^2]T}{\sigma\sqrt{T}} \right)$$

$$= S(0)e^{-\delta T} N(d_1)$$

This is the value of an asset-or-nothing option, equation (21.15), and it is the first term in the Black-Scholes formula.[14] Thus, we can view the first Black-Scholes term as a discounted risk-neutral probability with a change of numeraire.

If you hold both a share-denominated bet paying one share when $S(T) > K$, and also a bet that pays one share when $S(T) < K$, then you will for certain receive a share at time T. Thus, $Y^+ + Y^- = e^{-\delta T} S_0$, and we therefore have

$$Y^-[S(0), K, \sigma, r, T, \delta] = S(0)e^{-\delta T} - Y^+[S(0), K, \sigma, r, T, \delta]$$

$$= S(0)e^{-\delta T} - S(0)e^{-\delta T} N(d_1)$$

In the case of Joe and Sarah's bet, suppose that the share-price volatility is 30%, the continuously compounded risk-free rate is 6%, the time to expiration is 1 year, and the share pays no dividends. Joe bets that the share price will be above $106.184. The

....

[14]This argument linking the two terms in the Black-Scholes equation by changing the units of denomination is due to Geman et al. (1995).

value of this bet is

$$\text{Value of Joe's Bet} = Y^+[100, 106.184, 0.30, 0.08, 1, 0] = \$55.962$$

The opposite side of Joe's bet—receiving one share when $S(T) < \$106.184$—has the value $\$100 - \$55.962 = \$44.038$.

Sarah's bet pays $\$106.184$ if the price is below $\$106.184$; this bet has the value

$$\text{Value of Sarah's Bet} = e^{-0.08 \times 1} - V^+[100, 106.184, 0.30, 0.08, 1, 0] = \$55.962$$

The opposite side of Sarah's bet pays $e^{-.08} \times \$106.184 - \$55.962 = \$44.038$. Thus, both Sarah and Joe wish to denominate the bet in their favor. Moreover, Sarah and Joe's desired bets have the same value! 🌿

Problem 21.8 asks you to find the strike prices such that the cash and share-denominated bets have equal value. We will return to changes in the unit of denomination in Chapter 22 when we discuss more nonstandard options.

21.5 OPTION PRICING WHEN THE STOCK PRICE CAN JUMP

We discussed jumps in the stock price in Chapters 19 and 20. Jumps pose a problem for the Black-Scholes option pricing methodology. When the stock price can jump discretely as well as move continuously, a position that hedges against small moves will not also hedge against big moves. As we saw in Chapter 13, large moves in the stock typically cannot be hedged.

The fact that jumps cannot be hedged does not mean that option pricing is impossible; rather, it means that *risk-neutral* option pricing may be impossible. When moves in the option price cannot be hedged, we can still price the option by computing discounted expected payoffs using the actual probability density rather than the risk-neutral probability density. The problem is that the option has the risk of a leveraged position in the stock, and we do not know what discount rate is appropriate. Some assumption about appropriate discount rates (which is really an assumption about investor preferences) will then be necessary to price an option.[15]

Merton (1976) derived an option pricing formula when the stock price can jump by assuming that the jump risk is diversifiable. This assumption neatly sidesteps the discounting issue since diversifiable risk does not affect expected returns. While jump risk for a broad index is not diversifiable, arguably many of the discrete moves for individual stocks are. In that case, by holding a portfolio of delta-hedged positions, the market-maker can diversify the effects of jump risk.

---

[15]See Naik and Lee (1990) for an example of equilibrium option pricing when there are jumps that cannot be hedged.

Ultimately, the importance of jumps and their systematic component is an empirical issue. Nevertheless, Merton's formulas provide useful insights into the effects of jumps.

Merton's Solution for Diversifiable Jumps

Suppose that the stock follows the process

$$dS(t)/S(t) = (\alpha - \lambda k)dt + \sigma dZ + dq \tag{21.38}$$

where, over an interval dt, a jump occurs with probability λdt, and $dq = 0$ if there is no jump and $Y - 1$ if there is a jump. The jump magnitude, Y, is lognormally distributed such that

$$\ln(Y) \sim \mathcal{N}(\alpha_J, \sigma_J^2) \tag{21.39}$$

Thus, if the stock price is S before a jump, it is YS following the jump, where $Y - 1$ is the percentage change in the stock price due to the jump, and $k = E(Y - 1)$ is the expected percentage jump. Asume that the occurrence and magnitude of the jump are uncorrelated with the stock return.

Merton (1976) shows that with the stock following equation (21.38), and with jumps diversifiable, the Black-Scholes PDE becomes

$$V_t + \tfrac{1}{2}V_{SS}\sigma^2 S^2 + V_S(r - \delta - \lambda k)S + \lambda E_Y[V(SY, t) - V(S, t)] = rV \tag{21.40}$$

When jumps are lognormal, as in equation (21.39), Merton shows that the price of a European call is[16]

$$\sum_{i=0}^{\infty} \frac{e^{-\lambda'T}(\lambda'T)^i}{i!} \text{BSCall}\left(S, K, \sqrt{\sigma^2 + i\sigma_J^2/T}, r - \lambda k + i\alpha_J/T, T, \delta\right) \tag{21.41}$$

where $\lambda' = \lambda e^{\alpha_J}$. The price of a call is obtained by put-call parity.

Equation (21.41) provides the option value as an expectation of European option prices with respect to the probability of a given number of jumps occurring. Conditional on i jumps, we replace the variance, $\sigma^2 T$, with $\sigma^2 T + i\sigma_J^2$, a quantity that reflects the added variance from having i discrete lognormal price moves. We also replace the risk-free rate, r, with $(r - \lambda k)T + i\alpha_J$. The instantaneous drift, $r - \lambda k$, is increased by the cumulative mean of i jumps, $i\alpha_J$.[17]

An interesting special case occurs when the only possible jump that can occur is a jump of the stock price to zero. If the stock jumps to zero, a call option becomes worthless: $V(SY, t) = 0$, and $\lambda k = -\lambda$. Hence, with a jump to zero, the PDE for a call

---

[16]When jumps need not be lognormal, Merton (1976) shows that the solution for calls is obtained as an expected value of the Black-Scholes formula:

$$\sum_{i=0}^{\infty} \frac{e^{-\lambda T}(\lambda T)^i}{i!} E_i\left[\text{BSCall}\left(SY_n e^{-\lambda kT}, K, \sigma, r, T, \delta\right)\right]$$

where E_i denotes the expectation conditional on i jumps.

[17]We discussed in Chapter 19 the reason for subtracting λk.

becomes

$$V_t + \tfrac{1}{2}V_{SS}\sigma^2 S^2 + V_S(r + \lambda - \delta)S = (r + \lambda)V$$

Every occurrence of r is replaced by $r + \lambda$; hence, when the stock can jump to zero with instantaneous probability λdt, the value of a European call, BSCall_λ is

$$\text{BSCall}_\lambda(S, K, \sigma, r, T - t, \delta) = \text{BSCall}(S, K, \sigma, r + \lambda, T - t, \delta) \qquad (21.42)$$

The formula for a put, BSPut_λ, is then obtained by put-call parity:[18]

$$\text{BSPut}_\lambda(S, K, \sigma, r, T - t, \delta)$$
$$= \text{BSCall}(S, K, \sigma, r + \lambda, T - t, \delta, \lambda) - Se^{-\delta(T-t)} + Ke^{-r(T-t)}$$

We will discuss the Merton jump formula further in Chapter 23.

CHAPTER SUMMARY

The Black-Scholes equation, equation (21.11), characterizes the behavior of a derivative as a function of the price of one or more underlying assets. (The Black-Scholes equation also appeared in Chapter 13 as a break-even condition for delta-hedging market-makers.) We can interpret the Black-Scholes equation as requiring that a derivative earn an appropriate rate of return, which occurs when the delta, gamma, and theta of an asset satisfy a particular relationship. The Black-Scholes equation is thus a generalization of the idea, familiar from introductory finance, that zero-coupon bonds appreciate at the risk-free rate. Probabilities and partial expectations satisfy a related condition known as the backward equation. Along with the Black-Scholes equation, a derivative must satisfy an appropriate boundary condition.

A change of the units of an option payoff is called a change of numeraire. Proposition 21.1 shows that the price effect of a change of numeraire is accounted for with a simple transformation of the pricing formula.

FURTHER READING

In Chapter 22, we extend the Black-Scholes analysis to exotic options and in Chapter 24 to studying interest rates.

Two classic papers on option pricing are Black and Scholes (1973) and Merton (1973b). Merton (1976) extends the Black-Scholes model to allow diversifiable jumps in the stock price, and Naik and Lee (1990) develop a model to price options when

---

[18]For a put option, the solution does *not* entail replacing every occurrence of r with $r + \lambda$. The reason is that the PDE for the put option is different from the PDE for the call option in the case of a jump. There is a different boundary condition when the stock jumps to zero:

$$P(0, t) = Ke^{-rT}$$

rather than 0 in the case of a call.

jumps are systematic. The Heston model is described in Heston (1993). In addition to Bakshi et al. (1997) and Bates (2000), recent empirical studies of volatility skew include Benzoni (2001), Andersen et al. (2002), Eraker (2001), and Pan (2002).

Cox and Miller (1965) and Wilmott (1998, ch. 10) discuss the backward equation and its counterpart, the forward equation, which characterizes the probability density for S_t, conditional on S_T. Geman et al. (1995) studied the role of changing the numeraire as a pricing technique. Schroder (1999) extends their results, including examples with stochastic volatility and jump-diffusion models. Ingersoll (2000) provides some additional examples of the use of this technique. Marcus and Modest (1984, 1986) examine quantity uncertainty in agricultural production.

PROBLEMS

21.1. Verify that equation (21.12) satisfies the Black-Scholes equation. What is the boundary condition for which this is a solution?

21.2. Verify that $A S^a e^{\gamma t}$ satisfies the Black-Scholes PDE for

$$a = \left(\frac{1}{2} - \frac{r - \delta}{\sigma^2} \right) \pm \sqrt{\left(\frac{r - \delta}{\sigma^2} - \frac{1}{2} \right)^2 + \frac{2(r - \gamma)}{\sigma^2}}$$

21.3. Use the Black-Scholes equation to verify the solution in Chapter 20, given by Proposition 20.3, for the value of a claim paying S^a.

21.4. Assuming that the stock price satisfies equation (20.27), verify that $K e^{-r(T-t)} + S(t) e^{-\delta(T-t)}$ satisfies the Black-Scholes equation, where K is a constant. What is the boundary condition for which this is a solution?

21.5. Verify that $S(t) e^{-\delta(T-t)} N(d_1)$ satisfies the Black-Scholes equation.

21.6. Verify that $e^{-r(T-t)} N(d_2)$ satisfies the Black-Scholes equation.

21.7. Use the answers to the previous two problems to verify that the Black-Scholes formula, equation (12.1), satisfies the Black-Scholes equation. Verify that the boundary condition $V[S(T), T] = \max[0, S(T) - K]$ is satisfied.

21.8. Consider Joe and Sarah's bet in Examples 21.2 and 21.3.

    a. In this bet, note that $106.184 is the forward price. A bet paying $1 if the share price is above the forward price is worth less than a bet paying $1 if the share price is below the forward price. Why?

    b. Suppose the bet were to be denominated in cash. If we want the bet to pay x if $S > x$, what would x have to be in order to make the bet fair?

    c. Now suppose that we pay one share if $S > x$. What would x have to be in this case to make the bet fair?

21.9. Consider again the bet in Example 21.3. Suppose the bet is $S - \$106.184$ if the price is above $106.184, and $\$106.184 - S$ if the price is below $106.184. What is the value of this bet to each party? Why?

21.10. Suppose that a derivative claim makes continuous payments at the rate Γ. Show that the Black-Scholes equation becomes

$$V_t + \frac{1}{2}\sigma^2 S^2 V_{SS} + (r - \delta)SV_S + \Gamma - rV = 0$$

For the following four problems assume that S follows equation (21.5) and Q follows equation (21.35). Suppose $S_0 = \$50$, $Q_0 = \$90$, $T = 2$, $r = 0.06$, $\delta = 0.02$, $\delta_Q = 0.01$, $\sigma = 0.3$, $\sigma_Q = 0.5$, and $\rho = -0.2$. Use Proposition 21.1 to find solutions to the problems. *Optional:* For each problem, verify the solution using Monte Carlo.

21.11. What is the value of a claim paying $Q(T)^2 S(T)$? Check your answer using Proposition 20.4.

21.12. What is the value of a claim paying $Q(T)^{-1}S(T)$? Check your answer using Proposition 20.4.

21.13. You are offered the opportunity to receive for free the payoff

$$[Q(T) - F_{0,T}(Q)] \times \max[0,\, S(T) - K]$$

(Note that this payoff can be negative.) Should you accept the offer?

21.14. An agricultural producer wishes to insure the value of a crop. Let Q represent the quantity of production in bushels and S the price of a bushel. The insurance payoff is therefore $Q(T) \times V[S(T), T]$, where V is the price of a put with $K = \$50$. What is the cost of insurance?

APPENDIX 21.A: MULTIVARIATE BLACK-SCHOLES ANALYSIS

Consider a claim for which the payoff depends on the n asset prices, $S_1, S_2, \ldots, S_n$, where

$$\frac{dS_i}{S_i} = (\alpha_i - \delta_i)dt + \sigma_i dZ_i \tag{21.43}$$

The pairwise correlation between S_i and S_j is ρ_{ij}. Let $V(S_1, S_2, \ldots, S_n, t, T)$ be the value of this claim. Consider a portfolio consisting of the claim, the n assets, and bonds, W, such that

$$I = V + \sum_{i=1}^{n} N_i S_i + W$$

Using the multivariate version of Itô's Lemma (Proposition 20.2, Multivariate Itô's Lemma), the change in the value of the portfolio is

$$dI = V_t dt + \sum_{i=1}^{n} V_{S_i} dS_i + \frac{1}{2}\sum_{i=1}^{n}\sum_{j=1}^{n} dS_i dS_j V_{S_i S_j} dt + \sum_{i=1}^{n} N_i dS_i + dW$$

In order to delta-hedge V, set $N_i = -V_{S_i}$. Hold bonds to finance the residual such that $I = 0$. The same analysis used to derive equation (21.11) leads to the following PDE for V:

$$V_t + \sum_{i=1}^{n}(r - \delta_i)S_i V_{S_i} + \frac{1}{2}\sum_{i=1}^{n}\sum_{j=1}^{n}\sigma_i\sigma_j\rho_{i,j}S_iS_j V_{S_iS_j} = rV \qquad (21.44)$$

APPENDIX 21.B: PROOF OF PROPOSITION 21.1

In this section we will verify the solution in Proposition 21.1. We begin by assuming that we have a derivative price $V(S, \sigma, r, T - t, \delta)$, that satisfies

$$V_t + (r - \delta)SV_S + \tfrac{1}{2}\sigma^2 S^2 V_{SS} = rV \qquad (21.45)$$

By the multivariate Black-Scholes equation described in Appendix 21.A, the claim $Y(S, Q, t)$ must satisfy

$$Y_t + (r - \delta)SY_S + (r - \delta_Q)QY_Q + \tfrac{1}{2}\left(\sigma^2 S^2 Y_{SS} + \sigma_Q^2 Q^2 Y_{QQ} + 2\rho\sigma\sigma_Q SQ Y_{SQ}\right) = rY$$

Guess the solution $Y = Ae^{-(r-\delta^*)t}Q^b W$, where A is determined by boundary conditions, δ^* is to be determined, and W satisfies the same boundary condition as V. Compute the derivatives of this guess and substitute them into equation (21.44). After simplification (in particular, the Y multiplying every term divides out), this yields

$$\delta^* - r + b(r - \delta_Q) + \tfrac{1}{2}\sigma_Q^2 b(b - 1)$$
$$+ \frac{1}{W}\left\{W_t + [r - (\delta - b\rho\sigma\sigma_Q)]SW_S + \tfrac{1}{2}\sigma^2 S^2 W_{SS}\right\} = r \quad (21.46)$$

The term in braces is the same as equation (21.45), except that δ is replaced with $\eta = \delta - b\rho\sigma\sigma_Q$. Thus, W is the same as V except that δ is replaced by η. With this replacement, from equation (21.45), the term in parentheses equals rW. Equation (21.46) becomes

$$\delta^* - r + b(r - \delta_Q) + \tfrac{1}{2}\sigma_Q^2 b(b - 1) + \frac{rW}{W} = r$$

This equation is satisfied if $\delta^* = r - b(r - \delta_Q) - \tfrac{1}{2}\sigma_Q^2 b(b - 1)$. Thus, with the η and δ^* in Proposition 21.1, the candidate solution solves equation (21.44). The parameter A is set so, at the point the option is exercised, $A = e^{(r-\delta^*)t}$. For a European option, set $A = e^{(r-\delta^*)T}$ to solve the terminal boundary condition.

APPENDIX 21.C: SOLUTIONS FOR PRICES AND PROBABILITIES

Appendix available online at www.aw-bc.com/mcdonald.

CHAPTER 22

Exotic Options: II

Chapter 14 introduced exotic (or nonstandard) options, including barrier, gap, and outperformance options. In this chapter, we continue our study of exotic options. There are two main themes in this chapter. First, we introduce a variety of simple options such as all-or-nothing options that can be used as components for building more complex options. Second, we will examine options that depend on prices of more than one asset, such as quantos and rainbow options. The discussion in this chapter relies on material in Chapters 20 and 21.

Throughout this chapter, we will assume that there are two assets that follow the processes

$$\frac{dS}{S} = (\alpha - \delta)dt + \sigma dZ \tag{22.1}$$

$$\frac{dQ}{Q} = (\alpha_Q - \delta_Q)dt + \sigma_Q dZ_Q \tag{22.2}$$

The correlation between dZ and dZ_Q is ρdt.

22.1 ALL-OR-NOTHING OPTIONS

We begin with a discussion of simple all-or-nothing options, which pay the holder a discrete amount of cash or a share if some particular event occurs. These are described as all-or-nothing (also called *binary* or *digital* options) because the payoff can be thought of as 0 or 1: Either you receive the cash or share, or you do not.

Terminology

There are many different kinds of all-or-nothing options; payoffs can be contingent on the stock price at expiration, as well as on whether the stock price has hit a barrier over the life of the option. We are interested in these options in and of themselves, and also because they are building blocks, useful for constructing variants of ordinary puts and calls as well as barrier options.

Naming all of these options can be a complex task. Table 22.1 describes the naming scheme we will use. The terminology will make sense as we introduce the various claims.

TABLE 22.1	Option nomenclature used in this chapter.

Notation	Meaning
Asset	Payment at expiration is one unit of the asset
Cash	Payment at expiration is \$1
Call	Payment received if $S_T > K$
Put	Payment received if $S_T < K$
UI	Up and in: Payment received only if barrier $H > S_0$ is hit
DI	Down and in: Payment received only if barrier $H < S_0$ is hit
UO	Up and out: Payment received only if barrier $H > S_0$ is not hit
DO	Down and out: Payment received only if barrier $H < S_0$ is not hit
UR	Up rebate: Rebate received at the time the barrier, $H > S_0$, is hit
DR	Down rebate: Rebate received at the time the barrier, $H < S_0$, is hit
URDeferred	Same as UR, except \$1 paid at expiration
DRDeferred	Same as DR, except \$1 paid at expiration

To see how the naming scheme works, consider the cash-or-nothing option, a claim that we introduced in Chapter 21. One kind of cash-or-nothing option pays the holder \$1 at time T if the stock price is greater than K. The condition under which it pays off, $S_T > K$, is like that for an ordinary call option, but it is not an ordinary call because it pays \$1 instead of $S_T - K$. We will identify an option like this as a "cash call" (*CashCall*), i.e., a contract that pays cash under the same condition as a call—when $S_T > K$.

Some options make payments only if multiple events occur. For example, consider a cash-or-nothing call that pays \$1 only if $S_T > K$ and the barrier $H > S_0$ has not been hit. We will refer to this as a "cash up and out call" (*CashUOCall*): "Cash" because it pays \$1, "up and out" because payment does not occur if the stock price rises to the barrier, and "call" because payment requires $S_T > K$. Similarly we will use the terms "asset" to refer to options that pay off in shares and "put" to refer to options that pay off only when $S_T < K$. To simplify the formulas in this chapter, we will use the notation in Table 22.2.

Cash-or-Nothing Options

Recall from Chapter 18 that the risk-neutral probability that $S_T > K$ is given by $N(d_2)$ from the Black-Scholes formula. We know from Chapter 21 that discounted risk-neutral probabilities are prices of derivatives. Thus, the price for a **cash-or-nothing call**—which

TABLE 22.2	Definitions of expressions used in pricing formulas in this chapter.

$$d_1 = [\ln(S_t/K) + (r - \delta + 0.5\sigma^2)(T - t)]/\sigma\sqrt{T - t}$$

$$d_2 = d_1 - \sigma\sqrt{T - t}$$

$$d_3 = [\ln(H^2/S_t K) + (r - \delta + 0.5\sigma^2)(T - t)]/\sigma\sqrt{T - t}$$

$$d_4 = d_3 - \sigma\sqrt{T - t}$$

$$d_5 = [\ln(S_t/H) + (r - \delta + 0.5\sigma^2)(T - t)]/\sigma\sqrt{T - t}$$

$$d_6 = d_5 - \sigma\sqrt{T - t}$$

$$d_7 = [\ln(H/S_t) + (r - \delta + 0.5\sigma^2)(T - t)]/\sigma\sqrt{T - t}$$

$$d_8 = d_7 - \sigma\sqrt{T - t}$$

pays \$1 if $S_T > K$ and zero otherwise—is

$$\text{CashCall}(S, K, \sigma, r, T - t, \delta) = e^{-r(T-t)}N(d_2) \qquad (22.3)$$

where d_2 is defined in Table 22.2. Equation (22.3), multiplied by the strike price, K, is the second term in the Black-Scholes formula for a call option. If you were to be paid x if $S > K$, you could value this as x cash-or-nothing options:

$$xe^{-r(T-t)}N(d_2)$$

You could also have a security that pays \$1 if S is *less than* K. This is equivalent to a security that pays \$1, less a security that pays \$1 if S_T is greater than K. Such an option is called a **cash-or-nothing put.** The value is

$$\text{CashPut}(S, K, \sigma, r, T - t, \delta) = e^{-r(T-t)} - e^{-r(T-t)}N(d_2)$$
$$= e^{-r(T-t)}N(-d_2) \qquad (22.4)$$

Example 22.1   Suppose $S = \$40$, $K = \$40$, $\sigma = 0.3$, $r = 0.08$, $T - t = 0.25$, and $\delta = 0$. The value of a claim that pays \$1 if $S > K$ in 3 months is \$0.5129, computed using equation (22.3). The value of a claim that pays \$1 if $S < K$ is \$0.4673, using equation (22.4). The combined value of the two claims is $e^{-0.08 \times 0.25} = \$0.9802$.   ≋

We know that equations (22.3) and (22.4) are correct since, as discussed in Chapter 21, both formulas satisfy the Black-Scholes equation (equation (21.11)) and the appropriate boundary conditions.

Asset-or-Nothing Options

An **asset-or-nothing call** is an option that gives the owner a unit of the underlying asset if the asset price exceeds a certain level and zero otherwise. As discussed in Chapter 21, Propostion 21.1, the price of an asset-or-nothing call is obtained from the price of a cash-or-nothing by replacing the dividend yield, δ, in the cash-or-nothing formula with $\delta - \sigma^2$, and multiplying the result by the forward price for the stock. The result is

$$Se^{(r-\delta)(T-t)}e^{-r(T-t)}N\left(\frac{\ln[S_t/K]+[r-(\delta-\sigma^2)-0.5\sigma^2][T-t]}{\sigma\sqrt{T-t}}\right)$$

$$= Se^{-\delta(T-t)}N(d_1)$$

This is the first term in the Black-Scholes formula.

Thus, the formula for an asset-or-nothing call that pays one unit of stock is

$$\text{AssetCall}(S, K, \sigma, r, T-t, \delta) = e^{-\delta(T-t)}SN(d_1) \tag{22.5}$$

We could also have an option in which we receive the stock if $S_T < K$, in which case the value is

$$Se^{-\delta(T-t)} - Se^{-\delta(T-t)}N(d_1) = Se^{-\delta(T-t)}N(-d_1)$$

Thus, the value of the asset-or-nothing put is

$$\text{AssetPut}(S, K, \sigma, r, T-t, \delta) = e^{-\delta(T-t)}SN(-d_1)$$

Example 22.2 Suppose $S = \$40$, $K = \$40$, $\sigma = 0.3$, $r = 0.08$, $T - t = 0.25$, and $\delta = 0$. The value of a claim that pays one share if $S > K$ in 3 months is \$23.30, computed using equation (22.5). The value of a claim that pays one share if $S < K$ is \$16.70. The combined value of the two claims is \$40. ❧

Figure 22.1 graphs the maturity payoffs of cash and asset calls.

Ordinary Options and Gap Options

We can construct an ordinary call by buying a European asset-or-nothing call with strike price K and selling K European cash-or-nothing calls with strike price K. That is,

BSCall$(S, K, \sigma, r, T-t, \delta)$

$$= \text{AssetCall}(S, K, \sigma, r, T-t, \delta) - K \times \text{CashCall}(S, K, \sigma, r, T-t, \delta)$$

$$= Se^{-\delta(T-t)}N(d_1) - Ke^{-r(T-t)}N(d_2)$$

This is the Black-Scholes formula.

Similarly, we can construct a put:

BSPut$(S, K, \sigma, r, T-t, \delta)$

$$= K \times \text{CashPut}(S, K, \sigma, r, T-t, \delta) - \text{AssetPut}(S, K, \sigma, r, T-t, \delta)$$

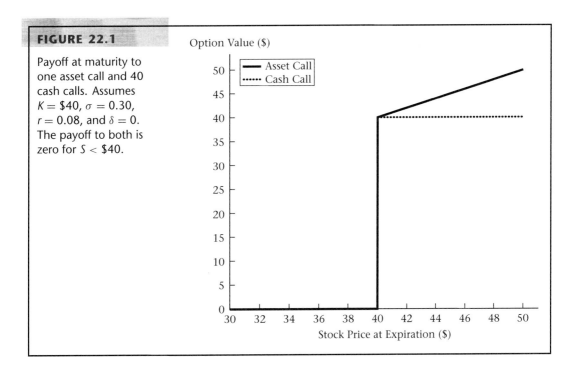

FIGURE 22.1

Payoff at maturity to one asset call and 40 cash calls. Assumes $K = \$40$, $\sigma = 0.30$, $r = 0.08$, and $\delta = 0$. The payoff to both is zero for $S < \$40$.

Finally, we can construct a gap option using asset-or-nothing options. Consider a call option that pays $S - K_1$ if $S > K_2$. The value of this is

$$\text{AssetCall}(S, K_2, \sigma, T - t, r, \delta) - K_1 \times \text{CashCall}(S, K_2, \sigma, T - t, r, \delta)$$

We buy an asset call and sell K_1 cash calls, both with the strike price K_2.

Example 22.3 Suppose $S = \$40$, $K = \$40$, $\sigma = 0.3$, $r = 0.08$, $T - t = 0.25$, and $\delta = 0$. The price of an ordinary call is an asset call less 40 cash calls. Using results in Examples 22.1 and 22.2, the price of the ordinary call is $\$23.30 - 40 \times \$0.5129 = \$2.7848$.

The price of a gap call in which the owner pays $20 ($K_1$) if the stock is greater than $40 ($K_2$) at expiration is $\$23.20 - 20 \times \$0.5129 = \$13.0427$.

Delta-Hedging All-or-Nothing Options

All-or-nothing options appear frequently in writings about options, but they are relatively rare in practice. The reason is that they are easy to price but hard to hedge. To understand why, think about the position of a market-maker when such an option is close to expiration. The nightmare scenario for a market-maker is that the option is close to

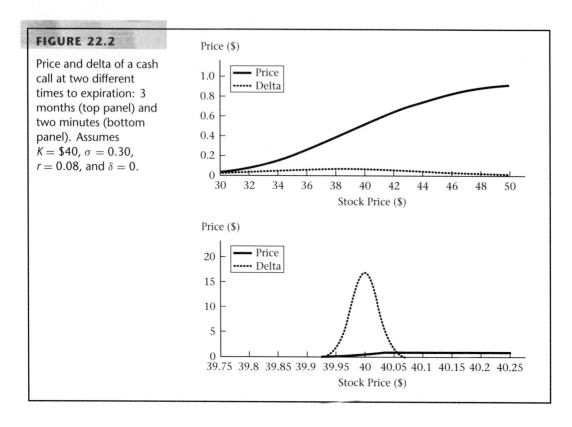

FIGURE 22.2

Price and delta of a cash call at two different times to expiration: 3 months (top panel) and two minutes (bottom panel). Assumes $K = \$40$, $\sigma = 0.30$, $r = 0.08$, and $\delta = 0$.

expiration *and* close to the strike price. In this case a small swing in the stock price can determine whether the option is in- or out-of-the-money, with the payoff changing discretely. This potential for a small price change to have a large effect on the option value is evident in Figure 22.1.

To assess hedging difficulty, Figure 22.2 graphs the price and delta of cash calls paying $1 with 3 months to expiration and two minutes to expiration. With 3 months to go, hedging is straightforward and delta is well-behaved. However, with 2 minutes to go until expiration, the cash call delta at $40 is 15. For the at-the-money option, delta and gamma approach infinity at expiration because an arbitrarily small change in the price can result in a $1 change in the option's value.

An ordinary call or put is easier to hedge because the payoff is continuous—there is no discrete jump at the strike price as the option approaches expiration. Supershares, discussed in the box on page 709, provide an alternative technology for creating complex payoffs.

Supershares

Hakannson (1976) proposed a concept known as **supershares,** which could be used to create exotic option-like payoffs without the need for delta-hedging by a dealer. The idea of a supershare is to create shares that pay $1 in particular circumstances, and to use these as building blocks for more complicated instruments. Supershares can be illustrated with a simple example.

Suppose that the risk-free rate is 10%, the market index is 100, and over the next year there are three possible values of the market index: $60, $110, and $160. (The use of three possible prices is just for simplicity.) Define three supershares that pay $1 if the market in 1 year is $60, $1 if the market is $110, and $1 if the market is $160. Call these shares "down," "middle," and "up."

We can create a fund with a $100 million investment in the index, and finance it by selling 60 million down shares, 110 million middle shares, and 160 million up shares.[1] If the market is $60 in 1 year, the entire $60 million is paid to the holders of the down shares. If the market is $160, the entire amount is paid to the holders of the up shares. Note that if you were to buy all of these shares, you would earn a return equivalent to a $100 million investment in the index. (You could also buy 6 down shares, 11 middle shares, and 16 up shares for a small position in the index.) If you bought 100 each of the down, middle, and up shares, you would have a risk-free zero-coupon bond paying $100. By buying just the down shares, you could replicate the payoff to a cash-or-nothing put, and so forth.

Although the supershare payoffs resemble the payoffs of cash-or-nothing options, the elegant simplicity of the supershare idea is that the shares are created as fully-collateralized contingent claims on a fund. No delta-hedging is required. Relative pricing of the components is determined by the willingness of investors to hold them, but the portfolios replicating a bond and the index must be priced correctly or else there would be arbitrage.

Supershares were actually brought to market in November 1992 by Leland, O'Brien, and Rubinstein (the first and third named principals are finance professors). The product consisted of exchange-traded money market and index funds, which could be decomposed into four supershares that could be traded individually at the Chicago Board Options Exchange. There were significant regulatory hurdles to introducing supershares, described in Lux (1992). Trading volume was weak and after several years the product was abandoned. The exchange-traded index fund, however, was the precursor to current popular products such as exchange-traded funds and SPDRs.

---

[1] In the examples in Hakannson (1976), shares are created paying returns every percentage point between −50% and +60%.

22.2 ALL-OR-NOTHING BARRIER OPTIONS

Barrier options, introduced in Chapter 14, are options in which the option comes into or goes out of existence if the price of the underlying asset hits a barrier.[2] There are down-and-out options, which become worthless if the stock price hits a barrier price below the initial stock price, as well as up-and-out, down-and-in, and up-and-in options. We can construct options such as these using *all-or-nothing barrier options*.

Suppose we take a cash-or-nothing call paying \$1 if $S_T > K$, but modify it by adding the additional requirement that it will only pay \$1 at expiration if the stock has also hit the barrier H sometime during the life of the option. If $H < S(0)$, this is a down-and-in cash call. Using the notation in Table 22.1, this would be a *CashDICall*. Just as we were able to construct ordinary options from digital options, we will also be able to construct barrier options from digital barrier options.

We will examine three different kinds of barrier options:

- A contract that pays \$1 contingent on either a barrier having or not having been reached (*cash-or-nothing barrier options*).

- A contract that pays a share of stock worth S contingent on either a barrier having or not having been reached (*asset-or-nothing barrier options*).

- A contract that pays \$1 at the time a barrier is reached (*rebate options*) or that pays \$1 at expiration as long as the barrier has been reached during the life of the option (*deferred rebate options*).

By valuing these pieces and adding them together we can price any standard barrier option. The assumption that the stock follows geometric Brownian motion makes it possible to derive relatively simple formulas for these options.

There are 16 basic kinds of all-or-nothing barrier options. First, consider cash-or-nothing barrier options that pay \$1 at expiration. Such options can knock-in or knock-out; they can be calls (pay cash if $S_T > K$) or puts (pay cash if $S_T < K$); and the barrier event can occur if the barrier is above the price (up-and-ins or up-and-outs) or below the price (down-and-ins or down-and-outs). This gives us $2^3 = 8$ basic cash-or-nothing barrier options to value. By the same reasoning there are also 8 basic asset-or-nothing barrier options, for a total of 16 all-or-nothing barrier options.

Cash-or-Nothing Barrier Options

We first consider the valuation of barrier cash-or-nothing options. To anticipate the results in this section, we will first see how to value one particular barrier cash-or-nothing option, a down-and-in cash call. From this one formula we will be able to value the remaining seven cash-or-nothing options and deferred rebate options.

---

[2] Three comprehensive discussions of barrier options are Rubinstein and Reiner (1991a), Rubinstein and Reiner (1991b), and Derman and Kani (1993).

Assume that the option is issued at time 0 and expires at time T. Let $\overline{S}_t$ denote the greatest stock price between times 0 and t (where $t \leq T$) and let $\underline{S}_t$ denote the lowest stock price between times 0 and t. Suppose the barrier is below the initial stock price, i.e., $H < S_0$. A cash down-and-in call (*CashDICall*) is an option that pays \$1 if two conditions are satisfied. First, at some point prior to maturity, the stock price drops to reach H, i.e., $\underline{S}_T \leq H$. Second, at expiration, the stock price is greater than the strike price, K.

We can analyze this option by first examining the risk-neutral probability that this joint event ($\underline{S}_T \leq H$ and $S_T \geq K$) occurs. This probability should satisfy three conditions:

1. Once the barrier has been hit ($\underline{S}_t \leq H$) the probability equals the probability that $S_T \geq K$ (the barrier at this point is irrelevant).

2. If at time T, $\underline{S}_T \leq H$ and $S_T \geq K$, the probability equals 1.

3. If at time T, $\underline{S}_T > H$ or $S_T < K$, the probability equals 0.

Assume that $H \leq K$, and consider this expression:

$$\text{Prob}(\underline{S}_T \leq H \text{ and } S_T > K) = \left(\frac{H}{S}\right)^{2\frac{r-\delta}{\sigma^2}-1} N(d_4) \tag{22.6}$$

The terms d_1 through d_8 are defined in Table 22.2. In Appendix 21.C, which is found on the book's Web site (www.aw-bc.com/mcdonald), we saw that an expression of this form solves the backward equation. We also want to verify that it satisfies the three boundary conditions described above.

First, at the point where $S_t = H$, equation (22.6) collapses to $N(d_2)$, which is the risk-neutral probability that $S_T > K$. (This occurs because when $H = S_t$, $d_1 = d_3$. You should examine equation (22.6) to verify that this happens.) Thus, once we hit the barrier, the barrier value H drops out of the expression because it is irrelevant. Second, if at expiration $\underline{S}_T \leq H$ and $S_T > K$, then equation (22.6) equals 1. The reason is that the probability equals $N(d_2)$ once the barrier is hit, and if $S_T > K$, $N(d_2) = 1$. Finally, if $\underline{S}_T > H$, i.e., S_t never reaches H, then at expiration $H^2 < S_T K$ (recall that $H \leq K$) and equation (22.6) collapses to 0. Thus, equation (22.6) both satisfies the backward equation and obeys the appropriate boundary conditions.

Equation (22.6) assumes that $H \leq K$. Why is this important? The answer is that if $H > K$, the boundary conditions may be violated. Consider the case where at expiration $S_T = \$55$, $K = \$45$, and $H = \$54$ (thus violating the condition $H \leq K$), and the boundary has not been hit. In this case a correct expression for the probability will evaluate to zero at expiration. However, $\ln(H^2/S_T K) = \ln(54^2/45 \times 55) = 0.164$, so equation (22.6) at maturity will equal 1 when the event has not occurred.

As a final comment on equation (22.6), you might ask why it is necessary to multiply $N(d_4)$ by the term $(H/S)^{2(r-\delta)/\sigma^2-1}$. The answer is simply that $N(d_4)$ by itself does not solve the backward equation, whereas equation (22.6) *does* solve the backward equation.

To handle the case where $H > K$ we need a more complicated version of equation (22.6). When $H > K$, we have

$$\text{Prob}(\underline{S}_T \leq H \text{ and } S_T > K) = N(d_2) - N(d_6) + \left(\frac{H}{S}\right)^{2\frac{r-\delta}{\sigma^2}-1} N(d_8) \qquad (22.7)$$

Problem 22.3 asks you to verify that this equation satisfies the boundary conditions. Note that when $S = H$, $N(d_6) = N(d_8)$; the formula again reduces to $N(d_2)$.

Down-and-in cash call   Equations (22.6) and (22.7) give us expressions for the probability that the barrier is hit and $S_T > K$. What is the value of a claim that pays \$1 when this event occurs? To answer this question we can use the result from Chapter 21 that discounted risk-neutral probabilities are prices of derivative claims. Discounting equations (22.6) and (22.7), we have

$$\text{CashDICall}(S, K, \sigma, r, T - t, \delta, H) =$$

$$\begin{cases} e^{-r(T-t)} \left(\frac{H}{S}\right)^{2\frac{r-\delta}{\sigma^2}-1} N(d_4) & H \leq K \\ e^{-r(T-t)} \left[N(d_2) - N(d_6) + \left(\frac{H}{S}\right)^{2\frac{r-\delta}{\sigma^2}-1} N(d_8)\right] & H > K \end{cases} \qquad (22.8)$$

Equation (22.8) gives us the value for a cash down-and-in call when $S_0 > H$. There are three closely related options we can now price: Cash down-and-out calls (*CashDOCall*), cash down-and-in puts (*CashDIPut*), and cash down-and-out puts (*CashDOPut*). We can value each of these using only the formula for the cash down-and-in call, equation (22.8). In addition, we can value a deferred down rebate option.

Deferred down rebate option   We first value a deferred down rebate, which is a claim that pays \$1 at time T as long as the barrier has been hit over the life of the option. The payoff to this claim does not depend on a strike price: It pays \$1 as long as the barrier has been hit. We will call this claim a **deferred down rebate.** It is a "down rebate" because it pays \$1 if we reach the barrier, and it is "deferred" because the payment is at expiration rather than at the time we reach the barrier. We obtain the value of this claim by setting $K = \$0$ in equation (22.8). Since we always have $S_T > 0$, the result is a claim that pays \$1 at T as long as $S_T \leq H$. Thus, we have[3]

$$\text{DRDeferred}(S, \sigma, r, T - t, \delta, H) = \text{CashDICall}(S, 0, \sigma, r, T - t, \delta, H) \qquad (22.9)$$

Note that since we set $K = 0$, the value of the deferred down rebate does not depend on the strike price.

Now we can compute the value of the remaining three options.

Down-and-out cash call   We can create a synthetic cash call by buying down-and-in and down-and-out cash calls with the same barrier; this combination is guaranteed to

---

[3]In peforming this calculation, to avoid a zero-divide error it is necessary to set K to be small, such as $K = \$0.000001$, rather than exactly \$0.

pay $1 if $S_T > K$. Thus, the value of a down-and-out cash call is

$$\text{CashDOCall}(S, K, \sigma, r, T - t, \delta, H) = \text{CashCall}(S, K, \sigma, r, T - t, \delta)$$
$$-\text{CashDICall}(S, K, \sigma, r, T - t, \delta, H) \tag{22.10}$$

Down-and-in cash put If you buy a down-and-in cash put with strike price K, you receive $1 if the barrier is reached and $S_T < K$. If you buy a down-and-in cash call, you receive $1 if the barrier is reached and $S_T \geq K$. Thus, if you buy *both* a down-and-in call and put, you receive $1 as long as the barrier is hit. This is the same payoff as a deferred rebate; thus, we have

$$\text{CashDIPut}(S, K, \sigma, r, T - t, \delta, H) = \text{DRDeferred}(S, \sigma, r, T - t, \delta, H)$$
$$-\text{CashDICall}(S, K, \sigma, r, T - t, \delta, H) \tag{22.11}$$

Down-and-out cash put Buying down-and-in and down-and-out cash puts creates an ordinary cash put. Thus, the value of the down-and-out put is

$$\text{CashDOPut}(S, K, \sigma, r, T - t, \delta, H) = \text{CashPut}(S, K, \sigma, r, T - t, \delta)$$
$$- \text{CashDIPut}(S, K, \sigma, r, T - t, \delta, H) \tag{22.12}$$

As a final point we can compute the risk-neutral probability that we reach the barrier. The deferred down rebate option pays $1 at expiration as long as the barrier is hit. Thus the price of this option is the present value of the risk-neutral probability that the barrier is reached. Therefore,

$$e^{r(T-t)}\text{DRDeferred}(S, 0, \sigma, r, T - t, \delta) \tag{22.13}$$

is the risk-neutral probability that the barrier is reached during the life of the option.

Example 22.4 Suppose $S = \$40$, $\sigma = 0.3$, $r = 0.08$, $\delta = 0$, and $T - t = 1$. The value of a claim that pays $1 if the stock hits the barrier $H = \$35$ over the next year is computed by setting $K = \$0$ in equation (22.8):

CashDICall($40, $0.0000001, 0.3, 0.08, 1, 0, $35) =

$$e^{-r(T-t)}\left[1 - N(d_6) + \left(\frac{H}{S}\right)^{2(r-\delta)/\sigma^2 - 1} N(d_8)\right] = \$0.574$$

The risk-neutral probability that the stock will hit the barrier is the undiscounted value of this claim, or $0.574 \times e^{0.08} = 0.622$.

The value of a claim that pays $1 if the stock hits the barrier, $35, and then is also greater than $K = \$35$ at the end of the year is

$$e^{-r(T-t)}\left(\frac{H}{S}\right)^{2(r-\delta)/\sigma^2 - 1} N(d_4) = \$0.309$$

This is the value of CashDICall($40, $35, 0.3, 0.08, 1, 0, $35). The risk-neutral probability of hitting the barrier and being above $35 is $0.309 \times e^{0.08} = 0.335$.   ❧

This example illustrates an interesting point. The value of the claim that pays $1 at expiration when the stock at expiration is greater than $35 and has hit the $35 barrier ($0.309), is approximately one-half the value of the claim that pays $1 at expiration as long as the stock has hit the $35 barrier ($0.574). The reason is that once the stock has hit $35, it subsequently has about a 50% chance of being above or below that value. This observation suggests that the probability of being above $35 conditional upon having hit $35 is $0.5 \times 0.622 = 0.311$. The actual probability is greater than that, however. The reason is that the lognormal drift is $r - 0.5\sigma^2 = 0.035$, which is positive. Thus, after having hit $35, the stock on average drifts higher.

To verify this intuition, suppose we set the lognormal drift equal to zero. We can do this by setting the risk-free rate to 0.045, which gives us $r - 0.5\sigma^2 = 0.045 - 0.5 \times 0.3^2 = 0$. We might expect that the value of a claim paying $1 at T if the barrier is hit is one-half the value of a claim paying $1 at T if the barrier is hit and the stock price at expiration is greater than the barrier. Put differently, when $r = 0.5\sigma^2$, the probability of hitting and ending up above $35 is half the unconditional probability of hitting $35. The next example shows that this intuition works.

Example 22.5   Suppose $S = \$40$, $\sigma = 0.3$, $r = 0.045$, $\delta = 0$, and $T - t = 1$. The value of a claim paying $1 if the stock hits the barrier $H = \$35$ over the next year is

$$e^{-r(T-t)} \left[1 - N(d_6) + \left(\frac{H}{S} \right)^{2(r-\delta)/\sigma^2 - 1} N(d_8) \right] = \$0.6274$$

The corresponding risk-neutral probability is $e^{0.045} \times 0.6274 = 0.6562$.

The value of a claim paying $1 if the stock hits the barrier and is then greater than $K = \$35$ at the end of the year is

$$e^{-r(T-t)} \left(\frac{H}{S} \right)^{2(r-\delta)/\sigma^2 - 1} N(d_4) = \$0.3137$$

This is one-half of $0.6274. The corresponding risk-neutral probability is $e^{0.045} \times 0.3137 = 0.3281$.   ❧

Up-and-in cash put   Now we consider cash-or-nothing options when the barrier is *above* the current stock price. First, consider the following formula for an up-and-in cash put, which pays $1 when $\bar{S}_T > H$ and $S_T < K$:

CashUIPut$(S, K, \sigma, r, T - t, \delta, H) =$

$$\begin{cases} e^{-r(T-t)} \left(\frac{H}{S} \right)^{2\frac{r-\delta}{\sigma^2} - 1} N(-d_4) & H \geq K \\[2ex] e^{-r(T-t)} \left[N(-d_2) - N(-d_6) + \left(\frac{H}{S} \right)^{2\frac{r-\delta}{\sigma^2} - 1} N(-d_8) \right] & H < K \end{cases} \tag{22.14}$$

If you compare this formula to equation (22.8), you will see that $N(d_2)$ is replaced with $N(-d_2)$, $N(d_4)$ with $N(-d_4)$, and so forth. We know from Appendix 21.C that these terms also solve the Black-Scholes equation. The effect of these changes is to reverse the effect of the d_i terms. As a consequence, equation (22.8), which prices a down-and-in cash call, is transformed into an equation pricing an up-and-in cash put. Problem 22.4 asks you to verify that equation (22.14) solves the appropriate boundary conditions for an up-and-in cash put.

Deferred up rebate Given equation (22.14), the procedure for obtaining the prices of the other three cash-or-nothing options when $H > S_0$ is analogous to that before. First, by setting $K = \infty$ in equation (22.14), we obtain the price of a claim paying \$1 at expiration as long as the barrier is reached:[4]

$$\text{URDeferred}(S, \sigma, r, T - t, \delta, H) = \text{CashUIPut}(S, \infty, \sigma, r, T - t, \delta, H) \quad (22.15)$$

With this equation, we can solve for the price of the other cash-or-nothing options.

Up-and-out cash put Buying up-and-in and up-and-out cash puts gives an ordinary cash put; hence,

$$\begin{aligned} \text{CashUOPut}(S, K, \sigma, r, T - t, \delta, H) = {}& \text{CashPut}(S, K, \sigma, r, T - t, \delta) \\ & - \text{CashUIPut}(S, K, \sigma, r, T - t, \delta, H) \end{aligned} \quad (22.16)$$

Up-and-in cash call Buying an up-and-in cash call and an up-and-in cash put yields the same payoff as a deferred up rebate. Thus, we have

$$\begin{aligned} \text{CashUICall}(S, K, \sigma, r, T - t, \delta, H) = {}& \text{URDeferred}(S, \sigma, r, T - t, \delta, H) \\ & - \text{CashUIPut}(S, K, \sigma, r, T - t, \delta, H) \end{aligned} \quad (22.17)$$

Up-and-out cash call Buying up-and-in and up-and-out cash calls gives an ordinary cash call; hence,

$$\begin{aligned} \text{CashUOCall}(S, K, \sigma, r, T - t, \delta, H) = {}& \text{CashCall}(S, K, \sigma, r, T - t, \delta) \\ & - \text{CashUICall}(S, K, \sigma, r, T - t, \delta, H) \end{aligned} \quad (22.18)$$

Asset-or-Nothing Barrier Options

We now wish to find the eight pricing formulas for asset-or-nothing options corresponding to those for the eight cash-or-nothing options. Fortunately, there is a simple way to do this. If we view asset-or-nothing options as cash-or-nothing options denominated in shares rather than cash, we can use Proposition 21.1, dealing with a change of numeraire, to transform the pricing formulas for cash-or-nothing options into formulas for

---

[4]To evaluate equation (22.14) at $K = \infty$, we simply set $N(-d_2) = 1$.

asset-or-nothing options. In each case, we replace δ by $\delta - \sigma^2$, and we multiply the cash-or-nothing formula by $S_0 e^{(r-\delta)(T-t)}$, the forward price for the stock. For example, we have

$$\text{AssetDICall}(S, K, \sigma, r, T - t, \delta, H)$$
$$= S e^{(r-\delta)(T-t)} \text{CashDICall}(S, K, \sigma, r, T - t, \delta - \sigma^2, H) \qquad (22.19)$$

The other seven asset-or-nothing pricing formulas—*AssetDOCall*, *AssetDIPut*, *AssetDOPut*, *AssetUICall*, *AssetUOCall*, *AssetUIPut*, and *AssetUOP*—can be created in exactly the same way.

Rebate Options

Rebate options pay \$1 if the barrier is hit. We have already seen how to price deferred rebate options, which pay the \$1 at expiration of the option. If the option pays at the time the barrier is hit, we will call the claim a **rebate option** (or *immediate rebate option*).

We have already seen in equations (22.9) and (22.15) how to price deferred rebates. The formulas for rebates paid when the barrier is hit are more complicated because the discount factor for the \$1 payment depends on the time at which the barrier is hit. In effect there is a random discount factor.

The formula for the price of a down rebate when $S > H$ is

$$\text{DR}(S, \sigma, r, T - t, \delta, H) = \left(\frac{H}{S}\right)^{h_1} N(Z_1) + \left(\frac{H}{S}\right)^{h_2} N(Z_2) \qquad (22.20)$$

where, letting

$$g = \sqrt{\left(r - \delta - \frac{1}{2}\sigma^2\right)^2 + 2r\sigma^2}$$

then

$$Z_1 = [\ln(H/S) + g(T - t)]/\sigma\sqrt{T - t}$$
$$Z_2 = [\ln(H/S) - g(T - t)]/\sigma\sqrt{T - t}$$
$$h_1 = \left(\frac{r - \delta}{\sigma^2} - \frac{1}{2}\right) + \sqrt{\left(\frac{r - \delta}{\sigma^2} - \frac{1}{2}\right)^2 + \frac{2r}{\sigma^2}}$$
$$h_2 = \left(\frac{r - \delta}{\sigma^2} - \frac{1}{2}\right) - \sqrt{\left(\frac{r - \delta}{\sigma^2} - \frac{1}{2}\right)^2 + \frac{2r}{\sigma^2}}$$

This formula satisfies (as it must) both the Black-Scholes equation and the boundary conditions for a rebate option. Suppose that the barrier is not hit over the life of the option. Then $H < S$ and both terms go to 0 as $t \to T$. At the point when the barrier is hit, $H = S$ and $\ln(H/S) = 0$. Because the normal distribution is symmetric around 0,

$$N\left[\frac{g(T - t)}{\sigma\sqrt{T - t}}\right] + N\left[\frac{-g(T - t)}{\sigma\sqrt{T - t}}\right] = 1$$

Thus, the formula evaluates to 1 when the barrier is hit.

The up-rebate formula is symmetric:

$$UR(S, \sigma, r, T - t, \delta, H) = \left(\frac{H}{S}\right)^{h_1} N(-Z_1) + \left(\frac{H}{S}\right)^{h_2} N(-Z_2) \qquad (22.21)$$

where all variables are defined as above for the down rebate.

If we let $T \to \infty$, the formulas for up and down rebates become the barrier present value formulas, equations (12.17) and (12.18), discussed in Chapter 12. (Problem 22.5 asks you to verify this.) The rebate formulas provide the value of $1 when the stock price hits a barrier, and this is exactly the calculation performed by barrier present value calculations, only for the case of infinitely lived claims.

22.3 BARRIER OPTIONS

At this point it is easy to construct the barrier option formulas from Chapter 14 using the preceding formulas. A down-and-out call, for example, can be valued as

$$CallDownOut(S, K, \sigma, r, T - t, \delta, H) = AssetDOCall(S, K, \sigma, r, T - t, \delta, H)$$
$$- K \times CashDOCall(S, K, \sigma, r, T - t, \delta, H)$$

Up-and-outs, down-and-ins, and so forth are all constructed analogously. See Table 22.3 for a listing of formulas for barrier calls and puts.

As another example of the use of all-or-nothing options as building blocks, **capped options** are single options that have the payoff of bull spreads, except that the option is exercised the first time the stock price reaches the upper strike price. An example of an American capped option is an option with a strike price of $100 and a cap of $120. When the stock hits $120, the option pays $20. If the option expires without the stock having hit $120, then the payoff is $\max(S_T - 100, 0)$. This option can be priced as the sum of the following two options:

- A rebate call, which pays the $20 when the stock hits $120 prior to expiration.

- A knock-out call with a strike of $100, which knocks out at $120.

If the stock reaches $120 prior to expiration, the rebate is triggered and the call knocks out. If the stock has not hit $120 prior to expiration but is above $100, the

TABLE 22.3	Formulas for barrier puts and calls. In each case, the arguments for the functions are $(S, K, \sigma, r, T - t, \delta, H)$.

	Call	Put
Up-and-In	AssetUICall $- K \times$ CashUICall	$K \times$ CashUIPut $-$ AssetUIPut
Up-and-Out	AssetUOCall $- K \times$ CashUOCall	$K \times$ CashUOPut $-$ AssetUOPut
Down-and-In	AssetDICall $- K \times$ CashDICall	$K \times$ CashDIPut $-$ AssetDIPut
Down-and-Out	AssetDOCall $- K \times$ CashDOCall	$K \times$ CashDOPut $-$ AssetDOPut

knock-out call pays $S - \$100$. The table below illustrates the payoffs, assuming that the option strike is K, the cap is H, and the option expires at T:

	H Hit	**H Not Hit**
Purchased Knock-Out	0	$\max(0, S_T - K)$
Rebate	$H - K$ at Hit	0
Total	$H - K$ at Hit	$\max(0, S_T - K)$

The table shows that we can price the American capped option above as a straight application of the rebate formula together with a knock-out. The holder owns a 100-strike call with a knock-out of $120, and a rebate call with a $20 rebate payable at $120. Note that a European capped option is much simpler to price. Since the payoff does not occur until expiration, this option is just an ordinary vertical spread (buy a 100-strike call and sell a 120-strike European call with the same times to expiration).

Example 22.6   Consider the capped call discussed in the text above and suppose that $S = \$100$, $\sigma = 0.3$, $r = 0.08$, $T - t = 1$, and $\delta = 0$. We can compute the price of an up-and-out call as

$$\text{CallUpOut}(S, K, \sigma, r, T - t, \delta, H) = \text{AssetUOCall}(S, K, \sigma, r, T - t, \delta, H)$$
$$- K \times \text{CashUOCall}(S, K, \sigma, r, T - t, \delta, H)$$

The price of the capped call is

$$20 \times \text{UR}(\$100, 0.3, 0.08, 1, 0, \$120) + \text{CallUpOut}(\$100, \$100, 0.3, 0.08, 1, 0, \$120)$$
$$= 20 \times \$0.5649 + \$0.4298 = \$11.73$$

The price of a European bull spread for the same parameters would be

$$\text{BSCall}(\$100, \$100, 0.3, 0.08, 1, 0) - \text{BSCall}(\$100, \$120, 0.3, 0.08, 1, 0)$$
$$= \$15.7113 - \$7.8966 = \$7.8147$$

The capped call is more expensive because all of the stock price paths that cross $120 and end up lower result in the maximum payout on the capped call but a lower payout on the bull spread.   ❧

22.4 QUANTOS

A U.S. investor wishing to invest in a foreign stock index can purchase the foreign index directly or hold futures based on that index. However, the investor then bears two risks: The risk of the foreign index and currency (exchange rate) risk.

For example, suppose that a U.S. investor wishes to invest in the Nikkei 225 index, expecting that it will increase over the next month. The investor can take a position in the

Nikkei by directly investing in the cash Nikkei index or by investing in yen-denominated futures, such as a Nikkei futures contract trading in Japan. Both strategies have a payoff denominated in yen. If the Nikkei appreciates but the yen depreciates, *the investor can lose money despite being correct about the movement of the Nikkei.*

You could try to reduce the problem of exchange rate risk by hedging the Nikkei investment using currency futures. However, the quantity of yen to be exchanged is high when the index has a high return and low when the index has a low return. Thus, *there is no way to know in advance how many yen to short.* This price uncertainty creates quantity uncertainty with respect to the yen exposure.

We could imagine a synthetic Nikkei investment in which the quantity of currency forwards depended upon the Nikkei's yen return. Such a contract would permit an investor in one currency to hold an asset denominated in another currency, without exchange rate risk. This contract is called an **equity-linked forward,** or **quanto.** For reasons that will become clear below, a quanto is also sometimes defined as a derivative having a payoff that depends on the product or ratio of two prices.

The Nikkei 225 index futures contract, traded at the Chicago Mercantile Exchange and discussed in Chapter 5, is an example of a quanto contract. This futures contract is marked-to-market daily in *dollars,* even though it settles based on a yen-denominated price.[5] There is also a yen-denominated Nikkei futures contract that trades in Osaka. Both futures are based on the Nikkei 225 contract, but they differ in currency of denomination. We will see in this section how their pricing differs. The box on page 728 discusses Nikkei put warrants, which were another example of a quanto contract. Table 22.4 lists the symbols and specific numbers used throughout the examples in this section.

TABLE 22.4   Parameters used in the Nikkei/yen quanto example.

Dollar-denominated interest rate	r	0.08
Yen-denominated interest rate	r_f	0.04
Current Nikkei index	Q_0	¥20,000
Nikkei dividend yield	δ_Q	0.02
Nikkei volatility (¥)	σ_Q	0.15
Current exchange rate ($/¥)	x_0	0.0100
Exchange rate volatility	s	0.1
Nikkei-exchange rate ($/¥) correlation	ρ	0.2
Time to expiration	T	1 year

[5]To illustrate dollar settlement, suppose the Nikkei 225 is at 22,000. Under the terms of the CME contract, a one point move corresponds to $5, so the notional value of one contract is $22,000 \times \$5 = \$110,000$. If instead the Nikkei had been 22,100, the notional value of the contract would be $110,500, a difference of $500.

FIGURE 22.3

Binomial trees for the dollar and the Nikkei index from the perspective of a yen-based investor. Both are forward trees constructed using the parameters in Table 22.4. The risk-neutral probabilities of up moves are 0.4750 in the dollar tree and 0.4626 in the Nikkei tree.

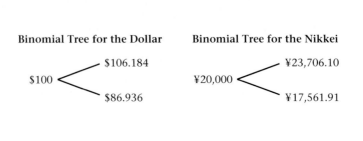

The Yen Perspective

The yen-based investor is interested in the yen price of $1 and, hence, faces an exchange rate of $1/x_0 = 100¥/\$$. Because the Nikkei index and the yen price of a dollar are both denominated in yen, we use the usual formulas to find forward prices for the yen and Nikkei. For the Nikkei, we have

$$\text{Nikkei forward (¥):} \quad F_{0,T}(Q) = Q_0 e^{(r_f - \delta_Q)T} \tag{22.22}$$

For the exchange rate, the dollar-denominated interest rate is the yield on dollars, so the forward price is

$$\text{Exchange rate forward (¥/\$):} \quad F_{0,T}(1/x) = \frac{1}{x_0} e^{(r_f - r)T} \tag{22.23}$$

These will be the forward prices observed in Japan.

A yen-based investor would construct binomial trees for the yen and Nikkei in the usual fashion. Figure 22.3 depicts trees for the dollar and Nikkei. The nodes on the dollar tree are constructed as

$$(1/x_T) = (1/x_0)e^{(r_f - r)T \pm s\sqrt{T}}$$

and on the Nikkei tree as

$$Q_T = Q_0 e^{(r_f - \delta_Q)T \pm \sigma_Q \sqrt{T}}$$

Example 22.7   Given the parameters in Table 22.4, the 1-year yen-denominated forward price for the Nikkei index is

$$F_{0,1}(Q) = ¥20,000e^{(0.04 - 0.02) \times 1} = ¥20,404.03$$

and that for the exchange rate is

$$F_{0,1}(1/x) = ¥100e^{(0.04-0.08)\times 1} = ¥96.079$$

We can also compute the forward prices on both trees as expected values. For the dollar tree we have

$$F_{0,1}(1/x) = 0.4750 \times \$106.184 + (1 - 0.4750) \times \$86.936 = \$96.079$$

For the Nikkei tree we have[6]

$$F_{0,1}(Q) = ¥0.4626 \times ¥23,706.10 + (1 - 0.4626) \times ¥17,561.91 = ¥20,404.03$$

The Dollar Perspective

Now we consider yen and Nikkei investments from the perspective of a dollar-based investor. The yen forward price is given by

$$\text{Exchange rate forward (\$/¥):} \quad F_{0,T}(x) = x_0 e^{(r-r_f)T} \qquad (22.24)$$

However, from the dollar perspective, the forward price of the Nikkei is not so straight-forward.

As discussed above, any Nikkei investment entails a combination of currency and index risk. To see why, suppose a dollar-based investor buys $e^{-\delta_Q T}$ units of the Nikkei and holds it for T years. The actual steps in this transaction are as follows:

1. Exchange $Q_0 x_0 e^{-\delta_Q T}$ dollars into yen (this is enough dollars to buy $e^{-\delta_Q T}$ units of the index).

2. Buy $e^{-\delta_Q T}$ units of the Nikkei index and hold for T periods.

3. Dividends are paid continuously over time and reinvested in the index; after T years we have an additional $e^{\delta_Q T}$ shares.

4. After T years sell the index and convert back into dollars.

The time-T value of the investment, denominated in dollars, is

$$Y(T) = x_T Q_T$$

The payoff is a *combination* of yen and Nikkei risk; we will call this investment the **currency-translated index.** Here is a point that is crucial for understanding what follows: *From the perspective of a dollar-based investor, the dollar-translated price of a yen-denominated asset, Y_T, is just like any other dollar-denominated asset.* However, Q_T is *not* the price of an asset for a dollar-based investor, because there is no simple way to obtain the risk of Q without also bearing currency risk.

---

[6]The calculation shown here uses rounded numbers and therefore does not exactly equal ¥20,404.03.

If you are not convinced that Y_T really is like any other dollar-denominated asset, consider the following thought experiment. Suppose you learn of a new stock, traded on a U.S. exchange, called "As American as Apple Pie, Inc." (AAAPI). The price is in dollars, just like any other domestic stock. You decide to investigate the stock and, to your surprise, you learn that the company is actually an American Depositary Receipt (ADR) for the Nikkei index.[7] The sole asset of this company is shares of the Nikkei, translated into dollars at the current exchange rate, and held in trust. The value at any time is $Y_t = x_t Q_t$ and it has a dividend yield of δ_Q. This ADR trades just like a dollar-denominated stock, because it *is* a dollar-denominated stock. Had you not investigated, you would never have known that you were holding a currency-translated yen-denominated stock.

This thought experiment is important, because it tells us that, for a dollar-based investor, the forward price for Y is given by[8]

$$F_{0,T}(Y) = Y_0 e^{(r-\delta_Q)T} \tag{22.25}$$

Since we can trade shares of AAAPI, we can undertake arbitrage if the forward price is anything other than equation (22.25). Similarly, the prepaid forward price on the currency-translated index is

$$F_{0,T}^P(Y) = x_0 Q_0 e^{-\delta_Q T} \tag{22.26}$$

In order to obtain Nikkei risk without currency risk, we need to combine the dollar-translated Nikkei with a position in forward yen contracts. Intuitively, we want to invest in Y and use currency contracts to hedge exchange rate risk. Let $V_{t,T}(Y_t, x_t; T)$ represent the price of a claim that, at maturity, pays the dollar value of the Nikkei. The boundary condition for this security is

$$V_{T,T}(Y_T, x_T; T) = \bar{x}\frac{Y_T}{x_T} \tag{22.27}$$

where $\bar{x}$ is an arbitrary exchange rate determined in advance. The boundary condition says that we will receive Y_T, the dollar-translated Nikkei, convert it to yen by multiplying by $1/x_T$, and then convert back to dollars at the rate $\bar{x}$. (Since the only purpose of $\bar{x}$ is to convert yen to dollars, the value is arbitrary and we can set it to 1. In practice the contract can call for any fixed exchange rate.) Prior to time T, the market-maker

---

[7]In simplest terms, an ADR is a claim to a trust containing a foreign stock. ADRs are a common means for investors in one country to buy a stock trading in another country.

[8]We saw in Chapter 20 that if S and Q are asset prices, then the forward price for SQ contained a covariance term. You may be wondering why there is no such covariance term in equation (22.26). In general, if an asset with price S_0 is traded and can be held by investors, then its forward price is $S_0 e^{(r-\delta)T}$. This is a no-arbitrage result. In the discussion in Chapter 20, we assume that S and Q are both prices of assets that can be held directly by investors. In that case SQ does not represent the price of an asset. In the discussion here, xQ is the price of an asset that can be held directly by investors, but Q cannot be held directly. In general, S, Q, and SQ cannot all simultaneously be the prices of traded assets.

hedges the value of the security using both the dollar-translated Nikkei and exchange rate contracts. Equation (22.27) makes it clear why quantos are said to be derivatives that depend on the ratio or product of two assets.[9]

We can price this contract by using Proposition 21.1. That proposition implies that we obtain the forward price for Y_T/x_T by multiplying the forward price for Y by the forward price for $1/x$, and adjusting the dividend yield to take account of the covariance between x and Y.

To apply Proposition 21.1 we need to know the forward price of $1/x$ for *dollar-denominated* investors. We can obtain the forward price for $1/x$ using Proposition 20.3. This gives[10]

$$F_{t,T}(1/x) = \frac{1}{x_0} e^{(r_f - r + s^2)(T-t)}$$

We also need to know the covariance between x and Y. Using Itô's Lemma, that covariance is

$$\frac{1}{dt}[dx - E(dx)][dY - E(dY)] = \rho s \sigma_Q + s^2 \tag{22.28}$$

In applying Proposition 21.1, we have $b = -1$; hence, when we compute the forward price for Q we replace δ_Q with $\delta_Q - (-1)(\rho s \sigma_Q + s^2)$.

Putting this all together, using Proposition 21.1 and with $\bar{x} = 1$ we have

$$V_{t,T}(Y_t, x_t; T) = \frac{1}{x_t} e^{(r_f - r + s^2)(T-t)} Q_t x_t e^{(r - \delta_Q - \rho s \sigma_Q - s^2)(T-t)}$$
$$= Q_t e^{(r_f - \delta_Q - \rho s \sigma_Q)(T-t)} \tag{22.29}$$

The dollar-denominated forward price for the Nikkei index is the same as the yen-denominated forward price, with a covariance correction. The prepaid quanto index forward price is thus

$$F_{0,T}^P(Q) = Q_0 e^{(r_f - \delta_Q - \rho \sigma_Q s - r)T} \tag{22.30}$$

The role of the covariance term in equation (22.29) is intuitive. Consider an investor who buys the cash Nikkei index and ultimately converts yen back to dollars. Suppose the index and the exchange rate (measured in dollars/yen) are positively

----

[9]If the market-maker hedges a claim with value V using x and Y, the claim value must satisfy the mulitvariate Black-Scholes equation. In this case, the equation is

$$0.5s^2 x^2 V_{xx} + 0.5(s^2 + \sigma^2 + 2\rho s \sigma)Y^2 V_{YY} + (s^2 + \rho s \sigma)Yx V_{Yx}$$
$$+ V_x(r - r_f)x + V_Y(r - \delta)Y + V_t - rV = 0$$

[10]In this calculation we start with the forward price for x from the dollar perspective and convert it to the forward price for $1/x$. As a result, the forward price for $1/x$ given here is different from that given by equation (22.23), which is the appropriate forward price given a yen perspective.

correlated. When the index does well, there are many yen to exchange. If ρ is positive, on average the exchange rate is favorable when there are many yen to exchange. When the index does poorly, there are fewer yen to exchange so the decline in the exchange rate does not matter as much. Thus, other things equal, the positive correlation systematically benefits the unhedged investment in the Nikkei relative to a contract with a fixed exchange rate. Consequently, if the exchange rate is fixed, as in a quanto contract, the price for the index settling in dollars will be lower in order to compensate the buyer for the loss of beneficial correlation between the index and exchange rate.

Example 22.8 Using equation (22.29) and the information in Table 22.4, the yen forward price is

$$F_{0,1} = x_0 e^{(r-r_f)t} = 0.01\$/\yen e^{(0.08-0.04)} = 0.010408\$/\yen$$

The forward price for the currency-translated Nikkei is

$$F_{0,1} = x_0 Q_0 e^{(r-\delta_Q)t} = 0.01\$/\yen \times \yen 20,000 e^{(0.08-0.02)} = \$212.367$$

Finally, using equation (22.29), the quanto forward price is

$$V_{0,1}(\$200, 0.01\$/\yen) = \yen 20,000 e^{(0.04-0.02-0.2\times 0.1\times 0.15)}$$

$$= \yen 20,342.91$$

This is lower than the yen-denominated Nikkei forward price of ¥20,404 in Example 22.7. ⚹

A Binomial Model for the Dollar-Denominated Investor

As another way to understand quanto pricing, we can construct a binomial tree that simultaneously models the currency-translated index and the exchange rate. In addition to this particular application of two-variable binomial trees, some options have prices that depend on two state variables.

In Figure 22.3 we constructed separate binomial trees for the yen-based investor. For the dollar-based investor we need to construct a tree that takes account of the correlation between the Nikkei and the yen. We can do so by first modeling the behavior of the yen in the usual way, and then, *conditional upon the yen*, model the movement in the Nikkei.[11] Since for each yen move there are two Nikkei moves, the tree will have four binomial nodes. We will denote these as $\{uu, ud, du, dd\}$, with the first letter denoting the yen move and the second the Nikkei move. We have a choice of constructing a joint tree for the yen and Nikkei or the yen and dollar-translated Nikkei, but we obtain the

---

[11]This is similar to the two-variable binomial model in Rubinstein (1994). See also Boyle et al. (1989) for a procedure to generate n-asset binomial trees.

same answer either way. Here we will model the yen and Nikkei. Problem 22.17 asks you to jointly model the yen and dollar-translated Nikkei.

The basic idea underlying the joint binomial model for x and Q is as follows. If x and Q are lognormal, they evolve like this:

$$x_h = x_0 e^{(r-r_f)h + s\sqrt{h}Z_1} \qquad (22.31a)$$

$$Q_h = Q_0 e^{(r-\delta_Q)h + \sigma_Q\sqrt{h}Z_2} \qquad (22.31b)$$

In the standard binomial model, we simply approximate Z_1 and Z_2 binomially, so that $Z_i = \pm 1$. However, we want to induce correlation between Z_1 and Z_2. We can create correlation by using the Cholesky decomposition discussed in Chapter 19. Begin by rewriting equation (22.31) using equation (19.17):

$$x_h = x_0 e^{(r-r_f)h + s\sqrt{h}\epsilon_1} \qquad (22.32a)$$

$$Q_h = Q_0 e^{(r_f-\delta_Q)h + \sigma_Q\sqrt{h}(\epsilon_1\rho + \epsilon_2\sqrt{1-\rho^2})} \qquad (22.32b)$$

Thus, $Z_1 = \epsilon_1$ and $Z_2 = \rho\epsilon_1 + \sqrt{1-\rho^2}\epsilon_2$. By construction, this Z_1 and Z_2 have correlation ρ. Now we construct the binomial tree by setting $\epsilon_1 = \pm 1$ (the exchange rate moves up or down) and $\epsilon_2 = \pm 1$ (the index moves up or down). There are four possible outcomes, which we will label A ($\epsilon_1 = 1; \epsilon_2 = 1$), B ($\epsilon_1 = 1; \epsilon_2 = -1$), C ($\epsilon_1 = -1; \epsilon_2 = 1$), and D ($\epsilon_1 = -1; \epsilon_2 = -1$).

For a dollar-based investor, the possible yen moves are

$$x_A = x_B = x_0 e^{(r-r_f)h + s\sqrt{h}} = x_0 u \qquad (22.33a)$$

$$x_C = x_D = x_0 e^{(r-r_f)h - s\sqrt{h}} = x_0 d \qquad (22.33b)$$

For each yen move, there are two Nikkei moves:

$$Q_A = Q_0 e^{(r_f-\delta_Q)h + \sigma_Q\sqrt{h}(\rho+\sqrt{1-\rho^2})} = Q_0 A \qquad (22.34a)$$

$$Q_B = Q_0 e^{(r_f-\delta_Q)h + \sigma_Q\sqrt{h}(\rho-\sqrt{1-\rho^2})} = Q_0 B \qquad (22.34b)$$

$$Q_C = Q_0 e^{(r_f-\delta_Q)h + \sigma_Q\sqrt{h}(-\rho+\sqrt{1-\rho^2})} = Q_0 C \qquad (22.34c)$$

$$Q_D = Q_0 e^{(r_f-\delta_Q)h + \sigma_Q\sqrt{h}(-\rho-\sqrt{1-\rho^2})} = Q_0 D \qquad (22.34d)$$

Finally, we have to determine the risk-neutral probabilities associated with the nodes. As in Chapter 10, the risk-neutral probability for an up move of the currency is

$$p = \frac{e^{(r-r_f)h} - d}{u - d} \qquad (22.35)$$

where u and d are implied by equation (22.33a) and (22.33b). The risk-neutral probability for an up move in the currency is 0.4750.

Recall that the risk-neutral probability arises from the requirement that an investment in the asset earn the risk-free rate. Specifically, for the currency, we consider an investment in the yen-denominated risk-free asset, hedged to remove currency risk when the investment is turned back into dollars. This investment earns the dollar-denominated risk-free return if the probability of an up move is given by equation (22.35).

FIGURE 22.4

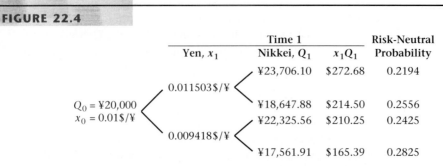

	Yen, x_1	Time 1 Nikkei, Q_1	$x_1 Q_1$	Risk-Neutral Probability
		¥23,706.10	$272.68	0.2194
	0.011503$/¥			
Q_0 = ¥20,000		¥18,647.88	$214.50	0.2556
x_0 = 0.01$/¥		¥22,325.56	$210.25	0.2425
	0.009418$/¥			
		¥17,561.91	$165.39	0.2825

The binomial process for the dollar/yen exchange rate (x) and the Nikkei (Q). The last two columns contain the value of the currency-translated Nikkei and the risk-neutral probability of each node, computed using equations (22.35) and (22.37).

We need a similar argument for the Nikkei. Since we cannot own the Nikkei index without bearing currency risk, we model an investment in the dollar-translated Nikkei. Let p^* denote the probability of an up move in the Nikkei, conditional on the move in the yen. We require that the dollar-translated Nikkei investment earn the dollar-denominated risk-free rate. This gives us

$$x_u Q_A p p^* + x_u Q_B p (1 - p^*) + x_d Q_C (1 - p) p^*$$
$$+ x_d Q_D (1 - p)(1 - p^*) = x_0 Q_0 e^{(r - \delta_Q)h} \quad (22.36)$$

Solving for p^* gives

$$p^* = \frac{x_0 Q_0 e^{(r - \delta_Q)h} - x_u Q_B p - x_d Q_D (1 - p)}{p x_u (Q_A - Q_B) + (1 - p) x_d (Q_C - Q_D)} \quad (22.37)$$
$$= \frac{e^{(r - \delta_Q)h} - u B p - d D(1 - p)}{p u (A - B) + (1 - p) d (C - D)}$$

This expression is a generalization of the one-variable formula for a risk-neutral probability, taking account of the two up and two down states for Q.

Figure 22.4 depicts the binomial tree constructed using equations (22.33) and (22.34), and probabilties of each node constructed using equations (22.35) and (22.37). The quanto forward price can be constructed as the expectation $E(Y_1/x_1)$.

Example 22.9   Using Figure 22.4 we can compute forward prices for the yen, the dollar-translated Nikkei, and the quanto Nikkei. The risk-neutral probability of an up move in the yen is 0.4750. The yen forward price is

$$F_{0,1}(x) = 0.4750 \times 0.011503\$/¥ + (1 - 0.4750) \times 0.009418\$/¥ = 0.010408\$/¥$$

The forward price for the currency-translated Nikkei is

$$F_{0,1}(xQ) = 0.2194 \times \$272.68 + 0.2556 \times \$214.50$$
$$+ 0.2425 \times \$210.25 + 0.2825 \times \$165.39 = \$212.367$$

Finally, the quanto forward price is

$$F_{0,1}(Q) = 0.2194 \times \frac{\$272.68}{0.011503\$/\yen} + 0.2556 \times \frac{\$214.50}{0.011503\$/\yen}$$

$$+0.2425 \times \frac{\$210.25}{0.009418\$/\yen} + 0.2825 \times \frac{\$165.39}{0.009418\$/\yen} = \yen20,342.91$$

All of the prices computed from the tree match those in Example 22.8. ≋

The tree in Figure 22.4 can be extended to multiple periods. Rubinstein (1994) shows that in general, with n steps, there are $(n+1)^2$ nodes; for example, with two steps there are nine nodes. To see why, if we add another binomial period to the tree, there are $4^2 = 16$ combinations of the up-down moves ($AA, AB, \ldots, DD$). The order of the moves is irrelevant, so, for example, $AB = BA$. This equivalence eliminates $n \times (n-1) = 6$ nodes, leaving 10. Further, from equation (22.34), $AB = CD$. Because $n = 2$, this leaves $(n+1)^2 = 9$ unique nodes.

22.5 CURRENCY-LINKED OPTIONS

There are several common ways to construct options on foreign assets, for which the return has an exchange rate component.[12] The different variants permit investors to assume different amounts of currency and equity risk. In this section we examine four variants and their pricing formulas. We will continue to use the notation and numbers from Table 22.4.

Before we discuss particular currency-linked options, recall the result from Chapter 12, equation (12.5), and Chapter 14, equation (14.16), that an option can be priced using only the prepaid forward prices for the underlying asset and strike asset, and the relative volatility of the two.[13] The intuition for this result is that a market-maker could hedge an option position using the two prepaid forwards, neither of which, by definition, makes any payouts. In the discussions to follow we will use this result to simplify the valuation of seemingly complex options.

------

[12]This section draws heavily from Reiner (1992), in particular adopting Reiner's terminology for the different kinds of options.

[13]To convince yourself of this, note that

$$\text{BSCall}(S, K, \sigma, r, T, \delta) = \text{BSCall}(Se^{-\delta T}, Ke^{-rT}, \sigma, 0, T, 0)$$

This equality will hold for any inputs you try.

Nikkei Put Warrants

An example of quanto options is the Nikkei 225 put warrants that traded on the American Stock Exchange beginning in 1990. Ryan and Granovsky (2000) provide an interesting account of the history of these options, in which Nikkei risk was repackaged and transformed several times by various global financial players.

Japanese institutional investors in the late 1980s bought Nikkei bull notes. These were bonds that carried a high coupon and contained an embedded written put spread: The note principal was not paid in full if the Nikkei fell below ¥32,000. The issuer of the notes was a European bank that sold the embedded put spread to an investment bank and entered into a currency swap to achieve dollar-denominated financing without any Nikkei risk. Japanese buyers were willing to pay a price that made it profitable for the European bank to issue the notes and hedge the resulting exposure.

The investment bank, having bought the put spread, had short exposure to the Nikkei. It sold dollar-denominated Nikkei puts to a European sovereign, which in turn sold dollar-denominated Nikkei puts to investors who wanted dollar-denominated Nikkei exposure in the form of SEC-registered securities without investment bank credit risk. (The sovereign issuer bore the investment bank credit risk and the notes carried sovereign risk.)

The net result of this chain of transactions was that Japanese institutional investors were betting—via the bull notes—that the Nikkei would rise. Buyers of the dollar-denominated Nikkei put warrants were betting that the Nikkei would fall. In the end, the Nikkei index suffered a long decline and the put warrant buyers won the bet.

Foreign Equity Call Struck in Foreign Currency

If we want to speculate on a foreign index, one possibility is to buy an option completely denominated in a foreign currency. The value of this option at expiration is

$$V(Q_T, T) = \max(0, Q_T - K_f)$$

where K_f denotes the strike denominated in the foreign currency.

As an example, we might have a 1-year call option to buy the Nikkei index by paying ¥19,500. An investor based in the foreign currency would use this kind of option; thus, it can be priced using the Black-Scholes formula from the perspective of the foreign currency. Only yen inputs—the yen-denominated interest rate and the Nikkei volatility and dividend yield—enter the pricing formula. The dollar price can be obtained by converting the option price at the current exchange rate.

$$C_{¥} = Q_0 e^{-\delta_Q t} N(d_1) - K_f e^{-r_f t} N(d_2) \tag{22.38}$$

$$d_1 = \frac{\ln(Q_0 e^{-\delta_Q t} / K_f e^{-r_f t}) + \frac{1}{2}\sigma_Q^2 t}{\sigma_Q \sqrt{t}}$$

$$d_2 = d_1 - \sigma_Q \sqrt{t}$$

Thus, we price this option by using the Black-Scholes formula with inputs appropriate for the asset being denominated in a different currency.

Example 22.10 Using the parameters in Table 22.4 and assuming a strike price of ¥19,500, we price the call by using the Black-Scholes formula and setting $S = ¥20,000$ (the current Nikkei index price), $K = ¥19,500$, $\sigma_Q = 0.15$ (the Nikkei volatility in yen), $r_f = 0.04$, $T - t = 1$, and $\delta_Q = 0.02$ (the dividend yield on the Nikkei). We obtain a call price of BSCall(¥20,000; ¥19,500; 0.15; 0.04; 1; 0.02) = ¥1632.16. The dollar price is $16.32. ≋

Foreign Equity Call Struck in Domestic Currency

Suppose we have a call option to buy the Nikkei but we denominate the strike, K, in *dollars*. If we exercise the option, we pay K dollars to acquire the Nikkei, which is worth $x_T Q_T$. Thus, at expiration, the option is worth

$$V(x_T Q_T, T) = \max(0, x_T Q_T - K)$$

In order to price this option, recognize that $Y(T) = x_T Q_T$, the currency-translated index, is priced like any domestic asset. The prepaid forward price for the currency-translated index is, from equation (22.26), $x_0 Q_0 e^{-\delta_Q T}$. The prepaid forward price for the strike is $K e^{-rT}$. The value of the option will depend upon the distribution of $x_T Q_T$; thus, the volatility that enters the option pricing formula is that of the currency-translated index. The volatility of $x_t Q_t$ is

$$v = \sqrt{\sigma_Q^2 + s^2 + 2\rho\sigma_Q s}$$

Using this volatility and the prepaid forward prices we have

$$C = x_0 Q_0 e^{-\delta T} N(d_1) - e^{-rt} K N(d_2) \tag{22.39}$$

$$d_1 = \frac{\ln(x_0 Q_0 e^{-\delta T} / e^{-rt} K) + \frac{1}{2}v^2 t}{v \sqrt{t}}$$

$$d_2 = d_1 - v\sqrt{t}$$

You can interpret this formula in terms of prepaid forward prices or as the Black-Scholes formula with $x_0 Q_0$ as the stock price, δ_Q as the dividend yield, v as the volatility, the domestic interest rate r as the risk-free rate, and K as the strike price.

Example 22.11   Using the parameters in Table 22.4, the volatility is

$$v = \sqrt{0.15^2 + 0.1^2 + (2 \times 0.2 \times 0.15 \times 0.1)} = 0.1962$$

and assuming a strike price of \$195, we price the call using prepaid forwards as

$$\text{BSCall}(x_0 Q_0 e^{-\delta T}, K e^{-rT}, v, 0, T, 0)$$
$$= \text{BSCall}(0.01\$/¥ \times ¥20{,}000 e^{-0.02}, \$195 \times e^{-0.08}, 0.1962, 0, 1, 0) = \$24.0719$$

❧

Fixed Exchange Rate Foreign Equity Call

Suppose we have a foreign equity call denominated in the foreign currency, but with the option proceeds to be repatriated at a predetermined exchange rate. This is a quanto option, analogous to the quanto forward, with the value of the option translated into dollars at a fixed exchange rate. Let $\bar{x}$ represent this rate. The payoff to this option with strike price K_f (denominated in the foreign currency) is

$$V(Q_T, T) = \bar{x} \times \max(0, Q_T - K_f)$$
$$= \max(0, \bar{x} Q_T - \bar{x} K_f)$$

Once again we can construct the pricing formula by thinking in terms of forward prices for the underlying and strike assets. From a dollar perspective, the underlying asset, $\bar{x} Q_T$, is a quanto index investment. The strike asset is simply a fixed number of dollars, translated at the rate $\bar{x}$. Since $\bar{x}$ is just a scale factor, we can set $\bar{x} = 1$.

Because the exchange rate is fixed, the volatility that affects the value of the option is that of the foreign-currency–denominated foreign index, σ_Q. We can obtain the pricing formula by using the prepaid forwards for the underlying and strike asset:

$$C = F_{0,T}^P(Q) N(d_1) - e^{-rT} K_f N(d_2) \tag{22.40}$$
$$d_1 = \frac{\ln[F_{0,t}^P(Q)/e^{-rT} K_f] + \frac{1}{2}\sigma_Q^2 T}{\sigma_Q \sqrt{T}}$$
$$d_2 = d_1 - \sigma_Q \sqrt{t}$$

The formula for $F_{0,T}^P(Q)$ is given in equation (22.30). Note that all values are dollar-denominated since $\bar{x}$ implicitly multiplies all prices. By substituting for $F_{0,t}^P$, equation (22.40) is the Black-Scholes formula with Q_0 as the stock price, $\delta_Q + \rho s \sigma_Q + r - r_f$ as the dividend yield, the domestic interest rate r as the risk-free rate, K_f as the strike, and σ_Q as the volatility.

Example 22.12   Using the parameters in Table 22.4 and assuming a strike price of ¥19,500 with a fixed exchange rate of $\bar{x} = 0.01\$/¥$, we price the call by using the

Black-Scholes formula. We obtain

$$\text{BSCall}(F^P_{0,T}(Q), K_f e^{-rT}, \sigma_Q, 0, T, 0) =$$
$$\text{BSCall}(0.01\$/¥ \times ¥20,000 \times e^{-(0.02+0.2\times0.1\times0.15+0.08-0.04)}, 0.01\$/¥ \times ¥19,500 e^{-0.08},$$
$$0.15, 0, 1, 0) = \$15.3187$$

Problem 22.6 asks you to verify that you obtain the same answer with $x_0 Q_0$ as the underlying asset and an appropriate choice of the dividend yield. ❧

Equity-Linked Foreign Exchange Call

If we invest in a foreign asset, we might like to insure against low exchange rates when we convert back to the domestic currency, while still having the ability to profit from favorable exchange rates. Buying an exchange rate put is insufficient because the quantity of currency to be exchanged is uncertain. What we want is an option that guarantees a minimum exchange rate *when we convert the asset value back to the domestic currency*. Such an option must therefore protect a variable quantity of currency. This is an *equity-linked foreign exchange option*, which is another example of a quanto option.

Let K be the minimum exchange rate. Then the payoff to such an insured position would be

$$Q_T x_T + Q_T \max(0, K - x_T) = Q_T K + Q_T \max(0, x_T - K)$$
$$= Q_T K + \max(0, Q_T x_T - Q_T K) \tag{22.41}$$

The expression to the left of the equal sign in equation (22.41) is the unprotected currency-translated Nikkei investment plus Q_T exchange rate puts with strike K. The equivalent expression on the right is a quanto investment with the fixed exchange rate equal to K, plus Q_T exchange rate calls. Either way, the protection entails receiving the payoff to a random number of options. All cash flows are denominated in the home currency.

There are at least two ways to value the payoff in equation (22.41): (1) By using Proposition 21.1 and (2) by using the prepaid forward approach. Using Proposition 21.1, we value $Q_T \times \max(0, x_T - K)$ as a currency call with a change of numeraire. We will pursue that approach; Problem 22.7 asks you to derive the same formula using prepaid forward prices.

The forward price for Q_T is the quanto forward price, equation (22.29). The put is a standard currency call denominated in the home currency. Since it is a currency option, the dividend yield is the foreign interest rate. To change the numeraire we subtract $\rho\sigma s$, the covariance between Q and x, from the dividend yield, r_f. Thus, we price the payoff $Q_T \times \max(0, x_T - K)$ by multiplying $Q_0 e^{(r_f - \delta_Q - \rho\sigma s)T}$, the quanto forward price, times the Black-Scholes currency call formula with r_f replaced by $r_f - \rho\sigma s$. This gives

$$C = Q_0 e^{(r_f - \delta_Q - \rho\sigma s)T} \left[x_0 e^{-(r_f - \rho\sigma s)T} N(d_1) - e^{-rT} K N(d_2) \right]$$
$$= x_0 Q_0 e^{-\delta_Q T} N(d_1) - K Q_0 e^{-(r + \delta_Q + \rho\sigma s - r_f)T} N(d_2) \tag{22.42}$$

$$d_1 = \frac{\ln(x_0/K) + (r - r_f + \rho\sigma s + 0.5s^2)T}{s\sqrt{T}}$$

$$d_2 = d_1 - s\sqrt{T}$$

This is the price of a call option with $x_0 Q_0$ as the stock price, $K Q_0$ as the strike price, $r + \delta_Q + \rho\sigma s - r_f$ as the risk-free rate, δ_Q as the dividend yield, and s as the volatility. It is perhaps surprising that only the volatility of the exchange rate matters. This occurs because the underlying option is a currency option and the change of numeraire does not affect the volatility.

Example 22.13 Using the parameters in Table 22.4 and assuming a strike price of 0.00975\$/¥, we price the call by using the Black-Scholes formula. The price of the underlying asset is $x_0 Q_0 = 0.01\$/¥ \times ¥20{,}000 = \$200$, the strike price is $0.00975\$/¥ \times ¥20{,}000 = \$195$, the risk-free rate is replaced by $r + \delta_Q + \rho\sigma s - r_f = 0.08 + 0.02 + 0.2 \times 0.15 \times 0.1 - 0.04 = 0.063$, and the dividend yield is $\delta_Q = 0.02$. The value of the option in equation (22.42) is

$$\text{BSCall}(\$200, \$195, 0.10, 0.063, 1, 0.02) = \$15.7287 \qquad ⚞$$

22.6 OTHER MULTIVARIATE OPTIONS

Quantos are a particular kind of claim with a payoff dependent on the price of two assets. There are many other options for which the payoff depends on two or more assets. In this section we examine several kinds of multivariate options that can be priced either by modifying the Black-Scholes formula or by using the bivariate normal distribution. We will also see how to price some of these options binomially. Throughout this section, we assume that the assets S and Q follow the processes given by equations (22.1) and (22.2).

Exchange Options

We saw in Section 14.6 that exchange options, in which the strike price is the price of a risky asset, can be priced with a simple modification of the Black-Scholes formula. Here we will use a change of numeraire to see why this is so.

At maturity, an exchange option with price $V(S_t, Q_t, t)$ pays

$$\begin{aligned} V(S_T, Q_T, T) &= \max(S_T - Q_T, 0) \\ &= Q_T \times \max(S_T/Q_T - 1, 0) \end{aligned} \qquad (22.43)$$

This payoff is like receiving a random number, Q_T, of options in which the underlying asset is S_T/Q_T and the strike price is \$1. We can price this option by applying Propositions 20.4 and 21.1.

First, consider the price of an option with S/Q as the underlying asset. We can price this option using the Black-Scholes formula with the lease rate for S/Q in place of the dividend yield and the variance of $\ln(S/Q)$ as the variance. Propositions 20.3 and 20.4 imply that the lease rate for S/Q is

$$\delta^* = r + \delta - \delta_Q - \sigma_Q^2 + \rho\sigma\sigma_Q \tag{22.44}$$

and the variance is

$$\hat{\sigma}^2 = \sigma^2 + \sigma_Q^2 - 2\rho\sigma\sigma_Q \tag{22.45}$$

Denote the value of this option by $W(S/Q, t)$. Its price is

$$W(S/Q, t) = S/Qe^{-\delta^*(T-t)}N(\hat{d}_1) - e^{-rt}N(\hat{d}_2) \tag{22.46}$$

$$\hat{d}_1 = \frac{\ln(S/Q) + (r - \delta^* + 0.5\hat{\sigma}^2)(T-t)}{\hat{\sigma}\sqrt{T-t}} \tag{22.47}$$

$$\hat{d}_2 = \hat{d}_1 - \hat{\sigma}\sqrt{T-t} \tag{22.48}$$

Now we want to value the option with payoff $Q \times W(S/Q, t)$. To do this we apply Proposition 21.1. The covariance between Q and S/Q is $\rho\sigma\sigma_Q - \sigma_Q^2$. Thus, applying Proposition 21.1, we replace δ^* with

$$\delta^* - (\rho\sigma\sigma_Q - \sigma_Q^2) = r + \delta - \delta_Q$$

Finally, multiplying W by $Qe^{(r-\delta_a)(T-t)}$ gives

$$V(S, Q, t) = Se^{-\delta(T-t)}N(\hat{d}_1) - Qe^{-\delta_Q(T-t)}N(\hat{d}_2) \tag{22.49}$$

$$\hat{d}_1 = \frac{\ln(S/Q) + (\delta_Q - \delta + 0.5\hat{\sigma}^2)(T-t)}{\hat{\sigma}\sqrt{T-t}}$$

$$\hat{d}_2 = \hat{d}_1 - \hat{\sigma}\sqrt{T-t}$$

This is the formula for an exchange option from Section 14.6. The risk-free rate is replaced by δ_Q and the volatility by $\hat{\sigma}$.

American exchange options can be valued using a two-state variable binomial tree, as in Section 22.4. However, it is also possible to value an American exchange option using a *one-variable* binomial tree. Rubinstein (1991b) shows that a standard binomial tree can be constructed setting the volatility equal to $\hat{\sigma}$, the dividend yield equal to δ, and the risk-free rate equal to δ_Q. This result can also be demonstrated by using arguments based on Propositions 20.4 and 21.1.

Options on the Best of Two Assets

Suppose an investor allocates a portfolio to both the S&P index and the currency-translated Nikkei. Allocating the portfolio to the index that the investor believes will obtain the highest return is called **market-timing.** A perfect market-timer would invest in the S&P when it outperformed the Nikkei and the Nikkei when it outperformed the

S&P. What is the value of being able to infallibly select the portfolio with the superior performance?

We can answer this question by valuing an option giving us the greater of the two returns. This option would have the payoff $\max(S_T, Q_T)$, where S is the S&P index and the Q the Nikkei index. Note that

$$\max(S_T, Q_T) = Q_T + \max(S_T - Q_T, 0)$$

Thus, an option on the best of two assets is the same as owning one asset plus an option to exchange that asset for the other asset. As discussed in Chapter 9, $\max(S_T - Q_T, 0)$ can be viewed either as a call on S with strike asset Q, or as a put on Q, with strike asset S.

An investor allocating funds between the S&P index and the Nikkei index might also want to include cash in the comparison, so that there is a guaranteed minimum return. If K represents this minimum return, the payoff for a perfect market-timer is then

$$\max(K, S_T, Q_T)$$

This option, called a **rainbow option,** has no simple one-variable solution. Instead, valuing this option requires the use of the bivariate normal distribution.[14] The bivariate normal distribution is defined as

$$\text{Prob}(z_1 < a, z_2 < b; \rho) = NN(a, b; \rho) \tag{22.50}$$

where z_1 and z_2 are standard normal random variables with correlation coefficient ρ. You may recall that we used the bivariate normal distribution in Chapter 14 to value compound options.

The formula for a rainbow option is

$$\text{RainbowCall}(S, Q, K, \sigma, s, \rho, \delta, \delta_Q, T - t)$$
$$= Se^{-\delta(T-t)} \left\{ N(d_{SQ}) - NN[-d_1(S), d_{SQ}, (\rho\sigma_Q - \sigma)/\hat{\sigma}] \right\}$$
$$+ Qe^{-\delta_Q(T-t)} \left\{ N(d_{QS}) - NN[-d_1(Q), d_{QS}, (\rho\sigma - \sigma_Q)/\hat{\sigma}] \right\} \tag{22.51}$$
$$+ Ke^{-r(T-t)} NN[-d_2(S), -d_2(Q), \rho]$$

where

$$d_1(S) = \frac{\ln(S/K) + (r - \delta + 0.5\sigma^2)(T - t)}{\sigma\sqrt{T - t}}$$

$$d_1(Q) = \frac{\ln(Q/K) + (r - \delta_Q + 0.5\sigma_Q^2)(T - t)}{\sigma_Q\sqrt{T - t}}$$

$$d_2(S) = d_1(S) - \sigma\sqrt{T - t}$$

$$d_2(Q) = d_1(Q) - \sigma_Q\sqrt{T - t}$$

---

[14] Stulz (1982) first valued a rainbow option. See also Rubinstein (1991c) for a discussion.

$$d_{SQ} = \frac{\ln(S/Q) + (\delta_Q - \delta + 0.5\hat{\sigma}^2)(T - t)}{\hat{\sigma}\sqrt{T - t}}$$

$$d_{QS} = \frac{\ln(Q/S) + (\delta - \delta_Q + 0.5\hat{\sigma}^2)(T - t)}{\hat{\sigma}\sqrt{T - t}}$$

$$\hat{\sigma} = \sqrt{\sigma^2 + \sigma_Q^2 - 2\rho\sigma\sigma_Q}$$

You can understand this daunting formula by recognizing that, at maturity, the option must be worth either S, Q, or K. By setting $t = T$, you can verify that the formula satisfies this boundary condition. The formula for an option that pays $\min(S, Q, K)$—a rainbow put—is obtained by putting a minus sign in front of each "d" argument in the normal and bivariate normal functions.

Certain related options can be valued using the rainbow option formula.[15] For example, consider an option on the maximum of two assets with the payoff

$$\max[0, \max(S, Q) - K]$$

This is equal to $\max(S, Q, K) - K$, which has the value

$$\text{RainbowCall}(S, Q, K, \sigma, \sigma_Q, \rho, \delta, \delta_Q, r, T - t) - Ke^{-r(T-t)}$$

Some options that seem as if they might be valued using the rainbow option formula, however, cannot be. For example, in Chapter 17 we discussed the valuation of peak-load electricity plants and encountered spread options, which have the payoff

$$\max(0, S - Q - K)$$

While there are approximations for valuing such an option (see Haug, 1998, pp. 59–61), more exact solutions require Monte Carlo or two-state binomial trees.

Basket Options

Basket options have payoffs that depend upon the average of two or more asset prices. Basket options are frequently used in currency hedging. A multinational firm dealing in multiple currencies, for example, might care only about hedging the average exchange rate, rather than each exchange rate individually. As another example, an option on the S&P index might pay off only if the S&P outperforms an average of the currency-translated Nikkei and Dax (German stock) indices. With equal weights on the Nikkei and Dax, the payoff to such an option would be

$$\max[0, S_{S\&P} - 0.5 \times (S_{Nikkei} + S_{Dax})]$$

You may be able to guess the problem with deriving a simple formula to value such a payoff. The arithmetic average of two indices does not follow geometric Brownian

---

[15]Rubinstein (1991c) provides a thorough discussion of these related options, as well as discussing which options *cannot* be valued as rainbow options.

motion. (In fact, if an index is an arithmetic average of stocks, the index itself does not follow geometric Brownian motion. We have been making the common, yet inconsistent, assumption that both stocks and indices containing those stocks follow geometric Brownian motion.)

Because the payoff can depend on many random variables and there is no easy formula, Monte Carlo is a natural technique for valuing basket options. Moreover, basket options provide a natural application for the control variate method to speed up Monte Carlo. A basket option based on the geometric average can be valued using Black-Scholes with appropriate adjustments to the volatility and dividend yield. This price can then serve as a control variate for the more conventional basket option based on an arithmetic average.

CHAPTER SUMMARY

It is possible to build new derivative claims by using simpler claims as building blocks. Important building blocks include all-or-nothing options, which pay either cash or an asset under certain conditions. Assuming that prices are lognormal with constant volatility, it is straightforward to value cash-or-nothing and asset-or-nothing options both with and without barriers. Cash-or-nothing claims can be priced as discounted risk-neutral probabilities, and a change of numeraire can then be used to price asset-or-nothing options. These claims can be used to create, among other things, ordinary options, gap options, and barrier options. While these options are straightforward to price, they may be quite difficult to hedge because of discontinuities in the payoff created by the all-or-nothing characteristic.

Quantos are claims for which the payoff depends on the product or quotient of two prices. They can be priced using arguments developed in Chapters 20 and 21. Quantos can be used to remove the currency risk from an investment in a foreign stock index and thus are used in international investing. It is possible to construct bivariate binomial trees to price quantos. International investors can also use currency-linked options to tailor their exposure to currency. The standard currency options can be priced using prepaid forwards and change of numeraire.

Other options, such as rainbow and basket options, have payoffs depending on two or more asset prices. Some of these options have simple pricing formulas; others must be valued binomially, using Monte Carlo, or in some other way.

FURTHER READING

Mark Rubinstein and Eric Reiner published a series of papers on exotic options in *Risk* magazine in the early 1990s. These provide a comprehensive discussion of pricing formulas on a wide variety of options. Some of the material in this chapter is based directly on those papers, which can be hard to obtain but are available on Mark Rubinstein's website (**http://www.in-the-money.com**). Ingersoll (2000) also provides examples of the use of all-or-nothing options as building blocks. An alternative approach to two-state binomial pricing is detailed in Boyle et al. (1989).

If you are interested in more pricing formulas, Haug (1998) presents numerous formulas and discusses approximations when those simple formulas are not available. Wilmott (1998) also has a comprehensive discussion emphasizing the use of partial differential equations (which, as we have seen, underlie all derivatives pricing). Zhang (1998) and Briys and Bellala (1998) discuss exotic options, including many not discussed in this chapter. In practice, the hitting of a barrier is often determined on a daily or other periodic basis. Broadie et al. (1997) provide a simple correction term that makes the barrier pricing formulas more accurate when monitoring of the barrier is not continuous. One class of options we have not discussed is lookback options, which pay out based on the highest (or lowest) price over the life of the option. These are discussed in Goldman et al. (1979a) and Goldman et al. (1979b) and are covered in Problems 22.13 and 22.14.

PROBLEMS

22.1. A **collect-on-delivery call** (COD) costs zero initially, with the payoff at expiration being 0 if $S < K$, and $S - K - P$ if $S \geq K$. The problem in valuing the option is to determine P, the amount the option-holder pays if the option is in-the-money at expiration. The premium P is determined once and for all when the option is created. Let $S = \$100$, $K = \$100$, $r = 5\%$, $\sigma = 20\%$, $T - t = 1$ year, and $\delta = 0$.

    a. Value a European COD call option with the above inputs. (*Hint:* Recognize that you can construct the COD payoff by combining an ordinary call option and a cash-or-nothing call.)

    b. Compute delta and gamma for a COD option. (You may do this by computing the value of the option at slightly different prices and calculating delta and gamma directly, rather than by using a formula.) Consider different stock prices and times to expiration, in particular setting t close to T.

    c. How hard is it to hedge a COD option?

22.2. A **barrier COD** option is like a COD except that payment for the option occurs whenever a barrier is struck. Price a barrier COD put for the same values as in the previous problem, with a barrier of \$95 and a strike of \$90. Compute the delta and gamma for the paylater put. Compare the behavior of delta and gamma with that for a COD. Explain the differences, if any.

22.3. Verify that equation (22.7) satisfies the appropriate boundary conditions for $\text{Prob}(\underline{S}_T \leq H \text{ and } S_T > K)$.

22.4. Verify that equation (22.14) (for both cases $K > H$ and $K < H$) solves the boundary conditions for an up-and-in cash put.

22.5. Verify that as $T \to \infty$ in equations (22.20) and (22.21) you obtain equations (12.17) and (12.18), discussed in Chapter 12.

22.6. Verify in Example 22.12 that you obtain the same answer if you use $x_0 Q_0$ as the stock price, $\delta_Q + \rho s \sigma_Q + r - r_f$ as the dividend yield, r as the interest rate, and σ_Q as the volatility.

22.7. Consider the equity-linked foreign exchange call in equation (22.42). In this problem we want to derive the formula for an option with the payoff $\max(0, Q_T x_T - Q_T K)$.

   a. What is the prepaid forward price for $Q_T x_T$?

   b. What is the prepaid forward price for $Q_T K$, where K is a dollar amount?

   c. What is the formula for the price of the option with the payoff $\max(0, Q_T x_T - Q_T K)$? Verify that your answer is the same as equation (22.42).

22.8. The quanto forward price can be computed using the risk-neutral distribution as $E(Y x^{-1})$. Use Proposition 20.4 to derive the quanto forward price given by equation (22.29).

22.9. In this problem we use the lognormal approximation (see equation 11.19) to draw one-step binomial trees from the perspective of a yen-based investor. Use the information in Table 22.4.

   a. Construct a one-step tree for the Nikkei index.

   b. Construct a one-step tree for the exchange rate (yen/dollars).

   c. Use the trees to price Nikkei and dollar forwards. Compare your answers with those in Example 22.7.

22.10. Suppose an option knocks in at $H_1 > S$, and knocks out at $H_2 > H_1$. Suppose that $K < H_2$ and the option expires at T. Call this a "knock-in, knock-out" option. Here is a table summarizing the payoff to this option (note that because $H_2 > H_1$ it is not possible to hit H_2 without hitting H_1):

H_1 Not Hit	H_1 Hit	
	H_2 Not Hit	H_2 Hit
0	$\max(0, S_T - K)$	0

What is the value of this option?

22.11. Suppose the stock price is \$50, but that we plan to buy 100 shares if and when the stock reaches \$45. Suppose further that $\sigma = 0.3$, $r = 0.08$, $T - t = 1$, and $\delta = 0$. This is a noncancellable limit order.

   a. What transaction could you undertake to offset the risk of this obligation?

   b. You can view this limit order as a liability. What is its value?

22.12. Covered call writers often plan to buy back the written call if the stock price drops sufficiently. The logic is that the written call at that point has little "upside," and, if the stock recovers, the position could sustain a loss from the written call.

    a. Explain in general how this buy-back strategy could be implemented using barrier options.

    b. Suppose $S = \$50$, $\sigma = 0.3$, $r = 0.08$, $t = 1$, and $\delta = 0$. The premium of a written call with a $50 strike is $7.856. We intend to buy the option back if the stock hits $45. What is the net premium of this strategy?

A European **lookback call** at maturity pays $S_T - \underline{S}_T$. A European **lookback put** at maturity pays $\overline{S}_T - S_T$. (Recall that $\overline{S}_T$ and $\underline{S}_T$ are the maximum and minimum prices over the life of the option.) Here is a formula that can be used to value both options:

$$W(S_t, \tilde{S}_t, \sigma, r, T - t, \delta, \omega) = \omega S_t e^{-\delta(T-t)} \left[N(\omega d_5') - \frac{\sigma^2}{2(r-\delta)} N(-\omega d_5') \right]$$

$$- \omega \tilde{S}_t e^{-r(T-t)} \left[N(\omega d_6') - \frac{\sigma^2}{2(r-\delta)} \left(\frac{S_t}{\tilde{S}_t} \right)^{1-2\frac{r-\delta}{\sigma^2}} N(\omega d_8') \right] \qquad (22.52)$$

where

$$d_5' = [\ln(S_t/\tilde{S}_t) + (r - \delta + 0.5\sigma^2)(T - t)]/\sigma\sqrt{T - t}$$
$$d_6' = d_5' - \sigma\sqrt{T - t}$$
$$d_7' = [\ln(\tilde{S}_t/S_t) + (r - \delta + 0.5\sigma^2)(T - t)]/\sigma\sqrt{T - t}$$
$$d_8' = d_7' - \sigma\sqrt{T - t}$$

The value of a lookback call is obtained by setting $\tilde{S}_t = \underline{S}_t$ and $\omega = 1$. The value of a lookback put is obtained by setting $\tilde{S}_t = \overline{S}_t$ and $\omega = -1$.

22.13. For the lookback call:

    a. What is the value of a lookback call as S_t approaches 0? Verify that the formula gives you the same answer.

    b. Verify that at maturity the value of the call is $S_T - \underline{S}_T$.

22.14. For the lookback put:

    a. What is the value of a lookback put if $S_t = 0$? Verify that the formula gives you the same answer.

    b. Verify that at maturity the value of the put is $\overline{S}_T - S_T$.

22.15. A European **shout option** is an option for which the payoff at expiration is $\max(0, S - K, G - K)$, where G is the price at which you shouted. (Suppose you have an XYZ shout call with a strike price of $100. Today XYZ is $130. If you shout at $130, you are guaranteed a payoff of $\max(\$30, S_T - \$130)$ at expiration.) You can only shout once, irrevocably.

a. Demonstrate that shouting at some arbitrary price $G > K$ is better than never shouting.

b. Compare qualitatively the value of a shout option to (i) a lookback option (which pays $\max[0, \overline{S}_T - K]$, where $\overline{S}_T$ is the greatest stock price over the life of the option) and (ii) a **ladder option** (which pays $\max(0, S - K, L - K)$ if the underlying hits the value L at some point over the life of the option).

c. Explain how to value this option binomially. (*Hint:* Think about how you would compute the value of the option at the moment you shout.)

22.16. Consider the Level 3 outperformance option with a multiplier, discussed in Section 16.2. This can be valued binomially using the single state variable $S_{Level3}/S_{S\&P}$, and multiplying the resulting value by $S_{S\&P}$.

a. Compute the value of this option if it were European, assuming the Level 3 stock price is $100, the S&P index is 1300, and the volatilities and dividend yields are 25% and 0 for the Level 3 and 16% and 1.8% for the S&P. The Level 3–S&P correlation is 0.4 and the option has 4 years to expiration.

b. Repeat the valuation assuming the option is American.

c. In the absence of a multiplier, would you expect the option ever to be early-exercised? Under what circumstances does early exercise occur with the multiplier?

22.17. Consider AAAPI, the Nikkei ADR in disguise. To answer this question, use the information in Table 22.4.

a. What is the volatility of Y, the price of AAAPI?

b. What is the covariance between Y and x, the dollar-yen exchange rate?

c. What is the correlation between Y and x, the dollar-yen exchange rate?

d. Using this information on the volatility of Y and the correlation between Y and x, construct a joint binomial tree for x and Y. Use this tree to price a Nikkei quanto forward.

CHAPTER 23

Volatility

Volatility is a critical input necessary for pricing options, but it is not directly observable and it is not constant over time. Consequently, both theorists and practitioners are concerned with the behavior of volatility and the construction of option pricing models in which volatility can change. Hedging volatility risk is also an important issue for market-makers.

In this chapter we will discuss specific techniques for measuring stock price volatility and also demonstrate how volatility models can be incorporated into the Black-Scholes pricing framework. The pricing models have the potential to explain observed prices better than the Black-Scholes formula, but the models are derived using the same pricing principles that we discussed in Chapter 21.

The chapter is divided into four general topics:

- Implied volatility: What information do option prices provide about volatility, both at a point in time and over time?

- Volatility estimation: Given the past history of stock returns, what can you say about volatility?

- Volatility hedging: What instruments are available to hedge volatility risk?

- Option pricing: How can we price options when volatility is stochastic?

You should keep in mind when reading this chapter that the distribution of asset prices remains an area in which there is significant ongoing research. Statistical techniques for measuring volatility continue to evolve, and there is ongoing research into the question of which pricing models best explain observed option prices.

23.1 IMPLIED VOLATILITY

To provide a context for the discussion in this chapter, we begin by revisiting implied volatility, a concept we discussed in Section 12.5. Figure 23.1 depicts implied volatilities for exchange-traded IBM options on January 18, 2001, an arbitrarily chosen date. The patterns are typical for equity options, with in-the-money (low strike) calls having higher implied volatilities than at-the-money and out-of-the-money calls. In addition, the implied volatility curve is flatter for options with longer time to maturity. You may

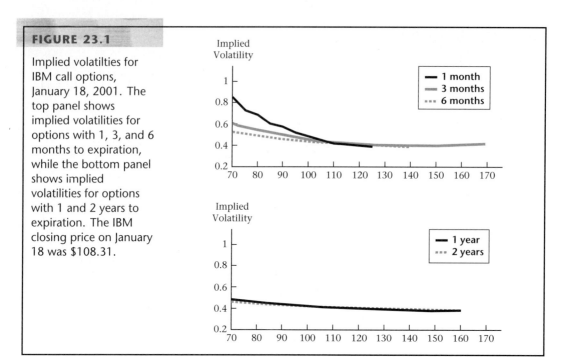

FIGURE 23.1

Implied volatilties for IBM call options, January 18, 2001. The top panel shows implied volatilities for options with 1, 3, and 6 months to expiration, while the bottom panel shows implied volatilities for options with 1 and 2 years to expiration. The IBM closing price on January 18 was $108.31.

Source: Optionmetrics

see volatilities plotted in a three-dimensional graph, with time to maturity on one axis and strike prices on a different axis. Such a plot is called a **volatility surface.**

The pattern of implied volatilities generally is referred to as the *volatility skew*. However, specific patterns are frequently observed. If you use your imagination, the implied volatility plot in Figure 23.1 resembles a lopsided grin or a smirk. The pattern in the figure is sometimes called a *volatility smirk*. When the plot of implied volatility against strike prices looks like a smile, it is called a **volatility smile.** *Volatility frowns* may also be observed.

Implied volatility may seem like a natural way to measure the volatility that is expected to prevail over a future period of time. However, the fact that implied volatilities are not constant across strike prices and over time raises at least two issues. First, it is common to measure implied volatility using the Black-Scholes model, which assumes that volatility is constant. The volatility skew may reflect pricing or specification error in the Black-Scholes model, which raises the question of what implied volatility actually measures. Second, since there is no single measure of implied volatility (for the same asset, implied volatilities differ across strikes and across option maturities), how should we interpret the implied volatility numbers? Should we look at volatility at a particular "moneyness"? Is there some way to average the different volatilities? We will see later in this chapter that some theoretical pricing models are able to account for implied volatility patterns such as those in Figure 23.1.

FIGURE 23.2

The top panel depicts the old VIX from 1986 to 2004. The bottom panel compares the new and old VIX indices during 2004.

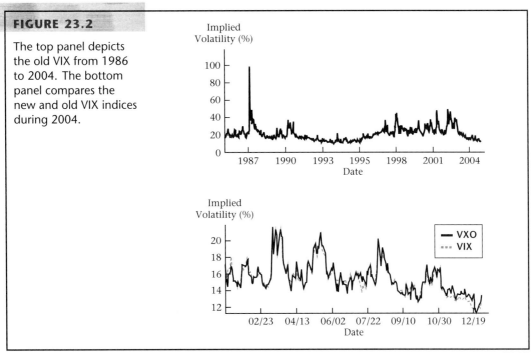

Source: CBOE

In addition to examining the pattern of implied volatilities at a point in time, it is also possible to track implied volatilities over time. Since 1993 the Chicago Board Options Exchange (CBOE) has reported an index of implied volatility for near-term S&P 100 index options. This index is called the "VIX," after its ticker symbol. Using this measure, we can track changes over time in implied volatility. Originally, the CBOE computed implied volatility by extracting implied volatility from near-the-money options, much as we discussed in Section 12.5. This index is called the "Old VIX," with ticker symbol VXO. However, beginning in 2003, the CBOE began computing implied volatility based on a new formula that we will describe later in this chapter.

Figure 23.2 plots the old VIX index from 1986 to 2004, and compares the new and old VIX for one year. The spike in the VIX in 1987 occurs on four days, October 19, 20, 22, and 26, when the VIX exceeded 100%. This period corresponds to the October 19, 1987, market crash, in which the Dow Jones index declined over 20% on one day.[1]

The bottom panel in Figure 23.2 compares the new and old VIX during one year, showing that while the two measures are not identical, they are generally quite close. At

[1] Plotting implied volatility over time raises the question of whether implied volatility is an accurate forecast of actual future volatility. Generally, implied volatility is a biased forecast of future volatility (e.g., see Bates, 2003).

the scale in the top panel, it would be difficult to detect any difference at all in the two series.

We will see in Section 23.3 below that the new VIX measure neatly finesses the problem of which particular option implied volatility to use by considering prices of *all* out-of-the-money options with a given time to maturity.

23.2 MEASUREMENT AND BEHAVIOR OF VOLATILITY

In this section we examine different ways to characterize and measure the behavior of volatility using only historical information about the asset price. In our examples we will concentrate on stock price volatility.

We take as a starting point the lognormal model of stock prices. Suppose the stock price follows this process:

$$dS_t/S_t = (\alpha - \delta)dt + \sigma(S_t, X_t, t)dZ \qquad (23.1)$$

where α is the continuously compounded expected return on the stock, δ is the continuously compounded dividend yield, and $\sigma(S_t, X_t, t)$ is the instantaneous volatility. This familiar looking equation is subtly different than the process we assumed in earlier chapters. In equation (23.1), volatility at a point in time can depend on the level of the stock price S, other variables, X, and time. By comparison, the standard Black-Scholes assumption is that $\sigma(S_t, X_t, t) = \sigma_0$, a constant. Equation (23.1) is an example of a stock price process with **stochastic volatility,** in which instantaneous volatility can change randomly.[2]

Given a series of stock prices that we observe every h periods, we can compute continuously compounded returns, ϵ:

$$\epsilon_{t+h} = \ln(S_{t+h}/S_t)$$

We will assume throughout this section that h is small, and therefore that we can ignore the mean return.

Historical Volatility

The natural starting point for examining volatility is historical volatility, which we compute using past stock returns. Suppose that we observe n continuously compounded stock returns over a period of length T, so that $h = T/n$. Under the assumption that volatility is constant, we can estimate the historical annual variance of returns, σ^2, as

$$\hat{\sigma}_H^2 = \frac{1}{h}\left[\frac{1}{(n-1)}\sum_{i=1}^{n}\epsilon_i^2\right] \qquad (23.2)$$

---

[2]Note that there are no jumps in equation (23.1), and we will assume that the volatility, $\sigma(S, X, t)$, also does not jump. It is possible to permit jumps for both; for example, see Duffie et al. (2000).

The multiplication by $1/h$ annualizes the variance estimate in square brackets.[3] This calculation differs from the usual formula for variance since it assumes the per-period mean is zero. This assumption makes little difference if h is small.

The top panel of Figure 23.3 displays the historical 60-day volatility for IBM and the S&P 500 index from 1991 to 2002. Each day, the preceding 60 trading days are used to compute the standard deviation of the continuously compounded daily return. Since

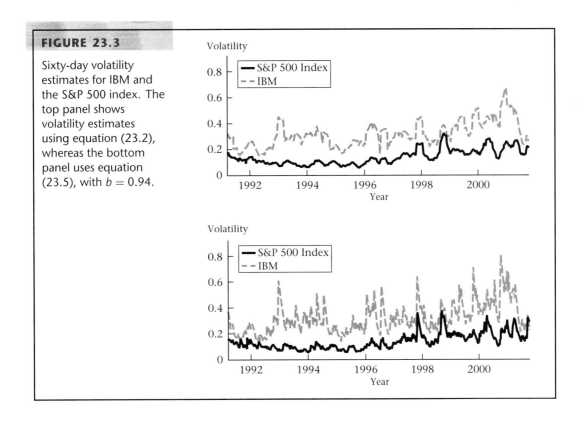

FIGURE 23.3

Sixty-day volatility estimates for IBM and the S&P 500 index. The top panel shows volatility estimates using equation (23.2), whereas the bottom panel uses equation (23.5), with $b = 0.94$.

---

[3] Suppose r_i is computed daily. It is important to annualize *after* computing the standard deviation of the daily returns, as opposed to annualizing the daily returns and then computing the standard deviation. To see why, let $\{r_i\}$ be the set of nonannualized daily returns. The annualized standard deviation is

$$\sqrt{252} \times \sqrt{\text{Var}(\{r_i\})}$$

If instead we first annualize the returns by multiplying them by 252 and then compute the standard deviation, we obtain

$$\sqrt{\text{var}(252 \times \{r_i\})} = 252 \times \sqrt{\text{Var}(\{r_i\})}$$

Annualizing returns before computing the standard deviation creates a return series that has too much volatility.

there are approximately 252 trading days in a year, the resulting standard deviation is multiplied by $\sqrt{252}$ to produce an annualized standard deviation.

The use of overlapping 60-day intervals induces smoothness in the series, since each day's return affects the next 60 days of volatility calculations. Even so, there is a great deal of variability in the standard deviation. For both series, volatility appears to have risen toward the end of the 1990s.

It is natural to estimate volatility using daily returns for all trading days. It is important to recognize, however, that not all calendar days, and not even all trading days, exhibit the same volatility. For example, if all days were the same, return volatility over a weekend (from Friday's close of trading to Monday's close of trading) should be $\sqrt{3}$ times the weekday volatility. However, French and Roll (1986) showed that returns from Friday to Monday were significantly less volatile than returns over three consecutive weekdays. More recently, Dubinsky and Johannes (2004) showed that individual stock price volatilities are greater on the days when firms make earnings announcements than on other days. Thus, while equation (23.2) provides an estimate of annualized volatility, the volatilities on individual days can vary.

Exponentially Weighted Moving Average

Because volatility in Figure 23.3 appears to be changing over time, it is natural to try to take this variation into account when estimating volatility. We might reason that if volatility is changing, we want to emphasize more recent observations at the expense of more distant observations. One way to do this is to compute an *exponentially weighted moving average* (EWMA) of the squared stock returns.

The EWMA formula computes volatility at time t as a weighted average of the time $t - 1$ EWMA estimate, $\hat{\sigma}^2_{\text{EWMA},t-1}$, and the time $t - 1$ squared stock price change, ϵ^2_{t-1}. Thus, we have

$$\hat{\sigma}^2_{\text{EWMA},t} = (1 - b)\epsilon^2_{t-1} + b\hat{\sigma}^2_{\text{EWMA},t-1} \qquad (23.3)$$

where b is the weight applied to the previous EWMA estimate. We can lag equation (23.3) and substitute the resulting expression for $\hat{\sigma}^2_{\text{EWMA},t-1}$ into the right-hand side of equation (23.3). Continuing in this way, we obtain the EWMA estimator as a weighted average of past squared returns:

$$\hat{\sigma}^2_{\text{EWMA},t} = \sum_{i=1}^{\infty} \left[(1 - b)b^{i-1} \right] \epsilon^2_{t-i} \qquad (23.4)$$

The term in square brackets in equation (23.5) is the weight applied to historical returns. The weights decline at the rate b, with the most recent return receiving the greatest weight. Because $\sum_{i=1}^{\infty}(1 - b)b^{i-1} = 1$, the weights on past squared returns sum to one.

It is also possible to use a moving window when estimating EWMA volatility. For example, we might use only the previous n days of data. In this case, equation (23.5) becomes

$$\hat{\sigma}^2_{\text{EWMA},t} = \sum_{i=1}^{n} \left[\frac{(1-b)b^{i-1}}{\sum_{j=1}^{n}(1-b)b^{j-1}} \right] \epsilon^2_{t-i}$$

$$= \sum_{i=1}^{n} \left[\frac{(1-b)b^{i-1}}{1-b^n} \right] \epsilon^2_{t-i} \quad (23.5)$$

Because $\sum_{i=1}^{n}(1-b)b^{i-1} = 1 - b^n$, the weights again sum to one.

There is also a simple updating formula, analogous to equation (23.3), in the case of a moving window estimate. Each period we add the latest observation and drop the oldest observation. Equation (23.5) is equivalent to

$$\hat{\sigma}^2_{\text{EWMA},t} = b\hat{\sigma}^2_{\text{EWMA},t-1} + \frac{1-b}{1-b^n} \left[\epsilon^2_{t-1} - b^n \epsilon^2_{t-1-n} \right] \quad (23.6)$$

Example 23.1 Suppose $b = 0.94$ and $n = 60$. We have $1 - b^n = 0.9756$. The first term in equation (23.6) is then

$$\frac{(1-0.94)}{0.9756} = 0.0615$$

This compares with a weight of $1/60 = 0.0167$ for each observation in the equal-weighted estimator in equation 23.2. Subsequent (earlier) observations have weights of 0.0578, 0.0543, 0.0511, etc.

The bottom panel in Figure 23.3 displays the EWMA estimate for $b = 0.94$ and $n = 60$ days. Note that the EWMA estimator is considerably more variable than the standard historical volatility estimate. This additional variability occurs because the most recent observation has four times the weight in the EWMA estimator as in the standard estimator. Thus a particularly large return will create a large effect on the estimate. This effect will then decay at the rate b. ≹

There are two problems with the EWMA estimator, one practical and one conceptual. First, if we use the EWMA estimator in equation (23.3) to forecast future volatility, we obtain a constant expected volatility at any horizon. The reason is that the forecast of ϵ^2_t is $\hat{\sigma}^2_{t-1}$, so that all forecasts of future volatility would equal $\hat{\sigma}^2_{t-1}$. Thus, the EWMA estimator does not forecast patterns in future volatility. Second, the EWMA estimator is not derived from a formal statistical model in which volatility can vary over time. ARCH and GARCH, which we discuss next, address both problems.

Time-Varying Volatility: ARCH

A casual examination of data, such as looking at historical volatilities (Figure 23.3), or looking at the behavior over time of implied volatilities (Figure 23.2), suggests that volatilities are not constant.[4] What do we do once we formally accept that volatilities change over time? Ideally we would have a statistical model that permits volatility changes to occur. Such a model could serve both to provide better estimates of volatility and also to provide a building block for better pricing models.

Research on the behavior of volatility shows that for many assets, there are periods of turbulence and periods of calm: high volatility tends to be followed by high volatility and low volatility by low volatility. Put differently, during a period when measured volatility is high, the typical day tends to exhibit high volatility. (High volatility could in principle also arise from an increased chance of large but infrequent price moves.) Figure 23.4 displays squared daily returns for the S&P 500 index and IBM. At a casual level, this figure exhibits this effect, with periods in which many of the daily squared returns are large, and periods when many are small. This is called **volatility clustering.**

If volatility is persistent, a volatility measure should weight recent returns more heavily than more distant returns. This difference in weighting is exactly how an EWMA volatility estimate differs from the ordinary equally weighted volatility measure. ARCH and GARCH models also give more weight to recent returns.

The ARCH model The autoregressive conditional heteroskedasticity (ARCH) model of Engle (1982) and the subsequent GARCH (Generalized ARCH) model of Bollerslev (1986) are important and widely used volatility models that attempt to capture statistically the ebb and flow of volatility.[5] Engle in fact won the 2003 Nobel Prize in economics for his work in this area (see the box on page 750). The basic idea motivating ARCH is that if volatility is high today it is likelier than average to be high tomorrow. Engle (1982) provided a statistical framework for modeling this effect.

A statistical model for asset prices could take the form

$$\ln(S_t/S_{t-h}) = (\alpha - \delta - 0.5\sigma^2)h + \epsilon_t \tag{23.7}$$

In this specification, the error term would have variance

$$\text{var}(\epsilon_t) = \sigma^2 h \tag{23.8}$$

---

[4]We can perform a back-of-the-envelope calculation by assuming that continuously compounded returns are normally distributed. In that case, the ratio of variances drawn from independent time periods has the the F distribution. If we estimate two annual volatilities using 252 observations, the ratio of the two estimated variances is distributed $F(\alpha, 251, 251)$. The 99.5% and 0.005% confidence levels are obtained from $F^{-1}(p, 251, 251)$, where $p = 0.995$ or $p = 0.005$. At a 1% significance level, the two bounds for the ratio of estimated variances are 1.386 and 0.722, corresponding to volatility ratios of 1.177 and 0.849. Thus, if volatility in one year is 15%, a subsequent measured volatility outside the range 12.74%–17.66% rejects the hypothesis of constant variance at a 1% significance level.

[5]Bollerslev et al. (1994) surveys the literature on ARCH and its variants. Two recent accessible introductions were written as a result of the 2003 Nobel prize: Diebold (2004) and Royal Swedish Academy of Sciences (2003). Nelson (1991) proposed exponential GARCH, which models the behavior of $\ln(\sigma^2)$.

FIGURE 23.4

Squared daily returns on the S&P 500 index (top panel) and IBM (bottom panel) from January 2, 1991, to October 24, 2001.

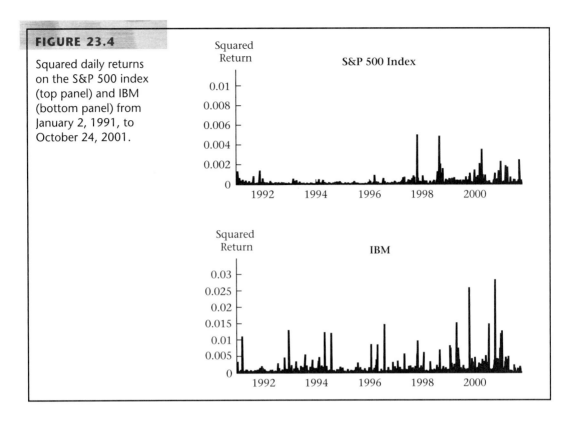

If σ^2 is constant over time, we say the error term, ϵ_t, is **homoskedastic.** Based on Figure 23.4, however, a more reasonable specification would be to assume that the variance of ϵ_t varies over time, in which case it is **heteroskedastic.**

If the time interval in equation (23.7) is short, then (as we saw in Chapter 20), the mean, $(\alpha - \delta - 0.5\sigma^2)h$ is small, and ϵ_t^2 is essentially the squared return. We will continue to assume that h is short enough so that we can ignore the drift in equation (23.7).

Let Ψ_t denote the information that is available up to and including time t, and therefore information that we have available at time t. The idea behind Engle's ARCH model is that squared returns have a variance that changes over time according to a statistical model. Specifically, let q_t be the conditional (upon information available at time $t - 1$) value of the return variance, i.e.,

$$q_t \equiv E(\epsilon_t^2 | \Psi_{t-1})$$

The ARCH model supposes that we can write

$$q_t = a_0 + \sum_{i=1}^{m} a_i \epsilon_{t-i}^2 \qquad (23.9)$$

A Nobel Prize for Volatility

The 2003 Nobel Prize in economics was awarded to Robert F. Engle and Clive Granger for their work in statistical methods in economics. Engle was cited for his work in studying the behavior of volatility. This quote, from the Royal Swedish Academy of Science press release announcing the award of the 2003 economics prize, describes Engle's contribution:

> Random fluctuations over time— volatility—are particularly significant because the value of shares, options and other financial instruments depends on their risk. Fluctuations can vary considerably over time; turbulent periods with large fluctuations are followed by calmer periods with small fluctuations. Despite such time-varying volatility, in want of a better alternative, researchers used to work

with statistical methods that presuppose constant volatility. Robert Engle's discovery was therefore a major breakthrough. He found that the concept of autoregressive conditional heteroskedasticity (ARCH) accurately captures the properties of many time series and developed methods for statistical modeling of time-varying volatility. His ARCH models have become indispensable tools not only for researchers, but also for analysts on financial markets, who use them in asset pricing and in evaluating portfolio risk.

Granger was cited for his work in cointegration, a statistical method important for studying the long-run behavior of economic time series.

where $a_0 > 0$, $a_i \geq 0$, $i = 1, \ldots, m$. Equation (23.9) is an ARCH(m) model, signifying that there are m lagged terms. In order for volatility to be well-behaved, we must have $\sum_{i=1}^{n} a_i < 1$. This model states that volatility at a point in time depends upon recent observed volatility.

At this point we can understand the meaning of "autoregressive conditional heteroskedasticty." *Autoregressive* means that the value at a point in time depends on past values. *Heteroskedasticity* means that variances are not equal. The unconditional variance is the variance estimated over a long period of time. The *conditional* variance is the variance estimated at a point in time, taking into account ("conditional upon") recent volatility. Thus, *autoregressive conditional heteroskedasticity* essentially means that the level of variance depends on recent past levels of variance. This is the behavior captured by equation (23.9).

ARCH volatility forecasts   An important practical question is how many lags we need in order to estimate equation (23.9). To better understand the behavior of an ARCH model, let's consider a single lag, where we set $a_1 > 0$ and $a_i = 0$, $i > 1$. The volatility equation is then

$$E(\epsilon_t^2|\Psi_{t-1}) = a_0 + a_1\epsilon_{t-1}^2 \qquad (23.10)$$

where $a_0 > 0$ and $a_1 < 1$. Equation (23.10) is an ARCH(1) model.

Suppose we forecast volatility at time $t+1, t+2$, etc., using only the information we have at time t. Equation (23.10) implies that for a one-period ahead forecast of q_t we have

$$E(\epsilon_{t+1}^2|\Psi_{t-1}) = a_0 + a_1 E(\epsilon_t^2|\Psi_{t-1})$$
$$= a_0 + a_1\left(a_0 + a_1\epsilon_{t-1}^2\right)$$

Similarly, for a two-period ahead forecast,

$$E(\epsilon_{t+2}^2|\Psi_{t-1}) = a_0 + a_1 E(\epsilon_{t+1}^2|\Psi_{t-1})$$
$$= a_0 + a_1\left[a_0 + a_1\left(a_0 + a_1\epsilon_{t-1}^2\right)\right]$$

Continuing in this way, for an n-period-ahead forecast, we have

$$E(\epsilon_{t+n}^2|\Psi_{t-1}) = a_0\left(1 + \sum_{i=1}^{n}a_1^i\right) + a_1^n\epsilon_{t-1}^2 \qquad (23.11)$$

This predicted pattern of volatility persistence is very specific and inflexible. A large squared return today implies larger squared returns at all future dates, but the effect decays per period by the factor a_1. Shocks to volatility are expected to die off at a constant rate.

Equation (23.11) implies that unconditional volatility (the value we would estimate as a long-run average) is

$$\bar{\sigma}^2 = a_0(1 + a_1 + a_1^2 + \ldots) = \frac{a_0}{1 - a_1} \qquad (23.12)$$

Thus, with estimates of a_0 and a_1 we can compute the unconditional volatility.

In practice, if markets become more turbulent, they may remain more turbulent for a period of time. Equation (23.9) with a single lag cannot account for a period of *sustained* high volatility. As you might guess, more than one lag—generally many lags—are necessary for ARCH to fit the data.

The GARCH Model

The GARCH model, due to Bollerslev (1986), is a variant of ARCH that allows for infinite lags yet can be estimated with a small number of parameters. The GARCH model has the form

$$q_t = a_0 + \sum_{i=1}^{m}a_i\epsilon_{t-i}^2 + \sum_{j=1}^{n}b_iq_{t-i} \qquad (23.13)$$

where $a_0 > 0, a_i \geq 0, i = 1, \ldots, m, b_i \geq 0, i = 1, \ldots, n$, and $\sum_{i=1}^{m}a_i + \sum_{i=1}^{n}b_i < 1$.

This model states that volatility at a point in time depends upon recent volatility as well as recent squared returns. Equation (23.13) is a GARCH(m,n) model.

GARCH(1,1) is frequently used in practice. The GARCH(1,1) model is

$$q_t = a_0 + a_1 \epsilon_{t-1}^2 + b_1 q_{t-1} \tag{23.14}$$

It is instructive to compare the GARCH(1,1) model to the ARCH(1) model, equation (23.10). To do this, we can rewrite equation (23.14) to eliminate q_{t-1} on the right-hand side. Lagging equation (23.14) and substituting the result for q_{t-1} on the right-hand side of equation (23.14), we obtain

$$q_t = a_0 + a_1 \epsilon_{t-1}^2 + b_1 \left(a_0 + a_1 \epsilon_{t-2}^2 + b_1 q_{t-2} \right)$$

Continuing in this way, we obtain

$$q_t = a_0 \sum_{i=0}^{\infty} b_1^i + a_1 \sum_{i=0}^{\infty} b_1^i \epsilon_{t-1-i}^2$$

$$= \frac{a_0}{1 - b_1} + \frac{a_1}{1 - b_1} \sum_{i=0}^{\infty} (1 - b_1) b_1^i \epsilon_{t-1-i}^2 \tag{23.15}$$

A GARCH(1,1) model is therefore equivalent to an ARCH(∞) model in which the lag coefficients decline at the rate b_1. Notice that the last term in equation (23.15) can be rewritten in terms of an EWMA volatility estimator (23.5):

$$q_t = \frac{a_0}{1 - b_1} + \frac{a_1}{1 - b_1} \hat{\sigma}_{\text{EWMA}}^2 \tag{23.16}$$

It is important to note that the parameter b_1 in the EWMA expression in equation (23.16) is not arbitrarily chosen, as in equation (23.3), but is estimated as part of the GARCH estimation procedure.

Maximum likelihood estimation of a GARCH model   Given the assumption that continuously compounded returns have a distribution that is conditionally normal, with variance q_t and mean zero, we can estimate a GARCH model using maximum likelihood.[6] The probability density for ϵ_t, conditional on q_t, is

$$f(\epsilon_t; q_t) = \frac{1}{\sqrt{2\pi q_t}} e^{-0.5\epsilon_t^2/q_t} \tag{23.17}$$

Since the ϵ_t are conditionally independent, the probability of observing the particular set of n returns is the product of the probabilities, which gives us the likelihood function:

$$\prod_{i=1}^{n} f(\epsilon_i | q_i) = \prod_{i=1}^{n} \frac{1}{\sqrt{2\pi q_i}} e^{-0.5\epsilon_i^2/q_i}$$

....

[6]Alexander (2001) discusses the estimation of GARCH models and is replete with examples.

For a GARCH(1,1), q_i is a function of a_0, a_1, and b_1. The maximum likelihood estimate is the set of parameters—a_0, a_1, and b_1—that maximizes the probability of observing the returns we actually observed. Typically it is easiest to maximize the log of the likelihood function, in which case maximizing the likelihood is the same as maximizing

$$\sum_{i=1}^{n} \left[-0.5 \ln(q_i) - 0.5\epsilon_i^2/q_i\right] \tag{23.18}$$

We omit the term $-0.5 \ln(2\pi)$ since it does not affect the solution. The maximization of equation (23.18) can be performed in statistical packages or even using Solver in Excel (see the chapter appendix).

Volatility forecasts   We can forecast volatility in the GARCH(1,1) model as we did in the ARCH(1) model. To understand the calculation, recognize that since $q_t = E(\epsilon_t^2|\Psi_{t-1})$, we then have $E(q_t|\Psi_{t-j}) = E(\epsilon_t^2|\Psi_{t-j})$ for $j \geq 1$. Thus, using equation (23.14), we have

$$\begin{aligned} E(q_{t+1}|\Psi_{t-1}) &= a_0 + a_1 E(\epsilon_t^2|\Psi_{t-1}) + b_1 E(q_t|\Psi_{t-1}) \\ &= a_0 + (a_1 + b_1) E(q_t|\Psi_{t-1}) \\ &= a_0 + (a_1 + b_1)(a_0 + a_1\epsilon_{t-1}^2 + b_1 q_{t-1}) \end{aligned}$$

The goal in this calculation is to express the forecasted value of q_{t+1} in terms of what we can observe at time t—namely, ϵ_{t-1} and q_{t-1}. Following the same procedure, we obtain

$$E(q_{t+2}|\Psi_{t-1}) = a_0 + a_0(a_1 + b_1) + (a_1 + b_1)^2(a_0 + a_1\epsilon_{t-1}^2 + b_1 q_{t-1})$$

For a k step-ahead forecast, we have

$$E(q_{t+k}|\Psi_{t-1}) = a_0 + a_0 \sum_{i=1}^{k}(a_1 + b_1)^i + (a_1 + b_1)^k(a_1\epsilon_{t-1}^2 + b_1 q_{t-1})$$

As we let k go to infinity, we obtain an estimate of unconditional volatility in the GARCH(1,1) model:

$$\bar{\sigma}^2 = a_0 \sum_{i=0}^{\infty}(a_1 + b_1)^i = \frac{a_0}{1 - a_1 - b_1} \tag{23.19}$$

Using equations (23.16) and (23.19), we can express the GARCH(1,1) equation in terms of the EWMA estimate of volatility:

$$q_t = \alpha\bar{\sigma}^2 + (1 - \alpha)\hat{\sigma}_{\text{EWMA}}^2 \tag{23.20}$$

where $\alpha = (1 - a_1 - b_1)/(1 - b_1)$. Thus, the GARCH(1,1) expected volatility at a point in time is a weighted average of the unconditional variance, $\bar{\sigma}^2$, and the current estimated EWMA volatility, $\hat{\sigma}_{\text{EWMA}}^2$.

Example 23.2   Estimating a GARCH(1,1) model for IBM using daily return data from January 1999 to December 2003 yields the GARCH volatility estimate

$$q_t = 0.000001305 + 0.0446\epsilon_{t-1}^2 + 0.9552q_{t-1}$$

The implied estimate of the unconditional annualized volatility is

$$\sqrt{\frac{0.000001305}{1 - 0.0446 - 0.9552} \times 252} = 1.5318$$

The historical volatility during this period was 39.85%. An estimated unconditional volatility of 153% suggests that the GARCH(1,1) model has trouble fitting the data. In this case, it turns out that the problem is caused by large returns on days during which IBM announced earnings.

During the 1999–2003 period there were four days on which the absolute one-day return exceeded 12%. On each of these days (April 21, 1999; October 20, 1999; July 19, 2000; and October 17, 2000), IBM announced earnings. The 153% volatility illustrates the GARCH model's difficulty in explaining these large magnitude returns under the assumption that returns are normally distributed. If we omit these four days from the sample, the estimated GARCH model is[7]

$$q_t = 0.000002203 + 0.0507\epsilon_{t-1}^2 + 0.9462q_{t-1}$$

These parameters imply an unconditional volatility of

$$\sqrt{\frac{0.000002203}{1 - 0.0507 - 0.9462} \times 252} = 0.4229$$

The other parameters do not change much, and this unconditional volatility estimate of 42.29% is more reasonable. This example illustrates that a GARCH model estimated using normally distributed returns can be sensitive to extreme data points. In addition to eliminating earnings announcement days, one could permit a fatter-tailed return distribution (e.g., see Bollerslev, 1987).

Figure 23.5 compares the GARCH volatility estimate with an EWMA estimate where $b = 0.94$. The two are not dramatically different, although the EWMA estimate exhibits more extreme behavior. An EWMA estimate with $b = 0.9462$ would be even closer to the GARCH estimate, because of the relation between GARCH and EWMA in equation (23.20).   ≋

---

[7]In order to obtain an unbiased estimate for nonearnings announcement days, the correct procedure would be to eliminate *all* earnings announcement days, not just those which, after the fact, exhibited high squared returns.

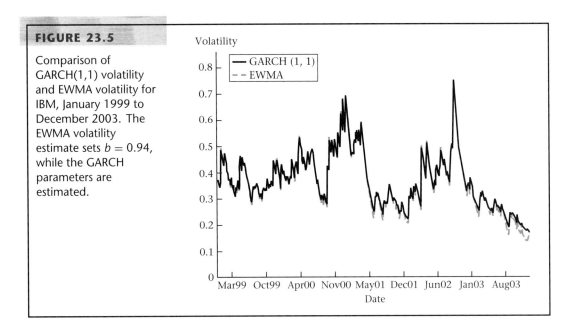

FIGURE 23.5

Comparison of GARCH(1,1) volatility and EWMA volatility for IBM, January 1999 to December 2003. The EWMA volatility estimate sets $b = 0.94$, while the GARCH parameters are estimated.

Realized Quadratic Variation

We saw in Chapter 20 that the quadratic variation (the sum of squared increments) of a Brownian motion from t to T is $T - t$. That is, suppose we frequently sample a diffusion process, $\sigma Z(t)$. Letting $n = (T - t)/h$ and $Z(i) = Z(t + ih)$, we have

$$\sum_{i=1}^{n} [\sigma Z(i + 1) - \sigma Z(i)]^2 \approx \sigma^2 (T - t)$$

Quadratic variation therefore provides an estimate of the total variance of the process over time.

Suppose stock returns are generated by equation (23.1), in which volatility varies over time. Consider what happens if we compute the quadratic variation of the log stock price. In order to do this, we would need to observe the stock price at a high frequency, for example, using multiple prices over the course of the trading day. Suppose we observe continuously compounded returns from time t to T every h periods. To simplify notation, let $S(t + ih) = S(i)$, and $\sigma(i) = \sigma(S_{t+ih}, X_{t+ih}, t + ih)$. The **realized quadratic variation** of the stock price from time t to time T is then the sum of squared, continuously compounded returns:[8]

$$\sum_{i=1}^{n} \ln[S(i)/S(i-1)]^2$$

$$= \sum_{i=1}^{n} \left\{ [\alpha - \delta - 0.5\sigma(i-1)^2]h + \sigma(i-1)[Z(i) - Z(i-1)] \right\}^2 \qquad (23.21)$$

$$\approx \sum_{i=1}^{n} \sigma(i-1)^2 h$$

When h is small, the drift term in the summation is small relative to the diffusion term (see Section 20.3.4), so that the squared change in $Z(t)$ dominates the summation.[9] The right-hand side is an estimate of the total stock price variance from time t to T.

One well-known difficulty with using high-frequency data is that some observed price movements occur simply because transactions alternate between customer purchases (made at the dealer's offer price) and customer sales (made at the dealer's bid price). The resulting up and down movement in the price is called "bid-ask bounce." Andersen et al. (2003) demonstrate a way to deal with intraday data when they use currency data to compare realized quadratic variation with other variance estimates, such as GARCH(1,1). They calculate realized quadratic variation as follows. At 30-minute intervals, they observe the bid and ask prices immediately preceding and following the 30-minute mark. They interpolate the averaged bid and ask prices to impute a price at 30-minute intervals. They then use this imputed price to measure the 30-minute continuously compounded return, from which they construct realized quadratic variation. In comparing forecasts based on realized quadratic variation with other methods of forecasting volatility, both in- and out-of-sample over one- and ten-day horizons, they find that realized quadratic variation is generally at least as good as other estimates.

---

[8]Unfortunately, there does not appear to be a standard terminology for the realized quadratic variation of an asset price. It is common to call σ the "volatility." It would seem consistent to refer to the sum of squared returns as the "realized variance," and the "realized volatility" would then be the square root of the realized variance. In practice, however, the sum of squared returns is sometimes called the "realized volatility." See, for example, Andersen et al. (2003). Moreover, the realized quadratic variation only measures the variance of the stock price diffusion, σ^2, under certain regularity conditions. Thus, for clarity, we will use the term "realized quadratic variation," which is unambiguous, albeit clumsy.

[9]You may wonder about the difference between estimating historical volatility and realized quadratic variation. Recall the historical variance estimate, equation (23.2). Multiplying by $1/h$ in equation (23.2) is the same as multiplying by n/T. Thus, the historical variance estimate can be rewritten as

$$\hat{\sigma}_H^2 = \frac{1}{T} \left[\frac{n}{(n-1)} \sum_{i=1}^{n} \epsilon_i^2 \right]$$

Apart from the $n/(n-1)$ term, this appears to be the same as annualized realized quadratic variation. In practice, the term "historical volatility" usually implies the use of daily or less frequent data over medium to long horizons, while "quadratic variation" implies the use of intraday data over short horizons.

FIGURE 23.6

Daily realized volatility for IBM, January, 1999 to December 2002, plotted against GARCH(1,1) volatility estimate.

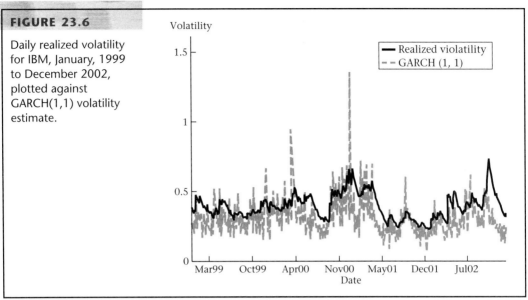

Source: Andersen et al. (2005).

Figure 23.6 plots daily realized quadratic variation for IBM (using returns computed at five-minute intervals from open to close) against the GARCH(1,1) volatility estimate using the parameters computed in Example 23.2. The GARCH estimate is a forecast of volatility, while realized quadratic variation measures actual volatility on a day. Thus, realized quadratic variation is considerably less smooth than the GARCH forecast. (Realized quadratic variation is smoother, on the other hand, than the squared daily returns depicted in Figure 23.4.) In intererpeting the graph of realized quadratic variation, it is important to recognize that if the price bounces around a great deal during the day, then realized volatility will be high even if the return for that day is not high. The empirical question is whether the magnitude of this intraday bouncing around of the price predicts volatility on subsequent days. The evidence in Andersen et al. (2003) is that it does.

23.3 HEDGING AND PRICING VOLATILITY

In this section we discuss derivative claims that have volatility as an underlying asset. We begin by discussing volatility and variance swaps (including one contract based on the VIX). We then look at an example of pricing a variance swap. Finally, we discuss the construction of the history of the VIX volatility index reported by the Chicago Board Options Exchange (CBOE). In this section we will let V denote measured volatility and V^2 measured variance.

Variance and Volatility Swaps

A **variance swap** is a forward contract that pays the difference between a forward price, $F_{0,T}(V^2)$, and some measure of the realized stock price variance, $\hat{V}^2$, over a period of time multiplied by a notional amount. The payoff to a variance swap is

$$[\hat{V}^2 - F_{0,T}(V^2)] \times N$$

where N is the notional amount of the contract. There are numerous measurement details that we have to specify in order to write the contract for a variance swap:

- How frequently the return is measured

- Whether returns are continuously compounded or arithmetic

- Whether the variance is measured by subtracting the mean or by simply squaring the returns

- The period of time over which variance is measured

- How to handle days on which, unexpectedly, trading does not occur

Most of these design issues are straightforward, but the last deserves some comment. Most futures contracts settle based upon a final observable price. A variance contract, by contrast, settles based upon a *series* of prices. Therefore, failing to observe a price (for example, because the market is unexpectedly closed) creates a problem for measuring the realized variance. If the market is unexpectedly closed on day t, then the next measured return will be a *two-day* return, which will have a greater expected variance than a one-day return. The following example shows how one contract deals with this issue.

Example 23.3   Three-month S&P 500 variance futures traded on the Chicago Futures exchange are an example of a variance swap. The payoff is based on the annualized sum of squared, continuously compounded daily returns over a three-month period, $\hat{V}^2$. The measured price is quoted as $\hat{V}^2 \times 10{,}000$, and by definition a one-unit change in this number (called a *variance point*) is worth $50.

For simplicity, we treat the payoff as if it were a forward contract, settling on one day. Let ϵ_i be the continuously compounded return on day i. The payoff at expiration is

$$\$50 \times \left[10{,}000 \times 252 \times \sum_{i=1}^{n_a-1} \frac{\epsilon_i^2}{n_e - 1} - F_{0,T}(V^2) \right]$$

In this formula, n_a is the actual number of S&P prices used in constructing V^2 (hence there are $n_a - 1$ returns), and n_e is the number of expected trading days at the outset of the contract. Thus, in the event of an unexpected trading halt, the sum of squared returns will be divided by a number larger than the number of squared returns. The reason for this is that the trading halt will not necessarily change the total variance over the period (if the trading halt is on a Tuesday, for example, the Monday to Wednesday return will typically reflect two days of volatility). Dividing the sum of squared returns by n_a would mechanically increase the measured variance when there is a trading halt. Dividing by n_e prevents this. ❧

A **volatility swap** is like a variance swap except that it pays based on volatility rather than variance. The payoff is

$$(\hat{V} - F_{0,T}(V)) \times N$$

where $F_{0,T}(V)$ is the forward price for volatility.

Example 23.4   The Chicago Board Options Exchange volatility index, the VIX, is the basis for a volatility futures contract that trades on the Chicago Futures Exchange. Unlike the variance futures contract, the volatility futures contract settles based upon the VIX index. The payoff is

$$1000 \times [\text{VIX}_T - F_{0,T}(V)]$$
❧

In comparing the volatility futures contract (Example 23.4) with the variance futures contract (Example 23.3), note that the two contracts are based on volatility measured over different periods of time. The variance contract settles based on realized quadratic variation over the period from 0 to T, and thus the futures price reflects volatility expectations from time 0 to time T. The VIX contract, since it is based on the VIX index, measures volatility expectations from time T to time $T + 30$ days. Thus, the volatility contract measures volatility going forward from the settlement date, while the variance contract looks backward from the settlement date.

There are at least two reasons that the variance contract is in some sense more "natural" than a volatility contract. First, we will see below that it is possible to price and hedge a variance forward contract (given some assumptions) using option prices. The pricing of a volatility forward contract is more complicated due to Jensen's inequality. Because the volatility is the square root of the variance, Jensen's inequality implies that the volatility forward price will be less than the square root of the variance forward price of the variance.

Second, variance swaps arise naturally from dealers hedging their option positions. Recall from Chapter 13, in particular equation (13.11), that the profit of a delta-hedging dealer depends on the squared stock price change. Dealers can hedge this risk in realized variance by using variance swaps. For example a dealer with a negative gamma position could enter a swap that pays the dealer when the stock has a large price change.

Pricing Volatility

We will see in this section one way to determine the fair price for a forward contract on variance.

Consider a variance contract that pays the sum of squared price changes from time 0 to time T. If price changes are measured over an interval of length $h = T/n$, the contract would have the payoff

$$\text{Payoff} = \sum_{i=1}^{n} \left(\frac{S_{(i+1)h} - S_{ih}}{S_{ih}} \right)^2 \qquad (23.22)$$

Note that, since arithmetic and continuously compounded returns are close over small intervals, this is the same as the realized quadratic variation measure discussed in the previous section. As h gets small, this equation (23.22) becomes

$$\text{Payoff} = \int_0^T \sigma(S_t, X_t, t)^2 dt \qquad (23.23)$$

where $\sigma(S, X, t)$ is the diffusion coefficient in equation (23.1). We want to answer two closely related questions. First, how is it possible to replicate the payoff to such a contract? Second, how should the contract be priced? As you might suspect, replicating the contract yields a way to price it.

In principle, the price of a forward contract on variance will be the expectation of equation (23.23) under the risk-neutral measure. In practice, how do we compute such an expectation? The following section will provide one answer.

The log contract   Neuberger (1994) pointed out that a forward contract that pays

$$\ln(S_T/S_0) \qquad (23.24)$$

could be used to hedge and speculate on variance. A claim with the payoff in equation (23.24) is a **log contract**. As of early 2005, there is no exchange-traded log contract in existence, but for the moment, suppose such a contract does exist.

Assuming the stock price follows equation (23.1), we can use Itô's Lemma to characterize the process followed by the log of the stock price. (Note that we assume that the stock price does not jump.) Equation (23.1) permits a wide range of processes for the volatility, but the prospective volatility over the next instant is known. Applying Itô's Lemma, we have

$$d[\ln(S_t)] = \frac{1}{S}dS - 0.5\frac{1}{S^2}dS^2$$

Thus,

$$0.5\sigma(t)^2 dt = \frac{1}{S}dS - d[\ln(S_t)]$$

Integrating this equation, we have

$$0.5\int_0^T \sigma^2(t)dt = \int_0^T \frac{1}{S}dS - \int_0^T d[\ln(S_t)]dt$$

The integral on the left-hand side is quadratic variation over 0 to T. Let $\hat{\sigma}^2$ denote annualized realized volatility from time 0 to time T. We can then rewrite this as

$$0.5T\hat{\sigma}^2 = \int_0^T \frac{1}{S}dS - \ln(S_T/S_0) \tag{23.25}$$

The right-hand side of equation (23.25) is the cumulative return to an investment in $1/S$ shares, less the return on a contract paying the realized continuously compounded return on the stock price from time 0 to time T. The left-hand side is annualized realized quadratic variation, which from equation (23.23) is also the payoff on a variance contract. Equation (23.25) demonstrates the connection between the payoff to the log contract and volatility.

Take expectations of both sides of equation (23.25) with respect to the risk-neutral stock price distribution. The expectation of dS/S under the risk-neutral distribution is rdt. Hence we obtain

$$0.5T E^*\left[\hat{\sigma}^2\right] = E^*\left[\int_0^T \frac{1}{S}dS - \ln(S_T/S_0)\right]$$
$$= rT - E^*\left[\ln(S_T/S_0)\right] \tag{23.26}$$

This expression seems to be of little help in pricing volatility. There is a trick, however, for pricing the log contract using other instruments.

Valuing the log contract Demeterfi et al. (1999) and Carr and Madan (1998) independently showed that it is possible to use a portfolio of options to replicate the payoff on the log contract. Note first that

$$\int_a^b \frac{1}{K^2}(K - S_T)dK = \left[\ln(K) + \frac{S_T}{K}\right]_a^b = \ln(b) - \ln(a) + \frac{S_T}{b} - \frac{S_T}{a}$$

Use this to obtain the following identity, for any S_T (see Demeterfi et al., 1999):[10]

$$-\ln\left(\frac{S_T}{S_*}\right) = -\frac{S_T - S_*}{S_*} + \int_0^{S_*} \frac{1}{K^2}\max(K - S_T, 0)dK + \int_{S_*}^\infty \frac{1}{K^2}\max(S_T - K, 0)dK$$

Notice that if we take expectations of both sides with respect to the risk-neutral distribution for S_T, the integrals on the right-hand side become undiscounted option prices, and the expected stock price is the forward price. We can add and subtract $\ln(S_0)$ to the

---

[10]To interpret the expression on the right-hand side, notice that for any given S_T, the value of the first integral is zero for K below S_T, and the value of the second integral is zero for K above S_T. Thus, the effective integration bounds are not 0 and ∞, but they instead depend upon S_T. For example, if $S_T = \bar{S} < K, S_*$, the equation becomes

$$-\ln\left(\frac{\bar{S}}{S_*}\right) = -\frac{\bar{S} - S_*}{S_*} + \int_{\bar{S}}^{S_*} \frac{1}{K^2}\max(K - \bar{S}, 0)dK + 0$$

left-hand side and then take expectations, to obtain

$$
- E^* \ln \left(\frac{S_T}{S_0} \right) + \ln \left(\frac{S^*}{S_0} \right)
$$

$$
= - \left[\frac{F_{0,T}(S) - S_*}{S_*} \right] + e^{rT} \left[\int_0^{S_*} \frac{1}{K^2} P(K) dK + \int_{S_*}^{\infty} \frac{1}{K^2} C(K) dK \right]
$$

Use this expression to substitute for $E^*[\ln(S_T/S_0)]$ in equation (23.26). The result is

$$
\hat{\sigma}^2 = \frac{2}{T} \left[rT - \ln \left(\frac{S_*}{S_0} \right) - \frac{F_{0,T}(S) - S_*}{S_*} \right.
$$

$$
\left. + e^{rT} \left(\int_0^{S_*} \frac{1}{K^2} P(K) dK + \int_{S_*}^{\infty} \frac{1}{K^2} C(K) dK \right) \right] \quad (23.27)
$$

Finally, note that if we set $S_* = F_{0,T}(S)$, the first three terms on the right-hand side of equation (23.27) vanish, and we have

$$
\hat{\sigma}^2 = \frac{2e^{rT}}{T} \left[\int_0^{F_{0,T}} \frac{1}{K^2} P(K) dK + \int_{F_{0,T}}^{\infty} \frac{1}{K^2} C(K) dK \right] \quad (23.28)
$$

Remarkably, this formula gives us an estimate of expected realized variance that we compute using the observed prices of out-of-the-money puts and calls! ("Out of the money" here is with respect to the forward price rather than the current stock price.) It is important to note that we have *not* assumed that options are priced using the Black-Scholes formula or any other specific model.

One important characteristic of equation (23.28) is that the variance estimate can be replicated by trading options. It is possible to buy the strip of out-of-the-money puts and calls, weighted by the inverse squared strike price, to create a portfolio that has the value of $\hat{\sigma}^2$.

To get a sense of why equation (23.28) works, we can examine the vega of a portfolio of options held in proportion to $1/K^2$. Figure 23.7 graphs vegas for a set of options and also displays the vega of a portfolio where the option holdings are weighted by the inverse squared strike price. The resulting portfolio has a vega that is not zero and is constant over a wide range of stock prices. If you hold such a portfolio, you make or lose money depending on volatility changes.

Computing the VIX   We can now explain the formula used to compute the CBOE's new volatility index. The calculation is based on equation (23.28). In practice, option strike prices are discrete and there may be no option for which the strike price equals the index forward price. The actual formula used by the CBOE is a discrete approximation to equation (23.28):

$$
\hat{\sigma}^2 = \frac{2}{T} \sum_{K_i \leq K_0} \frac{\Delta K_i}{K_i^2} e^{rT} \mathrm{Put}(K_i) + \frac{2}{T} \sum_{K_i > K_0} \frac{\Delta K_i}{K_i^2} e^{rT} \mathrm{Call}(K_i) - \frac{1}{T} \left[\frac{F_{0,T}}{K_0} - 1 \right]^2
$$

$$
(23.29)
$$

FIGURE 23.7

Solid lines depict vegas of options with (from left to right) strikes of 25, 30, 35, 40, 45, 50, and 55. The dashed line is the weighted sum of the vegas, with each divided by the squared strike price, times 600. The calculations assume $\sigma = 0.30$, $r = 0.08$, $T = 0.25$, and $\delta = 0$.

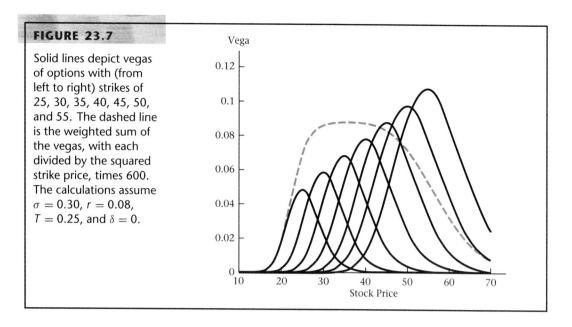

where K_0 is the first strike below the forward price for the index and $\Delta K_i = (K_{i+1} - K_{i-1})/2$.[11] The last term is a correction for the fact that there may be no option with a strike equal to the forward price.

23.4 EXTENDING THE BLACK-SCHOLES MODEL

In this section we examine three pricing models that are capable of generating volatility skew patterns resembling those observed in option markets. The goal is both to understand how the Black-Scholes model can be extended and also to gain a sense of how these extensions help us to better understand the data. We consider three models: (1) the Merton jump diffusion model, which relaxes the assumption that stock price moves are continuous; (2) the constant-elasticity of variance model, primarily due to Cox, which relaxes the assumption that volatility is constant; and (3) the Heston stochastic volatility model, which allows volatility to follow an Itô process that is correlated with the stock price process. These models have all been significantly generalized, but we can use them as touchstones for better understanding the economics of departures from the Black-Scholes lognormality assumption.

At the outset, note that the Black-Scholes model easily accommodates time-varying volatility if the volatility pattern is deterministic. Specifically, Merton (1973b) showed

[11]For the highest strike, ΔK_i is the difference between the high strike and the next highest strike. ΔK_i for the lowest strike is defined as the difference between the low strike and the next highest strike.

that if volatility is a deterministic function of time, then it is possible to price a European option with $T - t$ periods to maturity by substituting $\int_t^T \sigma^2(s)ds$ for $\sigma^2(T - t)$ in the Black-Scholes formula. We can think about this result in the context of a delta-hedging market-maker. As long as the market-maker knows the volatility at each point in time, the delta-hedge will work the same as if volatility were constant. What creates a problem is a *random* change in volatility.

Jump Risk and Implied Volatility

In Chapter 21 we presented Merton's valuation formula for an option when the underlying asset can jump. In this section we consider the special case of that model in which the stock price can jump only to zero (see equation 21.42); we show that the jump model generates a volatility skew. The intuition in this case is particularly clear.

Suppose that the stock can jump to zero with $\lambda = 0.5\%$ probability per year. If we let $S = \$40$, $K = \$40$, $\sigma = 30\%$, $r = 8\%$, $T - t = 0.25$, and $\delta = 0$, then we have call and put prices of $2.81 and $2.02, compared with the no-jump prices of $2.78 and $1.99. Now we do the following experiment: Generate "correct" option prices—i.e., prices properly accounting for the jump—for a variety of strikes and different times to maturity. We then ask what implied volatility we would compute for these options using the ordinary Black-Scholes formula. Table 23.1 shows the jump and no-jump prices for options at three different strike prices, along with the option vegas. The results are also graphed in Figure 23.8. Because of parity, puts and calls have the same implied volatility, so we need to graph only one of them.

In every case, out-of-the money puts (in-the-money calls) have higher implied volatilities than at-the-money options. We can see why this is happening by examining the numbers more closely. The small possibility of a jump causes all the option prices to increase from about 2.5 to 3.5 cents. If you are surprised that a call is more valuable when the stock can jump to zero, think about put-call parity. If the stock price remains

| **TABLE 23.1** | Option prices when the stock can and cannot jump. Assumes $S = \$40$, $\sigma = 30\%$, $r = 8\%$, $\delta = 0$, $\lambda = 0.5\%$, and $T - t = 0.25$. |

	Call Price				**Implied σ**
Strike ($)	**Jump**	**No Jump**	**Difference ($)**	**Call Vega**	**with Jump**
40	2.8104	2.7847	0.0257	0.0781	0.303
35	6.1704	6.1348	0.0356	0.0436	0.308
30	10.6679	10.6320	0.0359	0.0083	0.334

FIGURE 23.8

Implied volatilities computed using the Black-Scholes formula for three different times to maturity and different strike prices. The underlying option prices are generated when the stock can jump to zero with probability 0.5%/year. Assumes $S = \$40$, $\sigma = 30\%$, $r = 8\%$, $\delta = 0$.

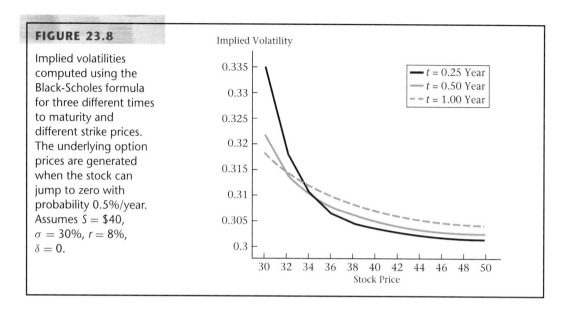

unchanged, the put will clearly be more valuable when the stock can jump to zero. Thus, by parity, the call must be more valuable as well.[12]

The standard implied volatility calculation uses the Black-Scholes formula without a jump adjustment to compute the implied volatility. The no-jump prices all have implied volatilities of 30%. What volatility in the no-jump model is required to generate the prices in the jump column? For the 40-strike option, vega is 0.0781, so a change in volatility of approximately $0.0257/0.0781 = 0.323$ percentage points, or a volatility of 0.30323, will generate the higher price of $2.81. For the 30-strike option, however, vega is only 0.0083. Thus, a change in volatility of approximately $0.0359/0.0083 = 4.3$ percentage points is required in order for the no-jump Black-Scholes model to explain the price of $10.6679. The actual implied volatility in this case is 0.334. When vega is lower, a larger change in volatility is required to explain a given change in the option price.

This example is at most suggestive. In practice, jumps can be positive or negative and of uncertain magnitude. If jumps can occur in both directions, then we would expect to see higher implied volatilities for both in-the-money and out-of-the-money options. Furthermore, jump risk is unlikely to be purely diversifiable since there can be market-wide moves. The example does, however, illustrate important intuition for why jumps can generate volatility smiles.

....

[12]For a more mechanical explanation, recall from Chapter 21 that when we incorporate the possibility of a jump to zero, we also increase the drift of the stock price by the expected jump magnitude times the instantaneous jump probability. This increase in the drift accounts for the rise in the option price.

Constant Elasticity of Variance

Cox (1975) proposed the constant elasticity of variance (CEV) model, in which volatility varies with the level of the stock price. Specifically, Cox assumed that the stock follows the process

$$dS = (\alpha - \delta)Sdt + \bar{\sigma}S^{\beta/2}dZ \tag{23.30}$$

Equation (23.30) describes the instantaneous dollar return on the stock. The instantaneous rate of return on the stock is

$$\frac{dS}{S} = (\alpha - \delta)dt + \bar{\sigma}S^{(\beta-2)/2}dZ \tag{23.31}$$

The instantaneous standard deviation of the stock return is therefore

$$\sigma(S) = \bar{\sigma}S^{(\beta-2)/2} \tag{23.32}$$

When $\beta < 2$, the CEV model implies that volatility is decreasing with the stock price. Volatility increases with the stock price when $\beta > 2$. When $\beta = 2$, the CEV model yields the standard lognormal process.

It is important to be clear that $\bar{\sigma}$ is a parameter that determines volatility, but the instantaneous rate of return volatility is $\bar{\sigma}S^{(\beta-2)/2}$. Thus, if we want the stock to have a volatility of σ_0 at the current stock price, S_0, we must then set $\bar{\sigma}$ so that $\sigma_0 = \bar{\sigma}S^{(\beta-2)/2}$, or

$$\bar{\sigma} = \sigma_0 S^{(2-\beta)/2}$$

From equation (23.30), the elasticity of the instantaneous stock price variance with respect to the stock price is a constant, β:

$$\frac{\partial(\bar{\sigma}^2 S^\beta)}{\partial S} \times \frac{S}{\bar{\sigma}^2 S^\beta} = \beta$$

This is where the name "constant elasticity of variance" comes from.

One motivation for the CEV model was the finding in Black (1976b) (see also Christie, 1982) that volatility increases when stock prices fall. One potential explanation for this stems from thinking about the effect on equity risk from a fall in leverage. As the stock price decreases, the debt-to-equity ratio rises, and the equity volatility should therefore increase. Thus, the negative correlation between stock prices and volatility is called the **leverage effect.**

A drawback of the CEV model may already have occurred to you. If the stock price declines and $\beta < 2$, the CEV model implies that volatility will increase *permanently*. In practice and in theory, such a deterministic relationship between volatility and the stock price level seems implausible. However, such a relationship seems more reasonable when modeling interest rates. The interest rate in the CIR model (see Section 24.2), for example, follows a CEV process.

The CEV pricing formula There is a relatively simple pricing formula for a European call when the stock price follows the CEV process.[13] Following Schroder (1989), define

$$\kappa = \frac{2(r - \delta)}{\bar{\sigma}^2 (2 - \beta) \left(e^{(r-\delta)(2-\beta)T} - 1 \right)}$$

$$x = \kappa S^{2-\beta} e^{(r-\delta)(2-\beta)T}$$

$$y = \kappa K^{2-\beta}$$

The CEV pricing formula for a European call is different for the cases $\beta < 2$ and $\beta > 2$. Let $Q(a, b, c)$ denote the noncentral chi-squared distribution function with b degrees of freedom and noncentrality parameter c, evaluted at a.[14] The CEV call price is given by

$$Se^{-\delta T} \left[1 - Q(2y, 2 + 2/(2 - \beta), 2x) \right] - Ke^{-rT} Q(2x, 2/(2 - \beta), 2y) \qquad \beta < 2 \tag{23.33}$$

$$Se^{-\delta T} \left[1 - Q(2x, 2/(\beta - 2), 2y) \right] - Ke^{-rT} Q(2y, 2 + 2/(\beta - 2), 2x) \qquad \beta > 2$$

Implied volatility in the CEV model When $\beta < 2$, the CEV model generates a Black-Scholes implied volatility skew curve resembling that in Figure 23.1: Implied volatility decreases with the option strike price. To understand why the CEV model generates this volatility skew, note from equation (23.31) that when $\beta < 2$ and the stock price falls, volatility increases. Thus compared with the case of a constant volatility, an out-of-the-money put option has a greater chance of exercise and is likely to be deeper in the money when it is exercised. The only way for the Black-Scholes model to account for this higher price is with a higher volatility. As the strike price increases, less of the option value is due to the stock price behavior at low prices, and volatility therefore need not increase as much.

Figure 23.9 plots implied volatility curves generated by using the Black-Scholes formula to compute implied volatility for prices generated by the CEV model. The top panel shows that, for the given parameters, the implied volatility curve is unaffected by changing time to maturity.

---

[13]Cox (1996) originally derived a pricing formula in terms of infinite series for the case $\beta < 2$. Emanuel and MacBeth (1982) generalized Cox's analysis to the case where $\beta > 2$. Schroder (1989) showed that both cases could be expressed more compactly in terms of the noncentral chi-squared cumulative distribution function. Davydov and Linetsky (2001) derive pricing formulas barrier and lookback options under a CEV process.

[14]The pricing formula is sometimes written in terms of the *complementary* noncentral chi-squared distribution, which is $1 - Q(a, b, c)$. The noncentral chi-squared distribution, unlike the chi-squared distribution, is not typically a standard function built into spreadsheets. However, it is available in software programs such as Matlab and Mathematica.

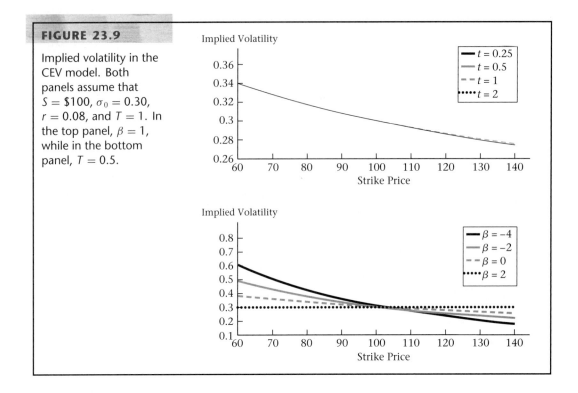

FIGURE 23.9

Implied volatility in the CEV model. Both panels assume that $S = \$100$, $\sigma_0 = 0.30$, $r = 0.08$, and $T = 1$. In the top panel, $\beta = 1$, while in the bottom panel, $T = 0.5$.

The Heston Model

In the CEV model, the instantaneous volatility of the stock evolves stochastically with the stock price, but volatility is a nonstochastic function of the stock price. A more general approach is to permit volatility to follow a stochastic process. The **Heston model** (Heston, 1993) allows volatility to vary stochastically but still to be correlated with the stock.[15] This generates a different option pricing model than the CEV process and also implies that market-makers must hedge both stock price and volatility risk. In the CEV model, market-makers need only hedge with the stock since volatility depends on the stock price.

Let $v(t)$ be the instantaneous stock return variance; hence, $\sqrt{v(t)}$ is the volatility. Suppose that the stock follows the process

$$\frac{dS}{S} = (\alpha - \delta)dt + \sqrt{v(t)}dZ_1 \tag{23.34}$$

---

[15]Earlier papers that modeled volatility as following a stochastic process included Hull and White (1987), Scott (1987), and Wiggins (1987). The Heston model has been generalized significantly by Duffie et al. (2000), who allow both jumps in the asset price and jumps in volatility.

Assume that the variance, $v(t)$, follows the mean-reverting process

$$dv(t) = \kappa[\bar{v} - v(t)]dt + \sigma_v\sqrt{v(t)}dZ_2 \tag{23.35}$$

We assume that $E(dZ_1dZ_2) = \rho dt$.

The interpretation of equations (23.34) and (23.35) is familiar. Equation (23.34) for the stock is the same as equation (21.5) except that the volatility, $\sqrt{v(t)}$, is random. The equation for volatility, equation (23.35), has two noteworthy characteristics. First, the instantaneous variance, $v(t)$, is mean-reverting, tending toward the value $\bar{v}$, with a speed of adjustment given by κ. Second, the volatility of variance, $\sigma_v\sqrt{v(t)}$, depends on the square root of $v(t)$, and variance is therefore said to follow a *square root process*.

Suppose that the risk premium for the risk $\sigma_v\sqrt{v(t)}dZ_2$ can be written as $v(t)\beta_v$, where we assume β_v is constant. This assumption that the risk premium is proportional to the level of the variance is analytically convenient. Given this assumption about the risk premium, the risk-neutral volatility process is

$$\begin{aligned} dv(t) &= \left\{\kappa[\bar{v} - v(t)] - v(t)\beta_v\right\}dt + \sigma_v\sqrt{v(t)}dZ_2^* \\ &= \kappa^*\left[\bar{v}^* - v(t)\right]dt + \sigma_v\sqrt{v(t)}dZ_2^* \end{aligned} \tag{23.36}$$

where $\kappa^* = \kappa + \beta_v$ and $\bar{v}^* = \bar{v}\kappa/(\kappa + \beta_v)$. This model of stochastic volatility is the Heston model.

Let $V[S(t), v(t), t]$ represent the price of a derivative on the stock when the stock price and volatility are given by equations (23.34) and (23.35). Suppose we proceed with the Black-Scholes derivation, in which we hold the option and try to hedge the resulting risk. We immediately encounter the problem that there are *two* sources of risk, dZ_1 and dZ_2. A position in the stock will hedge dZ_1, but what can we use to hedge risk resulting from stochastic volatility? Apart from other options, there will typically be no asset that is a perfect hedge for volatility.[16] In that case, we rely on the equilibrium approach to pricing the option. The PDE for the derivative $V[S(t), v(t), t]$ is then:

$$\begin{aligned} &\tfrac{1}{2}v(t)S^2V_{SS} + \tfrac{1}{2}\sigma_v^2 v(t)V_{vv} + \rho v(t)\sigma_v SV_{Sv} \\ &+ (r - \delta)SV_S + \left\{\kappa[\bar{v} - v(t)] - v(t)\beta_v\right\}V_v + V_t = rV \end{aligned} \tag{23.37}$$

This equation is the multivariate Black-Scholes equation, described in Appendix 21.A. The third term is due to the covariance between the stock return and volatility. Since there is no asset to hedge volatility, the coefficient on the V_v term has a correction for the risk premium associated with volatility.

Heston (1993) shows that equation (23.37) has an integral solution that can be evaluated numerically. Given this solution, we can see how implied volatility behaves when volatility is stochastic. Similar to the analysis of jumps in Section 21.5, we price options for different strikes and expirations under the stochastic volatility model and

---

[16]It might be possible to use other options on the same stock to hedge volatility, but the option would then be priced *relative* to the price of the option used as a hedge.

FIGURE 23.10

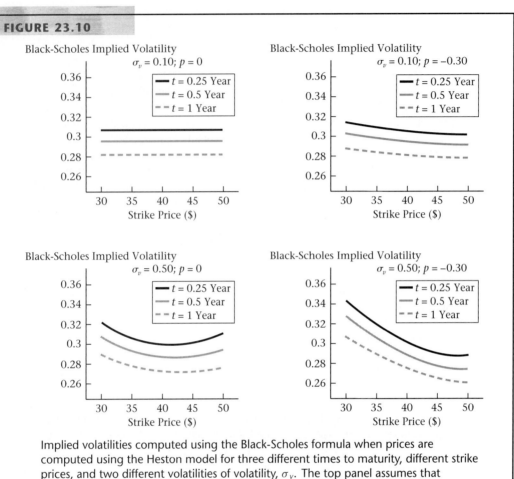

Implied volatilities computed using the Black-Scholes formula when prices are computed using the Heston model for three different times to maturity, different strike prices, and two different volatilities of volatility, σ_V. The top panel assumes that $\sigma_V = 0.10$, while the bottom panel assumes that $\sigma_V = 0.5$. In both panels, $\kappa^* = 2.0$, $v(t) = 0.32$, $\bar{v}^* = 0.25$, $r = 8\%$, and $\delta = 0$.

then use Black-Scholes to compute implied volatilities. We assume that the stock price is $40 and compute implied volatilities for options with strike prices ranging from $30 to $50 and with maturities from 3 months to 1 year.

Figure 23.10 shows the result of this experiment for two different values of σ_v and ρ. In the figure the long-run volatility, $\bar{v}^*$, is 25%, less than the current volatility, 32%. Because volatility reverts to the mean, implied volatility decreases with time to maturity in every case. In the panel where $\sigma_v = 0.10$ and $\rho = 0$, there is almost no skew, although the mean reversion in volatility is apparent. When $\sigma_v = 50\%$ and $\rho = 0$, the figure exhibits both symmetric skew and mean reversion. The asymmetric skew in both right-hand panels of Figure 23.10 arises from assuming a negative correlation between volatility and the stock price.

Evidence

The main challenge for an option pricing model is to match the observed volatility skew.[17] The literature investigating ways to do this is too large to adequately summarize here. Instead, we will sketch the nature of findings in the literature and highlight issues that arise when trying to match models to data.

The pricing models in this section illustrate ways in which modifying the Black-Scholes assumptions can enable a pricing model to better fit observed option prices. For example, all the pricing models we have discussed are capable of generating higher implied volatilities for in-the-money (low-strike) calls. The Merton jump model and the CEV model in the examples above both generate implied volatility curves that are flatter as time to maturity increases.[18] Combinations of the models, such as a Heston model that also allows jumps, seem able to reproduce *qualitative* features of Figure 23.1. However, matching models to data is a more involved exercise than just a visual comparison of implied volatility curves.

To illustrate the issues, suppose you want to match the Heston stochastic volatility model to data. There are a number of ways you might proceed. First, on a given day, you could find a set of model inputs that best matches the volatility curves for that day. This entails finding a return variance ($v(t)$), a volatility of volatility (σ_v), a mean reversion rate (κ^*), a long-run risk-neutral variance ($\bar{v}^*$), and a correlation between volatility and the stock return (ρ), that match the data for a particular day.

Matching implied volatilities across a set of options on a given day is a *cross-sectional* test of the model. Once you admit multiple days of data, the model has *time-series* implications as well. Equations (23.35) and (23.36) imply that volatility evolves over time in a specific way. If you look at the evolution of volatility over time, does it match equation (23.35)? Are the parameters that enable the model to fit the cross-section consistent with those implied by the volatility time series? When there is a risk premium in the equilibrium pricing model (as in the Heston model), it is potentially easier

----

[17]The true model should give equal implied volatilities for options at different strikes and maturities. For example, if the Heston stochastic volatility model were true and option prices were consistent with equation (23.37), then Black-Scholes implied volatilities would exhibit skew, but if the Heston model were used to compute implied volatility, then the options in Figure 23.10 would all have implied volatilities of 32%.

[18]It is not obvious how to interpret the change with respect to maturity in implied volatility curves such as those in Figures 23.1, 23.8, 23.9, and 23.10. The issue is that the economic distinction between a $50 strike and a $55 strike is greater with one week to expiration than with one year to expiration; therefore, other things equal, we might expect to see flatter volatility curves as time to expiration increases. Bates (2000) corrects for this effect by scaling strike prices by $\sigma \sqrt{T}$, effectively measuring distance between strikes in "standard deviation units."

to reconcile the behavior of the stock with option prices because there is an additional parameter. However, as Bates (2003) emphasizes, a risk premium must be plausible.

Bakshi et al. (1997) and Bates (2000) both asked whether option pricing models incorporating jumps and stochastic volatility can generate realistic volatility skew for options based on the S&P 500.[19] Both studies find greater volatility skew at short maturities than at long maturities. If you compare Figures 23.8 and 23.10, you can see that this pattern is generated by the jump model but not as obviously by the Heston model. This explains why, although Bakshi et al. (1997) found that the stochastic volatility model provided the best overall explanation of prices, they added jumps to account for skew at short maturities.[20] They also found that permitting stochastic interest rates (which can be added in the same fashion as stochastic volatility) helped explain prices at longer maturities.

Bates (2000) found that jump models (as in Figure 23.8) fit near-term option prices better but found the jump parameters implausible: the stock price does not appear to jump as often as implied by the estimates necessary to explain implied volatility. Bates also concluded that in order for the stochastic volatility model to explain skew, the volatility of volatility had to be implausibly large. However, Duffie et al. (2000) developed a pricing procedure that permitted jumps in both the asset price and the volatility, and noted that allowing jumps in volatility potentially addressed the problem of an implausibly large volatility of volatility.

Broadie et al. (2004) conclude that "models with jumps in returns drastically improve overall pricing performance ... [and] jumps in volatility offer a significant pricing improvement in the cross-section unless a model with jumps in returns is allowed to have a volatility-of-jump risk premium." In other words, jumps in at least some dimensions are important, and risk premia can be important as well.[21]

To add one more layer of complication, casual observation suggests that in some cases volatility changes deterministically over time. When a firm announces earnings, for example, volatility will be higher than on ordinary days. You can show that this is true by comparing the volatility of returns on earnings announcement days against that on other days. Dubinsky and Johannes (2004) show that this effect is also apparent in option prices, which imply a higher volatility before an earnings announcement than after.[22] This finding suggests that in addition to the use of increasingly sophisti-

---

[19] Bakshi et al. (1997) examined European options on the S&P 500 index while Bates (2000) examined options on the S&P 500 futures contract.

[20] Carr and Wu (2003) formalize the intuition that jumps matter more if there is a short time to expiration.

[21] It is possible to measure volatility risk premia directly by looking at the returns on portfolios that are hedged against stock price risk. For example, Coval and Shumway (2001) find negative returns on zero-delta written straddles on the S&P 100 and S&P 500 indexes. Since the written straddle loses money when volatility increases, this finding may be at least in part attributable to a volatility risk premium. Bakshi and Kapadia (2003) find smaller risk premia associated with delta-hedged individual stocks than with index options.

[22] In fact, we saw the effect of earnings announcements in Example 23.2 when we estimated a GARCH(1,1) model for IBM and found the estimates sensitive to the inclusion of four earnings announcement days.

cated mathematical pricing models, careful option pricing requires data sets that identify *anticipated* days of unusual volatility.[23]

CHAPTER SUMMARY

For options on a given underlying asset on a given day, implied volatility generally varies across option strikes and maturities. Implied volatility also varies over time. As a result there is great interest in measuring volatilities and in pricing options when volatility can vary.

Methods of measuring volatility using past data include historical volatility, exponentially weighted moving average volatility, ARCH, GARCH, and realized quadratic variation. ARCH and GARCH estimates are based upon a formal statistical model in which volatility is random. Realized quadratic variation exploits high frequency data to obtain a reliable volatility estimate using data from a short time horizon.

Both variance and volatility swaps permit hedging and speculation on volatility. The variance forward price can be obtained as a weighted sum of the prices of traded European options, a calculation that is the basis for the VIX measure of implied volatility.

The Black-Scholes model does not perfectly explain observed option prices; there is volatility skew, which means that implied volatility varies with the strike price and time to expiration. Two modifications to the model are to permit jumps in the stock price and to allow volatility to be stochastic. Both changes generate option prices that exhibit volatility skew and that better fit the data than the unmodified Black-Scholes model.

Attempts to explain prices of traded options suggest that it is important to account for jumps in both the asset price and volatility, and that risk premiums on one or both jumps may be important.

FURTHER READING

Early studies of stock returns (e.g., Fama, 1965) found that continuously compounded returns exhibit too many large returns to be consistent with normality. In recent years, research has focused on specifying stock price processes that give theoretical option prices consistent with observed prices. Introductions to GARCH models include Royal Swedish Academy of Sciences (2003), and Bollerslev et al. (1994). Alexander (2001) is a readable text for less technical readers. Realized quadratic variation as a measure of volatility is presented and applied in Andersen et al. (2003).

Demeterfi et al. (1999) present a clear and well-written discussion of volatility hedging, and the paper also develops the volatility measure used now to construct the VIX. See also Chicago Board Options Exchange (2003).

....

[23]This is not just an issue for individual firms. Governments make economic announcements on prespecified days at set times, and these announcements sometimes generate large moves in prices. For example, Hanweck (1994) shows that implied volatility in Eurodollar futures options is greater on days when the government announces aggregate employment.

The first papers to suggest alternative assumptions about the stock price for option pricing were Cox and Ross (1976), Cox (1996), and Merton (1976). Merton noted in his paper that the jump model had the potential to explain volatility skew patterns noted by practitioners at the time. The first stochastic volatility models were proposed by Hull and White (1987), Scott (1987), and Wiggins (1987). The Heston (1993) model has been generalized by Duffie et al. (2000), who develop a pricing framework that can accomodate jumps in volatility as well as in the stock price.

The empirical literature examining the ability of option pricing models to fit observed prices is rapidly evolving. Well-known papers include Bakshi et al. (1997), Bates (2000), and Pan (2002). Current research (which include citations to numerous other papers) include Andersen et al. (2005) and Broadie et al. (2004). Dubinsky and Johannes (2004) examine deterministic volatility changes, such as those due to earnings announcements.

PROBLEMS

For many of the first fifteen problems you will need to use data on the CD accompanying this book. The CD contains stock prices, option prices, and interest rates for a variety of maturities. If an interest rate you need is missing, use the rate for the nearest available maturity.

23.1. Using weekly price data (constructed Wednesday to Wednesday), compute historical *annual* volatilities for IBM, Xerox, and the S&P 500 index for 1991 through 2004. Annualize your answer by multiplying by $\sqrt{52}$. Also compute volatility for each for the entire period.

23.2. Compute daily volatilities for 1991 through 2004 for IBM, Xerox, and the S&P 500 index. Annualize by multiplying by $\sqrt{252}$. How do your answers compare to those in Problem 1?

23.3. For the period 1999–2004, using daily data, compute the following:

a. An EWMA estimate, with $b = 0.95$, of IBM's volatility using all data.

b. An EWMA estimate, with $b = 0.95$, of IBM's volatility, at each date using only the previous 60 days of data.

Plot both estimates. How different are they?

23.4. Estimate a GARCH(1,1) for the S&P 500 index, using data from January 1999 to December 2003.

23.5. Replicate the GARCH(1,1) estimation in Example 23.2, using daily returns from on IBM from January 1999 to December 2003. Compare your estimates with and without the four largest returns.

23.6. Use the following inputs to compute the price of a European call option: $S = \$100$, $K = \$50$, $r = 0.06$, $\sigma = 0.30$, $T = 0.01$, $\delta = 0$.

a. Verify that the Black-Scholes price is $50.0299.

b. Verify that the vega for this option is almost zero. Why is this so?

c. Verify that if you compute the option price with volatilities ranging from 0.05 to 1.00, you get essentially the same option price and vega remains about zero. Why is this so? What happens if you set $\sigma = 5.00$ (i.e., 500%)?

d. What can you conclude about difficulties in computing implied volatility for very short-term, deep in-the-money options?

23.7. Use the same inputs as in the previous problem. Suppose that you observe a bid option price of $50 and an ask price of $50.10.

a. Explain why you cannot compute an implied volatility for the bid price.

b. Compute an implied volatility for the ask price, but be sure to set the initial volatility at 200% or greater. Explain why the implied volatility for the ask price is extremely large.

c. (Optional) Examine the code for the *BSCallImpVol* function. Explain why changing the starting volatilty can affect whether or not you obtain an answer.

d. What can you conclude about difficulties in computing and interpreting implied volatilities for deep in-the-money options?

23.8. Use the following inputs to compute the price of a European call option: $S = \$50$, $K = \$100$, $r = 0.06$, $\sigma = 0.30$, $T = 0.01$, $\delta = 0$.

a. Verify that the Black-Scholes price is zero.

b. Verify that the vega for this option is zero. Why is this so?

c. Suppose you observe a bid price of zero and an ask price of $0.05. What answers do you obtain when you compute implied volatility for these prices. Why?

d. Why would market-makers set such prices?

e. What can you conclude about difficulties in computing and interpreting implied volatility for very short-term, deep out-of-the-money options?

23.9. Compute January 12 bid and ask volatilities (using the Black-Scholes implied volatility function) for IBM options expiring January 17. For which options are you unable to compute a plausible implied volatility? Why?

23.10. Compute January 12 bid and ask volatilties (using the Black-Scholes implied volatility function) for IBM options expiring February 21.

a. Do you observe a volatility smile?

b. For which options are you unable to compute a plausible implied volatility? Why?

23.11. Compute January 12 implied volatilities using the *average* of the bid and ask prices for IBM options expiring February 21 (use the Black-Scholes implied volatility function). Compare your answers to those in the previous problem. Why might someone prefer to use implied volatilities based on the average of the bid and ask prices, rather than the bid and ask volatilities individually?

23.12. In this problem you will compute January 12 bid and ask volatilties (using the Black-Scholes implied volatility function) for one-year IBM options expiring the following January. Note that IBM pays a dividend in March, June, September, and December.

   a. Compute implied volatilities ignoring the dividend.

   b. Take dividends into account using the discrete dividend correction to the Black Scholes formula, presented in Chapter 12. For simplicity, discount all observed future dividends at a 2% continuously compounded rate. How much difference does this correction make in implied volatility?

   c. Take dividends into account by computing a dividend yield for IBM based on its annualized dividend rate as of January 12. Use this dividend yield in the Black-Scholes model. How different are the implied volatilties from those you obtain in the previous part?

   d. Do you observe a volatility smile?

23.13. For this problem, use the implied volatilities for the options expiring in January 2005, computed in the preceding problem. Compare the implied volatilties for calls and puts. Where is the difference largest? Why does this occur?

23.14. Suppose $S = \$100$, $r = 8\%$, $\sigma = 30\%$, $T = 1$, and $\delta = 0$. Use the Black-Scholes formula to generate call and put prices with the strikes ranging from $40 to $250, with increments of $5. Compute the implied volatility from these prices by using the formula for the VIX (equation 23.29). What happens to your estimate if you use strikes that differ by $1 or $10, or strikes that range only from $60 to $200?

23.15. Explain why the VIX formula in equation (23.29) overestimates implied volatility if options are American.

   The following three problems use the Merton jump formula. As a base case, assume $S = \$100$, $r = 8\%$, $\sigma = 30\%$, $T = 1$, and $\delta = 0$. Also assume that $\lambda = 0.02$, $\alpha_J = -0.20$ and $\sigma_J = 0.30$.

23.16. Using the Merton jump formula, generate an implied volatility plot for $K = 50, 55, \ldots 150$.

   a. How is the implied volatility plot affected by changing α_J to -0.40 or -0.10?

   b. How is the implied volatility plot affected by changing λ to 0.01 or 0.05?

c. How is the implied volatility plot affected by changing σ_J to 0.10 or 0.50?

23.17. Using the base case parameters, plot the implied volatility curve you obtain for the base case against that for the case where there is a jump to zero, with the same λ.

23.18. Repeat problem 23.16, except let $\alpha_J = 0.20$, and in part (b) consider expected alternate jump magnitudes of 0.10 and 0.50.

    The following two problems both use the CEV option pricing formula. Assume in both that $S = \$100$, $r = 8\%$, $\sigma_0 = 30\%$, $T = 1$, and $\delta = 0$.

23.19. Using the CEV option pricing model, set $\beta = 1$ and generate option prices for strikes from 60 to 140, in increments of 5, for times to maturity of 0.25, 0.5, 1.0, and 2.0. Plot the resulting implied volatilties. (This should reproduce Figure 23.9.)

23.20. Using the CEV option pricing model, set $\beta = 3$ and generate option prices for strikes from 60 to 140, in increments of 5, for times to maturity of 0.25, 0.5, 1.0, and 2.0. Plot the resulting implied volatilties.

APPENDIX 23.A

Here is one way to set up a spreadsheet in order to estimate a GARCH model by maximum likelihood using Excel.

1. Enter daily prices in column B, beginning in B10.

2. Compute continuously compounded returns for a 5-year period in column C, beginning in row 11. Leave cells A1:C7 empty.

3. In column D compute the squared continuously compounded return. This will be ϵ^2.

4. In cell E11, enter the variance of the continuously compounded returns. This will be your starting value for q.

5. In cell E12, enter the formula =\$B\$1+\$B\$2*D12+\$B\$3*E11. Be sure to pay attention to which cells are absolute and which are relative references. Copy this formula down the length of your data.

6. In cell F13, enter the formula $= -\ln(E13) - D13/E13$. Copy this formula down. This is your log-likelihood function for each observation.

7. Suppose that your last return is in row 1200. In cell B4, enter the formula = SUM(F13:F1200). This is the log-likelihood function for your data.

8. In Solver, set up the following constraints: $B1 \geq 0.0000001$, $B2 \geq 0.00000001$, $B3 > 0$, $B2 \leq 0.99999999 - B3$.

9. In cell B5, enter the formula B1/(1-B2-B3). This is your unconditional variance estimate.

10. In cell B6, enter the formula SQRT(B5*252). This is your unconditional annualized standard deviation.

11. Set up Solver to maximize cell B4 (the likelihood) by varying cells B1:B3 (the parameters).

12. Solve!

Your solution will likely be quite sensitive to several factors: to starting values, to the Solver options, and to unusually large squared returns. You should change the tolerance (in Solver options) to 1% or less. You should also experiment with different starting values for the parameters.

CHAPTER 24

Interest Rate Models

O ur goal in this chapter is to understand how to price derivatives that have bonds and interest rates, rather than stocks, as the underlying asset. We begin by seeing how the Black-Scholes approach to option pricing, discussed in Chapter 21, applies to bonds. As with stocks, there is a partial differential equation that characterizes the behavior of bond prices and other functions of interest rates. The Vasicek and Cox-Ingersoll-Ross models illustrate the procedure for deriving bond prices from an assumed model of the short-term interest rate. Next we examine the pricing of bond and interest rate options using the Black model (the name for the version of the Black-Scholes model for which the underlying asset is a futures contract). The Black model assumes that forward interest rates are lognormally distributed and can be used to price interest rate caps as well as bonds. Finally we examine binomial interest rate models, in particular the Black-Derman-Toy model.

24.1 MARKET-MAKING AND BOND PRICING

In this section we examine market-making in bonds in order to better understand how the Black-Scholes option pricing framework applies to bonds. We begin by examining the hedging of one bond with another.

The Black-Scholes derivation of the option pricing model characterizes the fair option price for a delta-hedging market-maker. Vasicek (1977) used the same approach for pricing bonds. Consider a delta-hedging bond portfolio manager, like the market-maker who delta-hedged options in Chapters 13 and 21. Specifically, suppose the manager owns one bond with maturity T_2 and hedges this bond by buying N bonds with maturity T_1 (N can be negative). The position is financed using short-term bonds paying r. Hedging one bond with another is often called duration-hedging rather than delta-hedging. The intent of duration- and delta-hedging is the same, but as we will see, the two are generally *not* the same if we use the standard definition of duration from Section 7.8.

The logic of the Vasicek approach to pricing bonds is identical to the Black-Scholes approach to analyzing options: We think about the problem faced by a market-maker and see what it tells us about bond price behavior. We will focus on pricing zero-coupon bonds since, as discussed in Chapter 7, they are a building block for all fixed-income products.

The Behavior of Bonds and Interest Rates

Before discussing how a bond market-maker would delta-hedge, we first need to specify how bonds behave. Suppose we try to model a zero-coupon bond the same way we model a stock, by assuming that the bond price, $P(t, T)$ follows an Itô process:

$$\frac{dP}{P} = \alpha(r, t)dt + q(r, t)dZ \qquad (24.1)$$

In this equation, the coefficients α and q cannot be constants and in fact must be modeled rather carefully to ensure that the bond satisfies its boundary conditions. For example, the bond must be worth $1 at maturity. Also, the volatility of the bond price should decrease as the bond approaches maturity—a given change in interest rates affects the price of a long-lived bond more than the price of a short-lived bond. Neither of these restrictions is automatically reflected in equation (24.1). In order to accommodate such behavior α and q must be carefully specified functions of the interest rate and time.

An alternative to beginning with equation (24.1) is to model the behavior of the interest rate and *solve* for the bond price. If we follow this approach, the bond price will *automatically* behave in an appropriate way, as long as the interest rate process is reasonable.

Suppose we assume that the short-term interest rate follows the Itô process

$$dr = a(r)dt + \sigma(r)dZ \qquad (24.2)$$

This equation for the behavior of the interest rate is general, in that the drift and standard deviation are functions of r. Given equation (24.2), what is the bond price? We will see that different bond price models arise from different versions of this interest rate process.

An Impossible Bond Pricing Model

We will first look at a bond pricing model that is intuitive, appealing in its simplicity, and widely used informally as a way to think about bonds. We will assume that the yield curve is flat; that is, at any point in time, zero-coupon bonds at all maturities have the same yield to maturity. If the interest rate changes, yields for all bonds change uniformly so that the yield curve remains flat. Unfortunately, this model of the yield curve gives rise to arbitrage opportunities. It can be instructive, however, to see what doesn't work in order to better appreciate what does.

To analyze the flat-yield curve assumption, we assume that the interest rate follows equation (24.2). The price of zero-coupon bonds is given by

$$P(t, T) = e^{-r(T-t)} \qquad (24.3)$$

In this specification, every bond has yield to maturity r.

We now analyze the delta-hedging problem. If we buy one bond maturing at time T_2, hedge by buying N bonds maturing at time T_1, and finance the difference at the short-term interest rate, the bond portfolio has value

$$I = NP(t, T_1) + P(t, T_2) + W = 0 \qquad (24.4)$$

Since W is invested in short-term bonds, we have

$$dW = rWdt \qquad (24.5)$$

By Itô's Lemma, and using the formula for the bond price, equation (24.3), the change in the value of the portfolio is

$$dI = NdP(t, T_1) + dP(t, T_2) + dW$$

$$= N\left(-(T_1 - t)P(t, T_1)dr + \frac{1}{2}(T_1 - t)^2\sigma^2 P(t, T_1)dt + rP(t, T_1)dt\right) \quad (24.6)$$

$$+ \left(-(T_2 - t)P(t, T_2)dr + \frac{1}{2}(T_2 - t)^2\sigma^2 P(t, T_2)dt + rP(t, T_2)dt\right) + rWdt$$

We pick N to eliminate the effect of interest rate changes, dr, on the value of the portfolio. Thus, we set

$$N = -\frac{(T_2 - t)P(t, T_2)}{(T_1 - t)P(t, T_1)} \quad (24.7)$$

The delta-hedged portfolio has no risk and no investment; it should therefore earn zero:

$$dI = 0 \quad (24.8)$$

Combining equations (24.4), (24.6), (24.7), and (24.8), and then simplifying, gives us

$$\tfrac{1}{2}(T_2 - T_1)\sigma^2 = 0 \quad (24.9)$$

This equation cannot hold unless $T_1 = T_2$. Thus, we conclude that *the bond valuation model implied by equations (24.2) and (24.3) is impossible*, in the sense that arbitrage is possible if the yield curve is stochastic and always flat.

This example demonstrates the difficulties of bond pricing: A casually specified model may give rise to arbitrage opportunities. A crucial feature of bond prices is the nonlinearity of prices as a function of interest rates, a characteristic implicitly ignored in equation (24.3). The same issue arises in pricing stock options: The nonlinearity of the option price with respect to the stock price is critical in pricing options. This is another example of Jensen's inequality.

The example also illustrates that, in general, *hedging a bond portfolio based on duration does not result in a perfect hedge*. Recall that the duration of a zero-coupon bond is the bond's time to maturity. The hedge ratio, equation (24.7), is *exactly* the same as equation (7.13) in Chapter 7. The use of duration to compute hedge ratios assumes that the yield to maturity of all bonds shifts by the same amount, which is what we assumed in equation (24.3). However, this assumption gives rise to arbitrage opportunities. The use of duration to compute hedge ratios can be a useful approximation; however, bonds in equilibrium *must* be priced in such a way that duration-based hedging does not work exactly.

An Equilibrium Equation for Bonds

Let's consider again the bond-hedging problem, only this time we will not assume a particular bond pricing model. Instead we view the bond as a general function of the short-term interest rate, r, which follows equation (24.2).[1]

---

[1] The discussion in this section follows Vasicek (1977).

First, let's see how the bond behaves. From Itô's Lemma, the bond, which is a function of the interest rate and time, follows the process

$$dP(r, t, T) = \frac{\partial P}{\partial r} dr + \frac{1}{2} \frac{\partial^2 P}{\partial r^2} (dr)^2 + \frac{\partial P}{\partial t} dt$$

$$= \left[a(r) \frac{\partial P}{\partial r} + \frac{1}{2} \frac{\partial^2 P}{\partial r^2} \sigma(r)^2 + \frac{\partial P}{\partial t} \right] dt + \frac{\partial P}{\partial r} \sigma(r) dZ$$

(24.10)

This equation does not look like equation (24.1), but we can define terms so that it does. Let

$$\alpha(r, t, T) = \frac{1}{P(r, t, T)} \left[a(r) \frac{\partial P}{\partial r} + \frac{1}{2} \frac{\partial^2 P}{\partial r^2} \sigma(r)^2 + \frac{\partial P}{\partial t} \right] \qquad (24.11)$$

$$q(r, t, T) = \frac{1}{P(r, t, T)} \frac{\partial P}{\partial r} \sigma(r) \qquad (24.12)$$

We can now rewrite equation (24.10) as

$$\frac{dP(r, t, T)}{P(r, t, T)} = \alpha(r, t, T) dt + q(r, t, T) dZ \qquad (24.13)$$

By using equations (24.11) and (24.12) to define α and q, equations (24.1) and (24.13) are the same. Note that α and q depend on both the interest rate and on the time to maturity of the bond.

Now we consider again the delta-hedged bond portfolio, the value of which is given by equation (24.4). From Itô's Lemma, we have

$$dI = N \left[\alpha(r, t, T_1) dt + q(r, t, T_1) dZ \right] P(r, t, T_1)$$

$$+ \left[\alpha(r, t, T_2) dt + q(r, t, T_2) dZ \right] P(r, t, T_2) + r W dt$$

(24.14)

In order to eliminate interest rate risk, we set

$$N = -\frac{P(r, t, T_2)}{P(r, t, T_1)} \frac{q(r, t, T_2)}{q(r, t, T_1)} \qquad (24.15)$$

Note that by using the definition of q, equation (24.12), this can be rewritten

$$N = -\frac{P_r(r, t, T_2)}{P_r(r, t, T_1)}$$

If you compare this expression to equation (7.13), you will see that $P_r(r, t, T)$ replaces duration when computing the hedge ratio, N.

Substituting equation (24.15) into equation (24.14), and setting $dI = 0$ (equation (24.8)), we obtain

$$\frac{\alpha(r, t, T_1) - r}{q(r, t, T_1)} = \frac{\alpha(r, t, T_2) - r}{q(r, t, T_2)} \qquad (24.16)$$

This equation says that *the Sharpe ratio for the two bonds is equal*. Since both bond prices are driven by the same random term, dZ, they must have the same Sharpe ratio if they are fairly priced. (We demonstrated this proposition in Chapter 20.)

Denote the Sharpe ratio for dZ as $\phi(r, t)$. For any bond we then have

$$\frac{\alpha(r, t, T) - r}{q(r, t, T)} = \phi(r, t) \tag{24.17}$$

Substituting equations (24.11) and (24.12) for α and q then gives us

$$\boxed{\frac{1}{2}\sigma(r)^2 \frac{\partial^2 P}{\partial r^2} + [a(r) - \sigma(r)\phi(r, t)]\frac{\partial P}{\partial r} + \frac{\partial P}{\partial t} - rP = 0} \tag{24.18}$$

When the short-term interest rate is the only source of uncertainty, *this partial differential equation must be satisfied by any zero-coupon bond.* Different bonds will have different maturity dates and therefore different boundary conditions. All bonds solve the same PDE, however. The Black-Scholes equation, equation (21.11), characterizes claims that are a function of the stock price. Equation (24.18) is the analogous equation for derivative claims that are a function of the interest rate.

A difference between equation (24.18) and equation (21.11) is the explicit appearance of the risk premium, $\sigma(r, t)\phi(r, t)$, in the bond equation. Let's talk about why that happens.

In the context of stock options, the Black-Scholes problem entails hedging an option with a stock, which is an investment asset. The stock is expected to earn its risk premium, which we will call $\phi'\sigma$. Thus, for the stock, the drift term, which is analogous to $a(r)$, equals $r + \phi'\sigma$. The Black-Scholes delta-hedging procedure eliminates the risk premium on the stock. By subtracting the risk premium, we are left with the risk-free rate, r, as a coefficient on the $\partial V/\partial S$ term in equation (21.11).

The interest rate, by contrast, is not the price of an investment asset. The interest rate is a *characteristic* of an asset, not an asset by itself. The risk-neutral process for the interest rate is obtained by subtracting the risk premium from the drift. The risk-neutral process for the interest rate is therefore

$$\boxed{dr = [a(r) - \sigma(r)\phi(r, t)]dt + \sigma(r)dZ} \tag{24.19}$$

The drift in this equation is what appears in equation (24.18). You can also confirm that equation (24.18) is the same as equation (24.17).

Given a zero-coupon bond (which has a terminal boundary condition that the bond is worth $1 at maturity), Cox et al. (1985b) show that the solution to equation (24.18) is

$$P[t, T, r(t)] = E_t^* \left[e^{-R(t, T)} \right] \tag{24.20}$$

where E^* represents the expectation taken with respect to risk-neutral probabilities and $R(t, T)$ is the random variable representing the cumulative interest rate over time:

$$R(t, T) = \int_t^T r(s)ds \tag{24.21}$$

Thus, to value a zero-coupon bond, we take the expectation over all the discount factors implied by these paths. We will see the discrete time analogue of this equation when we examine binomial models.

Keep in mind that it is *not* correct to value the bond by discounting the bond payoff by the average interest rate, $\bar{R} = E^*[R(t, T)]$:

$$P(t, T, r) \neq e^{-\bar{R}}$$

Because of Jensen's inequality, this seemingly reasonable procedure gives a different bond price than equation (24.20).

Different bond price models solve equation (24.20), differing only in the details of how r behaves and the modeling of the risk premium.

To summarize, a consistent approach to modeling bonds is to begin with a model of the interest rate and then use equation (24.18) to obtain a partial differential equation that describes the bond price (this equation is really the same as the Black-Scholes equation), but with a time-varying interest rate. Using the PDE together with boundary conditions, we can determine the price of the bond. If this seems familiar, it should: It is *exactly* the procedure we used to price options on stock.

The derivation of equation (24.18) assumes that bond prices are a function of a single state variable, the short-term interest rate r. It is possible to allow bond prices to depend on additional state variables, and there is empirical support for having bond prices depend on more than one state variable. Litterman and Scheinkman (1991) estimate a factor model for Treasury bond returns and find that a three-factor model typically explains more than 95% of the variability in a bond's return. They identify the three factors as level, steepness, and curvature of the yield curve. The single most important factor, the level of interest rates, accounts for almost 90% of the movement in bond returns. The overwhelming importance of the level of interest rates explains why duration-based hedging, despite its conceptual problems, is widely used. We will focus on single-variable models in this chapter.

Delta-Gamma Approximations for Bonds

One interpretation of equation (24.18) is familiar from Chapter 21. Using Itô's Lemma, the expected change in the bond price under the risk-neutral distribtion of the interest rate, equation (24.19), is

$$\frac{1}{dt}E^*(dP) = \frac{1}{2}\sigma(r)^2\frac{\partial^2 P}{\partial r^2} + [a(r) - \sigma(r)\phi(r, t)]\frac{\partial P}{\partial r} + \frac{\partial P}{\partial t}$$

Equation (24.18) therefore says that

$$\frac{1}{dt}E^*(dP) = rP \qquad (24.22)$$

This is the same as equation (21.31) for options: Using the risk-neutral distribution, bonds are priced to earn the risk-free rate.

The fact that bonds satisfy equation (24.22) means that, as in Chapter 13, *the delta-gamma-theta approximation for the change in a bond price holds exactly if the interest rate moves one standard deviation.* However, the Greeks for a bond are not exactly the same as duration and convexity.

We discussed bond duration and convexity in Chapter 7. For a zero-coupon bond, duration is time to maturity and convexity is squared time to maturity. Conceptually it seems as if duration should be the delta of a bond and convexity should be gamma. However, this is true only in the "impossible" bond pricing model of equation (24.3). For any correct bond pricing model, duration and convexity will be different than P_r/P and P_{rr}/P. We will see examples of this in the next section.

24.2 EQUILIBRIUM SHORT-RATE BOND PRICE MODELS

In this section we discuss several bond pricing models based on equation (24.18), in which all bond prices are driven by the short-term interest rate, r. The three pricing models we discuss—Rendleman-Bartter, Vasicek, and Cox-Ingersoll-Ross—differ in their specification of $\alpha(r)$, $\sigma(r)$, and $\phi(r)$. These differences can result in very different pricing implications.

The Rendelman-Bartter Model

The simplest models of the short-term interest rate are those in which the interest rate follows arithmetic or geometric Brownian motion. For example, we could write

$$dr = a\,dt + \sigma\,dZ \qquad (24.23)$$

In this specification, the short-rate is normally distributed with mean $r_0 + at$ and variance $\sigma^2 t$. There are several objections to this model:

- The short-rate can be negative. It is not reasonable to think the *nominal* short-rate can be negative, since if it were, investors would prefer holding cash under a mattress to holding bonds.

- The drift in the short-rate is constant. If $a > 0$, for example, the short-rate will drift up over time forever. In practice if the short-rate rises, we expect it to fall; i.e., it is *mean-reverting*.

- The volatility of the short-rate is the same whether the rate is high or low. In practice, we expect the short-rate to be more volatile if rates are high.

The Rendleman and Bartter (1980) model, by contrast, assumes that the short-rate follows geometric Brownian motion:

$$dr = ar\,dt + \sigma r\,dz \qquad (24.24)$$

While interest rates can never be negative in this model, one objection to equation (24.24) is that interest rates can be arbitrarily high. In practice we would expect rates to exhibit mean reversion; if rates are high, we expect them on average to decrease. The Rendleman-Bartter model, on the other hand, says that the probability of rates going up or down is the same whether rates are 100% or 1%.

TABLE 24.1	Expected change in the interest rate in the Vasicek model. Assumes $a = 0.2$, $b = 0.1$, and $\sigma = 0.01$.

Short-Rate	Expected Change in Short-Rate
5%	0.01
10%	0
15%	−0.01
20%	−0.02

The Vasicek Model

The Vasicek model incorporates mean reversion:

$$dr = a(b - r)dt + \sigma dz \qquad (24.25)$$

This is an Ornstein-Uhlenbeck process (see Chapter 20). The $a(b - r)dt$ term induces mean reversion. Suppose we set $a = 20\%$, $b = 10\%$, and $\sigma = 1\%$. These parameters imply that a one-standard-deviation move for the short-rate is 100 basis points. The parameter b is the level to which short-term interest rates revert. If $r > b$, the short-rate is expected to decrease. If $r < b$, the short-rate is expected to rise. Table 24.1 illustrates mean reversion.

The parameter a reflects the speed with which the interest rate adjusts to b. If $a = 0$, then the short-rate is a random walk. If $a = 1$, the gap between the short-rate and b is expected to be closed in a year. If $a = 20\%$, we expect the rate to decrease in the first year by 20% of the gap.

Note also that the term multiplying dz is simply σ, independent of the level of the interest rate. This formulation implies that it is possible for interest rates to become negative and that the variability of interest rates is independent of the level of rates.

In the Rendleman-Bartter model, interest rates could not be negative because both the mean and variance in that model are proportional to the level of the interest rate. Thus, as the short-rate approaches zero, both the mean and variance also approach zero, and it is never possible for the rate to fall below zero. In the Vasicek model, by contrast, rates can become negative because the variance does not vanish as r approaches zero.

Why would anyone construct a model that permitted negative interest rates? Vasicek used equation (24.25) to illustrate the more general pricing methodology outlined in Section 24.1, not because it was a compelling empirical description of interest rates. The Vasicek model does in fact have some unreasonable pricing implications, in particular negative yields for long-term bonds.

We can solve for the price of a pure discount bond in the Vasicek model. Let the Sharpe ratio for interest rate risk be ϕ. With the Vasicek interest rate dynamics, equation

(24.25), equation (24.18) becomes

$$\frac{1}{2}\sigma^2\frac{\partial^2 P}{\partial r^2} + [a(b-r) - \sigma\phi]\frac{\partial P}{\partial r} + \frac{\partial P}{\partial t} - rP = 0$$

The bond price formula that solves this equation subject to the boundary condition $P(T, T, r) = 1$, and assuming $a \neq 0$, is[2]

$$P[t, T, r(t)] = A(t, T)e^{-B(t,T)r(t)} \qquad (24.26)$$

where

$$A(t, T) = e^{\bar{r}(B(t,T)+t-T)-B^2\sigma^2/4a}$$

$$B(t, T) = (1 - e^{-a(T-t)})/a$$

$$\bar{r} = b + \sigma\phi/a - 0.5\sigma^2/a^2$$

with $\bar{r}$ being the yield to maturity on an infinitely lived bond.

The Cox-Ingersoll-Ross Model

The Cox-Ingersoll-Ross (CIR) model (Cox et al., 1985b) assumes a short-term interest rate model of the form

$$dr = a(b-r)dt + \sigma\sqrt{r}dz \qquad (24.27)$$

The variance of the interest rate is proportional to the square root of the interest rate, instead of being constant as in the Vasicek model. Because of this subtle difference, the CIR model satisfies all the objections to the earlier models:

- It is impossible for interest rates to be negative. If $r = 0$, the drift in the rate is positive and the variance is zero, so the rate will become positive.

- As the short-rate rises, the volatility of the short-rate also rises.

- The short-rate exhibits mean reversion.

The assumption that the variance is proportional to $\sqrt{r}$ also turns out to be convenient analytically—Cox, Ingersoll, and Ross (CIR) derive bond and option pricing formulas using this model. The risk premium in the CIR model takes the form

$$\phi(r, t) = \bar{\phi}\sqrt{r}/\sigma \qquad (24.28)$$

---

[2]When $a = 0$, the solution is equation (24.26), with

$$A = e^{0.5\sigma\phi(T-t)^2+\sigma^2(T-t)^3/6}$$

$$B = T - t$$

When $a = 0$ the interest rate follows a random walk; therefore, $\bar{r}$ is undefined.

With this specification for the risk premium and equation (24.27), the CIR interest rate dynamics, the partial differential equation for the bond price is

$$\frac{1}{2}\sigma^2 r \frac{\partial^2 P}{\partial r^2} + [a(b-r) - r\bar{\phi}]\frac{\partial P}{\partial r} + \frac{\partial P}{\partial t} - rP = 0$$

The CIR bond price looks similar to that for the Vasicek dynamics, equation (24.26), but with $A(t, T)$ and $B(t, T)$ defined differently:

$$P[t, T, r(t)] = A(t, T)e^{-B(t,T)r(t)} \tag{24.29}$$

where

$$A(t, T) = \left[\frac{2\gamma e^{(a+\bar{\phi}+\gamma)(T-t)/2}}{(a+\bar{\phi}+\gamma)(e^{\gamma(T-t)} - 1) + 2\gamma}\right]^{2ab/\sigma^2}$$

$$B(t, T) = \frac{2(e^{\gamma(T-t)} - 1)}{(a+\bar{\phi}+\gamma)(e^{\gamma(T-t)} - 1) + 2\gamma}$$

$$\gamma = \sqrt{(a+\bar{\phi})^2 + 2\sigma^2}$$

With the CIR process, the yield on a long-term bond approaches the value $\bar{r} = 2ab/(a + \bar{\phi} + \gamma)$ as time to maturity goes to infinity.

Comparing Vasicek and CIR

How different are the prices generated by the CIR and Vasicek models? What is the role of the different variance specifications in the two models?

Figure 24.1 illustrates the yield curves generated by the Vasicek and by the CIR models, assuming that the current short-term rate, r, is 5%, $a = 0.2$ and $b = 10\%$. Volatility in the Vasicek model is 2% in the top panel and 10% in the bottom panel. The volatility, σ, has a different interpretation in each model. In the Vasicek model, volatility is absolute, whereas in the CIR model, volatility is scaled by the square root of the current interest rate. To make the CIR volatility comparable at the initial interest rate, it is set so that $\sigma_{CIR}\sqrt{r} = \sigma_{Vasicek}$, or 0.0894 in the top panel and 0.447 in the bottom panel. The interest rate risk premium is assumed to be zero.

The two models can exhibit very different behavior. The bottom panel has a relatively high volatility. For short-term bonds—with a maturity extending to about 2.5 years—the yield curves look similar. This is a result of setting the CIR volatility to match the Vasicek volatility. Beyond that point the two diverge, with Vasicek yields below CIR yields. The long-run interest rate in the Vasicek model is −0.025, whereas that in the CIR model is 0.0463. This difference is evident in Figure 24.1 as the Vasicek yields approach zero (in the long run approaching −0.025).

What accounts for the difference in medium to long-term bonds? As discussed earlier, the pricing formulas are based on *averages* of interest rate paths, as in equation (24.20). Some of the interest paths in the Vasicek model will be negative. Although

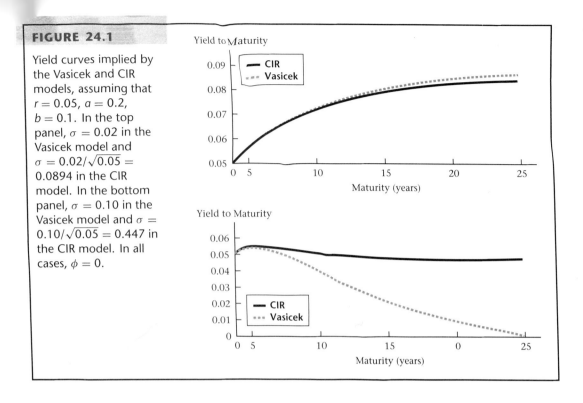

FIGURE 24.1

Yield curves implied by the Vasicek and CIR models, assuming that $r = 0.05$, $a = 0.2$, $b = 0.1$. In the top panel, $\sigma = 0.02$ in the Vasicek model and $\sigma = 0.02/\sqrt{0.05} = 0.0894$ in the CIR model. In the bottom panel, $\sigma = 0.10$ in the Vasicek model and $\sigma = 0.10/\sqrt{0.05} = 0.447$ in the CIR model. In all cases, $\phi = 0$.

the *typical* path will be positive because of mean reversion—rates will be pulled toward 10%—there will be paths on which rates are negative. Because of Jensen's inequality, these paths will be disproportionately important. Over sufficiently long horizons, large negative interest rates become more likely and this leads to negative yields. In the CIR model, this effect results in the long-run yield decreasing with volatility. Negative yields are impossible in the CIR model, however, since the short-term interest rate can never become negative.

In the top panel, with relatively low volatility, both yield curves are upward sloping. The effect of mean reversion outweighs that of volatility. In the long run, the Vasicek yield exceeds the CIR yield because volatility increases with the level of the interest rate in the CIR model. Consequently, the Jensen's inequality effect is more pronounced in the CIR model than in the Vasicek model.

We mentioned earlier that hedging in the context of this kind of interest rate ...na flowing is different from duration hedging. In the CIR and Vasicek models, delta convexity for a zero-coupon bond are based on the change in the short-ter~ example illustrates that the resulting hedge ratios can differ *f* as traditionally measured.

Example 24.1 Consider a 5-year zero-coupon bond priced using the CIR model, and suppose that $a = 0.2$, $b = 0.1$, $r = 0.08$, $\bar{\phi} = 0$, and $\sigma = 0.2$. The bond price is 0.667. Because it is a 5-year zero-coupon bond, duration is 5 and convexity is 25. However, in the CIR model with these parameters, $P_r = -1.918$ and $P_{rr} = 5.518$. The implied sensitivities to the short-term rate are $-P_r/P = 2.876$ (instead of 5) and $P_{rr}/P = 8.273$ (instead of 25). ⚜

24.3 BOND OPTIONS, CAPS, AND THE BLACK MODEL

We encountered the Black formula for pricing options on futures in Chapter 12. In this section we see how to use the Black model to price interest rate and bond options. The idea behind using the Black model in this context is that the forward price for a bond is the underlying asset, and we assume that this forward price is lognormally distributed.

We will begin by seeing how the Black model can be used to price an option on a zero-coupon bond. As in Chapter 7, let $P_t(T, T + s)$ denote the time-t price of a zero-coupon bond purchased at T and paying $1 at time $T + s$. If $t = T$, then $P_T(T, T + s)$ is the spot price of the bond and we will write $P(T, T + s)$ without a subscript. If $t < T$, then $P_t(T, T + s)$ is a forward price, which we will also represent as $F_{t,T}[P(T, T + s)]$.

Consider a call option with strike price K, expiring at time T, on a zero-coupon bond paying $1 at time $T + s$. The payoff of this option at time T is

$$\text{Call option payoff} = \max[0, P(T, T + s) - K] \tag{24.30}$$

We can price this option as an exchange option (see Sections 14.6 and 22.6). Recall that the time-t forward price of the bond deliverable at T is

$$F_{t,T}[P(T, T + s)] = P(t, T + s)/P(t, T) \tag{24.31}$$

The prepaid forward price of this bond at time t is $F_{t,T}[P(T, T + s)] \times P(t, T) = P(t, T + s)$, which is just the time-t price of the $T + s$ maturity bond. The time-t prepaid forward for the strike price is $KP(t, T)$.

The appropriate volatility for pricing this exchange option is the volatility of the ratio of the prepaid forward prices for the underlying asset and strike asset:

$$\text{Var}(\ln[P(t, T + s)/KP(t, T)]) = \text{Var}(\ln[P(t, T + s)/P(t, T)]$$
$$= \text{Var}(\ln(F_{t,T}[P(T, T + s)]))$$

at t the volatility that enters the pricing formula is the volatility of the forward price where the forward contract calls for time-T delivery of the bond maturing

If we assume that the bond forward price is lognormally distributed with constant volatility σ, we obtain the Black formula for a bond option:[3]

$$\boxed{C[F, P(0, T), \sigma, T] = P(0, T)[FN(d_1) - KN(d_2)]} \qquad (24.32)$$

where

$$d_1 = \frac{\ln(F/K) + 0.5\sigma^2 T}{\sigma\sqrt{T}}$$

$$d_2 = d_1 - \sigma\sqrt{T}$$

and where F is an abbreviation for the bond forward price $F_{0,T}[P(T, T + s)]$. Since $P(0, T)F = P(0, T + s)$, this formula simply uses the price of the $T + s$ bond as the underlying asset. The formula for a put can be obtained by put-call parity.

This use of the Black formula to price bond options is intuitively reasonable. The price of any particular bond varies over time. However, the value of a bond option depends upon the volatility of the *ratio* in the prices of bonds with different maturities. If today is time t and the option expires at time T, the interest rate from time t to time T affects the discounting of *both* the underlying asset (the bond maturing at time $T + s$) and the strike price (from time t to time T). Since the option price depends on $\ln[P(t, T + s)/P(t, T)]$, only the volatility of the bond forward price affects the price of the option.

The Black formula can be extended to price options on interest rates. Imagine that a floating rate borrower wishes to hedge the interest rate at time T for a loan with time to maturity s (therefore maturing at time $T + s$). We saw in Chapter 7 that the forward interest rate from time T to time $T + s$, $R_0(T, T + s)$, is

$$R_0(T, T + s) = \frac{P(0, T)}{P(0, T + s)} - 1 \qquad (24.33)$$

Notice that in equation (24.33), R is not annualized. If you invest \$1 at time T at the forward rate, after s periods you will have $1 + R_0(T, T + s)$.

One way for the borrower to hedge interest rate risk is by entering into a forward rate agreement (FRA), receiving at time $T + s$ the difference between the spot s-period rate, $R_T(T, T + s)$, and the forward rate, $R_0(T, T + s)$:

$$\text{Payoff to FRA} = R_T(T, T + s) - R_0(T, T + s)$$

As an alternative to hedging with an FRA, the borrower could enter into a call option on an FRA, with strike price K_R. This option, which is also called a **caplet**, at time $T + s$

---

[3] Note that we can write the option in terms of the bond prices as $P(0, T + s)N(d_1) - KP(0, T)N(d_2)$, where $d_1 = (\ln[P(0, T + s)/KP(0, T)] + 0.5\sigma^2 T)/\sigma\sqrt{T}$. Writing the formula as in equation (24.32) emphasizes that the relevant volatility is that of the forward bond price.

pays

$$\text{Payoff to caplet} = \max[0, R_T(T, T+s) - K_R] \tag{24.34}$$

The caplet permits the borrower to pay the time-T market interest rate if it is below K_R, but receive a payment for the difference in rates if the rate is above K_R. If settled at time T, the option would pay

$$\frac{1}{1 + R_T(T, T+s)} \max[0, R_T(T, T+s) - K_R] \tag{24.35}$$

Let R_T be shorthand for $R_T(T, T+s)$. We can rewrite equation (24.35) as

$$(1 + K_R) \max\left[0, \frac{R_T - K_R}{(1 + R_T)(1 + K_R)}\right]$$

$$= (1 + K_R) \max\left[0, \frac{1}{1 + K_R} - \frac{1}{1 + R_T}\right] \tag{24.36}$$

Note that $1/(1 + R_T)$ is the time-T price of a bond paying \$1 at time $T + s$. The expression on the right-hand side of equation (24.36) is therefore the expiration payoff to $1 + K_R$ bond put options with strike price $1/(1 + K_R)$. The bond option model, equation (24.32), can therefore be used to price caplets.

An interest rate **cap** is a collection of caplets. Suppose a borrower has a floating rate loan with interest payments at times t_i, $i = 1, \ldots, n$. A cap would make the series of payments

$$\text{Cap payment at time } t_{i+1} = \max[0, R_{t_i}(t_i, t_{i+1}) - K_R] \tag{24.37}$$

The value of the cap is the summed value of the individual caplets.

Example 24.2 One-year and 2-year zero-coupon bonds with a \$1 maturity value have prices of \$0.9091 and \$0.8116. The 1-year implied forward 1-year bond price is therefore \$0.8116/\$0.9091 = \$0.8928, with an implied forward rate of 12.01%. Suppose the volatility of the forward bond price is 10%. The price of a 1-year put option to sell the 1-year bond for a price of \$0.88 is

$$\text{BSPut}(\$0.8116, \$0.9091 \times \$0.88, 0.1, 0, 1, 0) = \$0.0267 \qquad ⩨$$

In practice, the implied volatility from the Black formula is convenient for quoting prices of caps and caplets. For example, the statement that caps are priced at about a 10% volatility (using the Black formula) gives a general sense of prices, even though there is likely to be a volatility skew across strikes.

Using the tree in Figure 24.2, we obtain the following valuation equations. For the one-period bond we have

$$P_0(0, 1; 0) = e^{-rh} \qquad (24.39)$$

The two-year bond is priced by working backward along the tree. In the second period, the price of the bond is $1. One year from today, the bond will have the price e^{-r_u} with probability p or e^{-r_d} with probability $1 - p$. The price of the bond is therefore

$$P_0(0, 2; 0) = e^{-rh} \left[pe^{-r_u h} + (1 - p)e^{-r_d h} \right] \qquad (24.40)$$

$$= e^{-rh} \left[p P_1(1, 2; 1) + (1 - p) P_1(1, 2; 0) \right] \qquad (24.41)$$

Thus, we can price the 2-year bond using either the interest rate tree or the implied bond prices.

Finally, the 3-year bond is again priced by traversing the entire tree. The price is $1 after 3 years. After 2 years, the price will be $1 discounted at r_{uu}, r_{ud}, r_{du}, or r_{dd}. Continuing in this way, the price is

$$P_0(0, 3; 0) = e^{-r} \left[pe^{-r_u} \left(pe^{-r_{uu}} + (1 - p)e^{-r_{ud}} \right) \right.$$
$$\left. + (1 - p)e^{-r_d} \left(pe^{-r_{du}} + (1 - p)e^{-r_{dd}} \right) \right] \qquad (24.42)$$

The 3-year bond calculation can be written differently. By collecting terms in equation (24.42), we can rewrite it as

$$P_0(0, 3; 0) = p^2 e^{-(r+r_u+r_{uu})} + p(1 - p)e^{-(r+r_u+r_{ud})}$$
$$+ (1 - p)p e^{-(r+r_d+r_{du})} + (1 - p)^2 e^{-(r+r_d+r_{dd})} \qquad (24.43)$$

This version of equation (24.42) makes clear that we can value the bond by considering separately each *path* the interest rate can take. Each path implies a realized discount factor. We then compute the expected discount factor, using risk-neutral probabilities. Denoting this expectation as E^*, the value of the zero-coupon bond is

$$E^* \left(e^{-(r_0+r_1+r_2)h} \right)$$

More generally, letting r_i represent the time-i rate, we have

$$\boxed{E^* \left(e^{-\sum_{i=0}^{n} r_i h} \right)} \qquad (24.44)$$

All bond valuation models implicitly calculate equation (24.44).

Example 24.3 Figure 24.2 constructs an interest rate tree assuming that the current 1-year rate is 10% and that each year the 1-year rate moves up or down 4%, with probability $p = 0.5$. We can use this tree to price 1-, 2-, and 3-year zero-coupon default-free bonds.

One-year bond: From equation (24.39), the price of the 1-year bond is

$$P(0, h) = e^{-0.10} = \$0.9048 \qquad (24.45)$$

Two-year bond: From equation (24.40), the two-period bond price is

$$P(0, 2) = e^{-0.10} \left(0.5e^{-0.14} + 0.5e^{-0.06} \right)$$
$$= \$0.8194$$

Three-year bond: Finally, from equation (24.42), the price of the 3-year bond is

$$P(0, 3) = e^{-0.10}\left[0.5e^{-0.14}\left(0.5e^{-0.18}+0.5e^{-0.10}\right)+0.5e^{-0.06}\left(0.5e^{-0.10}+0.5e^{-0.02}\right)\right]$$
$$= \$0.7438$$

Equation (24.44) also gives \$0.7438 as the price of the three-period zero-coupon bond.

We should note that the volatility of the bond price implied by Figure 24.3 is different from the behavior of a stock. With a stock, uncertainty about the future stock price increases with horizon due to the fact that the volatility of the continuously compounded return grows with the square root of time. With a bond, the volatility of the bond price initially grows with time. However, as the bond approaches maturity, volatility declines because of the boundary condition that the bond price approaches \$1. Just before maturity, volatility of the price must be essentially zero for a default-free bond. The binomial model in Figure 24.3 produces this behavior of volatility as a matter of course since it models the interest rate, not the bond price.

Yields and Expected Interest Rates

In Figure 24.3, we assume that $p = 0.5$ and the up and down moves are symmetric—the interest rate follows a random walk. Consequently, the expected interest rate at each node is 10%. The yields on the two- and three-period bonds, however, are *not* 10%. The yield on the two-period bond is

$$-\ln[P(0, 2)]/2 = -\ln(0.8194)/2 = 0.0996$$

The yield on the three-period bond is

$$-\ln[P(0, 3)]/3 = -\ln(0.7438)/3 = 0.0987$$

Yields are less than 10% on the two- and three-period bonds because of Jensen's inequality: The average of the exponentiated interest rates is less than the exponentiated average. Thus, as we discussed earlier, we cannot price a bond by using the expected interest rate. *Uncertainty causes bond yields to be lower than the expected average interest rate.* The discrepancy between yields and average interest rates increases with volatility. (Problem 24.7 asks you to verify this relationship by constructing a different

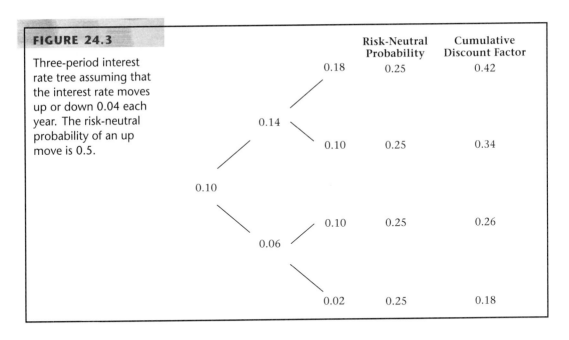

FIGURE 24.3

Three-period interest rate tree assuming that the interest rate moves up or down 0.04 each year. The risk-neutral probability of an up move is 0.5.

	Risk-Neutral Probability	Cumulative Discount Factor
0.18	0.25	0.42
0.10	0.25	0.34
0.10	0.25	0.26
0.02	0.25	0.18

interest rate tree and repeating the bond valuation.) This is another illustration of the effect of Jensen's inequality that was evident in the Vasicek–CIR comparison.

Option Pricing

Using the binomial tree to price a bond option works the same way as bond pricing. Suppose we have a call option with strike price K on a $(T - t)$-year zero-coupon bond, with the option expiring in $t - t_0$ periods. The expiration value of the option is

$$O(t, j) = \max[0, P_t(t, T; j) - K] \qquad (24.46)$$

To price the option we can work recursively backward through the tree using risk-neutral pricing, as with an option on a stock. The value one period earlier at the node j' is

$$O(t - h, j') = P_{t-h}(t - h, t; j') \\ \times \left[p \times O(t, 2 \times j' + 1) + (1 - p) \times O(m, 2 \times j') \right] \qquad (24.47)$$

The calculation here assumes there is a nonrecombining tree. Since each node generates two new nodes, if there are J nodes in one period, there will be $2 \times J$ nodes the next period. Thus, if we are at node j, we can potentially move to node $2 \times j$ or $(2 \times j) + 1$ in one period.[7] We continue in this way to obtain the option value in period 0. In the

---

[7]For example, from node 0, we move to node 0 or 1; from node 1, to node 2 or 3, and so forth.

same way, we can value an option on a yield, or an option on any instrument that is a function of the interest rate.

Delta-hedging works for the bond option just as for a stock option. In this case the underlying asset is a zero-coupon bond maturing at T, since that will be a $(T - t)$-period bond in period t. Each period, the delta-hedged portfolio of the option and underlying asset (the bond with $T - t_0$ to expiration) is financed by the short-term bond, paying whatever one-period interest rate prevails at that node.

Example 24.4   Suppose we have a two-year put on a 1-year zero-coupon bond and the strike price is \$0.88. The payoff in year 2 is

$$\max[0, \$0.88 - P(2, 3; 2, j)]$$

The option price is computed based on the 1-year bond price in year 2.

From Figure 24.3, there is only one node at which the put will be exercised, namely that where the interest rate is 0.18 and, hence, the bond price is $e^{-0.18} = \$0.8353$. Using the interest rates along the tree, and accounting for the 0.25 risk-neutral probability of reaching that one node, we obtain an option price of

$$(\$0.88 - \$0.8353)e^{-(0.14+0.10)} \times 0.25 = \$0.0088$$

24.5 THE BLACK-DERMAN-TOY MODEL

At any point in time we can observe the yield curve and the volatilities of bond options. Thus far we have ignored the important practical question of whether a particular interest rate model fits these data. For example, for any interest rate model, we can ask whether it correctly prices zero-coupon bonds (in which case it will correctly price forwards and swaps) and selected options. Matching a model to fit the data is called *calibration*.

Yield curves can have various shapes. The models we have examined, however, are not particularly flexible. For example, the binomial random walk model has two parameters: The starting interest rate and the volatility generating up and down moves. The CIR and Vasicek models have four parameters (a, b, r, and σ) and generate yield curves with particular stylized shapes that may not match the data. These models are arbitrage-free in a world consistent with their assumptions. In the real world, however, they will generate *apparent* arbitrage opportunities, in the sense that observed prices will not match theoretical prices. We then have a choice of concluding either that zero-coupon bonds are priced incorrectly or that the models are not accurate enough to capture reality.

Some models attempt to provide a rich characterization of the yield curve and the yield curve volatility. Notable papers describing these models include Ho and Lee (1986), Black et al. (1990), and Heath et al. (1992). We will focus on the Black-Derman-Toy (BDT) model to illustrate how calibration works.

| TABLE 24.2 | | Hypothetical bond-market data. Bond prices and yields are the observed prices and effective annual yields for zero-coupon bonds with the indicated maturity. Volatility refers to the volatility of the bond price 1 year from today. |

Maturity (years)	Yield to Maturity	Bond Price ($)	Volatility in Year 1
1	10%	0.9091	N/A
2	11%	0.8116	10%
3	12%	0.7118	15%
4	12.5%	0.6243	14%

The basic idea of the Black-Derman-Toy model is to compute a binomial tree of short-term interest rates, with a flexible enough structure to match the data. We will begin with sample data and demonstrate that a particular tree matches these data. We will then explain how to construct the tree. We assume in this discussion that the length of a binomial period is 1 year, although that is arbitrary.

Table 24.2 lists market information about bonds that we would like to match. We follow the Black-Derman-Toy paper in using effective annual yields rather than continuously compounded yields. Since the table contains prices of zero-coupon bonds, we can infer the term structure of implied forward interest rates. There is also information about the volatility of interest rates. The column headed "Volatility in Year 1" is the standard deviation of the natural log of the *yield* for that bond 1 year hence. (We could, if we wished, convert this into a standard deviation of the bond price in a year.) The volatility for the n-year bond tells us the uncertainty about the year-1 yield on an $(n-1)$-year bond. The volatility in year 1 of the 2-year bond is 10%; this tells us that the 1-year yield in year 1 will have a 10% volatility. Similarly, the volatility in year 1 of the 4-year bond (which will be a 3-year bond in year 1) is 14%. While the tree matches observed yields and volatilities, it makes no attempt to capture the evolution of the yield curve over time. The yield curve evolution is of course implicit in the tree, but the tree is not calibrated with this in mind.

The BDT approach provides enough flexibility to match this data. Black, Derman, and Toy describe their tree as driven by the short-term rate, which they assume is log-normally distributed. The general structure of the resulting tree is illustrated in Figure 24.4. We assume that the risk-neutral probability of an up move in the interest rate is 50%.

For each period in the tree there are two parameters. R_{ih} can be thought of as a rate level parameter at a given time and σ_i as a volatility parameter. These parameters can be used to match the tree with the data. In an ordinary lognormal stock-price tree,

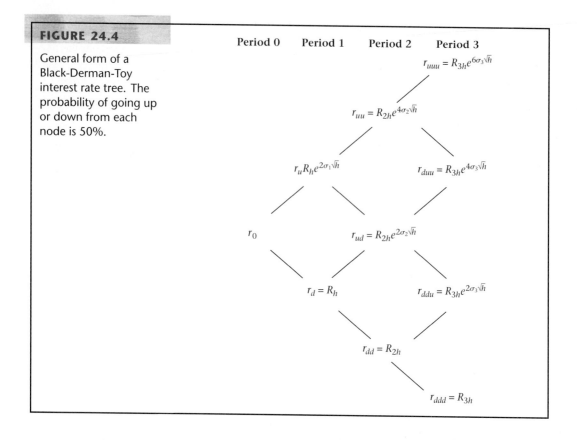

FIGURE 24.4

General form of a Black-Derman-Toy interest rate tree. The probability of going up or down from each node is 50%.

the ratio of the up node to the down node is $Ae^{\sigma\sqrt{h}}/Ae^{-\sigma\sqrt{h}} = e^{2\sigma\sqrt{h}}$. The ratio between adjacent nodes is the same in Figure 24.4.

The volatilities in Table 24.2 are measured in the tree as follows. Let the time-h price of a zero-coupon bond maturing at T when the time-t short-term rate is $r(h)$ be $P[h, T, r(h)]$. The yield of the bond is

$$y[h, T, r(h)] = P[h, T, r(h)]^{-1/(T-h)} - 1$$

At time h the short-term rate can take on the two values r_u or r_d. The annualized lognormal yield volatility is then

$$\text{Yield volatility} = 0.5 \times \ln\left[\frac{y(h, T, r_u)}{y(h, T, r_d)}\right] \tag{24.48}$$

We multiply by 0.5 since the distance between nodes is twice the exponentiated volatility.

The tree in Figure 24.5, which depicts 1-year effective annual rates, was constructed using the data in Table 24.2. The tree behaves differently from binomial trees

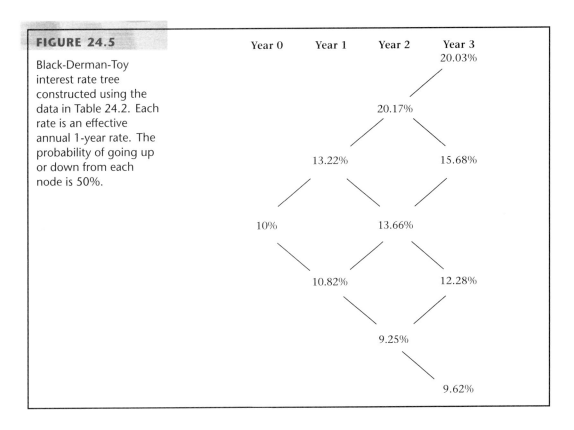

FIGURE 24.5

Black-Derman-Toy interest rate tree constructed using the data in Table 24.2. Each rate is an effective annual 1-year rate. The probability of going up or down from each node is 50%.

we have seen thus far. Unlike a stock-price tree, the nodes are not necessarily centered on the previous period's nodes. For example, in year 1, the lowest interest rate node is above the year-0 interest rate. If we track the minimum interest rate along the bottom of the tree, it increases, then decreases, then increases again. The maximum interest rate in year 3 is below the maximum rate in year 2.

These oddities arise because we constructed the tree to match the data in Table 24.2. Although bond yields steadily increase with maturity, volatilities do not. In order to match the pattern of volatilities given the structure of the BDT tree, rates must behave in what seems like an unusual fashion. Notice that in periods 2 and 3 the ratio of adjacent nodes in the same period is the same. For example, $r_{uuu}/r_{duu} = 20.03/15.68 = 15.68/12.28 = r_{duu}/r_{ddu}$.

Now let's verify that the tree in Figure 24.5 matches the data in Table 24.2. To verify that the tree matches the yield curve, we need to compute the prices of zero-coupon bonds with maturities of 1, 2, 3, and 4 years. To verify the volatilities, we need to compute the prices of 1-, 2-, and 3-year zero-coupon bonds at year 1, and then compute the yield volatilities of those bonds.

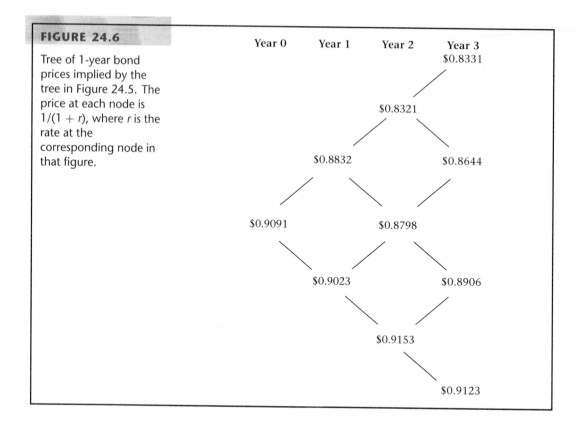

FIGURE 24.6

Tree of 1-year bond prices implied by the tree in Figure 24.5. The price at each node is $1/(1 + r)$, where r is the rate at the corresponding node in that figure.

	Year 0	Year 1	Year 2	Year 3

Verifying Yields

The rate at the first node is 10%, which corresponds to the current 1-year yield.

We can compute the price (and thus yield) of the 2-year zero-coupon bond by starting in year 2 and working backward. It is slightly more convenient to use the tree of 1-year bond prices in Figure 24.6. In year 1, the 2-year bond will be worth either $0.8832 (a yield of 13.22%) or $0.9023 (a yield of 10.82%). Thus, the discounted expected price at time 0 is

$$\$0.9091 \times (0.5 \times \$0.8832 + 0.5 \times \$0.9023) = \$0.8116$$

Figure 24.7 illustrates the tree corresponding to this calculation.

The price of the 3-year zero is computed in a similar way. Working backwards from the year-3 nodes we have

$$\$0.9091 \times [0.5 \times \$0.8832 \times (0.5 \times \$0.8321 + 0.5 \times \$0.8798)$$
$$+ 0.5 \times \$0.9023 \times (0.5 \times \$0.8798 + 0.5 \times \$0.9153)] = \$0.7118$$

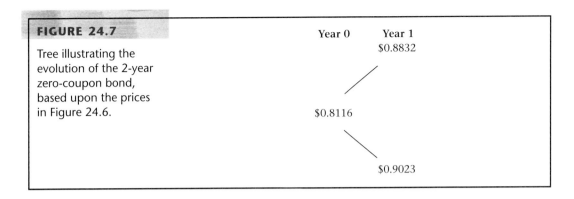

FIGURE 24.7

Tree illustrating the evolution of the 2-year zero-coupon bond, based upon the prices in Figure 24.6.

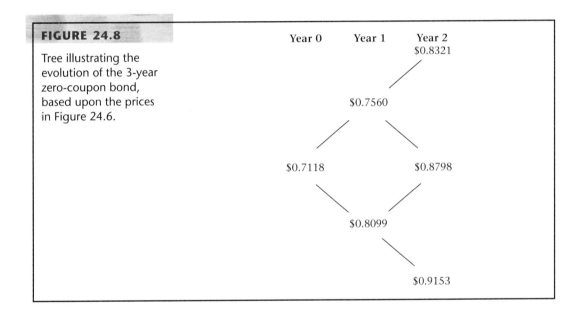

FIGURE 24.8

Tree illustrating the evolution of the 3-year zero-coupon bond, based upon the prices in Figure 24.6.

Figure 24.8 illustrates the tree showing the evolution of the 3-year bond. Problem 24.8 asks you to verify that the tree in Figure 24.6 generates the correct 4-year zero-coupon bond price.

Verifying Volatilities

Now we want to see what volatilities are implied by the tree. The volatilities in Table 24.2 are *yield* volatilities. Thus, for each bond, we need to compute implied bond yields in year 1 and then compute the volatility.

For the 2-year bond (1-year bond in year 1), the yield volatility using equation (24.48) is

$$0.5 \times \ln\left(\frac{0.8832^{-1} - 1}{0.9023^{-1} - 1}\right) = 0.1$$

From Figure 24.8, the 3-year bond in year 1 (which will be a 2-year bond) will be worth either $0.7560, with a yield of $0.7560^{-1/2} - 1 = 0.1501$ or $0.8099^{-1/2} - 1 = 0.1112$. The yield volatility is then

$$0.5 \times \ln\left(\frac{0.1501}{0.1112}\right) = 0.15$$

Both yields match the inputs in Table 24.2.

Problem 24.9 asks you to verify that the tree generates the correct 4-year yield volatility.

Constructing a Black-Derman-Toy Tree

We have verified that the tree in Figure 24.5 is consistent with the data in Table 24.2. Now we turn the question around: Given the data, how did we generate the tree in the first place? The answer is that we started at early nodes and worked to the later nodes, building the tree outward.

The first node is given by the prevailing 1-year rate. Therefore the 1-year bond price is

$$\$0.9091 = \frac{1}{1 + R_0} \tag{24.49}$$

Thus, $R_0 = 0.10$.

For the second node, the year-1 price of a 1-year bond is $P(1, 2, r_u)$ or $P(1, 2, r_d)$. We require that two conditions be satisfied:

$$\$0.8116 = \frac{1}{1 + 0.10}[0.5 \times P(1, 2, r_u) + 0.5 \times P(1, 2, r_d)]$$

$$= \frac{1}{1 + 0.10}\left(0.5 \times \frac{1}{1 + R_1 e^{2\sigma_1}} + 0.5 \times \frac{1}{1 + R_1}\right) \tag{24.50}$$

$$0.10 = 0.5 \times \ln([P(1, 2, r_u)^{-1} - 1]/[P(1, 2, r_d)^{-1} - 1])$$

$$= 0.5 \times \ln(R_1 e^{2\sigma}/R_1) \tag{24.51}$$

The second equation gives us $\sigma = 0.1$ and this value enables us to solve the first equation to obtain $R_1 = 0.1082$.

It is a bit messier to solve for the next set of conditions, but conceptually we are still fitting two parameters (R_2 and σ_2) to match two inputs (the 3-year yield and the 2-year yield volatility 1 year hence). The possible prices of a 2-year bond at the two nodes in year 1 are $P(1, 3, r_u)$ and $P(1, 3, r_d)$. Thus, we have the two conditions

$$\$0.7118 = \frac{1}{1 + 0.10} [0.5 \times P(1, 3, r_u) + 0.5 \times P(1, 3, r_d)]$$

$$= \frac{1}{1 + 0.10} \left[0.5 \times \frac{1}{1.1322} \left(0.5 \times \frac{1}{1 + R_2 e^{4\sigma_2}} + 0.5 \times \frac{1}{1 + R_2 e^{2\sigma_2}} \right) \right.$$

$$\left. + 0.5 \times \frac{1}{1.1082} \left(0.5 \times \frac{1}{1 + R_2 e^{2\sigma_2}} + 0.5 \times \frac{1}{1 + R_2} \right) \right] \tag{24.52}$$

$$0.15 = 0.5 \times \ln([P(1, 3, r_u)^{-1/2} - 1]/[P(1, 3, r_d)^{-1/2} - 1]) \tag{24.53}$$

By iterating, it is possible to solve R_2 and σ_2. In the same way, it is possible to solve for the parameters for each subsequent period.

Pricing Examples

In this section we use the interest rate tree in Figure 24.5 to compute several examples.

Caplets and caps As discussed in Section 24.3, an interest rate cap pays the difference between the realized interest rate in a period and the interest cap rate, if the difference is positive. To illustrate the workings of a cap, Figure 24.9 computes the cap payments on a \$100 3-year loan with annual interest payments, assuming a 12% cap settled annually. The payments in the figure are the *present value* of the cap payments for the interest rate at that node. For example, consider the topmost node in year 2. The realized interest rate is 20.173%. The cap payment made at the node, 2 years from today, is therefore

$$\text{Cap payment} = \frac{\$100 \times (0.2017 - 0.12)}{1 + 0.2017} = \$6.799$$

Since 20.17% is the observed 1-year rate 2 years from today, 3 years from today the borrower will owe an interest payment of \$20.17. The \$6.799 payment can be invested at the rate of 20.17%, so the net interest payment will be

$$\$20.17 - (\$6.799 \times 1.2017) = \$12.00$$

In the same way, we can compute the cap payment at the middle node in year 2, \$1.463. The payment at the bottom node is zero since 9.254% is below the 12% cap.

We can value the year-2 caplet binomially by working back through the tree in the usual way. The calculation is

$$\text{Value of year-2 cap payment} = \$0.9091 \times [0.5 \times \$0.8832 \times (0.5 \times \$6.799$$

$$+ 0.5 \times \$1.463) + 0.5 \times \$0.9023 \times (0.5 \times 1.463 + 0.5 \times 0)] = \$1.958$$

The value of the cap is the value of the sum of the caplets. Problem 24.10 asks you to verify that the value of the cap is \$3.909.

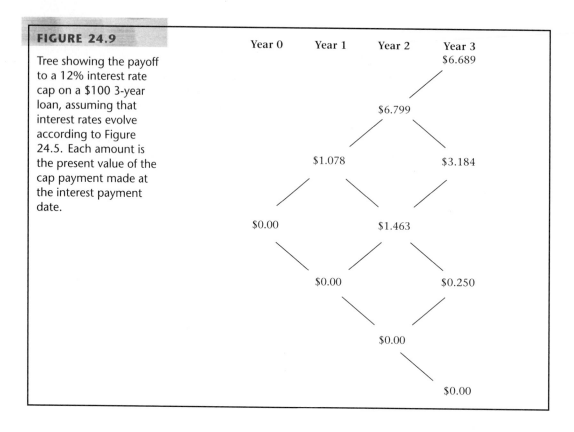

FIGURE 24.9

Tree showing the payoff to a 12% interest rate cap on a $100 3-year loan, assuming that interest rates evolve according to Figure 24.5. Each amount is the present value of the cap payment made at the interest payment date.

Forward rate agreements We discussed in Chapter 7 two different styles of settlement for a forward contract based on interest rates. The standard FRA calls for settlement at maturity of the loan, when the interest payment is made. (Equivalently, the FRA can be settled to pay the present value of this amount when the loan is made, with the present value computed using the prevailing interest rate.) Eurodollar-style settlement, by contrast, calls for payment at the time the loan is made. As we discussed in Chapter 7, the two settlement procedures generate different fair forward interest rates.

We can illustrate this difference with a simple example. Consider two contracts. Contract A is a standard forward rate agreement as described in Section 7.2. If $r(3, 4)$ is the 1-year rate in year 3, the payoff to contract A 4 years from today is

$$\text{Contract A payoff in year } 4 = r(3, 4) - \bar{r}_A \tag{24.54}$$

This is a forward rate agreement settled at maturity. We can compute $\bar{r}_A$ by taking the discounted expectation along a binomial tree of $r(3, 4)$ paid in year 4 and dividing by $P(0, 4)$. Since it is an implied forward rate, we can also value $\bar{r}_A$ as $P(0, 3)/P(0, 4) - 1$.

Contract B is a forward agreement that settles on the borrowing date in year 3:

$$\text{Contract B payoff in year 3} = r(3, 4) - \bar{r}_B \qquad (24.55)$$

This second contract resembles a Eurodollar futures contract. There is no marking-to-market prior to settlement, which would occur with a real futures contract, but the timing of settlement is mismatched with the timing of interest payments. The correlation between the contract payment and the interest rate discussed above and in Section 7.2 is therefore present in contract B. We can compute $\bar{r}_B$ by taking the discounted expectation along a binomial tree of $r(3, 4)$ paid in year 3, and dividing by $P(0, 3)$.

Example 24.5 We can value both contracts A and B using the interest rate tree in Figure 24.5. The rate on contract A is $\bar{r}_A = P(0, 3)/P(0, 4) - 1 = 0.7118/0.6243 - 1 = 0.140134$.

Contract B can be valued as follows. Suppose the forward rate on B is $\bar{r}_B$. In year 3, B makes the payment $r(3, 4) - \bar{r}_B$. We can value on the tree the payment $r(3, 4)$; the time $= 0$ value of $\bar{r}_B$ is simply $\bar{r}_B \times P(0, 3)$. Figure 24.10 depicts the payment for

FIGURE 24.10

Tree depicting value of a contract that pays the prevailing 1-year interest rate 3 years from today. Interest rates are from Figure 24.5. If the contract value at any node is $V(r)$, the amount at each node is $[0.5 \times V(r_u) + 0.5 \times V(r_d)]/(1 + r)$.

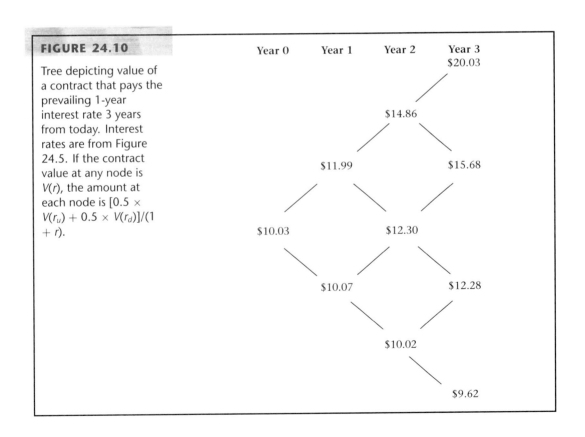

a \$100 notional amount. In the final period, we receive the prevailing 1-year rate times \$100. We then discount this payment back through the tree. The time-0 value is \$10.03. The implied rate is $\$10.03/P(0, 3) = \$10.03/\$71.18 = 0.1409$.

Thus, Eurodollar-style settlement in year 3 raises the forward rate from 14.01% to 14.09%. Problem 24.11 asks you to verify using the binomial tree that $\bar{r}_A = 14.0134\%$.

CHAPTER SUMMARY

Derivatives that are functions of interest rates can be priced and hedged in the same way as options. As with derivatives on stocks, prices of interest rate derivatives are characterized by a partial differential equation that is essentially the same as the Black-Scholes equation. The Vasicek and Cox-Ingersoll-Ross interest rate models are derived using this equation by assuming that the short-term interest rate follows particular means-reverting processes. These models generate theoretical yield curves but are too restrictive to match observed yield curves.

Under the assumption that the forward price for a bond is lognormally distributed, the Black model can be used to price bond and interest rate options, and therefore interest rate caps.

The Black-Derman-Toy tree is a binomial interest rate tree calibrated to match zero-coupon yields and a particular set of volatilities. This calibration ensures that it matches a set of observed market prices (for example the swap curve) but not necessarily the evolution of the yield curve. Valution of interest rate claims on a binomial interest rate tree is much like that on a stock-price tree.

FURTHER READING

Classic treatments of bond pricing with interest rate uncertainty are Vasicek (1977) and Cox et al. (1985b). These are examples of so-called "affine" term structure models, discussed more generally in Duffie and Kan (1996) and Dai and Singleton (2000).

Binomial treatments include Rendleman and Bartter (1980), Ho and Lee (1986), and Black et al. (1990). Heath et al. (1992) have been extremely influential insofar as they provide an equilibrium characterization of the evolution of forward rates. See also Brace et al. (1997) and Miltersen et al. (1997). More in-depth treatments of interest rate derivatives can be found in Hull (2000, chs. 20–22), Rebonato (1996), Jarrow (1996), and James and Webber (2001).

Litterman and Scheinkman (1991) is a classic study of factors affecting bond returns. Bliss (1997) surveys this literature.

PROBLEMS

For the first three problems, use the following information:

Bond maturity (years)	1	2	3	4
Bond price	0.9259	0.8495	0.7722	0.7020
1-Year forward price volatility		0.1000	0.1050	0.1100

24.1. **a.** What is the 1-year bond forward price in year 1?

   b. What is the price of a call option that expires in 1 year, giving you the right to pay $0.9009 to buy a bond expiring in 1 year?

   c. What is the price of an otherwise identical put?

   d. What is the price of an interest rate caplet that provides an 11% (effective annual rate) cap on 1-year borrowing 1 year from now?

24.2. **a.** What is the 2-year forward price for a 1-year bond?

   b. What is the price of a call option that expires in 2 years, giving you the right to pay $0.90 to buy a bond expiring in 1 year?

   c. What is the price of an otherwise identical put?

   d. What is the price of a interest rate caplet that provides an 11% (effective annual rate) cap on 1-year borrowing 2 years from now?

24.3. What is the price of a 3-year interest rate cap with an 11.5% (effective annual) cap rate?

24.4. Suppose the yield curve is flat at 8%. Consider 3- and 6-year zero-coupon bonds. You buy one 3-year bond and sell an appropriate quantity of the 6-year bond to duration-hedge the position. Any additional investment is in short-term (zero-duration) bonds. Suppose the yield curve can move up to 8.25% or down to 7.75% over the course of 1 day. Do you make or lose money on the hedge? What does the result tell you about the (impossible) flat-yield curve model discussed in Section 24.1?

24.5. Suppose the yield curve is flat at 6%. Consider a 4-year 5%-coupon bond and an 8-year 7%-coupon bond. All coupons are annual.

   a. What are the prices and durations of both bonds?

   b. Consider buying one 4-year bond and duration-hedging by selling an appropriate quantity of the 8-year bond. Any residual is financed with short-term (zero-duration) bonds. Suppose the yield curve can move up to 6.25% or down to 5.75% over the course of 1 day. What are the results from the hedge?

24.6. Consider two zero-coupon bonds with 2 years and 10 years to maturity. Let $a = 0.2$, $b = 0.1$, $r = 0.05$, $\sigma_{Vasicek} = 10\%$, and $\sigma_{CIR} = 44.721\%$. The interest rate risk premium is zero in each case. We will consider a position consisting of one $100 par value 2-year bond, which we will hedge with a position in the 10-year bond.

    a. Compute the prices, deltas, and gammas of the bonds using the CIR and Vasicek models. How do delta and gamma compare to duration and convexity?

    b. Suppose the Vasicek model is true. You wish to hedge the 2-year bond using the 10-year bond. Consider a 1-day holding period and suppose the interest rate moves one standard deviation up or down. What is the return on the duration-hedged position? What is the return on the Vasicek delta-hedged position?

    c. Repeat the previous part, only use the CIR model in place of the Vasicek model.

24.7. Construct a 4-period, 3-step (8 terminal node) binomial interest rate tree where the initial interest rate is 10% and rates can move up or down by 2%; model your tree after that in Figure 24.3. Compute prices and yields for 1-, 2-, 3-, and 4-year bonds. Do yields decline with maturity? Why?

24.8. Verify that the 4-year zero-coupon bond price generated by the tree in Figure 24.6 is $0.6243.

24.9. Verify that the 1-year yield volatility of the 4-year zero-coupon bond price generated by the tree in Figure 24.6 is 0.14.

24.10. Verify that the price of the 12% interest rate cap in Figure 24.9 is $3.909.

24.11. Using a binomial tree like that in Figure 24.10, verify that the 1-year forward rate 3 years hence in Figure 24.5 is 14.0134%.

For the next four problems, here are two BDT interest rate trees with effective annual interest rates at each node.

Tree #1

0.08000	0.07676	0.08170	0.07943	0.07552
	0.10362	0.10635	0.09953	0.09084
		0.13843	0.12473	0.10927
			0.15630	0.13143
				0.15809

Tree #2

0.08000	0.08112	0.08749	0.08261	0.07284
	0.09908	0.10689	0.10096	0.08907
		0.13060	0.12338	0.10891
			0.15078	0.13317
				0.16283

24.12. What are the 1-, 2-, 3-, 4-, and 5-year zero-coupon bond prices implied by the two trees?

24.13. What volatilities were used to construct each tree? (You computed zero-coupon bond prices in the previous problem; now you have to compute the year-1 yield volatility for 1-, 2-, 3-, and 4-year bonds.) Can you unambiguously say that rates in one tree are more volatile than the other?

24.14. For years 2–5, compute the following:

    a. The forward interest rate, r_f, for a forward rate agreement that settles at the time borrowing is repaid. That is, if you borrow at $t - 1$ at the 1-year rate $\tilde{r}$, and repay the loan at t, the contract payoff in year t is

$$(\tilde{r} - r_f)$$

    b. The forward interest rate, r_e, for a Eurodollar-style forward rate agreement that settles at the time borrowing is *initiated*. That is, if you borrow at $t - 1$ at the 1-year rate $\tilde{r}$, and repay the loan at t, the contract payoff in year $t - 1$ is

$$(\tilde{r} - r_e)$$

    c. How is the difference between r_f and r_e affected by volatility (you can compare the two trees) and time to maturity?

24.15. You are going to borrow $250m at a floating rate for 5 years. You wish to protect yourself against borrowing rates greater than 10.5%. Using each tree, what is the price of a 5-year interest rate cap? (Assume that the cap settles each year at the time you repay the borrowing.)

APPENDIX 24.A: THE HEATH-JARROW-MORTON MODEL

The Black-Derman-Toy model illustrates one particular way to construct a binomial tree from data. There are other ways to construct trees, such as the Ho and Lee (1986) model, which we do not discuss here. The Heath-Jarrow-Morton model (Heath et al., 1992) is notable for proposing a general structure for interest rate models, one which contains other models as a special case. Their basic insight is that no-arbitrage restrictions require that the evolution of forward rates (or equivalently, forward bond prices) hinges in a specific way on bond price volatilities. When you adopt a specific volatility model, you implicitly adopt a specific model for the evolution of forward interest rates.

To understand the link between volatilities and forward rates, suppose the single-state variable is the short-term interest rate, r, and we have two zero-coupon bonds with prices $P(t, T_1, r)$ and $P(t, T_2, r)$ with $T_2 > T_1$. The implied forward zero-coupon bond price between T_1 and T_2 is

$$F(t, T_1, T_2) = \frac{P(t, T_2, r)}{P(t, T_1, r)} \tag{24.56}$$

Under the risk-neutral distribution, all zero-coupon bond prices follow the equation

$$\frac{dP}{P} = r dt + q(t, T, r) dZ \tag{24.57}$$

Using Itô's Lemma, this equation implies that the forward bond price follows the process

$$\frac{dF}{F} = [q(t, T_1, r)^2 - q(t, T_1, r)q(t, T_2, r)]dt + [q(t, T_2, r) - q(t, T_1, r)]dZ$$

We can do this same calculation for every possible forward bond price. In every case, *only bond price volatilities affect the evolution of the forward curve.*

We can use equation (24.57) to derive the process that must be followed by forward interest rates. If the forward bond price is $F(t, T_1, T_2)$, then the implied forward interest rate is

$$f(t, T_1, T_2) = -\frac{\ln[F(t, T_1, T_2)]}{T_2 - T_1}$$

Using Itô's Lemma to compute df, we obtain

$$
\begin{aligned}
df &= -\frac{1}{T_2 - T_1}\left(\frac{dF}{F} - \frac{1}{2}\frac{(dF)^2}{F^2}\right) \\
&= \frac{\frac{1}{2}[q(t, T_2, r)^2 - q(t, T_1, r)^2]}{T_2 - T_1}dt + \frac{q(t, T_1, r) - q(t, T_2, r)}{T_2 - T_1}dZ
\end{aligned}
\tag{24.58}
$$

The intuition for the result that the forward rate process depends on volatilities is straightforward. For all bonds, the risk-neutral expected return is the risk-free rate, and in a one-factor world, the prices of all bonds are perfectly correlated. The forward bond price, $P(t, T_2)/P(t, T_1)$, varies *only* because of the volatility differences for the two bonds. Thus, the process for the forward bond price, and, hence, the forward interest rate, depends only on volatilities. This approach is more general than Black-Derman-Toy since a model of the volatility process can potentially be calibrated to the evolution of the yield curve as well as a snapshot at a point in time.

Jarrow (1996), Rebonato (1996), and James and Webber (2001) discuss empirical implementation of the model, which entails assuming and calibrating a model for bond volatilities.

CHAPTER 25

Value at Risk

A standard way to assess risk is to evelute the distribution of possible outcomes, with a focus on the worst that might happen. Insurance companies, for example, are in the business of assessing the likelihood of insured events, and the resulting possible losses for the insurer. Financial institutions must understand their portfolio risks in order to determine the capital needed to suppport their business.

In this chapter we use the framework and tools developed earlier in this book to understand this kind of risk assessment. Specifically, we discuss *value at risk*, which is a method frequently used to measure the possible losses on a portfolio of financial assets. Chapter 26 discusses the related problem of assessing credit risks.

25.1 VALUE AT RISK

A financial institution might have a complex portfolio containing stocks, bonds with different maturities and with various embedded options, and instruments denominated in different currencies. The form of these instruments could be simple notes or complex options. **Value at risk** (VaR) is one way to perform risk assessment for such a portfolio. The idea of value at risk is to estimate the losses on a portfolio that occur with a given probability.

With an estimate of the distribution of outcomes we can either ask about the probability of losing a given sum (e.g., what is the chance our loss exceeds $5m?) or ask, for a given probability, how much might we lose (what level of loss do we exceed with a 1% probability)? For example, a derivatives market-maker could estimate that for a given portfolio there is a 1% chance of losses in excess of $500,000. The amount $500,000 is then the 1-day value at risk with a 99% level of confidence.[1] In general, computing value at risk means finding the value of a portfolio such that there is a specified probability that the portfolio will be worth at least this much over a given horizon. The choice of horizon and probability will depend on how VaR is to be used. Regulators have

---

[1] In this example, the market-maker loses $500,000 with a 1% probability and performs better 99% of the time. It is common to speak of 99% as the "confidence level." Since VaR is always based upon tail probabilities, in practice it will be obvious that a "99% VaR" and a "1% VaR" refer to the same quantity.

proposed assessing capital using the 99% 10-day VaR (see the box on page 815 for more details). "Riskmetrics" (see J. P. Morgan/Reuters (1996)), developed by J. P. Morgan in the mid-1990s, is one comprehensive proposal for a value at risk methodology. Much of the discussion in this section, especially for bonds, follows the Riskmetrics methodology.

Before we discuss how to compute value at risk, recognize that the ideas underlying risk assessment matter in contexts other than measuring the riskiness of bank portfolios. For example, suppose a firm has $10m in capital and can pursue one of two investment opportunities, each costing $10 million. One year, investment A returns $12 million for sure, whereas investment B returns $24 million with probability one-half and $0 with probability one-half. Suppose the risk of investment B is idiosyncratic and the risk-free rate is 10%. Standard investment theory will assess both projects as having the same positive NPV. However, with investment B, half of the time the firm will lose its entire investment and therefore all of its capital. In order to make additional investments, the firm must raise additional capital, a costly process. Once we account for the costs associated with losing all capital, A and B may no longer seem equally attractive. More generally, managers will want to know how much of a firm's capital is at risk with a given project. Risk assessment can therefore affect project selection.[2]

Distributions of outcomes matter at the personal level as well. Suppose you are planning for retirement. You will need to decide both how much to save and how to allocate your savings among stocks, bonds, and other assets. For any strategy, a key question is: What is the probability that by following this strategy you will fail to achieve a desired minimum level of retirement savings by the time you retire?[3] This is not the only question to ask, but a strategy with a high probability of leaving you penniless— no matter how desirable on other grounds—should call for careful consideration. We will not discuss personal financial planning in this chapter, but the ideas underlying risk assessment can be used in making personal decisions as well as corporate decisions.

There are at least three uses of value at risk. First, as mentioned, regulators can use VaR to compute capital requirements for financial institutions. Second, managers can use VaR as an input in making risk-taking and risk-management decisions. Third, managers can also use VaR to assess the quality of the bank's models. For example, if the models say that there is a 5% chance that a particular trading operation will lose $1m over a 1-day horizon, then on average once every 20 days (5% of the time) the trading operation *should* lose $1m. If losses of this size occur more frequently, the models are assigning too little risk to the bank's activities. If such losses occur less frequently, the models are assigning too much risk.

Most of the examples in this section use lognormally distributed stocks and linear normal approximations to illustrate VaR calculations. Currencies and commodities can be modeled in this way as well. Although for long horizons it might not be reasonable

---

[2] See Stulz (1996) for a detailed discussion of the link between investment decisions and risk assessment.

[3] Bodie and Crane (1999) for example use Monte Carlo simulation to examine return distributions to assess the suitability of financial products for retirement savings.

VaR and Regulatory Capital

Regulators in most countries require that financial institutions maintain minimum levels of capital. The Basel Committee on Banking Supervision in 1996 outlined a framework for capital standards proposing that financial institutions use VaR in determining capital for *market risks*, defined as risk arising from stocks, commodities, interest rates, and foreign exchange. (Other categories of risk are *credit risk* and *operational risk*.) The proposal (Basel Committee on Banking Supervision, 1996) stated the following:

> Banks will have flexibility in devising the precise nature of their models, but the following minimum standards will apply for the purpose of calculating their capital charge. Individual banks or their supervisory authorities will have discretion to apply stricter standards.
>
> (a) "Value-at-risk" must be computed on a daily basis.
>
> (b) In calculating the value-at-risk, a 99th percentile, one-tailed confidence interval is to be used.
>
> (c) In calculating value-at-risk, an instantaneous price shock equivalent to a 10 day movement in prices is to be used, i.e., the minimum "holding period" will be ten trading days. . . .
>
> (d) The choice of historical observation period (sample period) for calculating value-at-risk will be constrained to a minimum length of one year. . . .
>
> (f) No particular type of model is prescribed. So long as each model used captures all the material risks run by the bank, ... banks will be free to use models based, for example, on variance-covariance matrices, historical simulations, or Monte Carlo simulations.

This approach to determining capital for market risks was reaffirmed in the 2004 revision of the Basel capital guidelines, known as *Basel II*.

to treat commodities as lognormally distributed, for short horizons this is generally a reasonable assumption. We ignore the possibility of jumps. We discuss bonds separately.

Value at Risk for One Stock

Suppose $\tilde{x}_h$ is the dollar return on a portfolio over the horizon h, and $f(x, h)$ is the distribution of returns. Define the value at risk of the portfolio as the return, $x_h(c)$, such that $\text{Prob}(\tilde{x}_h \leq x_h(c)) = c$. In other words, $x_h(c)$ is the c quantile of the return distribution over the horizon h.

Value at risk measures the loss that will occur with a given probability over a specified period of time. Notice that the definition of value at risk requires that we specify both a horizon, h, and a probability, c.

Suppose a portfolio consists of a single stock and we wish to compute value at risk over the horizon h. If the distribution of the stock price after h periods, S_h, is lognormal, we have

$$\ln(S_h/S_0) \sim N[(\alpha - \delta - 0.5\sigma^2)h, \sigma^2 h] \tag{25.1}$$

As we saw in Chapter 18, if we pick a stock price $\bar{S}_h$, then the probability that the stock price will be below $\bar{S}_h$ is

$$\text{Prob}(S_h < \bar{S}_h) = N\left(\frac{\ln(\bar{S}_h) - \ln(S_0) - (\alpha - \delta - 0.5\sigma^2)h}{\sigma\sqrt{h}}\right) \tag{25.2}$$

The complementary calculation is to compute the $\bar{S}_h(c)$ corresponding to the probability c. By the definition of $\bar{S}_h(c)$, we have

$$c = N\left(\frac{\ln(\bar{S}_h(c)) - \ln(S_0) - (\alpha - \delta - 0.5\sigma^2)h}{\sigma\sqrt{h}}\right) \tag{25.3}$$

We can solve for $\bar{S}_h(c)$ by using the inverse cumulative probability distribution, N^{-1}. Applying this function to both sides of equation (25.3), we have

$$N^{-1}(c) = \frac{\ln(\bar{S}_h(c)) - \ln(S_0) - (\alpha - \delta - 0.5\sigma^2)h}{\sigma\sqrt{h}} \tag{25.4}$$

Solving for $\bar{S}_h(c)$ gives

$$\bar{S}_h(c) = S_0 e^{(\alpha - \delta - 0.5\sigma^2)h + \sigma\sqrt{h}N^{-1}(c)} \tag{25.5}$$

This expression should look familiar from Chapter 18. In equation (25.5), $N^{-1}(c)$ takes the place of a standard normal random variable.

Example 25.1 Suppose we own \$3m worth of stock A, which has an expected return of 15% and a 30% volatility, and pays no dividend. Moreover, assume A is lognormally distributed. The value of the position in 1 week, V, is

$$V = \$3\text{m} \times e^{(0.15 - 0.5 \times 0.3^2)\frac{1}{52} + 0.3\sqrt{\frac{1}{52}}Z} \tag{25.6}$$

where $Z \sim N(0, 1)$.

Given this assumed stock price distribution, a 5% loss will occur if Z satisfies

$$\$3\text{m} \times e^{(0.15 - 0.5 \times 0.3^2)\frac{1}{52} + 0.3\sqrt{\frac{1}{52}}Z} = 0.95 \times \$3\text{m}$$

or

$$Z = \frac{\ln(0.95) - (0.15 - 0.5 \times 0.3^2)\frac{1}{52}}{0.3 \times \sqrt{\frac{1}{52}}} = -1.2815$$

We have

$$\text{NormSDist}(-1.2815) = 0.1000$$

Thus, we expect that 10% of the time there will be a weekly loss in excess of 5%.

With 95% probability, the value of the portfolio over a 1-week horizon will exceed

$$\$3m \times e^{(0.15-0.5\times0.3^2)\frac{1}{52}+0.3\sqrt{\frac{1}{52}}\times(-1.645)} = \$2.8072m$$

where $N^{-1}(0.05) = -1.645$. In this case, we would say the 95% value at risk is $\$2.8072m - \$3m = -\$0.1928m$. ≋

If the assumption of lognormality is valid and if the inputs are correct, a 1-week loss of this magnitude occurs on average once every 20 weeks.

In practice it is common to simplify the VaR calculation by assuming a normal return rather than a lognormal return. Recall from Chapter 20 that the standard lognormal model is generated by assuming normal returns over very short horizons. We can therefore approximate the exact lognormal result with a normal approximation:

$$S_h = S_0 \left(1 + \alpha h + z\sigma\sqrt{h}\right) \tag{25.7}$$

We could also further simplify by ignoring the mean:

$$S_h = S_0 \left(1 + z\sigma\sqrt{h}\right) \tag{25.8}$$

Both equations (25.7) and (25.8) become less reasonable as h grows.

Example 25.2 Using the same assumptions as in Example 25.1, equation (25.7) gives

$$\$3m \times \left[1 + \frac{0.15}{52} + \left(\frac{0.3}{\sqrt{52}} \times (-1.645)\right)\right] = \$2.8033m$$

VaR is therefore $\$2.8033m - \$3m = -\$0.1966m$. Ignoring the mean, equation (25.8) gives

$$\$3m \times \left(1 + \frac{0.3}{\sqrt{52}} \times (-1.645)\right) = \$2.7947m$$

VaR is $\$2.7947m - \$3m = -\$0.2053m$. ≋

Figure 25.1 compares the three models—lognormal, normal with mean, and normal without mean—over horizons of one day to one year. As you would expect, the approximation ignoring the mean (equation 25.8) is less accurate over longer horizons. In practice the mean is often ignored for two reasons. First, as we saw in Chapter 18, means are hard to estimate precisely. Second, as we saw in Chapter 20, for short horizons the mean is less important than the diffusion term in an Itô process.

VaR for Two or More Stocks

When we consider a portfolio having two or more stocks, the distribution of the future portfolio value is the sum of lognormally distributed random variables and is therefore

FIGURE 25.1

Comparison of VaR for a single stock over different horizons using the lognormal solution (equation (25.4)), normality with a positive mean (equation (25.7)), and normality assuming a zero mean (equation (25.8)). Assumes the same parameters as in Example 25.2.

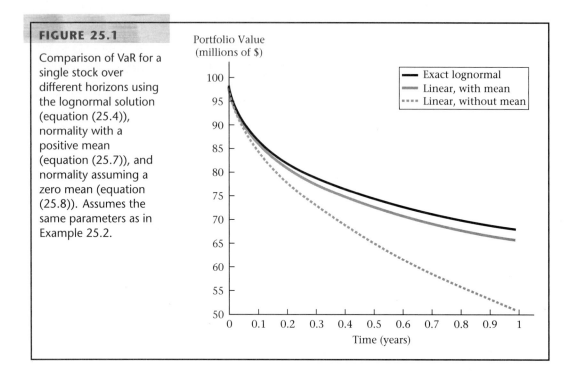

not lognormal. Since the lognormal distribution is no longer exact, we can use the normal approximation or we can use Monte Carlo simulation to obtain the exact distribution.

Let the annual mean and standard deviation of the realized return on stock i, $\tilde{\alpha}_i$, be α_i and σ_i, with the correlation between stocks i and j being ρ_{ij}. The dollar investment in stock i is W_i. The value of a portfolio containing n stocks is

$$W = \sum_{i=1}^{n} W_i$$

The return on the portfolio over the horizon h, R_h, is

$$\text{Portfolio return} = R_h = \frac{1}{W} \sum_{i=1}^{n} \tilde{\alpha}_{i,h} W_i$$

Assuming normality, the annualized distribution of the portfolio return is

$$R_h \sim \mathcal{N}\left(\frac{1}{W} \sum_{i=1}^{n} \alpha_i h W_i, \quad \frac{1}{W^2} \sum_{i=1}^{n} \sum_{j=1}^{n} \sigma_i \sigma_j \rho_{ij} h W_i W_j \right) \tag{25.9}$$

Example 25.3 Suppose we have $\alpha_1 = 0.15$, $\sigma_1 = 0.3$, $W_1 = \$3m$, $\alpha_2 = 0.18$, $\sigma_2 = 0.45$, $W_2 = \$5m$, and $\rho_{1,2} = 0.4$. The annual mean of the portfolio return is

$$\alpha_p = \frac{W_1\alpha_1 + W_2\alpha_2}{W_1 + W_2} = \frac{\$3m \times 0.15 + \$5m \times 0.18}{\$3m + \$5m} = 0.16875$$

The annual standard deviation of the portfolio return, σ_p, is

$$\sigma_p = \frac{\sqrt{W_1^2\sigma_1^2 + W_2^2\sigma_2^2 + 2W_1 W_2\sigma_1\sigma_2\rho_{1,2}}}{W_1 + W_2}$$

$$= \frac{\sqrt{(\$3m \times 0.3)^2 + (\$5m \times 0.45)^2 + (2 \times \$3m \times \$5m \times 0.3 \times 0.45 \times 0.4)}}{\$3m + \$5m}$$

$$= 0.34216$$

Using equation (25.7), there is a 95% probability that in 1 week, the value of the porfolio will exceed

$$\$8m \times \left[\left(1 + \left(0.16875 \times \frac{1}{52}\right) + \left(0.34216 \times \sqrt{\frac{1}{52}} \times (-1.645)\right)\right)\right] = \$7.40154m$$

The 1-week 95% VaR is therefore $\$7.40154m - \$8m = -\$0.5985m$. Using equation (25.8), which ignores the mean, we have a 95% chance that the value of the portfolio will exceed

$$\$8m \times \left(1 + 0.34216 \times \sqrt{\frac{1}{52}} \times (-1.645)\right) = \$7.3756m$$

The 1-week VaR ignoring the mean is therefore $\$7.3756m - \$8m = -\$0.6244m$. ≈

This example illustrates the effects of diversification. Although stock 2, which constitutes more than half of the portfolio, has a standard deviation of 45%, the portfolio standard deviation is only about 34%. Problem 25.5 asks you to consider the effects of different correlations.

If there are n assets, the VaR calculation requires that we specify at least the standard deviation (and possibly the mean) for each stock, along with all pairwise correlations.

VaR for Nonlinear Portfolios

If a portfolio contains options as well as stocks, it is more complicated to compute the distribution of returns. Specifically, suppose the portfolio consists of n different stocks with ω_i shares of stock i worth $\omega_i S_i = W_i$. There are also N_i options worth $C(S_i)$ for each stock i. The portfolio value is therefore $W = \sum_{i=1}^{n}[\omega_i S_i + N_i C_i(S_i)]$. We cannot easily compute the exact distribution of this portfolio; not only is the sum of the lognormally distributed stock prices not lognormal, but the option price distribution is complicated.

We will explore two different approaches to handling nonlinearity. First, we can create a linear approximation to the option price by using the option delta. Second, we can value the option using an appropriate option pricing formula and then perform Monte Carlo simulation to obtain the return distribution.[4]

Delta approximation   If the return on stock i is $\tilde{\alpha}_i$, we can approximate the return on the option as $\Delta_i \tilde{\alpha}_i$, where Δ_i is the option delta. The expected annual return on the stock and option portfolio is then

$$R_p = \frac{1}{W} \sum_{i=1}^{n} \alpha_i S_i (\omega_i + N_i \Delta_i) \tag{25.10}$$

The term $\omega_i + N_i \Delta_i$ measures the exposure to stock i. The variance of the return is

$$\sigma_p^2 = \frac{1}{W^2} \sum_{i=1}^{n} \sum_{j=1}^{n} S_i S_j (\omega_i + N_i \Delta_i)(\omega_j + N_j \Delta_j) \sigma_i \sigma_j \rho_{ij} \tag{25.11}$$

With this mean and variance, we can mimic the n-stock analysis. First, however, we will compute an example with a single stock for which we know the exact solution.

Example 25.4   Suppose we own 30,000 shares of a nondividend-paying stock and have sold 105-strike call options, with 1 year to expiration, on 25,000 shares. The stock price is $100, the stock volatility is 30%, the expected return on the stock is 15%, and the risk-free rate is 8%. The Black-Scholes option price is $13.3397 and the value of the portfolio is

$$W = 30{,}000 \times \$100 - 25{,}000 \times \$13.3397 = \$2{,}666{,}507$$

(Since the written options are a liability, we subtract their value in computing the value of the portfolio.) The delta of the option is 0.6003. Using equations (25.10) and (25.11), we obtain $R_p = 0.084343$ and $\sigma_p = 0.16869$. The written options reduce the mean and volatility of the portfolio. Therefore, there is a 95% chance that the value of the portfolio

---

[4]A third alternative is to use a delta-gamma approximation, which—as we saw in Chapter 13—is more accurate than a delta approximation. However, because the gamma term depends on the squared change in the stock price, the approximation is harder to implement than the delta approximation. The *Riskmetrics Technical Document* (Morgan/Reuters 1996, pp. 129–133) discusses an approach for implementing the delta-gamma approximation.

in 1 week will exceed

$$\$2{,}666{,}507 \times \left(1 + 0.084343 \times \frac{1}{52} + 0.16869 \times \sqrt{\frac{1}{52}} \times (-1.645)\right)$$

$$= \$2{,}568{,}220 \quad (25.12)$$

Value at risk using the delta approximation is therefore $\$2{,}568{,}220 - \$2{,}666{,}507 = -\$98{,}287$.

We can compute the exact value at risk by first determining the stock price that we will exceed with a 95% chance, and then computing the exact portfolio value at that price. With 95% probability, we will exceed the stock price

$$\$100 \times e^{(0.15-0.5\times0.3^2)\frac{1}{52}+0.3\sqrt{\frac{1}{52}}\times(-1.645)} = \$93.574$$

If this is the stock price 1 week later, the option price will be $\$9.5913$, and the value of the portfolio will be

$$(\$93.574 \times 30{,}000) - (\$9.5913 \times 25{,}000) = \$2{,}576{,}438$$

The exact 95% value at risk is therefore $\$2{,}576{,}438 - \$2{,}666{,}507 = -\$99{,}069$. ❧

Figure 25.2 compares the exact value of the portfolio as a function of the stock price 7 days later, compared to the value implied by the delta approximation. The delta approximation is close, but the VaR derived using delta is slightly low. The delta approximation also fails to account for theta—the time decay in the option position. Because the option is written, time decay over the 1-week horizon increases the return of the portfolio. This increased return is barely perceptible in Figure 25.2 as the exact portfolio value exceeds the delta approximation when the stock price is close to $100.

Example 25.5   Suppose we have two stocks along with written call options on those stocks. Information for the stocks and options is in Table 25.1. Using this information, we obtain a portfolio value of

$$W = (30{,}000 \times \$100) - (25{,}000 \times \$13.3397)$$
$$+ (50{,}000 \times \$100) - (60{,}000 \times 10.3511) = \$7{,}045{,}440$$

Using equations (25.10) and (25.11), the annual mean and standard deviation are 8.392% and 16.617%. There is a 95% chance that the portfolio value will exceed

$$W \times \left[1 + (R_p \times h) + (\sigma_p \times \sqrt{h} \times z)\right]$$

$$= \$7{,}045{,}440 \times \left[1 + 0.08392 \times \frac{1}{52} + 0.16617 \times \sqrt{\frac{1}{52}} \times (-1.645)\right] = \$6{,}789{,}740$$

FIGURE 25.2

Comparison of exact portfolio value after 1 week with a delta approximation. Assumes the position is long 30,000 shares of stock at $100 and short 25,000 call options with a strike price of $105. Value at risk is the difference between the original portfolio value and that at the 5% stock price.

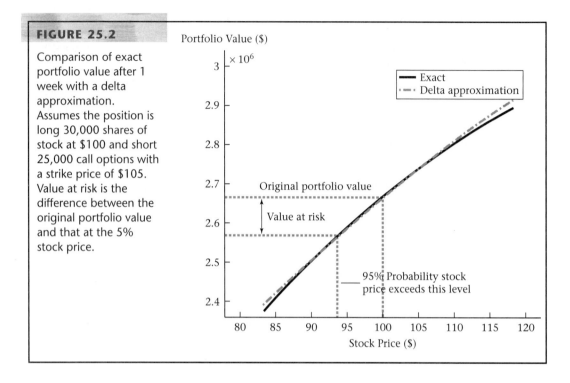

TABLE 25.1

Information about two stocks and call options on those stocks. Assumes the risk-free rate is 8% and that neither stock pays a dividend. The correlation between the stocks is 0.4.

| | Stock Information | | | | Option Information | | | | |
Stock	S	# Shares	α	σ	$C(S)$	Strike	Δ	Expiration	# Shares
# 1	$100	30,000	0.15	0.30	$13.3397	$105	0.6003	1.0	−25,000
# 2	$100	50,000	0.18	0.45	$10.3511	$110	0.4941	0.5	−60,000

The 95% value at risk over a 1-week horizon is therefore

$$\text{VaR} = \$6,789,740 - \$7,045,440 = -\$255,700$$

Monte Carlo simulation The delta approximation can work poorly for nonlinear portfolios. For example, consider an at-the-money written straddle (a written call and written put, both with the same strike price). The straddle suffers a loss if the stock price increases or decreases, which is not a situation suited to a linear approximation. Because of losses from stock moves in either direction, we need a two-tailed approach to VaR. Monte Carlo simulation works well in this situation since the simulation produces the distribution of portfolio values.

To use Monte Carlo simulation in the case of a single stock, we randomly draw a set of stock prices as discussed in Chapter 19. For multiple stocks, we can use the appropriate parameters for each stock and use the Cholesky decomposition (see Section 19.8) to ensure the appropriate correlation among stock prices. Once we have the portfolio values corresponding to each draw of random prices, we sort the resulting portfolio values in ascending order. The 5% lower tail of portfolio values, for example, is used to compute the 95% value at risk.

We will look at two examples in which we compute VaR for a position using Monte Carlo simulation. First we will examine a straddle on a single stock, and then a straddle-like position that contains a written call on one stock and a written put on the other.

Example 25.6   Consider the 1-week 95% value at risk of an at-the-money written straddle on 100,000 shares of a single stock. Assuming that $S = \$100$, $K = \$100$, $\sigma = 30\%$, $r = 8\%$, $T = 30$ days, and $\delta = 0$, the initial value of the straddle is $-\$685,776$. Because the underlying asset is a single stock, we can compute the VaR of the position directly without Monte Carlo simulation. Figure 25.3 graphs the exact value of the straddle after 1 week, compared with its initial value.[5] The expected return on the stock is 15% in this calculation.

Table 25.2 shows a subset of the values plotted in Figure 25.3. Examine the boxed entries in Table 25.2. If the stock price declines, there is a 0.9% probability that the value of the position will be less than $-\$942,266$. If the stock price rises, there is a 4% chance that the position value will be less than $-\$942,639$. Thus, in total, there is a 4.9% probability of a loss in excess of about $\$942,452$, which is the average of the boxed numbers. The 1-week 95% VaR is therefore approximately $-\$942,452 - (-\$685,776) = -\$256,676$. Even in this one-stock example, calculating the VaR for this two-tailed position is not as simple as computing the stock prices that are exceeded with 2.5% probability.

Monte Carlo simulation simplifies the analysis. To use Monte Carlo we randomly draw a set of $z \sim \mathcal{N}(0, 1)$, and construct the stock price as

$$S_h = S_0 e^{(\alpha - \delta - 0.5\sigma^2)h + \sigma\sqrt{h}z} \tag{25.13}$$

We compute the Black-Scholes call and put prices using each stock price, which gives us a distribution of straddle values. We then sort the resulting straddle values in ascending order. The 5% value is used to compute the 95% value at risk.

---

[5]The increase in value of the straddle if the stock price does not change is due to theta.

FIGURE 25.3

The value of a portfolio, as a function of the stock price, containing 100,000 written call options with a $100 strike and 100,000 written put options with a $100 strike. Assumes $\sigma = 30\%$, $r = 8\%$, $t = 23$ days and $\delta = 0$.

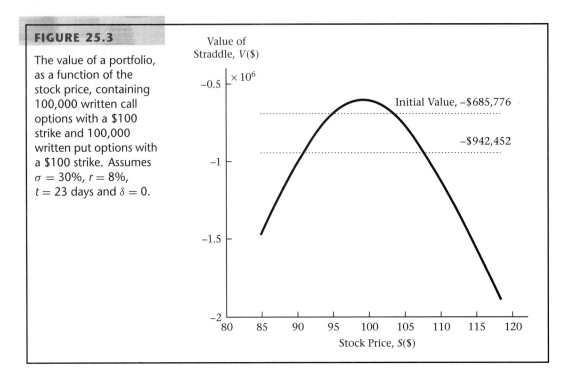

Figure 25.4 plots the histogram of values resulting from 100,000 random simulations of the value of the straddle. There is a 95% chance the straddle value will exceed $-\$943,028$; hence, value at risk is $-\$943,028 - (-\$685,776) = -\$257,252$. This result is very close to the value we inferred from Table 25.2. ❦

As a second example we suppose that instead of the written put and call having the same underlying stock, they have different, correlated underlying stocks.

Example 25.7 Suppose that there are two stocks. Stock 1 is the same as the stock in Example 25.6. Stock 2 has the same parameters and a correlation of 0.40 with stock 1. Because the stocks have the same volatility and dividend yield, the initial option values are the same and the written straddle has an initial value of $-\$685,776$. Based on 100,000 simulated prices for both stocks, the portfolio has a 95% chance of having a value greater than $\$1,135,421$. Hence, the 95% value at risk is $-\$1,135,421 - (-\$685,776) = -\$449,645$. The histogram for this calculation is in Figure 25.5. ❦

TABLE 25.2   Value of written straddle, V, for different stock prices, S. Values in the z column are standard normal values with the corresponding cumulative probabilities in the $N(z)$ column. Over 1 week there is approximately a 5% probability that the stock price will be outside the range $90.87 – $107.77. The option values are computed using the Black-Scholes formula with $\sigma = 30\%$, $r = 8\%$, $t = 23$ days, and $\delta = 0$. The stock price movement assumes $\alpha = 15\%$.

z	$S(\$)$	$V(\$)$	$N(z)$	z	$S(\$)$	$V(\$)$	$N(z)$
−2.50	90.30	−985970	0.006	1.70	107.55	−926472	0.955
−2.45	90.49	−971234	0.007	1.75	107.77	−942639	0.960
−2.40	90.68	−956663	0.008	1.80	107.99	−959111	0.964
−2.35	90.87	−942266	0.009	1.85	108.22	−975880	0.968
−2.30	91.06	−928050	0.011	1.90	108.44	−992939	0.971
−2.25	91.25	−914023	0.012	1.95	108.67	−1010281	0.974
−2.20	91.44	−900192	0.014	2.00	108.90	−1027900	0.977
−2.15	91.63	−886566	0.016	2.05	109.12	−1045788	0.980
−2.10	91.82	−873152	0.018	2.10	109.35	−1063938	0.982
−2.05	92.01	−859958	0.020	2.15	109.58	−1082345	0.984
−2.00	92.20	−846992	0.023	2.20	109.81	−1101000	0.986
−1.95	92.39	−834263	0.026	2.25	110.03	−1119898	0.988
−1.90	92.59	−821779	0.029	2.30	110.26	−1139031	0.989
−1.85	92.78	−809547	0.032	2.35	110.49	−1158393	0.991
−1.80	92.97	−797576	0.036	2.40	110.72	−1177978	0.992
−1.75	93.17	−785875	0.040	2.45	110.95	−1197780	0.993
−1.70	93.36	−774450	0.045	2.50	111.19	−1217792	0.994

A comparison of the results in Examples 25.6 and 25.7 shows that writing the straddle on two different stocks increases value at risk. If we examine the distributions in Figures 25.4 and 25.5, we can see why this happens.

Notice first that in Figure 25.4, the value of the portfolio never exceeds about −$597,000. The reason is that, since the call and put are written on the same stock, *stock price moves can never induce the two options to appreciate together.* They can appreciate due to theta, but a change in the stock price will induce a gain in one option

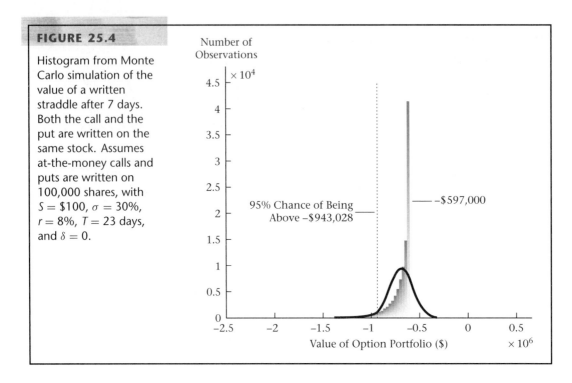

FIGURE 25.4

Histogram from Monte Carlo simulation of the value of a written straddle after 7 days. Both the call and the put are written on the same stock. Assumes at-the-money calls and puts are written on 100,000 shares, with $S = \$100$, $\sigma = 30\%$, $r = 8\%$, $T = 23$ days, and $\delta = 0$.

and a loss in the other. The same effect limits a loss, since the two options can never lose money together.

When the options are written on different stocks, as in Figure 25.5, it is possible for both to gain or lose simultaneously. As a result, the distribution of prices has a greater variance and increased value at risk.

As a final comment, all the value at risk calculations in this section assumed an expected return for the stocks that was positive and different from the risk-free rate. Because the horizon was only 7 days, the results are not too different from those obtained assuming the drift is zero or equal to the risk-free rate. For longer horizons the particular assumption about expected return would make more of a difference.

VaR for Bonds

In this section we see how to compute VaR for bonds, using information about the volatilities and correlations of yields for bonds at different maturities.

At any point in time there are numerous interest rate sensitive claims, including bonds, FRAs, and swaps, all of which can have different maturities and be denominated in different currencies. We can simplify the problem of risk modeling for interest-rate sensitive claims by recalling from Chapter 7 that all of these claims can be decomposed into zero-coupon bonds. Thus, the problem of assessing the risk of a bond, FRA, or

FIGURE 25.5

The value of a portfolio, as a function of the stock price, containing 100,000 written call options on one stock with a $100 strike and 100,000 written put options on a different stock with a $100 strike. For both stocks, assume $\sigma = 30\%$, $r = 8\%$, $T = 23$ days, and $\delta = 0$. The correlation between the two stocks is 40%.

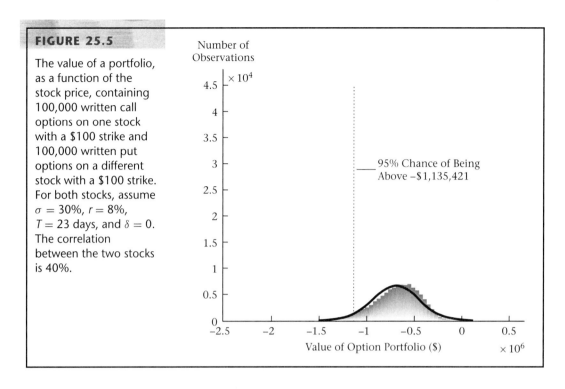

swap reduces to one of decomposing the claim into its constituent zero-coupon bonds and assessing the risk of these. The risk of the bond or other claim can then be measured as the risk of a portfolio of zero-coupon bonds.

With zero-coupon bonds and other finite maturity claims, the historical volatility of the claim is not necessarily a good measure of the future volatility of the claim. Other things being equal, bonds become less volatile as they approach maturity. A natural solution to this problem is to characterize risk in terms of the bond yield rather than the bond price. Yield uncertainty implies price uncertainty.

Here is an example of how to measure VaR for a zero-coupon bond. Suppose that a zero-coupon bond matures at time T and has price $P(T)$, and that the annualized yield volatility of the bond is σ_T. For a zero-coupon bond, duration equals maturity. Thus, if the yield changes by ϵ, the percentage change in the bond price will be approximately ϵT. Using this linear approximation based on duration, and ignoring the mean return on the bond, over the horizon h the bond has a 95% chance of being worth more than

$$P(T)[1 + \sigma_T T \sqrt{h} \times (-1.645)]$$

Example 25.8   Suppose a bond has $T = 10$ years to maturity. Its yield to maturity is 5.5% and the annualized yield volatility is 1%. The one-week VaR on a $10m position in these bonds is

$$\$10m \times \left[1 + 0.01 \times 10 \times \sqrt{\frac{1}{52}} \times (-1.645) \right] - \$10m = -\$228,120$$

Now suppose that instead of a single bond we have a portfolio of zero-coupon bonds. In particular, suppose we own W_1 of a bond maturing at T_1 with annualized yield volatility σ_{T_1} and W_2 of a bond maturing at T_2 with annualized yield volatility σ_{T_2}. Let ρ represent the correlation between the yields on the two bonds. (This yield volatility information could be estimated using historical data or using implied volatilities.) As with a portfolio of stocks, we can use the delta approximation, only here instead of two correlated stock returns we have two correlated bond yields.

Example 25.9 Let $T_1 = 10$, $T_2 = 15$, $\sigma_{T_1} = 0.01$, $\sigma_{T_2} = 0.012$ $\rho = 0.985$, $W_1 = \$6m$ and $W_2 = \$4m$. Since the portfolio is 60% invested in the 10-year bond and 40% invested in the 15-year bond, the variance of the bond portfolio is

$$(0.6 \times 0.01 \times 10)^2 + (0.4 \times 0.012 \times 15)^2$$
$$+ (2 \times 0.985 \times 0.6 \times 0.4 \times 0.01 \times 10 \times 0.012 \times 15) = 0.01729$$

The volatility is $\sqrt{0.01729} = 0.1315$. The 95% one-week VaR for this portfolio is therefore

$$\$10m \times [1 + 0.1315\sqrt{1/52} \times (-1.645)] - \$10m = -\$301,638$$

We discussed in Chapter 24 the shortcomings of duration as a measure of bond price risk, so you might be wondering about the use of duration in these examples. Duration here is used mechanically to compute the price change for a bond for a given change in the bond's own yield. This is a delta approximation to the actual bond price change. The conceptual problem with duration becomes problematic when we use duration to compute a hedge ratio for *two* bonds. The hedge ratio calculation assumes that the yield to maturity for the two bonds changes by the same amount. By contrast, in Example 25.9 each bond has a different yield volatility and there is an imperfect correlation between the two yields; thus, we do *not* assume that all yields to maturity change by the same amount—i.e., that there is a parallel yield curve shift. (For a parallel yield curve shift we would need each bond to have the same annualized yield volatility and $\rho = 1$.)

In general, if we are analyzing the risk of an instrument with multiple cash flows, the first step is to find the equivalent portfolio of zero-coupon bonds. A 10-year bond with semiannual coupons is equivalent to a portfolio of 20 zero-coupon bonds. Every interest rate claim is decomposed in this way into interest rate "buckets" containing the claim's constituent zero-coupon bonds. A set of bonds and swaps reduces to a portfolio of long and short positions in zero-coupon bonds. We need volatilities and correlations for all these bonds.

FIGURE 25.6

The probability distribution for S_T, the VaR price level $(\bar{S}(0.05))$, and the tail VaR price level $(E[S_T|S_T < \bar{S}(0.05)])$. Assumes the same parameters as in Example 25.1.

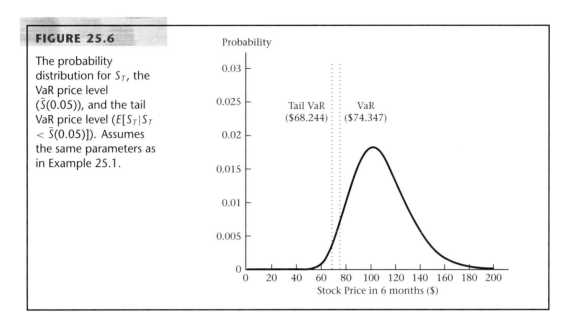

Thus, VaR is

$$\text{VaR} = \$100 - \$74.347 = \$25.653$$

The calculation of tail VaR is based on the expected stock price conditional upon $S_T < \$74.347$. Using equation (18.28), we obtain

$$E(S_T|S_T < \$74.347) = \frac{100 \times e^{0.15\times0.5}N(-\hat{d}_1)}{N(-\hat{d}_2)}$$
$$= \$68.244$$

where

$$\hat{d}_1 = -\frac{\ln(100/74.347) + (0.15 + 0.5 \times 0.30^2) \times 0.5}{0.30\sqrt{0.5}}$$
$$\hat{d}_2 = \hat{d}_1 - 0.30\sqrt{0.5}$$

Tail VaR is therefore

$$\text{Tail VaR} = \$100 - \$68.244 = \$31.756$$

Figure 25.6 depicts the probability density for the stock price in six months, the VaR price level, and the tail VaR price level. ≋

It is possible to interpret tail VaR as an average of VaRs with different confidence levels. We can approximate the conditional expectation of the stock price below $\bar{S}(c)$

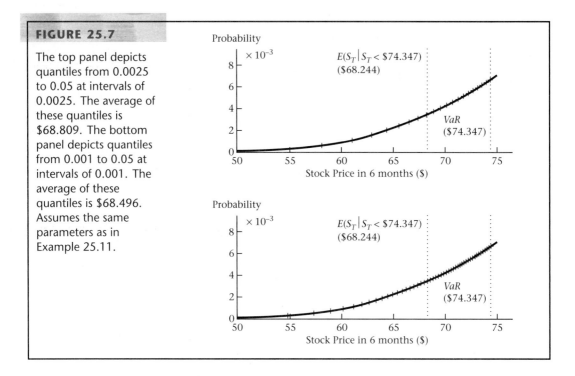

FIGURE 25.7

The top panel depicts quantiles from 0.0025 to 0.05 at intervals of 0.0025. The average of these quantiles is $68.809. The bottom panel depicts quantiles from 0.001 to 0.05 at intervals of 0.001. The average of these quantiles is $68.496. Assumes the same parameters as in Example 25.11.

by averaging the stock prices associated with VaRs at lower levels lower than c. For example, suppose we were to compute VaR at a series of different confidence levels: 0.005, 0.01, 0.015, etc. We would first compute a series of stock prices: $\bar{S}(0.005)$, $\bar{S}(0.01)$, $\bar{S}(0.015)$, etc. By definition, each of these stock prices is a quantile. While the probability that S_T is *below* each of these stock prices is different, there is an equal probability that S_T is approximately equal to any of these stock prices. More precisely, the probability of the stock price being between $\bar{S}(0.005)$ and $\bar{S}(0.01)$ is equal to the probability of S_T being between $\bar{S}(0.01)$ and $\bar{S}(0.015)$, etc. By averaging the stock prices $\bar{S}(0.005)$, $\bar{S}(0.01)$, $\bar{S}(0.015)$, . . . , $\bar{S}(0.05)$, we approximate the conditional expectation of the stock price below $\bar{S}(0.05)$, which is $68.244.

Figure 25.7 illustrates this calculation. The two panels show quantiles below 5%. The average of these quantiles is approximately equal to the conditional expectation of $68.244. As we average more quantiles, we approximate the conditional expectation more closely. In most applications there will be no simple formula for the conditional expectation. It is then possible to approximate tail VaR by averaging quantiles.

The cost of insurance   One application of VaR and VaR-like calculations is to compute the capital required to support a risky business. Capital is a resource that permits the firm to sustain losses and still meet its business obligations. As an alternative to capital, we could imagine a firm purchasing insurance against a loss. The capital required to undertake the business would then be the price of this insurance. The market price of this insurance provides another way to measure risk.

Returning to our example of a single stock portfolio, if we insure against losses due to a stock price below $\bar{S}(c)$, then the time T payoff on such an insurance policy will be

$$\max[0, \bar{S}(c) - S_T]$$

Thus, the insurance premium is the value of a put option with strike price $\bar{S}(c)$ and time to expiration T. We can obtain the value of the put by computing

$$e^{-rT} E^*[\bar{S}(c) - S_T | S_T < \bar{S}(c)] \times \text{Prob}^*[S_T < \bar{S}(c)]$$
$$= e^{-rT} \left\{ \bar{S}(c) \times -E^*[S_T | S_T < \bar{S}(c)] \right\} \times \text{Prob}^*[S_T < \bar{S}(c)] \quad (25.19)$$

where E^* and Prob^* represent the expectation and probability computed with respect to the risk-neutral distribution. The put price calculation appears similar to the conditional price calculation used in computing tail VaR, but the two calculations are not identical. One obvious difference is that tail VaR is computed using the conditional expectation of the stock price under the true distribution, while the option price uses the risk-neutral distribution. Note that while $\text{Prob}[S_T < \bar{S}(c)] = c$, $\text{Prob}^*[S_T < \bar{S}(c)] \neq c$ unless the risk premium on the asset is zero ($\alpha = r$). Also, the put price is discounted, while the tail VaR is not.

VaR horizons are often short, so that discounting may not be an important issue. Also, with a short horizon the difference between the risk-neutral and true distribution may not be large.[7]

Example 25.12 Assume the same parameters as in Example 25.11, and also that the risk-free rate is 8%. The price of a put with 6 months to expiration and a strike of $74.347 is

$$\text{BSPut}(100, 74.347, 0.30, 0.08, 0.50, 0) = \$0.4289$$ ≋

VaR and the Risk-Neutral Distribution

It might seem odd to you that we have mostly used the risk-neutral distribution in this book, but in discussing VaR we have concentrated on the true distribution. Using the foregoing examples, we can explore this difference.

....

[7]When prices move continuously and the hedging of risks is possible, the difference between the true and risk-neutral distributions depends upon the risk premium, $(\alpha - r)h$. When h is small, the risk premium will be small. When jumps are possible, the risk premium associated with the jump could create a significant difference between the risk-neutral and true distributions even over short horizons.

Let's try to interpret VaR and tail VaR in terms of insurance. If we are willing to accept losses less than the VaR level, then we can think of VaR as a deductible: It is the loss we willingly sustain before insurance pays anything. The difference between tail VaR and VaR is then the average payout from insurance; this payout occurs with true probability c. Since we are using the true distribution, the appropriate discount rate for a conditional expectation is unclear. (This is another manifestation of the problem of obtaining a "true" discount rate for an option.) Let γ denote the discount rate. A back-of-the-envelope calculation for the value of the average insurance payoff, assuming $\gamma = r$, is[8]

$$e^{-\gamma T} \text{[Tail VaR} - \text{VaR]} \times \text{Prob}[S_T < \bar{S}(c)] \qquad (25.20)$$
$$= e^{-\gamma T} \{S_0 - E[S_T|S_T < \bar{S}(c)] - [S_0 - \bar{S}(c)]\} \times c$$
$$= e^{-0.08 \times 0.50} \times (74.347 - \$68.244) \times 0.05$$
$$= 0.2932$$

The value of insurance inferred from the VaR calculations is substantially less than that computed using the Black-Scholes formula. There are two reasons why this calculation gives the wrong answer.

First, 5% is the VaR probability under the true distribution, not under the risk-neutral distribution. The risk-neutral probability that $S_T < 74.347$ is 6.945%. The risk-neutral probability is greater than the true probability because the 8% risk-free rate is less than the 15% expected return on the stock (i.e., $\alpha > r$).

Second, the conditional expected stock price under the risk-neutral distribution is less than that under the true distribution:

$$E^* \left(S_T | S_T < \$74.347\right) = \$67.919$$

Again, the true conditional expectation exceeds the risk-neutral conditional expectation because $\alpha > r$.

We can change the probability and conditional expectation to their risk-neutral values and repeat the calculation in equation 25.20. We then obtain

$$e^{-0.08 \times 0.50} \times (\$74.347 - \$67.919) \times 0.06945 = \$0.4289$$

This is the same as the put premium in Example 25.11.

As a final comment, note that the 5% VaR will also be different depending upon whether we use the true or risk-neutral distribution. In this discussion we continued to use $74.347—computed under the true distribution—as the VaR stock price.

The conclusion of this discussion is that we need to be cautious when interpreting VaR and tail VaR calculations. Economically, when $\alpha > r$, VaR-style calculations computed using the true stock price distribution understate the insurance cost because they fail to properly account for the risk premium as a component of the drift on the asset.

---

[8] If there is no risk premium on the stock—i.e., $\alpha = r$—this calculation produces the Black-Scholes put price.

The risk premium is compensation for the fact that when the stock earns a low return, investors generally have suffered losses on their investments (their marginal utility of consumption is high). Insurance hedges against this outcome and is therefore valuable to investors. The Black-Scholes calculation properly accounts for the role of the risk premium, while the back-of-the-envelope calculation using VaR does not.

Subadditive Risk Measures

Artzner et al. (1999) point out a conceptual problem with VaR. As we have discussed, a common use of a risk measure is to decide how much capital is required to support an activity. Artzner et al. argue that a reasonable risk measure (or measure of required capital) should have certain properties, among them **subadditivity**.[9] If $\rho(X)$ is the risk measure associated with activity X (the capital required to support activity X), then ρ is subadditive if for two activities X and Y

$$\rho(X + Y) \leq \rho(X) + \rho(Y) \tag{25.21}$$

This simply says that the risk measure for the two activities combined should be less than that for the two activities separately. Because combining activities creates diversification, the capital required to support two activities together should be no greater than that required to support the two separately. If capital requirements are imposed using a rule that is not subadditive, then firms can reduce required capital by splitting up activities.

VaR is not subadditive. To show this, Artzner et al. provide an example using European out-of-the-money cash-or-nothing options having the same time to expiration and written on a single stock. Option A, a cash-or-nothing call, pays $1 if $S_T > H$, while option B, a cash-or-nothing put, pays $1 if $S_T < L$. Represent the premiums of the two options as P_A and P_B and suppose that either option has a 0.8% probability of paying off. The probability that either option expires out-of-the-money is 99.2%, and the probability that *both* options expire out-of-the-money is 98.4%.

Consider a financial institution that *writes* such options. For either option considered alone, the bank is confident at a 99% level that the option will not be exercised, in which case the bank keeps the premium. Thus, VaR at a 99% confidence level is $-P_A$ (for option A) or $-P_B$ (for option B). VaR is *negative* because with 99% confidence, the option writer will keep the premium without the option being exercised.

Now suppose the institution sells both options. Because the two written options have the same underlying stock, they are perfectly negatively correlated. Therefore, the probability that one of the two options will be exercised is 0.8% + 0.8% = 1.6%. In the lowest 1% of the return distribution, one of the two options will be exercised. The VaR

[9]Artzner et al. (1999) define *coherent* risk measures as those satisfying four properties: (1) *subadditivity*; (2) *monotonicity*: if $X \leq Y$, $\rho(X) \geq \rho(Y)$ (if the loss is greater, the risk measure is greater); (3) *translation invariance*: $\rho(X + a) = \rho(X) - a$ (if you add $1 to the cash flow, the risk measure is reduced by $1); and (4) *positive homogeneity* $\rho(\lambda X) = \lambda \rho(X)$ for $\lambda > 0$ (if you multiply the risk by 10, the risk measure increases by 10).

at the 99% level for the writer of the two options is therefore $\$1 - P_A - P_B$. We have

$$\text{VaR}(-A - B) = \$1 - P_A - P_B > -P_A - P_B = \text{VaR}(-A) + \text{VaR}(-B)$$

This expression has the opposite inequality as equation (25.21), so VaR is not subadditive in this example. In words, the institution can eliminate risk, as measured by 99% VaR, by undertaking the two activities in separate entities.

As a different example that illustrates this point, suppose you are comparing activity C, which generates a $\$1$ loss with a 1.1% probability, with activity D, which generates a $\$1$m loss with a 0.9% probability. Any reasonable rule should assign greater risk (and require more capital) for activity D, but a 1% VaR would be greater for C than for D.

These examples highlight an intuitively undesirable property of VaR as a risk measure: a small change in the VaR probability can cause VaR to change by a large amount. For the written cash-or-nothing call in this example, a 0.81% VaR is $-P_A$, while the 0.79% VaR is $\$1 - P_A$.

In contrast with VaR, tail VaR and the cost of insurance are both subadditive. Intuitively, tail VaR takes into account the distribution of losses beyond the VaR level, so it does not change abruptly when we change the VaR probability. To see that it is subadditive in our examples, the tail VaRs at the 99% level for A and B are

$$\rho(A) = 0.8 \times (1 - P_A) + 0.2 \times (-P_A) = 0.8 - P_A$$
$$\rho(b) = 0.8 \times (1 - P_B) + 0.2 \times (-P_B) = 0.8 - P_B$$

With the same confidence level, tail VaR at the 99% level for A and B together is

$$\rho(A + B) = 1 - P_A - P_B$$

We then have

$$\rho(A + B) = 1 - P_A - P_B < \rho(A) + \rho(B) = 1.6 - P_A - P_B$$

Thus, tail VaR in this example is subadditive.

As for the subadditivity of insurance premiums, Merton (1973b) demonstrated that options on portfolios are no more expensive than a portfolio of options on the portfolio constituents. Insurance premiums are therefore subadditive.

CHAPTER SUMMARY

Value at risk (VaR) is used to measure and manage risk—for example, in computing capital requirements. VaR deals primarily with so-called "market risks": price changes of stocks, currencies, interest rates, and commodities. The value at risk of a portfolio is the level of loss that will be exceeded a given percentage of the time over a specified horizon. Computing value at risk requires approximating the return distribution of the portfolio, which in turn requires information on the variance and covariance of assets in the portfolio. When portfolios are simple—for example, containing only stocks—standard portfolio risk calculations can be used to compute VaR. When portfolios contain options and other nonlinear assets, Monte Carlo simulation is commonly used to assess the return distribution of the portfolio. It is possible to construct examples in which VaR is an ill-behaved risk measure. Tail VaR, which takes into account the distribution of losses beyond the VaR level, and the cost of insurance against losses exceeding the VaR level, may provide better alternatives.

FURTHER READING

The *Riskmetrics Technical Document* (J. P. Morgan/Reuters, 1996) is available from **www.riskmetrics.com**. It was distributed by J. P. Morgan—and now by Riskmetrics—to explain VaR, illustrate some of the calculations behind VaR, and review some of the judgments behind the particular set of calculations. The document was influential and remains worth reading.

Pearson (2002) provides an excellent overview of VaR, with very clear discussions of relevant mathematical techniques. Jorion (2001) provides a broad overview of the regulatory, practical, and analytical issues in computing VaR. Hendricks (1996) compares the results from computing VaR in a variety of different ways. Artzner et al. (1999) is an influential paper offering some important warnings about the use of VaR as a decision-making tool. Further explorations along these lines include Acerbi (2002) and Acerbi and Tasche (2002), and other papers in the July 2002 special issue of the *Journal of Banking and Finance*.

PROBLEMS

In the following problems, assume that the risk-free rate is 0.08 and that there are three stocks with a price of $100 and the following characteristics:

	α	σ	δ	Correlation with B	Correlation with C
Stock A	0.15	0.30	0.00	0.25	0.20
Stock B	0.18	0.45	0.02	1.00	0.30
Stock C	0.16	0.50	0.00	0.30	1.00

25.1. Consider the expression in equation (25.6). What is the exact probability that, over a 1-day horizon, stock A will have a loss?

25.2. Assuming a $10m investment in one stock, compute the 95% and 99% VaR for stocks A and B over 1-day, 10-day, and 20-day horizons.

25.3. Assuming a $10m investment that is 40% stock A and 60% stock B, compute the 95% and 99% VaR for the position over 1-day, 10-day, and 20-day horizons.

25.4. What are 95% and 99% 1-, 10- and 20-day VaRs for a portfolio that has $4m invested in stock A, $3.5m in stock B, and $2.5m in stock C?

25.5. Using the same assumptions as in Example 25.3, compute VaR with and without the mean assuming correlations of -1, -0.5, 0, 0.5, and 1. Is risk eliminated with a correlation of -1? If not, why not?

25.6. Using the delta-approximation method and assuming a $10m investment in stock A, compute the 95% and 99% 1-, 10-, and 20-day VaRs for a position consisting of stock A plus one 105-strike put option for each share. Use the same assumptions as in Example 25.4.

25.7. Repeat the previous problem, only use Monte Carlo simulation.

25.8. Compute the 95% 10-day VaR for a written strangle (sell an out-of-the-money call and an out-of-the-money put) on 100,000 shares of stock A. Assume the options have strikes of $90 and $110 and have 1 year to expiration. Use the delta-approximation method and Monte Carlo simulation. What accounts for the difference in your answers?

25.9. Using Monte Carlo, compute the 95% and 99% 1-, 10-, and 20-day tail VaRs for the position in Problem 25.2.

25.10. Compute the 95% 10-day tail VaR for the position in Problem 25.8.

25.11. Suppose you write a 1-year cash-or-nothing put with a strike of $50 and a 1-year cash-or-nothing call with a strike of $215, both on stock A.

   a. What is the 1-year 99% VaR for each option separately?

   b. What is the 1-year 99% VaR for the two written options together?

   c. What is the 1-year 99% tail VaR for each option separately and the two together?

25.12. Suppose the 7-year zero-coupon bond has a yield of 6% and yield volatility of 10% and the 10-year zero-coupon bond has a yield of 6.5% and yield volatility of 9.5%. The correlation between the 7-year and 10-year yields is 0.96. What are 95% and 99% 10-day VaRs for an 8-year zero-coupon bond that pays $10m at maturity?

25.13. Using the same assumptions as in Problem 25.12, compute the 10-day 95% VaR for a claim that pays $3m each year in years 7–10.

CHAPTER 26

Credit Risk

The risk that a counterparty will fail to meet a contractual payment obligation is known as **credit risk.** Such risk exists anytime one party promises to make a future payment to another. Credit risk arises with loans, corporate bonds, and derivative contracts, and market-making activities generally leave dealers exposed to credit risk. We will refer to the failure to make a promised payment as *default.* The term **credit event** is often used in contracts to refer to occurrences that suggest that a default is likely. Examples of credit events are declaration of bankruptcy, failure to make a bond payment, repudiation of an obligation, or a credit downgrade.[1]

In this chapter we present a framework for analyzing credit risk and we see how credit risk affects the prices of claims. We also discuss concepts and terminology that are essential for understanding credit risk. Finally, we look at the instruments used to modify, hedge, and trade credit risk, such as credit default swaps.

26.1 DEFAULT CONCEPTS AND TERMINOLOGY

In this section we introduce basic concepts and terminology related to default in the context of pricing a zero-coupon bond. Suppose that a firm with asset value A_0 issues a zero-coupon bond maturing at time T, with a promised payment of $\bar{B}$. Let B_T denote the market value of the bond at time T. At time T, there are two possible outcomes:

- $A_T > \bar{B}$. Since assets are worth more than the repayment owed bondholders, shareholders will repay bondholders in full, so $B_T = \bar{B}$.

- $A_T < \bar{B}$. Shareholders will walk away from the firm, surrendering it to bondholders. The value of the bonds at time T is then $B_T = A_T$.

Let $g^*(A_T; A_0)$ denote the risk-neutral probability density for the time T asset value, conditional upon the time 0 asset value, A_0. Then we can write the initial debt value,

---

[1]A company that fails to make a promised payment may seek court protection—or a quick resolution of its dilemma—by declaring bankruptcy. Specific bankruptcy rules vary by country. We will use the terms "default" and "bankruptcy" interchangably and without regard to their precise legal meaning.

B_0, as

$$B_0 = e^{-rT} \left[\int_0^{\bar{B}} A_T g^*(A_T; A_0) dA_T + \bar{B} \int_{\bar{B}}^{\infty} g^*(A_T; A_0) dA_T \right] \quad (26.1)$$

The first integral on the right-hand side is the risk-neutral partial expectation of the asset value, conditional on bankruptcy. The second integral is the risk-neutral probability that the firm is not bankrupt. Thus, we can rewrite the value of the bonds as

$$B_0 = e^{-rT} \{ E^*(A_T | \text{Default}) \times \text{Prob}^*(\text{Default}) + \bar{B} \times [1 - \text{Prob}^*(\text{Default})] \}$$

where E^* and Prob* are computed with respect to the risk-neutral measure. Since $B_T = A_T$ in default, we can also write this as

$$B_0 = e^{-rT} \{ E^*(B_T | \text{Default}) \times \text{Prob}^*(\text{Default}) + \bar{B} \times [1 - \text{Prob}^*(\text{Default})] \} \quad (26.2)$$

If we set the probability of default equal to zero, equation (26.2) yields the standard formula for the value of a default-free bond, $B_0 = e^{-rT} \bar{B}$. Equation (26.2) also illustrates that default introduces two new elements: the default probability (Prob*[Default]), and the payoff conditional on default ($E^*[B_T | \text{Default}]$).

The payoff conditional on default can be expressed in different ways. The **recovery rate** is the amount the debt-holders receive as a fraction of what they are owed. Thus, in the case where a firm issues a single zero-coupon bond, the risk-neutral expected recovery rate is

$$E^*(\text{Recovery rate}) = \frac{E^*(B_T | \text{Default})}{\bar{B}} \quad (26.3)$$

The **loss given default** is the difference between what the bondholders are owed and what they receive, as a fraction of the promised payment:

$$E^*(\text{Loss given default}) = 1 - E^*(\text{Recovery rate}) \quad (26.4)$$

Conventionally any such measure is expressed as a percentage.

Finally, we can express the **credit spread**—the difference between the yield to maturity on a defaultable bond and an otherwise equivalent default-free bond—in terms of the risk-neutral default probability and expected loss given default. In equation (26.2), divide both sides by $\bar{B}$ and take the natural logarithm of both sides. Recall that the annual yield to maturity on the bond, ρ, is

$$\rho = \frac{1}{T} \ln \left(\frac{\bar{B}}{B_0} \right)$$

After some rearrangement, we obtain the following expression from equation (26.2):

$$\rho - r = \frac{1}{T} \ln \left[\frac{1}{1 - \text{Prob}^*(\text{Default}) \times E^*(\text{Loss given default})} \right] \quad (26.5)$$

The left-hand side of equation (26.5) is the credit spread. Both the probability of default and the expected loss given default are less than one, so, as we would expect, the credit spread is greater than or equal to zero. If either the probability of default or the expected loss given default is zero, the bond yield equals the risk-free rate.

By taking a Taylor series expansion of the right-hand side of equation (26.5), we obtain

$$\rho - r \approx \frac{1}{T}\text{Prob}^*(\text{Default}) \times E^*(\text{Loss given default})$$

Thus, the credit spread approximately equals the annualized product of the risk-neutral default probability and the expected loss given default.

26.2 THE MERTON DEFAULT MODEL

In Section 16.1 we analyzed corporate securities as options. We saw that owning zero-coupon debt subject to default is the same thing as owning a default-free bond and writing a put option on the assets of the firm. This is an example of a *structural* approach to modeling bankruptcy: We create an explicit model for the evolution of the firm's assets, coupled with a rule governing default.

If we assume that the assets of the firm are lognormally distributed, then we can use the lognormal probability calculations of Chapter 18 to compute either the risk-neutral or actual probability that the firm will go bankrupt. This approach to bankruptcy modeling has come to be called the *Merton model* since Merton (1974) used continuous-time methods to provide a model of the credit spread. The Merton default model has in recent years been the basis for credit risk analyses provided by Moody's KMV.

Default at Maturity

Assume that the assets of the firm, A, follow the process

$$\frac{dA}{A} = (\alpha - \delta)dt + \sigma dZ \qquad (26.6)$$

where α is the expected return on the firm assets and δ is the cash payout made to claim holders on the firm. Suppose the firm has issued a single zero-coupon bond with promised payment $\bar{B}$, that matures at time T and makes no payouts. Default occurs at time T if $A_T < \bar{B}$. The probability of bankruptcy at time T, conditional on the value of assets at time t, is

$$\text{Prob}(A_T < \bar{B}|A_t) = N\left[-\frac{\ln(A_t/\bar{B}) + (\alpha - \delta - \frac{1}{2}\sigma^2)(T-t)}{\sigma\sqrt{T-t}}\right] \qquad (26.7)$$

$$= N(-\hat{d}_2)$$

In this equation, $\hat{d}_2$ is the Black-Scholes d_2 term with r replaced by α.

The expression $\hat{d}_2$ is called the **distance to default**, and measures the size (in standard deviations) of the random shock required to induce bankruptcy. To understand this interpretation, recall that when assets are lognormally-distributed, the expected log asset value at time T is

$$E[\ln(A_T)] = \ln(A_t) + (\alpha - \delta - 0.5\sigma^2)(T-t)$$

Thus, the distance to default is the difference between $E[\ln(A_T)]$ and the bankruptcy level $\bar{B}$, normalized by the standard deviation:[2]

$$\text{Distance to default} = \frac{E[\ln(A_T)] - \bar{B}}{\sigma\sqrt{T-t}}$$

$$= \frac{\ln(A_t) + (\alpha - \delta - 0.5\sigma^2)(T-t) - \ln(\bar{B})}{\sigma\sqrt{T-t}}$$

This is $\hat{d}_2$. The default probability is $N(-\text{distance to default})$.

The expected recovery rate, conditional on default, is

$$E(A_T | A_T < \bar{B}) = A_t e^{(\alpha-\delta)(T-t)} \frac{N\left[-\frac{\ln(A_t/\bar{B})+(\alpha-\delta+\frac{1}{2}\sigma^2)(T-t)}{\sigma\sqrt{T-t}}\right]}{N\left[-\frac{\ln(A_t/\bar{B})+(\alpha-\delta-\frac{1}{2}\sigma^2)(T-t)}{\sigma\sqrt{T-t}}\right]} \tag{26.8}$$

This is the same as equation (18.28).

It is important to notice that the calculations in equations (26.7) and (26.8) are performed under the true probability measure (also sometimes called the *physical measure*). Thus, these equations provide estimates of the empirically observed default probability and recovery rate, but we cannot use them in pricing calculations. In order to compute the theoretical credit spread, for example, we replace the actual asset drift, α, with the risk-free rate in equations (26.7) and (26.8). This gives us

$$\text{Prob}^*(A_T < \bar{B}; A_t) = N\left[-\frac{\ln(A_t/\bar{B}) + (r - \delta - \frac{1}{2}\sigma^2)(T-t)}{\sigma\sqrt{T-t}}\right] \tag{26.9}$$

and

$$E^*(A_T | A_T < \bar{B}) = A_t e^{(r-\delta)(T-t)} \frac{N\left[-\frac{\ln(A_t/\bar{B})+(r-\delta+\frac{1}{2}\sigma^2)(T-t)}{\sigma\sqrt{T-t}}\right]}{N\left[-\frac{\ln(A_t/\bar{B})+(r-\delta-\frac{1}{2}\sigma^2)(T-t)}{\sigma\sqrt{T-t}}\right]} \tag{26.10}$$

We can use these expressions to compute equation (26.5).

Example 26.1   Suppose that $\bar{B} = \$100$, $A_0 = \$90$, $\alpha = 10\%$, $r = 6\%$, $\sigma = 25\%$, $\delta = 0$ (the firm makes no payouts), and $T = 5$ years. As we saw in Example 16.2, which used the same assumptions, the theoretical debt value in this case is $62.928, which implies a yield of 9.2635%.

Using equations (26.7) and (26.9), the true and risk-neutral default probabilities are 33.49% and 47.26%. Thus, over a five-year horizon, we would expect to observe a

---

[2]The Moody's KMV model uses the different expression $(A_t - \bar{B})/\sigma A_t$ as a measure of distance to default. See Crosbie and Bohn (2003) for a discussion.

default one-third of the time. Under the risk-neutral measure, however, defaults occur almost half the time. The greater risk-neutral default probability is due to the assets growing more slowly under the risk-neutral measure.

Using equations (26.8) and (26.10), the expected asset value conditional on default is $71.867 under the true measure, and $68.144 under the risk-neutral measure. Expected recovery rates are therefore

$$E(\text{Recovery rate}) = \frac{71.867}{100} = 0.71867$$

under the true measure, and

$$E^*(\text{Recovery rate}) = \frac{68.144}{100} = 0.68144$$

under the risk-neutral measure. Note that the risk-neutral expected loss given default is

$$E^*(\text{Loss given default}) = 1 - 0.68144 = 0.31866$$

Using the risk-neutral default probability and loss given default, we can compute the theoretical debt yield. From equation (26.5), the credit spread is

$$\frac{1}{5} \ln \left[\frac{1}{1 - 0.4726 \times 0.31866} \right] = 0.032635$$

This implies a debt yield to maturity of $0.060 + 0.032635 = 0.092635$, which is the same answer as that using the Black-Scholes formula to compute the theoretical debt value. ≋

As the preceding example shows, historical data on *defaults* provides different information than historical data on *prices*. Historical default frequencies and recovery rates, which are observed under the true measure, correspond to equations (26.7) and (26.8). If we examine credit spreads, by contrast, we can infer the risk-neutral expected default frequency and recovery rate, which correspond to equations (26.9) and (26.10). Notice, however, that we would infer the same asset volatility from both sets of calculations.

Related Models

Suppose that the value of assets can jump to zero according to a Poisson process. Specifically, suppose that over an interval dt, the probability of a jump to zero is λdt, and that the occurrence of this jump is independent of the market and of other defaults. We saw in Section 23.4 that when a stock can independently jump to zero, the value of a European call is obtained by replacing the risk-free rate, r, with $r + \lambda$. As before, equity is a call option on the assets. If the firm makes no payouts, the value, B_t, of a single issue of zero-coupon debt maturing at time T is

$$B_t = A_t - \text{BSCall}(A_t, \bar{B}, \sigma, r + \lambda, T - t, 0) \tag{26.11}$$

The possibility that assets can jump to zero will raise the bond yield.[3]

There is a special case where the effect of the jump probability on the bond yield is particularly easy to interpret. When the bond is default-free except for the possibility of a jump, then the bond yield is $r + \lambda$: The yield increases one-for-one with the default probability.

Example 26.2   Suppose that a firm has a single issue of zero-coupon debt promising to pay \$10 in 5 years, and that $A_0 = \$90$, $\sigma = 30\%$, $r = 0.06$, and $\delta = 0$. From equation (26.11), when $\lambda = 0$, the value of the debt is

$$B_t = \$90 - \text{BSCall}(90, 10, 0.30, 0.06, 5, 0) = \$7.408$$

The yield on debt is $\ln(10/7.408)/5 = 0.06$. This bond is priced as if it were default-free.
When $\lambda = 0.02$, the price of the bond is

$$B_t = \$90 - \text{BSCall}(90, 10, 0.30, 0.06 + 0.02, 5, 0) = \$6.703$$

The yield is then $\ln(10/6.703)/5 = 0.08$: The yield increases by the default probability.

When a default is likely apart from jumps to zero, then the increase in the bond yield is less than λ. For example, when $\bar{B} = \$100$, the bond yield is 10.342% without jumps, and 11.588% with a 2% jump to zero.   ≋

The models we have discussed are relatively simple: There are no coupon payments and bankruptcy occurs only at maturity. In practice, firms typically have a mix of short-term and long-term coupon-paying debt, so that debt maturity is not well-defined and bankruptcy can occur at anytime. One solution in this case is to approximate the bankruptcy trigger as the face value of short-term debt plus one-half the face value of long-term debt (Vassalou and Xing, 2004).

With barrier option pricing formulas, binomial valuation, Monte Carlo, or other numerical methods, it is possible to create bankruptcy models that permit bankruptcy prior to a maturity date. The Black and Cox (1976) model is a variant of the Merton model in which bankruptcy occurs if assets fall to a predetermined level, $\underline{A}$, prior to maturity. This assumption mimics a debt covenant that triggers default if the firm's

---

[3]By differentiating the expression for yield to maturity $(\ln[\bar{B}/B_t]/T)$ with respect to λ, it is possible to show that the increase in yield from a 0.01 increase in λ is

$$\text{Yield increase} = \frac{\text{BSCallRho}(A_t, \bar{B}, \sigma, r + \lambda, T - t, \delta)}{\text{Bond price} \times T}$$

where "BSCallRho" is the formula for the rho (interest rate sensitivity) of a call.

finanical condition worsens sufficiently. Equity in this model is a call option that knocks out if $A_t \leq \underline{A}$.

26.3 BOND RATINGS AND DEFAULT EXPERIENCE

Bond ratings provide a measure of the credit risk for specific bonds. Such ratings, which are provided by third parties, attempt to measure the likelihood that a company will default on a bond.[4] In the United States, the Securities and Exchange Commission (SEC) identifies specific credit-rating firms as Nationally Recognized Statistical Rating Organizations (NRSROs). The history and significance of this designation was explained by the chairman of the SEC in congressional testimony:[5]

> The Commission originally used the term "Nationally Recognized Statistical Rating Organization," or NRSRO, with respect to credit rating agencies in 1975 solely to differentiate between grades of debt securities held by broker-dealers as capital to meet Commission capital requirements. Since that time, ratings by NRSROs have become benchmarks in federal and state legislation, domestic and foreign financial regulations and privately negotiated financial contracts.

Moody's rates bonds using the designations Aaa, Aa, A, Baa, Ba, B, Caa, Ca, and C. Within each ratings category, bonds may be further rated as a 1, 2, or 3, with 1 denoting the highest quality within a category. Standard and Poor's and Fitch have a similar rating system, using the designations AAA, AA, A, BBB, BB, B, CCC, CC, C.

The market distinguishes between "investment grade" (a rating of Baa/BBB or above) and "below-investment grade" or "speculative grade" (a rating below Baa/BBB) bond. Some investors are permitted to hold only investment grade bonds, and some contracts have triggers based upon whether a company's bond rating is investment grade. For example, prior to Enron's bankruptcy, some of the company's deals contained clauses requiring that Enron make payments if Enron lost its investment grade status. Enron's financial difficulties were worsened when its rating fell below investment grade.

Using Ratings to Assess Bankruptcy Probability

A company that goes bankrupt will typically have had ratings downgrades prior to bankruptcy. By looking at the frequency with which bonds experience a ratings change,

---

[4]Companies pay ratings agencies to have their bonds rated. Some have criticized this practice, arguing that payment for ratings creates a conflict of interest.

[5]"Testimony Concerning The State of the Securities Industry," by William H. Donaldson Chairman, U.S. SEC, U.S. Senate Committee on Banking, Housing, and Urban Affairs, March 9, 2005. As of mid-2005, five firms were recognized as NRSROs: Moody's Investor Services, Standard and Poor's, Fitch Ratings, Dominion Bond Rating Service, and A.M. Best.

TABLE 26.1		Moody's average 1-year credit ratings transition matrix, 1970 to 2004. "WR" stands for "withdrawn rating."								
Rating	Count	Aaa	Aa	A	Baa	Ba	B	Caa-C	Default	WR
Aaa	3,179	89.48	7.05	0.75	0.00	0.03	0.00	0.00	0.00	2.69
Aa	11,310	1.07	88.41	7.35	0.25	0.07	0.01	0	0	2.83
A	22,981	0.05	2.32	88.97	4.85	0.46	0.12	0.01	0.02	3.19
Baa	18,368	0.05	0.23	5.03	84.5	4.6	0.74	0.15	0.16	4.54
Ba	12,702	0.01	0.04	0.46	5.28	78.88	6.48	0.5	1.16	7.19
B	10,794	0.01	0.03	0.12	0.4	6.18	77.45	2.93	6.03	6.85
Caa-C	2,091	0	0	0	0.52	1.57	4	62.68	23.12	8.11

Source: Hamilton et al. (2005).

it is possible to estimate the ultimate bankruptcy probability. A change in ratings is called a **ratings transition.**

Table 26.1 is a *ratings transition matrix*, reporting the probability that a firm in a given ratings category will switch to another ratings category over the course of a year.[6] Firms rated Aaa, Aa, or A, all have about an 89% chance of retaining their rating over a one-year horizon, and almost no chance of suffering a default over that time. They do, however, have some chance of experiencing a downgrade, after which bankruptcy becomes likelier: The default probability increases as the rating decreases.

Given certain assumptions, we can use a short-term ratings transition matrix to compute the ultimate probability that a firm with a given rating will go bankrupt. Specifically, suppose we believe that a ratings transition matrix is constant over time and that the probability of moving from one rating to another in a given year does not depend on the rating in a previous year. Then we can use the matrix to compute the probability that a firm that is A-rated (for example) will move to any other rating, and the subsequent probability that it will move from one of the new ratings to a different rating, and so forth.

The following simple example will illustrate how to interpret and use a ratings transition matrix. Suppose that securities can be in one of three categories: Good, Bad, and Ugly. The matrix in Table 26.2 displays the probability that a firm with a rating in the left-hand column will, over the course of a year, move to a rating in the top row. For example, there is a 90% probability that a firm rated Good will still be Good one year later. There is a 3% chance that the Good firm will become Ugly.

---

[6]A rating can be withdrawn if the rated obligation has matured or if the ratings agency deems that there is insufficient information for a rating.

TABLE 26.2	Ratings transition matrix. The entry in the *i*th row and *j*th column is the probability that a firm will, over one year, move from type *i* to type *j*.

		To:		
		Good	**Bad**	**Ugly**
	Good	0.90	0.07	0.03
From:	Bad	0.15	0.75	0.10
	Ugly	0.06	0.14	0.80

Notice that each row sums to one. This means that after one year each firm must be in one of the three categories. By contrast, in Table 26.1, there is a "Withdrawn Rating" category, indicating that a firm has for some reason dropped out of the Moody's rating universe.

We can use the transition matrix to compute the probability that a firm rated Good will still be Good two years from now. To perform this calculation, recognize that there are three different paths by which a firm that is now Good can still be Good in two years.

- There is a 90% chance that a Good firm remains Good over one year. There is therefore an 81% (0.9×0.9) probability that the firm will be Good for both years.

- There is a 7% probability that the firm will be Bad next year, in which case there is a 15% chance the firm will be come Good the subsequent year. There is therefore a 1.05% (0.07×0.15) probability that the firm will go from Good to Bad and then back to Good.

- Finally, there is a 3% probability that the firm will become Ugly, and then a 6% probability that it will become Good again. There is therefore a 0.18% (0.03×0.06) probability that the firm become Ugly and then Good.

The total probablity that a Good firm will still be Good in two years is therefore 82.23%:

$$(0.90 \times 0.90) + (0.07 \times 0.15) + (0.03 \times 0.06) = 0.8223$$

In order to perform this calculation, it may at first seem necessary to enumerate the possible transitions. Notice, however, that the calculation entails multiplying each element of the the first row of the transition matrix by the corresponding element of the first column, and then summing the results. It turns out that if we wish to know all possible transitions over a two-year period, we can construct a new matrix from the one-year transition matrix, where the element in the *i*th row and *j*th column of the new matrix is created by multiplying the *i*th row of the original matrix by the *j*th column of the original matrix and summing the results. Table 26.3 shows the result.

TABLE 26.3		Ratings transition probabilities after two years.		
		To:		
		Good	**Bad**	**Ugly**
	Good	0.8223	0.1197	0.0580
From:	Bad	0.2535	0.5870	0.1595
	Ugly	0.1230	0.2212	0.6558

In order to compute the ratings distribution after three years, we can duplicate the procedure, only taking the two-year matrix and multiplying it by the one-year matrix. This is the same as multiplying the one-year matrix by itself twice.

In general, let $p(i, t; j, t + s)$ denote the probability that, over an s-year horizon, a firm will move from the rating in row i to that in column j. The entries in Table 26.1 give us $p(i, t; j, t + 1)$. Suppose there are n ratings. Over 2 years, the probability of moving from rating i to rating j is

$$p(i, t; j, t + 2) = \sum_{k=1}^{n} p(i, t; k, t + 1) \times p(k, t + 1; j, t + 2)$$

From the 2-year transitions we can go to 3 years, and then 4, and so on. Given the $s - 1$-year transition probabilities, the s-year transition probability is

$$p(i, t; j, t + s) = \sum_{k=1}^{n} p(i, t; k, t + s - 1) \times p(k, t + s - 1; j, t + s) \qquad (26.12)$$

Thus, a transition probability matrix can be used to tell us the probability that a firm will go bankrupt after a given period of time.

The long-term experience of bonds with a given rating is reported in Table 26.4. Note that if a bond has a Aaa rating, even after 20 years there is only a 1.54% chance it will have gone bankrupt. However, if a bond is below-investment grade, there is a 47% chance of bankrutpcy over a 20-year horizon.

Recovery Rates

There is also historical information about recovery rates. Table 26.5 displays historical average recovery rates for different kinds of bonds. As you would expect, bonds designated as more senior have higher recovery rates. When we modeled debt with different priorities in Section 16.1, we assumed that junior debt was not paid at all if senior debt was not completely repaid. This rule for assigning payments is called **absolute priority.**

TABLE 26.4 Cumulative default rates (in percent) for rated bonds, 1970–2004.

| | Years Since Rating | | | | | | |
Rating	1	2	3	5	10	15	20
Aaa	0	0	0	0.12	0.63	1.22	1.54
Aa	0	0	0.03	0.2	0.61	1.38	2.44
A	0.02	0.08	0.22	0.5	1.48	2.74	4.87
Baa	0.19	0.54	0.98	2.08	4.89	8.73	12.05
Ba	1.22	3.34	5.79	10.72	20.11	29.67	37.07
B	5.81	12.93	19.51	30.48	48.64	57.72	59.11
Caa-C	22.43	35.96	46.71	59.72	76.77	78.53	78.53
Investment grade	0.07	0.21	0.41	0.92	2.31	4.18	6.31
Below-investment grade	4.85	9.84	14.43	21.91	33.61	42.13	47.75
All rated	1.56	3.15	4.6	6.94	10.53	13.51	16.13

Source: Hamilton et al. (2005).

TABLE 26.5 Recovery rates (per $100 of par value) for different kinds of bonds, 1982–2003.

Priority	Mean ($)
Senior secured	57.40
Senior unsecured	44.90
Senior subordinated	39.10
Subordinated	32.00
Junior subordinated	28.90
All	42.20

Source: Hamilton et al. (2005).

If the bankruptcy process respects absolute priority, we expect more senior bonds to have higher recovery rates.

There is considerable variation in recovery rates across firms. Hamilton et al. (2005) report, for example, that for senior subordinated bonds in 2004, the mean recovery rate was 44.4%, but realized recovery rates ranged between 8% and 90%, with a standard deviation of 25%.

Reduced Form Bankruptcy Models

The existence of data on corporate bond ratings, ratings changes, and defaults, suggests that we could construct statistical pricing models designed to match the behavior of bond prices. Such models are called *reduced form models*.[7] In order to price bonds we require risk-neutral probabilities, so we cannot directly use historical data.

To understand how reduced form models work, consider the simplest version of such a model. Suppose a T-year bond promises to pay $\bar{B}$ at maturity and there is a zero recovery rate in the event of default. The risk-free rate is r and constant over time. If default follows a Poisson process with the risk-neutral intensity λ, then the bond price depends only on time and on the occurrence of the jump. From Section 21.5, the partial differential equation for pricing the bond is

$$\frac{\partial B(t)}{\partial t} - \lambda B(t) = r B(t)$$

With the boundary condition that $B(T) = \bar{B}$, the bond price is[8]

$$B(t) = \bar{B} e^{-(r+\lambda)(T-t)} \tag{26.13}$$

Given our strong assumptions that recovery rate is zero and interest rates are nonstochastic, it would seem a simple matter to price this bond by observing r and inferring λ from data on defaults. The problem, however, is that equation (26.13) presumes that λ is a risk-neutral jump probability. Thus, we can infer λ from bond prices but not from historical default data.

To understand the issue, suppose that bond defaults are idiosyncratic. In this case an investor can diversify default risk. We then expect λ in equation (26.13) to equal the historically observed λ.

If defaults are correlated, however, then even a portfolio containing numerous bonds will encounter systematic losses from correlated defaults. Defaults occur when firms perform poorly—i.e., when equity returns are low. Investors require a positive risk premium to hold such bonds, and therefore the risk-neutral default probability in equation (26.13) will exceed the historical default probability.

A more general approach than that in equation (26.13) uses ratings transitions. Equation (26.13) does not take into account that default becomes more likely as ratings decline. With risk-neutral ratings transitions, it is possible to price bonds taking into account the various paths by which default can occur. Jarrow et al. (1997) show how to use observed bond prices and historical ratings transitions to infer risk-neutral ratings transition probabilities.

....

[7]The reduced form approach was first used in Jarrow and Turnbull (1995). See Duffie and Singleton (2003) for a survey.

[8]Note that this is the same bond price solution we obtain in equation (26.11) when $B < A$, and $\sigma = 0$.

26.4 CREDIT INSTRUMENTS

The buyer of a corporate bond acquires both interest rate risk and the credit risk of a specific firm. A particular investor may wish to hold a different combination of these risks. There are ways to alter the mix: Investors can buy Treasury bonds instead of corporate bonds, thereby minimizing credit risk, or use interest rate derivatives to reduce or increase exposure to interest rate risk. More recently, it has become possible to use *credit derivatives* to trade the credit risk of a specific firm. In this section, we explain these instruments.

Collateralized Debt Obligations

A **collateralized debt obligation** (CDO) is a financial structure that repackages the cash flows from a set of assets. You create a CDO by pooling the returns from a set of assets and issuing financial claims to this pool. The CDO claims reapportion the returns on the asset pool. Typically, CDO claims are *tranched*, meaning that the different CDO claims have differing priorities with respect to the cash flows generated by the collateral. With a CDO, it is possible to take a group of risky bonds, for example, and create new claims, some of which are less risky than the original bonds, and others which are riskier.

Given this general description, there are many different ways a CDO can be structured. First, the asset pool can be a fixed set of assets, in which case the CDO is *static*. If instead a manager buys and sells assets, the CDO is *managed*. Second, the CDO claims can directly receive the cash flows generated by the pool assets; this is a *cash flow* CDO. Alternatively, the CDO claims can receive payments based on cash flows and the gain or loss from asset sales; this is a *market value* CDO.

There are at least two reasons for creating CDOs. First, financial institutions will sometimes want to securitize assets, effectively removing them from the institution's balance sheet by selling them to other investors. A CDO can be used to accomplish this, in which case it is a *balance sheet CDO*. Second, a CDO can be created in response to institutional frictions. For example, some investors are permitted to hold only investment grade bonds. As we will see below, CDOs can potentially be used to create investment grade bonds from a pool of noninvestment grade bonds. This is called an *arbitrage CDO*.

CDOs are relatively complex financial structures. The box included here provides an example of the legal arguments that sometimes result.

A CDO with independent defaults A simple example can illustrate how CDOs work. Suppose that there are three risky, speculative-grade bonds that each promise to pay $100 in one year. Defaults are independent and occur only at maturity of the bond. Each bond has a 10% risk-neutral probability of default and a 40% recovery rate, and the risk-free rate is 6%. The price of each bond is

$$e^{-0.06}\left[(1 - 0.1) \times \$100 + 0.1 \times \$40\right] = \$88.526$$

The yield on each bond is $\ln(100/88.526) = 0.1219$.

"Russian Doll" CDOs

Considering its giant size, the decade-old credit-derivatives market is remarkably free of public squabbles. ... [However] a battle in public would be of great interest to outsiders who would like to understand the market better. Such a fight is looming.

... Some CDOs, known as "Russian dolls," contain investments in other CDOs, making their monitoring extremely complicated. To make matters more difficult still, some CDOs are actively managed—i.e., the composition of the underlying portfolio can be changed by the asset manager.

In December 2000 Barclays, a big British bank, launched a Russian-doll CDO called Corvus (the Latin for "crow"), with a face value of $950m in tranches rated from AAA to B. Corvus performed badly, particularly after September 11th 2001. Fitch began to downgrade it in December 2002, and in early 2003 took the unprecedented step of publishing details of the Corvus portfolio on its web site. It included some unexpected stuff—for instance, exposure to airline leases and loans for prefabricated-housing in America. It also had exposure to other CDOs, all constructed by Barclays, some of which were never sold externally. By September 2003 the top three tranches of the CDO had fallen below a BBB rating (to "junk" status) [see Table 26.6]. The other four tranches were rated CCC or lower. A similar Barclays CDO, called Nerva, fared even worse. Investors were not amused: AAA ratings are not meant to deteriorate so rapidly. ...

If the case [a suit by HSH Nordbank, a German bank] does come to court, others will get to see how these complex financial instruments are put together and managed. One question for the court is whether Barclays correctly managed the potential conflict of interest when selecting credit risks from its own exposures for the CDO portfolio. Investors were not given details of each credit; Barclays argues that such disclosure was not required by the terms of the CDO. "The allegations in the suit are without merit," says a spokesman for the bank.[9]

Source: "Russian Doll," *The Economist*, September 23, 2004, p. 87.

Now suppose that there are investors wishing to invest in bonds, but some investors are happy to hold a speculative grade bond, while others seek safer bonds. We can create a CDO to rearrange the cash flows from a pool of bonds, in order to accomodate the different kinds of investors. The structure of the CDO is illustrated in Figure 26.1. The total promised payoff on the three bonds is $300; the CDO apportions this payoff among three tranches of unequal size. The senior tranche ($140) receives first claim to the bond payments, the mezzanine tranche ($90) has the next claim, and the subordinated tranche ($70) receives whatever is left. For the bond which is ith in line, with a promised

---

[9]The suit was settled out of court in February 2005.

TABLE 26.6   Rating of tranches of the Corvus portfolio.

Tranche	Amount (millions of US$)	Dec 2000	Dec 2002	Sep 2003
A1	550	AAA	A+	BB
A2	200	AAA	A+	BB
B	65	AA	BBB	BB
C	60	A	CCC+	CCC
D	40	BBB	CC	C
E	25	BB	C	C
F	10	B	C	C

FIGURE 26.1

Structure of a CDO.

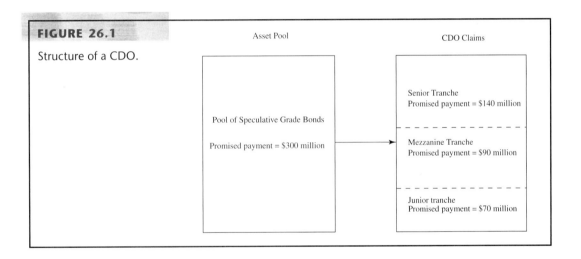

payment of $\bar{B}_i$, the payoff is

$$\text{Bond } i \text{ maturity payoff} = \min\left[\max\left(A_T - \sum_{j=1}^{i-1} \bar{B}_j, 0\right), \bar{B}_i\right] \qquad (26.14)$$

where A_T is the maturity value of the asset pool.

To understand the pricing of the CDO claims, recognize that there are four possible outcomes: no defaults ($0.90^3 = 72.9\%$ probability), one bond defaults ($3 \times 0.90^2 \times 0.10 = 24.3\%$ probability), two bonds default ($3 \times 0.90 \times 0.10^2 = 2.71\%$ probability),

TABLE 26.7   Pricing of CDO in Figure 26.1, assuming that bond defaults are uncorrelated. Promised payoffs to the bonds are $140 (senior), $90 (mezzanine), and $70 (subordinated).

Number of Defaults	Probability	Total Payoff	Bond Payoff Senior	Bond Payoff Mezzanine	Bond Payoff Subordinated
0	0.729	300	140	90	70
1	0.243	240	140	90	10
2	0.027	180	140	40	0
3	0.001	120	120	0	0
		Price	131.828	83.403	50.347
		Yield	0.0601	0.07613	0.3296
	Default probability		0.0010	0.0280	0.2710
	Average recovery rate		0.8571	0.4286	0.1281

and three bonds default ($0.10^3 = 0.1\%$ probability). To compute the price of a CDO tranche, we can compute the expected payoff of the tranche using the risk-neutral default probabilities.

The CDO pricing is illustrated in Table 26.7. Note that the senior tranche is almost risk-free. The only time the senior tranche is not fully paid is in the unlikely (0.1% probability) event that all three bonds default. In that case, the senior tranche receives $120, a recovery rate of 85.7%. Since it is almost paid in full, investors will pay $131.828 for the senior tranche, which is a yield of 6.02%.

The mezzanine tranche is fully paid if there is one default, but it is not fully paid if there are two or three defaults. The yield is 7.61% and the average recovery rate is $40/90 \times 0.027/0.028 = 0.4285$. Finally, the subordinated tranche receives less than full payment if there are any defaults. Consequently, it is priced to yield 32.96%. Note that the sum of the prices of the three tranches is $265.58. As you would expect, this is the same as the price of the three bonds put into the asset pool.

This example might remind you of the discussion of tranched debt in Chapter 16, especially Table 16.1. The idea is exactly the same, except that instead of valuing claims on corporate assets (the bonds in Chapter 16), we are valuing claims on a pool of corporate bonds.

A CDO with correlated defaults   In the preceding example we assumed that the bonds were uncorrelated. As you might have guessed, this is an important assumption. Table 26.8 shows how the CDO tranches are priced if the bonds are perfectly correlated—i.e.,

TABLE 26.8						Pricing of CDO in Figure 26.1, assuming that bond defaults are perfectly correlated. Promised payoffs to the bonds are $140 (senior), $90 (mezzanine), and $70 (subordinated).

Number of Defaults	Probability	Total Payoff	Bond Payoff		
			Senior	Mezzanine	Subordinated
0	0.9	300	140	90	70
1	0	240	140	90	10
2	0	180	140	40	0
3	0.1	120	120	0	0
		Price	129.963	76.283	59.331
		Yield	0.074	0.165	0.165
	Default probability		0.1	0.1	0.1
	Average recovery rate		0.857143	0	0

if at maturity, either all firms default or none do. A comparison of Tables 26.7 and 26.8 shows the importance of default correlation in the pricing of CDOs.

Given the structure of the CDO and the assumptions about the recovery rate, with perfect correlation of defaults, the mezzanine and subordinated tranches have the same yield. The senior tranche becomes riskier because the probability of three defaults—the only circumstance in which the senior tranche is not fully paid—is greater with perfect correlation.

Nth to default baskets   The previous examples showed that it is possible to pool risky bonds and create riskier and less risky claims. A particular variant of this strategy is the *Nth to default basket*.

Consider a CDO that contains equal quantities of N bonds. Over the life of the CDO there can be anywhere between 0 and N defaults. It is possible to create tranches where particular bondholders bear the consequences of a particular default.

The owner of the first-to-default tranche bears the most risk: If any of the bonds in the asset pool default, the first-to-default owner bears the loss from this default. The owner of the last-to-default generally bears the least risk, since all bonds must default in order for this claim to bear a loss.

Table 26.9 shows the pricing that results from this structure, assuming that the defaults are uncorrelated and occur only at time T. By comparing Table 26.9 with Table 26.7, you can observe a similarity between the subordinated tranche and the first-to-default on the one hand, and on the other, the senior tranche and the third to default.

TABLE 26.9			Pricing of Nth to default bonds. Assumes the bonds owned as assets have uncorrelated defaults.					
		Probability	**Payoffs**		**Expected**			
Default	**Probability**	**N or More**	**Default**	**No Default**	**Payoff**	**Price**	**Yield**	
First	0.243	0.271	40	100	83.74	78.863	0.237	
Second	0.027	0.028	40	100	98.32	92.594	0.077	
Third	0.001	0.001	40	100	99.94	94.120	0.061	

Figure 26.2 illustrates the pricing of Nth to default bonds for a 10-bond pool assuming default correlations of 0, 0.25, and 1.[10] Again, we assume defaults occur only at time T. The result for a default correlation of 1 is like that in Table 26.10: When one bond defaults, all bonds default, so all claims have the same yield. The graphs for correlations of 0 and 0.25 show significant differences for yields for low numbers of defaults. The first-to-default tranche, for example, has a yield of 16.02% when defaults are uncorrelated and 13.51% when the default correlation is 0.25. This again illustrates that Nth to default baskets are a way to speculate on default correlations.

Credit Default Swaps and Related Structures

Credit derivatives, which have existed since the early 1990s, are contracts that permit the trading and hedging of credit risk. Credit derivatives permit institutions to hedge credit risk, in much the same way that, for example, gold futures permit the hedging of gold price risk. Table 26.11 shows that the outstanding notional principal covered by credit default swaps, an important kind of credit derivative, has grown significantly over the

....

[10]How do we generate a default correlation of 0.25 among ten bonds? We can generate ten independent normally distributed random variables and create correlated normal random variables, z_i, using the Cholesky decomposition (equation 19.18). Following this procedure, each *pairwise* correlation is 0.25. Assuming a 10% unconditional default probability, a firm defaults if $z_i < -1.2816$. Note that once we use this method, we can also let z_i determine *when in time* the default occurs; we simply interpret a smaller z_i to mean that default occurs earlier. It is then necessary to specify a distribution for default times. For example, suppose default occurs with a constant Poisson intensity. Then the time to default is exponentially distributed, so that

$$\Pr(\text{default} < t) = 1 - e^{-ht}$$

Given this assumption, the default time is then $\tau = -\ln[N(z_i)]/h$. See Duffie and Yurday (2004a), Li (1999), and Watkinson and Roosevelt (2004) for a discussion of pricing credit tranches with default correlations modeled in this fashion.

FIGURE 26.2

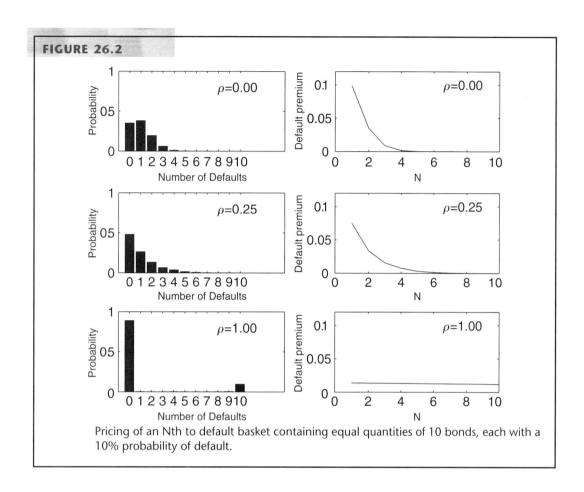

Pricing of an Nth to default basket containing equal quantities of 10 bonds, each with a 10% probability of default.

TABLE 26.10   Pricing of Nth to default bonds. Assumes the bonds owned as assets have perfectly correlated defaults.

Default	Probability	Probability N or More	Payoffs Default	No Default	Expected Payoff	Price	Yield
First	0.100	0.100	40	100	94.000	88.526	0.122
Second	0.100	0.100	40	100	94.000	88.526	0.122
Third	0.100	0.100	40	100	94.000	88.526	0.122

TABLE 26.11		Credit-default swaps outstanding, 2001–2004, billions of U.S. dollars.						
Year	06/01	12/01	06/02	12/02	06/03	12/03	06/04	12/04
Amount	631.50	918.87	1,563.48	2,191.57	2,687.91	3,779.40	5,441.86	8,422.26

Source: ISDA.

last few years. In addition to general growth, there has been a great deal of innovation in the credit derivatives market in the last few years.

Single name credit default swaps   A single name credit default swap (CDS) makes a payment when a specific company (the "single name") experiences a credit event. The buyer of the swap is the *protection buyer*. A corporate bondholder, for example, could use a CDS to buy protection against the credit risk of a company. The counterparty providing the credit insurance is the *swap writer* or *protection seller*.

If a credit event occurs, the protection buyer receives

$$\text{Protection buyer payoff} = \text{Bond par value} - \text{Bond market value} \qquad (26.15)$$

The bond market value is generally determined within 30 days of a credit event. The protection buyer pays to the seller a periodic insurance premium over time rather than a single amount initially. The premium payments stop once default occurs.

Figure 26.3 illustrates the cash flows and parties involved in a credit default swap on XYZ. Note in particular that there is no connection between XYZ and the swap writer. A default swap typically specifies an XYZ debt issue, called the *reference asset* or *reference obligation*. The reference asset is important because bonds from the same issuer with different seniority levels will have different prices after a default. Generally, the protection buyer can deliver any bond with payment rights equal to that of the reference asset.

If there is an actual default, the default swap could settle either financially or physically. In a financial (cash) settlement, the swap writer would pay the bondholder the value of the loss on the bond. In a physical settlement, the swap writer would buy the defaulted bond at the price it would have in the absence of default.

Financial settlement and physical settlement are economically equivalent in theory. However, the market for a defaulted corporate bond may not be liquid, and it may be difficult to determine a fair price upon which to base financial settlement. To avoid this problem, default swaps often call for, or at least permit, physical settlement. Nevertheless, cash settlement is increasingly common.

For many firms, it is possible to trade CDSs for a variety of different expirations. The set of prices with different maturities generates a *credit spread curve*, where, for example, you may observe that credit spreads are small at short horizons and substantially larger over five years. With this array of contracts it is possible to make sophisticated bets. For example, you could buy protection with a four-year horizon and sell protection with a five-year horizon; this is a bet that default will not occur in the fifth year.

FIGURE 26.3

Depiction of the cash flows in a credit default swap. The investor owns the reference asset, which was issued by XYZ. The investor buys a credit default swap and pays 40 basis points per year in exchange for the swap writer's payment in the event of a default by XYZ.

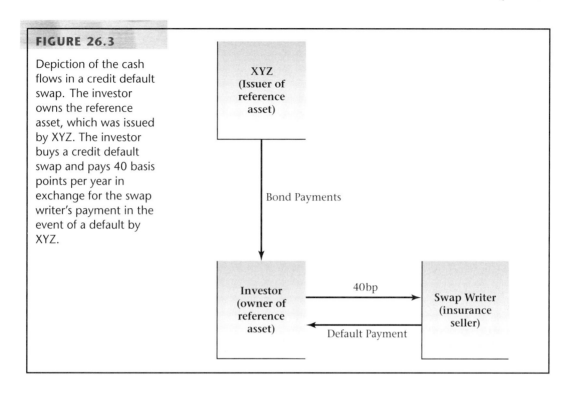

Finally, recognize that both parties to a default swap face credit risk from the swap itself. The protection buyer may default on premium payments, and protection seller could go bankrupt at the same time that a default occurs on the reference asset. Credit-linked notes, which we discuss below, are structured to eliminate counterparty credit risk.

CDSs versus CDOs   It may have already occurred to you that a CDO and a CDS are similar. Suppose that XYZ issues a bond promising to pay in one period $\$100 + c$, where c is the coupon. Suppose that a CDS guarantees the payment of both principal and the coupon, and that the protection buyer pays the CDS premium, ρ, under any circumstances. We can see the similarity between a CDO and a CDS by comparing the cash flows for the following two positions:

- The payoffs to a *protection writer* for a CDS on XYZ's bond.
- The payoff to the buyer of a single tranche CDO containing the XYZ bond (this is just the XYZ bond).

Table 26.12 compares the payoffs on the two positions.

Both the written CDS and the CDO bear the costs of a default. The difference between the two positions—in the last column of Table 26.12—is the payoff to a default-free bond. The difference between the CDO and written CDS, therefore, is that the CDO

TABLE 26.12 Comparison of a written CDS on XYZ's bond, and a CDO containing only an XYZ bond.

	Position		
Event	CDO Buyer	Written CDS	Difference (CDO − CDS)
No default	$100 + c$	ρ	$100 + c - \rho$
Default	B_1	$\rho - [(\$100 + c) - B_1]$	$100 + c - \rho$

is **funded,** meaning that the investor pays for it fully at the outset, while the CDS is **unfunded,** meaning that the investor pays nothing at the outset and can have payment obligations in the future. We can think of the CDO as analogous to a prepaid forward on the bond, while the written CDS is a forward contract on the bond.

Pricing a Default Swap

An investor who buys a bond and a default swap on the bond owns a synthetic default-free bond. This observation suggests that the default swap premium should approximately equal the default premium on the bond. To make this more precise, suppose we simultaneously undertake the following set of transactions:

- Buy protection with a CDS on $100 worth of senior bonds issued by XYZ. The default swap premium is ρ.

- Short-sell a $100 default-free floating rate note paying r. Suppose that we can short-sell the bond costlessly.

- Buy XYZ senior floating-rate notes paying $c = r + a$, with par value $100. The premium $a = c - r$ is constant over time.

The short-sale of the default-free note funds the purchase of the defaultable note. These transactions require no initial cash flow.

Each period prior to termination, the net cash flow on the position is $c - (r + \rho)$. XYZ either defaults or does not default prior to maturity of the CDS, so that the default swap terminates in either of two ways:

- If the CDS matures and XYZ has not defaulted, sell the XYZ floating rate bond and use the $100 proceeds to buy the default-free floating rate note in order to close the short sale. (By using floating rate notes, we ensure that both bonds are worth $100 if there is no default.)

- If XYZ defaults, under the terms of the CDS, surrender the defaulted floating rate notes in exchange for $100. Use the $100 proceeds to buy the default-free floating rate note in order to close the short sale.

In either case, there is no net cash flow.

Since we can enter and close the position with no net cash flow, the interim cash flows should also equal zero, which implies that $c - (r + \rho) = 0$, or

$$\rho = c - r \tag{26.16}$$

In other words, the default swap premium equals the credit spread.

Notice that we made very strong assumptions to reach this conclusion, so we should not expect equation (26.16) to hold exactly. In practice, we would need to take into account a variety of complications, including time variation in the credit spread, bonds having fixed coupons instead of being floating rate, and transaction costs (such as costs of short-selling). Duffie (1999) discusses the effects of many such complications.

An important question implicitly raised by this discussion is the definition of an "otherwise equivalent default-free bond." It seems natural to use government bonds as a benchmark, but government bonds can be unique in certain respects. Prices of government bonds may include a liquidity premium and sometimes reflect special tax attributes (for example, in the United States, federal government bonds are exempt from state taxes). Houweling and Vorst (2001) estimate a credit swap pricing model and find that, empirically, credit swap premiums are more related to the interest rate swap curve than to the government bond yield curve. This linkage between credit swaps and interest rate swaps suggests that the yield on an "equivalent default-free bond" is not the government bond curve, and in fact may not be directly observable. Rather the equivalent default-free yield may be inferred from the market for default swaps as the rate on the reference asset less the default swap premium.

Credit-linked notes A **credit-linked note** is a bond issued by one company with payments that depend upon the credit status (i.e., bankrupt or not) of a different company. For example, banks can issue credit-linked notes to hedge the credit risk of loans. To see how a credit-linked note works, suppose that bank ABC lends money to company XYZ. At the time of the loan, ABC creates a trust that issues notes: These are the credit-linked notes. The funds raised by the issuance of these notes are invested in bonds with a low probability of default (such as government bonds), which are held in the trust. If XYZ remains solvent, ABC is obligated to pay the notes in full. If XYZ goes bankrupt, the note-holders receive the XYZ loans and become creditors of XYZ. ABC takes possession of the securities in the trust. Thus, the credit-linked note is in effect a bond issued by ABC, which ABC does not need to repay in full if XYZ goes bankrupt. This structure eliminates a third-party insurance provider. Credit-linked notes can be rated and exchange-traded.

Because of the trust, the credit-linked notes can be paid in full even if ABC defaults. Thus, even though they are issued by ABC, the interest rate on the notes is determined by the credit risk of XYZ. An arrangement like this was used by Citigroup when it made loans to Enron in 2000 and 2001.[11] When Enron went bankrupt in late 2001, Citigroup

----

[11] See Daniel Altman, "How Citigroup Hedged Bets on Enron," *New York Times*, February 8, 2002, p. C1.

avoided losses on over $1 billion in loans because it had hedged the loans by issuing credit-linked notes.

Total rate of return swaps   Total rate of return swaps, discussed in Chapter 8, can also be used to hedge credit risk. These swaps are used less frequently than credit-default swaps. The difference between a total rate of return swap and the credit products we are discussing is that a total return swap for a bond makes payments based on changes in market value due to interest rate changes as well as due to credit changes. A CDS makes payments only if there is a credit event.

CDS Indices

A CDS index is an average of the premiums on a set of CDSs. Thus, a CDS index provides a way to track the overall market for credit. In this section we will discuss the kinds of structures and products that are traded.

To a first approximation, it is possible to replicate a CDS index by holding a pool of CDSs.[12] As with a single CDS, one party is a protection seller, receiving premium payments, and the other is a protection buyer, making the payments but receiving a payment from the seller if there is a credit event.

There are numerous ways in which a CDS index product can be structured and traded:

- A CDS index can be funded or unfunded. The unfunded version is like a credit default swap, except that the underlying asset is a basket of firms. The funded index is a note linked to the index with a collateral arrangement in case the note buyer had to make a payment.

- The claims are generally tranched in various ways, for example, simple priority or Nth to default.

- The underlying assets can represent different countries, currencies, maturities, or industries.

A 0–100% tranche on a CDS index can also be described as a *synthetic CDO*. The returns on a CDS index reflect the performance of the bonds in the index, just as the returns on a CDO reflect the performance of the bonds in the asset pool.

Credit indices have had a relatively brief history.[13] There are a number of potential challenges in trading credit risk. Historically, the corporate bond market has been less liquid than the stock market. Trading volume for bonds is lower than for stocks, and bid-ask spreads have been higher. A large firm can have dozens of different bond issues outstanding.

---

[12]The replication may not be exact since a default index can define a credit event differently than a single name CDS. For example, DJ TRAC-X, discussed below, specifies bankruptcy and failure to pay as credit events. A single name CDS can have a broader definition.

[13]See Duffie and Yurday (2004b) for an interesting account of the development of credit index products.

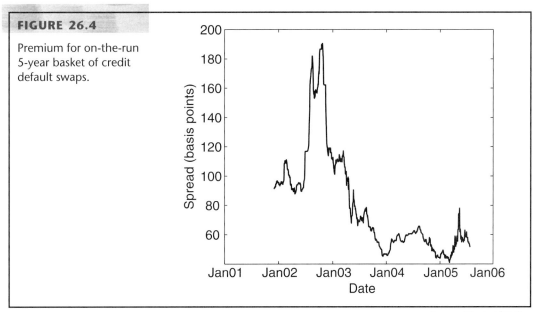

FIGURE 26.4

Premium for on-the-run 5-year basket of credit default swaps.

Source: Morgan Stanley.

Single name credit default swaps first traded in the mid 1990s. In 2001 Morgan Stanley introduced TRACERS, a basket of corporate bonds that investors could trade as a unit, much like an exchange traded fund. There were both funded and nonfunded TRACERS products. J. P. Morgan created a competing produce called HYDI. In 2003, Morgan Stanley and J. P. Morgan merged these products to create TRAC-X. Later in 2003, competing banks introduced CDX as an alternative credit index. In 2004, the TRAC-X and CDX products merged into Dow Jones CDX. These indices could be traded in both funded and nonfunded products.

Firms can drop out of an index due to bankruptcy or illiquidity, but otherwise the make-up of a given CDX offering is set for the life of the offering. A new CDX is currently offered every 6 months with 5- and 10-year maturities, with the most recent offering being the most heavily traded. For North America, there are versions of the index reflecting investment grade companies, high-volatility companies, and high-yield companies. The CDX North America index is an equally-weighted basket of 125 CDSs representing investment grade companies. There are also credit indices for North America, Europe, Asia, Japan, Australia, and emerging markets.

Figure 26.4 shows the CDS premium for the five-year on-the-run index. The series was constructed by Morgan Stanley from premiums on TRAC-X and CDX, and for years before TRAC-X, from data on credit default swaps from firms in the index. Credit default swap premia were four times larger in 2002 than at the beginning of 2005. This is due to the fact that a number of large companies defaulted during 2002, including Worldcom, Global Crossing, UAL Corp, Adelphia, and KMart, among others. The CDS premiums

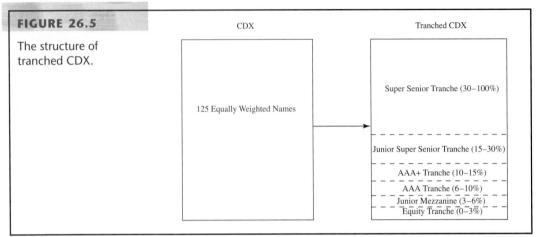

FIGURE 26.5

The structure of tranched CDX.

Source: Morgan Stanley.

for these companies would have been high prior to their defaults. In interpreting Figure 26.4, keep in mind that after a company defaults, it drops out of the index, so that other things equal, firms remaining in the index have a lower probability of default.

Tranched CDX and has a payoff structure illustrated in Figure 26.5. There are both funded and unfunded products based on this structure. As you would expect from our earlier discussion of CDOs and default correlation, the pricing of the various tranches is sensitive to correlation. In fact, tranche pricing is quoted using implied correlation in much the same way equity option premiums are quoted using implied volatility.

CHAPTER SUMMARY

A party to a contract may fail to make a required future payment. This possibility, which is called default, gives rise to credit risk. Credit risk is an important consideration in valuing corporate bonds, where two key inputs are the probability of default and the expected payoff to the bond if the firm does default. The Merton model uses option pricing to value debt subject to default. Credit agencies assign debt ratings to firms; these can be used to assess the probability of bankruptcy in the future.

There are various financial vehicles that permit the trading of credit risk. Collateralized debt obligations (CDOs) are claims to an asset pool. The claims are often structured (tranched) so as to create new claims, some of which are more and some of which are less sensitive to credit risk than the pool as a whole. The value of these claims depends importantly on the default correlation of the assets in the pool.

Credit default swaps pay to the protection buyer the loss on a corporate bond when there is a default. In exchange, the protection buyer makes a periodic premium payment to the seller. Baskets of credit default swaps are also called synthetic CDOs, since the holder of such a basket bears the default experience of the firms represented in the basket, as with a CDO. A synthetic CDO can be funded (the investor pays fully at the outset) or nonfunded (there is no initial payment).

The average premium on a basket of default swaps is effectively a credit index. These indices, such as Dow Jones CDX, serve as the basis for a variety of investment vehicles and investment strategies.

FURTHER READING

Both the actual traded credit contracts and pricing theory continue to evolve. Books with a practitioner perspective include Goodman and Fabozzi (2002) and Tavakoli (2001). Duffie (1999) discusses the pricing of credit default swaps. Frameworks for analyzing credit risk are discussed in Credit Suisse Financial Products (1997), J. P. Morgan (1997), Kealhofer (2003a,b) and white papers on the Moody's KMV Web site, **www.moodyskmv.com**. A debate between advocates and critics of the KMV approach is in the February 2002 issue of *Risk* (Kealhofer and Kurbat, 2002; Sobehart and Keenan, 2002).

Books with a more academic and theoretical perspective include Cossin and Pirotte (2001), Duffie and Singleton (2003), Meissner (2005), and Schönbucher (2003). Duffie and Yurday (2004b,a) provide a blended discussion of the history of some of the products, practical issues, and pricing models. Papers examining Merton-style models include Jones et al. (1984), Kim et al. (1993), Leland (1994), Leland and Toft (1996) and Longstaff and Schwartz (1995). Empirical studies of Merton-style models include Anderson and Sundaresan (2000), Bharath and Shumway (2004), and Eom et al. (2004). Shumway (2001) estimates hazard models of bankruptcy. Johnson and Stulz (1987), Hull and White (1995), and Klein (1996) consider how it affects prices of derivatives.

Data on bankruptcies are available from **www.bankruptcydata.com**. Simple summary data, such as the largest bankruptcies sorted by year, are available without charge.

PROBLEMS

For the first eight problems, assume that a firm has assets of $100, with $\sigma = 40\%$, $\alpha = 15\%$, and $\delta = 0$. The risk-free rate is 8%.

26.1. The firm has a single outstanding debt issue with a promised maturity payment of $120 in 5 years. What is the probability of bankruptcy? What is the credit spread?

26.2. Suppose the firm issues a single zero-coupon bond with maturity value $100.

a. Compute the yield, probability of default, and expected loss given default for times to maturity of 1, 2, 3, 4, 5, 10, and 20 years.

b. For each time to maturity compute the approximation for the yield:

$$\rho = r + \frac{1}{T} \times \text{Prob Default} \times \text{Expected loss given default}$$

How accurate is the approximation?

26.3. Suppose the firm issues a single zero-coupon bond with time to maturity 3 years and maturity value $110.

  a. Compute the price, yield to maturity, default probability, and expected recovery ($E[B_T|\text{Default}]$).

  b. Verify that equation (26.5) holds.

26.4. Suppose the firm issues a single zero-coupon bond.

  a. Suppose the maturity value of the bond is $80. Compute the yield and default probability for times to maturity of 1, 2, 3, 4, 5, 10, and 20 years.

  b. Repeat part (a), only supposing the maturity value is $120.

  c. Does default probability increase or decrease with debt maturity? Explain.

26.5. Repeat the previous problem, only compute the expected recovery value instead of the default probability. How does the expected recovery value change as time to maturity changes?

26.6. Suppose that there is a 3% per year chance that the firm's asset value can jump to zero. Assume that the firm issues 5-year zero coupon debt with a promised payment of $110. Using the Merton jump model, compute the debt price and yield, and compare to the results you obtain when the jump probability is zero.

26.7. Suppose the firm has a single outstanding debt issue with a promised maturity payment of $120 in 5 years. Assume that bankruptcy is triggered by assets (which are observable) falling below $40 in value at any time over the life of the bond—in which case the bondholder receives $40 at that time—or by assets being worth less than $120 at maturity, in which case the the bondholder receives the asset value. What is the probability of bankruptcy over the life of the bond? What is the credit spread?

26.8. Repeat the previous problem, except that the time to maturity can be 1, 2, 3, 4, 5, 10, or 20 years. How does the bond yield change with time to maturity?

For the next two problems, use this information on credit ratings. Suppose there are three credit ratings, F (first-rate), FF (future failure?), and FFF (fading, forlorn, and forsaken). The transition matrix between ratings looks like this:

	Rating To:		
Rating From:	**F**	**FF**	**FFF**
F	.9	.07	.03
FF	.15	.80	.05
FFF	.10	.30	.6

26.9. Consider a firm with an F rating.

  a. What is the probability that after 4 years it will still have an F rating?

  b. What is the probability that after 4 years it will have an FF or FFF rating?

  c. From examining the transition matrix, are firms tending over time to become rated more or less highly? Why?

26.10. Consider two firms, one with an FF rating and one with an FFF rating. What is the probability that after 4 years each will have retained its rating? What is the probability that each will have moved to one of the other two ratings?

26.11. Suppose that in Figure 26.7 the tranches have promised payments of $160 (senior), $50 (mezzanine), and $90 (subordinated). Reproduce the table for this case, assuming zero default correlation.

26.12. Repeat the previous problem, only assuming that defaults are perfectly correlated.

26.13. Using Monte Carlo simulation, reproduce Tables 26.9 and 26.10. Produce a similar table assuming a default correlation of 25%.

26.14. Following Table 26.9, compute the prices of first, second, and Nth-to-default bonds assuming that defaults are uncorrelated and that there are 5, 10, 20, and 50 bonds in the portfolio. How are the Nth-to-default yields affected by the size of the portfolio?

26.15. Repeat the previous problem, assuming that default correlations are 0.25.

PART SIX

Appendixes

APPENDIX A

The Greek Alphabet

The use of Greek letters is common in writing about derivatives and mathematics in general. Important concepts in this book are option characteristics that have the names of Greek letters such as "delta" and "gamma."

Table 1.1 presents the complete Greek alphabet, including both lowercase and uppercase forms. Some of the letters look like their Roman counterparts. Not all of these symbols will be used in the book.

TABLE 1.1			The Greek alphabet.		
alpha	α	A	nu	ν	N
beta	β	B	xi	ξ	Ξ
gamma	γ	Γ	omicron	o	O
delta	δ	Δ	pi	π	Π
epsilon	ϵ	E	rho	ρ	P
zeta	ζ	Z	sigma	σ	Σ
eta	η	H	tau	τ	T
theta	θ	Θ	upsilon	υ	Υ
iota	ι	I	phi	ϕ	Φ
kappa	κ	K	chi	χ	X
lambda	λ	Λ	psi	ψ	Ψ
mu	μ	M	omega	ω	Ω

APPENDIX B

Continuous Compounding

In this book we use both effective annual interest rates and continuously compounded interest rates. These are simply different conventions for expressing the same idea: If you invest $1 today, how much will you have after 1 year? One simple unambiguous way to answer this question is using zero-coupon bonds. If you invest $1 in zero-coupon bonds costing $P(0, T)$ for a $1 maturity payoff at time T, then at time T you will have $1/P(0, T)$ dollars. However, it is more common to answer the question using interest rates rather than zero-coupon bond prices.

Interest rates measure the rate of appreciation of an investment, but there are innumerable ways of quoting interest rates. Continuous compounding turns out to provide a particularly simple quoting convention, though it may not seem so simple at first. Since in practice option pricing formulas and other financial formulas make use of continuous compounding, it is important to be comfortable with it.

You might think that continuous compounding is not much used in the real world and, hence, there is no point in using it when studying derivatives. It is true that an auto dealer is likely to give you a blank stare if you inquire about the continuously compounded loan rate for your new car. However, continuous compounding does have advantages, and it is not often appreciated that almost *all* interest rate quoting conventions are complicated, some devilishly so. (If you doubt this, read Appendix 7.A).

B.1 THE LANGUAGE OF INTEREST RATES

We begin with definitions. There are two terms that we will use often to refer to interest rates:

- **Effective annual rate:** If r is quoted as an **effective annual rate**, this means that if you invest $1, n years later you will have $(1 + r)^n$. If you invest x_0 and earn x_n n years later, then the implied effective annual rate is $(x_n/x_0)^{1/n} - 1$.

- **Continuously compounded rate:** If r is quoted as an annualized **continuously compounded rate**, this means that if you invest $1, n years later you will have e^{rn}. If you invest x_0 and earn x_n n years later, then the implied annual continuously compounded rate is $\ln(x_n/x_0)/n$.

Let's look at this definition in more detail.

B.2 THE LOGARITHMIC
AND EXPONENTIAL FUNCTIONS

Interest rates are typically quoted as "$r\%$ per year, compounded n times per year." As every beginning finance student learns, this has the interpretation that you will earn an interest rate of r/n per period for n periods. Thus, if you invest \$1 today, in 1 year you will have

$$\left(1 + \frac{r}{n}\right)^n$$

In T years you will have

$$\left(1 + \frac{r}{n}\right)^{nT} \tag{B.1}$$

What happens if we let n get very large, that is, if interest is compounded many times a year (even daily or hourly)? If, for example, the interest rate is 10%, after 3 years we will have

- (\$1 + 0.1)^3 = \$1.331 with annual compounding,

- (\$1 + 0.1/12)^{36} = \$1.3482 with monthly compounding,

- (\$1 + 0.1/365)^{1095} = \$1.34980 with daily compounding, and

- (\$1 + 0.1/8760)^{26280} = \$1.349856 with hourly compounding.

The exponential function is e^x, where e is a constant approximately equal to 2.71828. If compounding is *continuous*—that is, if interest accrues every instant—then we can use the exponential function to compute future values. For example, with a 10% continuously compounded rate, after 3 years we will have a future value of

$$e^{0.1 \times 3} = \$1.349859$$

Notice that assuming continuous compounding gives us a result very close to that assuming daily compounding. In Excel, we compute continuously compounded results using the built-in exponential function, *exp*. The above example is computed as $\exp(0.1 \times 3)$.

Why does the exponential function work? The number e is *defined* as

$$e^{rT} \equiv \lim_{n \to \infty} \left(1 + \frac{r}{n}\right)^{nT} \tag{B.2}$$

Thus, the expression defining e is the same expression used for interest compounding calculations, equation (B.1)! By using e, you can compute a future value.

If you know how much you have earned from a \$1 investment, you can determine the continuously compounded rate of return by using the natural logarithm, ln. *Ln* is the *inverse* of the exponential function in that it takes a dollar amount and gives you a rate of return. In other words, if you apply the logarithmic function to the exponential function, you compute the original argument to the exponential function. Here is an example:

$$\ln(e^{rt}) = rt$$

Example B.1   Suppose you have a zero-coupon bond that matures in 5 years. The price today is $62.092 for a bond that pays $100. The annually compounded rate of return is

$$(\$100/\$62.092)^{1/5} - 1 = 0.10$$

The continuously compounded rate of return is

$$\frac{\ln(\$100/\$62.092)}{5} = \frac{0.47655}{5} = 0.09531$$

The continuously compounded rate of return of 9.53% corresponds to the annually compounded rate of return of 10%. To verify this, observe that

$$e^{0.0953} = 1.10$$

Finally, note that

$$\ln(1.10) = \ln(e^{0.0953}) = 0.0953 \qquad ≷$$

Changing Interest Rates

When we multiply exponentials, exponents add. So we have

$$e^x e^y = e^{x+y}$$

Suppose you can invest for 4 years, earning a continouuously compounded return of 5% the first 2 years and 6% the second 2 years. If you invest $1 today, after 4 years you will have

$$e^{2 \times 0.05} e^{2 \times 0.06} = e^{0.10+0.12} = \$1.2461$$

We could of course do the same calculation using effective annual rates. For the first 2 years we earn $e^{0.05} - 1 = 5.127\%$, and for the second 2 years, $e^{0.06} = 6.184\%$. The future value of $1 is

$$1.05127^2 1.06184^2 = \$1.2461$$

This calculation gives us the same answer.
What is the average annual rate earned over the 4 years? The average annual continously compounded rate is

$$\frac{1}{4}\ln(1.24608) = 0.055$$

which is the average of 5% and 6%.
However, if we express the answer in terms of effective annual rates, we get

$$1.24608^{0.25} - 1 = 5.6541\%$$

This is *not* the average of 5.127% and 6.184%, which is 5.6554. This makes calculations with continuous compounding easier.

Symmetry for Increases and Decreases

On March 4, 1999, the NASDAQ composite index closed at 2292.89. On March 10, 2000, the index closed at 5048.62. On January 2, 2001, the index closed at 2291.86, essentially the same level as in March 1999. The percentage increase from March 1999 to March 2000 was

$$\frac{5048.62}{2292.89} - 1 = 120.19\%$$

The subsequent decrease was

$$\frac{2291.86}{5048.62} - 1 = -54.60\%$$

When computing simple rates of return, a price can have an increase exceeding 100%, but its decrease can never be greater than 100%.

We can do the same calculations using continuous compounding. The continuously compounded increase from March 1999 to March 2000 was

$$\ln(5048.62/2292.89) = 78.93\%$$

while the subsequent decrease was

$$\ln(2291.86/5048.62) = -78.97\%$$

When using continuous compounding, increases and decreases are symmetric.

Moreover, if the index dropped to 1000, the continuously compounded return from the peak would be

$$\ln(1000/5048.62) = -161.91\%$$

Continuously compounded returns can be less than −100%.

PROBLEMS

B.1.   **a.** A bond costs $67,032 today and pays $100,000 in 5 years. What is its continuously compounded rate of return?

b. A bond costs $50 today, pays $100 at maturity, and has a continuously compounded annual return of 10%. In how many years does it mature?

c. An investment of $5 today pays a continuously compounded rate of 7.5%/year. How much money will you have after 7 years?

d. A stock selling for $100 is worth $5 1 year later. What is the continuously compounded return over the year? What if the stock price is $4? $3? $2? What would the stock price after 1 year have to be in order for the continuously compounded return to be −500%?

B.2. Suppose that over 1 year a stock price increases from $100 to $200. Over the subsequent year it falls back to $100.

a. What is the arithmetic return [i.e., $(S_{t+1} - S_t)/S_t$] over the first year? What is the continuously compounded return [i.e., $\ln(S_{t+1}/S_t)$]?

b. What is the arithmetic return over the second year? The continuously compounded return?

c. What do you notice when you compare the first- and second-year returns computed arithmetically and continuously?

B.3. Here are stock prices on 6 consecutive days: $100, $47, $88, $153, $212, $100. Note that the cumulative return over the 6 days is 0.

    a. What are the arithmetic returns from the first to the second day, the second to the third, and so forth?

    b. What are the continuously compounded returns from the first to the second day, the second to the third, and so forth?

    c. Suppose you want to compute the cumulative return over the 6 days. Suppose you don't know the prices, but only your answers to parts (a) and (b). How would you compute the cumulative return (which is 0) using arithmetic returns and continuously compounded returns?

APPENDIX C

Jensen's Inequality

The purpose of this appendix is to understand Jensen's inequality, which is a result cited frequently in this book. Suppose that x is a random variable with mean $E(x)$, and $f(x)$ is a convex function of x.

Proposition C.1 *Jensen's inequality* states that if $f(x)$ is convex, then for any probability distribution for x,

$$E[f(x)] \geq f[E(x)] \tag{C.1}$$

If $f(x)$ is concave, the inequality is reversed.

In order to understand this result we first need some definitions. A function is convex if it is curved like the cross-section of a bowl; a function is concave if it is curved like the cross section of an upside-down bowl.[1] We will provide some examples illustrating Jensen's inequality, and then provide a proof (including a more precise definition of convexity).

C.1 EXAMPLE: THE EXPONENTIAL FUNCTION

Figure C.1 shows a graph of the exponential function, $f(x) = e^x$. Note that e^x is convex. Let $x \sim \text{Binomial}(-1, 1; 0.5)$. We have

$$E(x) = (0.5 \times -1) + (0.5 \times 1) = 0$$

We also have

$$f(1) = e^1 = 2.7183$$
$$f(-1) = e^{-1} = 0.3679$$

---

[1] A way to remember this is that a con**vex** function has the shape of a "v" while a con**cave** function has the curvature of a **cave**.

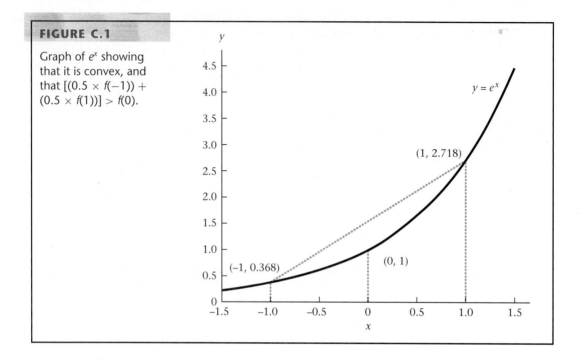

FIGURE C.1

Graph of e^x showing that it is convex, and that $[(0.5 \times f(-1)) + (0.5 \times f(1))] > f(0)$.

Thus,

$$f[E(x)] = e^{E(x)}$$
$$= e^0$$
$$= 1$$

and

$$E[f(x)] = (0.5 \times e^1) + (0.5 \times e^{-1})$$
$$= 1.5431$$

which is consistent with Jensen's inequality.

Graphically, the average of $f(1)$ and $f(-1)$ lies on the chord connecting those points, which is the straight line in Figure C.1. $f(0)$ is below the chord, which is what Jensen's inequality states.

C.2 EXAMPLE: THE PRICE OF A CALL

Here is an example of Jensen's inequality. Consider a call option with a strike price of $40. Suppose that x is the stock price, and that $x \sim$ Binomial$(35, 45; 0.5)$. Then

$$E(x) = (0.5 \times 35) + (0.5 \times 45) = 40.$$

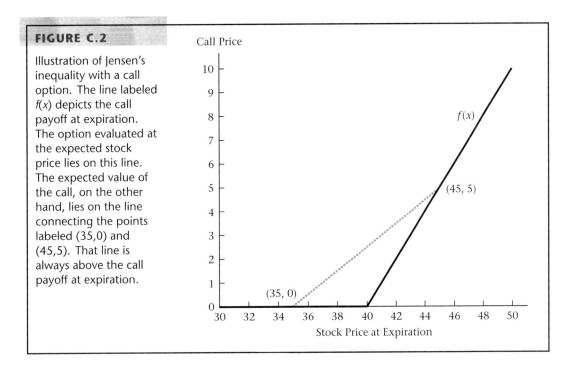

FIGURE C.2

Illustration of Jensen's inequality with a call option. The line labeled $f(x)$ depicts the call payoff at expiration. The option evaluated at the expected stock price lies on this line. The expected value of the call, on the other hand, lies on the line connecting the points labeled (35,0) and (45,5). That line is always above the call payoff at expiration.

Now let $f(x)$ be the value of the call at expiration:

$$f(x) = \max(x - K, 0)$$

When we evaluate the call price at the expected stock price, $f[E(x)]$, we have

$$f[E(x)] = \max[E(x) - 40, 0]$$
$$= 0$$

And when we evaluate the expected value of the the the call, $E[f(x)]$, we have

$$E[f(x)] = 0.5 \times f(45) + 0.5 \times f(35)$$
$$= 0.5 \times \max(45 - 40, 0) + 0.5 \times \max(35 - 40, 0)$$
$$= 0.5 \times 5 + 0 = 2.5$$

Since $2.5 > 0$, $E[f(x)] \geq f[E(x)]$, in accord with Jensen's inequality.

Figure C.2 displays this example graphically. The straight line connecting $f(35)$ and $f(45)$ represents $E[f(x)]$; this line always exceeds the payoff to the call option. This example illustrates in a purely mechanical fashion why uncertainty makes an option more valuable.

C.3 PROOF OF JENSEN'S INEQUALITY[2]

A mathematical way to state the definition of convexity is that $f(x)$ is convex if for any two points x and y, $0 \leq \lambda \leq 1$, and $z = \lambda x + (1 - \lambda)y$,

$$f(z) \leq \lambda f(x) + (1 - \lambda)f(y) \qquad (C.2)$$

If $f(x)$ is convex, then there is a line $L(x)$, running through the point $[z, f(z)]$ such that $L(z) = f(z)$ and for every x, $f(x) \geq L(x)$. Because $L(x)$ is a line, it can be written as $a + bx$, hence $E[L(x)] = L[E(x)]$. Define $L^*(x)$ as the tangent line at the point $\{E(x), f[E(x)]\}$. (In Figure C.1, this line would be the tangent line at the point $x = 0$.)

Now because $f(x) \geq L^*(x)$, we have $E[f(x)] \geq E[L^*(x)] = L^*[E(x)] = f[E(x)]$. (The last step is because we defined $L^*(x)$ to include the point $\{E(x), f[E(x)]\}$.) This proves Jensen's inequality.

PROBLEMS

C.1. The logarithmic function is $f(x) = \ln(x)$.

   a. Graph the logarithmic function in a spreadsheet. Observe that it is concave.

   b. Using whatever examples you wish, verify Jensen's inequality for the logarithmic function.

C.2. Do the following in a spreadsheet. Let σ vary from 0.05 to 1 in increments of 0.05, and let h vary from 1 month to 1 year in increments of 1 month.

   a. Compute $0.5(e^{\sigma\sqrt{h}} + e^{-\sigma\sqrt{h}})$

   b. Compute $0.5(e^{-0.5\sigma^2h+\sigma\sqrt{h}} + e^{-0.5\sigma^2h-\sigma\sqrt{h}})$

C.3. Let $x \sim \text{Binomial}(-a, a; 0.5)$. Using a spreadsheet, evaluate $E(e^{x-0.5a^2})$, for a's ranging from 0.025 to 1, in increments of 0.025.

C.4. Let $x \sim \text{Binomial}(-1, 2; 0.67)$. Verify Jensen's inequality for $f(x) = e^x$.

C.5. For the example of the call option in Section C.2, verify with a numerical example that the value of the call is increasing in the spread of the prices around the mean of $40.

C.6. Using the numerical example in Section C.2, verify Jensen's inequality for a put option.

---

[2]This proof is from Mood et al. (1974).

APPENDIX D

An Introduction to Visual Basic for Applications

Visual Basic for Applications, Excel's powerful built-in programming language, lets you incorporate user-written functions and subroutines into a spreadsheet.[1] You can easily calculate Black-Scholes and binomial option prices, for example. This appendix shows how to create user-written functions using VBA. You need not write complicated programs using VBA in order for it to be useful. At the very least, knowing VBA can make it easier for you to analyze relatively complex problems, and to create better-documented, more reliable spreadsheets.

This appendix presumes that you have a basic knowledge of Excel, including the use of built-in functions and named ranges. It does not presume that you know anything about writing macros or programming. The examples here are mostly related to option pricing, but the principles apply generally to any situation in which you use Excel as a tool for numerical analysis.

All of the examples here are contained in the Excel workbook *VBA_examples2.xls*.

D.1 CALCULATIONS WITHOUT VBA

Suppose you wish to compute the Black-Scholes formula in a spreadsheet. Suppose also that you have named cells[2] for the stock price (s), strike price (k), interest rate (r_), time to expiration (t), volatility (v), and dividend yield (d). You could enter the following into a cell:

```
s*Exp(-d*t)*NormSDist((Ln(s/k)+(r_-d+v^2/2)*t)/(v*t^0.5))
  -k*Exp(-r_*t)*NormSDist((Ln(s/k)+(r_-d-v^2 / 2)*t)/(v*t^0.5))
```

Typing this formula is cumbersome, though of course you can copy the formula wherever you would like it to appear. It is possible to use Excel's data table feature to create a table of Black-Scholes prices, but this is cumbersome and inflexible. If you

---

[1] This appendix is written for the versions of VBA in Office 2000 and Office XP. VBA changed dramatically between Office 95 and Office 97 and will change in the future as VBA is replaced with VBA.Net. When this happens, a guide will be available at the Web site for this book. There are numerous books on VBA.

[2] If you do not know what a named cell is, consult Excel's online help.

want to calculate option Greeks (e.g., delta and gamma), you must again enter or copy the formulas into each cell where you want a calculation to appear. And if you decide to change some aspect of your formula, you have to hunt down all occurrences and make the changes. When the same formula is copied throughout a worksheet, that worksheet potentially becomes harder to modify safely and reliably. When the worksheet is to be used by others, maintainability becomes even more of a concern.

Spreadsheet construction becomes even harder if you want to, for example, compute a price for a finite-lived American option. There is no way to do this in one cell, so you must compute the binomial tree in a range of cells and copy the appropriate formulas for the stock price and the option price. This is not so difficult with a three-step binomial calculation, but for 100 steps you will spend quite a while setting up the spreadsheet. If you decide you want to set up a binomial tree for pricing put options, it can be time-consuming to edit your call tree to price puts. If you plan ahead, you can make the formulas flexible and general with the use of "if" statements. But things would become much easier if you could create your own formulas within Excel. This is what Visual Basic for Applications permits you to do.

D.2 How to Learn VBA

Before delving into VBA, it is helpful to appreciate what learning VBA will entail. First, you will never learn VBA by reading about it; you must try to use it. Part of the challenge is that if a macro language is so powerful that it enables you to do everything, it is going to be too complex for you to memorize all the commands. A book or tutorial (like this one) will enable you to use VBA to solve specific problems. However, once you want to do more, you will have to become comfortable figuring out VBA by trial and error.

To facilitate learning VBA, you should use the macro recorder in Excel. When you use the macro recorder, the results of your actions will be recorded in VBA. Try this: Select Tools|Macro|Record New Macro in Excel. Then create a simple graph using the graph wizard. Look at the VBA code that Excel creates. (This example is described in more detail on page 904.) The result is daunting when you first look at it, but if you want to use VBA to create graphs, the recorded macro gives you a starting point that you can modify; you need not create the basic code from scratch.

The main objective of this tutorial is to help you create your own functions. While the examples here relate to option pricing, there are many other uses of VBA.

D.3 Calculations with VBA

In this section we will discuss functions and subroutines, which are techniques in VBA for performing calculations or automating actions.

Creating a Simple Function

With VBA, it is a simple matter to create your own function, say BSCall, which will compute a Black-Scholes option price. To do this, you must first create and open a macro module. Here are the steps required to open a new macro module and to create a simple formula:

1. *Open a blank workbook using File|New.*

2. *Select Tools|Macro|Visual Basic Editor from the Excel menu.*

3. *Within the VBA editor, select Insert|Module from the menu. You will find yourself in a new window, in which you can type macro commands.*

4. *Within the newly created macro module, type the following exactly (be sure to include the "_" at the end of the first line):*

```
' Here is a function to add two numbers _
Works well, doesn't it?

Function AddTwo(x, y)
  AddTwo = x + y
End Function
```

5. *Return to Excel. In cell A1 enter*

```
=AddTwo(3, 5)
```

6. *Hit <Enter>. You will see the result "8".*

These steps create an add-in function. Notice the following:

- You need to tell the function what to expect as input, hence, the list "(x, y)" following the name of the function.

- You specify the value of the function with a statement where you set the function name ("AddTwo") equal to a calculation ("x + y").

- An apostrophe denotes a comment, i.e., text that is not interpreted by VBA. You need not write comments, but they are very useful when you return to work you did several months ago.

- VBA is line-oriented. This means that when you start a comment with an apostrophe, if you press <Enter> to go to a new line, you must enter another apostrophe or else—since what you type will almost surely not be a valid command—VBA will report an error. You can continue a line to the next line by typing an underscore, i.e., "_" without the quotes. (You can test this by deleting the "_" in the example above.)

- When you entered the comment and the function, VBA automatically color-coded the text and completed the syntax (the line "End Function" was automatically inserted). Comments are coded green and the reserved words "Function" and "End" were coded in blue and automatically capitalized.

- The function you typed now appears in the function wizard, just as if it were a built-in Excel function. To see this, open the function wizard using Insert|Function. In the left-hand pane ("Function Category"), scroll to and highlight "User Defined".

Note that "AddTwo" appears in the right-side pane ("Function Name"). Click on it and Excel pops up a box where you are prompted to enter inputs for the function.

If you use a custom function in a spreadsheet, it will automatically recalculate when the spreadsheet recalculates.

A Simple Example of a Subroutine

A *function* returns a result. A *subroutine* (called a "sub" by VBA) performs an action when invoked. In the above example we used a function, because we wanted to supply two numbers and have VBA add them for us and tell us the sum. While functions recalculate automatically, subroutines are a set of statements that execute when the subroutine is explicitly invoked. Here are the steps to create a subroutine:

1. *Return to the Visual Basic Editor.*

2. *Click on the "Module1" window.*

3. *At the bottom of the module (i.e., below the function we just created) enter the following:*

```
Sub DisplayBox()
 Response = MsgBox("Greetings!")
End Sub
```

4. *Return to Excel.*

5. *Run the subroutine by using Tools|Macro|Macros, then double-clicking on "DisplayBox" out of the list.*

We have just created and run a subroutine. It pops up a dialog box that displays a message. The MsgBox function can be very useful for giving information to the spreadsheet user.

Creating a Button to Invoke a Subroutine

We ran the subroutine by clicking on Tools|Macro|Macros and then double-clicking on the subroutine name. If you are going to run the subroutine often, creating a button in the spreadsheet provides a shortcut to the subroutine. Here is how to create a button:

1. *Move the mouse to the Excel toolbar and right-click once.*

2. *You will see a list of toolbar names. Move the highlight bar down to "Forms" and left-click. A new toolbar will pop up.*

3. *The rectangular icon on this toolbar is the "Button" icon, which looks something like a button (of the software, not the clothing, variety). Click on it.*

4. *The cursor changes to a crosshair. Move the mouse to the spreadsheet, hold down the left mouse button, and drag to create a rectangle. When you lift your finger off the*

mouse button, a dialog box will pop up. One of the choices will be "DisplayBox."
Double-click on it.

5. *Now move the mouse away from the button you've created and click once (this de-*
selects the button). Move the mouse back to the button you created and left-click
once on it. Observe the dialog box that pops up, and click "OK" to get rid of the
dialog.

Some comments:

- This is a trivial example. However, if you have a calculation that is particularly time-consuming (for example, a Monte Carlo calculation), you might want to create a subroutine for it. Creating a button to activate the subroutine would be a natural adjunct.

- There is a more sophisticated version of the MsgBox function that permits you to customize the appearance of the dialog box. It is documented in the online help and an example of its use is contained in DisplayBox2 in the workbook. One nice feature of this more sophisticated version is that within the subroutine, we could have checked the value of the variable *Response* and had the subroutine perform different actions depending upon which button the user clicked. For an example of this, see the example DisplayBox2.[3]

Functions Can Call Functions

Functions can call functions. Here is an example.

1. *Enter this code in the "Module1" window.*

```
Function AddThree(x, y, z)
  AddThree = AddTwo(x, y) + z
End Function
```

2. *Now in cell A2, enter*

```
=AddThree(3, 5, 7)
```

The answer "15" will appear.

Illegal Function Names

Some function names are illegal, which means that you will receive an error message if you try to use them. You cannot use a number as a function name. You cannot use the following characters in a function name: space . , + - : ; " ' ` # $ % / \. If you try

---

[3] If you have examined the code for DisplayBox2, you may be puzzled by checking to see if *Response* = "vbYes". VbYes is simply an internal constant which VBA uses to check for a "yes" button response to a dialog box. The possible responses—documented in the help file—are vbOK, vbCancel, vbAbort, vbRetry, vbIgnore, vbYes, and vbNo.

to use any of these characters in a name, Visual Basic lets you know immediately that something is wrong. Note that you *can* use an underscore where you would like to have a space for readability of the function name. So BS_2, for example, is a legal function name.

Here is a more subtle issue. There are function names that are legal but that you should not use. BS2 is an example. This would be fine as the name of a subroutine, which is not called directly from a cell. But think about what happens if you give this name to a user-defined function. You enter, for example, "BS2(3)", in a cell. How does Excel understand this? The problem is that "BS2" *is also the name of a cell*. So if you try to use it as a function in the spreadsheet, Excel will become confused and return an error. This is why, later in this tutorial, you will see functions named BS_2, BS_3, and so on.

Differences between Functions and Subroutines

Functions and subroutines are *not* interchangeable and do not have the same capabilities. Think of subroutines as code meant to be invoked by a button or otherwise explicitly called, while functions return results and are meant to be inserted into cells (although functions can also be called by subroutines). Because of their different purpose, some VBA capabilities will work in one but not the other.

In a subroutine, for example, you can write to cells of the workbook. With a subroutine you could perform a calculation and have the answer appear in cell A1. However, if you invoke a function from a worksheet by entering it into a cell, you cannot write to cells from within that function. You cannot activate a worksheet or change anything about the display from within such a function. (On the other hand, if the function is invoked by a subroutine, but not invoked from a worksheet, it can do these things.) Subroutines, on the other hand, cannot be called from cells. These restrictions exist because functions and subroutines are intended for different purposes.

D.4 Storing and Retrieving Variables in a Worksheet

Suppose that there is a value in the spreadsheet that you want to include as input to your function or subroutine. (For instance, you might have a variable that determines whether the option to be valued is American or European.) Or suppose you create a subroutine that performs computations. You may want to display the output in the spreadsheet. (For example, you might wish to create a subroutine to draw a binomial tree.) Using VBA, how do you read and write values to the spreadsheet?

If you are going to read and write numbers to specific locations in the spreadsheet, you must identify those locations. The easiest way to identify a location is to use a named range. The alternatives—which we will examine below—require that you "activate" a specific location or worksheet within the workbook, and then read and write within this activated region.

There are at least three ways to read and write to cells:

- Range lets you address cells by name.
- Range().Activate and ActiveCell let you access cells by using traditional cell addresses (e.g., "A1").
- Cell lets you address cells using a row and column numbering scheme.

You may be thinking that it seems redundant to have so many ways to access cells, but each is useful at different times.

Using a Named Range to Read and Write Numbers from the Spreadsheet

1. *Enter the following subroutine in Module1:*

```
Sub ReadVariable()
 x = Range("Test")
 MsgBox (Str(x))
End Sub
```

2. *Select cell A1 in sheet "Sheet2"; then Insert|Name|Define, and type "Test"; then click OK. You have just created a named range.*

3. *Enter the value "5" in the cell you just named "Test".*

4. *Select Tools|Macro|Macros, then double-click on "ReadVariable".*

At this point you have just read from a cell and displayed the result. Note that "x" is a number in this example. Sometimes it is useful to be able to convert a number to its character equivalent (for example the character "7" rather than the number "7.0000000"). You can do this using VBA's built-in "Str" function.[4] It turns out this was not necessary in this example; entering "MsgBox(x)" would have worked as well.

As you might guess, you can use the Range function to write as well as read.

1. *Enter the following subroutine in Module1:*

```
Sub WriteVariable()
 Range("Test2") = Range("Test")
 MsgBox ("Number_copied!")
End Sub
```

2. *Give the name "Test2" to cell Sheet2.B2.*

3. *Enter a number in Sheet2.B2.*

4. *Go to Tools|Macro|Macros; then double-click on "WriteVariable."*

5. *The number from Test is copied to Test2.*

---

[4]You can locate the "Str" function by using the object browser, looking under VBA, then "Conversions."

Reading and Writing to Cells That Are Not Named

You can also access a specific cell directly. In order to do this, you first have to activate the worksheet containing the cell. Here is VBA code to read a variable:

```
Sub ReadVariable2()
 Worksheets("Sheet2").Activate
 Range("A1").Activate
 x = ActiveCell.Value
 MsgBox (Str(x))
End Sub
```

In this subroutine we first activate the worksheet named "Sheet2." Next we activate the cell "A1" within Sheet2. You will see that when you have finished calling this function, the cursor has moved to cell A1 in Sheet2. This is because the "active cell" is whatever cell the cursor happens to be on; the first two lines instruct the cursor to move to Sheet2.A1.

The active cell has properties, such as the font, color of the cell, and formatting. All of these properties may be accessed using the ActiveCell function. For fun, insert the line

```
ActiveCell.Font.Bold=True
```

after the MsgBox function. Then switch to Sheet2, run the subroutine, and watch the change in cell A1.

We can also assign a value to ActiveCell.Value; this is a way to write to a cell. Here is a macro that does this:

```
Sub WriteVariable2()
 Worksheets("Sheet2").Activate
 Range("A1").Activate
 x = ActiveCell.Value
 Range("B1").Activate
 ActiveCell.Value = x
End Sub
```

This subroutine reads the number from Sheet2.A1 and copies it to Sheet2.B1.

Using the Cells Function to Read and Write to Cells

There is yet another way to read and write to cells. The Cells function lets you address cells using a numerical row and column numbering scheme. Here is an example illustrating how Cells works:

```
Sub CellsExample()
 ' Make "Sheet2" the active sheet
 Worksheets("Sheet2").Activate
 ' The first entry is the row, the second is the column
```

```
' Write the number 1 into cell A3
Cells(3, 1) = 1
' Write the number 2 into cell A4
Cells(4, 1) = 2
' Copy the number from cell A3 into cell C3
Cells(3, 3) = Cells(3, 1)
' Copy the number from cell A4 into cell C4
Cells(4, 3) = Cells(4, 1)
End Sub
```

This subroutine reads the numbers 1 and 2 into cells A3 and A4, and it then copies the values into C3 and C4. Later we will use the Cells function to draw a binomial tree.

Reading from within a Function

It is possible to read from a worksheet from within a function. For example, consider these two functions:

```
Function ReadTest1(x, y)
 ReadTest1 = x + y + Range("Read_In_Function!A1").Value
End Function

Function ReadTest2(x, y)
 Application.Volatile
 ReadTest2 = x + y + Range("Read_In_Function!A1").Value
End Function
```

An interesting experiment is to create the sheet named "Read_In_Function," put the number "5" in cell A1, and enter ReadTest1(3,4) and ReadTest2(3,4) in cells A2 and A3. Both functions will return the value "12."

Now change the value in cell A1 to 20. *The function ReadTest2 will properly return the value 27, but ReadTest1 will not change.* Press the F9 key to recalculate the spreadsheet. *ReadTest1 will still not recalculate.* The problem is that Excel has no way of knowing that the value change in A1 affects either function. However, ReadTest2 recalculates because of the Application.Volatile statement at the beginning. This tells ReadTest2 to recalculate anytime *anything* changes. Obviously this will slow the worksheet, but it is necessary in this case.

Reading from the worksheet from within a function is possible, but, other things equal, it is preferable to pass values to the function explicitly as arguments.

D.5 Using Excel Functions from within VBA

VBA permits you to use most Excel functions within your own custom functions. Since Excel has a large number of built-in functions, this is a powerful feature.

Using VBA to Compute the Black-Scholes Formula

There is only one complicated piece of the Black-Scholes calculation: Computing the cumulative normal distribution (the "$N()$" function in the formula). Based on the example at the start of this appendix, we would like to do something like the following:

```
Function BS(s, k, v, r, t, d)
  BS=s*Exp(-d*t)*NormSDist((Ln(s/k)+(r-d+v^2/2)*t)/(v*t^0.5))  _
  -k*Exp(-r*t)*NormSDist((Ln(s/k)+(r-d-v^2/2)*t)/(v*t^0.5))
End Function
```

Unfortunately, this doesn't work. The reason it doesn't work is that VBA does not understand either "Ln" or "NormSDist." Though these are functions in Excel they are not functions in VBA, even though VBA is part of Excel. Instead of using "Ln," we can use "Log," which is the VBA version of the same function. However, there is no VBA version of NormSDist.

Fortunately, there is a way for you to tell VBA that NormSDist is located inside of Excel. The following example will show you the error you get if you fail to call NormSDist correctly:

1. *Click on the "Module1" tab.*

2. *Enter the following:*

```
Function BS(s, k, v, r, t, d)
  d1 = (Log(s / k) + (r - d + v ^ 2 / 2) * t) / (v * Sqr(t))
  d2 = d1 - v * Sqrt(t)
  BS = s*Exp(-d*t)*normsdist(d1)-k*Exp(-r*t)*NormSDist(d2)
End Function
```

Comment: To save a little typing and to make the function more readable, we are defining the Black-Scholes "d1" and "d2" separately. You will also notice that instead of entering "Ln," we entered "Log," which—as we noted above—is built into VBA.

3. *Enter into the spreadsheet*

```
=BS(40, 40, .3, .08, .25, 0)
```

Hit <Enter>. You will get the error message "sub or function not defined".

This error occurs because there is no version, however spelled, of "NormSDist" that is built in to VBA. Instead, we have to tell VBA where to look for "NormSDist." We do this by typing instead "WorksheetFunction.NormSDist" or "Application.NormSDist."[5]

....

[5]If you are curious about this, do the following: Select View|Object Browser or press F2. Click on the drop-down arrow under "Libraries/Workbooks"; then select "Excel." Under "Objects/Modules" click on "Application"; then under "Methods/Properties" scroll down to "NormSDist." You have now just located "NormSDist" as a method available from the application. If you scroll around a bit, you will see that there is an enormous and overwhelming number of functions available to be called from VBA.

With a correctly referenced NormSDist, the function becomes

```
Function BS(s, k, v, r, t, d)
  d1 = (Log(s / k) + (r - d + v ^ 2 / 2) * t) / (v * t ^ 0.5)
  d2 = d1 - v * t ^ 0.5
  BS = s*Exp(-d*t)*WorkSheetFunction.NormSDist(d1) _
    -k*Exp(-r*t)*WorkSheetFunction.NormSDist(d2)
End Function
```

The Black-Scholes function will now evaluate correctly to 2.78.

The Object Browser

The previous example illustrates an extremely powerful feature of VBA: It can access the functions built into Excel if you tell it where to find them. The way you locate other functions is to use the *Object Browser*, which is part of VBA. Here is how to use it:

1. *From within a macro module, press the F2 key. This will pop up a dialog box with the title "Object Browser."*

2. *In the top left you will see a drop-down box that says "All Libraries." Click on the down arrow at the right of this line. You will see a drop-down list with, at a minimum, "VBA" and "Excel" as two entries. (There may be other entries, depending upon how you have set up Excel.)*

3. *Click on VBA.*

4. *In the "Classes" list, click on "Math."*

5. *To the right, in the "Members of Math" box, you now have a list of all the math functions that are available in VBA. Note that "Log" is included in this list, but not "Ln" or "NormSDist." If you right-click on "Log" and then click on "Help," you will see that "Log" returns the natural logarithm.*

6. *Return to the top left box, which now says "VBA." Click on the down arrow at the right of this line.*

7. *Click on Excel.*

8. *In the "Classes" list, click on "WorksheetFunction."*

9. *To the right, in the "Members of WorksheetFunction" box, you now have a list of Excel built-in functions that may be called from a macro module by specifying "WorksheetFunction.functionname."[6] Note that both "Ln" and "NormSDist" are*

---

[6]By the way, you should not make the mistake of thinking that you can call any Excel function simply by prefacing it with "WorksheetFunction." Try it with "Sqrt" and it won't work. While most functions are accessible from VBA, the only way to know for sure which functions you can and cannot call is by using the object browser.

included in this list. Note also that "Log" is included in this list, but be aware that Excel's "Log" function is base 10 by default (you can specify a different base), whereas VBA's is base e.[7]

If you create any VBA functions that are even moderately ambitious, you will need to use the object browser. It is the heart and soul of VBA.

D.6 Checking for Conditions

Frequently, you want to perform a calculation only if certain conditions are met. For example, you would not want to calculate an option price with a negative volatility. It makes sense to check to see if your inputs make sense before proceeding with the calculation and aborting—possibly with an error message—if they do not.

The easy way to check if a condition exists is to use the construct *If . . . Then . . . Else*.[8] Here is an example of its use in checking for a negative volatility in the Black-Scholes formula:[9]

```
Function BS_2(s, k, v, r, t, d)
  If v > 0 Then
    BS_2 = BS(s, k, v, r, t, d)
  Else
    MsgBox ("Negative_volatility!")
    BS_2 = CVErr(xlErrValue)
  End If
End Function
```

This function checks to see if volatility is greater than 0; if it is, the function computes the Black-Scholes formula using the BS function we created earlier. If volatility is not greater than zero, then two things happen: (i) a message box pops up to inform you of the mistake and (ii) the function returns a value indicating that there is an error.

In general you should be cautious about putting message boxes into a function (as opposed to a subroutine), since every time the spreadsheet is recalculated the message box will pop up.

Because error-checking is often critically important (you would not want to quote a client a price on a deal for which you had accidentally entered a negative volatility), it is worth expanding a bit on the use of the CVErr function.

---

[7]Scroll down to the ":Log" entry and then click on the "?" button at the bottom left. If you use "Log" in a spreadsheet, or if you use "WorksheetFunction.log" in a function, you will get the base 10 logarithm. However, if you use "Log" in a function, you will get the base *e* logarithm. Note also that, as mentioned earlier, "Sqrt" is not included and, hence, is not available in VBA.

[8]There is also a *Case . . . Select* construct that we will not use but that is documented in VBA's help file.

[9]You need to be aware that VBA will expect the "If Then," "Else," and "End If" pieces to be on separate lines. If you write "Else" on the same line as "If Then," for example, the code will fail.

If the user enters a negative volatility, you *could* just have Excel return a nonsense value for the option, such as −99. This would be a bad idea, however. Suppose you have a complicated worksheet with many option calculations. If you failed to notice the error, the −99 would be treated as a true option value and propagated throughout your calculations.

Alternatively, you could have the function return a string such as "Oops, you entered a negative volatility." Entering a string in a cell when you should have a number could have unpredictable effects on calculations that depend on the cell. It is obvious that an addition between a string and a number will fail. However, suppose you are performing a frequency count. Are you sure what will happen to the calculation if you introduce a string among the numbers in your data?

Excel has built-in error codes that are documented in VBA's online help. For example, xlErrNA returns "#N/A," xlErrRef returns "#REF!," and xlErrValue returns "#VALUE!". By using CVErr along with one of the built-in error codes, you guarantee that your function will return a result that Excel recognizes as a numerical error. Excel programmers have already thought through the issues of how subsequent calculations should respond to a recognized error, and Excel usually does something reasonable in those circumstances.

D.7 ARRAYS

Often you will wish to use a single variable to store many numbers. For example, in a binomial option calculation, you have a stock price tree. After n periods, you have $n + 1$ possible stock prices. It can be useful to write the lowest stock price as $S(0)$, the next as $S(1)$, and the highest as $S(n)$. The variable S is then called an array—it is a single variable that stores more than one number. Each item in the array is called an *element*. Think of an array as a table of numbers. You access a specific element of the array by specifying a row and column number. Figure D.1 provides an example of an array.

Defining Arrays

When you create an array, it is necessary to tell VBA how big the array is going to be. You do this by using the Dim statement ("Dim" is short for "dimension"—the size of the array). Here are some examples of how to use Dim to create a one-dimensional array:

```
Dim P(2) As Double
```

This creates an array of three double-precision real numbers, with the array index running from 0 to 2. (By default, the first subscript in an array in VBA is 0.) If you had written

```
Dim P(3 to 5) As Double
```

you would have created a three-element array with the index running from 3 to 5. In this example we told Excel that the variable is type "Double." This was not necessary—we could have left the type unspecified and permitted Excel to determine the type automatically. It is faster and easier to detect mistakes, however, if we specify the type.

FIGURE D.1

Example of an array with 3 rows and 5 columns. By default, VBA numbers rows and columns start with 0. If the array is named X, the number "8" is retrieved as X(1, 3).

		Column Number				
		0	**1**	**2**	**3**	**4**
	0	12	3.91	−5	23	−33.183
Row Number	**1**	3	−82.5	1	8	24
	2	−19.8	44	6	17.2	7

You can also create arrays with multiple dimensions. For example, the following are valid Dim statements:

```
Dim X(3, 8)
Dim Y(1 to 4, -5 to 3)
Dim Z(1 to 4, -5 to 3, 25)
```

The first statement creates a two-dimensional array that has 4 rows and 9 columns—a 4×9 array. The second also creates a two-dimensional array with 4 rows and 9 columns. The third creates a three-dimsional array which is $4 \times 9 \times 25$. Since $4 \times 9 \times 25 = 900$, this last array has 900 spaces, or elements.

Here is a routine that defines a three-element one-dimensional array, reads numbers into the array, and then writes the array out into dialog boxes:

```
Sub UseArray()
  Dim X(2) As Double
  X(0) = 0
  X(1) = 1
  X(2) = 2
  MsgBox (X(0))
  MsgBox (X(1))
  MsgBox (X(2))
End Sub
```

You should enter this code and execute it to see what happens. The subroutine UseArray can also be written as follows:

```
Sub UseArray2()
  X = Array(0, 1, 2)
  MsgBox (X(0))
  MsgBox (X(1))
  MsgBox (X(2))
End Sub
```

The difference between UseArray and UseArray2 is the way arrays are declared. In UseArray, there is a dimension statement, and then array elements are created one by one. In UseArray2, there is *no* dimension statement, and the Array function (built into VBA) is used to set the initial values of the array elements (this is called *initializing* the array). UseArray will fail without the Dim statement, and UseArray2 will fail *with* the Dim statement.

Finally, notice the repetition in these examples. The statements that put numbers into the array are essentially repeated three times (albeit more compactly in UseArray2), and the statements that read numbers out of the array are repeated three times. If the array had 100 elements, it would take a long time to write the subroutine in this way. Fortunately, we can perform repetitive calculations by iteration.

D.8 ITERATION

Many option calculations are repetitive. For example, when we compute a binomial option price, we generate a stock price tree and then traverse the tree, calculating the option price at each node. Similarly, when we compute an implied volatility, we need to perform a calculation repeatedly until we arrive at the correct volatility. VBA provides us with the ability to write one or more lines of code that can be repeated as many times as we like.

A Simple *for* Loop

Here is an example of a *for* loop. This subroutine does exactly the same thing as the UseArray subroutine:

```
Sub UseArrayLoop()
  Dim X(2) As Double
  For i = 0 To 2
    X(i) = i
  Next i
  For i = 0 To 2
    MsgBox (Str(X(i)))
  Next i
End Sub
```

The following translates the syntax in the first loop above:

For i = 0 to 2 — Repeat the following statements three times, the first time setting $i = 0$, the next time $i = 1$, and finally $i = 2$.

X(i) = i — Set the ith value of X equal to i.

Next i — Go back and repeat the statement for the next value of i.

Creating a Binomial Tree

In order to create a binomial tree, we need the following information:

- The initial stock price.

- The number of time periods.

- The magnitudes up and down by which the stock moves.

Suppose we wish to draw a tree where the initial price is $100, we have 10 binomial periods, and the moves up and down are $u = 1.25$ and $d = 0.8$. Here is a subroutine, complete with comments explaining the code, that will create this tree. You first need to name a worksheet "Output", and then we will write the tree to this worksheet. The number of binomial steps and the magnitude of the moves are read from named cells, which can be in any worksheet. I have placed those named cells in Sheet1 in VBA_examples.xls.

```
Sub DrawBinomialTree()


ReDim Stock(2) ' provide default of 2 steps if no steps specified
Dim i As Integer
Dim t As Integer
n = Range("n") ' number of binomial steps
u = Range("u") ' move up
P0 = Range("P0") ' initial stock price
d = 1 / u ' move down
ReDim Stock(n + 1) ' array of stock prices
Worksheets("Output").Activate
' Erase any previous calculations
Worksheets("Output").Cells.ClearContents
Cells(1, 1) = P0
' We will adopt the convention that the column holds the
' stock prices for a given point in time. The row holds
' stock prices over time. For example, the first row
' holds stock prices resulting from all up moves, the
' second row holds stock prices resulting from a single
' down move, etc.

' The first loop is over time
For t = 2 To n
 Cells(1, t) = Cells(1, t - 1) * u
 ' The second loop is across stock prices at a given time
 For i = 2 To t
  Cells(i, t) = Cells(i - 1, t - 1) * d
 Next i
 Next t
End Sub
```

Several comments:

- There is a simple command to clear an entire worksheet, namely: Worksheets (*worksheetname*).Cells.ClearContents.

- The use of the Cells function means that you can perform the calculation exactly as you would if you were writing it down, using subscripts to denote which price you are dealing with. Think about how much more complicated it would be to use traditional row and column notation (e.g., "A1") to perform the same function.

- This subroutine does not price an option; it merely creates a binomial stock price tree.

Note that this subroutine uses the ReDim command to specify a flexible array size. Sometimes you do not know in advance how big your array is going to be. In this example you are unsure how many binomial periods the subroutine must handle. If you are going to use an array to store the full set of prices at each point in time, this presents a problem—how large do you make the array? You could specify the array to have a very large size, one larger than any user is ever likely to use, but this kind of practice could get you into trouble if memory is limited. Fortunately, with the ReDim statement VBA permits you to specify the size of an array using a variable.

Other Kinds of Loops

Although we will not discuss them, there are other looping constructs available in VBA. The following kinds of loops are available:

- *Do Until . . . Loop and Do . . . Loop Until*
- *Do While . . . Loop and Do . . . Loop While*
- *While . . . Wend*

If you ever think you need them, you can look these up in the online help. There is also a *For Each . . . In . . . Next* construct, which we discuss below.

D.9 READING AND WRITING ARRAYS

A powerful feature of VBA is the ability to read arrays as inputs to a function and also to write functions that return arrays as output.

Arrays as Output

Suppose you would like to create a single function that returns two numbers: The Black-Scholes price of a call option and the option delta. Let's call this function BS_3 and create it by modifying the function BS from Section D.5.1.

```
Function BS_3(s, k, v, r, t, d)
  d1 = (Log(s / k) + (r - d + 0.5 * v ^ 2) * t) / (v * t ^ 0.5)
  d2 = d1 - v * t ^ 0.5
  nd1 = WorksheetFunction.NormSDist(d1)
  nd2 = WorksheetFunction.NormSDist(d2)
  delta = Exp(-d * t) * nd1
```

```
   price = s * delta - k * Exp(-r * t) * nd2
  BS_3 = Array(price, delta)
End Function
```

The key section is the line

```
  BS_3 = Array(price, delta)
```

We assign an array as the function output, using the array function introduced in Section D.7.

If you just enter the function BS_3 in your worksheet in the normal way, in a single cell, it will return a single number. In this case, that single number will be the option price, which is the first element of the array. If you want to see both numbers as output from the function, you have to enter BS_3 as an array function spanning multiple cells: Select a range of two cells, enter the formula in the first, and then press Ctrl-Shift-Enter (instead of just Enter).

There is a 50% probability you just discovered a catch. The way we have written BS_3, the array output is *horizontal*. If you enter the array function in cells A1:A2, for example, you will see only the option price. If you enter the function in A1:B1, you will see the price and the delta. What happens if we want vertical output? The answer is that we transpose the array using the Excel function of that name, modifying the last line to read

```
  BS_3 = WorksheetFunction.Transpose(Array(price, delta))
```

This will make the output vertical.

There is also a way to make the output *both* horizontal and vertical. We just have to return a 2 × 2 array. Here is an illustration of how to do that:

```
Function BS_4(s, k, v, r, t, d)
  Dim temp(1, 1) As Double
  d1 = (Log(s / k) + (r - d + 0.5 * v ^ 2) * t) / (v * t ^ 0.5)
  d2 = d1 - v * t ^ 0.5
  nd1 = WorksheetFunction.NormSDist(d1)
  nd2 = WorksheetFunction.NormSDist(d2)
  delta = Exp(-d * t) * nd1
  price = s * delta - k * Exp(-r * t) * nd2
  temp(0, 0) = price
  temp(0, 1) = delta
  temp(1, 0) = delta
  temp(1, 1) = 0
  BS_4 = temp
End Function
```

Now it does not matter whether you select cells A1:A2 or A1:B1; either way, you will see both the price and the delta.[10]

....

[10]What do you see if you select cells A1:B2? What about A1:D4?

Arrays as Inputs

We may wish to write a function that processes many inputs, where we do not know in advance how many inputs there will be. Excel's built-in functions "sum" and "average" are two familiar examples of this. They both can take a *range* of cells as input. For example, you could enter in a worksheet "sum(a1:b8)." It turns out that it is easy to write functions that accept ranges as input. Once in the function, the array of numbers from the range can be manipulated in at least two ways: As a *collection*, or as an actual array with the same dimensions as the range.

The array as a collection   First, here are two examples of how to use a collection. Excel has built-in functions called SumSq and SumProd, which (as the names suggest) sum the squared elements of a range and sum the product of the corresponding elements of two or more arrays. We will see how to implement similar functions in VBA.

SumSq takes a set of numbers, squares each one, and adds them up:

```
Function SumSq(x)
  Sum = 0
  For Each y In x
   Sum = Sum + y ^ 2
  Next
  SumSq = Sum
End Function
```

The function SumSq can take a range (e.g., "A1:A10") as its argument. The *For Each* construct in VBA loops through each element of a collection without our having to know in advance how many elements the collection has.

There is another way to loop through the elements of a collection. The function SumProd takes two equally sized arrays, multiplies them element by element, and returns the sum of the multiplied elements. In this example, because we are working with two collections, we need to use a more standard looping construct. To do this, we need to first count the number of elements in each array. This is done using the Count property of a collection. If there is a different number of elements in each of the two arrays, we exit and return an error code.

```
Function SumProd(x1, x2)
  n1 = x1.Count
  n2 = x2.Count
  If n1 <> n2 Then
   'exit if arrays not equally sized
   SumProd = CVErr(xlErrNum)
  End If
  Sum = 0
  For i = 1 To n1
   Sum = Sum + x1(i) * x2(i)
  Next i
  SumProd = Sum
End Function
```

The array as an array   We can also treat the numbers in the range as an array. The only trick to doing that is that we need to know the dimensions of the array, i.e., how many rows and columns it has. The function RangeTest illustrates how to do this.

```
Function RangeTest(x)
  prod = 1
  r = x.Rows.Count
  c = x.Columns.Count
  For i = 1 To r
   For j = 1 To c
    prod = prod * x(i, j)
   Next j
  Next i
  RangeTest = WorksheetFunction.Transpose(Array(prod, r, c))
End Function
```

This function again multiplies together the cells in the range. It returns not only the product, but also the number of rows and columns.

When x is read into the function, it is considered by VBA to be an array.[11] Rows and Columns are properties of an array. The construct

```
x.Rows.Count
```

tells us the number of rows in the array. With this capability, we could multiply arrays, check to see whether two ranges have the same dimensions, and so on.

D.10 Miscellany

In this section we discuss miscellaneous topics.

Getting Excel to Generate Macros for You

Suppose you want to perform a task and you don't know how to program it in VBA. For example, suppose you want to create a subroutine to set up a graph. You can set up a graph manually and tell Excel to record the VBA commands that accomplish the same thing. You then examine the result and see how it works. To do this, select Tools|Macro|Record New Macro. Excel will record all your actions in a new module located at the *end* of your workbook, i.e., following Sheet16. You stop the recording by clicking the Stop button that should have appeared on your spreadsheet when you started recording. Macro recording is an *extremely* useful tool for understanding how Excel and VBA work and interact.

....

[11]You can verify this by using the VBA function IsArray. For example, you could write

```
y = IsArray(x)
```

and y will have the value "true" if x is a range input to the function.

For example, here is the macro code Excel generates if you use the chart wizard to set up a chart using data in the range A2:C4. You can see, among other things, that the selected graph style was the fourth line graph in the graph gallery, and that the chart was titled "Here is the title." Also, each data series is in a column and the first column was used as the *x*-axis ("CategoryLabels:=1").

```
' Macro1 Macro
' Macro recorded 2/17/99 by Robert McDonald
'
'
Sub Macro1()
Range("A2:C4").Select
ActiveSheet.ChartObjects.Add(196.5, 39, 252.75, 162).Select
Application.CutCopyMode = False
ActiveChart.ChartWizard Source:=Range("A2:C4"), Gallery:=xlLine, _
 Format:=4, PlotBy:=xlColumns, CategoryLabels:=1,SeriesLabels _
 :=0, HasLegend:=1, Title:="Here is the Title", CategoryTitle _
 :="X-Axis", ValueTitle:="Y-Axis", ExtraTitle:=""
End Sub
```

Using Multiple Modules

You can split up your functions and subroutines among as many modules as you like—functions from one module can call another, for example. Using multiple modules is often convenient for clarity.

Recalculation Speed

One unfortunate drawback of VBA—and of most macro code in most applications—is that it is slow. When you are using built-in functions, Excel performs clever internal checking to know whether something requires recalculation (you should be aware that on occasion it appears that this clever checking goes awry and something that should be recalculated isn't). When you write a custom function, however, Excel is not able to perform its checking on your functions, and it therefore tends to recalculate everything. This means that if you have a complicated spreadsheet, you may find *very* slow recalculation times. This is a problem with custom functions and not one you can do anything about.

If your calculation writes to the worksheet, you can significantly speed up your routine by turning off Excel's screen updating. You do this by

```
Application.ScreenUpdating=False
```

If you want to check the progress of your calculations, you can turn ScreenUpdating off at the beginning of your subroutine. Whenever you would like to see your calculation's progress (for example every 100th iteration), you can turn it on and then immediately turn it off again. This will update the display.

Finally, the keystroke Ctrl-Break will (usually) stop a recalculation. Ctrl-Break is more reliable if your macro writes output to the screen or spreadsheet.

Debugging

We will not go into details here, but VBA has sophisticated debugging capabilities. For example, you can set breakpoints (i.e., lines in your routine where Excel will stop calculating to give you a chance to see what is happening) and watches (which means that you can look at the values of variables at different points in the routine). Look up "debugging" in the online help.

Creating an Add-In

Suppose you have written a useful set of option functions and wish to make them broadly available in your spreadsheets. You can make the functions automatically available in *any* spreadsheet you write by creating an add-in. To do this, you simply save the file as an add-in, by selecting File|Save As and then selecting the type of file to be "Microsoft Excel Add-in (*.xla)." Excel will create a file with the .xla extension that contains your functions. You can then make these functions automatically available by Tools|Add-ins and browse to locate your own add-in module if it does not appear on the list. Any functions available through an add-in will automatically appear in the function list under the set of "User Defined" functions.

By default, a user of your add-in module will be able to see the VBA code by using the Visual Basic editor. You can password-protect the code from within the VBA editor by selecting Tools|VBAProject Properties. The protection tab gives you the option to "Lock Project for Viewing," which renders the code invisible.

GLOSSARY

Absolute priority   A procedure for a firm in bankruptcy in which junior creditors are not paid unless more senior creditors have been fully re-paid.

Accreting swap   A swap where the notional amount increases over the life of the swap.

Accrued interest   The pro-rated portion of a bond's coupon since the previous coupon date.

Alpha-porting   Using a futures overlay to transfer a portfolio alpha (a measure of superior performance) from one asset class to another.

American option   An option that may be exercised at any time during its life.

Amortizing swap   A swap where the notional amount declines over the life of the swap.

Antithetic variate method   A technique used in Monte Carlo valuation, in which each random draw is used to create two simulated prices from opposite tails of the asset price distribution.

Arbitrage   A transaction generating a positive cash flow either today or in the future by simultaneously buying and selling related assets, with no net investment of funds, and with no risk.

Arithmetic Brownian motion   A continuous stochastic process, $x(t)$, in which the increments are given as $dx(t) = \alpha\, dt + \sigma\, dZ$, where dZ is the increment to a Brownian process.

Asian option   An option in which the payoff at maturity depends upon an average of the asset prices over the life of the option.

Asian tail   A reference price that is computed as an average of recent prices. For example, an equity-linked note may have a payoff based on the average daily stock price over the last 20 days (the Asian tail).

Ask price   The price at which a dealer or market-maker offers to sell a security. Also called the *offer price*.

Asset swap   A swap, typically involving a bond, in which fixed bond payments are swapped for payments based on a floating rate.

Asset-or-nothing call   An option that pays a unit of the asset if the asset price exceeds the strike price at expiration or zero otherwise.

Asset-or-nothing option   An option that pays a unit of the asset if the option is in-the-money or zero otherwise.

Asset-or-nothing put   An option that pays a unit of the asset if the asset price is less than the strike price at expiration or zero otherwise.

Asymmetric butterfly spread   A butterfly spread in which the distance between strike prices is not equal.

At-the-money   An option for which the price of the underlying asset approximately equals the strike price.

Back-to-back transaction   A transaction where a dealer enters into offsetting transactions with different parties, effectively serving as a go-between.

Backward equation   See *Kolmogorov backward equation*.

Backwardation   A forward curve in which the futures prices are falling with time to expiration.

Barrier option   An option that has a payoff depending upon whether, at some point during the life of the option, the price of the underlying asset has moved past a reference price (the barrier). Examples are knock-in and knock-out options.

Basis   The difference between the cash price of the underlying asset and the futures price.

Basis point $1/100^{\text{th}}$ of 1%, i.e., one ten-thousandth (0.0001).

Basis risk   The possibility of unexpected changes in the difference between the price of an asset and the price of the contract hedging the asset.

Bear spread The sale of a call (or put) together with the purchase of an otherwise identical higher-strike call (or put).

Bermudan option An option that can only be exercised at specified times during its life.

Bid price The price at which a dealer or market-maker buys a security.

Bid-ask spread The difference between the bid price and the ask price.

Binary option An option that has a payoff that is a discrete amount—for example, $1 or one share. Also called a *digital option*.

Binomial tree A representation of possible asset price movements over time, in which the asset price is modeled as moving up or down by a given amount each period.

Black formula A version of the Black-Scholes formula in which the underlying asset is a futures price and the dividend yield is replaced with the risk-free rate. See equation (12.7) (p. 381).

Black-Scholes equation The partial differential equation, equation (21.11) (p. 682), relating price, delta, gamma, and theta, that must be satisfied by derivatives. The Black-Scholes *formula* solves the Black-Scholes *equation*.

Black-Scholes formula The formula giving the price of a European call option as a function of the stock price, strike price, time to expiration, interest rate, volatility, and dividend yield. See equation (12.1) (p. 377).

Bootstrapping This term has two meanings. First, it refers to the procedure where coupon bonds are used to generate the set of zero-coupon bond prices. Second, it means the use of historical returns to create an empirical probability distribution for returns.

Boundary condition The value of a derivative claim at a certain time, or at a particular price of the underlying asset. For example, a boundary condition for a zero-coupon bond is that the bond at maturity is worth its promised maturity value.

Box spread An option position in which the stock is synthetically purchased (buy call, sell put) at one price and sold (sell call, buy put) at a different price. When constructed with European options, the box spread is equivalent to a zero-coupon bond.

Brownian motion A stochastic process in which the random variable moves continuously and follows a random walk with normally distributed, independent increments. Named after the Scottish botanist Robert Brown, who in 1827 noticed that pollen grains suspended in water exhibited continual movement. Brownian motion is also called a *Wiener process*.

Bull spread The purchase of a call (or put) together with the sale of an otherwise identical higher-strike call (or put).

Butterfly spread A position created by buying a call, selling two calls at a higher strike price, and buying a fourth call at a still higher strike price, with an equal distance between strike prices. The butterfly spread can also be created using puts alone, or by buying a straddle and insuring it with the purchase of out-of-the-money calls and puts, or in a variety of other ways.

Calendar spread A spread position in which the bought and sold options or futures have the same underlying asset but different times to maturity.

Call option A contract giving the buyer the right, but not the obligation, to buy the underlying asset at a prespecified price.

Call protection A period during which a callable bond cannot be called.

Call schedule A contractual feature of a callable bond, specifying the price at which the company can buy the bond back from bondholders at different points in time.

Callable bond A bond where the issuer has the right to buy the bond back from bondholders by paying a prespecified amount.

Cap An options contract that serves as insurance against a high price. (See also *Interest rate cap*.)

Caplet A contract that insures a borrower against a high interest rate on a single date. A collection of caplets is an *interest rate cap*.

Capped option An option with a maximum payoff, where the option is automatically exercised if the underlying asset reaches the price at which the maximum payoff is attained.

Carry   Another term for owning an asset, typically used to refer to commodities. (See also *Carry market* and *Cost of carry*).

Carry market   A situation where the forward price is such that the return on a cash-and-carry is the risk-free rate.

Cash flow mapping   A procedure in which the cash flows of a given claim are assigned—or mapped—to a set of benchmark claims. This provides a way to approximate the claim in terms of the benchmark claims.

Cash settlement   A procedure where settlement entails a cash payment from one party to the other, instead of delivery of an asset.

Cash-and-carry   The simultaneous spot purchase and forward sale of an asset or commodity.

Cash-and-carry arbitrage   The use of a cash-and-carry to effect an arbitrage.

Cash-or-nothing call   An option that pays a fixed amount of cash if the asset price exceeds the strike price at expiration or zero otherwise.

Cash-or-nothing option   An option that pays a fixed amount of cash if the option is in-the-money or zero otherwise.

Cash-or-nothing put   An option that pays a fixed amount of cash if the asset price is less than the strike price at expiration or zero otherwise.

CDO   See *collateralized debt obligation*.

Central limit theorem   One of the most important results in statistics, which states that the sum of independent and identically distributed random variables has a limiting distribution that is normal.

Cheapest to deliver   When a futures contract gives the seller a choice of asset to deliver to the buyer, the asset that is most profitable for the short to deliver.

Cholesky decomposition   A formula used to construct a set of correlated random variables from a set of uncorrelated random variables.

Clean price   The present value of a bond's future cash flows less accrued interest.

Clearinghouse   A financial organization, typically associated with one or more exchanges, that matches the buy and sell orders that take place during the day and keeps track of the obligations and payments required of the members of the clearinghouse.

Collar   The purchase of a put and sale of a call at a higher strike price.

Collar width   The difference between the strike prices of the two options in a collar.

Collateralized debt obligation   a financial structure that consists of a pool of assets, financed by issuing financial claims that reapportion the return on the asset pool.

Collect-on-delivery option   An option where the premium is paid only when the option is exercised.

Commodity spread   Offsetting long and short positions in closely related commodities. (See also *Crack spread* and *Crush spread*.)

Compound option   An option that has an option as the underlying asset.

Concave   Shaped like the cross section of an upside-down bowl.

Constructive sale   A term in tax law describing the owner of an asset entering into an offsetting position that largely eliminates the risk of holding the asset.

Contango   A forward curve in which futures prices are rising with time to expiration.

Contingent convertible bond   A bond that becomes convertible once a contingency (for example, the share price is greater than $100 for 30 days) has occurred.

Continuation value   The value of leaving an option unexercised. You make an exercise decision by comparing the continuation value to the value of immediate exercise.

Continuously compounded interest rate   A way of quoting an interest rate such that if $1 is invested at a continuously compounded rate of r, the payoff in one year is e^r.

Control variate method   A technique used in Monte Carlo valuation in which simulated asset prices are used to compute two derivatives prices: The price of the derivative that is being valued, and the price of a related derivative for which the value is known. The error in valuing the derivative with a known price is used as a control for that with the unknown price.

Convenience yield   A nonmonetary return to ownership of an asset or commodity.

Conversion   A risk-free position consisting of an asset, a purchased put, and a written call.

Convertible bond   A bond which, at the option of the bondholder, can be surrendered for a specified number of shares of stock.

Convex   Shaped like the cross section of a bowl.

Convexity   The second derivative of a bond's price with respect to a change in the interest rate, divided by the bond price.

Cooling degree day   The greater of (i) 65 degrees Farenheit minus the average daily temperature, and (ii) zero.

Cost of carry   The interest cost of owning an asset, less lease or dividend payments received as a result of ownership; the net cash flow resulting from borrowing to buy an asset.

Covered call   A long position in an asset together with a written call on the same asset.

Covered interest arbitrage   A zero-investment strategy with simultaneous borrowing in one currency, lending in another, and entering into a forward contract to guarantee the exchange rate when the loans mature.

Covered write   A long position in an asset coupled with sale of a call option on the same asset.

Crack spread   The difference between the price of crude oil futures and that of equivalent amounts of heating oil and gasoline.

Credit derivative   A claim where the payoff depends upon the credit rating or default status of a firm.

Credit risk   Risk resulting from the possibility that a counterparty will be financially unable to meet its contractual obligations.

Credit spread   The difference between the yields on a bond that can default and on an otherwise equivalent default-free bond.

Credit-linked note   A bond that has payments determined at least in part by credit events (e.g., default) at a different firm.

Cross-hedging   The use of a derivative on one underlying asset to hedge the risk of another underlying asset.

Crush spread   The difference between the price of a quantity of soybeans and that of the soybean meal and oil that can be produced by those soybeans.

Cumulative distribution function   A function giving the probability that a value drawn from a distribution will be less than or equal to some specified value.

Cumulative normal distribution function   The cumulative distribution function for the normal distribution; $N(x)$ in the Black-Scholes equation.

Currency swap   A swap in which the parties make payments based on the difference in debt payments in different currencies.

Currency-translated index   An investment in an index denominated in a foreign currency, where the buyer bears both currency and asset risk.

Debenture   A bond for which payments are secured only by the general credit of the issuer.

Debt capacity   The maximum amount of debt that can be issued by a firm or secured by a specific asset.

Default premium   The difference between the yield on a bond and that on an otherwise equivalent default-free bond.

Default swap   A contract in which the swap buyer pays a regular premium; in exchange, if a default in a specified bond occurs, the swap seller pays the buyer the loss due to the default.

Deferred down rebate option   A deferred rebate option for which the current stock price is above the rebate barrier.

Deferred rebate option   A claim that pays $1 at expiration if the price of the underlying asset has reached a barrier prior to expiration.

Deferred swap   A swap with terms specified today, but for which swap payments begin at a later date than for an ordinary swap.

Deferred up rebate option   A deferred rebate option for which the current stock price is below the rebate barrier.

Delivery   The act of the seller (e.g., of a forward contract) supplying the underlying asset to the buyer.

Delta   The change in the price of a derivative due to a change in the price of the underlying asset.

Delta-gamma approximation   A formula using the delta and gamma to approximate the change in the derivative price due to a change in the price of the underlying asset.

Delta-gamma-theta approximation A formula using the delta, gamma, and theta to approximate the change in the derivative price due to a change in the price of the underlying asset and the passage of time.

Delta-hedging Hedging a derivative position using the underlying asset, with the amount of the underlying asset determined by the derivative's sensitivity (*delta*) to the price of the underlying asset.

Derivative A financial instrument that has a value determined by the price of something else.

Diff swap A swap in which payments are based on the difference in floating interest rates on a given notional amount denominated in a single currency.

Differential equation An equation relating a variable to its derivatives and one or more independent variables.

Diffusion process Generally, a continuous stochastic process in which uncertainty increases with time. Also used to describe the Brownian (random) part of an Itô process.

Digital option Another name for a binary option.

Dirty price The present value of a bond's future cash flows (this implicitly includes accrued interest).

Distance to default The distance between the current firm asset value and the level at which default occurs, measured in standard deviations.

Diversifiable risk Risk that is, in the limit, eliminated by combining a large number of assets in a portfolio.

Down-and-in A knock-in option for which the barrier is less than the current price of the underlying asset.

Down-and-out A knock-out option for which the barrier is less than the current price of the underlying asset.

Drift The expected change per unit time in an asset price.

Duration Generally, the weighted average life of the bond, which also provides a measure of the bond's sensitivity to interest rate changes. Two common duration measures are *modified duration* and *Macaulay duration*.

Effective annual interest rate A way of quoting an interest rate such that the quoted rate is the annual percentage increase in an amount invested at this rate. If $1 is invested at an effective annual rate of r, the payoff in one year is $1 + r$.

Elasticity The percent change in an option price for a 1% change in the price of the underlying asset.

Equity-linked forward A forward contract (e.g., for currency) where the quantity to be bought or sold depends upon the performance of a stock or stock index.

European option An option that can only be exercised at expiration.

Exchange option An option permitting the holder to obtain one asset by giving up another. Standard calls and puts are exchange options in which one of the two assets is cash.

Exercise The exchange of the strike price (or strike asset) for the underlying asset at the terms specified in the option contract.

Exercise price Under the terms of an option contract, the amount that can be exchanged for the underlying asset.

Exercise style The circumstances under which an option holder has the right to exercise an option. "European" and "American" are exercise styles.

Exotic option A derivatives contract in which an ordinary derivative has been altered to change the characteristics of the derivative in a meaningful way. Also called a *nonstandard option*.

Expectations hypothesis A term with multiple meanings, one of which is that the expected future interest rate equals the implied forward rate.

Expected Tail Loss The expected loss conditional upon the VaR loss being exceeded. Another name for Tail VaR.

Expiration The date beyond which an unexercised option is worthless.

Fair value Another name for the theoretical forward price: Spot price plus interest less the future value of dividends.

Financial engineering Creating new financial instruments by combining other derivatives, or more generally, by using derivatives pricing techniques.

Floor   An option position that guarantees a minimum price.

Forward contract   An agreement that sets today the terms—including price and quantity—at which you buy or sell an asset or commodity at a specific time in the future.

Forward curve   The set of forward or futures prices with different expiration dates on a given date for a given asset.

Forward premium   The annualized percentage difference between the forward price and the spot price.

Forward rate agreement   A forward contract for an interest rate.

Forward strip   Another name for the *forward curve*.

Funded   A position that is paid for in full at the outset. A prepaid forward, for example, is a funded position in a stock. See also *unfunded*.

Futures contract   An agreement that is similar to a forward contract except that the buyer and seller post margin and the contract is marked-to-market periodically. Futures are typically exchange-traded.

Futures overlay   Converting an investment in asset A into the economic equivalent of an investment in asset B by entering into a short futures position on asset A and a long futures position on asset B.

Gamma   The change in delta when the price of the underlying asset changes by one unit.

Gap option   An option where the option owner has the right to exercise the option at strike K_1 if the stock price exceeds (or, depending on the option, is less than) the price K_2. For an ordinary option, $K_1 = K_2$.

Geometric Brownian motion   A continuous stochastic process, $x(t)$, in which the increments are given as $dx(t)/x(t) = \alpha dt + \sigma dZ$, where dZ is the increment to a Brownian process.

Girsanov's theorem   A result that permits a change in the drift of an Itô process accompanied by a change in the probability distribution of the Brownian motion driving the process.

Greeks   A term generally referring to delta, gamma, vega, theta, and rho, all of which measure the change in the price of a derivative when there is a change in an input to the pricing formula.

Haircut   The collateral, over and above the market value of the security, required by the lender when a security is borrowed.

Heat rate   A measure of the efficiency with which heat can be used to produce electricity. Specifically, it is the number of British Thermal Units required to produce 1 kilowatt/hour of electricity.

Heating degree day   The greater of (i) the average daily temperature minus 65 degree Farenheit, and (ii) zero.

Hedge ratio   In a hedging transaction, the ratio of the quantity of the forward or futures position to the quantity of the underlying asset.

Hedging   An action—such as entering into a derivatives position—that reduces the risk of loss.

Heston model   An option pricing model in which the instantaneous variance of the stock return follows a mean-reverting square root process.

Heteroskedasticity   Data that is characterized by variances that are not equal, either over time or across different observations at a point in time.

Historical volatility   The standard deviation of the continuously compounded return on an asset, measured using historical prices.

Homoskedasticity   Data that is characterized by variances that are equal over time or across different observations at a point in time.

Hysteresis   The failure of an effect to reverse itself as the underlying cause is reversed.

Implied forward rate   The forward interest rate between time t_1 and time t_2 ($t_1 < t_2$) that makes an investor indifferent between, on the one hand, buying a bond maturing at t_2, and, on the other hand, buying a bond maturing at t_1 and reinvesting the proceeds at this forward interest rate.

Implied repo rate   The rate of return on a cash-and-carry.

Implied volatility   The volatility for which the theoretical option price (typically computed using the Black-Scholes formula) equals the observed market price of the option.

Interest rate cap A contract that periodically pays the difference between the market interest rate and a guaranteed rate, if the difference is positive.

In-the-money An option that would have value if exercised. For an in-the-money call, the stock price exceeds the strike price. For an in-the-money put, the stock price is less than the strike price.

Investment trigger price The price of an investment project (or the price of the good to be produced) at which it is optimal to invest in the project.

Itô process A continuous stochastic process that can be written in the form $dX(t) = \alpha[X(t), t]\,dt + \sigma[X(t), t]\,dZ(t)$, where $dZ(t)$ is the increment to a Brownian process.

Itô's Lemma If x follows an Itô process, Itô's Lemma describes the process followed by $f(x)$. For example, if x is a stock price and $f(x)$ an option price, Itô's Lemma characterizes the behavior of the option price in terms of the process for the stock.

Jensen's inequality If x is a random variable and $f(x)$ is convex, Jensen's inequality states that $E[f(x)] \geq f[E(x)]$. The inequality is reversed if $f(x)$ is concave.

Jump-diffusion model A process for an asset price in which the asset most of the time follows an Itô process but can also jump discretely, with occurrence of the jump controlled by a Poisson process.

Kappa Another name for *vega*.

Knock-in option An option in which there can only be a final payoff if, during a specified period of time, the price of the underlying asset has reached a specified level.

Knock-out option An option in which there can only be a final payoff if, during a specified period of time, the price of the underlying asset has *not* reached a specified level.

Kolmogorov backward equation A partial differential equation, (see equation (21.32) (p. 691), that is related to the Black-Scholes equation and that is satisfied by probability distributions for the underlying asset.

Kurtosis A measure of the peakedness of a probability distribution. For a random variable x with mean μ and standard deviation σ, kurtosis is the fourth central moment divided by the squared variance, $E(x - \mu)^4/\sigma^4$. For a normal random variable, kurtosis is 3.

Ladder option If the barrier $L > K$ is reached over the life of the option, a ladder option at expiration pays $\max(0, L - K, S_T - K)$. If the barrier is not reached, the option pays $\max(0, S_T - K)$.

Lambda Another name for *vega*.

Lattice A binomial tree in which an up move followed by a down move leads to the same price as a down move followed by an up move. Also called a *recombining tree*.

Law of one price The assertion that two portfolios generating exactly the same return must have the same price.

Lease rate The annualized payment required to borrow an asset, or equivalently, the annualized payment received in exchange for lending an asset.

Leverage effect A rise in the stock price volatility when the stock price declines.

LIBID London Interbank Bid Rate. See *LIBOR*.

LIBOR London Interbank Offer Rate. A measure of the borrowing rate for large international banks. The British Banker's Association determines LIBOR daily for different currencies by surveying at least 8 banks, asking at what rate they could borrow, dropping the top and bottom quartiles of the responses, and computing an arithmetic average of the remaining quotes. Since LIBOR is an average, there may be no actual transactions at that rate. Confusingly, LIBOR is also sometimes referred to as a lending rate. This is because a bank serving as a market-maker in the interbank market will offer to lend money at a high interest rate (LIBOR) and borrow money at a low interest rate (LIBID). (The difference between LIBOR and LIBID is the bid-ask spread in the interbank market.) A bank needing to borrow will thus pay LIBOR, and a bank with excess funds will receive LIBID.

Log contract A derivative contract that, at maturity, pays the natural log of an asset price.

Lognormal distribution A probability distribution in which the natural logarithm of the random variable is normally distributed.

Long A position is long with respect to a price if the position profits from an increase in that price. An owner of a stock profits from an increase in the stock price and, hence, is long the stock. An owner of an option profits from an increase in volatility and, hence, is long volatility.

Long forward The party to a forward contract who has an obligation to buy the underlying asset.

Lookback call See *Lookback option.*

Lookback option An option that, at maturity, pays off based on the maximum ($\overline{S}_T$) or minimum ($\underline{S}_T$) stock price over the life of the option. A *lookback call* has the payoff $S_T - \underline{S}_T$ and a *lookback put* has the payoff $\overline{S}_T - S_T$.

Lookback put See *Lookback option.*

Macaulay duration The percent change in a bond's price for a given percent change in one plus the bond's yield. This calculation can be interpreted as the weighted average life of the bond, with the weights being the percentage of the bond's value due to each payment.

Maintenance margin The level of margin at which the contract holder is required to add cash or securities to the margin account.

Mandatorily convertible bond A bond that makes payments in shares instead of cash, with the number of shares paid to the bondholder typically dependent upon the share price.

Margin A deposit required for both buyers and sellers of a futures contract, which indemnifies the counterparty against the failure of the buyer or seller to meet the obligations of the contract.

Margin call The requirement that the owner of a margined position add funds to the margin account. This can result from a loss on the position or an increase in the margin requirement.

Market corner Owning a large percentage of the available supply of an asset or commodity that is required for delivery under the terms of a derivatives contract.

Market-maker A trader in an asset, commodity, or derivative who simultaneously offers to buy at one price (the bid price) or to sell at a higher price (the offer price), thereby "making a market."

Market-timing The allocation of assets between stocks and bonds in an attempt to invest in whichever asset is going to have a higher return.

Mark-to-market The procedure of revaluing a portfolio or position to reflect current market prices.

Martingale A stochastic process for which $E[X(t+s)|\Phi(t)] = X(t)$, where $\Phi(t)$ is information available at time t.

Modified duration The percent change in a bond's price for a unit change in the yield. Modified duration is also Macaulay duration divided by one plus the bond's yield per payment period.

Monte Carlo valuation A procedure for pricing derivative claims by discounting expected payoffs, where the expected payoff is computed using simulated prices for the underlying asset.

Naked writing Selling options without an offsetting position in the underlying asset.

Net payoff Another term for *profit.*

Non-traded asset A cash flow stream that cannot be purchased directly in financial market. Many corporate investment projects are non-traded because they can only be acquired by buying the entire company.

Nondiversifiable risk Risk that remains after a large number of assets are combined in a portfolio.

Nonrecombining tree A binomial tree describing asset price moves in which an up move followed by a down move yields a different price than a down move followed by an up move.

Nonstandard option See *Exotic option.*

Normal distribution A bell-shaped, symmetric, continuous probability distribution that assigns positive probability to all values from $-\infty$ to $+\infty$. Sometimes called the "bell curve." (See also *Central limit theorem.*)

Notional amount The dollar amount used as a scale factor in calculating payments for a forward contract, futures contract, or swap.

Notional principal The notional amount for an interest rate swap.

Numeraire The units in which a payoff is denominated.

Offer price   The same as the *ask price*.

Off-market forward   A forward contract in which the forward price is set so that the value of the contract is not zero.

Off-the-run   A government bond that is not one of the recently issued bonds.

On-the-run   The most recently auctioned government bonds at the government's specific auction maturities.

Open interest   The quantity of a derivatives contract that is outstanding at a point in time. (One long and one short position count as one unit outstanding.)

Open outcry   A system of trading in which buyers and sellers in one physical location convey offers to buy and sell by gesturing and shouting.

Option elasticity   The percent change in an option price for a 1% change in the price of the underlying asset.

Option overwriting   Selling a call option against a long position in the underlying asset.

Option writer   The party with a short position in the option.

Order statistics   The n draws of a random variable sorted in ascending order.

Out-of-the-money   An option that would be exercised at a loss. An out-of-the-money call has the stock price less than the strike price. An out-of-the-money put has the stock price greater than the strike price.

Outperformance option   An option in which the payoff is determined by the extent to which one asset price is greater than another asset price.

Over-the-counter market   A term used generally to refer to transactions (e.g., purchases and sales of securities or derivatives contracts) that occur without the involvement of a regulated exchange.

Par bond   A bond for which the price at issue equals the maturity value.

Par coupon   The coupon rate on a par bond.

Partial expectation   The sum (or integral) of a set of outcomes times the probability of those outcomes.

Path-dependent   A derivative where the final payoff depends upon the path taken by the stock price, instead of just the final stock price.

Payer swaption   A swaption giving the holder the right to be the fixed-rate payer in a swap.

Paylater strategy   Generally used to refer to option strategies in which the position buyer makes no payments unless the option moves more into the money.

Payoff   The value of a position at a point in time. The term often implicitly refers to a payoff at expiration or maturity.

Payoff diagram   A graph in which the value of a derivative or other claim at a point in time is plotted against the price of the underlying asset.

Payout protected   A characteristic of a derivative where a change in the dividend payout on the underlying asset does not change the value of the derivative.

Perpetual option   An option that never expires.

Poisson distribution   A probability distribution that counts the number of events occurring in an interval of time, assuming that the occurrence of events is independent.

Positive-definite   An $n \times n$ matrix with elements $a_{i,j}$ is positive-definite if, for every $\omega_i \neq 0$, $i = 1, \ldots, n$, $\sum_{i=1}^{n} \sum_{j=1}^{n} \omega_i \omega_j a_{i,j} > 0$. A covariance matrix is positive-definite.

Power option   An option where the payoff is based on the price of an asset raised to a power.

Prepaid forward contract   A contract calling for payment today and delivery of the asset or commodity at a time in the future.

Prepaid forward price   The price the buyer pays today for a prepaid forward contract.

Prepaid swap   A contract calling for payment today and delivery of the asset or commodity at multiple specified times in the future.

Price limit   In futures markets, the size of a futures price move such that trading is halted temporarily.

Price participation   The extent to which an equity-linked note benefits from an increase in the price of the stock or index to which it is linked.

Price value of a basis point   The change in a bond price due to a 1-basis-point change in the yield of the bond. Frequently abbreviated PVBP.

Profit   The payoff less the future value of the original cost to acquire the position.

Profit diagram   A graph plotting the *profit* on a position against a range of prices for the underlying asset.

Proprietary trading　Taking positions in an asset or derivative to express a view—for example, that a stock price will rise or that implied volatility will fall.

Psi　The change in the price of a derivative due to a change in the dividend yield.

Purchased call　A long position in a call.

Purchased put　A long position in a put.

Put option　A contract giving the buyer the right, but not the obligation, to sell the underlying asset at a prespecified price.

Put-call parity　A relationship stating that the difference between the premiums of a call and a put with the same strike price and time to expiration equals the difference between the present value of the forward price and the present value of the strike price.

Puttable bond　A bond that the investor can sell back to the issuer at a predetermined price schedule.

Quadratic variation　The sum of squared increments to a Brownian motion.

Quantile　A data point is the xth quantile if $x\%$ of the data lies below that point.

Quanto　A derivatives contract with a payoff in which foreign-currency-denominated quantities are treated as if they were denominated in the domestic currency.

Quasi-arbitrage　The replacement of one asset or position with another that has equivalent risk and a higher expected rate of return.

Rainbow option　An option that has a payoff based on the maximum or minimum of two (or more) risky assets and cash. For example, the payoff to a rainbow call is $\max(S_T, Q_T, K)$, where S_T and Q_T are risky asset prices.

Random walk　A stochastic process, $X(t)$, in which increments, $\epsilon(t)$, are independent and identically distributed: $X(t) = X(t - h) + \epsilon(t)$.

Ratings transition　A change in the credit rating of a bond from one value to another.

Ratio spread　Buying m of an option at one strike and selling n of an otherwise identical option at a different strike.

Real options　The applications of derivatives theory to the operation and valuation of real (physical) investment projects.

Realized quadratic variation　The sum of squared continuously compounded asset returns, typically measured at a high frequency.

Realized volatility　Another term for realized quadratic variation.

Rebate option　A claim that pays \$1 at the time the price of the underlying asset reaches a barrier.

Receiver swaption　A swaption giving the holder the right to receive the fixed rate in a swap.

Recombining tree　A binomial tree describing asset price moves in which an up move followed by a down move yields the same price as a down move followed by an up move. Also called a *lattice*.

Recovery rate　The percentage of par value received by a bond holder in a bankruptcy.

Reference price　A market price or rate used to determine the payoff on a derivatives contract.

Repo　Another name for a *repurchase agreement*.

Repo rate　The annualized percentage difference between the original sale price and final repurchase price in a repurchase agreement.

Repricing　The replacement of an out-of-the-money compensation option with an at-the-money compensation option.

Repurchase agreement　The sale of a security coupled with an agreement to buy it back at a later date.

Reverse cash-and-carry　The simultaneous short-sale and forward purchase of an asset or commodity.

Reverse conversion　A short position in an asset coupled with a purchased call and written put, both with the same strike price and time to expiration. The position is equivalent to a short bond.

Reverse repo　Another name for *reverse repurchase agreement*.

Reverse repurchase agreement　The purchase of a security coupled with an agreement to sell it at a later date. The opposite of a repurchase agreement.

Rho　The change in value of a derivative due to a change in the interest rate.

Risk averse　A term describing an investor who prefers x to taking a risky bet with an expected value equal to x.

Risk management The active use of derivatives and other techniques to alter risk and protect profitability.

Risk neutral A term describing an investor who is indifferent between receiving x and taking a risky bet with an expected value equal to x.

Risk premium The difference between the expected return on an asset and the risk-free rate; the expected return differential that compensates investors for risk.

Risk-neutral measure The probability distribution for an asset transformed so that the expected return on the asset is the risk-free rate.

Risk-neutral probability In the binomial model, the probability of an up move in the asset price such that the expected return on the asset is the risk-free rate.

Self-financing portfolio A portfolio that retains specified characteristics (e.g., it is zero-investment and risk-free) without the need for additional investments in the portfolio.

Settlement The time in a transaction at which all obligations of both the buyer and the seller are fulfilled.

Share-equivalent The position in shares that has equivalent dollar risk to a derivative. (See also *Delta*.)

Sharpe ratio For an asset, the ratio of the risk premium to the return standard deviation.

Short A position is short with respect to a price if the position profits from a decrease in that price. A short-seller of a stock profits from a decrease in the stock price and, hence, is short the stock. A seller of an option profits from a decrease in volatility and, hence, is short volatility.

Short call A call that has been sold.

Short forward The party to a forward contract who has an obligation to sell the underlying asset.

Short put A put that has been sold.

Short rebate The rate of return paid on collateral when shares are borrowed.

Short-against-the-box The short-sale of a stock that the short-seller owns. The result of a short-against-the-box is that the short-seller has both a long and short position and, hence, bears no risk from the stock yet receives the value of the shares from the short sale.

Short-sale A transaction in which an investor borrows a security, sells it, and then returns it at a later date to the lender. If the security makes payments, the short-seller must make the same payments to the lender.

Shout option A shout call option expiring at time T has the payoff $\max(0, S_{\hat{t}} - K, S_T - K)$, where $\hat{t}$ is the time and $S_{\hat{t}}$ is the price at which the option holder "shouted," thereby guaranteeing an expiration payoff at least as great as $S_{\hat{t}} - K$.

Skewness A measure of the symmetry of a probability distribution. For a random variable x with mean μ and standard deviation σ, skewness is the third central moment divided by the cubed standard deviation, $E(x - \mu)^3/\sigma^3$. For a normal variable, skewness is 0. (See also *Volatility skew*.)

Spark spread The difference between the price of electricity and that of the quantity of natural gas required to produce the electricity.

Spot curve The set of zero-coupon bond prices with different maturities, usually inferred from government bond prices.

Spot price The current market price of an asset.

Spread Simultaneously buying and selling closely related derivatives. A spread in options is a position in which some options are bought and some are sold, and all options in the position are calls or all are puts. (See also *Calendar spread* and *Commodity spread*.)

Spread option An option with a payoff where a spread (the difference between prices) takes the place the of the underlying asset.

Stable distribution A probability distribution for which sums of random variables have the same distribution as the original random variable. The normal distribution is stable because sums of normally distributed random variables are normally distributed.

Stack and roll A hedging strategy in which an existing stack hedge with maturing futures contracts is replaced by a new stack hedge with longer dated futures contracts.

Stack hedge Hedging a stream of obligations by entering futures contracts with a *single* maturity, with the number of contracts selected so that changes in the *present value* of the future obligations are offset by changes in the value of this "stack" of futures contracts.

Static NPV   The net present value of a project at a point in time, ignoring the possibility of postponing adoption of the project.

Static option replication   The use of options to hedge options, with the goal of creating a hedging portfolio that has a delta that naturally moves in tandem with the delta of the option being hedged.

Stochastic differential equation   An equation characterizing the change in a variable in which one or more of the differential terms are increments to a stochastic process.

Stochastic process   A mathematical model for a random process as a function of time

Stochastic volatility   A process in which the instantaneous volatility can vary randomly, either as a function of the stock price or other variables.

Stock index   An average of the prices of a group of stocks. A stock index can be a simple average of stock prices, in which case it is *equally weighted*, or it can be a weighted average, with the weights proportional to market capitalization, in which case it is *value-weighted*.

Straddle   The purchase of a call and a put with the same strike price and time to expiration.

Straddle rules   Tax regulations controlling the circumstances in which a loss on a claim can be realized when a taxpayer continues to own related securities or derivatives.

Strangle   The purchase of a put and a higher-strike call with the same time to expiration.

Stratified sampling   A technique used in Monte Carlo valuation in which random numbers are drawn from each percentile (or other regular interval) of the distribution.

Strike price   Another term for *exercise price*.

Strip hedge   Hedging a stream of obligations by offsetting each individual obligation with a futures contract matching the maturity and quantity of the obligation.

STRIPS   Acronym for *Separate Trading of Registered Interest and Principal of Securities*. STRIPS are the interest and principal payments from Treasury bonds and notes traded as individual securities.

Structured note   A bond that makes payments that, at least in part, are contingent on some variable such as a stock price, interest rates, or exchange rates.

Supershare   A claim to a portfolio that pays the holder a portion of the portfolio only if a particular event occurs. (An example of an event would be the asset losing between 25% and 26% of its value.)

Swap   A contract calling for the exchange of payments over time. Often one payment is fixed in advance and the other is floating, based upon the realization of a price or interest rate.

Swap spread   The difference between the fixed rate on an interest rate swap and the yield on a Treasury bond with the same maturity.

Swap tenor   The lifetime of a swap.

Swap term   Another name for *swap tenor*.

Swaption   An option to enter into a swap.

Tail VaR   The expected loss conditional upon the VaR loss being exceeded.

Tailing   A reduction in the quantity of an asset held in order to offset future income received by the asset.

Tenor   Time to maturity or expiration of a contract, frequently used when referring to swaps.

Term repo   A repurchase agreement lasting for a specified period of time longer than one day.

Theta   The change in the value of a derivative due solely to the passage of time.

Time decay   Another term for *theta*.

Total return swap   A swap in which one party pays the total return (dividends plus capital gains) on a reference asset, and the other party pays a floating rate such as LIBOR.

Traded present value   The value an investment project would have once the investment was made; also called *twin security*.

Twin security   See *Traded present value*.

Underlying asset   The asset whose price determines the profitability of a derivative. For example, the underlying asset for a purchased call is the asset that the call owner can buy by paying the strike price.

Unfunded   A position that is not paid for at the outset, and for which cash inflows and outflows can later occur. A forward contract, for example, is an unfunded position in a stock. See also *funded*.

Up-and-in   A knock-in option for which the barrier exceeds the current price of the underlying asset.

Up-and-out   A knock-out option for which the barrier exceeds the current price of the underlying asset.

Value at risk   The level of loss that will be exceeded a given percentage of the time over a given horizon.

Vanilla   A standard option or other derivative. For example, ordinary puts and calls are "vanilla" options.

Variance swap   A forward contract that settles based on cumulative squared asset returns.

Vega   The change in the price of a derivative due to a change in volatility. Also sometimes called *kappa* or *lambda*.

Vertical spread   The sale of an option at one strike and purchase of an option of the same type (call or put) at a different strike, both having the same underlying asset and time to expiration.

Volatility   The standard deviation of the continuously compounded return on an asset.

Volatility clustering   The tendency of high volatility days to be followed by high volatility days.

Volatility skew   Generally, implied volatility as a function of the strike price. Volatility skew refers to a difference in premiums as reflected in differences in implied volatility. Skew is sometimes used more precisely to refer to a difference in implied volatilities between in-the-money and out-of-the-money options.

Volatility smile   A volatility skew in which both in-the-money and out-of-the-money options have a higher volatility than at-the-money options (i.e., when you plot implied volatility against the strike price, the curve looks like a smile).

Volatility surface   A three-dimensional graph in which volatility is plotted against strike price and time to maturity.

Volatility swap   A forward contract that settles based on some measure of the standard deviation of returns on an asset.

Warrant   An option issued by a firm with its own stock as the underlying asset. This term also refers more generally to an option issued in fixed supply.

Weather derivative   A derivative contract with a payment based on a weather-related measurement, such as heating or cooling degree days.

Wiener process   See *Brownian motion*.

Written call   A call that has been sold; a short call.

Written put   A put that has been sold; a short put.

Written straddle   The simultaneous sale of a call and sale of a put, with the same strike price and time to expiration.

Yield curve   The set of yields to maturity for bonds with different times to maturity.

Yield to maturity   The single discount factor for which the present value of a bond's payments is equal to the observed bond price.

Zero-cost collar   The purchase of a put and sale of a call where the strikes are chosen so that the premiums of the two options are the same.

Zero-coupon bond   A bond that makes only a single payment, at maturity.

Zero-coupon yield curve   The set of yields to maturity for zero-coupon bonds with different times to maturity.

BIBLIOGRAPHY

Acerbi, C., 2002, "Spectral Measures of Risk: A Coherent Repreentation of Subjective Risk Aversion," *Journal of Banking and Finance*, 26(7), 1505–1518.

Acerbi, C. and Tasche, D., 2002, "On the Coherence of Expected Shortfall," *Journal of Banking and Finance*, 26(7), 1487–1503.

Acharya, V. V., John, K., and Sundaram, R. K., 2000, "On the Optimality of Resetting Executive Stock Options," *Journal of Financial Economics*, 57(1), 65–101.

Alexander, C., 2001, *Market Models*, Wiley, Chichester, England.

Allayannis, G., Brown, G., and Klapper, L. F., 2003, "Capital Structure and Financial Risk: Evidence from Foreign Debt Use in East Asia," *Journal of Finance*, 58, 2667–2709.

Allayannis, G., Lel, U., and Miller, D., 2004, "Corporate Governance and the Hedging Premium Around the World," Working Paper, Darden School, University of Virginia.

Allayannis, G. and Weston, J., 2001, "The Use of Foreign Currency Derivatives and Firm Market Value," *Review of Financial Studies*, 14(1), 243–276.

Andersen, T., Benzoni, L., and Lund, J., 2002, "An Empirical Investigation of Continuous-Time Equity Return Models," *Journal of Finance*, 57(3), 1239–1284, forthcoming.

Andersen, T. G., Bollerslev, T., Diebold, F. X., , and Labysd, P., 2003, "Modeling and Forecasting Realized Volatility," *Econometrica*, 71(2), 579–625.

Andersen, T. G., Bollerslev, T., Frederiksen, P. H., and Nielsen, M., 2005, "Jumps in Financial Markets," Unpublished, Kellogg School, Northwestern University.

Anderson, R. and Sundaresan, S., 2000, "A Comparative Study of Structural Models of Corporate Bond Yields: An Exploratory Investigation," *Journal of Banking and Finance*, 24(1-2), 255–269.

Arnason, S. T. and Jagannathan, R., 1994, "Evaluating Executive Stock Options Using the Binomial Option Pricing Model," Working Paper, Carlson School of Management, University of Minnesota.

Artzner, P., Delbaen, F., Eber, J.-M., and Heath, D., 1999, "Coherent Measures of Risk," *Mathematical Finance*, 9(3), 203–228.

Arzac, E. R., 1997, "PERCs, DECs, and Other Mandatory Convertibles," *Journal of Applied Corporate Finance*, 10(1), 54–63.

Asquith, P., 1995, "Convertible Bonds Are Not Called Late," *Journal of Finance*, 50(4), 1275–89.

Bakshi, G., Cao, C., and Chen, Z., 1997, "Empirical Performance of Alternative Option Pricing Models," *Journal of Finance*, 52(5), 2003–49.

Bakshi, G. and Kapadia, N., 2003, "Volatility risk Premium Embedded in Individual Options: Some New Insights," *Journal of Derivatives*, pp. 45–54.

Bartram, S. M., Brown, G. W., and Fehle, F. R., 2004, "International Evidence on Financial Derivatives Use," Working Paper, University of North Carolina.

Basel Committee on Banking Supervision, 1996, *Amendment to the Capital Accord to Incorporate Market Risks*, Technical report, Bank for International Settlements.

Bates, D. S., 2000, "Post-'87 Crash Fears the S&P 500 Futures Option Market," *Journal of Econometrics*, 94, 181–238.

Bates, D. S., 2003, "Empirical Option Pricing: A Retrospection," *Journal of Econometrics*, 116(1–2), 387–404.

Baubonis, C., Gastineau, G., and Purcell, D., 1993, "The Banker's Guide to Equity-Linked Certificates of Deposit," *Journal of Derivatives*, 1(2), 87–95.

Baxter, M. and Rennie, A., 1996, *Financial Calculus: An Introduction to Derivative Pricing*, Cambridge University Press, Cambridge, England.

Benzoni, L., 2001, "Pricing Options under Stochastic Volatility: An Empirical Investigation," Unpublished, University of Minnesota.

Bernstein, P. L., 1992, *Capital Ideas: The Improbable Origins of Modern Wall Street*, Free Press, New York.

Bernstein, P. L., 1996, *Against the Gods: The Remarkable Story of Risk*, John Wiley & Sons, New York.

Bettis, J. C., Bizjak, J. M., and Lemmon, M. L., 2001, "Managerial Ownership, Incentive Contracting, and the Use of Zero-Cost Collars and Equity Swaps by Corporate Insiders," *Journal of Financial and Quantitative Analysis*, 36(3), 345–370.

Bharath, S. T. and Shumway, T., 2004, "Forecasting Default with the KMV-Merton Model," Working Paper, University of Michigan.

Black, F., 1976a, "The Pricing of Commodity Contracts," *Journal of Financial Economics*, 3(1/2), 167–179.

Black, F., 1976b, "Studies of Stock Price Volatility Changes," *Proceedings of the 1976 Meetings of the American Statistical Association, Business and Economics Statistics Section*, pp. 177–181.

Black, F., 1989, "How We Came Up With the Option Pricing Formula," *Journal of Portfolio Management*, 15(2), 4–8.

Black, F. and Cox, J., 1976, "Valuing Corporate Securities: Some Effects of Bond Indenture Provisions," *Journal of Finance*, 31, 351–367.

Black, F., Derman, E., and Toy, W., 1990, "A One-Factor Model of Interest Rates and Its Application to Treasury Bond Options," *Financial Analysts Journal*, 46(1), 33–39.

Black, F. and Scholes, M., 1973, "The Pricing of Options and Corporate Liabilities," *Journal of Political Economy*, 81, 637–659.

Bliss, R. R., 1997, "Movements in the Term Structure of Interest Rates," *Federal Reserve Bank of Atlanta Economic Review*, 82(4), 16–33.

Bodie, Z., 1995, "On the Risk of Stocks in the Long Run," *Financial Analysts Journal*, 51(3), 18–22.

Bodie, Z. and Crane, D., 1999, "The Design and Production of New Retirement Savings Products," *Journal of Portfolio Management*, 25(2), 77–82.

Bodie, Z., Kaplan, R. S., and Merton, R. C., 2003, "For the Last Time: Stock Options Are an Expense," *Harvard Business Review*, pp. 3–11.

Bodie, Z. and Rosansky, V. I., 1980, "Risk and Return in Commodity Futures," *Financial Analysts Journal*, pp. 3–14.

Bodnar, G. M., Hayt, G. S., and Marston, R. C., 1998, "1998 Wharton Survey of Financial Risk Management by US Non-Financial Firms," *Financial Management*, 27(4), 70–91.

Bollerslev, T., 1986, "Generalized Autoregressive Conditional Heteroskedasticity," *Journal of Econometrics*.

Bollerslev, T., 1987, "A Conditional Heteroskedastic Time Series Model for Speculative Prices and Rates of Return," *Review of Economics and Statistics*, 69, 542–547.

Bollerslev, T., Engle, R. F., and Nelson, D. B., 1994, "ARCH Models," in R. F. Engle and D. L. McFadden, (eds.) "Handbook of Econometrics," volume 4 of *Handbooks in Economics*, chapter 49, pp. 2959–3038, Elsevier Science, B.V., Amsterdam.

Boyle, P. P., 1977, "Options: A Monte Carlo Approach," *Journal of Financial Economics*, 4(3), 323–338.

Boyle, P. P., Broadie, M., and Glasserman, P., 1997, "Monte Carlo Methods for Security Pricing," *Journal of Economic Dynamics and Control*, 21(8–9), 1267–1322.

Boyle, P. P. and Emanuel, D., 1980, "Discretely Adjusted Option Hedges," *Journal of Financial Economics*, 8(3), 259–282.

Boyle, P. P., Evnine, J., and Gibbs, S., 1989, "Numerical Evaluation of Multivariate Contingent Claims," *Review of Financial Studies*, 2(2), 241–250.

Brace, A., Gatarek, D., and Musiela, M., 1997, "The Market Model of Interest Rate Dynamics," *Mathematical Finance*, 7, 127–154.

Brealey, R. and Myers, S., 2003, *Principles of Corporate Finance*, Irwin McGraw-Hill, Burr Ridge, IL, 6th edition.

Brennan, M. and Schwartz, E., 1985, "Evaluating Natural Resource Investments," *Journal of Business*, 58, 135–157.

Brennan, M. J., 1991, "The Price of Convenience and the Evaluation of Commodity Contingent Claims," in D. Lund and B. Øksendal, (eds.) "Stochastic Models and Option Values: Applications to Resources, Environment and Investment Problems," Contributions to Economic Analysis, pp. 33–71, North-Holland, Amsterdam.

Brennan, M. J., 2000, "Real Options: Development and New Contributions," in Brennan and Trigeorgis (2000), chapter 1, pp. 1–10.

Brennan, M. J. and Schwartz, E. S., 1977, "Convertible Bonds: Valuation and Optimal Strategies for Call and Conversion," *Journal of Finance*, 32(5), 1699–1715.

Brennan, M. J. and Schwartz, E. S., 1990, "Arbitrage in Stock Index Futures," *Journal of Business*, 63(1), S7–31.

Brennan, M. J. and Trigeorgis, L., (eds.) 2000, *Project Flexibility, Agency, and Competition: New Developments in the Theory and Application of Real Options*, Oxford University Press, London.

Brys, E. and Bellala, M., 1998, *Options, Futures and Exotic Derivatives: Theory, Application and Practice*, Wiley Frontiers in Finance, John Wiley & Sons, Chichester, England.

Broadie, M., Chernov, M., and Johannes, M., 2004, "Model Specification and Risk Premiums: the Evidence from the Futures Options," Working Paper, Columbia University.

Broadie, M. and Detemple, J., 1996, "American Option Valuation: New Bounds, Approximations, and a Comparison of Existing Methods," *Review of Financial Studies*, 9(4), 1211–1250.

Broadie, M. and Glasserman, P., 1997, "Pricing American Style Securities by Simulation," *Journal of Economic Dynamics and Control*, 21, 1323–1352.

Broadie, M., Glasserman, P., and Kou, S. G., 1997, "A Continuity Correction for Discrete Barrier Options," *Mathematical Finance*, 7(4), 325–349.

Brown, G. W., 2001, "Managing Foreign Exchange Risk With Derivatives," *Journal of Financial Economics*, 60(2–3), 401–448.

Brown, G. W., Crabb, P. R., and Haushalter, D., 2003, "Are Firms Successful at Selectively Hedging?" Working Paper, University of North Carolina.

Bulow, J. and Shoven, J. B., 2004, "Accounting for Options," Working Paper, Stanford University, March 2004.

Burghardt, G. and Hoskins, W., 1995, "The Convexity Bias in Eurodollar Futures," *Risk*, 8(3), 63–70.

Campbell, J. Y., Lo, A. W., and MacKinlay, A. C., 1997, *The Econometrics of Financial Markets*, Princeton University Press, Princeton, NJ.

Carr, P. and Madan, D., 1998, "Towards a Theory of Volatility Trading," in R. Jarrow, (ed.) "Volatility," pp. 417–427, Risk Publications.

Carr, P. and Wu, L., 2003, "What Type of Process Underlies Options? A Simple Robust Test," *Journal of Finance*, 58(6), 2581–2610.

Casella, G. and Berger, R. L., 2002, *Statistical Inference*, Duxbury, Pacific Grove, CA, 2nd edition.

Chance, D. M., Kumar, R., and Todd, R. B., 2000, "The 'Repricing' of Executive Stock Options," *Journal of Financial Economics*, 57(1), 129–154.

Chicago Board of Trade, 1998, *Commodity Trading Manual*, Chicago Board of Trade.

Chicago Board Options Exchange, 2003, *VIX: CBOE Volatility Index*, Technical report, Chicago Board Options Exchange.

Christie, A. A., 1982, "The Stochastic Behavior of Common Stock Variances," *Journal of Financial Economics*, 10(4), 407–432.

Cochrane, J. H., 2001, *Asset Pricing*, Princeton University Press, Princeton, NJ.

Collin-Dufresne, P. and Solnik, B., 2001, "On the Term Structure of Default Premia in the Swap and LIBOR Markets," *Journal of Finance*, 56(3), 1095–1115.

Constantinides, G. M., 1978, "Market Risk Adjustment in Project Valuation," *Journal of Finance*, 33(2), 603–616.

Constantinides, G. M., 1984, "Warrant Exercise and Bond Conversion in Competitive Markets," *Journal of Financial Economics*, 13(3), 371–397.

Cooper, L., 2000, "Caution Reigns," *Risk*, 13(6), 12–14, south Africa Special Report.

Core, J. E. and Guay, W. R., 2001, "Stock Option Plans for Non-Executive Employees," *Journal of Financial Economics*, 61(2), 253–287.

Cornell, B. and French, K. R., 1983, "Taxes and the Pricing of Stock Index Futures," *Journal of Finance*, 38(3), 675–694.

Cornell, B. and Shapiro, A. C., 1989, "The Mispricing of US Treasury Bonds: A Case Study," *Review of Financial Studies*, 2(3), 297–310.

Cossin, D. and Pirotte, H., 2001, *Advanced Credit Risk Analysis*, Wiley, Chichester, UK.

Coval, J. D. and Shumway, T., 2001, "Expected Option Returns," *Journal of Finance*, 56(3), 983–1009.

Cox, D. and Miller, H. D., 1965, *The Theory of Stochastic Processes*, Chapman and Hall, London.

Cox, J. C., 1975, "Notes on Option Pricing I: Constant Elasticity of Variance Diffusions," Working Paper, Stanford University (reprinted in *Journal of Portfolio Management* 1996, 22, 15–17).

Cox, J. C., 1996, "The Constant Elasticity of Variance Option Pricing Model," *Journal of Portfolio Management*, (22), 15–17.

Cox, J. C., Ingersoll, J. E., Jr., and Ross, S. A., 1981, "The Relation Between Forward Prices and Futures Prices," *Journal of Financial Economics*, 9(4), 321–346.

Cox, J. C., Ingersoll, J. E., Jr., and Ross, S. A., 1985a, "An Intertemporal General Equilibrium Model of Asset Prices," *Econometrica*, 53(2), 363–384.

Cox, J. C., Ingersoll, J. E., Jr., and Ross, S. A., 1985b, "A Theory of the Term Structure of Interest Rates," *Econometrica*, 53(2), 385–408.

Cox, J. C. and Ross, S. A., 1976, "The Valuation of Options for Alternative Stochastic Processes," *Journal of Financial Economics*, 3(1/2), 145–166.

Cox, J. C., Ross, S. A., and Rubinstein, M., 1979, "Option Pricing: A Simplified Approach," *Journal of Financial Economics*, 7(3), 229–263.

Cox, J. C. and Rubinstein, M., 1985, *Options Markets*, Prentice-Hall, Englewood Cliffs, NJ.

Crabbe, L. E. and Argilagos, J. D., 1994, "Anatomy of the Structured Note Market," *Journal of Applied Corporate Finance*, 7(3), 85–98.

Credit Suisse Financial Products, 1997, *CreditRisk+*, Technical report, Credit Suisse First Boston, London.

Crosbie, P. and Bohn, J., 2003, *Modeling Default Risk*, white paper, Moody's KMV.

Culp, C. L. and Miller, M. H., 1995, "Metallgesellschaft and the Economics of Synthetic Storage," *Journal of Applied Corporate Finance*, 7(4), 62–76.

Dai, Q. and Singleton, K. J., 2000, "Specification Analysis of Affine Term Structure Models," *Journal of Finance*, 55(5), 1943–1978.

D'Avolio, G., 2001, "The Market for Borrowing Stock," Graduate School of Business Administration, Harvard University.

Davydov, D. and Linetsky, V., 2001, "Pricing and Hedging Path-Dependent Options Under the CEV Process," *Management Science*, 47(7), 949–965.

DeGroot, M. H., 1975, *Probability and Statistics*, Addison-Wesley, Reading, MA.

Demeterfi, K., Derman, E., Kamal, M., and Zou, J., 1999, "A Guide to Volatility and Variance Swaps," *Journal of Derivatives*, 6(4), 9–32.

Derman, E. and Kani, I., 1993, "The Ins and Outs of Barrier Options," Goldman Sachs Quantitative Strategies Research Notes.

Diebold, F. X., 2004, "The Nobel Memorial Prize for Robert F. Engle," NBER Working Paper 10423.

Dixit, A., 1989, "Entry and Exit Decisions Under Uncertainty," *Journal of Political Economy*, 97, 620–638.

Dixit, A. K. and Pindyck, R. S., 1994, *Investment Under Uncertainty*, Princeton University Press, Princeton, N.J.

Dubinsky, A. and Johannes, M., 2004, "Earnings Announcements and Equity Options," Unpublished, Columbia Graduate School of Business.

Duffie, D., 1996, *Dynamic Asset Pricing Theory*, Princeton University Press, Princeton, NJ, 2nd edition.

Duffie, D., 1999, "Credit Swap Valuation," *Financial Analysts Journal*, 55(1), 73–87.

Duffie, D. and Kan, R., 1996, "A Yield-Factor Model of Interest Rates," *Mathematical Finance*, 6(4), 379–406.

Duffie, D., Pan, J., and Singleton, K., 2000, "Transform Analysis and Asset Pricing for Affine Jump-Diffusions," *Econometrica*, 68(6), 1343–1376.

Duffie, D. and Singleton, K. J., 2003, *Credit Risk*, Princton University Press, Princeton, NJ.

Duffie, D. and Yurday, E. C., 2004a, *TRAC-X Derivatives: Structured Credit Index Products and Default Correlation*, Case F-269, Stanford Graduate School of Business.

Duffie, D. and Yurday, E. C., 2004b, *TRAC-X: Emergence of Default Swap Index Products*, Case F-268, Stanford Graduate School of Business.

Eberhart, A. C., 2005, "Employee Stock Options as Warrants," *Journal of Banking and Finance*, 29(10), 2409–2433.

Edwards, F. R. and Canter, M. S., 1995, "The Collapse of Metallgesellschaft: Unhedgeable Risks, Poor Hedging Strategy, or Just Bad Luck?" *Journal of Applied Corporate Finance*, 8(1), 86–105.

Edwards, F. R. and Ma, C. W., 1992, *Futures and Options*, McGraw-Hill, New York.

Emanuel, D. C., 1983, "Warrant Valuation and Exercise Strategy," *Journal of Financial Economics*, 12(2), 211–235.

Emanuel, D. C. and MacBeth, J. D., 1982, "Further Results on the Constant Elasticity of Variance Call Option Pricing Model," *Journal of Financial and Quantitative Analysis*, 17(4), 533–554.

Engle, R. F., 1982, "Autoregressive Conditional Heterodskedasticity With Estimates of the Variance of U.K. Inflation," *Econometrica*, 50, 987–1008.

Eom, Y. H., Helwege, J., and Huang, J.-Z., 2004, "Structural Models of Corporate Bond Pricing: An Empirical Analysis," *Review of Financial Studies*, 17(2), 499–544.

Eraker, B., 2001, "Do Stock Prices and Volatility Jump? Reconciling Evidence from Spot and Option Prices," Unpublished, Duke University.

Fama, E. F., 1965, "The Behavior of Stock Prices," *Journal of Business*, 38(1), 34–105.

Faulkender, M., 2005, "Hedging or Market Timing? Selecting the Interest Rate Exposure of Corporate Debt," *Journal of Finance*, 60(2), 931–962.

Fleming, I., 1997, *Goldfinger*, Fine Communications, New York.

Fleming, M. J. and Garbade, K. D., 2002, "When the Back Office Moved to the Front Burner: Settlement Fails in the Treasury Market After 9/11," *FRBNY Economic Policy Review*, 8(2), 35–57.

Fleming, M. J. and Garbade, K. D., 2003, "The Repurchase Agreement Refined: GCF Repo," *Current Issues in Economics and Finance*, 9(6), 1–7.

Fleming, M. J. and Garbade, K. D., 2004, "Repurchase Agreements with Negative Interest Rates," *Current Issues in Economics and Finance*, 10(5), 1–7.

Forster, D. M., 1996, "The State of the Law After *Procter & Gamble v. Banker's Trust*," *Derivatives Quarterly*, 3(2), 8–17.

French, K. R., 1983, "A Comparison of Futures and Forward Prices," *Journal of Financial Economics*, 12(3), 311–342.

French, K. R. and Roll, R., 1986, "Stock Return Variances: the Arrival of Information and the Reaction of Traders," *Journal of Financial Economics*, 17(1), 5–26.

Froot, K., Scharfstein, D., and Stein, J., 1994, "A Framework for Risk Management," *Journal of Applied Corporate Finance*, 7(3), 22–32.

Froot, K. A., 2001, "The Market for Catastrophe Risk: A Clinical Examination," *Journal of Financial Economics*, 60(2–3), 529–571.

Froot, K. A. and O'Connell, P. G. J., 1999, "The Pricing of U.S. Catastrophe Reinsurance," in K. A. Froot, (ed.) "The Financing of Catastrophe Risk," pp. 195–231, University of Chicago Press, Chicago.

Fuller, K. P., 2003, "Why Some Firms Use Collar Offers In Mergers," *Financial Review*, 38(1), 127–150.

Galai, D. and Masulis, R. W., 1976, "The Option Pricing Model and the Risk Factor of Stock," *Journal of Financial Economics*, 3(1/2), 53–81.

Garman, M. B. and Kohlhagen, S. W., 1983, "Foreign Currency Option Values," *Journal of International Money and Finance*, 2(3), 231–237.

Gastineau, G. L., Smith, D. J., and Todd, R., 2001, *Risk Management, Derivatives, and Financial Analysis Under SFAS No. 133*, The Research Foundation of AIMR and Blackwell Series in Finance.

Géczy, C., Minton, B. A., and Schrand, C., 1997, "Why Firms Use Currency Derivatives," *Journal of Finance*, 52(4), 1323–1354.

Geman, H., Karoui, N. E., and Rochet, J.-C., 1995, "Changes of Numeraire, Changes of Probability Measure and Option Pricing," *Journal of Applied Probability*, 32, 443–458.

Geske, R., 1979, "The Valuation of Compound Options," *Journal of Financial Economics*, 7, 63–81.

Glasserman, P., 2004, *Monte Carlo Methods in Financial Engineering*, number 53 in Applications of Mathematics, Springer-Verlag, New York.

Goldman, B. M., Sosin, H. B., and Gatto, M. A., 1979a, "Path Dependent Options: Buy at the Low, Sell at the High," *Journal of Finance*, 34(5), 1111–1127.

Goldman, B. M., Sosin, H. B., and Shepp, L. A., 1979b, "On Contingent Claims That Insure Ex-post Optimal Stock Market Timing," *Journal of Finance*, 34(2), 401–413.

Goodman, L. S. and Fabozzi, F. J., 2002, *Collateralized Debt Obligations: Structures and Analysis*, Wiley.

Gorton, G. and Rouwenhorst, K. G., 2004, "Facts and Fantasies About Commodity Futures," NBER Working Paper 10595.

Graham, J. R. and Rogers, D. A., 2002, "Do Firms Hedge in Response to Tax Incentives?" *Journal of Finance*, 57, 815–839.

Graham, J. R. and Smith, C. W., Jr., 1999, "Tax Incentives to Hedge," *Journal of Finance*, 54(6), 2241–2262.

Grenadier, S. R., 1996, "The Strategic Exercise of Options: Development Cascades and Overbuilding in Real Estate Markets," *Journal of Finance*, 51(5), 1653–1679.

Grenadier, S. R., 1999, "Information Revelation through Option Exercise," *Review of Financial Studies*, 12(1), 95–129.

Grinblatt, M. and Longstaff, F. A., 2000, "Financial Innovation and the Role of Derivative Securities: An Empirical Analysis of the Treasury STRIPS Program," *Journal of Finance*, 55(3), 1415–1436.

Grossman, S. J. and Stiglitz, J. E., 1980, "On the Impossibility of Informationally Efficient Markets," *American Economic Review*, 70(3), 393–408.

Guay, W. and Kothari, S. P., 2003, "How Much Do Firms Hedge with Derivatives?" *Journal of Financial Economics*, 70, 423–462.

Güntay, L., Prabhala, N., and Unal, H., 2004, "Callable Bonds, Interest Rate Risk, and the Supply Side of Hedging," Working Paper, University of Maryland, Smith School of Business.

Gupta, A. and Subrahmanyam, M. G., 2000, "An Empirical Examination of the Convexity Bias in the Pricing of Interest Rate Swaps," *Journal of Financial Economics*, 55(2), 239–279.

Hakannson, N. H., 1976, "The Purchasing Power Fund: A New Kind of Financial Intermediary," *Financial Analysts Journal*, 32(6), 49–59.

Hamilton, D., Varma, P., Ou, S., and Cantor, R., 2005, *Default and Recovery Rates of Corporate Bond Issuers: A Statistical Review of Moody's Ratings Performance 1920-2004*, Technical report, Moody's Investor's Services.

Hanweck, G. A., 1994, *Essays on Interest-Rate Volatility and the Pricing of Interest-Rate Derivative Assets*, Ph.D. thesis, Department of Managerial Economics and Decision Sciences, Kellogg School, Northwestern University.

Harris, M. and Raviv, A., 1985, "A Sequential Signalling Model of Convertible Debt Call Policy," *Journal of Finance*, 40(5), 1263–1281.

Harrison, J. M. and Kreps, D. M., 1979, "Martingales and Arbitrage in Multiperiod Securities Markets," *Journal of Economic Theory*, 20, 381–408.

Haug, E. G., 1998, *The Complete Guide to Option Pricing Formulas*, McGraw Hill, New York.

Haushalter, G. D., 2000, "Financing Policy, Basis Risk, and Corporate Hedging: Evidence from Oil and Gas Producers," *Journal of Finance*, 55(1), 107–152.

Heath, D., Jarrow, R., and Morton, A., 1990, "Bond Pricing and the Term Structure of Interest Rates: A Discrete Time Approximation," *Journal of Financial and Quantitative Analysis*, 25(4), 419–440.

Heath, D., Jarrow, R., and Morton, A., 1992, "Bond Pricing and the Term Structure of Interest Rates: A New Methodology for Contingent Claims Valuation," *Econometrica*, 60(1), 77–105.

Hendricks, D., 1996, "Estimation of Value-at-Risk Models Using Historical Data," *Federal Reserve Bank of New York Economic Policy Review*, 2(1), 39–69.

Henriques, D. B., 1997, "The Wealthy Find New Ways to Escape Tax on Profits," *The New York Times*, Dec. 1, C1.

Heston, S. L., 1993, "A Closed-Form Solution for Options with Stochastic Volatility with Applications to Bonds and Currency Options," *Review of Financial Studies*, 6(2), 327–343.

Ho, T. S. Y. and Lee, S.-B., 1986, "Term Structure Movements and Pricing Interest Rate Contingent Claims," *Journal of Finance*, 41(4), 1011–1029.

Horowitz, J., 2001, "The Bootstrap," in J. J. Heckman and E. Leamer, (eds.) "Handbook of Econometrics," volume 5, pp. 3159–3228, Elsevier Science B. V., Amsterdam.

Horwitz, D. L., 1996, "*P&G v. Banker's Trust*: What's All the Fuss?" *Derivatives Quarterly*, 3(2), 18–23.

Houweling, P. and Vorst, T., 2001, "An Empirical Comparison of Default Swap Pricing Models," Erasmus University Working Paper.

Hsu, H., 1997, "Surprised Parties," *Risk*, 10(4), 27–29.

Huang, C. and Litzenberger, R., 1988, *Foundations for Financial Economics*, Elsevier Science Publishing Co., New York.

Huddart, S., 1998, "Patterns of Stock Option Exercise in the United States," in J. Carpenter and D. Yermack, (eds.) "Executive Compensation and Shareholder Value," chapter 8, pp. 115–142, Kluwer Academic Publishers, Norwell, MA.

Hull, J. C., 2000, *Options, Futures, and Other Derivatives*, Prentice-Hall, Upper Saddle River, NJ, 4th edition.

Hull, J. C. and White, A., 1987, "The Pricing of Options on Assets with Stochastic Volatilities," *Journal of Finance*, 42, 281–300.

Hull, J. C. and White, A., 1995, "The Impact of Default Risk on the Prices of Options and Other Derivative Securities," *Journal of Banking and Finance*, 19, 299–322.

Ingersoll, J. E., Jr., 1977, "A Contingent-Claims Valuation of Convertible Securities," *Journal of Financial Economics*, 4(3), 289–322.

Ingersoll, J. E., Jr., 2000, "Digital Contracts: Simple Tools for Pricing Complex Derivatives," *Journal of Business*, 73(1), 67–88.

J. P. Morgan, 1997, *CreditMetrics—Technical Document*, Technical report, J. P. Morgan & Co., New York.

J. P. Morgan/Reuters, 1996, *RiskMetrics—Technical Document*, Technical report, J. P. Morgan & Co., New York, 4th edn.

James, J. and Webber, N., 2001, *Interest Rate Modeling*, Wiley, Chichester, England.

Jarrow, R. A., 1996, *Modeling Fixed Income Securities and Interest Rate Options*, McGraw-Hill, New York.

Jarrow, R. A., Lando, D., and Turnbull, S. M., 1997, "A Markov Model for the Term Structure of Credit Risk Spreads," *Review of Financial Studies*, 10(2), 481–523.

Jarrow, R. A. and Oldfield, G. S., 1981, "Forward Contracts and Futures Contracts," *Journal of Financial Economics*, 9(4), 373–382.

Jarrow, R. A. and Rudd, A., 1983, *Option Pricing*, Richard D. Irwin, Homewood, Illinois.

Jarrow, R. A. and Turnbull, S. M., 1995, "Pricing Derivatives on Financial Securities Subject to Credit Risk," *Journal of Finance*, 50(1), 53–85.

Johnson, H. and Stulz, R., 1987, "The Pricing of Options With Default Risk," *Journal of Finance*, 42(2), 267–280.

Johnson, S. A. and Tian, Y. S., 2000a, "Indexed Executive Stock Options," *Journal of Financial Economics*, 57(1), 35–64.

Johnson, S. A. and Tian, Y. S., 2000b, "The Value and Incentive Effects of Nontraditional Executive Stock Option Plans," *Journal of Financial Economics*, 57(1), 3–34.

Jones, E. P., Mason, S. P., and Rosenfeld, E., 1984, "Contingent Claims Analysis of Corporate Capital Structures: An Empirical Investigation," *Journal of Finance*, 39(3), 611–25.

Jorion, P., 1995, *Big Bets Gone Bad: Derivatives and Bankruptcy in Orange County*, Academic Press, San Diego, CA.

Jorion, P., 2001, *Value at Risk*, McGraw-Hill, New York, 2nd edition.

Judd, K. L., 1998, *Numerical Methods in Economics*, MIT Press, Cambridge, MA.

Karatzas, I. and Shreve, S. E., 1991, *Brownian Motion and Stochastic Calculus*, Springer-Verlag, 2nd edition.

Karatzas, I. and Shreve, S. E., 1998, *Methods of Mathematical Finance*, number 39 in Applications of Mathematics: Stochastic Modelling and Applied Probability, Springer-Verlag, New York.

Karlin, S. and Taylor, H. M., 1981, *A Second Course in Stochastic Processes*, Academic Press, New York.

Kealhofer, S., 2003a, "Quantifying Credit Risk I: Default Prediction," *Financial Analysts Journal*, 59(1), 30–44.

Kealhofer, S., 2003b, "Quantifying Credit Risk II: Default Prediction," *Financial Analysts Journal*, 59(3), 78–92.

Kealhofer, S. and Kurbat, M., 2002, "Predictive Merton Models," *Risk*, 15(2), 67–71.

Kemna, A. G. Z. and Vorst, A. C. F., 1990, "A Pricing Method for Options Based on Average Asset Values," *Journal of Banking and Finance*, 14, 113–129.

Kim, I. J., Ramaswamy, K., and Sundaresan, S., 1993, "Does Default Risk in Coupons Affect the Valuation Of Corporate Bonds?: A Contingent Claims Model," *Financial Management*, 22(3), 117–31.

Klein, P., 1996, "Pricing Black-Scholes Options With Correlated Credit Risk," *Journal of Banking and Finance*, 20, 1211–1229.

Kulatilaka, N. and Marcus, A. J., 1994, "Valuing Employee Stock Options," *Financial Analysts Journal*, 50, 46–56.

Leland, H. E., 1994, "Corporate Debt Value, Bond Covenants, and Optimal Capital Structure," *Journal of Finance*, 49(4), 1213–52.

Leland, H. E. and Toft, K. B., 1996, "Optimal Capital Structure, Endogenous Bankruptcy, and the Term Structure of Credit Spreads," *Journal of Finance*, 51(3), 987–1019.

Lewis, M., 1989, *Liar's Poker*, Penguin, New York.

Li, D. X., 1999, "On Default Correlation: A Copula Function Approach," RiskMetrics Group.

Litterman, R. and Scheinkman, J., 1991, "Common Factors Affecting Bond Returns," *Journal of Fixed Income*, 1(1), 54–61.

Litzenberger, R. H., 1992, "Swaps: Plain and Fanciful," *Journal of Finance*, 47(3), 831–850.

Longstaff, F. and Schwartz, E., 1995, "A Simple "approach to Valuing Risky Fixed and Floating Rate Debt," *Journal of Finance*, 50(3), 789–819.

Longstaff, F. A. and Schwartz, E. S., 2001, "Valuing American Options by Simulation: A Least Squares Approach," *Review of Financial Studies*, 14(1), 113–147.

Lowenstein, R., 2000, *When Genius Failed: The Rise and Fall of Long-Term Capital Management*, Random House, New York.

Lux, H., 1992, "LOR's Big Gamble on SuperShares," *Investment Dealer's Digest*, 58(48), 12, 30.

Macaulay, F. R., 1938, *The Movement of Interest Rates, Bond Yields and Stock Prices in the United States Since 1856*, National Bureau of Economic Research.

Margrabe, W., 1978, "The Value of an Option to Exchange One Asset for Another," *Journal of Finance*, 33(1), 177–186.

McConnell, J. J. and Schwartz, E. S., 1992, "The Origin of LYONs: A Case Study in Financial Innovation," *Journal of Applied Corporate Finance*, 4(4), 40–47.

McDonald, R. L., 2000, "Real Options and Rules of Thumb in Capital Budgeting," in Brennan and Trigeorgis (2000), chapter 2, pp. 13–33.

McDonald, R. L., 2003, "Is it Optimal to Accelerate the Payment of Income Tax on Share-Based Compensation?" Unpublished, Northwestern University.

McDonald, R. L., 2004, "The Tax (Dis)Advantage of a Firm Issuing Options on Its Own Stock," *Journal of Public Economics*, 88(5), 925–955.

McDonald, R. L. and Siegel, D., 1986, "The Value of Waiting to Invest," *Quarterly Journal of Economics*, 101(4), 707–727.

McDonald, R. L. and Siegel, D. R., 1984, "Option Pricing When the Underlying Asset Earns a Below-Equilibrium Rate of Return: A Note," *Journal of Finance*, 39(1), 261–265.

McDonald, R. L. and Siegel, D. R., 1985, "Investment and the Valuation of Firms When There Is an Option to Shut Down," *International Economic Review*, 26(2), 331–349.

McMillan, L. G., 1992, *Options as a Strategic Investment*, New York Institute of Finance, New York, 3rd edition.

McMurray, S., 2001, "Ka-ching Around the Collar: "Costless collars" can cut execs' stock risk. But are they good for shareholders?" **http://www.business2.com/b2/web/articles/ 0,17863,513180,00.html**.

Meissner, G., 2005, *Credit Derivatives*, Blackwell Publishing, Malden, MA.

Mello, A. S. and Parsons, J. E., 1995, "Maturity Structure of a Hedge Matters: Lessons from the Metallgesellschaft Debacle," *Journal of Applied Corporate Finance*, 8(1), 106–120.

Merton, R. C., 1973a, "The Relationship Between Put and Call Option Prices: Comment," *Journal of Finance*, 28(1), 183–184.

Merton, R. C., 1973b, "Theory of Rational Option Pricing," *Bell Journal of Economics and Management Science*, 4(1), 141–183.

Merton, R. C., 1974, "On the Pricing of Corporate Debt: The Risk Structure of Interest Rates," *Journal of Finance*, 29(2), 449–470.

Merton, R. C., 1976, "Option Pricing When Underlying Stock Returns are Discontinuous," *Journal of Financial Economics*, 3(1), 125–144.

Merton, R. C., 1977, "On the Pricing of Contingent Claims and the Modigliani-Miller Theorem," *Journal of Financial Economics*, 5(2), 241–249.

Merton, R. C., 1990, "On the Mathematics and Economics Assumptions of Continuous-Time Models," in R. C. Merton, (ed.) "Continuous-Time Finance," chapter 3, pp. 57–93, Basil Blackwell, Cambridge, MA.

Merton, R. C., 1999, "Finance Theory and Future Trends: the Shift to Integration," *Risk*, 11(7), 48–51.

Miller, M. H., 1986, "Financial Innovation: The Last Twenty Years and the Next," *Journal of Financial and Quantitative Analysis*, 21(4), 459–471.

Miltersen, K. R., Sandmann, K., and Sondermann, D., 1997, "Closed Form Solutions for Term Structure Derivatives with Lognormal Interest Rates," *Journal of Finance*, 52(1), 409–430.

Mishkin, F. S. and Eakins, S. G., 2003, *Financial Markets + Institutions*, Addison-Wesley, Boston, MA, 4th edition.

Mitchell, M. and Pulvino, T., 2001, "Characteristics of Risk and Return in Risk Arbitrage," *Journal of Finance*.

Modest, D. M. and Sundaresan, M., 1983, "The Relationship between Spot and Futures Prices in Stock Index Futures Markets: Some Preliminary Evidence," *Journal of Futures Markets*, 3(1), 15–41.

Modigliani, F. and Miller, M., 1958, "The Cost of Capital, Corporation Finance, and the Theory of Investment," *American Economic Review*, 48(3), 261–297.

Mood, A. M., Graybill, F. A., and Boes, D. C., 1974, *Introduction to the Theory of Statistics*, McGraw-Hill, New York, 3rd edition.

Morgenson, G., 1998, "Trimming Stock Options' Sails: Accounting Proposal Would Lift the Cost of Repricing," *The New York Times*, August 20, D1.

Myers, S. C., 1977, "Determinants of Corporate Borrowing," *Journal of Financial Economics*, 5(2), 147–75.

Naik, V. and Lee, M., 1990, "General Equilibrium Pricing of Options on the Market Portfolio with Discontinuous Returns," *Review of Financial Studies*, 3(4), 493–521.

Neftci, S. N., 2000, *An Introduction to the Mathematics of Financial Derivatives*, Academic Press, San Diego, CA, 2nd edition.

Nelson, D. B., 1991, "Conditional Heterskedasticity in Asset Returns: A New Approach," *Econometrica*, 59, 347–370.

Neuberger, A., 1994, "The Log Contract," *Journal of Portfolio Management*, 20(2), 74–80.

Paddock, J. L., Siegel, D. R., and Smith, J. L., 1988, "Option Valuation of Claims on Real Assets: The Case of Offshore Petroleum Leases," *Quarterly Journal of Economics*, 103(3), 479–508.

Pan, J., 2002, "The Jump-Risk Premia Implicit in Options: Evidence from an Integrated Time-Series Study," *Journal of Financial Economics*, 63(1), 3–50.

Pearson, N. D., 2002, *Risk Budgeting: Portfolio Problem Solving with Value-at-Risk*, John Wiley & Sons, Inc.

Petersen, M. A. and Thiagarajan, S. R., 2000, "Risk Measurement and Hedging: With and Without Derivatives," *Financial Management*, 29(4), 5–29.

Petrie, K. N., 2000, "Why Some Firms Use Collar Offers In Mergers," Working Paper, Terry College of Business, University of Georgia.

Pindyck, R. S., 1993a, "Investments of Uncertain Cost," *Journal of Financial Economics*, 34(1), 53–76.

Pindyck, R. S., 1993b, "The Present Value Model of Rational Commodity Pricing," *The Economic Journal*, 103(418), 511–530.

Pindyck, R. S., 1994, "Inventories and the Short-Run Dynamics of Commodity Prices," *Rand Journal of Economics*, 25(1), 141–159.

Rebonato, R., 1996, *Interest Rate Option Models*, Wiley, Chichester, England, 2nd edition.

Reiner, E., 1992, "Quanto Mechanics," *Risk*, 5(3), 59–63.

Reinganum, M. R., 1986, "Is Time Travel Impossible? A Financial Proof," *Journal of Portfolio Management*, 13(1), 10–12.

Rendleman, R. J., Jr., 2002, *Applied Derivatives: Options, Futures, and Swaps*, Blackwell, Malden, MA.

Rendleman, R. J., Jr. and Bartter, B. J., 1979, "Two-State Option Pricing," *Journal of Finance*, 34(5), 1093–1110.

Rendleman, R. J., Jr. and Bartter, B. J., 1980, "The Pricing of Options on Debt Securities," *Journal of Financial and Quantitative Analysis*, XV(1), 11–24.

Richard, S. F. and Sundaresan, M., 1981, "A Continuous Time Equilibrium Model of Forward Prices and Futures Prices in a Multigood Economy," *Journal of Financial Economics*, 9(4), 347–371.

Ronn, A. G. and Ronn, E. I., 1989, "The Box Spread Arbitrage Conditions: Theory, Tests, and Investment Strategies," *Review of Financial Studies*, 2(1), 91–108.

Routledge, B. R., Seppi, D. J., and Spatt, C. S., 2000, "Equilibrium Forward Curves for Commodities," *Journal of Finance*, 55(3), 1297–1338.

Royal Swedish Academy of Sciences, 2003, *Time-Series Econometrics: Cointegration and Autoregressive Conditional Heteroskedasticity*, Technical report, Royal Swedish Academy of Sciences.

Rubinstein, M., 1991a, "Double Trouble," *Risk*, 5(1), 73.

Rubinstein, M., 1991b, "One for Another," *Risk*, 4(7), 30–32.

Rubinstein, M., 1991c, "Somewhere Over the Rainbow," *Risk*, 4(10), 63–66.

Rubinstein, M., 1994, "Return to Oz," *Risk*, 7(11), 67–71.

Rubinstein, M. and Reiner, E., 1991a, "Breaking Down the Barrier," *Risk*, 4(8), 28–35.

Rubinstein, M. and Reiner, E., 1991b, "Unscrambling the Binary Code," *Risk*, 4(9), 75–83.

Ryan, M. D. and Granovsky, R. J., 2000, "Nikkei 225 Put Warrants," in J. C. Francis, W. W. Toy, and J. G. Whittaker, (eds.) "The Handbook of Equity Derivatives," chapter 17, pp. 368–394, Wiley, New York, revised edition.

Saly, P. J., Jagannathan, R., and Huddart, S. J., 1999, "Valuing the Reload Features of Executive Stock Options," *Accounting Horizons*, 13(3), 219–240.

Samuelson, P. A., 1965, "Proof that Properly Anticipated Prices Fluctuate Randomly," *Industrial Management Review*, 6(2), 41–49.

Schönbucher, P., 2003, *Credit Derivatives Pricing Models*, Wiley.

Schroder, M., 1988, "Adapting the Binomial Model to Value Options on Assets with Fixed-Cash Payouts," *Financial Analysts Journal*, 44(6), 54–62.

Schroder, M., 1989, "Computing the Constant Elasticity of Variance Option Pricing Formula," *Journal of Finance*, 44(1), 211–219.

Schroder, M., 1999, "Changes of Numeraire for Pricing Futures, Forwards, and Options," *Review of Financial Studies*, 12(5), 1143–1163.

Schwartz, E. S., 1997, "The Stochastic Behavior of Commodity Prices: Implications for Valuation and Hedging," *Journal of Finance*, 52(3), 923–973.

Schwartz, E. S. and Moon, M., 2000, "Rational Valuation of Internet Companies," *Financial Analysts Journal*, 56(3), 62–75.

Scott, L. O., 1987, "Option Pricing when the Variance Changes Randomly: Theory, Estimation, and an Application," *Journal of Financial and Quantitative Analysis*, 22(4), 419–438.

Shao, J. and Tu, D., 1995, *The Jackknife and Bootstrap*, Springer-Verlag, New York.

Sharpe, W. F., 1976, "Corporate Pension Funding Policy," *Journal of Financial Economics*, 3(3), 183–193.

Sharpe, W. F., 1978, *Investments*, Prentice-Hall, Englewood Cliffs, NJ.

Shiller, R. J., 2003, *The New Financial Order: Risk in the 21st Century*, Princeton University Press, Princeton, New Jersey.

Shumway, T., 2001, "Forecasting Bankruptcy More Accurately: A Simple Hazard Model," *Journal of Business*, 74(1), 101–124.

Siegel, D. and Siegel, D., 1990, *Futures Markets*, Dryden Press, Chicago.

Siegel, J. J., 1998, *Stocks for the Long Run*, McGraw-Hill, 2nd edition.

Smith, C. W. and Stulz, R. M., 1985, "The Determinants of Firms' Hedging Policies," *Journal of Financial and Quantitative Analysis*, 20(4), 391–405.

Smith, D., 2002, "Two Common Textbook Misstatements About Bond Prices and Yields," Unpublished, Boston University School of Management.

Smith, D. J., 1997, "Aggressive Corporate Finance: A Close Look at the Procter & Gamble–Bankers Trust Leveraged Swap," *Journal of Derivatives*, 5(4), 67–79.

Sobehart, J. and Keenan, S., 2002, "The Need for Hybrid Models," *Risk*, 15(2), 73–77.

Spatt, C. S. and Sterbenz, F. P., 1988, "Warrant Exercise, Dividends, and Reinvestment Policy," *Journal of Finance*, 43(2), 493–506.

Srivastava, S., 1998, "Value at Risk Analysis of a Leveraged Swap," Working Paper, Carnegie-Mellon University.

Stein, J. C., 1992, "Convertible Bonds as Backdoor Equity Financing," *Journal of Financial Economics*, 32(1), 3–21.

Steiner, R., 1997, *Mastering Repo Markets*, FT Market Editions, Pitman Publishing, London.

Stigum, M., 1990, *The Money Market*, McGraw-Hill, New York, 3rd edition.

Stigum, M. and Robinson, F. L., 1996, *Money Market & Bond Calculations*, Richard D. Irwin, Inc., Chicago, IL.

Stoll, H. R., 1969, "The Relationship between Put and Call Option Prices," *Journal of Finance*, 24(5), 801–824.

Stoll, H. R., 1973, "The Relationship Between Put and Call Option Prices: Reply," *Journal of Finance*, 28(1), 185–187.

Stulz, R., 1982, "Options on the Minimum or the Maximum of Two Risky Assets," *Journal of Financial Economics*, 10(2), 161–185.

Stulz, R., 1996, "Rethinking Risk Management," *Journal of Applied Corporate Finance*, 9(3), 8–24.

Sundaresan, S., 2002, *Fixed Income Markets and Their Derivatives*, South-Western, Cincinnati, OH.

Tavakoli, J. M., 1998, *Credit Derivatives: A Guide to Instruments and Applications*, Wiley, New York.

Tavakoli, J. M., 2001, *Credit Derivatives & Synthetic Structures: A Guide to Instruments and Applications*, Wiley, New York, 2nd edition.

Thatcher, K. L., Flynn, T., Ehrlinger, J., and Reel, M., 1994, *Equity Put Warrants: Reducing the Costs and Risks of a Stock Repurchase Program*, Technical report, Salomon Brothers, New York.

Titman, S., 1985, "Urban Land Prices under Uncertainty," *American Economic Review*, 75(3), 505–514.

Triantis, A. and Borison, A., 2001, "Real Options: State of the Practice," *Journal of Applied Corporate Finance*, 14(2), 8–24.

Trigeorgis, L., 1996, *Real Options: Managerial Flexibility and Strategy in Resource Allocation*, MIT Press, Cambridge, MA.

Tsiveriotis, K. and Fernandes, C., 1998, "Valuing Convertible Bonds with Credit Risk," *Journal of Fixed Income*, 8(2), 95–102.

Tuckman, B., 1995, *Fixed Income Securities*, Wiley, New York.

Tufano, P., 1996, "Who Manages Risk? An Empirical Analysis of Risk Management Practices in the Gold Mining Industry," *Journal of Finance*, 51(4), 1097–1138.

Tufano, P., 1998, "The Determinants of Stock Price Exposure: Financial Engineering and the Gold Mining Industry," *Journal of Finance*, 53(3), 1015–1052.

Turnbull, S. M., 1987, "Swaps: Zero Sum Game?" *Financial Management*, 16(1), 15–21.

Vasicek, O., 1977, "An Equilibrium Characterization of the Term Structure," *Journal of Financial Economics*, 5(2), 177–188.

Vassalou, M. and Xing, Y., 2004, "Default Risk in Equity Returns," *Journal of Finance*, 59(2), 831–868.

Watkinson, L. and Roosevelt, D., 2004, *Correlation: The Layman's Guide to Implied Correlation*, Product note, Morgan Stanley Fixed Income, New York.

Wiggins, J. B., 1987, "Option Values Under Stochastic Volatilities," *Journal of Financial Economics*, 19, 351–372.

Wilmott, P., 1998, *Derivatives: The Theory and Practice of Financial Engineering*, John Wiley & Sons, Chichester, England.

Zhang, P. G., 1998, *Exotic Options: A Guide to Second Generation Options*, World Scientific, Singapore, 2nd edition.

Zwick, S. and Collins, D. P., 2004, "One Year In and the Jury is Still Out," *Futures*, 33(1), 66.

INDEX

Bold entries are defined in the glossary.

Absolute priority, 850–851
Accounting, for derivatives, 106–107
Accreting swap, 263
Accrued interest, 243
Acquisitions, collars in, 538–542
Adverse selection, 98
After-tax profit, as concave function of output
    price, 103
Alexander, C., 752n
Allayannis, G., 107
Allen, Paul, 491
All-or-nothing options, 685–686, 694, 703–709
    barrier options, 710–717
    delta-hedging of, 707–708
    terminology for, 703–704, 705
Alpha, of stocks, 151
Alphabet, Greek, 873
Alpha-porting, 151
Altman, Daniel, 863
American call option, binomial tree for pricing, 350
American-style option, 32, 293, 329, 330
    delta-hedging of, 430
    exercise of, 57, 294–297
    Monte Carl valuation of, 633–636
    parity bounds for, 310–311
    perpetual, 403–405
    strike prices for, 300
    time to expiration of, 297
Amortizing swap, 263
Andersen, T. G., 756
Antithetic variate method, 632
Appreciation, of land, 567
Arbitrage, 70, 129
    asymmetric butterfly spread and, 302, 303

    bear spread and, 301
    cash-and-carry, 137–138
    covered interest, 156–157
    forward pricing and, 175–176
    for mispriced option, 318–323
    no-arbitrage bounds and, 138–139
    on-the-run/off-the-run, 235, 236
    pricing commodity forwards by, 174–178
    pricing prepaid forward by, 129–130
    quasi-arbitrage, 139–140
    regulatory, 2–3
    S&P 500 index arbitrage, 147–149
    synthetic forwards and, 136–138
Arbitrage CDO, 853
ARCH (autoregressive conditional
    heteroskedasticity) model, 747–751
Arithmetic Asian option, Monte Carlo valuation
    and, 627–630
Arithmetic average, 446–447
Arithmetic Brownian motion, 653–654
    Ornstein-Uhlenbeck process and, 654–655
Arnason, S. T., 532
Arrays, VBA and, 897–899, 901–904
Arrow, Kenneth, 370n
Arrow-Debreu securities, 370n
Artzner, P., 837
Asian option, 48, 444–449
    on the average, 446–447
    based on geometric average, 466–467
    for CD structure, 485–486
    comparing, 447–448
    hedging strategies and, 445, 448–449
    Monte Carlo valuation and, 627–630
    payoff in, 683n
Asian tail, 445
Ask, origins of term, 12

Ask price, 11

Asset
as investment asset, 688–690
lease rate of, 14–15
Sharpe ratio and, 659–660
underlying, 21
valuation of, 558
volatility of, 510

Asset allocation
general, 151
as index futures use, 150–151

Asset-or-nothing call, 706

Asset-or-nothing option, 686
barrier options, 715–716

Asset price
average as, 446–447
distribution of, 608–612

Asset swap, 255

Asymmetry
in insurance purchase, 96–97
of zero-cost collar, 77

As-you-like-it option, 465

At-the-money call, 284

At-the-money geometric average price, 447

At-the-money option, 43, 530

At-the-money put, 76, 284

At-the-money written straddle, 822–823

Autoregressive, 750

Average price options, 466

Average strike options, 466–467

Back-to-back transaction, 250

Backwardation, 170

Backward equation, Kolmogorov, 691–692

Bakshi, G., 772

Balance sheet CDO, 853

Bankers Trust, Procter & Gamble swap with, 263, 264

Bankruptcy, 841n. *See also* Default
bond ratings and probability of, 847–850
hedging and, 103
reduced form models, 852

Banks, capital to cover losses, 495n

Barclays, Russian-doll CDO from, 854

Barrier COD option, 737

Barrier option, 449–453, 717–718
all-or-nothing, 710–717

asset-or-nothing, 715–716
cash-or-nothing, 710–715
defining barrier for, 450
types of, 450–451

Barrier present values, 403

Bartram, S. M., 107

Bartter, B. J., 313, 793n

Basel Committee on Banking Supervision, value at risk and, 815

Basis risk, 116, 196–198
in hedge with residual risk, 153n
in T-bond and T-note futures, 233

Basket options, 735–736

Bates, D. S., 743n, 771n, 772

Baxter, M., 662n, 674

Bear spread, 72, 300, 301

Below-investment grade bonds, 847

Benchmark, 459

Bernstein, P. L., 592n

Best, A. M., 847n

Beta, index futures and, 152

Bettis, J. C., 491

Bias
convexity, 219–221
futures price, by risk premium, 140–141

Bid, origins of term, 12

Bid-ask bounce, 12, 756

Bid-ask spread, 11–12

Bid price, 11

Bills. *See* Treasury bills

Binomial formula, graphic interpretation of, 319, 320

Binomial interest rate model, 793–798

Binomial model, 355, 528
Black-Scholes formula and, 375
for dollar-denominated investor, 724–727
Greeks in, 441–442
lognormality and, 355–358
origins of, 598
path dependence and, 444n
for pricing reload options, 532–534

Binomial option pricing, 313. *See also* Binomial tree
American options and, 329, 330
early exercise of option, 343–346
one-period binomial tree and, 313–323
options on other assets, 330–336
put options and, 328–329
two or more binomial periods and, 323–328

Binomial pricing formula, 315–318

Binomial tree, 314, 553, 555–556

    alternative, 358–359

    for American call option, 364

    Black-Derman-Toy model and, 798–808

    constructing, 321–322

    Cox-Ross-Rubinstein approach, 359

    for dollar and Nikkei index, 720

    generalization to many periods, 326–328

    lognormality and, 351–360

    nonrecombining tree, 324

    option Greeks and, 441–442

    path through, 356, 357

    prepaid forward and, 363–365

    for pricing of American call option, 331, 335, 350

    for pricing of American put option, 330, 333

    for pricing of European call option, 323, 324, 327, 349

    for pricing of European put option, 328

    for project value, 555–556

    recombining tree, 324

    stock price paths on, 356

    with two or more binomial periods, 323–328

    valuation with risk-neutral probabilities, 618, 619

    VBA for, 900–901

Binomial valuation, of callable noncovertible and convertible bonds, 518

Black, Fischer, 375, 376, 503, 798. *See also* specific formulas and models

Black-Cox model, 846

Black-Derman-Toy model, 779, 798–808

    constructing tree, 804–805

Black formula, 381–382, 560n

    bond options, caps, and, 790–792

Black-Scholes analysis

    Delta-hedging in practice and, 432

    multivariate, 700–701

    option pricing and, 70, 290n, 429–436, 679–698

Black-Scholes equation, 679–698

    equilibrium returns and, 686–688

    interest rate derivatives, for, 783

    jumps and, 696

    market-maker hedging claim and, 723n

    for pricing options, 679, 681–690

    risk-neutral pricing and, 690–691

Black-Scholes formula, 375–405. *See also* specific types of options

    applying to other assets, 379–382

    assumptions about, 379, 649–650

    binomial model and, 313–314

    for bonds, 779

    call provision and, 517

    for computing value of debt, 509

    computing with Visual Basic for Applications, 894–895

    derivation of, 585

    heuristic derivation of, 604–605

    history of, 376

    implied volatility and, 400–402

    inputs to, 377–378

    lognormal distribution of stock price and, 453

    market-makers and, 413

    Monte Carlo valuation and, 625

    option Greeks, 382–395

    for option premiums, 34n

    for payoffs to equity and debt, 505

    pricing formula for exchange option and, 460

    profit diagrams before maturity, 395–399

    value at risk and, 836

    value of options and, 524n

    for valuing bond convertible at maturity, 514–516

    volatility and, 763–773

Black-Scholes Greeks, 441–442

Black-Scholes-Merton methodology, 679n

Black-Scholes partial differential equation (PDE). *See* Black-Scholes equation

Bodie, Z., 172n, 299, 528, 814n

Bodnar, G. M., 107

Bohn, J., 844n

Bollerslev, T., 748, 751

Bond(s). *See also* specific types

    basics of, 205–214

    Black-Scholes equation for, 779

    boundary condition for, 680–681

    box spread alternative to, 74

    callable, 516–520

    catastrophe, 6

    cheapest to deliver, 231

    commodity-linked, 478–481

    contingent convertible, 520

    convertible, 84, 513–516

    coupon, 210–211, 475

    coupons and yields, 242–244

currency-linked, 481
as debenture, 504n
delta-gamma approximations for, 784–785
duration-hedging with, 779
with embedded options, 482–486
equilibrium equation for, 781–784
equity-linked, 476–478
features of, 520–522
high- and low-coupon, 233
interest rates and, 780
Marshall & Ilsley, 83–85
off-the-run, 206
on-the-run, 206
options on, 286–287, 335–336
par value of, 496
in payoff diagram, 61
price conventions for, 241–245
prices, yields, and conversion factors for, 232
recovery rates for, 850–851
Treasury-bond futures, 230–233
value at risk for, 826–830
valuing bond convertible at maturity, 514–516
verifying volatility for, 803–804
verifying yields for, 802–803
volatility for, 828–830
Wall Street Journal government bond listing, 207
zero-coupon, 28–29, 61, 206–208, 474–475, 794–796
Bond options
caps, Black model, and, 790–792
delta-hedging for, 798
Bond pricing, market-making and, 779–785
Bond ratings
bankruptcy probability and, 847–850
default and, 847–852
recovery rates for, 850–851
Bond valuation, based on stock price, 520
Bond volatility, 794–796, 812
Bootstrapping
bonds, 211
probability distributions, 831–832
Borrowers, rates by class of, 158n
Borrowing, 418
arbitrage and, 139
swaps and separation of, 263
Boundary condition, 680–681
of European call option, 680–681

for terminal boundary conditions, 686
Box spread, 72–73, 74
Boyle, P. P., 431, 630n, 632n, 633, 724n
Brealey, R., 105n
Brennan, M. J., 516n, 565n, 574n
Broadie, Mark, 622n, 633, 635, 636, 772
Brown, G. W., 107
Brownian motion, 649–674, 650
arithmetic, 653–654
continuous paths in, 672–674
geometric, 655–659
Girsanov's theorem and, 662–663
and Itô processes, 655–659
properties of, 652–653
quadriatic variation of, 652–653
risk-neutral process and, 660–663
Bull spread, 71–72, 300
Greeks for, 392
profit diagram for, 87
Bulow, J., 528, 529
Bulow-Shoven expensing proposal, 528, 529, 532
Burghardt, G., 258n
Butterfly spread, 81–82, 300
asymmetric, 82–83, 302, 303
profit diagram for, 87
Buyer
long as, 23
risk management by, 98–100
Buying
of index and put, 69
vs. short-selling, 14

Calendar spread, 397–399
Callable bonds, 516–520
convertible, 519–520
nonconvertible, 517–519
Call option, 31–38, 547, 558, 684–685. *See also*
  Purchased call option
asset-or-nothing, 706
at-the-money, 284
binomial tree for pricing European, 323
Black-Scholes formula for, 375–378
as cap, 62–63
cash-or-nothing, 704–705
in CD structure, 485
collar and, 73

down-and-out cash call, 712–713
elasticity for, 393
equity-linked foreign exchange call, 731–732
European call option, 293
exercising prior to dividend, 295–296
fixed exchange rate foreign equity call,
  730–731
formula for, 460
formulas for barrier, 717
gamma for, 384, 385
as high-beta security, 620–621
as insurance, 47–48, 99–100
insuring by selling, 95–96
on nondividend-paying stock, 294–295
payoff for, 33–37, 320
perpetual, 404
premium of, 60
price and Greek information for, 415
pricing of, 325–326
profit diagram and, 60–61
profit diagram of insured house and, 62
psi for, 388, 392
put-call parity and, 68–70
as puts, 289–290
selling of, 108–109
strike price properties for, 304
summary of, 52
up-and-in cash call, 715
up-and-out cash call, 715
written, 37–38
Call payoff, 35
Call profit, 35
Call protection, 516
Call schedule, 516
Cap, 62–63, 792, 805
  bond options, Black model, and, 790–792
  interest rate, 792
  selling of, 95
Capital
  insurance against loss and, 834–835
  insurance companies and, 437
  regulatory, 815
  short-seller needs for, 15
Capital Asset Pricing Model (CAPM), 659–660
Capital expenditure, research and development as,
  563–565
Capital gains, deferring, 490–495
Capital income, taxation of, 74

Capital loss, 490n
Capital management, long-term crisis in, 236
Caplets, 805
Cap level, collars and, 113
CAPM. *See* Capital Asset Pricing Model (CAPM)
Capped options, 717
Capped participation, for CD structure, 485–486
Carr, P., 433, 772n
Carry, 181
Carry market, 181–184
Cash-and-carry, 137
  reverse, 137
  transactions and cash flows for, 137
Cash-and-carry arbitrage, 137, 177
  lease rate and, 180
  with lending, 178
Cash call
  down-and-out, 712–713
  price and delta of, 708
  up-and-in, 715
  up-and-out, 715
Cash coupon payments, 477–478
Cash flow
  for company that borrows at LIBOR and swaps
    to fixed-rate exposure, 255
  in credit default swap, 861
  distribution through derivatives, 101
  for floating-rate borrower using swap, 256
  of market-makers hedging with forward rate
    agreements, 256
  portfolio and, 418–419
  short-selling and, 14
  standard discounted, 371
  stocks, puts, and, 283
  from swaps, 249
  on total return swap, 272, 273
  unhedged and hedged for dollar-based firm, 265
  valuing derivatives on, 552–554
Cash flow CDO, 853
Cash flow mapping, 829
Cash index, S&P's Depository Receipts (SPDRs)
  and, 148n
Cash interest, 479–480
Cash-or-nothing call, 647, 704–705
Cash-or-nothing options
  barrier options, 710–715
  supershare payoffs and, 709
Cash-or-nothing put, 705

Cash put
  down-and-in, 713
  up-and-in, 714–715
  up-and-out, 715
Cash-settled contract, S&P 500 as, 143
Cash settlement, 30
Catastrophe bonds, 6
CBT. *See* Chicago Board of Trade (CBT)
CDO. *See* Collateralized debt obligation (CDO)
CDs
  alternative structures for, 485–486
  economics of, 50–51
  equity-linked, 48–52, 483–485
  payoff on, 49, 50
CDS
  CDOs and, 861–862
  index, 864–866
CDX, 865
Central limit theorem, 592–593
Certainty
  single-barrel extraction under, 565–569
  valuation under, 679–681
CEV model. *See* Constant elasticity of variance
    (CEV) model
Cheapest to deliver bond, 231
Chicago Board of Trade (CBT)
  contracts traded annually at, 9
  futures contracts traded on, 10
  OneChicago and, 143
  quantity uncertainty contract and, 116n
Chicago Board Options Exchange (CBOE)
  index of implied volatility (VIX), 743, 757, 759
  OneChicago and, 143
  supershares and, 709
Chicago Mercantile Exchange (CME)
  contracts traded annually at, 9
  futures contracts traded on, 10
  OneChicago and, 143
Chi-squared distribution, 607n
Cholesky decomposition, 644, 657
Chooser option, 465
Cisco, 528n
Clean price, 243
Clearinghouse, 142, 144n
Clearing members, 142
CME. *See* Chicago Mercantile Exchange (CME)
Co-cos. *See* Contingent convertible bonds (co-cos)
Coherent risk measures, 837n

Collar, 73–75
  in acquisitions, 538–542
  CD structure as, 485, 420-440, 109
  price protection as, 503
  profit diagram for, 87
  short forward contract vs., 75
  strategies with, 112–113
  use and pricing and, 76–77
  zero-cost, 76, 110–112, 491–492
Collar width, 73
Collateral
  credit risk and, 30
  repurchase agreements and, 234
Collateralized debt obligation (CDO), 853
  CDO index and, 864–866
  CDS and, 861–862
  with correlated defaults, 856–857
  with independent defaults, 853–856
  Nth to default basket and, 857–858, 859
  types of, 853, 854
Collect-on-delivery call (COD), 737
Collin-Dufresne, P., 258n
Commodities
  lease rate for, 186
  options on, 334
  synthetic, 171
  value at risk calculations and, 814
Commodity extraction
  costs of, 568
  optimal, 566–567
  as option, 565–572
  with shut-down and restart options, 572–579
  single barrel under certainty, 565–569
  single barrel under uncertainty, 569–570
Commodity forwards, 169–184
  equilibrium pricing of, 171–172
  as hedging strategy, 196–200
  pricing by arbitrage, 174–178
Commodity futures
  as hedging strategy, 196–200
  as synthetic commodities, 172n
Commodity lease rate, 178–181
Commodity-linked bonds, 478–481
Commodity spreads, 195–196
Commodity swaps, 247–254, 268–270
  commodity swap price, 268–269
  with variable quantity and price, 269–270

Compensation options, 503, 523–538
    end of?, 526
    expensing option grants and, 528–531
    at Level 3 Communications, 534–538
    repricing of, 531–532
    selling of, 295n
    valuation inputs for, 527–528
    valuation of, 525–526
Compound call option, exercise decisions for, 453
Compounding, continuous, 875–879
Compound option parity, 454
Compound options, 453–456, 467–468
    currency hedging with, 456
Concave function, 103
Conditional expected price, 603–604
Confidence intervals, lognormal, 600–602
Constant elasticity of variance (CEV) model, 763,
    766–767
    implied volatility in, 767
    pricing formula for, 767
Constantinides, G. M., 689n
Constant maturity treasury (CMT) rate, 264
Constructive sale, 58, 491
Contango, 170–171, 298
Contingent convertible bonds (co-cos), 520,
    521–522
Contingent interest, bonds and, 520
Continuation value, 634–635
Continuous compounding, 875–879
Continuous dividends, 132–133, 134
Continuously compounded rate, 148n, 875
Continuously compounded returns, 353–354
Continuously compounded yields, 213–214
Control variate method, 630–632
Convenience yield, 182–184, 183
Convergence trades, 236
Conversion, 285
Conversion premium, 515
Convertible bond, 84, 482n, 495–498, 513–516
    callable, 519–520
    contingent, 520
Convexity, 224, 228–230
    delta-gamma approximation and, 423n
    strike price and, 304
Convexity bias, 219–221
Cooling degree-day, 200
Cooper, L., 486n

Core, J. E., 524
Corn, futures prices for, 190
Cornell, B., 235
Corn forward market, seasonality and, 188–191
Corporations
    derivatives issued by, 503–542
    tax deferral for, 492–495
Correlated Itô processes, 657
Correlated stock prices, simulating, 643–645
Correlation coefficient, computing, 154n
Correlations. *See also* Volatility
    historical, 831
    value at risk and, 828, 838–839
Cost(s)
    of commodity extraction, 568
    of hedging, 106
    storage, 181–182
Cost of carry, 141
Coupon bond, 210–211, 242–244, 475
    options in, 482–483
    as perpetuity, 480–481
    duration of, 225
    zero-coupon, 474–475
Coupon bond prices, zero coupon bond prices
    deduced from, 211–212
Covered call, 64–65
    profit from, 69
    selling, 63–64
    written put and, 65
Covered interest arbitrage, 156–157
Covered put, 65–66
Covered writing, 63–64
Cox, J. C., 292n, 313, 359, 650n, 690, 691n, 692n,
    763, 767n, 846
Cox-Ingersoll-Ross (CIR) model, 787–788
    Vasicek model and, 788–790
Cox-Ross-Rubinstein binomial tree, 359, 555–556
"Cracking" process, 195–196
Crack spread, 196
Crane, D., 814n
Credit default swaps, 858–862
    cash flows in, 861
    single name, 860–861
Credit event, 273, 841
Credit instruments, 853–866. *See also* specific
    types
Credit-linked notes, 863–864

Credit risk, 11, 15, 30–31, 841–867. *See also*
    Default
    of interest rate swap, 258n, 263
    in LIBOR rate, 258n
    swaps and, 263
    value at risk and, 815
Credit spread, 842
Credit spread curve, 860
Credit tranches, 858n
Crosbie, P., 844n
Cross-hedging, 114–116
    with imperfect correlation, 153
    with index futures, 151–154
    weather derivatives and, 199–200
Crush spread, 195
Cumulative normal distribution function, 589
Cumulative normal distribution, inverse, 622–623
Cumulative standard normal distribution function,
    409–410
Currencies
    LIBOR quotes in, 160
    options on, 286, 332, 381
    value at risk calculations and, 814
Currency contracts, 154–157
Currency hedging, 451–453
    with compound options, 456
Currency-linked bonds, 481–482
Currency-linked options, 727–732
Currency options, 290–292
Currency prepaid forward, 155–156
Currency risk, in Nikkei index, 726
Currency swaps, 264–268
    formulas for, 267
    types of, 267–268
Currency-translated index, 721
Currency translation, 693
Curves. *See also* specific types
    implied volatility, 741
    swap, 258–260, 270
    yield, 208

Daimler-Benz, dividend risk and, 434
Davydov, D., 767n
Dax index, 735
DCF. *See* Discounted cash flow (DCF)
Debenture, 504n

Debreu, Gerard, 370n
Debt
    conflict with equity, 510
    defaultable, 506
    of Enron, 252
    investment incentives harmed by, 510n
    leverage and expected return on, 506–510
    multiple debt issues and, 511–512
    as options, 503–510
    value at maturity, 505
Debt capacity, 105
Debt-to-asset ratio, as function of asset value of
    firm, 509–510
Decision trees, 557. *See also* Binomial tree
DECS (Debt Exchangeable for Common Stock),
    482n, 497
Default, 841
    bond ratings and, 847–852
    CDOs and, 853–856
    concepts and terminology of, 841–843
    cumulative rates of, 851
    by large companies in 2002, 865–866
    Merton model of, 843–845
    related models of, 845–847
Defaultable debt, 506
Default premium, 221
Default swaps, 273–274
    credit, 858–862
    pricing of, 862–864
    XYZ debt issue and, 860
Deferred capital gains, 490–495
Deferred down rebate option, 712
Deferred swap, 261–262
Deferred up rebate option, 715
DeGroot, M. H., 592n
Delivery, cash settlement and, 30
Delivery value, Treasury bonds, 231
Delta, 382, 383–384, 441
    formula for, 410
    as measure of exposure, 416–417
    put, 385
Delta approximation, of portfolio returns, 820–821,
    822
Delta-gamma approximation, 423, 424–425, 665
    for bonds, 784–785
    of portfolio returns, 820n
Delta-gamma-theta approximation, 442

Delta-hedged bond portfolio, 782
Delta-hedged positions, 435
Delta-hedging, 414, 417–422, 686n
    of all-or-nothing options, 707–708
    of American options, 430
    for bond option, 798
    market making and, 413–438
    mathematics of, 422–429
    in practice, 432–433
    profit calculation and, 418–419
    selling error in, 433
    for several days, 420–422
    supershares and, 709
    for two days, 417–418
Delta-neutral position, 433
Dependent bootstrap, 831
Derivative, 1
    construction from other products, 4
    corporate applications of, 503–542
    credit, 858–860
    financial firm use of, 106–107
    growth in trading of, 7–10
    nonfinancial firm use of, 107
    perspectives on, 3
    uses of, 2–3, 10–11
    valuing on cash flow, 552–554
    verifying formula for, 683–686
    weather derivatives as cross-hedging, 199–200
Derivative prices, as discounted expected cash
    flows, 692–693
Derman, E., 710n
Deutsche Bank, economic derivatives and, 6, 7
Deutsche Terminbörse (DTB) exchange, 434
Diagrams. *See* specific types
Diebold, F. X., 748n
Differential equations, and valuation under
    certainty, 679–681
Diff swap, 268
Diffusion process, 651
Digital cash option, 686n
Digital share option, 686n
Dirty price, for bond, 243
Discounted cash flow (DCF), 551–552
    standard, 371
    techniques for option prices, 350
    for valuing claim on S^a, 668
Discounted expected cash flows, derivative prices
    as, 692–693

Discounted expected value, option price as,
    617–621
Discounted present value, 129
Discrete dividends, 131, 134
    stocks with, 361–365
Discrete dividend tree, 362–363
Discrete probability distribution, Poisson
    distribution as, 636–638, 639
Disney, Roy, 492
Distance to default, 843
Distress costs, hedging and, 103
Distribution
    of asset prices, 608–612
    chi-squared, 607n
    exponential, 637n
    lognormal, 587–612
    normal, 587
    of payoffs, 617
    Poisson, 636–638, 639
    return, 831–832
    stable, 592
    two-parameter, 587
Diversifiable jumps, in Merton jump model,
    697–698
Diversifiable risk, 6
Diversification, in portfolio, 819
Dividend, 510
    binomial model and, 361–365
    continuous and forward price, 132, 134
    discrete and forward price, 131, 134
    on index, 28n
    liquidating, 297
    on options, 56–57
    option value and, 527n
    pricing prepaid forwards with, 131–133
Dividend-paying stocks, 681
    compound option model and, 455–456
Dividend risk, 434
Dixit, A., 574n, 578–579
Dollar-based investor, 719, 720, 721–724
Dollar-denominated call option, on euros, 290–291
Dollar-denominated investor, binomial model for,
    724–727
Dominion Bond Rating Service, 847n
Donaldson, William H., 847n
Down-and-in cash call, 712
Down-and-in cash put, 713
Down-and-in options, 450, 452

Down-and-out cash call, 712–713

Down-and-out option, 450

Down rebate option, deferred, 712

Drift

    geometric Brownian motion and, 656–657

    geometric random walk with, 663

Drugs, development process for, 563–565

Duffie, D., 650n, 674, 744n, 768n, 772, 852n, 858n, 863, 864n

Duration, 223–228

    delta-gamma approximation and, 423n

    hedging of bond portfolio and, 781

    Macaulay, 225

    as measure of bond price risk, 828

    modified, 225

Duration-hedging, with bonds, 779

Duration matching, 227–228

Dutch auction, 7

Early exercise of option, 343–346

Eberhart, A. C., 524

Economic derivatives, 6, 7

Economic observer perspective, on derivatives, 3

Effective annual rate, 148n, 875

Efficient Monte Carlo valuation, 630–633

Elasticity

    for call option, 393

    of defaultable bond, 507

    of equity, 507

    option, 389–395

    of portfolio, 395, 511–512

Elasticity of variance, constant, 766–767

Electricity

    nonstorability of, 172–174

    peak-load generation of, 559–563

Emanuel, D. C., 431, 767n

Embedded options

    bonds with, 482–486

    notes with, 488–489

End-user perspective, on derivatives, 3

Energy markets

    natural gas forward curve and, 194

    oil and, 194–195

Engle, Robert F., 748, 749, 750

Enron, 847

    hidden debt of, 252

Equilibrium equation, for bonds, 781–784

Equilibrium pricing, of commodity forwards, 171–172

Equilibrium returns, Black-Scholes equation and, 686–688

Equilibrium short-rate bond price models, 785–790

    Cox-Ingersoll-Ross model, 787–788

    Rendleman-Bartter model, 785–786

    Vasicek compared with Cox-Ingersoll-Ross, 788–790

    Vasicek model, 786–787

Equity

    conflict with debt, 510

    elasticity of, 507

    leverage and expected return on, 506–510

    as options, 503–510

    tax-deductible, 495–498

Equity call, foreign, 728–729

Equity-linked bonds, 476–478

Equity-linked CDs, 48–52

    reverse-engineering for, 51

    valuing and structuring, 483–485

Equity-linked foreign exchange call, 731–732

Equity-linked forward, 719

Equity-linked note, 48

    options in, 483

Equity-linked products, 48

Eurex, 9

Euribor (European Banking Federation) Interbank Offer Rate, 160

Euro-denominated put option on dollars, equivalence to dollar denominated call option on Euros, 290–291

Eurodollar contract, interest on, 160n

Eurodollar futures, 158–160, 218–223

Eurodollar prices, swap curve with, 258–259

Eurodollar strip, 158

    forward interest rate curve implied by, 260

    ten-year swap rate and, 261

Euro interest rate swap, 268

European call, Monte Carlo valuation of, 625–626

European call option, 684–685

    binomial tree for pricing, 323, 349

    Black-Scholes formula for, 375–378

    two-period, 323–326

European exchange option, electricity generation and, 560

European put option
 binomial tree for, 328
 Black-Scholes formula for, 378
European-style option, 32, 293. *See also* specific
  types
 Black-Scholes formula applied to, 379–380
 strike prices for, 298, 300
 time to expiration and value of, 297
EWMA. *See* Exponentially weighted moving
  average (EWMA)
Excel
 Monte Carlo valuation and, 622n
 Visual Basic for Applications (VBA), 885–906
Exchange option, 459–461, 732–733
 generalized parity and, 287–292
 infinitely lived, 468–469
Exchange rate
 Asian options and, 452
 history of changes in, 8
Exchange-traded contracts, credit risk and, 30, 31n
Exchange-traded index fund, 709
Exercise, 32
 moneyness and, 304
 of options, 57
Exercise price, 32
Exercise style, of option, 32
Exotic options, 443–461, 703–736
Expectations hypothesis, 213
Expected interest rates, yields and, 796–797
Expected return
 Black-Scholes equation and, 690
 on debt and equity, 506–510
 of lognormally distributed stock, 597
Expected return on equity, as function of asset
  value of firm, 509–510
Expected tail loss, 832
Expensing, of option grants, 524–525, 528–531
Expiration
 change in, effect on option price, 297–298
 of option, 32
Expiration date, 21
 of option, 32
Exponential distribution, 637n
Exponential function, 876–878
Exponentially weighted moving average (EWMA),
  746–747

Exposure, delta and gamma as measures of,
  416–417
External financing, hedging and, 103

Fair value, 134
Fama, Eugene, 376
FASB. *See* Financial Accounting Standards Board
  (FASB)
Faulkender, M., 107
Feynman-Kac solution, 692n
Financial Accounting Standards Board (FASB)
 on compensation options, 524
 contingent convertibles (co-cos) and, 521
 derivatives reporting requirements and, 10
 Statement of Financial Accounting Standards
  (SFAS) 123R, 525
Financial assets
 buying, 11–12
 short-selling, 12–14
Financial engineering, 3–4, 471, 473
 Modigliani-Miller theorem and, 474
 security design and, 473–498
 for tax and regulatory considerations, 490–498
Financial firms, derivatives used by, 106–107
Financial forwards. *See* Forward contracts
Financial markets
 impacts of, 4–5
 role of, 4–6
Financial options, real options and, 558
Financial policy, Modigliani-Miller theorem and,
  473–474
Financial products, routine categories of, 1
Financing
 hedging and, 103
 short-selling and, 13
 of zero-cost collar, 76–77
Financing cost, 60
Fitch Ratings, 847n
Fixed collar offer, 538
Fixed exchange rate foreign equity call, 730–731
Fixed-rate bonds, swaps and, 256
Fixed stock offer, 538
Floating collar offer, 538
Floating interest rates, currency swaps and, 268
Floating stock offer, 538
Floors, 59–62

Ford Motor Co., hedging for risk management by, 108

Foreign assets. *See also* Nikkei 225 index
    options on, 727–732

Foreign equity call, in foreign currency, 728–729

Foreign exchange call
    equity-linked, 731–732
    fixed exchange rate, 730–731

Foreign stock index. *See also* Nikkei 225 index
    foreign equity call and, 729–730
    risk of, 718–719

Formulas. *See* specific formulas

Forward
    commodity, 169–184, 196–200
    currency, 154–155, 156
    equity-linked (quanto), 719
    interest rate, 205–237
    prepaid, 727
    summary of, 52
    synthetic, 66–70, 112, 135–138

Forward contracts, 21–31, 125, 128, 279. *See also* Futures contracts
    canceling obligation to buy or sell, 142n
    collateralization and, 486n
    covered interest arbitrage for, 156–157
    currency prepaid forward, 155–156
    equating with futures, 166
    futures prices and, 146–147
    futures profits and, 146
    graphing payoff on, 25, 26
    hedging with, 92–93, 98–99
    long and short positions, 43
    off-market forward and, 69
    vs. outright purchase, 26–28
    over-the-counter, 142
    payoff on, 23–26
    as single-payment swap, 247
    on stock, 133–141
    synthetic, 135–136
    as zero-cost collar, 111–112

Forward curve, 169
    for natural gas, 193

Forward premium, 134–135

Forward price, 561
    for claim on S^a, 666–667
    cost of collar and, 77–78
    future price predicted by, 140–141
    of gold, 188
    lease rate and, 179–181
    premium for forward contract and, 134
    risk-neutral price as, 553
    for $S^a Q^b$, 670–672
    storage costs and, 181–182

Forward pricing formula, interpretation of, 141

Forward rate, implied, 208–210

Forward rate agreement (FRA), 214–215, 806–808, 826
    Eurodollar futures and, 219–221
    hedging with, 256
    settlement at time of borrowing, 215
    settlement in arrears, 215
    swap as, 258n
    synthetic, 216–218

Forward sale, hedging with, 92

Forward strip, 169

420-440 collar, 109

FRA. *See* Forward rate agreement (FRA)

French, K. R., 147n

Froot, K., 103n

Fuller, K. P., 538n

Fully leveraged purchase, of stock, 127

Funded CDO, 862

Funds, exchange-traded, 709

Future contracts, forward profits and, 146

Future interest rates, 221n

Future price, predicted by forward price, 140–141

Futures
    asset allocation use in, 150–151
    commodity, 196–200
    currency, 154–155
    Eurodollar, 218–223
    gold, 184–188
    index, 150–154
    interest rate, 205–237
    oil, 194
    options on, 381–382
    quanto contract and, 719
    stock-index, 22
    on terrorism, 24
    Treasury-bond, 230–233
    Treasury-note, 230–233

Futures contracts, 125, 142–150, 279. *See also* Forward contracts
    on CBT, CME, and NYMEX, 10
    equating with forward contracts, 166
    Eurodollar contract as, 258n
    Eurodollar futures, 158–160
    forward contracts and, 21

forward price and, 146–147
hedge quantity and, 153
index, 22
on individual stocks, 143
margin, marking to market, and, 144–146
mark-to-market proceeds and margin balance in, 146
Nikkei 225, 149–150
options on, 332–334
quantity uncertainty and, 116n
quanto index contracts and, 149–150
S&P 500, 143–144
S&P index arbitrage and, 147–149
traded on CBT, CME, and NYMEX, 10
Futures exchange, 9
Futures overlay, 151
Future value
forward price as, 133
in profit diagrams, 36
of option premium, 43

Gamma, 382, 384–386, 428, 442
to approximate change in option price, 423–424
call, 385
formula for, 410
hedging and, 420
as measure of exposure, 416
Gamma-hedging, 436
Gamma-neutrality, 433–436
Gap option, 457–459, 536, 686n, 706–707
GARCH (Generalized ARCH) model, 751–754, 755
comparison with EWMA volatility, 755
estimating using Excel, 777–778
exponential, 748
maximum likelihood estimation of, 752–753
volatility forecasts in, 753–754
Gastineau, G. L., 106n
Gates, Bill, on compensation options, 526
Géczy, C., 107
General collateral repurchase agreement, 234
Generalized parity, exchange options and, 287–292
Geometric average, 446–447
formulas for Asian options based on, 466–467
strike calls and puts, 447

Geometric Brownian motion, 649, 655–659
Black and Scholes and, 679, 681–682
Itô's Lemma and, 665
Geometric random walk, with drift, 663
Geman, H., 695n
Girsanov's theorem, 662
Glasserman, P., 630n, 633, 635, 636
Gold
extraction of, 568–569
forward price of, 188
gold-linked notes and, 486–488
investments in, 187
notes with embedded options and, 488–489
prepaid forward price of, 188
producer's perspective on risk management and, 91–98, 109–113
valuing future production of, 187–188
Gold futures, 184–188
Goldman Sachs, economic derivatives and, 6, 7
Gorton, G., 172n
Government securities, repos for, 234
Graham, J. R., 107
Granger, Clive, 750
Granovsky, R. J., 728
Graphical interpretation, of binomial formula, 319, 320
Greek alphabet, 873
Greeks
in binomial model, 441–442
for bull spread, 392
defined, 382–388
formulas for, 410–412
option, 382–395
as portfolio measures, 388–389
Griffin v. Citibank Investments Ltd., 74
Grossman, S. J., 130n
Guay, W. R., 524
Gupta, A., 258n
Guth, Robert A., 526

Haircut, 15, 234
Hakannson, N. H., 709
Hamilton, D., 851
Haug, E. G., 562n
Haushalter, G. D., 107
Heath, D., 793n, 794n, 798

Heath-Jarrow-Morton model, 811–812
Heating degree-day, 200
Heat rate, 560
Hedge
    basis risk in, 153
    cross-hedging and, 114–116
    stack, 197, 198
    strip, 197
    in swaps, 250–251
Hedged position, 4
Hedged profit, 93
Hedge funds, repos for, 235
Hedge ratio, 113–119, 114, 228n
    quantity uncertainty and, 116–119
    variance-minimizing, 118
Hedging, 2. *See also* Cross-hedging;
   Delta-hedging
    Asian options and, 445, 448–449
    barrier options and, 449
    of bond portfolio based on duration, 781
    commodity futures, using, 196–200
    currency, 451–453, 456
    delta-hedging, 417–422
    of diff swap, 268
    empirical evidence on, 106–107
    with Eurodollar contract, 160
    with forward contract, 92–93, 98–99
    with forward rate agreements, 256
    frequency of re-hedging and, 431–432
    of jet fuel with crude oil, 199
    by market-makers, 413
    option risk in absence of, 414–415
    reasons for, 100–101, 103–106
    reasons for not hedging, 106
    short-selling and, 13
    swaps and, 247
    value added by, 101–103
    volatility and, 741, 757–763, 769n
    zero-cost collar and, 111
Heston, S. L., 763
Heston model, 768–771
Heteroskedastic, 749, 750
High-beta security, call option as, 620–621
Histogram
    for assessing lognormality, 608–609
    jumps and, 642
    for risk-neutral stock price distribution, 628
Historical correlations, 831
Historical returns, of risk arbitrageurs, 541n

Historical volatility, 360, 361, 744–746, 756n
Ho, T. S. Y., 793n, 798
Home equity insurance, 6
Homeowner's insurance
    with house, 61–62
    as put option, 45–47
Homoskedastic error term, 749
Horowitz, J., 831n
Hoskins, W., 258n
Houweling, P., 863
Huddart, S., 527n
Hull, J. C., 768n
Hysteresis, 578–579

IASB. *See* International Accounting Standards
    Board (IASB)
IBM, volatilities for, 742, 745
Immediacy, as dealer service, 11n
Implicit borrowing and lending, in swap, 260–261
Implicit short position, 62n
Implied forward rate, 208–210
    expectations hypothesis and, 213
Implied repo rate, 135
Implied volatility, 400–402, 741–744
    in CEV model, 768
    computing, 400–402
    for IBM call options, 742
    jump risk and, 764–765
    over time, 743
    using, 402
Importance sampling, 633
Income-linked loans, 6
Index. *See also* Stock index; specific indexes
    buying of, 69
    currency-translated, 721
    for futures contracts, 22
    payoff from short-selling, 63
    profit from short-selling, 63
    put and, 59–62
Index futures. *See also* Futures contracts
    cross-hedging with, 151–154
    hedge rate determination, 152
    shorting of, 152
    uses of, 150–154
Individuals, tax deferral for, 491–492
Infinite investment horizon, evaluating project
    with, 558

Infinitely lived exchange option, 468–469
Ingersoll, J. E., Jr., 516n, 787–788
Inglis, Martin, 108
Insurance
    adjusting by changing strike, 96–98
    call option and, 47–48, 99–100
    homeowner's as put option, 45–47
    market-making as, 436–438
    minimum price guaranteed with put option,
        93–95
    options as, 45–48
    portfolio, for long run, 603
    by selling a call, 95–96
    selling of, 63–66
    strategies for, 59–66
    value at risk and, 834–835, 836–837
Intel, peak-load manufacturing at, 559
Interest, 418–419
    accrued, 243
    cash, 479–480
    contingent, 520
    on Eurodollar contract proceeds, 160n
Interest in-kind, 478, 480
Interest rate
    Black-Derman-Toy model and, 798–808
    Black formula to price options on, 791
    continuous compounding and, 875–879
    conventions for, 241–245
    determining, 15–16
    equilibrium short-rate bond price models,
        785–790
    futures and forward prices and, 146–147
    reasons for swapping, 262– 263
    S&P index arbitrage and, 147–148
    short-term, 783
    yields and expected rates, 796–797
Interest rate cap, 792
Interest rate curve, forward curve, 260
Interest rate forwards and futures, 205–237
Interest rate models, 779–808
    binomial, 793–798
    Cox-Ingersoll-Ross, 787–788
    Heath-Jarrow-Morton model for, 811–812
    Rendleman-Bartter, 785–786
    Vasicek, 786–787
Interest rate risk
    Eurodollar contract for hedging, 160
    swaps and, 263
Interest-rate sensitive claims and VaR, 826–827

Interest rate stacks, 223
Interest rate strips, 223
Interest rate swaps, 254–263
    euro swap, 268
    simple, 254–255
    swaps and, 256
Interest rate tree
    Black-Derman-Toy, 800, 801
    three-period, example, 793, 797
Internal rate of return, 208
International Accounting Standards Board (IASB)
    on compensation options, 524
    derivatives reporting requirements and, 10
    hedge accounting, 106–107
In-the-money option, 43, 304
Inverse cumulative normal distribution, 622–623
Investment. *See also* Net present value (NPV)
    in gold, 187
    in Nikkei 225 index, 728
    NPV rule and, 548–551
    in oil well, 572–578
    solving for optimal decision, 556–558
    staged, 564
    under uncertainty, 551–558
    when well shutdown is possible, 576–577
Investment asset, as underlying asset, 688–690
Investment cost, as strike price, 547
Investment grade bonds, 847
Investment horizon, evaluating project with 2-year
        horizon, 554–558
Investment project, 547
    as call option, 558
Investment trigger price, 551
Iomega Corporation, dividend of, 57
Itô process, 655–659
Itô's Lemma, 663–666
    Black and Scholes and, 679
    bond pricing model and, 781, 782
    log contract and, 663–666
    multivariate, 665–666
    applied to S^a, 667–668

Jagannathan, R., 532
James, J., 812
Jarrow, R., 812, 852
Jarrow-Rudd binomial tree, 359
Jensen's inequality, 103n, 370n, 594–595, 621n,
        663, 664, 665, 881–884
    bond pricing and, 784

exponential function and, 881–882
price of a call and, 882–883
proof of, 884
Jet fuel, hedging with crude oil, 199
Jorion, P., 1n
J. P. Morgan, 814
J. P. Morgan Chase, 526
Judd, K. L., 621n, 630n
Jump diffusion model, 763
Jump risk, implied volatility and, 764–765
Jumps
    multiple, 643
    option pricing with, 696–698, 772
    simulating with Poisson distribution, 639–643
    in stock price, 672–674
Junior bonds, 511–512
Junior tranche, 511

Kani, I., 710n
Kapadia, N., 772n
Karatzas, I., 650n, 652n, 662n, 664n, 674
Karlin, S., 691n, 692n
Kemna, A. G. Z., 630n
KMV model (Moody's), 844n
Knock-in options, 450
Knock-out options, 450
Kolmogorov backward equation, 691–692
Kulatilaka, N., 527n
Kurtosis of a distribution, 609, 643

Ladder option, 740
Land, as option, 567
Latin hypercube sampling, 633
Lattice, 325n
Lauder, Estee and Ronald, 491
Law of one price, 315
Lease market, for commodity, 178–179
Lease rate, 14, 479n
    of asset, 14–15
    cash-and-carry arbitrage and, 180
    commodity, 178–181
    forward prices and, 179–181
    for gold, silver, and other commodities, 186, 568–569
    storability and, 176–178
    storage costs and, 182
    for valuing claim on S^a, 669

Lee, M., 646, 696n
Lee, S.-B., 793n, 798
Leland, H. E., 709
Lending, of security, 12
    arbitrage and, 139
LEPO. *See* Low exercise price option (LEPO)
Leptokurtosis, 609
Level 3 Communications, compensation options at, 534–538
Leverage, and expected return on debt and equity, 506–510
Leverage effect, 766
Li, D. X., 858n
LIBOR. *See* London Interbank Offer Rate (LIBOR)
Linear regression, hedges and, 115n
Linetsky, V., 767n
Liquidating dividend, 297
Liquidity, of futures contracts, 142
Liquidity premium, 222
Loan balance, of swap, 260–261
Loans, income-linked, 6
Logarithmic function, 876–878
Log contract, 760–762
Lognormal confidence intervals, 600–602
Lognormal distribution, 587–612
    and the Black Scholes formula, 605
    estimating parameters of, 605–607
    probability calculations and, 598–605
    for value at risk calculations, 814
Lognormality
    binomial model and, 355–358
    binomial tree and, 351–360
    comparison with three-period binomial approximation, 357
    geometric Brownian motion and, 655–656
    histograms for assessing, 608–609
Lognormally distributed variable, 593–595
Lognormal model, of stock prices, 595–598, 744
Lognormal random variables, generating n correlated, 644–645
Lognormal stock prices, simulating, 623–624
Lognormal, binomial, tree, 359
London Interbank Offer Rate (LIBOR)
    computing, 258n
    Eurodollar futures and, 158–160, 218–221
    history 3-month LIBOR and 3-month T-bill yield, 222–223
    interest rate and, 147–148

three-month forward rates, 259
  vs. three-month T-bills, 221–223
Long (buyer), 23
Long call, profit, 53
Long forward, profit, 53
Long forward contract, synthetic, 67
Long forward position, 44, 52
Long position, bonds, repos, and, 235
Long positions, 12, 44, 52
  floors and, 59–62
  profit diagrams for, 44
Long put profit, 53
Long run, portfolio insurance for, 603
Long Term Capital Management, 236
Longstaff, F., 633, 635
Lookback call, European, 739
Lookback put, European, 739
Loops, in (VBA), 901
  for loop, 899
Losses
  capital, 490n
  with put and short forward, 40
Loss given default, 842
Low-coupon bonds, 233
Low discrepancy sequences, 633
Low exercise price option (LEPO), 133
Lublin, Joann S., 526
Lux, H., 709

Macaulay, Frederick, 225n
Macaulay duration, 225
  for zero-coupon bond, 229n
MacBeth, J. D., 767n
Madan, D., 433
Maintenance margin, 145
Managed CDO, 853
Mandatorily convertible bond, 84
Mapping, cash flow, 829
Marcus, A. J., 527n
Margin, 144
  maintenance, 145
  marking to market and, 144–146
  for written options, 57
Marginal utility, declining, 369–370
Margin balance, in futures contracts, 146
Margin call, 145
Market(s). *See also* specific types
  in contango, 170–171

economic derivatives, 6
over-the-counter, 10
for risk-sharing, 6
Market corner, 233
Market-maker, 4, 413–414
  bid price, offer price, and, 12
  delta-hedging all-or-nothing options and, 707–708
  dividend risk and, 434
  exposure in currency swaps, 266
  insurance and, 437–438
  overnight profit of, 421
  over-the-counter options and, 433n
  profit of, 427–429
  risk of, 414–417, 437–438
  and risk of extreme price moves, 432–433
  roles of, 413–414
  selling prepaid forward and, 130
Market-maker perspective, on derivatives, 3
Market-making, 413–438
  bond pricing and, 779–785
  as insurance, 436–438
  synthetic forwards in, 136–138
Market risks, value at risk and, 815
Market-timing, 733–734
Market value, of swaps, 253–254
Market value CDO, 853
Marking-to-market, 142, 415, 418
  margins and, 144–146
  proceeds and margin balance, 167
Mark-to-market proceeds, in futures contracts, 146
Married put, 58n
Marshall & Ilsley security, 83–85
  tax-deductible equity and, 495–498
Martingale, 651
"Matched book" transaction, 250
Mathematics, of delta-hedging, 422–429
Maturity
  default at, 843–844
  effect on option price, 297–298
  payoff for Marshall & Ilsley bond, 84–85
  profit diagrams before, 395–399
  yield to, 208
McDonald, R. L., 433n, 527n, 565n, 689n
McMurray, S., 491
Mean return, estimate of, 607
Mean reversion, in arithmetic Brownian process, 654–655
Measurement, of volatility, 744–757

Merger
  Northrop Grumman-TRW, 538–542
  options in agreements, 538–539
  price protection in, 503
Merrill Lynch, MITTS from, 48
Merton, Robert C., 1, 292n, 376, 403, 639, 641,
    650n, 664n, 673, 674, 679n, 696, 697, 843
  jump diffusion model, 763
  jump pricing model, 697–698
Merton default model, 843–845, 846
Metallgesellschaft A. G. (MG), 198
Mezzanine tranche, CDOs and, 854, 856
Microsoft, compensation options and, 524, 526,
    527–528
Miller, H. D., 650n, 691n
Miller, Merton, 376, 473. *See also*
    Modigliani-Miller theorem
Mispriced option, arbitrage for, 318–323
Mitchell, M., 541n
MITTS (Market Index Target Term Securities), 48
Mixture of normals model, 609, 647
Modeling, of discrete dividends, 361–362
Modified duration, 225, 237
Modigliani, Franco, 473
Modigliani-Miller theorem, 473–474, 507
Moneyness, exercise and, 304
Monotonicity, 837n
Monte Carlo valuation, 528, 617–645, 814n
  accuracy of, 626–627
  of American options, 633–636
  antithetic variate method, 632
  arithmetic Asian option and, 627–630
  for basket options, 736
  computing random numbers, 621–623
  control variate method of, 630–632
  efficient, 630–633
  of European call, 625–626
  importance sampling and, 633
  Latin hypercube sampling and, 633
  low discrepancy sequences and, 633
  naive, 631, 633
  for nonlinear portfolios, 822–826
  stratified sampling and, 632–633
  for value at risk of two or more stocks, 818
  of written straddle after 7 days, 826
Mood, A. M., 592n, 884n
Moody's
  bond ratings, 847

  Investor Services, 847n
  KMV model, 844n
Moon, M., 563n, 565
Moore, David, 559n
Moral hazard, 47n
Morgan Stanley, TRACERS and, 865
Morgenson, G., 531n
Moving average, exponentially weighted, 746–747
Multi-date swap, 247
Multiple debt issues, 511–512
Multivariate Black-Scholes analysis, 700–701
Multivariate Itô's Lemma, 665–666
Multivariate options
  basket options, 735–736
  exchange options as, 732–733
  options on best of two assets, 733–734
Myers, S., 105n
Myers, S. C., 510n

Naik, V., 646, 696n
Naive Monte Carlo valuation, 631, 633
Naked writing, 64
Nationally Recognized Statistical Rating
    Organizations (NRSROs), 847
Natural gas, seasonality, storage, and, 191–195
  futures contract, 191–194
Natural resources, commodity extraction and,
    565–572
Neftci, S. N., 652n, 662n, 674
Nelson, D. B., 748n
Net payoff, 28
Net present value (NPV)
  correct use of, 549–550
  investment and, 548–551
  static, 548–549
Netscape, 492–493, 498
Neuberger, A., 760
New York Mercantile Exchange (NYMEX)
  contracts traded annually at, 9
  futures contracts traded on, 10
  gold futures contracts on, 185
  light oil contracts on, 194
  natural gas futures on, 192
Nikkei 225 index, 735
  currency risk and, 726
  futures contracts and, 149–150, 268

investing in, 718–719, 720–724
    put warrants and, 728
No-arbitrage bounds, with transaction costs, 138–139
No-arbitrage pricing, 70
Noise term, geometric Brownian motion and, 656–657, 658
Nonconvertible bonds, callable, 517–519
Nondiversifiable risk, 6
Nonfinancial firms, derivatives used by, 107
Nonfinancial risk management, 105–106
Nonlinear portfolios, value at risk for, 819–826
Nonmonetary return, convenience yield as, 183
Nonrecombining tree, 325
Nonstandard option formulas, Black-Scholes equation and, 683–684
Nonstandard options, 443–461, 703–736
Nonstorablity, of electricity, 172–174
Normal density, 587–588
Normal distribution, 587–593
    cumulative function, 589
    cumulative inverse, 622–623
    standard, 409–410
Normal probability plots, 609–612, 610
    jumps and, 642–643
Normal random variables
    conversion to standard normal, 590–591
    sums of, 591–593
Northrop Grumman-TRW merger, 538–542
Notes. *See also* specific types
    with embedded options, 488–489
    equity-linked, 48, 483
    gold-linked, 486–488
    structured, 474
    Treasury note futures, 230–233
Notional amount of swap, 249
NPV. *See* Net present value (NPV)
NQLX. *See* OneChicago
Numeraire, 693–696
NYMEX. *See* New York Mercantile Exchange (NYMEX)

O'Brien, J., 709
OCC. *See* Options Clearing Corporation (OCC)
Offer price, 11
Offer structures, 538

Off-market forward, 69
Off-the-run bonds, 206, 236
Oil, 194–195
    hedging jet fuel with, 199
Oil extraction, 565–572
    with shut-down and restart options, 572–573
    valuing infinite oil reserve, 570–572
Oil futures, 194
Oil market, 198
Oil prices. *See also* Swap(s)
    derivatives markets and, 7
    producer price index for, 8
OneChicago, 143
One-period binomial tree, 313–323
On-the-run bonds, 206, 236
On-the-run/off-the-run arbitrage, 235, 236
Open interest, 144
Open outcry, 142
Operational risk, value at risk and, 815
Optimal investment decision, solving for, 556–558
Option(s). *See also* Investment; Parity; specific types
    all-or-nothing, 685–686, 703–709
    American-style, 32, 329, 330, 403, 404
    arbitrage for mispriced, 318–323
    Asian, 48, 444–449
    asset-or-nothing barrier options, 715–716
    on the average, 446–447
    barrier, 449–453, 717–718
    barrier COD, 737
    basket, 735–736
    on best of two assets, 733–734
    Black-Scholes analysis in pricing of, 429–436
    Black-Scholes equation for pricing of, 679–698
    on bonds, 286–287, 335–336
    bonds with embedded, 482–486
    Bulow-Shoven proposal and, 529
    buying, 34, 56–58
    call, 31–38
    capped, 717
    closing prices for S&P 500 Index from CBOT, 33
    on commodities, 334
    commodity extraction as, 565–572
    common debt and equity as, 503
    compensation, 503, 523–528
    compound, 453–456, 467–468
    in coupon bonds, 482–483

currency, 286, 290–292, 332, 381, 727–732
debt as, 503–510
distribution of returns in portfolio and, 819–820
on dividend-paying stocks, 455–456
embedded, 488–489
equity as, 503–510
equity-linked foreign exchange, 731–732
in equity-linked notes, 483
European-style, 32
European vs. American, 293
exchange, 288–289, 459–461
exercise of, 57, 279, 304
exotic, 443–461, 703–736
financial and real, 558
on futures, 332–334, 381–382
gamma to approximate change in, 423–424
gap, 457–459, 706–707
infinitely lived exchange options, 468–469
as insurance, 45–48
in-the-money, 43
ladder, 740
long and short positions, 43
maximum and minimum prices of, 293–294
multi-period example, 349–350
multivariate, 732–736
one-period binomial example, 348–349
outperformance, 459
overpriced arbitrage of, 318
path-dependent, 444
payoff and profit diagrams for, 33–43
perpetual, 403–405
power option, 690
pricing using real probabilities, 347–350
put, 38–43, 328–329
rainbow, 734–735
real, 547–580
rebate, 716–717
reload, 532–534
repricing of, 531–532
risk premium of, 394
Sharpe ratio of, 394–395
shout, 739
spreads of, 70–73
on stock index, 330–331
on stocks, 283–286
on stocks with discrete dividends, 380–381
style, maturity, and strike of, 292–304
summary of, 52

synthetic, 285–286
terminology for, 32–33
underpriced, 319
volatility of, 393–394
warrant and, 512
written, 37–38, 40–42
Option-based model, of debt, 511
Option elasticity, 389–395, 391
Option grants, expensing of, 528–531
Option Greeks, 382–395
formulas for, 410–412
Option overwriting, 63–64
Option premium
graphs for, 397, 398
Option price
computation with expected value and true
probabilities, 347–350, 620
computing, in one-period binomial model,
314–315
delta- and delta-gamma approximations of, 426
as discounted expected value, 347–350,
617–621
jumps and, 696–698, 764
taxes and, 341
Option pricing formula, for commodity extraction,
567–568
Option pricing model. *See also* Black-Scholes
formula; Binomial model
evidence of volatility skew in, 771–773
Option risk, in absence of delta hedging, 414–415
Options Clearing Corporation (OCC), 56–57, 434
Option writer, 37, 38
Order statistics, 610
Ordinary options, 706–707
Ornstein-Uhlenbeck process, 654–655
Vasicek model and, 786
Orwall, Bruce, 492n
OTC. *See* Over-the-counter market
Out-of-the-money options, 43
Outperformance feature, valuing, 535–536
Outperformance option, 459
stock option (OSO), 534
Outputs, arrays as in VBA, 901–902
Over-the-counter contracts
credit risk and, 30–31
forward contracts, 142
Over-the-counter market, 10
Over-the-counter options, market-makers and, 433n

Paddock, J. L., 565n
Palladium, Ford risk management and, 108
Par coupon, 210
Parity, 281. *See also* Option(s)
    bounds for American options, 310–311
    of compound options, 454
    generalized, and exchange options, 287–292
    put-call, 281–287
Partial expectation, 603–604
Par value of bond, 496
Path-dependent option, 444
    barrier options as, 449
    Monte Carlo valuation and, 627–628
Payer swaption, 271
Paylater strategy, 113, 114, 457n
Payoff, 23
    Asian option, 683n
    call, 35
    on CD, 49, 50
    combined index position and put, 59–62
    comparison of long position vs. forward
        contract, 27
    distribution of, 617
    at expiration, 36, 63, 65
    on forward contract, 23–25
    for future values of index, 25
    graphing on forward contract, 25, 26
    net, 28
    for purchased and written call option, 33–37
    for purchased and written put option, 39–42
    supershare, 709
Payoff diagram, 28
    for covered call, 66
    for covered put, 67
    for long forward contract, 29
    for purchased and written call option, 33–37
    for purchased and written put option, 39–40
    zero-coupon bonds in, 28–29
Payoff table, for arbitrage opportunity, 288
Payout-protected option, 57n
Peak-load electricity generation, 559–563
Peak-load manufacturing, at Intel, 559
PEPS (Premium Equity Participating Shares),
    482n, 493–494
Percentage risk, of option, 391–393
PERCS (Preferred Equity Redeemable for
    Common Stock), 482n
Perpetual calls, 404

Perpetual options, 403
Perpetual puts, 404–405
Perpetuities, 480–481
Petersen, M. A., 107
Pharmaceutical investments, 563–565
Physical measure, 844
PIBOR (Paris Interbank Offer Rate), 160
Pindyck, R. S., 565
Poisson distribution, 636–638, 639
    pricing options with, 694–696
    simulating jumps with, 639–643
Poisson process, 845
Portfolio
    elasticity of, 395, 511–512
    gold as asset in, 187
    Greek measures for, 388–389
    risk assessment for, 813
    risk premium of, 395
    value at risk for nonlinear, 819–826
Portfolio insurance, for long run, 299, 603
Positive-definite correlations, 644–645
Positive homogeneity, 837n
Positive lease rate, storability and, 176–178
Power option, 690
Premium, 32
    for call and put options, 39
    default, 221
    forward, 134–135
    future value of option premium, 43
    liquidity, 222
    option, 284, 300n
Premium for forward contract, forward price and,
    134
Prepaid forward, 727
    binomial tree with, 363–365
    currency prepaid, 155–156
Prepaid forward contract (prepay), 127, 684
    pricing by analogy, 128–129
    pricing by arbitrage, 129–130
    pricing by discounted present value, 129
    pricing with dividends, 131–133
    on stock, 128–133
Prepaid forward price
    for claim on S^a, 666–667
    of gold, 188
Prepaid swap, 248, 271
    Enron and, 252

Present value. *See also* Net present value (NPV)
  barrier values, 403
  calculations of, 684
  of cap payments, 805
  of future stock price, 179n
  pricing by discounted, 129
  of project, 547
  traded, 550
Price
  ask, 11
  bid, 11
  clean, 243
  dirty, 243
  futures and forward, 146–147
  guaranteeing with put option, 93–95
  offer, 11
  strike, 32, 97–98
Price bonds, denominated in stocks, commodities, and currencies, 471
Price limit, 142
Price options, average, 466
Price risk, derivatives and, 7–8
Price variability, derivatives markets and, 7–8
Probability
  of bankruptcy, 847–850
  distribution, to stock price, 593–603
  in high and low states of economy, 372
  log normal, 599–600
  normal plots, 609–612
  risk-neutral, 321, 618
  in value at risk assessment, 813
Probability calculations, for lognormal distribution, 598–605
Probability distribution
  for VaR and tail VaR, 833
Probability measure, 844
Procter & Gamble, swap with Bankers Trust, 263, 264
Producer, risk management by, 91–98
Producer price index, for oil (1947-2004), 8
Production, seasonality in, 188–191
Profit, 28
  call, 35
  daily calculation for market-maker, 422
  of delta-hedged market-maker, 428
  diagrams of, 53
  at expiration, 36, 63, 65
  for gold prices, 109

  hedged, 93
  from insurance on house, 46
  for long positions, 44
  overnight market-maker, 421
  for purchased call option, 33–37
  put, 39
  on short forward position, 92–93
  spark spread and, 560
  unhedged, 92
  for written put option, 40–42
  from written straddle, 80
Profit from delta hedging, interpreting, 418–419
Profit diagram, 28
  for bull spread, 72, 87
  for butterfly, 87
  for calendar spread, 399
  for collar, 87
  for covered call, 66
  for covered put, 67
  from holding call option, 398, 399
  of insured house, 62
  before maturity, 395–399
  for no arbitrage, 70n
  for ratio spread (2:1), 87
  for straddle, 79, 87
  for strangle, 87
  for unhedged buyer, long forward, and buyer hedged with long forward, 99
  zero-coupon bonds in, 28–29
Pro forma arbitrage calculation, 138n
Proprietary trading, 414
Psi, 383, 388, 411–412
  for call options, 392
Pulvino, T., 541n
Purchase, of stock, 127
Purchased call, gamma for, 384
Purchased call option, 396
  payoff and profit for, 33–37
  profit diagram for, 44
Purchased option, Greek for, 383–388
Purchased put, gamma for, 384
Purchased put option, 44–45
  payoff and profit for, 39–40
Purchase of shares, 418
Purchasing Manger's Index, 7
Put-call parity, 68–70, 71, 281–287, 530
  versions of, 305

Put option, 38–43, 328–329
  adjusting insurance with, 96–98
  Black-Scholes formula for, 376, 378
  buying of, 69
  calls as, 289–290
  cash-or-nothing, 705
  in CD structure, 485
  collar and, 73
  covered, 65–66
  delta for, 385
  down-and-in cash put, 713
  early exercise and, 296–297, 345–346
  gamma for, 384
  homeowner's insurance as, 45–47
  as insurance, 59
  payoff and profit for purchased, 39–40
  perpetual, 404–405
  premium for, 39
  risk of, 47
  strike price properties for, 304
  summary of, 52
  theta for, 390
  up-and-in cash put, 714–715
  up-and-out cash put, 715
Put premium, for gold options, 109
Put sales, as hedge, for share repurchase, 522
Put strikes, profit using various, 97
Puttable bonds, 520
Put warrants, 522–523, 728

Quadratic variation, 652–653
  realized, 755–757
Quantile, 611
Quantity uncertainty, 116–119, 694
Quanto, 116n, 149–150, 718–727, 719
Quanto option, equity-linked foreign exchange call
    as, 731–732
Quasi-arbitrage, 139–140

Rainbow option, 734–735
Random numbers, computing, 621–623
Random walk model, 351–352
  stock prices and, 352–353
Rate of return, 12
Ratings transition, 848–850
Ratio, hedge, 113–114

Rational option pricing theory, 292n
Ratio spread, 73
  profit diagram for, 87
Real assets, 547
Realized quadratic variation, 755–757
Realized returns, Sharpe ratio and, 395n
Realized volatility, 756n
  for IBM, 757
Real options, 547–580
Rebate
  deferred up, 715
  short, 16
Rebate option, 450, 716–717
Rebonato, R., 812
Receiver swaption, 271
Recombining tree, 324–325
Recovery rate, 842
  for bonds, 850–851
Reduced form bankruptcy models, 852
Reference asset (obligation), 860
Regression(s), hedges and, 115n
Regression beta, hedging and, 115n, 154
Regulation, financial engineering for, 490–498
Regulatory arbitrage, 2–3, 4
Regulatory capital, value at risk and, 815
Re-hedging, frequency of, 431–432
Reiner, E., 710n, 727n
Reinsurance, insurance companies and, 437
Reinvestment, dividend, 132
Reload option, 532–534
Rendleman, R. J., Jr., 313, 793n
Rendleman-Bartter model, 785–786
Rennie, A., 662n, 674
Repo rate, 16
  implied, 135
Repos (repurchase agreements), 233–235
  haircuts and, 234
  Long-Term Capital Management (LTCM) crisis
    (1998) and, 236
Repricing, 531–532
Repurchases, put sales as hedge against, 522
Research and development, as capital expenditure,
    563–565
Restart options, for oil production, 572–578
Return(s)
  continuously compounded, 353–354
  standard deviation of, 354–355
  variance of continuously compounded, 596

Return distributions, bootstrapping of, 831–832
Reverse cash-and-carry, 137
Reverse cash-and-carry arbitrage, 177
 apparent, 175–176
 lease rate and, 180
Reverse conversion, 285
Reverse repo, 234
Revlon stock, constructive sale of, 491
Rho, 383, 387–388, 411
Risk, 1. *See also* specific types
 basis, 116, 196–198
 bond price, 828
 of coupon bond, 225
 credit, 11, 15, 30–31, 815, 841–867
 diversifiable, 6
 dividend, 434
 duration as measure of, 237
 of extreme price moves, 432–433
 in foreign stock index, 718–719
 insurance purchases and, 97
 jump, 764–765
 market, 815
 of market-maker, 414–417
 nondiversifiable, 6
 operational, 815
 pooling of in insurance, 436
 of put options, 47
 in short-selling, 15
 swaps and, 263
 value at risk and, 813–839
 volatility, 741
Risk arbitrageurs, 541
Risk-averse investor, 105, 346
 declining marginal utility and, 369–370
 risk-neutral process and, 661
Risk-free bond, valuing, 372
Risk-free rate of return, Monte Carlo valuation and, 617–618
Risk management, 2, 91–119
 buyer's perspective on, 98–100
 cash-and-carry as, 137
 nonfinancial, 105–106
 producer's perspective on, 91–98
 reasons for, 100–107
 for stock-pickers, 154
Risk measures, subadditive, 837–838
Risk-neutral distribution, value at risk and, 835–837

Risk-neutral investor, 346–347
Risk-neutral measure, 662–663
Risk-neutral pricing, 320–321, 343, 346–350, 369–374, 690–693
 as forward price, 553
 reasons for success of, 373–374
 for valuing claim on S^a, 668
Risk-neutral probability, 321, 346, 347, 713, 725, 726
Risk-neutral process, 660–663
 for $dS^a Q^b$, 670–672
Risk-neutral valuation, of stock, 373
Risk premium
 forward contract earning of, 140
 forward price bias by, 140–141
 of option, 394
 of portfolio, 395
 Sharpe ratio and, 659
 value at risk and, 836–837
Risk-sharing, 5–6
Risky stock, valuing with real probabilities, 372
Rogers, D. A., 107
Roosevelt, D., 858n
Rosansky, V. I., 172n
Ross, S. A., 359, 555, 690, 787–788
Rouwenhorst, K. G., 172n
Rubinstein, M., 292n, 359, 555, 709, 710n, 724n, 727, 735n
Russian doll CDOs, 854
Ryan, M. D., 728

Sales, constructive, 491
Saly, P. J., 532, 534n
S&P 500 futures contract, 143–144
S&P 500 index
 arbitrage and, 147–149
 volatility estimates for, 745
S&P Depository Receipts (SPDRs), 148n
Scarcity, in short-selling, 15–16
Scholes, Myron, 375, 376, 503. *See also* Black-Scholes formula
Schwartz, E. S., 516n, 563n, 565, 565n, 574n, 633, 635
Scott, L. O., 768n
Seasonality
 corn forward market and, 188–191

in dividend payments, 132n
natural gas and, 191–195
SEC. *See* Securities and Exchange Commission (SEC)
Securities. *See also* specific types
Treasury, 205n
Securities and Exchange Commission (SEC), 847
derivatives reporting requirements and, 10
Security design, 4
financial engineering and, 473–498
Self-financing, 419
portfolio and, 422
Seller, short as, 23
Seniorities, of debt-holders, 511
Senior tranche, 511
CDOs and, 854, 856
SFAS. *See* Statement of Financial Accounting Standards (SFAS)
Shao, J., 831n
Shapiro, A. C., 235
Share(s), convertible bond exchanged for, 513
Share-equivalent of option, delta as, 383–384
Share repurchases, 510, 522
Sharpe, W. F., 313
Sharpe ratio, 395n, 659–660, 663, 688
bond pricing model and, 782–783
of option, 394–395
Shiller, Robert, 6
Shimko, David, 86n
Short (seller), 23
Short call profit, 53
Short forward contract, collar and, 75
Short forward position, 44–45
Short forward profit, 53
Short position, 12, 44–45, 52
bonds, repos, and, 235
insuring with cap, 62–63
Short put profit, 53
Short rebate, 16
Short-sale, 12–14
cash flows and, 14
risk and scarcity in, 15–16
of wine, 13–14
Short-term interest rate, 783
Shout option, European, 739
Shoven, J. B., 528, 529
Shreve, S. E., 650n, 652n, 662n, 664n, 674
Shut-down, of oil production, 572–578

Siegel, D. R., 115, 565n, 689n
Siegel, J. J., 299
Simulation, of lognormal stock prices, 623–624
Single-barrel extraction of oil
under certainty, 565–569
under uncertainty, 569–570
Single name credit default swaps, 860–861, 865
Single-payment swap, 247
Single stock futures, 143
Singleton, K. J., 852n
Smith, C. W., 103n, 107n
Smith, D., 243n
Smith, Randall, 492n
Solnik, B., 258n
Southwest Airlines, jet fuel hedging by, 199n
Spark spread, 560, 561
SPDRs. *See* S&P Depository Receipts (SPDRs)
Special collateral repurchase agreement, 234
Speculation, 2
financing with repos, 235
on foreign index, 728–729
short-selling and, 13
on volatility, using options, 78–85
Speculative grade bonds, 847
Spot price, 23
Spread, 70–73, 71
bear, 72
bid-ask, 11–12
box, 72–73
bull, 71
commodity, 195–196
crack, 196
crush, 195
ratio, 73
vertical, 71
Spread option, 562
Stable distribution, 592
Stack and roll, 198
Stack hedge, 197, 198
Staged investment, 564
Standard and Poor's, 847n. *See also* S&P 500 entries
Standard deviation
estimate of, 607
of returns, 354–355
Standard normal density, 587–588
Standard normal distribution, 409–410
Standard normal probability density function, 409

Standard normal variable, conversion of normal
    random variable to, 590–591
Statement of Financial Accounting Standards
    (SFAS)123R, 525, 527, 532, (SFAS) 133, 106
Static NPV, 548–549, 555
Static option replication, 433
Steiner, R., 233n
Stiglitz, J. E., 130n
Stochastic differential equations, 649
Stochastic process, 650, 768n
Stochastic volatility, 744, 763, 772
Stock
    alternative ways to buy, 127–128
    calls on nondividend-paying, 294–295
    cash flows for, 283
    with discrete dividends, 361–365
    forward contracts on, 133–141
    options to exchange, 288–289
    prepaid forward contract (prepay) on, 128–133
    risk management for picking, 154
    risk-neutral valuation of, 373
    short-selling, 14
    synthetic, 285
    value at risk for, 815–819
Stock index, 22–23
    forward contract vs. option and, 37
    option on, 330–331
Stock index futures, 22
Stock options. *See* Compensation options;
    Option(s)
Stock prices
    bond valuation based on, 520
    conditional expected price, 603–604
    current price as present value of future price,
        129, 179n
    jumps in, 672–674
    lognormal model of, 595–598
    portfolio value as function of, 827
    as random walk, 352–353
    simulating correlated, 643–645
    simulating jumps with Poisson distribution,
        639–643
    simulating sequence of, 623–624
    standard deviation correspondence and, 602
Stock price trees, option price trees and, 442
Stock purchase contract, 495–496
Storage
    as carry, 181

of corn, 189–190
    costs, forward prices, and, 181–182
    costs and lease rate, 182
    of electricity, 172–174
    of natural gas, 191–195
    positive lease rate and, 176–178
Straddle, 78–80
    at-the-money written, risk of, 822–823
    profit diagram for, 87
    on single stock, 823–824
    strangle and, 78–79, 80
    written, 79–80
Straddle rules, 58
Strangle, 78–79, 80, 87
Strategic options, 558
    future investment options as, 558
Stratified sampling, 632
Strike
    foreign equity call struck in domestic currency,
        729–730
    pricing options for, 769
Strike price, 32, 299–304, 547, 560
    average as, 446–447
    convexity and, 304
    effect on option price, 299–304
    risk management and, 97–98
Strike price convexity, 301
Strip, Eurodollar, 158
Strip hedge, 197
Strip, interest rate, 223
STRIPS, 206
Structured note, 474–482
Stulz, R., 814n
Style, of options effect on price, 293
Subadditivity, 837–838
Subordinated tranche, CDOs and, 854, 856
Subrahmanyam, M. G., 258n
Supershares, 709
Supply, of corn, 190
Swap(s), 125, 247, 279, 826
    accreting, 263
    amortizing, 263
    asset, 255
    cash flows from, 249
    collateralization and, 486n
    commodity, 247–254, 268–270
    computing rate, 257–258
    currency, 264–268

default, 273–274, 858–863
deferred, 261–262
financial settlement of, 248–249
as forward rate agreements, 258n
implicit loan balance of, 260–261
interest rate, 254–263
market value of, 253–254
physical settlement of, 248
prepaid, 248
total rate of return, 864
total return, 272–274
with variable quantity and price, 269–270
variance, 758–759
volatility, 759, 828–830
Swap counterparty, 250–251, 255–257
Swap curves, 258–260, 270
Swap price, 250
Swap-rate calculation, 274
Swap spread, 259–260
Swap tenor, 254
Swap term, 254
Swaptions, 271
Synthetic commodity, 171, 172n
Synthetic forwards, 66–70, 112, 135–136, 161
box spreads and, 72–73
in market-making and arbitrage, 136–138
Synthetic FRAs, 216–218
Synthetic Nikkei investment, 719
Synthetic options, 285–286
Synthetic stock, parity and, 285
Synthetic T-bills, 285

Tailing, 132
Tail VaR, 832, 836–837
Tax-deductible equity, 495–498
Taxes
box spreads and, 74
corporate deferral, 492–495
for derivatives, 58
on employee options, 527n
on equity-linked CD, 484n
financial engineering for, 490–498
hedging and, 104, 106
individual deferral, 491–492
option prices and, 341
Taylor, H. M., 691n, 692n
Taylor series expansion, of bond price, 228n

T-bills. *See* Treasury bills
Term repo, 234
Terrorism, futures on, 24
Theta, 383, 387, 428, 442
delta-hedging and, 425–426, 427
formula for, 410–411
hedging and, 420
for put options, 390
Thiagarajan, S. R., 107
TIBOR (Tokyo Interbank Offer Rate), 160
Times Mirror, 492–495
Time-varying volatility (ARCH), 747–751
T-note. *See* Treasury-note futures
Total rate of return swaps, 864
Total return payer, 272
Total return swap, 272–274
TRACERS, 865
TRAC-X, 865
Traded present value, 550
Trades, arbitrage and, 139
Trading
of derivatives, 7–10
proprietary, 414
Tranched CDO claims, 853
Tranched CDX, 866
Tranches, 511
ratings of, 854–856
Transaction costs, 2
in bonds, 233
future overlays and, 151
hedging and, 106
no-arbitrage bounds with, 138–139
Translation invariance, 837n
Treasury bill rate, monthly change in (1947–2004), 9
Treasury bills, 244–245
LIBOR vs. 3-month T-bills, 221–223
quotations for, 244
stocks and, 150
synthetic, 172n, 285
yield on, 147
Treasury bond(s). *See* Bonds; Treasury-bond futures
Treasury-bond futures, 230–233
Treasury-note futures, 230–233
Treasury securities. *See also* Treasury bills
issuance of, 205n
Trottman, Melanie, 199n

True probabilities
    pricing options with, 369
    valuation with, 619–621
Trust, tax-deductible equity and, 495–498
TRW. *See* Northrop Grumman-TRW merger
Tu, D., 831n
Tufano, P., 107
Turnbull, S. M., 852n
Twin security, 550
Two-parameter distribution, 587
Two-period European call, 323–326

Uncertainty
    discounted cash flow and, 551–552
    investment under, 551–558
    quantity, 116–119
    single-barrel extraction under, 569–570
Underlying asset, 21
Unfunded CDs, 862
Uniformly distributed random variables, sums of,
    622
U.S. Tax Code, on capital income, 74
Unit of denomination, numeraire as, 693
Up-and-in cash call, 715
Up-and-in cash put, 714–715
Up-and-in options, 450
Up-and-out cash call, 715
Up-and-out cash put, 715
Up-and-out-currency put options, 452
Up-and-out option, 450, 452
Upper DECS, 497
Upward-sloping yield curve, 107n
Utility-based valuation, 369–371
Utility weights, in high and low states of economy,
    372

Valuation. *See also* Monte Carlo valuation of
    American options, 633–636
    bond, 520
    under certainty, 679–681
    of claim on S^a, 666–672
    of claim on $S^a Q^b$, 670–672
    of compensation options, 524–525, 525–526
    of derivatives on cash flow, 552–554
    equation of, 680

of infinite oil reserve, 570–572
of log contract, 761–762
Monte Carlo, 617–645
of oil producing firm, 571
of option for electricity and gas production,
    560–563
of option to invest in oil, 571–572
of project with 2-year investment horizon,
    554–558
of project with infinite investment horizon, 558
with risk-neutral probabilities, 618, 619
with true probabilities, 619–621
utility-based, 369–371
Value at risk (VaR), 813–839
    alternative risk measures and, 832–835
    for bonds, 826–830
    estimating volatility in, 830–831
    Monte Carlo simulation for, 822–826
    for nonlinear portfolios, 819–826
    for one stock, 815–817
    regulatory capital and, 815
    risk-neutral distribution and, 835–837
    subadditive risk measures and, 837–838
    for two or more stocks, 817–819
    uses of, 814–815
VaR. *See* Value at risk (VaR)
Variable prepaid forward (VPF) contract, 492
Variance, constant elasticity of, 763, 766–767
Variance estimate, variability of, 607n
Variance swap, 758–759
Vasicek, O., 779, 781n
Vasicek model, 786–787
    Cox-Ingersoll-Ross model and, 788–790
Vassalou, M., 846
VBA. *See* Visual Basic for Applications (VBA)
Vega, 382, 386, 411
    for at-the-money 40-strike options, 386
Vertical spread, 71
Visual Basic for Applications (VBA), 885–906
    arrays and, 897–899
    Black-Scholes formula computation with,
        894–895
    checking for conditions and, 896–897
    creating button to invoke subroutine, 888–889
    differences between functions and subroutines,
        890
    functions can call functions, 889
    illegal function names, 889–890

iteration and, 899–901

object browser and, 895–896

storing and retrieving variables in worksheet, 890–893

subroutine in, 888

using Excel functions from within, 893–896

VIX volatility index, 743, 757, 762–763

Volatility, 741–773

    asymmetric butterfly spread and, 82–83

    averaging and, 447–448

    Black-Scholes model and, 763–773

    in bond pricing, 794–796

    for bonds and swaps, 828–830

    butterfly spreads and, 81–82

    deterministic changes over time, 772–773

    early exercise of option and, 343–346

    for electricity and natural gas, 560–562

    equity-holders and, 510

    estimating, 360, 361, 830–831

    Health-Jarrow-Morton model and, 812

    hedging and pricing, 757–763

    historical, 744–746

    for IBM and S&P 500 index, 745

    implied, 400–402, 741–744

    measurement and behavior of, 744–757

    of option, 393–394, 553n

    pricing of, 759–763

    speculating on, 78–85

    stochastic, 744

    straddles and, 78–80

    of various positions, 87

    verifying for bonds, 803–804

    zero, 322

Volatility clustering, 748

Volatility forecasts, in GARCH model, 753–754

Volatility frowns, 742

Volatility skew, 402

    in option pricing model, 771–773

Volatility smile, 742

Volatility smirk, 742

Volatility surface, 742

Volatility swap, 759

Vorst, A. C. F., 630n

Vorst, T., 863

Warrant, 512

    put, 522–523

Watkinson, L., 858n

Weather derivatives, 199–200

Webber, N., 812

Weston, J., 107

White, A., 768n

White, Gregory L., 108

Wiggins, J. B., 768n

Wilmott, P., 674

Writing

    of covered call, 64–65

    selling insurance and, 63–64

Written call option, 44–45, 96

    payoff and profit for, 37–38

    with different underlying stocks, 824–826

Written options. *See also* Written call option;
    Written put

    Greek for, 383–388

    margins for, 57

Written put

    covered call and, 65

    with different underlying stocks, 824–826

    payoff and profit for, 40–42

    profit diagram for, 42, 44

    with same underlying stock, 823–824

Written straddle, 79–80

    at-the-money, 822–823

    butterfly spread and, 81–82

Wu, L., 772n

Wyden, Ron, 24

Xing, Y., 846

XYZ debt issue, default swap and, 860

Yen-based investor, 719, 720–721

Yen forward contract, synthetic creation of, 157

Yield

    bond, 242–244

    continuously compounded, 213–214

    convenience, 182–184

    dividend, 132

    effective annual rate, continuously
        compounded rate, and, 148n

    expected interest rates and, 796–797

    verifying bond, 802–803

Yield curve, 208

    Black-Derman-Toy model and, 798

bond pricing model and, 780–781
    upward-sloping, 107n
    Vasicek and CIR models and, 789
Yield to maturity, 208, 241–245
Yurday, E. C., 858n, 864n

Zero-cost collar, 76–78, 110–111, 491–492
    financing of, 76–77
    forward contract as, 111–112
Zero-coupon bond, 206–208, 474–475, 779
    commodity-linked, 479
    default and, 841–843

    equity-linked, 476
    inferring price of, 211–212
    Macaulay duration and, 229n
    movement of, 829
    payoff, profit, and, 28–29, 61
    price of, 684
    STRIPS as, 206
    valuation of, 783
    value at risk for, 827–828
Zero-coupon bond prices, 794–796
Zero-coupon debt, 511
Zero premium, of forward contract, 69
Zero volatility, 322

MAGILL'S CHOICE

U.S. COURT CASES

Revised Edition

Volume 2

Court Cases:

*Geofroy v. Riggs —
Richmond v. J.A. Croson Co.*

Edited by
Thomas Tandy Lewis
St. Cloud State University

SALEM PRESS
Pasadena, California   Hackensack, New Jersey

∞ The paper used in these volumes conforms to the American National Standard for Permanence of Paper for Printed Library Materials, Z39.48-1992 (R1997).

Some of the essays in this work originally appeared in the following Salem Press sets: *Criminal Justice* (2006), *Encyclopedia of the U.S. Supreme Court* (2001), *Great Events from History: The Nineteenth Century* (2007), *Great Events from History: The Twentieth Century* (2008), *U.S. Court Cases* (1999), and *U.S. Supreme Court* (2007). New material has been added.

Library of Congress Cataloging-in-Publication Data

U.S. court cases / editor, Thomas Tandy Lewis. — Rev. ed.

   p. cm. — (Magill's choice)

Includes bibliographical references and index.

ISBN 978-1-58765-672-9 (set : alk. paper)

ISBN 978-1-58765-673-6 (vol. 1 : alk. paper)

ISBN 978-1-58765-674-3 (vol. 2 : alk. paper)

ISBN 978-1-58765-675-0 (vol. 3 : alk. paper)

   1. Law—United States—Cases. 2. Courts—United States. I. Lewis, Thomas T. (Thomas Tandy) II. Title: US court cases. III. Title: United States court cases.

  KF385.A4U15 2010

  347.73'1—dc22

                            2010019782

CONTENTS

U.S. Supreme Court Citation Numbers lvii
Complete List of Contents lix

Geofroy v. Riggs 437
Gertz v. Robert Welch 437
Gibbons v. Ogden 438
Gideon v. Wainwright 445
Gitlow v. New York 452
Gold Clause Cases 453
Goldberg v. Kelly 454
Goldfarb v. Virginia State Bar 455
Goldwater v. Carter 456
Gomez v. Perez 457
Gomillion v. Lightfoot 458
Gompers v. Buck's Stove and Range Co. 459
Gonzales v. Raich 460
Good News Club v. Milford Central School 461
Goodridge v. Department of Public Health 462
Goss v. Lopez 467
Graham v. Richardson 468
Gratz v. Bollinger/Grutter v. Bollinger 469
Graves v. New York ex rel. O'Keefe 471
Gray v. Sanders 472
Green v. Biddle 473
Green v. County School Board of New Kent County 474
Greer v. Spock 475
Gregg v. Georgia 477
Griffin v. Breckenridge 482
Griffin v. California 483
Griffin v. County School Board of Prince Edward
    County 484
Griggs v. Duke Power Co. 485
Griswold v. Connecticut 491
Grosjean v. American Press Co. 497
Grove City College v. Bell 498
Groves v. Slaughter 499

Grovey v. Townsend 500
Guinn v. United States 501

Hague v. Congress of Industrial Organizations 503
Hall v. DeCuir 504
Hamdan v. Rumsfeld 505
Hamling v. United States 507
Hammer v. Dagenhart 509
Harmelin v. Michigan 510
Harper v. Virginia State Board of Elections 512
Harris v. McRae 514
Harris v. New York 515
Harris v. United States 516
Hawaii Housing Authority v. Midkiff 518
Hayburn's Case 519
Hazelwood School District v. Kuhlmeier 520
Head Money Cases 521
Heart of Atlanta Motel v. United States 523
Helvering v. Davis 529
Hernández v. Texas 530
Herndon v. Lowry 531
Hirabayashi v. United States 533
Hodgson v. Minnesota 535
Holden v. Hardy 536
Holmes v. Jennison 537
Home Building and Loan Association v. Blaisdell 539
Hoyt v. Florida 541
Hudson v. Michigan 542
Hudson v. Palmer 543
Humphrey's Executor v. United States 544
Hurley v. Irish-American Gay, Lesbian, and Bisexual Group
   of Boston 545
Hurtado v. California 546
Hustler Magazine v. Falwell 548
Hutchinson v. Proxmire 548
Hutto v. Davis 549
Hylton v. United States 551

Illinois ex rel. McCollum v. Board of Education 552
Illinois v. Caballes 553
Illinois v. Gates 556

Illinois v. Krull 557
Illinois v. McArthur 559
Illinois v. Wardlow 561
Immigration and Naturalization Service v. Chadha 563
In re Baby M 564
In re Debs 565
In re Gault 567
In re Neagle 568
In re Winship 570
Insular Cases 571

Jackson v. Metropolitan Edison Co. 577
Jacobellis v. Ohio 578
Jacobson v. Massachusetts 579
Johnson and Graham's Lessee v. McIntosh 580
Johnson v. Louisiana 581
Johnson v. Santa Clara County 582
Johnson v. Zerbst 583
Joint Anti-Fascist Refugee Committee v. McGrath 584
Jones v. Alfred H. Mayer Co. 585
Jones v. Van Zandt 586

Kansas v. Hendricks 588
Kastigar v. United States 588
Katz v. United States 589
Katzenbach v. McClung 591
Katzenbach v. Morgan 591
Kelo v. City of New London 592
Kennedy v. Louisiana 594
Kent v. Dulles 596
Kentucky v. Dennison 597
Ker v. California 598
Keyes v. Denver School District No. 1 599
Keyishian v. Board of Regents 600
Keystone Bituminous Coal Association v. DeBenedictis 601
Kidd v. Pearson 602
Kilbourn v. Thompson 602
Kirkpatrick v. Preisler 604
Klopfer v. North Carolina 604
Knowles v. Iowa 605
Korematsu v. United States 607

Kunz v. New York 609
Kyllo v. United States 611

Lassiter v. Northampton County Board of Elections 612
Lau v. Nichols 613
Lawrence v. Texas 618
Lee v. Weisman 619
Legal Tender Cases 620
Lemon v. Kurtzman 621
License Cases 625
Local 28 of Sheet Metal Workers International Association v.
    Equal Employment Opportunity Commission 626
Lochner v. New York 627
Loewe v. Lawlor 633
Lone Wolf v. Hitchcock 634
Lorance v. AT&T Technologies 638
Louisiana ex rel. Francis v. Resweber 639
Louisville, Cincinnati, and Charleston Railroad Co. v. Letson 640
Louisville, New Orleans, and Texas Railway Co. v. Mississippi 641
Lovell v. City of Griffin 643
Loving v. Virginia 644
Lucas v. South Carolina Coastal Council 645
Luther v. Borden 646
Lynch v. Donnelly 648

McCleskey v. Kemp 650
McCleskey v. Zant 654
McConnell v. Federal Election Commission 655
McCray v. United States 656
McCulloch v. Maryland 657
McKeiver v. Pennsylvania 662
McLaurin v. Oklahoma State Regents for Higher Education 663
Mahan v. Howell 664
Maher v. Roe 665
Mallory v. United States 666
Malloy v. Hogan 667
Mapp v. Ohio 669
Marbury v. Madison 670
Marshall v. Barlow's 674
Martin v. Hunter's Lessee 675
Martin v. Mott 676

CONTENTS

Martin v. Wilks 677
Marvin v. Marvin 678
Maryland v. Buie 679
Maryland v. Craig 681
Massachusetts Board of Retirement v. Murgia 682
Massachusetts v. Mellon 684
Massachusetts v. Sheppard 685
Massiah v. United States 686
Masson v. New Yorker Magazine 688
Maxwell v. Dow 689
Memoirs v. Massachusetts 690
Meritor Savings Bank v. Vinson 691
Metro Broadcasting v. Federal Communications Commission 692
Meyer v. Nebraska 693
Miami Herald Publishing Co. v. Tornillo 695
Michael M. v. Superior Court of Sonoma County 696
Michigan Department of State Police v. Sitz 697
Michigan v. Long 698
Milkovich v. Lorain Journal Co. 699
Miller et al. v. Civil City of South Bend 700
Miller v. California; Paris Adult Theatre v. Slaton 701
Milliken v. Bradley 703
Minersville School District v. Gobitis 704
Minnesota v. Carter 705
Minnick v. Mississippi 706
Minor v. Happersett 708
Miranda v. Arizona 712
Mississippi University for Women v. Hogan 718
Mississippi v. Johnson 719
Missouri ex rel. Gaines v. Canada 720
Missouri v. Holland 721
Missouri v. Jenkins 722
Mistretta v. United States 723
Mobile v. Bolden 724
Monell v. Department of Social Services 725
Moore v. City of East Cleveland 725
Moore v. Dempsey 726
Moose Lodge v. Irvis 727
Morehead v. New York ex rel. Tipaldo 729
Morgan v. Virginia 729
Morrison v. Olson 730

Mueller v. Allen 731
Mugler v. Kansas 733
Mulford v. Smith 734
Muller v. Oregon 735
Munn v. Illinois 739
Murdock v. Memphis 740
Murdock v. Pennsylvania 741
Murphy v. Waterfront Commission of New York 742
Murray's Lessee v. Hoboken Land and Improvement Co. 743
Muskrat v. United States 744
Mutual Film Corp. v. Industrial Commission of Ohio 745
Myers v. United States 746

National Association for the Advancement
   of Colored People v. Alabama 747
National Association for the Advancement
   of Colored People v. Button 748
National Endowment for the Arts v. Finley 749
National Labor Relations Board v. Jones and Laughlin Steel Corp. . . . 753
National League of Cities v. Usery 755
National Treasury Employees Union v. Von Raab 756
Near v. Minnesota 757
Nebbia v. New York 759
Nebraska Press Association v. Stuart 760
New Jersey v. T.L.O. 761
New State Ice Co. v. Liebmann 763
New York State Club Association v. City of New York 764
New York Times Co. v. Sullivan 765
New York Times Co. v. United States 766
New York v. Belton 770
New York v. Ferber 771
New York v. Miln 773
Newberry v. United States 774
Nguyen v. Immigration and Naturalization Service 775
Nixon v. Administrator of General Services 776
Nixon v. Condon 777
Nixon v. Herndon 778
Nollan v. California Coastal Commission 780
Norris v. Alabama 782
Northern Securities Co. v. United States 783
Noto v. United States 790

CONTENTS

Ogden v. Saunders 791
O'Gorman and Young v. Hartford Fire Insurance Co.. 792
Ohio v. Akron Center for Reproductive Health 793
Olmstead v. United States. 794
Oregon v. Mitchell; Texas v. Mitchell; United States v. Arizona 796
Oregon Waste Systems v. Department of Environmental Quality 797
Orr v. Orr 798
Osborn v. Bank of the United States 799
Osborne v. Ohio 800
Ozawa v. United States 801

Pacific Mutual Life Insurance Co. v. Haslip 805
Pacific States Telephone and Telegraph Co. v. Oregon 806
Palko v. Connecticut 806
Palmer v. Thompson 809
Panama Refining Co. v. Ryan 810
Parents Involved in Community Schools v.
    Seattle School District No. 1. 811
Pasadena Board of Education v. Spangler 815
Passenger Cases 817
Patterson v. McLean Credit Union 817
Paul v. Virginia 818
Payne v. Tennessee 819
Payton v. New York 821
Penn Central Transportation Co. v. City of New York 822
Pennoyer v. Neff 823
Pennsylvania Coal Co. v. Mahon 824
Pennsylvania v. Nelson 825
Pennsylvania v. Wheeling and Belmont Bridge Co. 825
Penry v. Lynaugh 827
Personnel Administrator of Massachusetts v. Feeney 828
Phillips v. Martin Marietta Corp. 829
Pierce v. Society of Sisters 830
Planned Parenthood of Central Missouri v. Danforth 831
Planned Parenthood of Southeastern Pennsylvania v. Casey 833
Plessy v. Ferguson 835
Plyler v. Doe 841
Pointer v. Texas 844
Pollock v. Farmers' Loan and Trust Co. 845
Powell v. Alabama 847
Powell v. McCormick 848

Powers v. Ohio 849

Presser v. Illinois 850

Prigg v. Pennsylvania 851

Printz v. United States. 852

Prize Cases 853

Providence Bank v. Billings 854

Prudential Insurance Co. v. Benjamin 855

R.A.V. v. City of St. Paul 856

Reapportionment Cases 858

Red Lion Broadcasting Co. v. Federal Communications
    Commission 860

Redd v. State of Georgia 861

Reed v. Reed 862

Regents of the University of California v. Bakke 864

Reitman v. Mulkey 870

Reno v. American Civil Liberties Union 872

Reynolds v. Sims. 873

Reynolds v. United States 874

Rhodes v. Chapman. 876

Ricci v. DeStefano. 877

Richmond Newspapers v. Virginia 882

Richmond v. J. A. Croson Co.. 883

U.S. SUPREME COURT CITATION NUMBERS

Since the year 1876, official versions of U.S. Supreme Court decisions and opinions have appeared in volumes titled *United States Reports*, published by the federal government. Each standard citation listed in these volumes usually includes this information:

- names of the parties involved in the case, in italics
- volume number of *United States Reports* containing the case
- abbreviation "U.S."
- page number on which the case begins
- page number of quoted passage (where relevant)
- year in which the decision was made, in parentheses

This is a typical example: "*Brown v. Board of Education of Topeka*, 349 U.S. 294, at 342 (1954)."

For Supreme Court rulings earlier than 1876, each official government volume was published under the last name of the Court reporter who supervised its editing and publication. Standard citations to pre-1876 cases include the names of the reporters preceded by the numbers of the volumes within the series the reporters edited. The citations then give the volume numbers used by *United States Reports* in parentheses. This is a typical example: "*Marbury v. Madison*, 1 Cranch (5 U.S.) 137, at 146 (1803)."

Through 1875, the volumes were edited by seven different Court reporters whose names (Dallas, Cranch, Wheaton, Peters, Howard, Black, and Wallace) appear in citations. Howard (abbreviated How.) supervised the publication of the most volumes (twenty-four); Black the fewest (two).

The names given to U.S. Supreme Court decisions sometimes are different from the standard forms discussed above. For example, petitions for habeas corpus frequently do not include two parties; names of such cases typically include the Latin expression *Ex parte*, which means "in behalf of" or "for one party," as in "*Ex parte Milligan*, 71 U.S. 2 (1866)." Also, the Latin expression *In re*, which means "concerning" or "in the matter of" is frequently employed in judicial proceedings when there are no adversarial parties, as in "*In Re Gault*, 387 U.S. 1 (1967)."

After the Supreme Court hands down a ruling, its official version is generally not published until one or two years later. Consequently, until the decision is officially published, its page number in *United States Reports* cannot be known. Early publications of such cases are known as "slip opinions," and their citations utilize an underscore line to substitute for the volume number, as in "*Ricci v. DeStefano*, 555 U.S. ____ (2009)."

Although the vast majority of lawyers and legal writers refer to the federal government's official publications, some prefer to utilize one of the privately published and unofficial compilations, such as *Supreme Court Reporter* or *United States Supreme Court Reports, Lawyers' Edition*. Until the Court's official opinions are published in *United States Reports*, many writers cite numbers from these unofficial compilations. This is an example of a citation from the former publication: "*Reno v. American Civil Liberties Union*, 117 S.Ct. 2329 (1997)." In *United States Reports*, the same case is cited as "*Reno v. American Civil Liberties Union*, 521 U.S. 824 (1997)."

For more detailed information on citing court cases, one of the best resources is *The Bluebook: A Uniform System of Citation* (19 ed., 2010), an annually updated publication of the *Harvard Law Review*. Another useful publication is *ALWD Citation Manual: A Professional System of Citation* (2005) by Darby Dickerson and the Association of Legal Writing Directors.

COMPLETE LIST OF CONTENTS

Volume 1

Contents v
Publisher's Note xi
Contributors xv
U.S. Supreme Court Citation Numbers. xxi
Complete List of Contents. xxiii

Law and the Courts

Anglo-American Legal Systems 3
Law. 9
Jurisprudence 17
The U.S. Constitution 22
The Bill of Rights. 29
Constitutional Law 39
The U.S. Judicial System 45
State and Local Courts 53
The U.S. Supreme Court. 59
Judicial Review 68
Due Process of Law. 76

Court Cases

Abington School District v. Schempp 85
Ableman v. Booth 89
Abrams v. United States 91
Adair v. United States 92
Adamson v. California 98
Adarand Constructors v. Peña 99
Adderley v. Florida 104
Adkins v. Children's Hospital 105
Afroyim v. Rusk 111
Agostini v. Felton 112
Akron v. Akron Center for Reproductive Health 113
Albemarle Paper Co. v. Moody 114
Albertson v. Subversive Activities Control Board 115

Alcoa v. Federal Trade Commission 116
Alexander v. Holmes County Board of Education 123
Allegheny County v. American Civil Liberties Union Greater
    Pittsburgh Chapter 125
Allgeyer v. Louisiana 126
Alsager v. District Court. 127
American Booksellers Association, Inc. v. Hudnut. 128
American Communications Association v. Douds 130
Antelope, The. 131
Aptheker v. Secretary of State 132
Argersinger v. Hamlin 133
Arizona v. Fulminante. 134
Arlington Heights v. Metropolitan Housing
    Development Corp. 136
Ashcroft v. Free Speech Coalition 137
Ashwander v. Tennessee Valley Authority 138
Atkins v. Virginia 139
Atwater v. City of Lago Vista 142
Automobile Workers v. Johnson Controls 144

Bailey v. Drexel Furniture Co. 145
Baker v. Carr 146
Baker v. Vermont 150
Ballard v. United States 152
Ballew v. Georgia 153
Bank of Augusta v. Earle 153
Bank of the United States v. Deveaux 154
Barenblatt v. United States 155
Barker v. Wingo. 157
Barnes v. Glen Theatre, Inc. 158
Barron v. Baltimore. 160
Bates v. State Bar of Arizona 161
Batson v. Kentucky 162
Belle Terre v. Boraas 163
Benton v. Maryland 164
Berman v. Parker 170
Betts v. Brady 171
Bigelow v. Virginia 172
Bivens v. Six Unknown Named Agents 173
BMW of North America v. Gore 174
Board of Education of Oklahoma City v. Dowell. 175

Boerne v. Flores 176
Bolling v. Sharpe 177
Booth v. Maryland 179
Boumediene v. Bush 180
Bowe v. Colgate-Palmolive 185
Bowers v. Hardwick 186
Bowsher v. Synar 188
Boy Scouts of America v. Dale 189
Boyd v. United States 192
Bradwell v. Illinois 194
Brady v. United States 195
Brandenburg v. Ohio 196
Branzburg v. Hayes 198
Brecht v. Abrahamson 199
Breedlove v. Suttles 199
Briscoe v. Bank of the Commonwealth of Kentucky 200
Bronson v. Kinzie 201
Brown v. Board of Education 202
Brown v. Maryland 208
Brown v. Mississippi 209
Bryant v. Yellen 210
Buchanan v. Warley 215
Buck v. Bell 216
Buckley v. Valeo 217
Budd v. New York 219
Bunting v. Oregon 220
Burstyn v. Wilson 221
Burton v. Wilmington Parking Authority 222
Bush v. Gore 223
Butz v. Economou 225

Calder v. Bull 226
California v. Acevedo 228
California v. Cabazon Band of Mission Indians 229
California v. Greenwood 232
Cantwell v. Connecticut 234
Carroll v. United States 235
Carter v. Carter Coal Co. 236
Chambers v. Florida 238
Champion v. Ames 239
Chaplinsky v. New Hampshire 245

Charles River Bridge v. Warren Bridge. 247
Cherokee Cases. 248
Chicago v. Morales 253
Chicago, Burlington, and Quincy Railroad Co. v.
    Chicago 254
Chicago, Milwaukee, and St. Paul Railway Co. v.
    Minnesota 256
Chimel v. California. 257
Chinese Exclusion Cases 258
Chisholm v. Georgia 260
Church of Lukumi Babalu Aye v. Hialeah 261
Citizens United v. Federal Election Commission. 263
City of Renton v. Playtime Theaters 268
Civil Rights Cases 270
Clark Distilling Co. v. Western Maryland Railway Co. 275
Clinton v. City of New York 276
Clinton v. Jones 279
Cohen v. California 280
Cohen v. Cowles Media Co.. 281
Cohens v. Virginia. 282
Coker v. Georgia 283
Colegrove v. Green 284
Coleman v. Miller 286
Collector v. Day 287
Columbus Board of Education v. Penick. 288
Commonwealth v. Hunt 289
Communist Party v. Subversive Activities Control Board. 293
Cooley v. Board of Wardens of the Port of Philadelphia. 294
Cooper v. Aaron. 295
Corrigan v. Buckley 296
Counselman v. Hitchcock. 297
County of Washington v. Gunther 299
Cox v. Louisiana. 300
Cox v. New Hampshire 301
Coyle v. Smith 302
Craig v. Boren 303
Craig v. Missouri 304
Cruzan v. Director, Missouri Department of Health 305
Cumming v. Richmond County Board of Education 309
Cummings v. Missouri 310

Dames and Moore v. Regan. 311
Dandridge v. Williams. 312
Dartmouth College v. Woodward. 314
Davis v. Bandemer 315
Davis v. Beason 316
DeJonge v. Oregon 317
Dennis v. United States 318
DeShaney v. Winnebago County Department of
    Social Services 319
Diamond v. Chakrabarty 320
Dillon v. Gloss 326
District of Columbia v. Heller. 327
Dobbins v. Erie County 331
Dodge v. Woolsey 331
Doe v. Bolton 333
Dolan v. City of Tigard 334
Dombrowski v. Pfister 335
Dronenburg v. Zech 336
Duncan v. Kahanamoku 343
Duncan v. Louisiana 344
Dunn v. Blumstein 346
Duplex Printing Co. v. Deering. 347

Edelman v. Jordan 349
Edgewood Independent School District v. Kirby. 350
Edmonson v. Leesville Concrete Co. 355
Edwards v. Aguillard 356
Edwards v. California 357
Edwards v. South Carolina 359
Eisenstadt v. Baird. 360
Elfbrandt v. Russell 361
Elrod v. Burns 362
Employment Division, Department of Human Resources
    of Oregon v. Smith 364
Engel v. Vitale 365
Epperson v. Arkansas 368
Erie Railroad Co. v. Tompkins 369
Erznoznik v. Jacksonville 370
Escobedo v. Illinois 371
Euclid v. Ambler Realty Co.. 373
Evans v. Abney. 374

Everson v. Board of Education of Ewing Township 375
Ex parte Crow Dog 376
Ex parte McCardle 377
Ex parte Merryman 379
Ex parte Milligan 381
Ex parte Quirin 383
Ex parte Siebold 385
Ex parte Yarbrough 386
Ex parte Young 386

Fairfax's Devisee v. Hunter's Lessee 388
Faretta v. California 389
Fay v. Noia 391
Federal Trade Commission v. Procter & Gamble Co. 392
Fedorenko v. United States 397
Feiner v. New York 398
Feist Publications v. Rural Telephone Service Co. 399
Ferguson v. City of Charleston 400
Ferguson v. Skrupa 401
Firefighters Local Union No. 1784 v. Stotts et al. 402
First English Evangelical Lutheran Church of Glendale v.
    County of Los Angeles 408
First National Bank of Boston v. Bellotti 409
Flast v. Cohen 409
Fletcher v. Peck 410
Florida v. Bostick 416
Ford v. Wainwright 417
44 Liquormart, Inc. v. Rhode Island 418
Frank v. Mangum 420
Freedman v. Maryland 420
Frontiero v. Richardson 422
Frothingham v. Mellon 423
Fullilove v. Klutznick 424
Furman v. Georgia 425

Garcia v. San Antonio Metropolitan Transit Authority 432
Garrison v. Louisiana 433
Geduldig v. Aiello 433
Gelpcke v. Dubuque 434
General Electric v. Gilbert 435
Genesee Chief v. Fitzhugh 436

Volume 2

Contents xlix
U.S. Supreme Court Citation Numbers. lvii

Geofroy v. Riggs 437
Gertz v. Robert Welch. 437
Gibbons v. Ogden 438
Gideon v. Wainwright 445
Gitlow v. New York 452
Gold Clause Cases. 453
Goldberg v. Kelly 454
Goldfarb v. Virginia State Bar. 455
Goldwater v. Carter 456
Gomez v. Perez 457
Gomillion v. Lightfoot 458
Gompers v. Buck's Stove and Range Co. 459
Gonzales v. Raich 460
Good News Club v. Milford Central School 461
Goodridge v. Department of Public Health 462
Goss v. Lopez 467
Graham v. Richardson 468
Gratz v. Bollinger/Grutter v. Bollinger. 469
Graves v. New York ex rel. O'Keefe 471
Gray v. Sanders 472
Green v. Biddle 473
Green v. County School Board of New Kent County. 474
Greer v. Spock. 475
Gregg v. Georgia 477
Griffin v. Breckenridge 482
Griffin v. California 483
Griffin v. County School Board of Prince Edward County. 484
Griggs v. Duke Power Co.. 485
Griswold v. Connecticut. 491
Grosjean v. American Press Co.. 497
Grove City College v. Bell 498
Groves v. Slaughter 499
Grovey v. Townsend 500
Guinn v. United States 501

Hague v. Congress of Industrial Organizations 503
Hall v. DeCuir 504

Hamdan v. Rumsfeld 505
Hamling v. United States 507
Hammer v. Dagenhart 509
Harmelin v. Michigan. 510
Harper v. Virginia State Board of Elections 512
Harris v. McRae 514
Harris v. New York 515
Harris v. United States 516
Hawaii Housing Authority v. Midkiff 518
Hayburn's Case 519
Hazelwood School District v. Kuhlmeier 520
Head Money Cases 521
Heart of Atlanta Motel v. United States 523
Helvering v. Davis 529
Hernández v. Texas 530
Herndon v. Lowry. 531
Hirabayashi v. United States 533
Hodgson v. Minnesota 535
Holden v. Hardy 536
Holmes v. Jennison 537
Home Building and Loan Association v. Blaisdell 539
Hoyt v. Florida. 541
Hudson v. Michigan. 542
Hudson v. Palmer 543
Humphrey's Executor v. United States. 544
Hurley v. Irish-American Gay, Lesbian, and Bisexual Group
    of Boston. 545
Hurtado v. California 546
Hustler Magazine v. Falwell. 548
Hutchinson v. Proxmire 548
Hutto v. Davis 549
Hylton v. United States 551

Illinois ex rel. McCollum v. Board of Education 552
Illinois v. Caballes 553
Illinois v. Gates 556
Illinois v. Krull. 557
Illinois v. McArthur 559
Illinois v. Wardlow. 561
Immigration and Naturalization Service v. Chadha 563
In re Baby M 564

In re Debs 565
In re Gault 567
In re Neagle 568
In re Winship 570
Insular Cases 571

Jackson v. Metropolitan Edison Co. 577
Jacobellis v. Ohio 578
Jacobson v. Massachusetts 579
Johnson and Graham's Lessee v. McIntosh 580
Johnson v. Louisiana 581
Johnson v. Santa Clara County 582
Johnson v. Zerbst 583
Joint Anti-Fascist Refugee Committee v. McGrath 584
Jones v. Alfred H. Mayer Co. 585
Jones v. Van Zandt 586

Kansas v. Hendricks 588
Kastigar v. United States 588
Katz v. United States 589
Katzenbach v. McClung 591
Katzenbach v. Morgan 591
Kelo v. City of New London 592
Kennedy v. Louisiana 594
Kent v. Dulles 596
Kentucky v. Dennison 597
Ker v. California 598
Keyes v. Denver School District No. 1 599
Keyishian v. Board of Regents 600
Keystone Bituminous Coal Association v. DeBenedictis 601
Kidd v. Pearson 602
Kilbourn v. Thompson 602
Kirkpatrick v. Preisler 604
Klopfer v. North Carolina 604
Knowles v. Iowa 605
Korematsu v. United States 607
Kunz v. New York 609
Kyllo v. United States 611

Lassiter v. Northampton County Board of Elections 612
Lau v. Nichols 613

Lawrence v. Texas 618
Lee v. Weisman 619
Legal Tender Cases 620
Lemon v. Kurtzman 621
License Cases 625
Local 28 of Sheet Metal Workers International Association v.
    Equal Employment Opportunity Commission 626
Lochner v. New York 627
Loewe v. Lawlor 633
Lone Wolf v. Hitchcock 634
Lorance v. AT&T Technologies 638
Louisiana ex rel. Francis v. Resweber 639
Louisville, Cincinnati, and Charleston Railroad Co. v. Letson 640
Louisville, New Orleans, and Texas Railway Co. v. Mississippi 641
Lovell v. City of Griffin 643
Loving v. Virginia 644
Lucas v. South Carolina Coastal Council 645
Luther v. Borden 646
Lynch v. Donnelly 648

McCleskey v. Kemp 650
McCleskey v. Zant 654
McConnell v. Federal Election Commission 655
McCray v. United States 656
McCulloch v. Maryland 657
McKeiver v. Pennsylvania 662
McLaurin v. Oklahoma State Regents for Higher Education 663
Mahan v. Howell 664
Maher v. Roe 665
Mallory v. United States 666
Malloy v. Hogan 667
Mapp v. Ohio 669
Marbury v. Madison 670
Marshall v. Barlow's 674
Martin v. Hunter's Lessee 675
Martin v. Mott 676
Martin v. Wilks 677
Marvin v. Marvin 678
Maryland v. Buie 679
Maryland v. Craig 681
Massachusetts Board of Retirement v. Murgia 682

Massachusetts v. Mellon. 684
Massachusetts v. Sheppard 685
Massiah v. United States. 686
Masson v. New Yorker Magazine 688
Maxwell v. Dow 689
Memoirs v. Massachusetts. 690
Meritor Savings Bank v. Vinson. 691
Metro Broadcasting v. Federal Communications Commission 692
Meyer v. Nebraska. 693
Miami Herald Publishing Co. v. Tornillo. 695
Michael M. v. Superior Court of Sonoma County 696
Michigan Department of State Police v. Sitz 697
Michigan v. Long 698
Milkovich v. Lorain Journal Co. 699
Miller et al. v. Civil City of South Bend 700
Miller v. California; Paris Adult Theatre v. Slaton 701
Milliken v. Bradley 703
Minersville School District v. Gobitis 704
Minnesota v. Carter. 705
Minnick v. Mississippi 706
Minor v. Happersett. 708
Miranda v. Arizona 712
Mississippi University for Women v. Hogan 718
Mississippi v. Johnson 719
Missouri ex rel. Gaines v. Canada. 720
Missouri v. Holland 721
Missouri v. Jenkins 722
Mistretta v. United States 723
Mobile v. Bolden 724
Monell v. Department of Social Services 725
Moore v. City of East Cleveland. 725
Moore v. Dempsey 726
Moose Lodge v. Irvis 727
Morehead v. New York ex rel. Tipaldo 729
Morgan v. Virginia 729
Morrison v. Olson. 730
Mueller v. Allen 731
Mugler v. Kansas 733
Mulford v. Smith 734
Muller v. Oregon 735
Munn v. Illinois 739

Murdock v. Memphis 740
Murdock v. Pennsylvania 741
Murphy v. Waterfront Commission of New York 742
Murray's Lessee v. Hoboken Land and Improvement Co.. 743
Muskrat v. United States 744
Mutual Film Corp. v. Industrial Commission of Ohio 745
Myers v. United States. 746

National Association for the Advancement
    of Colored People v. Alabama. 747
National Association for the Advancement
    of Colored People v. Button. 748
National Endowment for the Arts v. Finley. 749
National Labor Relations Board v. Jones and Laughlin Steel Corp.. . . . 753
National League of Cities v. Usery 755
National Treasury Employees Union v. Von Raab 756
Near v. Minnesota. 757
Nebbia v. New York 759
Nebraska Press Association v. Stuart 760
New Jersey v. T.L.O.. 761
New State Ice Co. v. Liebmann 763
New York State Club Association v. City of New York 764
New York Times Co. v. Sullivan 765
New York Times Co. v. United States 766
New York v. Belton 770
New York v. Ferber 771
New York v. Miln 773
Newberry v. United States 774
Nguyen v. Immigration and Naturalization Service 775
Nixon v. Administrator of General Services 776
Nixon v. Condon 777
Nixon v. Herndon. 778
Nollan v. California Coastal Commission 780
Norris v. Alabama 782
Northern Securities Co. v. United States 783
Noto v. United States 790

Ogden v. Saunders 791
O'Gorman and Young v. Hartford Fire Insurance Co.. 792
Ohio v. Akron Center for Reproductive Health 793
Olmstead v. United States. 794

Oregon v. Mitchell; Texas v. Mitchell; United States v. Arizona 796
Oregon Waste Systems v. Department of Environmental Quality 797
Orr v. Orr 798
Osborn v. Bank of the United States 799
Osborne v. Ohio 800
Ozawa v. United States 801

Pacific Mutual Life Insurance Co. v. Haslip 805
Pacific States Telephone and Telegraph Co. v. Oregon 806
Palko v. Connecticut 806
Palmer v. Thompson 809
Panama Refining Co. v. Ryan 810
Parents Involved in Community Schools v.
     Seattle School District No. 1. 811
Pasadena Board of Education v. Spangler 815
Passenger Cases 817
Patterson v. McLean Credit Union 817
Paul v. Virginia 818
Payne v. Tennessee 819
Payton v. New York 821
Penn Central Transportation Co. v. City of New York 822
Pennoyer v. Neff 823
Pennsylvania Coal Co. v. Mahon 824
Pennsylvania v. Nelson 825
Pennsylvania v. Wheeling and Belmont Bridge Co. 825
Penry v. Lynaugh 827
Personnel Administrator of Massachusetts v. Feeney 828
Phillips v. Martin Marietta Corp. 829
Pierce v. Society of Sisters 830
Planned Parenthood of Central Missouri v. Danforth 831
Planned Parenthood of Southeastern Pennsylvania v. Casey 833
Plessy v. Ferguson 835
Plyler v. Doe 841
Pointer v. Texas 844
Pollock v. Farmers' Loan and Trust Co. 845
Powell v. Alabama 847
Powell v. McCormick 848
Powers v. Ohio 849
Presser v. Illinois 850
Prigg v. Pennsylvania 851
Printz v. United States. 852

Prize Cases 853
Providence Bank v. Billings 854
Prudential Insurance Co. v. Benjamin 855

R.A.V. v. City of St. Paul 856
Reapportionment Cases 858
Red Lion Broadcasting Co. v. Federal Communications
    Commission 860
Redd v. State of Georgia 861
Reed v. Reed 862
Regents of the University of California v. Bakke 864
Reitman v. Mulkey 870
Reno v. American Civil Liberties Union 872
Reynolds v. Sims. 873
Reynolds v. United States 874
Rhodes v. Chapman. 876
Ricci v. DeStefano 877
Richmond Newspapers v. Virginia 882
Richmond v. J. A. Croson Co.. 883

Volume 3

Contents. lxxxv

U.S. Supreme Court Citation Numbers. xci
Complete List of Contents xciii

Roberts v. United States Jaycees 885
Robinson v. California 886
Rochin v. California. 887
Roe v. Wade 888
Romer v. Evans 895
Rompilla v. Beard 899
Roper v. Simmons. 900
Rosenberg v. United States 903
Rosenfeld v. Southern Pacific. 904
Rostker v. Goldberg 905
Rotary International v. Duarte 906
Roth v. United States 912
Rowan v. U.S. Post Office Department 914
Rummel v. Estelle 916
Runyon v. McCrary 917

Rust v. Sullivan 919
Rutan v. Republican Party of Illinois 921

Safford Unified School District v. Redding. 922
San Antonio Independent School District v. Rodriguez 925
Santa Clara County v. Southern Pacific Railroad Co. 926
Santa Clara Pueblo v. Martinez 927
Santobello v. New York 928
Scales v. United States. 929
Schall v. Martin 931
Schechter Poultry Corp. v. United States. 932
Schenck v. United States 933
Scott v. Harris 935
Scott v. Sandford 937
Selective Draft Law Cases 943
Seminole Tribe v. Florida 944
Shapiro v. Thompson 945
Shaw v. Hunt 946
Shaw v. Reno 948
Shelley v. Kraemer 949
Sheppard v. Maxwell 951
Sherbert v. Verner. 953
Shreveport Rate Cases 954
Sierra Club v. Morton 955
Skinner v. Oklahoma 960
Skinner v. Railway Labor Executives' Association 961
Slaughterhouse Cases 962
Slochower v. Board of Education of New York City 963
Smith v. Allwright 964
Smyth v. Ames 968
Snepp v. United States 969
Solem v. Helm. 970
South Carolina v. Katzenbach 972
South Dakota v. Dole 973
Spallone v. United States 974
Springer v. United States 974
Standard Oil v. United States 976
Stanford v. Kentucky 982
Stanley v. Georgia 983
Stanton v. Stanton. 984
Steward Machine Co. v. Davis. 985

Stone v. Mississippi 986
Stone v. Powell 987
Strauder v. West Virginia 988
Strawbridge v. Curtiss 989
Stromberg v. California 990
Stuart v. Laird 991
Sturges v. Crowninshield 992
Swann v. Charlotte-Mecklenburg Board of Education 993
Sweatt v. Painter 999
Swift and Co. v. United States 1000
Swift v. Tyson 1007

Talton v. Mayes 1008
Taylor v. Louisiana 1008
Tennessee v. Garner 1009
Tennessee Valley Authority v. Hill 1011
Terminiello v. Chicago 1015
Terry v. Adams 1016
Terry v. Ohio 1017
Texas v. Hopwood 1018
Texas v. Johnson 1019
Texas v. White 1023
Thompson v. Oklahoma 1024
Thornburgh v. American College of Obstetricians
    and Gynecologists 1026
Thornhill v. Alabama 1027
Tilton v. Richardson 1028
Time v. Hill 1029
Times Film Corp. v. City of Chicago 1030
Tinker v. Des Moines Independent Community School District 1032
Tison v. Arizona 1034
Trop v. Dulles 1036
Truax v. Corrigan 1037
Twining v. New Jersey 1038
Tyson v. Banton 1039

Ullmann v. United States 1040
United Jewish Organizations of Williamsburgh v. Carey 1041
United Public Workers v. Mitchell 1042
United States Term Limits v. Thornton 1043
United States v. Alvarez-Machain 1044

United States v. American Tobacco Co.. 1045
United States v. Butler. 1052
United States v. California. 1053
United States v. Carolene Products Co.. 1054
United States v. Classic. 1056
United States v. Cruikshank 1057
United States v. Curtiss-Wright Export Corp.. 1058
United States v. Darby Lumber Co.. 1059
United States v. E. C. Knight Co. 1060
United States v. E. I. du Pont de Nemours and Co.. 1062
United States v. Eichman 1067
United States v. Guest 1068
United States v. Hudson and Goodwin 1070
United States v. Kagama 1070
United States v. Lanza 1071
United States v. Leon 1072
United States v. Lopez 1073
United States v. Lovett 1074
United States v. Nixon 1075
United States v. O'Brien 1076
United States v. Paramount Pictures, Inc.. 1077
United States v. Reese 1083
United States v. Richardson 1085
United States v. Robel 1086
United States v. Ross 1087
United States v. Shipp 1088
United States v. South-Eastern Underwriters
    Association 1089
United States v. United Mine Workers 1090
United States v. United States District Court 1091
United States v. United States Steel Corp. 1092
United States v. Ursery 1098
United States v. Virginia 1098
United States v. Wade 1099
United States v. Wong Kim Ark 1100
United Steelworkers of America v. Weber. 1105

Veazie Bank v. Fenno 1111
Vernonia School District 47J v. Acton 1112
Village of Skokie v. National Socialist Party of America 1116
Virginia v. Black 1118

Virginia v. Tennessee 1120
Virginia v. West Virginia 1120

Wabash, St. Louis, and Pacific Railway Co. v. Illinois 1121
Wallace v. Jaffree 1122
Walz v. Tax Commission 1124
Wards Cove Packing Co. v. Atonio 1124
Ware v. Hylton 1126
Washington v. Davis 1127
Washington v. Glucksberg 1128
Watkins v. United States 1130
Webster v. Reproductive Health Services 1131
Weeks v. Southern Bell 1137
Weeks v. United States 1138
Weems v. United States 1140
Weinberger v. Wiesenfeld 1140
Wesberry v. Sanders 1141
West Coast Hotel Co. v. Parrish 1143
West River Bridge Co. v. Dix 1144
West Virginia State Board of Education v. Barnette 1145
Weston v. Charleston 1151
Whitney v. California 1151
Whren v. United States 1152
Wickard v. Filburn 1154
Wiener v. United States 1156
Williams v. Florida 1157
Williams v. Mississippi 1157
Willson v. Blackbird Creek Marsh Co. 1158
Wilson v. Arkansas 1159
Wisconsin v. Mitchell 1161
Wisconsin v. Yoder 1163
Witherspoon v. Illinois 1166
Wolf v. Colorado 1168
Wolff Packing Co. v. Court of Industrial Relations 1170
Woodruff v. Parham 1171
Woodson v. North Carolina 1172
Worcester v. Georgia 1172
Wyatt v. Stickney 1174

Yakus v. United States 1180
Yates v. United States 1182

Yick Wo v. Hopkins 1184
Young v. American Mini Theatres. 1185
Younger v. Harris 1186
Youngstown Sheet and Tube Co. v. Sawyer 1187

Zablocki v. Redhail. 1188
Zadvydas v. Davis. 1189
Zelman v. Simmons-Harris 1191
Zorach v. Clauson 1192
Zurcher v. The Stanford Daily. 1193

Appendixes

Supreme Court Justices 1197
Bibliography. 1220
Glossary 1243
Time Line of Cases 1259
Categorized List of Entries 1277

Photo Index 1303
Subject Index 1305

U.S. COURT CASES
Revised Edition

GEOFROY V. RIGGS

Court: U.S. Supreme Court
Citation: 133 U.S. 258
Date: February 3, 1890
Issues: Immigration; Property rights; Treaties

- The U.S. Supreme Court upheld the right of French citizens to inherit property, thus expanding noncitizens' rights to transfer property.

French citizens had inherited real estate in the District of Columbia, but other descendants challenged the bequeathal on grounds that the property was located in the portion of the district carved out of Maryland, which had a ban on the transfer of real property to people who were not U.S. citizens. The French descendants argued that an 1853 treaty allowed French nationals to inherit real estate in all states where local laws permitted it. The Supreme Court unanimously upheld the right of aliens to inherit real property. Justice Stephen J. Field, in the opinion for the Court, found that the District of Columbia was a state for purposes of the treaty. The Court's ruling set a precedent in cases where the state law was ambiguous.

Richard L. Wilson

See also *Martin v. Hunter's Lessee; Pennoyer v. Neff; Plyler v. Doe.*

GERTZ V. ROBERT WELCH

Court: U.S. Supreme Court
Citation: 418 U.S. 323
Date: June 25, 1974
Issues: Freedom of the press

- The U.S. Supreme Court limited the broad protection from libel suits granted newspapers by its 1964 decision.

Robert Welch, Inc., publisher of the John Birch Society magazine, used its publication to make a number of false, strongly defamatory statements attacking Elmer Gertz, an attorney representing citizens in a civil suit against a police officer convicted of second-degree murder. Gertz sued but could not show actual malice as required by the existing holding of *New York Times Co. v. Sullivan* (1964). By a 5-4 vote, the Supreme Court ruled in favor of Gertz, holding that public officials and "public figures" had to show actual malice in order to recover damages for libel, but others, like Gertz, needed only to show some degree of fault. The Court limited its *Sullivan* ruling in *Gertz*, then limited *Gertz* in the case of *Dun and Bradstreet v. Greenmoss Builders* (1985). Later, in *Milkovich v. Lorain Journal Co.* (1990) and other cases, it effectively expanded *Gertz.* Chief Justice Warren E. Burger and Justices William O. Douglas, William J. Brennan, Jr., and Byron R. White dissented.

Richard L. Wilson

See also *Garrison v. Louisiana; Milkovich v. Lorain Journal Co.; New York Times Co. v. Sullivan; Time v. Hill.*

GIBBONS V. OGDEN

Court: U.S. Supreme Court
Citation: 22 U.S. 1
Date: March 2, 1824
Issues: Antitrust law; Congressional powers; Regulation of commerce; State sovereignty

• In supporting the federal license of a steamboat operator who challenged a state monopoly, the U.S. Supreme Court expanded federal control of commerce and laid the basis for many future Court rulings on commerce.

In order to provide the commercial relations of the United States with a sense of orderliness and uniformity that had been lacking before 1787, the U.S. Constitution empowered Congress to "regulate Commerce with foreign Nations, and among the several States, and with the Indian Tribes." Congress almost immediately took advantage of this power in the field of foreign commerce by providing for the regulation of ships and commerce from foreign countries and by enacting the National Coasting Licensing Act in 1793 for the licensing of vessels engaged in coastal trade. However, the Constitution was silent as to the meaning and scope of the commerce power. It was left to the Supreme Court, thirty years later, to make the first national pronouncement regarding domestic commerce in the case of *Gibbons v. Ogden.*

Steam Transportation

The catalyst for this decision was the development of the steamboat as a means of commercial transportation. This was accomplished in August of 1807, when Robert Fulton and Robert R. Livingston made a successful voyage up the Hudson River from New York to Albany. In April of 1808, the legislature of the state of New York responded to this success by giving Fulton and Livingston a monopoly to operate steamboats on New York waters for a period not to exceed thirty years. All other steam-powered craft were forbidden from navigating New York streams unless they were licensed by Fulton and Livingston. Any unlicensed vessels that were captured were to be forfeited to the same two men. A similar grant was obtained from the legislature of Orleans Territory in 1811, thus conferring upon Fulton and Livingston control over the two great ports of the United States, New York City and New Orleans.

As a practical matter, the commercial potential of steam transportation was too great to be left to the devices of two men. Rival companies soon came into being, and a commercial war reminiscent of the old Confederation era erupted. The state of New Jersey authorized owners of any boats seized under New York law to capture New York boats in retaliation. Connecticut would not allow Livingston and Fulton's boats to enter its waters. Georgia, Massachusetts, New Hampshire, Vermont, and Ohio enacted "exclusive privilege" statutes for operators of steamboats on their own waters. Finally, a number of New York citizens defied the state law and operated unlicensed steam vessels up the Hudson River. Among these was a man named Thomas Gibbons, who had a license granted under the federal Coasting Licensing Act of 1793. He was operating in competition with a former partner, Aaron Ogden, who had secured exclusive rights from Livingston and Fulton to navigate across the Hudson River between New York and New Jersey.

Fulton-Livingstone Monopoly

As early as 1812, the New York Court of Errors and Chief Justice James Kent, one of the most prominent U.S. jurists, had issued a permanent injunction against intruders on the Fulton-Livingstone monopoly. Gibbons persisted in the face of this injunction because he had a federal license, and Ogden sought a restraining order in New York Court of Chancery. Kent, who by then was state chancellor, upheld the monopoly once again, reasoning that

New York State chief
justice James Kent.
(Library of Congress)

a federal coasting license merely conferred national character on a vessel and
did not license it to trade, especially in waters restricted by state law. In short,
there was no conflict between the act of Congress and the actions of New York
State, for the power to regulate commerce was a concurrent one, existing on
both the federal and state levels. Nevertheless, Gibbons persisted in appealing
to the New York Court of Errors, where Kent's decision was upheld. This set
the stage for his final appeal to the U.S. Supreme Court.

It was expected that Gibbons's case would be heard during the 1821 term of
the Court, but for technical reasons it was delayed until February, 1824. The
oral arguments lasted four and one-half days that, by all accounts, resulted in
a great social and political occasion as well as one of the great moments in
U.S. constitutional history. Among the distinguished attorneys presenting the
case was Daniel Webster, champion of a strong national government and the
best-known orator of his time. Webster opened his argument in sweeping
terms by contending that the statutes of New York, and by implication all exclusive grants of others states, violated the U.S. Constitution: "The power of
Congress to regulate commerce is complete and entire," he argued. Individual states have no concurrent powers in this area; the federal government's
domain is exclusive. Webster left no doubt that commerce included navigation. Opposing counsel necessarily wished to limit the notion of commerce to
traffic or to the buying and selling of commodities, which would not include

navigation. The regulation of New York, he contended, was a matter of internal trade and navigation, the province of the states.

Congressional Powers

The case before the Court, however, dealt with far more than the conflict between New York State law and a federal coasting licensing act. In the weeks immediately preceding and during the argument in *Gibbons v. Ogden*, Congress was debating whether it had the power to build roads and canals, a debate in which the association of slavery with national control over commerce became apparent. If Congress could legislate over matters of internal commerce, it could easily prohibit the slave trade. Furthermore, Marshall's earlier decisions, particularly in *McCulloch v. Maryland* (1819) and *Cohens v. Virginia* (1821), were under fire in Congress, from the president, and in the press.

In a sense, the forces arguing the two sides of the *Gibbons* case represented national power and the potential for emancipation (some would add those who supported the protective tariff) on one hand, and, on the other, state sovereignty and the fear of emancipation (with some free trade proponents)—a not altogether logical set of alliances. It was in this context, however, that one month later, on March 2, 1824, John Marshall delivered the decision of the Court.

Typically, the opinion was a broad one, loaded with gratuitous comments or representations, and not typically as nationalistic as expected, or as Webster would have desired. Marshall began by agreeing with Webster's definition of commerce:

> Commerce, undoubtedly, is traffic, but it is something more; it is intercourse. It describes the commercial intercourse between nations, and parts of nations, in all its branches, and is regulated by prescribing rules for carrying on that intercourse. The mind can scarcely conceive a system for regulating commerce between nations, which shall exclude all laws concerning navigation, which shall be silent on the admission of the vessels of the one nation into the ports of the other and be confined to prescribing rules for the conduct of individuals, in the actual employment of buying and selling, or of barter.

What did the Constitution mean when it said that Congress had the power to regulate such commerce among the several states?

> The word "among" means intermingled with. A thing which is among others is intermingled with them. Commerce among the States cannot stop at the external boundary line of each State, but may be introduced into the interior.

After having laid the logical groundwork for claiming complete and exclusive federal power to regulate such commerce, which was Webster's argument, Marshall then retreated, stating:

> It is not intended to say that these words comprehend that commerce which is completely internal, which is carried on between man and man in a State, or between different parts of the same State, and which does not extend to or affect other States. . . . Comprehensive as the word "among" is, it may very properly be restricted to that commerce which concerns more States than one. . . .

The federal power over commerce was not exclusive, as Webster maintained, although in this instance, the state law was in violation of the federal coasting act. The one concurring opinion in the case given by Associate Justice William Johnson, ironically a Republican appointed by Thomas Jefferson, was stronger and more nationalistic than Marshall's. Johnson contended that the power of Congress "must be exclusive; it can reside but in one potentate; and hence, the grant of this power carries with it the whole subject, leaving nothing for the state to act upon."

Federal Supremacy

For Marshall, if it was clear that the "acts of New York must yield to the Law of Congress," it was also evident that the "completely internal commerce of a state, then, may be considered as reserved for the state itself." The nationalist chief justice had unwittingly laid the basis for a multitude of legal perplexities by making a distinction between intrastate and interstate commerce (terms he did not use); and it would fall to less subtle judicial minds to interpret this as meaning commerce that does not cross state lines. Lest anyone misunderstand his position on the general enumerated powers of the Congress and on the theory of strict construction of the Constitution adopted by Ogden's counsel and by Chancellor Kent, Marshall concluded his opinion with these words:

> Powerful and ingenious minds, taking, as postulates, that the powers expressly granted to the government of the union are to be contracted, by construction, into the narrowest possible compass, and that the original powers of the states are retained, if any possible construction will retain them, may, by a course of well digested, but refined metaphysical reasoning, founded on these premises, explain away the construction of our country, and leave it a magnificent structure indeed, to look at, but totally unfit for use. They may so entangle and perplex

the understanding, as to obscure principles which were before thought quite plain, and induce doubts where, if the mind were to pursue its own course, none would be perceived. In such a case, it is peculiarly necessary to recur to safe and fundamental principles. . . .

In other words, the courts should construe the Constitution and the powers of Congress broadly.

In immediate practical terms, Marshall finally had rendered a popular decision. The steamboat monopoly had come to an end, and state fragmentation of commerce was prevented. *Gibbons v. Ogden* was the first great antitrust decision given at a time when monopolies were decidedly unpopular. Lost in the public euphoria over the end of "exclusive grants," save to a few Jeffersonian Republicans, was the fact that Marshall had made the Supreme Court the future arbiter of matters involving congressional power over commerce and intervention into state police and taxing powers. In so doing, he had struck one more blow for a broad view of the Constitution and of national power. Only when steam came to be used for land transportation would the full commercial implications of the Gibbons decision be clear. If, as many maintain, half of the Constitution is the commerce clause (the other half being the due process clause of the Fourteenth Amendment), the *Gibbons v. Ogden* case has been correctly termed the "emancipation proclamation of American commerce."

Significance

Chief Justice John Marshall's opinion in *Gibbons v. Ogden* provided the starting point for all subsequent interpretations of the Constitution's commerce clause. Initially, Marshall's conception was demanded by the needs of a developing nation and an expansive approach to federal authority. The breadth and elastic nature of his definition of commerce, however, justified the extensive commercial enterprises in which the national government has been engaged since, including regulation of new forms of commercial activity brought about by technological changes, inventions, and advances in communications and transportation. During the twentieth century, the commerce power was used to justify various types of economic legislation (interstate and intrastate), including a presidential wage and price freeze under the Economic Stabilization Act of 1970 and noneconomic matters such as civil rights, kidnapping, and pollution control.

Further refinements of the definition of commerce and the types of activities that it encompasses evolved in a series of cases. Since 1937, the commerce clause has been understood to permit congressional regulation of intrastate activities that have a close and substantial relation to interstate commerce, so that their control is essential for protection from burdens and obstruction. In *United States v. Lopez* (1995), for example, the Supreme Court held that a purely intrastate activity is subject to congressional regulation only if it "substantially affects" interstate commerce. The case dealt with enactment of a 1990 criminal law banning possession of a gun within one thousand feet of a school. According to the Court, such noncommercial enterprise was unrelated to commerce, however broadly it is defined.

Cecil L. Eubanks, updated by Marcia J. Weiss

Further Reading

Baxter, Maurice G. *The Steamboat Monopoly: Gibbons v. Ogden, 1824*. New York: Alfred A. Knopf, 1970. A narrative and assessment of the case in which the Supreme Court had its first opportunity to interpret the commerce clause of the Constitution.

Faulkner, Robert K. *The Jurisprudence of John Marshall*. Princeton, N.J.: Princeton University Press, 1968. A comprehensive critique of Marshall's juridical thought. Places *Gibbons v. Ogden* in perspective with regard to Marshall's legal philosophy.

Frantz, John P. "The Reemergence of the Commerce Clause as a Limit on Federal Power: *United States v. Lopez*." *Harvard Journal of Law and Public Policy* 19, no. 1 (Fall, 1995): 161-174. A scholarly analysis of the *Lopez* case within the framework of the commerce clause, discussing its evolution.

Levinson, Isabel Simone. *Gibbons v. Ogden: Controlling Trade Between States*. Springfield, N.J.: Enslow, 1999. Concise analysis of the *Gibbons* case and its legal ramifications.

Lewis, Thomas T., and Richard L. Wilson, eds. *Encyclopedia of the U.S. Supreme Court*. 3 vols. Pasadena, Calif.: Salem Press, 2001. Comprehensive reference work on the Supreme Court that contains substantial discussions of *Gibbons v. Ogden, United States v. Lopez*, John Marshall, the commerce clause, and many related subjects.

Newmyer, R. Kent. *John Marshall and the Heroic Age of the Supreme Court*. Baton Rouge: Louisiana State University Press, 2001. Examination of Marshall's legal philosophy, with analyses of many Court decisions.

_____. *The Supreme Court Under Marshall and Taney*. Arlington Heights, Ill.: Harlan Davidson, 1968. Contains detailed information and presents Marshall's philosophy. Places *Gibbons v. Ogden* and the commerce power in historical context.

Schwartz, Bernard. *A History of the Supreme Court*. New York: Oxford University Press, 1993. Comprehensive in scope, this scholarly work details the Marshall Court and its influence on U.S. politics and society.

Smith, Craig R. *Daniel Webster and the Oratory of Civil Religion*. Columbia: University of Missouri Press, 2005. Biography focusing on Webster's legendary rhetorical ability, which he employed in the *Gibbons* case.

See also *Champion v. Ames*; *Cohens v. Virginia*; *McCulloch v. Maryland*; *New York v. Miln*; *United States v. Lopez*; *Willson v. Blackbird Creek Marsh Co.*

GIDEON V. WAINWRIGHT

Court: U.S. Supreme Court
Citation: 372 U.S. 335
Date: March 18, 1963
Issues: Right to counsel

• The U.S. Supreme Court's decision in *Gideon v. Wainwright* held that the Sixth Amendment's right-to-counsel provision required a lawyer to be provided free of charge to any defendant in a state criminal trial who could not afford an attorney.

The evidence is convincing that the provision in the Sixth Amendment to the U.S. Constitution guaranteeing that "the accused . . . in all criminal prosecutions shall enjoy the right . . . to have the Assistance of Counsel for his defense" meant, at the time of its adoption, no more than the right of a defendant to employ an attorney. This provision was in advance of the practice in contemporary England, where the assistance of counsel was allowed only in misdemeanor, but not in felony, cases, except for treason. Congress required by statute, starting in 1790, that the federal courts appoint counsel at the defendant's request in treason and other capital cases.

In state criminal prosecutions, practice varied from state to state. The United States Supreme Court would not define the meaning of the right-to-counsel clause even at the federal level until 1938. As for its application to the states, the generally accepted view before the Civil War—affirmed by Chief Justice John Marshall in *Barron v. Baltimore* (1833)—was that the first eight amendments applied only to the federal government and not to the states. The adoption of the Fourteenth Amendment reopened the question, but the Supreme Court balked at extending any of the provisions of the Bill of Rights to the states via the Fourteenth Amendment until 1925, when the Court ruled that states must protect the freedom of speech. A majority of the justices continued to resist extending the criminal law provisions of the Bill of Rights to states.

The first suggestion that a defendant had a constitutional right to be offered counsel if he or she could not afford an attorney came in *Powell v. Alabama* (1932). That decision was an outgrowth of the famous Scottsboro trials, in which seven black youths had been convicted in Alabama of the rape of two white women. The case against the boys rested on dubious testimony.

The Due Process Clause

Speaking for the Supreme Court in overturning the convictions, Justice George Sutherland rested the decision not upon the Sixth Amendment but upon the due process clause of the Fourteenth Amendment, which barred the states from depriving "any person of life, liberty, or property, without due process of law." Due process, Sutherland reasoned, required a fair hearing. Failure to provide the Scottsboro boys with lawyers denied them a fair hearing. Sutherland carefully limited the scope of his holding to the facts in the case: Due process required a state court to provide effective assistance of counsel in a capital case if the defendant is unable to employ counsel and is incapable adequately of making his own defense because of ignorance, feeble-mindedness, illiteracy, or the like.

The Supreme Court did not give its definitive interpretation of the meaning of the Sixth Amendment's right-to-counsel clause until 1938, in *Johnson v. Zerbst*. Ignoring the historical evidence regarding the provision, Justice Hugo L. Black wrote in his opinion that the Sixth Amendment required the appointment of counsel for poor defendants in federal criminal trials. Although the defendant could waive the right to have counsel assigned. The trial judge had the duty to make sure that the defendant fully understood the right to have legal assistance and had knowingly and intelligently waived that right. Did the same rule apply to state criminal trials via the Fourteenth Amendment?

The issue came before the Supreme Court in 1942 in *Betts v. Brady*, a case involving a conviction for robbery, a noncapital felony. At his trial in state court, the defendant, an unemployed farm laborer described by the Supreme Court as a person of "ordinary intelligence," had requested appointment of counsel, but his request had been denied. In the trial itself, the defendant had actively participated by examining his own witnesses and cross-examining the prosecution's. Justice Hugo L. Black strongly argued that the Fourteenth Amendment had been intended to incorporate as limits upon the states all the provisions of the Bill of Rights. Even apart from the Sixth Amendment, he held that due process required provision of counsel for those too poor to retain their own.

Justice Owen J. Roberts, writing for the 6-3 majority, held that the Fourteenth Amendment did not incorporate the Sixth Amendment as such. It was only "in certain circumstances, or in connection with other elements" that denial of a specific provision of the Bill of Rights was a violation of the due process of law guaranteed by the Fourteenth Amendment. He went on to conclude that there was nothing in history or contemporary practice to justify holding that due process required the appointment of counsel in every state criminal trial. Rather, the question in each case was whether, in the totality of circumstances, appointment of counsel was required to assure "fundamental fairness." Given the relatively simple issues involved in the case before the Court, the majority ruled that the lack of counsel had not denied the defendant a fair trial.

Aftermath

In the years that followed, the Court overturned most state convictions that were appealed because of a failure to assign counsel, but it shied away from laying down a blanket rule requiring the appointment of counsel. The one exception was the requirement of appointment of counsel in all capital cases, laid down in *Bate v. Illinois* (1948). By the early 1960's, the Court had turned against the totality-of-circumstances approach. There was growing unhappiness in the legal community with the lack of uniformity in the practices of different states. Many state judges and prosecutors complained about the uncertainty resulting from lack of a clearly defined rule. A majority of Earl Warren's Supreme Court was committed to extending most of the provisions of the Bill of Rights to the states and to promoting a larger degree of egalitarianism in American life. At the beginning of the Court's 1961 term, Warren instructed his law clerks to look through the petitions for review for a suitable right-to-counsel case that would give the Court an opportunity to reverse Betts. The petition selected was from Clarence Earl Gideon.

Gideon was a fifty-one-year-old drifter who had previously served four prison terms for felonies. He was charged in 1961 with breaking and entering the Bay Harbor Poolroom in Panama City, Florida, and stealing a pint of wine and some coins from a cigarette machine. When he went on trial in the Circuit Court of Bay County, Florida, on August 4, 1961, he asked the judge to appoint a lawyer for him because he could not afford to retain one himself. The judge refused, because Florida law provided for such appointment only in capital cases. After his appeal had been turned down by the Florida Supreme Court, Gideon submitted from prison a petition handwritten in pencil on lined paper to the United States Supreme Court. He argued that his conviction had violated the due process guarantee of the Fourteenth Amendment because of the trial judge's refusal to appoint counsel. The Constitution, he

Clarence Earl Gideon.
(AP/Wide World Photos)

wrote, required that "all citizens tried for a felony crime should have aid of counsel."

The Supreme Court granted review on June 1, 1962, and explicitly instructed counsel to discuss whether *Betts v. Brady* should be "reconsidered." In response to a follow-up petition from Gideon asking that the court appoint an attorney to argue his case, Warren suggested and his fellow justices agreed that Abe Fortas, one of the foremost lawyers in Washington, D.C., whom President Lyndon B. Johnson would later appoint to the Supreme Court, be named. The justices were unanimous in reversing Gideon's conviction and overruling Betts.

Separate concurring opinions were written by Justices William O. Douglas, Tom C. Clark, and John M. Harlan II. In a symbolic gesture, Chief Justice Warren picked Justice Black, who had angrily dissented in *Betts v. Brady*, to write the majority opinion. In his ruling, handed down on March 18, 1963, Black held that the right-to-counsel provision of the Sixth Amendment was "subsumed" in the Fourteenth Amendment, and thus its requirement of assignment of counsel for poor defendants applied to state criminal trials. "The right of one charged with crime to counsel may not be deemed fundamental and essential to fair trials in some countries," he concluded, "but it is in ours."

Significance

At his retrial in Florida after the Supreme Court overturned his conviction, Gideon was acquitted. Thereafter, he stayed clear of the law except for a vagrancy arrest. Ten years after his death in 1972, the American Civil Liberties Union arranged for a stone to mark his grave in Hannibal, Missouri, where he had been born. Gideon was not the only one freed by the Supreme Court ruling. The new Gideon rule was applied not only prospectively to future criminal trials but also retrospectively to persons in prison who had been tried without counsel.

Before *Gideon v. Wainwright*, in most instances when the court assigned counsel the attorney so named received no, or at most minimal, compensation. The result was that the lawyers typically assigned were beginners or hacks. Worse, they lacked the resources for presenting the most effective defense (for example, the ability to conduct pretrial investigations). Gideon gave a powerful stimulus to improving this situation. Congress, in the Criminal Justice Act of 1964, instituted a system of compensated legal assistance in the federal courts. Many states and localities established or expanded taxsupported public-defender or legal-aid offices.

Gideon was one of the Warren Court's most popular criminal law decisions. There was wide support for guaranteeing poor defendants minimal legal assistance in criminal trials. More controversial were the court's extensions of the Gideon principle. Although the opinion in Gideon did not explicitly limit the ruling to felony trials, that was the general assumption. Accordingly, many states did not provide for appointment of counsel for so-called petty offenses (typically where the punishment was no more than six months imprisonment). The Court, in *Argersinger v. Hamlin* (1972), ruled that an unrepresented defendant could not be jailed for any term unless he or she had waived counsel at the trial. In 1967's *In re Gault*, the Court recognized a right to counsel in state juvenile court delinquency proceedings.

A second area of extension was to post-trial situations. *Douglas v. California* (1963) upheld the right to appointed counsel for appeal from a conviction; *Mempa v. Rhay* (1967) extended that right to a postconviction deferred sentence or probation revocation proceeding. What most provoked attack was the extension of Gideon to the pretrial area. *Escobedo v. Illinois* (1964) barred the police from preventing a suspect from consulting with a lawyer until interrogation had been completed. *United States v. Wade* (1967) and *Gilbert v. California* (1967) held that suspects had the right to counsel, retained or appointed, at a police line-up because of the danger of faulty identification.

A series of decisions—among them *Massiah v. United States* (1964), *Brewer v. Williams* (1977), and *United States v. Henry* (1980)—appear to have taken the position that the government could not approach a defendant for evidence of his guilt in the absence of counsel any time after the initiation of judicial proceedings by an indictment or other in-court proceedings. Most controversial was the 5-4 decision in *Miranda v. Arizona* (1966) requiring state and federal officers to advise suspects before any questioning of their right to remain silent, to consult with a lawyer, to have that lawyer present at the interrogation, and to have a lawyer provided.

Backlash

The backlash against what many people thought was too much protection for the criminal at the expense of society led the Supreme Court, beginning in the 1970's, to move back from some of the extensions of Gideon. In *Scott v. Illinois* (1979), the Court sustained the conviction of an unrepresented defendant facing prosecution for an offense punishable by time and/or imprisonment who received only a money fine. *Ross v. Moffitt* (1974) held that the right to assigned counsel was limited to the first-level appeal and did not extend to discretionary appeals in the state courts or applications for review to the United States Supreme Court. *Gagnon v. Scarpelli* (1973) held that counsel need not be appointed at a hearing for revocation of probation or parole unless special circumstances required legal assistance; *Lassiter v. Department of Social Services* (1981) applied the same rule to indigent mothers in proceedings to terminate their parental rights. A series of rulings have chipped away at the Miranda protections regarding the questioning of suspects in the absence of counsel, and the Court has largely rebuffed appeals challenging the effectiveness of counsel.

John Braeman

Further Reading

Allen, Francis. "The Judicial Quest for Penal Justice: The Warren Court and the Criminal Cases." *University of Illinois Law Forum* 4 (1975): 518-542. Generally sympathetic appraisal of the Warren Court's criminal law decisions.

Braeman, John. *Before the Civil Rights Revolution: The Old Court and Individual Rights*. New York: Greenwood Press, 1988. A survey of the Supreme Court's decision making in the area of civil liberties and civil rights up to the post-1937 revolution in constitutional law.

Cole, David. "*Gideon v. Wainwright* and *Strickland v. Washington*: Broken Promises." In *Criminal Procedure Stories*, edited by Carol S. Steiker. New York: Foundation Press/Thomson/West, 2006. Essay examining the legacy of Gideon and failures of the criminal justice system to live up to the obligations placed on it by the Court. Bibliographic references.

Cook, Joseph G. *Constitutional Rights of the Accused.* 2d ed. 3 vols. Rochester, N.Y.: Lawyers Co-operative, 1985-1986. A comprehensive guide to current constitutional law regarding criminal procedure. Right-to-counsel issues are dealt with primarily in volume 2.

Fridell, Ron. *Gideon v. Wainwright: The Right to Free Counsel.* Tarrytown, N.Y.: Marshall Cavendish Benchmark, 2007. Part of its publisher's Supreme Court Milestones series designed for young-adult readers, this volume offers an accessible history and analysis of the *Gideon* case that examines opposing sides in the case, the people involved, and the case's lasting impact. Includes bibliography and index.

Graham, Fred P. *The Self-Inflicted Wound.* New York: Macmillan, 1970. This volume by *The New York Times*'s Supreme Court correspondent is the fullest and most balanced account of the Warren Court's criminal law decisions.

Israel, Jerold. "Criminal Procedure, the Burger Court, and the Legacy of the Warren Court." *Michigan Law Review* 75 (June, 1977): 1319-1425. Concludes that complaints that the Court under Chief Justice Warren Burger was guilty of reversing the criminal law decisions of the Warren Court have been grossly exaggerated.

_____. "*Gideon v. Wainwright*: The Art of Overruling." In *The Supreme Court Review, 1963*, edited by Philip B. Kurland. Chicago: University of Chicago Press, 1963. A critical appraisal of Justice Black's opinion in *Gideon* as failing to offer a persuasive rationale for overruling *Betts* "consistent with the accepted image of judicial review."

Kamisar, Yale. "*Betts v. Brady* Twenty Years Later: The Right to Counsel and Due Process Values." *Michigan Law Review* 61 (December. 1962): 219-282. A critical appraisal of the unfairness and problems resulting from the totality-of-circumstances approach.

Schwartz, Bernard. *Super Chief Earl Warren and His Supreme Court: A Judicial Biography.* New York: New York University Press, 1983. A look at the behind-the-scenes workings of the Supreme Court, based upon the private papers and notes of many of the justices and interviews with court members and their law clerks. Its weakness is the author's worshipful admiration for Warren.

Taylor, John B. *The Right to Counsel and Privilege Against Self-Incrimination: Rights and Liberties Under the Law.* Santa Barbara, Calif.: ABC-CLIO, 2004. Examination of Gideon in the context of both constitutional history and common-law history. Bibliographic references and index.

See also *Argersinger v. Hamlin; Barron v. Baltimore; Betts v. Brady; In re Gault; Johnson v. Zerbst; Massiah v. United States; Miranda v. Arizona; Powell v. Alabama; United States v. Wade.*

GITLOW V. NEW YORK

Court: U.S. Supreme Court
Citation: 268 U.S. 652
Date: June 8, 1925
Issues: Freedom of speech

- This decision weakened protection for free speech by establishing a "bad tendency" test for judging whether a person can be sent to prison for words advocating the overthrow of the government by force or violence.

World War I and the Russian Revolution brought about a Red Scare in the United States. This was a period of feverish antiradicalism characterized by mass deportations of aliens and the adoption by many states of criminal syndicalism or criminal anarchy statutes. Benjamin Gitlow was the general secretary of the left-wing section of the Socialist Party, whose headquarters were in New York. He supervised the publication of sixteen thousand copies of a paper called *The Revolutionary Age*, which contained a "Left-Wing Manifesto." The manifesto attacked the moderate Socialists and advocated militant and revolutionary socialism based on the class struggle. It called for mass industrial revolts and strikes for the purpose of conquering and destroying the parliamentary state.

Gitlow was indicted and convicted for violating New York State's criminal anarchy statute. This act defined criminal anarchy as a doctrine that organized government should be overthrown by force or violence. Advocacy of criminal anarchy was made a felony. At trial Gitlow argued that his publication was protected by the First Amendment. There had been no evidence that the "Left-Wing Manifesto" had any effect. Gitlow insisted that his conviction could not stand unless the state showed that a "clear and present danger" resulted from the publication. After losing in the New York courts, Gitlow appealed to the U.S. Supreme Court of the United States.

The Supreme Court held against Gitlow by a vote of seven to two. The majority's opinion, written by Justice Edward T. Sanford, limited the application of the "clear and present danger" test to cases not involving a direct legislative prohibition of particular kinds of speech. Under the test, utterances whose "natural tendency and probable effect" is to bring about revolutionary or violent activity are punishable by law. When the legislature does act to proscribe particular speech, a person may be punished for utterances which tend to bring about the evil whether there is any real danger. The Court's decision elicited a powerful dissenting opinion by Justice Oliver Wendell Holmes, Jr., with which Justice Louis D. Brandeis concurred.

The dissenting opinion attacks the majority for failing to distinguish between discussion and advocacy; only advocacy may be punished and even then only when it presents a clear and present danger of bringing about evil consequences which the legislature has the right to prevent. Justices Holmes and Brandeis often found themselves joining in dissent in free speech cases; their opinions collectively, and Holmes's dissent in this case, are the most powerful and compelling arguments for freedom of speech in the American legal canon.

Although this case was decided against Gitlow, the Court's assumption that freedom of speech is protected against invasion by state governments was a significant milestone in the development of free speech rights. In effect the Court held that freedom of speech is among the liberties protected against infringement by state government by the due process clause of the Fourteenth Amendment.

Robert Jacobs

See also *Dennis v. United States; Elfbrandt v. Russell; Lovell v. City of Griffin; Noto v. United States; Scales v. United States; Whitney v. California; Yates v. United States.*

Gold Clause Cases

Norman v. Baltimore and Ohio Railroad Co.; Nortz v. United States; Perry v. United States

Court: U.S. Supreme Court

Citations: 294 U.S. 240; 294 U.S. 317; 294 U.S. 330

Date: February 18, 1935

Issues: Fiscal and monetary powers

• The U.S. Supreme Court's ruling allowed Congress to pass laws abrogating various contracts that called for payment in gold because the contracts, if honored, would have harmed the U.S. economy.

All three cases were argued and decided together, with Chief Justice Charles Evans Hughes writing the opinion for the 5-4 majority. In fighting the Great Depression, Congress passed laws allowing the abrogation of contracts requiring payment in gold, allowing them to be paid in devalued currency. Bondholders challenged these laws as depriving them of property without due process and as a breach of contract. Writing for the Court, Hughes stated that the gold clause simply provided for payment in money. He further stated that Congress had the constitutional authority to regulate the monetary system and its enactments were within the scope of that authority, although he did find Congress erred in rescinding the gold clauses in its own government bonds. These must be paid, but the bondholders could recover only nominal damages and could not use the court of claims to pursue their loss. Justice James C. McReynolds dissented vehemently in each case, calling this abrogation of contracts a seizure of property and suggesting financial chaos would result.

Richard L. Wilson

See also *Briscoe v. Bank of the Commonwealth of Kentucky*; *Craig v. Missouri*; *Legal Tender Cases*.

GOLDBERG V. KELLY

Court: U.S. Supreme Court
Citation: 397 U.S. 254
Date: March 23, 1970
Issues: Due process of law

• The U.S. Supreme Court held that the due process clause of the Fourteenth Amendment requires that state agencies must provide welfare recipients with evidentiary hearings before ending their benefits.

In conformity with state law, New York welfare officials terminated the public assistance of a recipient, with notice that the action could be challenged in a posttermination hearing. By a 5-4 vote, the Supreme Court held that a recipient must have the right to a pretermination hearing. Although not requiring the hearing to be a formal judicial proceeding, Justice William J. Brennan, Jr.'s majority opinion did specify that the recipient must be allowed to confront witnesses, to retain a lawyer, and to bring oral evidence before an impartial official. Brennan reasoned that a statutory entitlement to welfare was a form of property that helped poor people to survive and participate in the life of the community.

In subsequent decisions, the Court expanded the *Goldberg* principle to related situations. In *Gross v. Lopez* (1975), for example, the Court held that suspension of students from public schools constituted deprivation of property within the meaning of the Fourteenth Amendment. In *Mathews v. Eldridge* (1976), however, the Court shifted toward a balancing test when it approved of a policy of not providing opportunity for a hearing for recipients of Social Security disability payments before termination of benefits.

Thomas Tandy Lewis

See also *Dandridge v. Williams; Gomez v. Perez; Graham v. Richardson; Shapiro v. Thompson.*

Goldfarb v. Virginia State Bar

Court: U.S. Supreme Court
Citation: 421 U.S. 773
Date: June 16, 1975
Issues: Antitrust law

- The U.S. Supreme Court promoted price competition in legal services when it held that the Sherman Antitrust Act of 1890 prohibited state bar associations from setting minimum fees for legal services.

The Virginia Bar Association enforced minimum fee schedules for services set by the county bar associations. Lawyers were threatened with disciplinary action for regularly charging less than the posted fees. The Goldfarbs sued the state bar association for illegal price fixing after they were unable to find a lawyer to perform a real estate title examination for less than the minimum rate. Speaking for an 8-0 majority, Chief Justice Warren E. Burger upheld the challenge and rejected the association's contention that the Sherman Antitrust Act did not apply to the "learned professions." He noted that many of the funds for purchasing homes came from other states, and therefore, the issue fell under the purview of the commerce clause. The *Goldfarb* decision was primarily significant in regard to relatively routine legal services.

Thomas Tandy Lewis

See also *Bates v. State Bar of Arizona; In re Debs; Loewe v. Lawlor; Northern Securities Co. v. United States; United States v. E. C. Knight Co.*

GOLDWATER V. CARTER

Court: U.S. Supreme Court
Citation: 444 U.S. 996
Date: December 13, 1979
Issues: Presidential powers; Treaties

- The U.S. Supreme Court refused to decide whether President Jimmy Carter had the authority to terminate a treaty without the approval of the Senate, but the majority could not agree about why the issue was nonjusticiable.

In December, 1979, President Jimmy Carter announced that he was establishing full diplomatic relations with the People's Republic of China, an action that required terminating the Mutual Defense Treaty with Taiwan. In view of the U.S. Constitution's requirement that a treaty must be approved by a two-thirds majority of the Senate, Senator Barry Goldwater and twenty-four other members of Congress filed a suit contesting the president's right to unilaterally terminate a treaty. A federal court of appeals ruled in favor of the president.

By a 6-3 vote, the Supreme Court summarily vacated the ruling and dismissed the complaint. In one concurring opinion, Justice William H. Rehnquist, joined by three other justices, argued that a disagreement between the president and members of Congress was a nonjusticiable political controversy. In another concurrence, Justice Lewis F. Powell, Jr., found that the issue was "not ripe for judicial review" because a congressional majority had not opposed the president's policy. Justice Thurgood Marshall concurred without writing or joining an opinion. In a dissent, two justices insisted that the Court should not render a decision about justiciability without first hearing oral arguments. In another dissent, Justice William J. Brennan, Jr., argued that the Court should uphold the judgment of the court of appeals.

Thomas Tandy Lewis

See also *Baker v. Carr; McCulloch v. Maryland; Mississippi v. Johnson; Missouri v. Holland; Nixon v. Administrator of General Services; United States v. Alvarez-Machain; United States v. Nixon; Wiener v. United States.*

GOMEZ V. PEREZ

Court: U.S. Supreme Court
Citation: 409 U.S. 535
Date: June 17, 1973
Issues: Children's rights; Equal protection of the law;
Welfare rights

• This U.S. Supreme Court decision ruled that states may not deprive children born out of wedlock of important benefits that are generally accorded to other children.

This case originated when a Texas man named Francisco Perez refused to provide support for his illegitimate child, Zoraida Gomez. When the child's natural mother sued Perez, the state courts ruled that a biological father had no legal obligation to make payments for an illegitimate child. The decision was based on both the statutes and common law in the state of Texas. The case was then appealed to the U.S. Supreme Court, whose justices declared that the relevant state's law was unconstitutional because it violated the equal protection clause of the Fourteenth Amendment.

In a *per curiam* opinion, the Court ruled that states were prohibited from invidiously discriminating against illegitimate children by depriving them of essential benefits that were generally available to other children. The Court noted that fathers were required to support all legitimate children even when they did not maintain custody and that it was "illogical and unjust" not to extend the same benefits to those children whose biological parents were not married. Expanding upon earlier precedents, the case of *Gomez v. Perez* acknowledged that if states recognized judicially enforceable rights for children generally, the U.S. Constitution mandated that equal rights must be extended to the children of unmarried parents.

Thomas Tandy Lewis

See also *Nguyen v. Immigration and Naturalization Service; Zablocki v. Redhail.*

GOMILLION V. LIGHTFOOT

Court: U.S. Supreme Court
Citation: 364 U.S. 339
Date: November 14, 1960
Issues: Reapportionment and redistricting

• The U.S. Supreme Court struck down racial gerrymandering in Tuskegee, Alabama, opening the door for a reconsideration of the justiciability of redistricting cases.

Justice Felix Frankfurter wrote the unanimous opinion of the Court overturning the arbitrary redrawing of the city limit lines in Tuskegee, Alabama, in such a way as to eliminate all but four or five African American voters while eliminating no white voters. In doing so, Frankfurter had to get around his own opinion in *Colegrove v. Green* (1946) in which he had concluded that legislative redistricting was a political question best left to the legislature. He did not drop his opposition to general judicial review of legislative districts, using the Fifteenth Amendment's voting rights principle rather than the Fourteenth Amendment in his reasoning in *Gomillion*. He defended his *Colegrove* opinion in his dissent in *Baker v. Carr* (1962). Justices William O. Douglas and Charles E. Whittaker concurred but said they would have struck down the gerrymandering on Fourteenth Amendment grounds, foreshadowing the overturning of *Colegrove* by *Baker.*

Richard L. Wilson

See also *Baker v. Carr; Colegrove v. Green; Gray v. Sanders; Kirkpatrick v. Preisler; Mahan v. Howell; Wesberry v. Sanders.*

GOMPERS V. BUCK'S STOVE AND RANGE CO.

Court: U.S. Supreme Court
Citation: 221 U.S. 418
Date: May 15, 1911
Issues: Freedom of speech; Labor law

• Although the U.S. Supreme Court overturned the conviction of union leaders on criminal contempt, it clearly indicated the Court's lack of support for labor unions.

The American Federation of Labor (AFL) supported the striking employees of Buck's Stove and Range Company by organizing a boycott of the manufacturer's products. The company got an injunction against the boycott, and the union planned an appeal. The AFL published the company's name on a list of companies engaging in unfair practices, and the company responded by seeking to cite the union leaders with criminal contempt. The Supreme Court unanimously reversed the criminal contempt citation on a technicality. However, in his opinion for the Court, Justice Joseph R. Lamar rejected the union's claim that its publication of the list was a legitimate exercise of free speech and strongly indicated the Court's support for the rights of employers against labor unions.

Richard L. Wilson

See also *Gitlow v. New York; Schenck v. United States; Stromberg v. California; Whitney v. California.*

GONZALES V. RAICH

Court: U.S. Supreme Court
Citation: 545 U.S. 1
Date: June 6, 2005
Issues: Illegal drugs; Regulation of commerce

- The U.S. Supreme Court recognized the federal government's authority to enforce federal laws outlawing marijuana in all circumstances, even in those states that have legalized the substance for some medical purposes.

In 1996, California legalized the use of marijuana for medicinal purposes in the so-called Compassionate Use Act, which was similar to the statutes in ten other states. All such statutes conflicted with the federal Controlled Substances Act (1970), which criminalized the possession of marijuana for any purpose. After agents of the Drug Enforcement Administration (DEA) destroyed the marijuana and cannabis plants grown by Angel Raich in her garden, Raich joined with other concerned parties to sue the attorney general and the DEA in federal district court.

The Ninth Circuit Court of Appeals ruled that the DEA's application of the federal statute was unconstitutional insofar as it applied to the intrastate, non-commercial possession and cultivation of a substance for medical use as recommended by a physician. The court pointed to the *United States v. Lopez* (1995), in which the Supreme Court had held that federal power did not extend to the regulation of purely local activities.

The Supreme Court, however, upheld the federal government's position by a 6-3 vote. In the opinion for the majority, Justice John Paul Stevens wrote that the commerce clause empowered Congress to prohibit the local cultivation and use of controlled substances, despite state laws to the contrary. He argued that the commerce clause authorized Congress to regulate any "class of activities" that substantially affects interstate commerce. The case was different from *Lopez*, which related to a noneconomic activity having no significant impact on interstate commerce. Because of the difficulty in distinguishing between marijuana cultivated locally and marijuana grown elsewhere, Stevens affirmed that Congress acted rationally in placing this class of activities within the larger regulatory scheme. He also observed that marijuana has a high potential for abuse and no generally recognized medical use.

Thomas Tandy Lewis

See also *California v. Acevedo; Hutto v. Davis; Illinois v. Caballes; Illinois v. McArthur; Ker v. California; Kyllo v. United States; New Jersey v. T.L.O.; United States v. Lopez.*

GOOD NEWS CLUB V. MILFORD CENTRAL SCHOOL

Court: U.S. Supreme Court
Citation: 533 U.S. 98
Date: June 11, 2001
Issues: Education; Establishment of religion

• The U.S. Supreme Court held that all public schools must open their doors for after-school religious activities on the same basis that school policy permits other after-hours activities.

In an earlier decision, *Lamb's Chapel v. Center Moriches Union Free School District* (1993), the Supreme Court had held that public high school property must be open to groups with religious messages so long as they could be used by other groups. Since the *Lamb's Chapel* case had involved an adult activity during evening hours, the Court had not addressed whether the same analysis would apply to activities involving young children as soon as the regular school day ends. When a school district in New York followed a policy of not allowing "quintessentially religious" subjects to be taught in elementary school buildings, an evangelical Christian organization for young boys and girls, the Good News Club, sued the district in federal court. The appeals court in Manhattan ruled in favor of the district, emphasizing the special susceptibility of young children to indoctrination.

Reversing the lower court's ruling by a 6-3 vote, the Supreme Court reaffirmed that the expression of religious viewpoints is protected by the First Amendment against discrimination on school property. Writing for the majority, Justice Clarence Thomas relied on the Court's well-established neutrality principle, and he argued that the danger that young children might misperceive an open-door policy as an endorsement of religion was no greater "that they might perceive a hostility toward the religious viewpoint if the club were excluded from the public forum." With Justice Stephen Breyer writing an equivocal concurring opinion, five members of the Court appeared not to make any distinctions among religious speech, worship services, and recruitment activities.

Thomas Tandy Lewis

See also *Edwards v. Aguillard; Engel v. Vitale; Everson v. Board of Education of Ewing Township; Illinois ex rel. McCollum v. Board of Education; Lemon v. Kurtzman; Minersville School District v. Gobitis; Wallace v. Jaffree; Zorach v. Clauson.*

Goodridge v. Department of Public Health

Court: Massachusetts Supreme Judicial Court
Citation: 798 N.W. 2d 941
Date: November 18, 2003
Issues: Gay and lesbian rights; Marriage

• The high court of Massachusetts held that the state's refusal to issue marriage licenses to same-sex couples violates the state constitution's guarantee of individual equality and liberty. As a result of the decision, Massachusetts became the first state in the country to give legal recognition to same-sex marriage.

The issue of same-sex marriage emerged as a controversial public issue during the last decade of the twentieth century. In 1993, the Supreme Court of Hawaii held that the refusal to recognize same-sex marriages violated the state's constitution, but five years later voters approved a constitutional amendment that authorized the state legislature to reserve marriage for heterosexual couples. In 1996, the controversy prompted the U.S. Congress to enact the Defense of Marriage Act (DOMA), which specified that the federal government did not recognize same-sex marriages and that states would not be required to recognize those made in another state. In 1999, California became the first state in the union to offer same-sex couples "domestic partnerships," which guaranteed a number of the enumerated privileges of traditional marriage. Also that year, the Vermont's supreme court ruled in *Baker v. Vermont* that same-sex couples under the state constitution were entitled to the same legal benefits and responsibilities as married other-sex couples. The legislature responded with the creation of civil unions, which offered essentially the same entitlements found in marriage.

Proponents of same-sex marriage frequently referred to the case of *Loving v. Virginia* (1967), in which the U.S. Supreme Court had ruled that the refusal to allow marriage among persons of different races was inconsistent with both the equal protection and due process clauses of the Fourteenth Amendment. In *Loving*, the Court had declared that the freedom to marry is "one of the vital personal rights essential to the orderly pursuit of happiness by free men." During the last decade of the twentieth century, the membership of the Supreme Court was relatively conservative, and it appeared unlikely that the justices were ready to extend the *Loving* precedent to gay and lesbian couples. However, in *Romer v. Evans* (1996) the Court struck down a provisions in Nebraska's constitution that would have prohibited antidiscriminatory policies based on sexual orientation. Then in *Lawrence v. Texas* (2003), the Court disallowed the criminalization of homosexual practices among consenting adults in private homes.

Gay Rights in Massachusetts

Massachusetts has long been one of the states with a strong movement advocating gay and lesbian rights. In March and April of 2001, seven same-sex couples from five Massachusetts counties attempted to obtain marriage licenses from their local city and town clerk offices. In each instance their applications were denied, with the explanation that the state had not authorized licenses for couples of the same sex. The fourteen persons then filed a complaint in state court, alleging that the state's policy of exclusion violated the state constitution of Massachusetts. The plaintiffs represented a large variety of professions, including lawyers, doctors, teachers, bankers, and factory workers. Many of them were active in civil organizations, community affairs, and churches throughout the state. Two of the plaintiffs were Hillary Goodridge and Julie Goodridge, who had been in a committed relationship for thirteen years and lived with their five-year-old daughter.

On November 18, 2003, the Massachusetts Supreme Judicial Court decided, by a 4-3 margin, that barring individuals from the protections, benefits, and obligations of civil marriage solely because the persons marry partners of the same sex violates the Massachusetts constitution. State chief justice Margaret Marshall defended the court's position in a fifty-page document, building upon the premise that the state's constitution affirms the dignity and equality of all individuals and forbids creation of second-class citizens. The right to marry a person of one's choice was not a privilege conferred by the state, but "a fundamental right that is protected against unwarranted State interfer-

Julie and Hillary Goodridge celebrating their marriage at Boston's Unitarian Universalist Church on May 17, 2004, six months after their court victory. (AP/Wide World Photos)

ence." She went on to say that although the court must defer to the legislature to decide social and policy issues, denial of fundamental rights requires a compelling rationale, and the state "has failed to identify any constitutionally adequate reason" for this particular denial.

Massachusetts state laws did not disqualify infertile couples from obtaining marriage licenses, because "it is the exclusive and permanent commitments of the marriage partners to one another, not the begetting of children, that is the *sine qua non* of civil marriage." Claiming that the ruling "does not disturb the fundamental value of marriage in our society," Marshall remarked that gays and lesbians were simply seeking an equal right to participate in an institution that currently exists, and they were not asking for polygamous relationships or other radical changes in the law. Because the decision was based on the state's constitution, rather than the Fourteenth Amendment, it could not be appealed to the U.S. Supreme Court.

Dissenting Opinions

The major argument of the dissenters was the traditional meaning of marriage: for at least two thousand years of Western civilization, marriage has been defined as a union between one man and one woman. Justice Robert Cordy, whose opinion was endorsed by the two other dissenters, wrote that the majority's conclusions were insupportable in light of basic principles of constitutional democracy: the judiciary should not "substitute its notion of correct policy for that of a popularly elected legislature," and it should respect the "presumption of constitutional validity and significant deference afforded to legislative enactment." He emphasized that since same-sex marriage was not deeply rooted in the nation's history, the state's policy required only a "rational basis," not a compelling state interest, and that the legislature could rationally conclude that restricting marriage to heterosexual couples furthers the legitimate state purpose of "enduring, promoting, and supporting an optimal social structure for the bearing and raising of children."

The issue before the Massachusetts court was not "government intrusion into matters of personal liberty," but rather the issue was whether the state must "endorse and support" the choice of a minority to the extent of redefining an important social institution that had existed during Massachusetts's entire history. In a separate dissent, Justice Martha Sosman wrote that since there was no scientific consensus about whether a redefinition of marriage might adversely affect the institution of marriage. It was, therefore, rational for the legislature to keep the traditional definition of marriage "until such time as it is certain that redefinition will not have unintended and undesirable social consequences."

Soon after the decision was announced, Republican governor Mitt Romney issued a statement in support of a constitutional amendment defining marriage as exclusively a union between a man and woman. Following a contentious debate, a narrow majority of the state legislature approved a proposed amendment that would have limited marriage to opposite-sex couples while establishing a system of civil unions for same-sex couples. However, the Massachusetts constitution requires that an amendment cannot be put before voters until approved by joint sessions of two consecutive legislative sessions, and opponents of the proposal were able to defeat it during the 2005-2006 session. The *Goodridge* ruling went into effect in 2004. Within two years, about eight thousand same-sex couples had exchanged marriage vows in Massachusetts, and forty-five couples, including Hillary and Julie Goodridge, were legally divorced.

The legalization of same-sex marriages in Massachusetts encouraged members of the gay and lesbian community to seek the right to marry elsewhere in the country. By the end of 2009, the supreme courts of three additional states—Connecticut, Iowa, and New Hampshire—had issued rulings that legalized same-sex marriage, and one state, Vermont, authorized the institution through legislation. Eight other states had civil unions or domestic partnerships that allowed same-sex couples most of the rights in marriage law.

In 2008, the Supreme Court of California issued a ruling that was very similar to *Goodridge*, but a voter referendum approved a constitutional amendment that overturned the court's ruling. In 2009, the Maine legislature passed a bill almost identical to the one in Vermont, but voters struck down the legislation in a referendum. That same year, however, the city council of the District of Columbia approved a bill to allow couples of the same sex to marry in the nation's capital. Several states were considering similar measures, and it was almost certain that Congress would approve. Many state legislatures were debating the issue, and Congress appeared ready to repeal the Defense of Marriage Act. Without the impetus of *Goodridge v. Department of Public Health*, it is doubtful that the issue would have advanced so rapidly.

Thomas Tandy Lewis

Further Reading

Badgett, M. V. Lee. *When Gay People Get Married: What Happens When Societies Legalize Same-Sex Marriage.* New York: New York University Press, 2009. Concludes that legal recognition has not harmed heterosexual marriage and that some same-sex couples have benefited.

Baird, Robert M., and Stuart E. Rosenbaum, eds. *Same-Sex Marriage: The Moral and Legal Debate.* New York: Prometheus Books, 1997. Valuable collection of differing reactions to the *Goodridge* opinion, including emotional reactions, philosophical arguments, and case studies.

Gerstmann, Evan. *Same-Sex Marriage and the Constitution.* New York: Cambridge University Press, 2007. Clear and fair-minded analysis of the strengths and weaknesses of the major arguments in favor and against the legal recognition of same-sex marriage.

Kahn, Karen, Patricia Gozemba, and Marilyn Humphries. *Courting Equality: A Documentary History of America's First Legal Same-Sex Marriages.* Boston: Beacon, 2007. Chronicles the path to the *Goodridge* decision, argues that it has had entirely positive results for everyone in Massachusetts, and celebrates the marriages that have occurred.

Nussbaum, Martha. *From Disgust to Humanity: Sexual Orientation and Constitutional Law.* New York: Oxford University Press, 2010. Argues that most gay and lesbian discrimination has been based on disgust and finds no justification for denying full equality on matters such as marriage and employment.

Phy-Olsen, Allene. *Same-Sex Marriage.* Westport, Conn.: Greenwood Press, 2006. Examines historical attitudes toward homosexuality and marriage throughout history and presents the strongest arguments on both sides of the debate.

See also *Baker v. Vermont; Lawrence v. Texas; Loving v. Virginia; Romer v. Evans.*

Goss v. Lopez

Court: U.S. Supreme Court
Citation: 419 U.S. 565
Date: January 22, 1975
Issues: Due process of law; Education

- The Court held 5-4 that states must provide some elements of due process of law in school disciplinary proceedings that can result in suspension. The decision stands for the proposition that schoolchildren are also entitled to at least some elementary procedural guarantees and evidentiary rules in school disciplinary proceedings.

During a period of unrest in the Columbus, Ohio, school system, Dwight Lopez was a student at Central High School. He was suspended from school for ten days for allegedly participating in a demonstration in the school cafeteria. There was some physical damage to the lunch room. Lopez received no hearing prior to his suspension. He later testified that he himself had not participated in the disturbance.

The U.S. Supreme Court held, in a 5-4 decision written by Justice Byron R. White, that Lopez and the other nine suspended appellants were entitled to a hearing prior to suspension so that the charges against them could be assessed. The state of Ohio's argument that it was constitutionally entitled not to offer public education at all and could thus manage the system as it pleased was rejected by the Court; having established the system and given the public rights in it, Ohio could not deprive people of due process by later depriving them of that right. The dissenting justices in this case argued that the penalty was too insignificant to warrant a hearing.

Robert Jacobs

See also *New Jersey v. T.L.O.*; *Safford Unified School District v. Redding*; *Tinker v. Des Moines Independent Community School District*.

Graham v. Richardson

Court: U.S. Supreme Court
Citation: 403 U.S. 365
Date: June 14, 1971
Issues: Equal protection of the law; Immigration; Welfare rights

- In this case, the U.S. Supreme Court declared alienage, like race, a "suspect classification" under the Fourteenth Amendment, thus subjecting state classifications based on alienage to strict scrutiny, under which states must promote a compelling government interest.

Carmen Richardson, a Mexican citizen, was lawfully admitted to the United States in 1956. From that time, she resided continuously in Arizona, where she became permanently disabled. When she applied to the state for welfare benefits, she was denied them because she had not met Arizona's requirement that welfare beneficiaries who are not United States citizens must have resided in the state for fifteen years. Richardson brought a class action on behalf of other similarly situated individuals against the Arizona commissioner of public welfare, claiming that the residency requirement violated their right to equal protection under the Fourteenth Amendment. She won her case in federal court, and the state appealed to the Supreme Court, claiming that limited public resources justified states favoring their own residents over aliens.

The Supreme Court unanimously upheld the lower court's decision. The Court agreed with the finding that residency requirements such as that at issue in *Graham v. Richardson* violate the Fourteenth Amendment's equal protection clause and that government classifications based on alienage, like those based on race, can only be upheld if they are closely related to a compelling state interest. Arizona's interest in husbanding its financial resources was clearly not compelling enough. In addition, the Court provided an alternate ground for striking down the Arizona statute: Because the Constitution empowers the federal government to control the conditions under which aliens reside in the United States, state laws addressing the same concerns were preempted because of the supremacy clause (Article VI of the Constitution).

The Court subsequently created a series of exceptions to *Graham*. In *Sugarman v. Dougall* (1973), for example, the Court indicated that states could bar aliens from certain posts in government. In *Foley v. Connelie* (1978), it employed only ordinary scrutiny (requiring the state to meet a much lower burden of proof) in upholding a New York statute barring aliens from becoming state troopers. Subsequent Supreme Court cases followed the political job function argument of *Foley* to uphold state laws barring aliens from employment as public school teachers (*Ambach v. Norwick*, 1979) and as deputy probation officers (*Cabell v. Chavez-Salido*, 1982).

In the seminal case *Plyler v. Doe* (1982), although the Court voted five to four to invalidate a Texas law withholding public education from children of aliens who had migrated to the U.S. outside legal channels, it lowered the burden of proof to that of intermediate scrutiny. Thus a different standard of proof was made to apply in cases involving so-called illegal aliens than to those concerning lawful resident aliens. Unlike discriminatory racial classifications, which are inherently suspect, alienage has proven to be a more protean concept.

Lisa Paddock

See also *Plyler v. Doe*; *Reed v. Reed*; *San Antonio Independent School District v. Rodriguez*; *Slaughterhouse Cases*.

GRATZ V. BOLLINGER/ GRUTTER V. BOLLINGER

GRATZ V. BOLLINGER

Court: U.S. Supreme Court
Citation: 539 U.S 306
Date: June 23, 2003

GRUTTER V. BOLLINGER

Court: U.S. Supreme Court
Citation: 539 U.S. 244
Date: June 23, 2003
Issues: Affirmative action; Civil rights and liberties; Education

- Declaring that government has a compelling interest in promoting student diversity, the Supreme Court upheld the constitutionality of narrowly tailored affirmative action programs for admissions into highly competitive universities.

In the seminal case of *Regents of the University of California v. Bakke* (1978), the Supreme Court endorsed admissions programs that provided limited preferences for members of underrepresented groups. The use of such programs became one of the most controversial issues in American society. The future of the programs became doubtful after the Court in *Adarand Constructors v. Peña* (1995) held that the programs would henceforth be evaluated according to the strict scrutiny standard. Applying this standard in 1996, the Court of Appeals for the Fifth Circuit announced that all race-based admissions policies were unconstitutional. The Supreme Court declined to review the decision.

The admissions policy at the University of Michigan Law School continued to provide racial preferences in order to achieve a "critical mass" of underrepresented minority students. After Barbara Grutter, a white student with a 3.8 undergraduate grade point average and an LSAT score of 161, failed to gain admission to the school, she sued with the argument that the preferences violated the equal protection clause and the 1964 Civil Rights Act. Although she won at the district court level, the appellate court upheld the university's affirmative action policy.

In a 5-4 decision, to the surprise of many observers, the Supreme Court also upheld the policy. Delivering the majority opinion, Justice Sandra Day O'Connor argued that the policy was "narrowly tailored" to further a compelling interest in seeking the benefits of a diverse student body. She emphasized that each student was individually reviewed, that factors other than race and ethnicity were considered, that the goal of a "critical mass" was not equivalent to a quota, and that the preferences did "not unduly harm majority students." Finally, she wrote of her expectation that the preferences would no longer be necessary after the passage of twenty-five years.

On the same day that the *Grutter* ruling was announced, the Court also announced *Gratz v. Bollinger*, in which the university's admissions policy for minorities was found unconstitutional by a 6-3 margin. For selecting undergraduates, the university had simply added a 20 percent increase in the number of points to every underrepresented minority applicant without any individualized assessment. Chief Justice William H. Rehnquist declared that because the automatic preferences were not narrowly tailored, they did not survive a review according to the strict scrutiny standards.

Thomas Tandy Lewis

See also *Adarand Constructors v. Peña; Green v. County School Board of New Kent County; Keyes v. Denver School District No. 1; Lau v. Nichols; Parents Involved in Community Schools v. Seattle School District No. 1; Regents of the University of California v. Bakke; Texas v. Hopwood; United Steelworkers of America v. Weber.*

GRAVES V. NEW YORK EX REL. O'KEEFE

Court: U.S. Supreme Court
Citation: 306 U.S. 466
Date: March 27, 1939
Issues: Taxation

- The U.S. Supreme Court gave the authority to the federal government to tax the salaries of state employees.

New York imposed a tax on the salary paid to a federal worker who resided in that state. The worker paid the tax and appealed, arguing intergovernmental immunity. The Supreme Court, by a 7-2 vote, overruled *Collector v. Day* (1871) and established the right of the federal government to collect taxes on the salaries paid to state employees. Until *Graves,* state employees had been immune from federal taxes and federal employees immune from state taxes. This mutual tax immunity was reinforced by the Court in *Pollock v. Farmers' Loan and Trust Co.* (1895). However, in his opinion for the Court, Justice Harlan Fiske Stone rejected the idea that a tax on income is equivalent to a tax on the income's source. The Public Salary Tax Act of 1939 specifically allowed the states to tax the salaries of federal employees and permitted the federal government to tax the incomes of state employees.

Richard L. Wilson

See also *Collector v. Day; Dobbins v. Erie County; Pollock v. Farmers' Loan and Trust Co.*

GRAY V. SANDERS

Court: U.S. Supreme Court
Citation: 372 U.S. 368
Date: March 18, 1963
Issues: Voting rights

- The U.S. Supreme Court invalidated a Georgia election system as not representative of its voters and introduced the one person, one vote concept.

By an 8-1 vote, the Court invalidated Georgia's county unit primary election system, which severely impacted urban areas, finding it to be unconstitutional under the equal protection clause of the Fourteenth Amendment. Justice William O. Douglas wrote the majority opinion with separate concurrences by Justices Potter Stewart and Tom C. Clark. Douglas viewed *Gray* as a voting rights case without legislative reapportionment implications, a view that Stewart and Clark underscored. Douglas also introduced the one person, one vote concept, declaring that equality of representation was necessary for political equality. *Gray* proved to be a critical link between *Baker v. Carr* (1962) and *Reynolds v. Sims* (1964), one of a group of reapportionment cases. In *Gray*, Justice John M. Harlan II dissented as he would in the reapportionment cases, arguing that this issue plunged justices further into the political thicket and that the superiority of the federal to state courts had not been proven.

Richard L. Wilson

See also *Baker v. Carr; Colegrove v. Green; Kirkpatrick v. Preisler; Mahan v. Howell; Reapportionment Cases; Reynolds v. Sims; Wesberry v. Sanders.*

GREEN V. BIDDLE

Court: U.S. Supreme Court
Citation: 21 U.S. 1
Date: decided March 5, 1821; redecided February 27, 1823
Issues: Freedom of contract; Land law

- The U.S. Supreme Court expanded the contracts clause to include public as well as private contracts.

The 1792 Virginia-Kentucky compact stipulated that Kentucky land titles were to be decided by the preexisting Virginia laws, which protected a number of absentee landowners. However, Kentucky passed a law allowing its settlers to recover the value of improvements they made on land they occupied even if they were not the owners under Virginia law. Virginia objected and took the case to the Supreme Court. In his 1821 opinion for the Court, Justice Joseph Story expanded the contracts clause to include public as well as private agreements and ruled that the contracts clause of the U.S. Constitution prevailed over the Kentucky statute. Kentucky was outraged and forced the Court to withdraw the Story decision. Upon rehearing, Justice Bushrod Washington found essentially the same as Story, but Kentucky continued to enforce its own laws, and the political disagreement over the powers of the Court continued in Congress for some time.

Richard L. Wilson

See also *Bronson v. Kinzie; Dartmouth College v. Woodward; Home Building and Loan Association v. Blaisdell; Keystone Bituminous Coal Association v. DeBenedictis; Providence Bank v. Billings; Stone v. Mississippi.*

Green v. County School Board of New Kent County

Court: U.S. Supreme Court
Citation: 391 U.S. 430
Date: May 27, 1968
Issues: Desegregation; Education

- In this case, the U.S. Supreme Court determined for the first time that school boards have an affirmative duty to desegregate their schools and disallowed "freedom-of-choice" desegregation plans that do not result in substantial pupil mixing.

In the wake of the Supreme Court's 1954 decision in *Brown v. Board of Education* that outlawed school segregation, few southern school boards took action to integrate their schools. Finally, in the mid-1960's, under the threat of federal fund cutoffs and adverse court decisions, most southern school boards made some effort to integrate their schools. Many such school boards did so by adopting an assignment system whereby students were permitted to choose which school they wished to attend. Most such "freedom of choice" plans resulted in little racial integration. Black students typically chose to attend traditionally black schools, whereas white students chose to attend traditionally white schools. As a result, schools remained racially segregated in many southern school districts following the introduction of free-choice plans.

One school district that adopted a free-choice plan during the 1960's was the school district in New Kent County, Virginia. New Kent County is a rural county; its student population was about half black and half white, with blacks and whites scattered throughout the county. Prior to 1965, the schools in New Kent County had been completely segregated, with all the black students attending the county's one black school and all the white students attending the county's one white school. In 1965, the school board adopted a free-choice plan whereby every student was permitted to choose between the two schools. As a result of the free choice, all the white students chose to remain in the white school and 85 percent of the black students chose to remain in the black school.

A group of black parents, with the assistance of the National Association for the Advancement of Colored People (NAACP) Legal Defense and Educational Fund, filed a lawsuit challenging this free-choice plan. These parents contended that the plan was deficient because it did not effectively dismantle the old dual school system. The Supreme Court, faced with thirteen years of southern school board recalcitrance on school desegregation, agreed that the school board's free-choice plan did not satisfy constitutional standards and announced that the school board had an affirmative duty to devise a desegregation plan that actually resulted in substantial pupil mixing.

This decision, the Supreme Court's most important school desegregation decision since the 1954 *Brown* decision, helped transform school desegregation law by forcing school boards to devise assignment plans that resulted in greater integration. In the wake of the *Green* decision, lower courts throughout the South required school boards to take additional action to integrate their schools.

Davison M. Douglas

See also *Alexander v. Holmes County Board of Education*; *Brown v. Board of Education*; *Griffin v. County School Board of Prince Edward County.*

GREER V. SPOCK

Court: U.S. Supreme Court
Citation: 424 U.S. 828
Date: March 24, 1976
Issues: Censorship; Military law; Political campaigning

- This case upheld the principal that censorship rules on military bases can differ from those in public forums.

Fort Dix, New Jersey, an army training facility, long operated under the exclusive jurisdiction of the federal government, which encompassed all state and county roads passing through the facility. Regulations promulgated by the base commander permitted free and open civilian access to certain areas of the base, but simultaneously prohibited distribution of literature without prior approval by military officials. The regulations also banned partisan political speeches and demonstrations anywhere on military property.

In 1972 Dr. Benjamin Spock, the famous pediatrician, author, and antiwar activist, was the left-leaning People's Party candidate for president of the United States. Together with his vice presidential running mate, several political activists who had previously been evicted from the base for distributing unapproved political literature, and the candidates for president and vice president of the Socialist Workers Party, Spock petitioned Fort Dix's commanding officers for permission to hold a political meeting on the base and to distribute campaign literature there.

Pursuant to standing regulations, the base commander rejected the request and barred the previously evicted activists from re-entering the base. Spock and his cohort filed a lawsuit, seeking to enjoin enforcement of the regulations, alleging violations of the First and Fifth amendments to the U.S. Constitution. They were partially successful when an appeals court enjoined the military from enforcing the regulations to the extent that they prevented the four actual candidates (but not the accompanying activists) from making political speeches and distributing campaign leaflets in the parts of Fort Dix that were otherwise generally open to the public.

On appeal to the U.S. Supreme Court, Solicitor General Robert Bork (later an unsuccessful Supreme Court nominee) successfully argued the government's case. Justice Potter Stewart, writing for the majority on the divided court, reversed the appeals court, upholding the right of the military to enforce the regulations that censored political activity and speech on military bases. The Supreme Court ruled that although Fort Dix admitted the public to certain areas of the base, the base had neither abandoned nor ceded control to nonmilitary authorities.

The Court declared that the fundamental business of a military installation was to train soldiers, not to provide a censorship-free public forum. Although municipal streets and parks had "traditionally served as a place for free public assembly and communication of thoughts by private citizens" without government censorship, the Court expressed a fear that if it failed to uphold the military's authority to insulate itself from any appearance of endorsing partisan political causes, the American constitutional tradition of a politically neutral military establishment under civilian control could be undermined.

A vigorous dissent, written by Justice William J. Brennan, Jr., and joined by Justice Thurgood Marshall argued that the military's training mission and the important principle of military neutrality could both be protected without such blanket prohibitions and censorship regulations.

David G. Hicks

See also *Hazelwood School District v. Kuhlmeier; Snepp v. United States.*

Gregg v. Georgia

Court: U.S. Supreme Court
Citation: 428 U.S. 153
Date: July 2, 1976
Issues: Capital punishment; Cruel and unusual punishment

- After declaring execution unconstitutional in 1972, the U.S. Supreme Court reinstated the death penalty contingent on protection against its arbitrary and capricious imposition.

The death penalty is a method of punishment that historically has been applied globally for both serious and relatively minor crimes against state, person, and property. During the medieval and early modern periods of European history, the death sentence was used as punishment for many crimes and usually was administered in public, often accompanied by torture of the most painful and gruesome kind. The greatest abuse of the use of the death penalty was probably reached in eighteenth century England when it was decreed, although not regularly applied, for several hundred offenses, most representing crimes against property.

The increased use of the death penalty and the resulting public desensitization, accompanied by the humanitarian movement in the West known as the Age of Enlightenment, led to a growing reaction to its use, especially among the intellectuals of the age. The most famous early attack on the death penalty came from an Italian, Cesare Beccaria, whose treatise *Dei delitti e delle pene* (1764; essay on crimes and punishments) led to a rapidly growing demand for reform. The results were quick to come. During the French Revolution, for example, the guillotine was used as a more humane instrument of execution than the less swift and sure ax or sword. By the 1830's, the number of cases in England for which the death penalty could be imposed had been reduced from the hundreds of a few decades earlier to fifteen. The same trends followed in the United States, although the death penalty had never been imposed widely there.

By the middle of the twentieth century, the use of the death penalty had declined even further throughout most of the world, especially in Europe and the Americas. However, a large majority of the states in the United States still legislated its potential use in court sentences, although it seldom was actually imposed. A continuous attack on the imposition of the death penalty in criminal cases accompanied this decline in capital punishment. The opponents of the death penalty were never a majority, however, and all their arguments were countered by its proponents.

Arguments for and Against Capital Punishment

Generally, arguments for and against capital punishment can be divided into two basic categories—one based on religious belief and emotions, and the other founded on utilitarian or practical arguments. Supporters have argued, for example, that it is ordained by God as a means by which humans act as God's agents in ridding the world of the grossly undesirable, whereas opponents have held that justice belongs to God alone and cannot be delegated to people. In the category of practicality, supporters have held that capital punishment is a deterrent, protecting the community, prison staffs, and fellow prisoners from dangerous criminals. They also argue that those prisoners who receive the penalty of life imprisonment instead of death are an economic liability to the state. Opponents have countered these arguments by asserting that there is no proof that the threat of death deters criminals from committing capital offenses. Rehabilitation in prison rather than punishment could mitigate the problem of the dangerous criminal to society, prison staff, and prisoners. Also, in well-run prisons, prisoners can be economic assets instead of liabilities. Most important, critics of the death penalty have argued that judicial error can and has led to the execution of innocent persons, and that the imposition of the death penalty often has been socially and racially arbitrary and discriminatory. It was essentially on these arguments that the U.S. Supreme Court made its decisions on the death penalty in 1972 and 1976.

In 1972, two petitioners from Georgia, William Henry Furman and Lucious Jackson, Jr., and a petitioner from Texas, Elmer Branch, brought suit in federal court against their respective states. Georgia state courts had convicted Furman and Jackson of murder and rape, respectively, and the men had been sentenced to death by juries that had discretion over whether to impose the death penalty. Their sentences had been upheld by the Georgia Supreme Court. Branch had been sentenced to death for rape in Texas by a jury with the same discretionary power, and his sentence had been upheld by the Texas Court of Criminal Appeals. The U.S. Supreme Court, in a 5-4 decision, reversed the judgment of the state courts and remanded the cases for further proceedings. The cases were consolidated for argument and decision.

Furman, the plaintiff in the most renowned case, was an African American man who had attempted to enter a private home at night. He had shot and killed the home owner through a closed door. Furman was twenty-six years of age and had a sixth-grade education. Prior to trial, Furman was committed to the Georgia Central State Hospital for a psychiatric examination on his plea of insanity. The hospital superintendent reported a diagnosis of mental deficiency with psychotic episodes. Although not psychotic at the time, Furman was not capable of cooperating with the defense counsel, and they believed he needed further treatment. The superintendent later amended the report, saying Furman knew right from wrong and could cooperate with counsel.

The Majority Argument

Justices William O. Douglas, William J. Brennan, Potter Stewart, Byron White, and Thurgood Marshall composed the majority. They held that the death penalty, as it had been applied in these three cases, violated the Eighth and Fourteenth Amendments' prohibition of cruel and unusual punishment because, under the laws of Georgia and Texas, juries had an untrammeled discretion to impose or withhold the death penalty. In his opinion, Douglas held that the death penalty was cruel and unusual because, since it was imposed at the discretion of the jury, it had been applied selectively in a discriminatory fashion to members of a minority. Brennan, probably in an attempt to counter strict constructionists of the Constitution, held that the Eighth Amendment's prohibition of cruel and unusual punishment should not be considered as limited to torture or to punishments considered cruel and unusual at the time the Eighth Amendment was ratified. The prohibition should include all punishments that did not comport with the concept of human dignity held by society as a whole. Since society, according to Brennan, did not regard so severe a punishment as acceptable, its imposition represented a violation of the Eighth Amendment. It was now up to Georgia, Texas, and states with similar death penalty laws either to abolish capital punishment or to draft new laws that could be in agreement with the Court's decision in these three cases.

After the Supreme Court decision in *Furman v. Georgia*, thirty-five states and the federal government revised their capital punishment statutes to eliminate the equal protection problems. The revised statutes fell into two categories: those that made the death penalty mandatory for certain crimes and those that allowed the judge or jury to decide, under legislative guidelines, whether to impose the death penalty. Georgia, for example, amended its laws regarding imposition of the death penalty and attempted to make them fair, nondiscriminatory, and nonarbitrary. Under the new law, guilt or innocence was to be determined either by a jury, or by a trial judge in a case where there was no jury. In a jury trial, the judge was required to instruct the jury on lesser included offenses supported by the evidence.

After either a verdict, a finding, or a plea of guilty, a presentence hearing was to be conducted, at which the jury or judge would hear arguments and additional evidence in order to determine the punishment. At least one of two aggravating circumstances specified in the laws had to be found to exist beyond a reasonable doubt and had to be stated in writing before a jury or judge could impose the death penalty. The death sentence then was appealed automatically to the Supreme Court of Georgia, which would determine if the sentence had been imposed under the influence of passion, prejudice, or any other arbitrary factor; whether the evidence supported the finding of a legally aggravating circumstance; and whether the sentence was excessive or disproportionate to the penalty imposed in similar cases. If the Georgia Supreme Court affirmed the death sentence, its decision was required to include reference to similar cases that the court had considered.

A case to test these revised Georgia statutes, *Gregg v. Georgia*, was argued before the U.S. Supreme Court in March, 1976, and decided on July 2, 1976. Troy Leon Gregg and a companion were picked up by two motorists while hitchhiking in Florida. The bodies of the two motorists later were found beside a road near Atlanta, Georgia. When arrested the next day, a .25-caliber pistol was found in Gregg's possession and subsequently identified as the murder weapon. Gregg confessed, but claimed self-defense. Gregg had been convicted by a jury in a Georgia state court of two counts of armed robbery and two counts of murder. Throughout the trial and in the appeals process, the new Georgia statutes had been followed. The Georgia Supreme Court affirmed the conviction and the imposition of the death sentence for murder, although it vacated the sentence for the two counts of armed robbery.

Significance

The U.S. Supreme Court affirmed the decision of the Georgia Supreme Court. In a decision announced by Justices Stewart, Lewis F. Powell, Jr., and John Paul Stevens, seven of the nine justices held that in this case, the imposition of the death penalty did not violate the prohibition of the infliction of cruel and unusual punishment under the Eighth and Fourteenth Amendments. The right of states to impose and implement the death penalty had been affirmed, so long as a state's statutes were fair, nondiscriminatory, and nonarbitrary. Although the restrictions had been lifted, society has continued to approach the death penalty with resistance, hesitation, and confusion.

J. Stewart Alverson and Janice G. Rienerth

Further Reading

Atwell, Mary Welek. *Evolving Standards of Decency: Popular Culture and Capital Punishment.* New York: Peter Lang, 2004. Referring to Chief Justice Warren's criterion of society's evolving standards of decency; Atwell explores views on the acceptability of capital punishment in the nation's popular culture.

Edelman, Bryan. *Racial Prejudice, Juror Empathy, and Sentencing in Death Penalty*

Cases. New York: LFB Scholarly Press, 2006. Based on interviews, Edelman's book concludes that white jurors are especially prone to render death sentences in cases with white victims and black offenders.

Isenberg, Irwin, ed. *The Death Penalty.* New York: H. W. Wilson, 1977. A compilation of writings on the constitutional, legal, ethical, and philosophical aspects of capital punishment, taken from a wide variety of sources, mainly periodicals.

Jenkins, Nicholas. "Dirty Needle." *The New Yorker,* December 19, 1994, 5-6. Arguing against capital punishment, the article looks at different methods used to execute and the implications these methods have for society.

Johnson, Robert. *Condemned to Die: Life Under Sentence of Death.* Prospect Heights, Ill.: Waveland Press, 1989. An easily readable text with implications for current criminological thought. It deals with the warehousing of condemned prisoners.

Keplan, David. "Anger and Ambivalence." *Newsweek,* August 7, 1995, 24-28. Examines the contradiction between the growing popularity of capital punishment and the number of inmates who actually are put to death.

Latzer, Barry. *Death Penalty Cases: Leading U.S. Supreme Court Cases on Capital Punishment.* 2d ed. Burlington, Mass.: Butterworth-Heinemann, 2002. Contains excerpts from 25 court cases, including *Gregg v. Georgia.* Designed as an introductory text.

_____. *Death Penalty in a Nutshell.* St. Paul, Minn.: Thomson/West, 2005. A clearly written overview of death penalty arguments and cases. Discusses special topics such as race and gender bias and execution of the innocent.

Nygaard, Richard. "Vengeance Is Mine, Says the Lord." *America* 8 (October, 1994): 6-8. Argues that revenge is the only reason for which a society uses the death penalty.

Parrish, Michael. *The Supreme Court and Capital Punishment.* Washington, D.C.: CQ Press, 2009. Includes a valuable historical account of the topic and analyses important issues such as the influence of race, public opinion, and financial resources available to defendants.

Reitan, Eric. "Why the Deterrence Argument for Capital Punishment Fails." *Criminal Justice Ethics* 12 (1993): 26-33. Examines the faults of the deterrence argument for capital punishment.

See also *Atkins v. Virginia; Coker v. Georgia; Furman v. Georgia; McCleskey v. Kemp; Woodson v. North Carolina.*

GRIFFIN V. BRECKENRIDGE

Court: U.S. Supreme Court
Citation: 403 U.S. 88
Date: June 7, 1971
Issues: Civil rights and liberties; Right to travel

- This decision extended federal civil rights guarantees of equal protection of the law to the protection of personal rights not only from state action but from personal conspiracies as well.

On July 2, 1966, a group of African Americans who were suspected of being civil rights workers were halted on a Mississippi highway near the Alabama border by Lavon and Calvin Breckenridge, whose car purposely blocked the road. The Breckenridge group forced the African Americans from their vehicle and then subjected them to intimidation with firearms. The travellers were clubbed about their heads, beaten with pipes and other weapons, and repeatedly threatened with death. Although terrorized and seriously injured, the African Americans (who included Griffin) survived. They subsequently filed a suit for damages, charging that Breckenridge and others had conspired to assault them for the purpose of preventing them and "other Negro-Americans" from enjoying the equal rights, privileges, and immunities of citizens of the state of Mississippi and of the United States, including the rights to free speech, assembly, association, and movement and the right not to be enslaved.

A federal district court dismissed the complaint by relying on a previous U.S. Supreme Court decision, *Collins v. Hardyman* (1951), which in order to avoid difficult constitutional issues had held that federal law extended only to "conspiracies" condoned or perpetrated by states. That is, the Court tried to avoid opening questions involving congressional power or the content of state as distinct from national citizenship, or interfering in local matters such as assault and battery cases or similar illegalities that clearly fell under local jurisdiction.

The Collins case, however, had been decided a decade before the nationwide Civil Rights movement of the 1960's, a period marked by the enactment of a new series of federal civil rights laws as well as by attentive regard by the U.S. Supreme Court of Chief Justice Warren Burger to cases involving civil rights violations. The Burger court heard the Griffin case on appeal.

The Supreme Court's unanimous decision in *Griffin* was delivered by Justice Potter Stewart on June 7, 1971. The Court broadly interpreted the federal statute under which Griffin brought damages, Title 42 of the U.S. Code, section 1985. Section 1985 stipulated that if two or more persons conspired or went in disguise on public highways with the intent to deprive any person or any class of persons of equal protection of the laws or of equal privileges and immunities under the laws, a conspiracy existed and damages could be brought.

The Court waived consideration of whether the Collins case had been correctly decided. Instead, reviewing previous civil rights legislation, starting in 1866, the justices determined that the language of the federal statute clearly indicated that state action was not required to invoke federal protection of constitutionally guaranteed personal rights from impairment by personal conspiracies. *Griffin* effectively extended federal safeguards of civil rights to reach private conspiracies under the Thirteenth Amendment as well as under congressional powers to protect the right of interstate travel.

Clifton K. Yearley

See also *Civil Rights Cases*; *Gratz v. Bollinger/Grutter v. Bollinger*; *Hernández v. Texas*; *Jones v. Alfred H. Mayer Co.*; *Massachusetts Board of Retirement v. Murgia*; *Robinson v. California*; *Shelley v. Kraemer.*

GRIFFIN V. CALIFORNIA

Court: U.S. Supreme Court
Citation: 380 U.S. 609
Date: April 28, 1965
Issues: Self-incrimination

• The U.S. Supreme Court held that prosecutors or judges cannot make negative comments about a defendant's invoking the Fifth Amendment and that this protection against self-incrimination applies to the states under the due process clause.

No one can stop a juror from drawing an inference regarding guilt or innocence from a defendant's declining to take the stand in his or her own defense. However, the Supreme Court ruled that a negative comment regarding the defendant's decision to remain silent, when made by the prosecutor or judge in front of the jury, tends to make the jurors disregard the defendant's presumption of innocence. The Court, in a 7-2 decision that overruled *Adamson v. California* (1947), declared that the right against self-incrimination was a fundamental right protected by the due process clause of the Fourteenth Amendment and that even a mention of the defendant's refusal to testify in a criminal case was an unconstitutional deprivation of the defendant's rights. William O. Douglas wrote the opinion for the Court, with Potter Stewart and Byron R. White dissenting.

Richard L. Wilson

See also *Adamson v. California; Benton v. Maryland; Boyd v. United States; Counselman v. Hitchcock; Kastigar v. United States; Kilbourn v. Thompson; Murphy v. Waterfront Commission of New York; Olmstead v. United States.*

GRIFFIN V. COUNTY SCHOOL BOARD OF PRINCE EDWARD COUNTY

Court: U.S. Supreme Court
Citation: 180 U.S. 609
Date: May 25, 1964
Issues: Desegregation; Education

• The U.S. Supreme Court ruled against a Virginia county that closed public schools rather than desegregate.

Contrary to the ruling in *Brown v. Board of Education II* (1955), Prince Edward County, Virginia, followed state law, closed its public schools, and provided tax credits and tuition grants to whites-only private schools. The Supreme Court unanimously rejected the county's policies. In the opinion for the Court, Justice Hugo L. Black stated that time had "run out" for the "all deliberate speed" in desegregating schools called for in *Brown II*. Black ruled that district courts could issue injunctions against the use of tuition tax credits and grants, control a noncomplying school board's taxing and appropriating power, and reopen public schools on an integrated basis. Tom C. Clark and John M. Harlan II disagreed with the majority on these latter points, without saying why. This was the first hint of a break in the united wall that had been presented since the first *Brown* decision in 1954 and may have influenced the somewhat more guarded language used in *Green v. County School Board of New Kent County* (1968).

Richard L. Wilson

See also *Brown v. Board of Education; Columbus Board of Education v. Penick; Green v. County School Board of New Kent County; Milliken v. Bradley; Pasadena Board of Education v. Spangler; Plessy v. Ferguson; Swann v. Charlotte-Mecklenburg Board of Education.*

GRIGGS V. DUKE POWER CO.

Court: U.S. Supreme Court
Citation: 401 U.S. 424
Date: March 8, 1971
Issues: Civil rights and liberties; Employment discrimination; Labor law; Racial discrimination

- In *Griggs v. Duke Power Company,* the U.S. Supreme Court ruled that employers could not require qualifications for jobs that were discriminatory in effect unless those qualifications were proved necessary for the job.

Legal challenges to the constitutionality of Title VII of the federal Civil Rights Act of 1964 brought the *Griggs* case before the U.S. Supreme Court for argument in December, 1970. The Court's decision, read by Chief Justice Warren E. Burger, was rendered on March 8, 1971.

Beginning in 1866, Congress enacted a series of civil rights laws that ostensibly safeguarded citizens' nonpolitical rights, notably those personal liberties guaranteed to U.S. citizens by the Thirteenth and Fourteenth Amendments to the Constitution. The Civil Rights Act of 1964 became law amid the turbulence of the 1960's associated with the Civil Rights movement, campaigns for women's rights, battles for alternative lifestyles, environmentalism, and bitter debate over the Vietnam War. The act represented the most sweeping legislation of its kind up to that time.

President John F. Kennedy launched the civil rights bill in June, 1963, five months before his assassination. Anxious to build the Great Society, President Lyndon B. Johnson, Kennedy's successor, was deeply committed both personally and politically to the principles embodied in the bill. So, too, were liberal members of the Congress, some of whom, including Hubert H. Humphrey, Mike Mansfield, and Estes Kefauver, were veteran civil libertarians, whereas others, including Sam Ervin, had become dedicated converts.

The real initiatives for fresh civil rights legislation lay outside the White House and Congress, most notably among black leaders. By 1963, Martin Luther King, Jr., and his young associates such as Jesse Jackson had begun their dramatic peaceful assaults on segregation in various cities of the American South. Almost simultaneously, they had launched Operation Breadbasket, a grassroots effort to bring an end to discriminatory practices that kept substantial numbers of African Americans out of the workforce and gravely handicapped their economic opportunities. It was this type of discrimination in particular that was dealt with in Title VII of the 1964 Civil Rights Act.

Hiring Discrimination

Although hiring discrimination affected many groups, the plight of African Americans, the nation's largest minority, was singularly bad in the early 1960's, and in some regards it was worsening. Long a leader against discrimination in trade unions and a proponent of equal employment opportunities, A. Philip Randolph, president of the Brotherhood of Sleeping Car Porters, outlined the effects of hiring and job discrimination to a U.S. Senate subcommittee in 1962. Randolph pointed to the relatively small number of skilled black workers in the nation, to segregation and racial barriers in trade unions and in apprenticeship programs, to a disproportionate concentration of black workers in unskilled occupations, and to new technologies that were diminishing industry's need for unskilled labor. He noted that the percentages of black carpenters, painters, bricklayers, and plasterers, for example, had declined precipitously since 1950. In addition, the unemployment rate for black workers was nearly three times the rate for whites.

Such was the background against which Willie S. Griggs and thirteen fellow black coworkers at the Duke Power Company's Dan River Steam Station in Draper, North Carolina, brought a class-action suit against their employer. All the black workers at the Dan River Plant worked in the Labor Department, in which the highest-paying jobs paid less than the lowest-paying jobs that whites held in the plant's four other departments. Promotions within departments were normally made on the basis of seniority, and transferees into a department usually began in the lowest positions.

In 1955, the Duke Power Company began requiring a high school diploma for assignment to any department except Labor. When the company eliminated its previous policies of segregation and stopped restricting black workers to the Labor Department, a high school diploma remained a prerequisite for transfer to other departments. In 1965, the company announced that for new employees, placement in any department except Labor was dependent on the achievement of adequate scores on two professionally designed high school equivalency tests. It was in this regard that the *Griggs* case invoked Title VII of the 1964 Civil Rights Act. The workers argued that black workers were less likely than whites to pass the tests but that performance on the tests was unrelated to ability to perform jobs.

The longest debate in American legislative history had preceded passage of the Civil Rights Act. Congress had laboriously made clear its intent in regard to Title VII: It was to achieve equality of employment opportunities and to remove previous barriers that had favored identifiable groups of white workers. No part of the act barred employers from utilizing "neutral" tests, practices, or procedures in selecting or promoting employees.

Burger's Opinion

Delivering the opinion of the Supreme Court in the case, Chief Justice Burger reiterated these congressional objectives. Speaking for a unanimous

Chief Justice Warren E. Burger. (Robert Oakes/Collection of the Supreme Court of the United States)

Court, Burger declared that even when an employer's tests, procedures, or practices were "neutral" in their intent, they could not be maintained if their effect was to freeze the status quo of prior discriminatory employment practices. What the Civil Rights Act and Title VII proscribed were any "artificial, arbitrary, and unnecessary barriers to employment" when such barriers served to discriminate on the basis of race, color, religion, sex, or any other impermissible classification. Burger acknowledged that the test requirements instituted by the Duke Power Company were intended to improve the overall quality of its workforce. The chief justice noted, however, that employment practices that could not be shown to be related to job performance and that disproportionately excluded black workers from employment opportunities were clearly prohibited. An employer's good intent or absence of discriminatory intent, Burger continued, did not redeem employment procedures or testing mechanisms that operated as "built-in headwinds" for minority groups and were unrelated to measurements of job performance. Burger emphasized that the purpose of Title VII was to protect the employer's right to insist that any job applicant, black or white, must meet the applicable job qualifications. Title VII in fact was designed to facilitate hiring on the basis of job qualifications rather than on the basis of race or color.

Significance

Title VII of the Civil Rights Act of 1964, however strongly President Johnson and liberal members of Congress felt about its objectives, did not miraculously abolish ingrained discriminatory hiring and employment practices. Despite the vast powers that Johnson derived from being the head of the country's largest employer, the federal government itself, and from having some control over billions of dollars in federal contracts, his power was circumscribed. The federal bureaucracy, many observers noted, was lethargic, and the country's great corporations and unions could not lightly be antagonized, particularly because the president required their support to attain other goals of his Great Society. After appointing Vice President Hubert H. Humphrey, one of the country's leading civil libertarians, to lead the President's Committee on Equal Employment Opportunity in February, 1965, Johnson abruptly removed him the following September. Taking this as a signal of presidential will, the agencies charged with implementing fair employment policies tended to drift.

There were gains, most notably in the changed public attitudes about race. Whereas in 1944 only 45 percent of whites polled believed that African Americans should have as good a chance as whites to secure jobs, in 1963, 80 percent espoused that belief. The U.S. Civil Service Commission increased the percentage of black workers in government jobs, principally in the U.S. Post Office. The Civil Rights Commission, however, found that the enforcement of nondiscrimination provisos in government contracts was almost nonexistent, and the Equal Employment Opportunity Commission (EEOC) that had been created to oversee applications of Title VII struggled without enforcement powers. Operation Breadbasket, initiated by Martin Luther King, Jr., and conducted largely by his aide, Jesse Jackson, had boycotted businesses until they opened jobs to black workers, but its efforts and success gradually diminished. Black unemployment ran four to five times as high as unemployment among whites. The problem was especially severe in inner cities.

Improving Conditions

By the early 1970's, there were signs of improvement. Enforced or not, the Civil Rights Act of 1964 encouraged employers to hire more black workers. This cause was aided by labor shortages of the 1960's as well as improvements in the education of black labor force entrants. Moreover, by 1972, Congress had granted the EEOC power to initiate legal action against businesses showing evidence of employment discrimination, and major offenders were soon forced to comply with Title VII's mandates. For these reasons, among others, black men nearly tripled their employment in white-collar jobs. Black women also gained in employment generally, with strong gains in white-collar jobs. Accordingly, the gap in income between white and black Americans narrowed significantly. The median income of black employees, for example, had been 59 percent of that of whites in 1959. By 1969, the proportion had risen to 69 percent. Employed black women, during the same period, raised their median income to 93 percent of that of white female employees, although women generally were paid less than were men.

By March, 1971, when Chief Justice Burger delivered the Court's decision in the *Griggs* case, some observers believed that despite the Civil Rights Act of 1964, the gap in opportunities between blacks and other Americans was widening. Increases in the numbers of black high school dropouts, black welfare recipients, and black women giving birth out of wedlock, as well as in venereal disease, drug abuse, and crime among African Americans, seemed to substantiate such assertions. According to some observers, the African American population had taken on the configurations of a distinct underclass.

As indicated above, however, there was heartening evidence that black workers were closing economic gaps between themselves and mainstream white society. Challenges to hiring and promotional barriers through Title VII and an empowered EEOC were important contributing factors to the hastening of this process. The liberal position taken by the Burger Supreme Court in giving specific weight to Title VII's objectives in the *Griggs* case also undoubtedly strengthened federal and state attacks on employment discrimination. To many black leaders, such decisions proved the worth of the 1964 Civil

Rights Act. As Roy Wilkins noted in a speech at the fifty-fifth annual convention of the National Association for the Advancement of Colored People (NAACP), the principal value of the act was the recognition by Congress that African Americans are constitutional citizens, recognition necessary to begin the pursuit of happiness through political, social, and economic progress. Wilkins might have gone further. As legal scholars observed, the *Griggs* decision went beyond the Constitution. The Constitution prohibited only intentional discrimination, and the illegality of such discrimination had for decades been beyond legal question. After the *Griggs* opinion, legislation such as the 1964 Civil Rights Act's Title VII was interpreted to prohibit de facto discriminatory effects of employment practices as well.

Clifton K. Yearley

Further Reading

Auerbach, Jerold S., ed. *American Labor: The Twentieth Century.* Indianapolis: Bobbs-Merrill, 1969. Commentary and documents clearly presented by a labor historian and other specialists. Part 4 is particularly relevant, dealing with civil and economic rights, race, segregation, employer and union job discrimination, and the impacts of automation. Part 3 also deals with major labor legislation.

Berger, Morroe. *Equality by Statute: The Revolution in Civil Rights.* New York: Octagon Books, 1978. A clearly written, intelligent survey of subject. Chapter 4 examines efforts to reduce employment discrimination in New York State as a mirror of national problems. Chapter 1 details creation of the EEOC and increments to its powers. Chapter 5 is an acute analysis of the effects of law in controlling prejudice and discrimination.

Blasi, Vincent, ed. *The Burger Court: The Counter-Revolution That Wasn't.* New Haven, Conn.: Yale University Press, 1983. The main thesis linking these expert analyses of the Burger Court is that it continued its work much in the same liberal spirit in regard to civil rights as its predecessor, led by Chief Justice Earl Warren. The *Griggs* case is treated in chapters 6 and 7, in context with analogous cases. Contains photos and biographies of Burger Court justices.

Grofman, Bernard, ed. *Legacies of the 1964 Civil Rights Act.* Charlottesville: University Press of Virginia, 2000. Nineteen scholars, lawyers, and statisticians address the history and evolution of the landmark legislation.

Matusow, Allen J. *The Unraveling of America: A History of Liberalism in the 1960's.* New York: Harper & Row, 1984. Outstanding survey is richly detailed and critical but well balanced. Places the *Griggs* case in context with a gamut of racial and employment problems. A fine historical survey, clearly written and engaging.

Mayer, Robert H., ed. *The Civil Rights Act of 1964*. San Diego, Calif.: Greenhaven Press, 2004. Overview of the act, its history, the debate surrounding the legislation, and its evolution. Includes essays written around that time as well as more recent essays. Recommended for grades 9-12.

Schwartz, Bernard, comp. *Civil Rights*. 2 vols. New York: Chelsea House, 1970. Consists of federal legislation, extracts from congressional debates, and Supreme Court decisions, with commentary by the compiler. An outstanding work for the background and context of Title VII.

Whalen, Charles, and Barbara Whalen. *The Longest Debate: A Legislative History of the 1964 Civil Rights Act*. Washington, D.C.: Seven Locks Press, 1985. Written by an outstanding congressman and civil libertarian with his columnist wife. This is an informative, engaging commentary and excerpting of testimony on an extraordinarily complex and politically difficult bill. Ample discussion of the EEOC and Title VII.

See also *Firefighters Local Union No. 1784 v. Stotts et al.*; *United Steelworkers of America v. Weber*; *Wards Cove Packing Co. v. Atonio*; *Washington v. Davis*.

GRISWOLD V. CONNECTICUT

Court: U.S. Supreme Court
Citation: 381 U.S. 479
Date: June 7, 1965
Issues: Reproductive rights; Right to privacy; Women's issues

- The U.S. Supreme Court decision in *Griswold v. Connecticut* prevented states from banning the sale or use of contraceptives, contributing to the sexual revolution of the 1960's. It also set an important legal precedent by declaring for the first time that the U.S. Constitution protects the right to privacy, a right that is not explicitly spelled out in that document.

Attempts to prevent conception have existed in human evolution and medical practice for thousands of years. Even in societies scorning birth control and sterility, the desire to control reproduction has existed. Only since the late nineteenth century, however, has there been a planned, organized effort to educate the general population about contraception.

In preliterate societies, abortion and infanticide were the chief practices limiting population growth; contraception was relatively infrequent. When attempts at contraception were undertaken, mixtures of potions, herbs, and powders were ingested, or complete abstinence or withdrawal were practiced. Egyptian papyri dating from about 1850 B.C.E. and 1300 B.C.E. speak of contraception in the form of combining physical and chemical features to prevent or interrupt pregnancy. The ancient Hebrews also practiced such contraceptive techniques as coitus interruptus and the use of intravaginal spongy substances, potions, and violent movements. The Egyptian and Hebrew techniques were passed on to the Greeks and Romans, whose writers, physicians, and encyclopedists spoke knowledgeably of contraception. Abortion is also mentioned in the Hippocratic oath. Diffusion of information among citizens, however, remained virtually nonexistent. Contraceptive advances in Asian cultures were even less rapid.

History of Birth Control

Prior to modern developments in birth control technology, contraception was primarily the responsibility of the male. Use of the condom to prevent the spread of syphilis was first described in 1564. By the 1720's, condoms were used for contraception in Europe.

Female contraception historically involved various violent gestures, ingestion of potions, and the insertion of vaginal plugs and solutions, some with spermicidal effects. Pessaries and sponges were among the oldest contraceptive devices. The cervical cap and diaphragm were developed during the nineteenth century. It was in nineteenth century England, Germany, and France that contraceptive practices spread most rapidly, in part as a result of social changes, attitude shifts, and other forces such as industrialization, urbanization, and "democratization" of contraceptive knowledge. The less privileged in society gained knowledge formerly in the possession solely of the upper class.

The European influence spread to the United States, where such pioneers in birth control and women's rights as Margaret Sanger sought to establish a system of clinics where women could obtain reliable birth control services. Such clinics also served as educational centers where private medical practitioners were instructed in contraceptive technique, a subject not taught in medical schools at that time. Other important contributions to the birth control movement in the United States were made by Charles Knowlton, Robert Dale Owen, Robert Latou Dickinson, and Clarence James Gamble. It was through their efforts, individually and collectively, that educational programs on contraception and contraceptive research were created and medical investigation conducted. The birth control movement reflected the changing social environment and growing emancipation and independence of women.

Opposition to Birth Control

At the same time, a countermovement condemning contraceptive practice became active. Led by Anthony Comstock, director and organizer of the New York Society for the Suppression of Vice, a relentless and vigorous campaign ensued initially against birth controllers and later against gamblers. In 1873, the U.S. Congress passed the Comstock Act, which prohibited interstate transport of contraceptive information and devices.

Comstock used the power of his governmental position as special agent of the U.S. Post Office to travel around the country making arrests of those acting in violation of the law. Fear of prosecution inhibited development and dissemination of birth control knowledge and quelled freedom of expression. Sections of medical treatises containing information on birth control methods had to be excised. In 1926, twenty-four states had anticontraception laws modeled on the Comstock Act; in twenty-two other states obscenity laws were interpreted to include a ban on contraception. Constitutionality of the act was not questioned, and no clear judicial trend emerged. The act's clause on contraception was not specifically repealed until 1971.

It was in this climate that Estelle Griswold and Charles Lee Buxton sought to challenge a state law of Connecticut that outlawed contraceptives and made their use a criminal offense. Connecticut had not generally enforced its law against individual physicians, sellers, or married couples. The law affected the poor, prohibiting them from receiving the same birth control information and supplies available to the middle class. Two prior attempts to challenge the law had failed.

The case was instigated on November 1, 1961, when Griswold and Buxton opened their clinic amid maximum publicity. Within ten days, they were arrested for dispensing birth control information and instructions to a married couple in violation of the General Statutes of Connecticut. The parties were found guilty by the Connecticut state courts and fined one hundred dollars each. They appealed their case to the United States Supreme Court, urging it to declare the Connecticut law unconstitutional. The Court overturned their conviction and caused Connecticut to repeal its birth control statute (called an "uncommonly silly law" by Associate Justice Potter Stewart). At the same time, the Court for the first time recognized the existence of a constitutional right of privacy and gave it legal protection.

Right to Privacy

Privacy as a complex and multidimensional legal concept had not been explicitly defined in the Constitution, but the Ninth Amendment stated that the people of the United States retained some rights that were not constitutionally enumerated. The right to personal privacy is thus a more nebulous right than are those explicitly mentioned in the Bill of Rights, one whose scope continues to be developed and clarified. Privacy denotes the right "to be let alone" (Justice Louis Brandeis) or the autonomy to make decisions without undue interference from others. Privacy may also mean physical separation from others. Protecting one's reputation from defamatory public disclosure of private facts and control over information about oneself (for example, credit records, bank statements, or tax returns) are other aspects of privacy. Finally, privacy as security from intrusion on the intimacies of life, including family-planning decisions, was the focus of the *Griswold* decision.

In a 7-2 decision issued June 7, 1965, the Court held that the Connecticut law forbidding the use of contraceptives intruded on the right of marital privacy guaranteed under the Constitution. It remained for the Court to define this right, as it is not specifically enumerated in the Constitution. Justice William O. Douglas, writing for the majority, stated that "specific guarantees in the Bill of Rights have penumbras, formed by emanations from those guarantees that help give them life and substance. . . . Various guarantees create zones of privacy." He recognized that the marital relationship at issue lay within a zone of privacy derived from the First, Third, Fourth, Fifth, Ninth, and Fourteenth Amendments to the Constitution and should be protected from state and federal interference. In upholding the sanctity of marriage, Justice Douglas termed it "an association that promotes a way of life." A law forbidding use of contraceptives rather than regulating their manufacture or sale, he concluded, seeks to achieve its goals by means having a maximum destructive impact on that relationship. Such a law was unacceptable and had to be struck down.

Significance

The immediate consequence of the Court's decision was the repeal of birth control statutes in Connecticut and thirteen other states and a dramatic increase in the number of women who had access to birth control devices and counseling. In *Griswold v. Connecticut*, the Supreme Court recognized as a right what had been considered as such by the general populace—a right lying within the spirit of other freedoms expressed in the Constitution even though the right itself is not specified in the Constitution. *Griswold* was confined to traditional notions of contraception for married persons. In 1972, however, the Supreme Court held that the privacy guarantee extended protection to contraception for single persons; in 1977, it was held to cover minors.

These decisions demonstrated a general legal response to a changing social environment. Restrictive birth control prohibitions were replaced by more flexible regulation or none at all. A general permissiveness ensued in society. The women's movement gained momentum; college dormitories were sexually integrated, and unmarried people openly began cohabiting. The landmark legal concept of a right of privacy in sexual matters was extended in 1973, in *Roe v. Wade,* to encompass a woman's right to choose to terminate her pregnancy through abortion without governmental interference and has also been used in "right to die" or termination of treatment cases. These controversial issues have divided the United States along moral and religious lines. They have also colored political debate. Public demonstrations often surrounded birth control and abortion facilities. Public funding for birth control and greater access to educational information on contraception, family planning, and genetic counseling remained issues of concern.

Birth control technology and capability have expanded rapidly, with the introduction of methods ranging from the intrauterine device (IUD) and the oral contraceptive ("pill") to injectable contraceptives, subdermal implants, "morning-after" pills, medicated vaginal rings containing steroids absorbed into the bloodstream, and biodegradable systems. The pill, developed by Gregory Pincus and first approved for use in June, 1960, revolutionized contemporary birth control methods as a result of its accessibility, ease of use, simplicity, and effectiveness. Within twenty years of its advent, an estimated ten to fifteen million American women and eighty to one hundred million women worldwide were using oral contraceptives for birth control.

The principles first articulated in *Griswold* and followed in succeeding related cases suggest that unless the state can demonstrate a compelling interest that out-weighs individual human rights, it may not interfere with social mores—a person's marriage, home, children, and lifestyle. In 1967, a state ban on interracial marriages was repealed; in 1968, state law forbidding private possession of obscene materials in one's home was overturned. When these fundamental privacy interests are invoked, courts will require a state's demonstration of a higher burden of justification or "compelling interest" viewed with "strict scrutiny" before these interests can be abridged.

Marcia J. Weiss

Further Reading

Dienes, C. Thomas. *Law, Politics, and Birth Control.* Urbana: University of Illinois Press, 1972. Excellent coverage of the issues from the latter part of the eighteenth century to the 1970's. Detailed research on Comstock and Sanger, and much information about legal cases. Contains copious primary and secondary source material including cross-references, notes, appendixes, and an extensive bibliography. Written in a scholarly manner.

Garrow, David J. *Liberty and Sexuality: The Right to Privacy and the Making of Roe v. Wade.* Berkeley: University of California Press, 1998. Follows the history of U.S. legislation and court decisions relating to the right to privacy, birth control, and abortion. Bibliographic references and index.

Himes, Norman E. *Medical History of Contraception*. New York: Schocken Books, 1970. Covers historic, anthropologic, economic, and sociologic aspects of contraception. Thorough coverage and meticulous detail. Written for the lay reader.

Knight, James W., and Joan C. Callahan. *Preventing Birth: Contemporary Methods and Related Moral Controversies*. Salt Lake City: University of Utah Press, 1989. An excellent account of contraception and a discussion of its political and philosophical implications. Various chapters discuss human reproductive anatomy, physiology, and endocrinology, as well as giving a detailed overview of the moral debate and social policy concerns surrounding elective abortion. Contains notes and an extensive bibliography.

Reed, James. *The Birth Control Movement and American Society: From Private Vice to Public Virtue*. Princeton, N.J.: Princeton University Press, 1983. Detailed account of contributions of early birth control crusaders and the entire movement from the nineteenth century to the 1970's. The emphasis is on the role of Margaret Sanger. Written in a clear and direct fashion with numerous notes and bibliographical essays.

Stotland, Nada Logan. *Social Change and Women's Reproductive Health Care: A Guide for Physicians and Their Patients*. New York: Praeger, 1988. Historical and social context of issues of reproduction. Discussion of changing attitudes on controversial topics of sexuality, reproduction, parenting, and medical care, with case examples. Also includes suggested readings. Written in a simple manner.

Tribe, Laurence H. "Right of Privacy and Personhood." In *American Constitutional Law*. 3d ed. New York: Foundation Press, 2000. Informative treatise on constitutional law. Locates the concept of privacy within the total scheme of constitutional law. Numerous footnotes and case references. Written for an audience with a legal orientation. Also includes material on abortion, death and dying, patients' rights, and association.

Tushnet, Mark, ed. *I Dissent: Great Opposing Opinions in Landmark Supreme Court Cases*. Boston: Beacon Press, 2008. Collection of dissenting opinions in thirteen major Supreme Court cases, including *Marbury v. Madison*, *Brown v. Board of Education*, *Griswold v. Connecticut*, and *Lawrence v. Texas*. Tushnet places each case in its historical perspective, with an overview of the principal issues at stake.

See also *Adamson v. California*; *Eisenstadt v. Baird*; *Ferguson v. Skrupa*; *Lawrence v. Texas*; *Olmstead v. United States*; *Pierce v. Society of Sisters*; *Roe v. Wade*.

GROSJEAN V. AMERICAN PRESS CO.

Court: U.S. Supreme Court
Citation: 297 U.S. 233
Date: February 10, 1936
Issues: Freedom of the press

- The U.S. Supreme Court held that a special tax on large newspapers was invalid because it abridged the freedom of the press guaranteed by the First and Fourteenth Amendments.

When Louisiana's largest newspapers were critical of Senator Huey Long, his supporters in the legislature imposed a special license tax on all newspapers with more than twenty thousand subscribers. The tax applied to only 13 of

Justice George Sutherland arriving for a session of the Supreme Court in October, 1937. (Harris & Ewing Collection/Library of Congress)

the 163 newspapers in the state, and 12 of the 13 had actively opposed Long's policies. Speaking for a unanimous Court, Justice George Sutherland concluded that the tax was "a deliberate and calculated device" aimed at limiting the circulation of information about public affairs. Sutherland argued that "certain fundamental rights safeguarded in the first eight amendments" were applicable to the states through the Fourteenth Amendment and that the Framers of the First Amendment had wanted to prevent all forms of prior restraint on either publication or circulation, including restraints through taxation.

Sutherland's opinion observed that newspapers were not immune from nondiscriminatory general taxation. The Court emphasized this principle in *Minnesota Star and Tribune Co. v. Minnesota Commissioner of Revenue* (1983).

Thomas Tandy Lewis

See also *Branzburg v. Hayes; Cohen v. Cowles Media Co.; Miami Herald Publishing Co. v. Tornillo; Near v. Minnesota; Richmond Newspapers v. Virginia.*

GROVE CITY COLLEGE V. BELL

Court: U.S. Supreme Court
Citation: 465 U.S. 555
Date: February 28, 1984
Issues: Sex discrimination

• The U.S. Supreme Court banned sex discrimination in postsecondary schools receiving federal funds.

Justice Byron R. White wrote the opinion for the Supreme Court for this 6-3 decision in which there was a wide, conflicting array of dissents and concurrences. This ruling declared that Title IX of the 1972 Educational Amendments to the 1964 Civil Rights Act banned gender discrimination in postsecondary schools receiving federal funds. Although Grove City College did not receive federal funds, enough students attended the college under the Basic Educational Opportunity Grants to justify the school's inclusion under Title IX. The Justice Department's original position was that all Grove City's programs needed to comply with Title IX before the school received any federal funds; however, when President Jimmy Carter was replaced by the more conservative Ronald Reagan, the government's stance against Grove City softened. The 1984 Court ruling did not broadly cut off funds to all programs but only those that were discriminatory. Civil rights and women's groups reacted strongly. Their efforts resulted in the passage of the 1987 Civil Rights Restoration Act—over Reagan's veto—to correct the Grove City ruling. The act applied Title IX if any part of the institution received federal funding and mandated that all programs be free from discrimination.

Richard L. Wilson

See also *Bradwell v. Illinois; County of Washington v. Gunther; Frontiero v. Richardson; Geduldig v. Aiello; Hoyt v. Florida; Mississippi University for Women v. Hogan; Phillips v. Martin Marietta Corp.; Rosenfeld v. Southern Pacific; Stanton v. Stanton.*

GROVES V. SLAUGHTER

Court: U.S. Supreme Court
Citation: 15 Pet. (40 U.S.) 449
Date: March 10, 1841
Issues: Interstate commerce; Slavery

- The U.S. Supreme Court held that an amendment to the Mississippi state constitution that banned bringing slaves into the state for sale was not valid in the absence of legislation to enforce it, but the majority could not agree on the constitutional issues of the case.

The state of Mississippi added a constitutional prohibition against the importing of slaves into the state for sale in 1832 but did not enact any legislation to enforce the amendment. A seller of slaves argued that the prohibition was void because it conflicted with federal authority over interstate commerce. The Supreme Court, in a 5-2 majority decision, held that the amendment to the Mississippi constitution was not binding because it was not implemented by legislation. By ruling that the amendment was not self-executing, the Court did not resolve the explosive issue of whether the federal government or the states had control over the slave trade. In concurring opinions, Justice John McLean of Ohio wrote that the federal government had jurisdiction over slaves transported in interstate commerce, and Chief Justice Roger

Brooke Taney insisted that states had control of all questions relating to slavery and African Americans. The deep divisions on the Court reflected the growing sectional controversy in the country.

Thomas Tandy Lewis

See also *Jones v. Van Zandt; Kentucky v. Dennison; Scott v. Sandford.*

GROVEY V. TOWNSEND

Court: U.S. Supreme Court
Citation: 295 U.S. 45
Date: April 1, 1935
Issues: Equal protection of the law; Racial discrimination;
Voting rights

- The U.S. Supreme Court upheld "whites only" primaries when approved by state party conventions without any involvement or encouragement from the state legislature.

One of the most successful devices in eliminating black voters in the South was the white primary. Since the Democratic Party dominated the solid South, whoever won the Democratic primary went on to win the general election. If blacks could not participate in the primaries, they were denied any real choice in selecting public officials.

In *Newberry v. United States* (1921), the U.S. Supreme Court held that primary elections were not constitutionally protected. Although the *Newberry* case took place in Michigan and involved the issue of vote fraud rather than racial discrimination, the South immediately took advantage of the ruling. In 1924 the Texas legislature passed a law that barred blacks from participation in that state's primary elections. Three years later, a unanimous Supreme Court struck down the Texas law in *Nixon v. Herndon* (1927), finding the actions of the Texas legislature a clear violation of the equal protection clause of the Fourteenth Amendment.

The Texas legislature then passed a law authorizing the executive committees of the political parties to determine eligibility for voting in primary elections. As expected, the executive committee of the Texas Democratic party excluded blacks from the primary. In *Nixon v. Condon* (1932), in a 5-4 decision, the U.S. Supreme Court ruled that the executive committee had acted as the agent of the state. As such, the attempt to bar black participation in the primary still violated the equal protection clause.

Texas succeeded on its third attempt to ban black voting. Immediately after the *Condon* decision, the Texas Democratic Party convention, without any authorization from the legislature, adopted a resolution restricting party membership to whites. R. R. Grovey, a black resident of Houston, brought suit against the county clerk who refused to give him a primary ballot. On April 1, 1935, a unanimous U.S. Supreme Court upheld the actions of the state party convention. According to the Court, there was no violation of the equal protection clause because there was no state action involved. The Democratic Party was a voluntary association of individuals who acted in their private capacity to exclude blacks from primary elections.

In 1941 the U.S. Supreme Court reversed *Newberry* in *United States v. Classic* (1941). The *Classic* decision brought primary elections under constitutional protection for the first time. *Classic* also paved the way for *Smith v. Allwright* (1944), the Supreme Court case banning white primaries.

Darryl Paulson

See also *Newberry v. United States; Nixon v. Condon; Nixon v. Herndon; Smith v. Allwright; United States v. Classic.*

GUEST, UNITED STATES V. *See* UNITED STATES V. GUEST

GUINN V. UNITED STATES

Court: U.S. Supreme Court
Citation: 238 U.S. 347
Date: June 21, 1915
Issues: Racial discrimination; Voting rights

• The decision in this case overturned Oklahoma's grandfather clause and marked a first step in the National Association for the Advancement of Colored People's campaign to use the courts to combat racial discrimination.

Though the Fifteenth Amendment supposedly prohibited racial discrimination in voting, during the late nineteenth and early twentieth centuries Southern and border states found ways to prevent African Americans from voting in significant numbers. One method was the literacy test. One potential drawback to this practice, however, was that such a test would also prevent poorly educated whites from voting. A number of states solved this problem by adopting "grandfather" clauses, provisions that allowed anyone registered before a certain date or anyone descended from such a person to vote regardless of literacy. Since the date selected was usually set at a point when there would have been few black voters (1866 was popular), very few blacks would qualify. Thus a measure that was nonracial on the surface was decidedly discriminatory in its effects.

Many grandfather laws had only temporary application, and most Southern states moved away from them in the early twentieth century. In 1910, however, Oklahoma enacted a literacy test requirement with a permanent grandfather clause. The measure threatened not only black voting rights but also the position of the state's Republican Party. Fearing the loss of several thousand black votes, the U.S. attorney brought suit under the Reconstruction-era Enforcement Acts and won a conviction against state officials who were trying to enforce the literacy test.

The state appealed the case to the U.S. Supreme Court, attracting the attention of the National Association for the Advancement of Colored People (NAACP), which was just beginning to use litigation as a strategy for combating racial discrimination. Moorfield Story of the NAACP filed a brief in support of the government. In a unanimous decision, the Court upheld the convictions and ruled that the grandfather clause was a clear attempt to thwart the Fifteenth Amendment's ban on racial discrimination in voting.

The decision had relatively little immediate impact: Only one other state still had a grandfather clause at the time, and the Court carefully avoided declaring literacy tests themselves discriminatory. Nevertheless, the decision was not without its significance. Not only did it mark a modest revival of the Fifteenth Amendment, but it also encouraged the NAACP to continue its strategy of using litigation to put the Constitution on the side of racial equality.

William C. Lowe

See also *Ex parte Yarbrough; Mobile v. Bolden; Nixon v. Condon; Shaw v. Hunt; South Carolina v. Katzenbach; Terry v. Adams.*

HAGUE V. CONGRESS OF INDUSTRIAL ORGANIZATIONS

Court: U.S. Supreme Court
Citation: 307 U.S. 496
Date: June 5, 1939
Issues: Freedom of assembly and association; Freedom of expression

- The U.S. Supreme Court introduced the public forum doctrine, which required that streets, parks, and other public places must be accessible for public assembly and the discussion of public issues.

A local ordinance of Jersey City, New Jersey, required a permit in order to hold public meetings or distribute literature in public areas. Mayor Frank Hague, an opponent of labor unions, had union members arrested for passing out pamphlets, and he refused to grant members the necessary permit for speaking on public property. By a 5-2 vote, the Supreme Court found that the city ordinance was unconstitutional. Speaking for a ruling plurality, Justice Owen J. Roberts defended the public forum doctrine in terms of the privileges, immunities, and liberties of citizens. Officials might regulate the use of public places in ways "consonant with peace and good order," but not abridge or arbitrarily deny their use because of disagreement with the content of the ideas discussed. The Court explicitly incorporated the First Amendment's freedom of petition into the due process clause of the Fourteenth Amendment, making it binding on state and local governments.

Thomas Tandy Lewis

See also *Cox v. New Hampshire; Edwards v. South Carolina; Greer v. Spock.*

HALL V. DECUIR

Court: U.S. Supreme Court
Citation: 95 U.S. 485
Date: January 14, 1878
Issues: Desegregation; Interstate commerce;
Private discrimination

- The U.S. Supreme Court held that a state law prohibiting segregation could not be applied to carriers engaged in interstate commerce, which was under the exclusive supervision of Congress.

During Reconstruction, the Louisiana legislature passed a statute forbidding public carriers in the state from segregating passengers according to race. Josephine DeCuir, a black woman, was traveling in a steamboat between two Louisiana cities on the Mississippi River when she was refused admission into

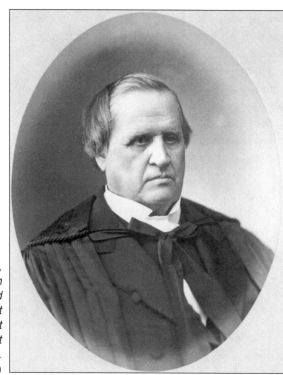

*Justice Nathan Clifford,
whose dissent in
Hall v. DeCuir anticipated
the "separate but
equal" doctrine that
the Supreme Court
would later articulate.*
(Library of Congress)

a cabin reserved for whites. After she won a damage award in state court, the company appealed the award.

Speaking for a unanimous Supreme Court, Chief Justice Morrison R. Waite held that the relevant carrier was involved in interstate commerce because it traveled to a neighboring state. Waite wrote, "If the public good requires such legislation, it must come from Congress and not from the states." Justice Nathan Clifford's concurring opinion anticipated the separate but equal doctrine. A few years later, the Court disregarded *Hall*'s broad view of interstate commerce when it overturned a federal ban on private discrimination in the *Civil Rights Cases* (1883).

Thomas Tandy Lewis

See also *Champion v. Ames; Morgan v. Virginia; Penn Central Transportation Co. v. City of New York; Plessy v. Ferguson.*

HAMDAN V. RUMSFELD

Court: U.S. Supreme Court
Citation: 548 U.S 557
Date: June 29, 2006
Issues: Habeas corpus; Military law; Presidential powers; Warfare and terrorism

- In this ruling, the U.S. Supreme Court held that the president did not have the authority to establish military commissions to try foreign nationals without congressional authorization. In addition, the Court held that foreign detainees had the rights guaranteed by the Geneva Convention on Prisoners of War.

After the terrorist attacks of September 11, 2001, the Bush administration launched its war on terrorism, targeting members of the al-Qaeda organization in Afghanistan. The U.S. military captured hundreds of foreign nationals, many of whom were taken to the detention center at the U.S. military base at Guantánamo Bay, Cuba. The administration argued that these prisoners lacked prisoner of war status because they were not fighting in uniform for an organized country. The administration insisted that the prisoners were therefore not entitled to the protections of the Geneva Convention of

1949. The prisoners were kept in indefinite detention, without counsel and usually without specific charges of illegal acts. In *Rasul v. Bush* (2004), the Court ruled that the detainees had the right to petition for writs of habeas corpus relief in federal courts.

In a presidential order of 2001, the Bush administration had made plans to have foreign nationals accused of war crimes to be tried before special military commissions. To defend the legality of the order, the administration referred to the inherent powers of the president as commander in chief and to the congressional Authorization for the Use of Military Force (AUMF) of 2001. In addition, administration lawyers pointed to the precedents of World War II, when the Court had approved trials of such a policy. Civil libertarians disliked several aspects of the commissions. They noted that the commissions were not entirely independent of the executive; in addition, the commissions could use evidence obtained by torture, as well as secret evidence that the defendant's lawyer could not examine. The commissions' verdicts, moreover, could not be appealed to civilian courts.

Salim Ahmed Hamdan, a Yemeni national who had worked as a driver for Osama bin Laden, was one of the suspected terrorists captured in Afghanistan and detained at Guantánamo Bay. He and nine other detainees were charged with conspiracy to commit acts of terrorism. Hamdan's lawyers petitioned for a writ of habeas corpus, arguing that the commissions were illegal, that Hamdan was entitled to all the protections of a prisoner of war under the Geneva Convention, and that he should not be tried until his status was determined. The district court partly ruled in his favor, but the Court of Appeals endorsed the government's position.

Reviewing Hamdan's habeas corpus petition, the Supreme Court rendered the administration a major setback in *Hamdan v. Rumsfeld*, which held, by 5-3 vote, that the special commissions were illegal under both the Geneva Convention and the Uniform Code of Military Justice (UCMJ). Writing the majority opinion, Justice John Paul Stevens further found that Congress's AUMF did not expand presidential war powers. Even if special commissions were later to be authorized by congressional authority, they would have to include all the procedures of the UCMJ and the Geneva Convention. Stevens firmly rejected the administration's claim that the detainees did not merit the protections of the Geneva Convention because they lacked the status of lawful combatants. He insisted that each detainee was entitled to the convention's full protections until a court ruled him not to be a prisoner of war. The three dissenting justices were sharply critical of the majority's ruling.

Although most observers expected that Congress would eventually authorize the creation of military commissions, the Court's 2006 decision was still important, for it helped to clarify the constitutional prerogatives of the president as commander in chief of the military.

Thomas Tandy Lewis

See also *Boumediene v. Bush; Dames and Moore v. Regan; Ex parte Quirin; Goldwater v. Carter; Humphrey's Executor v. United States; McCulloch v. Maryland; Martin v. Mott.*

HAMLING V. UNITED STATES

Court: U.S. Supreme Court
Citation: 418 U.S. 87
Date: June 24, 1974
Issues: Censorship; Pornography and obscenity

- This U.S. Supreme Court decision clarified the test for obscenity adopted in *Miller v. California* (1973) by ruling that distributors of obscene materials need not know that such materials are in fact obscene.

During the early 1970's, a small group of individuals and businesses mailed thousands of copies of a brochure advertising a book called *The Illustrated Presidential Report of the Commission on Obscenity and Pornography*—which was described as a companion to the official report of the President's Commission on Obscenity and Pornography. The illustrated report was essentially the same as its nonillustrated counterpart, with the addition of numerous photographs. The brochure itself contained graphic photographs of men and women engaged in a variety of heterosexual and homosexual acts. The distributors of the brochure were convicted of mailing and conspiring to mail obscene material in violation of a federal statute. Some of the defendants received prison sentences, others were fined.

The defendants appealed their convictions on several grounds. Between the time of their conviction and their appeal to the U.S. Supreme Court, the Court issued a decision in *Miller v. California* (1973) that reformulated the test for determining what constituted obscene material. Prior to the *Miller* decision, the test used for obscenity was one that the Court had articulated in *Memoirs v. Massachusetts* (1966). In that case, the Court held that in order for material to be deemed obscene, it must as a whole appeal to a prurient interest in sex. Further, it had to be patently offensive by affronting contemporary community standards relating to descriptions or representations of sexual matters. Finally, it had to be utterly without redeeming social value. In the *Hamling* case the Court concluded that the trial jury had not erred in finding the illustrated brochure obscene under the *Memoirs* test.

The Court reformulated its test for obscenity in its 1973 *Miller* decision, holding that material is obscene if the average person, applying contemporary community standards, would find that the work taken as a whole appeals to the prurient interest. It also had to depict or describe, in a patently offensive way, sexual conduct specifically described by applicable state law. Finally, the work, taken as a whole, had to lack serious literary, artistic, political, or scientific value. The defendants in the *Hamling* case argued that their convictions could not be upheld under the *Miller* test because the trial court had instructed their jury that the community standard against which its members should evaluate the allegedly obscene material was a national one. The Court refused to overturn the convictions on this ground because the instruction regarding the national standard was harmless error.

The defendants also argued that the federal statute under which they had been convicted was unconstitutionally vague because it did not give the same definition of obscenity as the *Miller* decision. However, the Court found that the statute did not need to follow the exact wording of the *Miller* decision and rejected that argument.

Finally, the defendants argued that the government should have been required to show that the defendants knew the materials were unlawfully obscene when they mailed them. The trial court had concluded that the jury must find only that the defendants knew the materials were mailed and knew the character and nature of the materials. The Supreme Court held that whether the defendants believed the materials to be obscene was not relevant. Hence, the Court affirmed the conviction of the defendants and in the process gave greater clarity to its *Miller* decision.

Davison M. Douglas

See also *Fletcher v. Peck; Memoirs v. Massachusetts; Miller v. California; New York v. Ferber.*

HAMMER V. DAGENHART

Court: U.S. Supreme Court
Citation: 247 U.S. 251
Date: June 3, 1918
Issues: Children's rights; Congressional powers; Labor law

- In this case the U.S. Supreme Court strictly limited the federal government's power to bring about industrial and economic reform under its power to regulate interstate commerce. Over the powerful and now classic dissent of Justice Oliver Wendell Holmes, Jr., the Court held the first federal child labor law unconstitutional because its purpose was to regulate manufacturing practices, even though on its face the statute only reached interstate transportation.

In September, 1916, Congress passed the Child Labor Act. This law prohibited the shipment in interstate commerce of goods made by a factory or mill in which children under certain specified ages had been employed within the previous thirty days. The law was challenged by Roland Dagenhart, whose two sons were employed in a cotton mill in North Carolina. Dagenhart argued that the purpose of the law was actually to regulate manufacturing and production. At that time, such regulation was beyond the direct power of Congress. A federal district court held for Dagenhart, and the United States appealed to the Supreme Court.

The Supreme Court ruled five to four in Dagenhart's favor in 1918. Justice William R. Day held that the real purpose of the act was not to regulate the shipment of goods in interstate commerce but to standardize the ages at which children could be employed. In other cases in which transportation in interstate commerce had been prohibited by the federal government, it was because the goods had been harmful or because the transportation was necessary to bring about the evil. According to the majority, that element was wanting in this case.

Day's opinion was countered by a brilliant dissent by Justice Oliver Wendell Holmes, Jr. In attacking the general premise of the majority opinion, that the government's commerce power must be read narrowly, Holmes argued that the majority was attempting to write laissez-faire economics into the Constitution. He insisted that the Court had been inconsistent in dealing with commerce limitation cases because every limit on interstate transportation affects business in some way. To Holmes it did not matter whether an evil preceded or followed the transportation. Congress could regulate the transportation regardless: "It is not for this court to pronounce when prohibition is necessary to regulation if it ever may be necessary—to say that it is permissible, as against strong drink, but not as against the product of ruined lives."

The rule established by the Court in *Hammer v. Dagenhart* was to last for about twenty years. It significantly limited industrial and economic reform measures from World War I to the early New Deal years. Holmes's dissent ultimately prevailed. In 1941 *Hammer v. Dagenhart* was explicitly overruled by *United States v. Darby Lumber Co.*, and Holmes's view, which had caught the imagination of the public, the press, and most of the bar, was vindicated.

Robert Jacobs

See also *Bailey v. Drexel Furniture Co.*; *Champion v. Ames*; *United States v. Darby Lumber Co.*

HARMELIN V. MICHIGAN

Court: U.S. Supreme Court
Citation: 501 U.S. 957
Date: June 27, 1991
Issues: Cruel and unusual punishment; Illegal drugs

• Upholding a Michigan drug possession law that carried a mandatory term of life imprisonment, the U.S. Supreme Court rejected the plaintiff's argument that the sentence was cruel and unusual punishment and therefore in violation of the Eighth Amendment.

Under Michigan law, the petitioner, Ronald Allen Harmelin, was convicted of possessing 672 grams of cocaine and sentenced to mandatory life imprisonment because the amount was in excess of the 650-gram threshold specified in the law for imposing the mandatory sentence. The Michigan State Court of Appeals upheld the sentence, rejecting Harmelin's claim that the sentence violated the protection against "cruel and unusual punishment" guaranteed by the Constitution. Harmelin argued that the sentence violated that restriction because it was "disproportionate" to his crime and, further, that because it was mandatory it provided for no "mitigating circumstances" that would allow a judge any latitude in sentencing.

Harmelin's appeal to the U.S. Supreme Court was denied and his sentence upheld. Justice Antonin Scalia delivered the Court's principal opinion. It concluded that because there is no proportionality provision in the Eighth Amendment, a sentence cannot be deemed cruel or unusual on the basis that it is disproportionate to the crime involved. Furthermore, it argued that Harmelin's claim that his mandatory sentence deprived him of his right to a consideration of mitigating circumstances had no precedent in constitutional law. It observed that mandatory penalties, though they could be harsh or extreme, were common enough in the history of the United States and had never been construed as cruel and unusual in the constitutional sense of that phrase.

While granting that Harmelin's argument had support in the so-termed individualized capital-sentencing doctrine of the Court's death-penalty legal theory, the majority dismissed Harmelin's claim because of the qualitative difference between execution and all other forms of punishment.

Justice Anthony Kennedy, joined by Justices Sandra Day O'Connor and David Souter, although concurring with the judgment against Harmelin, claimed that the Eighth Amendment's cruel and unusual punishment provision does encompass "a narrow proportionality principle that applies to noncapital sentences." Citing various precedents, these justices argued that the Court, though not clearly or consistently, had previously determined the constitutionality of noncapital punishments based on that principle, although said precedents had taken under review only the length of a punishment's term, not its type.

Having again broached the issue of proportionality, the Supreme Court was likely to face more challenges to mandatory sentencing. From state to state, in statutes imposing mandatory sentences, there is no uniform-sentencing code governing types of punishment or their length. Although in *Harmelin* the Court argued that state legislatures must retain the prerogative of establishing their own penal codes, where there is a wide discrepancy between mandatory penalties imposed for the same crime by one state and another, plaintiffs may seek relief from enforcement of the more severe penalty.

John W. Fiero

See also *Furman v. Georgia; Hudson v. Palmer; Hutto v. Davis; Rhodes v. Chapman; Robinson v. California; Rummel v. Estelle; Solem v. Helm.*

HARPER V. VIRGINIA STATE BOARD OF ELECTIONS

Court: U.S. Supreme Court
Citation: 383 U.S. 663
Date: March 24, 1966
Issues: Voting rights

- The Court's decision in this case eliminated the use of poll taxes in state and local elections.

Poll taxes, or the payment of a fee in order to vote, were widely used in southern states as a means to restrict the electorate, and in particular black voters. Because poll taxes led to corruption—as candidates and political organizations would pay the taxes of their supporters—and because there were more effective ways of eliminating black voters, many southern states started to repeal their poll taxes.

Opposition to the poll tax was led by the National Committee to Abolish the Poll Tax and the National Association for the Advancement of Colored People (NAACP). On five occasions the House of Representatives passed legislation to ban the tax, but southern senators filibustered, blocking its passage in the Senate. In 1964, the Twenty-fourth Amendment to the Constitution was ratified, eliminating the use of poll taxes in federal elections. Five states— Alabama, Arkansas, Mississippi, Texas, and Virginia—continued to use poll taxes in state and local elections. Arkansas dropped its poll tax in 1964 after the passage of the Twenty-fourth Amendment.

In 1965 the U.S. House of Representatives passed a poll tax ban in state elections as part of the 1965 voting rights bill. The Senate failed to support the ban, however, and the final version of the Voting Rights Act of 1965 merely stated that the poll tax "denied or abridged" the constitutional right to vote.

Blacks in Virginia brought suit against that state's $1.50 annual poll tax as a requirement for voting in state and local elections. The U.S. district court, citing the 1937 case *Breedlove v. Suttles*, dismissed the claim. In *Breedlove*, the U.S. Supreme Court had held that, except where constrained by the Constitution, the states may impose whatever conditions on suffrage that they deem appropriate. On appeal, a 6-3 majority in the Supreme Court overruled

During a World War II victory parade, the National Association for the Advancement of Colored People displayed a monkey in a cage to protest poll taxes. (Library of Congress)

Breedlove and held that the payment of a fee in order to vote violated the Constitution.

Interestingly, although the plaintiffs were black, the ruling was based on economic discrimination rather than racial discrimination. "To introduce wealth or payment of a fee as a measure of a voter's qualifications," wrote Justice William Douglas in the majority opinion, "is to introduce a capricious or irrelevant factor." In the view of the court's majority, voter qualifications had no relationship to wealth. The three dissenters believed that a "fairly applied" poll tax could be a reasonable basis for the right to vote. The *Harper* decision actually had little direct impact. Since only four states used poll taxes as a condition for voting at the time of the *Harper* decision, the ban on poll taxes barely generated a ripple on the surface of American politics.

Darryl Paulson

See also *Breedlove v. Suttles; Heart of Atlanta Motel v. United States; Lassiter v. Northampton County Board of Elections; Shaw v. Reno; Smith v. Allwright.*

HARRIS V. MCRAE

Court: U.S. Supreme Court
Citation: 448 U.S. 297
Date: June 30, 1980
Issues: Reproductive rights

• The U.S. Supreme Court upheld the Hyde Amendment (1976) to the Medicaid program, which prohibited federal funding for abortions except where the woman's life would be endangered or in cases of rape or incest.

The Medicaid program, which began in 1965, provides the states with funds to help pay for the medical needs of poor people. When the Supreme Court struck down restrictive abortion laws in *Roe v. Wade* (1973), the federal government at first allowed Medicaid funds to pay for abortion services. Most of

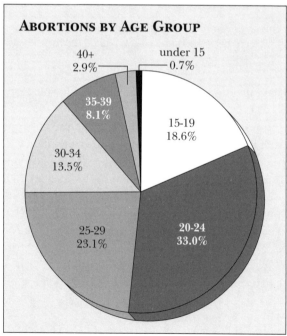

ABORTIONS BY AGE GROUP

40+ 2.9%
under 15 0.7%
35-39 8.1%
15-19 18.6%
30-34 13.5%
25-29 23.1%
20-24 33.0%

Source: Public Agenda, 2004. Figures are based on an estimated total of 1,313,300 abortions in the United States in 2000.

this funding ended in 1976, when Congress enacted the Hyde Amendment. A 7-3 majority of the Court endorsed a portion of Hyde's policy in *Maher v. Roe* (1977), approving a Connecticut welfare regulation that forbad payment for abortions not deemed "medically necessary." Justice Lewis F. Powell, Jr., reasoned that the state had not placed any direct obstacles in the pregnant woman's path to an abortion; therefore, it had not deprived her of the liberty guaranteed by the Fourteenth Amendment. Because no suspect classification or fundamental right was at issue, the Court applied the standard of rational scrutiny, concluding that the state had a "strong and legitimate interest in encouraging normal childbirth."

Soon after *Maher*, Norma McRae, a resident of New York, was denied assistance for an abortion deemed medically necessary. Because the denial was based on the Hyde Amendment, McRae claimed that the federal government was depriving her of a fundamental right guaranteed by the due process clause of the Fifth Amendment. By a 5-4 vote, the Court rejected her claim. Relying on the *Maher* precedent, Justice Potter Stewart wrote that the due process clause protects the liberty to make "certain private decisions" without "unwarranted governmental interference" but that it does not confer "an entitlement to such funds as might be necessary to realize all the advantages of that freedom." The dissenters argued that the law unconstitutionally discriminated against poor women.

The Court has reaffirmed the principles of *Maher* and *Harris* on many occasions. However, several state supreme courts have ruled that their state constitutions prohibit restrictions on abortions when state funds are used.

Thomas Tandy Lewis

See also *Akron v. Akron Center for Reproductive Health; Bigelow v. Virginia; Doe v. Bolton; Maher v. Roe; Roe v. Wade; Rust v. Sullivan; San Antonio Independent School District v. Rodriguez; Thornburgh v. American College of Obstetricians and Gynecologists; Webster v. Reproductive Health Services.*

HARRIS V. NEW YORK

Court: U.S. Supreme Court
Citation: 401 U.S. 222
Date: February 24, 1971
Issues: Confessions; Illegal drugs; Miranda rights

- The U.S. Supreme Court held that confessions excluded because of an absence of Miranda warnings could be used to impeach the credibility of a criminal defendant who takes the stand to testify.

When Viven Harris was arrested for selling heroin, he made incriminating statements before he was properly informed of his constitutional rights, as required by *Miranda v. Arizona* (1966). At trial, Harris testified in his own defense, and the prosecutor impeached his credibility by referring to his statements at the time of arrest. On appeal, his counsel argued that any reference to the improperly obtained evidence was invalid. By a 5-4 vote, however, the Supreme Court disagreed. Chief Justice Warren E. Burger's opinion for the majority reasoned that the defendant had an obligation to speak truthfully on the witness stand and that the *Miranda* precedent did not provide a license to use perjury without any "risk of confrontation with prior inconsistent utterances." The *Harris* decision was the first case in which the Court began to chip away at the *Miranda* ruling. It demonstrated that the majority of the justices regarded *Miranda* as a "prophylactic" device rather than as an integral part of the Fifth Amendment.

Thomas Tandy Lewis

See also *Arizona v. Fulminante; Brecht v. Abrahamson; Brown v. Mississippi; Escobedo v. Illinois; Faretta v. California; Gideon v. Wainwright; Mallory v. United States; Massiah v. United States; United States v. Wade.*

HARRIS V. UNITED STATES

Court: U.S. Supreme Court
Citation: 390 U.S. 234
Date: March 5, 1968
Issues: Search and seizure

- This case established the principle that if evidence of a crime is in "plain view" of a law-enforcement officer while the officer is fulfilling authorized duties, its use in criminal proceedings does not violate a defendant's constitutional protection against unlawful search and seizure.

EXCEPTIONS TO THE PLAIN VIEW DOCTRINE

The plain view doctrine does not apply when certain sense-enhancing technology is used in protected areas. For example, most courts do not permit thermal imaging and high-powered telescopes to qualify as "plain view." Use of basic items, such as flashlights and eyeglasses, is acceptable for the plain view doctrine to apply. Viewing evidence from aircraft is also acceptable, so long as the aircraft are flying in legal airspace.

James H. Harris, the petitioner, prior to his appeal to the U.S. Supreme Court, was tried for robbery in the U.S. District Court for the District of Columbia. Evidence used against him included his victim's automobile registration card, which the police found on the metal strip under the door of Harris's car after it had been impounded for its protection while Harris was being held as the robbery suspect. During his trial, Harris moved to have that evidence suppressed on the grounds that it was obtained through unlawful search. The district court denied the request, and Harris was convicted and sentenced to prison. Thereafter, a panel of the Court of Appeals for the District of Columbia reversed the conviction, concluding that the registration card had been obtained by unlawful search; however, it also granted the government's petition for a rehearing before the full court of appeals, which subsequently overturned the panel's determination, ruling that the conviction did not violate the petitioner's rights.

On *certiorari*, the U.S. Supreme Court upheld the decision, affirming the admissibility of the questionable evidence. Seven justices concurred in the majority opinion, arguing that nothing in the Fourth Amendment protects a suspect from the use of incriminating evidence found as a result of normal safeguards taken while a suspect's property is in police custody. According to the opinion, objects in the "plain view" of police officers authorized to be in a position to view the objects cannot be construed as the products of a search, are therefore subject to seizure, and may be introduced as evidence.

Various Supreme Court cases, including *Ker v. California* (1963), had established the right of law-enforcement agents to seize objects in plain view to be used as criminal evidence, but none addressed the issue of whether evidence secured from a defendant's property while it was in police custody constituted an illegal search. Jurists concerned with the protection of an accused individual's rights argue that the *Harris* decision erodes the Fourth Amendment guarantees against illegal search and seizure. Because the circumstances were somewhat unusual, however, the application of *Harris* to other attempts to suppress evidence is likely to be fairly limited. Nevertheless, the ruling does reflect the Supreme Court's increasing unwillingness to broaden its interpretation of constitutional guarantees in favor of the accused to the disadvantage of criminal investigators and prosecutors.

John W. Fiero

See also *Chimel v. California; Ker v. California; Maryland v. Buie, United States v. Ross; Whren v. United States.*

HAWAII HOUSING AUTHORITY V. MIDKIFF

Court: U.S. Supreme Court
Citation: 467 U.S. 229
Date: May 30, 1984
Issues: Land law; Takings clause

• The U.S. Supreme Court ruling in this Hawaii property case almost entirely eliminated public use as a limit on the government taking private property in condemnation proceedings.

A Hawaii law, designed to lessen the power of oligopoly landowners, allowed lessees of single family homes to invoke eminent domain and buy the property they leased. The landowners challenged the law, saying that the condemnation was not for public use because the government immediately turned the land over to the former lessee. Justice Sandra Day O'Connor wrote the unanimous opinion in this landmark case, quite clearly setting out that the Supreme Court would no longer use "public use" as a limit on future eminent domain actions. If a governmental body legislated the condemnation of private property, a public use occurred even if the property was immediately turned over to another private party. The public character of the government body making the condemnation was all that was required to give the action a public character. Justice Thurgood Marshall did not participate in this case.

Richard L. Wilson

See also *Barron v. Baltimore*; *Berman v. Parker*; *Dolan v. City of Tigard*; *First English Evangelical Lutheran Church of Glendale v. County of Los Angeles*; *Kelo v. City of New London*; *Penn Central Transportation Co. v. City of New York*; *West River Bridge Co. v. Dix*.

HAYBURN'S CASE

Court: U.S. Supreme Court
Citation: 2 U.S. 409
Date: August 11, 1792
Issues: Judicial powers; Judicial review

- In this early case, the U.S. Supreme Court asserted its power to find laws enacted by Congress unconstitutional and to decline to enforce them.

Congress passed a law in 1792 requiring the U.S. circuit court justices to hear veteran's disability claims and forward recommendations to the secretary of war, who could decline to accept them. Five of the original six justices declined to do this, asserting in various ways that the law violated separation of powers by giving them nonjudicial duties in the executive branch. Some objected that Congress, rather than being bound by a judicial judgment, could decline to follow their findings. Congress later revised the law to avoid these difficulties. Although ambiguous, scholars regard this case as an early assertion of the Supreme Court's powers of judicial review and justiciability because of concerns about the results of the justices' deliberations.

Richard L. Wilson

See also *Budd v. New York*; *Calder v. Bull*; *Chicago, Milwaukee, and St. Paul Railway Co. v. Minnesota*; *Fletcher v. Peck*; *Hylton v. United States*; *Marbury v. Madison*; *Mistretta v. United States*; *Stuart v. Laird*; *Yakus v. United States*.

Hazelwood School District v. Kuhlmeier

Court: U.S. Supreme Court
Citation: 484 U.S. 260
Date: January 13, 1988
Issues: Censorship; Education; Freedom of speech

- The Hazelwood decision, giving school administrators the power of prior restraint censorship, reversed a long-time trend of First Amendment support for freedom of expression on high school campuses.

This case involved the direct censorship of a school newspaper, the *Spectrum*, at East Hazelwood High School near St. Louis, Missouri, in 1983. The school's principal removed two pages he considered inappropriate from the newspaper prior to its distribution. The pages contained articles about teenage pregnancy and the impact of divorce on children. None of the students quoted in the two articles was identified.

The principal's censorship of the newspaper was upheld by a federal district court but overturned by a court of appeals. The appellate court decision was then reversed by the U.S. Supreme Court in January, 1988, when it ruled that the censorship was permissible under the First Amendment. The Supreme Court's ruling stunned First Amendment supporters, for it reversed a long-time trend of First Amendment support for freedom of expression issues on high school campuses. Further, it joined the *Pentagon Papers* case and *The Progressive*'s "H-bomb" case as a classic example of a particularly onerous form of censorship by prior restraint.

In writing for the majority of the Court in the 5-3 decision, Justice Byron White said: "We hold that educators do not offend the First Amendment by exercising editorial control over the style and content of student speech in school-sponsored expressive activities so long as their actions are reasonably related to legitimate pedagogical concerns." The ruling opened the door for widespread censorship by giving administrators the power to censor student publications and other school-sponsored activities, such as drama productions, in advance. The decision also contradicted the earlier landmark ruling in *Tinker v. Des Moines Independent School District* (1969), which had permitted campus censorship only if it served to protect the rights of other students or to quell a threatened campus disruption—neither of which was the case with *Hazelwood.*

Justice William J. Brennan, Jr., wrote the dissenting opinion, in which he and two other justices condemned the message by the court's majority: "Instead of teaching children to respect the diversity of ideas that is fundamental to the American system . . . the Court today teaches youth to discount important principles of our government as mere platitudes."

If the intent of the 1988 *Hazelwood* ruling was to intimidate student journalists, it appears to have succeeded. An analysis of high school journalism by the Freedom Forum in 1994 reported that 70 percent of 270 high school newspaper advisers admitted that school principals had rejected newspaper articles or required changes. In 1995 the Student Press Law Center reported that many student journalists "harbor feelings of anger or confusion" when they are not permitted to write about issues they feel are important. In many cases, as the censorship becomes routine, such feelings are replaced by indifference.

Carl Jensen

See also *Freedman v. Maryland; Grosjean v. American Press Co.; Kunz v. New York; Lovell v. City of Griffin; Near v. Minnesota; Nebraska Press Association v. Stuart; Snepp v. United States; Times Film Corp. v. City of Chicago; Tinker v. Des Moines Independent Community School District.*

HEAD MONEY CASES

Court: U.S. Supreme Court
Citation: 112 U.S. 580
Date: December 8, 1884
Issues: Congressional powers; Immigration; Taxation

• The U.S. Supreme Court approved a statute allowing Congress to levy a head tax on immigrants, thereby establishing congressional power over immigration and taxes imposed for other purposes.

Early immigration was handled by the states, some of which imposed a head tax on every immigrant a shipper delivered to the United States to create a fund to alleviate immigrants in financial distress. The Supreme Court struck

Puck *editorial cartoon depicting the Supreme Court's overworked justices in 1885—the year after the Court handled the* Head Money *cases.* (Library of Congress)

down these state laws as an interference with congressional power in the *Passenger Cases* (1849). To help the states deal with the financial burden of indigent immigrants, Congress passed a per capita tax on immigrants, which it collected and gave to the affected states. Litigants challenged the tax, claiming that Congress could not impose a tax unless it was for the common defense or general welfare of the people. Justice Samuel F. Miller wrote the unanimous opinion rejecting their claim. He maintained that immigration was a form of commerce over which Congress had broad authority and the tax in this case was really a fee associated with regulating commerce.

Richard L. Wilson

See also *Immigration and Naturalization Service v. Chadha; Passenger Cases.*

HEART OF ATLANTA MOTEL V. UNITED STATES

Court: U.S. Supreme Court
Citation: 379 U.S. 241
Date: December 14, 1964
Issues: Civil rights and liberties; Desegregation; Private discrimination;
Racial discrimination; Right to travel

- The U.S. Supreme Court endorsed laws forbidding private discrimination by hotels, restaurants, and other places of public accommodation in the case of *Heart of Atlanta Motel v. United States.*

The Fourteenth Amendment to the U.S. Constitution was enacted in 1868 to provide protection for the newly freed slaves. After the Civil War, Congress passed several broad statutes aimed at protecting African Americans against racial discrimination in housing and contracts. These laws were needed because, although they were freed from slavery, African Americans still suffered from severe discrimination in all aspects of American life. The Supreme Court took a narrow view of congressional power in 1883, however, and issued a decision that prevented Congress from attempting to stop private individuals and companies from engaging in racial discrimination. The Supreme Court said that Congress could enact laws aimed only at governmental discrimination. In effect, the Supreme Court declared that African Americans could be victims of blatant discrimination by private entities without any interference from the law. As a result, many African Americans' lives changed little from their experience as slaves. They were still forced to work as agricultural laborers because they were not permitted to be trained and hired for other jobs.

Legacy of Discrimination

Because no federal laws could prevent private discrimination, until 1964 African Americans were deprived of many opportunities readily enjoyed by white people. If they wished to travel, African Americans frequently could not find motels that would accept them or restaurants that would serve them. African Americans were forced to carry their own food if they went on bus trips and often had to knock on doors in African American neighborhoods in order to find families that would put them up for the night in private homes. For example, when professional baseball teams had spring training in Florida every year, the white players stayed in hotels while their African American teammates rented rooms in the homes of local African American families. Similar circumstances arose when northern college sports teams traveled to the South for games. Racial segregation and discrimination were so severe that bus stations had separate waiting rooms, rest rooms, and drinking fountains for African American passengers. In many cities, black and white friends could dine together only in African American-owned restaurants, because African Americans were not allowed to eat in white-owned establishments. In sum, it was very difficult for African Americans to travel and shop because they were denied access to so many business establishments.

Beginning in the 1940's, members of Congress made repeated attempts to enact antidiscrimination legislation. The structure of Congress, however, gave members power according to seniority. Because southerners had the most seniority, they controlled many of the legislative committees. Thus, by keeping bills tied up in committee hearings, they could prevent Congress from considering proposed legislation. Southern congressmembers were very successful in ensuring that only weak civil rights laws, if any, were enacted by Congress.

Beginning in the 1940's and 1950's, many African Americans organized boycotts, marches, and other protests to challenge racial discrimination. Peaceful protesters were often met by violent mobs of whites or were attacked,

"White only" signs were common sights in the South and in many northern cities during the segregation era. (Library of Congress)

beaten, and arrested by all-white police forces. Shortly after highly publicized demonstrations against racial discrimination in Alabama during May, 1963, President John F. Kennedy decided to send a major civil rights bill to Congress. Title II of the proposed legislation that eventually became the Civil Rights Act of 1964 prohibited private discrimination in places of public accommodation, including hotels, motels, restaurants, and theaters. President Kennedy was assassinated in November, 1963, while the bill was working its way through Congress. Upon succeeding to the presidency, Lyndon Johnson made the civil rights bill his major legislative priority. Within days of Kennedy's assassination, President Johnson asked a joint session of Congress to enact the Civil Rights Act as a memorial to President Kennedy.

When the Senate held hearings to consider the proposed legislation, questions arose concerning congressional power to outlaw private discrimination. The Supreme Court had clearly stated in 1883 that Congress lacked such power under the Fourteenth Amendment. Attorney General Robert F. Kennedy testified that Congress possessed the power to outlaw discrimination in public accommodations through its constitutional authority to regulate interstate commerce. Kennedy and his assistants argued that racial discrimination in public accommodations hampered the national economy because it prevented African Americans from traveling freely. Moreover, it deterred northern companies from expanding into the South because they did not wish to subject their African American employees to severe discrimination.

Senator Strom Thurmond of South Carolina, one of the consistent opponents of civil rights legislation, questioned Attorney General Kennedy closely. From the repeated questioning, it was clear that the Civil Rights Act's supporters were not completely certain about precisely which private businesses would be prevented from discriminating under the law. Although a national bus company could clearly be regulated under congressional power over interstate commerce, it was not clear whether establishments such as neighborhood diners and barbershops were subject to federal laws governing commerce. If these small businesses were involved only in the local economy and did not affect interstate commerce, then Congress presumably would be unable to prevent them from engaging in racial discrimination.

Challenges to Civil Rights Act

When the Civil Rights Act was enacted in 1964, it was immediately challenged by southern businesses that wished to continue engaging in racial discrimination. The Heart of Atlanta Motel claimed that it was not engaged in interstate commerce because it provided services at one location inside Georgia. The motel wished to continue its practice of refusing to rent rooms to African American customers, so it filed a legal action seeking to have federal judges declare that the Civil Rights Act was invalid. Although it usually takes several years for cases to work their way through the judicial system in order to reach the Supreme Court, the high court took up the issue of discrimination in public accommodations without delay in late 1964.

In opposition to the motel's arguments, Archibald Cox, the solicitor general of the United States, argued to the Supreme Court that congressional power to regulate interstate commerce should be construed broadly to cover all businesses which affect commerce in any way. Even if a business appeared to be limited to local customers, Cox argued that it would have links to interstate commerce. For example, a neighborhood barbershop's equipment inevitably includes a chair, a pair of scissors, or other equipment that was manufactured in another state.

On December 14, 1964, only two months after hearing oral arguments, the Supreme Court issued a unanimous decision that endorsed congressional power to outlaw private discrimination in public accommodations. The Court's opinion in *Heart of Atlanta Motel v. United States*, written by Justice Tom C. Clark, acknowledged that racial discrimination had prevented African Americans from enjoying their right to travel. Because the Heart of Atlanta Motel served many travelers from outside Georgia, it was found to affect interstate commerce and therefore to come under the antidiscrimination laws. In this and other decisions concerning Title II of the Civil Rights Act, the Supreme Court interpreted congressional power to regulate interstate commerce so broadly that virtually every private business, no matter how localized in nature, was barred from engaging in racial discrimination. Scholars argue that the Court dispensed with legal arguments concerning technical limitations on congressional power because the justices were committed to endorsing all governmental efforts to combat racial discrimination.

Significance

After the Supreme Court's decision in *Heart of Atlanta Motel*, the United States Department of Justice initiated hundreds of investigations into racial discrimination complaints concerning places of public accommodation. The Court's decision clearly confirmed the federal government's authority to prosecute businesses that failed to end discriminatory practices.

Through the combined efforts of Congress, the president, and the Supreme Court, African Americans could finally enjoy access to theaters, motels, and restaurants. The deeply entrenched practices of racial discrimination had been dealt a powerful blow by the federal government. As a result, African Americans who traveled could find motels and restaurants that would serve them. Many proprietors of public accommodation businesses initially resisted implementation of the antidiscrimination law by declining to serve African

Americans or by being rude to African American customers. Over time, however, the American public, including business owners in the South, accepted the idea that all people should have equal access to public accommodations. Only a tiny number of businesses were so opposed to desegregation that they turned themselves into private clubs in order to avoid application of the Civil Rights Act.

Title II of the Civil Rights Act of 1964 is regarded as one of the most effective civil rights laws ever enacted. Unlike laws concerning employment, in which there are controversies concerning proof of discrimination, Title II addresses a very straightforward subject. In the employment context, there might be many legally acceptable reasons why a particular individual did not receive a particular job. Thus, a minority applicant may find it difficult to discover whether illegal racial discrimination played a role in the hiring decision. In public accommodations, the question is much simpler. Were the customers provided with the services that they requested and for which they were willing to pay? Because discrimination in public accommodations, unlike that in employment, is very difficult to disguise, businesses throughout the United States have generally eliminated any vestiges of the formal discrimination that was previously so prevalent. In fact, proprietors of restaurants and other places of public accommodation have discovered that it is good for their businesses to seek African American customers. Previously, they not only deprived African Americans of services and the ability to travel but also deprived themselves of customers in a growing segment of the American population. Eventually, racial discrimination in public accommodations was pushed so firmly into the past that many establishments owned or controlled by whites developed advertising campaigns aimed specifically at African American consumers.

The Supreme Court's decision in the *Heart of Atlanta Motel* case indicated that all three branches of the federal government were committed to dismantling racial discrimination and segregation. The message sent by this decision not only warned segregationist interests that their power had been diminished but also helped mobilize and encourage civil rights supporters actively to pursue additional antidiscrimination statutes and favorable judicial decisions in areas such as housing and voting.

Christopher E. Smith

Further Reading

Abraham, Henry J., and Barbara A. Perry. *Freedom and the Court: Civil Rights and Liberties in the United States*. 8th ed. Lawrence: University Press of Kansas, 2003. Thorough review of the Supreme Court's cases interpreting the Bill of Rights and the Fourteenth Amendment. Contains good coverage of the cases and legal issues concerning the interpretation of the Civil Rights Act of 1964.

Cortner, Richard C. *Civil Rights and Public Accommodations: The Heart of Atlanta Motel and McClung Cases.* Lawrence: University Press of Kansas, 2001. A work dedicated to the Supreme Court case on racial discrimination in public accommodations. Highly recommended.

Cox, Archibald. *The Warren Court: Constitutional Decision as an Instrument of Reform.* Cambridge, Mass.: Harvard University Press, 1968. Discussion of how Supreme Court decisions affect social issues. Contains commentary about the design of particular arguments presented to the Supreme Court in the *Heart of Atlanta Motel* case by the lawyer who presented those arguments.

Griffin, John Howard. *Black Like Me: The Definitive Griffin Estate Edition, Corrected from Original Manuscripts.* 1961. San Antonio, Tex.: Wings Press, 2004. First-person account by a white writer who had his skin medically "darkened" to travel throughout the South in 1959. Describes the discrimination and harassment that faced African Americans prior to passage of the Civil Rights Act. A classic text, and widely read.

Loevy, Robert D. "'To Write It in the Books of Law': President Lyndon B. Johnson and the Civil Rights Act of 1964." In *Lyndon Baines Johnson and the Uses of Power,* edited by Bernard J. Firestone and Robert C. Vogt. New York: Greenwood Press, 1988. Detailed account of the events leading to the passage of the Civil Rights Act of 1964. Provides insights into the role played by Johnson in pushing the legislation past opponents in Congress.

Nieman, Donald G. *Promises to Keep: African-Americans and the Constitutional Order, 1776 to the Present.* New York: Oxford University Press, 1991. Discussion of racial discrimination in the United States. Provides a thorough history of the ways in which courts and other government institutions failed to provide African Americans with the rights guaranteed by the Constitution.

See also *Civil Rights Cases; Louisville, New Orleans, and Texas Railway Co. v. Mississippi; Moose Lodge v. Irvis.*

HELVERING V. DAVIS

Court: U.S. Supreme Court
Citation: 301 U.S. 619
Date: May 24, 1937
Issues: Congressional powers

- The U.S. Supreme Court affirmed the constitutionality of the Social Security Act of 1935.

By a 7-2 vote, the Supreme Court upheld the old-age benefits provisions of the Social Security Act of 1935. Justice Benjamin N. Cardozo, in the opinion for the Court, adopted a broad view of the federal congressional power to tax and spend under Article I, section 8, of the U.S. Constitution. Cardozo rejected the argument that the Tenth Amendment traditionally held that taxing and spending on welfare was the province of the states, not the federal

Charles E. Wyzanski, a Department of Justice attorney, immediately after winning a victory for the Roosevelt administration in Helvering v. Davis. (Harris & Ewing Collection/Library of Congress)

government. He noted that the Social Security Act was, in part, a response to a national calamity to which Congress surely had the power to respond.

Richard L. Wilson

See also *Collector v. Day; Steward Machine Co. v. Davis; United States v. Butler; Weinberger v. Wiesenfeld.*

HERNÁNDEZ V. TEXAS

Court: U.S. Supreme Court
Citation: 347 U.S. 475
Date: May 3, 1954
Issues: Equal protection of the law; Juries; Racial discrimination

- In this ruling, the U.S. Supreme Court struck down state policies that discriminated against Mexican Americans in jury selection, a ruling that helped pave the way for later decisions forbidding ethnic discrimination.

In 1950, Pete Hernández was charged with murder in Jackson County, Texas. He was tried, convicted, and sentenced to life imprisonment. Hernández argued at trial that persons of Mexican descent were systematically excluded from the jury, thus denying him the equal protection of the laws guaranteed by the Fourteenth Amendment.

It had long been established that exclusion of jurors of a defendant's race or color was unconstitutional. Texas argued that Hispanics are "whites" in the interpretation of Texas statutes; consequently, there had been no racial exclusion of jurors in this case. Despite Hernández's showing that no juror with a Spanish surname had served on a Jackson County jury during the prior twenty-five years, he lost in the Texas Court of Criminal Appeals. On Hernández's petition, the U.S. Supreme Court agreed to hear the case.

In an opinion written by Chief Justice Earl Warren, the Court unanimously reversed Hernández's conviction. There was clear evidence that Hispanics were treated as a separate class in Texas and that they had been systematically excluded from service on both grand and petit juries. This ruling stated that Hernández's Fourteenth Amendment right to the equal protection of the laws had been violated.

This decision was an important victory for Hispanic civil rights as it established that anti-Hispanic discrimination is unconstitutional despite the earlier Caucasian-African American bent of state law and federal cases. *Hernández v. Texas* was an important precedent until 1971, when Hispanics were accepted as a discrete minority group in *Cisneros v. Corpus Christi ISD*.

Robert Jacobs

See also *Ballard v. United States; Batson v. Kentucky; Norris v. Alabama; Powers v. Ohio; Strauder v. West Virginia; Taylor v. Louisiana; Williams v. Mississippi.*

HERNDON V. LOWRY

Court: U.S. Supreme Court
Citation: 301 U.S. 242
Date: April 26, 1937
Issues: Freedom of expression

- One of the first U.S. Supreme Court cases to reverse a state conviction on First Amendment grounds, *Herndon v. Lowry* limited the states' ability to prosecute political dissidents.

Angelo Herndon, a black organizer for the Communist Party in the South, was convicted of an "attempt to incite insurrection" under a Georgia statute that defined insurrection as "any combined resistance to the lawful authority of the state . . . when the same is manifested by acts of violence." Herndon's conviction rested on a booklet found in his possession that listed the aims of the Communist Party. The Georgia court found that none of these was criminal on its face but that one of them—"equal rights for the Negroes and self-determination of the Black Belt"—showed criminality because the aim could not be accomplished without violence. Georgia argued that this "extrinsic fact" proved criminality.

The Supreme Court reversed Herndon's conviction in a 5-4 vote. The reversal rested partly on the First Amendment and partly on grounds of vagueness. Justice Owen Roberts' majority opinion emphasized that there was no evidence that Herndon had ever advocated forcible subversion. Unless it could be shown that Herndon had advocated violence, the dangerous tendency of his words could not be made the basis of a criminal conviction. If it

Justice Owen J. Roberts in 1938. (Harris & Ewing Collection/Library of Congress)

were otherwise, anyone who solicited members for a political party that the state believed might later turn to violence could be convicted and—since the Georgia statute was capital—put to death.

The Court also attacked the statute on vagueness grounds. The law defined no specific acts that could be said to be criminal. As construed by the Georgia courts, a conviction under the law could rest on a jury's determination that any political speech might have a "dangerous tendency." Thus every speaker or party organizer must calculate whether some chain of causation might lead to violence. Justice Roberts said that "the law as construed and applied, amounts merely to a dragnet which may enmesh anyone who agitates for a change of government if a jury can be persuaded that he ought to have foreseen his words would have some effect on the future conduct of others." The Court insisted that this is so vague that it violates the guarantees of liberty contained within the Fourteenth Amendment.

Herndon v. Lowry is significant because it narrows state governments' powers to punish their political opponents. It is one of the first cases in which the Supreme Court overturned a state statute on First Amendment grounds. This case (and other cases of the 1930's in which speech convictions were overturned) left many free speech questions unsettled, however, and provided little guidance to the courts or to Congress when free speech issues were confronted again after World War II.

Robert Jacobs

See also *Albertson v. Subversive Activities Control Board; American Communications Association v. Douds; Aptheker v. Secretary of State; Communist Party v. Subversive Activities Control Board; DeJonge v. Oregon; Dennis v. United States; Pennsylvania v. Nelson; Scales v. United States; United States v. Robel.*

HIRABAYASHI V. UNITED STATES

Court: U.S. Supreme Court
Citation: 320 U.S. 81
Date: June 21, 1943
Issues: Antigovernment subversion; Due process of law;
Equal protection of the law

- The U.S. Supreme Court ruled that the exigencies of war justified a military curfew which was applied almost exclusively to Japanese Americans.

After the United States entered into a war against Japan, many Americans feared that Japanese Americans living on the West Coast might engage in subversive activities, especially if there were a bombing raid or an invasion. In addition to racial prejudice, there was a widespread belief that persons of Japanese background in Hawaii had helped prepare for the invasion of Pearl Harbor. At the urging of military and political leaders, President Franklin D. Roosevelt in early 1942 issued Executive Order No. 9066, authorizing the secretary of war to prescribe "military areas" from which any civilians might be excluded, and Executive Order No. 9102, establishing an executive agency for the purpose of interning the estimated 120,000 persons of Japanese ancestry, citizens and noncitizens alike. Soon thereafter, the Congress enacted a statute implementing the executive orders.

Acting under presidential authority, General John DeWitt of the Western Defense Command imposed a curfew on all persons of Japanese ancestry and also on German and Italian nationals. In addition, he ordered every Japanese American to report to a local civilian assembly center for assignment to an internment camp. Gordon Hirabayashi, a Japanese American student at the University of Washington, intentionally disobeyed both the curfew and the reporting order. For these two offenses, he was prosecuted and given concurrent three-month sentences.

Japanese Americans boarding a train in San Pedro, California, that would take them to the Manzanar relocation camp in the eastern Sierras in 1942. (National Japanese American Historical Society)

By a 9-0 vote, the Supreme Court held that the curfew was constitutionally permitted under the combined congressional and presidential war powers. Because of the concurrent sentences, the Court refused to examine the constitutionality of the relocation program. Writing for the Court, Chief Justice Harlan Fiske Stone emphasized the gravity of the national emergency and found justification for suspecting Japanese Americans of continued loyalty to Japan. Although Stone wrote that racial discrimination was "odious to a free people whose institutions are founded upon the doctrine of equality," he noted that the Fifth Amendment contained no equal protection clause and concluded that the principles of due process did not prohibit the government from taking race into account when relevant to national security in time of war. In upholding the curfew, Stone declared that the Court was not deciding whether more severe policies would be acceptable.

Three members of the Court wrote concurring opinions that narrowed the scope of the decision. Justice Frank Murphy, who almost registered a dissent, wrote, "Distinctions based on color and ancestry are utterly inconsistent with our traditions and our ideals." In *Korematsu v. United States* (1944), the justices voted six to three to approve of the exclusion and reporting orders. Ironically, the *Hirabayashi* and *Korematsu* opinions would later be quoted to support the idea that the due process clause of the Fifth Amendment includes an equal protection requirement.

Thomas Tandy Lewis

Further Reading

Harth, Erica. *Last Witnesses: Reflections on the Wartime Internment of the Japanese.* New York: Palgrave Macmillan, 2003.

Hosokawa, Bill. *Nisei: The Quiet Americans.* Rev. ed. Boulder: University Press of Colorado, 2002.

Irons, Peter. "*Gordon Hirabayashi v. United States.*" In *The Courage of Their Convictions.* New York: Free Press, 1988.

See also *Korematsu v. United States; Ozawa v. United States.*

HODGSON V. MINNESOTA

Court: U.S. Supreme Court
Citation: 497 U.S. 417
Date: June 25, 1990
Issues: Parental rights; Reproductive rights

• The U.S. Supreme Court's rulings regarding requirements that both parents of an unmarried minor be notified before the young woman obtains an abortion indicated that the Court would approve some restrictions on abortion rights.

The Supreme Court struck down a two-parent notification requirement without a judicial bypass for an unmarried minor to obtain an abortion, but the Court approved of a two-parent notification requirement that included an opportunity for a judicial bypass. In ruling the first option unconstitutional, a 5-4 majority of the justices found that many minors did not live with both parents, and often the absent parent had limited contact with the child. A different 5-4 majority approved of the judicial bypass option as a reasonable way to determine when parental notification is not in the best interests of the young woman. Justice Sandra Day O'Connor provided the fifth vote in both of the decisions.

Thomas Tandy Lewis

See also *Akron v. Akron Center for Reproductive Health; Doe v. Bolton; Harris v. McRae; Planned Parenthood of Central Missouri v. Danforth; Planned Parenthood of Southeastern Pennsylvania v. Casey; Roe v. Wade; Rust v. Sullivan; Thornburgh v. American College of Obstetricians and Gynecologists; Webster v. Reproductive Health Services.*

HOLDEN V. HARDY

Court: U.S. Supreme Court
Citation: 169 U.S. 366
Date: February 28, 1898
Issues: Constitutionalism; Freedom of contract; Labor law; Regulation of business

• In an age of laissez-faire constitutionalism, the U.S. Supreme Court recognized that a state, under its police power, could place some restrictions on freedom of contract.

During the 1890's Albert Holden was convicted of violating a Utah statute that had established the eight-hour workday in mines and smelters. In ap-

Justice Henry B. Brown.
(Library of Congress)

pealing his conviction, Holden argued that the law deprived both employees and employers of their constitutionally protected liberty to enter into contracts. Only one year earlier, in *Allgeyer v. Louisiana* (1897), the Supreme Court had overturned a state law that had been found to violate this unenumerated right, which was based on a substantive reading of the due process clause of the Fourteenth Amendment. In the *Holden* case, however, the Court voted six to two to uphold the Utah law. Justice Henry B. Brown explained that the freedom of contract was subject to limitation by the state's police power, which authorized the state to protect the safety, health, and morals of the public. While accepting the need for regulations in dangerous occupations such as mining, Brown's opinion suggested that the Court in the future would require a strong rationale for all governmental restrictions on the freedom of contract. The significance of Brown's reasoning would become much clearer when the Court overturned a maximum-hour law in *Lochner v. New York* (1905).

Thomas Tandy Lewis

See also *Allgeyer v. Louisiana*; *Lochner v. New York*; *West Coast Hotel Co. v. Parrish*.

HOLMES V. JENNISON

Court: U.S. Supreme Court
Citation: 39 U.S. 540
Date: March 4, 1840
Issues: Foreign policy; Treaties

• Although the U.S. Supreme Court dismissed this case involving a state's extradition of a suspect to Canada, Roger Brooke Taney's opinion is a memorable assertion of federal control of foreign affairs.

The governor of Vermont had a Canadian resident wanted for murder in Canada arrested, with the intent of sending him back to Canada, although no extradition treaty existed. The Supreme Court, split four to four, was forced to dismiss this case. Chief Justice Roger Brooke Taney wrote for himself and Justices Joseph Story, John McLean, and James M. Wayne. Justices Smith Thompson, Henry Baldwin, Philip P. Barbour, and John Catron wrote opinions in disagreement. Justice John McKinley was absent. McKinley's fre-

Justice John McKinley, who was notorious for his absences from the Court. (Library of Congress)

quent absenteeism and lack of contribution gave him the reputation as one of the weakest members of the Court. Although the case was dismissed, the positions of the justices are important.

Taney offered the nationalist view that the federal government controlled foreign affairs and that the Vermont governor did not have the right to arrest someone who was wanted by a country with whom the United States did not have a treaty. The four who disagreed believed that the Court lacked jurisdiction to hear a habeas corpus petition. Thompson joined Taney in stating that the Vermont governor did not have the right of arrest, making five justices who did not believe the governor acted properly. Noting that, the Vermont Supreme Court decided to release the Canadian suspect although the Supreme Court did not take the case.

Richard L. Wilson

See also *Dames and Moore v. Regan; Martin v. Mott; United States v. Alvarez-Machain; United States v. Curtiss-Wright Export Corp.*

HOME BUILDING AND LOAN ASSOCIATION V. BLAISDELL

Court: U.S. Supreme Court
Citation: 290 U.S. 398
Date: June 8, 1934
Issues: Freedom of contract; Regulation of commerce

- This interpretation of the U.S. Constitution's contract clause recognized an emergency power in government that would be able to deal with the crisis of the Great Depression.

During the Great Depression, many states enacted debtor relief statutes that postponed the obligations of borrowers to repay their home mortgage loans. The Minnesota Mortgage Moratorium Act of 1933 authorized state courts to exempt property from foreclosure by the lender for two years, so long as the borrower paid the reasonable rental value of the property and taxes into the court. The statute prevented the lender from immediately taking back the property and reselling it upon the borrower's default.

The contract clause of the Constitution (Article I, section 10) provides: "No State shall pass any law impairing the obligation of contracts." This clause, along with the other clauses in this section, expresses a general mistrust of retroactive legislation, which is a statute passed after people's expectations are agreed on and settled. Between the Declaration of Independence of 1776 and the Constitution of 1787, debtor relief legislation was common in the states. This legislation caused immediate problems for creditors, who lost their investments. The Framers of the Constitution were more worried about the long-term creditworthiness of the new nation, however, which needed capital from foreign investors, so the contract clause amounted to a federal guarantee of debts. Chief Justice John Marshall used the contract clause during his tenure to assert federal authority to protect vested interests in property.

The historical background, as well as earlier U.S. Supreme Court precedents, seemed to require that the Mortgage Moratorium Act be struck down. Instead, Chief Justice Charles Evans Hughes wrote for a five-member majority upholding the law. He explained that the prohibition of the contract clause is not an absolute and should not be read so literally that it interferes with the state's police power to legislate for the public good. While an emergency such as the Great Depression did not create additional legislative power, Hughes said, such a serious emergency was the occasion for the legislative exercise of a reserved power equal to dealing with the economic crisis.

The four dissenters argued that the original historical understanding of the contract clause and the Supreme Court's consistent interpretations of the prohibition could not be ignored because of political exigency. To this argument Hughes remarked, "If by the statement that what the Constitution meant at the time of its adoption it means to-day, it is intended to say that the great clauses of the Constitution must be confined to the interpretation which the Framers, with the conditions and outlook of their time, would have placed upon them, the statement carries its own refutation."

This holding rendered the contract clause a rather inconsequential limitation on the legislative prerogative. The majority opinion was also an early example of judicial interpretation to "keep the Constitution in tune with the times."

Thomas E. Baker

See also *Bronson v. Kinzie; Edwards v. California; Gold Clause Cases; Nebbia v. New York; Schechter Poultry Corp. v. United States; United States v. Butler.*

Chief Justice Charles Evans Hughes taking a walk on his seventy-seventh birthday in April, 1939. (Harris & Ewing Collection/ Library of Congress)

Hoyt v. Florida

Court: U.S. Supreme Court
Citation: 368 U.S. 57
Date: November 20, 1961
Issues: Sex discrimination

- The U.S. Supreme Court upheld a woman's murder conviction, denying her claim that an all-male jury prevented her from receiving a fair trial.

In the only sex discrimination case to come before the Supreme Court under Chief Justice Earl Warren, the Court unanimously upheld the conviction of Gwendolyn Hoyt for murdering her husband even though she claimed an all-male jury denied her a fair trial. According to Florida law, women were not included on jury lists unless they specifically asked to be considered. Because men were automatically included, women were a very small portion of the jury pool. Hoyt claimed that the statute prevented her from receiving equal protection of the law. In his opinion for the Court, Justice John M. Harlan II wrote that Florida was merely trying to accommodate the community view that a woman's place was in the home, a view unlikely to be expressed later. The Court overturned the *Hoyt* ruling in *Taylor v. Louisiana* (1975).

Richard L. Wilson

See also *County of Washington v. Gunther; Frontiero v. Richardson; Geduldig v. Aiello; Grove City College v. Bell; Meritor Savings Bank v. Vinson; Taylor v. Louisiana.*

Hudson and Goodwin, United States v. *See* United States v. Hudson and Goodwin

HUDSON V. MICHIGAN

Court: U.S. Supreme Court
Citation: 547 U.S. 586
Date: June 15, 2006
Issues: Common law; Evidence; Search and seizure

- In a major departure from previous rulings on the exclusionary rule, the U.S. Supreme Court allowed the use of criminal evidence that was the fruit of a search conducted contrary to the "knock-and-announce" rule.

From colonial times, American courts have subscribed to the common law requirement that police, before using force to enter a private home, should knock and announce their identity and purpose. In *Wilson v. Arkansas* (1995), the Supreme Court explicitly affirmed that the Fourth Amendment incorporates this requirement, even though the ruling allowed exceptions for "exigent circumstances," leaving it to the states to decide the details. In *Richards v. Wisconsin* (1997), the Court explained that a no-knock entry is justified when the police have a "reasonable suspicion" that announcing their presence would be dangerous or "inhibit the effectiveness" of police efforts. If the police were to conduct no-knock entries without adequate justification, however, any evidence obtained by the search would be suppressed according to the exclusionary rule.

In 1998, Detroit police officers obtained a regular warrant (with no exemption from the knock-and-announce rule) to search for drugs and weapons in the home of Booker T. Hudson. Without knocking, the officers announced their presence and waited only three or four seconds before entering through an unlocked door. They found guns and cocaine. At trial, Hudson's lawyers argued that the evidence should be suppressed because the police had violated the "knock-and-announce" rule. Although agreeing that the rule had not been followed, the judge nevertheless allowed the evidence to be admitted, and Hudson was sentenced to eighteen months' probation.

The U.S. Supreme Court voted five to four to uphold the conviction. Speaking for the majority, Justice Antonin Scalia acknowledged that the knock-and-announce rule was an ancient common law principle, but he argued that the suppression of evidence should be a last resort because "it generates substantial social costs which sometimes include setting the guilty free and the dangerous at large." He further asserted that there was no causal connection between the constitutional violation (the failure to knock) and the discovery of evidence. The "increasing professionalism of the police," moreover, minimized the need to deter misconduct. In a concurring opinion, Justice Anthony M. Kennedy wrote that the *Hudson* ruling should be viewed narrowly, for it was not meant to diminish either the knock-and-announce principle or the exclusionary rule.

Speaking for the four-member minority, Justice Stephen Breyer wrote a heated dissent, charging that the majority had departed from the Court's "basic principles" and had destroyed the major legal incentive of the police to comply with the knock-and-announce requirement. He took particular exception to Scalia's causality argument for disregarding the exclusionary rule, which he wrote could make the Fourth Amendment unenforceable.

Thomas Tandy Lewis

See also *Boyd v. United States*; *Illinois v. Krull*; *Ker v. California*; *Mapp v. Ohio*; *United States v. Leon*; *Weeks v. United States*; *Wilson v. Arkansas*; *Wolf v. Colorado*.

HUDSON V. PALMER

Court: U.S. Supreme Court
Citation: 468 U.S. 517
Date: July 3, 1984
Issues: Incarceration; Right to privacy; Search and seizure

• The U.S. Supreme Court held that prison inmates lack the rights to privacy and protection against searches under the Fourth Amendment.

A Virginia prison inmate named Palmer claimed prison officer Hudson conducted an improper search of his locker and cell, during which he destroyed some of Palmer's personal property and generally harassed him unnecessarily. The officer discovered a ripped pillow case and charged him with destroying state property. By a 5-4 vote, the Supreme Court determined that incarcerated convicts do not have a right to privacy or Fourth Amendment protection against "unreasonable searches and seizure." In the opinion for the Court, Chief Justice Warren E. Burger used *Katz v. United States* (1967) to dismiss Palmer's claim to a privacy right and protection against unreasonable searches and seizures and used *Parratt v. Taylor* (1981) to reaffirm that an inmate had no due process claim against negligent loss of property if the state provided a reasonable remedy for the loss. Justice Sandra Day O'Connor concurred on different grounds. Justice John Paul Stevens, William J. Brennan, Jr., Thurgood Marshall, and Harry A. Blackmun concurred in part and dissented in part.

Richard L. Wilson

See also *Katz v. United States; Rhodes v. Chapman; Robinson v. California.*

HUMPHREY'S EXECUTOR V. UNITED STATES

Court: U.S. Supreme Court
Citation: 295 U.S. 602
Date: May 27, 1935
Issues: Presidential powers; Separation of powers

- The U.S. Supreme Court ruled that the president could not remove members of independent regulatory commissions on policy grounds before their terms had expired.

In *Myers v. United States* (1926), the Supreme Court upheld the authority of the president to remove a postmaster before his term had expired. A dictum (statement of opinion or belief) in the opinion suggested that the president would also have power to remove officials within the independent regulatory agencies. In 1931, President Herbert Hoover appointed William Humphrey, a conservative Republican, to serve a second six-year term on the Federal Trade Commission (FTC). The FTC Act authorized the president to remove a commissioner only for inefficiency, malfeasance, or neglect of duty. Nevertheless, when Franklin D. Roosevelt became president, he fired Humphrey in order to replace him with a supporter of New Deal policies.

By a 9-0 vote, the Court held that Roosevelt had exceeded his powers. Justice George Sutherland's opinion for the Court reasoned that Congress possessed the authority to create regulatory agencies with quasi-legislative and quasi-judicial functions, designed to act independently of executive interference. That authority included the power to fix a term of office because the commissioners could not act independently if they served at the pleasure of the president. The ruling narrowed the *Myers* precedent so that the president had only "the unrestrictable power" to remove executive officials performing purely executive functions.

Although controversial at the time, the *Humphrey's Executor* decision remains good law. In *Wiener v. United States* (1958), the Court held that the president could not remove a member of a regulatory commission unless explicitly authorized by Congress.

Thomas Tandy Lewis

See also *Ballard v. United States; Dames and Moore v. Regan; Goldwater v. Carter; McCulloch v. Maryland; Martin v. Mott; Myers v. United States; Nixon v. Administrator of General Services; United States v. Nixon.*

Hurley v. Irish-American Gay, Lesbian, and Bisexual Group of Boston

Court: U.S. Supreme Court
Citation: 515 U.S. 557
Date: June 19, 1995
Issues: First Amendment guarantees; Symbolic speech

• The U.S. Supreme Court held that the organizers of a Saint Patrick's Day parade did not have to include a gay group and that Massachusetts violated the parade organizer's First Amendment right by forcing it to allow the gay group to march.

Justice David H. Souter wrote the unanimous decision of the Supreme Court, holding that a private group that organized a parade did not have to include groups whose message changed the character of the parade. For the state of Massachusetts to require the veteran's group organizers of the Saint Patrick's Day parade to include the Irish-American Gay, Lesbian, and Bisexual Group of Boston would be to violate the First Amendment rights of the organizers. Souter found that one important characteristic of freedom of speech is that a speaker may decide what not to say. In this case, the parade was an expressive event—symbolic speech—and Massachusetts was forcing the veterans to say something they did not want to say when the state insisted that the gay group be included.

Richard L. Wilson

See also *New York State Club Association v. City of New York; Roberts v. United States Jaycees; Texas v. Johnson; Tinker v. Des Moines Independent Community School District; United States v. O'Brien.*

HURTADO V. CALIFORNIA

Court: U.S. Supreme Court
Citation: 110 U.S. 516
Date: March 3, 1884
Issues: Due process of law; Incorporation doctrine

- For the first time the U.S. Supreme Court indicated that the due process clause of the Fourteenth Amendment might apply some provisions of the Bill of Rights to the states.

After Joseph Hurtado learned that his wife was having an affair, he shot and killed his rival. California authorities charged him with murder by filing an information—a formal accusation by a public prosecutor—in a state court. He was tried, convicted, and sentenced to death.

Hurtado appealed to the U.S. Supreme Court. He noted that the Fifth Amendment would have prevented the federal government from putting him on trial unless he had been indicted by a grand jury. He claimed that the Fourteenth Amendment's prohibition against a state's depriving "any person of life, liberty, or property without due process of law" meant that the state of California was bound to observe the same procedural limitations imposed on the federal government by the Fifth Amendment. The Supreme Court rejected his claim.

The Fifth Amendment contains a list of specific prohibitions on the federal government. It may not subject anyone to double jeopardy, self-incrimination, or trial without prior indictment by a grand jury. In addition it prohibits the federal government from depriving anyone of "life, liberty, or property without due process of law." Noting that the Constitution contained no superfluous language, the Court reasoned that had the Framers of the Fifth Amendment meant "due process of law" to include the right to be indicted before trial, they would not have listed indictment as a separate, additional requirement.

The Fourteenth Amendment protects against state deprivation of due process of law. The Court ruled that the phrase has the same limitations it has in the Fifth Amendment. Consequently the Fourteenth Amendment due process clause does not prohibit the state's use of an information instead of an indictment.

Due process of law means that states cannot impose "arbitrary power" on their subjects. "Law," said the Court, "is something more than mere will exerted as an act of power." It excludes "acts of attainder, bills of pains and penalties, acts of confiscation . . . and other similar special, partial, and arbitrary exertions of power."

Justice John Harlan disagreed with the majority's interpretation of the due process clauses. He said that the Framers of the Fifth Amendment listed certain prohibitions not because they were something other than due process of law but because they were essential to it.

Hurtado v. California is important for two reasons. Though the Court ruled that the due process clause of the Fourteenth Amendment did not incorporate the indictment requirement of the Fifth Amendment, it opened the door to incorporation by stating that certain standards of justice—some of which might be found in the Bill of Rights—did apply against the states. In addition the majority opinion is a classic statement distinguishing the rule of law from the arbitrary exercise of power.

William H. Coogan

See also *Barron v. Baltimore; Edwards v. South Carolina; Maxwell v. Dow; Pointer v. Texas; Presser v. Illinois.*

HUSTLER MAGAZINE V. FALWELL

Court: U.S. Supreme Court
Citation: 485 U.S. 46
Date: February 24, 1988
Issues: Censorship; Pornography and obscenity

• The U.S. Supreme Court ruled against a religious leader's libel claim, providing a right of parody for the press.

Publisher Larry Flynt's *Hustler* magazine printed an issue containing a parody of Jerry Falwell, in which the conservative religious leader was depicted having sex with his mother in an outhouse. A Virginia federal district court jury rejected Falwell's libel claim because it believed that no reasonable person would believe the parody was truthful but awarded Falwell $200,000 for "intentional infliction of emotional distress"—a ruling that did not require that a false statement was made. By an 8-0 vote, the Supreme Court overturned the lower court's decision. In the opinion for the Court, Chief Justice William H. Rehnquist wrote that a public figure could not recover for intentional infliction of emotional harm absent a libelous statement made with actual malice. Public figures such as Falwell must expect robust criticism because the press protection under the First Amendment takes precedence over their emotional loss from nonlibelous statements.

Richard L. Wilson

See also *Garrison v. Louisiana; Gertz v. Robert Welch; Milkovich v. Lorain Journal Co.; New York Times Co. v. Sullivan; Time v. Hill.*

HUTCHINSON V. PROXMIRE

Court: U.S. Supreme Court
Citation: 443 U.S. 111
Date: June 26, 1979
Issues: Congressional powers; Immunity from prosecution

• The U.S. Supreme Court held that the speech and debate clause applied only to statements made on the floor of the House or Senate and that members of Congress could be sued for allegedly libelous statements contained in press releases and newsletters to their constituents.

Senator William Proxmire regularly announced Golden Fleece awards in order to publicize the issue of wasteful government spending. One of the awards was bestowed on psychologist Ronald Hutchinson for his work on aggression in monkeys. Hutchinson sued for libel damages, claiming that the publicity had harmed his professional reputation and had caused him emotional anguish. By a 7-1 vote, the Supreme Court allowed the suit to proceed, holding that congressional immunity under Article I of the U.S. Constitution did not apply to press releases or newsletters because such activities were not essential to congressional deliberations. In addition, the Court found that Hutchinson was not a public figure, which meant that he could prevail under a less rigorous standard of proof than the actual malice standard required of public figures.

Thomas Tandy Lewis

See also *Kilbourn v. Thompson; New York Times Co. v. Sullivan; United Public Workers v. Mitchell; Weston v. Charleston.*

Hutto v. Davis

Court: U.S. Supreme Court
Citation: 454 U.S. 370
Date: January 11, 1982
Issues: Cruel and unusual punishment; Illegal drugs

• Narrowly interpreting the Eighth Amendment, the Court upheld a prison sentence of forty years for the possession and distribution of small amounts of illegal drugs.

In 1973, Virginia police officers with a valid search warrant raided the home of Roger Davis, where they seized nine ounces of marijuana with a street value of two hundred dollars. The police already possessed a tape recording of Davis selling marijuana and other illicit drugs to a police informant. Davis was tried and found guilty in state court for the sale and distribution of illicit drugs, and his penalty was forty years' imprisonment and a fine of twenty thousand dollars. The federal district court, however, overturned the penalty, declaring that it was so "grossly out of proportion to the severity of the crime as to constitute cruel and unusual punishment in violation of the Eighth Amendment." The court of appeals agreed that the penalty was unconstitutional.

About the same time, the U.S. Supreme Court was taking a more conservative view of the Eighth Amendment; the majority in *Rummel v. Estelle* (1980) upheld a sentence of life imprisonment, with possibility of parole, for three offenses of fraud involving about $230. *Rummel* established the principle that federal courts should be most reluctant to use the proportionality doctrine to overturn legislatively mandated prison terms. In spite of *Rummel*, however, the court of appeals in 1981 reaffirmed that Davis's sentence was a cruel and unusual punishment. Virginia appealed the ruling to the Supreme Court.

The Court voted six to three to reverse the judgments of the lower federal courts. Following the logic of the *Rummel* precedent, the majority insisted in a *per curiam* opinion that the length of prison terms was a matter for legislative discretion and that any use of the doctrine of proportionality to overturn such sentences should be "exceedingly rare."

In a strong dissent, Justice William J. Brennan argued that Davis's sentence was cruel and unusual compared with other punishments for similar offenses. He observed that in Virginia at the time the average sentence involving marijuana was about three years and that even the district attorney who prosecuted Davis considered the penalty of forty years to be "grossly unjust."

The *Hutto* decision seemed to indicate that in the foreseeable future the Supreme Court would not allow the application of the proportionality doctrine to overturn penalties except in cases of the death penalty. Less than two years later, however, the majority of the Court in *Solem v. Helm* (1983) would make use of the doctrine to overturn a sentence of life imprisonment without possibility of parole. *Solem* did not appear to mark a long-term change in the Court's view of the Eighth Amendment, for in *Harmelin v. Michigan* (1991) the majority approved a lifetime sentence, without the possibility of parole, for possession of slightly over 650 grams of cocaine.

Thomas Tandy Lewis

See also *Furman v. Georgia; Harmelin v. Michigan; Hudson v. Palmer; Louisiana ex rel. Francis v. Resweber; Rhodes v. Chapman; Rummel v. Estelle; Solem v. Helm.*

HYLTON V. UNITED STATES

Court: U.S. Supreme Court
Citation: 3 U.S. 171
Date: March 8, 1796
Issues: Judicial review; Taxation

- The U.S. Supreme Court's agreement to hear a case in which it was asked to review the constitutionality of a tax levied by Congress is regarded as implying that the Court had the power of judicial review.

Marbury v. Madison (1803) is generally accepted as the first case in which the Supreme Court both asserted its power of judicial review and used that power to strike down a congressional enactment. Because judicial review is not explicitly mentioned in the Constitution, the Court's argument was, in part, that it was so widely understood that the Court was to have that power that no specific mention was necessary. Later legal experts have searched for evidence of this claim before *Marbury*. This evidence can be found in *Hylton* and *Hayburn's Case* (1792).

Daniel Hylton defended himself for nonpayment of a congressionally enacted carriage tax, asserting it was an unconstitutional direct tax and, in effect, asking the Court to use the power of judicial review to declare the tax unconstitutional. Justices Samuel Chase, William Paterson, and James Iredell all wrote seriatim (separate) opinions but agreed the tax was constitutional because it was indirect and therefore not prohibited by Article I of the U.S. Constitution. They were the only justices available to hear the case, but their agreeing to hear the case implied that the Court had the power of judicial review.

Richard L. Wilson

See also *Hayburn's Case*; *Marbury v. Madison*; *Springer v. United States*; *Veazie Bank v. Fenno*.

ILLINOIS EX REL. MCCOLLUM V. BOARD OF EDUCATION

Court: U.S. Supreme Court
Citation: 333 U.S. 203
Date: March 8, 1948
Issues: Establishment of religion

- The U.S. Supreme Court disallowed a released-time religious instruction program in public schools, helping define the meaning of the First Amendment's establishment of religion clause.

By an 8-1 vote, the Supreme Court found unconstitutional a released-time religious education program in the Illinois public schools. Under the Illinois program, Protestant, Roman Catholic, and Jewish instructors—not paid with public funds but approved by the superintendent of schools—came into the schools to teach thirty- to forty-five-minute religious training programs and kept records of those attending. Any student not wishing to participate could participate in supervised alternative activities elsewhere in the building. In his opinion for the Court, Justice Hugo L. Black found the use of the school buildings to be excessive public support for religion under his earlier opinion in *Everson v. Board of Education of Ewing Township* (1947). Justice Felix Frankfurter concurred in an opinion joined by four other justices that argued there was a historical record against intermixing religious and secular activities in the United States. The separationist views that dominated this case were modified by *Zorach v. Clauson* (1952). Justice Stanley F. Reed dissented, arguing that the establishment of religion clause should be treated more narrowly to allow the state's incidental support of religion, a position close to the one taken by Justice Potter Stewart in later cases.

Richard L. Wilson

See also *Abington School District v. Schempp; Engel v. Vitale; Epperson v. Arkansas; Everson v. Board of Education of Ewing Township; Zorach v. Clauson.*

Illinois v. Caballes

Court: U.S. Supreme Court
Citation: 543 U.S. 405
Date: January 24, 2005
Issues: Police powers; Right to privacy; Search and seizure

- The U.S. Supreme Court held that the Fourth Amendment does not prohibit a police officer from conducting a dog sniff to detect illegal drugs in an automobile that has been validly stopped for a traffic violation so long as the dog sniff does not prevent the motorist from leaving for an unreasonable length of time.

In 1998, a state trooper pulled over Roy Caballes for speeding. While the trooper was writing out a warning, an officer with the state's drug interdiction squad unexpectedly arrived with a drug-sniffing dog and walked the dog around Caballes's car. The dog alerted the officers to an odor emanating from the car's trunk, in which they discovered marijuana valued at over $250,000. The entire incident took place within about ten minutes.

When Caballes was tried in state court, his lawyer claimed that the use of a "canine sniff" without a minimum of reasonable suspicion violated the Fourth Amendment. After the trial court refused to suppress the seized evidence, Caballes was found guilty and sentenced to twelve years imprisonment. However, the Illinois Supreme Court held that the evidence was inadmissible, declaring that without "specific and articulable facts" to suggest illegal activity, the use of the dog "unjustifiably enlarged the scope of a routine traffic stop into a criminal investigation." The state appealed the case to the U.S. Supreme Court.

Admissibility of Evidence

The question of the admissibility of the seized contraband in prosecuting Caballes raised a number of complex questions relating to the Supreme Court's relevant precedents interpreting the subjective phrase, "unreasonable searches and seizures." According to the logic of *Terry v. Ohio* (1968) and other cases, a traffic stop is classified as a "seizure," requiring "reasonable suspicion" that the motorist has committed a traffic offense. Even if the seizure of the driver is reasonable at its beginning, it becomes unreasonable if the driver is detained for an unreasonably long period of time. In *United States v.*

Place (1983), the Court had held that subjecting a person's luggage to a canine sniff in an airport did not constitute a search under the Fourth Amendment. There was some question, however, about whether a private automobile might have more of an "expectation of privacy" than a public airport. In *Kyllo v. United States* (2001), in contrast to *Place*, the Court held that the police must acquire a search warrant in order to use a heat detector to detect patterns of heat coming from a private home. However, since its 1925 *Carroll v. United States* ruling, the Court had consistently ruled that the privacy interests in an automobile has less sweeping protection than does a person's home. Following a review of the *Caballes* case, the Supreme Court voted six to two to reverse the ruling by Illinois's highest court and held that the evidence taken in Caballes's car trunk was admissible at trial.

In the official opinion for the Court, Justice John Paul Stevens wrote a relatively short but cogent analysis. First, he referred to *United States v. Jacobsen* (1984), which had recognized that if police conduct does not compromise "any legitimate interest in privacy," it does not constitute a search subject to Fourth Amendment restrictions. Secondly, since possession of contraband is not a legitimate interest, actions by the police that can only reveal such possession do not compromise any "legitimate privacy interest." Third, the *Place* ruling had recognized that well-trained dogs detect only contraband, not other items that might be subject to an expectation of privacy. Fourth, the dog sniff had been conducted from the exterior of Caballes's automobile while he was "lawfully seized" for a violation of traffic laws. Fifth, the dog sniff had not significantly prolonged the time that Caballes was required to wait in place.

Privacy Issues

Finally, the privacy interests in this case, as in the earlier *Place* ruling, were much less from those in *Kyllo* for two reasons: first, the special sanctity of a private home; second, the fact that a heat detector might be able to reveal intimate details in addition to the presence of contraband. In view of all these considerations, therefore, Justice Stevens wrote that a canine sniff "conducted during a concededly lawful traffic stop that reveals no information other than the location of a substance that has no individual has any right to possess does not violate the Fourth Amendment."

Both of the two dissenters, Justices David Souter and Ruth Bader Ginsburg, wrote dissenting opinions that exposed some logical and factual weaknesses in the majority opinion. Souter declared that the time had come to reconsider whether the *Place* ruling was based on valid information. Because statistical evidence proved that dogs trained to sniff particular items are not infallible, he argued that it was possible for a dog sniff to result in a false positive, thereby allowing the police to intrude into places having a reasonable expectation of privacy. Souter also argued that when the police stop a car for a traffic offense, a search of the automobile, unless conducted for the officer's safety, requires reasonable suspicion unrelated to the reason for the stop. Justice Ginsburg was primarily concerned about the possible implications of the majority's opinion, which appeared to clear "the way for suspicionless, dog-accompanied drug sweeps of parked cars along sidewalks and in parking lots."

Thomas Tandy Lewis

Further Reading

Clancy, Thomas K. *The Fourth Amendment: Its History and Interpretation.* Durham, N.C.: Carolina Academic Press, 2008. Comprehensive guide to the historical jurisprudence relating to search and seizure.

McInnis, Thomas. *The Evolution of the Fourth Amendment.* Lanham, Md.: Lexington Books, 2009. Describes and analyzes the different approaches of the Supreme Court in interpreting the prohibition on unreasonable searches and seizures.

Roberson, Cliff. *Constitutional Law and Criminal Justice.* New York: Taylor & Francis, 2009. Includes a wealth of information about principles and practices relating to the Fourth Amendment and the exclusionary rule.

Savage, David. *The Supreme Court and Individual Rights.* 5th ed. Washington, D.C.: CQ Press, 2009. Excellent analysis of the *Caballes* ruling within the broader context of the Fourth Amendment.

Waksman, David, and Debbie Goodman. *The Search and Seizure Handbook.* Englewood Cliffs, N.J.: Prentice Hall, 2009. Clearly written guide explaining Fourth Amendment principles for law-enforcement officers working in the current criminal justice system.

Zalman, Marvin. *Criminal Procedure: Constitution and Society.* Saddle River, N.J.: Prentice Hall, 2007. Central tenets of criminal procedure with helpful chapters on search warrants, the exclusionary rule, and related topics.

See also *Carroll v. United States*; *Kyllo v. United States*; *Terry v. Ohio*.

Illinois v. Gates

Court: U.S. Supreme Court
Citation: 462 U.S. 213
Date: June 8, 1983
Issues: Police powers; Search and seizure

- This U.S. Supreme Court decision on search warrants overruled the stringent standards of the "two-prong" test—also known as the *Aguilar-Spinelli* test—in favor of the "totality of the circumstances" test. In so doing, law-enforcement officers were given more flexibility in establishing probable cause when requesting a search warrant.

On May 3, 1978, city police in Bloomingdale, Illinois, received an anonymous letter stating that Lance and Susan Gates were involved in illegal drug trafficking. The letter delineated how the Gateses allegedly transported narcotics from Florida to Illinois. Specifically, Susan Gates was said to have driven a car to Florida so the trunk could be loaded with drugs. Lance flew to Florida a few days later and drove the car back to Illinois. The letter also stated that the defendants had approximately $100,000 worth of drugs in their basement.

Subsequently, the police found the Gateses' home address and verified that Lance had recently made a plane reservation for May 5, a few days after the police received the letter. Investigators later confirmed Lance had flown to Florida and stayed overnight in a hotel room registered in Susan's name. Based upon the anonymous letter and the information gathered by the police, a judge issued a search warrant. When the Gateses returned to Illinois, their car and home were searched, and large amounts of drugs and weapons were seized. The Illinois Supreme Court suppressed the evidence by ruling sufficient probable cause for a search had been established because the police could not verify whether the author of the anonymous letter was credible, thus satisfying analytical standards established in *Aguilar v. Texas* and *Spinelli v. United States*, known as the *Aguilar-Spinelli* test. The state of Illinois appealed to the U.S. Supreme Court.

In the *Gates* case, the U.S. Supreme Court ruled that the *Aguilar-Spinelli* test was excessively rigid in that it failed to incorporate the basis of knowledge that law-enforcement agents possessed when applying for a warrant. The Court determined that although the letter itself could not establish probable cause, the fact that law-enforcement agents were able to confirm some of the activity described in the letter to be accurate was sufficient to establish probable cause and justify issuance of a search warrant. The Court reversed the lower court ruling and established that the test for probable cause would be based upon the "totality of the circumstances."

Heidi Jo Blair-Esteves

Further Reading

Horwitz, Morton J. *The Warren Court and the Pursuit of Justice.* New York: Hill and Wang, 1998. Examines segregation, the Civil Rights movement, McCarthyism, and other issues of democratic culture.

Schwartz, Bernard, ed. *The Burger Court: Counter-Revolution or Confirmation?* New York: Oxford University Press, 1998. Essays included are written by justices, journalists, feminists, and lawyers.

Yarbrough, Tinsley E. *The Burger Court: Justices, Rulings, and Legacy.* Santa Barbara, Calif.: ABC-CLIO, 2000. Describes major decisions rendered by Warren E. Burger's court and their impact.

See also *California v. Greenwood; Maryland v. Buie; Miller v. California; Skinner v. Railway Labor Executives' Association; United States v. Leon; United States v. Ross; United States v. United States District Court.*

═══════════════════════════════

ILLINOIS V. KRULL

Court: U.S. Supreme Court
Citation: 480 U.S. 340
Date: March 9, 1987
Issues: Evidence; Search and seizure

• In this case the U.S. Supreme Court held that the "good-faith exception," sometimes allowing the courtroom use of evidence seized illegally, could apply to certain warrantless searches.

Illinois businesses that buy and sell used automobile parts or that process automobile scrap metal were required by a 1981 statute to obtain a business license, maintain detailed records of their transactions, and make these records and the business premises available to the state for inspection at any reasonable time to determine the accuracy of the records.

On July 5, 1981, the Chicago police entered the premises of Action Iron & Metal, Inc., an automobile wrecking yard, to inspect its records and examine the vehicle identification numbers of cars in the yard. The clerk at the wrecking yard was unable to produce any records other than a paper pad on which approximately five vehicle purchases were listed. The inspection of the wrecking yard disclosed that three of the cars were stolen and a fourth car had no vehicle identification number. Two men (Krull, who held the license for Action Iron & Metal, Inc., and the clerk) were charged with various criminal violations of the Illinois motor vehicle statutes.

On July 6, 1981, a federal court held that the Illinois statute was an unconstitutional administrative search law. Based on this decision, the Illinois trial court held that the search was illegal. The Illinois trial court also held that the *United States v. Leon* (1984) good-faith exception to the exclusionary rule did not apply because it was limited to circumstances in which a warrant was issued by a neutral magistrate. The Illinois Supreme Court affirmed the trial court's decision. The U.S. Supreme Court, however, in a 5-4 vote, reversed the decision. It stated that the *Leon* good-faith exception to the exclusionary rule could apply when a police officer's reliance on the constitutionality of a statute authorizing the search was objectively reasonable, even though the statute is subsequently declared unconstitutional.

In Justice Harry Blackmun's majority opinion, the Court noted that *Leon* had reaffirmed that the purpose of the exclusionary rule is to deter future unlawful police conduct, not to provide a cure for past unlawful police conduct. Because the exclusion of evidence undermines the truth-finding process of a criminal trial, the exclusionary rule remedy should be imposed only when the likelihood of deterring future unlawful police conduct outweighs the cost to the criminal justice system's primary purpose: determining the guilt or innocence of a defendant.

The statutory authorization for the warrantless search functions like the warrant for three reasons, the Court said. First, there is no evidence that legislators ignored the requirements of the Fourth Amendment in passing such legislation. Second, members of the legislature, like neutral magistrates, have no direct stake in the day-to-day conduct of law enforcement, so there is little incentive for them to overstep the limits of the Fourth Amendment. Third, no proof was offered that the application of the exclusionary rule would deter legislators from enacting statutes which may be declared unconstitutional or that exclusion of evidence in these cases will significantly deter future unlawful police conduct. Therefore, any marginal deterrent benefit in applying the exclusionary rule to cases such as this is outweighed by the cost of excluding reliable and relevant evidence from the process of determining guilt.

In this case the police acted in a reasonable manner in relying on the statute as authorizing a lawful search, because the Supreme Court had approved warrantless administrative searches in similar cases. In closing, the Court limited its decision by noting that if there was proof that the legislature wholly abandoned its responsibility to enact constitutional laws under the Fourth Amendment, or if a reasonable officer should have known the statute was unconstitutional, then the exclusionary rule should apply. Despite the caveat at the close of the opinion, the *Krull* case significantly expanded the scope of the decision in *Leon* by leaving open the possibility that it could be applied to other warrantless search circumstances.

Johnny C. Burris

See also *Massachusetts v. Sheppard; United States v. Leon.*

ILLINOIS V. MCARTHUR

Court: U.S. Supreme Court
Citation: 531 U.S. 326
Date: February 20, 2001
Issues: Illegal drugs; Police powers; Right to privacy; Search and seizure

- The U.S. Supreme Court's decision in *Illinois v. McArthur* allows police officers with probable cause to believe that criminal evidence is located in a private home to use reasonable means to prevent destruction of that evidence while they are waiting for a search warrant.

In *Illinois v. McArthur,* Tera McArthur requested and received police protection when she moved out of the trailer where she had been living with her husband, Charles McArthur. After relocating, she informed officer John Love that she had seen her husband hide marijuana under the sofa. When Charles McArthur refused to consent to a search of the trailer, Love instructed his colleague to obtain a search warrant. While waiting for the warrant, Love refused to allow McArthur, who was standing on the front porch, to reenter the trailer, except under supervision. Whenever McArthur went into the trailer, Love stood in the doorway, where he could see the sofa. About two hours later, armed with a warrant, police officers found and seized a small amount of marijuana and a marijuana pipe.

When Charles McArthur was prosecuted for misdemeanor possession of an illegal drug and paraphernalia, his attorneys moved to suppress the evidence. They argued that the porch constituted part of the trailer home and that the refusal to allow McArthur free access to his home was inconsistent with a primary purpose of the Fourth Amendment—to secure the privacy of persons in their homes. The trial court granted the motion, and an appellate court upheld the judgment. The state's supreme court denied the petition for a review.

The U.S. Supreme Court, however, by an 8-1 vote, held that the restriction on McArthur had been reasonable in the light of the circumstances. Writing for the Court, Justice Stephen Breyer balanced privacy considerations with concerns of law enforcement and made six points. First, the police had probable cause to believe that criminal evidence existed in a particular place. Second, there was good reason to expect that McArthur, unless supervised, would destroy the evidence. Third, the officers did not violate McArthur's personal privacy beyond the extent necessary to secure the evidence. Fourth, the restraint did not continue any longer than necessary. Fifth, earlier precedents had recognized that a person standing in an open doorway was in a "public place." Sixth, in contrast to *Welsh v. Wisconsin* (1984), the offenses at issue in this case were jailable crimes.

In a concurring opinion, Justice David Souter wrote that if Charles McArthur had not stepped outside the trailer, the threat of his destroying evidence would have constituted exigent circumstances to justify a prompt, warrantless search of the trailer. In a dissenting opinion, Justice John Paul Stevens argued that the majority struck the wrong balance, and he praised the Illinois jurists for placing a higher value on the sanctity of a private home than on the prosecution of a petty offense.

The *McArthur* decision did not break any new ground, but it helped clarify the extent to which police officers, when acting reasonably and with sensitivity, might intrude into the privacy of a home in order to prevent the destruction of criminal evidence.

Thomas Tandy Lewis

Further Reading

Epstein, Lee, and Thomas Walker. *Constitutional Law for a Changing America.* 5th ed. Washington, D.C.: CQ Press, 2003.

O'Brien, David M. *Constitutional Law and Politics.* 6th ed. New York: W. W. Norton, 2005.

See also *Carroll v. United States; Illinois v. Gates; Knowles v. Iowa; Marshall v. Barlow's; Maryland v. Buie; Tennessee v. Garner; United States v. Ross; Whren v. United States.*

ILLINOIS V. WARDLOW

Court: U.S. Supreme Court
Citation: 528 U.S. 119
Date: January 12, 2000
Issues: Police powers; Search and seizure

- This U.S. Supreme Court decision expanded the powers of police to stop and frisk suspects by holding that taking flight in high-crime areas gives police enough evidence to undertake such actions.

In 1995, two police officers were working in a special operations unit of the Chicago Police Department going into an area of the city known for high drug trafficking. There they noticed a man named Wardlow, who was carrying an opaque bag. After looking in their direction, Wardlow immediately fled. The officers then gave chase and eventually caught him. On the basis of his belief that people in high-crime neighborhoods often carry arms, one of the officers conducted a pat-down search of Wardlow and found a gun.

Wardlow was later convicted of unlawful possession of a firearm by a felon. Prior to his trial, Wardlow moved to suppress having his gun submitted as evidence, arguing that the officers had no basis for pursuing him in the first

A primary justification for permitting police to frisk, or "pat down," suspects is to ensure their safety by allowing them to determine whether the suspects are carrying dangerous weapons. (Brand-X Pictures)

place. Since their chase was illegal, he argued, so, too, was their frisking of him. Thus, the evidence should be suppressed because of the exclusionary rule.

Wardlow lost his argument at the trial level, but his conviction was overturned by the Illinois Supreme Court, which held his contention that his gun should have been suppressed as evidence, because his actions did not give the officers reasonable suspicion to stop him. After the state appealed this ruling, the case went to the U.S. Supreme Court, which overruled Illinois's supreme court.

Writing in the majority opinion for the Court, Chief Justice William H. Rehnquist contended that while an individual's presence in a high-crime area was not by itself sufficient to justify the arresting officer's reasonable suspicion, it was a factor that could be considered. Moreover, the chief justice noted, the defendant's "unprovoked flight" in that area should also be considered a factor in determining whether reasonable suspicion existed. In short, while neither flight nor presence in a high-crime area by itself was sufficient to constitute reasonable suspicion, the two combined were sufficient.

Wardlow was one of a series of cases in which the Supreme Court sought to define what constituted a level of evidence sufficient to form the "reasonable suspicion" to permit officers to stop and frisk. In its earlier decision in *Brown v. Texas* (1979), the Court held that the mere presence of an individual in a high-crime area was not enough to create a reasonable suspicion of criminal activity. In *Florida v. Royer* (1983), the Court had ruled that refusal of a citizen to stop to talk to police did not create the necessary reasonable suspicion to validate a stop. In the view of many, the Supreme Court's decision in *Wardlow* broadened the definition of "reasonable suspicion" and, hence, expanded law enforcement's right to stop individual citizens.

David M. Jones

Further Reading

Amar, Akhil Reed. *The Constitution and Criminal Procedure.* New Haven, Conn.: Yale University Press, 1997.

Bloom, Robert M. *Searches, Seizures, and Warrants.* Westport, Conn.: Praeger Publishing, 2003.

Yarborough, Tinsley. *The Rehnquist Court and the Constitution.* Oxford, England: Oxford University Press, 2000.

See also *California v. Acevedo; Carroll v. United States; Knowles v. Iowa; Maryland v. Buie; Terry v. Ohio; Whren v. United States.*

Immigration and Naturalization Service v. Chadha

Court: U.S. Supreme Court
Citation: 462 U.S. 919
Date: June 23, 1983
Issues: Immigration; Separation of powers

• By overturning congressional use of the legislative veto, the U.S. Supreme Court, in this single decision, overturned more combined laws than it had in its entire history.

Jagdish Chadha, a Kenyan of Asian Indian descent carrying a British passport, entered the United States on a student visa in the 1960's. When his student visa expired, he was denied reentry into either Great Britain or Kenya and applied for permanent residency in the United States. After lengthy deliberations, the Immigration and Naturalization Service (INS) granted his application to stay, only to have the House of Representatives veto the INS decision, leaving Chadha to face deportation.

Both liberals and conservatives saw the case as a chance to overcome the burgeoning practice of Congress passing laws containing legislative veto provisions. These enactments allowed one or both houses of Congress to act jointly or independently to cancel executive branch regulations made pursuant to some vague delegation of power.

Liberal public interest groups played the more public role as Ralph Nader's consumer advocate litigation group took over Chadha's case in the Supreme Court. The liberal public interest group's interest in the case stemmed from the explosion of congressional enactments of legislative vetoes. After having fought for the passage of regulatory legislation on the environment, consumer protection, worker safety, or similar causes, these liberal groups often were frustrated by the bureaucratic regulatory process. If they succeeded in the bureaucracy, they then were frustrated by the actions of their more wealthy opponents, who would persuade one or both houses of Congress to kill offending regulations with a legislative veto. Those conservatives who opposed both excessive delegations of power and legislative vetoes had no apparent vehicle for participation.

Conservative Chief Justice Warren E. Burger wrote the 7-2 majority opinion, which cut across liberal and conservative opinion and ended the use of the congressional veto. A moderate Lewis F. Powell, Jr., concurred. Moderately conservative Justice Byron R. White dissented, upholding the use of legislative vetoes, and conservative Justice William H. Rehnquist also dissented. The diversity of opinion continues. The Court seemed willing to push further in the direction of *Chadha* in *Bowsher v. Synar* (1986), but seemed to withdraw from *Chadha's* advanced stand in *Morrison v. Olson* (1988) and *Mistretta v. United States* (1989).

Richard L. Wilson

See also *Bowsher v. Synar; Mistretta v. United States; Morrison v. Olson; Panama Refining Co. v. Ryan.*

In re Baby M

Court: New Jersey Supreme Court
Citation: 537 A.2d 1227, 109 N.J. 396
Date: February 3, 1988
Issues: Children's rights; Parental rights;
Reproductive rights

• A state supreme court ruled for the first time in the case *In re Baby M* on whether a surrogate-parenting contract was enforceable.

Baby M raised questions regarding contract law, reproductive rights, and social and sexual equality. At issue was whether a contract signed between Mary Beth Whitehead, a "surrogate" mother, William Stern, a sperm donor, and the Infertility Center of New York (ICNY), the surrogacy broker, was enforceable. The New Jersey U.S. Supreme Court's decision affirmed in part, reversed in part, and remanded for further proceedings a lower trial court's decision.

Citing the "best interests of the child," the lower court had granted the Sterns custody of Baby M. Finding that only a state-approved agency can terminate parental rights, the New Jersey Supreme Court identified Whitehead as the natural mother, revoked the term "surrogate mother," and restored her parental rights. The surrogacy contract was declared unenforceable and illegal because of multiple conflicts with New Jersey's laws and public policies—for example, laws against baby selling. Furthermore, the court found that by privileging the father's rights over the mother's, the contract violated the state's laws regarding equal parental rights. While the court did not declare surrogacy itself criminal, it did find that an exchange of money for surrogacy services was illegal, thus rendering surrogacy contracts unenforceable and potentially undesirable. By 1992 eighteen states had outlawed or restricted surrogacy operations.

Steve J. Mazurana and Dyan E. Mazurana

See also *Alsager v. District Court*; *Ohio v. Akron Center for Reproductive Health*; *Zablocki v. Redhail.*

IN RE DEBS

Court: U.S. Supreme Court
Citation: 158 U.S. 564
Date: May 27, 1895
Issues: Antitrust law

- The U.S. Supreme Court upheld a federal injunction against a labor union in order to protect the U.S. mails and to preserve the orderly movement of interstate commerce. Also, the Court implicitly permitted lower courts to apply the Sherman Antitrust Act (1890) to labor unions.

During the famous Pullman strike in Chicago, members of the American Railway Union throughout the nation refused to handle trains carrying Pullman cars. When this resulted in firings, the union declared new strikes. President Grover Cleveland's administration sought and obtained a federal injunction against the strikers. The circuit court justified the injunction under the Sherman Antitrust Act of 1890 and the authority of the federal government to deliver the mails. With the spread of violence, Cleveland sent federal troops to Chicago to preserve order. When Eugene Debs, president of the union, refused to honor the injunction, he was held in contempt and given a sentence of six months in jail. He appealed to the Supreme Court on a writ of habeas corpus.

Eugene Debs.
(Library of Congress)

Speaking for a unanimous Court, Justice David J. Brewer upheld the injunction and the contempt citation of Debs. Brewer reasoned that the national government possessed a broad constitutional mandate to remove obstacles to interstate commerce and movement of the mails and that it might choose to use either military power or the equity jurisdiction of the federal courts. By maintaining silence about the lower court's reliance on the Sherman Antitrust Act, Brewer's opinion left the door open for antitrust injunctions against union activities in interstate commerce. In *Loewe v. Lawlor* (1908), the Court explicitly ruled that the Sherman Antitrust Act applied to combinations of workers. The Clayton Act of 1914 exempted labor unions from antitrust injunctions, but the use of injunctions to stop strikes continued until the New Deal period.

Thomas Tandy Lewis

See also *Abrams v. United States; Adair v. United States; Duplex Printing Co. v. Deering; Gompers v. Buck's Stove and Range Co.; Loewe v. Lawlor.*

In re Gault

Court: U.S. Supreme Court
Citation: 387 U.S. 1
Date: May 15, 1967
Issues: Children's rights; Evidence; Juvenile justice; Right to counsel

- This decision established that juvenile court procedures must include the most basic procedural rights and evidentiary rules.

In re Gault was the result of the 1964 arrest of Gerald Gault in Gila County, Arizona, for making a lewd telephone call to a neighbor. Gault, who was then fifteen years old, was on probation for an earlier minor offense. Although the state produced no evidence at Gault's hearing, the juvenile judge found him to be delinquent.

The basis of the finding was evidently police rumors about him and statements elicited from him in the absence of his parents or his lawyer. He was committed to a state industrial school until his eighteenth birthday. Had an adult committed the same crime, the maximum penalty that could have been assessed under Arizona law would have been a fifty-dollar fine and two months' imprisonment.

Gault's appeal to the Arizona Supreme Court was unsuccessful, and he brought the case to the U.S. Supreme Court. He argued that the Arizona juvenile code was unconstitutional on its face because it gives the judge almost unlimited discretion to take juveniles from their parents and commit them to an institution without notice of the charges, the right to counsel, the right to confront and cross-examine witnesses, the right to a transcript of the proceedings, or the right to an appeal. Arizona argued that because the main purpose of juvenile proceedings is to protect juvenile defendants from the full rigor and consequences of the criminal law, informal procedures are required. In Arizona's view, Gault's commitment to a state institution was protective rather than punitive.

The Court's Ruling

The Supreme Court decided for Gault by a vote of eight to one. In an opinion by Justice Abe Fortas, the Court held that the due process clause of the Fourteenth Amendment requires that juvenile defendants are at least entitled to notice of the charges, right to counsel, right to confrontation and cross-examination of witnesses, the privilege against self-incrimination, a transcript of the proceedings, and appellate review. Justice Fortas insisted that these are the minimal guarantees necessary to assure fairness. He argued that the guarantees would not unduly interfere with any of the benefits of less formal procedures for juveniles.

Justice John M. Harlan wrote a separate concurrence agreeing with the result but suggesting that the crucial minimum guarantees should be limited to notice of the charges, the right to counsel, including assigned counsel for indigent families, a transcript, and the right to appeal. In dissent, Justice Potter Stewart argued that because juvenile proceedings are not adversary criminal actions the court is unwise to fasten procedural guarantees upon them.

In re Gault forces states to provide juvenile defendants with the central procedural guarantees of the Fifth Amendment. The possibility that young defendants will be unfairly judged to have committed crimes or been delinquent was substantially reduced.

Robert Jacobs

Further Reading

Gold, Susan Dudley. *In re Gault: Do Minors Have the Same Rights as Adults?* Tarrytown, N.Y.: Marshall Cavendish Benchmark, 2008. Part of its publisher's Supreme Court Milestones series designed for young-adult readers, this volume offers an accessible history and analysis of the *Gault* case that examines opposing sides in the case, the people involved, and the case's lasting impact. Includes bibliography and index.

See also *Gideon v. Wainwright; In re Winship; McKeiver v. Pennsylvania; Schall v. Martin.*

In re Neagle

Court: U.S. Supreme Court
Citation: 135 U.S. 1
Date: April 14, 1890
Issues: Federal supremacy

- This case, involving an attack on U.S. Supreme Court Justice Stephen J. Field, expanded federal power by making certain acts committed under color of federal law subject to the jurisdiction of federal law rather than state criminal law.

While sitting as a circuit court judge in his native California in 1888, Justice Stephen J. Field delivered an opinion invalidating the purported marriage between William Sharon, a wealthy Nevada mine owner, and Sarah Althea Hill. During Sharon's federal action to nullify a state court award to Hill of a judgment of divorce and alimony, he died, and Hill married David S. Terry, one of Field's former colleagues on the California Supreme Court. Hill and Terry were outraged by Field's ruling, precipitating a courtroom brawl that resulted in Field citing them for contempt and sentencing them to jail.

Terry began a campaign of public vilification of Field, going so far as to threaten to kill him. Against all warnings, in 1889 Field returned to California for circuit duties. He traveled with David Neagle, a federal marshal who had been assigned to protect him. While eating breakfast on his way to Los Angeles, where he was to hold court, Field was attacked by Terry, who struck him twice. Neagle, who believed Terry to be reaching for a weapon, drew his own gun and shot Terry dead.

Neagle was arrested by state officials and charged with murder under California law. He appealed to the federal circuit court for a writ of habeas corpus, which federal law authorized if a person was being held against federal law. California then appealed the grant of the writ, and the release of Neagle, to the U.S. Supreme Court.

Justice Stephen J. Field.
(Library of Congress)

Justice Field did not participate in the case, which by a 6-2 vote upheld the lower court's grant of the writ. While the majority interpreted the authority under which the writ was granted to mean that federal "law" included Neagle's performance of his assigned duties as a federal marshal, the minority objected that this was a strained interpretation formulated solely to justify the intrusion of the federal government into the jurisdiction of state criminal law.

To be sure, the Court wanted to save Neagle—who had possibly saved the life of one of their own in the course of doing his job—from the vagaries of California law. In effect, however, the Supreme Court decided that the federal circuit court had the authority, on the basis of a petition for a writ of habeas corpus and without benefit of the fact-finding process afforded by a trial, to make a determination that Terry's murder had been justifiable homicide. The majority of laws governing criminal behavior are promulgated by individual states, and when criminal matters come before federal courts, customarily it is state law that applies. *In re Neagle* thus expanded federal judicial and executive power into a realm normally reserved for the states.

Lisa Paddock

See also *Dombrowski v. Pfister; Ex parte Young; Martin v. Hunter's Lessee; Murdock v. Memphis; Younger v. Harris.*

In re Winship

Court: U.S. Supreme Court
Citation: 397 U.S. 358
Date: March 31, 1970
Issues: Juvenile justice

• The U.S. Supreme Court ruled that any judicial proceeding involving a possible loss of liberty, including juvenile courts, must use the standard of guilt beyond a reasonable doubt.

In the landmark case, *In re Gault* (1967), the Supreme Court ruled that juvenile courts must apply the fundamental procedural guarantees of due process that are enjoyed by adults in criminal trials. In conformity with New York state law, nevertheless, a family court judge used the preponderance of evidence standard when sentencing twelve-year-old Samuel Winship to a school for juvenile delinquents. By a 6-3 vote, the Supreme Court overturned the sentence. Writing for the Court, Justice William J. Brennan, Jr., declared that the reasonable doubt standard is among "the essentials of due process and fair treatment." Throughout the nation's legal history, he argued, there had been "virtual unanimous adherence" to this demanding burden of proof. In dissent, Justice Hugo L. Black accused the majority of amending the Bill of Rights, which was silent about the standard of proof necessary for a criminal conviction. The next year, in *McKeiver v. Pennsylvania* (1971), the Court decided that juveniles did not have the right to a trial by jury.

Thomas Tandy Lewis

See also *Brecht v. Abrahamson; In re Gault; Johnson v. Louisiana; McKeiver v. Pennsylvania.*

INSULAR CASES

DeLIMA v. BIDWELL

Court: U.S. Supreme Court
Citation: 182 U.S. 1
Date: May 27, 1901

DOWNES v. BIDWELL

Court: U.S. Supreme Court
Citation: 182 U.S. 244
Date: May 27, 1901
Issues: Treaties

• In the two *Insular Cases*, the U.S. Supreme Court determined the constitutional status of overseas possessions of the United States.

In 1898, the United States acquired an overseas empire. Hawaii was annexed by joint resolution of both houses of Congress, and Puerto Rico, Guam, and the Philippine Islands were ceded to the United States by Spain under the terms of the Treaty of Paris, which ended the Spanish-American War. In a series of decisions known as the *Insular Cases*, or *Insular Tariff Cases*, the U.S. Supreme Court was called on to fashion a constitutional compromise whereby the territorial acquisitions desired by the national political forces would be rendered legitimate. The litigation is an excellent example of the flexibility of constitutional and statutory interpretation that the Supreme Court enjoys.

The drive to acquire foreign territory was led by Republican chieftains such as Theodore Roosevelt and Senator Henry Cabot Lodge, whereas opponents of "imperialism" were primarily Democrats. Much of the debate focused on the question of Senate advice and consent to the peace treaty negotiated by President William McKinley with Spain. One of the chief constitutional arguments used by the opponents of expansion was the slogan "The Constitution follows the flag," which was designed to dramatize the impractical nature of the annexation of territory that offered no prospect of being organized into states. Anti-imperialists such as Senator George G. Vest of Missouri and Senator George Hoar of Massachusetts argued that the Constitution did not give the federal government the power to acquire territories to be held permanently in subjugation as colonies. The power to acquire territories, they claimed, was inextricably connected with the responsibility to organize those territories into prospective states.

Moreover, they argued that imperialism by its very nature was contrary to the republican form of government established under the Constitution. Anti-imperialists also cited the Declaration of Independence as a general indictment of colonial arrangements. Vest made another constitutional argument against acquisition of colonies when he interpreted the Fourteenth Amendment's declaration that "all persons born or naturalized in the United States, and subject to the jurisdiction thereof, are citizens of the United States."

The advocates of expansion contended that the success of the United States in the Spanish-American War destined the nation for a major role in world affairs and that it was naïve to postpone the acquisition of colonies. Apologists for acquisition argued that colonies would provide the growing United States with outposts essential to the nation's security, ensure its control of the seas, and underwrite the steady growth of its burgeoning industry.

Arguments in the Case
Arguments in what the Court called the *Insular Tariff Cases* were heard for six days in January, 1901, and the Court's opinions were announced on May 27, 1901. The principles set forth at that time also determined the outcomes of two other cases that had been argued in December, 1899. In *DeLima v. Bidwell* (1901), the Court divided five to four on the question of the application of the general tariff laws (the Dingley Tariff) to imports from Puerto Rico following the proclamation of the treaty with Spain. In stating the majority

opinion, Justice Henry B. Brown said, "We are therefore of the opinion that at the time these duties were levied, Puerto Rico was not a foreign country within the meaning of the tariff laws but a territory of the United States, that the duties were illegally exacted, and that the plaintiffs are entitled to recover them back."

In a dissenting opinion, Justice Joseph McKenna, supported by Justices George Shiras and Edward D. White, contended that Puerto Rico's status as a foreign or nonforeign country had nothing to do with whether the tariff laws were applicable. It was clear, argued McKenna, that the island was not a part of the United States, and therefore the tariff laws should apply. Justice Horace Gray wrote a separate brief dissent.

The justices who dissented in *DeLima v. Bidwell* were joined by Justice Brown in the companion case of *Downes v. Bidwell* and, as if to dramatize the judicial confusion, Justice Brown again delivered the lead opinion. The question in *Downes v. Bidwell* concerned the validity of a special tariff law applicable only to Puerto Rico (the Foraker Act, also known as the Organic Act of 1900). Justice Brown concluded a long opinion surveying the applicable precedents and practices with the declaration that the judiciary must be careful not to impede the development of "the American Empire." The annexation of distant possessions "inhabited by alien races, differing from us in religion, customs,

Justice Joseph McKenna.
(Library of Congress)

laws, methods of taxation and modes of thought," might some day be desirable. He continued:

> The question at once arises whether large concessions ought not to be made for a time, that, ultimately, our own theories may be carried out, and the blessings of a free government under the Constitution extended to them. We decline to hold that there is anything in the Constitution to forbid such action.

Brown went on to rule that Puerto Rico was a "territory appurtenant and belonging to the United States, but not a part of the United States within the revenue clauses of the Constitution" and that the Foraker Act was, therefore, constitutional.

In a concurring opinion supported by Shiras and McKenna, Justice White introduced his theory of incorporation, which subsequently came to be the prevailing doctrine. According to White, "Whilst in an international sense Puerto Rico was not a foreign country, since it was subject to the sovereignty of and was owned by the United States, it was foreign to the United States in a domestic sense, because the island had not been incorporated into the United States, but was merely appurtenant thereto as a possession." It followed from this, said White, that the constitutional requirement that duties be uniform throughout the United States was not applicable to Congress in legislating for the island. Justice Gray solitarily concurred and argued that the law was valid because Puerto Rico was in a transitional stage from conquered territory to statehood.

Dissenting Opinions

Chief Justice Melville W. Fuller's dissenting opinion in *Downes v. Bidwell* was supported by the three justices who, along with Brown, had made up the *DeLima v. Bidwell* majority: John Marshall Harlan, David J. Brewer, and Rufus W. Peckham. Fuller urged that the Constitution did indeed follow the flag, that Puerto Rico was not a foreign country, and that Congress had violated the constitutional requirement that all taxes, duties, and imposts be uniform throughout the United States. Justice Harlan wrote a separate dissenting opinion that, among other things, attacked White's theory of incorporation.

Many constitutional scholars consider Harlan's dissent to be one of the great opinions in the history of the U.S. Supreme Court. Harlan asserted that it was not legitimate to argue, as the majority did, that Congress could take away some or any rights from territories of the United States. He held that the Constitution was in force wherever the U.S. flag had been planted. In the case of Puerto Rico and the Philippines, that meant residents of those islands had full constitutional rights and protections from the moment the Senate ratified the treaty making them U.S. possessions. That had been accomplished in 1899, with ratification of the treaty with Spain ending the Spanish-American War. Justice Harlan rejected the racist argument raised by some members of the Court, that the Filipinos and Puerto Ricans were "alien races" not covered by the Anglo-Saxon-inspired Constitution. He concluded his dissent with a warning: "The Constitution is not to be obeyed or disobeyed as the circumstances of a particular crisis in our history may suggest. . . . The People have decreed that it shall be the supreme law of the land at all times."

The majority did not accept Harlan's view that once a territory becomes part of the United States, its people must have all the protections enjoyed by all citizens. Residents of the new island territories were denied equal protection of the law, chiefly because they were considered to be racially inferior and unready for most democratic rights. Thus, contrary to what Harlan believed to be the ideas of the Framers of the Constitution, the Court supported a policy that allowed people to be governed without their consent.

Significance

In subsequent cases dealing with the question of the Constitution's applicability to territories, the Court was presented with questions having to do with the rights of criminal defendants within the rights of constitutional guarantees. Justice Brown again employed the extension theory in *Hawaii v. Mankichi* (1903) in finding that Congress had not extended the guarantees of the Bill of Rights to Hawaii. It was permissible, therefore, for Hawaii to try the defendant on the basis of any information instead of a grand jury indictment and to convict him on the strength of only nine guilty votes out of a jury of twelve. On the basis of his incorporation theory, Justice White agreed with this opinion, and this time he was joined by Justice McKenna.

The next year, in *Dorr v. United States* (1904), White's incorporation theory was adopted by a Court majority; it held that until the Philippines were incorporated into the United States by Congress, the latter could administer the territory under its general power to govern territory and without honoring all of the applicable constitutional guarantees. Subsequently, the Court held that Alaska had been sufficiently incorporated to warrant application of the Fifth, Sixth, and Seventh Amendments; in *Rasmussen v. United States* (1905) the Court reversed a conviction of a defendant found guilty on the basis of a six-person jury. In *Dowdell v. United States* (1911), the Court applied the same logic but reached the conclusion that the Philippines were not incorporated; therefore, it was permissible for territorial authorities to employ juries of fewer than twelve persons. Finally, in *Puerto Rico v. Tapia* (1918), the Court ruled that the congressional grant of citizenship to Puerto Ricans did not necessarily mean that these citizens were protected by the traditional constitutional guarantees.

Alaska and Hawaii, the two territories that the Supreme Court found to have been incorporated, became states of the Union on January 3 and August 21, 1959, respectively. The Philippines, Puerto Rico, and the Virgin Islands have not been incorporated, but the inhabitants of the two West Indian territories have been declared U.S. citizens. Incorporation was never an issue insofar as the other minor possessions were concerned.

James J. Bolner and Leslie V. Tischauser

Further Reading

Acosta-Belén, Edna, and Carlos Enrique Santiago. *Puerto Ricans in the United States: A Contemporary Portrait.* Boulder, Colo.: Lynne Rienner, 2006. Richly descriptive account of Puerto Rican lives in the United States through the early twenty-first century.

Cabán, Pedro A. *Constructing a Colonial People: Puerto Rico and the United States, 1898-1932.* Boulder, Colo.: Westview Press, 1999. Addresses how the relationship between the United States and Puerto Rico was formed following U.S. acquisition of the territory. Includes discussion of the impacts of the Supreme Court's decisions in the *Insular Cases.*

Gould, Lewis L. *The Spanish-American War and President McKinley.* Lawrence: University Press of Kansas, 1980. Provides useful background material on the acquisition of U.S. colonies. Discusses attitudes of U.S. leaders that led to denial of equal treatment for Filipinos and Puerto Ricans.

Henkin, Louis. *Foreign Affairs and the U.S. Constitution.* 2d ed. New York: Oxford University Press, 1996. Discusses how interpretations of the Constitution affect the ways in which the United States conducts foreign affairs. Includes information on the impacts of the *Insular Cases* on U.S. policy.

Kerr, James E. *The Insular Cases: The Role of the Judiciary in American Expansionism.* Port Washington, N.Y.: Kennikat Press, 1982. A detailed guide to the intricacies of the Court's decision making. Discusses the attitudes of all nine justices.

LaFeber, Walter. *The New Empire: An Interpretation of American Expansion, 1860-1898.* 35th anniversary ed. Ithaca, N.Y.: Cornell University Press, 1998. Describes the attitudes and beliefs of the supporters of expansion. A good summary of events leading to the *Insular* decisions.

Ringer, Benjamin B. *"We the People" and Others: Duality and America's Treatment of Its Racial Minorities.* New York: Tavistock, 1983. Massive work discusses the constitutional significance of the denial of rights in the *Insular* decisions. Describes the impact of those decisions on the peoples in the Philippines and Puerto Rico.

Thompson, Winfred Lee. *The Introduction of American Law in the Philippines and Puerto Rico, 1898-1905*. Fayetteville: University of Arkansas Press, 1989. Excellent guide to the Supreme Court's various decisions and to the impact of the Court's views on the citizens of U.S. island possessions.

See also *Duncan v. Kahanamoku; Reynolds v. United States; Scott v. Sandford; Worcester v. Georgia.*

JACKSON V. METROPOLITAN EDISON CO.

Court: U.S. Supreme Court
Citation: 419 U.S. 345
Date: December 23, 1974
Issues: Due process of law

• The U.S. Supreme Court, in a ruling involving a utility company, set a standard for determining when actions by private entities were public enough to fall under the constitutional limitations applied to the government.

A Pennsylvania resident claimed that Metropolitan Edison Co., a private utility company, failed to provide adequate notice and a public hearing before terminating her electrical service, thus violating her due process rights. The resident argued that the utility was an extensively regulated partial monopoly, but the Supreme Court did not find the company to be sufficiently public to merit the burden of the constitutional limits placed on governments. The due process clause, the Court argued, applies only to state actions, not those of a private entity such as the utility. This ruling was never overturned, but it was limited by a number of legislative enactments.

Richard L. Wilson

See also *Ashwander v. Tennessee Valley Authority; Chicago, Milwaukee, and St. Paul Railway Co. v. Minnesota; Smyth v. Ames; Wolff Packing Co. v. Court of Industrial Relations.*

Jacobellis v. Ohio

Court: U.S. Supreme Court
Citation: 378 U.S. 184
Date: June 22, 1964
Issues: Pornography and obscenity

- The U.S. Supreme Court ruled that a French film was not obscene and could not be banned but was divided as to its reasoning.

Justice William J. Brennan, Jr., wrote the opinion for the 5-3 majority, which held that a particular French film was not obscene by national standards and could not be banned—obscene or not—without violating freedom of expression. In his opinion, Brennan stated that the "community standards" used to determine obscenity were those of "society at large." In addition, to be obscene, material must be "utterly without redeeming social importance." Although Brennan wrote the majority opinion, all eight justices wrote either concurring or dissenting opinions. Justice Brennan and Justices Potter Stewart and Arthur J. Goldberg determined that the film was not obscene. In his opinion, Justice Stewart said he found it difficult to define obscenity; however, he stated, "I know it when I see it." Justices Hugo L. Black and William O. Douglas had no opinion on whether the film was obscene or not; however, they found that it would violate the First Amendment to ban the file regardless of the question of obscenity. Chief Justice Earl Warren and Justices Tom C. Clark and John M. Harlan II dissented, finding the film obscene. Justice Byron R. White did not participate in the decision.

Richard L. Wilson

See also *Memoirs v. Massachusetts; Miller v. California; New York v. Ferber; Roth v. United States.*

JACOBSON V. MASSACHUSETTS

Court: U.S. Supreme Court
Citation: 197 U.S. 11
Date: February 20, 1905
Issues: Constitutionalism

- The U.S. Supreme Court limited people's ability to make general claims that their rights were protected by the "spirit" of the Constitution's preamble or body.

Henning Jacobson refused to submit to a smallpox vaccination pursuant to a duly passed Massachusetts state law and Cambridge city ordinance and was fined five dollars. At trial, Jacobson insisted that the "spirit" of the Constitution's preamble and the wording of the Fourteenth Amendment meant he did not have to submit to vaccination. He further attempted to assert that there might be unfavorable health consequences to vaccination, the risk of which he should not be required to endure.

By a 7-2 vote, the Supreme Court rejected Jacobson's claim that he could use the "spirit" of the Constitution's preamble or the "spirit" of the body of the Constitution to assert rights, noting that the specific words of the document were all that could be used to invalidate a state statute. In the opinion for the Court, Justice John Marshall Harlan noted that Jacobson could not show specific harm was likely to follow from his being vaccinated. The Court further asserted that a state did not have to show that every vaccination would be a complete success in order to impose on its citizens a medical procedure that had been shown to be more helpful than harmful to the vast majority of the population in a situation involving a disease that was potentially epidemic. Justices David J. Brewer and Rufus W. Peckham dissented.

Richard L. Wilson

See also *Griswold v. Connecticut*; *McCulloch v. Maryland*; *Martin v. Hunter's Lessee*; *Muller v. Oregon*.

JOHNSON AND GRAHAM'S LESSEE V. MCINTOSH

Court: U.S. Supreme Court
Citation: 21 U.S. 543 (8 Wheat)
Date: March 10, 1823
Issues: Land law; Native American sovereignty

- Going back to the rights of discovery and conquest, the U.S. Supreme Court upheld the U.S. government's ultimate authority to extinguish title of occupancy and to convey title in the soil.

In 1775 Thomas Johnson purchased land in Illinois from the Piankeshaw tribe, but Virginia conveyed the land to the federal government for the public domain in 1783. In 1818 William McIntosh purchased part of this Illinois land from the federal government, but the Johnson family claimed to be the legitimate owner. By a 7-2 vote, the Supreme Court ruled in favor of McIntosh and held that the tribe had not possessed an absolute right to sell its land.

Writing for the Court, Chief Justice John Marshall paid homage to the idea of natural justice, while deciding on the basis of positive law and actual practice. He found that the property rights of natives, although not entirely disregarded, were "to a considerable extent, impaired." The discovering European nations had exercised "ultimate dominion" to decide questions of land ownership. Native Americans had been mere "occupants" of the land. Conquest had given "a title which the courts of the conqueror cannot deny," and it superseded any consideration for "original justice." British authority over land title, moreover, had been transferred to the government of the United States. Although the rhetoric changed, subsequent Court decisions upheld Marshall's position on congressional authority over tribal land claims.

Thomas Tandy Lewis

See also *California v. Cabazon Band of Mission Indians; Cherokee Cases; Employment Division, Department of Human Resources of Oregon v. Smith; Ex parte Crow Dog; Santa Clara Pueblo v. Martinez; Talton v. Mayes; United States v. Kagama; Worcester v. Georgia.*

JOHNSON V. LOUISIANA

Court: U.S. Supreme Court
Citation: 400 U.S. 356
Date: January 10, 1972 and May 22, 1972
Issues: Common law; Juries

- The U.S. Supreme Court held that convictions based on nonunanimous jury verdicts in state criminal trials do not violate the due process clause of the Fourteenth Amendment.

In the common law tradition, criminal convictions were based on the unanimous agreement of twelve-member juries. In 1968 the Supreme Court required states to provide jury trials in criminal cases, but it did not specify whether all of the common-law requirements were applicable to the states. In *Williams v. Florida* (1970), the Court approved the use of six-person juries in noncapital state trials. The state of Louisiana had a statute that allowed convictions based on nine jurors out of twelve in noncapital cases. Oregon had a similar law. The Court considered the constitutionality of the Louisiana law in the *Johnson* case, and it reviewed the Oregon law in the companion case of *Apodaca v. Oregon* (1972).

By a 5-4 vote, a divided Court surprised many observers when it departed from the unanimity rule. In a plurality opinion, Justice Byron R. White argued that nine out of twelve votes was a "substantial majority" and that the "disagreement of three jurors does not alone establish reasonable doubt." Justice Lewis F. Powell, Jr., joined the majority ruling in regard to state trials, but he argued in a concurring opinion that the Sixth Amendment, based on history and precedent, required a unanimous jury in federal trials. The four dissenters insisted that the same standards should apply to federal and state trials and that a nonunanimous verdict was inconsistent with the "beyond a reasonable doubt" standard.

The *Johnson* and *Apodaca* decisions, in view of *Williams*, left observers wondering about the relationship between jury size and the unanimity principle. The Court met that issue in *Burch v. Louisiana* (1979), requiring that unanimous verdicts are required in six-member juries.

Thomas Tandy Lewis

See also *Ballew v. Georgia; Williams v. Florida.*

JOHNSON V. SANTA CLARA COUNTY

Court: U.S. Supreme Court
Citation: 480 U.S. 616
Date: March 25, 1987
Issues: Affirmative action

- The U.S. Supreme Court rejected a reverse discrimination claim in which a female employee was promoted over a white male employee who was judged slightly more qualified.

In *United Steelworkers of America v. Weber* (1979), the Supreme Court ruled that Title VII of the Civil Rights Law of 1964 did not prohibit race-conscious affirmative action to eliminate racial imbalance in traditionally segregated job categories. In 1978 the Transportation Agency of Santa Clara County, California, adopted a voluntary plan to address gender and racial disparity in job classifications. Although women made up 76 percent of the agency's office and clerical staff, there were no women among its skilled craft workers. In a competition for promotion to road dispatcher, both Diane Joyce and Paul Johnson were rated as well qualified, but Johnson had slightly higher scores on the exams. When Joyce was promoted, Johnson sued for gender discrimination under Title VII.

The Court rejected Johnson's claim by a 6-3 vote. Speaking for the majority, Justice William J. Brennan, Jr., using the reasoning in the *Weber* precedent, held that a limited gender preference was an appropriate means to remedy the imbalance between men and women in skilled job classifications. Brennan emphasized three points: First, Santa Clara's plan used flexible goals rather than rigid quotas; second, gender was only one factor in the promotion choice; and third, men were not completely barred from future promotions in the agency. The decision was based on Title VII rather than the Fourteenth Amendment; therefore, there was no need to discuss the standards of strict or intermediate scrutiny. In a spirited dissent, Justice Antonin Scalia argued that Title VII's purpose was to guarantee that race and sex would not be the basis for employment determinations.

In the 1990's there was a strong movement against the continuing use of gender and race preferences in employment. In 1997 the Court refused to consider a challenge to California's constitutional amendment prohibiting such preferences. Nevertheless, the *Johnson* decision continued to be good law except in states with constitutional prohibitions against preferences.

Thomas Tandy Lewis

See also *Martin v. Wilks; Regents of the University of California v. Bakke; United Jewish Organizations of Williamsburgh v. Carey; United Steelworkers of America v. Weber.*

Johnson v. Zerbst

Court: U.S. Supreme Court
Citation: 304 U.S. 458
Date: May 23, 1938
Issues: Right to counsel

• The U.S. Supreme Court held that indigent defendants have a constitutional right to be represented by counsel in federal criminal proceedings.

In examining an appeal of a person convicted of counterfeiting, the Supreme Court ruled, by a 6-2 margin, that the Sixth Amendment prohibits the federal government from depriving any person of life or liberty unless the person has or waives the assistance of counsel. In the case of an indigent defendant, therefore, the federal government has the obligation of appointing and paying for a competent attorney. The *Johnson* requirement was later extended to state criminal proceedings in *Gideon v. Wainwright* (1963) and *Argersinger v. Hamlin* (1972).

Thomas Tandy Lewis

See also *Argersinger v. Hamlin; Betts v. Brady; Edwards v. California; Gideon v. Wainwright; Miranda v. Arizona; Powell v. Alabama.*

Joint Anti-Fascist Refugee Committee v. McGrath

Court: U.S. Supreme Court
Citation: 341 U.S. 123
Date: April 30, 1951
Issues: Antigovernment subversion; Freedom of assembly and association

- During a period of hostility to civil liberties, the U.S. Supreme Court issued a ruling regarding a list of allegedly subversive organizations that favored freedom of association.

In March, 1947, President Harry S. Truman issued an executive order creating a list of subversive organizations. Seventy-eight allegedly subversive organizations were placed in six classifications on the attorney general's list. The organizations were placed on the list without a hearing and were not given the opportunity to appeal or ask for a judicial review. Three groups, including the Joint Anti-Fascist Refugee Committee, objected to being declared unpatriotic, which caused them to be severely criticized in various public and private settings. Although lower courts found for the federal government, the Supreme Court, by a 5-3 vote, determined that the government had violated the constitutional rights of these groups. The Court found that the manner in which various groups had been placed on the attorney general's list of subversive organizations violated their constitutional rights. The five justices in the majority wrote separate opinions, thereby weakening the impact of the majority holding. Chief Justice Fred M. Vinson and Justices Sherman Minton and Stanley F. Reed dissented. Justice Tom C. Clark did not participate.

Richard L. Wilson

See also *Chaplinsky v. New Hampshire; Communist Party v. Subversive Activities Control Board; Noto v. United States; United States v. Robel.*

JONES V. ALFRED H. MAYER CO.

Court: U.S. Supreme Court
Citation: 392 U.S. 409
Date: June 17, 1968
Issues: Civil rights and liberties; Private discrimination; Slavery

• Reversing many precedents, the Court held that the 1866 Civil Rights Act prohibited both private and state-backed discrimination and that the Thirteenth Amendment authorized Congress to prohibit private acts of discrimination as "the badges of slavery."

Joseph Lee Jones, alleging that a real estate company had refused to sell him a house because he was African American, sought relief in a federal district court. Since the case appeared before the passage of the Civil Rights Act of 1968, Jones and his lawyer relied primarily on a provision of the 1866 Civil Rights Act that gave all citizens the same rights as white citizens in property transactions. Both the district court and the court of appeals dismissed the complaint based on the established view that the 1866 law applied only to state action and did not address private acts of discrimination. The U.S. Supreme Court, however, accepted the case for review.

All the precedents of the Supreme Court supported the conclusions of the lower courts. In the *Civil Rights Cases* (1883) the Court had ruled that the Thirteenth Amendment allowed Congress to abolish "all badges and incidents of slavery," but the Court had narrowly interpreted these badges or incidents as not applying to private acts of discrimination. In *Hodges v. United States* (1906) the Court held that Congress might prohibit only private actions that marked "a state of entire subjection of one person to the will of another," and even in *Shelley v. Kraemer* (1948) the Court recognized the right of individuals to make racially restrictive covenants.

In *Jones,* however, the Court surprised observers by voting seven to two to overturn its precedents. Writing for the majority, Justice Potter Stewart asserted that Congress under the Thirteenth Amendment possessed the power "to determine what are the badges and incidents of slavery, and the authority to translate that determination into effective legislation." In addition, the majority reinterpreted the 1866 law so that it proscribed both governmental and private discrimination in property transactions—an interpretation that is questioned by many authorities.

Justice John M. Harlan wrote a dissenting opinion which argued that the majority was probably wrong in its interpretation of the 1866 law. Harlan also wrote that the passage of the Fair Housing Act of 1968 eliminated the need to render this decision that relied on such questionable history.

Since the *Jones* decision was based on the Thirteenth rather than the Fourteenth Amendment, it was important in diluting the Court's traditional distinction between state and private action, and it appeared to grant Congress almost unlimited power to outlaw private racial discrimination. *Jones* became a precedent for new applications of the almost forgotten post-Civil War statutes in cases such as *Griffin v. Breckenridge* (1971) and *Runyon v. McCrary* (1976). In the quarter-century after *Jones*, however, the Congress did not pass any major legislation based upon the authority of the Thirteenth Amendment.

Thomas Tandy Lewis

See also *Civil Rights Cases; Griffin v. Breckenridge; Patterson v. McLean Credit Union; Runyon v. McCrary; Shelley v. Kraemer; United States v. Guest.*

JONES V. VAN ZANDT

Court: U.S. Supreme Court
Citation: 46 U.S. 215
Date: March 5, 1847
Issues: Slavery

• The U.S. Supreme Court upheld the 1793 Fugitive Slave Act, declaring that slavery was a political question for the states to decide.

A conductor on the Underground Railroad, John Van Zandt, was accused of hiding and assisting fugitive slaves in violation of the 1793 Fugitive Slave Act. Salmon P. Chase, attorney and future chief justice, defended Van Zandt before the Supreme Court, arguing that Congress had no enforcement power with regard to slavery and that the act was unconstitutional. However, the Court unanimously upheld the constitutionality of the 1793 act. In the opinion for the Court, Justice Levi Woodbury rejected all the abolitionist arguments presented by the petitioners for the fugitive slaves. He stated that slavery was one of the "sacred" compromises that led to the adoption of the U.S.

Poster cautioning free blacks living in Boston in 1851 against dealing with the authorities lest they be mistaken for fugitive slaves and returned to slavery. (Library of Congress)

Constitution and, therefore, was beyond reach of the Court. The legitimacy of slavery as an institution was a political question to be determined by the states, not the Court.

Richard L. Wilson

See also *Ableman v. Booth; Antelope, The; Groves v. Slaughter; Kentucky v. Dennison; Scott v. Sandford.*

KAGAMA, UNITED STATES V. *See* UNITED STATES V. KAGAMA

Kansas v. Hendricks

Court: U.S. Supreme Court
Citation: 521 U.S. 346
Date: June 23, 1997
Issues: Double jeopardy

- The U.S. Supreme Court held that violent sexual predator legislation did not violate the Fourteenth Amendment's substantive due process clause nor did it trigger criminal protections, such as those against ex post facto laws and double jeopardy.

At issue was whether the Kansas violent sexual predator legislation was in effect criminal legislation that violated Leroy Hendricks's rights by imposing double jeopardy or ex post facto punishments. If the legislation was purely civil, then the question was whether the statute violated the substantive due process protections of the Fourteenth Amendment. By a 5-4 vote, the Supreme Court found that the legislation was not criminal and, therefore, the Court did not need to rule on the double jeopardy or ex post facto questions. The Court found that the statute was permissible under the Fourteenth Amendment. All justices conceded that Hendricks was a violent sexual predator with a record of multiple cases of child molestation.

Richard L. Wilson

See also *Benton v. Maryland; Calder v. Bull; Cummings v. Missouri; Fletcher v. Peck; Palko v. Connecticut; United States v. Lanza; United States v. Ursery.*

Kastigar v. United States

Court: U.S. Supreme Court
Citation: 406 U.S. 441
Date: May 22, 1972
Issues: Immunity from prosecution; Self-incrimination

- The U.S. Supreme Court upheld grants of use immunity as well as of transactional immunity as falling within the Fifth Amendment protection against self-incrimination.

By a 5-2 vote, the Supreme Court upheld a 1970 congressional enactment requiring witnesses to testify before grand juries under use immunity grants. Use immunity means the government cannot use any testimony or information obtained from testimony against the person granted immunity in any subsequent prosecution. Transactional immunity offers more protection because it covers any offenses related to testimony. Kastigar based his challenge on the idea that the protection against self-incrimination in the Fifth Amendment required at minimum transactional immunity, but the Court held that use immunity was sufficient. By upholding use immunity, the Court strengthened the hand of prosecutors. Subsequently, grants of use immunity for grand jury testimony increased dramatically.

Richard L. Wilson

See also *Albertson v. Subversive Activities Control Board; Boyd v. United States; Counselman v. Hitchcock; Griffin v. California; Kilbourn v. Thompson; Malloy v. Hogan; Murphy v. Waterfront Commission of New York.*

KATZ V. UNITED STATES

Court: U.S. Supreme Court
Citation: 389 U.S. 347
Date: December 18, 1967
Issues: Right to privacy; Search and seizure

- The U.S. Supreme Court determined that electronic surveillance constitutes a search subject to the Fourth Amendment's warrant and probable cause provisions.

Katz was convicted of transmitting wagering information over the telephone on the basis of information he gave over a public telephone which he habitually used. The Federal Bureau of Investigation gained access to this information by attaching an external listening device to the telephone booth. The lower court concluded that since the booth had not been physically invaded, this investigative method did not constitute a "search" within the meaning of the Fourth Amendment, which requires an antecedent showing of probable cause and the issuance of a warrant. The Supreme Court, however, finding that the government had violated Katz's "legitimate expectation" of privacy, declared that the government's methods did indeed constitute a search and reversed the ruling.

Katz v. United States substituted a "reasonable expectation of privacy" test for the physical intrusion test the Court had previously used to determine if a police search and seizure was constitutional. This new test was cogently phrased in Justice John M. Harlan's concurring opinion: "[T]here is a twofold requirement, first that a person have exhibited an actual (subjective) expectation of privacy and, second, that the expectation be one that society is prepared to recognize as 'reasonable.'" Harlan's opinion was used by lower courts to parse the meaning of *Katz*, but as he himself later recognized in *United States v. White* (1971), any evaluation of a questionable search must of necessity "transcend the search for subjective expectations." The government could, for example, defeat any expectation of privacy in telephone conversations by issuing a declaration that all such conversations are subject to third-party eavesdropping.

The reasonableness requirement may mean that an expectation of privacy in a particular realm must be shared by a majority of Americans. It could also mean that although there are areas in which reasonable individuals might legitimately expect to maintain their privacy, such expectations can be superseded by more important policy considerations, such as the need for railroad engineers to give blood and urine specimens for purposes of drug testing.

In *White*, Harlan defined searches as "those more extensive intrusions that significantly jeopardize the sense of security which is the paramount concern of Fourth Amendment liberties," but the Supreme Court has applied the *Katz* doctrine narrowly. In *United States v. Miller* (1976), for example, the Court ruled that persons do not have a reasonable expectation of privacy as to bank records of their financial transactions. In *Smith v. Maryland* (1979), the Court found that while individuals might reasonably expect the content of their telephone conversations to remain private, they cannot entertain a similar expectation as to the telephone numbers they call. In both cases, the Court based its decision on the fact that the information plaintiffs claimed to be off limits to police was already accessed by others—bank employees and telephone companies, respectively.

Lisa Paddock

See also *Chimel v. California; Hudson v. Palmer; Skinner v. Railway Labor Executives' Association.*

Katzenbach v. McClung

Court: U.S. Supreme Court
Citation: 379 U.S. 294
Date: December 14, 1964
Issues: Racial discrimination; Regulation of commerce

• This decision represents the broadest interpretation of the commerce clause ever issued by the U.S. Supreme Court.

Early in U.S. history, the Supreme Court made a distinction between interstate commerce, which was regulated by the federal government, and intrastate commerce, which was the province of the states. Starting with *National Labor Relations Board v. Jones and Laughlin Steel Corp.* (1937), the Court began abandoning the distinction, and, by the time of *Katzenbach*, it was virtually gone. In *Katzenbach*, Ollie's Barbecue, a family-owned restaurant that bought its food locally and served people from the area, refused to seat African Americans. The Court ruled that the commerce clause applied, giving Congress power to regulate discrimination, because even a small portion of the food served may have moved in interstate commerce. The Court also found that the restaurant's discriminatory practices violated the public accommodations provision of the 1964 Civil Rights Act. This decision considerably broadened the powers of Congress to regulate commerce.

Richard L. Wilson

See also *Buchanan v. Warley; Heart of Atlanta Motel v. United States; National Labor Relations Board v. Jones and Laughlin Steel Corp.*

Katzenbach v. Morgan

Court: U.S. Supreme Court
Citation: 384 U.S. 641
Date: June 13, 1966
Issues: Voting rights

• The U.S. Supreme Court recognized the right of Congress to enforce its own interpretation of Fourteenth Amendment rights.

A New York statute required passage of an English literacy test in order to register to vote. In *Lassiter v. Northampton County Board of Elections* (1959), the Court had held that such literacy requirements did not violate the Fourteenth Amendment. New York's attorney general argued that Congress could not invoke the enforcement provision of the Fourteenth Amendment to prohibit implementation of a state law when that law had not been judged unconstitutional by the judicial branch.

However, by a 7-2 vote, the Court upheld a provision of the Voting Rights Act of 1965, providing that no person who had completed the sixth grade in an accredited Puerto Rican school could be denied the right to vote because of an inability to read or write English. Speaking for the majority, Justice William J. Brennan, Jr., argued that the Framers of the Fourteenth Amendment intended section 5 to give Congress broad powers to enforce the rights enumerated in the amendment. Brennan wrote, moreover, that Congress had the prerogative of interpreting the U.S. Constitution in ways that expanded on the rights that were recognized by the courts. Justice John M. Harlan II's dissent warned that if Congress could expand on the Court's interpretations of constitutional rights, it could logically also restrict some guarantees. Most commentators have concluded that the majority of the justices rejected Brennan's expansive view of congressional prerogatives in *Oregon v. Mitchell* (1970).

Thomas Tandy Lewis

See also *Lassiter v. Northampton County Board of Elections*; *Oregon v. Mitchell*; *South Carolina v. Katzenbach*.

KELO V. CITY OF NEW LONDON

Court: U.S. Supreme Court
Citation: 545 U.S. 469
Date: June 23, 2005
Issues: Land law; Property rights; Takings clause;
Taxation

- The U.S. Supreme Court held that government may use its power of eminent domain to seize private property against an owner's will for the purpose of transferring the property to private developers to promote economic development and increase the tax base.

When the city government of New London, Connecticut, became alarmed that the tax base was continually decreasing, it authorized a private entity, the New London Development Corporation (NLDC), to devise plans for economic development. When the Pfizer Corporation built a plant near the Fort Trumbull neighborhood, which contained mostly older homes, the city approved an NLDC plan to acquire the neighborhood in order to encourage economic activity. Among the owners of 115 residential and commercial lots, fifteen property owners refused to sell their lots. The city chose to exercise its power of eminent domain and authorized the NLDC to seize the lots. The controversy attracted national attention because such seizures were becoming increasingly common.

Susette Kelo and the other property owners sued the city, arguing that the Fifth Amendment only authorized the taking of property for a "public use," not to sell the land to private developers. The city countered that the concept of public use was broad enough to include considerations of employment and the alleviation of the city's economic distress. The Connecticut Supreme Court agreed with the city's position.

The U.S. Supreme Court upheld the ruling by a 5-4 margin. Defending the decision, Justice John Paul Stevens argued that the taking of land in New London was not simply for the private benefit of a few private individuals, but rather it was part of a development plan to promote the public's interest in overcoming economic difficulties. Rather than a narrow and "literal" reading of the takings clause, Stevens defended a "broader and more natural interpretation of public use as 'public purpose.'"

Justice Sandra Day O'Connor characterized the majority decision as a "reverse Robin Hood" action, taking from the poor to give to the rich. Justice Clarence Thomas wrote that the development plan appeared to give special consideration to the needs of the Pfizer Corporation. Throughout the country, property owners indicated strong agreement with the Court's minority. Minnesota and other states responded to the Court's ruling with legislation that significantly restricted applications of the eminent domain power.

Thomas Tandy Lewis

See also *Barron v. Baltimore; Berman v. Parker; Hawaii Housing Authority v. Midkiff; Nollan v. California Coastal Commission; West River Bridge Co. v. Dix.*

Kennedy v. Louisiana

Court: U.S. Supreme Court
Citation: 554 U.S. ____
Date: June 25, 2008
Issues: Capital punishment; Children's rights; Cruel and unusual punishment

- In an opinion that infuriated many people, the U.S. Supreme Court ruled that the Eighth Amendment does not permit the states to execute an offender for the crime of rape, even when the victim is a young child, at least when the child does not die and the offender did not intend to kill the child.

When Patrick Kennedy, a resident of New Orleans, Louisiana, reported the rape of his eight-year-old stepdaughter, he initially tried to blame two neighborhood boys for the crime. The incident was extraordinarily shocking: The sexual assault had torn the girl's perineum from the opening of her vagina to her anal opening, and it badly ripped the interior of her vagina, which was partially penetrated into her rectum. When the evidence against Kennedy became overwhelming, he refused to accept the offer of a plea bargain that would have spared him from the death sentence. At trial, he was found guilty and sentenced to death under a 1995 Louisiana law that allowed the penalty for the rape of children younger than twelve.

Appealing the sentence, Kennedy argued that it was inconsistent with the constitutional ban on cruel and unusual punishments. The Louisiana Supreme Court, however, rejected the challenge, based on their readings of the U.S. Supreme Court's precedents. First, *Coker v. Georgia* (1977) had disallowed executions for the rape of an adult, based on the theory that the punishment was grossly disproportionate. One U.S. Supreme Court justice, Lewis F. Powell, Jr., had only concurred to the extent that the crime had not been committed with excessive brutality. The Louisiana court concluded that capital punishment was not excessive for the brutal rape of a young child. In two other precedents, *Atkins v. Virginia* (2002) and *Roper v. Simmons* (2005), the U.S. Supreme Court had suggested that the death penalty might be permissible under conditions of a national consensus, and the Louisiana court argued that the fact that five other states had capital punishment laws like the one in Louisiana was sufficient evidence of a consensus. The Louisiana decision was appealed to the nation's highest court.

The Court's Ruling

After the U.S. Supreme Court reviewed the case, the judges split, five to four, to overturn the Louisiana court's ruling, holding that it is unconstitutional to impose the death penalty simply for the crime of rape, regardless of the victim's age. In the opinion for the Court, Justice Anthony Kennedy addressed the two major justifications that the Louisiana court had used. Concerning the issue of a national consensus, Kennedy declared that six out of fifty states did not constitute such a consensus. Secondly, he considered whether the death penalty was excessive for the violent rape of a child, and he concluded that it was. Even if the crime in this case was "devastating" to the young girl, its "severity and irrevocability" did not compare to the crime of intentional murder. Justice Kennedy was determined not to depart from the principle that "the death penalty should not be expanded to instances where the victim's life was not taken." Curiously, however, the opinion left open the possibility that the Eighth Amendment might not disallow capital punishment for "treason, espionage, terrorism, and drug kingpin activity, which are offenses against the state."

In a dissenting opinion, Justice Samuel Alito accused the majority of usurping the role of the legislatures. Finding no evidence of a national consensus that the execution of a child rapist was a cruel and unusual punishment, he charged that the decision prevented a full debate on "whether the death penalty for the targeted offense of raping a young child is consistent with prevailing standards of decency." He vehemently disagreed with a "blanket rule" that barred the death penalty in all cases regardless of circumstances, such as the victim's age, the sadistic nature of the incident, and the number of times that the offender might have committed a similar offense.

Only a few days after the Court's ruling was announced, an Internet blogger named Dwight Sullivan publicized the fact that the Supreme Court had not been informed that two years earlier that Congress had revised the Uniform Code of Military Justice, adding child rape on the list of crimes punishable by death. After journalist Linda Greenhouse pointed out this fact in *The New York Times*, eighty-five members of Congress petitioned the Supreme Court to rehear the case in light of the congressional action. On October 1, 2008, however, the Court declined reconsideration. One of the dissenting justices, Antonin Scalia, concurred with the denial, asserting that public views on the death penalty for child rape were "irrelevant to the majority's opinion in this case." However, he took pleasure in adding that the congressional act "utterly destroys the majority's claim to be discerning a national consensus and not just giving effect to the majority's own preference."

Because *Kennedy v. Louisiana* was announced during the midst of a presidential campaign, it was not surprising that candidates commented on the controversial ruling. Both the Democratic and Republican presidential candidates, Barack Obama and John McCain, indicated that they strongly disagreed with the decision. Obama, who had studied constitutional law at the University of Chicago, criticized the Court's "blanket prohibition" and declared that the rape of a small child is a "heinous crime" and if a state decides that under well-defined circumstances the death penalty is potentially applicable, such a decision "does not violate our Constitution." McCain found it "profoundly disturbing" that "there is a judge anywhere in America who does not believe that the rape of a child represents the most heinous of crimes, which is deserving of the most serious of punishments."

Thomas Tandy Lewis

See also *Atkins v. Virginia; Coker v. Georgia; Roper v. Simmons.*

Kent v. Dulles

Court: U.S. Supreme Court
Citation: 357 U.S. 116
Date: June 16, 1958
Issues: Right to travel

- The U.S. Supreme Court ruled that the right to travel was part of the liberty guaranteed by the due process clause of the Fifth Amendment and that Congress had not authorized the secretary of state to deny passports because of beliefs or political affiliations.

In 1948 the Department of State established a policy of not issuing passports to communists, communist sympathizers, or individuals considered security risks. When Rockwell Kent was denied a passport, he argued that the policy was unconstitutional. Speaking for a 5-4 majority, Justice William O. Douglas held that the Immigration and Nationality Act of 1952 did not authorize the secretary of state to withhold passports from citizens because of their beliefs or political activities. Douglas reasoned that the right to domestic and international travel was a constitutional right; therefore, the Court would have to assume that Congress would not have attempted to curtail the right without an explicit statute. In order to get Justice Felix Frankfurter to join the majority, Douglas did not consider the constitutional powers of Congress to restrict travel. As a result of the decision, nevertheless, passport application forms ceased to ask questions about Communist Party membership. Expanding on *Kent*, the Court limited the authority of Congress to restrict travel in *Aptheker v. Secretary of State* (1964).

Thomas Tandy Lewis

See also *Afroyim v. Rusk; Aptheker v. Secretary of State; Edwards v. California; Immigration and Naturalization Service v. Chadha; Shapiro v. Thompson.*

KENTUCKY V. DENNISON

Court: U.S. Supreme Court
Citation: 65 U.S. 66
Date: March 14, 1861
Issues: Slavery

• The U.S. Supreme Court ruled that it had no power to force state governors to extradite accused persons from their states, a decision that lasted until 1987.

A free black Ohioan helped a Kentucky slave escape to Ohio. The Kentucky governor asked two Ohio governors, first Salmon P. Chase then William Dennison, to extradite the Ohioan to Kentucky to stand trial for violating the fugitive slave laws, but both refused. The Kentucky governor sued Dennison under the Supreme Court's original jurisdiction involving suits between two states. Chief Justice Roger Brooke Taney was strongly proslavery but was apparently reluctant—in the emotionally charged days before the Civil War—to have the Court order the state governors to do anything. In writing the unanimous decision for the Court, Taney criticized the Ohio governors severely but held that the Court could not force them to extradite fugitives from one state to another. This ruling stood until *Puerto Rico v. Branstad* (1987).

Richard L. Wilson

See also *Ableman v. Booth; Antelope, The; Groves v. Slaughter; Jones v. Van Zandt; Scott v. Sandford.*

KER V. CALIFORNIA

Court: U.S. Supreme Court
Citation: 374 U.S. 23
Date: June 10, 1963
Issues: Search and seizure

- The U.S. Supreme Court defined the extent to which the federal rules covering searches and seizures should apply to the states.

California authorities entered the apartment of George and Diane Ker using a passkey and conducted a warrantless search during which they found and seized marijuana. In a 5-4 decision, the Supreme Court upheld their convictions, but the Court was divided about the facts of the case. Eight justices held that the state was required to adhere to federal standards, but a plurality of four, in an opinion written by Tom C. Clark, held that California had met those standards. Justice John M. Harlan II concurred in the result, but apparently was the only justice who thought that states should be held to a more flexible standard than the federal government. Chief Justice Earl Warren and Justices William J. Brennan, Jr., Arthur J. Goldberg, and William O. Douglas agreed that the states should be held to the same strict standards as the federal government when conducting searches and seizures but did not believe the actions of the California authorities should qualify under federal standards. The exclusionary rule applied in the *Mapp v. Ohio* (1961) decision remained a weapon for use by the Court even after this decision.

Richard L. Wilson

See also *Chimel v. California; Harris v. United States; Mapp v. Ohio; Marshall v. Barlow's; New York v. Belton; Wolf v. Colorado.*

Keyes v. Denver School District No. 1

Court: U.S. Supreme Court
Citation: 413 U.S. 189
Date: June 21, 1973
Issues: Desegregation; Education

- In its first school desegregation case involving a major city outside the South, the U.S. Supreme Court held that a district-wide busing plan was an appropriate remedy for a situation in which official policies had encouraged the establishment of racially segregated schools in any section within the district.

A federal district judge ordered a desegregation plan for the Park Hill section of Denver, Colorado, after he concluded that school officials had adopted policies promoting and encouraging segregation of the schools in that section. The judge did not require a citywide desegregation plan because of a lack of proof that other neighborhood schools were segregated as a result of intentional policy.

Speaking for a 7-1 majority, Justice William J. Brennan, Jr., held that a finding of deliberate segregation in one significant portion of a district is sufficient to shift the burden to school officials to prove that segregation elsewhere in the district is not also a result of official policy. School officials could avoid the imposition of a desegregation plan for the entire district only if they could prove that the district had not promoted segregation in some places through its choices of school construction sites, its drawing of attendance zones, and its pursuance of other such policies. Without such evidence, said Brennan, the school board had "an affirmative duty to desegregate the entire system, 'root and branch.'" Rejecting the arguments of two justices, the majority endorsed the continuing validity of the de jure/de facto distinction in school desegregation cases. The case was sent back to the district court, which adopted a system-wide busing plan.

The controversial *Keyes* decision allowed an expansion of court-ordered busing plans into many urban districts that were primarily segregated on a de facto basis. In *Milliken v. Bradley* (1974), however, the Court decided not to extend the reasoning of *Keyes* to a large urban region that was divided into many school districts.

Thomas Tandy Lewis

See also *Board of Education of Oklahoma City v. Dowell; Brown v. Board of Education; Columbus Board of Education v. Penick; Lemon v. Kurtzman; Milliken v. Bradley; Parents Involved in Community Schools v. Seattle School District No. 1; Swann v. Charlotte-Mecklenburg Board of Education.*

KEYISHIAN V. BOARD OF REGENTS

Court: U.S. Supreme Court
Citation: 385 U.S. 589
Date: January 23, 1967
Issues: Antigovernment subversion; Loyalty oaths

- The U.S. Supreme Court struck down loyalty oaths for public school teachers.

Justice William J. Brennan, Jr., wrote the decision for the 5-4 majority that struck down a New York law requiring public school teachers to swear a loyalty oath certifying that they were not communists or members of allegedly subversive organizations. The Supreme Court ruled that the law deprived them of their free speech rights and meant a citizen had improperly to risk losing constitutional rights in order to accept public employment. A major part of the law's failing was its unconstitutional vagueness that did not separate advocacy of an abstract doctrine from actual incitement to violence. Justices Tom C. Clark, John M. Harlan II, Potter Stewart, and Byron R. White dissented.

Richard L. Wilson

See also *Aptheker v. Secretary of State; Communist Party v. Subversive Activities Control Board; Dennis v. United States; Scales v. United States; Yates v. United States.*

KEYSTONE BITUMINOUS COAL ASSOCIATION V. DEBENEDICTIS

Court: U.S. Supreme Court
Citation: 480 U.S. 470
Date: March 9, 1987
Issues: Freedom of contract; Takings clause

• The U.S. Supreme Court held that a Pennsylvania law prohibiting underground mining that causes damage to surface structures does not violate either the takings clause or the contracts clause.

In 1966 the Pennsylvania legislature enacted a law prohibiting coal mining that caused subsidence damage to preexisting public buildings, dwellings, and cemeteries. Based on *Pennsylvania Coal Co. v. Mahon* (1922), the Keystone Bituminous Coal Association argued that it should be paid compensation for its inability to mine coal in certain places. The company also alleged that the law prevented the enforcement of its existing contracts that waived liability for surface damage.

Speaking for a 5-4 majority, Justice John Paul Stevens reasoned that a state could exercise its police power to protect the public's safety and welfare and that no Fifth Amendment taking occurs when landowners are not deprived of all economic use of their property. Observing that the statute deprived the company of less than 2 percent of its coal, Stevens found that Court precedents did not allow the company to divide property parcels into component parts when deciding whether the government was required to pay compensation. In regard to the contracts clause challenge, Stevens found that established precedents allowed contractual impairments judged reasonable and necessary for achieving important public purposes. "It is well-settled," he wrote, "that the prohibition against impairing the obligation of contracts is not to be read literally."

Thomas Tandy Lewis

See also *Lucas v. South Carolina Coastal Council; Nollan v. California Coastal Commission; Pennsylvania Coal Co. v. Mahon.*

KIDD V. PEARSON

Court: U.S. Supreme Court
Citation: 128 U.S. 1
Date: October 22, 1888
Issues: Regulation of commerce

- The U.S. Supreme Court's ruling created a distinction between manufacturing and commerce that survived many years but is no longer valid.

An Iowa law that prohibited companies from manufacturing liquor for sale outside the state was challenged as an unconstitutional attempt by a state to regulate interstate commerce. The Supreme Court upheld the statute, making a distinction between manufacturing and commerce. It ruled that under the commerce clause, congressional regulatory power did not extend to the manufacture of products. The Court stated that the police power of states was sufficient for them to regulate the manufacture of a potentially dangerous product such as alcohol without interfering with federal powers. This distinction survived for many years but was gradually abandoned by later Courts as they expanded federal control over commerce.

Richard L. Wilson

See also *Heart of Atlanta Motel v. United States*; *Katzenbach v. McClung*; *National Labor Relations Board v. Jones and Laughlin Steel Corp.*; *Wickard v. Filburn.*

KILBOURN V. THOMPSON

Court: U.S. Supreme Court
Citation: 103 U.S. 168
Date: February 28, 1881
Issues: Congressional powers

- The U.S. Supreme Court declared that Congress's investigative power and its derivative contempt power were limited to legislative not judicial purposes.

Justice Samuel F. Miller wrote the unanimous opinion of the Supreme Court in this decision, holding that Congress may conduct investigations to obtain information only for future legislation and not for judicial purposes. For this reason, the congressional attempt to subpoena Hallett Kilbourn, hold him in contempt, and imprison him were improper. In later decisions, the Court did allow for punishment for contempt of Congress and also allowed a broader definition of the scope of legislative investigation.

Richard L. Wilson

See also *Barenblatt v. United States; Ex parte McCardle; Helvering v. Davis; Kidd v. Pearson; Panama Refining Co. v. Ryan; Schechter Poultry Corp. v. United States; Yakus v. United States.*

Justice Samuel F. Miller.
(Library of Congress)

KIRKPATRICK V. PREISLER

Court: U.S. Supreme Court
Citation: 394 U.S. 526
Date: April 7, 1969
Issues: Reapportionment and redistricting

- The U.S. Supreme Court's decision regarding a Missouri congressional redistricting act established that legislative districts should be as mathematically equal as possible.

The Supreme Court, by a 6-3 vote, upheld a federal district court's overturning of a 1967 Missouri congressional redistricting statute. In the opinion for the Court, Justice William J. Brennan, Jr., held that there is no minimum population variance acceptable between districts in redistricting cases involving the House of Representatives. The one-person, one-vote principle means that all districts must be as precisely equal as possible, thereby ending the last of the arguments in legislative redistricting that a small variation should be acceptable. This case was broadly worded and was thought to apply to state legislative district cases as well, but the Court made it clear in *Mahan v. Howell* (1973) that state legislatures had greater latitude in redistricting themselves. Justices John M. Harlan II, Potter Stewart, and Byron R. White dissented.

Richard L. Wilson

See also *Colegrove v. Green; Gray v. Sanders; Mahan v. Howell; Reynolds v. Sims; Wesberry v. Sanders.*

KLOPFER V. NORTH CAROLINA

Court: U.S. Supreme Court
Citation: 386 U.S. 213
Date: March 13, 1967
Issues: Trial by jury

- The U.S. Supreme Court applied the Sixth Amendment's promise of a speedy trial to the states through the Fourteenth Amendment's due process clause under the incorporation doctrine.

Klopfer had been indicted by North Carolina for criminal trespass for taking part in a sit-in demonstration in a restaurant. At Klopfer's trial, the jury failed to reach an agreement, and the judge declared a mistrial. This meant the state could retry Klopfer, but the state prosecutor elected to persuade a court to delay the trial indefinitely. Klopfer sued and appealed in all relevant North Carolina courts without success. Finally he appealed to the Supreme Court, which ruled against North Carolina. The 6-3 majority opinion, written by Chief Justice Earl Warren, stated the uncertainty and delay that inevitably resulted from the state's procedure had deprived Klopfer of his liberty without due process of law. The Court also used the incorporation doctrine to apply the Sixth Amendment guarantee of speedy trial to the states. Justices John M. Harlan II and Potter Stewart dissented. In later cases, the Court often used a balancing test that generally favors the prosecution, as it did in *Barker v. Wingo* (1972).

Richard L. Wilson

See also *Barker v. Wingo; Brown v. Mississippi; Duncan v. Louisiana; Sheppard v. Maxwell.*

KNIGHT CO., UNITED STATES V. *See* UNITED STATES V. E. C. KNIGHT CO.

KNOWLES V. IOWA

Court: U.S. Supreme Court
Citation: 525 U.S. 113
Date: December 8, 1998
Issues: Police powers; Search and seizure

- This U.S. Supreme Court decision limited the authority of police to search cars while conducting routine traffic stops. Police could no longer search cars after traffic stops without either consent or probable cause.

Starting with its decision in *Carroll v. United States* (1925), the U.S. Supreme Court recognized that police can stop and search vehicles without the benefit of a warrant. The mobility of automobiles would allow for the destruction of evidence before the police could obtain a lawful warrant. Police do not, however, have a free hand in searching cars, as seen in *Knowles v. Iowa*.

A man named Knowles was pulled over for speeding by an Iowa state policeman. The officer wrote Knowles a citation for speeding, then conducted a search of Knowles's car without his consent. The officer did not have probable cause for conducting the search and had not arrested Knowles. The search turned up drug paraphernalia, and Knowles was arrested and convicted on drug charges in Iowa state court. Knowles appealed, claiming the search of his car violated the Fourth Amendment's ban on unreasonable search and seizure. Knowles's appeals were denied by Iowa appellate courts, and he appealed the case to the U.S. Supreme Court.

The Supreme Court overturned the conviction. In writing the opinion for a unanimous court, Chief Justice William Rehnquist noted that police could search automobiles either with the consent of the owner during a lawful arrest or to protect evidence of a crime. Rehnquist stated that the officer had only conducted a routine traffic stop and had not suspicion nor probable cause to believe Knowles was engaged in illegal activity. Without such cause, the officer had no reason to search the car.

According to Rehnquist, after writing the traffic citation for speeding, the officer was required to allow Knowles to continue on his way without a search. Conducting a routine traffic stop did not provide the officer with the basis for a full search of the automobile. Because the search was illegal under the Fourth Amendment, the drug evidence was to be excluded from any trial of Knowles.

The Knowles decision cut back on the authority of police to search cars on public highways. The Rehnquist court, which usually ruled for police in such cases, instead noted that the Fourth Amendment did prohibit searches that were not linked to an arrest or some probable cause. The ruling created a clearer definition of the circumstances under which police could use traffic stops as a reason for conducting full-blown searches of automobiles and people.

Douglas Clouatre

Further Reading

Franklin, Paula. *The Fourth Amendment.* New York: Silver Burdett Press, 2001.
    Study of the limitations placed on police powers by the Fourth Amendment.

Wetterer, Charles M. *The Fourth Amendment: Search and Seizure.* Springfield, N.J.: Enslow, 1998. Discusses the various aspects of search and seizure law and how the courts have interpreted the amendment.

See also *California v. Acevedo; Carroll v. United States; Harris v. United States; Illinois v. Caballes; Illinois v. Krull; United States v. Ross.*

======

KOREMATSU V. UNITED STATES

Court: U.S. Supreme Court
Citation: 323 U.S. 214
Date: December 18, 1944
Issues: Due process of law

- Based on the argument of military necessity, the U.S. Supreme Court upheld the exclusion of persons of Japanese ancestry from the West Coast and the requirement that they report to assembly centers, which almost always resulted in assignment to internment camps.

After the United States entered into a war with Japan, President Franklin D. Roosevelt issued executive orders authorizing a military program that removed persons of Japanese descent from the West Coast and resettled them in internment centers. Congress enacted a statute that implemented the executive orders. In *Hirabayashi v. United States* (1943), the Court unanimously upheld the military's curfew that applied almost exclusively to persons of Japanese ethnicity, but the Court refused to even consider the more fundamental issues of exclusion and resettlement.

Fred Korematsu was a Japanese American who tried to evade the evacuation program in order to live and work in California. When discovered, he was prosecuted for two crimes: remaining in the restricted area and not reporting to an assembly center for assignment under the program. He was sentenced to five years in prison but was paroled and sent to an internment camp in Utah. Korematsu claimed that his conviction violated the due process clause of the Fifth Amendment.

By a 6-3 vote, the Supreme Court rejected Korematsu's claim. Writing for the majority, Justice Hugo L. Black accepted the military's argument that the presence of Japanese Americans on the West Coast presented a danger to national security, and he insisted that their "temporary exclusion" was based on military necessity rather than any racial hostility. Although Black accepted the exclusion program without any solid evidence of sabotage or espionage, he nevertheless wrote that "all legal restrictions that curtail the rights of a single racial group are immediately suspect" and must be given "the most rigid scrutiny." Ironically, this statement helped establish the Court's use of the strict scrutiny test in cases involving racial restrictions. Because Korematsu was not convicted under the internment portion of the program, Black avoided any consideration of internment, and he examined only the constitutionality of the exclusion and reporting requirements.

The three dissenters emphasized the issue of racial discrimination and worried about future applications of the *Korematsu* precedent. Justice Frank Murphy wrote an especially strong dissent challenging "this legalization of racism" and insisted that investigations of Japanese Americans should have

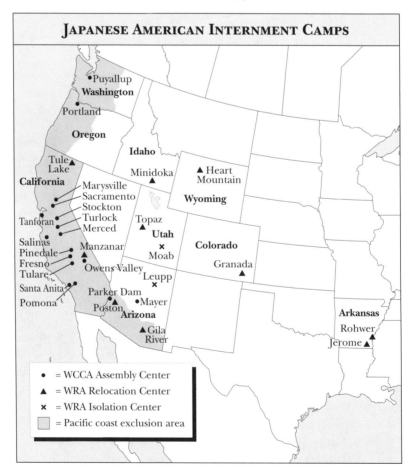

been conducted "on an individual basis" as had been done in cases involving persons of German and Italian ancestry.

In *Ex parte Endo*, announced the same day as *Korematsu*, the Court narrowly ruled that the War Relocation Authority must release any person whose loyalty to the United States had been clearly established. Because of the difficult burden of proof requirements in the *Endo* decision, this did not help Korematsu and most other Japanese Americans. In the 1980's lawyer Peter Irons discovered that the military had concealed evidence about Korematsu and others from the courts, and their convictions were overturned.

Thomas Tandy Lewis

See also *Ex parte Milligan*; *Hirabayashi v. United States*; *Ozawa v. United States*.

Ku Klux Klan case. *See* Ex parte Yarbrough

Kunz v. New York

Court: U.S. Supreme Court
Citation: 340 U.S. 290
Date: January 15, 1951
Issues: Freedom of speech

• The U.S. Supreme Court held that government statutes regulating speech must be narrowly drawn so that they do not unduly restrict freedom of expression.

Carl Kunz was a Baptist minister convicted of preaching on the New York City streets without a permit. Kunz, who had been accused of "scurrilous attacks on other religions" during earlier street preaching incidents, was denied a permit even though the ordinance contained no standards for determining the criteria for denying a permit. The Supreme Court judged the New York ordinance to be vague and overbroad, both constitutional defects, and reversed Kunz's conviction. The Court found that the New York ordinance,

*Justice Robert H.
Jackson.* (Harris &
Ewing/Collection of the
Supreme Court of the
United States)

which gave officials the authority to prevent people from speaking, constituted an unacceptable prior restraint on speech, in violation of the First
Amendment. Chief Justice Fred M. Vinson wrote the opinion for the 8-1 majority, with Justices Hugo L. Black and Felix Frankfurter concurring in the result only. Justice Robert H. Jackson dissented, stating the majority had missed
the point of the case entirely because the facts indicated that the defendant
had used profanity or "fighting words," which were not entitled to free speech
protection.

Richard L. Wilson

See also *Brandenburg v. Ohio; Feiner v. New York; Gitlow v. New York; Schenck v.
United States.*

KYLLO V. UNITED STATES

Court: U.S. Supreme Court
Citation: 533 U.S. 27
Date: June 11, 2001
Issues: Illegal drugs; Police powers; Right to privacy; Search and seizure

- In a decision that limited the use of modern privacy-threatening technology, the U.S. Supreme Court held that police must have a search warrant in order to use a thermal imager to detect patterns of heat coming from a private home.

In 1992, federal agents aimed a sensitive heat detector, the Agema Thermovision 210, at Danny Kyllo's home in Florence, Oregon. The agents were acting on the basis of tips and utility bills suggesting the possibility that Kyllo might be growing marijuana indoors under high-intensity lamps. After the instrument registered suspicious-looking hot spots, the agents obtained a warrant to enter and search the home, where they discovered more than one hundred marijuana plants growing under lamps. Although Kyllo agreed to plead guilty of a misdemeanor requiring one month in jail, he contested the validity of the search.

The Supreme Court, by a 5-4 margin, agreed with Kyllo's contention that the warrantless use of the thermal imager had violated his "reasonable expectation of privacy." Writing the opinion for the Court, Justice Antonin Scalia argued that the most fundamental purpose of the Fourth Amendment was to keep private homes "safe from prying government eyes," and he emphasized the importance of not "leaving the homeowner at the mercy of advancing technology." In a surprising dissent, Justice John Paul Stevens, who was often called the Court's most liberal justice, wrote that the use of the device outside the home "did not invade any constitutionally protected interest in privacy."

The Kyllo ruling highlighted the unpredictable nature of the Court's line drawing when applying Fourth Amendment principles. The previous year, in *Bond v. United States*, a 7-2 majority of Court had found that the police had engaged in an unconstitutional search when they walked down the aisle of a bus and squeezed a passenger's luggage to look for contraband. In that case, Stevens had voted with the majority, while Scalia had dissented.

Thomas Tandy Lewis

See also *California v. Acevedo; California v. Greenwood; Carroll v. United States; Chimel v. California; Illinois v. McArthur; Knowles v. Iowa; Marshall v. Barlow's; Payton v. New York; United States v. Leon; United States v. United States District Court.*

LANZA, UNITED STATES V. *See* UNITED STATES V. LANZA

LASSITER V. NORTHAMPTON COUNTY BOARD OF ELECTIONS

Court: U.S. Supreme Court
Citation: 360 U.S. 45
Date: June 8, 1959
Issues: Voting rights

- The U.S. Supreme Court upheld the states' right to impose literacy tests for voting.

An African American challenged a state literacy test that applied to voters of all races. The Supreme Court did not infer that the test was being used to discriminate against minorities and unanimously upheld the state law. In his opinion for the Court, Justice William O. Douglas wrote that states had wide latitude in passing laws establishing conditions for suffrage. This decision would seem to have stood in the way of the 1964 Civil Rights Act, which dispatched federal registrars to southern states that had often used literacy tests as a way to prevent African Americans from voting. The Court avoided that problem by asserting in *South Carolina v. Katzenbach* (1966) that the pattern of segregation justified special measures under the Fifteenth Amendment.

Richard L. Wilson

See also *Guinn v. United States; Katzenbach v. Morgan; South Carolina v. Katzenbach; United States v. Reese.*

LAU V. NICHOLS

Court: U.S. Supreme Court
Citation: 414 U.S. 563
Date: January 21, 1974
Issues: Civil rights and liberties; Education; Immigration

- The U.S. Supreme Court ruled that school districts must provide bilingual education to limited-English-speaking students. In 1975, the Office for Civil Rights established informal guidelines for four bilingual programs that would enable school districts to come into compliance with the Court's ruling.

In 1954, the U.S. Supreme Court ruled in *Brown v. Board of Education of Topeka, Kansas* that the Fourteenth Amendment to the U.S. Constitution forbade school systems to segregate students into separate schools for only whites or African Americans. The decision effectively overturned a previous Court ruling, in *Plessy v. Ferguson* (1896), that such facilities could be "separate but equal." Instead of desegregating, however, school systems in the American South engaged in massive resistance to the Court's order during the next decade. Congress then passed the Civil Rights Act of 1964, which prohibits many types of discrimination. Title VI of the law bans discrimination by recipients of federal financial assistance, including school systems.

In 1965, Congress adopted the Immigration and Nationality Act Amendments, under which larger numbers of Asian immigrants arrived in the United States than ever before, and their non-English-speaking children enrolled in public schools. In the San Francisco Unified School District, students were required to attend school until sixteen years of age, but in 1967, 2,856 students could not adequately comprehend instruction in English. Although 433 students were given supplemental courses in English on a full-time basis and 633 on a part-time basis, the remaining 1,790 students received no additional language instruction. Nevertheless, the state of California required all students to graduate with proficiency in English and permitted school districts to provide bilingual education, if needed. Except for the 433 students in the full-time bilingual education program, Chinese-speaking students were integrated in the same classrooms with English-speaking students but lacked sufficient language ability to derive benefit from the instruction. Of the 1,066 students taking bilingual courses, only 260 had bilingual teachers.

Some parents of the Chinese-speaking children, concerned that their children would drop out of school and experience pressure to join criminal youth gangs, launched protests. Various organizations formed in the Chinese American community, which in turn made studies, issued proposals, circulated leaflets, and tried to negotiate with the San Francisco Board of Education. When the board refused to respond adequately, a suit was filed in federal district court in San Francisco on March 25, 1970. The plaintiffs were Kinney Kinmon Lau and eleven other non-English-speaking students, mostly U.S. citizens born of Chinese parents. The defendants were Alan Hammond Nichols, president of the San Francisco Board of Education, the rest of the Board of Education, and the San Francisco Board of Supervisors.

On May 25, 1970, the Office for Civil Rights (OCR) of the U.S. Department of Health, Education, and Welfare issued the following regulation pursuant to its responsibility to monitor Title VI compliance: "Where inability to speak and understand the English language excludes national-origin minority group children from effective participation in the educational program offered by a school district, the district must take affirmative steps to rectify the language deficiency in order to open its instructional program to these students." OCR had sided with the Chinese-speaking students.

One day later, the court ruled that the school system was violating neither Title VI nor the Fourteenth Amendment; instead, the plaintiffs were characterized as asking for "special rights above those granted other children." Lawyers representing the Chinese Americans then appealed, this time supported by a friend-of-the-court brief filed by the U.S. Department of Justice. On January 8, 1973, the court of appeals also ruled adversely, stating that there was no duty "to rectify appellants' special deficiencies, as long as they provided these students with access to the same educational system made available to all other students." The appeals court claimed that the children's problems were "not the result of law enacted by the state . . . but the result of deficiency created by themselves in failing to learn the English language."

The Court's Ruling

On June 12, 1973, the Supreme Court agreed to hear the case. Oral argument was heard on December 10, 1973. On January 21, 1974, the Supreme Court unanimously overturned the lower courts. Justice William O. Douglas delivered the majority opinion, which included this memorable statement: "There is no equality of treatment merely by providing students with the same facilities, textbooks, teachers, and curriculum; for students who do not understand English are effectively foreclosed from any meaningful education." The Court returned the case to the district court so that the school system could design a plan of language-needs assessments and programs for addressing those needs. In a concurring opinion, Chief Justice Warren E. Burger and Justice Harry A. Blackmun observed that the number of underserved non-English-speaking, particularly Chinese-speaking, students was substantial in this case, but the justices would not order bilingual education for "just a single child who speaks only German or Polish or Spanish or any language other than English."

Significance

The Supreme Court's decision in *Lau* ultimately resulted in changes to enable Chinese-speaking students to obtain equal educational opportunity in San Francisco's public schools, although it was more than a year before such changes began to be implemented. The greatest impact has been among Spanish-speaking students, members of the largest language-minority group in the United States.

Subsequently, Congress passed the Equal Educational Opportunities Act in 1974, a provision of which superseded *Lau* by requiring "appropriate action to overcome language barriers that impede equal participation," which a federal district court later applied to the need for new methods to deal with speakers of Black English in *Martin Luther King, Jr., Elementary School Children v. Michigan Board of Education* (1979). Also in 1974, the Bilingual Education Act of 1968 was amended to provide more federal funds for second-language instruction so that school districts could be brought into compliance with *Lau*. Bilingualism was further recognized when Congress passed the Voting Rights Act of 1975, which established guidelines for providing ballots in the languages of certain minority groups.

In 1975, OCR established informal guidelines for four bilingual programs that would enable school districts to come into compliance with the Supreme Court ruling. The main requirement was first to test students to determine language proficiency. Students with no English proficiency at all were to be exposed to bilingual/bicultural programs or transitional bilingual education programs; secondary schools also had the option of providing "English as a second language" or "high intensive language training" programs. If a student had some familiarity with English, these four programs would be required only if testing revealed that the student had low achievement test scores.

Because the OCR guidelines were not published in the *Federal Register* for public comment and later modification, they were challenged on September 29, 1978, in the federal district court of Alaska (*Northwest Arctic School District v. Califano*). The case was settled by a consent decree in 1980, when the federal agency agreed to publish a "Notice of Proposed Rulemaking"; however, soon after Ronald Reagan took office as president, that notice was withdrawn. By 1985, a manual to identify types of language discrimination was compiled to supersede the 1975 guidelines, but it also was not published in the *Federal Register* for public comment. Meanwhile, methods for educating limited-English-speaking students evolved beyond the OCR's original conceptions, and further litigation followed. In 1981, a U.S. circuit court ruled in *Castañeda v. Pickard* that a bilingual educational program is lawful when it satisfies three tests: The program is recognized by professionals as sound in educational theory, the program is designed to implement that theory, and the program actually results in students' overcoming language barriers.

During the presidency of Ronald Reagan, federal civil rights monitoring focused more on "reverse discrimination" than on violations of equal educational opportunities. Congressional hearings were held to goad OCR into action. Although in 1991 OCR's top priority was equal educational opportunities for national-origin minority and Native American students with limited-English proficiency (LEP) or non-English proficiency (NEP), results were difficult to discern, and a movement to make English the official language of the United States (the "English-only" movement) threatened to overturn *Lau* and related legislation. California's Proposition 227, which was adopted in 1998 by popular vote, curtailed bilingual education in favor of mainstreaming. Arizona voters followed with a similar and even more restrictive measure calling for implementation of total immersion programs in 2000, indicating a popular backlash against bilingual programs in at least some states most affected by immigration.

Michael Haas

Further Reading

Biegel, Stuart. "The Parameters of the Bilingual Education Debate in California Twenty Years After *Lau v. Nichols.*" *Chicano-Latino Law Review* 14 (Winter, 1994): 48-60. The status of *Lau* in light of the 1990's English-only movement.

Blanton, Carlos Kevin. *The Strange Career of Bilingual Education in Texas, 1836-1981.* College Station: Texas A&M Press, 2004. Historical account of Texas's bilingual tradition and how various immigrant groups, including Spanish-speaking Tejano groups, adapted to or resisted government laws to assimilate into the mainstream English-speaking culture.

Bull, Barry L., Royal T. Fruehling, and Virgie Chattergy. *The Ethics of Multicultural and Bilingual Education.* New York: Columbia University Teachers College Press, 1992. Contrasts how liberal, democratic, and communitarian approaches to education relate to bilingual and multicultural education.

Fineberg, Elliot M., et al. "The Problems of Segregation and Inequality of Educational Opportunity." In *One Nation Indivisible: The Civil Rights Challenge for the 1990's,* edited by Reginald C. Govan and William L. Taylor. Washington, D.C.: Citizens' Commission on Civil Rights, 1989. Reviews underenforcement of laws dealing with language-minority students during the Reagan years.

Moran, Rachel F. "Of Democracy, Devaluation, and Bilingual Education." *Creighton Law Review* 26 (February, 1993): 255-319. Contrasts special-interest bargaining and bureaucratic rule-making methods for dealing with needs for bilingual education.

Newman, Terri Lunn. "Proposal: Bilingual Education Guidelines for the Courts and the Schools." *Emory Law Journal* 33 (Spring, 1984): 577-629. Legal requirements of *Lau* presented as guidelines for school systems in establishing bilingual programs.

Orlando, Carlos J., Mary Carol Combs, and Virginia P. Collier. *Bilingual and ESL Classrooms: Teaching in Multicultural Contexts.* 4th ed. New York: McGraw-Hill, 2006. Discusses the need for bilingual education, alternative approaches available, and resources required.

San Miguel, Guadalupe. *Contested Policy: The Rise and Fall of Federal Bilingual Education in the United States, 1960-2001.* Denton: University of North Texas Press, 2004. Traces the evolution of the contentious program, focusing on the years after 1978. Includes bibliographic references and index.

United States Commission on Civil Rights. *A Better Chance to Learn: Bilingual-Bicultural Education.* Washington, D.C.: Author, 1975. Assesses the national impact of *Lau*; contains the text of the Supreme Court decision and related documents.

Wang, L. Ling-chi. "*Lau v. Nichols*: History of Struggle for Equal and Quality Education." In *Asian-Americans: Social and Psychological Perspectives,* edited by Russell Endo, Stanley Sue, and Nathaniel N. Wagner. Palo Alto, Calif.: Science & Behavior Books, 1980. Describes how the *Lau* case was pursued, especially the resistance to implementation.

See also *Brown v. Board of Education; Meyer v. Nebraska; Plessy v. Ferguson.*

LAWRENCE V. TEXAS

Court: U.S. Supreme Court
Citation: 539 U.S. 558
Date: June 26, 2003
Issues: Gay and lesbian rights; Right to privacy

• In overturning a Texas statute that had outlawed homosexual conduct, the U.S. Supreme Court extended the Constitution's protection of "liberty interests" to gays and lesbians.

After the watershed case of *Griswold v. Connecticut* (1965), the Court emphasized that the due process clauses of the Fifth and Fourteenth Amendments protected a substantive right of generic liberty (or privacy), especially in intimate sexual relationships. The justices, however, often disagreed about the contours of this protection, and in *Bowers v. Hardwick* (1986), the Court held that Georgia's criminalization of homosexual sodomy did not violate the Constitution. The majority of the justices accepted the theory that the due process clauses protected only those liberties that had been recognized in the history and traditions of the United States.

In 1998, a Texas police officer, responding to a report of a weapons disturbance, entered the private apartment of John Lawrence. The officer observed Lawrence and another man in an act that was forbidden by Texas's antisodomy statute. The two men were found guilty and fined $125 each. The Texas Supreme Court upheld the judgment, based primarily on the *Hardwick* precedent.

When the case reached the U.S. Supreme Court, however, the justices, in a 5-1-3 decision, ruled that the Texas antisodomy law was unconstitutional. Speaking for five of the justices, Anthony M. Kennedy directly overturned *Hardwick* and recognized the liberty of consenting adults to make decisions about intimate relationships within the privacy of their homes. He argued that the Court's precedents since 1986 had expanded the scope of constitutional protection for liberty and that the decision of *Romer v. Evans* (1996) had weakened *Bowers* as a precedent. Kennedy noted that only thirteen states retained antisodomy statutes, with only four of these states actively enforcing those laws. Observing that the Court in *Bowers* had referred to Western traditions, he wrote that most Western countries no longer provided criminal penalties for homosexual practices. His opinion included expansive rhetoric about the need to respect gays and lesbians.

Although Justice Sandra Day O'Connor did not join Kennedy's opinion, she agreed that the law was unconstitutional. Her reasoning was that it violated the principle of equal protection because it punished only homosexual conduct, not heterosexual conduct. In a short dissent, Justice Clarence Thomas rejected the entire notion of a "general right of privacy." Justice Antonin Scalia's long dissent denounced the majority for supporting the "homosexual agenda." He warned that the logic of the decision might have broad consequences, such as forcing states to recognize same-sex marriages and requiring admission of openly gay persons into the military.

Thomas Tandy Lewis

See also *Bowers v. Hardwick*; *Griswold v. Connecticut*; *Romer v. Evans*.

LEE V. WEISMAN

Court: U.S. Supreme Court
Citation: 505 U.S. 577
Date: June 24, 1992
Issues: Establishment of religion

- The U.S. Supreme Court declared that public schools could not conduct prayer exercises at graduation ceremonies.

Graduation ceremonies at a high school in Providence, Rhode Island, were voluntary. When inviting local clergy to offer nonsectarian invocations and benedictions, the principal would give them guidelines suggesting the use of "inclusiveness and sensitivity." The principal took care to invite a diversity of local clergy—Protestant, Roman Catholic, Jewish, and others if available. Daniel Weisman, the father of two students, asked for a court order prohibiting the practice. In response, a federal appellate court ruled that the ceremony constituted an "advancement of religion" without a secular purpose, which was contrary to *Lemon v. Kurtzman* (1971). When the case was appealed to the Supreme Court, the administration of President George H. W. Bush submitted a brief asking the Court to overturn the *Lemon* precedent.

By a 5-4 vote, the Court upheld the lower court's judgment. Justice Anthony M. Kennedy emphasized the element of government coercion to participate in the ceremony, with social pressures on students to attend, to stand,

and to maintain respectful silence. In presenting clergy with guidelines for the prayers, moreover, the principal "directed and controlled the content of the prayer." Justice Antonin Scalia's dissent endorsed Kennedy's standard of coercion but found no coercion in this instance. The *Weisman* opinion did not limit the extent to which speakers at school events might discuss religious themes, and it did not address the question of whether students might organize prayer ceremonies without the involvement of public officials.

Thomas Tandy Lewis

See also *Agostini v. Felton; Brown v. Board of Education; Everson v. Board of Education of Ewing Township; Lemon v. Kurtzman; Swann v. Charlotte-Mecklenburg Board of Education.*

LEGAL TENDER CASES

HEPBURN V. GRISWOLD; PARKER V. DAVIS; AND KNOX V. LEE

Court: U.S. Supreme Court
Citations: 75 U.S. 603 (*Hepburn*); 79 U.S. 457 (*Parker* and *Knox*)
Date: February 7, 1870 (*Hepburn*); May 1, 1871 (*Parker* and *Knox*)
Issues: Fiscal and monetary powers; Freedom of contract; Takings clause; Warfare and terrorism

• With its decisions in these three cases, the U.S. Supreme Court clearly established the right of the U.S. government to pay its debts in paper money.

After a long tradition of rejecting the use of paper money as legal tender, the United States—including former secretary of the treasury and later chief justice Salmon P. Chase—found it necessary to use paper money temporarily during the Civil War. The Legal Tender Act of 1862 meant the paper money, called "greenbacks," had to be accepted in payment of debt, or debts could be forfeited. However, the paper currency depreciated compared with gold coins. In *Hepburn v. Griswold*, the Supreme Court, by a 4-3 vote, overturned the 1862 statute. Chase, who wrote the opinion for the Court, attempted with his decision to return to the earlier sound money era by holding that congressional enactment of the 1862 act violated the Fifth Amendment's due process clause as a taking and also violated the "spirit" of the contract clause. This case was heard by less than a full Court as the result of the machinations surrounding the Civil War and its aftermath.

After President Ulysses S. Grant was given an opportunity to appoint two members to the Court, the case was reheard. In *Parker v. Davis* and *Knox v. Lee*, decided a year later by a 5-4 vote, the Court reversed the *Hepburn* decision. Justice William Strong wrote the majority opinion with Justices Chase, Nathan Clifford, and Stephen J. Field dissenting. Important practical realities—and the principle of avoiding retroactive changes in obligations—led Justice Strong to write a decision that upheld congressional control of the currency as a legitimate implied power under the Constitution. Congressional power was upheld but the Court's prestige suffered.

Richard L. Wilson

See also *Briscoe v. Bank of the Commonwealth of Kentucky; Craig v. Missouri; Gold Clause Cases; Ware v. Hylton.*

LEMON V. KURTZMAN

Court: U.S. Supreme Court
Citation: 403 U.S. 602
Date: June 28, 1971
Issues: Education; Establishment of religion

- In *Lemon v. Kurtzman*, the U.S. Supreme Court established a three-part test to uphold the separation of church and state. Any government-sponsored act or legislation needed to pass the "*Lemon* test" to show that its intent was pervasively secular, that it did not prefer or inhibit any one religion over another, and that it did not produce excessive entanglement between government and religion.

Controversies over school busing and government support of parochial schools provided the background for *Lemon v. Kurtzman.* In the 1960's, Alton J. Lemon was one of many parents suing the state of Pennsylvania for violation of the U.S. Constitution, in particular the establishment clause of the First Amendment. Lemon was a resident of Pennsylvania whose child attended public school. Lemon claimed to have purchased a ticket at a horse track, thereby paying the Pennsylvania tax providing revenue for the Nonpublic Elementary and Secondary Education Act that diverted funds to largely Roman Catholic schools in the state.

In the 1947 case of *Everson v. Board of Education*, the Supreme Court upheld a law that reimbursed bus transportation costs to parents of children attending private schools. However, Justice Hugo L. Black wrote that the decision to support the law carried the Court to the limit of unconstitutionality. By allowing public money to go to families sending children to Catholic schools, the Court in *Everson* raised the question of whether the government was showing preference to one particular religion.

One impetus for the rise of private schools was the beginning of school desegregation following *Brown v. Board of Education of Topeka, Kansas* (1954), in which the Court ruled that the unfair policy of "separate but equal" schools for African American children and all other races was unconstitutional. The Court ordered that desegregation of schools take place beginning in 1955, but busing children of different races across school jurisdiction boundaries did not begin in earnest until 1971, following *Swann v. Charlotte-Mecklenburg Board of Education*. The growth of the suburbs also caused many white families to move away from cities and to choose private, church-sponsored schools if their children were required to be bused to racially diverse schools. Well before then, especially in the South and Midwest, private schools sponsored by the Roman Catholic Church and Protestant denominations had offered parents an alternative to the public schools. The private schools argued that they were responding to parents' requests for a more conservative, Bible-based curriculum, though it was often the case that parents were displeased with the prospect of their children riding buses to racially mixed schools.

Traditionally, the financial strength of public schools was based on the real estate tax revenues of each independent district. The reality of *Brown v. Board of Education* was that segregation, though illegal, still occurred along economic lines. African American populations tended to live in less prosperous, urban areas where property values were lower than for white, suburban families. More tax revenues thus flowed into public schools in wealthier districts.

Issues in the Case

At issue in *Lemon v. Kurtzman* were two similar state statutes from Pennsylvania and Rhode Island that allowed for transfer of public education funds to financially weaker religious schools. The Pennsylvania law was called the Nonpublic Elementary and Secondary Education Act. After the act was passed in 1968, the state of Pennsylvania's superintendent of public instruction, David H. Kurtzman, was authorized to reimburse private schools (most of which were Roman Catholic) for required textbooks and materials that did not pertain to religious subjects. The Rhode Island statute was called the Salary Supplement Act (1969), which allowed for a 15 percent supplementary increase to be given to private school teachers in school districts spending below state averages for per-student funding in the pubic schools. Most of these schools were also Roman Catholic. The Rhode Island supplement could be given only to teachers offering nonreligious courses common in the public schools.

The Court ruled that both the Pennsylvania and Rhode Island laws were unconstitutional because they violated the establishment clause and the free exercise clause of the First Amendment of the U.S. Constitution, which state, "Congress shall make no law respecting an establishment of religion, or prohibiting the free exercise thereof." Chief Justice Warren E. Burger wrote that the wording of the religion clauses is vague and difficult to interpret compared with the precision of most of the First Amendment. The First Amendment authors did not make absolutely illegal the future establishment of a state church, but they were well aware of the dangers of mixing religion and government. Burger wrote that the main injury the First Amendment authors wanted to prevent was government involvement in private religious groups.

The *Lemon* Test

Lemon v. Kurtzman established the so-called *Lemon* test, which outlines the limits of future legislation and government activity with reference to religion. According to the *Lemon* test, any law, act, or public display by the government must abide by three principles: It must be secular in purpose, it must not promote or prevent the practice of any one religion, and it must not become excessively entangled with religion. In the opinion written by Chief Justice Burger, the Supreme Court stated that the parochial school system in Rhode Island was "an integral part of the religious mission of the Catholic Church" and that the payments to private school teachers could be seen as "excessive entanglement" between church and state.

The Court's interpretation of "excessive entanglement" came about in the Rhode Island statute because the Catholic Church regulated the parochial school teachers. The Court held that religiously affiliated teachers could not be relied upon to deliver state-mandated secular curricula, especially in the early grades. The Court also held that the Rhode Island and Pennsylvania laws encouraged entanglement because the state superintendents were required to supervise instruction in secular subjects in church-related schools. Kurtzman's attorneys argued that the government upholds tax exemptions for places of religious worship, but the Court decided that the Rhode Island

and Pennsylvania laws were not based on generally accepted practice. These programs threatened to become self-perpetuating and self-expanding; if the programs continued unchecked, more religious groups might be encouraged to support educational ventures expecting government financial support.

Significance

Lemon v. Kurtzman was the definitive case for arguments about the separation of church and state in the late twentieth century. The Court ruled that government funding of any kind for religious education was illegal, but the *Lemon* test has neither been clearly defined nor consistently enforced over the years. States are not allowed to contribute to the salaries of teachers in private, religious schools; they cannot redirect money toward the maintenance of parochial school buildings or help to finance field trips or religious instructional materials; and they cannot reimburse parents for private school tuition. However, in some cases, states have been allowed to help finance the construction of new buildings intended for secular purposes at colleges with a religious affiliation, and states have been allowed to lend general textbooks to students in religious schools. Rather than submitting each new law to a rigorous screening to determine whether it passes the three-pronged test, the Court has allowed generally accepted practices to continue. Separation between church and state is not absolute simply because of building regulations, fire inspections, programs for school lunches, health services, transportation, and provision of textbooks. The Court has recognized that religion is important to the lives of many Americans even as it attempts to uphold the religion clauses of the Constitution.

Jonathan L. Thorndike

Further Reading

Bravin, Jess. "Court Hears Cases on Public Display of Commandments." *The Wall Street Journal,* March 3, 2005, p. A2. Reviews cases in Texas and Kentucky that affirmed the *Lemon* test and said that government references to religion must not advance or inhibit the practice of any religion.

Coyle, Marcia. "Justices Struggle with a 'Lemon.'" *National Law Journal,* July 3, 2000, p. A1. The U.S. Supreme Court is not willing to get rid of the *Lemon* test even though most justices believe that the landmark ruling is not a good constitutional test for violations of the separation between church and state.

Farish, Lean. *Lemon v. Kurtzman: The Religion and Public Funds Case.* Berkeley Heights, N.J.: Enslow, 2000. Accessible study that covers the background of the case but lacks energy and controversy.

See also *Abington School District v. Schempp; Allegheny County v. American Civil Liberties Union Greater Pittsburgh Chapter; Brown v. Board of Education; Edwards v. Aguillard; Everson v. Board of Education of Ewing Township; Mueller v. Allen; Swann v. Charlotte-Mecklenburg Board of Education; Zelman v. Simmons-Harris.*

Leon, United States v. *See* United States v. Leon

LICENSE CASES

Court: U.S. Supreme Court
Citation: 46 U.S. 504
Date: January 21, 1847
Issues: Interstate commerce; Police powers

• The U.S. Supreme Court unanimously upheld the validity of state taxes on the sale of imported liquor, but the justices disagreed about the basis of the ruling.

During the antebellum period, the Supreme Court found it difficult to harmonize federal authority over interstate commerce with the states' police powers. The legislatures of Massachusetts, Rhode Island, and New Hampshire enacted sales taxes on imported liquors, to the benefit of local retailers. In nine separate opinions, the justices were in general agreement that state taxes for police purposes might have an incidental effect on interstate commerce. Chief Justice Roger Brooke Taney and three other justices argued that states were free to regulate commerce in the absence of federal legislation. The other three justices viewed the state relations as a legitimate exercise of the state's police power to protect public health and morality. The *License Cases* influenced the development of the doctrine of selective exclusiveness, as articulated in *Cooley v. Board of Wardens of the Port of Philadelphia* (1852).

Thomas Tandy Lewis

See also *Brown v. Maryland; Cooley v. Board of Wardens of the Port of Philadelphia; Woodruff v. Parham.*

LOCAL 28 OF SHEET METAL WORKERS INTERNATIONAL ASSOCIATION V. EQUAL EMPLOYMENT OPPORTUNITY COMMISSION

Court: U.S. Supreme Court
Citation: 478 U.S. 421
Date: July 2, 1986
Issues: Affirmative action

- The U.S. Supreme Court approved a federal district court's order requiring a hiring goal and a timetable for the employment of minority workers as a remedy for a union's past discrimination.

A federal district court found that a labor union had discriminated against nonwhite workers in violation of Title VII of the Civil Rights Act of 1964. The court ordered the union to cease its discriminatory practices and to achieve a membership of 29 percent nonwhite workers, which would be equal to the percentage in the relevant labor pool. Speaking for a 5-4 majority, Justice William J. Brennan, Jr., concluded that Title VII did not prohibit courts from providing "make-whole" relief that included quotas and preferences affecting individuals who had not been the actual victims of discrimination. Although the Supreme Court under William H. Rehnquist subsequently decided to scrutinize affirmative action programs from a more critical perspective, the *Local 28* decision was never overturned.

Thomas Tandy Lewis

See also *Firefighters Local Union No. 1784 v. Stotts et al.; Griggs v. Duke Power Co.; Martin v. Wilks; Ricci v. DeStefano; United Steelworkers of America v. Weber; Wards Cove Packing Co. v. Atonio; Washington v. Davis.*

LOCHNER V. NEW YORK

Court: U.S. Supreme Court
Citation: 198 U.S. 45
Date: April 17, 1905
Issues: Labor law

• By ruling that maximum hours laws were unconstitutional in *Lochner v. New York*, the U.S. Supreme Court upheld the freedom of contract and severely limited the ability of states to enact workplace reform legislation.

On April 17, 1905, the U.S. Supreme Court ruled five to four in the case of *Lochner v. New York* that maximum hours laws were an unreasonable interference with the liberty of contract. The Court ruled that the power of the state to regulate did not outweigh the freedom of contract. The ruling struck down an 1895 New York statute that had limited the number of work hours for any employee in any bakery or confectionery establishment to no more than ten hours in a day or sixty hours in a week. New York's labor law was an example of the aggressive interventionist and experimental policies that several states had begun pursuing around the beginning of the twentieth century. The Court held that New York's experiment had been a "meddlesome interference" and an undue infringement on the right of free contract and thus of the private rights of the employer. In a powerful and eloquent dissent, Associate Justice Oliver Wendell Holmes, Jr., held that the states had the authority to pursue their own social experiments and enact reform legislation.

New York's Bakeshop Act had been enacted in an effort to regulate and improve the often dreadful working and health conditions in the state's cramped bakeshops, establishments that often employed only a handful of workers and frequently were located in the basements of tenement buildings. Passed as an act to regulate the manufacture of flour and meal food products, the Bakeshop Act established maximum hours and required that bakeries be drained and plumbed; that products be stored in dry and airy rooms; that walls and floors be plastered, tiled, or otherwise finished; and that inspections be carried out by officials.

Labor Laws

The law was not the first attempt to set limits on hours worked. Among the earliest efforts to regulate hours of work was an executive order signed by President Martin Van Buren in 1840 that limited the daily hours of labor in government navy yards to ten. Most early efforts to set limits on hours of labor concerned the employment of women and children. Massachusetts and Connecticut both passed laws limiting the number of hours for children employed in manufacturing establishments as early as 1842. By the late nineteenth century, laws limiting hours for women, children, or both had been passed in New Hampshire, Maine, Pennsylvania, New Jersey, Rhode Island, Ohio, Illinois, Missouri, and Wisconsin.

Those who supported limiting the hours of work argued that doing so would enhance the efficiency or productivity of labor and improve public health. Proponents of maximum hours legislation asserted that limits on the length of daily labor would lead to qualitative as well as quantitative improvements. Clearly, any bakeshop laborer who toiled long hours in cramped sweatshop conditions stood to gain some benefit, but proponents argued that there were also potential benefits for the consumers of baked goods. The principal arguments against such legislation were simply that it was an overextension of the police powers of the state and that it infringed on the right of freedom of contract. Moreover, proponents of the theories of social Darwinism and laissez-faire economics insisted that such government intervention constituted an unjustified and inefficient disruption of the free market.

Joseph Lochner owned and operated a small bread bakery in Utica, New York. After being twice found guilty of violating New York's Bakeshop Act, he was fined fifty dollars. He appealed his conviction to the New York Supreme Court and the New York Court of Appeals, losing each time. His case ultimately made its way to the U.S. Supreme Court. Why this case emerged as the test case for a host of reform legislation is unclear; Lochner's bakery was a small and relatively obscure establishment. An ongoing clash between Lochner and the Utica branch of the journeyman bakers' union may have led to his fine and kept this case alive on appeal.

The Majority Opinion

The majority opinion in Lochner was written by Associate Justice Rufus W. Peckham. Peckham was known for his staunch support of laissez-faire policies and his contempt for government regulation, stances that would lead others to link Peckham with the writings of Herbert Spencer, an influential scientist and philosopher who was one of the most outspoken champions of social Darwinism. In the Court's ruling in the 1897 case of *Allgeyer v. Louisiana*, Peckham had written the opinion that held a law unconstitutional for depriving a

The son of the distinguished nineteenth century writer Oliver Wendell Holmes, Justice Oliver Wendell Holmes, Jr., himself wrote opinions that were noted for their elegant style.
(Library of Congress)

person of liberty of contract. Any contract suitable to the operation of a lawful business was thus afforded protection under the Fourteenth Amendment. The doctrine of liberty of contract, established in *Allgeyer*, was advanced in *Lochner*.

In *Lochner*, Peckham held that there was no reasonable ground for interfering with the liberty of a person or the right of free contract by determining the hours of labor in this particular case. Although he acknowledged the power of states to protect the health and morals of citizens in specific situations, he questioned the need for protection of bakers. Laboring long hours in a bakery, although perhaps unpleasant and posing some health risks, was neither as arduous nor as unsafe as working at many other occupations. By restricting the freedom of contract, New York's Bakeshop Act had violated the due process clause of the Fourteenth Amendment and as such was unconstitutional. Because the connection between bakeries and health remained shadowy, the states were not free to exercise police or regulatory powers under the guise of conserving morals, health, or safety.

In a dissenting opinion, Associate Justice John Marshall Harlan held that New York's Bakeshop Act was not in conflict with the Fourteenth Amendment and that the states had the "power to guard the health and safety of their citizens by such regulations as they in their wisdom deem best." Justice Harlan held that it was clearly within the discretionary power of the states to enact laws regarding health conditions and that such statutes should be enforced unless they could be demonstrated to have plainly violated the "fundamental law of the Constitution." In Harlan's opinion, the use of the Fourteenth Amendment to invalidate New York's statute would in effect cripple the states in their ability to ensure the well-being of their citizens.

In a forceful and eloquent dissent, Associate Justice Oliver Wendell Holmes, Jr., held that the majority decision in *Lochner* was based on an economic theory rather than on law and that a "constitution is not intended to embody a particular economic theory." In this well-known dissent, Justice Holmes criticized the majority for extending the doctrine of liberty of contract and for defining too narrowly the states' police power. Holmes went on to write that a constitution is written for people of fundamentally differing views and that the "Fourteenth Amendment does not enact Mr. Herbert Spencer's Social Statistics."

Significance

The immediate impact of the U.S. Supreme Court's decision in *Lochner* was to restrict, or at least postpone, the ability of states to regulate such economic issues as maximum hours and minimum wages. Exactly how the Court would define the regulatory role of the states was an issue of great interest to reform-minded legislatures as well as to employers and their employees. The use of legislative reform was becoming more common, but such legislation often faced hostile review by the generally conservative courts.

Within a matter of a few years, the movement for shorter hours appeared to have won, lost, and then won again in significant cases before the Supreme Court. In 1898, the Court upheld a limitation on hours for Utah miners and smelters in *Holden v. Hardy*. In 1905, it reversed Joseph Lochner's conviction as an illegal and unwarranted interference with the liberty of contract, but in 1908 it upheld an Oregon law limiting hours for women in factories and laundries in *Muller v. Oregon*.

The Court's majority apparently viewed *Lochner* differently from the other two cases because its members saw no good reason bakers should be singled out; if bakers' hours were regulated, then regulations on others would follow. Exceptions could be made for inherently dangerous occupations or in the case of women and children, but a general limitation on hours was not yet to be accepted. A 1917 ruling, in *Bunting v. Oregon*, accepted a ten-hour day for men and women on the grounds of preserving the health and safety of workers, but only because the legislation did not apply to all workers; it applied only to workers in certain inherently dangerous industries.

Impact of the Ruling

The implications of the Court's ruling in *Lochner* obviously extended far beyond Joseph Lochner and the treatment of bakers in Utica bakeshops. The Court's decision signified an ardent acceptance by the Court majority of the doctrine of laissez-faire capitalism and a belief that reform legislation and the regulatory movement could be suspended by the courts. By ruling against the state of New York, the Court sent a clear message of hostility to any reform-minded legislative body. Liberty of contract, in this case the right of Joseph Lochner to make his own contracts and control his property, took precedence over the right of the state to exercise its police powers.

Up until the economic crisis of the Great Depression, the mostly conservative justices of the Supreme Court used the doctrine of liberty of contract to limit the ability of states to enact workplace reform legislation. Specific contracts could always be struck down, but only in those cases with narrowly defined public purposes. A notable example of prevailing judicial temperament can be seen in the 1908 case that outlawed "yellow-dog contracts," *Adair v. United States.* A law protecting union members by prohibiting yellow-dog contracts, under which employees promised not to join a union, was judged by the Court to be an unreasonable invasion of personal liberty and property rights. This reliance on liberty of contract and devotion to laissez-faire economic doctrines remained a marked feature of the Court for some years. However, not all scholars agree that the Court was as hostile to regulatory legislation and as antilabor as a few of these decisions might imply.

The decision in *Lochner* ranks among the most famous of all Supreme Court rulings, but for dubious reasons. Many consider it now, as Justice Holmes considered it then, an insensible ruling that ignored the hardships of sweatshop labor and launched a misguided assault on reform legislation. The premise of the decision later came into question. Rather than removing labor relations from the domain of politics, the decision resulted in eventual general acceptance of the notion that public debate and legislative action on economic issues are appropriate uses of police powers.

Social change is often a difficult and lengthy process. The necessary adjustments of an emerging industrial and increasingly urban society, with its resulting conflicts in labor relations, raised perplexing issues. Progressive reformers, and later New Dealers, who sought change through legislative enactments found, as in *Lochner,* that the courts were often unsympathetic. The realities and the pressures of the Great Depression led to a pervasive revision of judicial, political, and economic philosophies. New and inventive attempts were made to revitalize the economy, and legislatures were generally given more freedom to exercise regulatory powers.

Timothy E. Sullivan

Further Reading

Commons, John R., ed. *History of Labor in the United States, 1896-1932.* Vol. 3 in History of Labor in the United States. New York: Macmillan, 1935. Includes Don D. Lescohier's "Working Conditions" and Elizabeth Brandeis's "Labor Legislation," which are particularly helpful for placing *Lochner v. New York* in context. Thoroughly documented, with extensive bibliography and index. The set of which this volume is a part is a pioneering work of American labor history.

Hall, Kermit L., ed. *The Oxford Companion to the Supreme Court of the United States.* New York: Oxford University Press, 1992. Provides a detailed and useful outline of the history of the Court, major decisions and doctrines that have guided and influenced Court rulings dating back to 1789, and brief biographies of every justice who has served on the Court, as well as other historically significant characters. Concise but detailed entries help to make landmark cases and legal terms accessible to a variety of users.

Kens, Paul. *Judicial Power and Reform Politics: The Anatomy of Lochner v. New York.* Lawrence: University Press of Kansas, 1990. Presents a well-written and well-documented analysis of the issues surrounding the Lochner case, bakeries at the beginning of the twentieth century, the politics of reform legislation, and the ramifications of the Court's decision.

Lerner, Max, and Robert G. McCloskey. "The Supreme Court and American Capitalism." In *Essays in Constitutional Law.* New York: Alfred A. Knopf, 1957. Originally published in 1933, this is an interpretation of the Supreme Court as the institution that links the nation's supreme law and its economic system of capitalism. Not quite a theory of economic determinism, it fit the *Lochner* era well and explained the views of Justices Holmes and Harlan, as well as Peckham, but would not accommodate an activist, rights-oriented Court such as existed in the 1960's.

Nichols, Egbert Ray, and Joseph H. Baccus, eds. *Selected Articles on Minimum Wages and Maximum Hours.* New York: H. W. Wilson, 1936. Outlines and defines the debate over whether Congress has the power to fix minimum wages and maximum hours for workers. Reprints of editorials and comments offer a variety of legal, political, and economic interpretations.

Siegan, Bernard H. *Economic Liberties and the Constitution.* 2d ed. New Brunswick, N.J.: Transaction, 2005. An examination of changing judicial policy and the Court's review of economic legislation. Offers an explanation of alternative views of substantive due process and the protection of economic liberties.

Skocpol, Theda, and Gretchen Ritter. "Gender and the Origins of Modern Social Policies in Britain and the United States." *Studies in American Political Development* (Spring, 1991): 36-93. This long, well-documented article explains how differing governmental and class structures led to paternalistic social policies in Great Britain and maternalistic social policies in the United States in the early twentieth century. In relation to the United States, it offers an interesting discussion of the role of women's clubs.

U.S. Supreme Court. *Lochner v. New York. United States Reports* 198 (1905): 45. The case itself is the best source of information on the views of the justices. It is relatively brief and within the grasp of readers without a legal background.

See also *Adair v. United States; Allgeyer v. Louisiana; Bunting v. Oregon; Holden v. Hardy; Muller v. Oregon; West Coast Hotel Co. v. Parrish.*

LOEWE V. LAWLOR

Court: U.S. Supreme Court
Citation: 208 U.S. 274
Date: February 3, 1908
Issues: Antitrust law

• In the so-called Danbury Hatters' case, the U.S. Supreme Court held that a boycott against a manufacturer of hats, initiated in an attempt to force unionization, was an illegal restraint of trade.

Reacting to a secondary boycott sponsored by the American Federation of Labor, an employer brought suit against individual members of the United Hatters of America. The union claimed that the Sherman Antitrust Act of 1890 was designed for business corporations, not labor unions. Speaking for a unanimous Supreme Court, Chief Justice Melville W. Fuller ruled in favor of the employer. Fuller concluded that the Sherman Antitrust Act applied to all combinations in restraint of trade, and he found no evidence that Congress had intended to exempt labor unions from coverage. The Danbury Hatters' decision greatly increased the vulnerability of labor unions to injunctions and damage suits, but the Clayton Act of 1914 provided unions with partial relief.

Thomas Tandy Lewis

See also *Gompers v. Buck's Stove and Range Co.; In re Debs; Northern Securities Co. v. United States; Standard Oil v. United States; United States v. American Tobacco Co.*

LONE WOLF V. HITCHCOCK

Court: U.S. Supreme Court
Citation: 187 U.S. 553
Date: January 5, 1903
Issues: Land law; Native American sovereignty; Property rights; Treaties

- In *Lone Wolf v. Hitchcock* the U.S. Supreme Court decided that Congress has plenary power over Native American property and may dispose of such property at its discretion.

In 1887, after years of agitation and controversy, Congress passed the General Allotment Act (also known as the Dawes Act or Dawes Severalty Act). Under the terms of this legislation, the president was authorized to allot all tribal land in the United States to individual Native Americans. The standard share was 160 acres to each head of a family, with smaller amounts to unmarried men and children. Negotiations were to be carried on with Native American tribes for the sale to the federal government of the land remaining after the allotments were made and for the opening of the land to Euro-American settlement.

The allotment policy, which dominated relations between the U.S. government and Native Americans for more than fifty years, proved to be disastrous for Native Americans. It transformed Native American landownership from collective to individual holdings, thus severing the Indians' connections with communal tribal organizations; exposed Indians to wholesale exploitation by land speculators; pushed them onto land that was often arid and unproductive; and led ultimately to their loss of control over two-thirds of their lands. Deceit, duplicity, and coercion undermined the honest, but naïve, objectives of the U.S. reformers who espoused allotment prior to its enactment.

Tribal Sovereignty

Tribal sovereignty, the allotment policy, and Native American treaty rights came before the U.S. Supreme Court in *Lone Wolf v. Hitchcock* in 1902. In 1867, the U.S. government had signed the Medicine Lodge Creek Treaty with the Kiowas and Comanches, whereby the two tribes relinquished claims to 90 million acres in exchange for 2.9-million-acre reservations in western Oklahoma. A separate treaty placed the plains Apaches on the same reservation. Article XII of the Medicine Lodge Creek Treaty provided that no further cession of any part of the new reservation could be made without the written consent of three-quarters of the adult male members of the three tribes. The commitment to Article XII of the treaty lasted twenty-five years. In 1892, the Jerome Commission, composed of a former governor of Michigan and two judges, was able—through fraud and counterfeit signatures—to secure the necessary three-quarters consent to an agreement for the allotment of land to individual tribesmen and for the purchase of 2.15 million acres of what was denominated as surplus land at a price of approximately ninety-three cents per acre.

Almost immediately after the signing of the new agreement, representatives of the Kiowas, Comanches, and plains Apaches claimed that assent had been obtained through fraudulent misrepresentation of the agreement's terms by the interpreters and that three-quarters of the adult males had not consented to the cession. The U.S. House of Representatives ignored their arguments and voted to execute the agreement, but the Senate viewed their claims more sympathetically and defeated the bill in January, 1899.

In July, 1900, however, Congress passed an act that allowed the United States to take title to 2,991,933 acres of the Kiowa, Comanche, and plains Apache reservation. After 480,000 acres were set aside as common grazing lands, 445,000 acres were allotted to individual members of the three tribes, and 10,000 acres were committed to agency, schools, and religious purposes. Two million acres were left to be purchased by the federal government and opened to white settlement.

Although some Native Americans approved of the act, Lone Wolf, a Kiowa chief, and others were intent on challenging the act's constitutionality. They retained William McKendree Springer, formerly chief justice of the Court of Appeals for the Indian Territory, to litigate their case before the federal courts. Springer argued that the congressional act violated the property rights of the three tribes and was, therefore, repugnant to the due process clause of the Fifth Amendment to the Constitution. After losing in the Supreme Court of the District of Columbia and in the Court of Appeals for the district, Springer appealed to the U.S. Supreme Court.

Lone Wolf v. Hitchcock was argued in the Supreme Court in October, 1901, and reargued the following year. The decision was handed down on January 5, 1903. In the Court, attorney Hampton L. Carson, a prominent member of the Indian Rights Association, joined Springer as cocounsel; the Department of the Interior was represented by Willis Van Devanter of Wyoming, who later became a U.S. Supreme Court justice.

The Court's Ruling

The unanimous decision of the Supreme Court, written by Associate Justice Edward D. White of Louisiana, was characterized by a later commentator as the "Indian's Dred Scott decision," and January 5, 1903, as "one of the blackest days in the history of the American Indians." Justice White spoke of Native Americans in condescending terms, as an "ignorant and dependent race," "weak and diminishing in number," and "wards of the nation." These contemptuous phrases were not original to White; they were epithets that had long been used in the opinions of Supreme Court justices in relation to Native Americans. More important, White ruled that Congress possessed a paramount authority over the property of Native Americans "by reason of its exercise of guardianship over their interests." In exercising such power, Congress could abrogate provisions of a treaty with a Native American tribe.

Justice White then went on to argue that the congressional act of 1900 represented only "a mere change in the form of investment of Indian tribal property from land to money" even though the price paid was below the market value. White held that Congress had made a good-faith effort to compensate the Kiowas for their lands; therefore, there was no violation of the Fifth Amendment. "If injury was occasioned," White concluded, "which we do not wish to be understood to imply by the use made by Congress of its power, relief must be sought by an appeal to that body for redress and not to the courts."

Even before the Supreme Court had ruled in *Lone Wolf v. Hitchcock*, President William McKinley issued a proclamation opening the Kiowa lands to white settlement on August 6, 1901. Lone Wolf watched with chagrin as thousands of potential settlers camped on Kiowa lands near Fort Sill, waiting to register for a lottery; during a two-month period, 11,638 homestead entries were made at the land office.

Significance

The importance of the Supreme Court decision in *Lone Wolf* should not be underestimated. Justice White's opinion legitimated the long history of broken promises, of treaties made and treaties ignored, as well as the assertion of plenary authority of Congress over Indian lands. The opinion justified the alienation, between 1887 and 1934, of eighty-six million acres of Native American property; it also denied Native Americans recourse to the courts to seek redress for the coerced separation from their land and its purchase at bargain prices.

In *Lone Wolf*, Justice White told the Kiowas and associated tribes that they would have to seek relief for their alleged injuries in Congress, and the Kiowas had no alternative but to go to the federal legislature to secure redress. It was not until 1955 that the Indian Claims Commission awarded the Kiowas, Comanches, and plains Apaches $2,067,166 in compensation for the lands taken under the congressional act of 1900. It was not until 1980, in *United States v. Sioux Nation of Indians*, that Justice Harry Blackmun, in a majority opinion, held that the *Lone Wolf* doctrine was "discredited" and "had little to commend it as an enduring principle."

David L. Sterling

Further Reading

Clark, Blue. *Lone Wolf v. Hitchcock: Treaty Rights and Indian Law at the End of the Nineteenth Century*. Lincoln: University of Nebraska Press, 1994. A short but comprehensive study of the background and implications of the most significant Native American court case of the early twentieth century.

Duthu, N. Bruce. *American Indians and the Law*. New York: Penguin Books, 2008. Concise and accessible summary of Native American law, including a useful summary of the court decisions relevant to modern casinos.

Hagan, William T. *The Indian Rights Association: The Herbert Welsh Years, 1882-1904*. Tucson: University of Arizona Press, 1985. An account of the organization that participated in the litigation of the *Lone Wolf* case.

Highsaw, Robert B. *Edward Douglass White: Defender of the Conservative Faith*. Baton Rouge: Louisiana State University Press, 1981. An analysis of the judicial record of the writer of the Supreme Court opinion in *Lone Wolf v. Hitchcock*.

Johansen, Bruce E., ed. *Enduring Legacies: Native American Treaties and Contemporary Controversies*. New York: Praeger, 2004. Represents an attempt to maintain a "national conversation" on Native American treaties through discussion of related contemporary laws and issues.

Legters, Lyman, and Fremont J. Lyden, eds. *American Indian Policy: Self-Governance and Economic Development*. Westport, Conn.: Greenwood Press, 1994. A collection of articles detailing trends in Native American life and law in the late twentieth century.

Prucha, Francis Paul. *American Indian Treaties: The History of a Political Anomaly*. Berkeley: University of California Press, 1994. An exhaustive examination of the legal relationship between Native American tribes and the U.S. government since the time of the American Revolution.

Vinzant, John Harlan. *The Supreme Court's Role in American Indian Policy*. El Paso, Tex.: LFB Scholarly Publications, 2009. Study of the U.S. Supreme Court's role in reducing the sovereignty of Native American tribes.

Wilkins, David E., and K. Tsianina Lomawaima. *Uneven Ground: American Indian Sovereignty and Federal Law*. Norman: University of Oklahoma Press, 2002. Reviews the often inconsistent federal legal precedents related to issues concerning Native Americans. Chapter 5, "'Justices Who Bent the Law': The Doctrine of Implied Repeals," addresses the Supreme Court's political policy-making role in Indian affairs, as particularly illustrated in *Lone Wolf v. Hitchcock*.

See also *California v. Cabazon Band of Mission Indians; Cherokee Cases; Employment Division, Department of Human Resources of Oregon v. Smith; Ex parte Crow Dog; Johnson and Graham's Lessee v. McIntosh; Santa Clara Pueblo v. Martinez; Talton v. Mayes*.

LOPEZ, UNITED STATES V. *See* UNITED STATES V. LOPEZ

LORANCE V. AT&T TECHNOLOGIES

Court: U.S. Supreme Court
Citation: 490 U.S. 900
Date: June 12, 1989
Issues: Sex discrimination; Women's issues

- This U.S. Supreme Court opinion strictly interprets federal legislation limiting the time an individual has to file an Equal Employment Opportunity Commission (EEOC) complaint regarding unfair employment practices.

In a 1979 collective bargaining agreement, Local 1942 of the International Brotherhood of Electrical Workers and AT&T Technologies, Inc., changed the way in which the seniority of employees was calculated. Prior to that time, hourly employees were ranked solely by number of years employed in the plant. Individuals promoted to higher-paying "tester" positions were allowed to keep their seniority. A tester's seniority after 1979, however, was not based on length of plantwide service but on time as a tester, although one could regain plantwide seniority after five years.

Patricia Lorance, a tester when the new agreement became policy, was demoted in 1982 when her employer cut its workforce. Lorance and other female employees filed charges with the EEOC in 1983, followed by action in a district court alleging that the seniority system implemented in 1979 violated Title VII of the Civil Rights Act of 1964. The women claimed that the system in place protected male employees and discriminated against female employees, who had only recently become testers in increasing numbers.

The Supreme Court held that Lorance had no claim because she had not filed a charge with the EEOC within 180 days of the alleged unfair employment practice, as required by law. Critics of the decision say this opinion harms victims of discrimination: Because some of the claimants were not employed in the division when the policy was adopted, they would have to anticipate discrimination before it occurred.

Donald C. Simmons, Jr.

See also *Albemarle Paper Co. v. Moody; Bowe v. Colgate-Palmolive; Firefighters Local Union No. 1784 v. Stotts et al.; Griggs v. Duke Power Co.; Heart of Atlanta Motel v. United States; United Steelworkers of America v. Weber.*

LOTTERY CASE. *See* CHAMPION V. AMES

LOUISIANA EX REL. FRANCIS V. RESWEBER

Court: U.S. Supreme Court
Citation: 329 U.S. 459
Date: January 13, 1947
Issues: Cruel and unusual punishment

• After an electric chair failed to kill a convicted murderer because of a mechanical failure, the U.S. Supreme Court decided that a second trip to the electric chair would not violate the Eighth Amendment's proscription against cruel and unusual punishment.

Willy Francis, a fifteen-year-old African American, was found guilty of murdering a white druggist and was sentenced to death by electrocution. After the electric chair malfunctioned and a two-minute jolt of electricity failed to kill Francis, his lawyers argued that a second electrocution would involve so much mental anguish that it would constitute cruel and unusual punishment. Speaking for a 5-4 majority, Justice Stanley F. Reed's majority opinion rejected the argument and found that the unsuccessful attempt at execution was simply "an unforeseeable accident." Reed noted that an execution would be unconstitutional only if it involved barbarous practices or unnecessary pain.

Thomas Tandy Lewis

See also *Furman v. Georgia; Gregg v. Georgia; Harmelin v. Michigan; Hudson v. Palmer; Hutto v. Davis; Rhodes v. Chapman; Rummel v. Estelle; United States v. Carolene Products Co.*

Louisville, Cincinnati, and Charleston Railroad Co. v. Letson

Court: U.S. Supreme Court
Citation: 43 U.S. 497
Date: March 7, 1844
Issues: Diversity jurisdiction

- The U.S. Supreme Court's ruling enhanced the power of the federal courts by changing the definition of state residency for corporations.

Under diversity jurisdiction, New York resident Letson sued the Louisville, Cincinnati, and Charleston Railroad Co., chartered in South Carolina, in federal circuit court for breach of contract. The railroad claimed that the federal court lacked jurisdiction because the railroad had shareholders in New York. In *United States v. Deveaux* (1809), the Supreme Court stated that, for purposes of diversity jurisdiction, a corporation's home was the same as that of all its shareholders. Justice James M. Wayne wrote the unanimous 5-0 decision of the Court, overturning its 1809 decision and granting jurisdiction. Wayne held that a corporation had its home only in the state in which it was chartered, thereby opening the federal courts to corporations to sue and be sued. This had both advantages and disadvantages for corporations, but its immediate impact was to increase the jurisdictional power of federal courts. This jurisdiction was later restricted somewhat. This decision was rendered by a smaller than usual number of justices because Justice Smith Thompson had died. Chief Justice Roger Brooke Taney and Justices Peter V. Daniel and John McKinley did not participate.

Richard L. Wilson

See also *Bank of Augusta v. Earle; Bank of the United States v. Deveaux; Citizens United v. Federal Election Commission; Northern Securities Co. v. United States; Paul v. Virginia; Santa Clara County v. Southern Pacific Railroad Co.*

LOUISVILLE, NEW ORLEANS, AND TEXAS RAILWAY CO. V. MISSISSIPPI

Court: U.S. Supreme Court
Citation: 133 U.S. 587
Date: March 3, 1890
Issues: Racial discrimination; Regulation of commerce

• The U.S. Supreme Court upheld a Mississippi law mandating separate but equal accommodations on a railroad, despite its effect on interstate commerce.

By a 7-2 vote, the Supreme Court upheld a Mississippi statute requiring railroads to provide "equal, but separate accommodations" for African Americans and whites. The Louisville, New Orleans, and Texas Railway Company found this expensive and alleged the statute interfered with interstate commerce, but Justice David J. Brewer, who wrote the majority opinion, could see nothing wrong with requiring a railroad to add a car every time it crossed

Justice David J. Brewer.
(Library of Congress)

over into Mississippi. Brewer, as typical of the Court in that age, did not even comment on Mississippi's position that this law affected only intrastate commerce. Justice John Marshall Harlan dissented, maintaining that the state was interfering with the federal government's right to regulate commerce.

Richard L. Wilson

See also *Cumming v. Richmond County Board of Education; Hall v. DeCuir; McLaurin v. Oklahoma State Regents for Higher Education; Missouri ex rel. Gaines v. Canada; Plessy v. Ferguson; Sweatt v. Painter.*

LOVELL V. CITY OF GRIFFIN

Court: U.S. Supreme Court
Citation: 303 U.S. 444
Date: March 28, 1938
Issues: First Amendment guarantees; Freedom of speech

• The U.S. Supreme Court held that a city ordinance prohibiting the distribution of pamphlets without a permit violated the freedom of speech guaranteed by the First Amendment.

Alma Lovell, a member of the Jehovah's Witness Church, was prosecuted for distributing religious literature in Griffin, Georgia, without the required permission from the city commissioner. The Supreme Court had earlier applied the First Amendment guarantee of free speech to the states through the Fourteenth Amendment in *Gitlow v. New York* (1925), but the Court had never ruled that the federal guarantee for religious freedom was binding on the states.

Speaking for an 8-0 majority, Chief Justice Charles Evans Hughes wrote that the ordinance constituted a system of prior restraint on the expression of ideas. He emphasized that the First Amendment freedom of press extended to pamphlets and other modes of disseminating information and that the freedom to circulate materials was just as essential as the freedom to publish them. Hughes found that it was not necessary to consider the issue of religious freedom. A similar case, *Schneider v. Irvington* (1939), was also decided under the freedom of speech and press guarantees. It was not until the third case involving the Jehovah's Witnesses, *Cantwell v. Connecticut* (1940), that the Court incorporated the freedom of religious exercise into the Fourteenth Amendment.

Thomas Tandy Lewis

See also *Cantwell v. Connecticut; Gitlow v. New York; Near v. Minnesota.*

LOVETT, UNITED STATES V. *See* UNITED STATES V. LOVETT

LOVING V. VIRGINIA

Court: U.S. Supreme Court
Citation: 388 U.S. 1
Date: June 12, 1967
Issues: Marriage; Racial discrimination; Women's issues

- In this decision the U.S. Supreme Court struck down the antimiscegenation laws of several states that prohibited interracial couples from marrying or living together while not married.

In 1958 Virginia and several other states outlawed interracial marriage and sex between unmarried interracial partners. All such laws prohibited whites and African Americans from intermarrying; some also applied to members of other races.

Richard Loving, a white man, and Mildred Jeter, an African American woman, lived in Virginia and wanted to be married. They went to the District of Columbia, where they were married legally. When they returned to their home in Virginia, however, they were arrested. The circuit court of Caroline County, Virginia, found them guilty and sentenced them to one year in jail, a sentence which would be suspended if they agreed to leave the state.

The Lovings moved to Washington, D.C., and filed an appeal against the Virginia court decision. In 1967 the case reached the U.S. Supreme Court. The Court's justices unanimously sided with the Lovings, overturning the Virginia statute and those similar to it. By denying interracial couples the right to do something that other couples were allowed to do, antimiscegenation laws violated these citizens' right to the equal protection of the laws as guaranteed by the Fourteenth Amendment of the U.S. Constitution. This decision removed the legal stigma some states had attached to interracial unions, and it prohibited states from punishing people as criminals for loving someone of a different race.

Roger D. Hardaway

Further Reading

Gold, Susan Dudley. *Loving v. Virginia: Lifting the Ban Against Interracial Marriage.* Tarrytown, N.Y.: Marshall Cavendish Benchmark, 2008. Part of its publisher's Supreme Court Milestones series designed for young-adult readers, this volume offers an accessible history and analysis of *Loving v.*

Virginia that examines opposing sides in the case, the people involved, and the case's lasting impact. Includes bibliography and index.

See also *Baker v. Vermont*; *Goodridge v. Department of Public Health*; *Plessy v. Ferguson.*

Lucas v. South Carolina Coastal Council

Court: U.S. Supreme Court
Citation: 505 U.S. 1003
Date: June 29, 1992
Issues: Property rights; Takings clause

- In this case, the Court held for the first time that a state land-use regulation violated the Fifth Amendment's prohibition against taking private property without "just compensation" because, although it did not physically take property or transfer title, it reduced the land's value without compensation to the owner.

In 1986, David Lucas, a South Carolina real estate developer, paid almost a million dollars for two oceanfront lots zoned for single-family residential construction. Two years later, before Lucas built, the state legislature changed its coastal regulations, moving the construction line inland. Lucas's lots, on each of which he had planned to build a house, were stranded seaward of that line.

Lucas sued, alleging that the Beachfront Management Act of 1988 (BMA), the legislation that revised the regulations, had effected a taking of the value of his property without just compensation. The trial court agreed that Lucas had suffered a total loss of the value of his property and concluded that a regulatory taking had occurred. On appeal, the South Carolina Supreme Court reversed the decision, on the grounds that the BMA had been passed to prevent serious public harm. Lucas petitioned the U.S. Supreme Court to review the matter, and the Court sided with Lucas in a 6-2 opinion. Justices Harry Blackmun and John Paul Stevens dissented, and a separate statement was written by Justice David Souter.

Writing for the majority, Justice Antonin Scalia stated that it was impossible to ascertain whether the BMA had been designed to prevent harm or to obtain a free public benefit. Instead, he turned to the common-law principle that the right to use one's property is limited by the equal right of one's neighbor to an equivalent freedom of use. If a neighbor can bar a landowner's plan to put a nuclear plant on an earthquake fault, for example, the legislature may also act without compensation. However, if a use is one permitted between private landholders—such as the construction of a private residence—the legislature cannot bar such a use without compensating the owner for its loss, at least when the loss is total. The use Lucas sought to make of his property fell into the category of such an "essential use" and hence could not be barred without compensation. The Court's opinion thus endorsed the proposition that the common law of private nuisance is the appropriate guide to the constitutionality of land-use regulation.

The Supreme Court's holding in *Lucas* applies only to total loss of value, an uncommon situation. The logic of the *Lucas* opinion, however, is not limited to the case of total loss. If the difference between a regulation that prevents harm and one that confers a benefit is indeterminate, it is so whether or not the loss caused by the regulation is total. Indeed, Justice Scalia, challenged by Justice Stevens to explain why a total loss would be compensated but a 95 percent loss would not, could give no principled reason for restricting the scope of the opinion. Such uncertainty suggests that a later court may further restrict the legislative power to enact incompensable land use and environmental regulation.

Louise A. Halper

See also *Dolan v. City of Tigard; Euclid v. Ambler Realty Co.; First English Evangelical Lutheran Church of Glendale v. County of Los Angeles; Kelo v. City of New London; Keystone Bituminous Coal Association v. DeBenedictis; McCray v. United States; Penn Central Transportation Co. v. City of New York; Pennsylvania Coal Co. v. Mahon.*

LUTHER V. BORDEN

Court: U.S. Supreme Court
Citation: 7 48 U.S. 1
Date: January 3, 1849
Issues: Congressional powers

- By refusing to take sides in a dispute between two rival governments in Rhode Island, the U.S. Supreme Court held that the meaning of "a Republican form of government" is a political question and thus a responsibility of Congress rather than the courts.

Following the Dorr Rebellion of 1842, two competing groups claimed to be the lawful government of Rhode Island. One claim was based on a democratic referendum; the other was based on a colonial charter of 1663. The charter government, supported by President John Tyler, declared martial law and reestablished its authority. A Dorrite reformer, Martin Luther, argued in federal district court that the charter government's nondemocratic arrangements and procedures violated the "republican form" guarantee in the U.S. Constitution. The court dismissed Borden's claims and upheld the government in power.

Speaking for an 8-1 majority on the Supreme Court, Chief Justice Roger Brooke Taney affirmed the decision of the lower court. Taney announced the political question doctrine, which gives the legislative and executive branches responsibility to decide on political controversies absent a clear legal issue.

President John Tyler.
(Library of Congress)

The determination of the legitimacy of a state government did not fall within judicial competence. Taney did recognize that a federal court could inquire whether the use of martial law was consistent with the guarantee clause, but held that in this case, because martial law was temporary, Rhode Island had not violated the Constitution.

Thomas Tandy Lewis

See also *Ex parte McCardle; Helvering v. Davis; Kidd v. Pearson; Kilbourn v. Thompson; Pacific States Telephone and Telegraph Co. v. Oregon; Panama Refining Co. v. Ryan; Schechter Poultry Corp. v. United States; Yakus v. United States.*

LYNCH V. DONNELLY

Court: U.S. Supreme Court
Citation: 465 U.S. 668
Date: March 5, 1984
Issues: Establishment of religion

• The Court ruled that the inclusion of a Christian symbol in a city-sponsored display did not violate the Constitution's prohibition of religious establishment.

For at least four decades, the city of Pawtucket, Rhode Island, had used public funds to erect and maintain a nativity scene, or crèche, as part of the Christmas exhibit in its shopping district. In addition to the crèche, which contained figures of Jesus, Mary, Joseph, shepherds, and angels, the display included figures and symbols of a secular nature, including a reindeer pulling Santa's sleigh, a clown, and a Christmas tree. A local resident, Daniel Donnelly, joined with the American Civil Liberties Union to bring suit against Pawtucket mayor Dennis Lynch in federal court. The challengers argued that the nativity scene created both the appearance and the reality of a governmental endorsement of a particular religion, contrary to the establishment clause of the First Amendment. Both the district court and the court of appeals ruled in favor of the challengers, and the city of Pawtucket appealed the case to the U.S. Supreme Court.

A sharply divided court voted five to four to reverse the lower court's ruling and to allow Pawtucket to continue its Christmas display. Writing for the majority, Chief Justice Warren Burger began with the argument that rather than requiring a complete separation of church and state, the First Amendment "affirmatively mandates accommodation, not merely tolerance, of all religions, and forbids hostility toward any." He observed that the first Congress of 1789 employed members of the clergy as official legislative chaplains and that historically the three branches of the federal government had not hesitated to acknowledge the role of religion in American life. Burger found that the display had the secular motive of encouraging community spirit, promoting downtown business, and depicting the historical origins of a national holiday, and that any benefit to religion was "indirect, remote, and incidental."

In a vigorous dissent, Justice William J. Brennan answered that the crèche retained a specifically Christian meaning and that Pawtucket's action was an unconstitutional endorsement of a particular faith. He quoted from the city leaders to show that their intent was to "keep Christ in Christmas."

In the *Lynch* decision, the Court allowed governments much discretion to accommodate the majority's religious culture by allowing governmental acts that appeared to encourage that culture. A few years later, however, the Court narrowed the importance of the decision in *Allegheny County v. American Civil Liberties Union, Greater Pittsburgh Chapter* (1989), a case involving a county-sponsored nativity scene that was not diluted with secular symbols and that proclaimed, "Glory to God in the Highest." In the *Allegheny County* case, the majority found the more pious crèche to be an unconstitutional endorsement of religion. The idea that a religious display is considered constitutional if it is accompanied by secular images is sometimes referred to as the "reindeer rule."

Thomas Tandy Lewis

See also *Allegheny County v. American Civil Liberties Union Greater Pittsburgh Chapter; Flast v. Cohen; Lemon v. Kurtzman; Walz v. Tax Commission.*

MCCARDLE, EX PARTE. *See* EX PARTE MCCARDLE

McCleskey v. Kemp

Court: U.S. Supreme Court
Citation: 481 U.S. 279
Date: April 22, 1987
Issues: Capital punishment; Equal protection of the law;
Racial discrimination

• Despite evidence showing that race has a statistical impact on whether or not a jury recommends the death penalty, the U.S. Supreme Court concluded that the existence of statistical disparity did not violate the principles of the Eighth and Fourteenth Amendments to the U.S. Constitution.

In 1978, Warren McCleskey, a thirty-one-year-old African American man, joined with three accomplices to plan and carry out the robbery of a furniture store. Entering the store from different doors, all four of the men were armed. After rounding up the customers and employees, they forced the customers to lie face down on the floor and tied up the employees with tape. Before the robbery was completed, a white police officer, responding to a silent alarm, entered the store. Almost immediately, two shots were fired at the officer, with one hitting him fatally in the head. The four robbers then fled from the store with a small amount of stolen money and property.

A few weeks later, when McCleskey was arrested for an unrelated crime, he confessed to having participated in the robbery, but he denied that he had shot the officer. Investigators, however, discovered that at least one of the bullets striking the officer was fired from a .38 caliber Rossi revolver that matched the description of the gun that McCleskey carried. Investigators also found two witnesses who testified that they had heard him boast about firing at the officer.

Later that year, at the Superior Court of Fulton County, Georgia, McCleskey was tried on charges of two counts of robbery and one count of first-degree murder. The jury was composed of eleven white jurors and one black juror. Based on the evidence, they unanimously agreed that McCleskey was guilty beyond a reasonable doubt. At the penalty phase of the trial, after considering both the mitigating and aggravating circumstances of the crime, the jurors unanimously recommended the death penalty, a recommendation that was accepted by the court.

Constitutionality of Capital Punishment

At the time of the trial, the constitutionality of capital punishment was extremely controversial. Just six years earlier, in *Furman v. Georgia* (1972), the Supreme Court had ruled that the procedures then used in capital cases violated the Eighth Amendment to the U.S. Constitution. In the case of *Gregg v. Georgia* (1976), however, the Supreme Court decided that capital punishment was constitutionally permissible so long as the conviction was based on established principles of due process. These principles included competent counsel, opportunities for appeal, a bifurcated trial, and consideration of mitigating circumstances at the sentencing phase.

For his appeal, McCleskey had attorneys from the Legal Defense Fund of the National Association for the Advancement of Colored People (NAACP). In seeking legal reasons for an appeal, the attorneys were unable to discover any major violations of due process, but they did find some encouragement in the case of *Coker v. Georgia* (1977), in which the Court prohibited death sentences for the crime of rape, based on the principle that the Eighth Amendment prohibited punishments that are disproportionate to the crime. This ruling indicated that the Court might be open to a constitutional challenge relating to the particular circumstances of McCleskey's case.

McCleskey's petition for a writ of habeas corpus in federal court argued that Georgia's process of capital sentencing was cruel and unusual because it was racially discriminatory in violation of the equal protection clause of the Fourteenth Amendment. To support the claim, the petition referred to a massive statistical study by Professor David C. Baldus of the University of Iowa. Based on two thousand Georgia murder cases, the Baldus study found that the defendants charged with killing white victims were eleven times more likely to be sentenced to death than were defendants charged with killing black victims. Even when the results were adjusted for 230 nonracial variables, moreover, Baldus found that defendants charged with killing white victims were 4.3 times more likely than those accused of killing black victims to receive the death penalty.

The race of the defendant also had some impact on sentencing. Death sentences were given in 22 percent of cases with black defendants and white victims, in 3 percent of cases with white defendants and black victims, in 8 percent of cases when both parties were white, and in only 1 percent of cases in which both parties were black.

The Court's Ruling

When the Supreme Court finally decided the case in *McCleskey v. Kemp* in 1987, the justices rejected McCleskey's claim by a 5-4 majority. In the majority opinion, Justice Lewis F. Powell, Jr., referred to precedents requiring that to prevail under the equal protection clause, the defendant would have to prove that the conviction was a result of discriminatory motivation by either the Georgia legislature or by the officials involved in the trial. Emphasizing that there was no specific evidence of racial discrimination in McCleskey's trial, Powell argued that the Baldus study's discovery of statistical disparity in capital sentencing could not be used as proof of discrimination in particular cases and that the mere evidence of such statistics was not inconsistent with "evolving standards of decency." In Powell's view, the data in the study should be considered by legislatures rather than by the courts.

Four justices disagreed with the majority. In a lengthy dissent, Justice William J. Brennan postulated that the death penalty, in contrast to other punishments, should be assessed with "heightened rationality" because of its irrevocable nature. He further argued that Baldus's demonstration of racial disparity implied the real possibility of discriminatory treatment against black defendants like McCleskey, which meant that Georgia's application of the death penalty could not survive the test of heightened rationality. Justice Harry A. Blackmun also wrote a dissent echoing Brennan's concern for possible racial bias. Justice Thurgood Marshall, the only black member of the Court, joined both dissents. Justice John Paul Stevens was not willing to conclude that the Baldus study had proven the unconstitutionality of the death penalty, but he

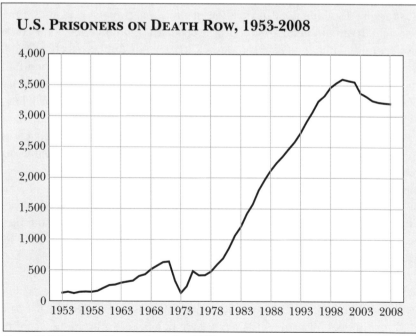

U.S. Prisoners on Death Row, 1953-2008

Source: U.S. Bureau of Justice Statistics, 2009.

wanted to remand the case back to the lower courts to consider the validity of the study and its implications.

Significance

Reaffirming the constitutionality of capital punishment, the *McCleskey* ruling established that the existence of statistical racial disparity in capital sentencing violated neither the Eighth Amendment nor the Fourteenth Amendment's requirement of equal protection. Because the case was decided by a narrow 5-4 vote, however, the decision could be overturned if a future majority of justices were to have more liberal views on the issues involved. The closeness of the decision was highlighted in a 1994 biography about Justice Powell, in which Powell was quoted as having said that if he could change his vote in any case, it would be *McCleskey v. Kemp.*

Since this ruling, the Supreme Court has not examined any major cases challenging the constitutionality of capital punishment in a comprehensive sense. Attorneys for several defendants, however, have convinced the Court that the Eighth Amendment prohibits the execution of particular categories of persons, including the insane (*Ford v. Wainwright,* 1986), the mentally retarded (*Atkins v. Virginia,* 2002), and persons who were younger than eighteen at the time of their crimes (*Roper v. Simmons,* 2005). In the case of *Wiggins v. Smith* (2003), moreover, the Court made it clear that it will give special scrutiny to the effectiveness of counsel in capital cases. Although the Court has never officially endorsed Justice Brennan's standard of heightened rationality, most justices have implicitly accepted the idea that capital sentences should be assessed more rigorously than other kinds of punishments.

Thomas Tandy Lewis

Further Reading

Baldus, David, Charles Pulaski, and George Woodworth. *Equal Justice and the Death Penalty: A Legal and Empirical Analysis.* Boston: Northeastern University Press, 1990. Classic of social science research, with the thesis that the victim's race has a major impact on whether defendants are sentenced to death.

Coyne, Randall, et al. *Capital Punishment and the Judicial Process.* Durham, N.C.: Carolina Academic Press, 2006. Provides a historical overview and analyzes all the major Supreme Court cases relating to the topic.

Edelman, Bryan. *Racial Prejudice, Juror Empathy, and Sentencing in Death Penalty Cases.* New York: LFB Scholarly Press, 2006. Based on interviews, Edelman's book concludes that white jurors are especially prone to render death sentences in cases with white victims and black offenders.

Latzer, Barry. *Death Penalty Cases: Leading U.S. Supreme Court Cases on Capital Punishment.* 2d ed. Boston: Butterworth-Heinemann, 2002. Contains introductions to most of the Supreme Court opinions in *McCleskey* and twenty-four other cases.

Mandery, Evan. *Capital Punishment in America: A Balanced Examination.* Sudbury, Mass.: Jones & Bartlett, 2004. Comprehensive assessment that gives multiple sides to the constitutional and moral issues relating to the controversial topic.

Melusky, Joseph, and Keith Pesto. *Cruel and Unusual Punishment Under the Law.* Santa Barbara, Calif.: ABC-CLIO, 2003. Useful guide with an excellent historical summary of the topic, with original documents and cogent analysis of *McCleskey* and other cases.

Ogletree, Charles, and Austin Sarat, eds. *From Lynch Mobs to the Killing State: Race and the Death Penalty in America.* New York: New York University Press, 2006. An outstanding collection of interesting essays, including much analysis of the *McCleskey* ruling.

Wright, Bruce. *Black Robes, White Justice: Why Our Legal System Doesn't Work for Blacks.* New York: Carol Publishing Group, 1993. An experienced lawyer and judge argues that the judiciary system is fundamentally discriminatory against African Americans in all areas, including application of capital punishment.

See also *Atkins v. Virginia; Coker v. Georgia; Ford v. Wainwright; Furman v. Georgia; Gregg v. Georgia; Roper v. Simmons; Washington v. Davis.*

McCleskey v. Zant

Court: U.S. Supreme Court
Citation: 499 U.S. 467
Date: April 16, 1991
Issues: Habeas corpus

• The U.S. Supreme Court significantly restricted the conditions under which federal courts were allowed to accept second habeas corpus petitions by state prisoners sentenced to death.

During the 1960's the Court had expanded the scope of federal habeas corpus reviews of state criminal convictions. One consequence was that death row inmates were able to file several habeas corpus petitions, each raising a different constitutional claim. After William H. Rehnquist became chief justice, however, the Court grew intolerant of long procedural delays in such cases. Following the Court's rejection of Warren McCleskey's first challenge to his death sentence, his lawyers filed a second habeas corpus petition, alleging that prosecutors at his trial had used incriminating statements that were made without assistance of counsel.

By a 6-3 vote, the Court rejected the claim. Justice Anthony M. Kennedy, in the opinion for the majority, insisted that a defendant must include all of his constitutional arguments in the first petition to the federal courts. To prevent abuse, the Court adopted the "cause and prejudice" standard, requiring the defendant to show that he or she had not raised the claim earlier because of a cause beyond his or her control and to demonstrate that the alleged errors resulted in actual prejudice. Exceptions to the cause and prejudice standard would be allowed only when the defendant could show that an error was so fundamental that it had resulted in the conviction of an innocent person.

In the Antiterrorism and Effective Death Penalty Act of 1996, Congress made it even more difficult for defendants to file second habeas corpus petitions. The Court upheld the constitutionality of the statute in *Felker v. Turpin* (1996).

Thomas Tandy Lewis

See also *Boumediene v. Bush*; *Brecht v. Abrahamson*; *Bunting v. Oregon*; *Duncan v. Kahanamoku*; *Ex parte Merryman*; *Frank v. Mangum*; *Moore v. Dempsey*; *Stone v. Powell*.

McConnell v. Federal Election Commission

Court: U.S. Supreme Court
Citation: 540 U.S. 93
Date: December 10, 2003
Issues: Political campaigning

- In what was a review of the Campaign Finance Reform Act of 2002, the U.S. Supreme Court upheld the constitutionality of the act's limits on contributions to political parties.

In 1974, Congress amended federal election campaign laws by limiting the amount that citizens could contribute to political candidates. In *Buckley v. Valeo* (1976), the Supreme Court upheld the amendment as only a minimal restriction on speech, but it also held on free speech grounds that government could not put a limit on expenditures in campaigns. The federal law did not put any limits on "soft money," which referred to donations to political parties for activities such as educating voters.

In 2002, Congress enacted the Bipartisan Campaign Reform Act (BCRA; also called the McCain-Feingold Law), which, among its provisions, restricted the amount that could be contributed to national political parties, and it also prohibited advertisements by special-interest groups sixty days before an election. That same year, the District of Columbia Court of Appeals ruled that the BCRA's limit on donations to political parties violated constitutional rights of free speech.

The Supreme Court voted five to four to uphold the two main provisions of the federal law: the control of soft money and the time regulation on issue ads. On the soft-money issue, Justices Sandra Day O'Connor and John Paul Stevens wrote that the restriction on free expression was minimal and that the limits furthered the government's legitimate interest in opposing both corruption and the appearance of corruption that resulted from large contributions.

The dissenters argued that the majority had erred in not applying a "strict scrutiny" standard to the law. Justice Antonin Scalia wrote that the majority's decision was based on the fallacy that money is not speech. Justice Clarence Thomas characterized the decision as the most significant abridgment of free speech since the Civil War.

Thomas Tandy Lewis

See also *Buckley v. Valeo*; *Citizens United v. Federal Election Commission*.

McCray v. United States

Court: U.S. Supreme Court
Citation: 195 U.S. 27
Date: May 31, 1904
Issues: Regulation of commerce; Taxation

• The U.S. Supreme Court established that the federal tax power could be used to regulate commerce.

Congress had passed a law to regulate the production of oleomargarine. Defendant McCray, convicted for buying colored oleomargarine at a lower than legal price, claimed that Congress had exceeded its proper power to tax for revenue purposes. McCray maintained that the law violated the Tenth Amendment, which gave the states the right to tax on those matters not within the proper scope of the federal government, as well as his rights to due process and just compensation for an improper taking under the Fifth Amendment.

As with *McCulloch v. Maryland* (1819), the question was which level of government had the power to take the action. The Supreme Court, by a 6-3 vote, ruled against McCray. Following *McCulloch,* Justice Byron R. White, in his opinion for the Court, noted there was no explicit ban on Congress levying an excise tax, and therefore, it could be "necessary and proper" within the meaning of Article I, section 8, of the Constitution. White, while reserving the Court's power to look into abuses, found Congress had a broad taxing power beyond mere revenue generation. With this conclusion, there would be no proper objections from the states under the Tenth Amendment and no proper individual objections under the Fifth Amendment. This ruling was restricted somewhat in the 1920's but restored in the 1930's. Chief Justice Melville W. Fuller and Justices Henry B. Brown and Rufus W. Peckham dissented.

Richard L. Wilson

See also *Bailey v. Drexel Furniture Co.*; *Gibbons v. Ogden*; *McCulloch v. Maryland*; *United States v. Lopez.*

McCulloch v. Maryland

Court: U.S. Supreme Court
Citation: 17 U.S. 316
Date: March 6, 1819
Issues: Federal supremacy

• In this landmark decision, the U.S. Supreme Court recognized the doctrine of implied powers, which gave the federal government broad authority over state governments and irrevocably established the principle of federal supremacy.

From the time of its framing in 1787, the U.S. Constitution has stirred controversy over the nature of the union that it created and the extent of federal authority. The Civil War (1861-1865) would in 1865 settle certain outstanding questions as to the nature of the union, but a more articulate consideration of the problem was provided by the Supreme Court of the United States in 1819 in the landmark case of *McCulloch v. Maryland*.

The Issues

The arguments surrounding the case were as old as the Constitution itself. Although the Constitutional Convention of 1787 had considered and rejected the proposal that Congress be empowered to charter corporations, a classic constitutional debate took place during the first administration of President George Washington over the question of chartering the First Bank of the United States. In memoranda they wrote at the president's request, Secretary of the Treasury Alexander Hamilton and Secretary of State Thomas Jefferson presented diametrically opposed advice on the question of whether the president should approve the bill chartering the First Bank of the United States. Hamilton urged a broad interpretation of the Constitution's "necessary and proper" clause, contending that Congress had the power to make all laws that it considered expedient or convenient. Jefferson insisted on a stricter interpretation of that clause, which, he argued, authorized Congress to pass only those laws that were necessary to give effect to its specifically delegated powers.

Washington took Hamilton's advice, and the bank was chartered in 1791. The bank's charter expired in 1811, and the adverse economic impact of the War of 1812, coupled with the abuses and irresponsibility of state-chartered banks, led to the chartering in 1816 of the Second Bank of the United States. The chartering of the First Bank of the United States had prompted a movement in favor of a constitutional amendment to restrict Congress's powers under the "necessary and proper" clause, and the chartering of the Second Bank of the United States led many states to adopt laws designed to suppress the bank's operations.

Hostility toward the bank rested on a number of factors. First, it was regarded as a Federalist-controlled enterprise, much of whose stock was held by foreign investors. Moreover, the operations of the First Bank of the United States had tended to undercut the success of the state banks, and many blamed the bleak economic conditions following the War of 1812 on the policies of the First Bank of the United States. Champions of the new bank regarded renewal of its charter as the only hope of improving economic conditions.

In certain states, antibank sentiment was rampant. Indiana, Illinois, Tennessee, Georgia, North Carolina, Kentucky, Ohio, and Maryland adopted laws designed to curtail or prohibit the operation of the Bank of the United States. The momentum of the antibank movement was encouraged by the mismanagement and fraud of the managers of the Second Bank of the United States. The growing anxiety over the deteriorating state of the economy made an appeal to the courts an attractive way of settling the question of the legitimacy of the state burdens that were being imposed on the bank's operations. This was the immediate motivation for the litigation that led to *McCulloch v. Maryland.*

John James, an agent of the state of Maryland, called on James W. McCulloch, the cashier of the Baltimore branch of the bank, and demanded that McCulloch comply with the state law. The Maryland law, adopted in February, 1818, required all banks chartered outside Maryland to pay a tax of one hundred dollars on all notes issued or, alternatively, to pay an annual sum of fifteen thousand dollars into the state's treasury. McCulloch refused to comply with this prohibitive state law. When he was prosecuted for his refusal, the Maryland courts ruled against him. In September, 1818, his case was appealed to the U.S. Supreme Court.

The Supreme Court heard arguments in the case for nine days. Appearing on behalf of the bank were Attorney General William Wirt, William Pinkney, and Daniel Webster. Luther Martin, the fiery attorney general of Maryland who had expedited the bringing of the case to the Supreme Court; Joseph Hopkinson; and Walter Jones were the lawyers appearing for Maryland.

The Court's Ruling

On March 6, 1819, the Supreme Court handed down its decision, only three days after completion of arguments and while there was much activity in Congress aimed at revoking the bank's charter. The opinion by Chief Justice John Marshall is regarded by most scholars as his most important pronouncement in constitutional law and the one most important to the future of the United States. The Constitution, said Marshall, established a truly national government that "is emphatically and truly a government of the people. In form and in substance it emanates from them, its powers are granted by them, and are to be exercised directly on them, and for their benefit."

Much of the remainder of Marshall's opinion is an extension and application of this "national" theory of the Constitution's foundations. Sovereignty is divided between federal and state governments. When state power conflicts with national power, the former must yield because national sovereignty is supreme. The judiciary, Marshall wrote, is constitutionally required to construe

Congress's enumerated powers broadly. The "necessary and proper" clause, sometimes called the "elastic" clause, was designed to empower Congress to exercise its delegated powers by any convenient and expedient methods not prohibited by the Constitution itself. Marshall found that the "necessary and proper" clause gave rise to what have come to be called "implied powers":

> A constitution, to contain an accurate detail of all the subdivisions of which its great powers will admit, and all of the means by which they may be carried into execution, would partake of the prolixity of a legal code, and could scarcely be embraced by the human mind. It would probably never be understood by the public. Its nature, therefore, requires that only its great outlines should be marked, its important objects designated, and the minor ingredients which compose those objects be deduced from the nature of the objects themselves.

By focusing on the ends sought to be achieved by the Constitution's Framers, Marshall ensured that Congress neither overstepped its bounds nor was denied any powers involved with its responsibilities. That flexible approach allowed Congress to select the means by which to implement its powers. Both the spirit and the language of the Constitution supported that view. The Framers had "omitted to use any restrictive term which might prevent its receiving a fair and just interpretation. In considering this question, then, we must never forget, that it is a constitution we are expounding."

Significance

McCulloch v. Maryland was the Supreme Court's earliest and most renowned implied powers case. In its ruling, the Court upheld the constitutionality of the federal government to incorporate a national bank in Baltimore. In doing so, it accomplished three important goals: It clarified the power of state taxation and congressional authority in economic policy making, reinforced the principles of U.S. federalism, and specified that the necessary and proper clause of the Constitution grants Congress certain implied powers that extend beyond its enumerated powers.

After the *McCulloch* decision, the implied powers were used to expand and contract governmental power in *Gibbons v. Ogden* in 1824 and in *United States v. Lopez* in 1995. Although many cases decided by the Court have dealt with economic policies, the Court has also addressed crime prevention programs, federalism cases, and the implied powers of the presidency. Indeed, the majority of presidential powers are based on authority implicit in such enumerated, yet vague, powers as the commander-in-chief- and executive-power clauses of the Constitution.

During the twentieth century, Supreme Court Justice Felix Frankfurter asserted that Marshall's words were the most important ever uttered by a United States judge, acknowledging an expansive source of power and an extension of that power beyond those expressly named sources. "Let the end be legitimate, let it be within the scope of the Constitution, and all means are appropriate, which are plainly adopted to that end, which are not prohibited, but consist with the letter of the Constitution, are constitutional. . . ." As a precedent for future assertions of national authority, the opinion asserted that legitimate uses of national power took priority over state authority and that the "necessary and proper" clause was a broad grant of national authority.

Luther Martin had insisted in his argument that even if Congress had the authority to establish the Bank of the United States, a state could still levy the tax in question. Marshall rejected his argument and laid down the general principle that the central government had constitutional power to "withdraw any subject from the action" of the states. "The power to tax," he declared, "involves the power to destroy." To permit Maryland to tax the bank's operations would place all federal programs at the mercy of the states. This facet of the *McCulloch* opinion gave rise to the doctrine of intergovernmental tax immunity.

James J. Bolner, updated by Marcia J. Weiss

Further Reading

Barron, Jerome A., and C. Thomas Dienes. *Constitutional Law in a Nutshell.* 6th ed. St. Paul, Minn.: West, 2005. Compact reference on the law for those with a legal or political science background.

Cox, Archibald. *The Court and the Constitution.* Boston: Houghton Mifflin, 1987. The former U.S. solicitor general and Watergate special prosecutor chronicles issues and debates in each era of constitutional history.

Gold, Susan Dudley. *McCulloch v. Maryland: State v. Federal Power.* Tarrytown, N.Y.: Marshall Cavendish Benchmark, 2008. Part of its publisher's Supreme Court Milestones series designed for young-adult readers, this volume offers an accessible history and analysis of *McCulloch v. Maryland* that examines opposing sides in the case, the people involved, and the case's lasting impact. Includes bibliography and index.

Gunther, Gerald, ed. *John Marshall's Defense of McCulloch v. Maryland.* Stanford, Calif.: Stanford University Press, 1969. A compilation of the debates surrounding Marshall's decision. Contains the newspaper battle with ideological opponents of the Supreme Court, as well as Marshall's replies. Introduction by the editor.

Johnson, Herbert A. *The Chief Justiceship of John Marshall, 1801-1835.* Columbia: University of South Carolina Press, 1997. Excellent biography of Marshall that closely examines his work on the Supreme Court.

Lewis, Thomas T., and Richard L. Wilson, eds. *Encyclopedia of the U.S. Supreme Court.* 3 vols. Pasadena, Calif.: Salem Press, 2001. Comprehensive reference work on the Supreme Court that contains substantial discussions of *McCulloch v. Maryland*, implied powers, John Marshall, and many related subjects.

McCloskey, Robert G. *The American Supreme Court.* 2d ed. Revised by Sanford Levinson. Chicago: University of Chicago Press, 1994. A detailed treatment of the Marshall Court. Contains additional resources in a bibliographical essay.

Newmyer, R. Kent. *John Marshall and the Heroic Age of the Supreme Court.* Baton Rouge: Louisiana State University Press, 2001. Focuses on Marshall's legal philosophies, analyzing some of his Supreme Court decisions and placing his beliefs in historical context.

Petit, Charles E., and Bonnie Pettifor. *McCulloch v. Maryland: When State and Federal Powers Conflict.* Berkeley Heights, N.J.: Enslow, 2004. Designed for young-adult readers, this volume examines the issues leading up to *McCulloch v. Maryland*, people involved in the case, the legal development of the case, and the historical impact of the ruling. Includes chapter notes, further reading list, and index.

Smith, Jean E. *John Marshall: Definer of a Nation.* New York: Henry Holt, 1996. One of the best biographies of Marshall yet published.

See also *Champion v. Ames; Collector v. Day; Dobbins v. Erie County; Gibbons v. Ogden; McCray v. United States; Osborn v. Bank of the United States; United States v. Lopez; Weston v. Charleston.*

MCKEIVER V. PENNSYLVANIA

Court: U.S. Supreme Court
Citation: 403 U.S. 528
Date: June 21, 1971
Issues: Juvenile justice; Trial by jury

• The U.S. Supreme Court narrowed the broad due process protection given to juveniles in state proceedings in 1967.

When the Supreme Court rendered its 1967 *In re Gault* decision, the Sixth Amendment's jury trial guarantee had not yet been applied to the states by incorporation. After the Court incorporated that right for adults in *Duncan v. Louisiana* (1968), the question arose of whether this guarantee should also be applied to juveniles. In *McKeiver*, which involved several cases regarding juvenile proceedings in North Carolina and Pennsylvania, the Court answered in the negative, deciding that *Gault* did not require strict conformity to the Sixth Amendment right to trial by jury but that "fundamental fairness" was all that was required. Despite some scholarly and legal criticism, the ruling in *McKeiver* remains valid law.

Richard L. Wilson

See also *Duncan v. Louisiana; Gideon v. Wainwright; In re Gault; In re Winship; Miranda v. Arizona.*

McLaurin v. Oklahoma State Regents for Higher Education

Court: U.S. Supreme Court
Citation: 339 U.S. 637
Date: June 5, 1950
Issues: Education; Racial discrimination

• The U.S. Supreme Court overruled a state policy of admitting African Americans to a public university's graduate program on a segregated basis.

In 1938, the Supreme Court held that states must provide equal opportunities for education in legal matters within the borders of the state. George McLaurin, a black teacher who was sixty-eight years old, was admitted to the University of Oklahoma's graduate program because no other program within the state offered a Ph.D. in education. The Oklahoma legislature passed a statute requiring segregation within all graduate programs that admitted African American students. McLaurin was required to sit at designated desks in classrooms and in the library. By a 9-0 vote, the Court found that such a policy of isolation detracted from McLaurin's educational experience, in violation of the equal protection clause of the Fourteenth Amendment. The Court held that after admitting a student to a state university, the state may not afford the student different treatment solely because of the person's race.

The *McLaurin* case was argued and decided simultaneously with a companion case, *Sweatt v. Painter* (1950). In *Sweatt*, the Court ruled that a law school for African Americans in Texas was unconstitutional because it did not offer educational opportunities that were substantially equal to those offered to whites. The *McLaurin* and *Sweatt* decisions helped prepare the way for *Brown v. Board of Education* (1954).

Thomas Tandy Lewis

See also *Brown v. Board of Education; Missouri ex rel. Gaines v. Canada; Sweatt v. Painter.*

MAHAN V. HOWELL

Court: U.S. Supreme Court
Citation: 410 U.S. 315
Date: February 15, 1973
Issues: Reapportionment and redistricting

• The U.S. Supreme Court relaxed mathematical equality standards for state legislative redistricting.

A Virginia state legislative redistricting plan was challenged because of deviations in district population that the state argued were the result of following county and city boundaries where possible. Justice William H. Rehnquist wrote the 5-3 majority decision for the Supreme Court maintaining that the one-person, one-vote standard in *Reynolds v. Sims* (1964) gave greater flexibility for deviations from exact mathematical equality in state legislative redistricting than in congressional redistricting. *Mahan* was one of four decisions in 1973 that allowed greater variances in state legislative than in congressional redistricting cases, for which the mathematical exactness standard of

Kirkpatrick v. Preisler (1969) continued to apply. Justices William J. Brennan, Jr., William O. Douglas, and Thurgood Marshall dissented.

Richard L. Wilson

See also *Colegrove v. Green; Gray v. Sanders; Kirkpatrick v. Preisler; Reynolds v. Sims; Wesberry v. Sanders.*

MAHER V. ROE

Court: U.S. Supreme Court
Citation: 432 U.S. 464
Date: June 20, 1977
Issues: Reproductive rights; Women's issues

- The Court ruled that while a woman's right to abortion is constitutionally protected, states are not required to provide Medicaid funding for abortions that are not "medically necessary."

Connecticut adopted a law which refused Medicaid support for abortions for poor women which were not "medically necessary"—necessary to protect the life or health of the mother. To receive state funding, the hospital or clinic performing the abortion had to submit physician certification that the abortion was medically necessary. A case was filed on behalf of indigent women in U.S. district court against Edward Maher, the Connecticut commissioner of social services. The suit argued that the law violated Title XIX of the Social Security Act (Medicaid) and the constitutional rights of poor women, including the Fourteenth Amendment guarantees of due process and equal protection under the law. It further argued that by providing Medicaid support for childbirth but not abortion the state was favoring some procedures pertaining to pregnancy over others, thus limiting poor women's free choice. The district court found in favor of Roe, and the case was appealed to the U.S. Supreme Court.

In a 6-3 decision, the Court found in favor of Maher and the state of Connecticut. The majority argued that while *Roe v. Wade* (1973) guaranteed a woman's right to abortion, the Constitution does not require state funding of pregnancy-related medical procedures for indigent women. It ruled that states have the right to decide what will be covered under Title XIX. Additionally, it qualified *Roe v. Wade* by stating that it did not affirm an unconditional right to abortion but only required that states not impose undue burdens on women attempting to obtain an abortion. The majority argued that poverty may constitute a burden, but it is not caused by the state and so the state is not required to alleviate the hardships pertaining to access to abortion that poverty causes.

In response to the objection that Connecticut favored childbirth over abortion, the Court cited the trimester provision of *Roe v. Wade*, arguing that states do, indeed, have a vested interest in potential (fetal) life and may enact policies that encourage childbirth over abortion. Finally, the majority held that a statement from the attending physician attesting the medical necessity of a Medicaid-funded abortion was appropriate. The minority opinion objected that failure to fund elective abortions for the poor makes it almost "impossible" for many of them to obtain safe abortions and so violates their constitutional rights. The case is one of many which has qualified the right to abortion first affirmed in the *Roe v. Wade* decision.

Charles L. Kammer

See also *Akron v. Akron Center for Reproductive Health; Bigelow v. Virginia; Doe v. Bolton; Harris v. McRae; Planned Parenthood of Central Missouri v. Danforth; Roe v. Wade; Rust v. Sullivan; Thornburgh v. American College of Obstetricians and Gynecologists; Webster v. Reproductive Health Services.*

MALLORY V. UNITED STATES

Court: U.S. Supreme Court
Citation: 354 U.S. 449
Date: June 24, 1957
Issues: Confessions

• The U.S. Supreme Court reaffirmed its power to create rules of evidence that apply in federal criminal cases.

In *McNabb v. United States* (1943), the Supreme Court ruled that any statements an accused made while being improperly detained could not be used against that person at trial, thereby dramatically reducing the prospect of coerced confessions. In *Mallory,* Justice Felix Frankfurter wrote the unanimous opinion for the Court, sustaining the *McNabb* rule for use in federal criminal cases, but not extending the rule to state criminal cases under the incorporation doctrine of the Fourteenth Amendment. The Court can only set aside state criminal convictions for violation of the Fourteenth Amendment's due process clause, but it can directly create rules for the federal courts. At one point, it seemed the Court might apply the *McNabb* rule to the states through the Fourteenth Amendment incorporation doctrine, but the Court chose to rely instead on the *Miranda v. Arizona* (1966) rule to achieve the comparable purpose. The *McNabb* rule was not constitutional law, so it could be changed by congressional action. It was effectively eliminated in the late 1960's.

Richard L. Wilson

See also *Gideon v. Wainwright; Hudson v. Michigan; In re Gault; Miranda v. Arizona; Weeks v. United States; Wolf v. Colorado.*

MALLOY V. HOGAN

Court: U.S. Supreme Court
Citation: 378 U.S. 1
Date: June 15, 1964
Issues: Self-incrimination

- The U.S. Supreme Court reversed prior decisions by holding that the privilege against self-incrimination is safeguarded by the due process clause of the Fourteenth Amendment.

William Malloy was arrested during a gambling raid in Connecticut in 1959. After pleading guilty to a gambling misdemeanor he received a light jail sentence, was fined five hundred dollars, and was placed on probation. Sixteen months later he was summoned to testify before a state court referee—a procedure similar to a grand jury investigation—on his gambling activities.

Several questions were asked regarding the events surrounding his arrest and conviction. He refused to answer any question on the ground that to answer "may tend to incriminate me." The Superior Court held him in contempt and sentenced him to prison until he was willing to answer the questions. Malloy appealed to Connecticut's Supreme Court of Errors, which held that the Fifth Amendment's privilege against self-incrimination did not apply to state proceedings and that the Fourteenth Amendment's due process clause did not confer such a privilege. Malloy petitioned the Supreme Court for a hearing on the issue.

The Supreme Court reversed the state court's decision. Justice William J. Brennan, Jr., wrote the opinion for the majority. In it he argued that the right not to incriminate oneself is fundamental to an adversary system of justice. Therefore, it is one of the rights which operate against state governments through the due process clause of the Fourteenth Amendment. Brennan held that the Fifth Amendment self-incrimination clause in its entirety limits state governments.

The question in the case then became whether Malloy had in fact been asked to incriminate himself. The questions he had been asked had to do with the identity of the person or persons who employed him at the time of his gambling convictions. Connecticut was trying to find out who was in charge of the gambling operation. The state argued that Malloy was in no danger of incriminating himself: He had already been convicted and could not be tried again for the same crime. Justice Brennan's opinion argued that Malloy's answers might furnish a link in a chain of evidence which might convict him of some new crime or more recent crime, particularly if he were still connected to the person who was running the gambling operation. Because "injurious disclosure" might result, Malloy was protected by the privilege against self-incrimination.

Four members of the Court dissented in two separate dissenting opinions. Justice John M. Harlan's dissent begins by pointing out that this issue was first encountered by the Supreme Court in 1908 in *Twining v. New Jersey. Twining*, and all the Court's subsequent cases regarding the privilege against self-incrimination, left it to the states to decide the extent of the self-incrimination privilege. Harlan argued that the Court should adhere to the precedents. First, it is not absolutely clear that the right is "fundamental." It is not necessarily unfair to ask a person to give an accounting of himself or even to compel an answer by legal means. Second, the decision fastens federal criminal procedure to the states, depriving them of the ability to experiment or to establish procedures that their own citizens wish to have. Finally, Harlan argued, Malloy's commitment for contempt would have been proper even under the federal standard espoused by the majority. Even if Malloy had answered the questions he would not have incriminated himself.

Malloy v. Hogan has had an immense impact on state legal procedures. As a result of this case, states have far less power to compel witnesses to testify in grand jury or other investigatory proceedings.

Robert Jacobs

See also *Adamson v. California; Miranda v. Arizona; Murphy v. Waterfront Commission of New York; Rochin v. California; Twining v. New Jersey.*

Mapp v. Ohio

Court: U.S. Supreme Court
Citation: 367 U.S. 643
Date: June 19, 1961
Issues: Evidence; Pornography and obscenity; Right to privacy

• The Court required that illegally obtained evidence must be excluded from criminal trials in state courts, a rule that previously had been applied to federal trials in 1914.

In 1957, Cleveland police officers went to the home of Dollree Mapp, acting on information that a suspect in a recent bombing and related paraphernalia were located in her home. After Mapp refused to admit them, the officers forcibly entered, conducted a widespread search of the house, and discovered some illegal pornography. Mapp was arrested and convicted of violating Ohio's antiobscenity statute. Unable to demonstrate that the officers had possessed a valid search warrant, the state of Ohio argued that even if the search had been illegal, precedents of the U.S. Supreme Court did not forbid the admission of the resulting evidence in a state trial.

For many years the Supreme Court had been debating the issue of the so-called exclusionary rule. Earlier in the century, in *Weeks v. United States* (1914), the Court had required that illegally obtained evidence be excluded from federal prosecutions. Thirty-five years later, in *Wolf v. Colorado* (1949), the Supreme Court applied the Fourth Amendment right of privacy to the states through the due process clause of the Fourteenth Amendment, but the Court decided against imposing the exclusionary rule as an essential element of that right. By 1961, nevertheless, about half the states had adopted the *Weeks* rule.

In *Mapp v. Ohio*, the Court ruled 5-3 to make the exclusionary rule binding on the states. In the majority opinion, Justice Tom Clark declared that the rule was "an essential part" of the constitutional rights of individuals, but he also pointed to the rule's deterrence as a justification for the decision. Experience demonstrated, he wrote, that other remedies were "worthless and futile" in preventing officials from disobeying the prohibition against unreasonable searches and seizures.

Three members of the Court were opposed to overruling the *Wolf* precedent. They objected that the briefs and oral arguments of the case had dealt more with the obscenity issue than with the exclusionary rule, but even more, they insisted that the principle of federalism should allow states to have flexibility in devising alternative remedies to deter unreasonable searches and seizures. Justice Potter Stewart wanted to decide the case on the basis of the First Amendment and refused to join with either the majority or the minority.

The *Mapp* decision, a landmark of the Warren Court years, has been one of the most controversial opinions ever rendered by the Supreme Court. Since most criminal prosecutions take place in state courts, the decision's impact was much greater than that of *Weeks*. Many state officials resented *Mapp* as an intrusion into the traditional prerogatives of the states, and members of the public had difficulty understanding why there were not other means to enforce the right to privacy implicit in the Fourth Amendment. In later cases such as *Massachusetts v. Sheppard* (1984), the majority of justices of the Court have accepted the deterrent rationale for the exclusionary rule, and this has resulted in flexibility in its application.

Thomas Tandy Lewis

See also *Escobedo v. Illinois; Ker v. California; Massachusetts v. Sheppard; Robinson v. California; Rochin v. California; Weeks v. United States; Wolf v. Colorado.*

MARBURY V. MADISON

Court: U.S. Supreme Court
Citation: 5 U.S. 137
Date: February 24, 1803
Issues: Judicial review

• For the first time, the U.S. Supreme Court declared that a congressional statute was unconstitutional and therefore invalid.

Before 1803, there was a great deal of debate about whether the Supreme Court possessed the authority to make binding decisions in regard to the constitutionality of statutes, especially those of the federal government. Many jurists argued that this prerogative, now called judicial review, was implied in the Constitution, and the majority of the delegates at the Constitutional Convention accepted the prerogative—narrowly conceived—as legitimate. Alexander Hamilton, in *The Federalist* (1788), No. 78, emphasized the importance of judicial review within a system of limited government. The

Court, in *Ware v. Hylton* (1796), did not hesitate to strike down a state statute that contradicted the "supreme law of the land," a national treaty in this particular case. Likewise, in upholding the constitutionality of a federal tax in *Hylton v. United States* (1796), the Court clearly assumed that it had the power to exercise judicial review over the statutes enacted by Congress.

Nevertheless, critics of the judiciary, including Thomas Jefferson, argued that each of the three coordinate branches of the national government had an equal right to decide on questions of constitutionality for itself.

The seminal *Marbury* decision evolved out of a bitter political conflict between the Federalist Party, which had held power since 1789, and the emerging Republican Party (Democratic-Republicans), headed by Thomas Jefferson. In the election of 1800, Jefferson defeated President John Adams, and Republicans gained firm control of both houses of Congress. The lame-duck president and Congress, horrified at the prospects of a Republican government, attempted to expand Federalist dominance over the national judiciary before Jefferson's inauguration. The strategy included three elements: the installation of John Marshall as chief justice, the Judiciary Act of 1801 (which created new circuit court judgeships), and the Organic Act (which authorized Adams to appoint forty-one justices of the peace for the District of Columbia).

President Thomas Jefferson. (White House Historical Society)

Undelivered Commissions

As late as March 3, 1801, the day before Jefferson became president, the Senate was still confirming the last of the so-called "midnight judges." President Adams had to sign the commissions, which he then sent to Secretary of State Marshall, who had the duties of attaching the Great Seal of the United States and of dispatching the completed commissions to the appointees. Because of the confusion associated with a change of administrations, a number of the commissions never left the executive office building. Once Jefferson was installed as president, he was so infuriated by the stacking of the judiciary that he instructed his secretary of state, James Madison, to withhold the undelivered commissions from the appointees. Somewhat later, the Republican Congress repealed the Judiciary Act of 1801 and postponed the Supreme Court's next meeting until 1803.

Although William Marbury, a well-connected Federalist, had been appointed to a five-year term as justice of the peace, he was among the appointees who never received a commission. Marbury and three associates decided to seek a court order, called a writ of mandamus, directing the secretary of state to turn over their commissions as required by law. They based their suit

John Marshall.
(Rembrandt Peale/
Collection of the
Supreme Court of the
United States)

on section 13 of the Judiciary Act of 1789, which authorized the Supreme Court to issue writs of mandamus to federal office holders. The *Marbury* case created a dilemma for Chief Justice Marshall and his fellow justices. If the Court ordered the secretary of state to deliver the commissions, it would give Jefferson an occasion to refuse, exercising his theory about the Court's lack of authority over a coordinate branch. On the other hand, if the Court declined to issue a writ without providing a good rationale, the Court would then implicitly appear to give confirmation to Jefferson's theory. Marshall was able to find a satisfactory solution.

The Court's Response

For a unanimous Court, Marshall declared that the Court had no authority to issue the requested writ of mandamus because of a constitutional principle of jurisdiction. He explained that Article III of the Constitution limited the Court's original jurisdiction to cases involving a state or a foreign diplomat. Marshall's most important point was that section 13 of the 1789 statute, which authorized the writs, contradicted the Constitution and was void. Referring to both constitutional principles and the constitutional text, Marshall insisted that it "is emphatically the province and duty of the judicial department to say what the law is." In a lengthy *obiter dictum* (an opinion not essential to the ruling), Marshall declared that Marbury and his associates were legally entitled to their commissions, and that the secretary of state, in withholding them, was "in plain violation" of the law. Because Marshall did not order Madison to do anything, however, it was impossible for him to disobey a Court ruling.

Modern commentators are often critical of two aspects of Marshall's interpretations in *Marbury*. In reference to the constitutional issue of original jurisdiction, Marshall could have concluded that the "exceptions" clause of Article III provided Congress with discretion for dealing with both original and appellate jurisdiction. This interpretation, however, was unacceptable to Marshall, because it would have forced the Court to exercise jurisdiction in the case. In regard to section 13 in the 1789 statute, Marshall could have interpreted the language to mean that the Court was authorized to issue only those writs that were proper according to the accepted principles of the law. Such an interpretation was not attractive to Marshall, because it would have prevented him from establishing a precedent of judicial review. In deciding the way he did, the chief justice was taking advantage of an opportunity to refute Jefferson's theory of "tripartite balance."

From the perspective of later history, the *Marbury* decision established the principle that the Court's interpretations of the law are binding on the other two coordinate branches of the national government. At the time, however, not many people recognized the significance of the case. After *Marbury*, with

Congress threatening impeachment, the Marshall Court used considerable restraint when ruling on federal statutes. In *Stuart v. Laird* (1803), announced just six days later, the Court upheld the Republicans' constitutionally suspect law that displaced judges of the circuit courts. It was not until the infamous *Scott v. Sandford* decision of 1857 that a future Court would exercise the power of "coordinate branch" judicial review for the second time. In contrast, when scrutinizing the constitutionality of state laws, nineteenth century justices tended to be much more aggressive.

Further Reading

Clinton, Robert. *Marbury v. Madison and Judicial Review.* Lawrence: University Press of Kansas, 1989.

Garraty, John. *Marbury v. Madison.* In *Quarrels That Have Shaped the Constitution.* New York: Harper & Row, 1987.

Haines, Charles. *The American Doctrine of Judicial Supremacy.* New York: Da Capo, 1973.

Levy, Leonard. *Judicial Review: History and Democracy.* New York: Harper & Row, 1967.

Newmyer, R. Kent. *John Marshall and the Heroic Age of the Supreme Court.* Baton Rouge: Louisiana State University Press, 2001.

Robarge, David. *A Chief Justice's Progress: John Marshall from Revolutionary Virginia to the Supreme Court.* Westport, Conn.: Greenwood Press, 2000.

Sloan, Cliff, and David McKean. *The Great Decision: Jefferson, Adams, Marshall, and the Battle for the Supreme Court.* New York: PublicAffairs, 2009.

Thomas Tandy Lewis

See also *Budd v. New York; Calder v. Bull; Chicago, Milwaukee, and St. Paul Railway Co. v. Minnesota; Fletcher v. Peck; Hayburn's Case; Hylton v. United States; Mississippi v. Johnson; Scott v. Sandford; Stuart v. Laird.*

MARSHALL V. BARLOW'S

Court: U.S. Supreme Court
Citation: 436 U.S. 307
Date: May 23, 1978
Issues: Search and seizure

- The U.S. Supreme Court found that warrantless inspections or "searches" by Occupational Safety and Hazards Act inspectors violated the Fourth Amendment.

A 5-3 majority of the Court in this case declared warrantless searches of businesses by 1970's Occupational Safety and Hazards Act (OSHA) inspectors to be violations of the Fourth Amendment. Although the Court had allowed warrantless searches of gun and liquor dealers because of the special nature of those businesses, the Court found that obtaining warrants would not impose an undue burden on OSHA inspectors. In *Camara v. Municipal Court* (1967), the Court found that historical notions of probable cause do not have to be found before a warrant is issued if an inspection follows "reasonable legislative or administrative standards." In *Barlow's*, the Court held that OSHA inspection warrants must be issued for a specific business as a result of a reasonable, neutral, general plan.

Richard L. Wilson

See also *Atwater v. City of Lago Vista*; *Boyd v. United States*; *Chimel v. California*; *Illinois v. Krull*; *Ker v. California*; *Kyllo v. United States*; *Maryland v. Buie*; *United States v. Leon*; *United States v. Ross*.

Martin v. Hunter's Lessee

Court: U.S. Supreme Court
Citation: 14 U.S. 304
Date: March 20, 1816
Issues: Federal supremacy; Judicial powers; Land law

- For the first time, the U.S. Supreme Court asserted its appellate jurisdiction to review decisions by state supreme courts.

During the American Revolution, Virginia confiscated the land estate of loyalist Lord Fairfax and sold it to private interests. Virginia also enacted a law denying the right of foreign subjects to inherit land in the state. Fairfax's English heir, Denny Martin, argued in court that the Virginia law was inconsistent with treaties between the United States and Great Britain. In *Fairfax's Devisee v. Hunter's Lessee* (1813), the Supreme Court ruled in favor of Martin.

The high court of Virginia, headed by Spencer Roane, refused to honor the decision and declared that section 25 of the Judiciary Act of 1789, which authorized the Court's review of state court decisions, was an unconstitutional violation of Virginia's sovereignty. The case was returned to the Supreme Court, renamed as *Martin v. Hunter's Lessee.*

Speaking for a unanimous Court, Justice Joseph Story repeated the earlier decision, and his forty-page opinion on behalf of federal judicial review is considered a masterpiece. Story insisted that section 25 of the Judiciary Act was "supported by the letter and spirit of the Constitution." For the purposes of national union and uniformity, it was imperative for the Court to have the final authority to interpret treaties, federal statutes, and the Constitution. Story's landmark opinion strengthened national sovereignty and the supremacy of the federal judiciary. The major ideas of *Martin* were reaffirmed in several cases, especially *Cohens v. Virginia* (1821).

Thomas Tandy Lewis

See also *Cohens v. Virginia; Ex parte Young; Fairfax's Devisee v. Hunter's Lessee; Younger v. Harris.*

MARTIN V. MOTT

Court: U.S. Supreme Court
Citation: 25 U.S. 19
Date: February 2, 1827
Issues: Presidential powers

• The U.S. Supreme Court, in the first of a long series of cases, granted the president broad powers to deal with war and foreign affairs.

When President James Madison called out the state militia during the War of 1812, Jacob Mott refused an order issued by his state's governor to assemble for duty. Duly convicted, he appealed the penalty, which was the seizure of his property. The state court initially held for Mott, but the Supreme Court found the Constitution gave Congress the power to authorize the statute under which the president acted and that the president was the sole authority as to whether the terms of the statute required his action. Justice Joseph Story wrote the unanimous decision for the seven-member Court.

Richard L. Wilson

See also *Dames and Moore v. Regan; Goldwater v. Carter; Humphrey's Executor v. United States; McCulloch v. Maryland; Mississippi v. Johnson; Myers v. United States; United States v. Curtiss-Wright Export Corp.; United States v. Nixon; Youngstown Sheet and Tube Co. v. Sawyer.*

MARTIN V. WILKS

Court: U.S. Supreme Court
Citation: 490 U.S. 755
Date: June 12, 1989
Issues: Employment discrimination

- The U.S. Supreme Court held that a group complaining of employment discrimination must include all other relevant groups in its complaint; this ruling was largely overturned by the 1991 Civil Rights Act.

Chief Justice William H. Rehnquist wrote the decision for the 5-4 majority, holding that African American firefighters who complained of hiring and promotion discrimination should have included all white firefighters in their original complaint. The African Americans did not, and the lower court ruled that the white firefighters attempted to intervene too late in the proceedings. The lower court allowed a consent decree to be entered which the white firefighters regarded as a form of reverse discrimination. The Supreme Court overturned the consent decree favoring the African American employees, but Congress believed that the Court went too far and amended the Civil Rights Act in 1991 to make it marginally easier for African Americans to file employment discrimination complaints. Justice John Paul Stevens wrote a strong dissent in which he was joined by Justices Thurgood Marshall, William J. Brennan, Jr., and Harry A. Blackmun.

Richard L. Wilson

See also *Citizens United v. Federal Election Commission; Firefighters Local Union No. 1784 v. Stotts et al.; Local 28 of Sheet Metal Workers International Association v. Equal Employment Opportunity Commission; Ricci v. DeStefano; United Steelworkers of America v. Weber; Washington v. Davis.*

Marvin v. Marvin

Court: California Supreme Court
Citation: 18 Cal. 3d 660
Date: December 27, 1976
Issues: Marriage; Women's issues

- The *Marvin* case began a trend that recognized the right of unmarried cohabitants to enter into express contracts to pool resources and acquire property. Express agreements between unmarried adults living together are unenforceable only to the extent that they are based explicitly on unlawful "meretricious" (sexual) services.

Plaintiff Michelle Triola Marvin, a Las Vegas dancer and supper club singer, met actor Lee Marvin and moved in with him in 1964. When they split up seven years later, she claimed that she had cooked and cleaned for him and had taken care of him after he had been drinking. She claimed that he told her, "What I have is yours and what you have is mine," that they agreed to hold themselves out to the general public as husband and wife, and that he agreed to support her.

California law required that married persons split the assets of their marriage (community property). Although the Marvins were not formally married, Michelle believed that she was entitled to money from Lee because she fulfilled her obligations under the agreement and gave up her career as an entertainer in order to devote herself to the defendant. When Lee disagreed, the dispute went to court. Celebrity divorce lawyer Marvin Mitchelson asserted Michelle's claim to Lee Marvin's earnings of more than one million dollars. The so-called palimony suit produced widespread media publicity.

The case demonstrated that courts may inquire into the conduct of the parties in order to determine whether it indicates an implied contract or implied agreement of partnership or joint venture, thereby setting an important legal precedent. Moreover, a nonmarital partner may recover in *quantum meruit* (the reasonable value) of the household services rendered minus the reasonable value of support received if he or she can prove that the services were rendered with the expectation of monetary reward. The suit relied on a doctrine in contract law known as "quasi" or "implied" contract, in which courts may infer a legally enforceable agreement from the circumstances of the parties' dealings, even though they had not entered into any written agreement.

The right of spouses to support and property arises from the spouses' status as married persons. The *Marvin* court case expressly declined to treat unmarried cohabitants like married persons. Rather, it ruled that a nonmarital partner's right to support or to property is dependent upon proof of some underlying basis, such as the existence of an express or implied contract or some other legal claim. Although the case applied specifically only in California, other states have since applied the same principles to contracts between unmarried couples, both heterosexual and homosexual.

The case was sent back to the trial court for further proceedings. In 1981, the trial court in *Marvin II* found that the parties had never agreed to share their property and that Lee Marvin did not agree to support Michelle. Nonetheless, the court awarded Michelle $104,000 for the purpose of rehabilitation or training to learn new employable skills.

Marcia J. Weiss

Further Reading

Ball, Howard. *The U.S. Supreme Court in the Intimate Lives of Americans: Birth, Sex, Marriage, Childrearing, and Death.* New York: New York University Press, 2002.

Booth, Alan, and Ann C. Crouter, eds. *Just Living Together: Implications of Cohabitation for Children, Families, and Social Policy.* Mahwah, N.J.: Lawrence Erlbaum, 2002.

See also *Orr v. Orr; Stanton v. Stanton.*

MARYLAND V. BUIE

Court: U.S. Supreme Court
Citation: 494 U.S. 325
Date: February 28, 1990
Issues: Police powers; Search and seizure

• The U.S. Supreme Court's ruling in *Maryland v. Buie* expanded the power of police officers to conduct warrantless sweeps of premises while making in-house arrests, thereby increasing their opportunities to seize evidence found in plain view.

The Supreme Court's finding in *Maryland v. Buie* established two separate rules. First, following an in-house arrest, police may—without a search warrant—conduct a protective sweep of the entire premises if there is reasonable suspicion to believe that dangerous third parties are present. In addition to authorizing protective sweeps, the ruling also established that absent a search warrant or any suspicion, incident to an arrest, the police may automatically look into other spaces, including closets or rooms, in which a dangerous third person might be found, provided that such areas immediately adjoin the place of arrest. Under either rule, evidence found in plain view may be seized.

The *Maryland v. Buie* case originated in 1986. Following an armed robbery in Maryland by two men, one of whom was wearing a red running suit, police obtained arrest warrants for Buie and his suspected accomplice, Allen. Police in Prince George's County executed the warrant at Buie's house and arrested Buie when he emerged from his basement. After the arrest, the police performed a cursory check of Buie's basement for the purpose of locating dangerous persons and found a red running suit lying in plain view. A police officer seized the suit, which was later admitted as evidence at Buie's trial for armed robbery. Buie was convicted.

After Buie's conviction, Maryland's Court of Appeals reversed the lower trial court and appellate court decisions because those courts had accepted the running suit as evidence. The high court disallowed the suit because the police who had conducted the sweep that found it lacked probable cause to believe that a dangerous third party might be present in Buie's home.

Because a protective sweep is a search, it falls under the limitations of the Fourth Amendment, which requires that searches be reasonable. Under most circumstances, the U.S. Supreme Court has found that for searches to be considered reasonable, they require warrants and probable cause. However, the Court has dispensed with those two requirements in cases in which there has been risk of immediate physical danger to police officers performing their official duties. For example, the Court has held that in the interest of safety, "stop and frisk" searches on the street and roadside searches of automobile passenger compartments—equivalent to "frisking" a vehicle—are permissible under the Fourth Amendment.

In *Buie*, the Supreme Court drew on its earlier findings in *Terry v. Ohio* (1968) and *Michigan v. Long* (1983) to find analogous risks of immediate physical danger to police officers while making in-house arrests. Those risks justify protective sweeps with search warrants or probable cause. However, the fact that the Court's ruling permits officers to look in adjoining spaces allows police making in-house arrests *always* to presume that dangerous third parties may be present. That aspect of the Court's ruling thus made it easier for police to collect evidence found in plain view.

LaVerne McQuiller Williams

Further Reading

Katz, Lewis R. *Questions and Answers: Criminal Procedure I and II.* Newark, N.J.: LexisNexis, 2003.

Loewy, Arnold H. *Criminal Procedure: Cases, Materials and Questions.* Cincinnati: Anderson Publishing, 2002.

See also *Harris v. United States; Marshall v. Barlow's; Michigan v. Long; Terry v. Ohio; United States v. Ross.*

Maryland v. Craig

Court: U.S. Supreme Court
Citation: 497 U.S. 836
Date: June 27, 1990
Issues: Children's rights

- In this case, which upheld a Maryland statute permitting a child to testify via one-way, closed-circuit television, the U.S. Supreme Court determined that the witness-confrontation rights of defendants guaranteed by the Sixth Amendment are neither absolute nor an indispensable part of criminal hearings.

In 1986, Sandra Ann Craig, an operator of a Maryland child-care center and kindergarten, was indicted for sexually abusing a six-year-old child in her care and was subsequently convicted. Under a state statute, the victim and other children were allowed to testify on a closed-circuit television without directly confronting the defendant. On the grounds that the law violated a defendant's right to face an accuser, guaranteed by the Sixth Amendment, Craig appealed the conviction. Although the Maryland Court of Special Appeals upheld the conviction, the next higher court, the Court of Appeals of Maryland, ordered a new trial, finding that the state prosecutors had not sufficiently justified their use of the closed-circuit television procedure. It also questioned the statute's constitutionality but did not determine it per se.

On *certiorari*, the U.S. Supreme Court vacated the lower court's order and remanded, holding that the confrontation clause of the Sixth Amendment did not invalidate the Maryland statute's procedure. Justice Sandra Day O'Connor, writing the 5-4 majority opinion, argued that under "narrow circumstances," when there are "competing interests," dispensing with witness-confrontation rights is warranted. Further, the Court stated that the term "confront" as used in the Sixth Amendment cannot be defined simply as "face-to-face." A state's concern for the psychological and physical well-being of a child abuse victim, as reflected in the Maryland statute, was deemed important enough to supersede a defendant's right to face an accuser. The majority also argued that in previous cases other Sixth Amendment rights had been interpreted "in the context of the necessities of trial and the adversary process."

A vigorous dissenting opinion, presented by Justice Antonin Scalia, argued that "confront" as used in the Sixth Amendment clearly means "face-to-face," whatever else it may also mean. The majority was also chided for distorting explicit constitutional text to suit "currently favored public policy." Although granting that the procedure authorized by the Maryland statute may be fair, the dissenters maintained that it violated the constitutional protection afforded defendants in the confrontation clause of the Sixth Amendment.

A controversial case, *Maryland v. Craig* left in its wake the likelihood of additional problems of interpretation precisely because it held a constitutional guarantee to be less than absolute and incontrovertible. Determining which "narrow circumstances" will validate a suspension of a defendant's right to a face-to-face confrontation with an accuser will be an ongoing issue in jurisprudence, because it must be decided virtually on a case-by-case basis.

John W. Fiero

See also *Counselman v. Hitchcock; Kastigar v. United States; Pointer v. Texas.*

MASSACHUSETTS BOARD OF RETIREMENT V. MURGIA

Court: U.S. Supreme Court
Citation: 427 U.S. 307
Date: June 25, 1976
Issues: Civil rights and liberties; Equal protection of the law

• In this age discrimination case, the Court restrained extensions of previously expanded categories of discrimination and the applicability of the equal protection clause to them.

Robert Murgia was a fifty-year-old uniformed officer with the Massachusetts State Police. Annual medical examinations required by the state had consistently shown him to be in excellent physical and mental health. Health notwithstanding, Murgia, like all uniformed officers, was subject to a state statute that mandated retirement on his fiftieth birthday. Murgia challenged the law, arguing that his compulsory retirement by Massachusetts discriminated against him on the basis of his age and therefore violated the equal protection clause of the U.S. Constitution's Fourteenth Amendment.

A three-judge federal district court upheld Murgia's challenge, concluding that the Massachusetts statute "lacked a rational basis in furthering any substantial state interest." The Massachusetts Board of Retirement, however, appealed to the U.S. Supreme Court, then headed by President Richard Nixon's appointee, Chief Justice Warren Burger, who had succeeded Chief Justice Earl Warren. Unlike Warren, Burger was a moderate conservative who advocated judicial restraint, in which he often was supported by Justices William Rehnquist, Lewis Powell, Byron R. White, and Harry Blackmun. By the mid-1970's, however, the Burger Court was in a difficult position. Through the 1960's, the Warren Court's antidiscrimination rulings had lent a literal interpretation to the equal protection clause, namely that no state should deny to any person within its jurisdiction equal protection of the laws. The clause was therefore applied to an increasing number of alleged civil rights discriminations.

This represented a significant shift for the Court. Previously the equal protection clause had been invoked almost exclusively in cases involving the civil rights of blacks. Thus the Warren Court launched so-called substantive due process and substantive equal protection. Under the Fourteenth Amendment, people's federally protected rights were also applied to violations of those rights by the states. Under Burger, the Court sought rational grounds to restrain this process by "strict judicial scrutiny." It was in this context that the Murgia appeal came before the Court.

In a 7-1 decision, the Court ruled against Murgia. It did not deny the adverse effects that premature retirement can have on individuals, nor did it suggest that the Massachusetts statute was well drafted or wise. Rather, it decided that drawing lines that created distinctions—age, in this case—was a legislative task, that the statute was rational, and that the Massachusetts legislature had not denied Murgia equal protection of the laws. Determining the appropriate applications of substantive equal protection has continued to trouble the Supreme Court.

Clifton K. Yearley

See also *Albemarle Paper Co. v. Moody; Bowe v. Colgate-Palmolive; Firefighters Local Union No. 1784 v. Stotts et al.; Lorance v. AT&T Technologies; Martin v. Wilks; Washington v. Davis.*

MASSACHUSETTS V. MELLON

Court: U.S. Supreme Court
Citation: 262 U.S. 447
Date: June 4, 1923
Issues: Standing; State sovereignty

- By deciding that the issue of noncoercive federal grants to the states was a political controversy and therefore nonjusticiable, the U.S. Supreme Court tacitly announced that such programs did not have any constitutional objections.

The Sheppard-Towner Act of 1921 provided federal subsidies for state programs promoting infant and maternal health. Massachusetts asserted in federal court that the act undermined state sovereignty by extending federal power into functions properly reserved to the states under the Tenth Amendment. Although acceptance of a subsidy was voluntary, Massachusetts argued that the financial penalty for nonacceptance was so great that states were coerced into accepting the federal funds.

By a 9-0 vote, the Supreme Court held that the case presented no "justiciable controversy." In the opinion for the Court, Justice George Sutherland concluded that the states were not coerced into accepting federal funds and that the program was financed by individual taxpayers. A state had no judicial standing to sue the federal government on behalf of its citizens. Although Sutherland wrote that the Court had no authority to make hypothetical judgments about "abstract questions," his opinion included an *obiter dictum* strongly suggesting that federal grants-in-aid were entirely constitutional. In a companion case, *Frothingham v. Mellon* (1923), the Court held that taxpayers did not have standing to challenge federal spending programs. The two *Mel-*

lon decisions were important because they removed a potential obstacle to the great expansion of federal grants that occurred during the New Deal period.

Thomas Tandy Lewis

See also *Alcoa v. Federal Trade Commission; Frothingham v. Mellon; United States v. Richardson.*

MASSACHUSETTS V. SHEPPARD

Court: U.S. Supreme Court
Citation: 468 U.S. 981
Date: July 5, 1984
Issues: Evidence; Search and seizure

• The Court ruled that, the Fourth Amendment notwithstanding, a search authorized by a defective warrant was proper because the police had acted in good faith in executing what they thought was a valid warrant.

Osborne Sheppard was convicted in a Massachusetts state court of first-degree murder. Sheppard appealed his conviction to the Massachusetts Supreme Judicial Court on the basis that the police had knowingly searched his residence with a defective search warrant.

Boston police detective Peter O'Malley had drafted an affidavit to support an application for an arrest warrant and a search warrant authorizing the search of Sheppard's residence. The affidavit stated that the police wanted to search for such items as the victim's clothing and a blunt instrument that might have been used on the victim. The affidavit was reviewed and approved by the district attorney.

Unable to find a proper warrant application form, O'Malley found a previously used warrant form used in another district to search for controlled substances. After making some changes on the form, it and the affidavit were presented to a judge at his residence. The judge was made aware of the defective warrant form, and he made further changes before he signed it. He did not change the substantive portion, however, which continued to authorize a search for controlled substances, nor did the judge alter the form to incorporate the affidavit.

The police believed that the warrant authorized the search, and they proceeded to act in good faith. The trial judge ruled that the exclusionary rule did not apply in this case because the conduct of the officers was objectively reasonable and largely error free. On appeal, Sheppard argued that the evidence obtained pursuant to the defective warrant should have been suppressed. The Supreme Judicial Court of Massachusetts agreed and reversed the lower court's conviction of Sheppard. The court held that it did not recognize a good-faith exception to the exclusionary rule.

Massachusetts filed a petition for writ of *certiorari*. Speaking for the U.S. Supreme Court, Justice Byron White stated that the police officers who conducted the search should not be punished. They acted in good faith in executing what they reasonably thought was a valid warrant—one that was subsequently determined invalid—issued by a detached and neutral magistrate (*United States v. Leon*, 1984). The exclusionary rule, White said, did not apply because it was adopted to deter unlawful searches by police, not to punish the errors of judges. He stated that an error of constitutional dimension may have been committed by the judge who did not make the necessary changes, but not the police. Judgment of the Supreme Judicial Court was therefore reversed and remanded for further proceedings consistent with the U.S. Supreme Court's opinion.

Bill Manikas

See also *United States v. Leon*; *United States v. United States District Court.*

MASSIAH V. UNITED STATES

Court: U.S. Supreme Court
Citation: 377 U.S. 201
Date: May 18, 1964
Issues: Confessions; Evidence; Right to counsel

• This U.S. Supreme Court ruling on the right to counsel expanded the exclusionary rule to disallow the prosecution from using any evidence that the police have deliberately elicited from an indicted defendant when not in the presence of a lawyer.

A federal grand jury indicted Winston Massiah and a codefendant on charges of illegally trafficking in cocaine. Massiah retained a lawyer and was released on bail. Unknown to Massiah, his codefendant agreed to cooperate with federal officers in exchange for a reduced sentence. In a private conversation with the codefendant, Massiah made incriminating statements that were overheard by an agent operating a transmitter.

At the subsequent trial, the judge allowed the agent to testify about Massiah's statements, which were tantamount to a confession. Based on this evidence, the jury quickly decided that Massiah was guilty. In appealing the conviction, defense lawyers pointed to the precedent of *Spano v. New York* (1959), in which the Supreme Court had held that the prosecution may not make use of a confession that police officers obtained by intimidating a defendant who had already been indicted. In getting Massiah to confess, however, the police had used only trickery, not threats or other forms of coercion.

The Supreme Court, by a 6-3 vote, overturned Massiah's conviction. Writing for the majority, Justice Potter Stewart held that once adversarial proceedings have been initiated, any statements deliberately elicited by government agents outside the presence of a defense lawyer must be excluded from a criminal trial, except if the defendant had explicitly waived his Sixth Amendment right to counsel. The justices in the majority made a linkage between this right and the Fifth Amendment privilege against self-incrimination, which they interpreted to mean that confessions not given voluntarily and intentionally are inadmissible as evidence. In this case, therefore, it was irrelevant that the police had not forcefully compelled Massiah to made incriminating statements to his colleague.

The *Massiah* holding applied only to statements obtained by law-enforcement officers after a person has been formally charged with a crime. Later that year, in *Escobedo v. Illinois*, the Court recognized that a suspect yet to be indicted has a right to counsel when in custody for the purpose of interrogation. The famous case of *Miranda v. Arizona* (1966) obligated the police to inform suspects of this right before interrogation. The Court further expanded the prohibition against using trickery to elicit information from detained suspects outside the presence of counsel in *Brewer v. Williams* (1977). In *United States v. Henry* (1980), the Court suppressed a conversation in which an incarcerated defendant made incriminating statements to a cellmate cooperating with the police, even though the cellmate had simply listened and had not encouraged the defendant to discuss the crime.

Thomas Tandy Lewis

Further Reading

Taylor, John B. *Right to Counsel and Privilege Against Self-Incrimination: Rights and Liberties Under the Law.* Santa Barbara, Calif.: ABC-CLIO, 2004.

Whitebread, Charles, and Christopher Slobogin. *Criminal Procedures: An Analysis of Cases and Concepts.* 4th ed. New York: Foundation Press, 2000.

See also *Arizona v. Fulminante; Escobedo v. Illinois; Gideon v. Wainwright; Miranda v. Arizona.*

MASSON V. NEW YORKER MAGAZINE

Court: U.S. Supreme Court
Citation: 501 U.S. 496
Date: June 20, 1991
Issues: Freedom of the press

• The U.S. Supreme Court held that the First Amendment allows for public persons to win libel suits against journalists who deliberately distort the meaning of their statements.

Janet Malcolm, a contributor to *The New Yorker* magazine, published a two-part article that was highly critical of psychoanalyst Jeffrey Masson, a former director of the Sigmund Freud Archives. In a libel suit against Malcolm and the magazine, Masson claimed that many of the statements attributed to him in quotation marks were fabrications. Because he was a public person, *New York Times Co. v. Sullivan* (1964) was applicable to the suit, and therefore, Masson had the burden of proving actual malice, which meant either knowledge of falsity or a reckless disregard for truthful reporting. The lower federal courts dismissed the suit, holding that interpretations of actual statements did not constitute actual malice.

By a 7-2 vote, the Supreme Court rejected the lower courts' judgment and remanded the case for a jury trial. Justice Anthony M. Kennedy's opinion for the majority held that a "deliberate alteration of words" in a statement constitutes a knowledge of falsity if it materially changes "the meaning conveyed by the statement." In the upcoming trial, therefore, the jury would have the task

of deciding whether the meaning of Masson's statements had been sufficiently altered to satisfy the *Sullivan* standard. The *Masson* decision provided
notice to writers and publishers to be very careful when using quotation
marks that appear to denote a person's actual words.

Thomas Tandy Lewis

See also *Gertz v. Robert Welch; Hustler Magazine v. Falwell; New York Times Co. v.
Sullivan.*

MAXWELL V. DOW

Court: U.S. Supreme Court
Citation: 176 U.S. 581
Date: February 26, 1900
Issues: Juries

• The U.S. Supreme Court's decision in this case, in which it ignored
the due process clause, is most notable for the dissent by Justice John

Justice John Marshall Harlan.
(Library of Congress)

Marshall Harlan, which can be seen as a precursor to the Fourteenth Amendment incorporation doctrine.

A man convicted of robbery challenged his conviction because of the use of a presentment rather than a grand jury indictment and a jury composed of eight rather than twelve members. The Supreme Court upheld his conviction, eight to one, and summarily dismissed the defendant's objections. As in the *Slaughterhouse Cases* (1873), the Court ignored the Fourteenth Amendment's due process clause and the privileges and immunities clause. To justify its decision, the Court sought out a precedent from a state court in a case taken before the passage of the Fourteenth Amendment. Justice John Marshall Harlan dissented eloquently about the importance of the states being required to follow the Fifth and Sixth Amendment's requirements for a fair trial and due process, thereby presaging the incorporation of the Bill of Rights through the Fourteenth Amendment in the twentieth century.

Richard L. Wilson

See also *Ballew v. Georgia; Barron v. Baltimore; Slaughterhouse Cases; Williams v. Florida.*

MEMOIRS V. MASSACHUSETTS

Court: U.S. Supreme Court
Citation: 383 U.S. 413
Date: March 21, 1966
Issues: Pornography and obscenity

• The U.S. Supreme Court strengthened the protection of freedom of speech by restricting the scope of what was obscene.

Writing for a six-vote majority, Justice William J. Brennan, Jr., ruled that each of the three elements of the national obscenity test announced in *Roth v. United States* (1957) had to be met for a book to be declared obscene. John Cleland's eighteenth century erotic classic, *Fanny Hill: Memoirs of a Woman of Pleasure* (1749), which was reprinted during the 1960's, dealt with a prostitute's sexual adventures and had been judged obscene in the early nineteenth century. However, because it did not meet all three *Roth* tests, it could not be banned. This decision strengthened the First Amendment protection of freedom of speech by restricting the government's power to ban allegedly obscene materials to only those cases in which the three tests of *Roth* could be satisfied simultaneously.

Richard L. Wilson

See also *Hamling v. United States; Miller v. California; Roth v. United States; Stanley v. Georgia.*

MERITOR SAVINGS BANK V. VINSON

Court: U.S. Supreme Court
Citation: 477 U.S. 57
Date: June 19, 1986
Issues: Sex discrimination; Women's issues

- This case found the U.S. Supreme Court holding that sexual harassment was discrimination and that a hostile working environment constituted harassment.

Mechelle Vinson was hired by Meritor Savings Bank in 1974 and proceeded up the ladder from teller-trainee to teller to head teller to assistant branch manager. In September, 1978, she took an indefinite sick leave and was discharged on November 1, 1978, for excessive use of that leave. Vinson sued, claiming sexual harassment in violation of Title VII of the Civil Rights Act of 1964, which bars discrimination in the workplace based on several factors, including sex. Vinson described the cause of her leave: She said that her supervisor had invited her out to dinner, then suggested they go to a motel to have sexual relations. At first, she had refused, but then for fear of losing her job, she agreed. Afterward, her supervisor made repeated demands for sexual favors, and they had intercourse forty or fifty times over the next several years. She also accused him of other forms of sexual harassment.

The position of the bank was that the law was only concerned with tangible loss of an economic character, not purely psychological aspects of the workplace environment, but Justice William Rehnquist, for a unanimous Court, disagreed. He said that the Equal Employment Opportunity Commission (EEOC) issued guidelines in 1980 holding that sexual harassment is a form of discrimination, and it includes a hostile or abusive work environment. If the sex-related conduct was unwelcome, the law was broken.

The implications of *Meritor Savings Bank v. Vinson* were that sexual harassment is illegal and that a hostile environment is harassment. Also, the voluntary nature of the act was not the issue, but whether it was unwelcome.

Robert W. Langran

See also *Clinton v. Jones; County of Washington v. Gunther; Frontiero v. Richardson; Geduldig v. Aiello; Grove City College v. Bell; Hoyt v. Florida; Phillips v. Martin Marietta Corp.; Rosenfeld v. Southern Pacific; Stanton v. Stanton.*

MERRYMAN, EX PARTE. *See* EX PARTE MERRYMAN

METRO BROADCASTING V. FEDERAL COMMUNICATIONS COMMISSION

Court: U.S. Supreme Court
Citation: 497 U.S. 547
Date: June 27, 1990
Issues: Affirmative action

• The U.S. Supreme Court ruled that Congress had the broad authority to enact affirmative action policies designed to increase minority participation in the broadcasting industry, but the Court overturned the ruling five years later.

By a 5-4 majority, the Supreme Court used the important governmental interest standard when upholding a Federal Communications Commission (FCC) policy designed to increase broadcast diversity. The decision surprised observers, because in *Richmond v. J. A. Croson Co.* (1989), the Court ruled that state and local affirmative action programs must be judged by the strict scrutiny standard, which almost certainly would have disqualified the FCC's policy. Apparently, the majority of the justices concluded that federal programs were entitled to a greater presumption of validity. In *Adarand Constructors v. Peña* (1995), however, a 5-4 majority of the justices repudiated the *Metro Broadcasting* approach and held that all affirmative action programs—federal, state, or local—must be reviewed under the demanding strict scrutiny standard.

Thomas Tandy Lewis

See also *Adarand Constructors v. Peña; Fullilove v. Klutznick; Richmond v. J. A. Croson Co.*

MEYER V. NEBRASKA

Court: U.S. Supreme Court
Citation: 262 U.S. 390
Date: June 4, 1923
Issues: Parental rights; Right to privacy

- The U.S. Supreme Court first applied the doctrine of substantive due process to strike down a law for infringing upon a noneconomic liberty.

Shortly after World War I, the Nebraska legislature passed a statute that prohibited schools from teaching any modern non-English language to children before the eighth grade. Meyer, who taught German in a Lutheran school, was convicted of disobeying the law. By a 7-2 vote, the Supreme Court ruled that the law violated the due process clause of the Fourteenth Amendment. Writing for the majority, Justice James C. McReynolds explained that the amendment protected long-recognized liberties such as the right to marry, to acquire knowledge, and to raise children. The law was "arbitrary" and "without reasonable relation" to a legitimate governmental purpose. In dissent, Justice Oliver Wendell Holmes, having often criticized the use of substantive due process to protect a freedom of contract, argued that the state had a reasonable interest in promoting a common language. *Meyer* was never

Justice James C.
McReynolds in 1914,
the year he joined the
Supreme Court. (Harris &
Ewing Collection/
Library of Congress)

overturned, and forty years later, it became an important precedent in the development of a constitutional right of privacy.

Thomas Tandy Lewis

See also *Lau v. Nichols; Pierce v. Society of Sisters.*

MIAMI HERALD PUBLISHING CO. V. TORNILLO

Court: U.S. Supreme Court
Citation: 418 U.S. 241
Date: June 25, 1974
Issues: Freedom of the press

- The U.S. Supreme Court strengthened the power of newspapers by holding that states cannot require newspapers to grant a right of reply to political candidates they criticize.

Florida passed a right-of-reply statute requiring newspapers to grant equal space to political candidates whom the newspaper had criticized. The *Miami Herald* denied equal space to Pat Tornillo, a local teachers' union leader, whom the paper had criticized twice editorially, and he sued. State courts upheld the right-of-reply law, but the Supreme Court struck it down as an infringement on the First Amendment freedom of the press. Chief Justice Warren E. Burger, in the unanimous opinion for the Court, wrote that choosing the content of a paper and determining how it portrayed public figures and issues was an exercise in editorial control and judgment, in which the government could not interfere without violating the constitutional guarantee of a free press. Justices William J. Brennan, Jr., William H. Rehnquist, and Byron R. White concurred.

Richard L. Wilson

See also *Branzburg v. Hayes; Cohen v. Cowles Media Co.; Garrison v. Louisiana; Grosjean v. American Press Co.; Richmond Newspapers v. Virginia; Time v. Hill.*

Michael M. v. Superior Court of Sonoma County

Court: U.S. Supreme Court
Citation: 450 U.S. 464
Date: March 23, 1981
Issues: Sex discrimination

- The U.S. Supreme Court upheld state laws saying men could commit statutory rape but women could not.

California law held men culpable for statutory rape but not women, even if both parties were within a narrow underage range, arguing that such a law acted more as a deterrent to pregnancy than a gender-neutral law would because the young woman was needed as a witness to the crime. A Supreme Court plurality of four accepted this view, upheld the statute, and sustained the conviction of "Michael M." The Court was anything but unified on the case. Justice Harry A. Blackmun concurred in the result but did not join in the opinion, thereby creating a 5-4 vote but only a four-member plurality opinion. Based on his quotation of lengthy extracts from the trial Blackmun appeared to feel that the case was a hard-to-prove forcible rape case. Potter Stewart wrote a separate concurrence. Justice William J. Brennan, Jr., dissented and was joined by Byron R. White and Thurgood Marshall. They argued that California had not proved its law was a greater deterrent to pregnancy than a more gender-balanced law would have been. Justice John Paul Stevens dissented separately, arguing that a law that punished one of two parties to a consensual act was illogical, and this problem could perhaps be avoided if the law punished the aggressor or more willing party.

Richard L. Wilson

See also *County of Washington v. Gunther*; *Frontiero v. Richardson*; *Geduldig v. Aiello*; *Grove City College v. Bell*; *Hoyt v. Florida*; *Meritor Savings Bank v. Vinson*; *Phillips v. Martin Marietta Corp.*; *Rosenfeld v. Southern Pacific*; *Stanton v. Stanton*.

MICHIGAN DEPARTMENT OF STATE POLICE V. SITZ

Court: U.S. Supreme Court
Citation: 496 U.S. 444
Date: June 14, 1990
Issues: Search and seizure

• The U.S. Supreme Court upheld the use of drunken driving checkpoints under certain conditions.

A group of licensed drivers sued Michigan, challenging the constitutionality of a state law and program that set up drunken driving checkpoints designed to catch people driving under the influence. They argued that the checkpoints constituted an illegal search and seizure under the Fourth Amendment. Lower courts ruled against the program, but by a 6-3 vote, the Supreme Court upheld the Michigan statute and program. The Court maintained that the lower courts had misread the relevant cases, *United States v. Martinez-Fuerte* (1976) and *Brown v. Texas* (1979). In the opinion for the Court, Chief Justice William H. Rehnquist agreed that Michigan had a legitimate interest in trying to curb drunken driving. Justice Harry A. Blackmun concurred, and Justices William J. Brennan, Jr., Thurgood Marshall, and John Paul Stevens dissented.

Richard L. Wilson

See also *Mapp v. Ohio; Maryland v. Buie.*

MICHIGAN V. LONG

Court: U.S. Supreme Court
Citation: 463 U.S. 1032
Date: July 6, 1983
Issues: States' rights

• The U.S. Supreme Court declared that it would assume that state courts relied on federal law unless the courts clearly demonstrated otherwise.

By a 6-3 vote, the Supreme Court attempted to unravel the perplexing question of how to interpret the "independent and adequate state grounds" issue. The case sprang from a Michigan Supreme Court decision about automobile searches. The ambiguity concerning just what constitutional provisions were involved in the lower court's decision led the Court to declare that it would regard state decisions as being based on federal law in most cases. In her opinion for the Court, Justice Sandra Day O'Connor stated that federal law was assumed to be the guiding model unless the state court clearly indicated that "federal cases were only being used for guidance" and the decision rested on "adequate and independent" state grounds. Justice Harry A. Blackmun concurred. Justices William J. Brennan, Jr., Thurgood Marshall, and John Paul Stevens dissented.

Richard L. Wilson

See also *Erie Railroad Co. v. Tompkins*; *Gelpcke v. Dubuque*; *Maryland v. Buie*; *Swift v. Tyson.*

MILKOVICH V. LORAIN JOURNAL CO.

Court: U.S. Supreme Court
Citation: 497 U.S. 1
Date: June 21, 1990
Issues: Freedom of the press

• The U.S. Supreme Court ruled that a trial could be held in a libel case against a newspaper, thereby increasing the complexity of libel litigation.

In 1975, a *Lorain Journal* sports commentator suggested that a high school coach might have lied in an investigation of a fight that took place after a sports event, and the coach sued. For fifteen years, the libel case was considered in various courts before the newspaper obtained a summary judgment from an Ohio court that the article was a constitutionally protected opinion. By a 7-2 vote, the Supreme Court dismissed the court's summary judgment of the fifteen-year-old suit and ordered that a trial must be held, thereby increasing the time needed to resolve the case.

Justice William H. Rehnquist, in his opinion for the Court, concluded that the Ohio court had mistakenly assumed that *Gertz v. Robert Welch* (1974) created a special, protected press category labeled "opinion." The Court emphasized that even public officials (the least protected of all) could sue for libel for false defamatory statements, and trials could be held. Naturally, a newspaper had all of the other protections granted it under the current complex libel law. Justice Thurgood Marshall joined Justice William J. Brennan, Jr., in dissent, agreeing that there was no special privilege for opinion, but that this article was protected because it was conjecture.

Richard L. Wilson

See also *Garrison v. Louisiana; Gertz v. Robert Welch; New York Times Co. v. Sullivan; Time v. Hill.*

MILLER ET AL. V. CIVIL CITY OF SOUTH BEND

Court: U.S. Court of Appeals for the Seventh Circuit
Citation: 904 F.2d 1081, 1120
Date: May 25, 1990
Issues: First Amendment guarantees; Pornography and obscenity;
Symbolic speech

- This decision held that nonobscene barroom nude dancing constituted "expressive activity," as opposed to "mere conduct," and thus deserved First Amendment protection.

This case represents an attempt to navigate the First Amendment's often elusive boundary between expression and conduct. The suit was originally brought in 1985 by several adult-entertainment entrepreneurs and dancers in an effort to prevent the state of Indiana from enforcing its public indecency law, which banned nudity in public places, against them. The plaintiffs challenged the statute as an unconstitutional infringement on their First Amendment rights of expression. In rebuttal, the state justified its law as an attempt to protect the public morality and family structure.

In an earlier case, the same statute had been challenged before the Indiana Supreme Court on overbreadth grounds. In that 1979 suit, the plaintiffs claimed that in addition to its permissible restrictions, Indiana's statute restricted constitutionally protected rights of free speech and expression. The Indiana U.S. Supreme Court had rejected this contention and interpreted the statute to apply to conduct alone and not to forms of expressive activity. Moreover, the court held that barroom dancing was "mere conduct," which could be constitutionally prohibited by the state.

In this later case, the district court for the Northern District of Indiana was asked to consider the statute as applied to nonobscene nude dancing. The court was able to skirt the definition of "obscenity" because the state conceded that the activity in question was not obscene. Instead, the state argued that the activity in question was "mere conduct," outside the realm of First Amendment protection. After viewing a videotape of the challenged activity, the district court agreed and held that nude barroom dancing was not expressive activity and thus could be prohibited by the state. *Miller et al. v. Civil City of*

South Bend marked an appeal from that ruling.

The U.S. Court of Appeals for the Seventh Circuit reversed the Indiana district court to find that nude barroom dancing, when performed for entertainment, was a form of expression deserving of First Amendment protection. The appeals court reached this result by relying on several strands of U.S. Supreme Court precedent. Most important, in its 1981 decision, *Schad v. Mt. Ephraim*, the Supreme Court had invalidated a zoning ordinance that prohibited all live entertainment and confirmed the First Amendment's protection of live entertainment. The Supreme Court clarified that nudity, or sexual content, does not automatically remove an activity or material from the ambit of First Amendment protection, although nudity alone, when not combined with some form of expressive conduct, was not protected.

In its invalidation of Indiana's public nudity statute as applied to nude barroom dancing, the appeals court rejected the dissent's suggestion that courts should distinguish between "high" and "low" art, on the grounds that such a determination risks affording unpopular forms of expression no constitutional protection at all. Instead, the court reiterated the principles at the heart of First Amendment protection: All expression is presumptively protected against government interference and restraint, and the government cannot prohibit the expression of an idea simply because the idea is offensive or distasteful.

Elizabeth Van Schaack

See also *Barnes v. Glen Theatre, Inc.*; *Erznoznik v. Jacksonville*; *Osborne v. Ohio*; *Safford Unified School District v. Redding*.

MILLER V. CALIFORNIA; PARIS ADULT THEATRE V. SLATON

Court: U.S. Supreme Court
Citations: 413 U.S. 15; 413 U.S. 49
Date: June 21, 1973
Issues: Pornography and obscenity; Right to privacy

- Reaffirming that obscenity was not protected by the First Amendment, the U.S. Supreme Court formulated a three-pronged test as a guide for determining what kinds of sexually explicit materials might be proscribed by the government.

Marvin Miller was prosecuted and convicted of a misdemeanor under California's antiobscenity statute after he conducted a mailing campaign to advertise the sale of sexually explicit materials. When the Supreme Court accepted Miller's petition for review, it also agreed to review a companion case, *Paris Adult Theatre v. Slaton*. After the landmark case of *Roth v. United States* (1957), the Court had consistently ruled that the First and Fourteenth Amendments did not protect hard-core obscenity but did protect nonobscene pornography and "indecency." Under Chief Justice Earl Warren, the Court had made it very difficult to prosecute obscenity cases. In *Jacobellis v. Ohio* (1964) and *Memoirs v. Massachusetts* (1966), the Court held that erotic materials could not be proscribed unless the average person applying standards of "the society at large" found the content to be "utterly without redeeming social importance."

Although Chief Justice Warren E. Burger, writing for a 5-4 majority, began by recognizing the "inherent dangers" of restricting any form of expression, he then formulated a three-part test for obscenity that was considerably more restrictive than the *Jacobellis/Memoirs* test. Obscene materials might be proscribed if three elements were present: first, the average person, applying "contemporary community standards," would consider the work, taken as a whole, to appeal to the "prurient interest in sex"; second, the material must involve "patently offensive" conduct that is specifically defined by applicable state law; and third, the work, taken as a whole, must be lacking in "serious literary, artistic, political, or scientific value."

The most controversial prong of the *Miller* test has been its community standards approach. When a Georgia community attempted to bar the film *Carnal Knowledge*, the Court held, in *Jenkins v. Georgia* (1974), that only "patently offensive hard core sexual conduct" could be proscribed, regardless of the views of the local community. In addition, in *Pope v. Illinois* (1987), the Court held that the third prong of the test, the serious literary, artistic, political, or scientific value element, must be measured by national standards and the perceptions of "a reasonable person" rather than "an average person." Although the Court has made these two modifications, the basic approach of the *Miller* test continues to be good law.

In *Miller's* companion case, *Paris Adult Theatre v. Slaton*, the Court upheld the conviction of an Atlanta theater owner for showing obscene films. Burger's majority opinion included three general ideas. First, the constitutional right of privacy did not encompass any right to watch obscene movies in places of public accommodations. Second, the state had the authority to promote "a decent society" even if this meant restricting the free choices of consenting adults. Third, the legislature of Georgia could reasonably determine, without conclusive evidence, that "a connection does or might exist" between antisocial behavior and obscene material. In contrast, Justice William J. Brennan, Jr., joined by two other dissenters, argued that the concept of obscenity was so vague that, except in situations involving juveniles or nonconsenting adults, efforts to suppress it violated constitutional rights.

Thomas Tandy Lewis

See also *Ashcroft v. Free Speech Coalition; Hamling v. United States; Jacobellis v. Ohio; Memoirs v. Massachusetts; Reno v. American Civil Liberties Union; Roth v. United States.*

Milligan, Ex parte. *See* Ex parte Milligan

Milliken v. Bradley

Court: U.S. Supreme Court
Citation: 418 U.S. 717
Date: July 25, 1974
Issues: Desegregation; Education

- The U.S. Supreme Court held that federal judges could not order the busing of students across school district lines into districts that had done nothing to promote racial segregation.

A federal district judge ordered a desegregation plan for the greater Detroit area, which included the predominantly black central city and fifty-three suburban school districts in which the students were mostly white. The judge had found that the Detroit school board had been guilty of practices that constituted de jure segregation. Although there was no evidence that any of the other districts had promoted segregation, he decided that a Detroit-only plan was inadequate to achieve school desegregation. He justified his order by referring to *Swann v. Charlotte-Mecklenburg Board of Education*

(1971), in which the Court had upheld a massive busing plan designed to desegregate an entire urban school district, even though only portions of the large district had been found to have engaged in discriminatory practices.

By a 5-4 margin, the Supreme Court held that the district judge had exceeded his authority. Speaking for the Court, Chief Justice Warren E. Burger emphasized that the remedy of busing was appropriate only when a particular district had been found to have engaged in discriminatory practices or policies. Burger observed that the record in the case did not present any evidence that the suburban districts had either caused or contributed to school segregation. Thus, the *Milliken* decision reaffirmed the validity of the de facto/de jure distinction and established a presumption against the use of interdistrict busing remedies.

Milliken defused the criticism directed at the Court because of the busing issue, but it did not entirely eliminate controversial interdistrict desegregation plans. In Boston and other cities, court-ordered busing produced intense hostility and even violence. In the 1990's, however, controversy about the issue decreased as busing became much less common.

Thomas Tandy Lewis

See also *Board of Education of Oklahoma City v. Dowell; Brown v. Board of Education; Columbus Board of Education v. Penick; Keyes v. Denver School District No. 1; Lemon v. Kurtzman; Parents Involved in Community Schools v. Seattle School District No. 1; Swann v. Charlotte-Mecklenburg Board of Education.*

MINERSVILLE SCHOOL DISTRICT V. GOBITIS

Court: U.S. Supreme Court
Citation: 310 U.S. 586
Date: June 3, 1940
Issues: Freedom of religion; Freedom of speech

- In this case, the U.S. Supreme Court upheld a compulsory flag salute, but the ruling was overturned in a very short time because some justices in the original decision changed their minds.

Numerous states required compulsory flag salutes at the beginning of every school day. In Pennsylvania in 1936, two young Jehovah's Witnesses were expelled from school for refusing to salute the flag. Their parents politely sought an exemption but were refused. They sued in federal district court on free exercise of religion grounds but were turned down by the court. The Supreme Court, by a vote of eight to one, ruled that religious freedom did not exempt people from otherwise valid laws and governmentally imposed political obligations. Justice Harlan Fiske Stone dissented.

Although one might expect that patriotic sentiment would lead Americans to support the Supreme Court, amazingly, there was a broad and profound negative reaction to the ruling. Newspapers and journals strongly opposed the Court's decision. In one of the more unusual happenings in Court history, some justices who had voted against the Jehovah's Witnesses announced in open court that they had been wrong and were prepared to change their minds if they were given another opportunity. The Court reversed itself three years later in *West Virginia State Board of Education v. Barnette* (1943).

Richard L. Wilson

See also *Brandenburg v. Ohio; Cohen v. California; Texas v. Johnson; Tinker v. Des Moines Independent Community School District; United States v. O'Brien; West Virginia State Board of Education v. Barnette.*

Minnesota v. Carter

Court: U.S. Supreme Court
Citation: 523 U.S. 83
Date: December 1, 1998
Issues: Right to privacy

- The U.S. Supreme Court held that guests in a private home had no expectation of privacy if they had no personal relationship with the householder and were in the home for a few hours purely to conduct a business transaction.

Responding to a tip, a Minnesota police officer looked through a gap in a closed blind located in a ground floor apartment and observed three men bagging white powder that looked like cocaine. The two guests were arrested after they left the apartment. At trial, their lawyers moved to suppress the evidence on the grounds that the initial observation was an unreasonable search that violated the Fourth Amendment. They referred to *Minnesota v. Olson* (1990), in which the Supreme Court held that an overnight guest had a legitimate expectation of privacy within the home visited. In other cases, in contrast, the Court had held that the expectation of privacy in commercial property was less than in a private home.

Writing for a 6-3 majority, Chief Justice William H. Rehnquist emphasized the commercial purpose of the visit, the relatively short time the visitors were in the building, and the lack of any previous connection between them and the householder. Because the visitors had no legitimate expectation of privacy in the home, the Court did not make a decision about whether the officer's observation constituted a search. Justice Anthony M. Kennedy spoke for at least five justices in his concurring opinion, noting that "almost all social guests" would have a legitimate expectation of privacy in a host's home.

Thomas Tandy Lewis

See also *Katz v. United States; Kyllo v. United States; National Treasury Employees Union v. Von Raab; Safford Unified School District v. Redding; Skinner v. Railway Labor Executives' Association.*

MINNICK V. MISSISSIPPI

Court: U.S. Supreme Court
Citation: 498 U.S. 146
Date: December 3, 1990
Issues: Confessions; Miranda rights; Right to counsel;
Self-incrimination

- The U.S. Supreme Court found that a reinitiated interrogation of a murder suspect who had been advised of his Miranda rights and received counsel still violated the suspect's Fifth Amendment rights because it was conducted without counsel being present.

Robert S. Minnick, the petitioner, sought reversal of his conviction for murder in the circuit court of Lowndes County, Mississippi, on the grounds that his constitutional rights against self-incrimination had been violated when his confession was taken during an interrogation conducted without counsel present. Minnick, a fugitive from prison, had been arrested and held in a California jail, where two federal agents, after reading the Miranda warnings to him, began an interrogation on a Friday. He requested that they return on the following Monday, when he would have counsel present. The agents complied, breaking off their questioning.

An appointed attorney then advised Minnick to speak to no one about the charges against him. After an interview with the agents on Monday, Minnick was questioned by a deputy sheriff from Mississippi. The deputy advised Minnick of his Miranda rights, and the accused, who refused to sign a waiver of those rights, confessed to the murder for which he was subsequently tried and sentenced to death.

At Minnick's murder trial in Mississippi, he filed a motion to suppress the confession, but his request was denied. The conviction was then upheld by the Supreme Court of Mississippi, which ruled that Minnick's right to counsel, as set forth in the Fifth Amendment, had been granted in accordance with the guidelines established in *Edwards v. Arizona* (1981), which stipulates that a defendant who requests counsel during questioning cannot be subjected to further interrogation until the counsel is "made available" to the defendant. According to the Mississippi Supreme Court, that condition had been met when Minnick consulted with his appointed attorney.

The U.S. Supreme Court, on *certiorari*, reversed and remanded in a 6-2 decision. In the majority opinion, written by Justice Anthony Kennedy, the justices ruled that in a custodial interrogation, once counsel is provided, questioning cannot be resumed without counsel being present. It stipulated that the *Edwards v. Arizona* ruling regarding protection against self-incrimination is not met, nor is that protection terminated or suspended, by the mere provision of counsel outside the interrogation process. The majority found that Minnick's confession to the Mississippi deputy sheriff should have been inadmissible at his murder trial. In a dissenting opinion, Justice Antonin Scalia argued the contrary, holding that the *Edwards v. Arizona* rule excluding self-incrimination without counsel was not applicable after Minnick's first interview with his appointed attorney.

The Court's relatively narrow interpretation of what constitutes right to counsel leaves a legacy of stringent procedural requirements on law-enforcement agencies, which must comply with a suspect's right to have counsel present during custodial interrogations that had been broken off and later resumed. From the point of view of such agencies, its practical effect is to inhibit an expeditious interrogation of suspects.

John W. Fiero

See also *Arizona v. Fulminante; Brown v. Mississippi; Chambers v. Florida; Faretta v. California; Gideon v. Wainwright; Mallory v. United States; Massiah v. United States; United States v. Wade.*

Minor v. Happersett

Court: U.S. Supreme Court
Citation: 88 U.S. 162
Date: March 29, 1875
Issues: Sex discrimination; Voting rights; Women's issues

- In this setback to the woman suffrage movement, the U.S. Supreme Court held that states could constitutionally forbid women to vote, despite their holding U.S. citizenship.

Long before the concerted effort for woman suffrage developed during the nineteenth century, American women had exercised the right to vote. In January, 1648, Margaret Brent had petitioned the Maryland assembly for permission to vote in their proceedings, and the assembly agreed. The governor of Maryland vetoed the decision, and Brent lodged an official protest. In the same decade, in Rhode Island and New York, women participated in community affairs by voting. In 1776, in New Jersey, all references to gender were omitted from suffrage statutes. During the first fourteen years after the laws were passed, women did not vote, thinking that the laws referred only to men. By 1800, women were voting throughout New Jersey. However, a legislature made up entirely of white men voted in 1807 to change the New Jersey law to include only white male voters, with the strange argument that allowing women to vote produced a substantial amount of fraud.

During the first half of the nineteenth century, some U.S. women joined with the abolitionist movement in an attempt to blend their search for legal rights for themselves with rights for the slaves. At the time, these women were more concerned with obtaining rights to own property and to enter into contracts than with the right to vote. At the women's first convention in Seneca Falls, New York, in 1848, Elizabeth Cady Stanton did mention as part of the platform that women should have the right to vote, but this right did not become a paramount issue until after the Civil War (1861-1865). At that time, when the slaves were freed and all male citizens were given the right to vote, women were shocked to discover that in spite of all the work that they had done on behalf of the slaves, they themselves had been denied that right. The right to vote thus became the central issue to concerned women over the next seventy years.

Woman suffrage was an issue that divided the country along race, gender, religious, and political lines. Among the many men opposed to granting women the right to vote was Horace Bushnell, who wrote *Women's Suffrage; The Reform Against Nature* (1869). In that tract, he argued a traditional nineteenth century position that men and women lived in separate spheres, public and private. Men inhabited the public sphere, women, the private. If women entered into the public sphere, the moral nature of current life would be jeopardized. He asserted that it was a historic fact, extending back to biblical times, that women were unsuited to any role in the government of countries. Last, he argued that granting suffrage to women would have a negative effect upon married life. Because men were the accepted heads of households at that time, to grant women the right to vote might threaten this arrangement. Such thinking exemplified that of many men who opposed woman suffrage.

The noted nineteenth century essayist Ralph Waldo Emerson rejected such thinking. He believed that because all humans are fallible and biased about one issue or another, granting women the right to vote would only be correcting the biases. He believed that if one brought together all of the various opinions existing in the country, such a franchise would produce something better.

Two parties existed that women could join in their fight for suffrage. One, the American Party, remained a single-issue party. The other, the Nationals, opened itself to other issues, so as to attract wider membership. Among the people it attracted were the sisters Victoria Woodhull and Tennessee Celeste Claflin. Woodhull advocated women's rights, in addition to free love, spiritualism, and faith healing, and argued before Congress that women already had the right to vote under the privileges and immunities clause of the Fourteenth Amendment to the Constitution. Claflin wrote a treatise in support of woman suffrage, *Constitutional Equality*. She argued that women and men should not exist in separate spheres, and that if it were feared that the entrance into politics would corrupt women, it was time that women entered into, discovered, and exposed what was so corrupting about politics. She also argued that the refusal of men to relinquish their claims to dominance over women was selfishness on their part.

For a time, both parties published newspapers. In 1869, *The Revolution*, the newspaper of the Nationals, published a set of resolutions that stated, as Woodhull had declared before Congress, that the Constitution already conferred the right to vote upon women because of its privileges and immunities

In early 1872, Thomas Nast pilloried Victoria Woodhull in this cartoon by depicting her as a devil offering salvation through free love. (Library of Congress)

clause. Francis Minor, an attorney from St. Louis, Missouri, wrote the resolution. His wife, Virginia Louisa Minor, was president of the Missouri Woman Suffrage Association. When Virginia was turned away from the polls by registrar Reese Happersett in November, 1872, she and Francis, who was required to participate in any legal action his wife might bring, petitioned the courts of St. Louis for damages in the amount of ten thousand dollars.

While Minor's suit was making its way through the courts, other suffragists were challenging the law. In 1871 and 1872, at least 150 other women tried to vote in various states throughout the country. Among these was Susan B. Anthony, who headed a group of sixteen women in Rochester, New York, in first registering and then voting in the presidential election of 1872. The women did this knowing that they risked being fined up to three hundred dollars and imprisoned for up to three years. Anthony was not allowed to testify at her trial and was denied the right to a genuine decision by the jury when the judge directed the jury to return a guilty verdict. After the jury returned the verdict, the judge refused to commit Anthony to jail. She therefore lost the right she would have had to appeal her case to the U.S. Supreme Court.

The Supreme Court, however, did eventually hear the *Minor* case and passed down its ruling on March 9, 1875. However, it summarily rejected the couple's claims under the Fourteenth Amendment's privileges and immunities clause. The Court held that Virginia Minor, like all American women, was a citizen of the United States, but it dismissed her additional claim that citizenship conveyed upon her the right to vote. This right was not intended as part of the privileges and immunities clause in the Constitution, according to the Court's decision.

Significance

The Supreme Court's ruling ignored the social factors that were at the root of arguments over whether women should have the vote. These factors, as expressed by Bushnell, Emerson, and Claflin, for example, continued to disturb the country after the *Minor* case was decided and until women achieved suffrage in 1920. The *Minor* case merely indicated to those who were determined to obtain woman suffrage how far they had to go before achieving that right.

Jennifer Eastman

Further Reading

Agonito, Rosemary. "Ralph Waldo Emerson." In *History of Ideas on Woman: A Source Book*. New York: G. P. Putnam's Sons, 1977. Emerson, a firm suffragist, believed that the right to vote for women was an inevitable and positive change in society.

Baker, Jean H., ed. *Votes for Women: The Struggle for Suffrage Revisited*. Oxford, England: Oxford University Press, 2002. Scholarly history of the woman suffrage movement.

Bushnell, Horace. *Women's Suffrage: The Reform Against Nature*. New York: Charles Scribner, 1869. Opposes woman suffrage on the grounds that it would undermine women's natural and moral position in society, that is, the private sphere of domesticity.

Claflin, Tennessee C. *Constitutional Equality: A Right of Woman*. New York: Woodhull, Claflin, 1871. This early feminist tract expounded on woman's right to equality and to vote in a world where men and women would share the same life, if men would allow it.

Flexner, Eleanor. *Century of Struggle: The Woman's Rights Movement in the United States*. Cambridge, Mass.: Belknap Press of Harvard University Press, 1959. Comprehensive study of the women's movements of the nineteenth and early twentieth centuries, which places the struggle for woman suffrage in a historical context.

Frost-Knappman, Elizabeth, and Kathryn Cullen-DuPont. *Women's Suffrage in*

America: An Eyewitness History. New York: Facts On File, 1992. Contains many primary sources concerning woman suffrage, including the *Minor* petition to the lower courts and the later opinion in the *Minor* case by the Supreme Court.

Goldstein, Leslie Friedman. *The Constitutional Rights of Women: Cases in Law and Social Change.* Rev. ed. Madison: University of Wisconsin Press, 1988. Includes little-known commentary on woman suffrage, as well as the Supreme Court opinion in the *Minor* case.

Lewis, Thomas T., and Richard L. Wilson, eds. *Encyclopedia of the U.S. Supreme Court.* 3 vols. Pasadena, Calif.: Salem Press, 2001. Comprehensive reference work on the Supreme Court that contains substantial discussions of *Minor v. Happersett* and many related subjects.

McFadden, Margaret, ed. *Women's Issues.* 3 vols. Pasadena, Calif.: Salem Press, 1997. Comprehensive reference work with numerous articles on Susan B. Anthony, woman suffrage, and related issues.

See also *Breedlove v. Suttles; Mobile v. Bolden; Phillips v. Martin Marietta Corp.*

MIRANDA V. ARIZONA

Court: U.S. Supreme Court
Citation: 384 U.S. 436
Date: June 13, 1966
Issues: Confessions; Right to counsel; Self-incrimination

- In this case the U.S. Supreme Court decided that arrested persons must be informed of their rights to remain silent and to counsel before police interrogation may begin.

Miranda v. Arizona was one of a series of landmark Supreme Court cases of the mid-1960's establishing new guarantees of procedural fairness for defendants in criminal cases. The Court's decision in *Miranda* sprang from two different lines of precedents under the Fourteenth Amendment.

One of these lines was the right-to-counsel cases: *Powell v. Alabama* (1932), in which the Court held that indigent defendants had to be afforded counsel in capital cases; *Gideon v. Wainwright* (1963), which extended the right to counsel for indigent defendants to all felony cases; and *Escobedo v. Illinois* (1964), in which the Court held that a confession obtained from a defendant who had asked for and been denied permission to speak to an attorney was inadmissible. By 1964, the right to counsel had expanded to include mandatory representation for indigents at trial in all felonies and also gave potential defendants the right to representation during questioning while in custody if they requested it.

The second line of cases culminated with *Malloy v. Hogan* (1964), in which the Court had held that the privilege against self-incrimination applied to the states. Moreover, prior to the *Miranda* case, a long series of Supreme Court decisions had established that neither physical coercion nor certain forms of psychological coercion could be used by police to obtain confessions from accused persons. Thus, on the eve of *Miranda,* constitutional rules barred the admission of confessions which had been coerced through either physical or psychological pressures or which had been obtained from an in-custody defendant who had requested the attendance of an attorney.

By then it was also clear that the entire body of the Fifth Amendment's self-incrimination clause was to be applied to the states through the due process clause of the Fourteenth Amendment. Like the other cases mentioned, *Miranda* rests on the due process clause of the Fourteenth Amendment, which requires that criminal procedure in state courts be fundamentally fair.

Miranda's Case

Ernesto Miranda's case involved a confession to rape and kidnapping which was elicited from him in a police interrogation room after his arrest. In addition to his oral admissions to the investigating officers, Miranda wrote out by hand a short statement, which he signed. The questioning, by two Phoenix detectives, involved neither physical nor psychological coercion as these had been defined in the earlier cases. The transcript of Miranda's interview showed that he answered the officers' questions freely, and that after an initial denial, he readily admitted abducting the victim and raping her. The entire interrogation and the preparation of Miranda's written statement took less than two hours.

At trial, Miranda's oral admissions and his written statement were admitted into evidence over his objection; the victim testified against him as well. The jury found Miranda guilty of rape in the first degree and kidnapping, and he was sentenced to prison for a term of twenty to thirty years. He appealed to the Supreme Court of Arizona. After losing in that court, he appealed to the U.S. Supreme Court, which decided to hear the case in 1965. *Miranda* and three companion cases were argued February 28-March 1, 1966. On June 13, 1966, the Court decided in Miranda's favor by a 5-4 vote.

Chief Justice Earl Warren wrote for the majority, which consisted additionally of Justices Hugo Black, William O. Douglas, William J. Brennan, Jr., and Abe Fortas. Warren's opinion focused on the coercive elements present in any custodial interrogation. He argued that an accused person is isolated from friends, family, and his or her attorney and is often fearful of the police. The police, as contemporary text-books on interrogation showed, were schooled in a variety of tricks and techniques which are designed to overbear the will of an arrested person and induce confession.

Warren's Opinion

These techniques, according to Chief Justice Warren's opinion, skirt the edge of improper physical or psychological coercion and demonstrate that custodial interrogation is inherently coercive. Consequently, an accused person does not have a free opportunity to use the Fifth Amendment right not to incriminate himself or herself or the Sixth Amendment right to counsel. Accordingly, the Court held that before any custodial interrogation can take place, an arrested person must be given a four-fold warning—what has become known as the Miranda warning. Under this rule, a suspect in custody has to be informed of the right to remain silent, of the potential use of his or her words in evidence against him or her, of the right to consult an attorney before questioning, and of the right to an assigned attorney if he or she is indigent.

Any statement elicited by the authorities is inadmissible at trial unless the defendant has been given the warning and has freely and knowingly waived these rights. Moreover, if during questioning the defendant has asked at any point that interrogation cease or that he or she be allowed to consult an attorney, any subsequent statements obtained by the police are also inadmissible.

Justice John Marshall Harlan's dissenting opinion in this case argued that the Court was searching for a kind of "utopian" voluntariness. The dissenters believed that Miranda's statement had been voluntarily given. No physical brutality or discomfort had been visited upon him, nor did the investigating officers use any special psychological tricks or deceptions. The record showed that Miranda freely gave a statement about the crimes of which he was accused. By the standards of 1963, the Phoenix police had acted properly. Harlan argued that the admissibility of Miranda's confession was supported by precedent; moreover, in Miranda's brief interrogation, there was "a legitimate purpose, no perceptible unfairness, and certainly little risk of injustice." Justices Byron White and Potter Stewart adhered to Harlan's opinion; Justice Tom Clark submitted a separate dissenting opinion.

Aftermath

The immediate result of *Miranda v. Arizona* was to reverse Miranda's conviction for kidnapping and rape. The Arizona authorities persevered in the

Miranda Warnings

Minimal warning, as outlined in the *Miranda v Arizona* case:

> You have the right to remain silent. Anything you say can and will be used against you in a court of law. You have the right to speak to an attorney, and to have an attorney present during any questioning. If you cannot afford a lawyer, one will be provided for you at government expense.

Full warning:

> You have the right to remain silent and refuse to answer questions. Do you understand?
> Anything you do or say may be used against you in a court of law. Do you understand?
> You have the right to consult an attorney before speaking to the police and to have an attorney present during questioning now or in the future. Do you understand?
> If you cannot afford an attorney, one will be appointed for you before any questioning if you wish. Do you understand?
> If you decide to answer questions now without an attorney present you will still have the right to stop answering at any time until you talk to an attorney. Do you understand?
> Knowing and understanding your rights as I have explained them to you, are you willing to answer my questions without an attorney present?

prosecution, and in 1969, at his second trial, Miranda was again convicted. Although the confession was not introduced against him this time, the victim's testimony alone was enough to persuade the jury of his guilt. In consequence of this conviction he served a prison term from which he was paroled in 1972. Ernesto Miranda was killed in a barroom fight in 1976; ironically, the man who stabbed him to death was given the Miranda warning when arrested.

The larger consequence of this controversial case was to require police officers all over the United States to provide themselves with "Miranda cards" which embodied the warning required by the Supreme Court. Once a person has been detained, no questioning may take place unless the detainee has been given the warning and has waived the rights to silence and to consult counsel before responding to questions. If a detainee does request the assistance of an attorney, interrogation must stop until he or she has had the opportunity to consult with a lawyer. Treatment of arrested persons changed significantly after *Miranda v. Arizona*. Because the Court's decision placed on the state the burden of demonstrating knowing and voluntary waiver of the right to silence, police must persuade the defendant to agree if they wish to elicit a statement. The atmosphere in which an arrested person finds himself or herself in the crucial moments after arrest has changed substantially as a result of the Court's decision.

There has been much discussion of the impact of this rule on American law enforcement. In most criminal cases, the defendant's words constitute a significant part of the case against him or her. Police and prosecutors feared that the Court's holding in *Miranda* would cripple their efforts; they argued that the new rule would make it impossible for investigators to get the kinds of inculpatory statements necessary to obtain criminal convictions. Once a defendant had consulted counsel, they believed, no further statements of any kind would be forthcoming, since any competent lawyer would immediately urge silence on the client.

Despite these fears, which were shared by large portions of the public, *Miranda* does not seem to have crippled the work of the police and criminal courts. There have been a number of empirical studies of the behavior of arrested persons. Most criminal defendants do give statements—often incriminating statements—even after receiving the Miranda warning. Moreover, there have been as many successful prosecutions in relation to the number of arrests after the Miranda case as before.

Miranda also accomplished something else very important to the protection of the rights of arrested persons. There are signs that since *Miranda* the incidence of brutal or abusive police practices has diminished. Most observers of law-enforcement practices in the United States believe police brutality is much less common than before this case. One strong indication is the rarity of claims of coerced confession in trials where the "coercion" involves police practices more abusive than violations of the Miranda rule itself.

In the largest sense this is the real significance of *Miranda*: By forcing the police to attend to a rigid technical requirement which respects the defendant's rights, the opportunity for abusive behavior is lessened. Moreover, the increased professionalism of police that has resulted from *Miranda* and the other cases of the 1960's has benefited both police and prosecutors in preparing good cases. In this light, *Miranda* represents an important step toward actualizing the rights of accused persons regardless of whether it achieves Chief Justice Warren's stated aim, which was "to assure that the individual's right to choose between silence and speech remains unfettered throughout the interrogation process."

Robert Jacobs

Further Reading

Baker, Liva. *Miranda: The Crime, the Law, and the Politics.* New York: Atheneum, 1983. Excellent essays about the *Miranda* case, blending the legal and political issues raised.

Hook, Sidney. *Common Sense and the Fifth Amendment.* New York: Criterion, 1959. Argument *against* the privilege against self-incrimination. Hook argues that one can correctly infer guilt from a defendant's silence most of the time. Written in the context of the Red Scare of the 1950's.

Israel, Jerold, and Wayne LaFave. *Criminal Procedure.* 3d ed. St. Paul, Minn.: West Publishing, 1980. Good discussion of the rules for police interrogation and a summary of empirical evidence regarding the efficacy of the Miranda rule in giving potential defendants a free choice whether or not to speak.

Jacobs, Robert. *"Miranda:* The Right to Silence." *Trial* 11 (March/April, 1975): 69-76. An analysis and critique of the logic underlying the Court's decision in *Miranda,* as well as a discussion of the psychology of confession.

Kamisar, Yale. *Police Interrogation and Confessions: Essays in Law and Policy.* Ann Arbor: University of Michigan Press, 1980. Kamisar, a professor of law, presents this series of essays which emphasize the actualities of police questioning.

Levy, Leonard. *Origins of the Fifth Amendment: The Right Against Self-Incrimination.* New York: Oxford University Press, 1968. Discussion of the historical purposes and original meaning of the Fifth Amendment.

Lewis, Anthony. *Gideon's Trumpet.* New York: Random House, 1964. A study of the case of Clarence Earl Gideon, whose handwritten appeal to the Supreme Court resulted in the decision entitling all indigent defendants to assigned counsel. This book is particularly strong on Supreme Court procedure and on the issues raised by Gideon's appeal.

Medalie, Richard, Leonard Zeitz, and Paul Alexander. "Custodial Interrogation in Our Nation's Capital: The Attempt to Implement *Miranda.*" *Michigan Law Review* 66 (1968): 1347. Empirical study of interrogations in Washington, D.C., subsequent to the Court's decision in *Miranda.*

Mendelson, Wallace. *The American Constitution and Civil Liberties.* Homewood, Ill.: Dorsey Press, 1981. This text has a strong chapter on constitutional theory and practice as applied to criminal procedure.

See also *Arizona v. Fulminante; Brecht v. Abrahamson; Chambers v. Florida; Faretta v. California; Gideon v. Wainwright; Harris v. New York; Malloy v. Hogan; Massiah v. United States; Powell v. Alabama.*

Mississippi University for Women v. Hogan

Court: U.S. Supreme Court
Citation: 458 U.S. 718
Date: July 1, 1982
Issues: Sex discrimination

- The U.S. Supreme Court required women's schools to admit male students.

Justice Sandra Day O'Connor wrote the decision—her first on the Supreme Court—for the 5-4 majority, upholding a young man's claim that he was discriminated against by not being admitted to a women's nursing school. Hogan, a young man who lived in Mississippi, claimed the state-supported school's women-only policy violated his right to equal protection. O'Connor applied an intermediate standard of review, the test developed in *Craig v. Boren* (1976), and found the state was not persuasive in saying it was trying to

Justice Sandra Day O'Connor wrote her first opinion for the Supreme Court in Mississippi University for Women v. Hogan. *(Library of Congress)*

redress discrimination against women with its policy, for O'Connor could not see how this policy would help redress the grievances of women. She also ruled that the policy did not further the state's objective because men were allowed to audit classes. Chief Justice Warren E. Burger and Justices Harry A. Blackmun, Lewis F. Powell, Jr., and William H. Rehnquist dissented.

Richard L. Wilson

See also *Bradwell v. Illinois*; *Craig v. Boren*; *Edwards v. Aguillard*; *Grove City College v. Bell*; *United States v. Virginia*.

MISSISSIPPI V. JOHNSON

Court: U.S. Supreme Court
Citation: 71 U.S. 475
Date: April 15, 1867
Issues: Presidential powers

• The U.S. Supreme Court held that the courts could not stop the president from enforcing a law that was allegedly unconstitutional.

President Andrew Johnson, pictured here, vehemently opposed the Reconstruction Act and regarded Mississippi's motion against him as a threat to presidential power. (Library of Congress)

Congress enacted the Reconstruction Act in 1867 over the veto of President Andrew Johnson. The act gave president-appointed military commanders power over the ten former Confederate states and required the states to make new constitutions giving former slaves the right to vote. Mississippi challenged the act's constitutionality and tried to stop its enforcement. In *Marbury v. Madison* (1803), the Supreme Court had commanded executive officials to do their duty. However, Chief Justice Salmon P. Chase, writing for a unanimous Court, argued that *Marbury* covered only ministerial acts and the Court could not stop a president from carrying into effect an unconstitutional act. Once the president had acted, Chase noted, his actions were subject to legal challenges in the courts.

Richard L. Wilson

See also *Dames and Moore v. Regan*; *Humphrey's Executor v. United States*; *McCulloch v. Maryland*; *Martin v. Mott*; *Myers v. United States*; *United States v. Curtiss-Wright Export Corp.*; *United States v. Nixon*; *Wiener v. United States.*

Missouri ex rel. Gaines v. Canada

Court: U.S. Supreme Court
Citation: 305 U.S. 337
Date: December 12, 1938
Issues: Education; Racial discrimination

• Chipping away at the separate but equal doctrine, the U.S. Supreme Court ruled that states must provide equal opportunities for legal education within the borders of the state.

The state of Missouri, like other southern states, had no law schools that admitted African Americans. The state claimed to provide separate but equal opportunity by offering a few scholarships to help pay expenses for African Americans to attend law schools in other states. The state also indicated that it would begin a separate law school for African Americans if there were sufficient demand. Lloyd Gaines, an African American resident of the state, sued the registrar of the University of Missouri, S. W. Canada, after being denied admission to the law school because of his race.

By a 6-2 vote, the Supreme Court held that Missouri's scholarship policy fell short of the demands of the equal protection clause of the Fourteenth Amendment. Chief Justice Charles Evans Hughes, for the majority, wrote that the policy denied African Americans the equal right to obtain a legal education without leaving the state. Hughes noted that the state, if it wished, might fulfill its constitutional obligations "by furnishing equal facilities in separate schools." The *Gaines* decision suggested that the Court would henceforth disapprove of segregated schools unless they met standards of near-absolute equality.

In *Sweatt v. Painter* (1950), the Court built upon *Gaines* when it held that an all-black law school in Texas was inadequate because it did not provide "substantial equality" of educational opportunities available to white persons.

Thomas Tandy Lewis

See also *Cumming v. Richmond County Board of Education; Hall v. DeCuir; Louisville, New Orleans, and Texas Railway Co. v. Mississippi; McLaurin v. Oklahoma State Regents for Higher Education; Plessy v. Ferguson; Sweatt v. Painter.*

MISSOURI V. HOLLAND

Court: U.S. Supreme Court
Citation: 252 U.S. 416
Date: April 19, 1920
Issues: Foreign policy; Treaties

• The U.S. Supreme Court created a new federal power to act in accordance with treaties.

The state of Missouri tried to prevent the enforcement of a statute resulting from the Migratory Bird Treaty Act of 1918, charging that the law intruded on the rights reserved to the states under the Tenth Amendment. By a 7-2 vote, the Supreme Court upheld the federal law enacted in compliance with the migratory bird treaty. An earlier decision not involving a treaty had held that states owned the birds within their borders, but in his opinion for the Court, Justice Oliver Wendell Holmes found that the federal government had to have the power to comply with treaties that, under the supremacy clause of Article VI, were the supreme law of the land. Controversial at the time, this decision lost its significance beginning in the 1930's as federal power in the domestic area was greatly expanded. Justices Willis Van Devanter and Mahlon Pitney—alone among the conservatives—dissented, upholding the traditional states' rights viewpoint.

Richard L. Wilson

See also *Goldwater v. Carter; Martin v. Hunter's Lessee; United States v. Alvarez-Machain; Ware v. Hylton.*

MISSOURI V. JENKINS

Court: U.S. Supreme Court
Citation: 495 U.S. 33
Date: April 18, 1990
Issues: Desegregation; Education; Taxation

• The U.S. Supreme Court's ruling restricted the powers of the federal judiciary in imposing new taxes on states in desegregation cases.

Justice Byron R. White wrote the unanimous decision of the Supreme Court overturning a tax imposed on a Kansas City school district by the local federal district judge. As a part of a desegregation plan, the judge had ordered the construction of a luxurious magnet school costing half a million dollars that would have required a substantial increase in local taxes. The Court disallowed the plan on grounds of fairness without touching on constitutional issues by approving an indirect remedy to allow the district to raise the funds. Justice Anthony M. Kennedy, joined by Chief Justice William H. Rehnquist and Justices Sandra Day O'Connor and Antonin Scalia, concurred but maintained that federal judges should not impose taxes on states and localities directly or indirectly.

Richard L. Wilson

See also *Edgewood Independent School District v. Kirby; Lemon v. Kurtzman; San Antonio Independent School District v. Rodriguez; Swann v. Charlotte-Mecklenburg Board of Education.*

Mistretta v. United States

Court: U.S. Supreme Court
Citation: 488 U.S. 361
Date: January 18, 1989
Issues: Judicial powers; Separation of powers

• The U.S. Supreme Court upheld the 1984 creation of the Criminal Sentencing Commission, despite its mixture of judicial and executive functions and personnel.

In order to provide more uniformity in sentencing of criminals, Congress passed the 1984 Sentencing Reform Act, which created the Sentencing Commission. The president appointed seven members to the commission, three of whom had to be federal judges selected from a list of six forwarded by the Judicial Conference. The commission was to create guidelines for improving uniformity of sentencing of criminals by federal judges, who previously had broad discretion. Although the law and commission raised separation of powers issues, the Supreme Court upheld the act by a vote of eight to one. In his opinion for the Court, Justice Harry A. Blackmun wrote that he did not see an essential conflict in the complex appointment arrangements and activities of the commission, departing from the example of *Hayburn's Case* (1792). Justice Antonin Scalia dissented, arguing that this act unconstitutionally allowed federal judges to participate in executive branch activities.

Richard L. Wilson

See also *Hayburn's Case; Immigration and Naturalization Service v. Chadha; Yakus v. United States.*

MOBILE V. BOLDEN

Court: U.S. Supreme Court
Citation: 446 U.S. 55
Date: April 22, 1980
Issues: Voting rights

• Reaffirming that the Fourteenth and Fifteenth Amendments prohibit only "purposeful discrimination," the U.S. Supreme Court upheld an at-large system of voting in which no African American had ever been elected.

The three-member city commission of Mobile, Alabama, had been elected on a citywide basis since 1911. Although African Americans made up almost 40 percent of the population, none had ever been elected to the commission. A district court found that the at-large system was unconstitutional, but the Supreme Court, by a 6-3 margin, reversed the judgment. In evaluating Mobile's electoral system according to the demands of the Fourteenth and Fifteenth Amendments, Justice Potter Stewart's plurality opinion simply followed the Court's many precedents indicating that a state policy that is neutral on its face does not violate the Constitution unless it is "motivated by a racially discriminatory purpose." In an angry dissent, Justice Thurgood Marshall accused the Court of being "an accessory to the perpetuation of racial discrimination" and argued that voting rights should be judged according to a discriminatory effects test rather than a discriminatory intent standard.

In *Rogers v. Lodge* (1982), the Court used the *Bolden* standard to strike down an at-large electoral scheme in Georgia. The Court's ruling in *Bolden*, however, became almost irrelevant after Congress passed the 1982 extension of the Voting Rights Act, which allows plaintiffs to prevail in voting dilution cases on the basis of a modified discriminatory effects test.

Thomas Tandy Lewis

See also *Ex parte Yarbrough; Grovey v. Townsend; Guinn v. United States; Nixon v. Condon; Nixon v. Herndon; South Carolina v. Katzenbach; Terry v. Adams; United States v. Classic.*

MONELL V. DEPARTMENT OF SOCIAL SERVICES

Court: U.S. Supreme Court
Citation: 436 U.S. 658
Date: June 6, 1978
Issues: Local government

• The U.S. Supreme Court held that municipalities could be sued in federal court for policies that allegedly violate constitutional rights.

By a 7-2 vote, the Supreme Court upheld the right of plaintiffs to pursue civil suits challenging New York City's policy of requiring pregnant female employees to take medically unnecessary leaves. The Court's decision involved an interpretation of Title 42, section 1983, of the U.S. Code and overturned a major part of *Monroe v. Pape* (1961). Municipalities were relieved to learn that the *Monell* decision limited their liability to damages relating to official policy and did not hold them liable for the illegal acts of their employees.

Thomas Tandy Lewis

See also *Automobile Workers v. Johnson Controls*; *Ferguson v. City of Charleston*; *Geduldig v. Aiello*.

MOORE V. CITY OF EAST CLEVELAND

Court: U.S. Supreme Court
Citation: 431 U.S. 494
Date: May 31, 1977
Issues: Due process of law; Right to privacy

- The U.S. Supreme Court used the doctrine of substantive due process to strike down a local zoning ordinance that prohibited extended families from living together in a single-unit residence.

A residential suburb of Cleveland, Ohio, wanting to maintain its character as a single-family neighborhood, enacted a zoning ordinance that restricted each dwelling to a single family. The ordinance defined a family so narrowly that it did not allow Inez Moore, a grandmother, to live with her two grandsons. When Moore refused to comply with the ordinance, she was sentenced to five days in jail and fined twenty-five dollars.

By a 5-4 vote, the Supreme Court held that the ordinance violated the due process clause of the Fourteenth Amendment. In a plurality opinion, Justice Lewis F. Powell, Jr., emphasized the importance of "personal choice in matters of marriage and the family," and he argued that the Fourteenth Amendment protects those liberties that are "deeply rooted in our history and tradition." He concluded that this tradition was broad enough to encompass various forms of extended families. Powell's opinion significantly extended the scope of the substantive due process approach, and his history and tradition standard has often served as a rationale for subsequent decisions.

Thomas Tandy Lewis

See also *Belle Terre v. Boraas; Euclid v. Ambler Realty Co.; First English Evangelical Lutheran Church of Glendale v. County of Los Angeles; Griswold v. Connecticut; Young v. American Mini Theatres.*

MOORE V. DEMPSEY

Court: U.S. Supreme Court
Citation: 261 U.S. 86
Date: February 19, 1923
Issues: Habeas corpus; Trial by jury

- The landmark Moore decision marked two constitutional developments: the U.S. Supreme Court's actual utilization of the due process clause of the Fourteenth Amendment as a limitation on state criminal proceedings and the federal courts' supervision of state proceedings by way of habeas corpus petitions.

In 1919 a violent racial clash in Phillips County, Arkansas, resulted in the deaths of scores of African Americans and five whites. More than one hundred African Americans, and no whites, were prosecuted. Swift trials took place in a lynch-mob atmosphere, with large angry crowds intimidating the juries.

Six defendants sentenced to death petitioned the federal district court for a habeas corpus hearing. As recently as *Frank v. Mangum* (1915), however, the Supreme Court had refused federal relief for a defendant convicted of murder in state court under mob-influenced conditions similar to those of Phillips County. Therefore, the district court dismissed the petition.

By a 6-2 vote, the Supreme Court reversed the ruling and instructed the lower court to hold a habeas corpus hearing. Speaking for the Court, Justice Oliver Wendell Holmes, Jr., observed that a trial influenced by the threat of mob violence was manifestly inconsistent with the constitutional requirements for due process of law. The state courts had the obligation to guarantee fair trials for the defendants, but if evidence indicated a failure to meet this obligation, the federal courts then had the duty to review the record and determine whether the convictions should be overturned. The two dissenters expressed concern that the ruling would result in excessive federal interference in state proceedings.

Thomas Tandy Lewis

See also *Boumediene v. Bush; Fay v. Noia; Frank v. Mangum; McCleskey v. Zant; Stone v. Powell.*

Moose Lodge v. Irvis

Court: U.S. Supreme Court
Citation: 407 U.S. 163
Date: June 12, 1972
Issues: Equal protection of the law; Racial discrimination;
Right to privacy

• The U.S. Supreme Court held that a state agency did not violate the equal protection clause of the Fourteenth Amendment when it issued a liquor license to a private club that practiced racial discrimination.

Moose Lodge No. 107, a private club in Harrisburg, Pennsylvania, allowed only white men to use its premises. One member of the club tried to bring Leroy Irvis, a prominent African American politician, as a guest. After Irvis was refused service, he brought a civil suit in federal court. He contended that the state, by providing the club with a license, was unconstitutionally participating in the club's policy of racial exclusion. Irvis pointed to *Burton v. Wilmington Parking Authority* (1961), in which the Court had ruled that a state agency did not have the right to lease property to a restaurant practicing racial segregation.

By a 6-3 vote, the Supreme Court rejected Irvis's claim. Speaking for the majority, Justice William H. Rehnquist interpreted the doctrine of state action narrowly and concluded that the mere licensing of the lodge did not constitute enough state involvement to bring the lodge's policies under the umbrella of the Fourteenth Amendment. The state played "absolutely no part" in determining the membership or guest policies of organizations receiving state licenses. The circumstances were considered different from the "symbiotic relationship" that had existed between a lessor and a lessee in the *Burton* case. Because states commonly provide regulations for many necessary services, Rehnquist feared that a ruling upholding Irvis's claim would "utterly emasculate" the long-standing distinction between private conduct and state action.

Dissenting, Justice William J. Brennan, Jr., argued that the state was an "active participant" in the Moose Lodge bar, and he noted that the liquor licensing laws included "pervasive regulatory schemes" for many aspects of the licensee's business. Justice William O. Douglas emphasized that liquor licenses were very scarce and that therefore the state's policy restricted the equal access of African Americans to liquor. Ironically, Irvis was able to find recourse under Pennsylvania's public accommodations law.

Thomas Tandy Lewis

See also *Burton v. Wilmington Parking Authority*; *Civil Rights Cases*; *Shelley v. Kraemer*.

MOREHEAD V. NEW YORK EX REL. TIPALDO

Court: U.S. Supreme Court
Citation: 298 U.S. 587
Date: June 1, 1936
Issues: Freedom of contract

• The U.S. Supreme Court, in this unpopular decision, overturned 1930's minimum-wage legislation.

By a 5-4 vote, the Supreme Court struck down a 1930's New York law that established minimum wages for women and children. Writing for the Court, Justice Pierce Butler said the law violated the freedom of employees to contract for work established by the due process clause of the Fourteenth Amendment. This was a terribly unpopular decision that drew heavy criticism from almost all newspapers in the country that commented on the case. Of more than three hundred editorials, only ten supported the Court. Even the Republican Party criticized the Court's decision, which was overturned in *West Coast Hotel Co. v. Parrish* (1937). Justices Charles Evans Hughes, Harlan Fiske Stone, Louis D. Brandeis, and Benjamin N. Cardozo dissented.

Richard L. Wilson

See also *Adkins v. Children's Hospital; Bunting v. Oregon; National League of Cities v. Usery; United States v. Darby Lumber Co.; West Coast Hotel Co. v. Parrish.*

MORGAN V. VIRGINIA

Court: U.S. Supreme Court
Citation: 328 U.S. 373
Date: June 3, 1946
Issues: Civil rights and liberties; Desegregation; Regulation of commerce

- The U.S. Supreme Court struck down segregation in interstate public transportation because it created an improper burden on interstate commerce.

Justice Stanley F. Reed wrote the opinion for the 7-1 majority, striking down a Virginia law that mandated segregation in bus transportation. The National Association for the Advancement of Colored People urged the Supreme Court to use a nineteenth century civil rights law to end the practice of segregation in interstate bus travel as an improper restraint on interstate commerce. Following *Hall v. DeCuir* (1878), the Court struck down a Virginia law and, by implication, those of all the other southern states. As a practical matter, segregation in bus transportation continued as the southern officials simply ignored the Court unless a ruling was directed specifically at their jurisdictions. Justices Hugo L. Black, Felix Frankfurter, and Wiley B. Rutledge concurred. Justice Harold H. Burton dissented. Justice Robert H. Jackson, active in the Nuremberg trials, did not participate.

Richard L. Wilson

See also *Hall v. DeCuir; Louisville, New Orleans, and Texas Railway Co. v. Mississippi; Plessy v. Ferguson.*

MORRISON V. OLSON

Court: U.S. Supreme Court
Citation: 487 U.S. 654
Date: June 29, 1988
Issues: Separation of powers

- The U.S. Supreme Court upheld the constitutionality of the independent counsel statute.

Chief Justice William H. Rehnquist wrote the opinion for the 7-1 majority, upholding the constitutionality of the independent counsel statute. The statute, adopted in 1978, provided for an independent counsel to investigate possible federal criminal violations made by senior executive officials such as the president. The counsel is appointed by a special court on the attorney general's application and is removable by the attorney general only for good cause. Although Justice Antonin Scalia was the lone dissenter in this case, the wisdom of his position was praised subsequently as abuses of the process became clear. Scalia took a strong separation of powers position under which the judiciary was unconstitutionally involved in the activities of the executive branch—a view the Supreme Court itself took in *Bowsher v. Synar* (1986) and *Immigration and Naturalization Service v. Chadha* (1983). In these cases, the Court backed away from an abstract formulation and accepted the temporary political popularity of the statute.

Richard L. Wilson

See also *Bowsher v. Synar; Immigration and Naturalization Service v. Chadha; Mistretta v. United States.*

MUELLER V. ALLEN

Court: U.S. Supreme Court
Citation: 463 U.S. 388
Date: June 29, 1983
Issues: Education; Establishment of religion; Parental rights; Taxation

- The U.S. Supreme Court upheld a state law that allowed taxpayers to deduct educational expenses that mostly benefited parents of children in private religious schools.

A Minnesota statute authorized state taxpayers to deduct up to seven hundred dollars from their gross income for expenses incurred in school tuition, textbooks, and transportation for dependents who attended elementary or secondary schools in the state. Although the law extended the benefits to parents of children attending both public and private schools, more than 95 percent of the benefits went to those whose children were in religious schools. Several Minnesota taxpayers contested the law in federal court, arguing that it violated the separation of church and state required by the establishment clause of the First Amendment. After the trial and appellate courts ruled that the law was constitutional, the plaintiffs took their case to the U.S. Supreme Court.

The precedents of the Court appeared to suggest that the statute would be ruled unconstitutional. In *Committee for Public Education and Religious Liberty v.*

Nyquist (1973), the Court had struck down a New York law that had provided tuition grants and tax credits for parents of children in church-related institutions. *Nyquist* and other precedents had established that a state may not aid parochial schools either by direct grants or by indirect tax credits to the parents.

In *Mueller,* however, the Court voted five to four to uphold the Minnesota law. Writing for the majority, Chief Justice William Rehnquist argued that the law was consistent with the three-pronged test of *Lemon v. Kurtzman* (1971). First, the law had the secular purpose of educating children and promoting diversity of educational institutions; second, it was religiously neutral, because it was designed to benefit parents of children in both public and private schools; third, it did not result in "excessive entanglement" between church and state, since there was no program for monitoring instructional materials.

The three dissenters argued that the Minnesota law was unconstitutional because it had the effect of providing financial assistance to sectarian schools. They emphasized that parents of public school children were unable to claim large deductions for tuition and textbooks, and that 95 percent of the law's financial benefits went to parents with children in religious schools. Also, they observed that the statute did not restrict private schools to books approved for the public schools, with the result that the state became entangled in religious questions when deciding which books might qualify for tax exemption.

The *Mueller* decision was important because the majority of the Court went further than in perhaps any other case toward allowing an indirect subsidy for religious education. In *Aguilar v. Felton* (1985), however, the Court appeared to return to the idea of strict separation. Few observers expected that future cases would consistently defend either the state's right to accommodate religion or the duty to maintain a high wall of separation.

Thomas Tandy Lewis

See also *Agostini v. Felton; Everson v. Board of Education of Ewing Township; Flast v. Cohen; Lemon v. Kurtzman; Zelman v. Simmons-Harris.*

Mugler v. Kansas

Court: U.S. Supreme Court
Citation: 123 U.S. 623
Date: December 5, 1887
Issues: Regulation of business

- In a transitional decision, the U.S. Supreme Court approved of a statute limiting the manufacture and sale of alcoholic beverages but warned that there were limits to a state's police power.

In the 1880's Peter Mugler was fined and imprisoned for continuing to manufacture beer after the Kansas legislature passed a statute forbidding its sale or manufacture without a license. In appealing the conviction, Mugler argued that Kansas had no authority to prevent him from manufacturing beer for his private consumption or for sale outside the state. Although Mugler contended that the state law constituted a deprivation of property without due process, the state maintained that the law was a valid exercise of its police power, designed to protect the safety, health, morality, and welfare of its citizens.

Although the Supreme Court voted eight to one to uphold the Kansas law, Justice John Marshall Harlan wrote for the majority that the Court had a duty to scrutinize governmental regulations to determine whether they had a "substantial relation" to the legitimate ends of the police power. He observed, moreover, that "there were limits beyond which legislation cannot rightfully go." In dissent, Justice Stephen J. Field vigorously argued that the law violated Mugler's rights to substantive liberty and property under the due process clause of the Fourteenth Amendment. Together, Harlan's opinion and Field's dissent helped prepare the way for the triumph of the substantive due process doctrine in *Allgeyer v. Louisiana* (1897).

Thomas Tandy Lewis

See also *Allgeyer v. Louisiana*; *Clark Distilling Co. v. Western Maryland Railway Co.*; *License Cases.*

MULFORD V. SMITH

Court: U.S. Supreme Court
Citation: 307 U.S. 38
Date: April 17, 1939
Issues: Regulation of commerce

- The U.S. Supreme Court used a broad interpretation of the commerce clause to uphold the constitutionality of the Agricultural Adjustment Act of 1938.

In striking down the Agricultural Adjustment Act of 1933 in *United States v. Butler* (1936), the Court held that Congress could not use its taxing powers to regulate agricultural production, a power that was reserved to the states by the Tenth Amendment. The Agricultural Adjustment Act of 1938, like the earlier act, attempted to increase farm prices by limiting productivity. In passing the 1938 law, however, Congress did not pay for the program with a special tax. The major provision of the law was a system of assigning marketing quotas for commodities that were destined to be sold in interstate commerce.

Writing for a 7-2 majority, Justice Owen J. Roberts reasoned that the second act was only a regulation of the commodities that flow into interstate commerce. He found that the objective of the law was not to control production but rather to prevent the injury of depressed prices that occurred when an excessive level of commodities flooded the interstate market. By avoiding any consideration of the Tenth Amendment, Roberts managed to uphold the second act without directly reversing his written opinion in *Butler.* Expanding on the *Mulford* ruling in *Wickard v. Filburn* (1942), the Court abandoned the indirect/direct distinction, and defended the agricultural act because of its "substantial economic effect" on interstate commerce.

Thomas Tandy Lewis

See also *Bailey v. Drexel Furniture Co.*; *United States v. Butler*; *United States v. Darby Lumber Co.*; *Wickard v. Filburn*.

MULLER V. OREGON

Court: U.S. Supreme Court
Citation: 208 U.S. 412
Date: February 24, 1908
Issues: Constitutionalism

- In *Muller v. Oregon*, the U.S. Supreme Court established the validity of "sociological jurisprudence," the principle that economic and social considerations are as significant as legal precedents in deciding the constitutionality of social legislation.

In his famous brief before the U.S. Supreme Court in the case of *Muller v. Oregon* in 1908, Louis D. Brandeis of Boston established the validity of "sociological jurisprudence" in the determination of constitutional questions. According to sociological jurisprudence, economic and social considerations are as significant as legal precedents in judicial decision making concerning the constitutionality of social legislation. In *Muller v. Oregon*, Brandeis (who later served on the Supreme Court himself) presented a brief that became a legal model for lawyers, judges, and social welfare proponents who were determined to humanize industrial working conditions.

Under attack was an Oregon law that limited a workday for women workers in an industry to ten hours. The law's critics claimed that it was unconstitutional because it contradicted legal precedent as established by the case of *Lochner v. New York* (1905). Because many members of the bar and the judiciary were hostile toward social welfare legislation, it was expected that the courts would uphold the claim of unconstitutionality. Many, if not most, lawyers and judges at the beginning of the twentieth century believed in natural economic laws and the primacy of property rights over human rights. For the government to attempt to control the use of property, they maintained, was not only unconstitutional but also contrary to the natural order.

Judges in the United States are entitled to review legislation to determine whether it violates state or federal constitutions; as a result, advocates of social welfare legislation viewed the decisions of judges who opposed such legislation as the greatest threat to progress. Federal courts had frequently nullified social welfare legislation enacted by the states. In addition, the U.S. Supreme Court had embraced the concept that corporations had the status of persons under the Fourteenth Amendment. No state, the Court held, could deprive a

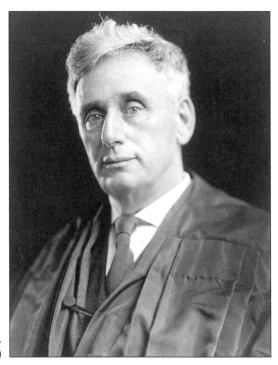

Justice Louis D. Brandeis.
(Library of Congress)

corporation—in this case, a particular industry—of life, liberty, or property without due process of law. In social welfare legislation, "liberty" generally meant the freedom to contract.

In 1905, the Supreme Court set specific limitations on how far a state could go in legislating hours and other working conditions for its industrial laborers. In *Lochner v. New York*, the Court ruled that New York laws that limited bakers to working ten hours per day and sixty hours per week were "mere meddlesome interferences with the rights of the individual." A state could not interfere with the freedom of the employer and employee to make a labor contract unless obvious and overriding reasons existed, such as matters of health. The Court asserted that if the state had been able to prove that longer hours had negative health effects on the workers, the Court would have upheld the statute.

The Issues
The stage was thus set for litigation of the Oregon ten-hour law for women. Two social justice reformers, Florence Kelley, who was chief factory inspector of Illinois and general secretary of the National Consumers League, and Josephine Goldmark, a leader of the National Consumers League and Brandeis's sister-in-law, hired Brandeis to defend the law. Known as "the people's attor-

ney," Brandeis had tried for years to minimize what Thorstein Veblen had called the "discrepancy between law and fact." The law, Brandeis argued, often did not correspond to the new economic and social facts of life in the United States. Lawyers and judges who blindly adhered to legal precedents and arguments about natural law actually knew little about twentieth century industrial conditions. Lawyers who did not understand economic and social realities were apt to become "public enemies." In his brief in *Muller v. Oregon*, which was researched in large part by Kelley and Goldmark, Brandeis sought to make clear the economic and social realities of the women workers' lives.

Brandeis's legal argument took up merely two pages of his brief. He devoted more than one hundred pages to demonstrating that Oregon had adopted its ten-hour law in order to safeguard the public health, safety, and welfare of women. "Long hours of labor are dangerous for women," Brandeis contended, because of the physiological differences between men and women. "Overwork . . . is more dangerous to the health of women than of men, and entails upon them more lasting injury." Fatigue in working women, Brandeis asserted, often resulted in general deterioration of health, anemia, the destruction of nervous energy, difficulties in childbearing, and industrial accidents. He further argued that the effect of overwork on morals was closely related to poor health. A breakdown in the health and morals of women, moreover, would inevitably lower the entire community physically, mentally, and morally. The rise of infant mortality was an obvious example. In contrast, the good of the entire community was actually promoted by women working hours that did not cause the deterioration of health and morals. Brandeis marshaled his economic and social data so impressively that the Court was convinced to uphold the Oregon ten-hour law for women. In his majority opinion, delivered on February 24, 1908, Justice David J. Brewer made reference to the uniqueness and efficacy of the Brandeis brief.

Significance

Brandeis's brief opened the way for the U.S. Supreme Court to examine factors other than legal precedents in reaching decisions. These other factors—social and economic data—which Brandeis called "what any fool knows," became part of subsequent briefs propounding equitable labor conditions. In the long term, it was not only in labor cases that sociological jurisprudence became an accepted principle in the law. In 1954, in the landmark case *Brown v. Board of Education* of Topeka, Kansas, the Court relied on sociological data in determining that segregation of the races in education is unconstitutional.

Several years after *Muller v. Oregon*, Felix Frankfurter called the case "epochmaking" because of Brandeis's approach. This approach, based on "the logic of facts," has been an intrinsic part of legal and constitutional practice ever since, paving the way for so-called judicial activism and the entry of the courts into the "political thicket." Opponents of this trend see judicial activism as the judicial system's usurpation of the powers of the legislative and executive branches of government.

William M. Tuttle and Jennifer Eastman

Further Reading

Amar, Akhil Reed. *America's Constitution: A Biography.* New York: Random House, 2005. Examines in turn each article of the Constitution and explains how the Framers drew on English models, existing state constitutions, and other sources in structuring the three branches of the federal government and in defining the relationship of that government to the states.

Barron, Jerome A., and C. Thomas Dienes. *Constitutional Law in a Nutshell.* 6th ed. St. Paul, Minn.: West, 2005. Compact reference on the law for those with a legal or political science background.

Blumberg, Dorothy R. *Florence Kelley: The Making of a Social Pioneer.* New York: Augustus M. Kelley, 1966. Biography provides little information about *Muller v. Oregon* but traces the influences that caused Kelley to become a social reformer.

Breyer, Stephen. *Active Liberty: Interpreting Our Democratic Constitution.* New York: Alfred A. Knopf, 2005. In this book, which is based on the Tanner Lectures on Human Values that he delivered at Harvard University in November, 2004, Stephen Breyer, associate justice of the United States, defines the term "active liberty" as a sharing of the nation's sovereign authority with its citizens.

Carrington, Paul D. *Stewards of Democracy: Law as a Public Profession.* Boulder, Colo.: Westview Press, 1999. Discusses the role of lawyers in U.S. social and political history. Focuses on a number of individual attorneys who have practiced law with an awareness of a responsibility to the public. Chapter 15 is devoted to Brandeis. Includes references and index.

Frankfurter, Felix, ed. *Mr. Justice Brandeis.* New Haven, Conn.: Yale University Press, 1932. Articles by Felix Frankfurter, Max Lerner, Charles Evans Hughes, and Donald R. Richberg; introduction by Justice Oliver Wendell Holmes, Jr.

Goldmark, Josephine. *Impatient Crusader: Florence Kelley's Life Story.* Urbana: University of Illinois Press, 1953. A sympathetic study of the militant and socially conscious women reformers who pioneered efforts for the abolition of child labor and shorter hours and higher pay for women.

Mason, Alpheus Thomas. *Brandeis: A Free Man's Life.* New York: Viking Press, 1946. An intimate portrait of Brandeis and the four stages of his career. Concise description of his participation in *Muller v. Oregon.*

Paper, Lewis J. *Brandeis*. Englewood Cliffs, N.J.: Prentice-Hall, 1983. A detailed
biography with an accurate account of Brandeis's involvement with *Muller
v. Oregon*.

Sklar, Kathryn Kish. *Florence Kelley and the Nation's Work: The Rise of Women's Political Culture, 1830-1900*. New Haven, Conn.: Yale University Press, 1995.
Biography covers the first forty years of Kelley's life and also serves as a political history of the United States during a time when women were becoming increasingly active in opposition to workplace abuses.

Strum, Philippa. *Louis D. Brandeis: Justice for the People*. New York: Schocken
Books, 1984. Discusses Brandeis and his importance in the legal world. Includes a detailed account of *Muller v. Oregon* and the Brandeis brief.

See also *Brown v. Board of Education*; *Bunting v. Oregon*; *Lochner v. New York*.

MUNN V. ILLINOIS

Court: U.S. Supreme Court
Citation: 94 U.S. 113
Date: March 1, 1877
Issues: Regulation of business

• This historic U.S. Supreme Court ruling recognized that a state
might exercise its police power to regulate private businesses.

In the 1870's the Illinois legislature, responding to demands of the Patrons
of Husbandry (the Grange), passed a statute limiting the maximum charges
for the storage of grain in warehouses located in cities of 100,000 or more.
The operators of several Chicago warehouses argued that the law violated
two provisions in the Constitution: the commerce clause and the due process
clause of the Fourteenth Amendment. By a 7-2 vote, however, the Supreme
Court upheld the legislation. Chief Justice Morrison R. Waite's majority
opinion concluded that the law's effect on interstate commerce was only incidental, and it rejected the doctrine of substantive due process. Recognizing that the states possessed an inherent police power to protect the safety,
welfare, and morality of the public, Waite concluded that this authority extended to the regulation of private property that is "affected with a public interest." Ironically, the concept of "affected with a public interest" was later

used to prohibit regulation of businesses that were small and of limited influence—a practice finally abandoned in *Nebbia v. New York* (1934).

Munn is remembered not only for the majority opinion but also for Justice Stephen J. Field's vigorous dissent, which defended almost a laissez-faire position on private property. Field charged that the majority opinion was dangerous to liberty because it implied that "all property and all business in the state are held at the mercy of the legislature." Field's dissent included a coherent argument in favor of a substantive reading of the due process clause—an interpretation later accepted by the Court in *Allgeyer v. Louisiana* (1897).

Thomas Tandy Lewis

See also *Allgeyer v. Louisiana; Budd v. New York; Chicago, Milwaukee, and St. Paul Railway Co. v. Minnesota; Nebbia v. New York.*

MURDOCK V. MEMPHIS

Court: U.S. Supreme Court
Citation: 87 U.S. 590
Date: January 11, 1875
Issues: Federal supremacy

• The U.S. Supreme Court upheld a key provision of dual federalism.

Justice Samuel F. Miller wrote the opinion for the 5-3 majority, upholding the concept that a state's top appellate court, not the U.S. Supreme Court, was the final arbiter of the meaning of that state's constitution and laws. This was originally specified in the 1789 Judiciary Act, but that provision had been omitted from the 1867 amendment. The question was whether the congressional omission meant that the Court had state jurisdiction, but Miller found that such an important question could not be decided by congressional silence alone. The previous provision remained in effect. Justices Joseph P. Bradley, Nathan Clifford, and Noah H. Swayne dissented. Chief Justice Morrison R. Waite did not participate.

Richard L. Wilson

See also *National League of Cities v. Usery; Robinson v. California; United States v. Darby Lumber Co.*

MURDOCK V. PENNSYLVANIA

Court: U.S. Supreme Court
Citation: 319 U.S. 105
Date: May 3, 1943
Issues: First Amendment guarantees

- The U.S. Supreme Court established the concept that the First Amendment guarantees of freedom of religion, press, and speech occupied a preferred position in U.S. constitutional law.

Justice William O. Douglas wrote the opinion for the 5-4 majority, striking down a city ordinance that required the Jehovah's Witnesses, a religious group, to pay a license tax to go door to door distributing literature and soliciting funds. *Murdock v. Pennsylvania* was one of a series of cases commonly known as the Jehovah's Witnesses cases in which the Supreme Court struck down a wide range of limits on the group's activities as prior restraints on its freedom of religion, speech, and press. Justices Felix Frankfurter, Stanley F.

William O. Douglas with his son, William O. Douglas, Jr., shortly after he joined the Supreme Court in 1939. One of the youngest persons ever appointed to the Court, Douglas would serve on it for more than thirty-six years—the longest term of any justice. (Harris & Ewing Collection/Library of Congress)

Reed, Robert H. Jackson, and Owen J. Roberts dissented, maintaining that municipalities had the right to levy reasonable, nondiscriminatory taxes on the sale of religious literature.

Richard L. Wilson

See also *Cantwell v. Connecticut; Cox v. New Hampshire; Hague v. Congress of Industrial Organizations; Lovell v. City of Griffin; Minersville School District v. Gobitis; West Virginia State Board of Education v. Barnette.*

Murphy v. Waterfront Commission of New York

Court: U.S. Supreme Court
Citation: 378 U.S. 52
Date: June 15, 1964
Issues: Self-incrimination

• The U.S. Supreme Court prohibited federal prosecutors from using incriminating evidence compelled by the state, citing the privilege against self-incrimination.

Justice Arthur J. Goldberg wrote the unanimous opinion for the Supreme Court, holding that incriminating evidence obtained under compulsion by one level of government may not be used by another in criminal prosecutions. This decision overruled *Feldman v. United States* (1944) and was handed down on the same day as *Malloy v. Hogan* (1964), which had applied the Fifth Amendment's protection against self-incrimination to the states. The logic of *Malloy* is evident in this decision. The protection against self-incrimination is not absolute, but grants of use immunity must be as broad as the original protection in the Fifth Amendment. This decision was limited by the Court's ruling in *Kastigar v. United States* (1972).

Richard L. Wilson

See also *Albertson v. Subversive Activities Control Board; Boyd v. United States; Counselman v. Hitchcock; Griffin v. California; Kastigar v. United States; Kilbourn v. Thompson; Malloy v. Hogan.*

MURRAY'S LESSEE V. HOBOKEN LAND AND IMPROVEMENT CO.

Court: U.S. Supreme Court
Citation: 59 U.S. 272
Date: February 19, 1856
Issues: Due process of law; Search and seizure

- In its first sustained definition of "due process of law," the U.S. Supreme Court ruled that the Treasury Department did not violate the Fifth Amendment when it used administrative warrants to recover embezzled funds.

The accounts of a customs collector, Samuel Swartwout, were short more than a million dollars. The Treasury Department used a congressional law of 1820 to place a lien on his property without prior judicial approval. Swartwout claimed that seizing his property without a judicial proceeding violated the due process requirements of the Fifth Amendment.

Justice Benjamin R. Curtis.
(Albert Rosenthal/Collection of the Supreme Court of the United States)

Speaking for a unanimous Supreme Court, Justice Benjamin R. Curtis upheld the constitutionality of both the action and the 1820 law. To determine the meaning of "due process," the Court must examine the Constitution itself, then look to the "settled usages and modes of proceedings existing in the common and statute law of England," as modified under U.S. conditions. According to this tradition, judicial proceedings were not required in order for the government to recover its funds. However, Curtis put the government on notice that the due process clause "cannot be so construed as to leave Congress free to make any process 'due process of law' by its mere will." The interpretation of due process in *Murray's Lessee* greatly influenced U.S. law, especially during the second half of the nineteenth century.

Thomas Tandy Lewis

See also *Adamson v. California; Hudson v. Palmer; Hurtado v. California; Safford Unified School District v. Redding.*

MUSKRAT V. UNITED STATES

Court: U.S. Supreme Court
Citation: 219 U.S. 346
Date: January 23, 1911
Issues: Judicial powers

• The U.S. Supreme Court maintained that the federal courts should hear only genuine cases and controversies and not offer advisory opinions.

Very early in its history, the Supreme Court decided that the fundamental principle that courts should hear only genuine conflicts between parties (or cases and controversies) meant that the Court could not give advisory opinions. *Muskrat v. United States* is an almost classic attempt to bring a mock case or a friendly lawsuit between parties before the Supreme Court for the purpose of getting an advisory opinion. Congress had passed legislation affecting Native Americans and sought to discover whether it was constitutional. Congress specified that the U.S. government would be represented by the attorney general and that the Native Americans would be represented by counsel paid for by the U.S. Treasury. The Court, down to seven members because

Justices Willis Van Devanter and Lucius Q. C. Lamar did not participate, rendered a unanimous decision denying the Court's jurisdiction; the opinion was written by Justice William R. Day.

Richard L. Wilson

See also *Santa Clara Pueblo v. Martinez; Talton v. Mayes.*

MUTUAL FILM CORP. V. INDUSTRIAL COMMISSION OF OHIO

Court: U.S. Supreme Court
Citation: 236 U.S. 230
Date: February 23, 1915
Issues: Censorship; Freedom of speech; Local government; Pornography and obscenity

• This U.S. Supreme Court decision—and *Mutual Film Corporation v. Kansas*, which the Court decided at the same time—upheld the constitutionality of 1913 Ohio and Kansas laws allowing the states to censor films on the grounds that motion picture films were not protected forms of speech under the First Amendment; these decisions opened the door to decades of government censorship of films.

At stake in *Mutual*'s suits against Ohio and Kansas was the right of states to allow public officials to review films for their moral content before permitting them to be shown to the general public. Under Ohio's and Kansas's laws, films found to be "sacrilegious, obscene, indecent, or immoral," or that might "corrupt the morals," could be banned from being shown in public. In appealing an earlier decision against it to the Supreme Court, the Mutual Film Corporation claimed that state review of films was a violation of "the freedom to say, write or publish whatever one will on any subject." In defense of their right to act as censors, the states of Ohio and Kansas argued that film censorship was a legitimate exercise of the authority of the state to protect public morality.

In deciding in the states' favor, the Court reflected for the first time on the question of just what a motion picture was. Possibly influenced by the popular press, which reported on the infant film industry as though it were primarily a source of cheap mass entertainment, the Court determined that films fell into the category of entertainment designed to make a profit. Although films certainly contain ideas, the Court explained, they are not a means of communicating them. With that distinction in mind, the Court decided for Ohio on the grounds that state censorship of films did not violate any personal liberties covered by the First Amendment. Using the same line of reasoning, it also ruled in Kansas's favor.

Coming at a time when films were new, these decisions had a powerful impact. They made film censorship possible, allowing for state and local governments to control what films were shown in theaters. They also opened up a wide latitude for the censorship of films, which could be banned as "immoral" for many different reasons. The decisions enabled private pressure groups, particularly religious organizations such as the Legion of Decency, to bring pressure and influence to bear on the decisions of public censorship boards. It took more than thirty-five years for the Supreme Court, ruling in *Burstyn v. Wilson* (1952), a case relating to the imported Italian film *The Miracle* (*L'amore*, 1948), to overturn this decision by ruling that films did indeed communicate ideas and thus were entitled to constitutional protection.

Diane P. Michelfelder

See also *Burstyn v. Wilson*; *City of Renton v. Playtime Theaters*; *Freedman v. Maryland*; *Times Film Corp. v. City of Chicago*.

MYERS V. UNITED STATES

Court: U.S. Supreme Court
Citation: 272 U.S. 52
Date: October 25, 1926
Issues: Presidential powers

• The U.S. Supreme Court held that the president possessed an inherent power to remove members of the executive branch and that a law requiring senatorial approval was unconstitutional.

In 1920 President Woodrow Wilson fired Frank Myers, a postmaster in Oregon, before his term had expired. In so doing, Wilson ignored a statute requiring the Senate's advice and consent before removing postmasters. Myers filed a suit for back pay. The Supreme Court, by a 6-3 margin, denied the claim. In a sweeping opinion for the majority, Chief Justice William H. Taft confirmed the president's unqualified discretion to remove anyone that he had appointed to the executive branch. Because presidents had the constitutional responsibility to execute the laws faithfully, they must be able to exercise control over subordinates who act under their authority. Taft also argued that the president's removal power was logically implied by the separation of powers doctrine. Three justices wrote vigorous dissents. Although the *Myers* precedent was never overturned, the Court in *Humphrey's Executor v. United States* (1935) limited the precedent so that it does not apply to officials with quasi-legislative and quasi-judicial functions within the independent regulatory agencies.

Thomas Tandy Lewis

See also *Dames and Moore v. Regan*; *Goldwater v. Carter*; *McCulloch v. Maryland*; *Martin v. Mott*; *Mississippi v. Johnson*; *Nixon v. Administrator of General Services*; *United States v. Curtiss-Wright Export Corp.*; *United States v. Nixon*; *Wiener v. United States*.

NATIONAL ASSOCIATION FOR THE ADVANCEMENT OF COLORED PEOPLE V. ALABAMA

Court: U.S. Supreme Court
Citation: 357 U.S. 449
Date: June 30, 1958
Issues: Civil rights and liberties; Freedom of assembly and association

- The U.S. Supreme Court explicitly recognized that a freedom of association was implied in the First Amendment's guarantee of free expression and free assembly and was an "inseparable aspect" of the liberty guaranteed by the due process clause of the Fourteenth Amendment.

As the Civil Rights movement started in the 1950's, several southern states tried to limit the activities of groups like the National Association for the Advancement of Colored People (NAACP). Alabama had a law that required out-of-state businesses to register with the state and disclose their membership list in order to do business in the state. A state court concluded that the NAACP was a business rather than a nonprofit organization and ordered the group to turn over the names of its members to the state attorney general. The NAACP refused and argued that the disclosure of rank-and-file members would lead to reprisals and public hostility, placing unacceptable burdens on the right of members to belong to the association and to support its goals.

The Supreme Court unanimously upheld the NAACP's position. Writing for the Court, Justice John M. Harlan II declared that the Constitution prohibited the states from limiting the ability of the members of a legal and nonsubversive organization "to pursue their collective efforts to foster beliefs which they admittedly have a right to advocate." Because the freedom to participate in an association is a fundamental right, Harlan instructed courts to use the closest scrutiny when examining state actions that have the effect of curtailing this freedom. In numerous cases since 1958, the Court upheld restrictions on the freedom of association whenever a group is engaged in criminal activities or invidious discrimination.

Thomas Tandy Lewis

See also *DeJonge v. Oregon; Guinn v. United States; National Association for the Advancement of Colored People v. Button; Nixon v. Herndon; Shelley v. Kraemer; Smith v. Allwright; Sweatt v. Painter.*

NATIONAL ASSOCIATION FOR THE ADVANCEMENT OF COLORED PEOPLE V. BUTTON

Court: U.S. Supreme Court
Citation: 371 U.S. 415
Date: January 14, 1963
Issues: Freedom of assembly and association

- In this landmark ruling, the U.S. Supreme Court held that the First and Fourteenth Amendments protected the right of an organization to use the courts in promoting its organizational mission.

The Virginia legislature enacted a "barratry" statute that threatened to disbar attorneys who represented an organization sponsoring a judicial proceeding without having a "pecuniary interest" in the outcome. The purpose of the statute was to prevent the National Association for the Advancement of Colored People and other civil rights organizations from sponsoring antisegregation litigation. By a 6-3 majority, the Supreme Court ruled that the statute was unconstitutional. Justice William J. Brennan, Jr.'s opinion for the Court emphasized that litigation is a protected form of political expression and is often the most effective means for an association to promote its goals as well as the only practical way for a minority to petition the government for a redress of grievances. In addition, a state may not ignore constitutional rights under the guise of prohibiting professional misconduct. In dissent, Justice John M. Harlan II argued that litigation was primarily conduct rather than First Amendment expression and therefore was subject to reasonable regulations.

Thomas Tandy Lewis

See also *DeJonge v. Oregon; Guinn v. United States; National Association for the Advancement of Colored People v. Alabama; Nixon v. Herndon; Shelley v. Kraemer; Smith v. Allwright; Sweatt v. Painter.*

NATIONAL ENDOWMENT FOR THE ARTS V. FINLEY

Court: U.S. Supreme Court
Citation: 524 U.S. 569
Date: June 25, 1998
Issues: Censorship; First Amendment guarantees; Pornography and obscenity

- After the U.S. Congress passed legislation requiring the National Endowment for the Arts to consider general standards of decency before awarding new grants, performance artist Karen Finley and three other artists challenged the law in the courts, arguing that it gave government the power to censor artists whose works were seen as unacceptable because of their disturbing style or unpopular political messages. The U.S. Supreme Court, however, upheld the decency law.

The U.S. Congress established the National Endowment for the Arts (NEA) in 1965 to support artistic accomplishment and community involvement in the arts. Through grants to individuals and museums, the NEA typically supports artists whose work may not be commercially successful. Public arguments about "decency" in the work of NEA-funded artists came to the surface in the late 1980's, when influential politicians learned of NEA support for the work of Andres Serrano and Robert Mapplethorpe. Serrano was a visual artist whose works included *Piss Christ*, a photograph showing a plastic crucifix immersed in a small fish tank filled with Serrano's urine. This photograph was displayed at a contemporary art museum exhibit in Winston-Salem, North Carolina, that was partially funded by the NEA. Mapplethorpe was a photographer whose controversial black-and-white images included scenes depicting homosexual behavior and sadomasochistic sexuality. Mapplethorpe's work appeared in many books and museum exhibits in Philadelphia and Chicago.

Opposition to the NEA

Led by Republican U.S. senator Jesse Helms of North Carolina, a group of politicians with the support of conservatives, including many on the Christian Right, lambasted the NEA for supporting what they saw as morally corrupt and blasphemous art with taxpayers' dollars. In response to pressure, the Corcoran Gallery of Art in Washington, D.C., withdrew plans to host Mapplethorpe's exhibition *The Perfect Moment* in 1989. The Mapplethorpe show traveled to several other cities, where it received mixed reviews but no attempts were made to censor it. When the show reached the Contemporary Arts Center in Cincinnati, Ohio, in 1990, however, the Hamilton County sheriff closed down the exhibit. Public resentment against unregulated government funding of controversial works of art was growing, and some politicians wanted complete abolishment of the NEA because it placed the federal government in the role of unregulated patron of the arts.

When the U.S. Congress reviewed the NEA annual budget for reauthorization in 1990, it placed clear conditions of review on the agency's funding of future artists and exhibitions. Congress passed U.S. Code 954, which states that the chairperson of the NEA is required to ensure that "artistic excellence and artistic merit are the criteria by which [grant] applications are judged, taking into consideration general standards of decency and respect for the diverse beliefs and values of the American public." Furthermore, the law states that the NEA needs to employ funding review procedures that clearly indicate that obscenity is without artistic merit, is not protected speech, and shall not be funded. The new law prevented artists, productions, workshops, and exhibitions that are determined to be generally in violation of standards of decency from receiving any financial support from the NEA.

Artists Holly Hughes, John Fleck, Tim Miller, and Karen Finley had all received small amounts of NEA grant money in the past, but their work seemed to violate the new decency guidelines. This group became known as the NEA Four because theirs was the first artistic work to test the new guidelines. Hughes was a playwright whose work embraced lesbian and feminist themes and had been termed pornographic by some observers. Fleck was a writer and performance artist who had been accused of acts of public indecency, including urination and masturbation. Miller was a gay actor and writer. Finley was a controversial performance artist.

Finley had become famous for works in which she covered her body with yams or chocolate while delivering verbal tirades about female sexuality and oppression of women. She had developed a style of performance in which she challenged audiences about their stereotypes and biases against women. During her monologues, Finley would break out of character to argue with people who laughed at the wrong time or tried to leave before a performance's conclusion. Another performance art project by Finley consisted of people dialing a telephone number to talk with each other. In her work, Finley tried to bring attention to the status of women and to bring oppressed voices into the open. She felt that women were marginalized, sanitized, and taught to sound safe and domesticated, like the voices of characters in novels by Barbara Pym or Jane Austen.

When Finley, Hughes, Fleck, and Miller applied to the NEA again for funding after the new law was passed, the agency's board of directors initially approved them. However, new NEA director John Frohnmayer then vetoed the recommendations of the board and denied funding to the four artists on the grounds that their work was blatantly sexual and controversial and seemed to go against community standards of decency. In response, the NEA Four brought a lawsuit against the NEA, claiming that Frohnmayer's veto went against the 1965 NEA original charter to support artists. They also asserted that the new grant review process limited their freedom of expression, in violation of the First Amendment of the U.S. Constitution.

The Court's Ruling

By a vote of eight to one, the U.S. Supreme Court held that the NEA could reference community standards of decency in making budgetary decisions about funding artists and exhibitions. In writing for the majority, Justice Sandra Day O'Connor stated that upholding decency standards does not constitute an act of censorship or a violation of free speech guaranteed in the First Amendment. O'Connor wrote that the NEA law is not absolute in nature but only advisory, just one consideration in a complicated and subjective review process. The law does not deliberately exclude future works of art that some might perceive as indecent, nor does it discourage future artistic accomplishment or support of artists, exhibits, and museums. O'Connor also wrote that the law does not violate artists' First Amendment rights and does not violate constitutional prohibitions against vagueness.

Significance

During the 1980's and the presidency of Ronald Reagan, the political climate in the United States turned away from the uncritical liberalism of the 1960's and 1970's. The U.S. Supreme Court finding in *National Endowment for the Arts v. Finley* had a chilling effect on performance artists and exhibitions of art that embraced controversial, disturbing, and sexual themes, although in the short term the case brought added attention to the artists of the NEA Four. Although Karen Finley complained of government censorship and suppression of free speech, the notoriety of the case guaranteed large audiences at her future performances.

Many observers asserted that accountability and public oversight of the NEA were long overdue. The federal law requiring consideration of standards of decency was based on common sense, even though Senator Helms tended to sound alarmist and his arguments struck fear into the hearts of liberals and patrons of the arts. The Supreme Court's ruling did not challenge the integrity of the guarantee of freedom of speech in the First Amendment because the Court viewed the NEA guidelines as advisory. The decency requirement was only one of many factors the NEA board needed to consider when reviewing grant applications, and the requirement was never meant to apply more broadly to all displays of art or public art galleries. Controversial artists such as Finley were understandably upset by the ruling, but the increased publicity and vociferous political attacks against the NEA that surrounded the case actually brought out advocates on the other side and helped the government agency in its mission of supporting art and artists.

Jonathan L. Thorndike

Further Reading

Mey, Kerstin. *Art and Obscenity.* New York: I. B. Tauris, 2007. Examines reactions to the works of twentieth century artists who have created art that some deem obscene or unacceptable.

Scholossman, David A. *Actors and Activists: Performance, Politics, and Exchange Among Social Worlds.* New York: Garland, 2001. Provides a good overview of the issues involved in the NEA controversy, with chapters on critical theory, performance art, the NEA Four, and issues surrounding the production of the musical *Miss Saigon.*

Yenawine, Philip, Marianne Weems, and Brian Wallis, eds. *Art Matters: How the Culture Wars Changed America.* New York: New York University Press, 1999. Collection of essays discusses visual art, popular culture, arts funding, censorship, and the nature of controversial artwork that explores racially and sexually challenging ideas.

Zeigler, Joseph Wesley. *Arts in Crisis: The National Endowment for the Arts Versus America.* Pennington, N.J.: A Cappella Books, 1994. Provides a historical overview of American public and government attitudes about funding in the arts. Includes a foreword by Garrison Keillor titled "Thanks for Attacking the NEA" and a chapter on the NEA Four.

See also *Cohen v. Cowles Media Co.; In re Neagle; Miller et al. v. Civil City of South Bend; Near v. Minnesota; New York v. Ferber.*

===============================

NATIONAL LABOR RELATIONS BOARD V. JONES AND LAUGHLIN STEEL CORP.

Court: U.S. Supreme Court
Citation: 301 U.S. 1
Date: April 12, 1937
Issues: Freedom of contract; Regulation of commerce

• In upholding the National Labor Relations Act (NLRA), the U.S. Supreme Court departed from its precedents prohibiting governmental interference with freedom of contract and also rejected its earlier distinctions between commerce and manufacturing and between direct and indirect burdens on interstate commerce.

The NLRA (also called the Wagner Act) of 1935 was one of the most important statutes enacted during President Franklin D. Roosevelt's New Deal. The statute guaranteed the right of labor unions to bargain collectively and authorized the National Labor Relations Board (NLRB) to investigate and prevent unfair labor practices. When a steel manufacturer fired ten employees for engaging in union activities, the NLRB obtained a court order compelling their reinstatement. Lawyers for the company argued that the NLRA was unconstitutional for two reasons: It interfered with the freedom of contract and invaded the reserved powers of the states when it regulated manufacturing activities.

Writing for a 5-4 majority, Chief Justice Charles Evans Hughes held that Congress had the authority to prohibit unfair labor practices as an appropriate means of promoting the smooth and peaceful flow of interstate commerce, which was threatened by strikes and other labor-management conflicts. He found that Congress had plenary power to protect interstate commerce from whatever sources of dangers might threaten it. In regard to the freedom of contract objection, Hughes found that protecting the right of workers to organize for collective bargaining was reasonable given the unequal relationship between workers and management. Therefore, he concluded that the NLRA did not arbitrarily interfere with the freedom to negotiate contracts. An interesting feature of Hughes's opinion is its emphasis on using statutory interpretations that uphold rather than overturn statutes.

The *Jones and Laughlin* decision signaled that the majority of the justices were ready to accept New Deal legislation by using a broad interpretation of the commerce clause and a narrow defense of the freedom of contract doctrine. The Court further expanded the authority of Congress to regulate productive activities in *United States v. Darby Lumber Co.* (1941) and *Wickard v. Filburn* (1942).

Thomas Tandy Lewis

See also *Katzenbach v. McClung*; *United States v. Darby Lumber Co.*; *Wickard v. Filburn*.

NATIONAL LEAGUE OF CITIES V. USERY

Court: U.S. Supreme Court
Citation: 426 U.S. 833
Date: June 24, 1976
Issues: Local government; Regulation of commerce; State sovereignty

• The U.S. Supreme Court resurrected and expanded the concept of state sovereignty under the Tenth Amendment when it held that Congress had no authority to require state and local governments to pay the minimum wage to public employees, but the Court overturned this decision in 1985.

In 1974 Congress amended the Fair Labor Standards Act so that its minimum-wage and maximum-hour standards were binding on state and local governments. By a 5-4 vote, the Supreme Court held that the amendments unconstitutionally infringed on the sovereign powers reserved to the states in the Tenth Amendment. Speaking for the Court, Chief Justice William H. Rehnquist, who had long been a proponent of states' rights, argued that Congress could not use its powers over interstate commerce to regulate the "States as States," and that "one undoubted attribute of state sovereignty" is the right of the states to decide the salaries to be paid to state employees. In a dissent, Justice William J. Brennan, Jr., denounced the decision as "a catastrophic judicial body blow at Congress' power under the Commerce Clause." The *Usery* decision was of great symbolic importance because it appeared to resurrect notions of pre-1937 dual federalism.

In *Garcia v. San Antonio Metropolitan Transit Authority* (1985), Justice Harry A. Blackmun switched his position, so that the justices voted five to four to reverse the *Usery* holding. The Court, however, resurrected the Tenth Amendment as a restraint on Congress in *United States v. Lopez* (1995) and *Printz v. United States* (1997).

Thomas Tandy Lewis

See also *Garcia v. San Antonio Metropolitan Transit Authority*; *Printz v. United States*; *United States v. Lopez.*

NATIONAL TREASURY EMPLOYEES UNION V. VON RAAB

Court: U.S. Supreme Court
Citation: 489 U.S. 656
Date: March 21, 1989
Issues: Illegal drugs; Labor law; Right to privacy

- In this case the U.S. Supreme Court expanded the scope and discretion of public employers to utilize mandatory drug testing in their efforts to promote a drug-free work environment.

The rules of the drug-testing program of the U.S. Customs Service required a very closely monitored urine test for employees seeking transfers or promotions to specified job classifications. Positions covered included those involved with classified materials, drug interdiction, and the carrying of firearms. The National Treasury Employees Union (NTEU) challenged these rules in federal district court on the grounds that they called for an unlawful search, a violation of employees' Fourth Amendment rights.

The court agreed, arguing that the drug testing was an overly intrusive violation of the employees' privacy and an unlawful search, given the lack of any actual evidence of drug abuse. An injunction was issued to keep the Customs Service from implementing the rules.

This injunction was later vacated by the circuit court of appeals, which, while it agreed that the testing did represent a "search," in the meaning of the Fourth Amendment, concluded that the Customs Service rules were "reasonable." This conclusion was based on the Customs Service's strong law-enforcement function and its related need to maintain public confidence that key employees were drug free.

The U.S. Supreme Court, in a 5-4 decision, upheld the majority of the testing program, based largely on the rationale of *Skinner v. Railway Labor Executives' Association* (1989). The Court ruled that there must be a balance between an employee's legitimate expectation of privacy and the government's legitimate public policy interest, a balance that must be evaluated on a case-by-case basis. Thus, for example, the Court excluded the drug-testing procedures for Customs Service positions dealing with "classified materials," concluding that the term was too vaguely defined.

The ongoing need to strike a balance was further demonstrated by the dissenting opinion of Justice Antonin Scalia. Though he had voted with the majority in *Skinner,* Scalia argued that in this instance the Customs Service did not adequately demonstrate a potential for great harm in the absence of drug testing and thus the government's interest in this case should not supersede the employees' Fourth Amendment protection.

NTEU v. Von Raab, in conjunction with *Skinner,* established that the Fourth Amendment does not exclude all drug testing of employees. Rather, some searches are "reasonable" and are therefore lawful. On the other hand, the government employer does not have an unfettered right to impose drug testing. The government must, in each instance, demonstrate that there is a rational connection between drug testing and the broader public interest. Properly and reasonably crafted drug-testing procedures are legal, and thus *NTEU v. Von Raab* both expanded and defined the scope of public sector drug testing.

David Carleton

See also *Skinner v. Railway Labor Executives' Association; Vernonia School District 47J v. Acton.*

NEAGLE, IN RE. *See* IN RE NEAGLE

NEAR V. MINNESOTA

Court: U.S. Supreme Court
Citation: 283 U.S. 697
Date: June 1, 1931
Issues: Censorship; Freedom of the press; Pornography and obscenity

• In this case the U.S. Supreme Court held for the first time that injunctions on the press to prevent publication are presumptively unconstitutional "prior restraints" and that the parties seeking them have a heavy burden to overcome; however, it also suggested that prior restraints could be acceptable under certain circumstances.

Based on a statute that allowed a court to enjoin (prohibit) the publication of a newspaper if it was detrimental to public morals and general welfare, a Minnesota district attorney requested an injunction against the *Saturday Press* because of its anti-Semitic and racist remarks. The trial court concluded that the publication was chiefly devoted to malicious, scandalous, and defamatory articles and enjoined the editors from publishing, editing, producing, and circulating their publication. The Supreme Court of Minnesota affirmed this decision, but the Supreme Court of the United States reversed it.

The Court held that the statute amounted to a prior restraint in violation of the First Amendment. Since the effect of the application of the statute was the suppression of information, the Court held that it operated as a system of censorship. The Court suggested that prior restraints are the most dangerous infringement on freedom of the press because their effect is to suppress speech totally and because of the inability of the press to challenge the constitutionality of the order by disobeying it. The Court suggested, however, that prior restraints could be acceptable in limited circumstances, including cases of obscene material, cases of fighting words and incitement to violence or to

Justice Pierce Butler.
(Library of Congress)

overthrow the government, and cases of national security during war where the information to be published could endanger U.S. troops or the success of a mission. The Court offered no explanation for these exceptions.

Justice Pierce Butler wrote a dissenting opinion joined by three other justices. They argued that the original court order did not have the effect of a prior restraint but of punishment imposed after publication to preserve law and order. They also emphasized the fact that the statute did not authorize administrative, licensing, or censorship control by the government. Therefore, they suggested, the statute did not amount to censorship.

The decision of the Court stated clearly for the first time that by issuing an injunction against the media prior to publication the state would be abridging freedom of the press. In reaching this conclusion, the Court gave the concept of prior restraint a much broader meaning than it had been afforded before. Traditionally, the phrase "prior restraint" was used to describe an administrative licensing system which allowed the state to determine in advance what could be published.

The Minnesota statute did not create a licensing system; the decision to enjoin a publication was made by a court after a hearing and not by an administrative licenser or censor prior to publication. However, the Court declared that the primary purpose of the First Amendment is to protect against governmental actions that have the ultimate effect of a prior restraint, whatever their character might be. Since *Near v. Minnesota*, therefore, the doctrine against prior restraints on the media has been related to the effects on speech notwithstanding the method used by the government in regulating it.

Alberto Bernabe-Riefkohl

See also *Branzburg v. Hayes*; *Cohen v. Cowles Media Co.*; *Grosjean v. American Press Co.*; *Miami Herald Publishing Co. v. Tornillo*; *New York Times Co. v. United States*; *Richmond Newspapers v. Virginia.*

NEBBIA V. NEW YORK

Court: U.S. Supreme Court
Citation: 291 U.S. 502
Date: March 5, 1934
Issues: Regulation of business

- Reversing several precedents, the U.S. Supreme Court held that the Fourteenth Amendment did not prohibit the states from regulating most aspects of any business open to the public.

Responding to the decline of milk prices during the Great Depression, the New York legislature passed the Milk Control Law of 1933, which created a board to fix the retail prices of milk. Leo Nebbia, proprietor of a small grocery store in Rochester, was convicted for selling two quarts of milk below the established price of nine cents each. By a 5-4 vote, the Supreme Court upheld both the conviction and the constitutionality of the law. Writing for the majority, Justice Owen J. Roberts abandoned the "affected with a public interest" doctrine, which had prevented states from regulating numerous categories of business establishments. Although Roberts wrote that "a state is free to adapt whatever economic policy may reasonably be deemed to promote public welfare," the decision did not reject the freedom of contract doctrine in regard to labor policy.

In dissent, Justice James C. McReynolds invoked the doctrine of substantive due process, and he argued that the New York statute interfered arbitrarily with the liberty of small businesspeople and consumers to negotiate prices in an open market.

Thomas Tandy Lewis

See also *Munn v. Illinois; Tyson v. Banton; Wolff Packing Co. v. Court of Industrial Relations.*

NEBRASKA PRESS ASSOCIATION V. STUART

Court: U.S. Supreme Court
Citation: 427 U.S. 539
Date: June 30, 1976
Issues: Freedom of the press

- The U.S. Supreme Court rejected the use of gag orders to protect the rights of those accused of crimes.

This case involved an unusually perverted mass murder and sex crime in a small town in Nebraska. At the preliminary hearing, a confession and note written by the defendant were made available to the press. In an attempt to provide the accused with an impartial, fair trial, the local court issued an injunction against not only the police and attorneys but also the members of the press who were present at the hearing in order to prevent the press from publishing the lurid details contained in the confession and note.

The Supreme Court unanimously overturned the lower court's gag order. It found that the Sixth Amendment's guarantee of the right to an open trial (which means the press has access to the information from the trial) is a long-standing constitutional right that should be balanced against freedom of the press, but balancing should not include prior restraint. When balancing, the lower courts should use the method with the "least means" of disturbing either of the rights (but especially the freedom of the press). One practical result of this case was the increased practice of sequestering juries in dramatic cases and closing preliminary hearings to the press, thereby avoiding the issuance of injunctions that violate the ban against prior restraint. Newspapers continue to object to various aspects of this treatment, but generally the Court has upheld the right of courts to keep certain information out of the hands of the press.

Richard L. Wilson

See also *Near v. Minnesota; New York Times Co. v. United States; Richmond Newspapers v. Virginia.*

New Jersey v. T.L.O.

Court: U.S. Supreme Court
Citation: 469 U.S. 325
Date: January 15, 1985
Issues: Education; Right to privacy; Search and seizure

- This decision established the standards by which the protections of the Fourth Amendment apply to searches of students by school officials.

A teacher at Piscataway High School in New Jersey found two students smoking cigarettes in a school restroom in violation of the school's rules. After being sent to the school office, one of the students, "T.L.O.," a fourteen-year-old freshman, denied smoking. Based on the report he had received from the teacher, the assistant vice principal searched T.L.O.'s purse and discovered a pack of cigarettes. As he reached for the cigarette pack, he then noticed other items, including cigarette rolling papers, which he associated with marijuana use. He then searched the purse more thoroughly and discovered marijuana, a pipe, plastic bags, a large sum of money in single dollar bills, a list of students who owed T.L.O. money, and two letters which suggested T.L.O. was involved in marijuana sales. School officials notified T.L.O.'s mother and the police.

On the basis of this evidence and a later confession, the state brought delinquency charges against T.L.O. T.L.O. appealed the charges, arguing that because the search of her purse was improper under the Fourth Amendment, the evidence was inadmissible. The U.S. Supreme Court, however, ruled that the search was conducted within the constitutional standards of the Fourth Amendment. In its opinion, the Court established standards to be used by school officials in searches of students' pockets, purses, and other items associated with the student's person. The Court specifically did not address searches of school lockers.

Until this case, public school officials had typically relied on the doctrine of in loco parentis, whereby school officials had broad search powers akin to those of a student's parents. The U.S. Supreme Court rejected this argument and held that when public school officials conduct a search of a student, they may be held to the same Fourth Amendment standards as government officials. In its analysis, the Court recognized that public school students maintain an expectation of privacy in their personal effects even on a public school campus, but the Court did not go so far as to hold school officials to exactly the same standards as police officers in conducting searches.

While police officers are usually required to show they had probable cause to believe the person has violated the law, the Court allowed that school officials may need to show only that they had a reasonable suspicion that a search would produce evidence that the student had violated a school code. The Court justified this relaxed standard for school officials by citing the major social problems evident in schools nationwide and a school's need to maintain an educational environment.

Paul Albert Bateman

See also *Safford Unified School District v. Redding; Vernonia School District 47J v. Acton; Zurcher v. The Stanford Daily.*

New State Ice Co. v. Liebmann

Court: U.S. Supreme Court
Citation: 285 U.S. 262
Date: March 21, 1932
Issues: Antitrust law; Regulation of business

- Overturning a state law that conferred a monopoly on existing businesses, the U.S. Supreme Court confirmed its commitment to free-market competition.

Responding to a surplus of ice producers throughout the state, an Oklahoma statute of 1925 forbade issuance of new licenses to sell ice except when a necessity could be shown in a particular community. The effect of the law was to prevent the establishment of new ice companies. When Liebmann, an Oklahoma businessman, began to sell ice in Oklahoma City without a license, the New State Ice Company used the statute to put him out of business. The Supreme Court, voting six to two, found that the license requirement was an unconstitutional violation of the substantive liberty protected by the due process clause of the Fourteenth Amendment. Justice George Sutherland, an articulate defender of economic freedom, emphasized that the effect of the statute was to shut out new enterprises and to confer a monopoly on existing companies. In a long dissent, Justice Louis D. Brandeis responded that state legislatures should have discretion to determine whether there was a need to eliminate destructive competition. It was necessary, moreover, to allow legislatures to experiment in order "to meet changing social and economic needs."

Although *New State Ice* was never directly overturned, it soon disappeared as the Court moved in the direction favored by Brandeis, recognizing a broad legislative authority to regulate business. At the end of the twentieth century, communities commonly restricted the numbers of licenses issued for the sale of alcoholic beverages or for the operation of taxi services. Nevertheless, the decision remained controversial. Proponents of free-market economics view the Oklahoma law as a prime example of the kind of unnecessary legislation that protects vested interests and stifles competition.

Thomas Tandy Lewis

See also *Adkins v. Children's Hospital; Ferguson v. Skrupa; Hammer v. Dagenhart; Holden v. Hardy; Munn v. Illinois.*

New York State Club Association v. City of New York

Court: U.S. Supreme Court
Citation: 487 U.S. 1
Date: June 20, 1988
Issues: First Amendment guarantees; Freedom of assembly and association; Sex discrimination

- The U.S. Supreme Court upheld a New York City law that prohibited racial, religious, or sex discrimination in private clubs having more than four hundred members as long as the clubs served meals to guests and regularly received payments from nonmembers for the advancement of trade or business.

In the landmark decision *Roberts v. United States Jaycees* (1984), the Supreme Court ruled that the First Amendment did not prohibit application of a state nondiscrimination law to a large national club that provided career and business opportunities for its members. In response, the New York City council made its nondiscrimination laws applicable to almost all private clubs, excluding only those that were small and did not receive payments from nonmembers. By a 9-0 majority, the Court upheld the law. Justice Byron R. White's majority opinion emphasized that the law did not prevent clubs from restricting their membership on the basis of viewpoint and that private organizations advocating particular viewpoints might be able to demonstrate that application of the law would interfere with their First Amendment rights.

In subsequent decisions, however, the Court refused to reject all free association claims for private organizations. For example, in *Hurley v. Irish-American Gay, Lesbian, and Bisexual Group of Boston* (1995), the Court held that the state could not compel a private organization to promote a message of which it disapproved.

Thomas Tandy Lewis

See also *County of Washington v. Gunther; Frontiero v. Richardson; Grove City College v. Bell; Hoyt v. Florida; Meritor Savings Bank v. Vinson; Phillips v. Martin Marietta Corp.; Rosenfeld v. Southern Pacific; Stanton v. Stanton.*

New York Times Co. v. Sullivan

Court: U.S. Supreme Court
Citation: 376 U.S. 254
Date: March 9, 1964
Issues: Freedom of the press

• The U.S. Supreme Court redefined freedom of the press by requiring that someone wishing to recover damages from a newspaper for a false story had to show that the newspaper had actual malice or a reckless disregard for the truth.

The New York Times printed an advertisement appealing for funds for civil rights organizations that included technically false statements about Montgomery, Alabama, police commissioner Sullivan. The Supreme Court was asked to rule on a half-million dollar civil damage award to Sullivan. There was no showing that the *Times* had any actual malice or reckless disregard for the truth in printing the statements. The most that could be alleged was that the *Times* was negligent.

The Court's unanimous decision in favor of the newspaper gave vastly greater protection to the news media from libel suits resulting from the publication of factual errors. In his opinion for the Court, Justice William J. Brennan, Jr., pointed out that allowing the damage award from the Alabama courts would provoke greater fear than criminal prosecution. Sullivan could show no monetary loss, but the newspaper would face a loss one thousand times greater than the maximum fine under Alabama criminal statutes. Because double jeopardy protection does not exist in civil litigation, other awards could be levied against the newspaper for the same advertisement. Fear of successive monetary losses would stifle the press, Brennan argued. The Court prohibited public officials from recovering damages for a defamatory falsehood relating to their official conduct unless they proved that the statement was made with actual malice—that is, with knowledge it was false or with a reckless disregard for whether it was false or not.

As a result, it became extraordinarily difficult for public officials to ever win a damage suit against a newspaper or television station, no matter how false or defamatory the statements against them were. The same situation also confronts those people who are defined as "public figures." A public figure, for purposes of defamation law, is a person who "thrusts himself into a public controversy in order to affect its outcome." An otherwise little-known person unwillingly caught up in a matter of public interest is not a public official and thus need prove only negligence (not actual malice) to prevail against a defamer, according to *Wolston v. Reader's Digest Association* (1979). "Public figure" is a more vague term than "public official," and for that reason, the Court has had to deal with a large number of libel suits involving people who believe they are ordinary citizens but whom the newspapers claim are public figures. Generally speaking, a public figure would be a movie star, a sports hero, or some other well-known person who had been mentioned in the press before a controversy arose. Presumably, the laws of libel apply to any ordinary citizen who is libeled or defamed by a newspaper, and private people are able to recover damages from newspapers or magazines.

Richard L. Wilson

Further Reading

Gold, Susan Dudley. *New York Times Co. v. Sullivan: Freedom of the Press or Libel?* Tarrytown, N.Y.: Marshall Cavendish Benchmark, 2007. Part of its publisher's Supreme Court Milestones series designed for young-adult readers, this volume offers an accessible history and analysis of the *Sullivan* case that examines opposing sides in the case, the people involved, and the case's lasting impact. Includes bibliography and index.

See also *Chaplinsky v. New Hampshire; Garrison v. Louisiana; Gertz v. Robert Welch; Masson v. New Yorker Magazine; Milkovich v. Lorain Journal Co.; Time v. Hill.*

NEW YORK TIMES CO. V. UNITED STATES

Court: U.S. Supreme Court
Citation: 403 U.S. 713
Date: June 30, 1971
Issues: Censorship; Warfare and terrorism

- In an emergency session, the U.S. Supreme Court refused to uphold lower court decisions directing *The New York Times* to refrain from publishing the Pentagon Papers, a history of the Vietnam War that revealed the duplicity and missteps of several presidential administrations in dealing with the conflict.

In 1967, U.S. secretary of defense Robert McNamara directed a study of the American military and political involvement in Vietnam since World War II. Leslie Gelb, a civilian staff official in the Department of Defense, headed up a team of dozens of military and civilian scholars who assembled seven thousand pages of documents in forty-seven volumes; the collection was classified top secret. One of those working on the project was Daniel Ellsberg, an employee of the RAND Corporation who was growing to distrust the government's public assessment of the progress of the war in Vietnam. He felt the documents exposed the ineptitude of several presidential administrations in dealing with affairs in Southeast Asia and also highlighted the government's efforts to keep embarrassing information from the American people.

After gaining access to the RAND Corporation's set of these volumes, in 1971 Ellsberg and fellow RAND employee Anthony J. Russo made copies; immediately Ellsberg began seeking ways to have them released to the public. When he failed in attempts to have Senator J. William Fulbright of Arkansas share them with Congress, Ellsberg gave them to *The New York Times* after the newspaper agreed to do an extensive series based on the documents.

On June 13, 1971, the *Times* began publishing what was projected to be a ten-part series. Although the stories could not directly embarrass the Richard M. Nixon administration, since the documents on which they were based covered the period from 1954 to 1968, President Nixon felt it was important for the government to block further disclosure of classified information. Almost immediately, attorneys from the U.S. Department of Justice went before Federal District Judge Murray I. Gurfein in New York to obtain a court order to stop publication. Gurfein directed that the *Times* halt publication until the matter could be argued more fully in court.

Several days later, however, *The Washington Post* began a similar series. Again, Nixon administration lawyers went to court, appealing to Federal District Judge Gerhard A. Gesell in Washington, D.C., to enjoin the *Post* from continuing its series. Unlike Gurfein, however, Gesell did not order the *Post* to cease publishing the series. In both cases, lawyers for the government argued that information in these documents, popularly titled the Pentagon Papers, was highly sensitive; they claimed that publication would hurt efforts to end the war in Vietnam and would place lives in jeopardy. They also pointed out that in 1931 the Supreme Court had ruled in *Near v. Minnesota* that prior restraint (a form of censorship used by the government to prevent a statement from being published) was permissible when national security was threatened.

The Issues

Both sides in the case, and the judges in the federal court system, realized that the issues with which they were dealing had serious First Amendment implications. The *Times* appealed Judge Gurfein's ruling; the government appealed Judge Gesell's. Both cases proceeded on parallel tracks through the federal system very quickly, the government insisting that national security was threatened by publication of the Pentagon Papers while the newspapers' attorneys argued that their clients were protected from prior restraint of publication by the First Amendment. In the meantime, other newspapers across the country began carrying stories that reprinted material from the Pentagon Papers, further publicizing the government's long-standing secret activities in Southeast Asia.

On June 25, 1971, having lost in the lower courts, the *Times* appealed to the U.S. Supreme Court. Because the *Post* had won in the lower courts, the Justice Department brought its case against the Washington, D.C., paper to the Supreme Court as well. The cases were combined and heard as *New York Times Co. v. United States* before the Court in an emergency session. Two noted constitutional scholars represented the opposing parties: Yale professor Alexander Bickel argued on behalf of the newspapers, and the government's arguments were presented by the solicitor general of the United States, Erwin Griswold. The government reiterated its argument that national security was endangered, but Bickel pointed out that the Justice Department had not identified for any federal court specific information that national security was being threatened.

On June 30, in a 6-3 ruling, the Supreme Court justices affirmed that prior restraint was not appropriate in this case. Each justice wrote a separate opinion indicating his reasons for voting as he did. Three thought that prior restraint was called for, but six argued that, since the government could not prove how release of this information would specifically damage the nation, the newspapers were protected under the First Amendment to publish what they wished. Several justices emphasized, however, that the government could bring criminal charges against newspaper officials and others involved in making public the classified information contained in the Pentagon Papers.

By this point, however, the American public had already seen enough of these documents to know that what was really being protected were the reputations of political officials who had gotten the country deep into the quagmire in Southeast Asia. Further, on the eve of the Supreme Court decision,

Alaska senator Mike Gravel, an opponent of the war, had obtained a copy of the Pentagon Papers and began reading them at a congressional subcommittee meeting, thus entering them into the *Congressional Record* as public documents.

Significance

The immediate impact of the Supreme Court's ruling was to permit American newspapers to continue publishing information from the Pentagon Papers that revealed the government's behind-the-scenes activities in dealing with the Vietnam War. Legally, the justices actually upheld the principle that prior restraint of publication is sometimes permissible, but by refusing to stop publication of the Pentagon Papers they set a high standard for the government to meet in requesting prior restraint in the future.

The court case also made public some embarrassing facts about the government's classification system. During hearings, it became clear that some information that government lawyers were trying to suppress had in fact long been available to the public. Worse, testimony revealed that there was no definitive rule for assigning levels of classification to government documents; individual judgment by midlevel bureaucrats was often the only standard for determining the sensitivity of a document. This revelation, combined with the release of information that exposed attempts by several presidential administrations to mislead the American people, fueled widespread distrust of government.

The indirect impact of the Pentagon Papers case was even more significant. Although no charges were filed against the newspapers, the government brought criminal charges against Ellsberg and Russo in 1971 for leaking the classified documents. Charges were dismissed in 1973, but the Nixon administration's aggressive attempts to prosecute Ellsberg and to prevent future leaks of classified information led to the establishment of a clandestine group known as the "Plumbers." One of this group's first actions was to break into the office of Ellsberg's psychiatrist to steal information that might damage the RAND analyst's credibility. Later, the Plumbers would reprise their tactics at the offices of the Democratic National Committee in the Watergate complex in Washington, D.C. The discovery of their activities, and the revelation that President Nixon had personally authorized their activities, led to the resignation of the thirty-seventh president of the United States.

Laurence W. Mazzeno

Further Reading

Gold, Susan Dudley. *The Pentagon Papers: National Security or the Right to Know?* Tarrytown, N.Y.: Marshall Cavendish Benchmark, 2005. Part of its publisher's Supreme Court Milestones series designed for young-adult readers, this volume offers an accessible history and analysis of *New York Times Co. v. Sullivan* that examines opposing sides in the case, the people involved, and the case's lasting impact. Includes bibliography and index.

Prados, John, and Margaret Pratt Porter, eds. *Inside the Pentagon Papers*. Lawrence: University Press of Kansas, 2004. Examines the impact the release of the Pentagon Papers had in 1971 and subsequently. Includes interviews with many who were directly involved in producing the documents or in the court cases involving their release, and a chapter on the legal battles that emerged over publication of these documents.

Rudenstine, David. *The Day the Presses Stopped: A History of the Pentagon Papers Case*. Berkeley: University of California Press, 1996. Explains how and why the Pentagon Papers were released; concentrates on the legal issues surrounding the U.S. government's efforts to prevent public disclosure. Discusses the impact of this incident on American legal and political history.

Ungar, Sanford J. *The Papers and the Papers*. New York: E. P. Dutton, 1972. Chronicles the creation of the Pentagon Papers and Ellsberg's efforts to have them made public; describes legal actions taken to prevent publication.

Wells, Tom. *Wild Man: The Life and Times of Daniel Ellsberg*. New York: Palgrave, 2001. Account of Ellsberg's work on the Pentagon Papers, his efforts to obtain a copy of the complete document, and his campaign to release the documents in an effort to help halt hostilities in Vietnam. Also describes his indictment and trial.

See also *Branzburg v. Hayes; Cohen v. Cowles Media Co.; Grosjean v. American Press Co.; Miami Herald Publishing Co. v. Tornillo; Near v. Minnesota; Richmond Newspapers v. Virginia.*

New York v. Belton

Court: U.S. Supreme Court
Citation: 453 U.S. 454
Date: July 1, 1981
Issues: Search and seizure

• The U.S. Supreme Court expanded the range of warrantless automobile searches.

New York police officers stopped an automobile for speeding and ordered the occupants to step out of the car. The officers found cocaine in the pocket of a coat that had been left in the car and belonged to one of the car's occupants. Citing *Chimel v. California* (1969), the Supreme Court upheld the search by a vote of six to three because the coat had been within the reach of the occupant while he was in the car. This ruling arguably expanded the permissible areas to be searched by police without a warrant. Justices William J. Brennan, Jr., and Byron R. White dissented, arguing that the majority had misunderstood the case on which they were relying. In *Chimel*, the Court had permitted searches of the immediate area only to protect the police officer and prevent evidence from being destroyed. In addition, the area searched had to be within the reach of the accused at the time of the arrest, not simply an area that could have been reached at some point.

Richard L. Wilson

See also *Chimel v. California; Katz v. United States; Mapp v. Ohio; Olmstead v. United States; Weeks v. United States.*

NEW YORK V. FERBER

Court: U.S. Supreme Court
Citation: 458 U.S. 747
Date: July 2, 1982
Issues: Censorship; Children's rights; Freedom of speech;
Pornography and obscenity

• The U.S. Supreme Court ruled that pornography depicting the sexual performances of children was a category of material not protected by the First Amendment.

The state of New York, like nineteen other states, had a statute that criminalized the dissemination of material depicting sexual conduct of children under the age of sixteen, regardless of whether the material satisfied the legal definition of obscenity. The owner of a Manhattan adult bookstore, Paul Ferber, was tried and convicted under the statute for selling films that depicted young boys masturbating. The New York Court of Appeals, however, reversed the conviction, holding that the statute violated the

First Amendment because it was inconsistent with the recognized legal standard of obscenity. The state then appealed the case to the U.S. Supreme Court.

The Court voted unanimously to uphold the conviction of Ferber under the New York statute. Justice Byron White, writing for the Court, proclaimed that child pornography was "a category of material outside the protection of the First Amendment." He emphasized five points. First, the state had a compelling interest in safeguarding minor children from sexual exploitation and abuse. Second, the distribution of materials depicting the sexual activity of juveniles was intrinsically related to their sexual abuse. Third, the advertising and selling of child pornography provided an economic motive for an activity that was everywhere illegal. Fourth, child pornography was of very modest literary, scientific, or educational value. Finally, the recognition of a category of material outside the protection of the First Amendment was compatible with earlier decisions of the Court. White concluded that the test for child pornography was much less demanding than the three-part test in *Miller v. California* (1973), but he also wrote that the prohibited conduct must be adequately defined in state law.

The most important aspect of the *Ferber* decision was that all the justices agreed that the state's interest in protecting children was sufficiently compelling to justify more discretion in criminalizing child pornography than when dealing with other forms of pornography. The majority of the Court was unwilling to consider the possibility of constitutional protection of any material depicting juveniles engaged in sexual conduct. A liberal minority cautioned, however, that such material would be protected by the First Amendment if its depictions were found to contain serious literary, artistic, scientific, or medical value.

Thomas Tandy Lewis

See also *Ashcroft v. Free Speech Coalition; Miller v. California; Osborne v. Ohio.*

New York v. Miln

Court: U.S. Supreme Court
Citation: 36 U.S. 102
Date: February 16, 1837
Issues: Admiralty law; Immigration; Regulation of commerce;
Right to travel

• In the first commerce clause case before the Taney Court, the U.S. Supreme Court found that state police powers could cover people on boats traveling in inland waterways.

A New York law required ship captains to provide a list of passengers, post a bond for poor passengers, and carry away any undesirable aliens on board. The Supreme Court's ruling in *Gibbons v. Ogden* (1824) seemed to make the law unconstitutional, but the proslavery majority on the Court ignored *Gibbons* in its desire to preserve the rights of slave states to regulate the entrance of abolitionists, antislavery propagandists, and free blacks into their jurisdictions. The Supreme Court ruled six to one that although commerce covered only goods, state police power could cover the flow of people into a state, thereby expanding the power of the southern states to control immigration from other states on economic status grounds. Justice Joseph Story dissented, maintaining that this ruling interfered with the federal government's commerce power. The ruling remained valid until the *Edwards v. California* case in 1941, in which the Court found that this ruling wrongly allowed legislatures to limit personal travel on grounds of economic status.

Richard L. Wilson

See also *Champion v. Ames*; *Edwards v. California*; *Genesee Chief v. Fitzhugh*; *Gibbons v. Ogden*.

NEWBERRY V. UNITED STATES

Court: U.S. Supreme Court
Citation: 256 U.S. 232
Date: May 2, 1921
Issues: Political campaigning; Voting rights

• The U.S. Supreme Court concluded that the federal government lacked the constitutional authority to regulate party primaries, a ruling that had the unintended consequence of disfranchising black citizens in the single-party South.

In 1918, Truman H. Newberry, Republican candidate for the U.S. Senate, was tried in Michigan, along with more than one hundred associates, for conspiring to violate the Federal Corrupt Practices Act of 1910. The statute violated had set a limit on campaign financing, and the indictment claimed that Newberry had exceeded this limit in primary and general election expenditures. Newberry and his associates were found guilty in the U.S. District Court for the Western District of Michigan.

The U.S. Supreme Court reversed the conviction and sent the case back to the lower court, finding that the statute on which Newberry's conviction rested had no constitutional authority. The Court argued that prior to the Seventeenth Amendment, the only part of the Constitution empowering Congress to regulate the election process was to be found in Article I, section 4, which pertained only to the time, place, and manner of holding general elections and failed to address such matters as party primaries and conventions, additions to the election process unforeseen by the Framers of the Constitution. Consequently, the Court ruled that in the relevant section of the Corrupt Practices Act, Congress had exceeded its authority.

The Court also maintained that because the statute antedated the ratification of the Seventeenth Amendment, which extended congressional authority, it was invalid at the time of its enactment. The Court held that a power later acquired could not, *ex proprio*, validate a law that was unconstitutional at the time of its passing. The Court did not question a state's right to regulate primaries and campaign financing, claiming that "the state may suppress whatever evils may be incident to primary or convention."

The *Newberry* ruling imposed an important barrier to the enfranchisement of black Americans in the single-party South. Although the Court would strike down laws expressly prohibiting African Americans from voting in primaries, as late as 1935, in *Grovey v. Townsend*, it upheld legal measures taken in Texas to bar blacks from participating in the state Democratic convention, arguing that such "private" discrimination did not come under constitutional purview. *Grovey* and *Newberry* were finally successfully challenged in *United States v. Classic* (1941), which held that Congress had the authority to regulate both primary and general elections for federal offices.

Three years later a final legal blow to de jure disfranchisement of African Americans was dealt in *Smith v. Allwright* (1944), which held that laws governing all elections—local, state, and federal—could be invalidated if they violated Article I, section 4 of the Constitution. Sponsored by the National Association for the Advancement of Colored People, the plaintiff argued that Texas Democratic Party officials had denied him a primary ballot because of his race. The Supreme Court concurred, noting that state laws regulated both primary and general elections and were therefore responsible for barriers to the ballot box erected on racial grounds.

John W. Fiero

See also *Grovey v. Townsend; Nixon v. Herndon; Smith v. Allwright; United States v. Classic.*

NGUYEN V. IMMIGRATION AND NATURALIZATION SERVICE

Court: U.S. Supreme Court
Citation: 533 U.S. 53
Date: June 11, 2001
Issues: Children's rights; Citizenship; Immigration

- The Nguyen ruling upheld a federal law giving a gender-based preference in rights to citizenship of illegitimate children who are born abroad when only one parent is a U.S. citizen.

Tuan Anh Nguyen, who was born out of wedlock in Vietnam, was the son of an American father and a Vietnamese mother. At the age of five, the boy was brought to the United States and raised by his father. When he was twenty-two years old, Nguyen was found guilty of sexually abusing a young child. Under U.S. law, a child born to an unmarried American mother was automatically considered a natural-born citizen, whereas a child born to an unmarried father was not a citizen unless the father proved paternity with a blood test and formally claimed paternity before the child's eighteenth birthday. Because the father had not satisfied these requirements, the Immigration and Naturalization Service (INS) ruled that Nguyen was not a citizen and therefore deportable. Nguyen argued in federal court that the gender distinction in the law was discriminatory and therefore unconstitutional.

By a 5-4 margin, the U.S. Supreme Court held that Nguyen could be deported and that the gender distinction in the law was "consistent with the constitutional guarantee of equal protection." Writing for the majority, Justice Anthony Kennedy explained that such distinctions are permissible if they serve "important governmental objectives" and employed means that are "substantially related to the achievement of those objectives." While the majority concluded that the law satisfied the two standards because of different relationships between children with their mothers and fathers, Justice Sandra Day O'Connor and three other justices vigorously disagreed.

Thomas Tandy Lewis

See also *Afroyim v. Rusk; Fedorenko v. United States; Geofroy v. Riggs; Graham v. Richardson; Immigration and Naturalization Service v. Chadha; Zadvydas v. Davis.*

Nixon, United States v. *See* United States v. Nixon

Nixon v. Administrator of General Services

Court: U.S. Supreme Court
Citation: 433 U.S. 425
Date: June 28, 1977
Issues: Presidential powers; Separation of powers

• The U.S. Supreme Court upheld the Presidential Recordings and Materials Preservation Act of 1974, which authorized the General Services Administration (GSA) to take control of former president Richard M. Nixon's nonprivate presidential papers and to make them available to the public.

Following President Richard M. Nixon's resignation, Congress enacted the relevant statute in order to protect historically important tapes and papers. Nixon argued that the statute was an unconstitutional bill of attainder because it singled him out for punishment by depriving him of the traditional right of presidents to control their presidential papers. He also asserted that the law violated the separation of powers doctrine as well as his personal rights to privacy. Writing for a 7-2 majority, Justice William J. Brennan, Jr., reasoned that the law was not a bill of attainder because it was not punitive in either result or intent. Given the circumstances, he found that Congress had sufficient justification to treat Nixon's public papers differently from those of other presidents. In addition, Brennan reaffirmed a flexible interpretation of the separation of powers doctrine and concluded that the statute contained necessary safeguards allowing Nixon to defend his legal rights.

Thomas Tandy Lewis

See also *Bank of Augusta v. Earle; Dames and Moore v. Regan; Goldwater v. Carter; McCulloch v. Maryland; Martin v. Mott; Myers v. United States; United States v. Lovett; Wiener v. United States; Youngstown Sheet and Tube Co. v. Sawyer.*

NIXON V. CONDON

Court: U.S. Supreme Court
Citation: 286 U.S. 73
Date: May 2, 1932
Issues: Racial discrimination; Voting rights

• In the second round of the white primary cases, the U.S. Supreme Court struck down an exclusion of African Americans from primary elections by a party's executive committee, holding that the committee was acting as an agent of the state.

In *Nixon v. Herndon* (1927), the Supreme Court unanimously overturned a law that directly excluded African Americans from voting in the primaries. The Texas legislature responded by authorizing the parties' executive committees to set qualifications for primary elections. The Democratic committee quickly limited the primaries to whites only. When A. L. Nixon, an African American physician, challenged his exclusion, the Democratic Party asserted that the equal protection clause of the Fourteenth Amendment did not apply to private organizations.

Speaking for a 5-4 majority, Justice Benjamin N. Cardozo ruled narrowly that state action was involved because a state statute had vested the executive committee with its authority to set voting qualifications. The discrimination, therefore, violated the Fourteenth Amendment. The Texas legislature responded by repealing all primary election statutes and giving full control over the primaries to the political parties. This approach to African American disfranchisement would continue until *Smith v. Allwright* (1944).

Thomas Tandy Lewis

See also *Grovey v. Townsend; Newberry v. United States; Nixon v. Herndon; Smith v. Allwright.*

NIXON V. HERNDON

Court: U.S. Supreme Court
Citation: 273 U.S. 536
Date: March 7, 1927
Issues: Racial discrimination; Voting rights

• The U.S. Supreme Court voided an attempt by the Texas legislature to restrict black participation in primary elections.

In 1921, the U.S. Supreme Court ruled in *Newberry v. United States* that Congress lacked authority to regulate primary elections. Southern state legislatures immediately took advantage of this decision to prohibit black participation in state primary elections. "White primaries" were quickly adopted throughout the South. Texas, during the first half of the twentieth century, was part of the Democrat-dominated South. The only competition that mattered was within the Democratic Party, so if blacks were not allowed to participate in the Democratic primary they would effectively be denied any meaningful choice in the electoral process.

In 1924, the Texas legislature passed a law barring African Americans from voting in the Democratic primary. L. A. Nixon, a black resident of El Paso, attempted to vote in the primary and was refused by Herndon, an election judge. Nixon and the National Association for the Advancement of Colored People (NAACP) claimed that the Texas law violated the Fourteenth and Fifteenth Amendments. The Supreme Court did not deal with the issue of the Fifteenth Amendment, but a unanimous Court found that the Texas white primary law violated the equal protection clause of the Fourteenth Amendment.

The NAACP won the battle but temporarily lost the war. Texas responded to the Court's decision by engaging in the strategy of "legislate and litigate." By passing a different white primary law after their defeat in *Nixon v. Herndon*, the Texas legislature forced the NAACP to institute another attack on the white primary. When the second law was declared unconstitutional in *Nixon v. Condon* in 1932, Texas came up with a third variation of the white primary. This time, in *Grovey v. Townsend* (1935), the U.S. Supreme Court upheld the Texas white primary, arguing that no state discrimination was present. According to the Court, the Texas Democratic Party, a private voluntary association, decided to exclude blacks from voting in the primary elections. It was not until *Smith v. Allwright* (1944) that a unanimous Supreme Court declared that the Fifteenth Amendment could be used as a shield to protect the right to vote in primary elections.

From the passage of the first white primary law in 1924 until the final abolition of white primaries in the *Smith* case in 1944, blacks were denied the right to vote in Democratic Party primaries, the only election of significance at that time. The white primary cases illustrate one of the dilemmas in using the federal courts—the fact that justice delayed is justice denied.

Darryl Paulson

See also *Grovey v. Townsend; Newberry v. United States; Nixon v. Condon; Smith v. Allwright.*

Nollan v. California Coastal Commission

Court: U.S. Supreme Court
Citation: 483 U.S. 825
Date: June 26, 1987
Issues: Land law; Property rights; Takings clause

- In this case, the U.S. Supreme Court substantially expanded the protection of property rights by limiting the power of states to force land owners to consent to physical occupations of their property by third parties as a precondition to obtaining government permission to develop the property.

James and Marilyn Nollan planned to demolish a dilapidated bungalow and replace it with a three-bedroom house on a beachfront lot in California located between two public beaches to the north and south. Pursuant to state law, the Nollans sought a development permit from the California Coastal Commission to enable them to proceed. The Coastal Commission conditioned the granting of the permit on the Nollans' agreeing to create an easement that would allow the public to cross their beachfront to gain better access to the adjacent public beaches. The Nollans challenged this condition in state court on the grounds that it violated the Fourteenth Amendment by "taking" their property without the payment of just compensation. When the state court of appeal ruled against them, the Nollans sought review from the U.S. Supreme Court.

In a 5-4 decision, the Supreme Court held that the Coastal Commission had violated the Constitution and reversed the ruling of the court of appeal. Justice Antonin Scalia, writing for the majority, argued that the commission could not directly require property owners to grant an easement to the public to cross their land unless the state paid the owners just compensation as the Constitution required. The issue before the Court in *Nollan* was whether the state could avoid the constitutional obligation of paying for this property interest by denying the owners the right to develop their property unless they agreed to grant the sought-after easement to the public without receiving compensation in return.

The Court conceded that a state agency might impose lawful conditions on the development of property even to the point of requiring owners to dedicate easements to the public. Such conditions would comply with the takings clause of the Fifth Amendment, made applicable to the states by incorporation into the Fourteenth Amendment, if the condition mitigated or offset some externality caused by the proposed development. Thus, if the anticipated use of private property resulted in a burden to the community in which the property was located, the state could refuse to allow the development of the property to protect the public from the anticipated externality, or it could condition the development on the owners taking appropriate steps to reduce or eliminate the problems their development would cause.

Without this "essential nexus" between the conditions placed on development permits and some legitimate state interest in avoiding harms caused by the development, however, the state's demand for concessions from the property owner amounted to a constitutionally impermissible use of the state's regulatory power to take property interests without paying for them.

The majority did not find the required "nexus" in the facts before the Court. There seemed to be no connection whatsoever between any burden to the public that might result from the construction of the house and the public easement the Coastal Commission was requiring. The Nollans' house would not interfere with the public's rightful access to any public beach. Therefore, the easement could not be upheld as a legitimate regulatory response. If the Coastal Commission still wanted a public easement on the Nollans' land, it would have to acquire it through the power of eminent domain and pay for it.

Nollan is an important land use decision because many states and cities throughout the United States regularly impose land dedication conditions on property owners as a way of offsetting the burden on municipal services and infrastructure created by new land development in a community. *Nollan* is the first case in which the Supreme Court indicated that this "dealmaking" form of land use regulation is limited by constitutional constraints. Subsequent cases, particularly *Dolan v. City of Tigard* (1994), expanded on this foundation and further limited the state's ability to regulate land use by placing conditions on development permits.

Alan E. Brownstein

See also *Dolan v. City of Tigard; Pennsylvania Coal Co. v. Mahon.*

NORRIS V. ALABAMA

Court: U.S. Supreme Court
Citation: 294 U.S. 587
Date: April 1, 1935
Issues: Juries

- In its second Scottsboro rape decision, the U.S. Supreme Court held that the African American defendants had been denied a fair trial because African Americans had been systematically excluded from juries.

In *Powell v. Alabama* (1932), the Supreme Court ruled that the conviction of the "Scottsboro boys," a group of young African American men, without effective assistance of counsel violated the Fourteenth Amendment's due process requirement. After defendant Clarence Norris was sentenced to death in a second trial, his lawyers presented evidence of systematic racial exclusion from both the grand jury and trial jury. Writing for a unanimous Court, Chief Justice Charles Evans Hughes reversed the conviction as inconsistent with the due process and equal protection clauses. In both *Powell* and *Norris*, the justices ruled on the basis of immutable principles of justice and declined the opportunity to make the Sixth Amendment explicitly binding on the states through the Fourteenth Amendment.

Thomas Tandy Lewis

See also *Bates v. State Bar of Arizona; Duncan v. Louisiana; Powell v. Alabama.*

NORTHERN SECURITIES CO. V. UNITED STATES

Court: U.S. Supreme Court
Citation: 193 U.S. 197
Date: March 14, 1904
Issues: Antitrust law; Regulation of commerce

- By prosecuting and ordering dissolution of the Northern Securities Company, the U.S. government showed that it would regulate corporations and set the precedent for later antitrust cases.

On March 14, 1904, the U.S. Supreme Court of the United States ordered the dissolution of the Northern Securities Company. One of the first large-scale holding companies, Northern Securities had been formed in November, 1901, by James Jerome Hill, Edward H. Harriman, and J. P. Morgan as a way to gain greater control over and increase the efficiency of three railroad companies: the Great Northern Railroad, the Northern Pacific Railroad, and the Chicago, Burlington, & Quincy Railroad lines. Responding to the general antitrust sentiment of the time, in March, 1902, President Theodore Roosevelt instructed Attorney General Philander C. Knox to bring suit against the Northern Securities Company for violation of the Sherman Antitrust Act of 1890. The case eventually went to the U.S. Supreme Court and ultimately ended in 1904 with *Northern Securities Co. v. United States.* The Supreme Court found the Northern Securities Company to be in violation of the Sherman antitrust law and ordered it to be dissolved.

The Northern Securities case came at the end of a great consolidation period in U.S. business history; from 1896 to 1900, nearly two thousand business mergers occurred. General suspicion of large corporations had been growing among the American public, as evidenced by support for the Interstate Commerce Act of 1887 and the growth of the reform-minded Populist Party. These concerns, and consequent political movements, had pressured Congress into passing the Sherman Antitrust Act of 1890, which made illegal "every contract, combination in the form of trust or otherwise, or conspiracy, in restraint of trade or commerce."

Any hopes that this law would control corporations, however, were undermined by the probusiness laissez-faire policies of the legislative, executive, and judicial branches of the federal government at the time. The Sherman Act had very little real effect on corporations in the United States for more than a decade after its passage. Between 1893 and 1903, the federal government initiated fewer than two dozen cases under the Sherman Act. Furthermore, the Supreme Court decision in the case of *United States v. E. C. Knight Company* (1895) undermined the strength and credibility of the Sherman Act. In that case, the Supreme Court ruled that the American Sugar Company and its subsidiary, the E. C. Knight Company, although perhaps a monopoly in manufacturing, had not monopolized or restrained interstate commerce. This was a very strict and limited interpretation of the Sherman Act.

Railroad Competition

In May, 1901, James J. Hill of the Great Northern Railroad and Edward H. Harriman of the Union Pacific Railroad engaged in a competition to purchase controlling stock in the Northern Pacific Railroad. That railroad company in turn held a controlling interest in the Chicago, Burlington, & Quincy Railroad, the tracks of which provided a highly desirable line into Chicago and ran throughout the northern Midwest region. Harriman worked through the Kuhn Loeb investment house, with the backing of the Rockefeller family; Hill enlisted the considerable financial services of J. P. Morgan. As Hill and Harriman fought for control of Northern Pacific, the price of its stock soared to one thousand dollars per share. In their efforts to obtain liquid capital to purchase Northern Pacific shares, Hill and Harriman dumped other holdings at very low prices. These actions caused stock prices to fluctuate wildly, generally disrupting the stock market.

Neither Hill nor Harriman was able to gain a controlling interest in Northern Pacific, and the two men decided that cooperation would be preferable to market disorder. In November, 1901, they had Morgan arrange for the incorporation of the Northern Securities Company, a $400 million holding company that would, they hoped, bring order and efficiency to the northwestern railroad market by bringing their combined interests—the Great Northern Railroad, the Northern Pacific Railroad, and the Chicago, Burlington, & Quincy Railroad lines—under the aegis of one board of directors. Morgan had a history of improving rail systems through his own reorganization and consolidation efforts. In the sixteen years since 1885, Morgan had worked to make thousands of miles of railroads throughout the East more efficient, including saving the New York Central Railroad from financial collapse. In his book *Highways of Progress* (1910), Hill stated that the formation of the Northern Securities Company was "a device contributing to the welfare of the public by assuring in the management of great properties that security, harmony and relief from various forms of waste out of which grow lower rates just as surely as dividends." He argued that consolidation was in the public interest, as it contributed to efficiency.

To the public and much of the rest of the business world, however, the actions of Hill, Harriman, and Morgan appeared to be the very worst of the disruptive, careless, and crude abuses of power attributed to the "robber barons" of that era. Public opinion was further enraged by the fact that the episode had resulted in one of the largest holding companies yet formed in this era of large business trusts. Even *The Wall Street Journal* criticized Harriman and Hill for their actions. Responding to these pressures, in March, 1902, President Roosevelt instructed Attorney General Knox to bring suit against the Northern Securities Company.

Working with the governor and attorney general of Minnesota, the home of Hill's Great Northern Railroad, Knox filed the federal suit in a circuit court in St. Paul on March 10, 1902. The federal circuit court ruled against the Northern Securities Company on April 9, 1903. The company then appealed to the U.S. Supreme Court, and on March 14, 1904, the Court found the Northern Securities Company to be in violation of the Sherman Antitrust Act. In a 5-4 decision, the Court affirmed the decision of the lower court and ordered the dissolution of the Northern Securities Company.

President Theodore Roosevelt in 1903.
(Library of Congress)

Significance

The prosecution and dissolution of the Northern Securities Company sent shock waves through the business world. It may have slowed the growth of mergers, but the trend continued through both of Theodore Roosevelt's administrations. Mergers decreased dramatically from 1902 to 1904 but increased from 1904 to 1906. The fact that by 1909 just 1 percent of the industrial firms in the United States were producing nearly half of the nation's manufactured goods illustrates how large the largest firms had become.

By successfully prosecuting the Northern Securities Company, Roosevelt and Knox gave meaning and legitimacy to the Sherman Antitrust Act that it had not had since its passage in 1890. They also built up the legitimacy and the credibility of the Justice Department, which before the Northern Securities case had been nothing more than a small team of independent lawyers. In his efforts to prosecute the case, Knox built within the Justice Department the legal machinery necessary to bring antitrust suits in the future. Roosevelt stated that Knox had "done more against trusts and for the enforcement of the antitrust law than any other man we have ever had in public life." Vigorous presidential action also influenced the jurisprudence of the Supreme Court, making it more sympathetic to the cause of antitrust in the future.

The dissolution of the Northern Securities Company opened the door for many other prosecutions by the Justice Department for antitrust violations. Just after the Justice Department brought suit against the Northern Securities Company in 1902, Roosevelt instructed Knox to bring suit against the "beef trust," which was made up of a number of Chicago packinghouses, including Swift & Co. Like the Northern Securities case, the suit against the beef trust was supported by widespread public opinion, especially given that meat prices were on the rise. In the 1905 case of *Swift & Co. v. United States*, the Supreme Court enjoined the beef trust from engaging in collusive practices that kept prices stable or rising. This case was significant in that it expanded federal jurisdiction to include manufacturing combinations whose products were later traded in interstate commerce, a line of argument that the Court had rejected in the E. C. Knight case.

Other Antitrust Suits

In 1906 and 1907, Roosevelt had the Justice Department bring suit against the American Tobacco Company, the E. I. du Pont Chemical Corporation, the New Haven Railroad, and the Standard Oil Company. The Supreme Court subsequently ordered the dissolution of American Tobacco (1911) and Standard Oil (1911). In the years between 1890 and 1905, the Department of Justice brought twenty-four antitrust suits. Theodore Roosevelt's administrations brought fifty-four suits, and the single administration of William Howard

Taft prosecuted ninety antitrust cases. In the decade from 1905 to 1915, at least eighteen antitrust cases were prosecuted each year.

Perhaps the most important impact of the Northern Securities case was that it answered the question of whether the federal government had the ability and willingness to regulate large corporations aggressively. Roosevelt later wrote that in 1902 the question had not been how large corporations should be controlled. "The absolutely vital question," said Roosevelt, "was whether the government had power to control them at all." Before the federal government could compose the rules and create the agencies needed for regulation, it had to show that it had the willingness and ability to do so. The prosecution and dissolution of the Northern Securities Company proved that the federal government had both.

In addition to proving that the federal government could regulate and punish large corporations, the Northern Securities case set the precedent for federal intervention in the national economy. The Hill-Harriman battle had disrupted the stock market, and the overwhelming pressure of public opinion provided a favorable arena for the reform philosophy of Roosevelt and Knox. Just after he announced the antitrust suit against the Northern Securities Company, Roosevelt said that the prosecution aimed to prevent violent fluctuations and disaster in the market. In April, 1902, Roosevelt stated that "after the combinations have reached a certain stage it is indispensable to the general welfare that the Nation should exercise . . . the power of supervision and regulation."

Roosevelt did not oppose the fact of large corporations. He believed that with their ability to provide economies of scale, vertically integrated operations, and consolidations that prevented ruinous competition, corporations could achieve a degree of organizational efficiency that smaller concerns could not. Roosevelt believed in an increased regulatory role for the federal government, one that involved policing corporate behavior and actions rather than size itself. A few days after he announced the suit against the Northern Securities Company, Roosevelt told J. P. Morgan, who was concerned for his much larger United States Steel Corporation, that U.S. Steel would be prosecuted only if it had "done something that we regard as wrong."

Perhaps because of Roosevelt's accommodationist regulatory policy, the trend toward large corporations grew at the same time that the number of antitrust cases increased. The economic concentration that had increased dramatically in the late nineteenth century continued to rise in the early twentieth century. In addition, in the cases concerning Standard Oil and American Tobacco, the Supreme Court ruled that not every restraint of trade is illegal in terms of the Sherman Act, thus encouraging merger activity.

In the case regarding Standard Oil, the U.S. Supreme Court noted that it would determine through the "rule of reason" whether combinations were restraining trade unreasonably and thus violating the Sherman Act. Congress passed the Clayton Antitrust Act of 1914 in part to eliminate interlocking directorates but also to create statutory specifics on antitrust prohibitions so that the government need not rely on the shifting opinions of the federal judiciary. The Clayton Act was supplemented by the Robinson-Patman Act of 1936, which sought to clarify and codify further the types of illegal price discrimination. The Celler-Kefauver Act of 1950 again sought to reinforce the Clayton Act, in much the same manner as had the Robinson-Patman Act. In 1976, Congress passed the Hart-Scott-Rodino Act, also known as the Concentrated Industries Act, a mild reform law that attempted to strengthen provisions of existing antitrust laws.

Merger Trend

The trend toward business mergers and economic concentration continued. With the war efforts of both World War I and World War II, the federal government accepted the economic and industrial concentration necessary to keep production levels high. This was also true of the federal efforts to deal with the Great Depression in the 1930's. The laissez-faire policies of the 1920's were born of political philosophy rather than of necessity. Finally, the economic prosperity that followed World War II also lessened desire for antitrust regulation, as the system seemed to be working for the benefit of most.

Several important antitrust cases, however, did reach the courts following the main period of antitrust prosecution. In 1945, the Aluminum Company of America (Alcoa) was found to be in violation of the Sherman Antitrust Act. In 1948, the federal government forced a number of major U.S. film studios to divest themselves of studio-owned movie theaters. In 1961, the Supreme Court ordered the Du Pont Corporation to divest itself of its holdings in General Motors Company. In 1967, the Federal Communications Commission ordered the American Telephone and Telegraph Company (AT&T) to lower its rates. In 1982, under continuing federal pressure, AT&T agreed to be broken up, and a number of rival telephone companies entered the market to challenge AT&T's control. In the late 1990's, the federal government pursued legal action against Microsoft Corporation for monopolistic practices in the computer software and Internet browser industries.

Bruce Andre Beaubouef

Further Reading

Areeda, Phillip, Louis Kaplow, and Aaron Edlin. *Antitrust Analysis: Problems, Text, Cases.* 6th ed. New York: Aspen, 2004. Textbook containing case studies of the major antitrust cases in American history. Bibliographic references and index.

Blum, John Morton. "Theodore Roosevelt and the Definition of Office." In *The Progressive Presidents: Theodore Roosevelt, Woodrow Wilson, Franklin D. Roosevelt, Lyndon Johnson.* New York: W. W. Norton, 1980. Good for an introduction to the Progressive policies and politics, as well as foreign policies, of Roosevelt and Wilson.

Clark, John D. *The Federal Trust Policy.* Baltimore: Johns Hopkins University Press, 1931. Analytic, detailed, and still brief enough to be of use both to readers seeking an introduction to antitrust policy at the federal level and to those seeking to expand their knowledge of the subject.

Gould, Lewis L. "Immediate and Vigorous Executive Action." In *The Presidency of Theodore Roosevelt.* Lawrence: University Press of Kansas, 1991. Excellent history of the foreign and domestic policies of Roosevelt's administrations. Good on the Northern Securities case. Focuses on the Roosevelt presidency, but also good for students beginning study of the Progressive Era.

Hill, James Jerome. *Highways of Progress.* 1910. Reprint. New York: Books for Business, 2001. Hill's own account of the process of railroad building in the United States is very useful. Provides an enlightening and different perspective on the Northern Securities case and the railroad industry in general.

Hylton, Keith N. *Antitrust Law: Economic Theory and Common Law Evolution.* New York: Cambridge University Press, 2003. Comprehensive text on economic principles behind antitrust and the development of American antitrust law over more than one hundred years of litigation. Includes a chapter on the Alcoa case. Bibliographic references and index.

Meyer, Balthasar Henry. *A History of the Northern Securities Case.* Madison: Bulletin of the University of Wisconsin, 1906. Reprint. New York: Da Capo Press, 1972. Meyer, a member of the Railroad Commission of Wisconsin, gives a valuable contemporary treatment of the Northern Securities case and the trust issue itself. Places the case in context by briefly describing the growth of the antitrust movement at the state and federal levels. Includes copies of relevant documents.

Peritz, Rudolph J. R. *Competition Policy in America: History, Rhetoric, Law.* Rev. ed. New York: Oxford University Press, 2001. Explores the influences on U.S. public policy of the concept of free competition. Discusses congressional debates, court opinions, and the work of economic, legal, and political scholars in this area.

Thorelli, Hans B. *The Federal Antitrust Policy: Origination of an American Tradition.* Baltimore: Johns Hopkins University Press, 1955. Comprehensive and penetrating treatment of U.S. antitrust policy. Covers economic, social, and political formation of the antitrust movement in the legislative, executive, and judicial branches of government in the late nineteenth and early twentieth centuries. For those seeking an advanced and detailed treatment of U.S. antitrust policy.

See also *Bank of Augusta v. Earle; Citizens United v. Federal Election Commission; Louisville, Cincinnati, and Charleston Railroad Co. v. Letson; Paul v. Virginia; Santa Clara County v. Southern Pacific Railroad Co.; Swift and Co. v. United States; United States v. E. C. Knight Co.*

===============

NOTO V. UNITED STATES

Court: U.S. Supreme Court
Citation: 367 U.S. 290
Date: June 5, 1961
Issues: Antigovernment subversion; Freedom of assembly and association

- The U.S. Supreme Court seriously undermined the anticommunist Smith Act (1940) by holding that mere membership in an alleged subversive group is not enough to show intent to commit conspiracy.

Freedom of association is often called into question by indictments for conspiracy because it is alleged that some associations are conspiracies to use violence to overthrow the U.S. government. After the South attempted to secede from the Union in the Civil War, it became illegal to attempt the violent overthrow of the U.S. government, and various Supreme Court decisions have held some associations are conspiracies that may be restrained as clear and present dangers to the nation. This phrase came from an attempt on the part of Justices Oliver Wendell Holmes, Jr., and Louis D. Brandeis to define a test for balancing liberty against order. They intended the clear and present danger test to be valid only if used with all the safeguards they set out.

Until the 1960's, the Court faced great difficulty defining "clear and present danger" and often employed a test that viewed the seriousness of the danger discounted by its improbability or used the bad tendency test. Justices Hugo L. Black and William O. Douglas expressed their conclusion in a series of dissents that the clear and present danger test violated the First Amendment and only an absolute standard should be used. In *Noto*, the Court took an important step in the direction of the Black-Douglas position when it held that Communist Party membership was not in itself evidence of conspiracy to overthrow the government. This made it more difficult for the government to harass the Communist Party under the provisions of the 1940 Smith Act.

Richard L. Wilson

See also *Albertson v. Subversive Activities Control Board; Communist Party v. Subversive Activities Control Board; Dennis v. United States; Elfbrandt v. Russell; Lovell v. City of Griffin; Scales v. United States; Whitney v. California; Yates v. United States.*

O'Brien, United States v. *See* United States v. O'Brien

Ogden v. Saunders

Court: U.S. Supreme Court
Citation: 25 U.S. 213
Date: February 19, 1827
Issues: Bankruptcy law; Freedom of contract

- The U.S. Supreme Court took a first important step in restricting the operation of the contract clause of the U.S. Constitution.

A New York State law, passed in 1801, gave relief to people who could not pay their debts. The Constitution forbids the states to "pass any . . . Law impairing the Obligation of Contracts." Therefore the New York law could not constitutionally be applied to contracts made prior to the passage of the law. *Ogden v. Saunders* tested whether the New York law could be applied to contracts made after the law's passage. It was argued that all contracts carry with them the state laws which prescribe the rules for the enforcement of contracts—including debtor relief provisions.

After elaborate and protracted argument in 1824, in which Daniel Webster and Henry Clay participated, the Supreme Court decided 4 to 3 that a state bankruptcy law such as the New York law does not impair the obligation of contracts which are entered into after passage of the law. The decision was accompanied by six separate extensive opinions by the justices, which revealed deep disagreements within the Court. Chief Justice John Marshall was in the minority in this case for the only time in his judicial career. Marshall's conservative view was that the constitutional grant of power to Congress to establish uniform bankruptcy rules necessarily excluded the operation of all state bankruptcy laws.

A second issue settled by *Ogden v. Saunders* was whether a debtor discharged under the New York State law could claim that discharge for a contract or debt owed to a citizen of another state. On this issue the Court split differently. Chief Justice Marshall and the other conservatives on the Court held that the debt was still collectible in a federal court. To hold otherwise would produce "a conflict of sovereign power and a collision with the judicial powers."

In sum, then, the Court decided that state bankruptcy and debtor relief laws are unconstitutional when applied to contracts entered into before passage of the law and constitutional with respect to contracts made after passage of the law. Second, such laws are unconstitutional if they attempt to invalidate a debt owed to a citizen of another state.

This decision began the restoration of state powers which had been restricted by the contract clause as the Court had previously interpreted it. *Ogden v. Saunders* presaged a broader view of the state's police powers, which soon became dominant and has prevailed in the United States ever since.

Robert Jacobs

See also *Adair v. United States; Bronson v. Kinzie; Sturges v. Crowninshield.*

O'GORMAN AND YOUNG V. HARTFORD FIRE INSURANCE CO.

Court: U.S. Supreme Court
Citation: 282 U.S. 251
Date: January 5, 1931
Issues: Due process of law

• The U.S. Supreme Court ceased to use the substantive due process concept to overrule legislative judgments in economic liberty cases.

Justice Louis D. Brandeis wrote the opinion for the 5-4 majority, upholding a New Jersey statute that regulated the fees insurance companies paid to their local agents. Previously, the Supreme Court would have struck down this statute as a violation of the substantive due process clause of the Fourteenth Amendment, but in this case, the Court ruled that legislative enactments were to be presumed constitutional and could be overturned only if there were a factual foundation in the record for unconstitutionality. Brandeis further argued that the Court should stop using the substantive due process concept to overrule legislatures in economic matters. Justices Willis Van Devanter, James C. McReynolds, George Sutherland, and Pierce Butler dissented vigorously, asserting freedom of contract and the protection of property required exactly the restraints on the legislative branch being abandoned by the majority in this case.

Richard L. Wilson

See also *Allgeyer v. Louisiana; Chicago, Burlington, and Quincy Railroad Co. v. Chicago; Chicago, Milwaukee, and St. Paul Railway Co. v. Minnesota; Pacific Mutual Life Insurance Co. v. Haslip; Paul v. Virginia; Prudential Insurance Co. v. Benjamin; United States v. South-Eastern Underwriters Association.*

Ohio v. Akron Center for Reproductive Health

Court: U.S. Supreme Court
Citation: 497 U.S. 502
Date: June 25, 1990
Issues: Parental rights; Reproductive rights

- The U.S. Supreme Court upheld a law requiring that one parent of an unmarried minor be notified before the performance of an abortion, unless the abortion was authorized by a court.

By a 6-3 margin, the Supreme Court found that the Ohio regulations did not place too many obstacles on applicants. In order to obtain a judicial bypass, a young woman was required to show by clear and convincing evidence that she was mature or that the abortion was in her best interest. The dissenters argued that the procedures were overly complicated and that approval could take longer than three weeks. On the same day, the Court approved of a two-parent notification requirement with a judicial bypass in *Hodgson v. Minnesota* (1990). The two rulings indicated that the justices were becoming somewhat more conservative on the issue of abortion rights.

Thomas Tandy Lewis

See also *Akron v. Akron Center for Reproductive Health; Bigelow v. Virginia; Doe v. Bolton; Harris v. McRae; Hodgson v. Minnesota; Maher v. Roe; Planned Parenthood of Central Missouri v. Danforth; Roe v. Wade.*

Olmstead v. United States

Court: U.S. Supreme Court
Citation: 277 U.S. 438
Date: June 4, 1928
Issues: Right to privacy; Search and seizure; Self-incrimination

- Although a majority of justices rejected the argument that government wiretaps on telephones constituted illegal searches and compelled self-incrimination, Justice Louis D. Brandeis' famous dissenting opinion laid the groundwork for the later development of a constitutional right to privacy.

During the Prohibition era, Roy Olmstead was convicted of being the general manager of a significant illegal smuggling operation that brought liquor to the United States from Canada in violation of federal law. Olmstead's illegal business had fifty employees and reportedly earned more than two million dollars each year. The evidence that produced the convictions of Olmstead and his associates was gathered through the use of wiretaps. Law-enforcement officials had attached wires to the telephone lines leading from Olmstead's residence and office. Officials had listened to and had stenographers take notes on the conversations secretly overheard through the telephone lines.

Olmstead and his codefendants challenged the use of such investigative techniques and evidence. They claimed that the wiretaps constituted an illegal search and seizure in violation of the Fourth Amendment and that the use

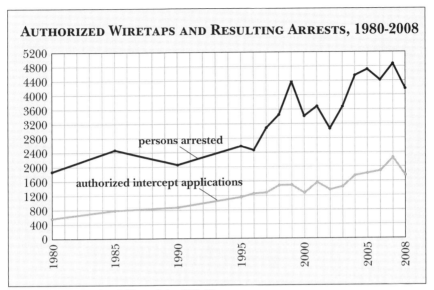

AUTHORIZED WIRETAPS AND RESULTING ARRESTS, 1980-2008

Source: Administrative Office of the U.S. Courts.

of private conversations as evidence violated the Fifth Amendment's prohibition on compelled self-incrimination.

In an opinion by Chief Justice William Howard Taft, the U.S. Supreme Court rejected Olmstead's arguments. Taft concluded that the Fourth Amendment protected only against unreasonable searches of material things and that telephone lines running between two people's property could not be considered protected against intrusion by government. Taft also declared that the defendants' conversations were voluntary and therefore could not be regarded as compelled self-incrimination.

In a famous dissenting opinion, Justice Louis D. Brandeis made an eloquent plea for the recognition of a constitutional right to privacy. According to Brandeis, the authors of the Constitution "sought to protect Americans in their beliefs, their thoughts, their emotions, and their sensations. They conferred, as against the government, the right to be let alone—the most comprehensive of rights and the right most valued by civilized men."

Brandeis was not the lone dissenter in the case; Justices Oliver Wendell Holmes, Jr., Pierce Butler, and Harlan F. Stone also found fault with Taft's conclusions. Brandeis, however, was the lone justice to place great emphasis on a general right of privacy. The other justices were also concerned about the definition of a search under the Fourth Amendment or the legality of police methods.

Brandeis could not manage to gain majority support for his ideas during his lifetime. Instead, his eloquent defense of a right to privacy stood for more than thirty years as the primary argument against government intrusions into citizens' private lives. Beginning in the 1960's, when the Supreme Court's composition had changed significantly, Brandeis's words were used by a generation of justices who followed his ideals and established the existence of a constitutional right to privacy in *Griswold v. Connecticut* (1965).

Christopher E. Smith

See also *Griswold v. Connecticut; Katz v. United States; United States v. United States District Court.*

OREGON V. MITCHELL; TEXAS V. MITCHELL; UNITED STATES V. ARIZONA

Court: U.S. Supreme Court
Citation: 400 U.S. 112
Date: December 21, 1970
Issues: Standing; Voting rights

- The confusion created by the U.S. Supreme Court's fragmented decision, which established different minimum voting ages for federal and state elections, was eliminated through the passage of the Twenty-sixth Amendment, which made the minimum voting age eighteen in all elections.

As a part of the 1970 amendments to the 1965 Voting Rights Act, Congress not only extended the act for five years but also attempted to standardize residency and age requirements for voting in elections at all levels. The act lowered the voting age to eighteen for federal, state, and local elections. However, because states had previously had the authority to set the minimum voting age, the act was challenged as a violation of federalism. By a 5-4 vote, the Supreme Court ruled that Congress could set the minimum voting age for federal elections but could not do so for state or local elections. Five opinions were filed in the case. Essentially, four justices believed Congress had the power to set the voting age in any election and four did not. Justice Hugo L.

Black, who cast the deciding vote, believed that Congress had the power in federal—but not state and local—elections. To eliminate the confusion and avoid complicated election procedures, Congress proposed the Twenty-sixth Amendment, which lowered the voting age to eighteen in all elections and was quickly ratified.

Richard L. Wilson

See also *Breedlove v. Suttles; Dunn v. Blumstein.*

Oregon Waste Systems v. Department of Environmental Quality

Court: U.S. Supreme Court
Citation: 510 U.S. 93
Date: April 4, 1994
Issues: Environmental issues and animal rights; Regulation of commerce

- The U.S. Supreme Court struck down a tax on an out-of-state solid waste fee that was three times higher than the in-state tax on solid waste.

Oregon placed a higher tax on solid wastes coming from out of state than those originating within the state. Oregon courts had determined that the tax was merely compensatory; however, the U.S. Supreme Court disagreed and ruled against the tax. Justice Clarence Thomas wrote the opinion for the 7-2 majority, holding that the Oregon tax was discriminatory on its face and violated the commerce clause. Thomas found that although states had broad authority to tax, taxation must not unduly affect interstate commerce or benefit their citizens except incidentally. The Oregon courts' conclusions found support in the dissenting opinion of Chief Justice William H. Rehnquist, who was joined by Justice Harry A. Blackmun.

Richard L. Wilson

See also *Bryant v. Yellen; Sierra Club v. Morton; Tennessee Valley Authority v. Hill.*

Orr v. Orr

Court: U.S. Supreme Court
Citation: 440 U.S. 268
Date: March 5, 1979
Issues: Equal protection of the law; Marriage; Standing

- The U.S. Supreme Court ruled that Alabama's law making husbands, but not wives, liable for alimony payments was a violation of the equal protection clause of the Fourteenth Amendment.

In *Craig v. Boren* (1976), the Court had announced that it would henceforth evaluate gender classifications according to a heightened scrutiny standard. The *Orr* decision was an early application of this standard. When William and Lillian Orr were divorced, William Orr was ordered to make alimony payments to his former wife. He argued that the state's differential requirements for men and women were discriminatory. The state responded that the law was justified by two important goals: providing for needy ex-wives and compensating them for the economic discrimination produced by the traditional marital role.

Speaking for a 6-3 majority, Justice William J. Brennan, Jr., ruled that the law was not "substantially related" to the state's legitimate objectives. Because alimony awards were based on individual circumstances, a gender-neutral law would give just as much help to needy ex-wives. Likewise, statutes designed to compensate for past discrimination must be "carefully tailored" not to discriminate unnecessarily and not to reinforce traditional "stereotypes about the 'proper place' of women and their need for special protection." The three dissenting justices argued that William Orr lacked standing to sue because a law based entirely on need would not have changed his financial obligations.

Thomas Tandy Lewis

See also *Craig v. Boren; In re Neagle; Reed v. Reed.*

OSBORN V. BANK OF THE UNITED STATES

Court: U.S. Supreme Court
Citation: 22 U.S. 738
Date: March 19, 1824
Issues: Taxation

- The U.S. Supreme Court overturned a state tax on a federal corporation, affirming the constitutionality of the Bank of the United States.

Chief Justice John Marshall wrote the opinion for the 6-1 majority, using an elaborate defense of federal judicial power to uphold the Supreme Court's decision in *McCulloch v. Maryland* (1819). As with *McCulloch*, this case involved a state (Ohio) opposed to the Bank of the United States that was attempting to impose a tax on a federal corporation. Ohio state auditor Ralph Osborn seized the assets of the bank but lost a countersuit in federal court. On appeal, the Court upheld the lower federal court, broadly interpreting the Constitution's phrase "cases arising under" the Constitution, thereby claiming that any case involving the mere possibility of a federal question could be carried to the federal courts. Justice William Johnson dissented, saying he thought this decision gave federal courts jurisdiction over too many potential questions.

Richard L. Wilson

See also *Dobbins v. Erie County; Dodge v. Woolsey; Graves v. New York ex rel. O'Keefe; McCray v. United States; McCulloch v. Maryland.*

OSBORNE V. OHIO

Court: U.S. Supreme Court
Citation: 495 U.S. 103
Date: April 18, 1990
Issues: Children's rights; Pornography and obscenity

- In this case, the U.S. Supreme Court upheld the states' rights to prohibit the possession and viewing of child pornography.

Clyde Osborne was convicted of possessing child pornography after police found sexually explicit photographs of a nude minor male in his home. Ohio law prohibited any person from possessing or viewing materials that include a nude minor who is not their child unless they have a "bona fide purpose" or written consent from the minor's parents for such materials. Sentenced to six months in prison, Osborne appealed on the contention that the First Amendment protected his right to possess and view the photographs. In 1990, the Supreme Court ruled six to three to uphold Ohio's law, although Osborne's conviction was reversed and a new trial ordered. Essentially, the case contained three elements: whether Ohio's law was constitutional; whether Ohio's law was overbroad; and whether Osborne was denied due process.

In appealing the constitutionality of Ohio's child pornography law, Osborne relied on the Supreme Court's 1969 ruling in *Stanley v. Georgia*, in which the court struck down the state's right to prohibit obscene materials. Justice Byron White, however, writing for the majority, pointed to the different underlying motivations for the Georgia and Ohio laws. In the case of *Georgia*, the state wished to prevent the "poisoning of the viewer's mind," while in Ohio's law, the motivation was to protect the victims of child pornography and to destroy the market for such materials. The Court ruled that the state's interest in this case was sufficiently compelling and deemed the law constitutional.

Osborne's second contention, that the Ohio law was overbroad, was also struck down by the Court. The Ohio statute prohibited only "lewd exhibition" or "graphic focus of the genitals" of a child who was not the child of the person charged. The court ruled that this interpretation was specific in its intentions and therefore denied Osborne's overbroad arguments. Osborne's due process arguments were noted, however, and the Court ruled that he should receive a new trial.

Justice William Brennan wrote the dissenting opinion, with Justices Thurgood Marshall and John Paul Stevens concurring. Brennan saw the Ohio law as overbroad, especially concerning its definition of "nudity." While the photographs were "distasteful," Brennan contended that Osborne had the right to possess the photographs under the protection of the First Amendment. The dissenting opinion also suggested that the state's interest was better served through other laws prohibiting the "creation, sale and distribution of child pornography."

Although somewhat weak in its ruling, the *Osborne* case is significant in its upholding of the states' rights to prohibit the possession of child pornography. As the dissenting opinion reveals, however, to stand up to further Supreme Court scrutiny, such laws need to be carefully worded to avoid overbroad interpretation.

Jennifer Davis

See also *Ashcroft v. Free Speech Coalition; New York v. Ferber; Stanley v. Georgia.*

Ozawa v. United States

Court: U.S. Supreme Court
Citation: 260 U.S. 178
Date: November 13, 1922
Issues: Citizenship; Immigration; Land law; Racial discrimination

- In *Ozawa v. United States*, the U.S. Supreme Court ruled that Japanese aliens did not qualify as "white" and therefore could not be naturalized as citizens.

In the early twentieth century, naturalization in the United States was under the effective control of local and state authorities. In California and other Pacific states, fears of the "yellow peril" or "silent invasion" of Asian immigrants were deeply entrenched and politically exploited. In these states, citizenship had been repeatedly denied to both Chinese and more recent Japanese settlers, although there were some rare exceptions. The prevailing belief among the nativist majority was that such settlers should be ineligible for U.S. citizenship.

Partly to test the Alien Land Act—a California law passed in 1913 that barred noncitizens from owning land in that state—Japanese immigrant Takao Ozawa sought U.S. citizenship in defiance of a 1906 law that limited naturalization to "free white persons," "aliens of African nativity," and "persons of African descent." Although he was born in Japan, Ozawa had been educated in the United States. He had graduated from high school in Berkeley and attended the local University of California campus for three years. He was aware that some Issei (first-generation Japanese immigrants) had been naturalized, even in California.

Specifically, Ozawa may have known of Isao Yoshikawa, the first Japanese immigrant to be naturalized in California. Yoshikawa had arrived in San Francisco from Japan in 1887. A law clerk in his homeland, he had studied U.S. law and served as a court translator in his adopted country. In 1889 he began the naturalization process, which, presumably, was completed five years later, although there is no extant record of his naturalization. His case was publicized because it broached such issues as mandatory citizenship renunciation and the legality of dual citizenship.

Regardless of Ozawa's knowledge of Yoshikawa, on October 16, 1914, Ozawa applied for U.S. citizenship before the district court for the territory of Hawaii. He argued that he had resided in the United States and its territory of Hawaii for a total of twenty years, had adopted the culture and language of his host country, had reared his children as Americans in heart and mind, and was, by character and education, wholly qualified for naturalization.

District Court Ruling

The district court ruled against Ozawa on the grounds that his Japanese ethnicity denied him access to naturalization. Ozawa then took his case to the Ninth Circuit Court of Appeals, which passed it to the U.S. Supreme Court for instruction. In turn, the Supreme Court upheld the laws that in effect declared Ozawa ineligible for citizenship.

Rather than questioning the justice of the racial restrictions on naturalization, the Court's opinion, written by Associate Justice George Sutherland, focused on clarifying the meaning of the term "white persons" and distinguishing between "Caucasian" and "white person." The Court determined that the latter term, although more inclusive than the former, is not so inclusive as to encompass persons of Asian extraction. The opinion concluded that "a person of the Japanese race" is not a "free white person" within the meaning of the 1906 law, and therefore is not eligible for naturalization as a U.S. citizen.

In tracing the history of the naturalization laws, the Court attempted to demonstrate that all statutes preceding the 1906 act contested by Ozawa had the same intent: the selective admission to citizenship based on the interpretation of "white," not as a racial appellation but as a reflection of character. It argued that the words "free white persons" do not indicate persons of a particular race or origin, but rather describe individuals who are fit for citizenship under the policy of the United States. According to that doctrine, any non-African alien, if desired by Congress, might be deemed "white."

Regardless of this race disclaimer, however, the Court, in reasoning through its arguments, distinguished between "whites" (all Europeans, for example) and "nonwhites" (such as the Chinese) on ethnic grounds pure and simple. In addition, the decision clearly sanctioned the seriously flawed assumption that character and racial heritage are inextricably interrelated.

Significance

The Supreme Court's ruling in *Ozawa v. United States* reflected the prevailing nativist bias against Asian immigrants, an attitude that was reflected in both law and policy throughout the first half of the twentieth century. In fact, no more formidable barriers to citizenship were erected than those devised to prevent the naturalization of Japanese, Chinese, and other Asian immigrants. In 1924, an isolationist Congress enacted an immigration law that placed numerical restrictions on immigrants allowed into the United States based on national origin. One provision of the Immigration Act of 1924, also known as the Johnson Act, excluded immigrants who were ineligible for naturalization. The law's obvious aim—to bar entry of Japanese aliens—quickly led to the deterioration of diplomatic relations between Japan and the United States.

The plight of Japanese already in the United States also worsened in this anti-Asian climate. In separate rulings, the Supreme Court went so far as to revoke citizenship that had been granted to some Issei. In 1925, the Court even ruled that service in the U.S. armed forces did not make Issei eligible for naturalization, overturning a policy that had previously been in effect. Not only were Issei barred from naturalization, but also in many states "alien land laws" prohibited them from owning land and even from entering some professions.

This sort of codified prejudice partly accounts for the terrible treatment Japanese Americans were subjected to during World War II, when 112,000 of them, including 70,000 Nisei (persons of Japanese descent born in the United States), were rounded up and incarcerated in detention centers that bore some grim similarities to the concentration camps of Europe. It was not until the passage of the McCarran-Walter Act in 1952 that the long-standing racial barriers to naturalization finally came down.

John W. Fiero

Further Reading

Bankston, Carl L., III, ed. *Encyclopedia of American Immigration.* 3 vols. Pasadena, Calif.: Salem Press, 2010. Comprehensive reference source on all aspects of American immigration history, with articles on individual laws, court cases, events, immigrant groups, and other subjects. Profusely illustrated with photographs, maps, charts, and graphs. Extensive appendix materials and bibliographical notes in every article.

Curran, Thomas J. *Xenophobia and Immigration, 1820-1930*. Boston: Twayne, 1975. Traces the origins of anti-immigrant movements in the United States and relates the xenophobic tradition to exclusionist laws and practices.

Daniels, Roger. *Guarding the Golden Door: American Immigration Policy and Immigrants Since 1882*. New York: Hill & Wang, 2004. Examines trends in and influences on U.S. immigration policy from late in the nineteenth century to the beginning of the twenty-first century. Includes tables and charts, bibliography, and index.

Hosokawa, Bill. *Nisei: The Quiet Americans*. Rev. ed. Boulder: University Press of Colorado, 2002. A good general study of Japanese Americans and their struggle against legal and social discrimination. Includes photographs.

O'Brien, David J., and Stephen Fugita. *The Japanese American Experience*. Bloomington: Indiana University Press, 1991. Scholarly study focuses on the legal and social problems that confronted Japanese Americans before World War II and the rapid acculturation this group experienced after the war.

Takaki, Ronald. *Iron Cages: Race and Culture in Nineteenth-Century America*. Rev. ed. New York: Oxford University Press, 2000. Provides insight into the origins of anti-Asian sentiment in the United States and its connection to legislation such as the alien land laws.

————. *Strangers from a Different Shore: A History of Asian Americans*. Rev. ed. Boston: Back Bay Books, 1998. Excellent and sensitive overview of Asian American history. Includes extensive notes and photographs.

Wilson, Robert Arden, and Bill Hosokawa. *East to America: A History of the Japanese in the United States*. New York: William Morrow, 1980. General history of Japanese migration to North America. Appendixes provide census statistics, the text of an exclusionist law, and a letter to President Woodrow Wilson pleading the Issei cause.

Yuji, Ichioka. "The Early Japanese Immigrant Quest for Citizenship: The Background of the 1922 Ozawa Case." *Amerasia* 4, no. 2 (1977): 12. Brief account of the reasons for Ozawa's legal action and his desire for citizenship.

See also *Afroyim v. Rusk; Fedorenko v. United States; Hirabayashi v. United States; Immigration and Naturalization Service v. Chadha; Korematsu v. United States; Nguyen v. Immigration and Naturalization Service; United States v. Wong Kim Ark.*

Pacific Mutual Life Insurance Co. v. Haslip

Court: U.S. Supreme Court
Citation: 499 U.S. 1
Date: March 4, 1991
Issues: Trial by jury

- In the face of a challenge brought by business, the U.S. Supreme Court upheld sizable punitive awards made by juries.

Justice Harry A. Blackmun wrote the opinion for the 7-1 majority, upholding a sizable punitive damage award made in Alabama. Earlier, the Supreme Court had rejected a challenge to such jury awards on Eighth Amendment grounds. In this case, the Court rejected the argument that the jury decision was so irrational and unrelated to the plaintiff's actual injuries as to run afoul of the Fourteenth Amendment's due process guarantee. Although Blackmun acknowledged there might be cases in which an exceedingly irrational jury award might violate due process protections, generally he defended the common-law process of judicial determinations and found that the Alabama courts had reasonably well provided for rational decision making. Justices Antonin Scalia and Anthony M. Kennedy concurred. Justice Sandra Day O'Connor dissented, finding that the Alabama procedure did not provide for "rational implementation."

Richard L. Wilson

See also *BMW of North America v. Gore*; *Cohen v. Cowles Media Co.*; *New York Times Co. v. Sullivan.*

PACIFIC STATES TELEPHONE AND TELEGRAPH CO. V. OREGON

Court: U.S. Supreme Court
Citation: 223 U.S. 118
Date: February 19, 1912
Issues: States' rights

• The U.S. Supreme Court upheld state use of the initiative and referendum to make laws as being compatible with the Constitution's promise of a republican form of government.

Oregon, along with other relatively new Western states, used initiatives and referendums to give voters the option of legislating directly on some questions. The state used this power to impose a tax on the phone companies. The phone companies could no longer use their lobbying power in the legislature effectively, so Pacific States Telephone and Telegraph Company sued, attempting to have practices such as the initiative and referendum declared contrary to the Constitution's promise of a republican form of government. Relying on *Luther v. Borden* (1849), the Supreme Court unanimously ruled that it lacked jurisdiction in this case. The Court was clearly unwilling to act contrary to a direct expression of popular will and refused to hear the case, holding that it was a political and not a judicial question.

Richard L. Wilson

See also *First National Bank of Boston v. Bellotti; Luther v. Borden.*

PALKO V. CONNECTICUT

Court: U.S. Supreme Court
Citation: 302 U.S. 319
Date: December 6, 1937
Issues: Double jeopardy; Incorporation doctrine

- In this case, while refusing to apply the Fifth Amendment right against double jeopardy to the states, the U.S. Supreme Court established an influential test for determining which fundamental rights contained within the Bill of Rights are incorporated into the Fourteenth Amendment's due process clause.

On the night of September 30, 1935, Bridgeport, Connecticut, police officers Wilfred Walker and Thomas J. Kearney were shot and killed. Frank Palka (his name was spelled "Palko" in court records) was charged with first-degree murder, a charge which carried a death sentence. On January 24, 1936, a trial jury found Palka guilty of only second-degree murder because the killings were not sufficiently premeditated. Palka received a sentence of life imprisonment.

On July 30, 1936, the Supreme Court of Errors of Connecticut ordered a new trial by finding that the trial judge gave improper instructions to the jury. On October 15, 1936, a second jury found Palka guilty of first-degree murder, and he was sentenced to death. Palka's case came to the U.S. Supreme Court with the claim that the second trial violated his Fifth Amendment right not to "be subject for the same offense [nor] to be twice put in jeopardy of life or limb." At the time, however, the Supreme Court had applied the Fifth Amendment right against double jeopardy only to criminal cases in federal, rather than state, courts.

For most of American history, the provisions of the Bill of Rights protected individuals only against actions by the federal government. The ratification of the Fourteenth Amendment in 1868 applied constitutional rights to protection against the states, but those rights were vaguely worded protections involving "due process" and "equal protection." People repeatedly brought cases to the Supreme Court asserting that the provisions of the Bill of Rights should apply against state as well as federal government officials. Beginning in 1925, the Supreme Court gradually incorporated a few rights—speech, press, and religion—into the Fourteenth Amendment's due process clause and thereby made those rights applicable to the states.

Unfortunately for Palka, the Court was unwilling to incorporate the Fifth Amendment's protection against double jeopardy in 1937. Thus Palka's conviction was affirmed, and he was subsequently executed for the murders. Justice Benjamin Cardozo's majority opinion, however, established a test for determining which rights to incorporate by declaring that only rights which are "fundamental" and "essential" to liberty are contained in the right to due process in the Fourteenth Amendment.

In analyzing Palka's case, Cardozo decided that many criminal justice rights contained in the Bill of Rights, such as trial by jury and protection

Justice Benjamin N. Cardozo. (Harris & Ewing/Collection of the Supreme Court of the United States)

against double jeopardy and self-incrimination, are not fundamental and essential because it is possible to have fair trials without them.

The importance of *Palko v. Connecticut* is that Cardozo's test established an influential standard for determining which provisions of the Bill of Rights apply against the states. Although justices in later decades disagreed with Cardozo's specific conclusions and subsequently incorporated double jeopardy and other rights for criminal defendants, most justices have continued to use Cardozo's basic approach of evaluating whether each specific right was fundamental and essential to liberty.

Christopher E. Smith

See also *Benton v. Maryland; Duncan v. Louisiana; Robinson v. California; Rochin v. California.*

PALMER V. THOMPSON

Court: U.S. Supreme Court
Citation: 403 U.S. 217
Date: June 14, 1971
Issues: Local government; Racial discrimination; Separation of powers

- The U.S. Supreme Court refused to seek out racially discriminatory intent in cases in which local government decisions were neutral on face.

Justice Hugo L. Black wrote the opinion for the 5-4 majority, upholding the decision of the city of Jackson, Mississippi, to close a public swimming pool rather than operate it as an integrated facility. Lower federal courts had ordered the pool to be integrated, and the city closed it rather than comply. African Americans thought this showed a clear discriminatory intent, but the Supreme Court was reluctant to go beyond the plausible nondiscriminatory reason the city offered for its decision. Chief Justice Warren E. Burger concurred, and Justices William O. Douglas, Byron R. White, Thurgood Marshall, and William J. Brennan, Jr., dissented, finding that there was sufficient evidence of discriminatory intent to justify overturning this local government decision as a violation of the Fourteenth Amendment's equal protection clause. The Court subsequently has moved more in the direction of the dissenters' point of view.

Richard L. Wilson

See also *Heart of Atlanta Motel v. United States; Plessy v. Ferguson; Rotary International v. Duarte; Swann v. Charlotte-Mecklenburg Board of Education.*

PANAMA REFINING CO. V. RYAN

Court: U.S. Supreme Court
Citation: 293 U.S. 388
Date: January 7, 1935
Issues: Congressional powers; Separation of powers

- The U.S. Supreme Court voided a congressional enactment on the grounds that it unconstitutionally made a vague delegation of power to executive branch agencies.

In *Panama Refining Co. v. Ryan, Schechter Poultry Corp. v. United States* (1935), and *Carter v. Carter Coal Co.* (1936), the Supreme Court attempted to limit the later widespread congressional practice of transferring its constitutional lawmaking responsibility by delegating the hard decisions or the actual wording to executive branch agencies. In *Panama*, the Court addressed only the single section challenged by the refining company, but the Court addressed broader issues in *Schechter.*

Chief Justice Charles Evans Hughes wrote the opinion for the 8-1 majority, holding that the 1933 National Industrial Recovery Act (NIRA) was unconstitutional in that Congress had delegated its lawmaking power to the executive branch through excessively vague legislation. Justice Benjamin N. Cardozo dissented, arguing that the national economic emergency of the Great Depression justified this vague delegation of power. The Court never overturned these three cases but later ignored its own rulings. From time to time, the Court appeared willing to take up the issue of vague delegation of lawmaking power as in *Immigration and Naturalization Service v. Chadha* (1983) and *Bowsher v. Synar* (1986), but it did not do so in any consistent fashion. These cases continue to be valid, but only on the narrow issues raised in those particular cases.

Richard L. Wilson

See also *Bowsher v. Synar; Carter v. Carter Coal Co.; Immigration and Naturalization Service v. Chadha; Mistretta v. United States; Morrison v. Olson; Schechter Poultry Corp. v. United States.*

Paramount Pictures, Inc., United States v. *See* United States v. Paramount Pictures, Inc.

Parents Involved in Community Schools v. Seattle School District No. 1

Court: U.S. Supreme Court
Citation: 551 U.S. 701
Date: June 28, 2007
Issues: Desegregation; Education; Equal protection of the law; Parental rights

• The U.S. Supreme Court held that the equal protection clause of the Fourteenth Amendment prohibits the assigning of students to particular public schools for the sole purpose of achieving statistical racial balance.

When the Supreme Court held that racial segregation of the public schools violates the Fourteenth Amendment in *Brown v. Board of Education* in 1954, the Court was directly referring only to the kind of segregation that is a consequence of governmental mandate or encouragement (called de jure segregation). Consequently, after that decision, many students continued to attend schools that were segregated solely as a result of racially imbalanced neighborhoods (called de facto segregation). In *Swann v. Board of Education* (1971), the Supreme Court authorized lower federal courts to require local school boards to utilize busing plans in an attempt to desegregate the schools when there was good evidence that segregation was partially due to governmental encouragement. By the late 1990's, there was almost no evidence that governmental action remained a major cause for the continuation of racial imbalance in the schools, and the majority of justices on the Supreme Court had become less committed to desegregation than the justices of previous decades. As a result of these two factors, statistics indicated a strong trend toward the resegregation of the schools on a de facto basis.

Some school boards were determined to establish policies that would increase the racial integration of the schools in their districts. One of the major tools for this purpose was to take race into account when assigning students to attend particular schools. Such a policy meant that some students were not allowed to attend the schools of their choice (usually the nearest to where they lived), and inevitably a number of parents strongly opposed the policy. Opponents of the policy argued that it was discriminatory to deny some students the right to attend the schools of their choice simply because of their race. Defenders insisted that assignments were necessary to counter the evils of racial isolation and separation. They also pointed out that assignment policies had been established by elected officials, and that the elections of the officials demonstrated that the majority of citizens in the region supported the policies.

Supreme Court Precedents

In deciding the case, the Supreme Court considered several of its own precedents. In *Adarand Constructors v. Peña* (1995), the Court had held by a 5-4 vote that all racial classifications must be assessed according to "strict scrutiny," requiring that they be "narrowly tailored" and that they must be justified by a "compelling governmental interest." In *Grutter v. Bollinger* (2003), on the other hand, the Court had held that racial diversity was a compelling interest that justified a policy of applying racial preferences in selecting students to attend a competitive law school. The policy was deemed to be "narrowly tailored" to promote diversity in higher education. It was not clear, however, whether the Supreme Court would find the affirmative action policy approved in *Grutter* to be comparable to the race-conscious assignment of seats in the public schools.

The school district of Seattle, Washington, was one of the districts that instituted a policy of making school assignments with the goal of promoting racial balance. Approximately 59 percent of the students attending district schools were nonwhite, and about 41 percent were classified as white. No distinction was made among Asian, African American, and Hispanic ancestry. In order for each high school to reflect approximately the district's racial balance, students at the beginning of the year were instructed to indicate their first choice of schools within the district. When a given school became oversubscribed, the district used a number of tie-breakers to decide which students would be allowed to attend the more popular schools.

A second important consideration for Seattle school assignments was a student's race. A nonprofit group, Parents Involved in Community Schools, took the district to court, arguing that assignments based on race violated both the equal protection principle of the Fourteenth Amendment and the Civil Rights Act of 1964. The federal District Court upheld the assignment policy, but the Court of Appeals ruled in favor of the parents. The school board appealed the case to the Supreme Court. A Kentucky case challenging a similar race-based assignment plan, *Meredith v. Jefferson County*, was appealed to the Court at about the same time, and the Court decided to consider the two cases together.

The Court's Ruling

In a 5-4 decision, the Supreme Court ruled that the two school programs violated the constitutional rights of the plaintiffs. Speaking for the majority, Chief Justice John Roberts began by observing that the Court's precedent required that when a government distributes "burdens or benefits based on individual racial classifications," its actions must be reviewed under *Adarand's* demanding standard of "strict scrutiny." He found that the school boards had failed to meet this difficult hurdle. Conceding that the Court's precedent in *Grutter* had recognized that a diverse student body is a compelling state interest in higher education, he argued that *Grutter* had insisted on individual assessment and that diversity was not as important in public schools as at the university level. He further wrote that the assignment plans in Seattle and Louisville had not been "narrowly tailored" to utilize the least restrictive means. By interpreting the *Swann* decision of 1971 as remedial action in response to de jure segregation, he claimed that the present ruling was entirely consistent with that precedent.

Chief Justice Roberts, joined by three other justices, wanted to go further and issue a "color-blind" interpretation of the Constitution, thereby prohibiting all racial classifications designed to promote desegregation. Roberts concluded his opinion with the words: "The way to stop discrimination on the basis of race is to stop discriminating on the basis of race." However, Justice Anthony Kennedy, the acknowledged swing-vote of the Court, would not join this portion of Roberts's opinion. Kennedy agreed that the Seattle and Louisville programs were unconstitutional because they were not narrowly tailored to promote diversity, but he was not willing to express opposition to all racially conscious government policies. He therefore wrote a separate opinion, emphasizing that *Grutter* had recognized that the promotion of racial diversity was "a compelling educational goal a school district may pursue." Among acceptable policies to promote diversity, Kennedy endorsed the redrawing of attendance zones, selection of strategic locations for new schools, and the use of special programs and magnate schools.

Justice Clarence Thomas, the only African American on the Court, wrote a concurring opinion that took issue with Kennedy's position. Defining racial imbalance as the failure of a district's individual schools to match or approximate the demographic makeup of the student population at large, Thomas denied that there was anything unconstitutional, or necessarily undesirable, about such an imbalance. Referring to a number of social science studies, he asserted that there was no evidence that racially balanced schools were more successful than imbalanced schools in academic outcomes or in improving racial attitudes and race relations. Denouncing governmental practices that are "race-based," he quoted John Marshall Harlan's statement, "Our constitution is color-blind, and neither knows nor tolerates classes among citizens."

Breyer's Dissent

Justice Stephen Breyer wrote a seventy-seven page dissent asserting that the majority decision was a "radical" departure from settled law that would take away tools communities need to counter the growing resegregation of the public schools. Conceding that Seattle and Louisville were not required to adopt the policies that were under review, he argued that *Swann* and other decisions had established the legal principle that a school district "may voluntarily adopt race-conscious measures to improve conditions of race even when it is not under a constitutional obligation to do so." Advocating a flexible application of strict scrutiny, he argued that none of the Court's precedents had ever held that "all racial classifications—no matter whether they seek to include or exclude—must in practice be treated the same." The school assignments under consideration, moreover, had been narrowly tailored, taking into account the students' choices and diminishing the need for mandatory busing. Breyer emphasized that one of the major goals of the Fourteenth Amendment was to bring about an end to "racial isolation," and he dismissed Kennedy's alternative proposals as ineffective. "This is a decision that the Court and the nation will come to regret," he declared.

Most observers expected that the Court's *Seattle* ruling would marginally increase the extent of racial segregation in the public schools. Districts making race-based assignments, such as those in Seattle and Louisville, would be required to terminate their practices, and other districts would no longer be faced with pressures to implement such polices. Although the ruling did not challenge race-based programs of affirmative action, it appeared to indicate that the Court's majority would likely take a very critical view of such programs. Because the controversial decision was based on a 5-4 vote, however, the future of the ruling appeared to be rather uncertain.

Thomas Tandy Lewis

Further Reading

Clotfelter, Charles T. *After Brown: The Rise and Retreat of School Desegregation.* Princeton, N.J.: Princeton University Press, 2006. Historical account of the attempts to promote racial segregation in the public schools since the landmark decision, *Brown v. Board of Education.*

Gaillard, Frye. *The Dream Long Deferred: The Landmark Struggle for Desegregation in Charlotte, North Carolina.* 3d ed. Columbia: University of South Carolina Press, 2006. Argues that the Supreme Court's *Swann* decision ordering busing in 1971 successfully promoted desegregation, but that neighborhood schools returned because of a judicial reversal in 1999.

Goldstein, Joel K. "Not Hearing History: A Critique of Chief Justice Roberts's Reinterpretation of *Brown.*" *Ohio State Law Journal* 69, no. 5 (2008): 791-846. Refuting Roberts's "color-blind" interpretation of the Fourteenth Amendment, Goldstein argues that a major effect of *Brown* was to combat the educational isolation of minority students.

Rossell, Christine H., David J. Armor, and Herbert J. Walberg, eds. *School Desegregation in the Twenty-first Century.* Westport, Conn.: Praeger, 2002. Arguing that mandatory busing and racial quotas had too many costs and too few benefits, the essays advocate compensatory programs and school-choice plans that do not use racial criteria.

See also *Adarand Constructors v. Peña; Board of Education of Oklahoma City v. Dowell; Brown v. Board of Education; Columbus Board of Education v. Penick; Keyes v. Denver School District No. 1; Lemon v. Kurtzman; Milliken v. Bradley; Swann v. Charlotte-Mecklenburg Board of Education.*

Pasadena Board of Education v. Spangler

Court: U.S. Supreme Court
Citation: 427 U.S. 424
Date: June 28, 1976
Issues: Desegregation; Education

• In this school desegregation case, the U.S. Supreme Court held that a federal district court exceeded its authority in ordering annual reassignments of students to facilitate changes in the racial makeup of schools caused by demographic shifts.

In 1968, several students and their parents filed suit against the Pasadena Unified School District in California, alleging that the district's schools were segregated as a result of official action on the part of the district. In 1970, the federal district court found for these plaintiffs, concluding that the district had engaged in segregation and ordering the district to adopt a plan to cure the racial imbalances in its schools. The federal court's order provided that no school was to have a majority of minority students. The district thereafter presented the court with a plan to eliminate segregation in the Pasadena schools; the court approved the plan, and the district subsequently implemented it.

Approximately four years later, the Pasadena Unified School District asked the district court to modify its original order and eliminate the requirement that no school have a majority of minority students. The district contended that though it had abandoned its racially segregative practices, changing racial demographics had created new racial imbalances in the district's schools. The federal district court refused to modify its original order, however, and the Ninth Circuit Court of Appeals upheld the district court's ruling.

Reviewing this decision, Justice William H. Rehnquist, joined by five other justices, concluded that the district court had abused its authority in refusing to remove the requirement that no district school have a majority of minority students. According to the Court, there had been no showing that changes in the racial mix of the Pasadena schools had been caused by the school district's policies. Since the school district had implemented a racially neutral attendance policy, the federal district court was not entitled to require a continual reshuffling of attendance zones to maintain an optimal racial mix. Justices Thurgood Marshall and William J. Brennan dissented from this holding, emphasizing the breadth of discretion normally allotted to federal district courts to remedy school segregation once a constitutional violation had been shown.

The majority's decision signaled that the broad discretion with which the Court previously had seemed to invest federal district courts was not without limits. It had been widely thought that once officially sanctioned or de jure segregation had been shown, a federal court had great latitude in eliminating not only such de jure segregation but also de facto segregation—that is, segregation not necessarily tied to official conduct. The majority's decision in this case, however, signified otherwise.

Timothy L. Hall

See also *Board of Education of Oklahoma City v. Dowell; Columbus Board of Education v. Penick; Keyes v. Denver School District No. 1; Lemon v. Kurtzman; Milliken v. Bradley; Swann v. Charlotte-Mecklenburg Board of Education.*

Passenger Cases

Court: U.S. Supreme Court
Citation: 48 U.S. 283
Date: February 7, 1849
Issues: Interstate commerce; Right to travel

• The U.S. Supreme Court banned taxes levied by states on incoming passengers, holding that such taxes directly regulated interstate commerce.

Smith v. Turner and *Norris v. Boston*, together known as the *Passenger Cases*, involved New York and Massachusetts taxes on inbound passengers, including citizens of other countries. By a 5-4 vote, a badly divided Supreme Court held that state taxes on alien passengers were direct regulations of interstate commerce and therefore void. Amid the confusion of eight separate opinions, the judges appeared to have decided that people were articles of commerce. The opinions demonstrated how strongly the justices disagreed concerning issues of slavery and federalism. In his dissent, Chief Justice Roger Brooke Taney wrote an influential statement about the right of citizens to travel throughout the country "without interruption."

Thomas Tandy Lewis

See also *Head Money Cases; License Cases; Woodruff v. Parham.*

Patterson v. McLean Credit Union

Court: U.S. Supreme Court
Citation: 491 U.S. 164
Date: June 15, 1989
Issues: Civil rights and liberties; Employment discrimination; Racial discrimination

- The U.S. Supreme Court reargued this racial discrimination case, apparently intending to overturn a remaining provision of the 1866 Civil Rights Act, but backed off in the face of widespread controversy.

In *Patterson*, the Supreme Court was asked to determine whether an African American woman's charge of racially motivated employment harassment was a cause of action under Title 42, section 1981, a surviving part of the 1866 Civil Rights Act. The Court had used this provision of the 1866 act as a way of stopping racial discrimination in private and contractual relationships in *Runyon v. McCrary* (1976) and *Jones v. Alfred H. Mayer Co.* (1968). The Court ordered a reargument and decided to determine whether *Runyon* should be overturned. Its action resulted in deep internal division and widespread criticism in the country. The majority believed there was need to issue a written defense of its reargument order in writing.

Upon reargument, the Court decided unanimously not to overturn *Runyon* but limited the scope of the ruling dramatically. The Court, however, ruled five to four that section 1981 did not apply to what an employer did after entering into a contract with an employee and, therefore, that the woman's claims of racial harassment after her hiring did not fall under section 1981. Not only were there four dissents on this issue, but Congress also quickly passed the 1991 Civil Rights Act, which restored the legal standard in use prior to the *Patterson* ruling.

Richard L. Wilson

See also *Buchanan v. Warley; Corrigan v. Buckley; Jones v. Alfred H. Mayer Co.; Katzenbach v. McClung; Reitman v. Mulkey; Runyon v. McCrary; Shelley v. Kraemer.*

PAUL V. VIRGINIA

Court: U.S. Supreme Court
Citation: 75 U.S. 168
Date: November 1, 1869
Issues: Citizenship; Regulation of commerce

- The U.S. Supreme Court upheld a state law placing special burdens on out-of-state insurance companies, ruling that a corporation was not protected by the privileges and immunities clause and that insurance sales were not transactions in interstate commerce.

During the nineteenth century, many states encouraged the growth of in-state insurance companies by charging special taxes and license fees on companies located in other states. A combination of insurance companies organized a test case to challenge the constitutionality of these discriminatory practices. Speaking for a unanimous Supreme Court, Justice Stephen J. Field ruled that corporations were not citizens for the purposes of the privileges and immunities clause of Article IV of the U.S. Constitution. In addition, insurance was held to be local in nature, and therefore, states had the authority to regulate the industry under their police powers.

Without directly reversing *Paul*, the Court ruled in 1886 that corporations were persons for purposes of the Fourteenth Amendment. The second portion of *Paul* was reversed in *United States v. South-Eastern Underwriters Association* (1944).

Thomas Tandy Lewis

See also *Bank of Augusta v. Earle; Citizens United v. Federal Election Commission; Louisville, Cincinnati, and Charleston Railroad Co. v. Letson; Northern Securities Co. v. United States; Santa Clara County v. Southern Pacific Railroad Co.; United States v. South-Eastern Underwriters Association.*

PAYNE V. TENNESSEE

Court: U.S. Supreme Court
Citation: 501 U.S. 808
Date: June 27, 1991
Issues: Capital punishment; Evidence

- In a dramatic departure from *stare decisis* (the practice of basing decisions on precedents of previous cases) the U.S. Supreme Court overruled two cases it had decided within the past four years and held that victim impact evidence would be permitted in capital sentencing hearings.

In 1987, the Supreme Court in *Booth v. Maryland* had held that prosecutors in capital cases would not be permitted to use victim impact evidence to persuade the jury that the defendant deserved to be executed. The five members of the *Booth* majority held that evidence about the personal characteristics of the murdered person and evidence about the impact of the crime on surviving family members were irrelevant to the jury's decision whether the character of the defendant and the circumstances of the crime should call for the death penalty or for some lesser punishment.

Because victim impact evidence focused the jury's attention on the victim and surviving family members, it diverted the jury's attention from the defendant. Most important, it created a risk that a death sentence might be based on arbitrary and capricious reasons, such as the willingness and ability of surviving family members to articulate their grief, or the relative worth of the murder victim to the community.

Four justices had sharply dissented. In their view, victim impact evidence was relevant to the defendant's moral blameworthiness because it gave the jury important information about the extent of the harm caused by the defendant.

The *Booth* decision was reaffirmed two years later in *South Carolina v. Gathers*, when another bare majority of the Court held that prosecutors could not present victim impact evidence to the jury during closing arguments in death penalty cases. By 1991, however, two members of the *Booth* majority had retired from the Court and had been replaced by more conservative justices. That same year, the Court agreed to reconsider its recent decisions and granted *certiorari* in *Payne v. Tennessee.*

Pervis Tyrone Payne had stabbed to death twenty-eight-year-old Charisse Christopher and her two-year-old daughter, Lacie. Payne also stabbed and left for dead Charisse's three-year-old son, Nicholas. Nicholas survived his stab wounds, several of which passed completely through his body. During Payne's trial, Nicholas's grandmother testified emotionally as to the effect of the murders on Nicholas. In addition, during closing arguments to the jury, the prosecutor strongly implied that returning a death sentence would somehow help Nicholas. The jury sentenced Payne to die.

In the Supreme Court, Payne argued that the grandmother's testimony and the prosecutor's argument to the jury constituted victim impact evidence and thereby violated *Booth* and *Gathers.* In a radical departure from past practice, the Supreme Court discarded those recent decisions and announced a new rule: Victim impact evidence would be permitted in capital sentencing proceedings. According to the majority, victim impact evidence gave the jury important information about the extent of the harm caused by the defendant.

Justice Thurgood Marshall, who voted with the majority in *Booth* and *Gathers*, was enraged and disheartened. Breaking tradition, Justice Marshall read his dissent from the bench on the last day of the Court's 1991 term. He said: "Neither the law nor the facts supporting *Booth* and *Gathers* underwent any change in the last four years. Only the personnel of this Court did." Within two hours of reading his dissent, Justice Marshall announced his resignation from the Court.

Randall Coyne

See also *Akron v. Akron Center for Reproductive Health; Booth v. Maryland; Church of Lukumi Babalu Aye v. Hialeah; Furman v. Georgia; Planned Parenthood of Southeastern Pennsylvania v. Casey; Thornburgh v. American College of Obstetricians and Gynecologists.*

PAYTON V. NEW YORK

Court: U.S. Supreme Court
Citation: 445 U.S. 573
Date: April 15, 1980
Issues: Search and seizure; Takings clause

• The U.S. Supreme Court declared that police need an arrest warrant before they make a nonconsensual entrance into an accused's residence to make an arrest.

Justice John Paul Stevens.
(Courtesy, the Supreme Court Historical Society)

Justice John Paul Stevens wrote the opinion for the 6-3 majority on the Supreme Court, declaring that an arrest warrant was needed before an arrest was made if the arrest required a nonconsensual entrance into a home. Exceptions could be made if there were exigent circumstances, such as if the police were in hot pursuit of a felon. The long-standing rule had been that a search warrant was necessary to make a nonconsensual search of a residence, but this principle had not been previously applied to the arrest itself. Some experts have argued that a search warrant should also be necessary in these circumstances. Still others, including the dissenters in *Payton*, would not have gone as far as the Court did in this case. Chief Justice Warren E. Burger and Justices Byron R. White and William H. Rehnquist dissented. Justice Harry A. Blackmun concurred separately.

Richard L. Wilson

See also *Atwater v. City of Lago Vista*; *California v. Greenwood*; *Knowles v. Iowa*; *Maryland v. Buie*; *New York v. Belton*; *Tennessee v. Garner*; *Terry v. Ohio*; *United States v. United States District Court*.

===

PENN CENTRAL TRANSPORTATION CO. V. CITY OF NEW YORK

Court: U.S. Supreme Court
Citation: 438 U.S. 104
Date: June 26, 1978
Issues: Takings clause

• The U.S. Supreme Court established several important principles governing the takings impact of regulations.

After a local preservation committee made New York's Grand Central Station a national landmark, Penn Central was denied the right to build a fifty-story building on arches over the train terminal. New York City allowed Penn Central certain "transferable development rights" to nearby transfer sites, but Penn Central was not satisfied and sued New York City, claiming that its inability to build constituted a taking and a denial of due process. By a 6-3 vote, the Supreme Court found the zoning restriction was not a taking because it did not excessively "frustrate distinct investment-backed expectations," a phrase created by the Court that found its way into subsequent cases. The Court did not take up transferable rights directly but suggested that such rights might either mitigate the situation so a taking would not occur or act as a form of compensation. It seems obvious that the Court had the value of historic preservation in its collective mind in reaching this unusual decision.

Richard L. Wilson

See also *Chicago, Milwaukee, and St. Paul Railway Co. v. Minnesota*; *Dolan v. City of Tigard*; *Euclid v. Ambler Realty Co.*; *First English Evangelical Lutheran Church of Glendale v. County of Los Angeles*; *Hawaii Housing Authority v. Midkiff*; *Kelo v. City of New London*; *Keystone Bituminous Coal Association v. DeBenedictis*; *Nollan v. California Coastal Commission*; *Payton v. New York*.

PENNOYER V. NEFF

Court: U.S. Supreme Court
Citation: 95 U.S. 714
Date: January 21, 1878
Issues: Diversity jurisdiction

- The U.S. Supreme Court established basic rules covering people who were not citizens or residents of states.

To secure judgment in a contract suit, a plaintiff in Oregon attached the real property of a noncitizen, nonresident of Oregon by constructive service through a legal notice in a local newspaper. By an 8-1 vote, the Supreme Court ruled against the plaintiff, holding that these steps were insufficient to secure jurisdiction over the defendant. The Court ruled that a state had jurisdiction over those within its borders and none over those outside its borders. This simple distinction became unworkable in the twentieth century because of modern transportation and communications and its failure to provide a basis for jurisdiction over corporations. *International Shoe Co. v. Washington* (1945) and *Burnham v. Superior Court* (1990) contain significant modifications. Justice Stephen J. Field wrote the opinion for the Court, and Justice Ward Hunt dissented.

Richard L. Wilson

See also *Bank of the United States v. Deveaux; Erie Railroad Co. v. Tompkins; Louisville, Cincinnati, and Charleston Railroad Co. v. Letson; Strawbridge v. Curtiss.*

PENNSYLVANIA COAL CO. V. MAHON

Court: U.S. Supreme Court
Citation: 260 U.S. 393
Date: December 11, 1922
Issues: Land law; Property rights; Regulation of commerce; Takings clause

• The U.S. Supreme Court first held that a regulation regarding land use may constitute a taking.

Justice Oliver Wendell Holmes wrote the opinion for the 8-1 majority. Holmes ruled that a Pennsylvania statute regulated land to such an extent that a coal company could not access the coal deposit for which it owned the mineral rights. The Supreme Court held that the regulation was a taking for which just compensation had not been offered. Justice Louis D. Brandeis dissented. *Keystone Bituminous Coal Association v. DeBenedictis* (1987) seems to modify *Pennsylvania Coal,* but neither holding determined exactly when such a regulation became a taking, and the controversy continued.

Richard L. Wilson

See also *Carter v. Carter Coal Co.; Keystone Bituminous Coal Association v. DeBenedictis; Penn Central Transportation Co. v. City of New York; United States v. California.*

Pennsylvania v. Nelson

Court: U.S. Supreme Court
Citation: 350 U.S. 497
Date: April 2, 1956
Issues: Freedom of assembly and association

• The U.S. Supreme Court began to move away from blanket approval of anticommunist legislation.

Chief Justice Earl Warren wrote the opinion for the 6-3 majority, upholding the Pennsylvania Supreme Court in overturning the conviction of Communist Party leader Steve Nelson on a state antisedition law. The Supreme Court decided that federal anticommunist legislation was so pervasive that the federal government had preempted the field. The domestic political reaction was so strong that the Court did not advance further in this direction in the 1950's. Justice Stanley F. Reed wrote a dissent in which he was joined by Justices Sherman Minton and Harold H. Burton.

Richard L. Wilson

See also *Albertson v. Subversive Activities Control Board; Aptheker v. Secretary of State; Communist Party v. Subversive Activities Control Board; Dennis v. United States; Scales v. United States; Yates v. United States.*

Pennsylvania v. Wheeling and Belmont Bridge Co.

Court: U.S. Supreme Court
Citation: 54 U.S. 518
Date: February 6, 1852
Issues: Regulation of commerce; Standing

• In this case, the result of an unusual chain of events, the U.S. Supreme Court set the standard for the height of bridges above navigable rivers throughout the second half of the nineteenth century.

By a 7-2 vote, the Supreme Court held that the bridge Virginia built from Wheeling (later West Virginia) to the western states was a nuisance because it interfered with large steamboat traffic in which Pennsylvania had a special interest. Having decided Pennsylvania had standing to sue, Justice John McLean ordered the bridge torn down or elevated. Chief Justice Roger Brooke Taney and Justice Peter V. Daniel dissented, arguing that the Court lacked jurisdiction because there was no federal statute on the question. Later, Congress passed a law making the bridge lawful at its existing height, and the Court—in a case by the same name—decided the bridge was not a nuisance because of the federal statute. This height of the bridge at the end of this case was used to determine the height of bridges above navigable rivers throughout the late nineteenth century.

Richard L. Wilson

See also *Garcia v. San Antonio Metropolitan Transit Authority; Gibbons v. Ogden; Hammer v. Dagenhart; Morgan v. Virginia; Penn Central Transportation Co. v. City of New York.*

Justice John McLean.
(Library of Congress)

Penry v. Lynaugh

Court: U.S. Supreme Court
Citation: 492 U.S. 302
Date: June 26, 1989
Issues: Capital punishment

- The U.S. Supreme Court upheld capital punishment for mentally retarded but legally sane people.

Defendant Penry was moderately mentally retarded but judged legally sane so that he could be tried, convicted, and sentenced to death for murder and rape in Texas. Justice Sandra Day O'Connor wrote the opinion for the Supreme Court, which was unanimous in its decision but divided on the reasons. Other justices concurred in part and dissented in part. On the narrow issue of this defendant's trial, the Court reversed his sentence to death for murder and rape because the jury had not been specifically instructed that it could consider mitigating circumstances such as his mental retardation. On the broader issue of whether a mildly or moderately mentally retarded individual could be sentenced to death, the Court found that the Eighth Amendment did not bar capital punishment in such cases. The Court did not disturb its conclusion in *Ford v. Wainwright* (1986) that legally insane individuals could not be executed.

Richard L. Wilson

See also *Atkins v. Virginia; Ford v. Wainwright.*

Personnel Administrator of Massachusetts v. Feeney

Court: U.S. Supreme Court
Citation: 442 U.S. 256
Date: June 5, 1979
Issues: Equal protection of the law; Military law; Sex discrimination;
Women's issues

- This case found the U.S. Supreme Court upholding a law that affected women adversely.

Under a Massachusetts law, all military veterans were given an absolute lifetime preference, which meant that as long as they passed the examination for classified civil service jobs, they were ranked above all other candidates. Since 98 percent of the veterans were male, the law was challenged as a violation of the Fourteenth Amendment's equal protection clause, which requires states to treat persons equally. In a 7-2 opinion, however, the U.S. Supreme Court upheld the law.

Justice Potter Stewart argued that veteran status is not uniquely male and that the nonveteran class is not substantially all-female. In fact, there are significant numbers of nonveterans who are men, and all nonveterans were placed at a disadvantage by the law. Since so many men were affected, the statute was not a pretext for preferring men over women. Nevertheless, since most veterans are men, there are adverse consequences of the law for women; but the law was not enacted to keep women in a stereotypic and predefined place in the Massachusetts civil service.

The impact of *Personnel Administrator of Massachusetts v. Feeney* was the formulation of a basic rule that a law adversely affecting women but not specifically classifying on the basis of sex does not fall within equal protection analysis.

Robert W. Langran

See also *Frontiero v. Richardson; Rosenfeld v. Southern Pacific; Rostker v. Goldberg; United States v. Virginia; Weeks v. Southern Bell.*

PHILLIPS V. MARTIN MARIETTA CORP.

Court: U.S. Supreme Court
Citation: 400 U.S. 542
Date: January 25, 1971
Issues: Civil rights and liberties; Employment discrimination;
Labor law; Sex discrimination; Women's issues

• This was the first Title VII case to reach the U.S. Supreme Court, and the outcome was a victory for women.

Title VII of the Civil Rights Act of 1964 prohibits discrimination in the workplace on the basis of a number of factors, including sex. The first Title VII case to reach the Supreme Court was the one in which Ida Phillips sued Martin Marietta Corporation over its refusal to hire her as an assembly trainee because she had preschool-aged children—although the company hired men with preschool-aged children for the same position. Both lower courts had rejected her complaint, holding that she was not refused the job because of her sex alone.

The Supreme Court, however, in a unanimous unsigned *per curiam* (by the Court) opinion, disagreed with the lower courts and in so doing rejected this "sex plus" reasoning. The Court held that discrimination on the basis of sex plus another characteristic does violate Title VII. The law does not allow a company to have one hiring policy for men and another for women.

Nevertheless, the Court then sent the case back to the lower court to determine whether sex was a bona fide occupational qualification (BFOQ) for the job, because the law does allow that exception. The company would have the chance to show that having preschool-aged children might significantly hamper a woman's job performance. If it could so prove, the company could refuse to hire women with small children.

The impact of *Phillips v. Martin Marietta Corp.* was that the Court did accept the argument that sex discrimination, even though accompanied by another factor, is a violation of the law.

Robert W. Langran

See also *County of Washington v. Gunther; Frontiero v. Richardson; Geduldig v. Aiello; Grove City College v. Bell; Hoyt v. Florida; Meritor Savings Bank v. Vinson; Rosenfeld v. Southern Pacific; Stanton v. Stanton.*

PIERCE V. SOCIETY OF SISTERS

Court: U.S. Supreme Court
Citation: 268 U.S. 510
Date: June 1, 1925
Issues: Education; Parental rights; Reproductive rights

- This case, which struck down state legislation requiring parents to send their children to public rather than private schools on grounds that such legislation violated the liberty clause of the Fourteenth Amendment, has provided important authority in U.S. Supreme Court cases in the areas of contraceptive, abortion, and homosexual rights.

In 1922, the state of Oregon adopted the Compulsory Education Act, which compelled general attendance at public schools by normal children between the ages of eight and sixteen. The Society of the Sisters of the Holy Names of Jesus and Mary, a private parochial school, challenged this legislation on the grounds that it conflicted with the right and liberty of parents to send their children to schools of their own choosing and violated the right of private schools and teachers therein to engage in a useful business and profession.

In a unanimous decision, the U.S. Supreme Court held that "the Act of 1922 unreasonably interferes with the liberty of the parents and guardians to direct the upbringing and education of children under their control." Justice James C. McReynolds, writing for the Court, explained that "rights guaranteed by the Constitution may not be abridged by legislation which has no reasonable relation to some purpose within the competency of the state."

This decision has since become a focal point for vigorous judicial debate over the application of the Ninth Amendment as authority for the invalidation of state legislation in such areas as contraceptive, abortion, and homosexual rights. That amendment states: "The enumeration in the Constitution, of certain rights, shall not be construed to deny or disparage others retained by the people." One judicial view, espoused by Justices Arthur Goldberg and William Brennan, is that the Ninth Amendment clearly implies that there are other rights, not specifically set forth in the Bill of Rights, which are protected from government infringement and that the Court may therefore strike down state legislation deemed to infringe upon such other rights as might be subsumed under the liberty clause.

An opposing view expresses alarm that the Ninth Amendment, adopted by the states as a means of ensuring that the federal government did not exceed its limited and enumerated powers, might be used in a way to expand federal veto power over state legislation. As Justice Potter Stewart stated in his dissenting opinion in *Griswold v. Connecticut* (1965), "The Ninth Amendment was passed, not to broaden the powers of this Court . . . but . . . to limit the federal government."

The former view has prevailed in cases such as *Roe v. Wade* (1973), in which the Court, upholding a woman's right to an abortion, cited *Pierce v. Society of Sisters* for the proposition that personal rights that can be deemed "implicit in the concept of ordered liberty" are guaranteed by the Constitution. In *Bowers v. Hardwick* (1986), however, the Court narrowly declined to find the freedom to engage in homosexual conduct as a right subsumed under the Fourteenth Amendment.

Robert M. Hardaway

See also *Bowers v. Hardwick*; *Griswold v. Connecticut*; *Wisconsin v. Yoder.*

===

PLANNED PARENTHOOD OF CENTRAL MISSOURI V. DANFORTH

Court: U.S. Supreme Court
Citation: 428 U.S. 52
Date: July 1, 1976
Issues: Parental rights; Reproductive rights; Right to privacy; Women's issues

- The Court ruled that states cannot require a spouse's consent for an abortion and upheld the right of minors to receive abortions without parental consent.

In June of 1974, the Missouri Abortion Act was passed. It required a woman to sign a consent form prior to abortion, spousal consent for abortions, and parental consent for abortions for minors. It also required that physicians make every effort to preserve the life of viable fetuses and prohibited the use of saline amniocentesis as a method of abortion. Planned Parenthood of Central Missouri filed a suit on behalf of itself, women seeking abortions, and physicians who perform abortions. The defendant was John Danforth, attorney general of Missouri. The U.S. District Court, Eastern Missouri, upheld most of the provisions of the law, leading to the case's appeal to the U.S. Supreme Court.

The Supreme Court, in a 5-4 decision, overturned the law's central provisions. It ruled that the law did not provide adequate definition of viability and, further, that the restrictions on physicians placed improper legal constraints in an area that was a matter of medical judgment. Drawing on its *Roe v. Wade* (1973) decision, the Court struck down the prohibition of saline amniocentesis as a method of abortion, following its earlier ruling permitting restriction on abortion methods during the second trimester only on the grounds of health risks to the mother. It found no serious health threats to maternal life from this procedure.

The Court also ruled that requiring parental consent for minors was improper, since such consent was not legally required for other medical procedures. Significantly, it argued that rights do not emerge at a certain age but that competent minors already have a "right to privacy" that assures them access to abortion. Its most far-reaching decision involved the denial of a right of spousal consent for abortion. The Court ruled that the woman's right to privacy takes precedence over any claims that others may have.

The minority opinion objected that the state's interest in developing fetal life, as articulated in *Roe v. Wade*, permitted states to require physicians to attempt to save viable fetal life. It also argued that the *Roe* decision did not establish an absolute right to abortion. Consequently, they supported provisions for spousal consent in cases where the spouse was willing to assume the burden of care for the child. Similarly, they indicated that parental consent for minors would be acceptable if there was provision for court intervention in the case of conflict or for court permission in lieu of parental consent in potentially abusive family situations. This last provision has been enacted in a number of subsequent state laws and upheld by the Court.

Charles L. Kammer

See also *Akron v. Akron Center for Reproductive Health; Bigelow v. Virginia; Doe v. Bolton; Harris v. McRae; Maher v. Roe; Roe v. Wade; Rust v. Sullivan; Thornburgh v. American College of Obstetricians and Gynecologists; Webster v. Reproductive Health Services.*

PLANNED PARENTHOOD OF SOUTHEASTERN PENNSYLVANIA V. CASEY

Court: U.S. Supreme Court
Citation: 505 U.S. 833
Date: June 29, 1992
Issues: Reproductive rights; Right to privacy; Women's issues

• The U.S. Supreme Court reaffirmed its holding in *Roe v. Wade* (1973) that the constitutional right of privacy protects a woman's right to choose to have an abortion before the fetus she is carrying becomes viable; a controlling plurality of the Court also determined that regulations making it more difficult for a woman to obtain an abortion will be upheld as long as they do not unduly burden the woman's decision to terminate her pregnancy.

Five medical clinics and one physician challenged the constitutionality of certain provisions of the Pennsylvania Abortion Control Act, which restricted access to abortion services. The Supreme Court, however, could not reach a consensus on the appropriate standard of review to apply to these regulations. Three justices wrote a joint opinion upholding all but one of the challenged provisions on the grounds that they did not unduly burden the right to have an abortion. Four other justices, arguing that the Constitution does not recognize a right to have an abortion, concurred in that result. Thus, seven justices voted to uphold the following abortion regulations: Prior to obtaining her informed consent to surgery, physicians must provide a woman seeking to have an abortion with specific information about the nature of an abortion, the risks associated with this medical procedure, and the gestational age of the fetus. A woman must wait twenty-four hours after receiving this information before she can obtain an abortion. A woman under the age of eighteen may not obtain an abortion without either the informed consent of one of her parents or the determination by a court that the woman is mature enough to make this decision for herself or that having an abortion is in her best interests.

The three-justice plurality struck down as unduly burdensome a regulation prohibiting a married woman from obtaining an abortion unless she first notifies her spouse of her decision to terminate her pregnancy. Two other justices, who argued that all abortion regulations should be strictly scrutinized, concurred in declaring this provision unconstitutional.

The Court's decision in *Casey*, particularly the plurality opinion of Justices David Souter, Anthony Kennedy, and Sandra Day O'Connor, appeared to reflect a constitutional compromise on the abortion issue. On the one hand, the right to have an abortion was explicitly affirmed by a majority of the Court out of respect for *stare decisis*, the obligation of judges to respect past precedent, if for no other reason. Under the authority of *Casey*, any law attempting to criminalize abortion, as many state laws did prior to the Court's decision in *Roe v. Wade* in 1973, would be declared unconstitutional on its face.

On the other hand, the "undue burden" standard applied by the plurality to determine the constitutionality of abortion regulations in *Casey* represented a significant retreat from the trimester framework and rigorous review the Court had applied during the twenty-year period after *Roe* was decided. Unlike the old approach, under which virtually any regulation of abortion during the first two trimesters of the gestation period would be struck down, regulations that increased the cost of having an abortion after *Casey* would be upheld unless plaintiffs challenging their constitutionality could demonstrate the severity of the resulting burden on a woman's right to choose to terminate her pregnancy.

This new standard of review not only was more lenient than its predecessor, but also seemed more ambiguous in its meaning and less predictable in its application. The plurality opinion in *Casey* defined an undue burden as "shorthand for the conclusion that a state regulation has the purpose or effect of placing a substantial obstacle in the path of a woman seeking an abortion of a nonviable fetus." Exactly what constituted a substantial-enough burden to justify a court's invalidating an abortion regulation remained unclear. The plurality's language left unanswered many important questions that could only be resolved by further litigation and additional judicial decisions.

Notwithstanding this criticism, the Court's decision in *Casey* did resolve one important constitutional question in unambiguous terms. The core holding of *Roe v. Wade* was not overruled. As the plurality stated emphatically, "a State may not prohibit any woman from making the ultimate decision to terminate her pregnancy before viability."

Alan E. Brownstein

See also *Akron v. Akron Center for Reproductive Health; Bigelow v. Virginia; Doe v. Bolton; Maher v. Roe; Planned Parenthood of Central Missouri v. Danforth; Roe v. Wade; Rust v. Sullivan; Thornburgh v. American College of Obstetricians and Gynecologists; Webster v. Reproductive Health Services.*

Plessy v. Ferguson

Court: U.S. Supreme Court
Citation: 163 U.S. 537
Date: May 18, 1896
Issues: Civil rights and liberties; Equal protection of the law;
Racial discrimination

- One of the most notorious decisions in the history of the U.S. Supreme Court, *Plessy v. Ferguson* not only upheld racial segregation in the United States, but it also lent the sanction of the Supreme Court and created the contentious doctrine of separate but equal that a later Court would eventually overturn as a self-contradiction.

On July 10, 1890, the Louisiana General Assembly, over the objection of its eighteen African American members, enacted a law that read, in part:

> . . . all railway companies carrying passengers in their coaches in this state shall provide equal but separate accommodations for the white and colored races, by providing two or more passenger coaches for each passenger train, or by dividing the passenger coaches by a partition so as to secure separate accommodations.

The Louisiana law empowered train officials to assign passengers to cars; passengers insisting on going into a car set aside for the other race were liable to a twenty-five-dollar fine and twenty days' imprisonment. In addition, the company could refuse to carry an obstreperous passenger and, if it were sued for doing so, was immune from damages in state courts. A third section outlined the penalties for noncomplying railroads and provided that "nothing in this act shall be construed as applying to nurses attending children of the other race."

At first the Separate Car Bill was stymied by the black legislators and by railroad officials who were as anxious to avoid the economic burden of providing separate facilities as they were to avoid a boycott of irate black passengers. After the black legislators had helped to override the veto of a major lottery bill, however, the legislature revived the Separate Car Bill and enacted it by a safe margin.

After its enactment, some of the railroad companies were inclined to disregard the law, and they apparently collaborated with black people to test its validity. In 1890, the railroads had unsuccessfully challenged a Mississippi separate but equal law; the Supreme Court of the United States had held in *Louisville, New Orleans, and Texas Railway Co. v. Mississippi* that such a law, when applied solely to travel within the state, did not encroach upon interstate commerce.

The prominent black community of New Orleans organized to mount a legal attack upon the new law. A group calling itself the Citizens' Committee to Test the Constitutionality of the Separate Car Law, led by Louis A. Martinet and Alexander A. Mary, organized to handle the litigation and enlisted the services of Albion Winegar Tourgée. Tourgée was to serve as chief counsel and devote his considerable talents to rallying public opposition to the Jim Crow system typified by the Louisiana law. The new counsel had served as a classical carpetbagger in North Carolina during Reconstruction and, among other accomplishments, had published a number of novels about the Reconstruction era, among them *A Fools Errand* (1879), *An Appeal to Caesar* (1884), and *Bricks Without Straw* (1880).

Louisiana Court Decision

Martinet engaged James Walker to assist in handling the Louisiana phase of the controversy. Before the first test of the Louisiana law (also featuring an African American who could "pass for white") could be settled, the Louisiana Supreme Court decided in *State ex rel. Abbott v. Hicks* (1892) that the 1890 law could not be applied to interstate travelers since it was an unconstitutional regulation of interstate commerce. The *Plessy* case, then, redefined the question raised in the 1890 Mississippi railroad case, but as a problem in the constitutional law of civil liberties rather than one of interstate commerce.

The person recruited to test the segregation law was Homer Adolph Plessy, a person of seven-eighths Caucasian and one-eighth African ancestry, in whom "the mixture of colored blood was not discernible." On June 7, 1892, holding a first-class ticket entitling him to travel on the East Louisiana Railway from New Orleans to Covington, Louisiana, Plessy took a seat in the car reserved for whites. The conductor, assisted by a policeman, forcibly removed Plessy and, charging him with violating the segregation law, placed him in the parish jail. The state prosecuted Plessy in the Orleans Parish criminal district court before Judge John H. Ferguson. Plessy's plea that the law was unconstitutional was overruled by Ferguson, who directed the defense to address itself to the questions of fact. Having no defense in the facts, Tourgée and Walker appealed Ferguson's ruling on the law's constitutionality to the Louisiana Supreme Court by asking that court to issue a writ of prohibition, which in effect would have directed Ferguson to reverse his ruling on the constitutional question.

On December 19, 1892, Associate Justice Charles E. Fenner of the Louisi-

Justices of Melville W. Fuller's Court who ruled in Plessy v. Ferguson. (Library of Congress)

ana Supreme Court ruled the law constitutional in an opinion that served as a model for that written later by Justice Henry B. Brown of the U.S. Supreme Court. After a delay of almost four years—a delay that Tourgée encouraged on the grounds that it gave the opponents of segregation needed time—the U.S. Supreme Court heard the arguments in Plessy's case on April 13, 1896. On May 18, 1896, Justice Brown handed down the majority opinion, supported by six other justices (Justice David Brewer did not participate, and Justice John Marshall Harlan dissented).

Justice Brown first disposed of Tourgée's argument that the segregation law was a "badge of servitude," a vestige of slavery prohibited by the Thirteenth Amendment (1865). Decisions in the 1872 *Slaughterhouse Cases* and the 1883 *Civil Rights Cases*, wrote Brown, indicated that it was because the Thirteenth Amendment barred only outright slavery, and not laws merely imposing "onerous disabilities and burdens," that the movement for the Fourteenth Amendment had been successful. Later in his opinion, Brown blended the "badge of servitude" argument of the Thirteenth Amendment with his treatment of the equal protection question:

> We consider the underlying fallacy of the plaintiff's argument to consist in the assumption that the enforced separation of the two races

stamps the colored race with a badge of inferiority. If this be so, it is not by reason of anything found in the act, but solely because the colored race chooses to put that construction upon it.

If the plaintiff was to gain any relief, it had to be from the Fourteenth Amendment, but that amendment, according to Brown

> merely . . . enforced the absolute equality of the two races before the law, but in the nature of things it could not have been intended to abolish distinctions based upon color, or to enforce social, as distinguished from political, equality, or a commingling of the two races upon terms unsatisfactory to either.

To support his point, Brown cited state school segregation and antimiscegenation laws and federal laws prescribing segregated schools for the District of Columbia. Special stress was placed on the 1849 decision of *Roberts v. Boston*, in which Chief Justice Lemuel Shaw of the Massachusetts Supreme Judicial Court had upheld the constitutionality of separate but equal schools for Boston. Brown did not mention that the Massachusetts legislature had repudiated Shaw's doctrine in 1855.

To the plaintiff's argument that the principle of segregation could be used by the state to enforce extreme and arbitrary forms of racial discrimination, Brown responded that every exercise of state power must be "reasonable, and extend only to such laws as are enacted in good faith for the promotion of the public good, and not for the annoyance or oppression of a particular class." There was nothing unreasonable about the Louisiana law according to the Court; in determining what is reasonable, state legislators could "act with reference to the established usages, customs, and traditions of the people, with a view to the promotion of their comfort, and the preservation of the public peace and good order." Finally, Brown in his opinion delivered a famous statement on the relationship between law, prejudice, and equality:

> The [plaintiff's] argument also assumes that social prejudice may be overcome by legislation, and that equal rights cannot be secured to the negro except by an enforced commingling of the two races. We cannot accept this proposition. If the two races are to meet on terms of social equality, it must be the result of natural affinities, a mutual appreciation of each other's merits, and a voluntary consent of individuals.

The law in question interfered with the "voluntary consent of individuals."

Sanctioning Segregation

Tourgée's fears were realized: The Court had sanctioned Jim Crowism. What comfort African Americans derived from the case had to be found in the strong dissenting opinion of Justice Harlan, who once again proved himself to be a staunch champion of a broad interpretation of the Reconstruction amendments. Harlan construed the ban on slavery to cover segregation laws; he insisted on Tourgée's thesis that a railroad was a public highway and that under the Fourteenth Amendment, government could make no racial distinctions—whether one considered the case under the privileges and immunities, due process, or equal protection clauses of that amendment.

Harlan attacked the Court's reliance on pre-Fourteenth Amendment precedents; his most memorable language appeared in connection with his charge that the majority usurped constitutional power by assuming authority to decide on the "reasonableness" of state social legislation:

> The white race deems itself to be the dominant race in this country. And so it is, in prestige, in achievements, in education, in wealth, and in power. So, I doubt not that it will continue to be for all time, if it remains true to its great heritage and holds fast to the principles of constitutional liberty. But in view of the Constitution, in the eye of the law, there is in this country no superior, dominant, ruling class of citizens. There is no caste here. Our Constitution is color-blind, and neither knows nor tolerates classes among citizens. In respect of civil rights, all citizens are equal before the law.

Harlan turned out to be a competent soothsayer:

> The destinies of the two races in this country are indissolubly linked together, and the interests of both require that the common government of all shall not permit the seeds of race hate to be planted under the sanction of law.

Significance

Despite Harlan's impassioned words, it would take the general public and the justices of the Supreme Court decades to adopt his views and interpretation of the Constitution. *Plessy v. Ferguson*'s strong sanction of segregation lasted formally in transportation until the Court's decision in *Henderson v. United States* (1950) and in education until *Brown v. Board of Education of Topeka, Kansas* (1954). Antimiscegenation laws were not outlawed until 1967 in *Loving v. Virginia.*

James J. Bolner, updated by Brian L. Fife

Further Reading

Axelrod-Contrada, Joan. *Plessy v. Ferguson: Separate But Unequal.* Tarrytown, N.Y.: Marshall Cavendish Benchmark, 2009. Part of its publisher's Supreme Court Milestones series designed for young-adult readers, this volume offers an accessible history and analysis of the *Plessy* case that examines opposing sides in the case, the people involved, and the case's lasting impact. Includes bibliography and index.

Fireside, Harvey. *Separate and Unequal: Homer Plessy and the Supreme Court Decision That Legalized Racism.* New York: Carroll & Graf, 2004. A detailed look at the legacy of the Court's decision in *Plessy v. Ferguson.*

Kauper, Paul G. "Segregation in Public Education: The Decline of *Plessy v. Ferguson.*" *Michigan Law Review* 52 (1954): 1137-1158. Kauper contends that the Court did not deal definitively with the validity of segregation legislation, relying instead on its view of "reasonableness."

Lofgren, Charles A. *The Plessy Case: A Legal-Historical Interpretation.* New York: Oxford University Press, 1987. In tracing the history of transportation law, Lofgren concludes that *Plessy* did not cause Jim Crow but instead confirmed the American racism of its era.

Mueller, Jean West, and Wynell Burroughs Schamel. "*Plessy v. Ferguson* Mandate." *Social Education* 53 (1989): 120-122. Traces the historical events leading to the Court's ruling and provides teaching strategies for instructors.

Rasmussen, R. Kent. *Farewell to Jim Crow: The Rise and Fall of Segregation in America.* New York: Facts On File, 1997. Accessible history of the origins of American segregation and the legal struggle to abolish it.

Roche, John P. "*Plessy v. Ferguson:* Requiescat in Pace?" *University of Pennsylvania Law Review* 103 (1954): 44-58. Roche believes that the *Plessy* decision reflected the political climate of its time and was a judicial attempt to deal with a social and political problem.

Woodward, C. Vann. *American Counterpoint: Slavery and Racism in the North-South Dialogue.* Boston: Little, Brown, 1971. Woodward discusses the irony of Justice Brown's and Harlan's positions, in the light of the origins of the two men.

See also *Brown v. Board of Education; Civil Rights Cases; Lau v. Nichols; Louisville, New Orleans, and Texas Railway Co. v. Mississippi; Loving v. Virginia; Swann v. Charlotte-Mecklenburg Board of Education; Sweatt v. Painter.*

Plyler v. Doe

Court: U.S. Supreme Court
Citation: 457 U.S. 202
Date: June 15, 1982
Issues: Citizenship; Education; Equal protection of the law; Immigration; Judicial review

- The U.S. Supreme Court extended the equal protection clause of the Fourteenth Amendment to the U.S. Constitution to guarantee the right of noncitizens to public social services.

In May, 1975, the Texas legislature enacted a law that denied financial support for the public education of the children of undocumented aliens. The state's local school districts, accordingly, were allowed to exclude such children from public school enrollment. The children of noncitizen aliens who henceforth paid for their public school education still were permitted to enroll. Despite the statute, Texas public school districts continued enrolling the children of undocumented aliens until 1977-1978, when, amid a continuing economic recession and accompanying budget tightening, the law was enforced. An initial challenge to the 1975 law arose in the Tyler Independent School District in Smith County, located in northeastern Texas, but similar challenges in other school districts soon produced a class-action suit.

The problem that had inspired the state law was the massive influx—principally of Mexicans but also of persons from Central American countries—into Texas, as well as into New Mexico, Arizona, and California. Some of these people entered the United States for seasonal agricultural jobs, while others, undocumented, remained. Most were poor and seeking economic opportunities unavailable to them in Mexico and Central America. Figures released by the U.S. Immigration and Naturalization Service estimated that when the *Plyler v. Doe* case arose, between two and three million undocumented aliens resided in Texas and other southwestern portions of the United States. Texas claimed that 5 percent of its population, three-quarters of a million people, were undocumented aliens, roughly twenty thousand of whose children were enrolled in Texas public schools. With recession adversely affecting employment, many of the state's taxpayers asked why they should bear the financial burdens of educating illegal aliens, as well as providing them with other benefits, such as food stamps and welfare payments.

The Court's Ruling

On June 15, 1982, on behalf of the U.S. Supreme Court's majority, Associate Justice William J. Brennan declared that the 1975 Texas statute rationally served no substantial state interest and violated the equal protection clause of the Fourteenth Amendment. Ratified along with the Thirteenth and Fifteenth Amendments during the post-Civil War Reconstruction era, the Fourteenth Amendment guaranteed "that no State shall . . . deny to any person within its jurisdiction the equal protection of the laws." Although the overriding concern of Reconstruction politicians, judges, and states in ratifying the Fourteenth Amendment was to afford protection to newly emancipated African Americans, the equal protection clause increasingly had been interpreted to mean what it stated: guaranteeing equal protection of the laws to any person—precisely the line of reasoning taken by Brennan. Brennan and the Court majority likewise disagreed with the Texas argument that undocumented aliens did not fall "within its jurisdiction," thus excluding them and their children from Fourteenth Amendment guarantees. Such an exclusion, Brennan declared, condemned innocents to a lifetime of hardship and the stigma of illiteracy.

The Supreme Court's 5-4 decision in *Plyler v. Doe* upheld a previous decision by the U.S. Fifth Circuit Court that had ruled for the plaintiffs. Chief Justice Warren E. Burger vigorously dissented from the majority opinion, along with Justices Byron White, William H. Rehnquist, and Sandra Day O'Connor.

Significance

The *Plyler* decision was novel in two important respects. It was the first decision to extend Fourteenth Amendment guarantees irrespective of a person's citizenship or immigration status. Second, the Court majority introduced a new criterion for determining the applicability of Fourteenth Amendment protections: the doctrine of heightened or intermediate scrutiny. The Court avoided applying its previous standard of strict scrutiny. It recognized that education is not a fundamental right and that undocumented aliens are not, as it had previously phrased it, a "suspect class," in the sense that they, like African Americans, historically had been victims of racial discrimination. Heightened scrutiny was warranted, Brennan and the majority agreed, because of education's special importance to other social benefits and because children of undocumented aliens are not responsible for their status.

Chief Justice Burger and the three other dissenting, generally conservative, justices, all staunch advocates of judicial restraint, strongly criticized Brennan and the majority for what the dissenters considered to be arguing political opinions instead of adhering to sound jurisprudence. The dissenters seriously questioned heightened scrutiny as a viable judicial standard and found that the Texas statute substantially furthered the state's legitimate interests.

The *Plyler* decision represented a significant departure from the decision rendered by Chief Justice Roger Brooke Taney in *Scott v. Sandford* (1857), a decision that the Fourteenth Amendment was designed in part to nullify. *Plyler*'s heightened standard of scrutiny, however, continued to be controversial and confusing, both within the Supreme Court and among legal observers. The issue of the applicability of the equal protection clause to cases not involving racial discrimination had been raised in *Buck v. Bell* (1927), when Justice Oliver Wendell Holmes, Jr., denounced such decision making as "the usual last resort of constitutional arguments."

In *Plyler*, Brennan and the majority saw no chance to apply the Court's already accepted classification of strict scrutiny to equal protection cases, because *Plyler*'s plaintiffs, the undocumented aliens, were not victims of institutionalized racial discrimination or of "reverse discrimination." They were illegal immigrants as a consequence of their own conscious actions. Nevertheless, as legal scholars observed, in order to prevent hardship and stigmas from afflicting schoolchildren—who were not responsible for their parents' actions—the *Plyler* majority introduced an intermediate level of classification with their standard of heightened scrutiny. Such a standard raised questions about whether undocumented aliens and their families enjoyed rights to other government benefits, such as welfare assistance, medical care, and food stamps.

Clifton K. Yearley

Further Reading

Aleinikoff, Thomas A., David A. Martin, and Hiroshi Motomura. *Immigration and Citizenship: Process and Policy.* 5th ed. St. Paul, Minn.: Thomson/West, 2003. A careful review of modern U.S. immigration policies. Discusses the problems posed by undocumented aliens and the difficulties faced by government policy makers in coping with undocumented people.

Bankston, Carl L., III, ed. *Encyclopedia of American Immigration.* 3 vols. Pasadena, Calif.: Salem Press, 2010. Comprehensive reference source on all aspects of American immigration history, with articles on individual laws, court cases, events, immigrant groups, and other subjects, including rights of noncitizens in the United States. Profusely illustrated with photographs, maps, charts, and graphs. Extensive appendix materials and bibliographical notes in every article.

Blasi, Vincent, ed. *The Burger Court.* New Haven, Conn.: Yale University Press, 1983. An authoritative yet readable analysis of the chief justiceship of Warren Burger, which did little to modify civil rights decisions of his predecessors. Also clarifies Brennan's attitudes and decisions.

Curtis, Michael Kent. *No State Shall Abridge: The Fourteenth Amendment and the Bill of Rights.* Durham, N.C.: Duke University Press, 1986. Provides clear, scholarly exposition of the role played by the Fourteenth Amendment and the Bill of Rights in modern U.S. jurisprudence, including civil and criminal rights, racial and reverse discrimination, and interpretations of due process.

Hull, Elizabeth. *Without Justice for All.* Westport, Conn.: Greenwood Press, 1985. A precise study bearing on the problems raised in *Plyler*, the historical plight of resident and illegal aliens and their families, and the varying status of their constitutional rights.

Mirandé, Alfredo. *Gringo Justice.* Notre Dame, Ind.: University of Notre Dame Press, 1990. A spirited, dismaying critique of U.S. judicial and political treatment of Hispanic immigrants by both the states and the federal government. Provides excellent context for understanding important aspects of the *Plyler* case.

Nelson, William E. *The Fourteenth Amendment: From Political Principle to Judicial Doctrine.* Cambridge, Mass.: Harvard University Press, 1988. An authoritative analysis of the evolution of the Fourteenth Amendment from a set of political principles to a vital part of twentieth century judicial decision making. Good analyses of the Supreme Court's standards of scrutiny, including the intermediate or "heightened" scrutiny applied in *Plyler*.

Soltero, Carlos R. *Latinos and American Law: Landmark Supreme Court Cases.* Austin: University of Texas Press, 2006. Survey of important Supreme Court cases, including *Plyler v. Doe*, that have impacted Hispanic Americans.

See also *Buck v. Bell; Graham v. Richardson; Scott v. Sandford.*

POINTER V. TEXAS

Court: U.S. Supreme Court
Citation: 380 U.S. 400
Date: April 5, 1965
Issues: Incorporation doctrine

- The U.S. Supreme Court applied the Sixth Amendment right of the accused to confront witnesses to the states through the incorporation doctrine.

An attorney for Pointer objected to the use during his trial of a transcript containing the testimony of a robbery victim who had moved out of state. The testimony was taken at a preliminary hearing in which Pointer was present but without counsel. Pointer was convicted largely on the basis of this transcript. Justice Hugo L. Black wrote the unanimous opinion for the Court, which overturned Pointer's conviction. The Court found that the Sixth Amendment's guarantee to the accused of the right to confront witnesses is so fundamental that it applies to the states through incorporation under the Fourteenth Amendment's due process clause. Justices Arthur J. Goldberg, John M. Harlan II, and Potter Stewart concurred separately.

Richard L. Wilson

See also *Counselman v. Hitchcock; Goldberg v. Kelly; In re Gault; Maryland v. Craig.*

POLLOCK V. FARMERS' LOAN AND TRUST CO.

Court: U.S. Supreme Court
Citation: 157 U.S. 429
Date: April 8, 1895, reheard and redecided on May 20, 1895
Issues: State sovereignty; Taxation

- In one of the most controversial decisions of the late nineteenth century, the U.S. Supreme Court ruled a peacetime federal income tax unconstitutional.

In the first decision, Chief Justice Melville W. Fuller wrote the opinion for the Supreme Court, which was unanimous 8-0 on one part, divided 6-2 on a second part, and tied 4-4 on a third part. Terminally ill Justice Howell E. Jackson did not participate in the first decision but traveled to Washington, D.C., to participate in the second decision. In the first decision, Justice Stephen J. Field concurred with Fuller; and Justice Edward D. White and Justices John

Justice George Shiras, Jr.
(Library of Congress)

Marshall Harlan, Henry B. Brown, and George Shiras, Jr., dissented. In the second decision, Fuller again wrote the opinion for the 5-4 majority, facing dissents from White, Harlan, Brown, and Jackson. Jackson's participation in the rehearing should have led to the upholding of the federal income tax, but apparently Shiras switched sides, and the Court struck down the tax.

At issue was the constitutionality of the 1894 income tax law, a statute imposing the first income tax that was not a wartime measure. The Court could have avoided hearing the case on the grounds that it was not a true case and controversy because the plaintiff was suing his bank to keep it from paying an income tax that it had no desire to pay anyway. However, instead of ducking the issue, the Court expedited the hearing of the case. The plaintiff's argument was more emotional and political than legal because the Court had already upheld a wartime income tax. The plaintiff argued that the income tax was a direct tax in contravention of the Constitution, but this position contradicted precedents in that the Court had long held that a direct tax was very narrowly construed. Other arguments—such as the contention that the income tax was a tax on the state and, therefore, a violation of state sovereignty—were asserted by the Court in the first decision but abandoned in the second decision, which rested mainly on the argument that the income tax was a direct tax that could be constitutionally valid only if apportioned according to the states' populations. This was an obvious impossibility. For all the controversy, this decision was set aside by the Sixteenth Amendment, which explicitly authorized an income tax; the case remains useful to show the laissez-faire point of view of the late nineteenth century Court regarding the Constitution.

Richard L. Wilson

See also *Graves v. New York ex rel. O'Keefe*; *Hylton v. United States*; *Springer v. United States.*

POWELL V. ALABAMA

Court: U.S. Supreme Court
Citation: 287 U.S. 45
Date: November 7, 1932
Issues: Capital punishment; Due process of law; Right to counsel

• The Court ruled that the concept of due process requires states to provide effective counsel in capital cases when indigent defendants are unable to represent themselves.

In 1931, Ozie Powell and eight other black youths whose ages ranged from twelve to nineteen, afterward known as the "Scottsboro boys," were tried and convicted before an all-white jury in Scottsboro, Alabama, charged with having raped two white women while traveling on a freight train. Although the Alabama constitution required the appointment of counsel for indigents accused of capital crimes, no lawyer was definitely appointed to represent the defendants until the day of their trial.

An atmosphere of racial hostility influenced the proceedings, and after a trial lasting one day, seven of the youths were sentenced to death, while the two youngest were transferred to the juvenile authorities. The trial attracted considerable attention, so that procommunist lawyers of the International Labor Defense volunteered to represent the young men on appeal. After the Alabama Supreme Court affirmed the convictions, the U.S. Supreme Court granted review.

The Court voted seven to two to reverse the conviction and to remand the case to Alabama for a new trial. Writing for the majority, Justice George Sutherland did not speak of the Sixth Amendment, which had not yet been made applicable to the states, but, he instead asked whether the defendants had been denied the right of counsel, contrary to the due process clause of the Fourteenth Amendment.

Sutherland noted that from the time of arraignment to the time of the trial, the defendants had not had "the aid of counsel in any real sense." The right to be heard implied the right to be heard with the assistance of counsel, for even most educated and intelligent persons would not have the training or experience to represent themselves in a criminal trial. Sutherland was impressed with "the ignorance and illiteracy of the defendants" and with the "circumstances of public hostility." In this particular case, therefore, the failure of the trial court to make "an effective appointment of counsel" was a denial of due process within the meaning of the Fourteenth Amendment.

The Scottsboro case represented transitional steps in three important directions. First, the decision came very close to incorporating the right to counsel into the meaning of the Fourteenth Amendment, so that this portion of the Sixth Amendment would apply to the states. Second, it recognized that at least in capital cases, the state must provide counsel for indigents unable to defend themselves. Third, it included the provocative suggestion that the state had the obligation to provide "effective" assistance of counsel. These three issues would become increasingly important in subsequent cases.

Thomas Tandy Lewis

See also *Betts v. Brady*; *Escobedo v. Illinois*; *Miranda v. Arizona*.

POWELL V. MCCORMICK

Court: U.S. Supreme Court
Citation: 395 U.S. 486
Date: June 16, 1969
Issues: Congressional powers

• The U.S. Supreme Court limited the power of Congress to expel its members.

African American politician Adam Clayton Powell, Jr., was reelected to his seat in the House of Representatives. However, because of some allegations regarding misuse of congressional funds based on some improperly filed expense reports, Congress sought to block him from taking his seat in the House. The Supreme Court, by a 7-1 vote, ruled that the House of Representatives could not add to the qualifications of its members any criteria other than those set forth in the Constitution, all of which Powell met. Further, Congress could expel a member only by a two-thirds vote. Had Congress prevailed in this case, its members would have been able to circumvent the expulsion process in many cases.

Richard L. Wilson

See also *District of Columbia v. Heller; Presser v. Illinois; United States v. Lopez.*

POWERS V. OHIO

Court: U.S. Supreme Court
Citation: 499 U.S. 400
Date: April 1, 1991
Issues: Racial discrimination

- The U.S. Supreme Court held that prosecutors cannot use peremptory challenges to exclude African Americans from juries in criminal trials.

Justice Anthony M. Kennedy wrote the opinion for the 7-2 majority, holding that prosecutors cannot attempt to pack the jury with jurors racially satisfactory to themselves by using peremptory challenges in jury selection in criminal cases. Kennedy held that this was true even if the accused and the excluded juror were of different races. The past practice of allowing the use of peremptory challenges affected not only the defendant's right to a fair trial but also the excluded juror's right to participate in the administration of justice. The defendant further was entitled to raise the excluded juror's right at trial. Dissenting, Justice Antonin Scalia argued that this decision was illogical, freeing a guilty defendant based on the fact that some other person's abstract right to participate in the judicial process was denied.

Richard L. Wilson

See also *Batson v. Kentucky; Duncan v. Louisiana; Norris v. Alabama; Strauder v. West Virginia; Williams v. Mississippi.*

Presser v. Illinois

Court: U.S. Supreme Court
Citation: 116 U.S. 252
Date: January 4, 1886
Issues: Incorporation doctrine; Right to bear arms

- The U.S. Supreme Court upheld an Illinois law that prohibited parading with arms by any groups other than the organized militia.

After Herman Presser was convicted for leading a parade of armed members of a fraternal organization, he asserted that the law violated the rights protected by the Second and Fourteenth Amendments. Writing for a unanimous Supreme Court, Justice William B. Woods held that the Second Amendment applied only to the federal government and not to the states. Woods also suggested in *dicta* (in an individual, nonbinding opinion) that the regulation in question did not appear to infringe on the right to keep and bear arms. *Presser* was never reversed. If the Court were to make the Second Amendment binding on the states, it is highly unlikely that this would preclude the states from making reasonable regulations to protect the public safety.

Thomas Tandy Lewis

Justice William B. Woods.
(Collection of the Supreme
Court of the United States)

See also *District of Columbia v. Heller; Hurley v. Irish-American Gay, Lesbian, and Bisexual Group of Boston; Powell v. McCormick; Village of Skokie v. National Socialist Party of America.*

PRIGG V. PENNSYLVANIA

Court: U.S. Supreme Court
Citation: 41 U.S. 539
Date: March 1, 1842
Issues: Federal supremacy; Regulation of commerce

• The U.S. Supreme Court held that slave owners had the constitutional right to take possession of their property, but state officials could not be required to assist their efforts.

In 1837 Edward Prigg, an agent of a Maryland slave owner, took possession of a runaway female slave in Pennsylvania. Because of the state's personal liberty law of 1826, he was not able to obtain legal authorization to remove the woman from the state, but he forcibly took her back to Maryland. After Pennsylvania indicted Prigg for kidnapping, the state of Maryland agreed to extradite him so that the Supreme Court might consider the legal issues of the case. Writing for an 8-1 majority, Justice Joseph Story made four rulings: First, the federal Fugitive Slave Law of 1793 was constitutional; second, the Pennsylvania personal liberty law was unconstitutional; third, the fugitive slave clause in the Constitution implied the right of slave owners to recapture runaway slaves; and fourth, the national government had no power to compel state officials to enforce federal law. Chief Justice Roger Brooke Taney, while joining with the rest of the opinion, disagreed with the fourth ruling.

Following the *Prigg* decision, some northern legislatures prohibited state officials from helping capture fugitive slaves or using state facilities for that purpose. Southern dissatisfaction with this situation contributed to the passage of the stringent Fugitive Slave Law of 1850.

Thomas Tandy Lewis

See also *Ableman v. Booth; Antelope, The; Groves v. Slaughter; Jones v. Van Zandt; Kentucky v. Dennison.*

PRINTZ V. UNITED STATES

Court: U.S. Supreme Court
Citation: 521 U.S. 898
Date: June 27, 1997
Issues: Right to bear arms; State sovereignty

- The U.S. Supreme Court held that a congressional statute intruded on the rights of the states when it required local law-enforcement officers to conduct background checks on prospective handgun purchasers.

Two law-enforcement officers, Sheriff Jay Printz of Montana and Sheriff Richard Mack of Arizona, challenged the constitutionality of a key provision of the Brady Handgun Violence Prevention Act of 1993. Speaking for a 5-4 majority, Justice Antonin Scalia held that Congress had no power to require the states to enforce a federal regulatory program absent a particularized constitutional authorization. Scalia argued that the Constitution established a system of dual sovereignty, and that the states, as an essential attribute of their retained sovereignty, are "independent and autonomous within their proper sphere of authority." In his dissent, Justice John Paul Stevens argued that the commerce clause authorized Congress to regulate interstate commerce in handguns and that nothing in the Tenth Amendment prohibits Congress from delegating enforcement to the states.

Although the *Printz* decision had many implications for federalism, it did not have much direct impact on the Brady bill. More than half the states had laws requiring background checks consistent with the federal statute, and the federal government was scheduled to conduct its own background checks on gun purchasers in late 1998.

Thomas Tandy Lewis

See also *District of Columbia v. Heller; National League of Cities v. Usery; United States v. Lopez.*

PRIZE CASES

Court: U.S. Supreme Court
Citation: 67 U.S. 635
Date: March 10, 1863
Issues: International law; Presidential powers; Regulation of commerce; Taxation; Warfare and terrorism

- Upholding President Abraham Lincoln's blockade of Confederate ports, the U.S. Supreme Court declared that the president had a great deal of flexibility when responding to emergency situations.

In April, 1861, President Abraham Lincoln declared that the actions of Southern states had created a state of insurrection and ordered the blockade and the seizure of ships doing business with the Confederacy. Although Congress later endorsed Lincoln's actions, it did not issue a declaration of war. The *Prize Cases* dealt with whether the government had legitimate claims over the foreign vessels seized under the blockade. The key issue was whether the

Justice Robert C. Grier.
(Handy Studios/
Collection of the
Supreme Court of
the United States)

blockade was legal according to the Constitution and the principles of international law.

Writing for a 5-4 majority, Justice Robert C. Grier wrote that the president was "bound to accept the challenge" of a domestic insurrection without waiting for any special legislative authorization. Faced with such a military emergency, it was up to the president, not to the Supreme Court, to decide what kinds of military measures were necessary. Grier also noted that Congress had subsequently ratified Lincoln's actions. In regard to international law, he found that the blockade was evidence that "a state of war existed." Thus, his opinion allowed the Union government to treat the conflict as an international war, without formally recognizing the existence of the Confederate government. The four justices in the minority insisted that the president had no power to proclaim a blockade without a congressional declaration of war.

The Court's decision in the *Prize Cases* gave the president a great deal of power to formulate and execute policies in a time of crisis. For domestic purposes, Lincoln could deal with the Civil War (1861-1865) as an insurrection, and he could announce to other countries that the Confederacy was a belligerent that could be legally blockaded. The Court's theory of the war appeared to justify Lincoln's other controversial measures, such as the suspension of habeas corpus and the Emancipation Proclamation.

Thomas Tandy Lewis

See also *Dames and Moore v. Regan*; *Goldwater v. Carter*; *McCulloch v. Maryland*; *Mississippi v. Johnson*; *Myers v. United States*; *United States v. Curtiss-Wright Export Corp.*; *Wiener v. United States*; *Youngstown Sheet and Tube Co. v. Sawyer.*

PROVIDENCE BANK V. BILLINGS

Court: U.S. Supreme Court
Citation: 29 U.S. 514
Date: March 22, 1830
Issues: Freedom of contract

- The U.S. Supreme Court limited the amount of protection granted to corporate charters under the contracts clause.

Rhode Island granted a bank charter to Providence Bank in 1791 and in 1822 sought to impose a tax on the capital stock of all banks including Providence, which claimed it was exempt because no tax was included in its charter. Providence claimed protection under the contracts clause of Article I of the Constitution, but the Supreme Court, by a 7-0 vote, held that the contracts clause protected only explicit contractual commitments. In his opinion for the Court, Chief Justice John Marshall wrote that because taxing was so basic to all governments, the government could not have been expected to abdicate its right to tax without making an explicit provision in a charter or contract. This view of strictly construed contracts was further developed in *Charles River Bridge v. Warren Bridge* (1837).

Richard L. Wilson

See also *Charles River Bridge v. Warren Bridge*; *Dartmouth College v. Woodward*; *McCulloch v. Maryland*.

PRUDENTIAL INSURANCE CO. V. BENJAMIN

Court: U.S. Supreme Court
Citation: 328 U.S. 408
Date: June 3, 1946
Issues: Regulation of commerce

• The U.S. Supreme Court upheld a state law when a congressional enactment explicitly delegated the right to regulate a federal activity to the states.

By an 8-0 vote, the Supreme Court upheld a South Carolina statute that imposed a tax on insurance premiums for policies written in South Carolina by foreign (out-of-state) insurance companies, but not on policies written by domestic companies. Prudential, a New Jersey company, sued, asserting that the South Carolina law interfered with an interstate commerce power that properly belonged to the federal government. Although supported by the Court's decisions in *United States v. South-Eastern Underwriters Association* (1944) and *Cooley v. Board of Wardens of the Port of Philadelphia* (1852), Prudential did not prevail because Congress had explicitly granted the right to regulate insurance to the states and not simply remained silent in the face of a state-based intrusion, as it had in previous cases.

Richard L. Wilson

See also *Allgeyer v. Louisiana; Cooley v. Board of Wardens of the Port of Philadelphia; Paul v. Virginia; United States v. South-Eastern Underwriters Association.*

Quirin, Ex parte. *See* Ex parte Quirin

R.A.V. v. City of St. Paul

Court: U.S. Supreme Court
Citation: 505 U.S. 377
Date: June 22, 1992
Issues: Symbolic speech

- This holding, invalidating an ordinance which made it a crime to burn a cross to harass African Americans, demonstrates how the U.S. Supreme Court affords a preferred status to First Amendment free speech, even reprehensible speech.

During the early morning hours of June 21, 1990, "R.A.V."—an unnamed seventeen-year-old, self-described as a white supremacist—and several other teenagers burned a makeshift wooden cross on the front lawn of the only African American family in their St. Paul, Minnesota, neighborhood. They were prosecuted for disorderly conduct in juvenile court under the city's "bias-motivated crime ordinance," which prohibited cross burning along with other symbolic displays that "one knows" or should know would arouse "anger, alarm or resentment in others on the basis of race, color, creed, religion, or gender."

The state trial court ruled that this ordinance was unconstitutionally overbroad because it indiscriminately prohibited protected First Amendment speech as well as unprotected activity. The Supreme Court of Minnesota reversed the lower court's decision and upheld the ordinance, which it interpreted to prohibit only unprotected "fighting words," face-to-face insults which are likely to cause the person to whom the words are addressed to attack the speaker physically.

The U.S. Supreme Court ruled unanimously in favor of R.A.V. and invalidated the ordinance, but the justices did not agree in their reasoning. Stating that they found the cross-burning reprehensible, Justice Antonin Scalia, writing for the majority, nevertheless concluded that the ordinance was unconstitutional because it criminalized only specified "fighting words" based on the content of the hate message and, consequently, the government was choosing sides. He noted that the ordinance would prohibit a sign that attacked Roman Catholics but would not prohibit a second sign that attacked those who displayed such an anti-Catholic bias.

Four justices concurred in the ruling of unconstitutionality, but Justice Byron White's opinion sharply criticized the majority opinion for going too far to protect racist speech. He reasoned that the ordinance was overbroad because it made it a crime to cause another person offense, hurt feelings, or resentment and because these harms could be caused by protected First Amendment speech. Justices Harry Blackmun and John Paul Stevens also wrote separate opinions complaining that hate speech did not deserve constitutional protection.

This holding calls into question numerous, similar state laws designed to protect women and minorities from harassment and discrimination. Some of these individuals and groups may still invoke long-standing federal civil rights statutes, however, which carry severe criminal penalties of fines and imprisonment. In 1993, *R.A.V.*'s significance was called into question by the *Wisconsin v. Mitchell* decision upholding a state statute that increased the sentence for a crime of violence if the defendant targeted the victim because of the victim's race or other specified status.

Thomas E. Baker

See also *Virginia v. Black; Wisconsin v. Mitchell.*

REAPPORTIONMENT CASES

REYNOLDS V. SIMS;
WMCA V. LOMENZO;
MARYLAND COMMITTEE FOR FAIR
REPRESENTATION V. TAWES;
DAVIS V. MANN;
ROMAN V. SINOCK;
LUCAS V. FORTY-FOURTH GENERAL
ASSEMBLY OF COLORADO

Court: U.S. Supreme Court
Citations: 377 U.S. 533; 377 U.S. 633; 377 U.S. 656; 377 U.S. 678;
377 U.S. 695; 377 U.S. 713
Date: June 15, 1964
Issues: Reapportionment and redistricting

• The U.S. Supreme Court's rulings in these six landmark cases regarding state legislatures are the cornerstone of the reapportionment revolution.

These six decisions built on the Supreme Court's *Baker v. Carr* (1962) ruling that legislative reapportionment would no longer be considered a political question to be left to legislatures to decide but would be justiciable, or capable of litigation by the federal courts. Preliminary decisions include *Gray v. Sanders* (1963), which struck down the unequal Georgia county unit system for electing governors and first set out the principle of one person, one vote; and *Wesberry v. Sanders* (1964), in which the Court resolved questions of the reapportionment of U.S. House of Representatives seats within state boundaries on the same one-person, one-vote basis. In the *Reapportionment Cases*, the Court addressed reapportionment of state legislatures. This was the most central issue of reapportionment because state legislatures drew all the lines—their own and those for congressional seats. It was also the most complicated because of the variations in districting across the fifty states. This complexity was reflected in the six cases and the pattern of support and dissent in the justices' varying responses to them.

Chief Justice Earl Warren wrote the majority opinion in all six cases, which were decided by varying margins and dissents. In a way, Warren's simple response to the complexity—one person, one vote—may have been the only consistent way to deal with the myriad circumstances found in the states. Equally consistent was Justice John M. Harlan II, who dissented in all six cases. Earlier, Harlan had had the support of the late Justice Felix Frankfurter in opposing the Court's entrance into what Frankfurter called the "political thicket." However, on *Reynolds*, Harlan stood alone against the Court. Harlan's charge was answered by Warren, who wrote that the pervasive denial of effective representation was a denial of constitutionally protected rights demanding judicial protection. Indeed, the Court's logic after footnote 4 of *United States v. Carolene Products Co.* (1938) was that the Court was the only institution capable of correcting certain wrongs. Malapportioned districts were certainly such an issue, because one could not expect the beneficiaries of malapportionment to vote themselves out of representation if they were voters, or out of a job if they were state legislators.

As the Court moved away from the facts of *Reynolds*, the justices' positions became more complex. In the Virginia case (*Davis v. Mann*), both Justices Tom C. Clark and Potter Stewart concurred with Warren, and Harlan dissented. In the Maryland (*Tawes*) and Delaware (*Sinock*) cases, Clark concurred with Warren; and Stewart, in essence, voted with Harlan without joining in the dissent. In the New York case (*WMCA v. Lomenzo*), Stewart and Clark joined Harlan in dissent. In the Colorado case (*Lucas*), Stewart and Clark not only joined Harlan but also offered spirited dissents because of the special factors in that case. The Colorado malapportionment had grown out of a plan and process embedded in the Colorado constitution and not simply as a result of legislative action. From the simple vantage point of one person, one vote, this made no difference, but from the point of view of those who appreciated that a political "thicket" did exist, the difference was important. The considerations included in the dissents in *Lucas* reappear in subsequent cases in which the Court pressed more relentlessly toward absolute mathematical equality, eventually leading a majority of the Court to rethink the rigidity of this position.

Richard L. Wilson

See also *Baker v. Carr; Colegrove v. Green; Gray v. Sanders; Kirkpatrick v. Preisler; Mahan v. Howell; Reynolds v. Sims; United States v. Carolene Products Co.; Wesberry v. Sanders.*

RED LION BROADCASTING CO. V. FEDERAL COMMUNICATIONS COMMISSION

Court: U.S. Supreme Court
Citation: 393 U.S. 367
Date: June 9, 1969
Issues: Freedom of speech

- The U.S. Supreme Court upheld the fairness doctrine that required television and radio broadcasters to provide reply time for those criticized on air.

A radio station broadcast an attack against Fred Cook, who had written a book criticizing Arizona senator Barry Goldwater, but the station refused to allow Cook time to respond. Justice Byron R. White wrote the unanimous 8-0 opinion (Justice William O. Douglas did not participate) upholding the fairness doctrine of the Federal Communications Commission (FCC). The Court held that the FCC could require broadcast licensees to allow time for a reply from those who had been criticized on broadcasts from that station. The Court found that the First Amendment had to be limited by the reality that there are a finite number of broadcast frequencies (unlike the unlimited channels of communication available through newspapers). In such circumstances, the interests of the viewing and listening public take precedence over the interests of the station owners and licensees. An attempt to codify the rule by congressional enactment was vetoed by President Ronald Reagan, and the FCC repealed the rule in 1987.

Richard L. Wilson

See also *Metro Broadcasting v. Federal Communications Commission.*

Redd v. State of Georgia

Court: Georgia Court of Appeals
Citation: 248 Ga. App. 312
Date: April 6, 1910
Issues: Censorship; Pornography and obscenity

• This Georgia court decision expanded the definition of public indecency, affirming the right of the state to regulate individual behaviors that society deems indecent.

The state of Georgia's 1895 penal code dictated that acts of public indecency were punishable as criminal misdemeanors. The plaintiffs in *Redd v. State of Georgia* had been convicted of public indecency for having deliberately displayed to a woman and her children a view of a bull and a cow copulating in an open field. The plaintiffs argued that their actions did not fall within the legal definition of public indecency, which, they asserted, "relates only to indecent exposure of the human person." Rejecting this interpretation, the court ruled that public indecency encompassed "all notorious public and indecent conduct, tending to debauch the public morals."

The Georgia court's interpretation was supported by an 1858 Indiana court decision, *McJunkins v. State.* Quoting from *McJunkins,* the court held that the term "public indecency" had no fixed legal meaning, that it was "vague and indefinite" and could not in itself imply a definite offense. The court's acceptance of this view, coupled with its refusal to limit acts of public indecency to those outlined in *McJunkins*—the inappropriate display of the human body or the production and distribution of obscene materials—allowed it to expand the legal definition of public indecency. The court ruled that the state's statute was "broad enough to cover all notorious public and indecent conduct, tending to debauch the public morals, even though it be unattended by an exposure of the human body."

Having expanded the legal definition of public indecency, the court went on to state that acts by themselves could not be considered indecent, unless "the time, the place, the circumstances, and the motives of the actors [are] considered." Accordingly, certain acts might be deemed decent in certain contexts and indecent in others. The court ruled that "a fair test to determine whether an act is notoriously indecent . . . is to consider whether the general run of the citizenry . . . would readily recognize it as such (all the attendant facts and circumstances and the motives of the actor being considered)."

Redd determined that individual behavior and the right to free expression were governed by contemporary social norms of decency. It supported assertions that individual behavior is open to public censure when it runs contrary to society's norms. Thus, the court classified the plaintiffs' behavior as indecent and open to censure because their deliberateness in displaying animal copulation to other people ran contrary to society's norms of decency at that time.

Thomas Aaron Wyrick

See also *Ashcroft v. Free Speech Coalition; Barnes v. Glen Theatre, Inc.; Miller et al. v. Civil City of South Bend; Miller v. California; National Endowment for the Arts v. Finley; Reno v. American Civil Liberties Union.*

REED V. REED

Court: U.S. Supreme Court
Citation: 404 U.S. 71
Date: November 22, 1971
Issues: Equal protection of the law; Sex discrimination; Women's issues

- Finding for the first time that a state law violated the Fourteenth Amendment because it discriminated against women, the Court insisted that gender classifications must be rationally related to a legitimate state objective.

When Richard Reed, a minor, died without a will in Idaho, his separated parents, Cecil Reed and Sally Reed, filed separate petitions in probate court, each seeking appointment to administer the deceased's estate. In a joint hearing, the probate court followed the Idaho Code, which required a preference to the father because he was a male. In applying the statute, the probate judge could give no consideration to the relative capabilities of the two applicants to administer an estate.

Sally Reed appealed the judgment with the argument that a mandatory preference to males violated the equal protection clause of the Fourteenth Amendment. After losing the case in the Idaho Supreme Court, she appealed for a review by the U.S. Supreme Court. The Court had earlier indicated that the equal protection clause might forbid some kinds of classifications based on gender, but in contrast to categories of race, the Court had allowed states broad discretion to legislate different treatment for men and women, based on traditional sex roles that had been accepted as reasonable.

Departing from its previous leniency in the matter, the Court unanimously supported Sally Reed's position and ruled that the statute was incompatible with the state's obligation to provide "each person" with the "equal protection of the laws." The case, therefore, was remanded to the Idaho courts for new proceedings consistent with the Court's decision. In writing the official opinion, Chief Justice Warren Burger insisted that classifications of persons must not be arbitrary and must have "a fair and substantial relation to the object of the legislation." Burger conceded that there was some legitimacy for using a gender preference to reduce the workloads of the probate courts, but he found this rationale not sufficient to justify a mandatory preference without a hearing to determine the relative merits of the two petitioners. There was no rational basis to assume that men were always more qualified than women to administer wills.

The *Reed* decision was a landmark case that marked the Court's first use of the equal protection clause to strike down a statute on account of gender discrimination. Based on the history of the clause, Burger declined to consider whether gender is a "suspect" classification requiring strict judicial scrutiny, and his use of the "rational relationship test" would allow states much discretion in making gender distinctions. In later cases such as *Craig v. Boren* (1976), however, the Court would develop a more demanding test with a heightened level of scrutiny.

Thomas Tandy Lewis

See also *Bradwell v. Illinois*; *Craig v. Boren*; *Frontiero v. Richardson*; *Weinberger v. Wiesenfeld*.

Reese, United States v. *See* United States v. Reese

Regents of the University of California v. Bakke

Court: U.S. Supreme Court
Citation: 438 U.S. 265
Date: June 28, 1978
Issues: Affirmative action; Civil rights and liberties; Education; Equal protection of the law

- The U.S. Supreme Court defined racial quotas in preferential admissions programs as unconstitutional yet also declared that an applicant's race could be a consideration.

During the 1950's and 1960's, the United States made substantial progress in civil rights, aided by decisions of the U.S. Supreme Court that found state-sponsored segregation of the races to be unconstitutional. With its decision in *Brown v. Board of Education of Topeka, Kansas* (1954), the Court signaled that the equal protection clause of the Fourteenth Amendment to the Constitution could not be reconciled with public policy that discriminated on the basis of race. The Civil Rights Act of 1964 enacted this idea into law. The 1960's also heralded the beginning of a new effort to correct the wrongs of racial discrimination through the adoption of affirmative action programs.

Supporters of affirmative action contended that the removal of legal barriers was inadequate to ensure equality of the races. For example, President Lyndon B. Johnson argued that the effects of years of discrimination could not be erased through the dismantling of legal segregation alone; affirmative action was necessary to aid those who had been the victims of that discrimination. Agencies throughout the federal bureaucracy adopted regulations requiring or encouraging the use of affirmative action programs by recipients of federal funds. In response to a regulation of this type established by the U.S. Department of Health, Education, and Welfare, many colleges and universities throughout the country altered their admissions policies to include affirmative action elements that would help them to recruit students who were members of minority groups.

The University of California at Davis Medical School (UCDMS) enrolled its first class in 1968. The class was made up of fifty students, three of whom were Asian American and none of whom were African American, Latino, or

American Indian. Almost immediately, the school decided to create a special-admissions program that would provide seats in each class for disadvantaged minorities. In 1970, eight seats were reserved for special admissions. In 1971, the total class size of the school doubled to one hundred, and the number of special admissions slots was doubled to sixteen. Applying for admission became a two-track process, with applicants indicating whether they wanted to be considered as disadvantaged minorities. Persons found to qualify for special-admissions competed against one another for the sixteen special seats, while all other applicants competed for the remaining seats. Applicants for special admissions did not have to meet the same requirements in terms of grade point averages and standardized test scores as those competing in the general admissions process. Between 1968 and 1973, the year Allan Paul Bakke first applied to UCDMS, the number of minority students enrolled in the medical school rose from three to thirty-one.

Allan Paul Bakke

Bakke was employed as an engineer with the National Aeronautics and Space Administration (NASA) in California when he decided to apply to medical school in the fall of 1972. He had come to the decision that his true calling was the practice of medicine. He applied to twelve medical schools that year and was rejected by all of them. Several of the schools cited Bakke's age, thirty-three, as the cause of their rejection. Bakke had an admissions interview at UCDMS and received high marks in the ranking of candidates for admission, but because his application was late, he missed by a few points the cutoff score for the few seats left at that time. Bakke visited the school after he was rejected and talked with an admissions officer who encouraged him to apply again the next year and to consider challenging the special-admissions program. Bakke believed that he would have been admitted to the school in 1973 if sixteen places had not been set aside for disadvantaged minorities.

Bakke applied for the 1974 class at UCDMS and was again rejected. This time it appeared that his views on the special-admissions program, which he had discussed with an administrator during his interview, were a factor in his rejection. Bakke decided to sue the medical school, arguing that the special-admissions program violated his constitutional equal protection rights because the sixteen special-admissions seats were allocated purely on the basis of race. Bakke's case brought to the limelight a new equal protection question: Can members of the white majority be the victims of racial discrimination? Bakke contended that affirmative action programs like the one at UCDMS created "reverse discrimination" and were no less a violation of the equal protection clause because the victim was a member of the majority race instead of a minority group member.

UCDMS argued that it had compelling reasons for creating the racial classification. It was seeking to remedy past societal discrimination that had kept minorities from becoming doctors. Additionally, the school asserted that on completion of their medical training, minority doctors would be likely to return to minority communities and provide much-needed medical care. Finally, the school contended that ethnic diversity was an important asset to the educational environment and that the special-admissions program helped ensure a more diverse student body.

Reverse Discrimination

The question of reverse discrimination had been before the courts only once before. In 1971, Marco DeFunis had challenged a similar special admissions program at the University of Washington Law School; he believed the program had kept him from being accepted at that school. The trial court agreed with DeFunis's claim and ordered the law school to admit him. The school complied but appealed the decision against its program. At the appeals level, the court sided with the school, and the case reached the U.S. Supreme Court in 1974, the same year Bakke began his suit. The *DeFunis v. Odegaard* case received considerable attention and clearly contributed to Bakke's decision to go ahead with his suit. In April, 1974, the Court decided to dismiss the *DeFunis* case as moot. DeFunis was about to graduate from the law school, and the Court held that no true legal controversy existed any longer. This decision opened the way for Bakke's case to be the standard-bearer for the "reverse discrimination" argument.

The Superior Court of California agreed with Bakke's position. It found that the special-admissions program constituted a racial quota in violation of the constitutions of the nation and the state and the Civil Rights Act of 1964. The court said that UCDMS could not take race into account in its admissions decisions. It refused, however, to order Bakke's admission to the school, finding no evidence that Bakke would have been admitted if no affirmative action program had been in place. Both Bakke and the medical school appealed the decision, and, in 1976, the Supreme Court of California ruled in Bakke's favor, holding that the special-admissions program was a violation of the equal protection clause of the Fourteenth Amendment. The court further ordered UCDMS to admit Bakke. The medical school appealed this decision to the U.S. Supreme Court.

U.S. Supreme Court Ruling

At the end of its 1977-1978 term, the Supreme Court announced its decision in the case of *Regents of the University of California v. Bakke*. Four of the nine justices, led by John Paul Stevens, believed the UCDMS program to be a violation of Title VI of the Civil Rights Act of 1964, which forbids discrimination on the basis of race in any program receiving federal funds. These justices believed that the Court should go no further than this in ruling on the case. Four other justices, led by William J. Brennan, argued that affirmative action programs were acceptable because they helped to remedy the effects on minorities of centuries of discrimination. These justices distinguished between invidious discrimination, which is forbidden by the Fourteenth Amendment, and what they saw as the benign discrimination at the root of affirmative action programs. They argued that some discrimination in favor of minorities was necessary if real equality, rather than theoretical equality, was the goal. Justice Harry A. Blackmun wrote: "In order to get beyond racism, we must first take account of race. . . . And in order to treat some persons equally, we must treat them differently."

Justice Lewis F. Powell, Jr., wrote the decision that, because it allowed each of the other justices to join in at least part, became the ruling of the Court. Powell found that the UCDMS special-admissions program was indeed unconstitutional. He argued that the equal protection clause prohibited policies based solely on racial factors unless there was some compelling state interest that could override the very high barrier to such classification. In examining the justifications offered by the medical school, he found only the academic interest in student-body diversity convincing. He rejected the argument that past societal discrimination justified affirmative action. To find that reverse discrimination had occurred, the Court required a showing that the agency practicing it (in this case, UCDMS) had in the past discriminated. Because the school had opened in 1968 and begun its special-admissions program in 1970, no such history of discrimination existed.

Powell also rejected the argument that the program was justified because it served the medical needs of disadvantaged minority communities. The medical school could provide no evidence that special-admissions doctors were any more likely than others to practice medicine in these communities after they completed their education. Powell held that the program could not stand. In this part of his opinion, he was joined by the four justices in the Stevens coalition, creating a majority to strike down the special-admissions program and compel Bakke's admission.

Powell did not rule out all affirmative action programs as violations of equal protection. In the medical school's third justification, the promotion of student-body diversity, he found some legitimacy because of the traditional freedom granted to academic institutions to set their educational goals. Powell said that the desire for diversity justified some consideration of race as a factor in admissions decisions. The flaw in the UCDMS program was that race appeared to be the only factor shaping decisions for the sixteen seats. In this part of his decision, Powell was joined by the four justices in the Brennan coalition, thus creating a majority for the position that race may be considered as one factor among others in admissions decisions.

Significance

The landmark *Bakke* case provided something for both opponents and supporters of affirmative action. While it accepted the idea of reverse discrimination asserted by Bakke and vindicated his rights, it refused to reject the concept of affirmative action altogether. For college admissions officers, the Court's decision in the case provided a road map for how they could go about pursuing affirmative action in admissions decisions without violating the equal protection clause. For policy makers in general, it warned against the use of numerical quotas for accomplishing affirmative action ends.

The division on the Court over the *Bakke* decision heralded an extended battle in the courts over which kinds of affirmative action programs would be found to be constitutional and which would not. In the years after *Bakke*, the courts struggled repeatedly, and contentiously, with questions regarding affirmative action in employment. *Bakke* raised more questions than it answered and brought to the forefront the breakdown of consensus on civil rights questions in the United States. When the issues of civil rights had been about the dismantling of legal barriers to equality, a broad consensus had existed about the justice of this course of action. It was generally agreed that the Constitution does not permit a legally segregated society. After the landmark desegregation decisions of the 1950's and 1960's, the questions became more complicated and the moral imperatives less clear. What kind of equality does the Constitution require? Once the legal requirements of segregation are removed, does society have any further affirmative obligation to remedy the wrongs of the past? To what extent can individuals who are not responsible for past discrimination be made to bear the burden for the past?

For Allan Bakke, the impact of the Supreme Court's decision was clear-cut. He enrolled in the University of California at Davis Medical School in the fall of 1978, and in the spring of 1982 he graduated to a loud round of applause from the audience. For thousands of minority students across the United States, the *Bakke* decision provided new opportunities in higher education. The Court's ruling permitting race to be considered as one factor ensured that special admissions programs would continue.

Katy Jean Harriger

Further Reading

Ball, Howard. *The Bakke Case: Race, Education, and Affirmative Action.* Lawrence: University Press of Kansas, 2000. A history of the case's litigation, introduced by a history of affirmative action in higher education and followed by chapters discussing the dynamics of Supreme Court decision making, affirmative action policy in the 1990's, and the legacy of *Bakke* as of the year 2000. Includes bibliographic essay and index.

Dreyfuss, Joel, and Charles Lawrence III. *The Bakke Case: The Politics of Inequality.* New York: Harcourt Brace Jovanovich, 1979. Written by journalists in a readable narrative style that is sympathetic to arguments for affirmative action. Suggests that the focus of debate on qualifications obscured the underlying economic issues in affirmative action and signaled a fundamental change in race relations in the United States.

Eastland, Terry, and William J. Bennett. *Counting by Race: Equality from the Founding Fathers to Bakke and Weber.* New York: Basic Books, 1979. A historical summary with an emphasis on the change from the goal of individual equality of opportunity to that of "numerical parity" for groups. The authors are very critical of the majority opinion in the *Weber* case.

Greenawalt, Kent. *Discrimination and Reverse Discrimination.* New York: Alfred A. Knopf, 1982. About two-thirds of this convenient little book is composed of Supreme Court opinions and other primary material, with an excellent introduction that defends racial preference. This is designed primarily as a text for college courses.

Gross, Barry. *Discrimination in Reverse: Is Turnabout Fair Play?* New York: New York University Press, 1978. Addresses the philosophical and ethical issues of preferential treatment, with limited material on the legal questions. Argues that such policies are ethically wrong and contrary to the goal of equal justice.

McPherson, Stephanie Sammartino. *The Bakke Case and the Affirmative Action Debate: Debating Supreme Court Decisions.* Berkeley Heights, N.J.: Enslow, 2005. Explanation of the case and of affirmative action in general is aimed at young-adult readers. Includes chapter notes and questions for discussion.

Nieman, Donald G. *Promises to Keep: African-Americans and the Constitutional Order, 1776 to the Present.* New York: Oxford University Press, 1991. Readable historical essay on African Americans and U.S. law includes a good chapter at the end dealing with the debate about affirmative action.

Schwartz, Bernard. *Behind Bakke: Affirmative Action and the Supreme Court.* New York: New York University Press, 1988. Provides behind-the-scenes insights into the decision-making process of the Court in this landmark case.

Sindler, Allan P. *Bakke, DeFunis, and Minority Admissions: The Quest for Equal Opportunity.* New York: Longman, 1978. Focuses on the issue of how to promote equal opportunity without engaging in reverse discrimination. Provides a useful detailed look at the underlying issues and court histories of the *Bakke* and *DeFunis* cases.

Stefoff, Rebecca. *The Bakke Case: Challenge to Affirmative Action.* Tarrytown, N.Y.: Marshall Cavendish Benchmark, 2006. Part of its publisher's Supreme Court Milestones series designed for young-adult readers, this volume offers an accessible history and analysis of the *Bakke* case that examines opposing sides in the case, the people involved, and the case's lasting impact. Includes bibliography and index.

Urofsky, Melvin. *A Conflict of Rights: The Supreme Court and Affirmative Action.* New York: Charles Scribner's Sons, 1991. About a fifth of this excellent book deals with the history of affirmative action, and the rest is devoted to the 1987 case of *Johnson v. Transportation Agency.* Presents a balanced and sympathetic evaluation of the opposing viewpoints on the controversial topic.

Wilkinson, J. Harvie, III. *From Brown to Bakke: The Supreme Court and School Integration, 1954-1978.* New York: Oxford University Press, 1979. Chronicles the role of the Supreme Court in the desegregation of education and argues that public support for Court decisions breaks down with the move from principle to the imposition of such remedies as busing and affirmative action.

Zelnick, Robert. "The Beginning of the End for *Bakke.*" *Hoover Digest,* no. 2 (2002): 101-109. Considers the *Bakke* case in the light of developments at the University of Michigan and their implications for affirmative action in higher education.

See also *Gratz v. Bollinger/Grutter v. Bollinger; Texas v. Hopwood; United Steelworkers of America v. Weber.*

Reitman v. Mulkey

Court: U.S. Supreme Court
Citation: 387 U.S. 369
Date: May 29, 1967
Issues: Civil rights and liberties; Equal protection of the law; Housing discrimination; Racial discrimination

• California's adoption of Proposition 14, which repealed the state's fair-housing laws, was struck down by the U.S. Supreme Court after the California Supreme Court interpreted the repeal as "authorizing" discrimination.

In 1959 and 1963, California established fair-housing laws. These statutes banned racial discrimination in the sale or rental of private housing. In 1964, acting under the initiative process, the California electorate passed Proposition 14. This measure amended the state constitution so as to prohibit the state government from denying the right of any person to sell, lease, or refuse to sell or lease his or her property to another at his or her sole discretion. The fair-housing laws were effectively repealed. Mr. and Mrs. Lincoln Mulkey sued Neil Reitman in a state court, claiming that he had refused to rent them an apartment because of their race. They claimed that Proposition 14 was invalid because it violated the equal protection clause of the Fourteenth Amendment. If Proposition 14 was unconstitutional, the fair-housing laws would still be in force. The Mulkeys won in the California Supreme Court, and Reitman appealed to the Supreme Court of the United States.

Justice Byron White's opinion for the five-justice majority admitted that mere repeal of an antidiscrimination statute would not be unconstitutional. In this case, however, the California Supreme Court had held that the intent of Proposition 14 was to encourage and authorize private racial discrimination. This encouragement amounted to "state action" that violated the equal protection clause of the Fourteenth Amendment.

The four dissenters in the case agreed on an opinion by Justice John M. Harlan. Harlan argued that California's mere repeal of its fair-housing laws did not amount to encouraging and authorizing discrimination. If the repeal were to be seen that way, then a state could never rid itself of a statute whose purpose was to protect a constitutional right, whether of racial equality or some other. Harlan also suggested that opponents of antidiscrimination laws would later be able to argue that such laws not be passed because they would be unrepealable. Indeed, several ballot measures which have reversed or repealed civil rights laws protecting gays and lesbians have been struck down on the basis of *Reitman v. Mulkey*.

Reitman v. Mulkey has not had a major effect on American civil rights law. The Supreme Court has not been disposed to expand the "authorization" and "encouragement" strands of constitutional thought. The principle of "state action"—which is all that the Fourteenth Amendment equal protection rules can reach—has not been further broadened. Nevertheless, the precedent remains, with its suggestion that there is an affirmative federal constitutional duty on state government to prevent private racial discrimination.

Robert Jacobs

See also *Buchanan v. Warley*; *Corrigan v. Buckley*; *Evans v. Abney*; *Runyon v. McCrary*; *Shelley v. Kraemer*; *Spallone v. United States*.

Reno v. American Civil Liberties Union

Court: U.S. Supreme Court
Citation: 521 U.S. 844
Date: June 26, 1997
Issues: Freedom of speech

- The U.S. Supreme Court struck down the Communications Decency Act of 1996, which had made it a felony to display "obscene or indecent" material over the Internet in ways that might make it available to minors.

After 1957 the Supreme Court often held that the First Amendment protected indecent materials but not obscene materials. Speaking for a 7-2 majority, Justice John Paul Stevens emphasized that the Communications Decency Act of 1996 did not adequately define obscenity and that it did not define indecency at all. Therefore, people using the Internet had no adequate notice of what specific communications were prohibited. The law's definition of obscenity, moreover, went beyond the Court's standards in *Miller v. California* (1973), and it did not guarantee protection for materials with serious political, scientific, or educational value. Although he recognized the government's legitimate interest in protecting children from inappropriate expression, Stevens wrote that this objective did not justify limiting the access of adults to only materials that are appropriate for children. The two dissenters would have sustained those portions of the law that prohibited indecent communications from an adult to one or more minors.

Thomas Tandy Lewis

Further Reading

Axelrod-Contrada, Joan. *Reno v. ACLU: Internet Censorship.* Tarrytown, N.Y.: Marshall Cavendish Benchmark, 2007. Part of its publisher's Supreme Court Milestones series designed for young-adult readers, this volume offers an accessible history and analysis of the *Reno* case that examines opposing sides in the case, the people involved, and the case's lasting impact. Includes bibliography and index.

See also *Miller v. California; National Endowment for the Arts v. Finley; Shaw v. Reno; Village of Skokie v. National Socialist Party of America.*

Reynolds v. Sims

Court: U.S. Supreme Court
Citation: 377 U.S. 533
Date: June 15, 1964
Issues: Reapportionment and redistricting; Voting rights

- For the first time taking action against state legislatures for ignoring constitutionally mandated requirements for redistricting, the Court specifically applied a "one-person, one-vote" solution to what it deemed to be inaccurate representation.

The 1960's witnessed a significant change in the apportionment of state legislative and congressional delegations. For the first time, the U.S. Supreme Court interfered with the apportionment practices of the states. The Court's action was an attempt to rectify what it deemed to be the malapportionment of a great majority of American state legislatures and of state delegations to the House of Representatives.

This situation had developed over the years because predominantly rural state legislatures continually ignored the population shifts that produced the tremendous growth of the country's cities in the twentieth century. In many cases, state legislatures, out of a fear that equitable redistricting would shift the rural-urban balance of power, deliberately ignored the provisions within their own state constitutions for periodic redistricting. The result was a constitutional abnormality that was distorting the democratic political process.

In a series of cases brought before the Court in the 1960's, the malapportionment problems were judicially corrected when the Court applied a "one-person, one-vote" principle. In 1964, a federal district court ordered the state of Alabama to reapportion and then nullified two plans that did not apportion the legislative districts solely on the basis of population. The state appealed to the Supreme Court, which held that the equal protection clause of the Fourteenth Amendment requires that the seats in both houses be equally apportioned.

The existing apportionment of the Alabama state legislature was struck down when the Court, in an 8-1 majority, applied the one-person, one-vote principle in the case. Writing for the majority, Chief Justice Earl Warren declared that restrictions on the right to vote "strike at the heart of representative government." The Court, he added, had "clearly established that the fundamental principle of representative government in this country is one of equal representation for equal numbers of people, without regard to race, sex, economic status, or place of residence within the state." The concept of one person, one vote was virtually a pure and intractable rule.

In his dissent, Justice John M. Harlan argued that the decision had the "effect of placing basic aspects of state political systems under the pervasive overlordship of the federal judiciary." This type of "judicial legislation" frightened not only Harlan but also a number of conservatives who did not want to see the Supreme Court become more active in producing equal voting rights.

The legacy of this case is clear: In *Reynolds* and several companion cases decided the same day, the Supreme Court determined that it had an obligation to interfere in the apportionment practices of the states in order to guarantee that no person was deprived of the right to vote. By guaranteeing those individual rights, *Reynolds* ensured that the state legislatures as well as the House of Representatives would more properly reflect the genuine complexion of American society.

Kevin F. Sims

See also *Baker v. Carr*; *Colegrove v. Green*; *Gray v. Sanders*; *Mahan v. Howell*; *Reapportionment Cases*; *Wesberry v. Sanders*.

REYNOLDS V. UNITED STATES

Court: U.S. Supreme Court
Citation: 98 U.S. 145
Date: May 5, 1879
Issues: Freedom of religion; Marriage

- Upholding a congressional prohibition of polygamy in the territories, the Court established the principle that the First Amendment protects all religious beliefs but does not protect religiously motivated practices that harm the public interest.

George Reynolds, a member of the Mormon church and a resident of the territory of Utah, was tried in a federal territorial court for committing the crime of bigamy, in violation of an 1862 statute. At his trial, Reynolds presented evidence that the accepted doctrine of his church was that every male member had the duty, circumstances permitting, to practice plural marriage and that failure to do so would be punished by "damnation in the life to come." He further argued that the First Amendment prohibited Congress from placing such limitations on the free exercise of religion. The trial judge refused to instruct the jury that the defendant should be exempted from the law for actions motivated by his religious beliefs, and the jury returned a guilty verdict. Reynolds appealed to the U.S. Supreme Court.

The Court unanimously ruled to uphold Reynolds's conviction. Writing the majority opinion, Chief Justice Morrison R. Waite recognized that Congress cannot pass a law that prohibits the free exercise of religion, but he made a distinction between religious beliefs and religious conduct. While beliefs or opinions were fully protected, Congress was free to punish "actions which were in violation of social duties or subversive of good order."

An obvious example, Waite pointed out, was the possible practice of human sacrifice. Historically, polygamy had always been punished as a crime in the common law and statutes of Great Britain, and this tradition had been uniformly followed in every state of the United States. In addition, Waite quoted several respected jurists who argued that polygamy promoted despotic government and had other undesirable consequences. Congress, therefore, possessed legitimate authority to criminalize polygamy in the territories, and there was no obligation to make an exception for those who followed different religious beliefs.

The *Reynolds* decision was the Court's first major consideration of a law that restrained the religious freedom of a minority, and it would become an important precedent because of Waite's formulation of the belief-conduct distinction. Implicitly, the Court acknowledged that Congress could not prohibit a religious practice without a legitimate state interest, but the Court did not try to articulate guidelines for the level of state interest required. In its later decisions, the Court would consistently follow *Reynolds* in its belief-conduct distinction, but the decision would not prove helpful in providing standards to determine what kinds of religious conduct might be protected.

The immediate impact of *Reynolds* was limited because the free-exercise clause did not then apply to state laws, but the Court would often refer to the case after the clause was made binding on the states in *Cantwell v. Connecticut* (1940).

Thomas Tandy Lewis

See also *Cantwell v. Connecticut*; *Davis v. Beason.*

RHODES V. CHAPMAN

Court: U.S. Supreme Court
Citation: 452 U.S. 337
Date: June 15, 1981
Issues: Cruel and unusual punishment; Incarceration

- In this case, the U.S. Supreme Court ruled that the "double-celling" of inmates at a maximum-security prison in Ohio did not violate constitutional safeguards against cruel and unusual punishment.

Rhodes v. Chapman evolved from a class-action suit brought by two inmates at the Southern Ohio Correctional Facility, a maximum-security prison in Lucasville. Cellmates Kelly Chapman and Richard Jaworski, citing a federal statute, maintained that incarcerating two inmates in the same cell violated the protection against cruel and unusual punishment guaranteed by the Eighth and Fourteenth Amendments. The U.S. District Court for the Southern District of Ohio, after an extensive investigation, concurred. Among other supporting reasons for its decision, the court argued that double-celling of long-term prisoners aggravated the various problems associated with close confinement. It further noted that the Ohio facility housed a prison population 38 percent larger than its designed capacity and that it failed to provide each inmate with the recommended standard of 50 to 55 square feet of living space. It found, too, that the prison had made double celling a practice rather than a temporary solution to crowded conditions.

After the United States Court of Appeals for the Sixth Circuit upheld the lower court's judgment, the case went to the Supreme Court, which reversed the lower courts' decisions and ruled that double-celling did not constitute cruel and unusual punishment. The Court stated that the district court's findings were insupportable and that the data on which it based its judgment were "insufficient to support its constitutional conclusion." The majority opinion, presented by Justice Lewis F. Powell, Jr., held that there was no real evidence that double-celling at the Ohio prison facility inflicted undue pain or imposed any hardship that was out of proportion to the crimes warranting the inmates' imprisonment. A concurring opinion, however, cautioned that the Court's decision should not be interpreted as an abrogation of its responsibility to scrutinize prison conditions to ensure that humane but realistic standards are maintained.

The lone dissenter, Justice Thurgood Marshall, argued that prison overcrowding and the double-celling of prisoners, unchecked, would eventually have a deleterious effect on the mental and physical health of prisoners, in total disregard of modern standards of human decency. Marshall also expressed concern that the Court's ruling might be construed as an admonition to district courts, enjoining them to adopt a laissez-faire position toward the administration of state prison systems.

For those individuals who believe that hardened felons have been mollycoddled and encouraged to seek legal redress for minor and even frivolous complaints, the *Rhodes* decision has landmark significance. It reflected the rising anger and fear of the nation regarding crime; by the early 1980's, the country was growing increasingly unsympathetic to the rights of prisoners.

John W. Fiero

See also *Furman v. Georgia*; *Hudson v. Palmer*; *Hutto v. Davis*; *Robinson v. California*; *Rummel v. Estelle*; *Stanford v. Kentucky*; *Trop v. Dulles*.

RICCI V. DESTEFANO

Court: U.S. Supreme Court
Citation: 557 U.S. _____
Date: June 29, 2009
Issues: Affirmative action; Civil rights and liberties; Employment discrimination; Equal protection of the law; Labor law; Racial discrimination

• In an important disparate-impact case, the U.S. Supreme Court held that if an employer fears a possible lawsuit by racial minorities because an employment practice has disqualified a disproportionate percentage of minorities, this fear does not justify the intentional discrimination against white employees, unless there is a "strong basis in evidence" that the minorities would likely prevail in a court of law.

Title VII of the Civil Rights Act of 1964 prohibits racial and other group-based discrimination in employment. In *Griggs v. Duke Power Company* (1971), the U.S. Supreme Court interpreted the law as prohibiting a "disparate impact" in the employment of protected classes. The ruling held that if an employment practice has a disproportionally negative effect on a group protected by the act, the employer then bears the burden of demonstrating a valid business necessity for the practice.

Following a long controversy about the interpretation of the 1964 statute, Congress amended Title VII with the Civil Rights Act of 1991, which explicitly incorporated the disparate-impact theory, requiring employers to show that all employment practices having a racially disparate impact are "job-related for the position in question and consistent with business necessity." Even if employers could make this demonstration, they might still lose in court if the challengers could prove that a valid alternative practice would result in less racial disparity. Critics of the 1991 statute charged that it tended to result in racial preferences, sometimes even in quotas, because of the many problems in proving that employment practices and qualifications are truly necessary and justified by the ambiguous concept of business necessity.

Background

The controversy that culminated in the *Ricci* decision began in 2003 when the fire department of New Haven, Connecticut, administered a combination of written and oral examinations in order to determine which of its firefighters would be promoted to the ranks of lieutenant and captain. The processes for the exam were based on the contract between the city and the firefighters' union. The city spent $100,000 to pay a prominent consulting firm that specialized in personnel selection, Industrial/Organizational Solutions (IOS), to develop and administer the examinations. In an attempt to ensure that the examinations would not unintentionally favor white candidates, the company wrote the questions below a tenth-grade reading level. Of 118 firefighters who took the exams, nineteen met the qualifications for promotion, including seventeen who were white and two Hispanics. None of the nineteen African American candidates scored high enough to be considered for promotion. Before the promotions could take effect, it was necessary for the Civil Service Board (CSB) to certify that the test results were not racially biased.

The CSB held a series of hearings to decide whether to certify the tests. Appearing at the hearings, a representative of Mayor John DeStefano and several lawyers and managers strongly advised the CSB not to certify the tests, warning that their disparate impact on minorities opened the city to a possible lawsuit under Title VII because of the possibility that there were alternative tests that would result in the promotion of a larger percentage of minorities. An IOS representative advised approval of the tests, which he claimed were "facially neutral" and well-designed to prevent bias. A representative from a rival company, however, testified that his company was able to design a test that would not have such an "adverse impact" on minority applicants. Black firefighters claimed that the exams were racially biased, whereas most of the white firefighters disagreed, saying that they were based on information taken from "nationally recognized" books and the fire department's own rules and standard operating procedures. Frank Ricci, who had obtained high scores, reported that he had studied eight to thirteen hours a day in preparation for the test and that because of his dyslexia, he had made flashcards and paid an acquaintance one thousand dollars to put materials on audiotape. At the conclusion of the hearings, the CBS voted two to two on the question of certification. The city decided to throw out the test results and not promote anyone, citing the possibility of a disparate-impact lawsuit.

The Firefighters' Grievances

Eighteen of the firefighters (seventeen whites and one Hispanic) who had passed the initial exam entered a federal lawsuit against the city and several officials, including Mayor DeStefano. Among other grievances, the plaintiffs alleged that by discarding the results of the exams, the defendants had engaged in racial discrimination in violation of both the equal protection clause of the Fourteenth Amendment and Title VII of the Civil Rights Act of 1964. The city and the named officials responded that if they had approved the test results, they might have been sued by the minority firefighters, based on the statutes and case law dealing with disparate impact.

At the federal district court, Judge Janet Arterton ruled in favor of the city and granted its motion for a summary judgment. When the case was appealed to the Court of Appeals for the Second Circuit, a three-judge panel that included Judge Sonia Sotomayor (who later became a justice on the U.S. Supreme Court) affirmed the district court's ruling in a summary order without a written opinion. However, when one judge on the Second Circuit requested that the Court review the case, the panel withdrew the summary order and instead issued a short *per curiam* opinion, characterizing the trial court's ruling as "thorough, thoughtful, and well reasoned." While expressing sympathy for the situation of the plaintiffs, particularly Frank Ricci, the panel concluded that the Civil Service Board had followed the law and lamented that there were "no good alternatives" in such a case. Although the judges on the Court of Appeals voted seven to six against a rehearing with all the judges of the court, two judges dissented and urged review by the U.S. Supreme Court, which granted *certiorari* and heard the oral arguments on April 22, 2009.

The Supreme Court's Ruling

The U.S. Supreme Court, by a 5-4 vote, reversed the rulings of the two lower courts and held that the city's action in discarding the test results constituted racial discrimination against the eighteen plaintiffs in violation of Title VII. Speaking for the majority, Justice Anthony Kennedy emphasized that the city did not have "a strong basis in evidence" that a lawsuit would be successful. He found that the record of the CSB hearing indicated that the city could have reasonably argued that the tests were job-related and consistent with business necessity, and that city officials had "turned a blind eye to evidence that supported the exams' validity." Fear of possible litigation "cannot justify an employer's reliance on race to the detriment of individuals who passed the tests and qualified for promotions." Kennedy concluded that once a process had been initiated with clear selection criteria based on good-faith attempts to avoid racial bias, the employer "may not then invalidate the test results, thus upsetting an employee's legitimate expectation not to be judged on the basis of race." To do so, without extremely good evidence that the test is discriminatory, "amounts to the sort of racial preference that Congress has disclaimed and is antithetical to the notion of a workplace where individuals are guaranteed equal opportunity regardless of race."

Although Justices Antonin Scalia and Samuel Alito joined the majority opinion, each wrote a separate concurrence. Scalia argued that the disparate-impact provisions of Title VII are inconsistent with the guarantee of equal protection in the Fourteenth Amendment. These provisions placed "a special thumb on the scales," mandating employers to base their employment policies on racial outcomes that are equivalent to "quotas." In conclusion, Scalia insisted that the government treat citizens as individuals, "not as simply components of a racial, religious, sexual, or national class." Justice Alito focused on the city's reason for throwing out the tests. Finding evidence in the record that New Haven's African Americans had put great pressure on the CSB and city officials, he concluded: "The City's real reason was illegitimate, namely, the desire to placate a politically important racial constituency."

Dissenting Opinions

In dissent, Justice Ruth Bader Ginsburg, joined by the three other dissenters, wrote that the eighteen plaintiffs had "no vested right to promotion" and that other persons had not received promotion in preference to them. Citing the racial disparities in the results of the tests, she argued that the record establishes that the city had cause to fear disparate-impact liability. The record showed, moreover, that the exams contained "multiple flaws" that would likely meet the "strong basis in evidence" standard in a lawsuit. Ginsburg also remarked that "the starkly disparate results" of the exams should be assessed against the background of historical and continuing inequality in the New Haven fire department, in which only one of the city's captains was an African American. She also questioned whether an emphasis on written exams was the best way to judge the effectiveness and leadership qualities of firefighters.

It appeared likely that the *Ricci* decision would have relatively minimal influence on the policies used in the hiring and promoting of employees. Under Title VII, employers would continue to have the obligation to defend all employment policies resulting in racially disparate outcomes by demonstrating that the policies are job-related and necessary for a successful business. Certainly *Ricci* gave warning to employers that they should not choose to disregard the results of a competitive test after it has been given, but employers concerned about a disparate-impact suit could always devise a different test in the future. One possible impact of the *Ricci* case was that its publicity appeared to increase the general public's disaffection with race-conscious policies in employment, especially among persons who worried about "reverse discrimination."

Thomas Tandy Lewis

Further Reading

Anderson, Terry H. *The Pursuit of Fairness: A History of Affirmative Action.* New York: Oxford University Press, 2004. Balanced account of race-conscious policies designed to increase the opportunities of underrepresented minorities.

Cathcart, David A., et al. *The Civil Rights Act of 1991.* Philadelphia: American Law Institute, 1993. Text and commentary concerning the complex law that forbids employment practices having an adverse impact on protected groups.

Player, Mack. *Federal Law of Employment Discrimination in a Nutshell.* 6th ed. St. Paul, Minn.: West, 2009. Reliable summary of laws relating to discrimination, including disparate impact and affirmative action.

Rutherglen, George A., and John J. Donohue III. *Employment Discrimination: Law and Theory.* 2d ed. New York: Foundation Press, 2009. Huge volume that includes a detailed analysis of laws and principles concerning disparate impact.

Zimmer, Michael, Charles Sullivan, and Rebecca White. *Cases and Materials on Employment Discrimination.* 7th ed. Austin, Tex.: Wolters Kluwer, 2008. Comprehensive text dealing with both legislation and case law.

See also *Firefighters Local Union No. 1784 v. Stotts et al.*; *Griggs v. Duke Power Co.*; *Martin v. Wilks*; *Washington v. Davis.*

RICHARDSON, UNITED STATES V. *See* UNITED STATES V. RICHARDSON

Richmond Newspapers v. Virginia

Court: U.S. Supreme Court
Citation: 448 U.S. 555
Date: July 2, 1980
Issues: Freedom of the press; Trial by jury

- The U.S. Supreme Court ruled that the First Amendment protects the right of the public and the press to attend criminal trials even if the defendant objects.

After *New York Times Co. v. United States* (1971) and *Nebraska Press Association v. Stuart* (1976), the broad rule was that the press could print any material it possessed without prior restraint, but the government and courts were entitled to keep materials secret if they could. The question remained whether the press had a right to have access to all trials. In *Gannett Co. v. DePasquale* (1979), a narrow majority on the Supreme Court held that the Sixth Amendment stipulated that only a defendant could insist on an open trial. In *Richmond Newspapers*, a local judge honored a defendant's request to exclude the press. When the case reached the Court, however, it ruled that the First and Fourteenth Amendments required that the trial be open to the press and public, but for widely different reasons. Chief Justice Warren E. Burger wrote the opinion for the 7-1 majority, and Justices William J. Brennan, Jr., Thurgood Marshall, Potter Stewart, Byron R. White, and John Paul Stevens each wrote concurrences. Justice William H. Rehnquist wrote a dissent, and Justice Lewis F. Powell, Jr., did not participate.

Richard L. Wilson

See also *Branzburg v. Hayes; Cohen v. Cowles Media Co.; Grosjean v. American Press Co.; Miami Herald Publishing Co. v. Tornillo; Near v. Minnesota; Nebraska Press Association v. Stuart; New York Times Co. v. Sullivan; New York Times Co. v. United States.*

RICHMOND V. J. A. CROSON CO.

Court: U.S. Supreme Court
Citation: 488 U.S. 469
Date: January 23, 1989
Issues: Affirmative action; Private discrimination

- *Richmond v. J. A. Croson Co.* made it much more difficult for cities and states to establish race-conscious affirmative action programs.

In 1983, the City Council of Richmond, Virginia, adopted a minority set-aside program for city contracting. Under the plan, 30 percent of all city construction subcontracts were to be granted to (or "set aside" for) minority-owned business enterprises. The J. A. Croson Company, a contracting firm which had been the low bidder on a city project, sued the city when its bid was rejected in favor of a larger bid submitted by a minority-owned firm. Croson's position was that the minority set-aside violated the equal protection clause of the Fourteenth Amendment by establishing a racial classification.

Richmond argued that the minority set-aside was valid as an attempt to remedy past discriminations. An earlier case, *Fullilove v. Klutznick* (1980), had approved a similar set-aside program for federal government contracts. The city pointed out that only 0.67 percent of its prime construction contracts had gone to minority firms between 1978 and 1983.

By vote of six to three, the U.S. Supreme Court decided for the Croson Company. The opinion of the Court was written by Justice Sandra Day O'Connor. Justice O'Connor argued that the earlier federal case was not relevant because the federal government has legislative authority to enforce the Fourteenth Amendment. State governments are limited by it. Race-conscious affirmative action programs are valid only where there is a showing of past discrimination by the state government itself. In the case of the Richmond statute, there was no such showing. It was undeniable that there had been discrimination against minority contractors, but that discrimination was by private firms, not by the city itself. While the city has the power to remedy private discriminations, she argued, it may not do so by setting up a quota system which is itself racially biased.

Justice Thurgood Marshall wrote the major dissenting opinion. He argued that the majority's view of the facts was too narrow. The extraordinary disparity between contracts let to minority and nonminority firms showed that there was systematic and pervasive discrimination which could only be remedied in practice by a set-aside or quota program of the kind passed in Richmond. He pointed out, as he had in earlier cases, the irony of a constitutional rule which forbids racial classifications for benign purposes, given the long history of constitutionally permitted racial classifications for discriminatory purposes. Justice Marshall insisted that the court should not scrutinize racial classifications strictly so long as the purpose of the classification is benign. Justices William Brennan, Jr., and Harry A. Blackmun joined Marshall in his dissent.

Richmond v. J. A. Croson Co. cast doubt on the future of race-conscious programs designed to remedy past discriminations. At the very least, it means that racial quotas, however well-meant, are likely to be held unconstitutional.

Robert Jacobs

See also *Adarand Constructors v. Peña; Fullilove v. Klutznick; Metro Broadcasting v. Federal Communications Commission.*

Robel, United States v. *See* United States v. Robel